THE LAW OF
DEMOCRATIC
GOVERNING

VOLUME II:
JURISPRUDENCE

Gregory Tardi, B.A., B.C.L., LL.B.

Senior Legal Counsel,
Office of the Law Clerk and Parliamentary Counsel
House of Commons, Parliament of Canada

Lecturer, Faculty of Law, McGill University

President, Political Law Development *Initiative* Inc.

With a Foreword by
John Reid,
Information Commissioner of Canada

THOMSON
*
TM
CARSWELL

National Library of Canada Cataloguing in Publication

Tardi, Gregory, 1949-
    The law of democratic governing / Gregory Tardi.
Includes bibliographical references.
Contents: v. 1. Principles — v. 2. Jurisprudence.
ISBN 0-459-24149-4 (v.1). — ISBN 0-459-24150-8 (v. 2)
1. Public law — Canada. 2. Public law — Canada — Cases.
I Title.
KE5015.T37 2004   342.71 C2004-904025-1
KF5402.T37 2004

Composition: Computer Composition of Canada Inc.

THOMSON
CARSWELL

One Corporate Plaza, 2075 Kennedy Road, Toronto, Ontario M1T 3V4
Customer Service:
Toronto 416-609-3800
Elsewhere in Canada/U.S. 1-800-387-5164
Fax (416) 298-5094
Website: www.carswell.com
E-mail: carswell.orders@thomson.com

To My Uncle Zoltan Kiss

*who was a model of extreme courage and generosity
in his career and throughout his life*

LAW REPORTS

CANADA

A.C.W.S.	All Canada Weekly Summaries
Admin.L.R.	Administrative Law Reports
Alta. L.R.	Alberta Law Reports
A.P.R.	Atlantic Provinces Reports
A.R.	Alberta Reports
B.C.A.C.	British Columbia Appeal Cases
B.C.L.R.	British Columbia Law Reports
B.R.	Banc de la Reine
C.A.	Cour d'Appel
C.C.C.	Canadian Criminal Cases
C.C.L.S.	Canadian Cases on the Law of Securities
C.C.E.L.	Canadian Cases on Employment Law
C.C.L.T.	Canadian Cases on the Law of Torts
C.E.L.R. (N.S.)	Canadian Environmental Law Reports (New Series)
C.L.R.	Construction Law Reports
C.N.L.R.	Canadian Native Law Reporter
C.P.C.	Carswell's Practice Cases
C.P.R.	Canadian Patent Reporter
C.R.	Criminal Reports
C.R.R.	Canadian Rights Reporter
C.T.C.	Canadian Tax Cases
D.L.R.	Dominion Law Reports
D.T.C.	Dominion Tax Cases
F.C.	Federal Court Reports
F.R.D.	Federal Rules Decisions
F.T.R.	Federal Trial Reports
G.S.T.C.	Canada GST Cases
Imm. L.R.	Immigration Law Reports
M.P.L.R.	Municipal Planning Law Reports
N.B.R.	New Brunswick Reports
Nfld. & P.E.I.R.	Newfoundland and Prince Edward Island Reports
N.R.	National Reporter
N.S.R.	Nova Scotia Reports
N.W.T.R.	Northwest Territories Reports
O.A.C.	Ontario Appeal Cases

O.J.	Ontario Judgments
O.R.	Ontario Reports
O.T.C.	Ontario Trial Cases
P.S.S.R.B.	Public Service Staff Relations Board Decisions
Qué. Q.B.	Québec Queen's Bench
REJB	Répertoire électronique de jurisprudence du Barreau
R.D.J.	Receuil de droit judiciaire
R.F.L.	Reports on Family Law
R.J.Q.	Recueils de jurisprudence du Québec
R.R.A.	Receuil en responsabilité et assurance
Sask. R.	Saskatchewan Reports
S.C.R.	Supreme Court Reports
W.A.C.	Western Appeal Cases
W.C.B.	Weekly Criminal Bulletin
W.D.C.P.	The Weekly Digest of Civil Procedure
W.W.R.	Western Weekly Reports

AUSTRALIA

A.L.R.	Australian Law Reports

COMMONWEALTH

L.R.C.	Law Reports of the Commonwealth
L.R.C. (Cons.)	Law Reports of the Commonwealth (Constitutional)

EUROPEAN COMMUNITY

E.H.R.R.	European Human Rights Reporter

HONG KONG

H.K.L.R.D.	Hong Kong Law Reports and Digest

INTERNATIONAL COURT OF JUSTICE

I.C.J.R.	International Court of Justice Reports

NEW ZEALAND

N.Z.L.R.	New Zealand Law Reports

PAKISTAN

P.L.D.   Pakistan Law Reports

SINGAPORE

S.L.R.   Singapore Law Reports

UNITED KINGDOM

A.C.   Appeal Cases
All E.R.   All England Reports
E.R.   English Reports
Hob.   Hobart
I.R.L.R.   Industrial Relations Law Reports
T.N.L.R.   Times Newspaper Law Reports
Ves. Sen.   Vesey, Senior

UNITED STATES

C.S.C.R.   Connecticut Superior Court Reports
F.   Federal Reporter
F. Supp.   Federal Supplement
L. Ed   Lawyers' Edition
Mass. L. Rep.   Massachussetts Law Reports
N.J.   New Jersey Reports
P.   Pacific Reporter
S.Ct.   Supreme Court Reports
U.S.   United States Reports

FOREWORD

When Gregory Tardi started to talk about his concept of Political Law some twenty years ago, I found this to be a suggestion worth following. At that time, I was involved with a number of legislative activities, reform of the *Canada Elections Act*, and the development of the *Election Expenses Act*, as well as Access to Government held Information by citizens and the Privacy Rights of Canadians in the new information age. The idea of a special branch of legal study focusing on questions of democracy, looking at the way in which constitutional law and conventions, administrative law, election law, Speaker's decisions, and other branches of the Canadian legal *corpus*, defined and affected the environment in which our democracy system operated, seemed to meet a felt need. For while there were many Canadian political science studies of the day, they described only the way in which the political system worked, but paid little or no attention to the way in which Canadian laws and judicial decisions laid out the ground rules for all participants in the system, from elected representatives, to public servants, to those served by government and to the electors themselves.

The menu for the study of Political Law is significantly larger than most would credit. When one examines its scope, Political Law becomes larger than it originally appeared. It cuts to the heart of our democracy and the way in which we govern ourselves. Political Law starts, of course, with the concept of the rule of law, and works its way through discussions of interactions between the law, policy and politics; between sovereignty, legitimacy and governance; to deal with elections, parties, campaigning and political promises; to examine the legislative system; the question of the legality by which government programmes are administered (the question of the rule of law or *raison d'État*); the litigation of political law cases, that is the use of the courts to advance political and partisan aims; and the question of the accountability of the players in the area of political law to the laws and the courts.

The case studies provided are both instructive and (for a non-lawyer) interesting. The focus, of course, is on Canadian and Provincial legal decisions (including Parliamentary decisions of the Speaker of the House of Commons). There are also some examples from the United States, Great Britain, France, the European Union, and from a variety of other jurisdictions. One can examine briefly the interplay of notions of Political Law within other countries to see where ideas and interpretations have been borrowed and integrated across jurisdictions. These excursions are helpful and useful in understanding trends in Canadian judicial decisions.

The material in the book poses a number of interesting questions. First, it is clear to the courts that the ideal of democracy has still not been totally defined; it is an evolving concept. I was struck by the obvious care and deep study that Canadian courts have given, not only to the ideal of democracy, but to its practical workings as well. There is also an awareness of the importance of the relationship between the courts and legislatures, which can be traced in decisions before and after the *Charter of Rights*.

Second, in a number of cases, the role of the Attorney General comes into play. While the question is never directly developed, what emerges from the case studies is the question of whether or not the Attorney General should be an elected representative in Cabinet. Because the Government, Federal or Provincial, is in court on a regular basis, and given the normal rules of Cabinet government, how much independence does the Attorney General have in legal matters or even in quasi-legal matters? This is one of the anomalies of our system.

Third, there is an interesting section on the activities of lawyers in Government: their position, what they do, and how they are or are not a part of the administrative system. Increasingly, there is criticism about the role of the Department of Justice, which apparently no longer sees its role as being to uphold the law and to speak truth to power, but rather to be the law firm of the government. The question of the rule of law versus administrative efficiency and/or convenience is one theme that appears consistently in the case studies.

As I read this book, I began to think about who might learn from it. The first group comprises those politically involved, including elected representatives, candidates for election and people working in politics—people with an abiding interest in politics. Moreover, this study illuminates areas of activities, which, to the ordinary citizen, must seem totally confusing. But for those involved in Canada's democratic governmental legal structures, this book is a guide through the maze, and provides a close look at many of the pitfalls of conflict with political law. All Civil Servants would find this book useful, and it could form the basis of courses Civil Servants should take in their formative years, with regular updates, so they would have an understanding of their status in law as opposed to the demand for loyalty to one's institution or superior only. Those interested in Political Science and History will find it of interest because the case studies throw light on a number of areas not studied deeply. And of course, lawyers might enjoy having it on their work table to dip into each day.

But I think that the group that would most enjoy this book would be Canadian judges. For those who think the decisions of various courts have deteriorated over time, a careful read of this book and its case studies, both old and new, will indicate that in this field of Political Law, Canadian courts have worked with great diligence and intelligence in a very difficult, controversial field.

Honourable John M. Reid, P.C.
Information Commissioner of Canada,
Ottawa, August 24, 2004

PREFACE

In 1992, when my first book, *The Legal Framework of Government: A Canadian Guide*, was published, I prefaced it as "an expression of a lifelong fascination with public affairs and the relevance of law to their conduct." In the decade since then, through intensified observation, further study and research, as well as writing and teaching, my fascination has turned into a genuine passion. I am convinced that learning the lessons and drawing conclusions from the myriad interactions of legality, public administration and political life is a more thorough way of understanding democratic governance than by carrying on any of the traditional but single-disciplinary avenues of examination and exploration. From this, grew the idea of an interdisciplinary perspective, combining the existing studies of political society. Similarly, I have come to believe that single-jurisdictional observation of the law/public administration/politics interaction is inadequate. For this reason, I have expanded my horizons to make this next phase of my work comparative in an international sense.

In the perspective I have adopted, democratic governance comprises bodies of binding rules arising from law, from public administration, and from politics. These bodies of rules represent diverse social and philosophical underpinnings of, and belief systems in, society; largely, they stem from different professions and elites among governing circles. Certainly, they express the ideals, ideas and objectives of those elites through instruments of governance that can be grouped in discrete categories, but which are susceptible of comparison:

- the first category comprises primarily the constitution of the State, laws and related regulations, and court judgments;
- the second consists of a variety of policies, guidelines, manuals, instructions, established practices and even recommendations in Royal Commission reports;
- the third encompasses the constitutions, platforms and resolutions of political parties, Speeches from the Throne, Budgets and Economic Statements, as well as constitutional conventions.

The notable criterion of comparison and analysis among all these types and forms of instruments of governance is that the rules emanating from them all are, or become, binding on the body politic. Some are inherently and autonomously binding and are backed by the principled power, might and majesty of the courts. Others become binding through systems of professional discipline, shared beliefs and values, public acceptance, usage, or mere acquiescence. However, all are binding in various manners and to various degrees in that they affect the conduct of public affairs, they impact on political society, and their breach is, generally, sanctioned.

Some instruments, most significantly national constitutions, belong to several categories simultaneously; in the case of such constitutions, they are both legal and political documents. Moreover, many sets of rules evolve over the cycles of public life; they begin as political declarations or documents, they are pragmatically transformed into policy instruments, and when the time is appropriate, they are sanctified into statute.

The interaction among these categories of instruments of governance is constant and vibrant.

In this portrait of governmental action and behaviour, the fundamental questions, posed in true interdisciplinary fashion, are to see, as systematically as possible, how the instruments creating the diverse sets of rules interact. Which set of rules guides what aspect of governance in what socio-political circumstances? How do the mutual interactions of the rules affect, or result from, the relations among the Legislative, Executive and Judicial Branches of Government? When, where and how does law prevail? What is the extent of the sway of public administration? How great is the impact of political interests, and the art of the possible, in and on governance?

Instinctive, superficial or cynical responses to the effect that politics and self-interest are forever dominant, are inadequate and insufficient in a study that is both scholarly and practical. Evidence must displace impressionistic beliefs and imprecise reporting.

A more refined aspect of the line of inquiry into the law/public administration/politics interaction is necessary in a system of governance that is democratic. Given that the underlying hypothesis is that law is the foundation of democracy, we must also inquire particularly as to what is the influence and impact of law on public administration and on politics.

Since the incorporation of the *Canadian Charter of Rights and Freedoms* into the Canadian constitutional fabric, many scholars have contributed significantly to a better understanding of Canada by examining the influence of politics on law or on specific aspects of law that are of current interest. In this study, the focus of inquiry is intended to be different in several respects. The scope of the examination involves not only law and politics, but more appropriately for a State with a highly sophisticated and extensive Public Service, the three-way relationship of law, public administration and politics. Moreover, the emphasis is not on the influence of politics on the legal and administrative components of public life, but rather on the mutual impacts of law, policy and politics in general, and in particular on the impact of law on public administration and on politics. Further, the attempt is made to examine the law/public administration/politics relationship both at the macro level, concentrating on the major aspects and functions of governance, as well as at the micro level, in terms of the interaction between and among specific instruments. In all of this, attention will remain on the State as a permanent set of institutions and processes, rather than on specific topics of current interest.

With this intellectual setting in mind, let us declare the precise aims of this volume.

First and foremost, this work seeks to fill a perceptible void in the specialized literature relating to statecraft. There is indeed a need for a Canadian-originated book that is both systematic and comprehensive on the legal aspects of government and politics. In order to accomplish this, the chapter headings follow neither the traditional categorization found in books of law, nor those which would be based on a look at public life on a ministerial portfolio-by-portfolio basis. Rather, the chapter headings here are drawn from a combination of legal, public administration as well as political science criteria. They reflect the institutions and the workings of the legislative, executive and judicial branches of the State all together.

Building on the theories first set out in *The Legal Framework of Government*, I would like to reaffirm that this study, and that indeed this subject-matter of political law, is more than the traditional "law and politics" program and that it even goes beyond the expanded version of "law, policy and politics." In my view, the study of the interaction of these social sciences, and of the influence and impact of law on public administration and on politics is a self-standing subject matter, conceptually situated at the convergence of the individual social sciences that lead into it. Considering that what we are dealing with is the analysis of the rules at play in the conduct of public affairs, this new subject is best entitled "political law," because it is concerned with the various types of binding rules applicable to the conduct of public affairs, most notably with the legally binding rules.

We should no longer be thinking of legal practice in a political environment, or the legal interface with politics, or the legal component of public administration or politics, nor even of legal rules for politics. The objective of this study is to change the perspective on the "rule of law," an aspect of public and especially of constitutional and administrative law, by adding to it the "role of law" as the interdisciplinary expression of those traditional topics.

Having set out in *The Legal Framework of Government* the foundations of this study and having conducted there an enumeration of some of its most notable instruments, I have taken in this book the necessary next step: assembling a collection of judicial and other similar decisions about the conduct of public affairs and about political life, showing the living and constantly evolving nature of the relationships prevailing in political law. These cases of course take account of the traditional categorizations used in treatises of constitutional law and administrative law. However, they are arranged in a manner more deliberately reflective of the interdisciplinary nature of this study. The chapters and the headings within them reflect a combination of legal, public administration and political science criteria. They are intended to illuminate the structure of the State, involving its legislative, executive and judicial functions, as well as the processes of governance and the major aspects of contemporary politics.

By contrast to earlier works on law, public administration and politics, I have cast my search for material wider than at just the final judgments of the senior courts. The practice of political law implies various other sources which, while they may not constitute *res judicata* or precedent in the traditional sense, do illustrate the issues, stresses and strains, and the coordination and conflict among legal, policy and political influences in the course of democratic governance. Thus, I have also included in this book judicial decisions that are unreported because others thought them not sufficiently significant; court cases that may still be pending; yet others that were abandoned or settled; or those in which the pleadings are more revealing than the actual or potential judgment, all with the idea that they are worth saving from a *1984*-like "memory hole" because they can indeed inform student and practitioners of political law. I have also looked at authoritative decisions from other quasi-judicial or quasi-legal sources, where they can contribute to a better understanding of the role of law in governance.

There is a deliberate attempt in this book to apply this method of research to several areas of interest for those studying the State, governance and politics, and which overlap the traditional conceptual boundaries between law and the social sciences related to it. Given the notion that legality is the central pillar of democratic governance, the collection of cases addresses, for example, what are the legal elements of democracy and democratization. Other avenues of exploration opened here deal with the rules, if any, regarding the choices public decision-makers face in selecting the type of instrument most appropriate for specific circumstances in government, and the litigation before the judiciary of issues that are fundamentally more political than legal.

Taking this line of reasoning further, one of the objectives of this book and of the study of political law in general must be the crystallization of the most significant form of accountability that democracy requires of governmental institutions and actors, namely accountability to law. This can more elaborately or more precisely be labelled as "legal accountability to democracy." I see this form of accountability as being intimately related to the constitutional and legal protection of civil and political rights, and their natural counterpoint. I have tried to set out the basic elements of this form of accountability through the most significant recent judgments and other similar decisions about it.

One other intended characteristic of this book needs mentioning. Political law as an aspect of the study of democracy cannot be properly examined in an exclusively jurisdictional mindset. It transcends provincial and national boundaries. The struggle to achieve democracy goes on in many countries and the effort to develop it is universal. Authoritative decisions that are about the subjects within the domain of political law, and that are worthy of attention, thus arise in a multitude of jurisdictions. In a world where globalization prevails not only in business, but also in intellectual ferment, we must be aware that examples drawn from other jurisdictions exert an ever-increasing influence on decision-makers, but also on perceptive practitioners, scholars and observers, despite differences of specifics. An exclusively Canadian framework for this study would therefore be inadequate. Alongside decisions from every Canadian jurisdiction, comparative material from a selection of like-minded countries has been included here. Where rulings from jurisdictions along the path to democracy are instructive, they have been added as well.

The reader may conclude by now, rightly, that this work is not a mere exercise, but that it has become a labour of love. My intention in developing *The Law of Democratic Governing* has been to contribute to the understanding of democracy and to demonstrate that government action, although not exclusively reliant on legality, must be based to an appropriate degree and extent on legality in order to constitute not only what the Canadian constitution entitles "Peace, Order and Good Government," but also to qualify as the democratic governance to which most of the world's peoples aspire. In my opinion no aspect of public affairs could be more interesting, or more meaningful, than this.

Having completed this phase of my exploration of the subject matter, I hope to continue the analysis of political law and its development as a self-standing study among the social sciences dealing with matters of State. I will continue to look at what the instruments dictate and what the actual practice reveals. The methodology for the study of political law has been established and the gathering of the evidence on the practice of political law is under way. I would next like to focus on determining the criteria that engender the impact of law on the conduct of public affairs. Through application of those criteria to ongoing public life, I would also hope to develop a complete perspective for analyzing the role and influence of law in the conduct of public affairs.

Gregory Tardi
Ottawa, August 24, 2004

ACKNOWLEDGEMENTS

I gratefully acknowledge the generosity of the Department of Justice of Canada. Without the assistance of their Grants and Contributions Unit, this book may well have remained a series of unexpressed ideas.

I am similarly indebted to Carol Forde, President of Simcoe Court Reporting, who translated a lengthy and time-consuming manuscript into word-processed text that, by becoming legible, is accessible to the world at large. Her perseverance, advice, and humour have been twelve-fold valuable.

Many colleagues and friends have placed ideas in my mind and documents on my desk, have participated in my classes at the Faculty of Law of McGill University, or have contributed to conferences and meetings of the Political Law Development *Initiative* Inc.; they have all notably improved this project. I would like to mention in particular Gaston Jorré, Senior Deputy Commissioner of Competition; Jason Reiskind, Warren Newman and Gail Sinclair of the Department of Justice; Yvon Tarte, Chair of the Public Service Staff Relations Board; Nathalie DesRosiers, Chair of the Law Commission of Canada; Hon. John Reid, P.C., Canada's Information Commissioner; Professor Sharon Sutherland of the School of Policy Studies at Queen's University, as well as Professor Gilles Paquet of the University of Ottawa; Barbara McIsaac of McCarthy Tétrault; and Benoit Duchesne of Perley-Robertson, Hill & McDougall. I have drawn greatly on the expertise of Professor William C. Banks of the Syracuse University College of Law, to whom I offer particular thanks. I would like to reserve a most notable word of appreciation to Rob Walsh, Law Clerk and Parliamentary Counsel of the House of Commons, who has strengthened this work through his unfailing encouragement and his astute sense that work and study function in tandem.

I am grateful to Dimitra Moudilos, a colleague, for extensive and lightning-fast legal research. At the Library of Parliament, Catherine Green and Irene Brown have been genuinely helpful in finding everything this book needed for completion.

During the time I have spent preparing *Law of Democratic Governing*, I have placed countless calls to parliamentarians, knowledgeable academics, lawyers involved in political litigation and sometimes their clients and court officials. My enquiries were always received with interest and in a spirit conducive to the expansion of knowledge and information. To everyone: Thank You!

My hope is that this book will prove interesting, instructive and especially provocative to all its readers. I thank them most of all!

INVITATION

The law is constantly evolving. With the combined trends of democratization, the legalization of political life in democratic countries and the consequentially increasing importance of accountability to law, as well as the gradual rapprochement among political/legal systems, political law is evolving particularly rapidly.

In this context, the present book requires expansion and updating in order to be relevant and useful to its readers and users.

In preparing this first edition of *Law of Democratic Governing*, I have tried to include both the most important cases that fall into the particular topics of study that come under the umbrella of political law, and a representative sampling of other cases that may be less-well known, but that still contribute to understanding of the linkages and influences at play. Despite my best intentions and dedication to development of this study, no individual alone can capture all significant cases that deserve either mention or analysis in this book.

Readers and users are therefore kindly invited to submit court decisions and other types of political law jurisprudence they believe merit the attention of scholars and practitioners. All such material is hereby gratefully acknowledged in advance.

Please send documents and information to:

Gregory Tardi
President, Political Law Development *Initiative* Inc.
2095 Chalmers Road
Ottawa, Ontario
Canada K1H 6K4

INTRODUCTION

This study presents and explores the linkages among law, public administration and politics that are fundamental to democratic governance. It focuses on the practical interactions among these three social sciences, as well as on the relationships and mutual influences among the various types of instruments of governance that arise from each of them.

Within that context, through the authoritative cases on point, this book sets out those relationships and interactions on the basis of the premises that they are, in turn,

- susceptible to comprehensive as well as detailed observation;
- liable to be characterized as a generally coherent body of practices, behaviours and rules;
- capable of giving rise to discernible criteria of analysis;
- subject to systematic analysis based on those criteria; and
- prone to sustaining general conclusions as to:
  - the nature of the interaction among the subject social sciences,
  - the three-way balance of power among law, public administration and politics, and
  - the quality and extent of the influence of law on public administration and politics.

The subject matter into which all phases and aspects of this analysis are woven together is entitled "political law."

The primary use of political law, the added intellectual value it seeks to assert, is to achieve a better understanding of the role and impact of law in the governance of democratic States.

This conceptual aspect should be publicized in order to inform and influence decision-makers. Deeper and broader understanding of political law can lead to strengthening of the democratic nature of governance in those States that acknowledge that democracy itself is founded upon the rule of law in administrative and political power.

Political scientists, public administrators, participants in political life, and, most of all, lawyers might be surprised by the notion and especially by the title of "political law." This label is indeed less commonly used today than it was in earlier times. It also has less currency in North America than in Europe. Both the concept and the term are valid, nonetheless.

The designation of political law is meant to tie the subject matter to the traditional areas of the legal study of matters relating to statecraft, namely constitutional law and administrative law. In political law, we are dealing with legal matters in the sense that we examine rules, some of which are legal rules, and fundamental ones at that. Rather than remaining within the pure realm of law, however, one of the objectives is to compare and contrast these rules of law with administrative and political rules, notably as to the difference in the binding nature of each type. Hence arises the adjectival part of the designation. The laws and other rules we examine here are all political in that they deal with the structure of the State and the conduct and processes of governance. In this sense, political law is thus also related to non-legal social sciences that analyze statecraft and propose solutions to issues and problems in the conduct of public affairs, namely political science and public administration.

This interdisciplinary perspective on the workings of the State is not without precedent or intellectual heritage. Indeed, its lineage as a modern study of government and governance can be traced back to the Enlightenment. No less a figure than Montesquieu, who analyzed the form of government that arose out of the English Revolution and who was one of the intellectual forebears of both the American and the French Revolutions used, and perhaps even coined the phrase to denote his conception of public life. The best way of rendering Montesquieu's thoughts is to quote him on this point directly and in the original.

CHAPITRE III
Des lois positives

. . .

Ces deux sortes d'états de guerre font établir les lois parmi les hommes.

. . .

Considérés comme vivants dans une société qui doit être maintenue, ils ont des lois dans le rapport qu'ont ceux qui gouvernent avec ceux qui sont gouvernés; et c'est le DROIT POLITIQUE.

. . .

Outre le droit des gens qui regarde toutes les sociétés, il y a un *droit politique* pour chacune. Une société ne saurait subsister sans un gouvernement. *La réunion de toutes les forces particulières*, dit très bien *Gravina*, forme ce qu'on appelle l'ÉTAT POLITIQUE.

. . .

La loi, en général, est la raison humaine, en tant qu'elle gouverne tous les peuples de la terre; et les lois politiques et civiles de chaque nation ne doivent être que les cas particuliers où s'applique cette raison humaine.

. . .

C'est ce que j'entreprends de faire dans cet ouvrage. J'examinerai tous ces rapports : Ils forment tous ensemble ce que l'on appelle l'ESPRIT DES LOIS.

Je n'ai point séparé les lois *politiques* des *civiles*. Car, comme je ne traite point des lois, mais de l'esprit des lois; et que cet esprit consiste dans les divers rapports que les lois peuvent avoir avec diverses choses; j'ai dû moins suivre l'ordre naturel des lois, que celui de ces rapports et de ces choses.

J'examinerai d'abord les rapports que les lois ont avec la nature et avec le principe de chaque gouvernement : et, comme ce principe a sur les lois une suprême influence, je m'attacherai à la bien connaître; et, si je puis une fois l'établir, on en verra couler les lois comme de leur source.[1]

Having acknowledged the intellectual inheritance upon which the modern version of political law that I am developing in this book is based, there is a requirement to set out an appropriate conceptual framework for this topic. This framework begins with a view of Canada as a modern, democratic State founded, as the *Constitution Act, 1982* declared, "upon principles that recognize the supremacy of God" (while retaining nonetheless the secular characteristic of the State) "and the rule of law."

The rule of law and its implicit and explicit links to the notion of democracy imply that the most fundamental type of instrument of governance is the legal kind. The words of the *Constitution Act, 1982,*

---

[1] Montesquieu, *De l'Esprit des Lois* (Collection GF Flammarion, Paris, 1979) at 127-129.

state that, "The Constitution of Canada is the supreme law of Canada. . .."[2] The necessary consequence of this provision is that some legal instruments are more binding than others, which are hierarchically inferior.

The modernity and highly developed nature of the Canadian State imply that in addition to democracy and the rule of law, pluralistic politics, administration and complex bureaucracy, as well as advanced civil society and a highly developed capitalist economy pervade society. Given the multiplicity of actors in, and influences upon, political, legal, social, sociological and economic development, law cannot be the only type of instrument of public governance. It is thus for the sake of conceptualization and ease of classification that I regroup the other types of instruments of public governance under the headings of (1) policies (generally arising from public administration); and (2) political instruments (generally arising from political life and Parliamentary activities). Combining the legal framework of governance with the administrative and political ones on a systemic level, and putting side-by-side the legal instruments of governance with the other two types, we have the basically interdisciplinary elements of a modern view of political law. As is true within the legal category alone, much of the interest of this scheme will be in determining from the evidence which type of rule is more binding in what circumstance. Following in the footsteps of this classical author, it is only natural that political law must, today, be approached not only in an interdisciplinary, but also in a comparative manner. The Canadian system is better understood if it is set out in contrast to that of other like-minded countries, or to that of countries along the path toward democratization.

The chart on the following page best illustrates this view. In this conception, the point of interest is to observe, analyze, appraise and draw conclusions from the centre of the picture, from the point at which law, public administration and politics actually interact in public life.

---

[2] *Constitution Act, 1982*, R.S.C. 1985, App. No. 44, s. 52.

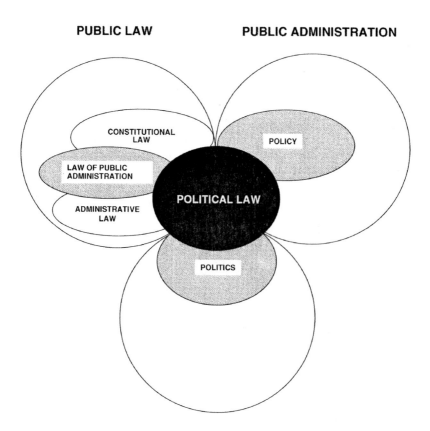

POLITICAL LAW
AND THE RELATED SOCIAL DISCIPLINES

The study of the conduct of public affairs in democratic States that is based on the conceptual framework expressed in the foregoing chart serves two general purposes.

GAINING MORE THOROUGH UNDERSTANDING

Over the centuries, legal scholarship has evolved into specific categories, which are now universally recognized. The main topics of public law are constitutional law and administrative law. Similarly, in the field of political science and its more recent derivative study, public administration, well-accepted ways of analyzing the State and what happens in it have developed. Curiously, the manner in which each and every one of these social sciences has focused on statecraft has left a gap in analysis. The legal aspects of the State and of political life, other than at the level of constitutional and administrative principles and practices, has never been systematically surveyed, or studied in a discrete and comprehensive manner, as a complement to the other social sciences.

Indeed, the evidence demonstrates the need for such a study and the growth of several elements that render such study more possible than ever before. What has been lacking so far is the conscious realization flowing from the evidence; namely that information about, knowledge of, and conclusions based upon, the legal aspects of the State and of political life are not merely disparate, self-standing or occasional items in the news, but that they form a cohesive and consistent body of learning and knowledge that is worth examining in a comprehensive manner.

Some of the elements enabling this type of exercise have been in place for a long time. *Hansard*, the revised and yearly collections of statutes and the law reports are long-standing sources of necessary information. At the highest level, based on section 17 of the statute establishing it,[3] the Supreme Court of Canada has published the reports of its decisions since its inception. In addition to this most traditional method of information, the Court has had an agreement in place with the Cable Parliamentary Channel (CPAC) since April 1994, for the gavel-to-gavel broadcasting of some of its hearings. Moreover, under the leadership of chief justices Dixon, Lamer and now McLaughlin,

---

[3] *Supreme Court Act*, R.S.C. 1985, c. S-26, s. 17.

working in coordination with the Canadian Judicial Council, the Court has adopted new policies on promoting knowledge of its workings, which result in various media interviews with justices.

It is noteworthy that there now exist many more law reports than in earlier decades and thus many more court judgments are readily available for public scrutiny. Some of these deal with elements of political life, even though they are classified under other categories. One has only to extract from all these sources the material relevant to and necessary for this study.

The Internet has, in the most literal sense, put laws, court judgments, as well as other pertinent political and legal information at one's fingertips at a scale unimaginable even a decade ago. The frequent use of sites containing this information is the best evidence of the thirst for knowledge about the legal aspects of public life across all international boundaries.

The somewhat older technology of television, which, for now, is still more widespread and more easily accessible than the Internet, is also an important element in gathering information about political life systematically. On the domestic level, such broadcast undertakings as Newsworld and RDI, and internationally, such global ventures as BBC World, CNN and TV5 all serve to inform and update the global audience about raw news. With their focus on public affairs, they also enable long-term viewers to grasp sufficient information about law and politics to establish patterns of conclusions about the role of law.

The important element in all of this is the general realization, and in particular, the realization by the organs of the State itself, that citizens should have constant and systematic information to become accultured in political and public legal affairs. The best illustration of this kind of realization on the Canadian stage is provided by the recent Public Notice No. 2001-115, in which the Commission announced that it would shortly require that all Canadian viewers be enabled to watch federal parliamentary proceedings live and in their own language.

CRTC TO GIVE CANADIANS ACCESS TO HOUSE OF COMMONS PROCEEDINGS IN OFFICIAL LANGUAGE OF THEIR CHOICE

OTTAWA-HULL — The Canadian Radio-television and Telecommunications Commission (CRTC) intends to make the televised proceedings of the House of Commons more accessible to Canadians in the official language of their choice. In the view of the Commission, this programming is vital to the public interest and an important part of the Canadian broadcast system.

Thanks to the voluntary efforts and monetary contributions of the Canadian broadcast distribution industry, the Cable Public Affairs Channel or CPAC, which carries the House of Commons proceedings, is already available in the language of the majority, to 95% of cable subscribers and over 1 million direct-to-home (DTH) subscribers. The Commission is now codifying what the distributors are already doing and employing a little-used, but largely available technology to enhance service to Canadians in the language of the minority.[4]

Background

1. The Cable Public Affairs Channel (CPAC) is a satellite-to-cable programming undertaking owned by members of the Canadian cable distribution industry. Its programming consists of two main elements: programming provided by the House of Commons Broadcasting Service, and public affairs programming produced by CPAC. The House of Commons programming includes gavel-to-gavel coverage of the proceedings of the House of Commons, and coverage of its various parliamentary committees. The proceedings are provided unedited with no editorial comment. They are available in three audio modes: English, French and "floor" sound (language of originating speaker). Under the terms of its agreement with the House of Commons, when the House is in session, CPAC must carry the proceedings live, and cannot pre-empt the coverage.

. . .

13. The intervention submitted by the Commissioner of Official Languages stated that access to the Debates of the House of Commons is essential to the healthy exercise of democracy, and therefore all Canadians should enjoy equal access to these debates in Canada's two official languages. In the Commissioner's opinion, when the House of Commons chooses to disseminate parliamentary debates by one method or another, it must respect the principle of equal access to the proceedings of Parliament, and the requirement for bilingualism which flows from that. The Commissioner further noted that both an English-language and a French-language version of the proceedings of the House of Commons and its committees should be distributed in an equivalent manner, on two separate television channels.

---

[4] "CRTC to Give Canadians Access to House of Commons Proceedings in Official Language of their Choice" CRTC News Release (6 November 2001).

. . .

27. CPAC's public affairs programming is regarded by the Commission
as a significant and valuable component which complements the proceedings of the House of Commons and its committees. At the same
time, the Commission is of the view that coverage of the proceedings
themselves is primarily what makes CPAC a unique and vital service. It
is this component that is essential to "safeguard, enrich and strengthen
the cultural, political, social and economic fabric of Canada." [*The Broadcasting Act*, s. 3 (1)(d)(i)].

28. Therefore, consistent with its recommendation in the Report, the
Commission has determined that its main objective in this matter should
be ensuring that a majority of Canadians have access to the proceedings
of the House of Commons and its committees, in the official language
of their choice.[5]

Taken together, the doctrinal books and scholarly writings about law,
public administration and politics, which, admittedly, may be of interest only to some readers, when supplemented by all the modern
tools and technologies available to the overwhelming majority of the
citizenry and the electorate, should put into peoples' hands sufficient
information to enable them to acquire the knowledge of the legal
aspects of public life that have been left unexplored by traditional
fields of study.

In *Reference re Secession of Quebec*,[6] the Supreme Court of Canada
informed us about the constitutional principles breathing life into the
present-day public and political life of Canada. In the federal general
election immediately following thereafter on November 27, 2000,[7] the
principal slogan of the Liberal Party of Canada, in office both before
and after the election, was "Canadian values." It does not appear an
exaggeration that these Canadian constitutional principles and the
remarkably similar Canadian values can achieve their full meaning
and relevance in the democratic sense only if the population, the
citizenry and the electorate become sufficiently aware and knowledgeable about their government, and in particular if they gain some
familiarity with the legal underpinning of that government, fulfilling
the maxim that bases democracy on the rule of law.

---

[5] "The distribution of the proceedings of the House of Commons" CRTC Public Notice
2001-115 (6 November 2001).

[6] (1998), 161 D.L.R. (4th) 385 (S.C.C.).

[7] 37th federal general election.

In these circumstances, where vast amounts of information about the legal aspects of the State and the legal components of governance are available, the task of a book such as this one are to define and refine the concept of political law, to organize it and structure it so that it may best be understood, and to develop the analytical framework for the best use of this information.

By contrast to the other domains of study to which we have already alluded, political law focuses on the precise subject matters that deal with the law/public administration/politics relationship illustrated at the centre of the chart that appears on page xxv above:

- the definition of the legal concept of democracy and the legal aspects of democratization;
- electoral processes and the life-cycle of political parties;
- the choice of instruments for governing;
- the balance of law and politics in legislative institutions and processes;
- the precedence of law and its accommodation with other types of instruments in government institutions and management;
- the litigation of State issues that are primarily political;
- the relative weight of legal and political influences in the adjudication of judicial disputes on matters of public governance; and
- the accountability to law of public officials and public institutions, as a democratic counterpart to civil and political rights.

These topics, in sum, can be collectively characterized as dealing with the role of law in the State. The systematic analysis of these subjects is particularly timely when, throughout the democratic world, there is a trend toward the legalization and judicialization of public life.

The next step on the Cartesian path to making political law usefully informative is to develop, based on the evidence gathered in all of the specialized subjects listed above, a general framework for the analysis of legality in democratic governance. This framework must include, first, a number of authoritative and objective criteria, which suitably blend political and legal considerations:

- the doctrine of democracy;
- constitutional principles;
- the inherent characteristics of law, namely its independence from politics and its autonomously binding nature;

- legislation and other legislative instruments;
- jurisprudence;
- the concept of *"raison de droit,"* as a counterbalance to *"raison d'État."*

The analytical framework must also take account of a second set of criteria, which, by contrast to the first, are discretionary and subjective:

- the agreement and acceptance of the rule of law by State officials;
- the public interest;
- politics;
- public opinion and attitudes;
- ideology and currently held public beliefs;
- education;
- governmental experience;
- managerial and administrative convenience and necessity;
- efficiency, effectiveness and economy in government; and
- *raison d'État.*

In order to develop the most comprehensive yet precise framework of analysis possible for legality in democratic governance, bearing in mind that we are within the realm of the social and not the exact sciences, these two sets of criteria need to be synthesized into a notion of legal legitimacy.

If political law can contribute something to the more thorough understanding of the State and of governance, it is the notion of an accountability to law and it is this form of analysis of legality.

While better understanding can be a benefit in itself, the translation of political law from an albeit interesting, but academic, exercise to a live influence in democratic public life would be its greatest contribution. This topic, and this book, should therefore be of particular interest and benefit to those active in government, whether elected, appointed to administer, or providing legal advice to members of the other two groups.

INDUCING BETTER GOVERNMENT

Legal training and the practice of law are not prerequisites for parliamentary life or public service. It is undeniable, however, that in every domain of statecraft, knowledge of legal principles is an indispensable and irreplaceable advantage. In no system of governance is this more true than in democracy, where the rule of law prevails; where Parliament, National Assembly, Legislative Assembly or Congress speaks through legal texts; where the courts interpret the substance of those texts and determine legal and political consequences that must necessarily flow from them; and where the government and the public service must, and generally speaking do, act primarily on the basis of those texts.

Where legal knowledge, awareness and experience are beneficial, the additional inspiration of political law can be even more salutary in providing public actors expertise in managing and developing those organs of the State that are placed in their trust.

The analysis of the relationship among diverse types of instruments and the use of a framework for realizing legality can first be of concrete assistance by informing the relations among the legislative, executive and judicial branches of government. The best characterization of the separation of governmental powers among these branches is that set out in Bradley's *Constitutional and Administrative Law*:

Meaning of separation of powers

As the strong contrast between the United States and France shows, the doctrine of separation of powers has a variety of meanings. The concept of "separation" may mean at least three different things:

(a) that the same persons should not form part of more than one of the three organs of government, for example that ministers should not sit in Parliament;

(b) that one organ of government should not control or interfere with the work of another, for example, that the judiciary should be independent of the executive;

(c) that one organ of government should not exercise the functions of another, for example, that ministers should not have legislative powers.

In considering each of these aspects of separation, it needs to be remembered that complete separation of powers is possible neither in theory nor in practice.[8]

The categories of membership in institutions, control of institutions and exercise of powers have particular meaning in the Canadian context, as long as we remember that our particular variation of the doctrine is best defined as distinction of functions, rather than being similar to the American model of more formal separation of powers with checks and balances.

Attention to political law can induce in members of each branch of government better decision-making, by providing them both context and substantive knowledge of the articulations of, and centrifugal and centripetal forces in, the system of government in which they have to carry out their respective functions.

The legislative branch functions in an atmosphere where political and partisan criteria prevail, but are framed by legal considerations. Its relations with the executive highlight the balance of power between politics and administrative policies. The current type of controversy here relates to the relevance of Parliament *vis-à-vis* the notable rise in the power of the executive and in particular the Prime Minister and the Prime Minister's Office.

The executive branch functions in an atmosphere where administrative priorities dominate, but they are circumscribed and even directed by political and legal considerations. Its relations with the judiciary highlight the balance of power between policies and jurisprudence, which is in fact the subjection of policies based on administrative benefit to legal norms arising from court judgments. The current topics of interest here relate to the degree and extent of the independence of the judiciary, the safeguarding of judges from instruction or interference by ministers, and the extent to which judges can or should issue law-mandated instructions as to how public administration should be conducted.

---

[8] E.C.S. Wade and A. W. Bradley, *Constitutional and Administrative Law*, 11th edition, edited by A. W. Bradley and K. D. Ewing (London and New York: Longman, 1995) at 58.

The judicial branch functions in an atmosphere where constitutional and legal considerations are the only valid ones, but where, in reality, the judges take some note of the political and administrative facts and circumstances and may even allow themselves to be influenced by them. Its relations with the legislative are the most intense of the three sets of relations in this Montesquieuan scheme, especially in the era of the *Charter*. This set of relations highlights the balance of power between law and politics, which is in fact the degree and extent of the subjection of politics to constitutional and legal norms. The current theory of interest here is the Hoggian dialogue between Parliament and the Supreme Court and the current topics of practical interest are the numerous instances of that dialogue. These range from the most basic, such as the questioning in some political and geographic quarters of Canada, of the validity of judicial review of legislation, to the actual *renvoi* between Parliament and the senior courts of various provisions dealing with statecraft and politics.

Preoccupation with political law also serves to examine and explain the nature and quality of the supremacy of legal norms over administrative and political ones, and hence the primacy of legal instruments over all the other ones used in governance. The supremacy of law needs to be explained, clarified and emphasized in order to influence decision-makers of all professions and in order to ensure that governance remains within its democratic and rule of law parameters. Such explanations would help counteract the fact that while law is not the required training for political life or the occupation of administrative functions, legal thinking and motivation seem not to be necessarily the prime factor in the actions. This is true for politicians and public administrators who are lawyers, and perhaps in some cases even of practicing government lawyers.

The most direct and most expressive explanation of this doctrine of supremacy is not found in a Canadian text, but in the writings of the French professor of administrative science, Charles Debbasch.

SECTION III – L'influence du système de droit

53. – Système de droit et système administratif. – Le pouvoir de l'administration dépend du système juridique dans lequel elle se trouve insérée. Les règles de droit définissent les prérogatives et les contraintes de l'administration, les principes de son organisation. Toute administration se trouve enserrée dans une réglementation juridique, formulation des principes du pouvoir politique. Ce système juridique peut être simplement un aménagement du fonctionnement *interne* de l'administration : en ce sens, il n'intéresse pas le problème du pouvoir de l'administration dans ses relations avec la société mais seulement la répartition du pouvoir à l'intérieur de la machine administrative. Le système de droit peut, au contraire, définir les principes régissant les *relations* de l'administration avec les citoyens, il s'agit d'une des données fondamentales du pouvoir de l'administration.

1. – La soumission au droit

54. – Le principe de légalité. – La soumission de l'administration à des règles de droit préétablies constitue un principe fondamental de l'État libéral. À l'inverse de la situation de l'État de police où l'administration est totalement libre de son action, l'État libéral est un État de droit. Les administrés disposent de droits à l'égard de l'administration et ils ont notamment le droit d'exiger que celle-ci respect les règles de droit en vigueur, principalement par l'exercice de recours juridictionnels. Les particuliers ont ainsi la garantie que l'action administrative sera conduite objectivement et non avec partialité. Dans la pratique, le principe de légalité n'est pas admis dans les pays révolutionnaires, il se trouve fortement cantonné, à l'époque actuelle, dans les démocraties libérales.

. . .

56. – 2e Démocraties libérales et légalité. – La conception de la légalité retenue à l'origine par les démocraties libérales est singulièrement restrictive. Elle signifie l'obligation pour l'administration de respecter la loi. Celle-ci apparaît comme une garantie nécessaire et suffisante de la soumission de l'administration au droit. Cette conception s'explique par la traditionnelle foi dans la loi, incarnation de la volonté générale. Elle s'appuie, également, sur l'impossibilité pour l'administration, instrument du pouvoir exécutif, de modifier la loi, fruit du Parlement. Le principe de légalité est ainsi le moyen de réaliser la subordination de l'administration au Parlement et, par là même, de protéger les citoyens contre les initiatives arbitraires de l'administration. Progressivement, la notion de légalité s'est *étendue*. Elle couvre aujourd'hui, l'ensemble des règles juridiques *y compris celles qui sont élaborées par l'administration elle-même*. Cette extension a eu à la fois des conséquences heureuses et néfastes. Elle a, tout d'abord, enrichi la légalité et, à ce titre, elle a permis que l'extension du pouvoir de réglementation autonome de l'administration ne ruine pas le principe de légalité. L'administration est soumise aussi bien au droit qu'elle forge qu'à celui élaboré par le Parlement. Elle a cependant masqué la différence de situation entre la subordination de l'administration à la loi et la subordination de l'administration aux règles édictées par elle-même. La première est *absolue*, la légalité étant extérieure à l'administration. La seconde est *relative*, l'administration auteur des règles détenant le pouvoir de les mod-

xxxviii / LAW OF DEMOCRATIC GOVERNING – VOLUME II: JURISPRUDENCE

ifier, la sécurité juridique est moins grande que dans un système de légalité *stricto sensu.*[9]

No matter the origin of the text, the thoughts set out here apply forcefully in the Canadian context, as they do for all other democratic States. Even, or perhaps especially, those parliamentarians and political figures who are elected in order to enact a specific program or to obtain particular results in public policy need to take account of these lines.

A further and extremely significant use of political law as a midwife of improved and more democratic governance is the popularization of the doctrine of accountability to law.

The evolution of democracy over the last half century has put attitudes to law into the sharpest contrast possible. On one hand are acquiescent public and political attitudes that the State and society should achieve political goals desired by leaders of the State apparatus, parties, factions or minority groupings within society organized for political victory, or merely the acquiescent masses of the people in general. In counterpoint one finds attitudes to the effect that society should act rightly, observing the humanity and dignity of as many as possible, whether such collective behaviour enables society to achieve defined ideological goals or not. The essence of democracies is that in their political lives, they have gradually replaced the notion of "might is right" with that of "collective political morality is right." In substance as well as in process, legality is the best vehicle for collective moral behaviour.

Along this path of socio-political development, the founding of the United Nations, the Nuremberg judgments, the incorporation of the *Canadian Charter of Rights and Freedoms* into the Canadian constitutional fabric, the adoption of various provincial bills of rights, the fall of Communism, and most recently the Pinochet judgments of the House of Lords, the establishment of the International Criminal Court as well as the eventual Milosevic judgment (in the expectation of his condemnation at the time of writing), are part of the same process of increasing the strength of legal principles in political life, to the det-

---

[9] Charles Debbasch, *Science Administrative: Administration publique* (Paris: Préciz Dalloz, 1980) at 65-66.

riment of the use of raw, unbridled political power against the very people that governments oversee.

We, observers, and more to the point, the political actors, must draw the inevitable conclusion from this trend. Political figures owe more than a political accountability to their electorates or to the political formations from which they draw their power. Similarly, public administrators in the service of their political masters owe more than mere bureaucratic, financial and administrative accountabilities to their respective hierarchies. Along with the judges and lawyers in the service of the public, they all are accountable to the law in the largest sense of that expression, including the principles arising from the constitution, statutes and court rulings. This accountability is the positive duty counterpart of the defence of human rights. Those in public life have the duty to avoid harming the human rights of citizens and electors; going beyond that, they have the positive obligation to abide by the law regarding the political and civic lives of their peoples. Nothing short of recognizing this form of accountability helps to ensure the democratic rule of law.

To date, this form of accountability has been expressed and applied by various courts but has not yet been codified in law. Such codification may not be far off, however. In a Private Member's Bill in the United Kingdom House of Commons,[10] the Labour M.P. and constitutional campaigner Graham Allen has attempted to codify the position of Prime Minister of his country. For purposes of our discussion, the most significant provision of this Bill deals with accountability to law and reads as follows:

8 Duty to behave lawfully

Nothing in this Act shall empower the Prime Minister, or any person acting under his authority, to disregard any provision of the Human Rights Act 1998, or any obligation under international law or treaty, under common law or equity or any other obligation to behave justly, fairly, reasonably and lawfully, or any published rules for the time being in force for ministers or civil servants in the conduct of public life, or to act in contempt of any resolution of the House of Commons.[11]

---

[10] *Prime Minister (Office, Role and Functions) Bill*, Bill 60, November 28, 2001.
[11] *Ibid.*, s. 8.

Mindful of the 1867-based rule that Canada has "a Constitution similar in Principle to that of the United Kingdom,"[12] with the necessary translations *mutatis mutandis*, this provision has enormous significance as a model for Canada especially, but also more generally for other democratic States. Notwithstanding that the British constitutional tradition against explicit statutory definition of the roles of senior officers of the State renders it unlikely that this Bill will be adopted, its service to the cause of defining accountability to law is great. The notable difference between this provision and that contained in the 1982 Canadian *Charter* is that while section 52 of the *Charter* deals only with the hierarchy among provisions of a constitutional and legal nature, Bill 60 in the United Kingdom ensures by codification the supremacy of legal norms over other types of instruments, including those arising from public administration and politics, in the work of the Prime Minister. Neither the Canadian *Charter*, nor Bill C-60 of 1978,[13] the last major pre-*Charter* constitutional amendment legislative proposal, went that far.

To what outcome should more thorough understanding and the inducement of more democratic governance bring us? The evidence of the last decade includes democratization as well as the inescapability of the linkage of democracy to legality.

In the most recent months, following the attack of September 11, 2001, political evolution in democratic States has shown first that in democracy, there is no alternative to government, notwithstanding passing phases of anti-Statism. With equal strength, events have demonstrated that in democracy, there is no alternative to legality in government. All democratic States have come face-to-face in the current crisis with the two ultimate ironies of democracy. Domestically, they have had to confront the question: "to what extent should democratic States use undemocratic methods in the defence of democracy, while seeking to retain their democratic nature?" Internationally, they have had to see "to what extent should or can democratic States attempt to export and implant democracy without resorting to means that threaten their democratic quality?"

The age-old dilemmas of democratic governance as well as these new ironies all point to the development, hopefully with the added assis-

---

[12] *Constitution Act, 1867*, R.S.C. 1985, App. No. 5, Preamble.
[13] *Constitutional Amendment Bill*, Bill C-60, First Reading, June 20, 1978.

tance that the study of political law can contribute, of a legal, political culture.

Summary Outline

1. DEFINITION OF THE BASIC CONCEPTS OF POLITICAL LAW

2. RELATION OF, AND RELATIVE INFLUENCE AMONG, LAW, POLICY AND POLITICS

3. LEGAL ELEMENTS OF DEMOCRACY

4. SOVEREIGNTY, LEGITIMACY AND GOVERNANCE

5. ELECTIONS

6. PARTIES, CAMPAIGNING AND POLITICAL PROMISES

7. CHOICE OF THE APPROPRIATE INSTRUMENT FOR GOVERNANCE

8. INTEGRITY OF THE LEGISLATIVE SYSTEM

9. LEGALITY IN GOVERNMENTAL MANAGEMENT

10. LITIGATION OF POLITICAL LAW ISSUES

11. LEGAL ACCOUNTABILITY TO DEMOCRACY

TABLE OF CONTENTS

LAW REPORTS v

FOREWORD ix

PREFACE xiii

ACKNOWLEDGMENTS xix

INVITATION xxi

INTRODUCTION xxiii

1. DEFINITION OF THE BASIC CONCEPTS OF POLITICAL LAW

1.1	General Principles	1
1.2	Constitution; "Constitution of Canada"	1
1.3	Law	8
	1.3.A—Definition of "Law"	8
	1.3.B—Rule of Law	22
	1.3.C—"Prescribed by Law"	22
	1.3.D—"Laws of Canada"	23
1.4	Public Law	27
1.5	Public Interest	30
1.6	Public Interest in Law	33
1.7	Justice	33
1.8	Policy	34
	1.8.A—Definition of Policy	34
	1.8.B—Characterization of Policy	35
	1.8.C—Policy Issues	50
	1.8.D—Varieties of Policy	50
	1.8.E—Guidelines	51
	1.8.F—Directives	51
1.9	Public Policy	52
1.10	Public Convenience and General Policy	58

1.11   Politics   58
1.12   Constitutional Convention   72
1.13   Government   76
        1.13.A—Definition of Government   76
        1.13.B—Branches of Government and
                Separation of Powers   89
1.14   Governmental Function, Government Action or
        Decision   89
1.15   Government Official   105
1.16   Public Sector   105
1.17   Public Authority   107
1.18   Public Service   107
1.19   Public Purpose   107
1.20   Political Trust   108
1.21   Uncertainty in the Characterization of
        Instruments: Is it Law, Policy or Politics?   109

2.   RELATION OF, AND RELATIVE INFLUENCE AMONG, LAW, POLICY AND POLITICS

2.1   General Principles   113
2.2   Law and Policy   113
       2.2.A—Authority to Create Policy Instruments ...   113
       2.2.B—Consistency of Policy Instruments with
               Constitutional Norms   114
       2.2.C—Application of Legal Norms to Policy
               Instruments   118
       2.2.D—Consistency of Legal Instruments with
               Public Policy   120
       2.2.E—Supremacy of Legal Norms Over Policy
               Instruments in Matters of Public
               Administration   121
       2.2.F—Supremacy of Legal Norms Over Policy
               Instruments in Criminal Matters   140
       2.2.G—Policy Instruments Inconsistent with
               Legal Norms   141
       2.2.H—Absence of Legal Norms Underlying
               Policy Instruments   143
       2.2.I—Absence of Policy Implying Resort to Law
                 144
2.3   Law and Policy Discretion   148
2.4   Law and Politics   148

2.5	Law and Political Science	....	177
2.6	Policy and Politics	....	177
2.7	Law, Policy and Politics	....	181

3. LEGAL ELEMENTS OF DEMOCRACY

3.1	General Principles	....	185
3.2	Recognition of the Democratic Nature of Canada		
		....	185
3.3	Consensus on the Political/Legal Regime	....	188
	3.3.A—Canada's Form of Government	....	188
	3.3.B —Canadian Unity and Sovereignty	....	198
	3.3.C—Inclusion of Aboriginals in Canadian		
	Statehood	....	208
3.4	Constitutionalism, Rule of Law, Legal System		
	Based on Fundamental Rights	....	219
3.5	Separation of Government and Party,		
	Multipartyism	....	223
3.6	Representative Democracy, Free and Fair		
	Electoral System and Administration	....	226
3.7	Leadership in Governance Through an Integral		
	Legislative System	....	243
3.8	Judiciary Independent of Political Influences	.....	247
3.9	Balance between the Legislative and Judicial		
	Branches	....	252
3.10	Particular Role of the Minister of Justice/		
	Attorney General Within Cabinet	....	259
3.11	Apolitical Criminal Law, Objective Prosecutorial		
	Authority	....	282
3.12	Non-Partisan Public Service and Armed Forces	..	287
	3.12.A—Candidacy of Public Servants for		
	Political Office	....	287
	3.12.B —Public Expression of Political Opinion		
	by Public Servants and Military		
	Personnel	....	291
	3.12.C—Incitement of Public Servants to Take		
	Political Positions	....	299
	3.12.D—Political Aspects of Public Servants'		
	Union Activities	....	302
3.13	Public Access to State Records and Proceedings		
		....	303
3.14	Impartial and Unfettered News Media	....	305

3.15   Foreign Relations Based on Popular Legitimacy
....   314
3.16   Acknowledgment of the Democratic Nature of a
Foreign Country   318
3.17   The Dilemmas of Democracy   323
3.17.A—The Internal Dilemma: The Trade-off
Between Human Rights for Domestic
Enemies of Democracy and National
Security   323
3.17.B —The External Dilemma: The Trade-off
Between the Export of Democratic Ideas
and the Forceful Imposition of
Democratic Institutions   323

4. SOVEREIGNTY, LEGITIMACY AND GOVERNANCE

4.1   General Principles   325
4.2   Characterization of "Canada"   325
4.3   Defence of Sovereignty by the State   335
4.4   Debate of Sovereignty Issues by Citizens   342
4.5   Limitation of Sovereignty   366
4.6   Legitimacy of a New Political / Legal Regime   367
4.7   Legitimacy of New Governmental Institutions ...   383
4.8   Formation and Composition of Governments
and Oppositions   389
4.9   Dismissal and Dissolution of Governments   394
4.10   Participation in Public Life   399
4.11   Legal Expression of the Expansion of the
Canadian Polity   416
4.11.A—Terms of Union with British Columbia
in 1871   416
4.11.B —Terms of Union with Prince Edward
Island in 1873   420
4.11.C—Terms of Union with Newfoundland in
1949   425
4.12   Principles of Constitutional Development   430
4.13   Latest Attempts at Constitutional Reform   433
4.13.A—Patriation   433
4.13.B —Meech Lake Accord   437
4.13.C—Charlottetown Accord   451
4.13.D—Senate Reform   458

5. ELECTIONS

5.1 General Principles 467
5.2 Electoral Systems, the Meaning of "Election"
and Political Representation 467
5.3 Drawing Electoral Boundaries 475
5.4 Valuation of the Right to Vote 497
5.5 Inclusion for Participation in the Electoral
Process 500
    5.5.A—Voting 500
    5.5.B—Candidacy for Office 505
    5.5.C—Incurring Election Expenses 511
5.6 Restraints on Participation in the Electoral
Process 518
5.7 Exclusion from Participation in the Electoral
Process 518
    5.7.A—Exclusion of Parties, Party Leaders and
Candidates 518
    5.7.B—Exclusion of Third Parties 519
5.8 Political Broadcasting and Advertising 526
5.9 Party Leaders' and Candidates' Debates 535
5.10 Public Opinion Polling 565
5.11 Integrity of Voting 567
5.12 Suspending Elections 567
5.13 Political Interference in Election Results 571

6. PARTIES, CAMPAIGNING AND POLITICAL PROMISES

6.1 General Principles 575
6.2 Legal Personality, Status and Powers of Political
Parties 575
6.3 Public and Proprietary Rights in a Political
Designation 587
6.4 Selection of Party Leadership and Candidates 594
    6.4.A—Party Leadership 594
    6.4.B—Candidates 601
6.5 Campaigning by Political Parties, Candidates
and Referendum Committees 613
6.6 Political Discourse and Rhetoric 616
    6.6.A—Characterization of Political Speech 616
    6.6.B—Political Speech About Public Servants ... 616
    6.6.C—Political Speech About Political Figures .. 616

6.6.D—Political Speech By Political Figures
About Each Other 629
6.6.E—Political Speech By Political Figures
About Third Parties 641
6.6.F—Political Speech of a Criminal Nature 641
6.7 Political Promises 642
6.7.A—Election Campaign Promises 642
6.7.B —Political Promises Made Otherwise than
in a Campaign 670
6.8 Variations of Political Allegiance 680
6.8.A—Changes of Individuals' Party Allegiance
.... 680
6.8.B —Merger of Parties 683
6.9 Political Books, Documents and Memoirs 691

7. CHOICE OF THE APPROPRIATE INSTRUMENT FOR
GOVERNANCE

7.1 General Principles 693
7.2 Constitutional Requirement to Legislate 693
7.3 Requirement to Use Legislation as the Proper
Instrument 696
7.4 Appropriate Instances for the Use of Legislation
as the Proper Instrument 701
7.5 Appropriate Instances for the Use of Policy as
the Proper Instrument 704
7.6 Appropriate Instances for the Use of a Program
as the Proper Instrument 706
7.7 Appropriate Instances for the Use of Politics as
the Proper Instrument 708

8. INTEGRITY OF THE LEGISLATIVE SYSTEM

8.1 General Principles 711
8.2 Legal Personality, Status and Powers of
Parliament 711
8.2.A—Parliament as a Whole 711
8.2.B —Senate 713
8.2.C—House of Commons 719
8.3 Protection of Legislative Institutions and
Legislators 725
8.4 Privilege: The Regime of Rules Applicable to
Parliamentary Bodies and Parliamentarians 743

8.5	Membership in Parliamentary Bodies	....	744
8.6	Work of the Legislative Branch	....	758
8.7	Unfettered Nature of the Legislative Process from Policy and Politics	....	778
8.8	Validity of the Legislative Process	....	785
8.9	Maintaining Invalid Legislation for Public Policy Purposes	....	795
8.10	Legal Support for the Work of Legislators	....	798
8.11	Employees of Parliament	....	802

9. LEGALITY IN GOVERNMENTAL MANAGEMENT

9.1	General Principles	....	803
9.2	Legal Personality, Status and Powers of Government Departments	....	803
9.3	Implementation of Government Policy Within Law	....	809
	9.3.A—Legally Valid Management	....	809
	9.3.B —Maladministration/Malfeasance/ Misfeasance; Abuse of Power; Breach of Trust by Public Officials	....	817
9.4	Legality in the Management of the Machinery of Government	....	818
9.5	Political Interference in State Appointments and Dismissals	....	835
9.6	Political Interference in Public Services	....	853
9.7	Legality in the Management of Social Policy	......	862
9.8	Legality in the Management of Economic Policy	....	865
	9.8.A—Major Economic Issues	....	865
	9.8.B —Government Contracting	....	879
9.9	Legality in the Management of Foreign Policy, Defence and Security	....	881
	9.9.A—National Boundaries and the National Interest	....	881
	9.9.B —Foreign Policy	....	884
	9.9.C—National Defence, Peace-Keeping and War	....	898
	9.9.D—Public Security	....	907
9.10	Legality in the Management of International Trade and Aid	....	908
	9.10.A—Bilateral and Multilateral Trade	....	908

| | 9.10.B —International Assistance and Assisted Export | 910 |
| 9.11 | Legality in the Management of the Financing of Government | 911 |

10. LITIGATION OF POLITICAL LAW ISSUES

10.1	General Principles	919
10.2	The Politically Neutral Nature of Judicial Functions	919
10.3	The Nature of Litigation	922
10.4	The Decision Whether to Initiate Litigation in Political Matters	923
10.5	The Decision Whether to Defend Litigation in Political Matters	934
10.6	Judicial Notice of Political Facts, Parliamentary Speeches and Public Administration	937
10.7	Use of Litigation for Political and Partisan Purposes	937
10.8	Litigation of Primarily Political and Partisan Issues	954
10.9	Reporting on Events and Figures in Political Life	980
10.10	Political Trials: Criminal Trials Based on Politically Motivated Offences	1000
10.11	Political Trials: Criminal Trials Based on Politically Motivated Defences	1009
10.12	Political Involvement in the Prosecution of Criminal Offences	1017
10.13	Use of Prosecution for Political and Partisan Motives	1026
10.14	Testimony by Political Figures in Litigation and in Trials	1030

11. LEGAL ACCOUNTABILITY TO DEMOCRACY

11.1	General Principles	1031
11.2	The Doctrine of Accountability to Law	1031
	11.2.A—The General Concept of Accountability to Law	1031
	11.2.B —Willingness to Abide by the Law	1032
	11.2.C—Willful Desire to Respect and Apply the Law	1034

11.3	Obligation of Public Servants to Observe Legal Norms	1036
	11.3.A—Subjection of Public Servants to Domestic Legal Norms	1036
	11.3.B —Subjection of Public Servants to Foreign Legal Norms	1046
	11.3.C—Subjection of Public Servants to Norms of International Law	1049
11.4	Professional Ethics of Public Servants	1049
11.5	Obligation of Parliamentarians to Observe Legal Norms	1051
11.6	Professional Ethics of Parliamentarians	1056
11.7	Obligation of Members of the Executive Government to Observe Legal Norms	1058
11.8	Professional Ethics of Members of the Executive Government	1072
11.9	Obligation of Heads of State and Government to Observe Legal Norms	1106
	11.9.A—Subjection of Heads of State and Government to Domestic Law	1106
	11.9.B —Subjection of Heads of State and Government to Foreign Law	1123
	11.9.C—Subjection of Heads of State and Government to International Law	1132
11.10	Professional Ethics of Heads of State, Government and International Institutions	1142
11.11	Obligation of Government to Observe Legal Norms	1169
	11.11.A—Prevalence of Legal Norms Over Other Written Norms	1169
	11.11.B —Application of Legal Norms Even in the Absence of Texts: «Principes Généraux du Droit»	1169
	11.11.C—Prevalence of Legal Norms Over Political Interests	1169
	11.11.D—Application of Domestic Legal Writ to Foreign Governments	1170
11.12	Difference Between Private Legal Obligation and Public Accountability to Law	1170
11.13	Political Unpopularity of Legal Norms	1172
11.14	Role of Lawyers in Government	1181

11.15   State Support for Public Participation in the
         Political/Legal System 1214

INDEX 1217

TABLE OF CASES

[Cases and other references appearing in **bold** are discussed in detail in this volume.]

2003 Extra-Parliamentary Ontario Budget Process, **Legal Opinions Submitted to the Government House Leader and to the Speaker of the Legislative Assembly** 766

A.U.P.E. v. Alberta (1996), 46 Alta. L.R. (3d) 44, 1996 CarswellAlta 940, [1996] A.J. No. 1060, 41 Admin. L.R. (2d) 33, 197 A.R. 1 (Alta. Q.B.) 829

Aaron v. Bouchard, Ontario Court (General Division), filed November 17, 1993, file no. 93-44891-CP, abandoned 342

Ability of President Color de Mello to be a candidate, Supreme Court of Brazil, December 3, 1997 518

Action by Agreement Democratic Unionist Party, [2001] NIEHC, November 5, 2001 393

Adams v. Clinton 475

Adbusters Media Foundation v. Canadian Broadcasting Corp. (1995), 13 B.C.L.R. (3d) 265, 1995 CarswellBC 953, [1996] 2 W.W.R. 698 (B.C. S.C.), affirmed (1997), 1997 CarswellBC 2376, 154 D.L.R. (4th) 404, 99 B.C.A.C. 19, 162 W.A.C. 19, 49 C.R.R. (2d) 168 (B.C. C.A.), leave to appeal refused (1998), 51 C.R.R. (2d) 188 (note), 227 N.R. 289 (note), 119 B.C.A.C. 319 (note), 194 W.A.C. 319 (note) (S.C.C.) 305

Adler v. Ontario, [1996] 3 S.C.R. 609, 1996 CarswellOnt 3989, 1996 CarswellOnt 3990, 30 O.R. (3d) 642 (note), 204 N.R. 81, 95 O.A.C. 1, 140 D.L.R. (4th) 385, 40 C.R.R. (2d) 1 (S.C.C.) 98

Affaire Demoiselle Arbouset, Conseil d'État, le 2 mars 1973 1169

Affaire Fédération nationale des syndicats de police, Conseil d'État, le 24 novembre 1961 1169

Affaire Syndicat général des ingénieurs-conseils, Conseil d'État, le 26 février 1959 1169

AFL-CIOV v. March Fong Eu, 686 P.2d 609 (Cal., 1984) 781

Ahenakew v. MacKay (2004), 235 D.L.R. (4th) 371, 2003 CarswellOnt 4930, [2003] O.J. No. 4821, 68 O.R. (3d) 277 (Ont. S.C.J.), additional reasons at (2004), 2004 CarswellOnt 1641 (Ont. S.C.J.), affirmed (2004), 2004 CarswellOnt 2246 (Ont. C.A.) 683

Aiken v. Ontario (Premier) (1999), 177 D.L.R. (4th) 489, [1999] O.J. No. 2866, 1999 CarswellOnt 2359, 45 O.R. (3d) 266 (Ont. S.C.J.) 641

Ainsley Financial Corp. v. Ontario (Securities Commission) **(1994), 121 D.L.R. (4th) 79, [1994] O.J. No. 2966, 1994 CarswellOnt 1021, 18 O.S.C.B. 43, 21 O.R. (3d) 104, 77 O.A.C. 155, 6 C.C.L.S. 241, 28 Admin. L.R. (2d) 1 (Ont. C.A.)** 45

Ainsworth Lumber Co. v. Canada (Attorney General), 85 B.C.L.R. (3d) 62, 2001 CarswellBC 278, [2001] B.C.J. No. 255, 2001 BCCA 105, 2001 D.T.C. 5136, 1 C.P.C. (5th) 49, 149 B.C.A.C. 263, 244 W.A.C. 263 (B.C. C.A.), reversing 2000 BCSC 1399, 2000 CarswellBC 1893, [2000] 4 C.T.C. 205 (B.C. S.C. [In Chambers]) 779

Air Canada v. British Columbia (Attorney General) (1986), [1986] 2 S.C.R. 539, 1986 CarswellBC 369, 1986 CarswellBC 762, [1987] 1 W.W.R. 304, 32 D.L.R. (4th) 1, 72 N.R. 135, 8 B.C.L.R. (2d) 273, 22 Admin. L.R. 153 (S.C.C.) 263

Akins v. Federal Election Commission, 141 L.Ed.2d 10 (1998) 72

Alberta Government Telephones v. Canada (Radio-Television & Telecommunications Commission), [1989] 2 S.C.R. 225, 1989 CarswellNat 699, 1989 CarswellNat 758, [1989] 5 W.W.R. 385, 61 D.L.R. (4th) 193, 98 N.R. 161, 68 Alta. L.R. (2d) 1, 26 C.P.R. (3d) 289 (S.C.C.) 848

Alberta Teachers' Assn. v. Alberta, 1 Alta. L.R. (4th) 361, 2002 CarswellAlta 300, 2002 ABQB 240, [2002] 6 W.W.R. 347, 40 Admin. L.R. (3d) 309, 310 A.R. 89 (Alta. Q.B.) 277, 1169

Alden v. Maine, 144 L.Ed.2d 636 (1999) 342

Aleksic v. Canada (Attorney General) (2002), 215 D.L.R. (4th) 720, 2002 CarswellOnt 2317, 13 C.C.L.T. (3d) 139, 24 C.P.C. (5th) 280, 165 O.A.C. 253 (Ont. Div. Ct.) 905

Alexander v. Daley, 90 F. Supp. 2d 27 (D.C.C., 2000) 475

Alfred Crompton Amusement Machines Ltd. v. Customs & Excise Commissioners (No. 2), **[1972] 2 All E.R. 353, [1972] 2 Q.B. 102 (Eng. C.A.), affirmed (1973), [1974] A.C. 405, [1973] 2 All E.R. 1169 (U.K. H.L.)** 1209

Algonquin College Student Association v. Cour du Québec, **chambre criminelle et pénale (1997), [1997] A.Q. No. 1011, 1997 CarswellQue 4006 (Que. S.C.)** 359

Allegation against the Canadian Alliance of Spying on the Government, April 7, 2001 629

Allegation of Unfair Cartooning by the Reform Party of Canada, **1997, litigation not initiated** 616

Allegations of Illegal Signage against the Alliance for the Preservation of English in Canada, **1997, prosecution not initiated** 619

Allegations of Racism Against the Reform Party, 1997, litigation not
   initiated 932

Allegations of Racism against the Reform Party, Hansard, February 4, 1997, pp.
   7645-6 and February 5, 1997, pp. 7716-7 631

*Alliance for Public Accountability et al. v. R.C.M.P. and Canada (Attorney
   General)*, Federal Court of Canada - Trial Division, filed February 28,
   2001, abandoned 835

American Coalition for Competitive Trade v. Clinton, 128 F.3d 761 (D.C. Cir.,
   1997) 910

Amertek Inc. v. Canadian Commercial Corp. (2003), 229 D.L.R. (4th) 419, [2003]
   O.J. No. 3177, 2003 CarswellOnt 3100, 39 B.L.R. (3d) 163 (Ont. S.C.J.),
   additional reasons at (2003), 2003 CarswellOnt 5142, 39 B.L.R. (3d) 287
   (Ont. S.C.J.), additional reasons at (2003), 2003 CarswellOnt 5143, [2003]
   O.J. No. 5246, 39 B.L.R. (3d) 290 (Ont. S.C.J.) 881

***Ammeter v. Perrier*, [1999] 10 W.W.R. 725, 1999 CarswellMan 324, [1999]
   M.J. No. 306, 3 M.P.L.R. (3d) 54, 139 Man. R. (2d) 214 (Man. Q.B.),
   affirmed (2000), 2000 CarswellMan 58, [2000] M.J. No. 71, 145 Man. R.
   (2d) 156, 218 W.A.C. 156, [2001] 6 W.W.R. 226 (Man. C.A.)** 635

Anderson v. Islamic Republic of Iran, 90 F. Supp.2d 107 (D.D.C., 2000) 1003

Andrews v. Law Society (British Columbia), [1989] 1 S.C.R. 143, 1989
   CarswellBC 16, 1989 CarswellBC 701, [1989] 2 W.W.R. 289, 56 D.L.R.
   (4th) 1, 91 N.R. 255, 34 B.C.L.R. (2d) 273, 25 C.C.E.L. 255, 36 C.R.R. 193,
   10 C.H.R.R. D/5719 (S.C.C.) 192

Ange v. Bush, 752 F.Supp. 509 (1990) 902

***Angus v. R.*, 72 D.L.R. (4th) 672, 1990 CarswellNat 16, 1990 CarswellNat
   699, 5 C.E.L.R. (N.S.) 157, [1990] 3 F.C. 410, 72 D.L.R. (4th) 672, 111 N.R.
   321 (Fed. C.A.)** 38, 84

Apotex Inc. v. Manitoba (Lieutenant-Governor in Council) (1994), 52 C.P.R. (3d)
   135, 1994 CarswellMan 439 (Man. Q.B.) 54

Application by West Toronto Junction Historical Society, Ontario Municipal
   Board, November 26, 1999, file no. PL990500 495

Application Under s. 83.28 of the Criminal Code, Re, 2003 BCSC 1172, [2003]
   B.C.J. No. 1749, 2003 CarswellBC 1823 (B.C. S.C.), affirmed 2004
   CarswellBC 1378, 2004 CarswellBC 1379, 2004 SCC 42 (S.C.C.) 907

Arar v. Syria and Jordan, case in progress 1170

***Arkansas Educational Television Commission v. Forbes*, 140 L.Ed.2d 875
   (1998)** 561

Arsenault-Cameron v. Prince Edward Island, [2000] 1 S.C.R. 3, 2000
   CarswellPEI 4, 2000 CarswellPEI 5, 70 C.R.R. (2d) 1, 2000 SCC 1, 249
   N.R. 140, 181 D.L.R. (4th) 1, 184 Nfld. & P.E.I.R. 44, 559 A.P.R. 44
   (S.C.C.) 175

Arthur (Village) v. Ontario **(1991), 1991 CarswellOnt 2343 (Ont. Gen. Div.)** 810

Asbestos Corp., Re (1992), 10 O.R. (3d) 577, 1992 CarswellOnt 948, 15 O.S.C.B. 4973, 58 O.A.C. 277, 1 C.C.L.S. 300, 97 D.L.R. (4th) 144 (Ont. C.A.), leave to appeal refused 157 N.R. 239 (note), 101 D.L.R. (4th) viii (note), 65 O.A.C. 78 (note), [1993] 2 S.C.R. x (S.C.C.) 32

Ashdown v. Telegraph Group Ltd., [2001] EWCA Civ 1142; July 18, 2001 (U.K.) 691

Assn. of Private Home Care (British Columbia) v. British Columbia (Attorney General), 144 D.L.R. (4th) 425, 1997 CarswellBC 806, 147 W.A.C. 178, 90 B.C.A.C. 178, 48 Admin. L.R. (2d) 71, 38 B.C.L.R. (3d) 114, [1997] 10 W.W.R. 256 (B.C. C.A.) 106

Atlantic Coast Scallop Fishermen's Assn. v. Canada (Minister of Fisheries & Ocean) (1996), 116 F.T.R. 81, 1996 CarswellNat 921 (Fed. T.D.) ... 877

Attorney General of Canada v. R.J. Reynolds Tobacco Holdings, Inc., 103 F. Supp.2d 134 (N.D.N.Y., 2000) and U.S.C.A. 2nd Cir., October 12, 2001 918

Attorney General of Cape Province v. P.W. Botha, currently being researched, December, 1997 (South Africa) 1120

Attorney General of Trinidad and Tobago and Another v. Phillip and Another, [1995] 1 A.C. 396 1003

Auditor General's Report on the Office of the Privacy Commissioner of Canada, September, 2003 817

Audziss v. Santa (2003), 223 D.L.R. (4th) 257, 2003 CarswellOnt 19, 33 M.P.L.R. (3d) 163, 167 O.A.C. 226 (Ont. C.A.), additional reasons at (2003), 2003 CarswellOnt 497 (Ont. C.A.) 500

Australia (Attorney General) v. Commonwealth (1975), 135 C.L.R. 1 (Australia H.C.) 233

Australian Capital Television Property Ltd. v. Commonwealth (No. 2), New South Wales v. Commonwealth of Australia (No. 2) (1992), 108 A.L.R. 577, 66 A.L.J.R. 695 (Australia H.C.) 71, 532

Australian Capital Television v. Commonwealth of Australia, New South Wales v. Commonwealth of Australia (1991), 104 A.L.R. 389 ..... 71, 532

Australian Communist Party v. The Commonwealth (1951), 83 C.L.R. 1 518

Authorson (Litigation Guardian of) v. Canada (Attorney General), 227 D.L.R. (4th) 385, 2003 CarswellOnt 2773, 2003 CarswellOnt 2774, [2003] S.C.J. No. 40, 306 N.R. 335, 175 O.A.C. 363, 4 Admin. L.R. (4th) 167, [2003] 2 S.C.R. 40, 66 O.R. (3d) 734 (note), C.E.B. & P.G.R. 8051, 2003 SCC 39, 36 C.C.P.B. 29 (S.C.C.) 108, 766

Aviation Portneuf Ltée c. Canada (Procureur général), 2001 FCT 1299, 2001 CarswellNat 2743, 2001 CarswellNat 3391, 2001 CFPI 1299 (Fed. T.D.) 779

Ayala v. U.S., 980 F.2d 1342 (10th. Cir., 1992) 58

Azak v. Nisga'a Nation, 2003 BCHRT 79 (B.C. Human Rights Trib.) 218

B.C. and Canadian bills to fix the date of elections 472

B.C. Citizens First Society v. British Columbia (Attorney General) (1999), [1999] B.C.J. No. 120, 1999 CarswellBC 115 (B.C. S.C.) and (1999), [1999] B.C.J. No. 662, 1999 CarswellBC 583 (B.C. S.C.) 213

B.C. Fisheries Survival Coalition v. Canada (1999), [1999] B.C.J. No. 109, 1999 CarswellBC 116 (B.C. S.C.) and (1999), [1999] B.C.J. No. 660, 1999 CarswellBC 572 (B.C. S.C.) 213

Babcock v. Canada (Attorney General), [2002] 3 S.C.R. 3, 2002 CarswellBC 1576, 2002 CarswellBC 1577, [2002] S.C.J. No. 58, 2002 SCC 57, 3 B.C.L.R. (4th) 1, [2002] 8 W.W.R. 585, 214 D.L.R. (4th) 193, 3 C.R. (6th) 1, 289 N.R. 341, 168 B.C.A.C. 50, 275 W.A.C. 50 (S.C.C.) 1209

Bacon v. Saskatchewan Crop Insurance Corp., [1997] S.J. No. 400, 1997 CarswellSask 423, [1997] 9 W.W.R. 258, 157 Sask. R. 199, 34 B.L.R. (2d) 39, 45 C.C.L.I. (2d) 181 (Sask. Q.B.), affirmed [1999] S.J. No. 302, 1999 CarswellSask 308, 65 C.R.R. (2d) 170, [1999] 11 W.W.R. 51, 180 Sask. R. 20, 205 W.A.C. 20 (Sask. C.A.), leave to appeal refused (2000), 2000 CarswellSask 358, 2000 CarswellSask 359, [1999] S.C.C.A. No. 437, 257 N.R. 396 (note), 203 Sask. R. 109 (note), 240 W.A.C. 109 (note) (S.C.C.) 33

Bacon v. Saskatchewan Crop Insurance Corp., [1999] 11 W.W.R. 51, [1999] S.J. No. 302, 1999 CarswellSask 308, 65 C.R.R. (2d) 170, 180 Sask. R. 20, 205 W.A.C. 20 (Sask. C.A.), leave to appeal refused (2000), 2000 CarswellSask 358, 2000 CarswellSask 359, [1999] S.C.C.A. No. 437, 257 N.R. 396 (note), 203 Sask. R. 109 (note), 240 W.A.C. 109 (note) (S.C.C.) 1031

Baie d'Urfé (Ville) c. Québec (Procureur général), 27 M.P.L.R. (3d) 295, 2001 CarswellQue 2633, 2001 CarswellQue 2634, 285 N.R. 194 (note 1), 285 N.R. 194 (note 2), 285 N.R. 195 (note 1), 285 N.R. 195 (note 2), 285 N.R. 196 (note), [2001] 3 S.C.R. xi (S.C.C.) 335

Baker v. Carr, 369 U.S. 186, 82 S.Ct. 691, 7 L.Ed.2d 663 (1962) 160, 229, 233, 976

Bal v. Ontario (Attorney General) (1994), 21 O.R. (3d) 681, 1994 CarswellOnt 164, 121 D.L.R. (4th) 96 (Ont. Gen. Div.), affirmed (1997), 1997 CarswellOnt 2610, 101 O.A.C. 219, 34 O.R. (3d) 484, 151 D.L.R. (4th) 761, 44 C.R.R. (2d) 356 (Ont. C.A.), leave to appeal refused (1998), 49 C.R.R. (2d) 188 (note), 227 N.R. 151 (note), 113 O.A.C. 199 (note) (S.C.C.) 115

Baldasaro v. Candidate Liaison Committee of the Progressive Conservative Party of Canada **(January 27, 2000), Doc. T-1566-98 (Fed. T.D.), not reported** 600

Banco Nacioinal de Cuba v. Sabbatino, 376 U.S. 398 (1964) 983

Bangoura v. Washington Post (2004), [2004] O.J. No. 284, 2004 CarswellOnt 340, [2004] O.J. No. 284, 235 D.L.R. (4th) 564 (Ont. S.C.J.), additional reasons at (2004), 2004 CarswellOnt 675 (Ont. S.C.J.) 616

Banning of Suharto's Golkar Party (Indonesia) 519

Banning of the Islamic Virtue Party, Constitutional Court of Turkey, June 22, 2001 518

Banning of the Islamic Welfare Party, Constititutional Court of Turkey, February 22, 1998 518

Barke v. Calgary (City) (1989), 98 A.R. 157, 1989 CarswellAlta 140, 69 Alta. L.R. (2d) 276 (Alta. Q.B.) 287

***Barreau (Montréal) c. Wagner* (1967), [1968] B.R. 235, 1967 CarswellQue 253 (Que. Q.B.)** 259

Basu v. R. (1991), [1992] 2 F.C. 38, 1991 CarswellNat 349, 1991 CarswellNat 819, 41 C.C.E.L. 130, 87 D.L.R. (4th) 85, 52 F.T.R. 4 (Fed. T.D.) 54

Bates v. Jones, 131 F.3d 843 (9th Cir., 1997) 518

***Bavarda v. Attorney General* (1988), L.R.C. (Cons.) 13 (Fiji)** 394

Bears and Grassroots for Day v. Grey, Alberta Queen's Bench, filed June 8, 2001, file no. 0101-11358, discontinued November 9, 2001 682

Beaudoin c. Banque de développement du Canada (2004), 2004 CarswellQue 208 (Que. S.C.) 862

Beaumier v. Brampton (City) (1998), 46 M.P.L.R. (2d) 32, 1998 CarswellOnt 1264 (Ont. Gen. Div.), affirmed (1999), 1999 CarswellOnt 3805, 7 M.P.L.R. (3d) 219, 128 O.A.C. 352 (Ont. C.A.) 613

Becker v. Federal Election Commission, 230 F.3d 381 (1st Cir., 2000) 564

***Bédard c. Québec (Procureur général)* (February 24, 1998), Doc. 500-05-039679-988 (Que. S.C.)** 435

***Bedford (Town) v. Nova Scotia (Law Amendments Committee)* (1993), 123 N.S.R. (2d) 355, 340 A.P.R. 355, 1993 CarswellNS 145 (N.S. C.A.)** ... 787

Bedford Service Commission v. Nova Scotia (Attorney General) (1976), 72 D.L.R. (3d) 639, 1976 CarswellNS 24, 18 N.S.R. (2d) 132, 20 A.P.R. 132, 1 M.P.L.R. 204 (N.S. C.A.), reversed 1977 CarswellNS 52, 1977 CarswellNS 52F, [1977] 2 S.C.R. 269, 24 A.P.R. 310, 19 N.S.R. (2d) 310, 14 N.R. 413, 80 D.L.R. (3d) 767 (S.C.C.) 865

Beit Sarrik Village Council v. The Government of Israel, HCJ 2056/04, Supreme Court of Israel, June 30, 2004 1169

Beno v. Canada (Somalia Inquiry Commission), 149 D.L.R. (4th) 118, 1997 CarswellNat 1001, 1997 CarswellNat 2676, [1997] 3 F.C. 784, 133 F.T.R. 81, 50 Admin. L.R. (2d) 111 (Fed. T.D.) 833

Benoit v. Canada, 2002 FCT 243, 2002 CarswellNat 448, [2002] F.C.J. No. 257, 2002 CarswellNat 4793, [2002] G.S.T.C. 22, 2002 D.T.C. 6896, [2002] 2 C.N.L.R. 1, [2002] 4 C.T.C. 295, 217 F.T.R. 1, 2002 CFPI 243 (Fed. T.D.), reversed [2003] F.C.J. No. 923, 2003 CarswellNat 1660, 2003 CarswellNat 1704, 307 N.R. 1, 242 F.T.R. 159 (note), 2003 FCA 236, 2003 CAF 236, 2003 G.T.C. 1659, [2003] 3 C.N.L.R. 20, 228 D.L.R. (4th) 1, [2003] G.S.T.C. 101, 2003 D.T.C. 5366 (Fed. C.A.), leave to appeal refused (2004), 2004 CarswellNat 1209, 2004 CarswellNat 1210 (S.C.C.) 1034

Berezovsky v. Michaels and others; Glouchkov v. Michaels and others, [2000] 2 All E.R. 986 1000

Bertrand c. Québec (Procureur général), 138 D.L.R. (4th) 481, 1996 CarswellQue 893, [1996] R.J.Q. 2393 (Que. S.C.) 348

Bertrand v. Québec (Premier ministre), [1998] R.J.Q. 1203 to 1221, 1998 CarswellQue 358, [1998] A.Q. No. 595, 1998 CarswellQue 1348 (Que. S.C.) 362

Bertrand v. Quebec (Procureur général), 127 D.L.R. (4th) 408, 1995 CarswellQue 131, [1995] R.J.Q. 2500 (Que. S.C.) 348

Bhaduria v. Standard Broadcasting Inc. (August 16, 1996), Doc. CP-12321-95, [1996] O.J. No. 2853 (Ont. Gen. Div.) 616

Bhaduria v. The Liberal Party of Canada and Chrétien, Ontario Court (General Division), filed October 1, 1996, file no 103091/96, discontinued 757

Bhatnager v. Canada (Minister of Employment & Immigration), [1990] 2 S.C.R. 217, 1990 CarswellNat 73, 1990 CarswellNat 737, 44 Admin. L.R. 1, 71 D.L.R. (4th) 84, 111 N.R. 185, 12 Imm. L.R. (2d) 81, 43 C.P.C. (2d) 213, 36 F.T.R. 91 (note) (S.C.C.) 1067

Bill 150 and the Québec General Election of 1994, litigation not initiated 1106

Bill C-218 of 2001 682

Bisaillon c. Keable, [1980] C.A. 316, 1980 CarswellQue 22, 62 C.C.C. (2d) 340, 17 C.R. (3d) 193, 127 D.L.R. (3d) 368 (Que. C.A.), reversed 1983 CarswellQue 28, 1983 CarswellQue 96, [1983] 2 S.C.R. 60, 2 D.L.R. (4th) 193, 51 N.R. 81, 4 Admin. L.R. 205, 7 C.C.C. (3d) 385, 37 C.R. (3d) 289 (S.C.C.) 260

Black v. Canada (Prime Minister) (2001), 199 D.L.R. (4th) 228, 2001 CarswellOnt 1672, 54 O.R. (3d) 215, 147 O.A.C. 141 (Ont. C.A.) 966

Blanco v. R., 2003 FCT 263, 2003 CarswellNat 552, 2003 CarswellNat 1596, 231 F.T.R. 3, 2003 CFPI 263 (Fed. T.D.) 905

Bland v. Canada (National Capital Commission), 41 F.T.R. 202, 1991 CarswellNat 784, 1991 CarswellNat 361, 41 F.T.R. 202, 4 Admin. L.R.

(2d) 171, [1991] 3 F.C. 325, 36 C.P.R. (3d) 289 (Fed. T.D.), reversed (1992), 1992 CarswellNat 162, 1992 CarswellNat 162F, 46 C.P.R. (3d) 21, [1993] 1 F.C. 541, 151 N.R. 10, 59 F.T.R. 319 (note) (Fed. C.A.) 303

Blencoe v. British Columbia (Human Rights Commission), [2000] 2 S.C.R. 307, 2000 SCC 44, 2000 CarswellBC 1860, 2000 CarswellBC 1861, [2000] S.C.J. No. 43, 2 C.C.E.L. (3d) 165, 81 B.C.L.R. (3d) 1, 190 D.L.R. (4th) 513, [2000] 10 W.W.R. 567, 23 Admin. L.R. (3d) 175, 2000 C.L.L.C. 230-040, 260 N.R. 1, 77 C.R.R. (2d) 189, 141 B.C.A.C. 161, 231 W.A.C. 161, 38 C.H.R.R. D/ 153 (S.C.C.) 816

Bloc Québécois c. National Post Company et al., Québec Superior Court, filed January 27, 2000, file no. 500-05-055603-003, in progress 993

Bob v. British Columbia, 2002 BCSC 733, 2002 CarswellBC 1414, 3 B.C.L.R. (4th) 135, [2002] 8 W.W.R. 621 (B.C. S.C. [In Chambers]) 218, 415

Bonneville v. Frazier, 12 M.P.L.R. (3d) 236, 2000 CarswellBC 565, [2000] B.C.J. No. 480, 2000 BCSC 416 (B.C. S.C.) 636

Bosnian Case against NATO Bombing of Serbia, European Court of Human Rights, filed October 24, 2001 (European Community) 1141

Bouchard and Best v. Arthur and Radiomédia et al., Québec Superior Court; filed July 20, 1995, file no. 500-05-007814-955, settled 988

Boucher v. Canada (Immigration Appeal Board) (1989), 105 N.R. 66, 1989 CarswellNat 712 (Fed. C.A.) 937

Bouzari v. Iran (Islamic Republic) (2002), [2002] O.J. No. 1624, 2002 CarswellOnt 1469 (Ont. S.C.J.), affirmed (2004), 2004 CarswellOnt 2681 (Ont. C.A.) 1170

Bovbel v. Canada (Minister of Employment & Immigration), [1994] 2 F.C. 563, 1994 CarswellNat 841, 1994 CarswellNat 1467, 18 Admin. L.R. (2d) 169, 167 N.R. 10, 113 D.L.R. (4th) 415, 77 F.T.R. 313 (note) (Fed. C.A.), leave to appeal refused (1994), 23 Admin. L.R. (2d) 320 (note), 115 D.L.R. (4th) vii (note), 179 N.R. 65 (note) (S.C.C.) 1191

Bowman v. United Kingdom (1998), 26 E.H.R.R. 1 (European Community) 584

Bown v. Newfoundland (Minister of Social Services) (1985), 54 Nfld. & P.E.I.R. 258, 1985 CarswellNfld 83, 160 A.P.R. 258 (Nfld. C.A.) 1036

Bowsher v. Synar, 92 L.Ed.2d 583 (1986) 918

Brantford (Township) v. Doctor (1995), 29 M.P.L.R. (2d) 300, 1995 CarswellOnt 790, [1996] 1 C.N.L.R. 49 (Ont. Gen. Div.) 121

"Bridging the Gap"; From Oblivion to the Rule of Law: Development and Vitality of the Francophone and Acadian Communities; A Fundamental Obligation for Canada, Report by Senator Jean-Marc Simard, November 16, 1999 933

British Columbia (Attorney General) v. Mount Currie Indian Band (1992),
18 B.C.A.C. 301, 31 W.A.C. 301, 1992 CarswellBC 580, 10 C.P.C. (3d)
366, [1994] 1 C.N.L.R. 61 (B.C. C.A.), leave to appeal refused (1992), 10
C.P.C. (3d) 366n (S.C.C.) 451

British Columbia (Minister of Forests) v. Okanagan Indian Band (2001), 208
D.L.R. (4th) 301, 2001 CarswellBC 2355, [2001] B.C.J. No. 2279, 2001
BCCA 647, 95 B.C.L.R. (3d) 273, [2002] 1 C.N.L.R. 57, 161 B.C.A.C. 13,
263 W.A.C. 13, 92 C.R.R. (2d) 319 (B.C. C.A.), leave to appeal allowed
2002 CarswellBC 2450, 2002 CarswellBC 2451, [2002] 4 C.N.L.R. iv
(note), 301 N.R. 400 (note), 181 B.C.A.C. 160 (note), 298 W.A.C. 160
(note) (S.C.C.), leave to appeal allowed (2002), 2002 CarswellBC 2452,
2002 CarswellBC 2453, [2001] S.C.C.A. No. 629, [2002] 4 C.N.L.R. iv
(note), 182 B.C.A.C. 160 (note), 300 W.A.C. 160 (note), 302 N.R. 197
(note) (S.C.C.), affirmed (2003), 2003 CarswellBC 3040, 2003 CarswellBC
3041, 2003 SCC 71, 43 C.P.C. (5th) 1, [2003] 3 S.C.R. 371, 313 N.R. 84,
[2004] 2 W.W.R. 252, 21 B.C.L.R. (4th) 209, 233 D.L.R. (4th) 577, [2004] 1
C.N.L.R. 7, 189 B.C.A.C. 161, 309 W.A.C. 161 (S.C.C.) 1215

British Columbia Civil Liberties Association v. British Columbia
(Attorney General), British Columbia Supreme Court, filed March 16,
1998, file 980711, Vancouver Registry, adjourned sine die June 6,
1999 467

British Columbia et al. v. United States et al., U.S. District Court for the
Western District of Washington, January 30, 1998, not reported, file
C97-1464C 881

Bromley London Borough Council v. Greater London Council, [1983] A.C.
768 670

Brown v. Alberta, [1999] 12 W.W.R. 330, [1999] A.J. No. 1006, 1999
CarswellAlta 819, 1999 ABCA 256, 177 D.L.R. (4th) 349, 72 Alta. L.R.
(3d) 69, 244 A.R. 86, 209 W.A.C. 86, 38 C.P.C. (4th) 19 (Alta. C.A.) ... 458

Brown v. British Columbia (Minister of Transportation & Highways), 112
D.L.R. (4th) 1, [1994] S.C.J. No. 20, 1994 CarswellBC 128, 1994
CarswellBC 1236, [1994] 4 W.W.R. 194, 20 Admin. L.R. (2d) 1, 89
B.C.L.R. (2d) 1, 19 C.C.L.T. (2d) 268, [1994] 1 S.C.R. 420, 42 B.C.A.C. 1,
67 W.A.C. 1, 2 M.V.R. (3d) 43, 164 N.R. 161 (S.C.C.) 118

Buchanan v. Federal Election Commission, 112 F. Supp.2d 58 (D.D.C.,
2000) 564

Buckley v. American Constitutional Law Foundation, 142 L.Ed.2d 599
(1999) 518

Burge v. Prince Edward Island (Human Rights Commission) (1991), 97 Nfld. &
P.E.I.R. 70, 1991 CarswellPEI 102, 91 C.L.L.C. 17,022, 308 A.P.R. 70, 15
C.H.R.R. D/417 (P.E.I. C.A.) 857

Burge v. Prince Edward Island (Liquor Control Commission) (1994), 123
Nfld. & P.E.I.R. 143, 382 A.P.R. 143, 1994 CarswellPEI 117, 94 C.L.L.C.

17,037, 24 C.H.R.R. D/349 (P.E.I. T.D.), reversed 1995 CarswellPEI 129, 96 C.L.L.C. 230-006, 135 Nfld. & P.E.I.R. 245, 420 A.P.R. 245, 24 C.H.R.R. D/364, [1995] 2 P.E.I.R. 77 (P.E.I. C.A.) 860

Burke v. Canada (Employment & Immigration Commission) **(1994), 79 F.T.R. 148, 1994 CarswellNat 626 (Fed. T.D.)** 113

Bush Plan for Middle East Peace, Speech by President George W. Bush in the Rose Garden, June 24, 2002 323

Bush v. Gore, 148 L.Ed.2d 388 (2000) 177

Bush v. Palm Beach County Canv. Bd., 148 L.Ed.2d 366 (2001) 573

C.U.P.E. v. Minister of National Revenue, **93 D.T.C. 5099, 1993 CarswellNat 854, [1993] 1 C.T.C. 185 (Fed. C.A.)** 114

C.U.P.E. v. Ontario (Minister of Labour), 2003 SCC 29, 2003 CarswellOnt 1770, 2003 CarswellOnt 1803, [2003] S.C.J. No. 28, [2003] 1 S.C.R. 539, 66 O.R. (3d) 735 (note), 2003 C.L.L.C. 220-040, 304 N.R. 76, 173 O.A.C. 38, 50 Admin. L.R. (3d) 1, 226 D.L.R. (4th) 193 (S.C.C.) 277

Cameron v. Boyle **(1994), 1994 CarswellOnt 2820 (Ont. Gen. Div.)** 597

Campaign for Nuclear Disarmament v. Prime Minister, [2002] EWHC 2712 Admin, December 5, 2002 and [2002] EWHC 2759 (Q.B.) (U.K.) 907

Campbell v. British Columbia (Attorney General), **[1999] 3 C.N.L.R. 1, 1999 CarswellBC 117, [1999] B.C.J. No. 121 (B.C. S.C.) and (1999), [1999] B.C.J. No. 233, 1999 CarswellBC 188 (B.C. S.C.) and 2000 BCSC 619, 2000 CarswellBC 809 (B.C. S.C.) and 189 D.L.R. (4th) 333, [2000] B.C.J. No. 1524, 2000 CarswellBC 1545, 2000 BCSC 1123, 79 B.C.L.R. (3d) 122, [2000] 8 W.W.R. 600, [2000] 4 C.N.L.R. 1 (B.C. S.C.), additional reasons at 2001 BCSC 1400, 2001 CarswellBC 2163, 11 C.P.C. (5th) 384 (B.C. S.C.)** 213

Campbell v. Clinton, 203 F.3d 19 (D.C. Cir., 2000) 907

Canada (Attorney General) v. Boutilier (1997), 31 P.S.S.R.B. 15, 1997 CarswellNat 3148, 65 L.A.C. (4th) 102 (Can. P.S.S.R.B.), reversed (1998), 1998 CarswellNat 2227, 1998 CarswellNat 2876, 154 F.T.R. 40, [1999] 1 F.C. 459, 35 C.H.R.R. D/141 (Fed. T.D.), affirmed (1999), 1999 CarswellNat 2540, 1999 CarswellNat 3100, 36 C.H.R.R. D/257, 2000 C.L.L.C. 230-009, 181 D.L.R. (4th) 590, [2000] 3 F.C. 27, 250 N.R. 181, 21 Admin. L.R. (3d) 12 (Fed. C.A.), leave to appeal refused (2000), 2000 CarswellNat 1943, 2000 CarswellNat 1944, 261 N.R. 197 (note) (S.C.C.) 21

Canada (Attorney General) v. British Columbia (February 5, 1999), Doc. Vancouver C974423 (B.C. S.C. [In Chambers]) 902

Canada (Attorney General) v. Canada (Information Commissioner), [2001] F.C.J. No. 282, 2001 FCA 25, 2001 CarswellNat 360, 268 N.R. 328, 12 C.P.R. (4th) 492, 32 Admin. L.R. (3d) 238, 200 F.T.R. 320 (note) (Fed. C.A.), leave to appeal refused (2001), 2001 CarswellNat 1897, 2001 CarswellNat 1898, [2001] S.C.C.A. No. 233, 278 N.R. 192 (note) (S.C.C.) 305, 809

Canada (Attorney General) v. Canada (Information Commissioner), [2002] 3 F.C. 606, 2002 CarswellNat 382, 2002 CarswellNat 3133, 2002 FCT 129, 18 C.P.R. (4th) 92, 216 F.T.R. 233 (Fed. T.D.), affirmed 2003 CarswellNat 3643, 2003 CarswellNat 1884, 2003 CAF 285, 311 N.R. 158, 2003 FCA 285, 26 C.P.R. (4th) 125 (Fed. C.A.) and 2004 FC 431, 2004 CarswellNat 860, 2004 FC 431 (F.C.) 305

Canada (Attorney General) v. Canada (Information Commissioner), 2003 FCA 285, 2003 CarswellNat 3643, 2003 CarswellNat 1884, 2003 CAF 285, 311 N.R. 158, 242 F.T.R. 318 (note), 26 C.P.R. (4th) 125 (Fed. C.A.) 305

Canada (Attorney General) v. P.S.A.C. (1993), 107 D.L.R. (4th) 178, 1993 CarswellNat 1970, 158 N.R. 301 (Fed. C.A.) 302

Canada (Attorney General) v. P.S.A.C. (1991), [1993] 1 S.C.R. 941, 1993 CarswellNat 805, 1993 CarswellNat 1379, 93 C.L.L.C. 14,022, 150 N.R. 161, 101 D.L.R. (4th) 673, 11 Admin. L.R. (2d) 59 (S.C.C.) 50

Canada (Attorney General) v. P.S.A.C., 80 D.L.R. (4th) 520, 1991 CarswellNat 753, 1991 CarswellNat 828, [1991] S.C.J. No. 19, 91 C.L.L.C. 14,017, 48 Admin. L.R. 161, [1991] 1 S.C.R. 614, 123 N.R. 161 (S.C.C.) 107

Canada (Attorney General) v. S.D. Myers Inc., 2001 FCT 317, 2001 CarswellNat 738 (Fed. T.D.), affirmed 2002 CarswellNat 227, 2002 FCA 39 (Fed. C.A.), leave to appeal refused (2002), 2002 CarswellNat 2733, 2002 CarswellNat 2734, 302 N.R. 398 (note) (S.C.C.) 910

Canada (Attorney General) v. S.D. Myers Inc., 2002 FCA 39, 2002 CarswellNat 227 (Fed. C.A.), leave to appeal refused (2002), 2002 CarswellNat 2733, 2002 CarswellNat 2734, 302 N.R. 398 (note) (S.C.C.) 910

Canada (Attorney General) v. Somerville, 184 A.R. 241, 122 W.A.C. 241, 1996 CarswellAlta 503, 39 Alta. L.R. (3d) 326, 37 C.R.R. (2d) 24, 136 D.L.R. (4th) 205, [1996] 8 W.W.R. 199 (Alta. C.A.) 60, 519

Canada (Auditor General) v. Canada (Minister of Energy, Mines & Resources), 61 D.L.R. (4th) 604, 1989 CarswellNat 593, 1989 CarswellNat 698, 97 N.R. 241, 40 Admin. L.R. 1, [1989] 2 S.C.R. 49 (S.C.C.) 818

Canada (Canadian Human Rights Commission) v. Lane, [1990] 2 F.C. 327, 1990 CarswellNat 630, 1990 CarswellNat 630F, 67 D.L.R. (4th) 745, 107 N.R. 124, 13 C.H.R.R. D/568 (Fed. C.A.) 802

Canada (Human Rights Commission) v. Canada (Minister of Indian Affairs & Northern Development) (1994), 89 F.T.R. 249, 1994 CarswellNat 519, 25 C.R.R. (2d) 230, [1995] 3 C.N.L.R. 28, 25 C.H.R.R. D/386 (Fed. T.D.) 137

Canada (Human Rights Commission) v. Taylor, 75 D.L.R. (4th) 577, 1990 CarswellNat 742, 1990 CarswellNat 1030, [1990] S.C.J. No. 129, [1990] 3

**S.C.R. 892, 3 C.R.R. (2d) 116, 117 N.R. 191, 13 C.H.R.R. D/435
(S.C.C.)** 582

Canada (Information Commissioner) v. Canada (Attorney General), [2001] F.C.J.
No. 926, 2001 CarswellNat 3965, 2001 CarswellNat 3966, 2001 FCT 599
(Fed. T.D.) 305

**Canada (Information Commissioner) v. Canada (Minister of External
Affairs), [1990] 3 F.C. 514, 1990 CarswellNat 660, 1990 CarswellNat
660F, 3 T.C.T. 5297 (Fed. T.D.)** 1038

Canada (Information Commissioner) v. Canada (Minister of National Defence)
(1996), 116 F.T.R. 131, 1996 CarswellNat 946, [1996] F.C.J. No. 927 (Fed.
T.D.) 305

Canada (Information Commissioner) v. Canada (Prime Minister) (1992), [1993] 1
F.C. 427, 1992 CarswellNat 161F, 1992 CarswellNat 185, [1992] F.C.J. No.
1054, 12 Admin. L.R. (2d) 81, 49 C.P.R. (3d) 79, 57 F.T.R. 180 (Fed.
T.D.) 303

Canada (Information Commissioner) v. Canada (Solicitor General), [1988] 3 F.C.
551, 1988 CarswellNat 714, [1988] F.C.J. No. 408, 1988 CarswellNat 664,
32 Admin. L.R. 103, 20 F.T.R. 314 (Fed. T.D.) 303

Canada Deposit Insurance Corp. v. Oland (1997), [1997] A.J. No. 931, 1997
CarswellAlta 797, 53 Alta. L.R. (3d) 192, 152 D.L.R. (4th) 509, 12 C.P.C.
(4th) 50, [1998] 1 W.W.R. 507, 206 A.R. 283, 156 W.A.C. 283 (Alta.
C.A.) 1070

Canada Post Corp. v. Post Office (2000), [2001] 2 F.C. 63, 2000 CarswellNat
2305, 2000 CarswellNat 3452, 8 C.P.R. (4th) 289, 191 F.T.R. 300 (Fed.
T.D.) 107

Canada v. Ahenakew, 2003 FCT 306, [2003] F.C.J. No. 429, 2003 CarswellNat
617, 2003 CarswellNat 1615, 2003 CFPI 306, [2003] 2 C.N.L.R. 131, 230
F.T.R. 29 (Fed. T.D.) 246

Canada v. Evans (1983), 1 D.L.R. (4th) 328, 1983 CarswellNat 485, 49 N.R.
189 (Fed. C.A.) 817

**Canada v. Pharmaceutical Society (Nova Scotia), 93 D.L.R. (4th) 36, 1992
CarswellNS 15, 1992 CarswellNS 353, [1992] S.C.J. No. 67, 15 C.R. (4th)
1, [1992] 2 S.C.R. 606, 43 C.P.R. (3d) 1, 74 C.C.C. (3d) 289, 10 C.R.R. (2d)
34, 139 N.R. 241, 114 N.S.R. (2d) 91, 313 A.P.R. 91 (S.C.C.)** 31

**Canada v. Prince Edward Island, 66 D.L.R. (3d) 465, 1976 CarswellNat 54,
1976 CarswellNat 54F, [1976] 2 F.C. 712 (Fed. T.D.), reversed (1977),
1977 CarswellNat 122, 1977 CarswellNat 122F, [1978] 1 F.C. 533, 20 N.R.
91, 83 D.L.R. (3d) 492, 14 Nfld. & P.E.I.R. 477, 33 A.P.R. 477 (Fed.
C.A.)** 708

Canadian Alliance Accusation of Partiality against Mr. Justice Silcoff, April 9,
2001 637

Canadian Council of Christian Charities v. Canada (Minister of Finance),
168 F.T.R. 49, 1999 CarswellNat 848, [1999] F.C.J. No. 771, 1999
CarswellNat 2844, 99 D.T.C. 5337, [1999] 3 C.T.C. 123, [1999] 4 F.C. 245
(Fed. T.D.), additional reasons at 1999 CarswellNat 1199, [1999] F.C.J.
No. 983, 99 D.T.C. 5408, [1999] 4 C.T.C. 45 (Fed. T.D.) 815

Canadian Disability Rights Council v. Canada [1988] 3 F.C. 622, 1988
CarswellNat 133, 1988 CarswellNat 133F, 21 F.T.R. 268, 38 C.R.R. 53
(Fed. T.D.) 500

Canadian Egg Marketing Agency v. Richardson, 166 D.L.R. (4th) 1, [1998]
S.C.J. No. 78, 1998 CarswellNWT 118, 1998 CarswellNWT 119, 57
C.R.R. (2d) 1, 223 A.R. 201, 183 W.A.C. 201, [1998] 3 S.C.R. 157, 231 N.R.
201 (S.C.C.) 807

Canadian Federation of Independent Business v. R. (1974), 49 D.L.R. (3d) 718,
1974 CarswellNat 106, 1974 CarswellNat 106F, [1974] 2 F.C. 443 (Fed.
T.D.) 709

Canadian Free Speech League v. R. (1992), [1992] F.C.J. No. 966, 1992
CarswellNat 1222 (Fed. T.D.) 937

Canadian Javelin Ltd., Re, [1982] 2 S.C.R. 686, 1982 CarswellNat 490, 1982
CarswellNat 490F, 44 N.R. 571, 141 D.L.R. (3d) 395, 68 C.P.R. (2d) 145
(S.C.C.) 1064, 1106

Canadian Jewish Congress v. Chosen People Ministries Inc., 231 D.L.R. (4th) 309,
2003 CarswellNat 1881, 2003 CarswellNat 2842, 311 N.R. 162, 2003 FCA
272, 2003 CAF 272 (Fed. C.A.) 89

Canadian Museum of Nature v. Bélanger (1995), 107 F.T.R. 241, 1995
CarswellNat 843 (Fed. T.D.) 51

Canadian National Railway v. Moffatt (2001), 207 D.L.R. (4th) 118, 2001
CarswellNat 2396, 2001 CarswellNat 3522, 2001 FCA 327, 278 N.R. 83,
[2002] 2 F.C. 249 (Fed. C.A.) 430

Canadian Pacific Ltd. v. Matsqui Indian Band (1992), 58 F.T.R. 23, 1992
CarswellNat 147, 1992 CarswellNat 147F, [1992] F.C.J. No. 927, [1993] 1
F.C. 74 (Fed. T.D.), reversed (1993), 1993 CarswellNat 218, 1993
CarswellNat 218F, 153 N.R. 307, [1994] 1 C.N.L.R. 66, [1993] 2 F.C. 641,
62 F.T.R. 270 (note) (Fed. C.A.), affirmed 1995 CarswellNat 264, 1995
CarswellNat 700, 26 Admin. L.R. (2d) 1, [1995] 2 C.N.L.R. 92, 122 D.L.R.
(4th) 129, 85 F.T.R. 79 (note), [1995] 1 S.C.R. 3, 177 N.R. 325
(S.C.C.) 120

Canadian Pacific Ltd. v. Quebec North Shore Paper Co. (1976), 71 D.L.R.
(3d) 111, 1976 CarswellNat 432, 1976 CarswellNat 432F, [1977] 2 S.C.R.
1054, [1976] 1 F.C. 646, 9 N.R. 471 (S.C.C.) 23, 326

*Canadian Reform Conservative Alliance Party Portage-Lisgar Constituency
Assn.v. Harms* (2003), 231 D.L.R. (4th) 214, [2003] M.J. No. 319, 2003

CarswellMan 371, 35 C.P.C. (5th) 261, 177 Man. R. (2d) 251, 304 W.A.C. 251, [2004] 3 W.W.R. 1, 2003 MBCA 112 (Man. C.A.) 584

Canadian Reform Conservative Alliance v. Western Union Insurance Co., 2001 BCCA 274, 2001 CarswellBC 700, [2001] B.C.J. No. 697, 87 B.C.L.R. (3d) 299, 26 C.C.L.I. (3d) 1, [2001] 5 W.W.R. 245, 12 C.P.R. (4th) 475, 153 B.C.A.C. 48, 251 W.A.C. 48 (B.C. C.A.) 666

Canadian Wildlife Federation Inc. v. Canada (Minister of the Environment) (1989), [1990] 2 W.W.R. 69, 1989 CarswellNat 130, 38 Admin. L.R. 138, 99 N.R. 72, 4 C.E.L.R. (N.S.) 1, 27 F.T.R. 159 (note) (Fed. C.A.) 13, 178

Canadian Wildlife Federation Inc. v. Canada (Minister of the Environment) (1989), [1990] 1 F.C. 595, 1989 CarswellNat 615, 1989 CarswellNat 615F, 32 F.T.R. 81 (Fed. T.D.) 24

Canadian Wildlife Federation Inc. v. Canada (Minister of the Environment) (1989), 31 F.T.R. 1, 1989 CarswellNat 11, 4 C.E.L.R. (N.S.) 201 (Fed. T.D.), affirmed (1990), 1990 CarswellNat 18, 1990 CarswellNat 725, 6 C.E.L.R. (N.S.) 89, [1991] 1 F.C. 641, 121 N.R. 385, 41 F.T.R. 318 (note) (Fed. C.A.) 1065, 1183

Canadian Wildlife Federation Inc. v. Canada (Minister of the Environment), [1989] 3 F.C. 309, 1989 CarswellNat 129, 1989 CarswellNat 640, 37 Admin. L.R. 39, 3 C.E.L.R. (N.S.) 287, [1989] 4 W.W.R. 526, 26 F.T.R. 245 (Fed. T.D.), affirmed (1989), 1989 CarswellNat 130, 38 Admin. L.R. 138, 99 N.R. 72, [1990] 2 W.W.R. 69, 4 C.E.L.R. (N.S.) 1, 27 F.T.R. 159 (note) (Fed. C.A.) 121

Canadian Wildlife Federation Inc. v. Canada (Minister of the Environment) (1990), 121 N.R. 385, 1990 CarswellNat 18, 1990 CarswellNat 725, 6 C.E.L.R. (N.S.) 89, [1991] 1 F.C. 641, 41 F.T.R. 318 (note) (Fed. C.A.) 177, 1031

Carey v. Ontario (1983), 1 D.L.R. (4th) 498, 1983 CarswellOnt 521, 43 O.R. (2d) 161, 38 C.P.C. 237, 3 Admin. L.R. 158, 7 C.C.C. (3d) 193 (Ont. C.A.), reversed 1986 CarswellOnt 1011, 1986 CarswellOnt 472, [1986] S.C.J. No. 74, 22 Admin. L.R. 236, [1986] 2 S.C.R. 637, 35 D.L.R. (4th) 161, 72 N.R. 81, 20 O.A.C. 81, 30 C.C.C. (3d) 498, 14 C.P.C. (2d) 10, 58 O.R. (2d) 352n (S.C.C.) 1169

Carey v. Ontario, [1986] 2 S.C.R. 637, 1986 CarswellOnt 1011, 1986 CarswellOnt 472, [1986] S.C.J. No. 74, 22 Admin. L.R. 236, 35 D.L.R. (4th) 161, 72 N.R. 81, 20 O.A.C. 81, 30 C.C.C. (3d) 498, 14 C.P.C. (2d) 10, 58 O.R. (2d) 352n (S.C.C.) 30

Carlsen v. Prime Minister, Danish High Court, Eastern Division, June 27, 1997 367

Carter v. Alberta, 2001 ABQB 429, 2001 CarswellAlta 669, 33 Admin. L.R. (3d) 149, 290 A.R. 127 (Alta. Q.B.), affirmed (2002), 2002 CarswellAlta 1601, 2002 ABCA 303, [2003] 2 W.W.R. 419, 222 D.L.R. (4th) 40, 46

Admin. L.R. (3d) 191, 317 A.R. 299, 284 W.A.C. 299, 9 Alta. L.R. (4th) 18 (Alta. C.A.), leave to appeal refused (2003), 2003 CarswellAlta 894, 2003 CarswellAlta 895, 18 Alta. L.R. (4th) 7, [2004] 1 W.W.R. 585 (S.C.C.), additional reasons at 2004 CarswellAlta 201, [2004] 5 W.W.R. 201, 2004 ABCA 99 (Alta. C.A.) 1087

Case of Prime Minister Sergei Kiriyenko, 1998, litigation not initiated (Russia) 389

Cavilla v. Canada (Chief Electoral Officer) (1993), 76 F.T.R. 77, 1993 CarswellNat 642 (Fed. T.D.) 599

CBS Inc. v. Federal Communications Commission, 453 U.S. 367 (1980) 532

CCH Canadian Ltd. v. Law Society of Upper Canada, 2004 SCC 13, [2004] S.C.J. No. 12, 2004 CarswellNat 446, 2004 CarswellNat 447, 236 D.L.R. (4th) 395, 317 N.R. 107, 30 C.P.R. (4th) 1 (S.C.C.) 1214

Cdn. Coalition on the Constitution Inc. v. R. (1988), 1988 CarswellNat 1264 (Fed. T.D.) 445, 447

Cencourse Project Inc. v. Ontario (1995), [1995] O.J. No. 3445, 1995 CarswellOnt 4764 (Ont. Gen. Div.) 789

Centre for Legal Research v. State of Kerala, [1987] L.R.C. (Cons.) 544 (India) 1215

Certification of the Amended Text of the Constitution of the Republic of South Africa, 1996, Constitutional Court, December 4, 1996, file CCT 37/ 96 370

Chair's Final Report After Commissioner's Notice, February 18, 2004 896

Chandler v. Director of Public Prosecutions (1962), [1964] A.C. 763, 46 Cr. App. R. 347, [1962] 3 All E.R. 142 (U.K. H.L.) 159

Chaouilli c. Québec (Procureur général) (2002), [2002] J.Q. No. 759, 2002 CarswellQue 598, [2002] R.J.Q. 1205 (Que. C.A.), leave to appeal allowed (2003), 2003 CarswellQue 850, 2003 CarswellQue 851 (S.C.C.) and (2002), [2002] J.Q. No. 763, 2002 CarswellQue 599 (Que. C.A.), leave to appeal allowed (2003), 2003 CarswellQue 850, 2003 CarswellQue 851 (S.C.C.) 864

Charlottetown (City) v. Prince Edward Island (1998), 169 Nfld. & P.E.I.R. 188, 521 A.P.R. 188, 1998 CarswellPEI 108, 168 D.L.R. (4th) 79 (P.E.I. C.A.), leave to appeal refused (1999), 251 N.R. 399 (note), 188 Nfld. & P.E.I.R. 182 (note), 569 A.P.R. 182 (note) (S.C.C.) 1053

Chaudhury v. Qarase and President of the Republic of Fiji Islands, Fiji Court of Appeal, February 15, 2002, Miscellaneous No 1/2001 393

Chavali v. Canada, 2001 FCT 268, 2001 CarswellNat 677, 34 Admin. L.R. (3d) 101, 202 F.T.R. 166 (Fed. T.D.), affirmed 2002 CarswellNat 1145, 2002 FCA 209, 291 N.R. 311 (Fed. C.A.) 921

Chesterfield v. Janssen (1750), 2 Ves. Sen. 125, 28 E.R. 82 70

Chipkar v. Xinchun, Ontario Superior Court of Justice, file No. 03-CV-253110CM1, endorsement February 3, 2004 1048

Chisom v. Roemer, United States v. Roemer, 115 L.Ed.2d 348 (1991) 921

Chopra v. Canada (Treasury Board) (2003), 2003 PSSRB 115, 2003 CarswellNat 4617, [2004] L.V.I. 3450-10 (Can. P.S.S.R.B.), on appeal to the Federal Court of Canada – Trial Division, file T-103-04 299

Cit-Can Foundation et al. v. Québec (Attorney General), Superior Court of Québec, filed August 6, 1997, file no. 500-05-034521-979, adjourned *sine die* 519

City of Boerne v. Flores, 138 L.Ed.2d 624 (1997) 252

Claim of False Advertising Regarding Unemployment Insurance Reforms, 1996, litigation not initiated 926

Clark v. Canada (Attorney General) (1977), 81 D.L.R. (3d) 33, 1977 CarswellOnt 642, 17 O.R. (2d) 593, 34 C.P.R. (2d) 91 (Ont. H.C.) 959

Clark v. R. (1979), 99 D.L.R. (3d) 454, 1979 CarswellBC 313, 15 B.C.L.R. 311 (B.C. S.C.) 1058

Clement v. McGuinty, [2000] O.T.C. 438, 2000 CarswellOnt 2252, [2000] O.J. No. 2466 (Ont. S.C.J.), additional reasons at (2000), 2000 CarswellOnt 2617, [2000] O.J. No. 2730 (Ont. S.C.J.), reversed (2001), 143 O.A.C. 328, 2001 CarswellOnt 1275, 18 C.P.C. (5th) 267 (Ont. C.A.) 637

Clement, Re, 44 D.L.R. 623, 1919 CarswellBC 5, [1919] 1 W.W.R. 372, 30 C.C.C. 309 (B.C. S.C.), reversed 1919 CarswellBC 94, [1919] 3 W.W.R. 309 (B.C. C.A.) 76

Clinton, President of the United States, et al v. Glavin et al, case no. 98-564 496

Clinton v. City of New York, 141 L.Ed.2d 393 (1998) 773

Clinton v. Jones, 137 L.Ed.2d 945, 520 U.S. 681, 117 S.Ct. 1636, 65 U.S.L.W. 4372, 70 Empl. Prac. Dec. 44,646 (U.S. Ark., 1997) 1114

Closure of British Columbia Human Rights Commission, 2002 835

Coalition of Citizens for a Charter Challenge v. Metropolitan Authority (1993), 122 N.S.R. (2d) 1, 338 A.P.R. 1, 1993 CarswellNS 33, 10 C.E.L.R. (N.S.) 257, 103 D.L.R. (4th) 409 (N.S. S.C. [In Chambers]), reversed (1993), 1993 CarswellNS 34, 12 C.E.L.R. (N.S.) 1, 125 N.S.R. (2d) 241, 349 A.P.R. 241, 108 D.L.R. (4th) 145, 20 Admin. L.R. (2d) 283 (N.S. C.A.), leave to appeal refused (1994), 12 C.E.L.R. (N.S.) 319 (S.C.C.) 32

Colt and Glover v. Bishop of Coventry and Litchfield, Hob. 140, 80 E.R. 290 175

Columbia Broadcasting System v. Democratic National Commission, 412 U.S. 94 (1973) 629

Colvin, Re, [1993] 2 F.C. 351, 1993 CarswellNat 213, 1993 CarswellNat 213F, 61 F.T.R. 210, 15 C.R.R. (2d) 131 (Fed. T.D.), affirmed 1994 CarswellNat

851, 1994 CarswellNat 1485, 25 Admin. L.R. (2d) 174, 173 N.R. 290, 81
F.T.R. 319 (note), [1994] 3 F.C. 562, 25 C.R.R. (2d) 186 (note) (Fed.
C.A.) 1041

Comeau's Sea Foods Ltd. v. Canada (Minister of Fisheries & Oceans), 142 D.L.R.
(4th) 193, 1997 CarswellNat 10, 1997 CarswellNat 11, 206 N.R. 363, 31
C.C.L.T. (2d) 236, 43 Admin. L.R. (2d) 1, [1997] 1 S.C.R. 12 (S.C.C.) .. 863,
879

*Comité pour la République du Canada - Committee for the Commonwealth
of Canada v. Canada*, **[1991] 1 S.C.R. 139 (S.C.C.), reconsideration
refused (May 8, 1991), Doc. 20334 (S.C.C.)** 40

Comité Provisoire pour le NON c. Ministre des Transports du Québec
**(September 21, 1995), n° 500-05-010066-957 (Que. S.C.), not
reported** 613

Comité spécial pour l'unité canadienne c. Conseil du referendum (17 décembre
1996), n° C.S. Montréal 500-05-012726-954, [1996] A.Q. No. 4240 (Que.
S.C.) and (16 novembre 2000), n° C.A. Montréal 500-09-004438-974,
[2000] J.Q. No. 5643 (Que. C.A.) 357

Commission for Public Complaints Against the R.C.M.P., Chair's Interim
Report on Events at the Summit of the Americas, Québec, April 20-22,
2001, October 29, 2003 896

Commission for Public Complaints Against the R.C.M.P., **Interim and
Final Report, July 31, 2001 and March 25, 2002, file No. PC 6910-
199801** 884

Commission of Inquiry Chaired by Mr. Justice Gomery, **established
February 19, 2004** ....

Commission of the European Communities v. Greece, European Court Reports,
2000, page I – 5047, Case C-387/97 1169

Commonwealth v. Woodward, 7 Mass. L. Rep. 449 (Mass. Super., 1997) .. 1181

Communist Party of Canada v. Canada (Attorney General), Ontario Court
(General Division), October 1, 1993, not reported 518

Communist Party of Chile v. Augusto Pinochet, Court of Appeal of Santiago,
January 12, 1998 1120

*Communist Party of the United States v. Subversive Activities Control Board No.
12*, 367 U.S. 1 (1961) 518

Complaint of Brill-Edwards to the Privacy Commissioner, Letter-decision; June
22, 1998 1041

*Complaint of Conflict of Interest by Peter Jenkins, M.L.A. against Hon. Pat
Duncan, First Minister of the Yukon*, Decision of the Commissioner under
the Conflict of Interest Act, November 29, 2001 637

*Concerned Citizens of Vinemont, Fruitland & Winona v. Canada Post
Corp.* **(1992), 58 F.T.R. 140, 1992 CarswellNat 1035 (Fed. T.D.)** 143

Condon v. Prince Edward Island, 2002 PESCTD 41, [2002] P.E.I.J. No. 56, 2002 CarswellPEI 57, 2002 C.L.L.C. 230-029, 214 Nfld. & P.E.I.R. 244, 642 A.P.R. 244, 95 C.R.R. (2d) 216, 43 Admin. L.R. (3d) 71, 43 C.H.R.R. D/433 (P.E.I. T.D. [In Chambers]) 853

Confirmation of John Ashcroft as Attorney General of the United States, Hearings in the United States Senate, February, 2001 282

Controversy Involving the Purchase of CIPRO by the Minister of Health, October–November, 2001 881

Conyers v. Reagan, 765 F.2d 1124 (C.A. D.C., 1985) 905

Cook v. Gralike, 149 L.Ed.2d 44 (2001) 518

Coon Come v. Commission Hydro-Électrique de Québec, [1991] R.J.Q. 922, 1991 CarswellQue 1013, [1991] 3 C.N.L.R. 40 (Que. C.A.) 209

Coorsh v. Decker (1955), [1956] Que. Q.B. 78 (Que. Q.B.) 758

Copello v. Canada (Minister of Foreign Affairs) (1998), 152 F.T.R. 110, 1998 CarswellNat 1762, [1998] F.C.J. No. 1301 (Fed. T.D.) and (2000), [2000] F.C.J. No. 1641, 2000 CarswellNat 2349, 196 F.T.R. 159 (note) (Fed. C.A.) and (2001), [2001] F.C.J. No. 1835, 2001 CarswellNat 3592, 2001 CarswellNat 2792, 2001 FCT 1350, 39 Admin. L.R. (3d) 89, [2002] 3 F.C. 24, 213 F.T.R. 272 (Fed. T.D.), affirmed 2003 CarswellNat 1955, 2003 CarswellNat 2594, 3 Admin. L.R. (4th) 214, 308 N.R. 175, 2003 FCA 295, 2003 CAF 295 (Fed. C.A.) 1047

Copps v. Hustler Magazine and Riverin, 1999, litigation not initiated 620

Corp. of the Canadian Civil Liberties Assn. v. Ontario (Minister of Education) (1990), 71 O.R. (2d) 341, 1990 CarswellOnt 1078, 65 D.L.R. (4th) 1, 46 C.R.R. 316, 37 O.A.C. 93, (Ont. C.A.) 115

Corriero v. Liberal Party of Ontario (August 31, 2001), Doc. 01-CV-216594-CM (Ont. S.C.J.), not reported 609

Coyne v. R. (July 30, 1993), Doc. T-381-93 (Fed. T.D.), not reported 453

Crédit Suisse v. United States District Court for the Central District of California, 130 F.3d 1342 (9th Cir., 1997) 1128

Cree Regional Authority v. Robinson, [1991] 3 F.C. 533, 1991 CarswellNat 354, 1991 CarswellNat 791, 1 Admin. L.R. (2d) 173, 81 D.L.R. (4th) 659, [1991] 3 C.N.L.R. 82, 127 N.R. 52, 43 F.T.R. 240 (note) (Fed. C.A.), leave to appeal refused (July 4, 1991), Doc. 22485, 22486 (S.C.C.) 17

Cross c. Teasdale, [1991] R.J.Q. 1826 à 1832, 1991 CarswellQue 15, 6 C.R. (4th) 343 (Que. C.A.) 1188

Croteau v. Canada (1995), 92 F.T.R. 288, 1995 CarswellNat 1061 (Fed. T.D.) 915

Crowe v. R., 2003 FCA 191, 2003 CarswellNat 982, 2003 CarswellNat 2492, [2003] 4 F.C. 321, 2003 D.T.C. 5288, [2003] 3 C.T.C. 271, 2003 CAF 191, 226 D.L.R. (4th) 685, 303 N.R. 305 (Fed. C.A.) 921

Currie v. MacDonald **(1949), 29 Nfld. & P.E.I.R. 294, 82 A.P.R. 294, 1949 CarswellNfld 12 (Nfld. C.A.)** 425, 954

Dagg v. Canada (Minister of Finance), [1997] 2 S.C.R. 403, 1997 CarswellNat 870, 1997 CarswellNat 869, [1997] S.C.J. No. 63, 213 N.R. 161, 148 D.L.R. (4th) 385, 46 Admin. L.R. (2d) 155, 132 F.T.R. 55 (note) (S.C.C.) 1031

Davis v. Bandemer, 106 S.Ct. 2797 (1986) 495

De Cosmos v. R. **(1883), 1 B.C.R. (Pt. 2) 26, 1883 CarswellBC 5 (B.C. S.C.)** 670

DeBané v. **Canadian Broadcasting Corporation, Ontario Court (General Division), filed May 31 1995, file 91722/95, not completed** 935

Décision 92-312, Traité de Maastricht sur l'Union européenne, Conseil Constitutionnel, le 2 septembre 1992 366

Décision 93-308, Traité de Maastricht sur l'Union européenne, Conseil Constitutionnel, le 9 avril 1992 366

Decision on the Lawlessness of the Communist Regime, **Pl. US 19/93, Constitutional Court (Czech Republic)** 223

Decision regarding the Referendum on Accession to NATO, **Constitutional Court, 2/1997.(X.14.) (Hungary)** 314

Decker v. Coorsh (1955), [1956] B.R. 78 (Que. Q.B.) 759

Declaration and Plan of Action to Strengthen Democracy, Organization of American States Summit of the Americas, Final Communiqué, April 22, 2001 323

Decock v. Alberta, 2000 ABCA 122, 2000 CarswellAlta 384, [2000] A.J. No. 419, 186 D.L.R. (4th) 265, 79 Alta. L.R. (3d) 11, [2000] 7 W.W.R. 219, 255 A.R. 234, 220 W.A.C. 234 (Alta. C.A.), leave to appeal allowed (2000), 2000 CarswellAlta 1366, 2000 CarswellAlta 1367, 266 N.R. 200 (note), 293 A.R. 388 (note), 257 W.A.C. 388 (note) (S.C.C.) 864

Delgamuukw v. British Columbia (1997), 153 D.L.R. (4th) 193, [1997] S.C.J. No. 108, 1997 CarswellBC 2358, 1997 CarswellBC 2359, 220 N.R. 161, 99 B.C.A.C. 161, 162 W.A.C. 161, [1997] 3 S.C.R. 1010, [1998] 1 C.N.L.R. 14, [1999] 10 W.W.R. 34, 66 B.C.L.R. (3d) 285 (S.C.C.) 212

Delisle c. Canada (Procureure générale), **[1998] R.J.Q. 2751 à 2767, 1998 CarswellQue 955, 1998 CarswellQue 2901 (Que. S.C.)** 505

Democracy Watch v. Chrétien et al., Federal Court of Canada – Trial Division; filed December 3, 2001 1165

Democratic Republic of the Congo v. Belgium, February 14, 2002 (International Court of Justice) 1071

Department of Commerce et al. v. United States House of Representatives et al., **142 L.Ed.2d 797 (1999)** 495

Desrosiers v. Gough (1998), 235 A.R. 127, 1998 CarswellAlta 1038 (Alta. Q.B.), additional reasons on (1998), 1998 CarswellAlta 1033, 235 A.R. 127 at 130 (Alta. Q.B.) 592

Dewar v. Ontario (1998), 156 D.L.R. (4th) 202, 1998 CarswellOnt 812, 37 O.R. (3d) 170, 108 O.A.C. 125, 37 C.C.E.L. (2d) 214, 7 Admin. L.R. (3d) 207 (Ont. C.A.) 845

Dick v. Dick (1993), 46 R.F.L. (3d) 219, 1993 CarswellOnt 320, [1993] O.J. No. 140 (Ont. Gen. Div.), additional reasons at (1993), 1993 CarswellOnt 4128 (Ont. Gen. Div.) 66

Dickerson v. United States, 166 F.3d 667 (4th Cir., 1999) and 120 S. Ct. 2326, 147 L.Ed.2d 405, 68 U.S.L.W. 4566, 530 U.S. 428 (U.S. Va., 2000) 277

Distribution Canada Inc. v. Minister of National Revenue, [1993] 2 F.C. 26, 1993 CarswellNat 803, 1993 CarswellNat 1305, [1993] F.C.J. No. 9, 10 Admin. L.R. (2d) 44, 99 D.L.R. (4th) 440, 149 N.R. 152, 60 F.T.R. 160 (note), 11 T.T.R. 186 (Fed. C.A.), leave to appeal refused (1993), 12 Admin. L.R. (2d) 280n (S.C.C.) 869

Dixon v. British Columbia (Attorney General), 59 D.L.R. (4th) 247, 1989 CarswellBC 43, 35 B.C.L.R. (2d) 273, [1989] 4 W.W.R. 393 (B.C. S.C.) 162, 226

Dixon v. Canada (Somalia Inquiry Commission), [1997] 2 F.C. 391, 1997 CarswellNat 307, 1997 CarswellNat 1571, 146 D.L.R. (4th) 156, 46 Admin. L.R. (2d) 245, 128 F.T.R. 249 (Fed. T.D.), reversed 1997 CarswellNat 1133, 1997 CarswellNat 2149, 149 D.L.R. (4th) 269, [1997] 3 F.C. 169, 218 N.R. 139, 3 Admin. L.R. (3d) 306 (Fed. C.A.), leave to appeal refused (1998), [1997] S.C.C.A. No. 505, 226 N.R. 400 (S.C.C.) 833

Dixon v. Canada (Somalia Inquiry Commission), [1997] 3 F.C. 169, 1997 CarswellNat 1133, 1997 CarswellNat 2149, 1 49 D.L.R. (4th) 269, 218 N.R. 139, 3 Admin. L.R. (3d) 306 (Fed. C.A.), leave to appeal refused (1998), [1997] S.C.C.A. No. 505, 226 N.R. 400 (S.C.C.) 833

Doe et al. v. Bush and Rumsfeld, 323 F.3d 133 (CA 1; March 13, 2003) and 322 F.3d 109 (CA 1; March 18, 2003) 907

Doern v. British Columbia (Police Complaint Commissioner), 203 D.L.R. (4th) 295, 2001 CarswellBC 1414, [2001] B.C.J. No. 1405, 2001 BCCA 446, 92 B.C.L.R. (3d) 76, [2001] 9 W.W.R. 216, 155 B.C.A.C. 105, 254 W.A.C. 105 (B.C. C.A.), leave to appeal allowed (2002), 2002 CarswellBC 541, 2002 CarswellBC 542, [2001] S.C.C.A. No. 504, 293 N.R. 195 (note), 173 B.C.A.C. 178 (note), 283 W.A.C. 178 (note), 227 D.L.R. (4th) 239 (S.C.C.), set aside/quashed (2003), 2003 CarswellBC 1068, 2003 CarswellBC 1069 (S.C.C.) 896

Dolphin Delivery Ltd. v. R.W.D.S.U., Local 580 (1986), [1986] 2 S.C.R. 573, 1986 CarswellBC 411, 1986 CarswellBC 764, [1986] S.C.J. No. 75, 38 C.C.L.T. 184, 71 N.R. 83, 9 B.C.L.R. (2d) 273, 87 C.L.L.C. 14,002, 33

D.L.R. (4th) 174, 25 C.R.R. 321, [1987] D.L.Q. 69 (note), [1987] 1 W.W.R. 577 (S.C.C.) 78

Doucet-Boudreau v. Nova Scotia (Department of Education), 2003 SCC 62, 2003 CarswellNS 375, 2003 CarswellNS 376, [2003] S.C.J. No. 63, 232 D.L.R. (4th) 577, [2003] 3 S.C.R. 3, 312 N.R. 1, 218 N.S.R. (2d) 311, 687 A.P.R. 311 (S.C.C.) 256

Douglas v. R. (1993), 98 D.L.R. (4th) 129, 1992 CarswellNat 156, 1992 CarswellNat 156F, 93 C.L.L.C. 17,004, 19 C.H.R.R. D/76, 12 C.R.R. (2d) 284, [1993] 1 F.C. 264, 58 F.T.R. 147 (Fed. T.D.) ....

Douglas/Kwantlen Faculty Assn. v. Douglas College **(1990), 77 D.L.R. (4th) 94, 1990 CarswellBC 278, 1990 CarswellBC 766, [1990] S.C.J. No. 124, 91 C.L.L.C. 17,002, [1990] 3 S.C.R. 570, [1991] 1 W.W.R. 643, 118 N.R. 340, 52 B.C.L.R. (2d) 68, 13 C.H.R.R. D/403, 50 Admin. L.R. 69, 2 C.R.R. (2d) 157 (S.C.C.)** 14, 87

Driskell v. Manitoba (Attorney General), **[1999] 11 W.W.R. 615, 1999 CarswellMan 366, 67 C.R.R. (2d) 147, 140 Man. R. (2d) 49 (Man. Q.B.)** 1179

Duggan v. Newfoundland **(1992), 99 Nfld. & P.E.I.R. 56, 315 A.P.R. 56, 1992 CarswellNfld 190, 91 D.L.R. (4th) 262 (Nfld. T.D.)** 803

Duggan v. Newfoundland **(1993), 107 Nfld. & P.E.I.R. 33, 336 A.P.R. 33, 1993 CarswellNfld 156, [1993] N.J. No. 84 (Nfld. T.D.)** 862

Dumont c. Johnson **(1994), [1994] A.Q. No. 604, 1994 CarswellQue 973 (Que. C.A.)** 551

Dunmore v. Ontario (Attorney General), 207 D.L.R. (4th) 193, 2001 CarswellOnt 4434, 2001 CarswellOnt 4435, [2001] S.C.J. No. 87, 2001 SCC 94, 13 C.C.E.L. (3d) 1, 2002 C.L.L.C. 220-004, 279 N.R. 201, 154 O.A.C. 201, 89 C.R.R. (2d) 189, [2001] 3 S.C.R. 1016 (S.C.C.) 1031

Durham (Town) v. Ontario (Attorney General) (1978), 23 O.R. (2d) 279, 1978 CarswellOnt 1318, 95 D.L.R. (3d) 327 (Ont. H.C.) 811

Dussault v. Palmer ....

Earle v. Coltsfoot Publishing Co., **Nova Scotia Supreme Court, February 10, 2000, not reported, file no. 129049** 996

East Timor prosecutions and litigation, started February 2000 (Indonesia) 1123

Elahi v. Islamic Republic of Iran, 124 F. Supp.2d 97 (D.D.C., 2000) 896, 897

Esquimalt & Nanaimo Railway v. Wilson (1920), [1922] 1 A.C. 202, 1921 CarswellBC 102, [[1921] 3 W.W.R. 817, 28 C.R.C. 296, 61 D.L.R. 1 (British Columbia P.C.) 151

Eurig Estate, Re **(1998), 165 D.L.R. (4th) 1, 1998 CarswellOnt 3950, 1998 CarswellOnt 3951, [1998] S.C.J. No. 72, 40 O.R. (3d) 160 (headnote** only), 231 N.R. 55, 23 E.T.R. (2d) 1, 114 O.A.C. 55, [1998] 2 S.C.R. 565, [2000] 1 C.T.C. 284 (S.C.C.) 107

Ex parte Attorney-General; Re the Constitutional Relationship between the Attorney-General and the Prosecutor-General (1995), 3 L.R.C. 507 (S.C.) (Namibia) 284

Ex parte Augusto Pinochet Ugarte, [1998] All E.R. (D) 629, October 28, 1998 1132

Ex parte Chairperson of the Constitutional Assembly, in re Certification of the Constitution of the Republic of South Africa, 1996, 1996 (4) SA 744 (CC) 370

Expulsion of John Nunziata, M.P. from the Caucus of the Liberal Party of Canada, 1996, litigation not initiated 929

Favreau v. Québec (Cour de Kahnawake), [1993] R.J.Q. 1450, 1993 CarswellQue 14, 22 C.R. (4th) 257 (Que. S.C.), affirmed [1995] R.J.Q. 2348 (Que. C.A.) 209

Federal Liberal Agency of Canada v. CTV Television Network Ltd. (1988), [1989] 1 F.C. 319, 1988 CarswellNat 141F, 1988 CarswellNat 141, 24 C.P.R. (3d) 466 (Fed. T.D.), affirmed (1988), 1988 CarswellNat 1000, 24 C.P.R. (3d) 466 at 470, 99 N.R. 74, 27 F.T.R. 160 (note) (Fed. C.A.), leave to appeal refused (1989), 24 C.P.R. (3d) 466n (S.C.C.) and (1988), [1989] 1 F.C. 324, 1988 CarswellNat 142F, 1988 CarswellNat 142, 24 F.T.R. 211, 24 C.P.R. (3d) 470 (Fed. T.D.), affirmed (1988), 99 N.R. 74, 27 F.T.R. 160 (note), 24 C.P.R. (3d) 470 at 478 (Fed. C.A.) 526

Fenton v. Service Plus Hospitality Ltd., Alberta Court of Queen's Bench, filed March 8, 2001, action no. 01100-00422 of 2001, settled May 2, 2001 ....

Ferranti-Packard Ltd. v. Cushman Rentals Ltd. (1980), 30 O.R. (2d) 194, 1980 CarswellOnt 444, 19 C.P.C. 132, 115 D.L.R. (3d) 691 (Ont. Div. Ct.), affirmed (1981), 1981 CarswellOnt 781, 31 O.R. (2d) 799, 123 D.L.R. (3d) 766 (Ont. C.A.) 91

Ferrell v. Ontario (Attorney General) (1997), 149 D.L.R. (4th) 335, 1997 CarswellOnt 3046, [1997] O.J. No. 2765, 45 C.R.R. (2d) 177, 97 C.L.L.C. 230-034, 36 O.T.C. 384 (Ont. Gen. Div.), affirmed (1998), 1998 CarswellOnt 4754, 58 C.R.R. (2d) 21, 99 C.L.L.C. 230-005, 168 D.L.R. (4th) 1, 116 O.A.C. 176, 42 O.R. (3d) 97 (Ont. C.A.), leave to appeal refused (1999), 252 N.R. 197 (note), 134 O.A.C. 199 (note) (S.C.C.) .. 101

Ferrell v. Ontario (Attorney General) (1998), 42 O.R. (3d) 97, 1998 CarswellOnt 4754, 58 C.R.R. (2d) 21, 99 C.L.L.C. 230-005, 168 D.L.R. (4th) 1, 116 O.A.C. 176 (Ont. C.A.), leave to appeal refused (1999), 252 N.R. 197 (note), 134 O.A.C. 199 (note) (S.C.C.) 693

Figueroa v. Canada (Attorney General) (1997), 147 D.L.R. (4th) 765, 1997 CarswellOnt 1782, 100 O.A.C. 232, 34 O.R. (3d) 59 (Ont. Div. Ct.) and (1999), 170 D.L.R. (4th) 647, 1999 CarswellOnt 665, 43 O.R. (3d) 728, 61

C.R.R. (2d) 91 (Ont. Gen. Div.), varied (2000), 2000 CarswellOnt 2885, [2000] O.J. No. 3007, 189 D.L.R. (4th) 577, 50 O.R. (3d) 161, 137 O.A.C. 252, 67 O.R. (3d) 440 (note) (Ont. C.A.), leave to appeal allowed (2001), 2001 CarswellOnt 766, 2001 CarswellOnt 767, [2000] S.C.C.A. No. 511, 269 N.R. 206 (note), 149 O.A.C. 199 (note) (S.C.C.), reversed 227 D.L.R. (4th) 1, [2003] S.C.J. No. 37, 2003 CarswellOnt 2462, 2003 CarswellOnt 2463, 176 O.A.C. 89, 108 C.R.R. (2d) 66, [2003] 1 S.C.R. 912, 2003 SCC 37, 306 N.R. 70 (S.C.C.) 584

Figueroa v. Canada (Attorney General), 227 D.L.R. (4th) 1, [2003] S.C.J. No. 37, 2003 CarswellOnt 2462, 2003 CarswellOnt 2463, 176 O.A.C. 89, 108 C.R.R. (2d) 66, [2003] 1 S.C.R. 912, 2003 SCC 37, 306 N.R. 70 (S.C.C.) 518

Final Report of the Walkerton Inquiry, Hon. Dennis O'Connor, issued January 18, 2002 817

Finlay v. Canada (Minister of Finance) (1986), [1986] 2 S.C.R. 607, 1986 CarswellNat 104, 1986 CarswellNat 741, [1987] 1 W.W.R. 603, 33 D.L.R. (4th) 321, 71 N.R. 338, 23 Admin. L.R. 197, 17 C.P.C. (2d) 289, 8 C.H.R.R. D/3789 (S.C.C.) 911

First National Properties Ltd. v. Highlands (District), 198 D.L.R. (4th) 443, 2001 CarswellBC 884, [2001] B.C.J. No. 925, 2001 BCCA 305, 88 B.C.L.R. (3d) 125, 17 M.P.L.R. (3d) 80, 152 B.C.A.C. 83, 250 W.A.C. 83, 9 C.C.L.T. (3d) 34 (B.C. C.A.), leave to appeal refused (2001), [2001] S.C.C.A. No. 365, 2001 CarswellBC 2807, 2001 CarswellBC 2808, 285 N.R. 198 (note), 169 B.C.A.C. 320 (note), 276 W.A.C. 320 (note) (S.C.C.) 817

Fiske v. Nova Scotia (Attorney General), 2001 NSSC 99, 2001 CarswellNS 244, 195 N.S.R. (2d) 108, 609 A.P.R. 108 (N.S. S.C.) 862

Fitzgerald v. Muldoon, [1976] 2 N.Z.L.R. 615 (New Zealand S.C.) 667

Flatow v. Islamic Republic of Iran, 999 F. Supp.2d (D.D.C., 1998) 896

Flieger v. New Brunswick, [1993] 2 S.C.R. 651, 1993 CarswellNB 137, 1993 CarswellNB 151, 48 C.C.E.L. 1, 155 N.R. 1, 104 D.L.R. (4th) 292, 138 N.B.R. (2d) 161, 354 A.P.R. 161 (S.C.C.) 829

Florida Prepaid Postsecondary Education Expense Board v. College Saving Bank, 144 L.Ed.2d 575 (1999) 105

Fogal v. Canada (1999), 161 F.T.R. 121, 1999 CarswellNat 55, [1999] F.C.J. No. 39 (Fed. T.D.) and (1999), 30 C.P.C. (4th) 13, 1999 CarswellNat 164, [1999] F.C.J. No. 129, 164 F.T.R. 99 (Fed. T.D.), affirmed (2000), 2000 CarswellNat 1229, [2000] F.C.J. No. 916, 258 N.R. 97, 184 F.T.R. 160 (note) (Fed. C.A.), leave to appeal refused (2001), 2001 CarswellNat 1196, 2001 CarswellNat 1197, 273 N.R. 400 (note) (S.C.C.) and (1999), 167 F.T.R. 266, 1999 CarswellNat 939, [1999] F.C.J. No. 788, 38 C.P.C. (4th) 159 (Fed. T.D.), affirmed (2000), 2000 CarswellNat 1229, [2000] F.C.J. No. 916, 258 N.R. 97, 184 F.T.R. 160 (note) (Fed. C.A.), leave to

appeal refused (2001), 2001 CarswellNat 1196, 2001 CarswellNat 1197, 273 N.R. 400 (note) (S.C.C.) 908

Foret v. British Columbia (Attorney General) (1996), 48 C.P.C. (3d) 165, 1996 CarswellBC 424, 21 B.C.L.R. (3d) 179, 73 B.C.A.C. 25, 120 W.A.C. 25 (B.C. C.A.) 519

Forget c. Québec (Commission des valeurs mobilières), [1993] R.J.Q. 2145 à 2170, [1993] R.R.A. 623 (Que. S.C.) 806

Forghanian-Arani, Re (1991), 50 F.T.R. 1, 1991 CarswellNat 296 (Fed. T.D.) 222

Formea Chemicals Ltd. v. Polymer Corp., [1968] S.C.R. 754, 1968 CarswellOnt 33, 38 Fox Pat. C. 116, 55 C.P.R. 38, 69 D.L.R. (2d) 114 (S.C.C.) 77

Foster v. Love, 139 L.Ed.2d 369 (1997) 473

Fourteenth Report of the Standing Committee on Procedure and House Affairs, May 9, 2001 277

Francis v. Mohawk Council of Akwesasne (1993), 62 F.T.R. 314, 1993 CarswellNat 423, [1993] F.C.J. No. 369 (Fed. T.D.) 567

Francis v. Mohawk Council of Kanesatake, 2003 FCT 115, 2003 CarswellNat 235, 2003 CarswellNat 2792, 227 F.T.R. 161, [2003] 3 C.N.L.R. 86, 2003 CFPI 115 (Fed. T.D.) 532

Fraser v. Canada (Treasury Board, Department of National Revenue) (1985), 23 D.L.R. (4th) 122, 1985 CarswellNat 669, 1985 CarswellNat 145, [1985] 2 S.C.R. 455, 63 N.R. 161, 18 Admin. L.R. 72, 9 C.C.E.L. 233, 86 C.L.L.C. 14,003, 19 C.R.R. 152, [1986] D.L.Q. 84 (note) (S.C.C.) 291, 302

Fraser v. Nova Scotia (Attorney General) (1986), 30 D.L.R. (4th) 340, 1986 CarswellNS 287, 74 N.S.R. (2d) 91, 180 A.P.R. 91, 24 C.R.R. 193 (N.S. T.D.) 287

Friends of Democracy v. Northwest Territories (Commissioner) (1999), 171 D.L.R. (4th) 551, 1999 CarswellNWT 33 (N.W.T. S.C.), leave to appeal refused (1999), 1999 CarswellNWT 73, 176 D.L.R. (4th) 661 (N.W.T. C.A.) 491

Friends of the Athabaska Environmental Assn. v. Alberta (Director of Standards & Approvals) (1992), 131 A.R. 129, 25 W.A.C. 129, 1992 CarswellAlta 90, 3 Alta. L.R. (3d) 275, 6 Admin. L.R. (2d) 6 (Alta. C.A.), leave to appeal refused (1993), 9 Admin. L.R. (2d) 100 (note), 7 Alta. L.R. (3d) liii (note), 151 N.R. 160 (note), 141 A.R. 319 (note), 46 W.A.C. 319 (note) (S.C.C.) 853

Friends of the Island Inc. v. Canada (Minister of Public Works) [1993] 2 F.C. 229, 1993 CarswellNat 5, 1993 CarswellNat 1310, 10 C.E.L.R. (N.S.) 204, 102 D.L.R. (4th) 696, 61 F.T.R. 4 (Fed. T.D.), reversed (1995), 1995 CarswellNat 782, 191 N.R. 241, 131 D.L.R. (4th) 285, 106 F.T.R. 320 (note)

(Fed. C.A.), leave to appeal refused (1996), [1996] S.C.C.A. No. 80, 138
D.L.R. (4th) vii (note), 206 N.R. 76 (note) (S.C.C.) 425

Friends of the Oldman River Society v. Canada (Minister of Fisheries & Oceans)
(1998), 1998 CarswellNat 2856, 29 C.E.L.R. (N.S.) 315 (Fed. T.D.) 879

Friends of the Oldman River Society v. Canada (Minister of Transport),
**[1992] 1 S.C.R. 3, [1992] S.C.J. No. 1, 1992 CarswellNat 649, 1992
CarswellNat 1313, [1992] 2 W.W.R. 193, 3 Admin. L.R. (2d) 1, 7 C.E.L.R.
(N.S.) 1, 84 Alta. L.R. (2d) 129, 88 D.L.R. (4th) 1, 132 N.R. 321, 48 F.T.R.
160 (S.C.C.)** 17, 130

Friesen v. Hammell, **28 B.C.L.R. (3d) 354, 1997 CarswellBC 329, [1997] 4
W.W.R. 268 (B.C. S.C.) and (1997), 47 B.C.L.R. (3d) 308, 1997
CarswellBC 2316 (B.C. S.C.), additional reasons at (1998), 45 B.C.L.R.
(3d) 319, 1997 CarswellBC 2811, 15 C.P.C. (4th) 301, 4 Admin. L.R. (3d)
115 (B.C. S.C.), affirmed 57 B.C.L.R. (3d) 276, 1999 CarswellBC 88, 117
B.C.A.C. 1, 191 W.A.C. 1, [1999] 5 W.W.R. 345, 29 C.P.C. (4th) 241 (B.C.
C.A.), leave to appeal refused (2000), 252 N.R. 397 (note), 139 B.C.A.C.
155 (note), 227 W.A.C. 155 (note) (S.C.C.) and 190 D.L.R. (4th) 210, 2000
CarswellBC 1620, 2000 BCSC 1185, 78 B.C.L.R. (3d) 317 (B.C. S.C.),
additional reasons at 2002 CarswellBC 1956, 2002 BCSC 1103, 22 C.P.C.
(5th) 320 (B.C. S.C.)** 471, 653

Frobisher Bay Municipal Election, Re, [1986] N.W.T.R. 183, 1986
CarswellNWT 13 (N.W.T. S.C.) 1051

Furey v. Conception Bay Centre Roman Catholic School Board (1993), 108 Nfld.
& P.E.I.R. 328, 339 A.P.R. 328, 1993 CarswellNfld 116, 104 D.L.R. (4th)
455, 17 Admin. L.R. (2d) 46 (Nfld. C.A.) 50

Gabais v. Assemblée législative du Québec (May 3, 1965), Doc. 138-195 (Que.
S.C.) 720

Gaboriault v. Tecksol Inc., [1992] 3 F.C. 566, 1992 CarswellNat 207, 1992
CarswellNat 608, 92 C.L.L.C. 14,057, 8 Admin. L.R. (2d) 113, 146 N.R.
388 (Fed. C.A.), leave to appeal refused (1993), 149 N.R. 238 (note), 149
N.R. 320 (note) (S.C.C.) 105

Gairy and another v. Attorney General of Grenada, [2002] 1 A.C. 167 1071

Galati v. McGuinty (1999), [1999] O.J. No. 2171, 1999 CarswellOnt 1802, 64
C.R.R. (2d) 1 (Ont. S.C.J.), affirmed (1999), 1999 CarswellOnt 3770, 127
O.A.C. 161 (Ont. C.A.), leave to appeal refused (2001), 2001 CarswellOnt
2776, 2001 CarswellOnt 2777, 275 N.R. 391 (note), 153 O.A.C. 198 (note)
(S.C.C.) 609

***Gallant v. R.* (1948), [1949] 2 D.L.R. 425, 1948 CarswellPEI 4, 23 M.P.R. 48,
93 C.C.C. 237 (P.E.I. C.A.)** 785

Gauthier c. Canada (Conseil de la Radiodiffusion & des Télécommunications)
(2001), [2000] C.S.C.R. No. 575, 2001 CarswellNat 1293, 2001

CarswellNat 1294, 278 N.R. 199 (note) (S.C.C.), Federal Court of Appeal, file A-11-00 334

Gay v. Council, Township of Keppel (November 27, 1997), (Ont. Gen. Div.), not completed 139

Gazette (The) c. Conseil du Référendum, [2000] R.J.Q. 1082, 2000 CarswellQue 546 (Que. C.A.), leave to appeal refused (2001), 2001 CarswellQue 183, 2001 CarswellQue 184, 267 N.R. 400 (note) (S.C.C.) 243

Geiger v. London Monenco Consultants Ltd. (1992), 9 O.R. (3d) 509, 1992 CarswellOnt 959, 43 C.C.E.L. 291, 57 O.A.C. 222, 94 D.L.R. (4th) 233, 18 C.H.R.R. D/118, 92 C.L.L.C. 17,038 (Ont. C.A.), leave to appeal refused (1993), 151 N.R. 390n (S.C.C.) 52

George v. Harris (2003), 32 C.P.C. (5th) 134, 2003 CarswellOnt 80, 102 C.R.R. (2d) 316 and (2003), 2003 CarswellOnt 3548 (Ont. S.C.J.), additional reasons at (2003), 2003 CarswellOnt 1710 (Ont. S.C.J.) .. 1112

Geraghty v. Minister for Local Government (1975), I.R. 300 1212

Gerrard v. Manitoba (1992), 98 D.L.R. (4th) 167, 1992 CarswellMan 139, [1993] 1 W.W.R. 182, 81 Man. R. (2d) 295, 30 W.A.C. 295, 13 C.C.L.T. (2d) 256 (Man. C.A.) 817

Glitter v. Anders, Levant and Anderson, Court of Queen's Bench of Alberta, issued October 20, 1998, file no. 9801-14126, settled 631

GHZ Resource Corp. v. Vancouver Stock Exchange (1993), 1 C.C.L.S. 229, 1993 CarswellBC 1222, [1993] B.C.J. No. 3106 (B.C. C.A.), affirmed (1993), 1993 CarswellBC 1223, 1 C.C.L.S. 246 (B.C. C.A.) 144

Gil v. Canada (Minister of Employment & Immigration) (1994), [1995] 1 F.C. 508, 1994 CarswellNat 165, 1994 CarswellNat 1438F, [1994] F.C.J. No. 1559, 25 Imm. L.R. (2d) 209, 119 D.L.R. (4th) 497, 174 N.R. 292 (Fed. C.A.) 1001

Girard v. R. (1994), 79 F.T.R. 219, 1994 CarswellNat 631 (Fed. T.D.) ....

Glacier View Lodge Society v. British Columbia (Minister of Health), 136 B.C.A.C. 198, 2000 CarswellBC 723, [2000] B.C.J. No. 702, 2000 BCCA 242, 75 B.C.L.R. (3d) 373, 222 W.A.C. 198 (B.C. C.A.) 175

Gleason v. Lethbridge Community College (1995), 179 A.R. 130, 1995 CarswellAlta 790, 36 Alta. L.R. (3d) 103, [1996] 3 W.W.R. 377, 38 Admin. L.R. (2d) 137 (Alta. Q.B.) 144

Goddard v. Day (2000), 194 D.L.R. (4th) 559, 2000 CarswellAlta 1516, 80 C.R.R. (2d) 107, [2001] 5 W.W.R. 651, 90 Alta. L.R. (3d) 142, 282 A.R. 349 (Alta. Q.B.) 641

Goddard v. Day, 194 D.L.R. (4th) 551, 2000 CarswellAlta 1302, 2000 ABQB 822, 276 A.R. 185, 10 C.P.C. (5th) 337 (Alta. Q.B.) and (2000), 194 D.L.R. (4th) 559, 2000 CarswellAlta 1516, 80 C.R.R. (2d) 107, [2001] 5 W.W.R. 651, 90 Alta. L.R. (3d) 142, 282 A.R. 349 (Alta. Q.B.) and 200 D.L.R. (4th) 752, 2000 CarswellAlta 1623, [2000] A.J. No. 1612, 276 A.R. 180, 2000

ABQB 735 (Alta. Q.B.) and 2000 ABQB 799, 2000 CarswellAlta 1259, [2000] A.J. No. 1340, 86 Alta. L.R. (3d) 293, 276 A.R. 358, 5 C.P.C. (5th) 140 (Alta. Q.B. [In Chambers]) and (2000), 2000 ABQB 820, 2000 CarswellAlta 1301, 276 A.R. 304, 4 C.C.L.T. (3d) 125, 86 Alta. L.R. (3d) 300, [2001] 5 W.W.R. 501 (Alta. Q.B.) and 2000 ABQB 970, 2000 CarswellAlta 1495, [2000] A.J. No. 1580, 276 A.R. 279, 10 C.P.C. (5th) 133, 95 Alta. L.R. (3d) 112 (Alta. Q.B.), settled December, 2000 1087

Goddard v. Day, 200 D.L.R. (4th) 752, 2000 CarswellAlta 1623, [2000] A.J. No. 1612, 276 A.R. 180, 2000 ABQB 735 (Alta. Q.B.) 177

Godlewski v. McGurk and Whetung, Ontaraio Court (General Division) Toronto Registry, court file 95-CO-81 599

Goggin v. The State of Colorado et al. and U.S. Term Limits, Inc., 951 P.2d 911 (Colo., 1998) 780

Goh Chok Tong v. Joshua Benjamin Jeyaretnam (1998), 3 S.L.R. 337 (Singapore) 518

Gombu v. Ontario (Assistant Information & Privacy Commissioner) (2002), 59 O.R. (3d) 773, 2002 CarswellOnt 1599, [2002] O.J. No. 1776, 214 D.L.R. (4th) 163, 160 O.A.C. 105, 31 M.P.L.R. (3d) 277, 21 C.P.R. (4th) 96 (Ont. Div. Ct.), additional reasons at (2002), 2002 CarswellOnt 2132, [2002] O.J. No. 2570, 163 O.A.C. 185 (Ont. Div. Ct.), leave to appeal allowed (2002), 2002 CarswellOnt 2874 (Ont. C.A.) 243

Goose Bay Outfitters Ltd. v. Newfoundland (Minister of Tourism, Culture & Recreation) (2002), 214 Nfld. & P.E.I.R. 326, 2002 CarswellNfld 149, 642 A.P.R. 326 (Nfld. T.D.) 817

Gosselin c. Québec (Procureur général), [2002] 4 S.C.R. 429, 2002 CarswellQue 2706, 2002 CarswellQue 2707, [2002] S.C.J. No. 85, 2002 SCC 84, 298 N.R. 1, 221 D.L.R. (4th) 257, 100 C.R.R. (2d) 1, 44 C.H.R.R. D/363 (S.C.C.) 864

Gouriet v. Union of Post Office Workers (1977), [1978] A.C. 435, [1977] 3 W.L.R. 319, [1977] 3 All E.R. 70, [1977] 3 W.L.D. 300, [1977] 2 W.L.R. 310, [1977] Q.B. 729 (U.K. H.L.) 33

Government of British Columbia v. David Black Newspapers, Decision of the British Columbia Press Council; January 15, 1999 313

Government of Germany v. Krenz, Leipzig Court, November 7, 1999 1120

Gravel v. U.S., 408 U.S. 606 (1972) 740

Green Party Political Assn. of British Columbia v. Canadian Broadcasting Corp. (October 8, 1991), Doc. Vancouver C916786 (B.C. S.C.), Collver J., 29 A.C.W.S. (3d) 539 540

Grieve v. Sir Alec Douglas Hume, 1965 S.C. 315 at 318 556

Guenette v. Canada (Attorney General) (2002), 216 D.L.R. (4th) 410, 2002 CarswellOnt 2554, [2002] O.J. No. 3062, 2002 C.L.L.C. 220-038, 19 C.C.E.L. (3d) 36, 60 O.R. (3d) 601, 162 O.A.C. 371 (Ont. C.A.) 1041

Guerin v. R. (1985), 13 D.L.R. (4th) 321, 1984 CarswellNat 813, 1984
CarswellNat 693, [1984] 6 W.W.R. 481, [1984] 2 S.C.R. 335, 55 N.R. 161,
[1985] 1 C.N.L.R. 120, 20 E.T.R. 6, 36 R.P.R. 1, 59 B.C.L.R. 301
(S.C.C.) 108

Hagelin et al v. Federal Election Commission et al, Civil Action 96-2132 558

Haider v. Pelinka (Austria) 670

Haig v. R., **[1993] 2 S.C.R. 995, 105 D.L.R. (4th) 577, 1993 CarswellNat 1384,**
1993 CarswellNat 2353, 156 N.R. 81, 66 F.T.R. 80 (note), 16 C.R.R. (2d)
193 (S.C.C.) 233

Hamilton v. Al-Fayed, [2000] 1 A.C. 395 and [2000] E.W.J. No. 6960 782

Hamilton-Wentworth (Regional Municipality) v. Ontario (Minister of
Transportation) (1991), 2 O.R. (3d) 716, 1991 CarswellOnt 45, [1991]
O.J. No. 439, 45 C.L.R. 257, 34 M.V.R. (2d) 276, 49 Admin. L.R. 169, 78
D.L.R. (4th) 289, 46 O.A.C. 246 (Ont. Div. Ct.), leave to appeal refused
(1991), [1991] O.J. No. 3201, 4 Admin. L.R. (2d) 226 (Ont. C.A.) 811,
866

Hammond et al. v. The Queen, Federal Court of Canada - Trial Division,
April 22, 1991, file T-210-91, not reported 898

Harper v. Canada (Attorney General) (2002), 223 D.L.R. (4th) 275, [2002]
A.J. No. 1542, 2002 CarswellAlta 1664, 2002 ABCA 301, 320 A.R. 1, 288
W.A.C. 1, 14 Alta. L.R. (4th) 4, [2003] 8 W.W.R. 595 (Alta. C.A.), leave to
appeal allowed (2003), 2003 CarswellAlta 1287, 2003 CarswellAlta 1288
(S.C.C.), reversed 2004 CarswellAlta 646, 2004 CarswellAlta 647, 2004
SCC 33 (S.C.C.) and presently before the Supreme Court of
Canada 520

Harris v. Globe and Mail 1114

Harris v. R. (1998), [1999] 2 F.C. 392, 1998 CarswellNat 2468, 1998
CarswellNat 3027, 99 D.T.C. 5018, [1999] 1 C.T.C. 115, 161 F.T.R. 288
(Fed. T.D.), affirmed 2000 CarswellNat 1047, 2000 CarswellNat 1048,
[2000] F.C.J. No. 729, 2000 D.T.C. 6373, [2000] 3 C.T.C. 220, 187 D.L.R.
(4th) 419, [2000] 4 F.C. 37, 256 N.R. 221 (Fed. C.A.), leave to appeal
refused (2000), 2000 CarswellNat 2664, 2000 CarswellNat 2665, 264 N.R.
391 (S.C.C.) 915

Harrison v. University of British Columbia, 49 D.L.R. (4th) 687, 1988
CarswellBC 1, [1988] B.C.J. No. 13, 21 B.C.L.R. (2d) 145, [1988] 2 W.W.R.
688, 40 C.R.R. 205, 9 C.H.R.R. D/4557 (B.C. C.A.), reversed (1990), 1990
CarswellBC 764, 1990 CarswellBC 279, 91 C.L.L.C. 17,001, 52 B.C.L.R.
(2d) 105, [1991] 1 W.W.R. 681, 77 D.L.R. (4th) 55, [1990] 3 S.C.R. 451, 13
C.H.R.R. D/317, 2 C.R.R. (2d) 193, 120 N.R. 1 (S.C.C.), leave to appeal
allowed [1988] 4 W.W.R. lxxii (S.C.C.) 93

Harvey v. New Brunswick (Attorney General), [1996] 2 S.C.R. 876, 1996
CarswellNB 467, 1996 CarswellNB 468, 137 D.L.R. (4th) 142, 201 N.R. 1,

37 C.R.R. (2d) 189, 178 N.B.R. (2d) 161, 454 A.P.R. 161 (S.C.C.) 743, 754

Hawkes v. The Toronto Sun Publishing Corporation, Alberta Queen's Bench, filed February 2, 1994, file 9401-01702 (1994), settled 986

Haydon v. Canada (Treasury Board), 2004 FC 749, 2004 CarswellNat 1590 (F.C.) 299

Haydon v. R. (2000), [2001] 2 F.C. 82, 2000 CarswellNat 2024, 2000 CarswellNat 3450, [2000] F.C.J. No. 1368, 192 F.T.R. 161 (Fed. T.D.) 299, 817

Hébert et al. v. Canada (Attorney General), Federal Court of Canada - Trial Division, filed December 6, 1991, file T-3035-91, settled 825

Henderson v. Villeneuve & Mouvement de Libération Nationale du Québec, Superior Court of Québec, filed December 10, 1997 518

Henderson v. Villeneuve, Québec Superior Court, filed December 10, 1997, file no. 500-05-037916-978, not completed 359

Her Majesty's Advocate v. Megrahi and Fhimah, High Court of Justiciary at Camp Zeist, January 31, 2001, Case No: 1475/99 and Appeal No. C104/01, March 13, 2002 (Netherlands/Scotland) 1003

Hervieux-Payette c. Société St-Jean Baptiste de Montréal (1997), [1998] R.J.Q. 131 à 153, 1997 CarswellQue 3077, [1998] R.R.A. 221 (Que. S.C.), reversed 2002 CarswellQue 1170, [2002] J.Q. No. 1607, [2002] R.R.A. 727, [2002] R.J.Q. 1669 (Que. C.A.) 620

Herzig v. Canada, 2001 FCT 39, 2001 CarswellNat 253, [2001] F.C.J. No. 180, 200 F.T.R. 161 (Fed. T.D.), affirmed 2002 CarswellNat 232, 2002 CarswellNat 1256, 2002 FCA 36, 2002 CAF 36, 287 N.R. 105 (Fed. C.A.), leave to appeal refused (2002), 2002 CarswellNat 2191, 2002 CarswellNat 2192, 301 N.R. 394 (note) (S.C.C.) and 2001 PSSRB 68 (Can. P.S.S.R.B.) and 2002 FCA 36, 2002 CarswellNat 232, 2002 CarswellNat 1256, 2002 CAF 36, 287 N.R. 105 (Fed. C.A.), leave to appeal refused (2002), 2002 CarswellNat 2191, 2002 CarswellNat 2192, 301 N.R. 394 (note) (S.C.C.) 1209

Hesford v. General Council of the Bar, [1999] T.N.L.R. No. 617 (U.K.) .. 757

Hewat v. Ontario (1998), 37 O.R. (3d) 161, 1998 CarswellOnt 806, [1998] O.J. No. 802, 156 D.L.R. (4th) 193, 108 O.A.C. 117, 98 C.L.L.C. 220-037, 41 C.L.R.B.R. (2d) 54, 35 C.C.E.L. (2d) 32, 7 Admin. L.R. (3d) 257 (Ont. C.A.) 847

Hilao v. Estate of Marcos, 95 F.3d 848 (9th Cir., 1996) 1123

Hill v. Church of Scientology of Toronto, [1995] 2 S.C.R. 1130, 1995 CarswellOnt 396, 1995 CarswellOnt 534, [1995] S.C.J. No. 64, 25 C.C.L.T. (2d) 89, 184 N.R. 1, 126 D.L.R. (4th) 129, 24 O.R. (3d) 865 (note), 84 O.A.C. 1, 30 C.R.R. (2d) 189 (S.C.C.) 95

Hlavaty v. Canada (Minister of Employment & Immigration) (1993), 69 F.T.R. 259, 1993 CarswellNat 155, 22 Imm. L.R. (2d) 176 (Fed. T.D.) 318

Hoeppner v. Hermanson, December, 2000 and (2001) Ontario Court of Appeal, April 19, 2001 637

Hoeppner v. Manning et al., Manitoba Court of Queen's Bench, file No. CI 04-01-36726, in progress 609

Hoeppner v. Shaker, personally and on behalf of all other Executive Councillors of the Reform Party of Canada who voted on October 15, 1999, in favour of a resolution to revoke the applicant's membership in the Reform Party of Canada, Manitoba Queen's Bench, file C1 99- 01-15378, filed November 8, 1999, abandoned December 3, 1999 680

Hogan v. Newfoundland (Attorney General) (1998), 156 D.L.R. (4th) 139, 1998 CarswellNfld 6, 162 Nfld. & P.E.I.R. 132, 500 A.P.R. 132, 17 C.P.C. (4th) 300, 4 Admin. L.R. (3d) 59 (Nfld. T.D.) 427, 789

Hogan v. Newfoundland (Attorney General), 183 D.L.R. (4th) 225, 2000 CarswellNfld 47, [2000] N.J. No. 54, 2000 NFCA 12, 72 C.R.R. (2d) 1, 189 Nfld. & P.E.I.R. 183, 571 A.P.R. 183 (Nfld. C.A.), leave to appeal refused (2000), 2000 CarswellNfld 337, 2000 CarswellNfld 338, 264 N.R. 395 (note), 201 Nfld. & P.E.I.R. 179 (note), 605 A.P.R. 179 (note) (S.C.C.) 428, 531

Hogan v. Newfoundland (School Boards for Ten Districts) (1997), 149 D.L.R. (4th) 468, 1997 CarswellNfld 129, 154 Nfld. & P.E.I.R. 121, 479 A.P.R. 121 (Nfld. T.D.) 427

Hollinger Inc. and Black v. Nystrom, Ontario Superior Court of Justice, issued February 7 2000, file no. 00-CV-184764, discontinued 641

Hong Kong Special Administrative Region v. Ma Wai Kwan, Daniel and Others (1997), HKLRD 761 370

Hopkinson v. Canada (Commissioner of Patents) (1997), 1997 CarswellNat 1207, [1997] F.C.J. No. 848, 74 C.P.R. (3d) 332, 133 F.T.R. 241 (Fed. T.D.), reversed (2000), 2000 CarswellNat 681, [2000] F.C.J. No. 492, 5 C.P.R. (4th) 414, 254 N.R. 331, 181 F.T.R. 157 (note) (Fed. C.A.) 831

Horgan v. Taoiseach [2003 No. 3739P], (Transcript), April 28, 2003 (Ireland) 907

House of Sga'nisim v. Canada, 2000 BCCA 260, 2000 CarswellBC 866, [2000] B.C.J. No. 821 (B.C. C.A.) 218

House of Sga'Nisim v. Canada, 2000 BCSC 659, 2000 CarswellBC 873, [2000] B.C.J. No. 831 (B.C. S.C.) and 2000 BCCA 260, 2000 CarswellBC 866, [2000] B.C.J. No. 821 (B.C. C.A.) 213

Human Rights Institute of Canada v. Goldie (1999), [2000] 1 F.C. 475, 1999 CarswellNat 1766, 1999 CarswellNat 3009, 68 L.C.R. 81, 176 F.T.R. 225 (Fed. T.D.) 905

Hupacasath First Nation v. British Columbia, British Columbia Supreme Court, March 27, 2002, unreported and 2002 BCCA 238, 2002 CarswellBC 959, [2002] 2 C.N.L.R. 141, 169 B.C.A.C. 12, 276 W.A.C. 12 (B.C. C.A.) and 2002 BCSC 802, 2002 CarswellBC 2122 (B.C. S.C. [In Chambers]) 218, 415

I.B.E.W., Local 894 v.Ellis-Don Ltd., 194 D.L.R. (4th) 385, 2001 CarswellOnt 99, 2001 CarswellOnt 100, [2001] S.C.J. No. 5, 2001 SCC 4, 265 N.R. 2, 52 O.R. (3d) 160 (note), 2001 C.L.L.C. 220-028, 26 Admin. L.R. (3d) 171, 140 O.A.C. 201, [2001] 1 S.C.R. 221, [2001] O.L.R.B. Rep. 236, 66 C.L.R.B.R. (2d) 216 (S.C.C.) 50

Idaho v. Coeur d'Alene Tribe of Idaho, 138 L.Ed.2d 438 (1997) 8, 219

Idziak v. Canada (Minister of Justice), [1992] 3 S.C.R. 631, 1992 CarswellOnt 113, 1992 CarswellOnt 1000, 17 C.R. (4th) 161, 9 Admin. L.R. (2d) 1, 12 C.R.R. (2d) 77, 59 O.A.C. 241, 77 C.C.C. (3d) 65, 97 D.L.R. (4th) 577, 144 N.R. 327 (S.C.C.), reconsideration refused (1992), 9 Admin. L.R. (2d) 1n (S.C.C.) 263

Illahi Bux Soomro (Pakistan Muslim League) et al. v. General Pervez Musharraf et al., Supreme Court of Pakistan, May 11, 2000, Constitutional Petitions 62/99, 63/99, 53/99, 57/99, 3/2000, 66/99 and 64/99 380

Impeachment of President Boris Yeltsin, **Duma of the Russian Federation, May 15, 1999** 951

Impeachment of President Raul Cubas, Congress of the Republic of Paraguay, March, 1999 950

Impeachment of President William Clinton, **United States Congress, February 12, 1999** 943

In re Article 55 of the Constitution, [2003] N.R.S.C., Constitutional Reference No. 1 of 2003, Supreme Court of Nauru, January 11 and January 17, 2003 398

In Re Estate of Ferdinand E. Marcos Human Rights Litigation, Trajano v. Marcos, 978 F.2d 493 (9th Cir., 1992) 1123

In re Fayed, 91 F. Supp.2d 137 (D.D.C., 2000) 980

In re: Sealed Case No. 99-3091, United States Court of Appeal – D.C. Circuit, September 13, 1999 1213

In the Matter of Complaints under the Human Rights Act, Board of Inquiry Decision, July 23, 1999 1032

Independent Contractors & Business Assn. (British Columbia) v. British Columbia, [1995] 7 W.W.R. 159, 1995 CarswellBC 258, 6 B.C.L.R. (3d) 177, 31 Admin. L.R. (2d) 95 (B.C. S.C.) 141

Infolink v. LeDrew ....

Inshore Fishermens' Bonafide Defense Fund Assn. v. Canada (1994), 132
N.S.R. (2d) 370, 376 A.P.R. 370, 1994 CarswellNS 78, 28 C.P.C. (3d) 291,
117 D.L.R. (4th) 56 (N.S. C.A.) 874

Inuit Tapirisat of Canada v. Canada (Attorney General), [1980] 2 S.C.R.
735, 1980 CarswellNat 633, 1980 CarswellNat 633F, 115 D.L.R. (3d) 1, 33
N.R. 304 (S.C.C.) 148, 446

*Investigations of the Groupaction Contracts and the Sponsorship
Program*, Special Audit Report of the Auditor General of Canada to
the Minister of Public Works and Government Services on Three
Contracts Awarded to Groupaction, May, 2002 1102

Investigations of the Management of the Office of the Privacy Commissioner,
Annual Report of the Privacy Commissioner to Parliament for 2002-
2003 817

Irwin Toy Ltd. c. Québec (Procureur general), [1989] 1 S.C.R. 927 (S.C.C.) .. 731

Iscar Ltd. v. Karl Hertel GmbH (1988), 19 C.P.R. (3d) 385, 1988
CarswellNat 1024, 18 F.T.R. 264 (Fed. T.D.) 778

J.E. Verreault & Fils Ltée v. Quebec (Attorney General) (1975), 57 D.L.R.
(3d) 403, 1975 CarswellQue 38, 1975 CarswellQue 38F, [1977] 1 S.C.R.
41, 5 N.R. 271 (Fr.), 8 N.R. 72 (S.C.C.) 89

Jebanayagam v. Canada (Solicitor General) (1994), 30 Imm. L.R. (2d) 19,
1994 CarswellNat 1569, [1994] F.C.J. No. 1435, 85 F.T.R. 277 (Fed. T.D.),
reconsideration refused (1995), 30 Imm. L.R. (2d) 194, 1995
CarswellNat 1118, 91 F.T.R. 193, 32 Admin. L.R. (2d) 268 (Fed.
T.D.) 27

Jenner v. Sun Oil Co., [1952] O.R. 240, 1952 CarswellOnt 199, [1952] O.W.N.
151, 16 C.P.R. 87, [1952] 2 D.L.R. 526 (Ont. H.C.), leave to appeal allowed
[1952] O.W.N. 370 (Ont. H.C.) 982

Jepson and Dyas-Elliott v. The Labour Party, [1996] I.R.L.R. 116 609

Jerram v. Canada (Minister of Agriculture), [1994] 3 F.C. 17, 1994 CarswellNat
845, 1994 CarswellNat 1474, 76 F.T.R. 161, 24 Admin. L.R. (2d) 305 (Fed.
T.D.) 148

Johnson c. Arcand, [2002] R.J.Q. 2802, [2002] J.Q. No. 4591, 2002 CarswellQue
2063, [2002] R.R.A. 1153 (Que. S.C.), varied (2004), 2004 CarswellQue
117 (Que. C.A.) 629

Johnson v. British Columbia (Securities Commission) (1999), 67 B.C.L.R. (3d)
145, 1999 CarswellBC 987, [1999] B.C.J. No. 552, 67 B.C.L.R. (3d) 145, 64
C.R.R. (2d) 275 (B.C. S.C. [In Chambers]), reversed 206 D.L.R. (4th) 711,
2001 CarswellBC 2164, 2001 BCCA 597, [2001] 10 W.W.R. 635, 94
B.C.L.R. (3d) 233, 158 B.C.A.C. 69, 258 W.A.C. 69 (B.C. C.A.) 33

Johnston v. Li Preti (October 12, 1993), Doc. 93-CQ-43281 (Ont. Gen. Div.),
not reported 601

Johnston v. Prince Edward Island (1989), 73 Nfld. & P.E.I.R. 222, 229
A.P.R. 222, 1989 CarswellPEI 144 (P.E.I. C.A.) 1182

Jones v. Bennett (1967), 59 W.W.R. 449, 1967 CarswellBC 32 (B.C. S.C.),
reversed (1968), 1968 CarswellBC 16, 63 W.W.R. 1, 66 D.L.R. (2d) 497
(B.C. C.A.), reversed (1968), 1968 CarswellBC 181, [1969] S.C.R. 277, 2
D.L.R. (3d) 291, 66 W.W.R. 419 (S.C.C.) 641, 835

Jones v. Canada (Attorney General) (1974), [1975] 2 S.C.R. 182, 1974
CarswellNB 14, 1974 CarswellNB 14F, 16 C.C.C. (2d) 297, 1 N.R. 582, 7
N.B.R. (2d) 526, 45 D.L.R. (3d) 583 (S.C.C.) 325

Jones v. Canada (Attorney General), **British Columbia Supreme Court,
filed December 8, 1997, case no. C976571, Vancouver registry,
discontinued** 884

Jones v. Chrétien and Axworthy, **British Columbia Supreme Court, filed
September 29, 1998, case no. C984928, Vancouver registry,
discontinued** 884

Jones v. Clinton, **36 F. Supp.2d 1118 (E.D. Ark., 1999)** 1166

Jones v. Clinton, **57 F. Supp.2d 719 (E.D. Ark., 1999)** 1166

Jose Pereira E Hijos S.A. v. Canada (Attorney General), 2002 FCA 470, 2002
CarswellNat 3344, 2002 CarswellNat 4195, [2002] F.C.J. No. 1658, 2002
CAF 470, 299 N.R. 154, 235 F.T.R. 158 (note) (Fed. C.A.) 881

Kadenko v. Canada (Solicitor General) **(1996), 1996 CarswellNat 2216,
[1996] F.C.J. No. 1376, 206 N.R. 272, 124 F.T.R. 160 (note), 143 D.L.R.
(4th) 532 (Fed. C.A.), leave to appeal refused (1997), 218 N.R. 80 (note)
(S.C.C.)** 321

Kealey v. R. **(1991), [1992] 1 F.C. 195, 1991 CarswellNat 352, 1991
CarswellNat 799, [1991] F.C.J. No. 403, 1 Admin. L.R. (2d) 138, 46 F.T.R.
107 (Fed. T.D.), leave to appeal allowed (1991), 1991 CarswellNat 865,
139 N.R. 189 (Fed. C.A.)** 26, 728

Kearney v. R. **(1992), 70 C.C.C. (3d) 507, 1992 CarswellNB 7, 40 C.C.E.L. 56,
13 C.R. (4th) 41, 122 N.B.R. (2d) 282 (N.B. C.A.), reversed 1992
CarswellNB 248, 1992 CarswellNB 9, 76 C.C.C. (3d) 480, 18 C.R. (4th)
237, 130 N.B.R. (2d) 177, 328 A.P.R. 177, [1992] 3 S.C.R. 807, 144 N.R.
305 (S.C.C.)** 1188

Keating v. Canada (Minister of Fisheries & Oceans), 2002 FCT 1174, 2002
CarswellNat 3290, 224 F.T.R. 98, 49 Admin. L.R. (3d) 145 (Fed.
T.D.) 879

Kelly v. Liberal Party of Canada **(1994), 120 D.L.R. (4th) 746, [1994] O.J.
No. 2808, 1994 CarswellOnt 128 (Ont. Gen. Div.)** 601

Kilosbayan Inc., Santiago et al. v. Commission on Elections et al., Supreme Court
of the Philippines; October 16, 1997, case no. GR128054 518

Kindler v. Canada (Minister of Justice), [1991] 2 S.C.R. 779, 1991 CarswellNat 3, 1991 CarswellNat 831, 8 C.R. (4th) 1, 67 C.C.C. (3d) 1, 84 D.L.R. (4th) 438, 129 N.R. 81, 6 C.R.R. (2d) 193, 45 F.T.R. 160 (note) (S.C.C.) 263

Klein v. Law Society of Upper Canada (1985), 16 D.L.R. (4th) 489, 1985 CarswellOnt 1566, 50 O.R. (2d) 118, 8 O.A.C. 161, 13 C.R.R. 120 (Ont. Div. Ct.) 616

Kohl v. Canada (Department of Agriculture) (1994), 81 F.T.R. 35, 1994 CarswellNat 860, 28 Admin. L.R. (2d) 38 (Fed. T.D.), reversed (1995), 1995 CarswellNat 1315, 185 N.R. 149, 99 F.T.R. 319 (note), 34 Admin. L.R. (2d) 34 (Fed. C.A.) 110

Labrador Inuit Assn. v. Newfoundland (Minister of Environment & Labour) (1997), 25 C.E.L.R. (N.S.) 232, 1997 CarswellNfld 171, [1997] N.J. No. 223, 152 D.L.R. (4th) 50, 155 Nfld. & P.E.I.R. 93, 481 A.P.R. 93 (Nfld. C.A.) 879

Lalonde v. Ontario (Commission de restructuration des services de santé) (2001), 208 D.L.R. (4th) 577, [2001] O.J. No. 4768, 2001 CarswellOnt 4275, 2001 CarswellOnt 4276, [2001] O.J. No. 4767, 56 O.R. (3d) 505 (Eng.), 56 O.R. (3d) 577 (Fr.), 89 C.R.R. (2d) 1, 153 O.A.C. 1, 38 Admin. L.R. (3d) 1 (Ont. C.A.), additional reasons at (2002), 2002 CarswellOnt 336 (Ont. C.A.) 331

Lamarche v. Canada (Attorney General), Federal Court of Canada – Trial Division; case no. T-299-04 817

Landry c. Diffusion Métromédia C.M.R. Inc. and The Gazette, REJB 1999-12769, settled January 4, 2002 629

Lange v. Australian Broadcasting Corp. (1997), 145 A.L.R. 96, 189 C.L.R. 520, 71 A.L.J.R. 818 (Australia H.C.) 997

Large v. Stratford (City) Police Department, 14 C.C.E.L. (2d) 177, 1995 CarswellOnt 796, 1995 CarswellOnt 1173, 128 D.L.R. (4th) 193, 24 C.H.R.R. D/1, 86 O.A.C. 81, 188 N.R. 124, 26 O.R. (3d) 160 (note), 95 C.L.L.C. 230-033, [1995] 3 S.C.R. 733, [1995] L.V.I. 2720-1 (S.C.C.), reconsideration refused (January 25, 1996), Doc. 2400 (S.C.C.) 864

Larouche c. Gouvernement du Québec (1997), 1997 CarswellQue 1362, 1997 CarswellQue 3078 (Que. S.C.) 433

LaSalle (Ville) c. Lavigne, [1993] R.J.Q. 1419 (Que. S.C.) to 1431 148

Lau Kong Yung v. The Director of Immigration, [1999] HKCFA 78, December 3, 1999 378

Lavigne v. O.P.S.E.U., [1991] 2 S.C.R. 211, 1991 CarswellOnt 1038, 1991 CarswellOnt 1038F, 91 C.L.L.C. 14,029, 48 O.A.C. 241, 4 C.R.R. (2d) 193, 126 N.R. 161, 81 D.L.R. (4th) 545, 3 O.R. (3d) 511 (note) (S.C.C.), reconsideration refused (1991), 4 O.R. (3d) xii (S.C.C.) 302

Lavoie v. Canada (1999), [2000] 1 F.C. 3, 1999 CarswellNat 962, [1999] F.C.J. No. 754, 1999 CarswellNat 3054, 174 D.L.R. (4th) 588, 242 N.R. 278, 163

F.T.R. 251 (note), 64 C.R.R. (2d) 189 (Fed. C.A.), leave to appeal allowed
2000 CarswellNat 873, 2000 CarswellNat 874, 257 N.R. 199 (note), [2000]
1 S.C.R. xiv (S.C.C.), affirmed 2002 CarswellNat 406, 2002 CarswellNat
407, [2002] S.C.J. No. 24, 2002 SCC 23, 210 D.L.R. (4th) 193, 284 N.R. 1, 15
C.C.E.L. (3d) 159, 92 C.R.R. (2d) 1, 2002 C.L.L.C. 210-020, 22 Imm. L.R.
(3d) 182, [2002] 1 S.C.R. 769 (S.C.C.) 69

**Law Society of Upper Canada v. Ontario (Attorney General) (1995), 21
O.R. (3d) 666, 1995 CarswellOnt 800, 121 D.L.R. (4th) 369, 31 Admin.
L.R. (2d) 134 (Ont. Gen. Div.)** 55

Lawpost v. New Brunswick (1999), 182 D.L.R. (4th) 167, 1999 CarswellNB 468,
3 C.P.R. (4th) 247, 220 N.B.R. (2d) 146, 565 A.P.R. 146, 40 C.P.C. (4th) 123
(N.B. C.A.), leave to appeal refused (2000), 2000 CarswellNB 330, 2000
CarswellNB 331, 260 N.R. 400 (note), 226 N.B.R. (2d) 400 (note), 579
A.P.R. 400 (note) (S.C.C.) 921

Lawpost v. New Brunswick (1999), 214 N.B.R. (2d) 297, 1999 CarswellNB 183,
1 C.P.R. (4th) 112, 33 C.P.C. (4th) 396, 547 A.P.R. 297 (N.B. Q.B.),
affirmed (1999), 182 D.L.R. (4th) 167, 1999 CarswellNB 468, 3 C.P.R. (4th)
247, 220 N.B.R. (2d) 146, 565 A.P.R. 146, 40 C.P.C. (4th) 123 (N.B. C.A.),
leave to appeal refused (2000), 2000 CarswellNB 330, 2000 CarswellNB
331, 260 N.R. 400 (note), 226 N.B.R. (2d) 400 (note), 579 A.P.R. 400 (note)
(S.C.C.) 722

Leat v. Thunder Bay (City) (2004), [2004] O.J. No. 108, 2004 CarswellOnt 105
(Ont. S.C.J.) 567

**Leblanc v. Canada (1991), 80 D.L.R. (4th) 641, 1991 CarswellOnt 838, [1991]
O.J. No. 84, 3 O.R. (3d) 429, 47 O.A.C. 391 (Ont. C.A.)** 749

**Lederman and Morley v. MacLellan and Dingwall, Supreme Court of
Nova Scotia, Trial Division, filed August 14, 1994, file S.T. no. 05608,
abandoned** 839

**LeFrancois v. Canada (Attorney General) and Via Rail Canada Inc.,
Québec Superior Court; action no. 500-17-020104-041** 1102

Lee v. Globe & Mail (2001), 52 O.R. (3d) 652, [2001] O.J. No. 317, 2001
CarswellOnt 239, 6 C.P.C. (5th) 354 (Ont. S.C.J.) and (2002), [2002] O.J.
No. 16, 2002 CarswellOnt 42, 17 C.P.C. (5th) 342 (Ont. S.C.J.) 996

*Legal Consequences of the Construction of a Wall in the Occupied Palestinian
Territory; (Request for an Advisory Opinion)*, International Court of Justice,
hearings started February 23, 2004 1169

**Legality of the Use of Force (Yugoslavia v. Spain), I.C.J. Reports 1999,
(June 2, 1999),** 905

Legislative Proposal on Crossing the Floor of the House of Commons 682

LePen v. European Parliament (European Court of Human Rights) ....

**Les Artistes pour la Souveraineté v. Axworthy, Québec Superior Court,
filed May 20, 1997, file no. 500-05-032235-978, settled** 357

Letelier v. Republic of Chile, 488 F. Supp. 665 (1980) 907

Li Preti v. Chrétien (1993), 1993] O.J. No. 2205, 1993 CarswellOnt 4306 (Ont. Gen. Div.) 601

Libertarian Party v. Dalfen (September 3, 1992), Doc A-916-88 (Fed. C.A.), not reported 528

Libman c. Québec (Procureur général), 151 D.L.R. (4th) 385, 1997 CarswellQue 851, 1997 CarswellQue 852, [1997] S.C.J. No. 85, 46 C.R.R. (2d) 234, [1997] 3 S.C.R. 569, 3 B.H.R.C. 269 (S.C.C.) 520

Liebmann v. Canada (Minister of National Defence) (1993), [1994] 2 F.C. 3, 1993 CarswellNat 248, 1993 CarswellNat 248F, 69 F.T.R. 81 (Fed. T.D.) and (1996), 110 F.T.R. 284, 1996 CarswellNat 527 (Fed. T.D.) and (1998), [1999] 1 F.C. 20, 1998 CarswellNat 1794, 1998 CarswellNat 2806, 56 C.R.R. (2d) 152, 151 F.T.R. 303 (Fed. T.D.), reversed (2001), 203 D.L.R. (4th) 642, 2001 CarswellNat 1624, 2001 CarswellNat 3170, 2001 FCA 243, 273 N.R. 332, 2001 C.L.L.C. 230-040, [2002] 1 F.C. 29, 210 F.T.R. 160 (note) (Fed. C.A.) 902

Link Organization Plc. v. North Derbyshire Tertiary College, [1998] EWCA Civ 1400, August 14, 1998 (U.K.) 1170

Litigation by the Association for the Revendication of Political Rights, filed in Québec Superior Court, March 17, 2004 472

Little Sisters Book & Art Emporium v. Canada (Minister of Justice) (2000), [2000] 2 S.C.R. 1120, 2000 CarswellBC 2442, [1998] S.C.C.A. No. 448, 2000 CarswellBC 2452, [2000] S.C.J. No. 66, 2000 SCC 69, 83 B.C.L.R. (3d) 1, [2001] 2 W.W.R. 1, 38 C.R. (5th) 209, 150 C.C.C. (3d) 1, 193 D.L.R. (4th) 193, 263 N.R. 203, 145 B.C.A.C. 1, 237 W.A.C. 1, 28 Admin. L.R. (3d) 1, 79 C.R.R. (2d) 189 (S.C.C.) 816

Longley v. Minister of National Revenue, 2000 BCCA 241, 2000 CarswellBC 742, [2000] 2 C.T.C. 382, 73 B.C.L.R. (3d) 222, [2000] 5 W.W.R. 155, 184 D.L.R. (4th) 590, 138 B.C.A.C. 17, 226 W.A.C. 17, 74 C.R.R. (2d) 294 (B.C. C.A.), leave to appeal refused (2000), 2000 CarswellBC 2342, 2000 CarswellBC 2343, [2000] S.C.C.A. No. 256, 264 N.R. 398 (note), 152 B.C.A.C. 320 (note), 250 W.A.C. 320 (note) (S.C.C.) 915

Lord Gray's Motion, [2002] 1 A.C. 124 466

Lord Mayhew of Twysden's Motion, [2002] 1 A.C. 109 466

Lortie c. R., [1985] C.A. 451, 1985 CarswellQue 13, 46 C.R. (3d) 322, 21 C.C.C. (3d) 436 (Que. C.A.) 725

Lortie-Hinse v. Pageau & St.-Laurent (September 7, 1993), Doc. 500-05-011895-933 (Que. S.C.), not reported 608

Lougheed v. Canadian Broadcasting Corporation, Alberta Supreme Court, filed September 27, 1977, not completed, limited information available 930

Luscher v. Deputy Minister of National Revenue (Customs & Excise), 17 D.L.R. (4th) 503, 1985 CarswellNat 196, 1985 CarswellNat 612, [1985] 1 F.C. 85, 57 N.R. 386, 45 C.R. (3d) 81, 15 C.R.R. 167, [1985] 1 C.T.C. 246, 9 C.E.R. 229 (Fed. C.A.) 22

MacDonell v. Québec (Commission d'accès à l'information), [2002] 3 S.C.R. 661, 2002 CarswellQue 2172, 2002 CarswellQue 2173, [2002] S.C.J. No. 71, 2002 SCC 71, 44 Admin. L.R. (3d) 165, 219 D.L.R. (4th) 193, 294 N.R. 238, 22 C.P.R. (4th) 129, [2002] C.A.I. 469 (S.C.C.) 766

MacKay v. Attorney General of Nova Scotia, Nova Scotia Supreme Court, filed October 27, 1997, file S.H. no. 145553 C, settled September 20, 2001 851

MacKeigan v. Hickman (1988), 85 N.S.R. (2d) 126, 216 A.P.R. 126, 1988 CarswellNS 161, 31 Admin. L.R. 289 (N.S. T.D.), reversed (1988), 1988 CarswellNS 305, 86 N.S.R. (2d) 181, 218 A.P.R. 181, 53 D.L.R. (4th) 244 (N.S. C.A.) 251

MacLean v. Nova Scotia (Attorney General) (1987), 35 D.L.R. (4th) 306, 1987 CarswellNS 431, 76 N.S.R. (2d) 296, 189 A.P.R. 296, 27 C.R.R. 212 (N.S. T.D.) 744, 1051

MacLeod v. Canada (Canadian Armed Forces) (1990), [1991] 1 F.C. 114, [1990] F.C.J. No. 977, 1990 CarswellNat 6, 1990 CarswellNat 709, 2 C.R. (4th) 213, 38 F.T.R. 129 (Fed. T.D.) 223, 305

MacMillan Bloedel Ltd. v. Simpson (1993), 12 C.E.L.R. (N.S.) 81, [1993] B.C.J. No. 2869, 1993 CarswellBC 588 (B.C. S.C.), affirmed (1994), 113 D.L.R. (4th) 368, 1994 CarswellBC 162, [1994] B.C.J. No. 670, 90 B.C.L.R. (2d) 24, 43 B.C.A.C. 1, 69 W.A.C. 1, 89 C.C.C. (3d) 217, 21 C.R.R. (2d) 116 (B.C. C.A.), additional reasons at (1994), 1994 CarswellBC 948, 43 B.C.A.C. 136, 21 C.R.R. (2d) 109, 69 W.A.C. 136 (B.C. C.A.), additional reasons at (1994), 1994 CarswellBC 2252 (B.C. C.A.), affirmed (1995), 1995 CarswellBC 974, 1995 CarswellBC 1153, [1995] S.C.J. No. 101, [1995] 4 S.C.R. 725, [1996] 2 W.W.R. 1, 14 B.C.L.R. (3d) 122, 44 C.R. (4th) 277, 130 D.L.R. (4th) 385, 103 C.C.C. (3d) 225, 191 N.R. 260, 33 C.R.R. (2d) 123, 68 B.C.A.C. 161, 112 W.A.C. 161 (S.C.C.), leave to appeal refused (1994), 23 C.R.R. (2d) 192 (note), 55 B.C.A.C. 320 (note), 90 W.A.C. 320 (note), 179 N.R. 79 (note) (S.C.C.) 134

Made in the USA Foundation and United Steelworkers of America v. United States of America, 56 F. Supp.2d 1226 (N.D. Ala., 1999) and 242 F.3d 1300 (11th Cir., 2001) 910

Madzimbamuto v. Lardner-Burke (1968), [1969] 1 A.C. 645, [1968] 3 All E.R. 561 (Southern Rhodesia P.C.) 370

Mangat v. Canada (Attorney General), Supreme Court of British Columbia, filed September 30, 1993, file no. A933715, Vancouver Registry, abandoned 590

Marbury v. Madison, **5 U.S. 137, 1 Cranch 137 (U.S. Dist. Col., 1803)** ... 256

Marchiori v. Environmental Agency, [2002] EWCA Civ. 03; February 25, 2002 (U.K.) 907

Marshall v. Canada, [1999] 3 S.C.R. 456, 1999 CarswellNS 262, 1999 CarswellNS 282, [1999] S.C.J. No. 55, 177 D.L.R. (4th) 513, 246 N.R. 83, 138 C.C.C. (3d) 97, [1999] 4 C.N.L.R. 161, 178 N.S.R. (2d) 201, 549 A.P.R. 201 (S.C.C.), reconsideration refused [1999] 3 S.C.R. 533, 1999 CarswellNS 349, 1999 CarswellNS 350, [1999] S.C.J. No. 66, [1999] 4 C.N.L.R. 301, 247 N.R. 306, 179 D.L.R. (4th) 193, 139 C.C.C. (3d) 391, 179 N.S.R. (2d) 1, 553 A.P.R. 1 (S.C.C.) 816

Martel v. Samson Band (2000), [2001] 1 C.N.L.R. 173, 2000 CarswellNat 2893 (Fed. T.D.) 218

Martin v. Ontario, Superior Court of Justice, January 20, 2004, file No. 03-CV-249922-CM-3 766

Martinez v. Republic of Cuba, General Jurisdiction Division, 11th Judicial District, March 9, 2001, Case no. 99-18208 CA 20 1029

Massachussetts v. Laird, 451 F.2d 26 (1st Cir., 1971) 905

Masse v. Ontario (Minister of Community & Social Services) (1996), 134 D.L.R. (4th) 20, 1996 CarswellOnt 338, [1996] O.J. No. 363, 40 Admin. L.R. (2d) 87, 35 C.R.R. (2d) 44, 89 O.A.C. 81 (Ont. Div. Ct.), leave to appeal refused (1996), 1996 CarswellOnt 1453, [1996] O.J. No. 1526, 40 Admin. L.R. (2d) 87n, 89 O.A.C. 81n (Ont. C.A.), leave to appeal refused (1996), [1996] S.C.C.A. No. 373, 40 Admin. L.R. (2d) 87 (note), 39 C.R.R. (2d) 375 (note), 207 N.R. 78, 97 O.A.C. 240 (S.C.C.) 864

Matters Related to the Review of the Office of the Privacy Commissioner, Ninth Report of the Standing Committee on Government Operations and Estimates, November 2003 817

Matters Relating to the Office of the Privacy Commissioner, Fifth Report of the Standing Committee on Government Operations and Estimates, June 2003 817

Mayor of Toronto (City) v. Ontario (2000), 47 O.R. (3d) 177, 2000 CarswellOnt 217, 183 D.L.R. (4th) 546, 19 M.P.L.R. (3d) 142 (Ont. S.C.J.) 295

McCartan Turkington Breen v. Times Newspapers, [2000] 2 A.C. 277 1000

McConnell v. Federal Election Commission, 000 U.S. 02-1674 (2003) 517

McCutcheon v. Toronto (City) (1983), 41 O.R. (2d) 652, 1983 CarswellOnt 15, 147 D.L.R. (3d) 193, 20 M.V.R. 267, 22 M.P.L.R. 139, 6 C.R.R. 32 (Ont. H.C.) 8

McGonnell v. United Kingdom (2000), 30 E.H.R.R. 289 (European Community) 277

McKinney v. Liberal Party of Canada (1987), 43 D.L.R. (4th) 706, 1987 CarswellOnt 481, 21 C.P.C. (2d) 118, 61 O.R. (2d) 680, 35 C.R.R. 353 (Ont. H.C.) 92, 577, 739

McKinney v. University of Guelph (1987), 46 D.L.R. (4th) 193, 1987
CarswellOnt 951, 24 O.A.C. 241, 29 Admin. L.R. 227, 37 C.R.R. 44, 63
O.R. (2d) 1, 9 C.H.R.R. D/4573 (Ont. C.A.), affirmed 1990 CarswellOnt
1019F, 1990 CarswellOnt 1019, 91 C.L.L.C. 17,004, 2 O.R. (3d) 319 (note),
13 C.H.R.R. D/171, [1990] 3 S.C.R. 229, 2 C.R.R. (2d) 1, 45 O.A.C. 1, 118
N.R. 1, 76 D.L.R. (4th) 545 (S.C.C.) 80

McRae v. Canada (Attorney General) (1998), 61 B.C.L.R. (3d) 83, 1998
CarswellBC 2298, [1999] 7 W.W.R. 596, 9 C.C.L.I. (3d) 188 (B.C. S.C.),
additional reasons at (1998), 1998 CarswellBC 2774, 9 C.C.L.I. (3d) 215
(B.C. S.C.) 1203

Mercier c. Québec (March 23, 1994), Doc. C.A. Québec 200-10-000062-914
(Que. C.A.) 299

Mercier c. Québec (ministre du Conseil exécutif), REJB 1999-10883 853

Meredith v. Pratt (1999), [1999] F.C.J. No. 15, 1999 CarswellNat 83 (Fed.
T.D.) 631

Metropolitan Separate School Board v. Taylor (1994), 21 C.C.L.T. (2d) 316, 1994
CarswellOnt 934, [1994] O.J. No. 1870 (Ont. Gen. Div.) 922

Miami Herald Publishing Co. v. Tornillo, 418 U.S. 241, 94 S.Ct. 2831, 41
L.Ed.2d 730 (U.S. Fla., 1974) 629

Milosevic action in Dutch national court to prevent detention 1141

Miron v. Trudel, [1995] 2 S.C.R. 418, 1995 CarswellOnt 93, 1995 CarswellOnt
526, [1995] S.C.J. No. 44, 10 M.V.R. (3d) 151, 23 O.R. (3d) 160 (note),
[1995] I.L.R. 1-3185, 13 R.F.L. (4th) 1, C.E.B. & P.G.R. 8217, 181 N.R. 253,
124 D.L.R. (4th) 693, 81 O.A.C. 253, 29 C.R.R. (2d) 189 (S.C.C.) 29

Mitchell Estate v. Ontario (2003), [2003] O.J. No. 3313, 2003 CarswellOnt
3249, 175 O.A.C. 211, 66 O.R. (3d) 737 (Ont. Div. Ct.) 864

Mitchell v. Minister of National Revenue (2001), 199 D.L.R. (4th) 385, 2001 SCC
33, 2001 CarswellNat 873, 2001 CarswellNat 874, [2001] S.C.J. No. 33, 83
C.R.R. (2d) 1, 269 N.R. 207, [2001] 3 C.N.L.R. 122, [2001] 1 S.C.R. 911, 206
F.T.R. 160 (note), [2002] 3 C.T.C. 359 (S.C.C.) 218

M-Jay Farms Enterprises Ltd. v. Canadian Wheat Board (1997), [1998] 2 W.W.R.
48, 1997 CarswellMan 457, [1997] M.J. No. 462, 118 Man. R. (2d) 258, 149
W.A.C. 258 (Man. C.A.), leave to appeal refused (1998), 126 Man. R. (2d)
154 (note), 167 W.A.C. 154 (note), 227 N.R. 191 (note) (S.C.C.),
reconsideration refused (August 6, 1998), Doc. 26346 (S.C.C.) 305

Mohtarma Benazir Bhutto v. President of Pakistan, P.L.D. 1996 Sup. Ct.
388 398

**Monks v. Canada (Attorney General) (1992), 58 F.T.R. 196, 1992
CarswellNat 787 (Fed. T.D.)** 868

Montmigny c. Québec (Commission d'accès à l'information), [1986] R.L. 570,
1986 CarswellQue 126, [1986] A.Q. No. 861, 1 Q.A.C. 15, [1986] C.A.I.
217 (Que. C.A.) 303

Moores v. Canadian Broadcasting Corporation, **Ontario Court (General Division), filed February 13, 1996, file no. 96-CU-98875, not completed** 991

Morin v. Crawford **(1999), 29 C.P.C. (4th) 362, 1999 CarswellNWT 4, [1999] N.W.T.J. No. 5, 14 Admin. L.R. (3d) 287 (N.W.T. S.C.)** 1158

Morrissey v. The State of Colorado and U.S. Term Limits, Inc. 780

Motion of Loss of Confidence in the Attorney General, Vote by the British Columbia Law Society, May 22, 2002 277

Mugesera c. Canada (Ministre de la Citoyenneté & de l'Immigration) (2003), 232 D.L.R. (4th) 75, [2003] F.C.J. No. 1292, 2003 CarswellNat 2663, 2003 CarswellNat 2926, 309 N.R. 14, 31 Imm. L.R. (3d) 159, [2004] 1 F.C.R. 3, 2003 CAF 325, 2003 FCA 325 (Fed. C.A.), leave to appeal allowed (2004), 2004 CarswellNat 376, 2004 CarswellNat 377 (S.C.C.), additional reasons at 2004 CarswellNat 1105, 2004 CAF 157 (F.C.A.) 641

Muldoon v. R., **[1988] 3 F.C. 628, 1988 CarswellNat 134, 1988 CarswellNat 134F, 21 F.T.R. 154 (Fed. T.D.)** 501

Mulroney v. Canada (Attorney General) et al., **Québec Superior Court, file no. 500-05-012098-958, settled January 6, 1997** 1145

Mulroney v. Coates **(1986), 27 D.L.R. (4th) 118, 1986 CarswellOnt 560, 54 O.R. (2d) 353, 8 C.P.C. (2d) 109 (Ont. H.C.)** 1062

Munro v. Canada **(1992), 98 D.L.R. (4th) 662, 1992 CarswellOnt 706, [1992] O.J. No. 2453, 11 O.R. (3d) 1 (Ont. Gen. Div.), reversed (1993), 110 D.L.R. (4th) 580, 1993 CarswellOnt 3837, 16 O.R. (3d) 564 (Ont. Div. Ct.)** 1081

Munro v. Canada (Attorney General) **(1993), [1993] O.J. No. 2370, 1993 CarswellOnt 2785 (Ont. Gen. Div.), additional reasons at (1994), 1994 CarswellOnt 3254 (Ont. Gen. Div.)** 601

Munro v. Toronto Sun Publishing Corp. (1982), 39 O.R. (2d) 100, 1982 CarswellOnt 703, 21 C.C.L.T. 261 (Ont. H.C.) 982

Mushkegowuk First Nation v. Ontario, 184 D.L.R. (4th) 532, 2000 CarswellOnt 586, [2000] O.J. No. 641, 130 O.A.C. 88, [2000] 2 C.N.L.R. 79 (Ont. C.A.) 218

Nanoose Conversion Campaign v. Canada (Minister of Environment) (2000), 257 N.R. 287, 2000 CarswellNat 1349, 35 C.E.L.R. (N.S.) 89, 184 F.T.R. 84 (note) (Fed. C.A.) 905

Naskapi-Montagnais Innu Assn. v. Canada (Minister of National Defence), **[1990] 3 F.C. 381, 1990 CarswellNat 698, 1990 CarswellNat 17, 35 F.T.R. 161, 5 C.E.L.R. (N.S.) 287 (Fed. T.D.), additional reasons at (1990), 5 C.E.L.R. (N.S.) 287 at 313 (Fed. T.D.)** 61, 179

National Capital News Canada v. Canada (Speaker of the House of Commons), 2002 Comp. Trib. 38 (Competition Trib.) and 2002 Comp. Trib. 41, 2002 CarswellNat 4487, 23 C.P.R. (4th) 77 (Competition Trib.), affirmed 2004

CarswellNat 124, [2004] F.C.J. No. 83, 2004 CarswellNat 612, 2004 FCA 27, 2004 CAF 27, 29 C.P.R. (4th) 421 (F.C.A.) 996

National Citizens' Coalition Inc./Coalition nationale des citoyens Inc. v. Canada (Attorney General), **11 D.L.R. (4th) 481, 1984 CarswellAlta 87, 32 Alta. L.R. (2d) 249, [1984] 5 W.W.R. 436, 14 C.R.R. 61 (Alta. Q.B.)** 513

National Labour Relations Board v. Sears, Roebuck & Co., 421 U.S. 132 (1975) 1212

National Party of Canada v. Canadian Broadcasting Corp. **(1993), 106 D.L.R. (4th) 575, 1993 CarswellAlta 113, 13 Alta. L.R. (3d) 29, [1994] 1 W.W.R. 361, 145 A.R. 267, 55 W.A.C. 267, 19 C.P.C. (3d) 191n (Alta. C.A.), leave to appeal refused [1994] 2 W.W.R. lxv (note), 107 D.L.R. (4th) vii (note), 15 Alta. L.R. (3d) lii (note), 169 N.R. 160 (note), 162 A.R. 158 (note), 83 W.A.C. 158 (note) (S.C.C.)** 93, 542

National Party of Canada v. Stephenson **(1996), 124 F.T.R. 108, 1996 CarswellNat 2055 (Fed. T.D.), affirmed (1998), 1998 CarswellNat 1761, 230 N.R. 342, 154 F.T.R. 160 (note) (Fed. C.A.)** 597, 599

Native Women's Assn. of Canada v. R. **(1992), 97 D.L.R. (4th) 537, 1992 CarswellNat 152, 1992 CarswellNat 152F, [1993] 1 F.C. 171, 57 F.T.R. 115, 11 C.R.R. (2d) 244 (Fed. T.D.), affirmed (1992), 97 D.L.R. (4th) 548, 1992 CarswellNat 1014, 13 C.R.R. (2d) 382, 145 N.R. 253, 57 F.T.R. 27 (note) (Fed. C.A.)** 406

Native Women's Assn. of Canada v. R., **90 D.L.R. (4th) 394, 1992 CarswellNat 98F, 1992 CarswellNat 98, 53 F.T.R. 194, [1992] 4 C.N.L.R. 59, 2 F.C. 462, [1992] 2 F.C. 462 (Fed. T.D.), reversed 95 D.L.R. (4th) 106, 1992 CarswellNat 114, 1992 CarswellNat 114F, [1992] 3 F.C. 192, [1992] 4 C.N.L.R. 71, 10 C.R.R. (2d) 268, 146 N.R. 40, 57 F.T.R. 320 (note) (Fed. C.A.), reversed (1994), 119 D.L.R. (4th) 224, 1994 CarswellNat 1499, 1994 CarswellNat 1773, 173 N.R. 241, [1995] 1 C.N.L.R. 47, 84 F.T.R. 240 (note), 24 C.R.R. (2d) 233, [1994] 3 S.C.R. 627 (S.C.C.)** 406

Natural Law Party of Canada v. Canadian Broadcasting Corp. **(1993), [1994] 1 F.C. 580, 1993 CarswellNat 827, 1993 CarswellNat 1350, 52 C.P.R. (3d) 97, 77 F.T.R. 73, 21 Admin. L.R. (2d) 161 (Fed. T.D.)** 546

Natural Resources Defense Council v. Department of Energy, 191 F. Supp.2d 41, February 21, 2002 1071

Nawaz Sharif v. President of Pakistan, P.L.D. 1993 Sup. Ct. 473 398

Nebot v. Bucaram, Supreme Court of Ecuador, August 13, 1998, limited information available 641

Nelles v. Ontario, [1989] 2 S.C.R. 170, 1989 CarswellOnt 963, 1989 CarswellOnt 415, [1989] S.C.J. No. 86, 69 O.R. (2d) 448 (note), 60 D.L.R. (4th) 609, 98 N.R. 321, 35 O.A.C. 161, 41 Admin. L.R. 1, 49 C.C.L.T. 217, 37 C.P.C. (2d) 1, 71 C.R. (3d) 358, 42 C.R.R. 1 (S.C.C.) 1183

New Brunswick (Minister of Health & Community Services) v. G. (J.), 1999
CarswellNB 305, 1999 CarswellNB 306, [1999] S.C.J. No. 47, 26 C.R. (5th)
203, 244 N.R. 276, 177 D.L.R. (4th) 124, 50 R.F.L. (4th) 63, 66 C.R.R. (2d)
267, 216 N.B.R. (2d) 25, 552 A.P.R. 25, [1999] 3 S.C.R. 46, 7 B.H.R.C. 615
(S.C.C.) 1215

**New Brunswick Broadcasting Co. v. Nova Scotia (Speaker of the House of
Assembly), [1993] 1 S.C.R. 319, 1993 CarswellNS 417, 1993 CarswellNS
417F, [1993] S.C.J. No. 2, 146 N.R. 161, 13 C.R.R. (2d) 1, 100 D.L.R. (4th)
212, 118 N.S.R. (2d) 181, 327 A.P.R. 181 (S.C.C.)** 5, 74, 721, 735, 743

New Democratic Party of British Columbia v. Southam Inc., British Columbia
Supreme Court, Vancouver registry, No. C984790 filed September 21,
1988, dismissed November 18, 1999 419

New Partnership for Africa's Development; Africa Action Plan Highlights, 2002
G-8 Meeting, Final Communiqué, June 27, 2002 323

Newfoundland (Treasury Board) v. N.A.P.E., 221 D.L.R. (4th) 513, 2002
CarswellNfld 332, 2002 NLCA 72, 220 Nfld. & P.E.I.R. 1, 657 A.P.R. 1,
2003 C.L.L.C. 230-019, 103 C.R.R. (2d) 1 (N.L. C.A.), leave to appeal
allowed (2003), 2003 CarswellNfld 144, 2003 CarswellNfld 145, 105
C.R.R. (2d) 188 (note), 315 N.R. 199 (note), 233 Nfld. & P.E.I.R. 180
(note), 693 A.P.R. 180 (note) (S.C.C.) 252

Newfoundland Threat of Separation Over Fisheries, Proceedings of the House
of Assembly, Vol. XLIV, No. 18, May 7, 2003, http://www.gov.nf.ca/
hoa/business/hansard/44th,%205th/h03-05-07.htm 430

**Ng Ka Ling v. The Director of Immigration, [1999] HKCFA 11; January 29,
1999 and [1999] HKCFA 19, February 26, 1999** 373

Ng King Luen v. Rita Fan, (1997), HKLRD 757 383

Ng, Re, [1991] 2 S.C.R. 858, 1991 CarswellAlta 563, 1991 CarswellAlta 563F,
67 C.C.C. (3d) 61, 84 D.L.R. (4th) 498, 129 N.R. 177, 6 C.R.R. (2d) 252, 119
A.R. 300 (S.C.C.) 263

**Nguyen v. Canada (Minister of Employment & Immigration) (1993), [1994]
1 F.C. 232, 1993 CarswellNat 92, 1993 CarswellNat 1341, [1993] F.C.J.
No. 702, 20 Imm. L.R. (2d) 231, 156 N.R. 212, 16 Admin. L.R. (2d) 1, 66
F.T.R. 240 (note) (Fed. C.A.), leave to appeal refused (1994), 17 Admin.
L.R. (2d) 67 (note), 22 Imm. L.R. (2d) 159n (S.C.C.)** 132

Nieboer v. Canada (Attorney General) (1996), 121 F.T.R. 29, 1996 CarswellNat
1686 (Fed. T.D.) 51

Nielsen v. Canada (Canadian Human Rights Commission), [1992] 2 F.C. 561,
1992 CarswellNat 195, 1992 CarswellNat 589, 5 Admin. L.R. (2d) 278, 9
C.R.R. (2d) 289, 53 F.T.R. 216 (Fed. T.D.) 27

**Noreen Stevens v. Parker, Commissioner, Federal Court of Appeal, filed
December 16, 1987, file A-1277-87, withdrawn June 28, 1988** 1073

Northwest Territorries (Commissioner) v. Doyle, [1992] N.W.T.R. 279, 1992 CarswellNWT 14, 8 C.P.C. (3d) 196 (N.W.T. S.C.), additional reasons at (1992), 1992 CarswellNWT 15, 8 C.P.C. (3d) 209 (N.W.T. S.C.) 1049

Nunziata v. Toronto (City) (2000), 189 D.L.R. (4th) 627, 2000 CarswellOnt 3314, [2000] O.J. No. 3407, 50 O.R. (3d) 295, 14 M.P.L.R. (3d) 1, 78 C.R.R. (2d) 123, 137 O.A.C. 70 (Ont. C.A.), additional reasons at (2000), 2000 CarswellOnt 3698, 137 O.A.C. 70 (Ont. C.A.) 508

O.E.C.T.A. v. Essex (County) Roman Catholic Separate School Board (1987), 36 D.L.R. (4th) 115, 1987 CarswellOnt 944, 18 O.A.C. 271, 58 O.R. (2d) 545, 28 Admin. L.R. 39, 34 C.R.R. 146 (Ont. Div. Ct.), leave to appeal refused (1988), 51 D.L.R. (4th) vii, 65 O.R. (2d) x, 32 O.A.C. 80 (note), 93 N.R. 325 (note), 39 C.R.R. 384 (note) (S.C.C.) 10, 35

O.P.S.E.U. v. Ontario (Attorney General) (1979), 24 O.R. (2d) 324, 1979 CarswellOnt 881, 98 D.L.R. (3d) 168 (Ont. H.C.), affirmed (1980), 1980 CarswellOnt 1108, 81 C.L.L.C. 14,082, 31 O.R. (2d) 321, 118 D.L.R. (3d) 661 (Ont. C.A.), affirmed 1987 CarswellOnt 945, 1987 CarswellOnt 968, [1987] 2 S.C.R. 2, 41 D.L.R. (4th) 1, 77 N.R. 321, 23 O.A.C. 161, 28 Admin. L.R. 141, 87 C.L.L.C. 14,037, 59 O.R. (2d) 671 (note) (S.C.C.) 287

O.P.S.E.U. v. Ontario (Attorney General) (1980), 118 D.L.R. (3d) 661, 1980 CarswellOnt 1108, 81 C.L.L.C. 14,082, 31 O.R. (2d) 321 (Ont. C.A.), affirmed 1987 CarswellOnt 945, 1987 CarswellOnt 968, [1987] 2 S.C.R. 2, 41 D.L.R. (4th) 1, 77 N.R. 321, 23 O.A.C. 161, 28 Admin. L.R. 141, 87 C.L.L.C. 14,037, 59 O.R. (2d) 671 (note) (S.C.C.) 287

O.P.S.E.U. v. Ontario (Attorney General) (1988), 52 D.L.R. (4th) 701, 1988 CarswellOnt 881, 88 C.L.L.C. 14,051, 65 O.R. (2d) 689 (Ont. H.C.), reversed (1993), 1993 CarswellOnt 1183, 14 O.R. (3d) 476, 105 D.L.R. (4th) 157, 64 O.A.C. 385 (Ont. C.A.) 287

O.P.S.E.U. v. Ontario (Attorney General), 41 D.L.R. (4th) 1, 1987 CarswellOnt 945, 1987 CarswellOnt 968, [1987] 2 S.C.R. 2, 77 N.R. 321, 23 O.A.C. 161, 28 Admin. L.R. 141, 87 C.L.L.C. 14,037, 59 O.R. (2d) 671 (note) (S.C.C.) 287, 302

O.P.S.E.U. v. Ontario (Attorney General), Ontario Court of Appeal, March 26, 2002 921

O.T.F. v. Ontario (Attorney General) (1998), 39 O.R. (3d) 140, 1998 CarswellOnt 542, [1998] O.J. No. 545, 17 C.P.C. (4th) 58 (Ont. Gen. Div.) 227, 701

O.T.F. v. Ontario (Attorney General) (2000), 49 O.R. (3d) 257, 2000 CarswellOnt 1988, [2000] O.J. No. 2094, 188 D.L.R. (4th) 333, 74 C.R.R. (2d) 247, 132 O.A.C. 218 (Ont. C.A.), leave to appeal refused (2001), 2001 CarswellOnt 494, 2001 CarswellOnt 495, 80 C.R.R. (2d) 187 (note), 268 N.R. 195 (note), 147 O.A.C. 400 (note) (S.C.C.) 779

O'Connor v. Nova Scotia (Deputy Minister of the Priorities & Planning Secretariat) (2001), 209 D.L.R. (4th) 429, 2001 CarswellNS 322, [2001]

N.S.J. No. 360, 197 N.S.R. (2d) 154, 616 A.P.R. 154, 2001 NSCA 132, 39
Admin. L.R. (3d) 221 (N.S. C.A.), leave to appeal refused (2002), 2002
CarswellNS 256, 2002 CarswellNS 257, [2001] S.C.C.A. No. 582, 206
N.S.R. (2d) 202 (note), 645 A.P.R. 202 (note), 293 N.R. 197 (note)
(S.C.C.) 305

O'Donohue v. Canada (2003), 109 C.R.R. (2d) 1, 2003 CarswellOnt 2573 (Ont.
S.C.J.) 198

O'Sullivan v. R. (1991), [1992] 1 F.C. 522, 1991 CarswellNat 808, 1991
CarswellNat 495, 91 D.T.C. 5491, 7 C.R.R. (2d) 310, 84 D.L.R. (4th) 124,
45 F.T.R. 284, [1991] 2 C.T.C. 117 (Fed. T.D.) 21

Odhavji Estate v. Woodhouse, 233 D.L.R. (4th) 193, 2003 CarswellOnt 4851,
2003 CarswellOnt 4852, [2003] S.C.J. No. 74, 2003 SCC 69, 19 C.C.L.T.
(3d) 163, [2003] 3 S.C.R. 263, 312 N.R. 305, 180 O.A.C. 201 (S.C.C.) ... 817

Official Status for the British Columbia N.D.P. Opposition, Speaker's Ruling,
July 12, 2001 389

Olson v. R., [1996] 2 F.C. 168, 1996 CarswellNat 142, 1996 CarswellNat
1761, 34 C.R.R. (2d) 1, 107 F.T.R. 81 (Fed. T.D.), affirmed (1997), 1997
CarswellNat 2734 (Fed. C.A.), leave to appeal refused 46 C.R.R. (2d)
375 (note), 223 N.R. 399 (note), [1997] 3 S.C.R. xii (S.C.C.) 22

Olympia Interiors Ltd. v. R. (1999), [2000] 1 C.T.C. 256, 1999 CarswellNat
1978, [1999] F.C.J. No. 1474 (Fed. C.A.), leave to appeal refused (2000),
252 N.R. 393 (note) (S.C.C.), reconsideration refused (June 22, 2000),
Doc. 27550 (S.C.C.) 1207

Ontario (Attorney General) v. Dieleman (1993), 16 O.R. (3d) 39, 1993
CarswellOnt 468, 21 C.P.C. (3d) 49, 110 D.L.R. (4th) 343, 19 C.R.R. (2d)
345 (Ont. Gen. Div.), leave to appeal refused (1993), 1993 CarswellOnt
1832, 16 O.R. (3d) 39 at 46, 110 D.L.R. (4th) 349 (Ont. Gen. Div.) 937

Ontario (Attorney General) v. O.T.F. (1997), 36 O.R. (3d) 367, 1997
CarswellOnt 4375, 98 C.L.L.C. 220-005 (Ont. Gen. Div.) 270

Ontario (Chicken Producers' Marketing Board) v. Canadian Chicken
Marketing Agency (1992), [1993] 1 F.C. 116, 1992 CarswellNat 148, 1992
CarswellNat 148F, 58 F.T.R. 34 (Fed. T.D.) 806

Ontario (Human Rights Commission) v. Etobicoke (Borough), [1982] 1 S.C.R. 202
at 213-214, quoted at (1992), 9 O.R. (3d) 509 at 520 a-b 54

Ontario (Ministry of Community & Social Services) v. O.P.S.E.U. (1992), 11
O.R. (3d) 558, 1992 CarswellOnt 913, 93 C.L.L.C. 14,001, 10 Admin. L.R.
(2d) 59, 58 O.A.C. 292, 97 D.L.R. (4th) 173 (Ont. C.A.) 50

Ontario (Ministry of Finance) v. Ontario (Inquiry Officer) (1999), 118 O.A.C.
108, 1999 CarswellOnt 650, [1999] O.J. No. 484, 13 Admin. L.R. (3d) 1
(Ont. C.A.), leave to appeal refused (2000), [1999] S.C.C.A. No. 134, 252
N.R. 394 (note), 134 O.A.C. 196 (note) (S.C.C.) 342

Ontario (Speaker of the Legislative Assembly) v. Casselman **(March 18, 1996), Winkler J., [1996] O.J. No. 5343 (Ont. Gen. Div.)** 734

Ontario (Speaker of the Legislative Assembly) v. Ontario (Human Rights Commission) (2001), 201 D.L.R. (4th) 698, 2001 CarswellOnt 1985, [2001] O.J. No. 2180, 146 O.A.C. 125, 54 O.R. (3d) 595, 85 C.R.R. (2d) 170, 33 Admin. L.R. (3d) 123, 40 C.H.R.R. D/246 (Ont. C.A.) 743

Ontario Cattlemen's Assn. v. Thames Sales Yard Ltd. (2002), [2002] O.J. No. 1473, 2002 CarswellOnt 1358 (Ont. S.C.J.), affirmed (2003) 175 O.A.C. 104 (Ont. C.A.) 108

Ontario Debt After the 2003 General Election 666

Ontario Federation of Anglers & Hunters v. Ontario (Ministry of Natural Resources) (2002), 211 D.L.R. (4th) 741, [2002] O.J. No. 1445, 2002 CarswellOnt 1061, 158 O.A.C. 255, 93 C.R.R. (2d) 1 (Ont. C.A.), leave to appeal refused (2003), 2003 CarswellOnt 1067, 2003 CarswellOnt 1068, 313 N.R. 198 (note), 101 C.R.R. (2d) 376 (note), 181 O.A.C. 198 (note) (S.C.C.) 69, 1030

Ontario Liberal Response to Progressive Conservative Tax Cuts, **Statement by the Leader of the Ontario Liberal Party, December 18, 1996** 651

Ontario NDP Application for Standing, Ruling by the Walkerton Inquiry, September 12, 2000 111

Operation Dismantle Inc. v. R., **18 D.L.R. (4th) 481, 1985 CarswellNat 151, 1985 CarswellNat 664, [1985] S.C.J. No. 22, [1985] 1 S.C.R. 441, 59 N.R. 1, 12 Admin. L.R. 16, 13 C.R.R. 287 (S.C.C.)** 9, 156, 162

Organization for Quality of Government et al. v. Government of Israel, **High Court of Justice of Israel, June 15, 1997** 1119

Osborne v. Canada (Treasury Board), **82 D.L.R. (4th) 321, 1991 CarswellNat 348, 1991 CarswellNat 830, [1991] S.C.J. No. 45, 37 C.C.E.L. 135, 91 C.L.L.C. 14,026, 125 N.R. 241, 41 F.T.R. 239 (note), 4 C.R.R. (2d) 30, [1991] 2 S.C.R. 69 (S.C.C.)** 287, 302

Ottawa (City) v. Ontario (Minister of Municipal Affairs & Housing) (2002), 62 O.R. (3d) 503, 2002 CarswellOnt 5116, 41 M.P.L.R. (3d) 303, 44 O.M.B.R. 353 (Ont. Div. Ct.) and (2003), 63 O.R. (3d) 785, 2003 CarswellOnt 902, 170 O.A.C. 77 (Ont. Div. Ct.) 495

Ottawa (City) v. Ottawa (Chief Building Official) (2003), [2003] O.J. No. 1945, 2003 CarswellOnt 2033, 2003 CarswellOnt 2034, 3 C.E.L.R. (3d) 46, 39 M.P.L.R. (3d) 1 (Ont. S.C.J.) 862

Ouellet c. R. **(1976), 72 D.L.R. (3d) 95, 1976 CarswellQue 19, 36 C.R.N.S. 296, 32 C.C.C. (2d) 149, [1976] C.A. 788 (Que. C.A.)** 247

Oversight of Financial Institutions by the Alberta Minister of Consumer and Corporate Affairs 866

Özdep v. Turkey (2001), 31 E.H.R.R. 27 (European Community) 519

P.H.L.F. Family Holdings Ltd. v. R., [1994] G.S.T.C. 41, 1994 CarswellNat 49, 2 G.T.C. 1039 (T.C.C.) 918

P.I.P.S.C. v. Canada (Attorney General), [1995] 2 F.C. 73, 1995 CarswellNat 657, 1995 CarswellNat 657F, 95 C.L.L.C. 210-008, 89 F.T.R. 161 (Fed. T.D.) 58

P.S.A.C. v. Canada (House of Commons), 27 D.L.R. (4th) 481, 1986 CarswellNat 48F, 1986 CarswellNat 48, 66 N.R. 46, 86 C.L.L.C. 14,034, [1986] 2 F.C. 372 (Fed. C.A.) 719, 760

P.S.A.C. v. Canada (Treasury Board) (Ball, Reinhardt and Bonin) (October 28, 1985), Doc. 148-2-109, [1985] C.P.S.S.R.B. No. 239 (Can. P.S.S.R.B.) .. 1181

P.S.A.C. v. Canada, 38 D.L.R. (4th) 249, 1987 CarswellNat 904, 1987 CarswellNat 1103, 87 C.L.L.C. 14,022, [1987] 1 S.C.R. 424, 75 N.R. 161, 32 C.R.R. 114, [1987] D.L.Q. 230 (note) (S.C.C.) 243, 865

P.S.A.C. v. R. (2000), 192 F.T.R. 23, 2000 CarswellNat 1094 (Fed. T.D.) .. 795

Pacific Press v. British Columbia (Attorney General) (1997), 45 B.C.L.R. (3d) 235, 1997 CarswellBC 2630 (B.C. S.C.) and [2000] B.C.J. No. 308, 2000 CarswellBC 319, 2000 BCSC 248, 73 B.C.L.R. (3d) 264, [2000] 5 W.W.R. 219, 71 C.R.R. (2d) 255 (B.C. S.C.) 519

Pakistan Bar Council v. Federation of Pakistan, Constitutional Petition No. 12/2002, Supreme Court of Pakistan, April 27, 2002 383

Pakistan Lawyers' Forum v. General Pervez Musharraf, Constitutional Petition No. 6/2002, Supreme Court of Pakistan, April 27, 2002 383

Parizeau c. Lafferty, Harwood & Partners Ltd. (1999), 1999 CarswellQue 3973, [2000] R.J.Q. 81 (Que. S.C.) and [2000] R.R.A. 417, 2000 CarswellQue 472, [2000] J.Q. No. 682 (Que. S.C.), affirmed 2003 CarswellQue 2345, 19 C.C.L.T. (3d) 269, [2003] R.R.A. 1145, [2003] R.J.Q. 2758 (Que. C.A.), leave to appeal allowed (2004), 2004 CarswellQue 1073, 2004 CarswellQue 1074 (S.C.C.) 624

Parrish v. Cosgrove and National Post, Ontario Superior Court of Justice, filed April 23, 2003 629

Parti Union Nationale c. Côté, [1989] R.J.Q. 2502 (Que. S.C.) at 2505-2506 580

Payne v. Wilson (2002), 162 O.A.C. 48, 2002 CarswellOnt 2224, [2002] O.J. No. 2566 (Ont. C.A.) 69

Pearlberg v. Varty (Inspector of Taxes), [1972] 1 W.L.R. 534, [1972] 2 All E.R. 6, 48 T.C. 30 (U.K. H.L.) 150

Peat Marwick Thorne v. Canadian Broadcasting Corp. (1991), 5 O.R. (3d) 747, 1991 CarswellOnt 437, 84 D.L.R. (4th) 656, 4 C.P.C. (3d) 233, 39 C.P.R. (3d) 58 (Ont. Gen. Div.), affirmed (1991), 5 O.R. (3d) 759, 1991 CarswellOnt 3157, 40 C.P.R. (3d) 414, 87 D.L.R. (4th) 316 (Ont. Gen. Div.) 983

Peet v. Canada (Attorney General), [1994] 3 F.C. 128, 1994 CarswellNat 858, 1994 CarswellNat 1478, 78 F.T.R. 44, 26 Admin. L.R. (2d) 243 (Fed. T.D.) 42

Pelletier v. Canada (Attorney General), Federal Court of Canada–Trial Division; action no T-668-04 1102

Peltier v. Henman, 997 F.2d 461 (8th Cir., 1993) 722

Penikett v. R. (1987), 45 D.L.R. (4th) 108, 1987 CarswellYukon 3, 21 B.C.L.R. (2d) 1, [1988] N.W.T.R. 18, 45 D.L.R. (4th) 108, [1988] 2 W.W.R. 481, 2 Y.R. 314 (Y.T. C.A.), leave to appeal refused 3 Y.R. 159n, 46 D.L.R. (4th) vi, 27 B.C.L.R. (2d) xxxv (note), [1988] N.W.T.R. xliv, [1988] 6 W.W.R. lxix, 88 N.R. 320n (S.C.C.) 399, 411, 437

Pereira v. Canada (Minister of Citizenship & Immigration) (1994), 86 F.T.R. 43, 1994 CarswellNat 1579, 31 Imm. L.R. (2d) 294 (Fed. T.D.) .. 44

Perot et al. v. Federal Election Commission et al., 97 F.3d 553 (D.C. Cir., 1996) 557

Peter Kiewit Sons Co. v. Richmond (City) (1992), 1 C.L.R. (2d) 5, 1992 CarswellBC 630, 7 Admin. L.R. (2d) 124, 11 M.P.L.R. (2d) 110 (B.C. S.C.) 879

Petition on the Legality of the Communist Party, Russian Constitutional Court, June 26, 1992 518

Petravic v. Cullen, Superior Court of Justice, Small Claims Division, filed March 13, 2002 766

Petryshyn v. R., [1993] 3 F.C. 640, 1993 CarswellNat 135, 1993 CarswellNat 1333, 16 Admin. L.R. (2d) 247, 21 Imm. L.R. (2d) 303, 65 F.T.R. 38 (Fed. T.D.) 836

Pick v. Conservative Party of Canada (February 26, 2004), Doc. Q.B. No. 32 of 2004 (Sask. Q.B.), not reported 609

Pindling v. National Broadcasting Corp. (1984), 14 D.L.R. (4th) 391, 1984 CarswellOnt 479, 49 O.R. (2d) 58, 47 C.P.C. 18, 31 C.C.L.T. 251 (Ont. H.C.) 982

Plant v. British Columbia (Attorney General), Supreme Court of British Columbia, filed April 3, 1997, file No. 97 1582 Victoria Registry, discontinued 482

Police Raid on British Columbia Legislature Offices, December 12, 2003 1045

Political Interference in the Human Resources Development Canada (HRDC), Transitional Jobs Fund 862

Polling and the General Election of 1999, Supreme Court of India, September 14, 1999 565

Polsinelli v. Marzilli (1987), 60 O.R. (2d) 713, 1987 CarswellOnt 455, 42 C.C.L.T. 46, 21 C.P.R. (3d) 140, 20 C.P.C. (2d) 23 (Ont. H.C.), affirmed

(1987), 61 O.R. (2d) 799, 1987 CarswellOnt 583, 21 C.P.R. (3d) 145, 31
C.P.R. (2d) 214, 31 C.P.C. (2d) 214 (Ont. Div. Ct.) 587

Porter v. Magill (2001), [2002] 2 A.C. 357, [2001] UKHL 67, [2002] 2 W.L.R. 37
(U.K. H.L.) 817

Position of the Premier of Québec on Bilingual Signage, **Press conference
by The Rt. Hon. Lucien Bouchard, October 1, 1998** 812

Possibility of Litigation by Senator Pat Carney, 1997, litigation not
initiated 620

Potter c. Québec (Procureur général), [2001] R.J.Q. 2823, 2001 CarswellQue
2773 (Que. C.A.), leave to appeal refused (2002), 2002 CarswellQue 2259,
2002 CarswellQue 2260, 305 N.R. 395 (note) (S.C.C.) 432

Powell v. McCormack, Speaker of the House of Representatives et al., 395 U.S. 486
(1969) 757

Pratt v. Meredith (January 29, 1997), Doc. 99756/96 (Ont. Gen. Div.), settled
June 23, 1998 631

Prebble v. Television New Zealand, [1994] 3 N.Z.L.R. 1 629

***Premier of Ontario's Threat of Legal Challenge to NAFTA, October 13,
1993, litigation not initiated*** 923

Price v. Socialist People's Lybian Arab Jamahiriya, 110 F. Supp.2d 10 (D.D.C.,
2000) 896, 897

***Prime Minister's Office Complaint About CBC Reporting on APEC,
Complaint initiated October 16, 1998.*** 308

***Prince Edward Island (Minister of Transportation & Public Works) v.
Canadian National Railway (1990), 71 D.L.R. (4th) 596, 1990
CarswellNat 106, 1990 CarswellNat 106F, 110 N.R. 394, [1991] 1 F.C. 129
(Fed. C.A.)*** 424

Prior v. R., 88 D.T.C. 6207, 1988 CarswellNat 275, 1988 CarswellNat 690,
[1988] 1 C.T.C. 241, 18 F.T.R. 227, [1988] 2 F.C. 371 (Fed. T.D.), affirmed
1989 CarswellNat 302, 89 D.T.C. 5503, [1989] 2 C.T.C. 280, 28 F.T.R. 240n,
44 C.R.R. 110, 101 N.R. 401 (Fed. C.A.), leave to appeal refused (1990), 44
C.R.R. 110 (note), 105 N.R. 399 (note) (S.C.C.), reconsideration refused
(September 20, 1990), Doc. 21709 (S.C.C.) 911

*Progressive Conservative Party of Canada v. Canadian Reform Conservative
Alliance and Reform Party of Canada*, Federal Court of Canada – Trial
Division, filed May 2, 2000, file T-795-00, discontinued 594

*Progressive Conservative Party of Canada v. Canadian Reform Conservative
Alliance and Canada Alliance Fund*, Federal Court of Canada – Trial
Division, filed May 23, 2000, file T-911-00, discontinued 594

*Promises of Premier Bernard Lord for his First 200 Days in Office and plan for an
MLA Responsibility Act, 1993 Federal Liberal Promise regarding the Ethics
Counsellor*, Hansard, February 8 and 18, 2001 666

Proper Handling of Harassment in the Canadian Forces, Report of the Military
Ombudsman, August 14, 2001 817

Proposal for a Judicial Accountability Act, 2000, First Reading, Legislative
Assembly of Ontario, April 18, 2000 251

Prosecution of British Columbia Premier Campbell, January, 2003 (U.S.) ... 1132

Prosecution of Deputy Prime Minister Anwar Ibrahim, High Court of Malaysia,
September, 1998 – August, 2000, *limited* information available 1029

Prosecution of former President Kenneth Kaunda of Zambia, High Court of
Zambia, December, 1997 – March, 1999 1029

Prosecution of former President Suharto, started in 2000 (Indonesia) 1123

Prosecution of George Speight for treason, February 18, 2002 (Fiji) 393

Prosecution of José Barrionuevo, Supreme Court of Spain, July 29, 1998 ... 908

Prosecution of Minister of the Interior Abdollah Nouri, Clerical court in Teheran,
November 26, 1999, limited information available (Iran) 1029

Prosecution of Ministers Laurent Fabius, Edmond Hervé et Georgina Dufoix,
Cour de justice de la République, Arrêt du 21 juin 1999 1071

**Prosecution of NATO Secretary General Claes, Cour de Cassation of
Belgium, December 23, 1998** 1165

Prosecution of Palestinian Leader Yasser Arafat, December 20, 2001
(Belgium) 1132

Prosecution of President Jacques Chirac, Cour de Cassation, Assemblée
Plénière, Arrêt no. 481 du 10 octobre 2001 1123

Prosecution of President Muammar Khadafi, Cour de Cassation, Chambre
criminelle, Arrêt no. 1414 du 13 mars 2001 1139

Prosecution of President Saddam Hussein, June 29, 2001 (Belgium) 1132

Prosecution of Presidents Chun Doo Hwan and Roh Tae-woo, Supreme Court of
the Republic of Korea, December 16, 1996 1119

Prosecution of Prime Minister Ariel Sharon, November 19, 2001
(Belgium) 1132

**Prosecution of Prime Minister Mian Muhammad Nawaz Sharif, Anti-
Terrorism Court No. 1, Karachi, April 6, 2000, SPL. Case No. 385/1999
and Sindh High Court; October 22, 2000 (Pakistan)** 380

**Prosecution of Prince Norodom Ranariddh, Phom Penh Military Court,
March 4 and 17, 1998 (Cambodia)** 1120

**Prosecution of Slobodan Milosevic, started February 12, 2002
(International Criminal Tribunal for the Former Yugoslavia)** 1140

Proulx c. Québec (Procureur général), 206 D.L.R. (4th) 1, 2001 CarswellQue
2187, 2001 CarswellQue 2188, [2001] S.C.J. No. 65, 2001 SCC 66, 46 C.R.
(5th) 1, 7 C.C.L.T. (3d) 157, 159 C.C.C. (3d) 225, 276 N.R. 201, [2001] 3
S.C.R. 9 (S.C.C.) 277

Public Citizen v. United States Trade Representative, 782 F. Supp. 139 (D.D.C., 1992) and 970 F.2d 916 (D.C. Cir., 1992) and 822 F. Supp. 21 (D.D.C., 1993) and 5 F.3d 549 (D.C. Cir., 1993) 910

***Public Disavowal of Legal Advice by the Premier of Alberta*, March 11, 1998** 1195

Public Inquiry into the events surrounding the death of Dudley George, established November 12, 2003 1114

Public Service Commission Audit of the Office of the Privacy Commissioner, September 2003 817

Pulp, Paper & Woodworkers of Canada, Local 8 v. Canada (Minister of Agriculture) (1994), 174 N.R. 37, [1994] F.C.J. No. 1067, 1994 CarswellNat 2931, 84 F.T.R. 80 (note) (Fed. C.A.) 811

Québec – Labrador Boundary Dispute, 1999, litigation not initiated 932

Quebec (Attorney General) v. Blaikie, [1981] 1 S.C.R. 312, 1981 CarswellQue 100, 1981 CarswellQue 100F, 36 N.R. 120, 123 D.L.R. (3d) 15, 60 C.C.C. (2d) 524 (S.C.C.) 78

Québec (Attorney General) v. Canada (Attorney General), action commenced December 23, 1996, contact Justice HRDC 918

Quebec (Attorney General) v. Eastmain Band, [1992] 3 F.C. 800, 1992 CarswellNat 142, 1992 CarswellNat 142F, 148 N.R. 116, 98 D.L.R. (4th) 206 (Fed. C.A.) 937

Québec (Directeur général des élections) c. Fortin (1999), 1999 CarswellQue 3821 (Que. C.A.) 239

Québec (Procureur général) c. Collier, [1990] 1 S.C.R. 260, 1990 CarswellQue 101, 1990 CarswellQue 101F, 66 D.L.R. (4th) 575, 32 Q.A.C. 316, 107 N.R. 235 (S.C.C.) 760

Québec (Procureur général) c. Collier, 23 D.L.R. (4th) 339, 1985 CarswellQue 263, [1985] C.A. 559 (Que. C.A.), affirmed 1990 CarswellQue 101, 1990 CarswellQue 101F, 66 D.L.R. (4th) 575, 32 Q.A.C. 316, 107 N.R. 235, [1990] 1 S.C.R. 260 (S.C.C.) 760

Québec (Procureur général) c. Henderson, [2002] R.J.Q. 2435, 2002 CarswellQue 1711, 220 D.L.R. (4th) 691 (Que. S.C.) 366

Québec (Procureur général) v. Canada (Procureur général), [1982] 2 S.C.R. 793, 1982 CarswellQue 124, 1982 CarswellQue 124F, 140 D.L.R. (3d) 385, 45 N.R. 317 (S.C.C.) 73

Quebec Assn. of Protestant School Boards v. Quebec (Attorney General) (No. 2), [1984] 2 S.C.R. 66, 1984 CarswellQue 100, 1984 CarswellQue 100F, 10 D.L.R. (4th) 321, 54 N.R. 196, 9 C.R.R. 133 (S.C.C.) 219

Québec Prosecution of Mohawks for the Events of Oka in 1990, July 1992 209

Queremos Eligir c. Consejo Nacional Electoral, Tribunal Supremo de Justicia, May 25, 2000, Exp. No. 00-1642 (Venezuela) 569

R. c. Cogger, [1997] 2 S.C.R. 845, 1997 CarswellQue 621, 1997 CarswellQue 622, 116 C.C.C. (3d) 322, 148 D.L.R. (4th) 649, 127 N.R. 64, 8 C.R. (5th) 283 (S.C.C.) and (1998), 1998 CarswellQue 657, 1998 CarswellQue 2723 (C.Q.) 1057

R. c. Cross, [1992] R.J.Q. 1001 (Que. S.C.) 209

R. c. Foisy (May 17, 2000), Doc. Montréal 199 092 891, [2000] J.Q. No. 2990 (Que. Mun. Ct.) 624

R. c. Gosset, [1991] R.J.Q. 1567, 1991 CarswellQue 14, 1991 CarswellQue 121, 6 C.R. (4th) 239, 37 Q.A.C. 161, 67 C.C.C. (3d) 156 (Que. C.A.), affirmed 1993 CarswellQue 16, 1993 CarswellQue 162, [1993] S.C.J. No. 88, 23 C.R. (4th) 280, 157 N.R. 195, 105 D.L.R. (4th) 681, 83 C.C.C. (3d) 494, 57 Q.A.C. 130, 17 C.R.R. (2d) 77, [1993] 3 S.C.R. 76 (S.C.C.) 140

R. c. Lamothe, 58 C.C.C. (3d) 530, 1990 CarswellQue 168, [1990] R.J.Q. 973, 33 Q.A.C. 11 (Que. C.A.) 30

R. c. Lortie, [1986] R.J.Q. 2787 à 2797, 1986 CarswellQue 179, 1986 CarswellQue 20, 2 Q.A.C. 118, 54 C.R. (3d) 228 (Que. C.A.) 725

R. c. Montour, [1991] R.J.Q. 1470 (Que. S.C.), affirmed (1998), 1998 CarswellQue 888, 1998 CarswellQue 2831 (Que. C.A.), leave to appeal allowed (1999), 237 N.R. 399 (note), 132 C.C.C. (3d) vi (note) (S.C.C.) 1188

R. c. Robert (2000), 2000 CarswellQue 956, [2000] J.Q. No. 2919 (Que. Mun. Ct.) 624

R. v. Achtem (1979), 52 C.C.C. (2d) 240, 1979 CarswellAlta 67, 19 A.R. 338, 11 Alta. L.R. (2d) 151, 13 C.R. (3d) 199 (Alta. C.A.), leave to appeal refused (1979), 19 A.R. 339n, 31 N.R. 178n (S.C.C.) 78

R. v. Andrews, [1990] 3 S.C.R. 870, 1990 CarswellOnt 61, 1990 CarswellOnt 1011, 1 C.R. (4th) 266, 117 N.R. 284, 61 C.C.C. (3d) 490, 77 D.L.R. (4th) 128, 3 C.R.R. (2d) 176, 47 O.A.C. 293, 75 O.R. (2d) 481 (note) (S.C.C.) 580

R. v. Appleby (1990), 78 C.R. (3d) 282, 1990 CarswellOnt 107, [1990] O.J. No. 1329 (Ont. Prov. Ct.) 1021

R. v. Archer, [2002] EWCA Crim 1996, July 22, 2002 (U.K.) 758

R. v. Arseneau, [1979] 2 S.C.R. 136, 1979 CarswellNB 15, 1979 CarswellNB 15F, 95 D.L.R. (3d) 1, 25 N.B.R. (2d) 390, 51 A.P.R. 390, 45 C.C.C. (2d) 321, 26 N.R. 226 (S.C.C.) 1056

R. v. Asgari, Ontario Court (Provincial Division), September 1998, not reported, limited information available 1016

R. v. Ashini (1989), 51 C.C.C. (3d) 329, 1989 CarswellNfld 259, 79 Nfld. & P.E.I.R. 318, 246 A.P.R. 318 (Nfld. C.A.) 208

R. v. Baines (1908), [1909] 1 K.B. 258, 21 Cox C.C. 756 (Eng. K.B.) 1064

R. v. Barrow, [1987] 2 S.C.R. 694, 1987 CarswellNS 344, [1987] S.C.J. No. 84, 1987 CarswellNS 42, 87 N.S.R. (2d) 271, 222 A.P.R. 271, 45 D.L.R. (4th) 487, 81 N.R. 321, 38 C.C.C. (3d) 193, 61 C.R. (3d) 305 (S.C.C.) .. 580

R. v. BBC (Ex parte Prolife Alliance), [2003] UKHL 23 535

R. v. Behrens (2001), [2001] O.J. No. 245, 2001 CarswellOnt 5785 (Ont. C.J.) 740

R. v. Bonadie (1996), 109 C.C.C. (3d) 356, 1996 CarswellOnt 2994 (Ont. Prov. Div.) 1046

R. v. Bow Street Metropolitan Stipendiary Magistrate (1999), [1999] 1 All E.R. 577, [1998] H.L.J. No. 52, [1999] 2 W.L.R. 272, 237 N.R. 201 (U.K. H.L.) 1132

R. v. Bow Street Metropolitan Stipendiary Magistrate (No. 3) (1999), [1999] 2 All E.R. 97, [1999] H.L.J. No. 12, [1999] 2 W.L.R. 827, [2000] 1 A.C. 147 (U.K. H.L.) 1132

R. v. Bow Street Metropolitan Stipendiary Magistrate, [1998] 4 All E.R. 897, [1998] H.L.J. No. 41, [1998] 3 W.L.R. 1456 (U.K. H.L.) 1132

R. v. Brown, 2001 PESCTD 6, [2001] P.E.I.J. No. 8, 2001 CarswellPEI 5, 197 Nfld. & P.E.I.R. 285, 591 A.P.R. 285 (P.E.I. T.D.) 629, 743

R. v. Bruneau (1963), [1964] 1 O.R. 263, 1963 CarswellOnt 22, 42 C.R. 93, [1964] 1 C.C.C. 97 (Ont. C.A.) 759

R. v. Bryan, 170 D.L.R. (4th) 487, 1999 CarswellMan 46, [1999] M.J. No. 49, 134 Man. R. (2d) 61, 193 W.A.C. 61, 133 C.C.C. (3d) 217, [1999] 6 W.W.R. 714, 16 Admin. L.R. (3d) 49 (Man. C.A.), leave to appeal refused (2000), 253 N.R. 194 (note), 145 Man. R. (2d) 320 (note), 218 W.A.C. 320 (note) (S.C.C.) 1177

R. v. Bryan, 2003 BCPC 39, [2003] B.C.J. No. 318, 2003 CarswellBC 369, 104 C.R.R. (2d) 364 (B.C. Prov. Ct.) and 233 D.L.R. (4th) 745, 2003 CarswellBC 2650, 2003 BCSC 1499 (B.C. S.C.), leave to appeal allowed 2004 BCCA 140, 2004 CarswellBC 486, 236 D.L.R. (4th) 340 (B.C. C.A. [In Chambers]) 567

R. v. Campbell, [1967] 2 O.R. 1, 1967 CarswellOnt 29, C.R. 270, [1967] 3 C.C.C. 250 (Ont. C.A.), affirmed (1967), 1967 CarswellOnt 21, 2 C.R.N.S. 403 (S.C.C.) 817

R. v. Campbell, [1997] 3 S.C.R. 3, [1997] S.C.J. No. 75, 1997 CarswellNat 3038, 1997 CarswellNat 3039, 11 C.P.C. (4th) 1, 150 D.L.R. (4th) 577, 118 C.C.C. (3d) 193, 46 C.R.R. (2d) 1, 206 A.R. 1, 156 W.A.C. 1, 217 N.R. 1, 156 Nfld. & P.E.I.R. 1, 121 Man. R. (2d) 1, 49 Admin. L.R. (2d) 1, [1997] 10 W.W.R. 417, 483 A.P.R. 1 (S.C.C.), additional reasons at 1998 CarswellNat 79, 1998 CarswellNat 114, 155 D.L.R. (4th) 1, 121 C.C.C. (3d) 474, 50 Admin. L.R. (2d) 273, 49 C.R.R. (2d) 1, [1998] 1 S.C.R. 3, 15 C.P.C. (4th) 306, 223 N.R. 21, 161 Nfld. & P.E.I.R. 124, 497 A.P.R. 124, 212 A.R. 161, 168 W.A.C. 161, 126 Man. R. (2d) 96, 167 W.A.C. 96 (S.C.C.) 251

R. v. Canadian Broadcasting Corp. (1992), 72 C.C.C. (3d) 545, 1992
CarswellOnt 887, 42 C.P.R. (3d) 252 (Ont. Gen. Div.), affirmed (1993),
1993 CarswellOnt 925, 84 C.C.C. (3d) 574, 51 C.P.R. (3d) 192 (Ont. C.A.),
leave to appeal refused (1994), 72 O.A.C. 158 (note), 174 N.R. 238
(note), 88 C.C.C. (3d) vi (note), 53 C.P.R. (3d) v (note) (S.C.C.) .. 64, 109,
117, 540

R. v. CFRB Ltd. (1976), 30 C.C.C. (2d) 386, 1976 CarswellOnt 934, 31 C.P.R.
(2d) 13 (Ont. C.A.) 58

R. v. Clark, [1943] O.R. 501, 1943 CarswellOnt 30, [1943] 3 D.L.R. 684 (Ont.
C.A.), leave to appeal refused (1943), 1943 CarswellOnt 93, [1944] S.C.R.
69, [1944] 1 D.L.R. 495 (S.C.C.) 744

R. v. Cote, 193 Sask. R. 1, 2000 CarswellSask 322, 2000 SKQB 36 (Sask.
Q.B.) 69

R. v. Curtis, Provincial Court of New Brunswick, case no. 07624605,
sentencing January 6, 2004 740

R. v. Dubas (June 26, 1992), Doc. Victoria 58997, [1992] B.C.J. No. 2935 (B.C.
S.C.), affirmed (1995), 1995 CarswellBC 516, 60 B.C.A.C. 202, 99 W.A.C.
202 (B.C. C.A.) 817

R. v. Gauvin (1984), 1984 CarswellOnt 1164, 2 O.A.C. 309, 11 C.C.C. (3d) 229
(Ont. C.A.), leave to appeal refused (1984), 57 N.R. 159n (S.C.C.) 535

R. v. Giguère, [1983] 2 S.C.R. 448, 1983 CarswellOnt 109, 1983 CarswellOnt
815, 37 C.R. (3d) 1, 50 N.R. 347, 3 D.L.R. (4th) 524, 8 C.C.C. (3d) 1
(S.C.C.) 78

R. v. Halpert (1984), 15 C.C.C. (3d) 292, 1984 CarswellOnt 1338, 48 O.R.
(2d) 249, 12 C.R.R. 201 (Ont. Co. Ct.) 963

R. v. Hinchey, [1996] 3 S.C.R. 1128, [1996] S.C.J. No. 121, 1996 CarswellNfld
253, 1996 CarswellNfld 254, 111 C.C.C. (3d) 353, 205 N.R. 161, 142 D.L.R.
(4th) 50, 3 C.R. (5th) 187, 147 Nfld. & P.E.I.R. 1, 459 A.P.R. 1
(S.C.C.) 1050

R. v. Jones, [1965] 3 C.C.C. 263, 1965 CarswellBC 25, 51 W.W.R. 303, 50
D.L.R. (2d) 477 (B.C. Co. Ct.) 105

R. v. Jones, [1996] 2 S.C.R. 821, 1996 CarswellOnt 3987, 1996 CarswellOnt
3988, 27 O.R. (3d) 95, 50 C.R. (4th) 216, 138 D.L.R. (4th) 204, [1996] 4
C.N.L.R. 164, 92 O.A.C. 241, 109 C.C.C. (3d) 275 (S.C.C.) 209

R. v. Kanayok, Nunavut Court of Justice, July 15, 1999, Rankin Inlet, file
199-59548 (N.C.J.), not reported 1214

R. v. Kevork (1986) 27 C.C.C. (3d) 523, 1986 CarswellOnt 2151, 27 C.C.C.
(3d) 523 (Ont. H.C.) 1009

R. v. Kevork (1986), 27 C.C.C. (3d) 271, 1986 CarswellOnt 2149, 20 C.R.R.
325 (Ont. H.C.) 1009

R. v. Kevork (1988), 29 O.A.C. 387, 1988 CarswellOnt 1095 (Ont. C.A.) 1009

R. v. Kormos (1997), 154 D.L.R. (4th) 551, 1997 CarswellOnt 4796, [1997] O.J. No. 4861, 12 C.R. (5th) 348, 36 O.R. (3d) 667 (Ont. Prov. Div.) 1026

R. v. Langlois, Superior Court of Québec, filed April 21, 1988, pending .. 432

R. v. Lords Commissioners of the Treasury (1872), L.R. 7 Q.B. 387 (Eng. Q.B.) 867

R. v. Lyons; R. v. Saunders; R. v. Parnes; R. v. Ronson, [2001] EWCA Crim 2860 (U.K.) 246

R. v. MacDougal, 138 C.C.C. (3d) 38, 1999 CarswellBC 1975, [1999] B.C.J. No. 2034, 27 C.R. (5th) 340, 67 C.R.R. (2d) 17, 178 D.L.R. (4th) 227, 128 B.C.A.C. 281, 208 W.A.C. 281, 1999 BCCA 509 (B.C. C.A.) 33

R. v. Marchese, Ontario Court (General Division), January 23, 1997, not reported, limited information available 1001

R. v. McGarry and Saniforth, Ontario District Court, 1978, limited information available 725

R. v. McSorley, 2000 BCPC 114, [2000] B.C.J. No. 2639 (B.C. Prov. Ct.) .. 1181

R. v. Morales, 17 W.C.B. (2d) 580, 1992 CarswellQue 18, 1992 CarswellQue 121, 17 C.R. (4th) 74, 12 C.R.R. (2d) 31, [1992] 3 S.C.R. 711, 77 C.C.C. (3d) 91, 144 N.R. 176, 51 Q.A.C. 161 (S.C.C.) 32

R. v. Munro (1991), 1991 CarswellOnt 3290 (Ont. Gen. Div.) 1080

R. v. Parliamentary Commissioner for Standards, ex parte Al-Fayed, [1998] 1 All E.R. 93 259

R. v. Peterson (October 1, 1997), Doc. CE87921-1 (Ont. Prov. Div.), not reported 530

R. v. Pilarinos, 2002 BCSC 1267, 2002 CarswellBC 1971, 216 D.L.R. (4th) 680, 167 C.C.C. (3d) 97 (B.C. S.C.) 1165

R. v. Pilarinos, 219 D.L.R. (4th) 165, 2002 CarswellBC 673, [2002] B.C.J. No. 609, 2002 BCSC 452, 93 C.R.R. (2d) 16, 168 C.C.C. (3d) 548 (B.C. S.C.) 1165

R. v. Powley, 47 O.R. (3d) 30, 2000 CarswellOnt 126, [2000] O.J. No. 99, [2000] 2 C.N.L.R. 233 (Ont. S.C.J.), leave to appeal allowed (2000), 2000 CarswellOnt 1062, [2000] O.J. No. 1063, 49 O.R. (3d) 94 (Ont. C.A. [In Chambers]), affirmed 2001 CarswellOnt 480, [2001] O.J. No. 607, 152 C.C.C. (3d) 97, 196 D.L.R. (4th) 221, 40 C.R. (5th) 221, 141 O.A.C. 121, 53 O.R. (3d) 35, 80 C.R.R. (2d) 1, [2001] 2 C.N.L.R. 291 (Ont. C.A.), leave to appeal allowed 2001 CarswellOnt 3490, 2001 CarswellOnt 3491, 86 C.R.R. (2d) 187 (note), [2001] 4 C.N.L.R. iv (note), 283 N.R. 397 (note), 158 O.A.C. 195 (note) (S.C.C.), leave to appeal allowed (2002), 2002 CarswellOnt 833, 2002 CarswellOnt 834, 301 N.R. 388, 170 O.A.C. 220

(S.C.C.), affirmed 2003 CarswellOnt 3502, 2003 CarswellOnt 3503, [2003] S.C.J. No. 43, 230 D.L.R. (4th) 1, 177 C.C.C. (3d) 193, [2003] 4 C.N.L.R. 321, 308 N.R. 201, 177 O.A.C. 201, 68 O.R. (3d) 255 (note), [2003] 2 S.C.R. 207, 110 C.R.R. (2d) 92, 2003 SCC 43, 5 C.E.L.R. (3d) 1 (S.C.C.) 1031

R. v. Prince Edward Island (1977) 83 D.L.R. (3d) 492, 1977 CarswellNat 122, 1977 CarswellNat 122F, [1978] 1 F.C. 533, 20 N.R. 91, 14 Nfld. & P.E.I.R. 477, 33 A.P.R. 477 (Fed. C.A.) 420

R. v. Prunelle, Court Martial Transcript Summaries, C.F.B. Valcartier, April 15, 1997, file 04/97 295

R. v. Pryce, Ontario Court (Provincial Division), April 27, 1998, not reported, limited information available 937

R. v. Regan, 209 D.L.R. (4th) 41 at 115, 2002 CarswellNS 61, 2002 CarswellNS 62, [2002] S.C.J. No. 14, 2002 SCC 12, 161 C.C.C. (3d) 97, 282 N.R. 1, 49 C.R. (5th) 1, 201 N.S.R. (2d) 63, 629 A.P.R. 63, 91 C.R.R. (2d) 51, [2002] 1 S.C.R. 297 (S.C.C.) 284

R. v. Reyat (1991), 1991 CarswellBC 1245, [1991] B.C.J. No. 2006 (B.C. S.C.), affirmed (1993), 1993 CarswellBC 491, 20 C.R. (4th) 149, 80 C.C.C. (3d) 210, 24 B.C.A.C. 161, 40 W.A.C. 161, 14 C.R.R. (2d) 282 (B.C. C.A.), leave to appeal refused (1993), 25 C.R. (4th) 125 (note), 83 C.C.C. (3d) vi (note), 159 N.R. 320 (note), 16 C.R.R. (2d) 383 (note), 33 B.C.A.C. 319 (note), 54 W.A.C. 319 (note) (S.C.C.) 1014

R. v. Rizzotto (1986), [1987] N.W.T.R. 63, 1986 CarswellNWT 52, [1986] 6 W.W.R. 679 (N.W.T. S.C.) 1051

R. v. Roach (1978), 25 O.R. (2d) 767, 1978 CarswellOnt 1393, 101 D.L.R. (3d) 736, 48 C.C.C. (2d) 405 (Ont. Co. Ct.) 511

R. v. S. (R.J.), [1995] 1 S.C.R. 451, 1995 CarswellOnt 2, [1995] S.C.J. No. 10, 1995 CarswellOnt 516, 36 C.R. (4th) 1, 26 C.R.R. (2d) 1, 177 N.R. 81, 21 O.R. (3d) 797 (note), 96 C.C.C. (3d) 1, 78 O.A.C. 161, 121 D.L.R. (4th) 589 (S.C.C.) 223

R. v. Saplys, 60 C.R.R. (2d) 287, 1999 CarswellOnt 468, [1999] O.J. No. 395, 90 O.T.C. 111, [1999] G.S.T.C. 22 (Ont. Gen. Div.) 814

R. v. Secretary of State for Foreign and Commonwealth Affairs, ex parte Rees-Mogg, [1994] 2 Q.B. 552 896

R. v. Secretary of State for the Home Department, [1995] 2 A.C. 513 (U.K. H.L.) 704

R. v. Shirose, [1999] 1 S.C.R. 565, 1999 CarswellOnt 948, 1999 CarswellOnt 949, [1999] S.C.J. No. 16, 237 N.R. 86, 133 C.C.C. (3d) 257, 42 O.R. (3d) 800 (note), 171 D.L.R. (4th) 193, 119 O.A.C. 201, 43 O.R. (3d) 256 (note), 24 C.R. (5th) 365 (S.C.C.) 284

R. v. Sparrow, 70 D.L.R. (4th) 385, 1990 CarswellBC 105, 1990 CarswellBC 756, [1990] S.C.J. No. 49, 111 N.R. 241, [1990] 1 S.C.R. 1075, [1990] 3

C.N.L.R. 160, 46 B.C.L.R. (2d) 1, 56 C.C.C. (3d) 263, [1990] 4 W.W.R. 410 (S.C.C.) 129

R. v. Valente (No. 2) (1985), [1985] 2 S.C.R. 673, 1985 CarswellOnt 948, 1985 CarswellOnt 129, [1985] S.C.J. No. 77, 37 M.V.R. 9, 64 N.R. 1, 14 O.A.C. 79, 23 C.C.C. (3d) 193, 19 C.R.R. 354, 52 O.R. (2d) 779, [1986] D.L.Q. 85, 24 D.L.R. (4th) 161, 49 C.R. (3d) 97 (S.C.C.) 249

R. v. Van Hee (June 21, 1991), Doc. Ottawa 91-11045 (Ont. Prov. Div.), not reported, limited information available 727, 1016

R. v. Vermette, 50 D.L.R. (4th) 385, 1988 CarswellQue 18, 1988 CarswellQue 138, 84 N.R. 296, 34 C.R.R. 218, 14 Q.A.C. 161, 64 C.R. (3d) 82, [1988] 1 S.C.R. 985, 41 C.C.C. (3d) 523 (S.C.C.) 1019

R. v. Yacoub, Ontario Court (General Division), April 30, 1990, file S.C.O. 269/89, not reported 1013

R.C.M.P. Investigation of Canadian Alliance Payment to Jim Hart, M.P. 518

Radiomutuel Inc. c. Wlihelmy (September 14, 1992), Doc. C.S. Québec 200-05-002998-925 (Que. S.C.) and (September 22, 1992), Doc. C.A. Québec 200-09-000619-921 (Que. C.A.) and (September 24, 1992), Doc. C.S. Québec 200-05-002998-925 (Que. S.C.) and (September 30, 1992), Doc. C.S. Québec 200-05-002998-925 (Que. S.C.) 291

Rai Muhammad Nawaz Karal v. Federation of Pakistan, Constitutional Petition No. 8/2002, Supreme Court of Pakistan, April 27, 2002 383

Raîche v. R., Federal Court of Canada – Trial Division; filed September 22, 2003, file T-1730-03, in progress 484

Raines v. Byrd, 138 L.Ed.2d 849 (1997) 773

Ramsden v. Peterborough (City), [1993] 2 S.C.R. 1084, [1993] S.C.J. No. 87, 1993 CarswellOnt 117, 1993 CarswellOnt 988, 16 M.P.L.R. (2d) 1, 156 N.R. 2, 23 C.R. (4th) 391, 106 D.L.R. (4th) 233, 66 O.A.C. 10, 16 C.R.R. (2d) 240, 15 O.R. (3d) 548 (note) (S.C.C.) 613

Ranta et al v. Alain et al, British Columbia Supreme Court, Vancouver Registry, Court file C950096 599

Reclamation Systems Inc. v. Ontario (1996), 27 O.R. (3d) 419, 1996 CarswellOnt 95, 19 C.E.L.R. (N.S.) 1 (Ont. Gen. Div.) 672

Reese v. Alberta (1992), [1993] 1 W.W.R. 450, 1992 CarswellAlta 138, [1992] A.J. No. 745, 5 Alta. L.R. (3d) 40, 9 C.E.L.R. (N.S.) 65, 133 A.R. 127, 13 C.P.C. (3d) 323, 11 Admin. L.R. (2d) 265n (Alta. Q.B.) 922

Refah Partisi (Welfare Party) v. Turkey (2002), 35 E.H.R.R. 3 (European Community) 519

Reference re Amendment to the Constitution of Canada, 125 D.L.R. (3d) 1, 1981 CarswellMan 110, 1981 CarswellMan 360, 11 Man. R. (2d) 1, [1981] 6 W.W.R. 1, [1981] 1 S.C.R. 753, 39 N.R. 1, 34 Nfld. & P.E.I.R. 1, 95 A.P.R. 1, 1 C.R.R. 59 (S.C.C.) 72, 177, 430, 750, 1031, 1034

Reference re Anti-Inflation Act, 1975 (Canada), [1976] 2 S.C.R. 373, 1976
CarswellOnt 405, 1976 CarswellOnt 405F, 9 N.R. 541, 68 D.L.R. (3d) 452
(S.C.C.) 243

Reference re Bill 30, an Act to amend the Education Act, [1987] 1 S.C.R. 1148,
1987 CarswellOnt 1049, 1987 CarswellOnt 1049F, 77 N.R. 241, 40 D.L.R.
(4th) 18, 22 O.A.C. 321, 36 C.R.R. 305 (S.C.C.) 98

Reference re Canada Assistance Plan (Canada), [1991] 2 S.C.R. 525, 1991
CarswellBC 168, 1991 CarswellBC 920, 58 B.C.L.R. (2d) 1, 1 Admin. L.R.
(2d) 1, 1 B.C.A.C. 241, 1 W.A.C. 241, 127 N.R. 161, [1991] 6 W.W.R. 1, 83
D.L.R. (4th) 297 (S.C.C.) 410, 913

Reference re Electoral Divisions Statutes Amendment Act, 1993 (Alberta)
(1994), 119 D.L.R. (4th) 1, 1994 CarswellAlta 232, 24 Alta. L.R. (3d) 1,
157 A.R. 241, 77 W.A.C. 241, 25 C.R.R. (2d) 347 (Alta. C.A.) 185, 479,
1172

Reference re Excise Tax Act, [1992] 2 S.C.R. 445, 1992 CarswellAlta 61, 1992
CarswellAlta 469, 2 Alta. L.R. (3d) 289, 20 W.A.C. 161, [1992] G.S.T.C. 2,
[1992] 4 W.W.R. 673, 138 N.R. 247, 127 A.R. 161, 94 D.L.R. (4th) 51, 5
T.C.T. 4165 (S.C.C.) 913

Reference re Firearms Act (Canada), [2000] 1 S.C.R. 783, 2000 CarswellAlta
517, 2000 CarswellAlta 518, [2000] S.C.J. No. 31, 2000 SCC 31, 185 D.L.R.
(4th) 577, 144 C.C.C. (3d) 385, 34 C.R. (5th) 1, [2000] 10 W.W.R. 1, 82
Alta. L.R. (3d) 1, 254 N.R. 201, 261 A.R. 201, 225 W.A.C. 201
(S.C.C.) 816

*Reference re Language Rights Under s. 23 of Manitoba Act, 1870 & s. 133 of
Constitution Act, 1867*, 19 D.L.R. (4th) 1, 1985 CarswellMan 183, 1985
CarswellMan 450, [1985] S.C.J. No. 36, [1985] 1 S.C.R. 721, [1985] 4
W.W.R. 385, 59 N.R. 321, 35 Man. R. (2d) 83 (S.C.C.) and (1985), 26
D.L.R. (4th) 767 (note) (S.C.C.) and [1990] 3 S.C.R. 1417, 1990
CarswellNat 749, 1990 CarswellNat 749F (S.C.C.) and [1992] 1 S.C.R. 212,
1992 CarswellMan 96, 1992 CarswellMan 219, [1992] 2 W.W.R. 385, 76
Man. R. (2d) 124, 10 W.A.C. 124, 88 D.L.R. (4th) 385, 133 N.R. 88
(S.C.C.) 19, 73, 161, 795

Reference re Legislative Authority of Parliament to Alter or Replace the
Senate (1979), 102 D.L.R. (3d) 1, 1979 CarswellNat 643F, 1979
CarswellNat 643, [1980] 1 S.C.R. 54, 30 N.R. 271 (S.C.C.) 1, 325, 711,
713

*Reference re Proposal for an Act Respecting Certain Aspects of Legal Capacity for
Marriage for Civil Purposes*, case in progress 864

Reference Re Provincial Electoral Boundaries, [1991] 2 S.C.R. 158, 1991
CarswellSask 188, 1991 CarswellSask 403, [1991] 5 W.W.R. 1, 127 N.R.
1, 81 D.L.R. (4th) 16, 5 C.R.R. (2d) 1, 94 Sask. R. 161 (S.C.C.) 186, 230,
475

Reference re Secession of Quebec, **161 D.L.R. (4th) 385, 1998 CarswellNat 1299, 1998 CarswellNat 1300, [1998] S.C.J. No. 61, 228 N.R. 203, 55 C.R.R. (2d) 1, [1998] 2 S.C.R. 217 (S.C.C.)** 6, 169, 326, 367, 919, 1034

Reference re ss. 26, 27 & 28 of Constitution Act, 1867, **78 D.L.R. (4th) 245, 1991 CarswellBC 27, 53 B.C.L.R. (2d) 335, [1991] 4 W.W.R. 97 (B.C. C.A.)** 747, 764

Reform Party Motion to Avoid Judicial Rulings on Legislation, **Hansard, June 8, 1998, p. 7677** 252

Reform Party of Canada v. Canada (Attorney General) (1992), [1993] 3 W.W.R. 139 (Alta. Q.B.), additional reasons at (1993), 7 Alta. L.R. (3d) 34 (Alta. Q.B.), reversed [1995] 4 W.W.R. 609 (Alta. C.A.), additional reasons at [1995] 10 W.W.R. 764 (Alta. C.A.) 548

Reform Party of Canada v. Canada (Attorney General), 165 A.R. 161, 89 W.A.C. 161, 1995 CarswellAlta 79, [1995] 4 W.W.R. 609, 123 D.L.R. (4th) 366, 27 C.R.R. (2d) 254, 27 Alta. L.R. (3d) 153 (Alta. C.A.), additional reasons at 1995 CarswellAlta 378, 32 Alta. L.R. (3d) 430, 174 A.R. 169, 102 W.A.C. 169, [1995] 10 W.W.R. 764 (Alta. C.A.) 530, 998

Reform Party of Canada v. Reform Party of Manitoba **(1991), 39 C.P.R. (3d) 440, 1991 CarswellMan 106 (Man. C.A.)** 589

Reform Party of the United States et al. v. Gargan et al., 89 F. Supp.2d 751 (W.D. Va., 2000) 600

Reform Party of the United States et al. v. Verney et al., U.S. District Court, Western District of Virginia, March 27, 2000, Case no. 6: 00CV00014/ 50012 600

Reform Party of the United States of America v. Hagelin et al., California Superior Court, County of Los Angeles, South District, September 15, 2000, Case no. NC 028469 600

Regina (Sivakuram) v. Secretary of State for the Home Department, [2001] EWCA Civ 1196, July 24, 2001 and November 11, 2001 (U.K.) 641

Regina v. H. M. Treasury, Ex parte University of Cambridge (October 17, 2000), Doc. Case C380/98 (European Ct. Just.) (European Community) 29

Regina v. Secretary of State for Employment, **Ex parte Equal Opportunities Commission [1995] 1 A.C. 1 (U.K. H.L.)** 366

Regina v. Secretary of State for Transport, Ex parte Factortame Ltd. (No. 2), [1991] 1 A.C. 603 (U.K. H.L.) 366

Registration of "Bloc Québécois" Name 594

Regular, Re **(1995), 132 Nfld. & P.E.I.R. 310, 140 A.P.R. 310, 1995 CarswellNfld 169 (Nfld. T.D.)** 33, 50

Reid (Next Friend of) v. Canada **(1994), 73 F.T.R. 290, 1994 CarswellNat 333, [1994] F.C.J. No. 99 (Fed. T.D.)** 504, 914

Report of a Commission of Inquiry into the Facts of Allegations of Conflict of Interest Concerning the Honourable Sinclair Stevens, **December 1, 1987** 1073

Report of the (Monnin) Commission of Inquiry into Allegations of Infractions during the 1995 Manitoba General Election, **March 29, 1999** 571

Report of the Auditor General of Canada to the House of Commons, **November 2003, Chapters 3, 4 and 5, on Government-Wide Audit of Sponsorship, Advertising and Public Opinion Research and** *Appointment of a Special Counsel for Financial Recovery*, **announced February 10, 2004** 1102

Report of the Commissioner of Conflict of Interest on the Activities of Don Morin, **November 24, 1998** 1158

Report of the Hutton Inquiry (U.K.) 907

Report of the National Commission on Federal Election Reform; July 31, 2001 573

Report of the Parliamentary Commissioner for Standards, **July, 1997 (England)** 782

Report of the Standing Committee on Procedure and House Affairs on the Letter to the Armed Forces by a Bloc Québécois Member of Parliament, **Hansard, June 18, 1996, p. 3988** 299

Report of the Westray Mine Public Inquiry, Justice K. Peter Richard, Commissioner, November, 1997 814

Republic of Fiji and Attorney General v. Prasad, [2001] 2 L.R.C. 743 383

Republican Party of Minnesota et al. v. Kelly et al., 996 F. Supp. 875 (1998) and U.S.C.A. (8th) Circ., November 2, 1998 and 63 F. Supp.2d 967 (1999) on appeal to the United States Supreme Court, Cert. December 3, 2001 922

Retention of outside counsel by the House of Commons, Hill Times, September 22, 1997 802

Review of the Nova Scotia Public Prosecution Service (Kaufman Inquiry), **Final Report, June 9, 1999** 1203

Reynolds v. Times Newspapers Ltd., [1999] 4 All E.R. 609, [1999] H.L.J. No. 45, [1999] 3 W.L.R. 1010 (U.K. H.L.) 1000

Rhéaume v. Canada (1992), **11 Admin. L.R. (2d) 124, 1992 CarswellNat 184, 153 N.R. 270 (Fed. C.A.), leave to appeal refused (1993), 11 Admin. L.R. (2d) 126n (S.C.C.)** 132

Riot at the Kingston Prison for Women, Report by a Commission of Inquiry, April 1, 1996 1041

Ripley v. Bastin et al., **Nova Scotia Supreme Court, August 5 and November 24, 1999, not reported** 623

Rizzuto c. Rocheleau, [1996] R.R.A. 448 (Que. S.C.) 629

RJR-Macdonald Inc. c. Canada (Procureur général), [1995] 3 S.C.R. 199, 1995 CarswellQue 119, 1995 CarswellQue 119F, [1995] S.C.J. No. 68, 127 D.L.R. (4th) 1, 100 C.C.C. (3d) 449, 62 C.P.R. (3d) 417, 31 C.R.R. (2d) 189, 187 N.R. 1 (S.C.C.) (at 328-329 [S.C.R.]) 1177

Roach v. Canada (Minister of State for Multiculturalism & Culture), [1994] 2 F.C. 406, 1994 CarswellNat 1463, 1994 CarswellNat 93, 23 Imm. L.R. (2d) 1, 113 D.L.R. (4th) 67, 164 N.R. 370, 72 F.T.R. 304 (note) (Fed. C.A.), leave to appeal refused (1994), 113 D.L.R. (4th) 67n (Fed. C.A.) 188

Robinson v. Canada (Attorney General) (August 8, 2001), Doc. 01-CV-215525SR (Ont. S.C.J.) 907

Roman Corp. v. Hudson's Bay Oil & Gas Co., [1973] S.C.R. 820, 1973 CarswellOnt 228, 36 D.L.R. (3d) 413 (S.C.C.) 181

Roncarelli v. Duplessis, 1959 CarswellQue 37, [1959] S.C.R. 121, 16 D.L.R. (2d) 689 (S.C.C.) 184, 1208

Rosales et al. v. Crédit Suisse and Swiss Bank Corporation, No. CV 96-6419 1128

Rowley et al v. Hewison et al., Ontario Court (General Division), filed November 6, 1991, file no. 3872991U, settled 594

Rowling v. Takaro Properties Ltd. (in receivership), [1988] 1 All E.R. 163 879

Rowswell & Associates Engineers Inc. v. Brandt (2001), 13 C.L.R. (3d) 114, 2001 CarswellOnt 4179 (Ont. S.C.J.), additional reasons at (2002), 2002 CarswellOnt 285 (Ont. S.C.J.) 1036

Rubin v. Canada (Clerk of the Privy Council), [1993] 2 F.C. 391, 1993 CarswellNat 810, 1993 CarswellNat 1312, [1993] F.C.J. No. 203, 14 Admin. L.R. (2d) 246, 63 F.T.R. 1, 48 C.P.R. (3d) 348 (Fed. T.D.), reversed 1994 CarswellNat 275F, 1994 CarswellNat 853, [1994] F.C.J. No. 316, 167 N.R. 43, 77 F.T.R. 320 (note), 25 Admin. L.R. (2d) 241, 113 D.L.R. (4th) 275, 54 C.P.R. (3d) 511, [1994] 2 F.C. 707 (Fed. C.A.), affirmed 1996 CarswellNat 420, 1996 CarswellNat 420F, 191 N.R. 394, 131 D.L.R. (4th) 608, 36 Admin. L.R. (2d) 131, [1996] 1 S.C.R. 6, 106 F.T.R. 240 (note), 66 C.P.R. (3d) 32 (S.C.C.) 303

Ruby v. Canada (Solicitor General), [2002] 4 S.C.R. 3, 2002 CarswellNat 3225, 2002 CarswellNat 3226, [2002] S.C.J. No. 73, 2002 SCC 75, 219 D.L.R. (4th) 385, 295 N.R. 353, 7 C.R. (6th) 88, 22 C.P.R. (4th) 289, 99 C.R.R. (2d) 324, 49 Admin. L.R. (3d) 1 (S.C.C.) 907

Ruffo c. Québec (Conseil de la magistrature), 130 D.L.R. (4th) 1, 1995 CarswellQue 183, 1995 CarswellQue 184, 190 N.R. 1, [1995] 4 S.C.R. 267, 35 Admin. L.R. (2d) 1, 33 C.R.R. (2d) 269 (S.C.C.) 251

Ruffolo v. Mulroney (June 28, 1988), Doc. York 363/88, [1988] O.J. No. 2670 (Ont. Prov. Ct.) 642

Rural Dignity of Canada v. Canada Post Corp. (1991), 78 D.L.R. (4th) 211,
1991 CarswellNat 370, 7 Admin. L.R. (2d) 242 at 246, 40 F.T.R. 255 (Fed.
T.D.), affirmed (1992), 1992 CarswellNat 204, 88 D.L.R. (4th) 191, 7
Admin. L.R. (2d) 242, 139 N.R. 203, 54 F.T.R. 80 (note) (Fed. C.A.), leave
to appeal refused (1992), 7 Admin. L.R. (2d) 242n, 92 D.L.R. (4th) vi
(note), 141 N.R. 399 (note) (S.C.C.) 820

Russow & The Green Party of Canada v. Canada (Attorney General) (May 1,
2001), Doc. 01-CV-210088 (Ont. S.C.J.) 472

S.E.I.U., Local 204 v. Ontario Realty Corp. (1997), 35 O.R. (3d) 345, 1997
CarswellOnt 4486, 151 D.L.R. (4th) 255, 97 C.L.L.C. 220-088, 38
C.L.R.B.R. (2d) 145, 6 Admin. L.R. (3d) 288, 40 O.T.C. 176 (Ont. Gen.
Div.) 862

S.G.E.U. v. McKenzie **(1991), 96 Sask. R. 22, 1991 CarswellSask 249, 1
Admin. L.R. (2d) 284 (Sask. Q.B.)** 822

Samson v. Canada (Attorney General) **(1998), 165 D.L.R. (4th) 342, 1998
CarswellNat 1653, [1998] F.C.J. No. 1208, 155 F.T.R. 137, 10 Admin. L.R.
(3d) 178 (Fed. T.D.)** 463

*Saskatchewan (Provincial Court Chief Judge) v. Saskatchewan (Human Rights
Commission)* (2003), 230 D.L.R. (4th) 493, 2003 CarswellSask 586, 236
Sask. R. 176, 37 C.P.C. (5th) 277, 111 C.R.R. (2d) 72, 47 C.H.R.R. D/344,
[2004] 3 W.W.R. 472, 2003 SKQB 369, 8 Admin. L.R. (4th) 288 (Sask.
Q.B.) 921

Sauvé v. Canada (Chief Electoral Officer) (1999), 180 D.L.R. (4th) 385, 1999
CarswellNat 2126, [1999] F.C.J. No. 1577, 1999 CarswellNat 3047, [2000]
2 F.C. 117, 170 F.T.R. 320 (note), 248 N.R. 267, 29 C.R. (5th) 242, 69 C.R.R.
(2d) 106 (Fed. C.A.), leave to appeal allowed (2000), 2000 CarswellNat
1724, 2000 CarswellNat 1725 (S.C.C.), reversed 2002 CarswellNat 2883,
2002 CarswellNat 2884, [2002] S.C.J. No. 66, [2002] 3 S.C.R. 519, 2002
SCC 68, 5 C.R. (6th) 203, 168 C.C.C. (3d) 449, 98 C.R.R. (2d) 1, 218 D.L.R.
(4th) 577, 294 N.R. 1 (S.C.C.) 504

Schachter v. Canada, [1992] 2 S.C.R. 679, 1992 CarswellNat 658, 1992
CarswellNat 1006, [1992] S.C.J. No. 68, 92 C.L.L.C. 14,036, 10 C.R.R. (2d)
1, 139 N.R. 1, 93 D.L.R. (4th) 1, 53 F.T.R. 240 (note) (S.C.C.) 223, 798

Schelin v. Grey, limited information available 682

Schreiber (Township) v. Superior Greenstone District School Board (2002), [2002]
O.J. No. 3303, 2002 CarswellOnt 2798, 164 O.A.C. 174 (Ont. Div. Ct.) .. 50

Schreiber v. C.B.C. (Alberta) 996

Schreiber v. C.B.C. (Ontario) 996

Schreiber v. Canada (Attorney General) (1999), [2000] 1 F.C. 427, 1999
CarswellNat 1610, 1999 CarswellNat 3015, 174 F.T.R. 221 (Fed.
T.D.) 1158

Schreiber v. Canada (Attorney General) (2000), 2000 CarswellOnt 1794, [2000]
O.J. No. 1813, 48 O.R. (3d) 521, 187 D.L.R. (4th) 146 (Ont. S.C.J.),
additional reasons at (2000), 2000 CarswellOnt 2118 (Ont. S.C.J.), leave to
appeal allowed (2000), 2000 CarswellOnt 4972 (Ont. Div. Ct.), affirmed
(2001), 2001 CarswellOnt 385, 152 C.C.C. (3d) 205, 196 D.L.R. (4th) 281,
52 O.R. (3d) 577, 142 O.A.C. 27, 4 C.P.C. (5th) 1 (Ont. C.A.), leave to
appeal allowed (2001), 2001 CarswellOnt 3162, 2001 CarswellOnt 3163,
[2001] S.C.C.A. No. 201, 276 N.R. 397 (note), 155 O.A.C. 200 (note)
(S.C.C.), affirmed [2002] S.C.J. No. 63, 2002 CarswellOnt 2921, 2002
CarswellOnt 2922, [2002] 3 S.C.R. 269, 2002 SCC 62, 167 C.C.C. (3d) 51,
216 D.L.R. (4th) 513, 22 C.P.C. (5th) 207, 61 O.R. (3d) 160 (note), 292 N.R.
250 (S.C.C.), reversed (2001), 2001 CarswellOnt 4298, 206 D.L.R. (4th)
577, 160 C.C.C. (3d) 131, 153 O.A.C. 137, 57 O.R. (3d) 316, 21 C.P.C. (5th)
1 (Ont. C.A.), leave to appeal refused (2002), 2002 CarswellOnt 2703,
2002 CarswellOnt 2704, 301 N.R. 392 (note), 172 O.A.C. 199 (note)
(S.C.C.) 881

Schreiber v. Lavoie (2002), 59 O.R. (3d) 130, 2002 CarswellOnt 1220 (Ont.
S.C.J.), additional reasons at (2002), 2002 CarswellOnt 3695 (Ont.
S.C.J.) 996

Scierie Amos inc. c. Lord (1999), [2000] 3 C.N.L.R. 78, 1999 CarswellQue 4022,
[2000] R.J.Q. 250, 42 C.E.L.R. (N.S.) 214 (Que. S.C.), leave to appeal
allowed (2000), 2000 CarswellQue 38 (Que. C.A.), reversed [2000] 3
C.N.L.R. 107, 2000 CarswellQue 842, [2000] R.J.Q. 1400, 42 C.E.L.R.
(N.S.) 202 (Que. C.A.), leave to appeal to the Supreme Court of Canada
refused 2001 CarswellQue 345, 2001 CarswellQue 346, 268 N.R. 394
(note), [2001] 2 C.N.L.R. iv (note) (S.C.C.) 251

Scott v. Fulton, 137 B.C.A.C. 77, 2000 CarswellBC 369, 2000 BCCA 124, 73
B.C.L.R. (3d) 392, 49 C.C.L.T. (2d) 196, 223 W.A.C. 77 (B.C. C.A.) 218,
637

**Scottish National Party v. Scottish Television et al, Scottish Court of
Session, April 4, 1997** 553

*Secretary of State for Education & Science v. Tameside Metropolitan Borough
Council* (1976), [1977] A.C. 1014, [1976] 3 All E.R. 665 (Eng. C.A.),
affirmed (1976), [1977] A.C. 1014 at 1036, [1976] 3 All E.R. 665 at 679
(U.K. H.L.) 670

Seminole Tribe of Florida v. Florida, 116 S.Ct. 1114 (1996) 342

Senate Speaker's Ruling on Official Opposition in the Senate, Senate Hansard,
February 6, 2001, p. 63 207

**Sethi v. Canada (Minister of Employment & Immigration), 52 D.L.R. (4th)
681, 1988 CarswellNat 698, 1988 CarswellNat 35, 31 Admin. L.R. 123, 87
N.R. 389, 5 Imm. L.R. (2d) 161, 16 C.E.R. 327, [1988] 2 F.C. 552 (Fed.
C.A.), leave to appeal refused (1988), 36 Admin. L.R. xl, 52 D.L.R. (4th)
681n, 92 N.R. 325 (note) (S.C.C.)** 762, 809

Sexton v. Holden, [2001] 6 W.W.R. 116, 2001 CarswellMan 61, 2001 MBCA 31, 153 C.C.C. (3d) 79, 17 M.P.L.R. (3d) 137, 153 Man. R. (2d) 248, 238 W.A.C. 248 (Man. C.A.) 614

Shade v. Canada (Attorney General), 2003 FCT 327, 2003 CarswellNat 713, 2003 CarswellNat 1725, 2003 CFPI 327, 2 Admin. L.R. (4th) 300 (Fed. T.D.) 779

Shaffer v. The Queen, Tax Court of Canada, September 8, 1994, not reported, file no. 94-539 [IT] I 1194

Sharples v. O'Shea & Anor. (1999), Q.S.C. 190 (Queensland) 584

Shell Canada Ltd. v. Canada (Director of Investigation & Research) (1975), 55 D.L.R. (3d) 713, 1975 CarswellNat 1, 22 C.C.C. (2d) 70, [1975] F.C. 184, 29 C.R.N.S. 361, 18 C.P.R. (2d) 155, 7 N.R. 157 (Fed. C.A.) 1212

Shell Canada Products Ltd. v. Vancouver (City), [1994] 1 S.C.R. 231, 1994 CarswellBC 115, 1994 CarswellBC 1234, [1994] S.C.J. No. 15, [1994] 3 W.W.R. 609, 20 M.P.L.R. (2d) 1, 20 Admin. L.R. (2d) 202, 110 D.L.R. (4th) 1, 88 B.C.L.R. (2d) 145, 163 N.R. 81, 41 B.C.A.C. 81, 66 W.A.C. 81 (S.C.C.) 884

Shewfelt v. Canada (1998), 1998 CarswellBC 2894 (B.C. C.A.), leave to appeal refused (1998), 234 N.R. 195 (note), [1998] S.C.C.A. No. 194, 57 C.R.R. (2d) 376 (note), 120 B.C.A.C. 160 (note), 196 W.A.C. 160 (note) (S.C.C.) 497

Sibbeston v. Northwest Territories (Attorney General), 45 D.L.R. (4th) 691, 1988 CarswellNWT 45, [1988] N.W.T.R. 38, [1988] 2 W.W.R. 501 (N.W.T. C.A.) 404, 442

Sierra Club of Canada v. Canada (Minister of Finance), 211 D.L.R. (4th) 193, 2002 CarswellNat 822, 2002 CarswellNat 823, [2002] S.C.J. No. 42, 2002 SCC 41, 18 C.P.R. (4th) 1, 44 C.E.L.R. (N.S.) 161, 287 N.R. 203, 20 C.P.C. (5th) 1, 40 Admin. L.R. (3d) 1, 93 C.R.R. (2d) 219, 223 F.T.R. 137 (note), [2002] 2 S.C.R. 522 (S.C.C.) 910

Simon v. Toronto (Metropolitan) (1993), 99 D.L.R. (4th) 11, 1993 CarswellOnt 511, 13 M.P.L.R. (2d) 301, 61 O.A.C. 389 (Ont. Div. Ct.) 34

Simpson v. Ontario (1999), [1999] O.J. No. 895, 1999 CarswellOnt 844, 118 O.A.C. 201 (Ont. C.A.) 833

Sinclair c. Québec (Procureur général) (1992), [1992] 1 S.C.R. 579, 1992 CarswellQue 48, 1992 CarswellQue 133, 89 D.L.R. (4th) 500, 134 N.R. 39, 10 M.P.L.R. (2d) 92, 47 Q.A.C. 59, [1991] 3 S.C.R. 134 (S.C.C.) 796

Sinclair Stevens v. Parker, Commissioner, Federal Court of Appeal, filed December 11, 1987, file A-1276-87, withdrawn May 13, 1988 1073

Sinclair v. Québec (Procureur général) (1992), [1992] 1 S.C.R. 579, 1992 CarswellQue 48, 1992 CarswellQue 133, 89 D.L.R. (4th) 500, 134 N.R.

39, 10 M.P.L.R. (2d) 92, 47 Q.A.C. 59, [1991] 3 S.C.R. 134 (S.C.C.) 18, 696

Singh v. Canada (Attorney General), [1999] 4 F.C. 583, 1999 CarswellNat 1289, [1999] F.C.J. No. 1056, 1999 CarswellNat 2952, 67 C.R.R. (2d) 81, 170 F.T.R. 215 (Fed. T.D.), affirmed 2000 CarswellNat 26, [2000] F.C.J. No. 4, 2000 CarswellNat 1752, 183 D.L.R. (4th) 458, 251 N.R. 318, [2000] 3 F.C. 185, 20 Admin. L.R. (3d) 168 (Fed. C.A.), leave to appeal refused (2000), 2000 CarswellNat 1720, 2000 CarswellNat 1721, 259 N.R. 400 (note) (S.C.C.) 22

Singh v. Canada (Attorney General), [2000] 3 F.C. 185, 2000 CarswellNat 26, [2000] F.C.J. No. 4, 2000 CarswellNat 1752, 183 D.L.R. (4th) 458, 251 N.R. 318, 20 Admin. L.R. (3d) 168 (Fed. C.A.), leave to appeal refused (2000), 2000 CarswellNat 1720, 2000 CarswellNat 1721, 259 N.R. 400 (note) (S.C.C.) 89, 896

Singh v. Canada (Minister of Employment & Immigration), 17 D.L.R. (4th) 422, 1985 CarswellNat 152, 1985 CarswellNat 663, [1985] 1 S.C.R. 177, 58 N.R. 1, 12 Admin. L.R. 137, 14 C.R.R. 13 (S.C.C.) 1060

Singh v. Comité des Québécoises et Québécois pour le Non et al., Conseil du Référendum, October 31, 1995, not reported 357

Singh v. Québec (Attorney General), Québec Superior Court, filed October 23, 1995, not completed 357

Socialist Party of Serbia v. Belgrade Election Commission, First Municipal Court in Belgrade, November 23, 1996 573

Société des Acadiens et des Acadiennes du Nouveau Brunswick et autres c. Canada (1997), 188 N.B.R. (2d) 330, 480 A.P.R. 330, 1997 CarswellNB 224 (N.B. Q.B.) 484

Society Promoting Environmental Conservation v. Canada (Attorney General), 2002 FCT 236, 2002 CarswellNat 597, 2002 CarswellNat 2766, 2002 CFPI 236, 46 C.E.L.R. (N.S.) 119, 77 L.C.R. 85, 217 F.T.R. 279 (Fed. T.D.), reversed [2003] F.C.J. No. 861, 2003 CarswellNat 1559, 2003 CarswellNat 2653, 228 D.L.R. (4th) 693, 305 N.R. 203, 80 L.C.R. 1, 4 Admin. L.R. (4th) 223, [2003] 4 F.C. 959, 2003 FCA 239, 2003 CAF 239 (Fed. C.A.) 905

Sommers v. R., 124 C.C.C. 241, 1959 CarswellBC 3, [1959] S.C.R. 678, 31 C.R. 36 (S.C.C.) 1072

Sommerville v. Canada (Attorney General), Alberta Court of Queen's Bench, June 25, 1993, unreported, file 9301-05393 987

Southam Inc v. Canada (Attorney General), [1990] 3 F.C. 465, 1990 CarswellNat 658, 1990 CarswellNat 658F, 73 D.L.R. (4th) 289, 114 N.R. 255, 1 C.R.R. (2d) 193, 38 F.T.R. 239 (note) (Fed. C.A.) 717

Speaker's Ruling in the Matter of Oaths of Office, Hansard, November 1, 1990, p. 14969 198

Speaker's Ruling on a Question of Privilege, **Official Report of Debates, Hansard, May 8, 2003, pp. 230-234** 766

Speaker's Ruling on Deborah Grey's Question of Privilege regarding seizure of computer files, Hansard, October 15, 2001, p. 6081 682

Speaker's Ruling on Disclosure of Ontario Liberal Caucus Meeting of February 25, 2004, Hansard, March 26, 2004, p. 1712 314

Speaker's Ruling on Display of the Flag in the House of Commons, **Hansard, March 16, 1998, p. 4902** 194

Speaker's Ruling on Official Opposition, **Hansard, February 27, 1996, p. 16** 203

Speaker's Ruling on the Application of the Progressive Conservative Democratic Representative Coalition for Recognition in the House of Commons, Hansard, September 24, 2001, p. 5489 682

Speaker's Ruling on the Duty of the Minister of Justice to the House of Commons in respect of the Introduction of Legislation, Hansard, March 19, 2001, p. 1839 277

Speaker's Ruling on the Duty of the Minister of Justice to the House of Commons in respect of the Introduction of Legislation, Hansard, October 15, 2001, pp. 6082-6085 277

Speaker's Ruling on the Nature of Parliamentary Privilege, Hansard, May 26, 3003, p. 6413 744

Speaker's Ruling on the Privacy Commissioner's Comments regarding the Information Commissioner, Hansard, May 28, 2001, pp. 4276-4277 802

Speaker's Ruling on the Role of Legislative Counsel, **Hansard, October 23, 1997, p. 1003** 796

Speakers' Rulings on the Use of Estimates to Establish Programs, **Hansard, March 25, 1981, p. 8600 and Hansard, November 25, 1997, p. 2208** 706

Speech from the Throne, July 24, 2001 and Constitution (Fixed Election Dates) Amendment Act, 2001, S.B.C. 2001, c. 36 243

Starr v. Ontario (Commissioner of Inquiry), **68 D.L.R. (4th) 641, 1990 CarswellOnt 998, 1990 CarswellOnt 1299, [1990] 1 S.C.R. 1366, 110 N.R. 81, 55 C.C.C. (3d) 472, 72 O.R. (2d) 701 (note), 41 O.A.C. 161 (S.C.C.)** 1142

Starr v. Ontario, **Ontario Court (General Division), filed July 5, 1990, file no. 51523/90, settled** 1142

Starrs v. Procurator Fiscal, Linlithgow, [1999] Scot HC 242, November 11, 1999 922

State of Washington ex rel. Public Disclosure Commission v. 119 Vote No! Committee, **957 P.2d 691 (Wash., 1998)** 637

Statement of Resignation of the Privacy Commissioner, June 23, 2003 817

Stevens v. Canada (Attorney General) and Conservative Party of Canada,
Federal Court of Canada – Trial Division, file No. T-2465-03, in
progress 683

Stevens v. Canada (Commission of Inquiry), [2003] F.C.J. No. 1589, 2003
CarswellNat 3373, 2003 CarswellNat 4239, 2003 FC 1259, 2003 CF 1259,
241 F.T.R. 108 (F.C.) 1073

Stevens v. Canada (Commissioner of Inquiry) (2000), [2001] 1 F.C. 156, 2000
CarswellNat 1717, 2000 CarswellNat 3290, 187 F.T.R. 228 (Fed. T.D.),
affirmed 2002 CarswellNat 276, 2002 FCT 2, 215 F.T.R. 228 (Fed.
T.D.) 1073

Stevens v. Canada (Prime Minister) [elsewhere reported as Stevens v.
Canada (Privy Council)], [1998] 4 F.C. 89, 1998 CarswellNat 1051, [1998]
F.C.J. No. 794, 1998 CarswellNat 2311, 161 D.L.R. (4th) 85, 228 N.R. 142,
147 F.T.R. 308 (note), 21 C.P.C. (4th) 327, 11 Admin. L.R. (3d) 169 (Fed.
C.A.) 1202

Stinson v. Cannis 631

Stoffman v. Vancouver General Hospital (1990), [1990] 3 S.C.R. 483, 1990
CarswellBC 277, 1990 CarswellBC 765, [1990] S.C.J. No. 125, 91 C.L.L.C.
17,003, [1991] 1 W.W.R. 577, 52 B.C.L.R. (2d) 1, 13 C.H.R.R. D/337, 76
D.L.R. (4th) 700, 118 N.R. 241, 2 C.R.R. (2d) 215 (S.C.C.) 306

Stoffman v. Vancouver General Hospital, 49 D.L.R. (4th) 727, 1988
CarswellBC 2, 21 B.C.L.R. (2d) 165, [1988] 2 W.W.R. 708, 40 C.R.R. 236,
9 C.H.R.R. D/4569 (B.C. C.A.), reversed (1990), 1990 CarswellBC 277,
1990 CarswellBC 765, [1990] S.C.J. No. 125, 91 C.L.L.C. 17,003, [1991] 1
W.W.R. 577, 52 B.C.L.R. (2d) 1, [1990] 3 S.C.R. 483, 13 C.H.R.R. D/337,
76 D.L.R. (4th) 700, 118 N.R. 241, 2 C.R.R. (2d) 215 (S.C.C.) 12, 82

Stopforth v. Goyer (1979), 23 O.R. (2d) 696, 1979 CarswellOnt 670, 97 D.L.R.
(3d) 369, 8 C.C.L.T. 172 (Ont. C.A.) 629

Suharto v. Time Asia Inc., litigation initiated July 5, 1999, Central District
Court, Jakarta, decision June 9, 2000, limited information available
(Indonesia) 954

Supreme Court Bar Association v. Federation of Pakistan, Constitutional
Petition No. 1/2002, Supreme Court of Pakistan, April 27, 2002 383

Suresh v. Canada (Minister of Citizenship & Immigration), 208 D.L.R. (4th) 1,
2002 CarswellNat 7, 2002 CarswellNat 8, [2002] S.C.J. No. 3, 2002 SCC 1,
18 Imm. L.R. (3d) 1, 281 N.R. 1, 90 C.R.R. (2d) 1, 37 Admin. L.R. (3d) 159,
[2002] 1 S.C.R. 3 (S.C.C.) 323

Swinamer v. Nova Scotia (Attorney General), 112 D.L.R. (4th) 18, 1994
CarswellNS 3, 1994 CarswellNS 433, [1994] S.C.J. No. 21, 19 C.C.L.T.
(2d) 233, 20 Admin. L.R. (2d) 39, 129 N.S.R. (2d) 321, 362 A.P.R. 321,
[1994] 1 S.C.R. 445, 2 M.V.R. (3d) 80, 163 N.R. 291 (S.C.C.) 118

T1T2 Ltd. Partnership v. Canada (1994), 23 O.R. (3d) 66, 1994 CarswellOnt
251, [1994] O.J. No. 2614, 35 C.P.C. (3d) 353, 19 B.L.R. (2d) 72 (Ont. Gen.
Div.) and (1995), 23 O.R. (3d) 81, 1995 CarswellOnt 356, 38 C.P.C. (3d)
167 (Ont. Gen. Div.), additional reasons at (1995), 1995 CarswellOnt
4367, 38 C.P.C. (3d) 167 at 180 (Ont. Gen. Div.), affirmed (1995), 1995
CarswellOnt 357, 38 C.P.C. (3d) 183, 24 O.R. (3d) 546 (Ont. C.A.) and
(1996), 48 C.P.C. (3d) 84, 1996 CarswellOnt 1703, 3 O.T.C. 127 (Ont. Gen.
Div.) and (1997), 8 C.P.C. (4th) 193, 1997 CarswellOnt 414, 23 O.T.C. 228
(Ont. Gen. Div.) 934

**Tafler v. British Columbia (Commissioner of Conflict of Interest) (1995), 5
B.C.L.R. (3d) 336, 1995 CarswellBC 231, 31 Admin. L.R. (2d) 1 (B.C.
C.A. [In Chambers])** 303

**Tafler v. British Columbia (Commissioner of Conflict of Interest) (1998),
161 D.L.R. (4th) 511, 1998 CarswellBC 1257, [1998] B.C.J. No. 1332, 108
B.C.A.C. 263, 176 W.A.C. 263, 49 B.C.L.R. (3d) 328, 11 Admin. L.R. (3d)
228 (B.C. C.A.)** 1083

Telezone Inc. v. Canada (Attorney General) and Manley (2004), [2004] O.J. No.
5, 2004 CarswellOnt 8, 180 O.A.C. 360, 235 D.L.R. (4th) 719 (Ont.
C.A.) 744

**Tetzlaff v. Canada (Minister of the Environment) (1991), 47 Admin. L.R.
290, 1991 CarswellNat 750 (Fed. T.D.)** 1070

**Thatcher v. Canada (Attorney General) (1996), 120 F.T.R. 116, 1996
CarswellNat 1708, 1996 CarswellNat 2621, [1997] 1 F.C. 289 (Fed.
T.D.)** 267

The Globe and Mail v. Ontario Ministry of Finance, January, 1999 305

**The Kingdom of Spain v. Augusto Pinochet Ugarte, Bow Street
Magistrates' Court, October 8, 1999, (2000) ILM 39, 135 (U.K.)** 1132

The Matter of Megawati Sukarnoputri, Litigation in 1996 – 1998, limited
information available (Indonesia) 518

The New Jersey Democratic Party et al.v. Hon. David Samson et al., 175 N.J. 178,
October 2, 2002 475

The Prosecutor v. Jean Kambanda, September 4, 1998, ICTR 97-23-S
(International Criminal Tribunal for Rwanda) 1132

The Socialist Party and Others v. Turkey (1998), 27 E.H.R.R. 51 (European
Community) 518

Therrien c. Québec (Ministre de la justice), 200 D.L.R. (4th) 1, 2001
CarswellQue 1013, 2001 CarswellQue 1014, [2001] S.C.J. No. 36, 155
C.C.C. (3d) 1, 2001 SCC 35, 43 C.R. (5th) 1, 270 N.R. 1, 30 Admin. L.R.
(3d) 171, 84 C.R.R. (2d) 1, [2001] 2 S.C.R. 3 (S.C.C.) 342

**Thibodeau v. Prince Edward Island (Human Rights Commission), 114
Nfld. & P.E.I.R. 119, 356 A.P.R. 119, 1993 CarswellPEI 50, 94 C.L.L.C.**

17,008, 23 Admin. L.R. (2d) 219, 26 C.H.R.R. D/132, [1993] 2 P.E.I.R. D-244 (P.E.I. T.D.) 856

Thomas et al. v. British Columbia and Canada (Attorney General) 740

Thomson Newspapers Corp. v Canada (Attorney General), [1998] 1 S.C.R. 877, [1998] S.C.J. No. 44, 1998 CarswellOnt 1981, 1998 CarswellOnt 1982, 159 D.L.R. (4th) 385, 226 N.R. 1, 51 C.R.R. (2d) 189, 38 O.R. (3d) 735 (headnote only), 109 O.A.C. 201, 5 B.H.R.C. 567 (S.C.C.) ... 164, 565, 998

Thorne's Hardware Ltd. v. R., 143 D.L.R. (3d) 577, 1983 CarswellNat 530, 1983 CarswellNat 530F, [1983] 1 S.C.R. 106, 46 N.R. 91 (S.C.C.) 152

Threat of Litigation by Candidate Lou Sekora, 1998, litigation not initiated 620

Threatened Prosecution of American Infantrymen, no prosecution initiated, April – May, 1999 (Yugoslavia) 1029

Timiskaming Indian Band v. Canada (Minister of Indian & Northern Affairs) (1997), [1997] F.C.J. No. 676, 1997 CarswellNat 906, 148 D.L.R. (4th) 356, 132 F.T.R. 106 (Fed. T.D.) 212

Timmons v. Twin Cities Area New Party, 137 L.Ed.2d 589 (1997) 682

Tito v. Waddell, [1977] 3 All E.R. 129, [1977] Ch. 106 (Eng. Ch. Div.) ... 677

Toronto Police Association v. Toronto Police Services Board, Divisional Court, filed February 1, 2000, file no. 58/2000, settled May 2, 2000 299

Toronto Police Services Board v. Toronto Police Assn., [2000] O.T.C. 327, [2000] O.J. No. 1674, 2000 CarswellOnt 1669 (Ont. S.C.J.) 295

Tremblay c. Québec (Commission de la Fonction publique), [1990] R.J.Q. 1386 (Que. S.C.) 282, 1185

Tremblay c. Québec (Procureur général), [2001] R.J.Q. 1293, 2001 CarswellQue 685 (Que. S.C.), leave to appeal refused (2001), 2001 CarswellQue 1573, 2001 CarswellQue 1574, 275 N.R. 389 (note) (S.C.C.) 966

Trial of the Leaders of the Khmer Rouge Movement (Cambodia) 1071

Trieger v. Canadian Broadcasting Corp. (1988), 54 D.L.R. (4th) 143, 1988 CarswellOnt 867, 66 O.R. (2d) 273 (Ont. H.C.) 537, 549

Trinh v. Chan (1997), 34 C.C.E.L. (2d) 293, 1997 CarswellBC 2349 (B.C. S.C.), additional reasons at (1998), 1998 CarswellBC 628, [1998] B.C.J. No. 720, 20 C.P.C. (4th) 142 (B.C. S.C.) 940

Trinity Western University v. College of Teachers (British Columbia), 199 D.L.R. (4th) 1, 2001 CarswellBC 1016, 2001 CarswellBC 1017, [2001] S.C.J. No. 32, 2001 SCC 31, 269 N.R. 1, 2001 C.L.L.C. 230-026, 151 B.C.A.C. 161, 249 W.A.C. 161, 31 Admin. L.R. (3d) 163, [2001] 1 S.C.R. 772, 82 C.R.R. (2d) 189, 39 C.H.R.R. D/357 (S.C.C.) 146

Tripp v. Executive Office of the President, 104 F. Supp.2d 30 (D.D.C., 2000) 1119

Tunda c. Canada (Ministre de la Citoyenneté & de l'Immigration) (1999),
[1999] F.C.J. No. 902, 1999 CarswellNat 3160, 1999 CarswellNat 3161,
190 F.T.R. 1 (Fed. T.D.), additional reasons at (1999), 1999 CarswellNat
1981, 1999 CarswellNat 1982, 177 F.T.R. 274, 70 C.R.R. (2d) 372 (Fed.
T.D.), affirmed 2001 CarswellNat 1064, 2001 CarswellNat 2805, 2001
CAF 151, 2001 FCA 151, 19 Imm. L.R. (3d) 42, 285 N.R. 386, 214 F.T.R.
159 (note) (Fed. C.A.) 794

*Turmel v. Canada (Canadian Radio-Television & Telecommunications
Commission)* (1980), 117 D.L.R. (3d) 697, 1980 CarswellNat 187F, 1980
CarswellNat 187, [1981] 2 F.C. 411, 60 C.P.R. (2d) 37 (Fed. T.D.), leave to
appeal refused (1983), 48 N.R. 80n (S.C.C.) 526

*Turmel v. Canada (Canadian Radio-Television & Telecommunications
Commission)* (1983), 48 N.R. 80n (S.C.C.) 535

**Turmel v. Canada (Radio-Television & Telecommunications Commission)
(1985) 16 C.R.R. 9, 1985 CarswellNat 929 (Fed. T.D.) 535**

**Turmel v. Cdn. Radio-Television & Telecommunications Comm. (1987), 14
F.T.R. 22, 1987 CarswellNat 272 (Fed. T.D.) 536**

**Turner v. Canada (April 26, 1990), Collier J. (Fed. T.D.), 21 A.C.W.S. (3d)
799** 805

Turner v. R., 93 D.L.R. (4th) 628, 1992 CarswellNat 125, 1992 CarswellNat
125F, 10 C.R.R. (2d) 376, [1992] 3 F.C. 458, 149 N.R. 218 (Fed. C.A.), leave
to appeal refused (1993), 148 N.R. 238n (S.C.C.) 787

Turner-Lienaux v. Nova Scotia (Attorney General) (1992), 115 N.S.R. (2d) 200,
1992 CarswellNS 147, [1992] N.S.J. No. 334, 314 A.P.R. 200 (N.S. T.D.),
affirmed (1993), 1993 CarswellNS 229, 48 C.C.E.L. 128, 122 N.S.R. (2d)
119, 338 A.P.R. 119 (N.S. C.A.), additional reasons at (1992), 115 N.S.R.
(2d) 200 at 211, 314 A.P.R. 200 at 211 (N.S. T.D.) 51

Turp c. Canada, 2003 FCT 301, 2003 CarswellNat 673, 2003 CarswellNat
2825, 2003 CFPI 301, 111 C.R.R. (2d) 184 (Fed. T.D.) 905

**Tyabji v. Sandana (1994), 112 D.L.R. (4th) 641, 1994 CarswellBC 654, [1994]
B.C.J. No. 469, 2 R.F.L. (4th) 265 (B.C. S.C.)** 67

U.S. Steel Corp. v. United States, 730 F.2d 1465 (1984) 1212

U.S. Term Limits Inc. v. Thornton, 131 L.Ed.2d 881 (1995) 518

U.S. Treatment of Al-Qaeda Prisoners, Report of the American Bar
Association Task Force, January 4, 2002 908

U.S. v. Doe, 332 F.Supp. 930 (Mass., 1971) 741

U.S. v. Doe, 455 F.2d 753 (1st Cir., 1972) 741

U.S. v. Munoz-Flores, 495 U.S. 385 (1990) 111

U.S. v. Nixon, 483 U.S. 203 (1974) 1114

U.S. v. Pitawanakwat, 120 F. Supp.2d 921 (D. Or., 2000) 1003

United Communist Party of Turkey v. Turkey (1998), 26 E.H.R.R. 121
(European Community) 518

United Parcel Service of America, Inc. v. Government of Canada, UNCITRAL/
NAFTA, filed April 19, 2001 809

United States v. Alvarez Machain, 504 U.S. 655 (1992) 1049

United States v. Burns, 195 D.L.R. (4th) 1, 2001 SCC 7, 2001 CarswellBC 272,
2001 CarswellBC 273, [2001] S.C.J. No. 8, 85 B.C.L.R. (3d) 1, 151 C.C.C.
(3d) 97, 39 C.R. (5th) 205, [2001] 3 W.W.R. 193, 265 N.R. 212, 148
B.C.A.C. 1, 243 W.A.C. 1, 81 C.R.R. (2d) 1, [2001] 1 S.C.R. 283
(S.C.C.) 277

**United States v. Houslander (1993), 13 O.R. (3d) 44, 1993 CarswellOnt 752
(Ont. Gen. Div.)** 1000

United States v. Monsalve (1993), [1993] O.J. No. 1180, 1993 CarswellOnt 2238
(Ont. Gen. Div.), affirmed (May 9, 1994), Doc. CA C16354, [1994] O.J.
No. 1099 (Ont. C.A.) 267

United States v. Noriega, 117 F.3d 1206 (11th Cir., 1997) 1128

United States v. Usama bin Laden et al., 160 F. Supp.2d 670 (S.D.N.Y.,
2001) 1016

United States v. Zacarias Moussaoui, 205 F.R.D. 183 (E.D. Virg., 2002) 1016

United States President's Executive Order on Presidential Papers, November 1,
2001 305

**University of New Brunswick Student Union (1996) Inc. v. New Brunswick
(Municipal Electoral Officer) (1999), 217 N.B.R. (2d) 322, 555 A.P.R. 322,
1999 CarswellNB 357 (N.B. Q.B.)** 942

Vancouver Island Peace Society v. Canada (1993), [1994] 1 F.C. 102, 1993
CarswellNat 822, 1993 CarswellNat 1340, 11 C.E.L.R. (N.S.) 1, 19 Admin.
L.R. (2d) 91, 64 F.T.R. 127 (Fed. T.D.), affirmed (1995), 1995 CarswellNat
4, 16 C.E.L.R. (N.S.) 24, 179 N.R. 106, 89 F.T.R. 136 (note) (Fed. C.A.),
leave to appeal refused (1995), [1995] S.C.C.A. No. 103, 17 C.E.L.R. (N.S.)
298 (note), 192 N.R. 80 (note) (S.C.C.) 902

**Vancouver Island Railway, An Act Respecting, Re, 114 D.L.R. (4th) 193,
1994 CarswellBC 188, 1994 CarswellBC 1239, [1994] 6 W.W.R. 1, 91
B.C.L.R. (2d) 1, 166 N.R. 81, 21 Admin. L.R. (2d) 1, 44 B.C.A.C. 1, 71
W.A.C. 1, [1994] 2 S.C.R. 41 (S.C.C.)** 416

*Vander Zalm v. British Columbia (Acting Commissioner of Conflict of
Interest)*, 56 B.C.L.R. (2d) 37, 1991 CarswellBC 95, 80 D.L.R. (4th) 291,
[1991] 6 W.W.R. 125, 1 Admin. L.R. (2d) 214 (B.C. S.C.) 1077

Vander Zalm v. Times Publishers, 96 D.L.R. (3d) 172, 1979 CarswellBC 662,
[1979] 2 W.W.R. 673, 8 C.C.L.T. 144 (B.C. S.C.), reversed 1980
CarswellBC 6, [1980] 4 W.W.R. 259, 12 C.C.L.T. 81, 18 B.C.L.R. 210, 109
D.L.R. (3d) 531 (B.C. C.A.) 980

VanKoughnet v. Conservative Party of Canada (February 20, 2004), Doc. 04-CV-026769 (Ont. S.C.J.), not reported 609

Various Federal Liberal Promises Relating to the Goods and Services Tax, Hansard, April 23, 1996, p. 1803 645

Venczel v. Assn. of Architects (Ontario) (1989), 45 Admin. L.R. 288, 1989 CarswellOnt 938, 42 C.L.R. 8, 41 O.A.C. 50, 74 O.R. (2d) 755 (Ont. Div. Ct.), additional reasons at (1990), 1990 CarswellOnt 2744, 42 C.L.R. 8 at 9, 41 O.A.C. 50 at 51, 74 O.R. (2d) 755 at 756, 45 Admin. L.R. 288 at 289 (Ont. Div. Ct.) 1187

Vennat v. Canada (Attorney General), Federal Court of Canada–Trial Division; action no. T-611-04 1102

Vennat v. Canada (Attorney General) and Federal Business Development Bank, Québec Superior Court; action no. 500-17-020135-045 1102

Victorian Council for Civil Liberties Incorporated v. Minister for Immigration & Multiculturalism Affairs & Ors., 2001 FCA 1297 (Fed. C.A.), (11 September 2001) (Australia) 922

Vieth v. Jubilier, United States Supreme Court, file 02-1580, in progress 496

Virginia v. Reno, 117 F. Supp.2d 46 (D.D.C., 2000) 496

Vivace Tavern Inc. v. Metropolitan Licensing Commission (1997), 96 O.A.C. 246, 1996 CarswellOnt 4840 (Ont. Div. Ct.) 33

Volker Stevin N.W.T. ('92) Ltd. v. Northwest Territories (Commissioner), [1994] 4 W.W.R. 236, 1994 CarswellNWT 18, 22 Admin. L.R. (2d) 251, [1994] N.W.T.R. 97, 113 D.L.R. (4th) 639 (N.W.T. C.A.) 872

Vriend v. Alberta (1998), 156 D.L.R. (4th) 385, 1998 CarswellAlta 210, 1998 CarswellAlta 211, [1998] S.C.J. No. 29, 50 C.R.R. (2d) 1, 224 N.R. 1, 212 A.R. 237, 168 W.A.C. 237, 31 C.H.R.R. D/1, [1998] 1 S.C.R. 493, 98 C.L.L.C. 230-021, 67 Alta. L.R. (3d) 1, [1999] 5 W.W.R. 451, 4 B.H.R.C. 140 (S.C.C.) 103

W.G. Knight & Associates Inc. v. Manitoba (Securities Commission) (1990), 47 Admin. L.R. 234, 1990 CarswellMan 22, 49 B.L.R. 256, 71 Man. R. (2d) 183 (Man. Q.B.) 130

Waddell v. British Columbia (Governor in Council), 126 D.L.R. (3d) 431, 1981 CarswellBC 194, [1981] 5 W.W.R. 662, 30 B.C.L.R. 127 (B.C. S.C.), affirmed (1982), 1982 CarswellBC 344, [1983] 1 W.W.R. 762, 41 B.C.L.R. 317, 142 D.L.R. (3d) 177 (B.C. C.A.), leave to appeal refused (1982), 1982 CarswellBC 752, 142 D.L.R. (3d) 177n, 46 N.R. 261 (S.C.C.) 759

Walker v. Cheney, 230 F. Supp.2d 51 1071

Walker v. Toronto (City) (1993), 14 O.R. (3d) 91, 1993 CarswellOnt 521, 15 M.P.L.R. (2d) 213 (Ont. Gen. Div.) 835

Walkerville Brewing Co. v. Mayrand, [1929] 2 D.L.R. 945, 63 O.L.R. 573 (Ont. C.A.) 52

Ward v. Clark (2001), 2001 BCCA 724, 2001 CarswellBC 2846, [2001] B.C.J. No. 2687, 95 B.C.L.R. (3d) 209, [2002] 2 W.W.R. 238, 161 B.C.A.C. 192, 263 W.A.C. 192 (B.C. C.A.), leave to appeal refused (2002), 2002 CarswellBC 1614, 2002 CarswellBC 1615, 295 N.R. 199 (note), 179 B.C.A.C. 160 (note), 295 W.A.C. 160 (note) (S.C.C.) 879

Ward v. Maracle (1995), 24 O.R. (3d) 148, 1995 CarswellOnt 1061, 32 Admin. L.R. (2d) 296 (Ont. Gen. Div.) 1031

Waterford v. Commonwealth (1987), 71 A.L.R. 673, 163 C.L.R. 54 (Australia H.C.) 1212

Wattan Party v. Federation of Pakistan, Constitutional Petition No. 7/2002, Supreme Court of Pakistan, April 27, 2002 383

Weatherill v. Canada (Attorney General) (1998), 143 F.T.R. 302, 1998 CarswellNat 183, 98 C.L.L.C. 210-010, 6 Admin. L.R. (3d) 137 (Fed. T.D.) and [1999] 4 F.C. 107, 1999 CarswellNat 940, 1999 CarswellNat 2614, 168 F.T.R. 161, 22 Admin. L.R. (3d) 192 (Fed. T.D.) 842

Weir v. Canada (Attorney General) (1991), 84 D.L.R. (4th) 39, 1991 CarswellNB 395, 119 N.B.R. (2d) 337, 300 A.P.R. 337 (N.B. C.A.) 752

Weir v. Secretary of State for Transport, High Court of Justice, Chancery Division (U.K.) 817

Weisfeld v. R. (1994), [1995] 1 F.C. 68, 1994 CarswellNat 1421, 1994 CarswellNat 1421F, 22 C.R.R. (2d) 1, 116 D.L.R. (4th) 232, 171 N.R. 28, 81 F.T.R. 320 (note) (Fed. C.A.) 730

Wells v. Newfoundland, 177 D.L.R. (4th) 73, 1999 CarswellNfld 214, 1999 CarswellNfld 215, [1999] S.C.J. No. 50, [1999] 3 S.C.R. 199, 245 N.R. 275, 99 C.L.L.C. 210-047, 180 Nfld. & P.E.I.R. 269, 548 A.P.R. 269, 46 C.C.E.L. (2d) 165, 15 Admin. L.R. (3d) 268 (S.C.C.) 848

Westlake v. R., 33 D.L.R. (3d) 256, [1973] S.C.R. vii (S.C.C.) 803

Whetung v. Boyle et al, British Columbia Supreme Court, Victoria Registry, Court file 94-4041 599

Wilson & Lafleur Ltée. c. Société québécoise d'information juridique (Soquij), [1998] R.J.Q. 2489, [1988] A.Q. No. 2762, 1998 CarswellQue 929, 1998 CarswellQue 2948 (Que. S.C.), reversed 2000 CarswellQue 513, [2000] R.J.Q. 1086 (Que. C.A.) 1214

Winterhaven Stables Ltd. v. Canada (Attorney General) (1988), 53 D.L.R. (4th) 413, 1988 CarswellAlta 492, [1988] A.J. No. 924, 62 Alta. L.R. (2d) 266, 91 A.R. 114, [1989] 1 W.W.R. 193, [1989] 1 C.T.C. 16 (Alta. C.A.), leave to appeal refused [1989] 3 W.W.R. lxxi, 66 Alta. L.R. (2d) xlix, 95 A.R. 236 (note), 55 D.L.R. (4th) viii, 101 N.R. 233 (note) (S.C.C.) 911

Winters v. Legal Services Society (British Columbia), 1999 CarswellBC 1969, 1999 CarswellBC 1970, [1999] S.C.J. No. 49, [1999] 9 W.W.R. 327, 137

C.C.C. (3d) 371, 244 N.R. 203, 177 D.L.R. (4th) 94, 27 C.R. (5th) 1, 66
C.R.R. (2d) 241, 128 B.C.A.C. 161, 208 W.A.C. 161, [1999] 3 S.C.R. 160, 73
B.C.L.R. (3d) 193 (S.C.C.) 1215

Wong v. R. (1996), [1997] 1 F.C. 193, 1996 CarswellNat 1699, 1996
CarswellNat 2608, 119 F.T.R. 306 (Fed. T.D.), affirmed (1997), 1997
CarswellNat 2506, 232 N.R. 4, 154 F.T.R. 39 (note) (Fed. C.A.), leave to
appeal refused (1998), 234 N.R. 195 (note) (S.C.C.) 21

**Yakhin v. Canada (Minister of Citizenship & Immigration) (1996), 1996
CarswellNat 1932 (Fed. T.D.)** 321

Yeung v. Canada (Minister of Employment & Immigration) (1992), 17 Imm. L.R.
(2d) 191, 1992 CarswellNat 54, 53 E.T.R. 205, 53 F.T.R. 205 (Fed.
T.D.) 50

**Yhap v. Canada (Minister of Employment & Immigration) (1989), 29 F.T.R.
223, 1989 CarswellNat 83, 9 Imm. L.R. (2d) 69 (Fed. T.D.)** 123

**Yhap v. Canada (Minister of Employment & Immigration), [1990] 1 F.C.
722, 1990 CarswellNat 102, 1990 CarswellNat 672, 9 Imm. L.R. (2d) 243,
34 F.T.R. 26 (Fed. T.D.)** 126

**Young & Rubicam Ltd. v. Progressive Conservative Party of Canada
(March 22, 1971), Doc. 803-933 (Que. S.C.), not reported** 575

Young v. Toronto Star Newspapers Ltd. (2003), 66 O.R. (3d) 170, [2003] O.J.
No. 3100, 2003 CarswellOnt 3073, 18 C.C.L.T. (3d) 244 (Ont. S.C.J.) .. 616

Zrig c. Canada (Ministre de la Citoyenneté & de l'Immigration), 229 D.L.R. (4th)
235, 2003 CarswellNat 924, 2003 CarswellNat 1978, 307 N.R. 201, [2003]
3 F.C. 761, 32 Imm. L.R. (3d) 1, 2003 CAF 178, 2003 FCA 178 (Fed.
C.A.) 1003

Zündel v. Liberal Party of Canada (2000), 46 O.R. (3d) 410, [1999] O.J. No.
4244, 1999 CarswellOnt 3532, 90 O.T.C. 395 (note), 127 O.A.C. 251, 181
D.L.R. (4th) 463, 69 C.R.R. (2d) 69 (Ont. C.A.), leave to appeal refused
(2000), 2000 CarswellOnt 2534, 2000 CarswellOnt 2535, 259 N.R. 399
(note), 139 O.A.C. 398 (note) (S.C.C.) 737

1

DEFINITION OF THE BASIC
CONCEPTS OF POLITICAL LAW

1.1 GENERAL PRINCIPLES

See Volume I, Chapter 1.

1.2 ISSUE: CONSTITUTION; "CONSTITUTION OF CANADA"[1]

---

§ 1.2.1[2]
Reference re Legislative Authority of Parliament
to Alter or Replace the Senate
Supreme Court of Canada; December 21, 1979
(1979), 102 D.L.R. (3d) 1

The constitution has always been a matter of intense preoccupation in Canada and it continues to be a central focus of debate in the country's public life. A clear understanding of the notion of "constitution" in general and that of the "Constitution of Canada" in particular is thus vital to the proper examination of political law.

The *Dictionary of Canadian Law* defines the term constitution as "1. The body of law which establishes the framework of government for a nation or an organization. 2. The supreme law of Canada..."[3] The

---

[1] Cross-reference to § 1.3.D and 4.2.
[2] Cross-reference to § 4.2.1, 8.2.A.1 and 8.2.B.1.
[3] Daphne Dukelow, *Pocket Dictionary of Canadian Law*, 3d ed. (Toronto: Carswell, 2002) at 93.

Civilians Henri Brun and Guy Tremblay refer, in their comprehensive textbook on *Droit Constitutionnel*,[4] to the constitution by the legislative definition set out in subsection 52(2) of the *Constitution Act, 1982*. Among common lawyers, Peter Hogg also bases his explanation of what the constitution is on that provision, but he goes on to point out that the section 52(2) definition speaks of the "Constitution of Canada" as including the elements listed there. The provision in question in fact reads as follows:

> (2) The Constitution of Canada includes
>> (a) the *Canada Act 1982*, including this Act;
>> (b) the Acts and orders referred to in the schedule; and
>> (c) any amendment to any Act or order referred to in paragraph (*a*) or (*b*).[5]

The definition provided by legal dictionaries and even those written by legal scholars are worthwhile, but they have proved to be neither sufficiently complete nor adequately authoritative. This lack of authoritativeness in particular illustrates the need for a comprehensive guide in political law to the pertinent statements of the courts that better complement the texts provided by the legislatures and that also give us binding interpretations of the meaning of legal expressions and legal norms in public administration and political life.

What, then, do the courts declare the constitution to be?

In the late 1970s, the government of Prime Minister Trudeau undertook a major effort toward reforming the Constitution of Canada with a view to modernizing the structures and institutions of the country. As part of this initiative, in June 1978 the government introduced the *Constitutional Amendment Bill, 1978*.[6] One of the centrepieces of this proposal was to reform the Senate, widely perceived as outmoded and ineffective, into a House of the Federation. This proposal became highly controversial and when the session of Parliament was prorogued on October 10, 1978, the Bill died on the Order Paper.

---

[4] Henri Brun et Guy Tremblay, *Droit Constitutionnel*, 2e édition (Cowansville, QC : les Editions Yvon Blais Inc., 1990).

[5] *Constitution Act, 1982*, R.S.C. 1985, Appendix II, Item No. 44, s. 52(2).

[6] Bill C-60, *Constitutional Amendment Bill, 1978*, 3rd Session, 30th Parliament.

Rather than abandon the idea of Senate reform altogether, the government decided to take an approach that would enable it to settle the legal aspects of the issue before developing another proposal or attempting to proceed again with Bill C-60. On November 23, 1978, it thus referred to the Supreme Court of Canada a series of questions that were essentially designed to ascertain whether the Parliament of Canada had legislative authority to abolish the Senate, as the Bill had proposed.

In formulating the replies to the questions referred to it, the court started by reminding us of the fundamental principle of the similarity of the constitution of this country to that of the United Kingdom. It went on to trace the evolution of constitutional amendments made since the enactment of the original *British North America Act* in 1867. This historical perspective led it to state that four general principles were at play in amending the constitution:

- amending action was taken by the United Kingdom Parliament only upon formal request from Canada;
- the sanction of Parliament was required for a request to be addressed to the British Parliament asking that the *British North America Act* be amended;
- no amendment to Canada's Constitution was made by the British Parliament on the request of a Canadian province without the approval of the federal Parliament; and
- the Canadian Parliament will not request an amendment directly affecting federal-provincial relationships without prior consultation and agreement with the provinces.

The finding of these principles showed the court's emphasis on the federal nature of Canada, implying the sharing of legislative and governmental authority between the federal and provincial levels.

The court then went on to stress particularly the other amendment to the *British North America Act*, made in 1949, which gave the Parliament of Canada authority to amend the Constitution of Canada in certain circumstances.[7] The change accomplished by that amendment was that in respect of what the court termed federal "housekeeping" matters alone, where there was no provincial involvement, the Parliament of Canada alone would thenceforth be able to enact changes to

---

[7] *British North America Act (No. 2), 1949*, R.S.C. 1985, Appendix II, Item No. 33.

the *British North America Act*, without the previously required legislative assent of Westminster. The focus of the ruling, as to whether Parliament could abolish the Senate, was considered in this light.

While the ratio of this case revolved around the matter of the abolition of the Senate, we can justifiably draw conclusions about what the court felt to be the concepts of "constitution" and "the Constitution of Canada."

The necessary implication of the use of terminology by the Supreme Court is that "constitution" means the legal text constitutive of the country, including its juristic units at both federal and provincial levels. Moreover, the fact that in developing the concept of constitution the court specifically listed the *British North America Act, 1867*, and all of the amendments that had been made to it until this case can only lead us to conclude that it saw the notion of "constitution" as including all legislative texts of a constitutional nature.

The court also defined in this case the concept of the "Constitution of Canada." By reference to the 17th amendment discussed above, the one made in 1949, as well as the definition of "Canada", the court was able to conclude that the "Constitution of Canada," as used in the *British North America Act*, was meant to indicate those elements of the legislation that dealt with the juristic federal unit; that is, the federal level of legislature and government alone. These were the parts that Parliament was, after 1949, authorized to amend alone.

It is interesting to note the somewhat arcane point that a thorough reading of the decision will show that while the expression "the Constitution of Canada" defines the federal level alone within the constitutional texts, the similar but slightly different expression "Canada's Constitution" can be taken to define the entire body of constitutional texts.

This case clearly demonstrates several fundamental realities of political law. First, it shows that the constitution, in the sense of the series of documents establishing the country and providing a framework for it, is intrinsically and inherently both a text of law and a political statement. Second, it indicates that in order to understand the concept of constitution in general or the specifics of the "Constitution of Canada" in particular, one must take an historical and comprehensive perspective, showing how these notions that combine legal and political aspects have evolved. Finally, it puts in perspective that the authoritative judgments of the courts—that is the determination of the correct interpretation of the law—occurs in a political environment and produces political consequences with profound influences on the reform process.

> It is a very static view to regard British constitutionalism as wedded to the principle of purely nominated or hereditary upper houses (compare Australia's directly elected Senate). In truth, the British House of Lords and the Canadian Senate are the exceptions—the constitutional aberrations, if you wish—in Commonwealth constitutionalism, where the clear trend is either to abolish upper houses or to legitimate them by election. The "radical change" so deplored by the Supreme Court would in fact accord with the best trends in modern liberal democratic constitutionalism.[8]

---

§ 1.2.2[9]
New Brunswick Broadcasting Co. v. Nova Scotia
(Speaker of the House of Assembly)
Supreme Court of Canada; January 21, 1993
[1993] 1 S.C.R. 319

The Nova Scotia House of Assembly allowed members of the press to attend to sittings in the gallery, but upon refusing the request of a Canadian Broadcasting Corporation affiliate to televise the proceedings, litigation ensued. The matter was framed before the Supreme Court of Canada in terms of whether the *Charter*, and in particular the section 2(b) freedom of expression, applied to a legislative body or whether the application of the *Charter* was barred in circumstances where parliamentary privilege was present. In that context, part of the argumentation related to the effect of the written Constitution on the unwritten part, and the court was consequentially led to examine the extent of the "Constitution of Canada." The discussion related to whether section 52(2) of the *Constitution Act, 1982*, was an exhaustive listing of constitutional instruments.

---

[8] Edward McWhinney, *Canada and the Constitution 1979-1982* (Toronto: University of Toronto Press, 1982).
[9] Cross-reference to § 1.12.2, 8.2.C.2 and 8.4.

The court concluded that the listing in section 52(2) was not limitative The preamble of the *Constitution Act, 1867* imparted into the constitution a number of principles derived from British constitutional practice and precedent that were unwritten and even unexpressed, but that nevertheless formed an integral part of Canada's constitutional fabric. These principles were not necessarily the same as those that apply in the United Kingdom today; their origin is the same, but the two countries have evolved differently. For the purposes of this case, the inherent privileges of Canadian legislative bodies "fall within the group of principles constitutionalized by virtue of this preamble."[10] More broadly, the meaning of the expression "Constitution of Canada" is not limited by the written part of the constitution set out in section 52(2); the unwritten part complements these instruments that are written.

---

§ 1.2.3[11]
Reference re Secession of Québec
Supreme Court of Canada; August 20, 1998
(1998), 161 D.L.R. (4th) 385

This case is of interest in political law study because it is the ultimate authoritative judicial pronouncement regarding the most politically and legally important issue in Canada's public life, namely the continued existence of the country as a genuine federal State and the balance of centrifugal and centripetal forces within it. It is also of supreme interest in that it is a fount of knowledge on a number of interrelated topics flowing from the nature of the secession controversy. The first of these topics is the definition of the notion of the "constitution of Canada" and the reaffirmation of the constitution's existence and validity.

Ever since the adoption of the *Constitution Act, 1982*, there had existed within some legal, and in particular political, circles in Québec a theory rendered fashionable by adherents of the sovereignty movement: that the *Constitution Act, 1982*, was not applicable to Québec. The source of this theory was the absence of Québec's delegates from among those political officials who came to an understanding, in

---

[10] [1993] 1 S.C.R. 319 at 377 g.
[11] Cross-reference to § 2.4.6, 3.1, 4.2.2, 4.3.1, 10.2.1 and 11.2.C.1.

November 1980, which would eventually lead to the constitutional amendment package of April 1982, which consisted of patriation, the *Charter* and the amending formula. The more generally accepted position is that while the absence of Québec from among those who agreed was generally regrettable and indeed politically damageable to the deal underlying the reform, it did not affect in any way the legal validity or, ultimately, the political validity of the 1982 constitutional reforms. Nevertheless, a political and quasi-legal myth had developed in Québec and had persisted throughout the period from 1982 until the time of this case, to the effect that the *Constitution* was alien to Québec. This was reflected in much of the political commentary within Québec and among members of the Bloc Québécois elected to the House of Commons; such expression as "their constitution" became common currency, along with "their court" and "their judges."

> A la démarche démocratique québécoise, le gouvernement libéral de l'époque, le premier ministre Pierre Trudeau, son ministre de la Justice, Jean Chrétien, ont répondu par un geste unilatéral: l'imposition d'une nouvelle constitution canadienne. Contre le voeu du gouvernement élu, contre le voeu de l'Opposition officielle, et malgré, le désaveu de l'Assemblée nationale, ils ont imposé au Québec une constitution qui, loin de répondre au programme autonomiste des fédéralistes du Québec, réduisait au contraire les pouvoirs de l'Assemblée nationale.
>
> . . .
>
> Le procureur du gouvernement du Canada, Me Yves Fortier, était lui-même un des partisans d'une déclaration unilatérale d'indépendendance pour le Canada. Il écrivait a l'époque que cette mesure « ne soulèverait aucun problème majeur sur le plan international ». En 1987, dans le cadre d'audiences sur l'accord du lac Meech, il a même déclaré ce qui suit, et je cite, « Politiquement, et j'irais jusqu'à dire moralement, la loi constitutionnelle de 1982 ne s'applique pas au Québec. Et ceux qui prétendent le contraire commettent des hérésies constitutionnelles. »[12]

The Supreme Court of Canada felt it necessary to set the record straight on this issue. In the initial paragraphs of its response to the

---

[12] Extracts of a speech delivered by Premier Lucien Bouchard at the Faculty of Law of the Université de Montréal on February 12, 1998, days before the hearing on the Reference was to begin.

first of the three questions that had been referred to it, the court defined the constitution of Canada in the following terms.

> The "Constitution of Canada" certainly includes the constitutional texts enumerated in s. 52(2) of the *Constitution Act, 1982*. Although these texts have a primary place in determining constitutional rules, they are not exhaustive. The Constitution also "embraces unwritten, as well as written rules"...
>
> ...These supporting principles and rules, which include constitutional conventions and the workings of Parliament, are a necessary part of our Constitution because problems or situations may arise which are not expressly dealt with by the text of the Constitution.[13]

Having informed us of the extent of the *Constitution* and thus leading readers into the discussion of constitutional principles that characterize the State [see § 4.2.2], the court gave a reminder, in short and stark terms, that the *Constitution* was alive and applicable throughout Canada.

> The *Constitution Act, 1982* is now in force. Its legality is neither challenged nor assailable...as we said in the *Patriation Reference*...the Constitution of Canada includes
>
>> the global system of rules and principles which govern the exercise of constitutional authority in the whole and in every part of the Canadian state.[14]

See also international reference *Idaho v. Coeur d'Alene Tribe of Idaho*,[15] 138 L.Ed.2d 438 (1997).

1.3 ISSUE: LAW

1.3.A—DEFINITION OF "LAW"

See *McCutcheon v. Toronto (City)* (1983), 41 O.R. (2d) 652 (Ont. H.C.).

---

[13] (1998), 161 D.L.R. (4th) 385 at 403, para. 32.
[14] *Ibid.*
[15] Cross-reference to § 3.3.C.5.

§ 1.3.A.1[16]
Operation Dismantle Inc. v. R.
Supreme Court of Canada; May 9, 1985
(1985), 18 D.L.R. (4th) 481

This is the first major case following the incorporation of the *Canadian Charter of Rights and Freedoms* into the legal and political system of Canada in which the concept of "law" was required to be analyzed and defined. This need arose from the fact that the terms of the *Charter* made that constitutional instrument applicable to the Parliament and government of Canada, as well as to their respective provincial counterparts.[17] To an even greater extent, the definition of the concept of "law" was necessary because of the constitutional provision established in the 1982 reform, pursuant to which the Constitution was defined as the supreme law of Canada and requiring every law to be consistent with it.[18]

The occasion that gave rise to this first consideration of the meaning of law in the new political legal regime of Canada was an application by Operation Dismantle Inc., a group of non-governmental organizations and unions, for declaratory relief against a Cabinet decision of July 15, 1983, to allow testing of cruise missiles by the United States within Canada. The Supreme Court of Canada rendered a judgment allowing a motion by the government to strike out the applicant's statement of claim on the grounds that it disclosed no reasonable cause of action, that it was frivolous and vexatious, and that it was an abuse of the court's process. As part of that decision, it commented on the "law" element of the proceedings.

The court noted that Operation Dismantle was relying on section 52(1) of the *Constitution Act* as the vehicle to have the Cabinet decision declared contrary to the *Charter*. Counsel for the applicant admitted that Parliament had not enacted a law, in the form of a statute, to express the authorization of the cruise missile testing. They argued, however, that they should not be prejudiced by the absence of a law authorizing, ratifying or implementing the agreement between Canada and the United States, because one should have been passed. The

---

[16] Cross-reference to § 2.4.3.
[17] S. 32(1).
[18] *Constitution Act, 1982*, R.S.C. 1985, Appendix II, Item No. 44, s. 52(1).

implication of the argument was that if the matter had been submitted to Parliament, it could have given rise to a public debate which, in the circumstances, had not taken place.

The court relied on the Labour Conventions case,[19] long-established precedent regarding the treaty-making power in Canada, to determine that legislation was not required here. This agreement took the form of an exchange of notes at the level of officials. As the substance of that agreement would not alter the domestic law of Canada, no legislation was needed for its implementation. Notwithstanding this distinction, as the outcome of the judgment hinged on other lines of argumentation, the court seemed to concede this point to the applicant.

> Although little, if any, argument has been in addressed in this case to the question whether the government's decision to permit testing of the cruise missile in Canada falls within the meaning of the word "law" as used in s. 52 of the *Constitution Act, 1982*, I am prepared to assume, without deciding, that it does.[20]

This was the beginning of the court's sustained attention to the issue of what is "law" in the *Charter* era of Canadian public life; the specific interest of the case is the argument that even if no law was enacted, if it should have been, recourse can be had to the constitutional provision declaring the Constitution to be supreme and requiring other laws to be consistent with it.

---

§ 1.3.A.2[21]
O.E.C.T.A. v. Essex (County) Roman Catholic Separate School Board
Ontario High Court of Justice, Divisional Court; February 3, 1987
(1987), 36 D.L.R. (4th) 115[22]

This is one of the early cases on the meaning of the concept of "law" that is interesting because of the thoroughness of its analysis. The subject matter is the retirement policy of a school board, requiring

---

[19] *Canada (Attorney General) v. Ontario (Attorney General)*, [1937] 1 D.L.R. 673, [1937] A.C. 326 (Canada P.C.).
[20] (1985), 18 D.L.R. (4th) 481 at 514.
[21] Cross-reference to § 1.8.B.1.
[22] Leave to appeal refused (1988), 51 D.L.R. (4th) vii (S.C.C.).

teachers to end their careers at age 65 along with the resolution by which the board terminated the employment of several such teachers. These teachers' action alleged that their forced retirement was contrary to the section 15(1) equality provision of the *Charter*.

The court first had to examine the nature and quality of the actor: was it a "legislature" or "government" in the sense of section 32 of the *Charter*? Given that the school board was created by statute and that it had a clearly defined role under the statute, this pre-condition was met.

The core of the ruling is the examination of the nature and quality of the action or activity. The court distinguished between the various types of activities undertaken by governmental actors and held that only some of them constituted "law." The exercise of a statutory power by a governmental actor is law; here, for example, if the board were to conduct an expropriation. By contrast, the exercise of an ordinary corporate power, such as a contract for cleaning of schools, is not law. The distinction depends on the nature of the action.

The board's actions in relation to the teachers' retirement are between the ends of this spectrum of actions. Determining where a particular action falls along that spectrum depends on criteria that this court set out. An employer's relations with its employees are not the same as those of the state with its subjects. There is no call for judicial intervention only because one of the parties to a dispute has a nexus with government. There is no cause to consider a matter "law" under the *Charter* when the matter at stake is essentially private. For all these reasons, the court held that this issue was not law and no remedy applied. The retirement policy was a statement of corporate intent rather than a regulation in the sense of statutory instrument.

> It seems to me an inescapable conclusion that s. 15(1) addresses itself to the rights and liabilities of the individual in relation to law in the sense of a rule of conduct made binding upon a subject by the State. Two dictionary definitions of "law" are helpful. The following is found in the Shorter Oxford Dictionary (1973): "The body of rules...which a state or community recognizes as binding on its members or subjects." See also Webster's New World Dictionary, Second College Edition (1978): "All the rules of conduct established and enforced by the authority, legislation, or custom of a given community, state or other group." Of course

the "law" might be a narrower kind; for example, an exercise of the right of eminent domain.[23]

The dissenting judge's contrary view was based on the binding nature of the instrument in question.

---

§ 1.3.A.3[24]
Stoffman v. Vancouver General Hospital
British Columbia Court of Appeal; January 6, 1988
(1988) 49 D.L.R. (4th) 727[25]

Physicians at the Vancouver General Hospital were subject to a regulation made pursuant to the *Hospital Act*,[26] which effectively forced them into retirement at age 65. Stoffman and others brought suit under section 15 of the *Canadian Charter of Rights and Freedoms*, the equality provision, in order to have the regulation declared to be of no force and effect. The principal issue addressed by the court was the substantive one; did the regulation entail discrimination and if it did, could such discrimination be retained as being justified in a free and democratic society? Before examining the constitutional validity of the physicians' retirement rule, the court dealt with two preliminary matters. Its analysis of whether the Vancouver General Hospital was a governmental body and whether the application of the regulation therefore constituted government action was one of these.

The issue that concerns us here is whether the regulation in question constitutes "law" in the sense of section 15 of the *Charter*. The British Columbia Court of Appeal considered this matter very briefly but its reply to the question is significant, because it took a very pragmatic as well as functional view. The court linked the concept of law to the rather broad category of the exercise of governmental powers. It based its holding on the opinion of the Supreme Court of Canada in the *Douglas/Kwantlen Teachers' Association* case and said:

> It is there stated that law comprehends a rule or system of rules formulated by government and imposed upon the whole or a segment of

---

23 (1987), 36 D.L.R. (4th) 115 at 135-136.
24 Cross-reference to § 1.13.A.5.
25 Reversed (1990), [1991] 1 W.W.R. 577 (S.C.C.).
26 R.S.B.C. 1979, c. 176.

society. As such, law may be made by the legislative, executive or administrative branches of government or by subordinate bodies exercising governmental powers.[27]

This holding clearly demonstrates how closely the courts have intertwined the three notions, related in law, of "law," "government" and "governmental powers."

---

§ 1.3.A.4[28]
Canadian Wildlife Federation Inc. v. Canada (Minister of Environment)
Federal Court of Appeal; June 22, 1989
(1989), [1990] 2 W.W.R. 69

This judgment provides irrefutable evidence of the binding nature of law as an instrument of governance. Not only did a three-member panel of the Federal Court of Appeal unanimously uphold a ruling of the Trial Division of the same court, but it also set out its opinion in such a short and direct ruling as to make the matter starkly clear.

The subject matter of the dispute was the construction of a dam on the Saskatchewan River. In order for the project to proceed, the *International River Improvements Act* required that the federal Minister of the Environment issue a licence. The Minister did so without conducting the environmental assessment and review about which rules were set out in the *Environmental Assessment and Review Process Guidelines Order* (EARPGO). This instrument had originally been drafted merely as a set of "Guidelines" but had subsequently been elevated into an "Order," thus a statutory instrument as defined in the *Statutory Instruments Act*.[29] The very purpose of this conversion from a policy instrument into a legal one had been to clarify and crystallize its binding nature, no matter how it was designated in its title.

The court first determined that the EARPGO was indeed subordinate legislation, validly made pursuant to the powers in the *Department of the Environment Act*. Next, it gave greater weight to the substance of the EARPGO to its title in determining whether it had binding quality. As the instrument directed the Minister by indicating repeatedly that

---

[27] (1988), 49 D.L.R.(4th) 727 at 732.
[28] Cross-reference to § 1.3.D.2, 2.2.E.1, 2.6.1, 11.7.4 and 11.14.2.
[29] R.S.C. 1985, c. S-22.

he "shall" take a course of action, the text was held to be mandatory. The use of the expression "Guidelines" in the title of the instrument was held to be neutral; that is, of insufficient importance to counteract or confuse the Order's mandatory nature.

Most importantly, the court held that if the Order was mandatory, the Minister of the Environment was obliged to follow it "just as he is obliged to follow any other law of general application."[30] On these grounds, despite the obstinate efforts of the appellant, the Saskatchewan Water Corporation, probably acting under the political direction of the provincial government, the licence for the project was set aside and quashed and *mandamus* was issued to compel the federal Minister of the Environment to comply with the guidelines.

---

§ 1.3.A.5[31]
Douglas/Kwantlen Faculty Assn. v. Douglas College
Supreme Court of Canada; December 6, 1990
(1990), 77 D.L.R. (4th) 94

This is a case in which the underlying legal issue was the mandatory retirement provision contained in a collective agreement between a college and the union representing its teachers. The question put before the courts was whether the clause was in contravention of section 15(1) of the *Charter*, in that it constituted discrimination. The issue from a political law perspective was whether the collective agreement was in fact law within the conceptual framework of the *Charter*, which at the time of this litigation, was still new.

The British Columbia Court of Appeal reasoned that law meant a rule or a system of rules formulated by government and imposed upon the whole or upon a segment of society. Moreover, it said that law may be made by a body exercising governmental power.

The Supreme Court of Canada followed in the tracks set out by that judgment and based its decision on the finding that the College was not only an emanation of government, but was also in fact government. This was the prerequisite basis upon which the highest court

---

[30] (1989), [1990] 2 W.W.R. 69 at 70.
[31] Cross-reference to § 1.13.A.7.

determined that the subject collective agreement was law within the *Charter*'s concept of that notion. The interest of the case is not only the resulting extension of the domain of law, but also the diverse ways in which several of the justices expressed their views on the nature of law.

In the majority opinion, Mr. Justice La Forest relied heavily on the finding of the British Columbia Court of Appeal and went on to state that "The fact that the collective agreement takes effect upon the approval of the commissioner under the *Compensation Stabilization Act* 'takes it out of the realm of a privately negotiated agreement and places it in the realm of law, subjecting it to scrutiny under s. 15(1) of the Charter.'"[32] What we are to retain from this is that, as in pre-*Charter* times, law is a public set of rules, not just the privately binding agreement of the parties. The novel element of La Forest's further analysis came in the linkage of the notion of binding rule with that of the rule being in furtherance of government policy. In the realm of *Charter* phraseology, that was the necessary link to render a rule law.

IS THE COLLECTIVE AGREEMENT "LAW"?

> For reasons discussed in *McKinney v. University of Guelph*, I am of the view that the collective agreement is law. It was entered into by a government agency pursuant to powers granted to that agency by statute in furtherance of government policy. The fact that the collective agreement was agreed to by the appellant association does not alter the fact that the agreement was entered into by government pursuant to statutory power and so constituted government action. To permit government to pursue policies violating Charter rights by means of contracts and agreements with other persons or bodies cannot be tolerated.[33]

A more thorough and deliberately purposive approach was taken by Justice Wilson, who wrote her concurring opinion obviously after having read La Forest's ruling. She started off with the view she had earlier expounded.

> Section 52 is animated by the doctrine of constitutional supremacy. As such, a wide view of "law" under that provision is mandated so that all

---

[32] (1990), 77 D.L.R. (4th) 94 at 109 e.
[33] *Ibid.* at 111 a-c.

exercises of state power, whether legislative or administrative, are caught by the Charter.[34]

She then went on to develop her views.

> As I stated in *McKinney* [at p. 601]:
>
>> I would agree with La Forest J. that if you have to find a "law" under s. 15 before the section is triggered, then "law" should be given a very liberal interpretation and should not be confined to legislative activity. It should also cover policies and practices even if adopted consensually.
>
> In this case, La Forest J. has adopted such a generous interpretation of the word "law." In his view, the collective agreement should be construed as "law" because to do otherwise would permit government to avoid its obligations under the Charter through the use of contracts. I agree with him that to sanction such practices by placing them beyond the purview of s. 15 would be intolerable and that therefore the fact that a Charter violation is contained within a collective agreement cannot insulate it from review by this court. If there must be a "law" involved before s. 15 is triggered, that law is found in the collective agreement and in particular art. 4.04.
>
> Alternatively, another such "law" may be found in the college's enabling statute which contains a provision specifically conferring power on the board to terminate contracts of employment.[35]

It is plain that the purposive approach of the court expands the concept of law from that of only statutes and statutory instruments to include other instruments made in execution of a governmental purpose. It is also patent that this expansion blurs the distinction between law and what were earlier considered other types of instruments.

Specifically on the point of the meaning of law, Justice Sopinka disagreed, however.

> I respectfully disagree that the consensual nature of the policies in question may be so discarded in the examination as to whether they constitute "law".

---

[34] *Ibid.* at 103, citing from *Canada (Director of Investigation & Research, Combines Investigation Branch) v. Southam Inc.* (1984), 11 D.L.R. (4th) 641 (S.C.C.).

[35] (1990), 77 D.L.R. (4th) 94 at 104 b-e.

. . .

> While I do not dispute that "law" is not confined merely to legislative activity, I am of the view that an element of coercion must be present even in government "activity" or "program" for such to be reasonably characterized as law. This element of imposition or prescription by the state distinguishes law from voluntarily-assumed rights and obligations.[36]

Notwithstanding this dissent, the effect of the *Charter* was to broaden the scope of law and its application.

See also *Cree Regional Authority v. Robinson*, [1991] 3 F.C. 533 (Fed. C.A.), leave to appeal refused (July 4, 1991), Doc. 22485, 22486 (S.C.C.).

---

§ 1.3.A.6[37]
Friends of the Oldman River Society v. Canada (Minister of Transport)
Supreme Court of Canada; January 23, 1992
[1992] 1 S.C.R. 3

This was, to date, the last of the great and complex cases to grow out of the interpretation of the legal or other nature of the *Environmental Assessment and Review Process Guidelines Order* (EARPGO).[38] The project in question was the construction of a dam at a site called Livingston Gap on the Oldman River in Alberta. Its origins can be traced back to 1958 but it was in February 1988 that the contract for the construction of the dam was awarded. By the time the plaintiff Society took the matter to court in April 1989, the project was 40 per cent complete. It was only then that they sought by way of *certiorari* and *mandamus* in the Federal Court of Canada – Trial Division to have the work stopped. That court dismissed the action but the Federal Court of Appeal allowed it.

This background gave the Supreme Court of Canada the opportunity to adjudicate definitively on the nature of the EARPGO, and to thereby lay down the parameters of the characteristics of instruments that are law. The way the court phrased the principal question was

---

[36] *Ibid.* at 127 f-h.
[37] Cross-reference to § 2.2.E.6.
[38] SOR/84-467.

to ask whether the EARPGO was authorized by section 6 of the *Department of Environment Act*.[39] It relied on several precedents in the train of jurisprudence dealing with the question of the legal nature of subordinate instruments, notably the *Canadian Wildlife Federation* case [see § 2.2.E.1]. It then defined the test as follows. The designation of "guideline," or for that matter any other designation or label on the instrument to be analyzed is not what matters. That designation, by itself, is a neutral matter in this regard. Rather, the courts ought to look first at whether the text of law pursuant to which the instrument was enacted can support a power to enact subordinate legislation, with the emphasis on the binding nature of that instrument. Moreover, the courts also need to look at the legislative intent of Parliament. Did Parliament intend to have enacted something that is "clearly mandatory in nature"?[40] Where these two parts of the test are met, the rights thereby created are enforceable by the courts because the subject instrument is "law." The alternative is that an instrument that is not legal in nature is administratively enforceable only and that is what, in that study, is entitled "policy."

The key expressions, in sum, are "binding," "mandatory" and, consequentially "legally enforceable."

Here, again, the EARPGO was held to be law.

---

§ 1.3.A.7[41]
Sinclair v. Québec (Procureur général)
Supreme Court of Canada; February 27, 1992
[1992] 1 S.C.R. 579

It is clear that a statute enacted by a Parliament or another legislative body is "law" and therefore an instrument of governance of a legislative nature. Considering, however, that legislators and drafters have devised a broad range of other instruments for the purpose of achieving the same results as statute law, which depend on the existence of underlying statute law and which derive their own existence from that statute law, the question of "what is law?" takes on significance. The *Sinclair* case is fundamental in setting out basic rules to

---

[39] R.S.C. 1985, c. E-10.
[40] [1992] 1 S.C.R. 3 at 35 a.
[41] Cross-reference to § 7.3.1 and 8.9.1.

determine which instruments of governance other than statutes are legislative in nature and hence constitute law.

This case arose out of the rather complicated mechanism provided for the amalgamation of the adjacent cities of Rouyn and Noranda in Québec, by a statute entitled *An Act Respecting the Cities of Rouyn and Noranda*.[42] Essentially, the process was to consist of an agreement between the two municipalities, followed by a referendum. In the absence of agreement, the citizens involved would vote on the contents of an Order issued by the Minister of Municipal Affairs, which Order would set out the terms and conditions of the amalgamation. The union of the two cities into Rouyn-Noranda took place by the second of these methods. In the course of following the steps set out in the Act, the Government of Québec issued and published a number of the required instruments in the French language only.

Sinclair, who opposed the amalgamation, sued on the ground that the establishment of the new, combined city was invalid, on the ground that the instruments required had been made in French only and that this was contrary to section 133 of the *Constitution Act, 1867*. The Attorney General of Québec defended, alleging that each instrument was separately valid and not subject to the requirement of bilingualism of section 133. This led the Supreme Court of Canada to review the entire process and gave it an opportunity to declare the state of the law as to what constitutes law.

The court set out first to determine the basic issue of what is law. It provided its analysis primarily on the last paragraph of section 133, which states, "The Acts of the Parliament of Canada and of the Legislature of Quebec shall be printed and published in both of those languages."[43]

It was to these "Acts" that the requirement of section 133 applied, and the task of the court was to determine the extent of the meaning of the expression "Act." Basing itself on one of its earlier rulings in a language case arising out of Manitoba,[44] the court determined that the concept of "law" comprises not only statutes but also all other

---

[42] S.Q. 1985, c. 48, previously Bill 190 of 1985.
[43] *Constitution Act, 1867*, s. 133, as quoted in [1992] 1 S.C.R. 579 at 587.
[44] *Reference re Language Rights Under s. 23 of Manitoba Act, 1870 & s. 133 of Constitution Act, 1867*, [1985] 1 S.C.R. 721 at 739.

instruments of a legislative nature. It also declared that the test to be applied as to the legislative nature of an instrument is not one of form but is based, rather, on the degree of connection between the legislature and the instrument. This matter is so capital to the understanding of political law that the explanation given by the Supreme Court merits reproduction *in extenso*:

> Section 133, therefore, must be read to apply not only to statutes in the strict sense, but equally to all other instruments of a legislative nature. In the 1992 *Manitoba Language Reference*, we decided that the class of instruments having a legislative character might include certain orders in council and documents incorporated into statutes by reference. More generally, we decided that it is not the form of the instrument, but, rather, the degree of "connection between the legislature and the instrument [which] is indicative of a legislative nature" (p. 233).

> With respect to the content and effect of an instrument, we decided that the following characteristics are further badges of its legislative character (at p. 233):

> 1. The instrument embodies a rule of conduct;

> 2. The instrument has the force of law; and

> 3. The instrument applies to an undetermined number of persons.

> The Attorney General of Quebec does not dispute this general definition. Indeed, in its factum, the following definition of legislative instruments, as opposed to executive acts is adopted from the *Regulations Act*, R.S.Q., c. R-19.1, s. 1:

> A normative instrument of a general and impersonal nature, made under an Act and having force of law when it is in effect.

> The question, therefore, is whether the instruments in question in this appeal possess these characteristics.[45]

The court not only laid out the foregoing ground rules; in a further determination of principle, it also indicated how these rules are to be interpreted and used by legislators. It said that:

> At the outset, however, and prior to embarking upon an examination of the five instruments here in question, we should point out that, as we

---

[45] [1992] 1 S.C.R. 579 at 587 d to 588 a.

said in the 1992 *Manitoba Language Reference*, the courts will not permit the circumvention of s. 133 by means of a disingenuous division of a legislative act into a number of discrete parts—for instance, a "shell" statute incorporating by reference some other "non-legislative" unilingual document. To do otherwise would be to invite the triumph of form over substance. As we told the Government of Manitoba, if the net effect of a series of discrete acts has a legislative character, then each of these component acts will also be imbued with this same character.[46]

The court's final clarification on that point was to indicate that the character of each part of a legislative scheme is governed by the nature of the whole.

> As we have already emphasized, it is not permissible to assess the character of the component parts of the legislative process individually and in isolation in order to determine whether s. 133 of the *Constitution Act, 1867* has been complied with. Rather, it is the character of the whole which determines the nature of the parts.[47]

In the present instance, the court applied these tests to each of the instruments used in the process of amalgamating Rouyn and Noranda that were in question. It found every one of them to be legislative in character and therefore subject to the section 133 requirement. The judgment induced the authorities of Quebec to correct the mistakes they had made in establishing the new municipal government.

While the definition of law and the prohibition on attempts to avoid the effects and consequences of that definition arose here on the basis of one particular constitutional circumstance, the findings of the Supreme Court of Canada on these issues are so important that they are to be generally applied to the political legal system.

See also *O'Sullivan v. R.* (1991), [1992] 1 F.C. 522 (Fed. T.D.); *Wong v. R.* (1996), [1997] 1 F.C. 193 (Fed. T.D.), affirmed (1997), 232 N.R. 4 (Fed. C.A.), leave to appeal refused (1998), 234 N.R. 195 (note) (S.C.C.) and *Canada (Attorney General) v. Boutilier* (1997), 31 P.S.S.R.B. 15 (Can. P.S.S.R.B.), reversed (1998), 154 F.T.R. 40 (Fed. T.D.), affirmed (1999), 36 C.H.R.R. D/257 (Fed. C.A.), leave to appeal refused (2000), 261 N.R. 197 (note) (S.C.C.).

---

[46] *Ibid.* at 588 b-c.
[47] *Ibid.* at 590 a-b.

1.3.B—RULE OF LAW

See *Singh v. Canada (Attorney General)*, [1999] 4 F.C. 583 (Fed. T.D.), affirmed [2000] F.C.J. No. 4 (Fed. C.A.), leave to appeal refused (2000), 259 N.R. 400 (note) (S.C.C.).

1.3.C—"PRESCRIBED BY LAW"

See *Luscher v. Deputy Minister of National Revenue (Customs & Excise)*, 17 D.L.R. (4th) 503 (Fed. C.A.).

---

§ 1.3.C.1
Olson v. R.
Federal Court of Canada – Trial Division; February 9, 1996
[1996] 2. F.C. 168[48]

A comprehensive perspective on the notion of "law" in the context of the various types of instruments of governance requires not only the examination of what law itself is, but also an understanding of what is a law-based norm. In order to distinguish this type of norm from others, such as norms based on policy, the *Canadian Charter of Rights and Freedoms* used the expression "prescribed by law"[49] to indicate that limits on the guaranteed rights and freedoms would be valid only if they were based on legal norms or standards. What are such norms and how are they recognizable?

In 1982, Olson was convicted of 11 murders and sentenced to life imprisonment. During his first decade in prison, he was thought to be attracting too much media attention. Therefore, in 1993, his access to members of the media was restricted. The Warden of the Saskatchewan Penitentiary took this action as part of a correctional plan tailored for Olson and designed for the public's protection, in particular the families of Olson's victims, and for the inmate's rehabilitation. These goals and actions were based on the *Corrections and Conditional*

---

[48] Affirmed (1997), 1997 CarswellNat 2734 (Fed. C.A.), leave to appeal refused [1997] 3 S.C.R. xii (S.C.C.).

[49] This expression is used in the *Charter*, at s. 1.

Release Act[50] and the *Corrections and Conditional Release Regulations* made thereunder.[51]

Olson applied to the Federal Court for declaratory relief, alleging that his *Charter* section 2(b) freedom of expression, section 2(d) freedom of association, and section 15(1) (equality) rights had been infringed. The application was dismissed. The Crown submitted that the expression "prescribed by law" in section 1 of the *Charter* was synonymous with "having the force of law." Governmental actions have the force of law where they are based on legal texts such as statutes and regulations and where they are intended to carry out the goals enunciated in those legal texts. The actions of the Warden were found by the court to have been taken pursuant to the body of correctional legislation. The limitations imposed on Olson's access to publicity also followed the texts, the goals and the spirit of that body of legislation and it was reasonable in light of the requirements of the correctional system and commensurate to the situation of this particular inmate. Based on these criteria, the judgment was that the limit on Olson's rights was "prescribed by law."

1.3.D—"LAWS OF CANADA"[52]

---

§ 1.3.D.1
Canadian Pacific Ltd. v. Quebec North Shore Paper Co.
Supreme Court of Canada; June 29, 1976
(1976), 71 D.L.R. (3d) 111

This case was part of the struggle to delineate the jurisdiction of the Federal Court of Canada following the reconstitution of the Exchequer Court into the Federal Court in 1971. The litigants had contracted that as part of an overall scheme relating to the transportation of newsprint a rail-car terminal be built at Sept-Isles, Québec. Non-performance of this term of the contract led to an action for breach, which in turn led to a motion to strike out the jurisdiction of the Federal Court in favour of the Superior Court of Québec.

---

[50] S.C. 1992, c. 20.
[51] SOR/92-620.
[52] Cross-reference to § 1.2 and 4.2.

In examining the issue, the Supreme Court of Canada looked at section 23 of the *Federal Court Act*, establishing the jurisdiction of the Trial Division, in light of the constitutional provision that enabled the federal authorities to set up courts, namely section 101 of the *British North America Act, 1867*. That section held the key phrase, authorizing courts to be established "for the better Administration of the Laws of Canada." Did the phrase "laws of Canada" refer only to statutes or to law in its broader meaning? Was the phrase intended to encompass federal law alone, or all law made in Canada by legislative bodies? The Supreme Court took a restrictive view of the concept of "laws of Canada" and held that the Federal Court lacked jurisdiction to hear the case. While the judgment seems to admit the existence of a federal common law, it draws a clear federal distinction, favouring an interpretation of the phrase "laws of Canada" as requiring a link to the federal Parliament.

> It should be recalled that the law respecting the Crown came into Canada as part of the public or constitutional law of Great Britain, and there can be no pretence that that law is provincial law. In so far as there is a common law associated with the Crown's position as a litigant it is federal law in relation to the Crown in right of Canada, just as it is provincial law in relation to the Crown in right of a Province, and is subject to modification in each case by the competent Parliament or Legislature. Crown law does not enter into the present case.[53]

The effect of this judgment was reaffirmed by the Supreme Court of Canada in the *Québec Secession Reference*.[54]

---

§ 1.3.D.2[55]
Canadian Wildlife Federation Inc. v. Canada (Minister of Environment)
Federal Court – Trial Division; November 30, 1989
(1989), [1990] 1 F.C. 595

The same parties had litigation earlier on the matter of the licenses required for the construction of the Rafferty-Alameda damming project. In that case, as in this one, the Saskatchewan Water Corporation was one of the named defendants. The proceedings in both cases

---

[53] (1976), 71 D.L.R. (3d) 111 at 118.
[54] (1998), 161 D.L.R. (4th) 385 at 395.
[55] Cross-reference to § 1.3.A.4, 2.2.E.1, 2.6.1, 11.7.4 and 11.14.2.

were pursuant to section 18 of the *Federal Courts Act*,[56] which deals with the exclusive jurisdiction of the Trial Division. In a rather unusual manner, the court in that instance called into question its own jurisdiction over the Saskatchewan Water Corporation, a provincially constituted body. This led it to look not only at its own statute, but also at section 101 of the *Constitution Act, 1867*,[57] which dealt with the establishment of courts for the better administration of Canadian laws. The court noted the significance of the provision as having enabled Canada to achieve autonomy from the United Kingdom in the judicial field. Basing itself on an earlier decision of the Supreme Court, the Federal Court held that in order for it to have jurisdiction, the case it was considering must be based on a law of Canada. Here, that requirement was met because the litigation revolved around the *International River Improvements Act*[58] and the *Environmental Assessment and Review Process Guideline Order*.[59] The court's jurisdiction also needed to be based on an existing body of federal law that was essential to the disposition of the case. It felt that this criteria was also met, without further explanation.

The specificity of this case is that the court not only dealt with the "laws of Canada," part of the phrase originating in section 101 of the Constitution, but also with the entire term "better administration of the laws of Canada." In determining whether it had jurisdiction, the court held that its own establishment had been for the better administration of those laws, not merely for the due administration thereof. It even added that it was certainly not for the "crippled" administration of those laws.

This ruling of the Trial Division was struck down by the Federal Court of Appeal. The Trial Division, in the face of the rule of *stare decisis*, restored the first ruling but that was struck down again.[60] Nevertheless, the Federal Court of Appeal did not dispute the analysis of the lower court's treatment of the concept of "law of Canada."

---

[56] R.S.C. 1985, c. F-7.
[57] 30 and 31 Vict. c. 3 (U.K.); R.S.C. 1985, Appendix II, No. 5.
[58] R.S.C. 1985, c. I-20.
[59] SOR/84-467.
[60] (1992), 134 N.R. 57 at 64.

§ 1.3.D.3[61]
Kealey v. R.
Federal Court of Canada – Trial Division; May 2, 1991
(1991), [1992] 1 F.C. 195[62]

Kealey, who alleged that he had been cheated by the government of Canada in a commercial matter at the instance of then Prime Minister Mulroney, had for some time been protesting near the entrance to Parliament that the Prime Minister regularly used. Effective March 1, 1990, the *Public Works Nuisance Regulations* were amended so as to prohibit noise, disruption and demonstration near the entrances of Parliament. Kealey was arrested and held for several days. Subsequently, the proceedings against him were stayed. Three months thereafter, Kealey brought suit against the Crown, the Prime Minister, the Minister of Public Works, the Minister of Justice, the Commissioner of the R.C.M.P. and the arresting R.C.M.P. officer, alleging breach of statutory duty, wrongful arrest, abuse of process, and malicious prosecution. He also based his actions on the plea that the *Public Works Nuisance Regulations*, as amended, violated his constitutional rights, thereby bringing into issue the *Charter*.

This ruling of the Federal Court focused primarily on whether the court had jurisdiction to hear the case. The rules on jurisdiction had been settled by earlier jurisprudence and one of the criteria which the plaintiff would have to meet in order to show that the court did indeed have jurisdiction was that the law on which the case is based must be a "law of Canada" as that phrase is used in section 101 of the *Constitution Act, 1867*. This gave the court, albeit within a very limited circumstance and for a specific purpose, the opportunity to examine whether the *Charter* could be considered to be a law of Canada.

In response to Kealey's argument of breach of constitutional rights, the Prime Minister, the Minister of Public Works and the Minister of Justice submitted together that the *Charter* did not fit within the requisite ambit of section 101 and that reliance on it could not satisfy the test for granting the Federal Court jurisdiction to hear that part of the case. Without any explanation, the court agreed with the submission.

---

[61] Cross-reference to § 8.3.4.

[62] Leave to appeal allowed (1991), 139 N.R. 189 (Fed. C.A.).

It said that while the *Charter* would not suffice to constitute a body of law to the statutory grant of jurisdiction, once the court had identified an existing body of federal law, it would have jurisdiction over the *Charter* issues, as these issues would be part of the same matter. Here, the existing body of federal law was held to be "federal common law." This leaves us with the rather strange circumstance that at least for some purposes, the most vital part of the Constitution of Canada is not to be qualified as a "law of Canada."

1.4 ISSUE: PUBLIC LAW[63]

See *Nielsen v. Canada (Canadian Human Rights Commission)*, [1992] 2 F.C. 561 (Fed. T.D.) and *Douglas v. R.* (1993), 98 D.L.R. (4th) 129 (Fed. T.D.).

---

§ 1.4.1
Jebanayagam v. Canada (Solicitor General) [No. 1]
Federal Court of Canada – Trial Division; September 30, 1994
(1994), 30 Imm. L.R. (2d) 19
-and-
Jebanayagam v. Canada (Solicitor General) [No. 2]
Federal Court of Canada – Trial Division; March 9, 1995
(1995), 30 Imm. L.R. (2d) 194

Both these judgments arise out of the application of Antan Jebanayagam, a Sri Lankan Tamil, to be accepted as a convention refugee pursuant to Canada's immigration legislation. In a decision of August 4, 1994, the Convention Refugee Determination Division (CRDD) of the Immigration and Refugee Board (IRB) rejected the application. The applicant then took the next step mandated by law, seeking a judicial review by the Federal Court of Canada – Trial Division. As part of that proceeding, the two Cabinet officers involved, the Attorney General and the Minister of Immigration and Citizenship, filed a consent to judgment, agreeing with the applicant that the CRDD decision be set aside and asking to have the matter re-determined by a different panel of the same body. They did not support their position with reasons and in the first ruling, on September 30, 1994, the Federal

---

[63] Cross-reference to § 3.10, 3.11, 11.12, 11.13.

Court denied the application. Pursuant to the rules of procedure of the court, the applicant sought reconsideration of that decision. On March 9, 1995, the same judge heard the matter again and reaffirmed the refusal to grant judicial review. In both instances, the issue at the heart of the case was the absence of reasoning tendered by the officers of the State for not defending the relevant provisions of the *Immigration Act*.

The court motivated its rejection of the State's acquiescence to Jebanayagam's applications on the ground of the distinction between private law and public law. It gave examples of private law cases as being ones dealing with personal injury, debt and contract suits and said that in such cases, "the litigation 'belongs' to the litigants and they may settle or concede as they will subject to [the rules of the court]."[64] In such cases involving private parties, as long as the remedy granted by means of a trial, the court may make the consent of the parties to a judgment the basis of its ruling and it need not look beyond the terms of a judgment so agreed upon. The nature of private law renders this method of ruling applicable even if the State is one of the parties to such a case.

The court proceeded to draw clear distinctions between the private obligations, rights and matters of litigants, and issues touching on the general welfare of the population. First, it qualified public law as "a matter of the state's laws of general application for the public benefit"[65] and went on to explain the concept in greater detail. It emphasized that "Public law is different from private law. Public law involves the administration and enforcement of public statutes in which the general public have an enduring interest or those statutes' due and unbiased enforcement, without fear or favour."[66]

It also held that legislation on immigration and refugees is certainly part of this category of public law. This characterization of public law was reinforced by reference to section 101 of the *Constitution Act, 1867*,[67] which provided for the establishment of courts for the better

---

[64] (1994), 30 Imm. L.R. (2d) 19 at 23.
[65] *Ibid.* at 24.
[66] (1995), 30 Imm. L.R. (2d) 194 at 198.
[67] "**101.** The Parliament of Canada may, notwithstanding anything in this Act, from Time to Time provide for the Constitution, Maintenance, and Organization of a General Court of Appeal for Canada, and for the Establishment of any additional Courts for the better Administration of Laws of Canada."

administration of Canadian laws. The mandate of the Federal Court was said to include the better administration and the interpretation of the *Immigration Act*, an authentic law of Canada.

Several consequences derive from the public law character of statutes such as the *Immigration Act*. First, it strengthens the public expectation in the time-honoured adage that justice must not only be done but must also be seen to be done. In the specific instance, this means that the adjudicating system would operate in a fair and unbiased manner vis-à-vis the interests of refugee claimants as well as those of Canada. Further, in matters of public law, there is a requirement in avoiding the suspicion of improper interference in the course of justice and in negating the possibility of favouritism, through such processes as the submission to the court of a ministerial consent to judgment without sufficient grounds, or with "no questions asked."[68] Here, the arguments put forward by the Attorney General were alternatively qualified as "bare-bones," as "barren, anorexic," and as "sere and groundless."[69] In matters of public law, the court could not accept such unexplained abandonment of the administration and enforcement of public law; it could not allow ministers to abandon their duty to uphold the law.

In order to enable the minister to live up to the standard of conduct required of his office in a matter of public law, the court offered two courses of action. Preferably, he was to submit reasons in defence of impugned legislation "which the court finds to be cogent and appropriate for the better, or at least proper administration of the laws of Canada."[70] If, however, the minister could offer no such valid reasons, the court would be prepared here, as the Supreme Court of Canada had already done elsewhere, to appoint an *amicus curiae* to uphold the public law of Canada. In indication of its belief in the significance of matters of public law, the court even offered that such an *amicus curiae* be appointed at public expense, a step it held justifiable, even though wholly unnecessary.

See also *Miron v. Trudel*, [1995] 2 S.C.R. 418 (S.C.C.) and international comparison *Regina v. H. M. Treasury, Ex parte University of Cambridge* (October 17, 2000), Doc. Case C380/98 (European Ct. Just.).

---

[68] *Supra* note 66 at 198, 199.
[69] *Supra* note 66 at 197, 198.
[70] *Supra* note 64 at 26.

1.5   ISSUE: PUBLIC INTEREST

See *Carey v. Ontario*, [1986] 2 S.C.R. 637 (S.C.C.).

§ 1.5.1
R. c. Lamothe
Québec Court of Appeal; March 16, 1990
(1990), 58 C.C.C. (3d) 530

The concept of "public interest" in society is very broad and transcends any conceptual boundary that may exist between legal and political connotations of the expression. It is the subject of a number of interpretations by the courts, largely dependant on the context.

This decision deals with the interpretation of the concept of public interest in the criminal law context. The accused was awaiting trial on a charge of being an accessory after the fact to murder. The Superior Court denied his release on bail but the Québec Court of Appeal allowed it. The governing provision was section 515(10) of the *Criminal Code*, which stated that in considering an application for bail, the court's primary concern was to ensure the accused's attendance at trial and its secondary concern was the public interest and protecting the public's safety. The court's analysis of the scope of "public interest" makes this a difficult case, although a most interesting one, in that it contrasts the objective criteria that should guide judges with the subjective and contentious ones animating public opinion.

The first element of public interest in the circumstances of bail applications is the public perception in case of release. The court realizes that the public is not rational in that regard, and that it has a negative and emotional attitude towards criminals. Nevertheless, basing itself on the educational value of the criminal law, the court prescribes that judges aim their decisions at an informed public, judging unemotionally. It states, most significantly, that the public application of the constitutionally guaranteed presumption of innocence is the price that must be paid for living in a free and democratic society. Judges ought, it goes on, to also consider whether release would discredit the administration of justice. It is from these terms that we must start to extrapolate to develop a comprehensive view of judicial notions on the public interest.

---

§ 1.5.2
Canada v. Pharmaceutical Society (Nova Scotia)
Supreme Court of Canada; July 9, 1992
(1992), 93 D.L.R. (4th) 36

In this case more than in any other, the Supreme Court of Canada tied the notion of "public interest" to the difficulty of the vague nature of that expression and to the impact of that vagueness on the rule of law. The Nova Scotia Pharmaceutical Society was charged with conspiring to lessen competition unduly in respect of prescription drugs and dispensing services. Upon the application of the Society for a declaration that the provision of the *Combines Investigation Act*[71] under which it had been charged was of no force and effect, the highest court found that the section was indeed precise enough to meet the requirement of fundamental justice.

This case is more pertinent for the analysis it offers than the specific conclusions with respect to the particular defendant. The Supreme Court started by reminding us that the rule of law lies at the core of our political and constitutional tradition. While most judgments that cite foreign doctrine or precedent rely on British, American or Commonwealth jurisprudence, this one, significantly, goes further afield. "The criterion of absence of legal debate relates well to the rule of law principles that form the backbone of our policy. Here one must see the rule of law in the contemporary context. "Continental European studies on the 'État de droit' or 'Rechtsstat' are relevant."[72]

The essence of the judgment was that in law, there is a need for clarity and definition. As the court put it, vague provisions cannot fuel a legal debate and they do not offer a grasp to the judiciary. Nevertheless, where the provision in question contains an intelligible principle, one that has meaning and conceptual force, it is not invalid only because it is subject to interpretation.

---

[71] R.S.C. 1970, c. C-23.
[72] (1992), 93 D.L.R. (4th) 36 at 57.

§ 1.5.3
R. v. Morales
Supreme Court of Canada; November 19, 1992
17 W.C.B. (2d) 580

This case was a consideration of the notion of "public interest" in the context of the granting of bail to an accused in criminal proceedings. The majority of the Supreme Court held that the standard set out in section 515(10)(b) of the *Criminal Code*, namely that detention was justified for, among other reasons, the public interest, was contrary to the *Charter* because the principles of fundamental justice precluded the kind of "standardless sweep" implied by the undefined nature of the term. The court elaborated that:

> ...[t]he term "public interest" has not been given a constant or settled meaning by the courts. The term provides no guidance for legal debate. It authorizes a standardless sweep, as the court can order imprisonment whenever it sees fit....No amount of judicial interpretation would be capable of rendering it a provision that gives any guidance for legal debate.[73]

While the five justices of the majority, including the Chief Justice, found no guidance in the *Criminal Code* to define and refine the concept, the minority's very perceptive search for meaning led it to conclude that Parliament had used it to provide for social peace and order. "The concept of 'public interest' was broader than that of protection of the public and included interests which may not be properly included within the categories of public health or safety, such as avoiding interference with the administration of justice."[74] Thus, while the meaning of public interest may be more difficult for the lawyer to define than for the public administrator, specific criteria can be attached to it which have meaning in both disciplines.

See also *Asbestos Corp., Re* (1992), 10 O.R. (3d) 577 (Ont. C.A.), leave to appeal refused 157 N.R. 239 (note) (S.C.C.); *Coalition of Citizens for a Charter Challenge v. Metropolitan Authority* (1993), 122 N.S.R. (2d) 1 (N.S. S.C. [In Chambers]), reversed (1993), 12 C.E.L.R. (N.S.) 1 (N.S. C.A.), leave to appeal refused (1994), 12 C.E.L.R. (N.S.) 319 (S.C.C.);

---

[73] 17 W.C.B. (2d) 580 at page 431.
[74] *Ibid.* at page 432.

Bacon v. Saskatchewan Crop Insurance Corp., [1997] S.J. No. 400 (Sask. Q.B.), affirmed [1999] S.J. No. 302 (Sask. C.A.), leave to appeal refused (2000), [1999] S.C.C.A. No. 437 (S.C.C.); *R. v. MacDougal*, 138 C.C.C. (3d) 38 (B.C. C.A.); *Johnson v. British Columbia (Securities Commission)* (1999), 67 B.C.L.R. (3d) 145 (B.C. S.C. [In Chambers]), reversed 206 D.L.R. (4th) 711 (B.C. C.A.) and international comparison *Gouriet v. Union of Post Office Workers* (1977), [1978] A.C. 435 (U.K. H.L.).

1.6   ISSUE: PUBLIC INTEREST IN LAW

See *Vivace Tavern Inc. v. Metropolitan Licensing Commission* (1997), 96 O.A.C. 246 (Ont. Div Ct.).

1.7   ISSUE: JUSTICE

§ 1.7.1[75]
Regular, Re
Newfoundland Supreme Court – Trial Division; July 17, 1995
(1995), 132 Nfld. & P.E.I.R. 310

The Law Society of Newfoundland was called upon to adjudicate complaints of unprofessional conduct against one of its own members, Regular. It dismissed the complaints but refused to award the costs of Regular's defence to him and against either the complainant or the Law Society itself. Regular appealed to the Trial Division of the Newfoundland Supreme Court. Pursuant to subsection 95(5) of the *Law Society Act*, the judge sitting in appeal could make such order as he or she considered "just."

The court held that in administrative law terms, this wording gave it a wide scope of review, and in particular one that, contrary to other instances in which a court is called upon to review decisions of specialized tribunals, did not "indicate any legislative intention of deferral to the decision"[76] of the Law Society. The court also endeavou-

---

[75] Cross-reference to § 1.8.D.1.
[76] (1995), 132 Nfld. & P.E.I.R. 310, 410 A.P.R. 310 at 313.

red to define the notion of justice in a broader socio-political context. In determining the scope of its own adjudicative responsibility, the court held that a "just" order would be one made in accordance with law and justice, the latter term being taken as a synonym for being fair, proper and equitable. In order that the decision be just, the Trial Division went on, it had to "fairly consider the interests of both parties."[77] It would also have to bear in mind the public interest and the duty of the Bar to protect that interest. In the specific instance, a just decision would have to include consideration of the dissuasive effect of the imposition of costs on the filing of complaints.

1.8 ISSUE: POLICY

1.8.A—DEFINITION OF POLICY

§ 1.8.A.1

Simon v. Toronto (Metropolitan)

Ontario Court (General Division), Divisional Court; January 6, 1993

(1993), 99 D.L.R. (4th) 11

On February 26, 1992, the Toronto Metropolitan Council decided to amend the policy procedures of the Community Services Department so as to discontinue payment of the last month's rental deposit for apartments rented by welfare recipients. The reason for the decision was budgeting and financial restraint. The welfare scheme administered by the municipal government was based on federal legislation, namely the *Canada Assistance Plan*,[78] as well as provincial legislation, namely the *General Welfare Assistance Act*.[79]

Simon and others applied for judicial review of the decision, but the Ontario Court (General Division) denied their application. The central question the court formulated in analyzing the situation was whether the policy statement restricted the discretion of employees of the Community Services Department in even considering making such payments. It rejected this on the grounds that, "Given the prior

---

[77] *Ibid.* at 314

[78] R.S.C. 1985, c. C-1 and regulations made thereunder.

[79] R.S.O. 1990, c. G.6 and regulations made thereunder.

history of the making of such payments, it appears the policy state-ment is no more than the present statement of Metro's approach to this matter."[80]

Beyond the fundamental definition of a policy as a statement of ap-proach to a matter of governance, involving no legal component or obligation, the court offered the following additional explanation:

> In my view, courts should be very reluctant to interfere in decisions with policy and financial decisions made by any level of government in these difficult times. This is especially so when called upon to deal with iso-lated applications when the court has no knowledge or real understand-ing of the overall financial problems faced in making such decisions.[81]

1.8.B—CHARACTERIZATION OF POLICY

§ 1.8.B.1[82]

O.E.C.T.A. v. Essex (County) Roman Catholic Separate School Board
Ontario High Court of Justice (Divisional Court); February 3, 1987
(1987), 36 D.L.R. (4th) 115[83]

Section 52 of the *Canadian Charter of Rights and Freedoms* declares that the Constitution is the supreme law of Canada and that any law tainted with inconsistency is of no force and effect. This provision has often drawn the courts into an examination of whether a partic-ular instrument pursuant to which actions have been taken and are complained of, constitutes law or not. In conducting this type of analysis, the court can take one of two approaches. It can either generally define the category of instruments to which the particular instrument being scrutinized belongs, or it can more directly analyze whether the particular instrument constitutes law. In the present case, the Ontario High Court of Justice was asked to interpret a rule entitled a "policy" and to choose the second method. Thus, by a process of exclusion rather than outright definition, the court distinguished the notion of "policy" from that of "law." What makes the ruling addi-

---

[80] (1993), 99 D.L.R. (4th) 11 at 14h.
[81] *Ibid.* at 15a.
[82] Cross-reference to § 1.3.A.2.
[83] Leave to appeal refused (1988), 51 D.L.R. (4th) vii (S.C.C.).

tionally interesting is that the court used the "binding" quality of the subject rule to determine the category to which it belonged.

Mordowanec, a teacher with the Essex County Roman Catholic Separate School Board, was forced to follow the Board's policy and to retire after reaching age 65. The union to which he belonged applied on his behalf for judicial review of the Board's decision to apply the policy.

The court decided first that the applicant was entitled to judicial review under Ontario's *Judicial Review Procedure Act*.[84] The first part of the analysis was to look at the nature and quality of the action; was the Board a governmental actor? The court concluded that it was. The second and more important point to analyze was the nature and quality of the action or activity; was it law, so as to bring the *Charter* into play? In setting the parameters for its reply, the court distinguished between the Board's exercise of its statutory powers that are to be construed as "law" and its exercise of ordinary corporate powers, such as the power to contract, which are not "law."

The court situated this decision as falling somewhere between what it called these two extremes. In clarifying where along the spectrum of decision-making the decision to force a teacher's retirement stood, it said that

> It was the submission of counsel for the applicants that the policy statement was a "regulation" as that term is understood in common legal parlance, as, for example, subordinate legislation created by Order in Council pursuant to the provisions of an Act of the Legislature. In my view, there is no health in that argument. The policy statement is simply that: a statement of the board as to its policy with respect to retirement of its employees. Standing by itself it is of no force or effect and binds no one.[85]

The court supported this conclusion by various ways of crystallizing the concept of law. The most convincing of its arguments was that a law-based rule pertains to the relationship between the State and one of its subjects, which is not the kind of relation that tied Mordowanec to the School Board that had employed him. The court also relied on

---

[84] R.S.O. 1980, c. 224.
[85] (1987), 36 D.L.R. (4th) 115 at 132.

collateral material involving the binding nature of a legal rule of conduct.

> It seems to me an inescapable conclusion that s. 15(1) addresses itself to the rights and liabilities of the individual in relation to law in the sense of a rule of conduct made binding upon a subject by the State. Two dictionary definitions of "law" are helpful. The following is found in the Shorter Oxford Dictionary (1973): "The body of rules...which a state or community recognizes as binding on its members or subjects." See also Webster's New World Dictionary, Second College Edition (1978): "All the rules of conduct established and enforced by the authority, legislation, or custom of a given community, state, or other group." Of course the "law" might be a narrower kind; for example, an exercise of the right of eminent domain.[86]

Applying the criteria derived from those sources, the court concluded that, given the contractual rather than the State-subject nature of the relationship between this teacher and School Board, the Board's rule and its decision based on that rule could not be held to be law, despite the Board's nexus with the government. It held consequently that Mordowanec could not invoke section 15 of the *Charter* in place of what would have been the usual basis of such complaints for improper or discriminatory termination, namely lodging a complaint under his collective agreement, individual employment contract, or under the *Ontario Human Rights Act*.

While agreeing with the outcome of the case, one of the three judges on the panel dissented on the issue of whether the Board had made law. He wrote that the policy in question was "law" because it was intended to be binding upon the teachers. This, however, was not strong reasoning, as it could be interpreted as being based on the argument that the policy had never been challenged.

The task the court set itself here was to determine whether a particular rule of conduct constituted law and could thus be adjudicated. It is for this reason that the present case offers us only the barest definition of what is policy and indicates with greater clarity that policy is distinguishable from law. Moreover, while the case raises the pivotal issue of the binding characteristic of different types of rules as grounds on which to distinguish law from policy, its conclusion that law is binding while policy is not, is not quite accurate from the

---

[86] *Ibid.* at 135-136.

perspective of political law. It is more appropriate to say that the two types of rules are binding in different ways. Law is legally binding; it is a rule of general application on the State and in society, and it is the only type of rule for the enforcement of which the courts of law are established. Policy is a different kind of rule, an administrative rule that is binding on a particular category of institutions and individuals, those to whom the rule is directed. The binding nature of policy rules exists in the sense that there is an expectation that those at whom the rule is directed are to abide by it. The courts of law may recognize policy rules but their enforcement is assured by other, such as individual tribunals.

---

§ 1.8.B.2[87]

Angus v. R.

Federal Court of Appeal; July 4, 1990

(1990), 72 D.L.R. (4th) 672

In the period 1989-1990, the Progressive Conservative Government of Prime Minister Mulroney was at its zenith. As part of its reordering of the Canadian economy, it decided in the April 1989 federal budget to significantly downsize VIA Rail, the country's passenger rail service, for purposes of cost cutting. This decision was implemented through an Order in Council of the Governor in Council, dated October 4, 1989. The effect included eliminating just over half of the VIA network and abandoning service to various remote parts of the country. It is not surprising, therefore, that the principal plaintiff here is the New Democratic Member of Parliament for Thunder Bay-Atikokan, a sparsely populated constituency in the distant north-western part of Ontario.

The application is for *certiorari* to quash the Order in Council and the central issue to be determined is whether either the Governor in Council or the Minister of Transport were subject to the *Environmental Assessment and Review Process Guidelines Order* (EARPGO)[88] in making the service reduction Order in Council. The application was denied by both the Trial Division and the Federal Court of Appeal. This case offered the court an opportunity to examine the binding nature of the

---

[87] Cross-reference to § 1.13.A.6.

[88] SOR/84-467.

EARPGO and thus to characterize the nature of policy instruments. At the subject time, the EARPGO was an Order, meaning subordinate legislation and therefore a legal instrument. The case must therefore be read so as to give the characteristics of a policy instrument by contraindication to legal instruments.

Angus argued that EARPGO was mandatory, given that the service reduction was a "proposal" of "any department, board or agency of the Government," according to the terminology used in EARPGO.

> They therefore conclude that, by the phrase "any department, board or agency of the Government of Canada" (which is, in part, how "department" is defined in s. 2), Parliament intended to cover all instrumentalities through which the executive power of that government might be exercised even to the inclusion of the Governor in Council. A contrary interpretation would be inconsistent with the purpose of the enactment, it was said, and a large range of federal decision-making would be excluded from the requirement of environmental assessment and review notwithstanding Parliament's intention that all new federal proposals, undertakings and activities be so examined.
>
> In this contention, it seems to me, the court is confronted with an underlying political argument as to the desirability of universal environmental protection, a matter which, in the absence of statutory or other authority, is beyond the capacity of a court to judge.[89]

The court held that in the sense of the EARPGO in particular, rather than in the general sense, the Governor in Council was not a board or agency of the Government of Canada, because EARPGO did not contain clear language to provide for that meaning. Consequently, the Governor in Council was not subject to the mandatory requirement of the EARPGO Order. The conclusion we are to draw from this is that in order to subject an institution to a mandatory procedure, first a legal instrument is required and a policy instrument is insufficient and second, even in such legal instruments, precise language is required to submit an institution to legal requirements, language that a policy instrument cannot sustain.

By contrast, on the basis of the language of the EARPGO and of precedent,[90] the court found that all ministers of the Crown, and by

---

[89] (1990), 72 D.L.R. (4th) 672 at 682 d-g.
[90] *Friends of The Old Man River Society v. Canada (Minister of Transport)* (1990), 68 D.L.R.

implication all government departments, are indeed subject to the EARPGO Order.

§ 1.8.B.3
Comité pour la République du Canada – Committee for the Commonwealth of Canada v. Canada
Supreme Court of Canada; January 25, 1991
[1991] 1 S.C.R. 139[91]

This is a freedom of expression case, pursuant to section 2(b) of the *Canadian Charter of Rights and Freedoms*. At Dorval Airport in Montréal, two members of a political organization called the *Comité pour la République du Canada*—Committee for the Commonwealth of Canada spoke to members of the travelling public to provide them with information about their group and distributed publications of the Committee to them. They were asked by the R.C.M.P. to stop their activities. When they objected, the police brought them before airport management. The assistant manager of the airport advised them that they would be required to cease their activities, as these were prohibited by the *Government Airport Concession Operations Regulations*,[92] a statutory instrument made under the *Department of Transport Act*.[93] The Committee started an action against the Crown, alleging that its members' freedom of expression had been infringed and asking for declaratory judgment to that effect. The Federal Court of Canada – Trial Division and the Federal Court of Appeal both ruled in favour of the Committee. The Crown appealed to the Supreme Court of Canada and here also, the Committee's right to exercise freedom of speech was affirmed.

The primary interest of this case is its examination of freedom of political expression as an aspect of the rights and freedoms protected by the *Charter*. As such, it belongs most prominently in a volume on human rights. There is, however, one aspect of the judgment that is pertinent to political law study and that is the analysis of the instru-

---

(4th) 375 (Fed. C.A.), affirmed [1992] 2 W.W.R. 193 (S.C.C.) [see § 1.3.A.7 and § 2.2.E.6, which show that case at a later stage of appeal].
[91] Reconsideration refused (May 8, 1991), Doc. 20334 (S.C.C.).
[92] SOR/79-373.
[93] R.S.C. 1985, c. T-8.

ments involved in preventing the members of the Committee from exercising their activities.

The provision in the Regulations upon which the airport authorities relied in ordering the cessation of the Committee's activities reads as follows:

> 7. Subject to section 8, except as authorized in writing by the Minister, no person shall
>
> (a) conduct any business or undertaking, commercial or otherwise, at an airport;
> (b) advertise or solicit at an airport on his own behalf or on behalf of any person; or
> (c) fix, install or place anything at an airport for the purpose of any business or undertaking.[94]

The court gave this section a close reading and recalled the aims and objectives with which the members of the Committee had approached travellers at the airport, namely "to inform people on the premises of the existence of the Committee for the Commonwealth of Canada, and the ideology promoted by it."[95] On this basis, the court made one of the key determinations in its rather extensive judgment, to the effect that as "the mere fact of engaging in a discussion about a political ideology or of distributing political pamphlets to members of the public is not strictly speaking 'soliciting' within the meaning of s. 7(b) of the Regulations[,]"[96] section 7 of the Regulations did not apply to the facts of the case. As the airport authorities' decision was grounded on no other provision of statute or regulation than section 7, the court could then conclude only that the decision was not based on "law" in the sense of a reasonable limit on a fundamental freedom that could be "prescribed by law," as set out in section 1 of the *Charter*.

The court's line of reasoning gave rise to the question that if the decision to prevent the Committee's activities was not based on law, what was it based on? This, in turn, led the Chief Justice to define the concept of "policy" in the purest sense as that concept is intended to be understood in political law.

---

[94] *Government Airport Concession Operations Regulations*, s. 7, quoted at [1991] 1 S.C.R. 139 at 159i-160a.
[95] [1991] 1 S.C.R. 139 at 158 h.
[96] *Ibid.* at 161 j.

In my opinion, the limitation imposed on the respondents' freedom of expression arose from the action taken by the airport manager, a government official, when he ordered the respondents to cease their activities. Although this action was based on an established policy or internal directive, I do not think it can be concluded from this that there was in fact a "law" which could be justified under s. 1 of the *Charter*. The government's internal directives or policies differ essentially from statutes and regulations in that they are generally not published and so are not known to the public. Moreover, they are binding only on government officials and may be amended or cancelled at will. For these reasons, the established policy of the government cannot be the subject of the test under s. 1 of the *Charter*.[97]

Given this defining view, in the absence of a limit prescribed by law, the airport management's actions, based as they were on policy, the limitation under section 1 of the *Charter* could not be justified.

See also *Girard v. R.* (1994), 79 F.T.R. 219 (Fed. T.D.).

---

§ 1.8.B.4
Peet v. Canada (Attorney General)
Federal Court of Canada – Trial Division; April 20, 1994
[1994] 3 F.C. 128

While the informed observer would believe that the different characteristics of law and policy as instruments of governance result in divergent consequences arising out of their use, this is not always true. In order to do justice, the courts have, on occasion, ascribed to policy instruments elements drawn from the nature of legal instruments, in particular that of having a binding nature and of therefore being enforceable. Such rulings blur the law-policy distinction, but for the greater benefit of preventing the commission of an injustice or otherwise permitting an unjust result.

Peet, a federal public servant in what was at the material time the Department of Forestry, also established two companies. The Deputy Minister of Forestry made a finding on February 5, 1993, that Peet was in breach of the *Conflict of Interest and Post-Employment Code for the Public Service*. According to the Code, Peet would be required to

---

[97] *Ibid.* at 164 e-h.

divest or close down his private interests, or leave the Public Service. At first, Peet challenged the Deputy Minister's decision before the Public Service Staff Relations Board, but this tribunal held that it was without jurisdiction. Peet then made an application to the Federal Court, alleging that an unfair procedure was followed and that the Code was improperly applied. In the context of that litigation, the respondent made a motion to strike out Peet's application on the ground that the court did not have jurisdiction because the Code does not constitute law.

The matter for this court to decide was whether, even though the Code was not an instrument of law but of policy, it produced legal and therefore legally binding results. The court began its analysis by noting the fact that its decision would be clouded by the semantic difficulty. The predecessor instrument to the Code had been the *Public Servants Conflict of Interest Guidelines*,[98] promulgated by Order in Council and therefore without a doubt having the force of law.

> These were promulgated by order in council (SI/74-2, January 9, 1974) and thus there was no doubt they had the force of law. Counsel for the respondent argues that with the revocation of the Guidelines, and with the adoption in their place of the Code, conflict of interest ceased to be governed by provisions having the force of law. Counsel notes, ironically, that what carried the title of "Guidelines" had the force of law because they were promulgated as such, while what carries the title "Code" is not law because it has not been so established. A somewhat backwards use of language?[99]

By contrast, the newer Code was adopted upon the repeal of the Guidelines, pursuant to the Treasury Board's authority to act on matters of general administrative policy in the Public Service, and was definitely nothing more than a policy.

In support of its motion to strike out the application, the respondent relied on that law-policy distinction and pleaded that the court could engage in judicial review only of matters arising under instruments of law. The court added its own interpretation of the Department's motive for this: "The respondent's main concern, as I understand it,

---

[98] SI/74-2; January 9, 1974.
[99] [1994] 3 F.C. 128 at 133 a-c.

is that if decisions under the Code are reviewable, all managerial decisions within the civil service will also be reviewable."[100]

The court's first reason for decision was that it was not the name, or title, or designation of an instrument that was determinative of its characteristic as being enforceable or not, but rather whether the language it contained was mandatory or not. It illustrates this point by reference to the *Environmental Assessment and Review Process Guidelines Order* (EARPGO), which had been held to have the force of law despite being called "guidelines." The EARPGO was distinguished, however, because it was eventually promulgated by Order in Council.[101] Pursuing the matter further, the court relied on the judgment of the majority in the *Nguyen* case, which said that implied duties arising from policy instruments (such as in that case the Immigration Manual) could create an imposition of a duty on public officials and could thus give rise to the use of prerogative writs such as mandamus. The conclusion drawn from this reasoning in the *Nguyen* case, which the court adopted here, was that "Not all duties imposed by law are express. An implied duty is nonetheless enforceable."[102]

The court explained its force to impute the nature of a legally binding obligation to the Code by referring to the serious consequences that the Code's application could have on Peet. Decisions having such serious consequences were held to have traditionally been subject to judicial review. Thus, the Department's motion to strike out Peet's application was dismissed.

---

§ 1.8.B.5
Pereira v. Canada (Minister of Citizenship & Immigration)
Federal Court of Canada – Trial Division; October 12, 1994
(1994), 86 F.T.R. 43

Pereira, an immigrant from Portugal who fell into the "backlog group," was found by an immigration officer to have insufficient humanitarian and compassionate grounds to be granted permanent residence. The alternative was for her to apply for a visa in the normal

---

[100] *Ibid.* at 137 b.
[101] SOR/84-467.
[102] *Supra* note 99 at 136 e.

manner. The decision was made on the basis of notes made by the interviewing officers in the course of the review of Pereira's situation. Indeed, the notes were treated as the decision itself. Pereira applied for judicial review. The Federal Court dismissed.

One of the three arguments considered by the Federal Court of Canada – Trial Division related to the interviewing officers' use, in the notes, of language that was said to indicate fettering of their own discretion. The applicant relied on the discussion of departmental policy guidelines in the *Yhap* case [see § 2.2.E.3] as guidance regarding the exercise of discretion, trying to assimilate the effect of guidelines to that of laws. Here, the court reacted by saying that reliance on *Yhap* would imply that guidelines have the status of legal norms, and it concluded that they do not; they are "not more than guidance for officers, with the intent of seeking a reasonable measure of consistency in the exercise of discretion."[103] It then went on to clarify that guidelines cannot be established as equivalent to law. The interviewers' notes could thus not fetter their discretion.

---

§ 1.8.B.6
Ainsley Financial Corp. v. Ontario (Securities Commission)
Ontario Court of Appeal; December 21, 1994
(1994), 121 D.L.R. (4th) 79

It is one of the foundations of this study that, among the types of instruments available for governance, there is a qualitative difference between legal instruments and those based on the organizational intention and convenience of a public body, namely its policy-making power. That qualitative difference resides principally in the binding or non-binding nature of the instrument. In the eyes of the law, and therefore in the view of democracy, only legal instruments are inherently and fully binding. Is this assumption correct? The Ontario Court (General Division) and the Ontario Court of Appeal agree.

The Ontario Securities Commission was established by a statute of the Legislative Assembly[104] and given certain powers by that statute. The statute was supplemented by regulations. Both these types of instruments were compulsory and binding. In addition to them, the

---

[103] (1994), 86 F.T.R. 43 at 46, para. 11.
[104] *Securities Act*, R.S.O. 1990, c. S.5.

Commission issued Policy Statements intended for those who conducted business of the type regulated by the Commission. These
Policy Statements were being interpreted and used by the Commission so as to force certain companies to conduct their business in the
manner directed by the Commission. Among other things, one instrument in particular, Policy Statement No. 10, was "designed to
curb the hard-sell tactics of penny stockbrokers."[105] Ainsley and a
number of other companies sued the Ontario Securities Commission
to have Policy Statement No. 10 declared void.

The Ontario Court (General Division) looked first at the purpose of
the instrument. It noted that the Commission had found evidence of
abusive and unfair sales practices in the marketing of penny stocks,
which was contrary to the Commission's role in protecting the in-
vesting public and in preserving the integrity of the capital market.
Next, it examined the language of the instrument and found that it
was inconsistent with the powers of the Commission.

> Policy 1.10 in [sic] not a "guideline", in my view; it is a mandatory
> requirement of a regulatory nature.
>
> . . .
>
> In spite of the efforts of the commission to cast Policy 1.10 in the light of
> a mere guideline, the policy is mandatory and regulatory in nature, in
> my view. Its language, the practical effect of failing to comply with its
> tenets, and the evidence with respect to the expectations of the commis-
> sion and staff regarding its implementation, all confirm this.
>
> The policy is not simply, as it purports to be, "a guide to identify what
> the Commission believes are appropriate business practices to assist
> securities dealers and their employees in satisfying their obligations
> under the Act in connection with the sale of penny stocks", focusing in
> that respect on the use of two forms, namely the risk disclosure statement
> and the suitability statement. Its effect is to impose a positive obligation
> upon securities dealers to follow those practices, thus *creating their status*
> as "appropriate practices". Failure to comply raises the spectre of disci-
> plinary proceedings. The juxtaposition between the statement of the
> commission's belief that the business practices set out in the policy
> should be adopted in the public interest—to be found in the section of

---

[105] Thomas Claridge, "Judge quashes OSC policy," *The Globe & Mail*, August 14, 1993,
p. B-1.

the policy entitled "Purpose of the Policy"—and the reference to the Draconian powers of the commission under s. 27(1) of the Act—in the same paragraph—is telling in this respect.

This is regulation of the conduct of those engaging in the business of trading in penny stocks.[106]

The court of first instance was not satisfied to invalidate the offending policy statement on the ground that the Commission did not have jurisdiction to issue it, and that this constituted legislating by the back door. It went further, in framing the issue in terms of the rule of law. Citing first from a text on securities regulation, it said, "It is thus impossible to escape the conclusion that policy statements must not be used [to] create substantive legal requirements of a legislative or regulatory character. Any other conclusion would be inconsistent with the Rule of Law."[107]

The writing of an even more eminent legal scholar was referred to.

> *Every act of governmental power,* i.e. every act which affects the legal rights, duties or liberties of any person, *must be shown to have a strictly legal pedigree.* The affected person may always resort to the courts of law, and *if the legal pedigree is not found to be perfectly in order the court will invalidate the act,* which [the person] can then safely disregard. [Emphasis in original.][108]

In sum, what the court found was that the Policy Statement was invalid because the body applying it was using it as if it had a binding quality, which it in fact did not have. In this, the policy instrument was in breach of the principle that a legal rule must be based on the legal right to create that rule, even where the purpose of the rule is to apply good public policy.

The Commission appealed and the Ontario Court of Appeal declared that it would not rework the ground so fully tilled by the trial court. Nevertheless, it stated the law very explicitly on this issue. The court

---

[106] (1993), 106 D.L.R. (4th) 507 (Ont. Gen. Div. [Commercial List]) at 520 c, 520 e-521 a.

[107] *Ibid.* at 525 b, citing from Professor Jeffrey G. MacIntosh, "The Excessive Use of Policy Statements by Canadian Securities Regulators" (1992) 1 Corporate Financing 19.

[108] *Supra* note 106 at 528 f, citing from Wade, *Administrative Law* at 23-24.

gave to instruments such as the subject Policy Statement the collective title of "non-statutory statement." These were, it said, designed to inform, to guide and to further the goals of the Commission. It also held that bodies such as the Commission may issue such non-binding instruments for sound administrative practice, without specific statutory authority.

The court offered an authoritative characterization of such non-statutory instruments.

> Non-statutory instruments, like guidelines, are not necessarily issued pursuant to any statutory grant of the power to issue such instruments. Rather, they are an administrative tool available to the regulator so that it can exercise its statutory authority and fulfil its regulatory mandate in a fairer, more open and more efficient manner. While there may be considerable merit in providing for resort to non-statutory instruments in the regulator's enabling statute, such a provision is not a prerequisite for the use of those instruments by the regulator. The case law provides ample support for the opinion expressed by the Ontario Task Force on Securities Regulation: Responsibility and Responsiveness (June, 1994) at pp. 11-12:
>
>> A sound system of securities regulation is more than legislation and regulations. Policy statements, rulings, speeches, communiqués, and Staff notes are all valuable parts of a mature and sophisticated regulatory system.[109]

The conclusion to be drawn from this is that a guideline remains a guideline even if those at whom it is directed and who are affected by it voluntarily conform to it.

The important element of this court's analysis included reference to the language of instruments.

> There is no bright line which always separates a guideline from a mandatory provision having the effect of law. At the centre of the regulatory continuum one shades into the other. Nor is the language of the particular instrument determinative. There is no magic to the use of the word "guideline", just as no definitive conclusion can be drawn from the use of the word "regulate". An examination of the language of the instrument is but a part, albeit an important part, of the characterization pro-

---

[109] (1994), 121 D.L.R. (4th) 79 at 83 e-g.

cess. In analyzing the language of the instrument, the focus must be on the thrust of the language considered in its entirety and not on isolated words or passages.[110]

In addressing this issue, the court ventured into the confusion caused in political law that is more fully developed in section 1.17 of this text.

The vital element of the characterization of a "policy"-type instrument is its binding nature *vis-à-vis* legal instruments. Here also, this court provided a significant ruling:

> A non-statutory instrument can have no effect in the face of contradictory statutory provision or regulation:
>
> . . .
>
> Most importantly, for present purposes, a non-statutory instrument cannot impose mandatory requirements enforceable by sanction; that is, the regulator cannot issue *de facto* laws disguised as guidelines. Iacobucci J. put it this way in *Pezim* at p. 409:
>
>> However, it is important to note that the Commission's policy-making role is limited. By that, I mean that their policies cannot be elevated to the status of law; they are not to be treated as legal pronouncements absent legal authority mandating such treatment.[111]

Two factors were singled out in support of this characterization based on the effect of the subject instruments. The first is its format. While general statements of principles, standards, criteria or factors intended to elucidate and give direction to those intended to be addressed by the instrument are acceptable uses of policy-based instruments, detailed codes of conduct reading like statutes or regulations are not acceptable. The second factor is the coercive nature of the instrument. In order to remain a policy rather than, as here, crossing the line into becoming an unauthorized legal instrument, an instrument must not make a link between the power of the public body issuing the instrument to sanction in the public interest and its pronouncement that the practices set out in the instrument accord with

---

[110] *Ibid.* at 84 f-85 a.
[111] *Ibid.* at 84 a and c-d.

the public interest. Such a connection would give the policy a coercive tone and substance that it is not entitled to have.

In the end, the Policy Statement that the court looked at here failed because it imposed a *de facto* legislative scheme that the Securities Commission could not impose without statutory authority. As the court put it, it had crossed the Rubicon.

1.8.C—POLICY ISSUES

See *Yeung v. Canada (Minister of Employment & Immigration)* (1992), 17 Imm. L.R. (2d) 191 (Fed. T.D.); *Ontario (Ministry of Community & Social Services) v. O.P.S.E.U.* (1992), 11 O.R. (3d) 558 (Ont. C.A.); *Canada (Attorney General) v. P.S.A.C.*, [1993] 1 S.C.R. 941 (S.C.C.); *I.B.E.W., Local 894 v. Ellis-Don Ltd.*, 194 D.L.R. (4th) 385 (S.C.C.) and *Schreiber (Township) v. Superior Greenstone District School Board* (2002), [2002] O.J. No. 3303 (Ont. Div. Ct.).

1.8.D—VARIETIES OF POLICY

See *Furey v. Conception Bay Centre Roman Catholic School Board* (1993), 108 Nfld. & P.E.I.R. 328 (Nfld. C.A.).

---

§ 1.8.D.1[112]
Regular, Re
Newfoundland Supreme Court – Trial Division; July 17, 1995
(1995) 132 Nfld. & P.E.I.R. 310

Complaints of unprofessional conduct against Regular, a barrister and solicitor, were considered by the Law Society of Newfoundland. These complaints were dismissed. However, without giving reasons, the Law Society did not exercise its discretionary power under the *Law Society Act*, enabling it to award costs against the complainant or against the Law Society itself. Regular appealed that part of the Law Society's decision regarding costs to the Supreme Court of New-foundland – Trial Division.

---

[112] Cross-reference to § 1.7.1.

The *Law Society Act* does not declare that costs follow the cause. At trial, the Law Society testified that it did not have a policy concerning the payment of costs by lawyers against whom complaints had been filed, either in the event of a finding of guilt or if the facts indicated a not guilty finding. The evidence showed that of the complaints considered by the Law Society over the previous 20 years, it had made orders for the payment of costs by those lawyers against whom complaints had been, in the overwhelming majority of cases where there was a finding of guilt. No order was made in the remaining cases that concluded in findings of guilt, as well as in all of the cases where the finding was absence of guilt.

While the court accepted the evidence of the absence of a policy, it concluded that the consistency of the practices of the Law Society, which it went so far as to call "uniformity of results" could lead to the inference of the existence of one. This inferred policy affected the issue of whether the Law Society properly exercised its discretion in that if the Law Society started from the proposition that costs would normally not be ordered in the case of a finding of not guilty, the inferred policy fettered or pre-determined the exercise of the discretion. The court therefore sent the matter back to the Law Society to have it provide reasons for its decision.

See also *Nieboer v. Canada (Attorney General)* (1996), 121 F.T.R. 29 (Fed. T.D.).

1.8.E— GUIDELINES

See *Turner-Lienaux v. Nova Scotia (Attorney General)* (1992), 115 N.S.R. (2d) 200 (N.S. T.D.), affirmed (1993), 48 C.C.E.L. 128 (N.S. C.A.), additional reasons at (1992), 115 N.S.R. (2d) 200 at 211 (N.S. T.D.).

1.8.F— DIRECTIVES

See *Canadian Museum of Nature v. Bélanger* (1995), 107 F.T.R. 241 (Fed. T.D.).

1.9 ISSUE: PUBLIC POLICY

See *Walkerville Brewing Co. v. Mayrand*, [1929] 2 D.L.R. 945 (Ont. C.A.).

---

§ 1.9.1
Geiger v. London Monenco Consultants Ltd.
Ontario Court of Appeal; July 30, 1992
(1992), 9 O.R. (3d) 509[113]

This was a case involving the rights of workers protected under the Ontario *Human Rights Code, 1981*[114] (the Code) in which the court dealt with two issues, only one of which attracts the attention of those dealing with political law. That is the matter of public policy and of enactments that express public policy. The other issue was that of discrimination in employment.

In 1982, Geiger, an engineer, and Barboutsis, an architectural planner, were hired by London Monenco to work in a joint venture at an Ontario Hydro project at a remote site in Atikokan. Both men were bachelors. It was London Monenco's policy, which was reflected in its employment contracts, that only married employees would be reimbursed family related travel expenses. It was only in April 1983 that the two employees attended a human rights seminar sponsored by Ontario Hydro, at which they learned that the Code provided for equal treatment without discrimination because of marital status. They lodged a complaint, to which the employer's response was that at the time of hiring, both men were told what they could be entitled to and had accepted the terms of their respective contracts, as these had been offered to them. The claim was rejected by a board of inquiry and by the Divisional Court.

The Ontario Court of Appeal allowed the appeal that the Human Rights Commission raised to it on behalf of the complainants. It restated that the company's policy infringed the complainants' rights under the relevant provision of the Code, which, among other things, guaranteed equal treatment with respect to employment without dis-

---

[113] Leave to appeal refused (1993), 151 N.R. 390n (S.C.C.).
[114] S.O. 1981, c. 53, currently R.S.O. 1990, c. H.19.

crimination because of marital status. In the court's opinion, the critical question was whether the company's policy would be justified and whether marital status was a reasonable and *bona fide* qualification because of the nature of the employment. In formulating its reply, the court started off by characterizing the Code in terms of its objectives.

> In construing a provision of this nature in the context of the broad public policy purposes of the *Code*, the exception should be interpreted narrowly so as not to diminish or undermine the right to non-discrimination in employment and the effectiveness of the *Code* in this regard any more than the specific language of the provision compels.[115]

The court then went further, making several points of significance for this study. It declared that private parties such as the ones litigating here are not free to contract out of a public enactment. It also added the necessary corollary, namely that:

> A private contract agreeing to a discriminatory policy or practice contrary to the *Code* cannot serve as a ground for holding that the discriminatory policy or practice is not in violation of the *Code*.[116]

The implication of these holdings is to reinforce the binding nature of this law at the very least, and more generically of law in general. However, the ruling merits further examination for what it says about public policy.

The sense of the court's statements is that the Code, a statute, is a public policy statement or pronouncement. This is an element of explanation, if not quite definition of the notion of public policy, but it engenders pertinent questions. Are all laws statements of public policy, or only some? Moreover, if some or all laws are the parliamentary expression of public policy, does that imply that instruments of governance that are entitled policies can be considered governmental or executive expressions of public policy?

Beyond these thoughts, we are still left with the fundamental inquiry of what is public policy in the eyes of the courts. It is quite rare for a court to engage directly in an exercise of precise definition of a concept

---

[115] (1992), 9 O.R. (3d) 509 at 516 d.
[116] *Ibid.* at 519-520 a.

as vast as "public policy," especially as that concept permeates the bounds between law, public administration and politics. Observers must thus seek the meaning intended to be assigned to this type of concept from other methods of explanation used by the courts, in particular their reliance on precedent. In this case, in order to explain its understanding of the concept, the Ontario Court of Appeal referred to a decision of the Supreme Court of Canada in which the judiciary's most senior members came closest to a definition.

> Although the Code contains no explicit restriction on such contracting out, it is nevertheless a public statute and it constitutes public policy in Ontario as appears from a reading of the statute itself and as declared in the preamble. It is clear from the authorities, both in Canada and in England, that parties are not competent to contract themselves out of the provisions of such enactments and that contracts having such effect are void, as contrary to public policy...The *Ontario Human Rights Code* has been enacted by the Legislature of the Province of Ontario for the benefit of the community at large and of its individual members and clearly falls within that category of enactment which may not be waived or varied by private contract; therefore this argument cannot receive effect.[117]

The idea to be retained from this precedent is that the Code was enacted for the benefit of the community at large and for that of its individual members. We may therefore conclude that public policy is the complex of goals and objectives adopted by society for the benefit of the community and that of its individual members. We can also establish the link that law as enacted by the legislature constitutes the highest form of formalized expression of those goals and objectives.

See also *Basu v. R.* (1991), [1992] 2 F.C. 38 (Fed. T.D.) and *Apotex Inc. v. Manitoba (Lieutenant-Governor in Council)* (1994), 52 C.P.R. (3d) 135 (Man. Q.B.).

---

[117] *Ontario (Human Rights Commission) v. Etobicoke (Borough)*, [1982] 1 S.C.R. 202 at 213-214, quoted at (1992), 9 O.R. (3d) 509 at 520 a-b.

§ 1.9.2
Law Society of Upper Canada v. Ontario (Attorney General)
Ontario Court (General Division); January 6, 1995
(1995), 21 O.R. (3d) 666

The issue in this case is the determination of who in society, and within the State, is empowered to make public policy. In deciding this controversy, the court broke new ground by defining the distinctions between the functions of making public policy and of governance.

The Law Society of Upper Canada (the Society) has been a self-governing body since the time of its establishment in 1797.[118] In the early 1990s, as it approached its 200th anniversary, the Society wanted to change the way it elected its governing body, known as the benchers, to conduct its internal workings. There was some doubt as to whether this required a legislative amendment. The Society's preference in effecting this change was to rely on its rule-making powers above, rather than having to request an amendment to its current legislation.[119] The Attorney-General supported the Society's position. The Society obtained a legal opinion to the effect that it would be able to act according to its wish, but some members of the Society opposed this method of change. The Society thus applied to the Ontario Court (General Division) for a determination of the question of law involved. In dispute was section 62(1) of the *Law Society Act* and the formulation of the question was whether the Convocation, the meeting of the benchers convened for the purpose of transacting the business of the Society, had, under its power to make rules relating to the affairs of the Society, authority to make rules with respect to the regional election of benchers. The court expressed the focus of the question as follows: "The issue raised by this application is whether the legislature has conferred this power on Convocation to enable the Society internally, by its rule-making powers, to exercise it."[120]

One of the points of interest to be noted is that this is one of the rare cases in which all participants, clients, solicitors, the intervenor, as well as of course the judge, are all lawyers, with intimate knowledge

---

[118] *An Act For the Better Regulating the Practice of Law*, 37 Geo. III (1797), c. 13.
[119] *Law Society Act*, R.S.O. 1990, c. L.8.
[120] (1995), 21 O.R. (3d) 666 at 668 g.

of the subject matter and with a greater than usual stake in the out-come.

The court first noted that the procedural and technical aspects of bencher elections were abrogated from earlier versions of the *Law Society Act* and transferred to the jurisdiction of the Convocation only in 1970. It then looked closely at the provisions in the current text of that Act that deals with making rules relating to "the business of the Society" to see what, in its opinion, the legislature had meant by that phrase. It concluded that the business of the Society is the governance of the legal profession, which includes the matters obviously pertain-ing to the integral workings of the professional association, such as education, admission, discipline and a compensation fund. On this basis, the court reached the first ground of its conclusion, that bencher elections do not constitute business of the Society.

> In my view, the determination by Convocation that the election of bench-ers may take place on a regional basis does not constitute business of the Society. In a broad sense, the business of the Society is the governance of the legal profession which includes such obvious matters as the edu-cation, admission and discipline of the members of the Society, as well as the compensation fund. It is the benchers on whom the legislature has conferred the power of governance. However, the legislature has re-tained the power to determine how those that govern are to be elected by those whom they are empowered to govern. Therefore, the business of the Society does not encompass the very basic determination of how those that govern are to be elected. In other words, the composition of Convocation, by whom its members are to be elected and the regions of the province they are to represent, do not constitute business of the Society and, therefore, do not come within the general rule-making pow-ers conferred by s. 62(1). In this regard, one must not lose sight of the basic fact that in delegating to Convocation the legislative function of governing the legal profession, Convocation remains under the control of, and accountable to, the legislature.[121]

The court further defined its analysis by examining the scope of the rule-making power delegated by the Legislature to the Society. In its perception, the power of the Convocation was restricted to matters of administration and to the domestic affairs of the Society as well as to the matters of policy not contained in the *Law Society Act*. The key to the entire judgment is that by contrast to the foregoing category,

---

[121] *Ibid.* at 677 b-e.

the court held that the Legislature's role was in relation to the governance of the members of the Society, which it entitled "a fundamental matter of policy." This distinction can best be understood as being synonymous with a reservation of matters of public policy to the legislature. In the court's view, only the sovereign Legislature could deal with matters of public policy, in this instance relating to the legal profession. We should understand the distinction drawn by the court to mean that the public governance of the legal profession was a matter of public policy, reserved for the Legislature. What had been delegated to the Society was only the power over its internal governance.

This distinction can also be presented in a different fashion. The legislature's public policy domain consisted of substantive matters, while the Society's included only procedural ones.

In order to underline the critical importance of the question of who may make public policy, the ratio of the court merits being quoted directly.

> The governance of the members of the Society is a fundamental matter of policy which must be regulated by primary or subordinate legislation. As the members of the Society are governed by the benchers whom they elect, it follows that any fundamental or substantive change in how the benchers are to be elected is a matter of policy for the legislature.[122]

The judgment of the court in this matter had a direct and tangible outcome in respect to the Law Society of Upper Canada. The election of benchers that took place in April 1995 was conducted under the rules pre-existing the Society's application to the court. The next election was held in 1999 and by then the Society successfully amended the election system, but only on the basis of amendments to the *Law Society Act* sought of the Legislature.

The importance and influence of this case is, however, broader than its effect on the Society's electoral system above. The judgment can be held as authority for the principle that the legislature is the sole source of public policy in general. This is so in part because the court reached its conclusions comparatively, by reference to the statutes dealing with several other professional bodies. More to the point, it

---

[122] *Ibid.* at 678 d-e.

relied extensively on the McRuer Report.[123] That report contained a section on self-governing professions and occupations but its conclusions dealt with and affected the entire political/legal system of Ontario. Reliance on McRuer's conclusions shows the court's intention to arrive at conclusions of its own that can be generalized.[124]

See also international comparison *Ayala v. U.S.*, 980 F.2d 1342 (10th. Cir., 1992).

1.10 ISSUE: PUBLIC CONVENIENCE AND GENERAL POLICY

See *P.I.P.S.C. v. Canada (Attorney General)*, [1995] 2 F.C. 73 (Fed. T.D.).

1.11 ISSUE: POLITICS

§ 1.11.1
R. v. CFRB Ltd.
Ontario Court of Appeal; January 30, 1976
(1976), 30 C.C.C. (2d) 386

On October 21, 1971, a provincial general election was held in Ontario. The previous afternoon, a well-known and influential radio announcer discussed campaign issues and the likely outcome of the election on his program. Among other things, he commented that William Davis, the Provincial Premier and leader of the Progressive Conservative Party, which was again one of the contenders for office, was "a man of decision" and went on to state that this was "surely an asset in any leader." This statement was made in defiance of subsection 28(1) of the *Broadcasting Act*:

---

[123] Royal Commission of Inquiry into Civil Rights, Report, 1968.
[124] For an interesting analysis of this judgment, see "Legislative or Judicial Determination of Public Policy?" (1996) 5 R.A.L. 27.

Prohibitions and Offences

28. (1) No broadcaster shall broadcast, and no licensee or a broadcasting receiving undertaking shall receive a broadcast of a program, advertisement or announcement of a partisan character in relation to

(a) a referendum, or
(b) an election of a member of the House of Commons, the legislature or a province or the council of a municipal corporation

that is being held or is to be held within the area normally served by the broadcasting undertaking of the broadcaster or such licensee, on the day of any such referendum or election or on the one day immediately preceding the day of any such referendum or election.

In recognition of the influence of broadcasting on the outcome of election campaigns, this provision had been adopted in 1968 to avoid one-sided political commentary by broadcasters. In the particular medium under discussion, section 28 was reinforced by a provision in the *Radio (A.M.) Broadcasting Regulations* that contemplated radio time on an equitable basis for all political parties, thus hopefully eradicating unfair electoral advantage.[125]

CFRB was charged with having unlawfully broadcast a program or announcement of a partisan character in relation to an election. An initial defence based on the constitutional invalidity of section 28 failed. On the merits of the charge, the Provincial Court and then the Ontario Court of Appeal had to determine what elements constituted the partisan character of a broadcast. These courts' decisions were set against two larger issues: first, what is the nature of partisanship in political speech and political activity in general and, second, what is the link between directive legislation on partisan speech and the principle of freedom of expression.

The broadcaster's defence was based on the allegation that partisanship resulted from an affiliation or a nexus of the subject broadcast

---

[125] In the revision of the *Broadcasting Act* effected some years later by S.C. 1991, s. 28 was dropped. The reasoning was that other provisions relating to both political broadcasts and to broadcasting blackouts during election campaigns had been incorporated into the *Canada Elections Act*. Nevertheless, in the area of jurisdiction that remained with the Canadian Radio-Television and Telecommunications Commission, the agency regulating broadcasting, the Commission still applies the doctrine of equitable access to the airwaves among competing political parties.

with a political party or candidate. It also contended that the purpose of section 28 was a restrictive one, namely to prevent a party or a candidate "from introducing a new issue into the election without affording the other side an opportunity to reply."[126] It even tried to assimilate the quality of partisanship with inaccuracy.

Both courts rejected these arguments and established the test of partisanship on more objective criteria, thus helping to provide a judicially based understanding of politics. The Provincial Court declared that partisanship does not depend on the presence of a sponsor, but rather on the inherently one-sided, biased or prejudiced nature of the broadcast itself. The Court of Appeal added to this definition that even in the absence of a connection between the speaker and any political party or recognizable faction, a broadcast is partisan if it "intended to favour one candidate over the other or others, in an election, or to favour one point of view over another, in a referendum."[127] The judgment also distinguished between the reporting of news and the presentation of an individual's political commentary in which he expressed support for a specific candidate or party, indicating that only the latter was partisan. It clarified that the main characteristic of unpartisan statements is objectivity. As a final consideration, although not quite precise criterion, the court added that partisan comments are such as may have had an influence on voters, although the success or absence of influence would not determine the outcome of the case.

The application of this assessment, along with the court's reaction to the announcer's intentional defiance of section 28 as a stupid rule and one being discriminatory in favour of newspapers, resulted in the conviction being upheld.[128]

---

[126] (1976), 30 C.C.C. (2d) 386 at 388.

[127] *Ibid.* at 390-391.

[128] The aspect of s. 28 of the *Broadcasting Act* that operated as a blackout of partisan programming immediately prior to the conduct of polling, designed to afford voters a time for uninfluenced reflection on their political choice, also inspired what were then ss. 48 and 213 of the *Canada Elections Ac*, R.S.C. 1985, c. E-2. In these provisions, the blackout was expressed to be not on political broadcasts, but rather on political advertising. Section 213 was struck down by the Alberta Court of Appeal in *Canada (Attorney General) v. Somerville* (1996), 136 D.L.R. (4th) 205 (Alta. C.A.), as being contrary to § 2(b) (freedom of expression), and § 2(d) (freedom of association) of the *Canadian Charter of Rights and Freedoms*. The outcome of the CFRB case might also have been different if it had been decided after the *Charter's* adoption.

While this issue of partisanship is closely related to judicial consideration of the concept of politics and matters political, there are clear distinctions between the two notions. The courts hold the political domain to include the entire realm of public activity related to the securing and use of State power. Within that framework, partisan political activities are those undertaken by one of the competitors for power, on its own behalf. Nevertheless in actual practice, the expressions "political" and "partisan" are often used interchangeably.

---

§ 1.11.2
Naskapi-Montagnais Innu Assn. v. Canada (Minister of National Defence)
Federal Court of Canada – Trial Division; April 12, 1990
[1990] 3 F.C. 381[129]

While the earlier cases in this section deal with the definition of politics, in this instance, the court examined the nature of obligations arising from political life, although unfortunately in a too cursory manner, leaving it for alert observers to complete the thoughts so initially sketched out.

As long ago as 1976, Canada started to make it possible for its NATO partners to use the airspace over Labrador for training military pilots. On February 13, 1986, the Minister of National Defence took a decision to authorize the air forces of the United States, the United Kingdom, the Federal Republic of Germany, and the Netherlands to train out of Goose Bay and to overfly portions of Labrador and northern Québec for purposes of low-level training and target practice. As it was apparent that this project needed environmental assessment, the Minister of National Defence referred the matter to the Minister of the Environment. On July 8, 1986, the latter established a panel under the *Environmental Assessment and Review Process Guidelines Order* (EARPGO) and, pursuant to the procedures set out in that Order, the panel started its assessment.

The Minister of National Defence authorized the flights projected in the decision of February 13, 1986, to proceed prior to the conclusion of work by the environmental assessment panel and the issue by it of a final report. On this basis, the plaintiff, an association of native

---

[129] Additional reasons at (1990), 5 C.E.L.R. (N.S.) 287 at 315 (Fed. T.D.).

peoples, some of whom were customary hunters in the area to be overflown, presented an application to quash the decision of the Minister of National Defence and to prevent the Minister from making other decisions before the environmental assessment process mandated by the EARPGO was to have been completed.

The court accepted that the provisions of the EARPGO were mandatory. It determined that the more precise issue in this case was whether, once a referral had been made to a panel, "an obligation arises so that the initiating department or Minister must not proceed with the project under review, until the referral process and review has been completed."[130] The applicant argued that if a referral could be made to a panel and the project be allowed to proceed at the same time, the whole purpose of the Order would be undermined.

The court perceived that this case had arisen in the context of a disputed but as yet unsettled land claim. At first, it admitted its own hesitation but then it provided a remarkably subtle ruling. In a bow to the principle of the rational sequence of decisions in public administration, it held that the course of action advocated by the applicant would be the prudent one for a department to follow and that "in most cases, this might very well occur as a matter of practice."[131] Nevertheless, basing itself on the actual text of the Order, the court concluded that nothing in the EARPGO expressly required that a project be halted until the panel's review is completed. Indeed, the court used legal reasoning very similar to that prevailing in injunction cases. It contrasted the considerable prejudice that would ensue from issuing the order sought and the resulting damage to the air forces and on the residents of Goose Bay, with the minimal prejudice that the refusal of the order would cause to a small and undetermined number of natives when intermittently hunted in the area. On the basis of this reasoning, the court dismissed the application.

For the purpose of this study, the real significance of the case flows from that part of the *ratio* in which the court sets out the difference between obligations on the Minister of National Defence arising from legal sources, that is from the EARPGO, and from other obligations, of a political nature, also incumbent upon him.

---

130 [1990] 3 F.C. 381 at 398 (i).
131 *Ibid.* at 403 (b).

> In addition, an implied mandatory obligation to halt the proposal does not accord well with the general scheme of the Order and with its other provisions. Under the Order initiating departments and Ministers are able to ignore whatever recommendations a Panel might make. They, of course, do so at their peril in so far as public opinion is concerned. Under the scheme of the Order it is the watchful eye of public opinion which is to operate as the leverage to ensure that environmentally responsible decisions are taken. It is entirely consistent with this mechanism, then, that the regime which operates during the course of the panel review process, in so far as any obligation may exist not to proceed with the project is concerned, would be of a similar nature. In my view, any obligation not to proceed while the project is under review also depends for "enforcement" on the pressure of public opinion and the adverse publicity which will attach to a contrary course of action.[132]

As an institution of the State charged with applying and interpreting the law only, the court felt bound to limit itself to mentioning the existence of such obligations of a political nature as arise from public opinion and publicity; that is, from the political will of the people. Analysts of political law can allow themselves, however, to elaborate the concepts that flow naturally from the words of the judgment. Political obligations arise from the undertakings of public officials such as Ministers, even when they are implicit. Here, the actions of the two ministers in submitting the environmental assessment to a panel created implicit undertakings in public opinion; that is, in the political sphere. The submission of the project created a non-legal, political presumption that the panel would produce a result in the form of a recommendation to proceed or not, as well as a further presumption that the ministers would act on the basis of that resulting recommendation. The public opinion and publicity relating to the results of the panel's work would also support the enforcement of the recommendations.

While the court could not base its holding on the political obligations, it could note them prominently, thereby reminding the ministers not only that their breach of such obligations could entail a political price, but also that political obligations could be infused with ethical, perhaps quasi-legal, elements. It is thus possible to say that political obligations complement legal ones even if the courts regard them as subordinate to the law.

---

[132] *Ibid.* at 403 (h) to 404 (a).

§ 1.11.3[133]
R. v. Canadian Broadcasting Corp.
Ontario Court (General Division); May 12, 1992
(1992), 72 C.C.C. (3d) 545[134]

Canada's 34th federal general election was held on November 21, 1988. In preparation for that event, nationally televised debates of the leaders of the three traditionally major political parties were held on October 24 in French and October 25 in English. A member of another formation, the Green Party of Canada, brought a private prosecution against the Canadian Broadcasting Corporation and other broadcasting enterprises, alleging that their refusal to include the leader of this party in the debate constituted an infringement of section 8 of the *Television Broadcasting Regulations, 1987*. At trial, the judge dismissed the charge on the ground that the referenced provision did not apply to a nationally televised leaders' debate. In upholding the trial judgment, the Ontario Court (General Division) conducted an extensive review of the statutory and regulatory provisions relating to broadcasting of matters political. The construction of the true meaning of these texts of law offered the court an opportunity to define the concept of what broadcasts are "political." From this characterization of political broadcasts, we can glean a more general notion of what matters the courts consider to be political, at least in the electoral context.

Section 8 of the *Television Broadcasting Regulations, 1987* is worded as follows:

Political Broadcasts

8. During an election period, a licensee shall allocate time for the broadcasting of programs, advertisements or announcements of a partisan political character on an equitable basis to all accredited political parties and rival candidates represented in the election or referendum.

One of the central issues of this case was whether a debate among the leaders of some or all political parties constituted a program,

---

[133] Cross-reference to § 1.21.1 and 5.9.5.
[134] Affirmed (1993), 51 C.P.R. (3d) 192 (Ont. C.A.), leave to appeal refused (1994), 72 O.A.C. 158 (note) (S.C.C.).

advertisement or announcement of a partisan political character within the meaning of the section. The court held that it did not. It reached this conclusion on the basis of a distinction between politically partisan broadcasts and programs containing political content. Programming that is political in the sense of partisan was defined as being for the express purpose of conveying the policies of a party, designed to persuade voters to support it and its candidates. Such programs are "biased, prejudiced and one sided, intended to favour one party over the other or others in its presentation of a political viewpoint."[135] They are of a self-promotional nature, conceived, produced and controlled exclusively by or on behalf of a party.

By contrast, programs containing political content were described as being informational. These include reporting or coverage by way of newscasts, interviews, documentaries, public affairs programs, and on-the-spot coverage of news events such as political conventions and leaders' debates. A debate in particular "includes the expression of politically partisan points of view," but is not "devoted exclusively to the views of a single party or candidate."[136] Such broadcasts are conceived, written organized, edited, and produced by networks and broadcasts exercising their own editorial judgment.

This case can be taken as a direct elaboration of the one involving CFRB. The court has affixed the label of "political" to all broadcasts—that is, both partisan or persuasive ones as well as informational or analytical ones—that deal with the competition between opposing parties or factions for the achievement, exercise and maintenance of State power. We may therefore conclude that in the judicial view, not only in broadcasting but more generally as well, politics or "matters political" include the entire range of activities aiming at control of the State. This is precisely the meaning of politics and matters "political" that is applicable in the concept of political law. It is a comprehensive view of the concept, according to which politics is the entire sphere of activity relating to public power and to the State.

---

[135] (1992), 72 C.C.C. (3d) 545 at 574 a.
[136] *Ibid.* at 574 b.

§ 1.11.4
Dick v. Dick
Ontario Court (General Division); January 22, 1993
(1993), 46 R.F.L. (3d) 219[137]

This is a divorce case and proceedings under Ontario's *Family Law Act*,[138] regarding in particular the valuation of the pension of the ex-husband, a federal parliamentarian, and a Minister of the Crown. The financial arrangements determined by the court are not material to political law. What is of interest, however, as a result of the case, is the judicial determination that pursuing a political career has private law repercussions on the manner in which the valuation of one's assets is done.

The court heard expert testimony from three actuaries. It relied on that of the only one among them who devised a way to render it unnecessary for the court to engage in conjecture about factors in a political career that influence success or failure. It accepted the following testimony about the nature of parliamentary work:

> Being a Member of Parliament is a unique occupation. Generally speaking, people enter the House at a later age than they would begin a more traditional profession, and their continued employment is subject to being reelected at approximately four year intervals. Therefore, a typical career for an MP is both shorter and less certain that it is for most other professionals. The pension plan for MPs is designed with these facts in mind.[139]

The factors relating to the calculation of income from such a career were said by the court to include factors specific to political life, such as past success in being elected; the present and future political climate in Canada; being in government or in opposition; if in government, being in Cabinet or on the backbenches; and the Prime Minister's own career plans.

---

[137] Additional reasons at (1993), 1993 CarswellOnt 4128 (Ont. Gen. Div.).

[138] R.S.O. 1990, c. F.3.

[139] (1993), 46 R.F.L. (3d) 219 at 223.

---

§ 1.11.5
Tyabji v. Sandana
British Columbia Supreme Court; March 3, 1994
(1994), 112 D.L.R. (4th) 641

One would be surprised to uncover principles of political law from a judgment based essentially on private legal matters such as this one dealing with the custody of children in the context of a divorce. Yet, this case involving British Columbia political figures whose romance caused a minor scandal, is of more than anecdotal interest. In fact, this case offers insight into the nature of a life in politics and by that means sheds some further light on the concept of politics. While this case may not be rigorously on point in explaining politics as one of the types of instruments of governance, it does recognize the human dimension of the practice of statecraft.

The parties were already married when, in the October 17, 1991, general election, Tyabji was elected as the Liberal Member of the British Columbia Legislative Assembly (MLA) for Okanagan East. In the course of the 35th Legislature that followed that election, Tyabji became romantically involved with Gordon Wilson, the leader of her party and another MLA. This led to the break-up of her marriage and the action for custody by each ex-spouse, which was the subject of the present ruling. Prior to the judgment, the children had been with Tyabji and two court-appointed experts recommended that she continue as the custodial parent. The court rejected their analysis and awarded custody to the former husband, Sandana, while granting Tyabji generous visitation rights.

In this case, the mother's political career and its demands upon her became a fact in issue. Tyabji's own evidence was to the effect that her role as an MLA and her political career were full-time, taking up 24 hours a day, 7 days a week. There was also testimony from Wilson emphasizing the stress of politics on marriage. The judge quite properly defined custody as the placement of the children with the parent who presented the best prospect for their best interests, care and upbringing. He then applied these guidelines to the circumstances of the political environment presented to him. One factor in his decision was Tyabji's lack of permanence in the family home; that home was in Kelowna while the Legislature is located in Victoria, resulting in her prolonged absences. This situation was only partially resolved by the move of the children away from Tyabji's matrimonial home into one in which she cohabited with Wilson, her intended second husband. The most important consideration taken into account by the court was Tyabji's preoccupation with political life, both as an aspect of her ability to care for the children and in comparison with the ability of the ex-husband, Sandana, to care for them. This is where the court's pronouncement adds to our understanding of politics.

> I find, however; that the career paths followed by both the mother and by Mr. Wilson, entail their absences from the home to a much greater degree than does the father's occupation. That is particularly true of the periods each year when the provincial legislature will be in session. That is sometimes limited to a period of about three months in the spring, but that is not true of every year, and it cannot be predicted with certainty. The history for both the mother and Mr. Wilson shows that their respective political roles have occupied a great deal of their time out of the legislative sessions. Their fortunes have since changed, but they now face the prospect of establishing a new political base and I cannot think that is to be done without a great commitment of time and effort.[140]

The court also alluded to the uncertainty in both Tyabji's and Wilson's political careers after the next general elections, then expected to be held in 1996. With the explanation that Tyabji's political career agenda sidetracked her attention as a parent, and on the grounds that Sandana would be able to provide more continuity of care in the children's lives, the court ruled in his favour. In rendering this decision, the court also discounted Tyabji's attempt to politicize the matter of the claims for custody by introducing arguments that some testimony was based on adverse political motives.

The court acknowledged that the case had attracted media attention because of Tyabji's and Wilson's political profile. In fact, the press reaction to the judgment was not the least interesting aspect of the case. Some of the reporting and the consequential editorial comment were negative, alleging that the judgment would keep women out of politics. There were, however, stories that took a more balanced view in interpreting the judgment as putting children's interests first: "Male or female, married or single, would-be politicians should care-

---

[140] (1994), 112 D.L.R. (4th) 641 at 650 b-d.

fully consider the effects on their families before they let their names appear on a ballot."[141]

There can be no clearer statement of the absorbing intensity of political life than this judgment. The next provincial general election did in fact occur on May 28, 1996. Gordon Wilson who, in the meantime, had been expelled from the leadership of the Liberal Party for his association with Tyabji and who had formed a new party called the Progressive Democratic Alliance (PDA), was elected under that banner. Tyabji ran as a PDA candidate and lost. Tyabji and Wilson are now married.

Judy Tyabji's parental difficulties arising out of political life did not end with this judgment. In December 1999, while her second husband, Gordon Wilson, was campaigning to become Leader of British Columbia's NDP Party, Sandana raised a sexual abuse charge against Wilson's son Matthew, in respect of one of the children common to Sandana and Tyabji. This charge was immediately linked to Wilson's political campaign and the political context. The media used the opportunity to remind readers of the 1994 judgment and of the reasoning that preoccupation with politics had prevented Tyabji from good parenting.[142]

See also *R. v. Cote*, 193 Sask. R. 1 (Sask. Q.B.); *Lavoie v. Canada* (1999), [2000] 1 F.C. 3 (Fed. C.A.), leave to appeal allowed 257 N.R. 199 (note) (S.C.C.), affirmed [2002] S.C.J. No. 24 (S.C.C.); *Ontario Federation of Anglers & Hunters v. Ontario (Ministry of Natural Resources)*[143] (2002), 211 D.L.R. (4th) 741 (Ont. C.A.), leave to appeal refused (2003), 313 N.R. 198 (note) (S.C.C.) and *Payne v. Wilson* (2002), 162 O.A.C. 48 (Ont. C.A.).

---

[141] Editorial, *Vancouver Sun*, March 5, 1994, p. A-8.

[142] Michael Smyth, "Wife of NDP leadership hopeful Gordon Wilson says she has been denied access to her children because of sexual abuse allegations against Wilson's son," *Ottawa Citizen*, December 21, 1999, online: http://www.southam.com/ottawacitizen/cpfs/national991219/n121941.html (last consulted December 21, 1999).

[143] Cross-reference to § 10.14.

§ 1.11.6
Chesterfield v. Janssen
Court of the Lord Chancellor; February 4, 1750
(1750), 2 Ves. Sen. 125

This is the earliest judgment that could be found, in which a court in which judges engage in discussion of "politics" in the modern sense of that term. The matter concerns the repayment of a loan contracted in 1738 by John Spencer, whose executor was the Earl of Chesterfield, the plaintiff. The judgment is a rather exhaustive litany of reasons drawn from statute, case law and equity. There is also examination of whether rules of a legal nature can be set aside on "principles of policy or political reasoning." While the context indicates that the expression "political" is sometimes used in a manner that could, today, be mistaken for the terms "public policy" or "public benefit," it is also clear from the ruling that the judges have ideas that closely approximate those of their modern-day successors regarding the division between legislative and judicial functions, and between law as a set of rules based on the judiciary's understanding of independent principles, and politics as the rules regarding the structuring and conduct of public affairs determined through adversarial discussion and debate.

In his part of the judgment, Lord Chancellor Hardwicke defined the concept of politics then "admitted" or accepted in England as meaning that "it comprehends every thing that concerns the government of the country; of which the administration of justice makes a considerable part."[144]

This statement is refined by the distinction of the true meaning of politics from what the Chancellor calls the "common acceptation" or popularized version of the term, which he criticized the defendant for having introduced into the case, and which consisted here of the argument that the plaintiff had in part used political reasons, or reasoning drawn from public utility (and therefore not legally valid into the court). The thrust of the Lord Chancellor's argument may be taken to be that politics is a general term referring to the conduct of public affairs, what we could perhaps today call "governance." For

---

[144] (1750), 2 Ves. Sen. 125, 28 E.R. 82 at 100.

him, the administration of justice is a distinct part of this, but a part nevertheless.

---

§ 1.11.7[145]
Australian Capital Television v. Commonwealth of Australia
New South Wales v. Commonwealth of Australia
High Court of Australia; January 15, 1992
(1991), 104 A.L.R. 389
-and-
Australian Capital Television Property Ltd. v. Commonwealth (No.2)
New South Wales v. Commonwealth of Australia
High Court of Australia; September 30, 1992
(1992), 108 A.L.R. 577

This case grew out of the challenge by a broadcaster of provisions included in Australia's *Broadcasting Act* that was designed to prohibit political advertising during election campaigns and referenda, as well as to oblige broadcasters to provide free political broadcasting time during such periods. One of the issues raised in the course of the proceedings was the definition of "political matters." As in the case of *R. v. Canadian Broadcasting Corporation* there was a clear differentiation between the dissemination of political information, comment and argument as opposed to the broadcasting of news and current affairs items and talkback radio programs.

Political broadcasts were held by this court to be those that are intended to enable electors to form political judgements; that is, to influence their decisions, rather than to inform or enlighten them. The court accepted the intent of the legislation to arrive at this distinction on the basis of the actual words of the statute:

> **95B(6)** In this section:...
> "political matter" means...
>   (a) matter intended or likely to affect voting in the election or referendum concerned;...[146]

The court struggled with the extent of this definition. It queried whether the debate of a particular substantive topic in the political

---

[145] Cross-reference to § 5.8.5.
[146] *Broadcasting Act 1942* (Cth), as amended, s. 95B.

arena, such as, for example, multiculturalism, would render that topic political. Given the court's view that there was an implied freedom of communication in the Australian Constitution, it also considered whether political discussion of multiculturalism would extend freedom of communication as part of a campaign. In the end, the court held the restrictions imposed on political advertisements to be invalid.

See also *Akins v. Federal Election Commission*, 141 L.Ed.2d 10 (1998).

1.12 ISSUE: CONSTITUTIONAL CONVENTION

§ 1.12.1[147]
Reference re Amendment of the Constitution of Canada (Nos. 1, 2 and 3)
Supreme Court of Canada; September 28, 1981
(1981), 125 D.L.R. (3d) 1

Considering that the study of political law focuses on the interaction of binding roles of governance that arise from three sources, namely law, policy and politics, introducing the concept of "constitutional convention" is indispensable, in that it adds a further nuance to the categorization and the working together of the types of rules. Indeed, one recent author qualified such conventions as "The marriage of law and politics."[148]

Within this perspective, the present case arose out of the conflict between the federal government and those of several of the provinces regarding the plan developed in 1980 and 1981 by Ottawa to patriate the Constitution and to attach a Charter and an amending formula to it. Three provinces referred a series of questions to their various courts of appeal, from which a unified case went forward to the Supreme Court of Canada for determination. It was in this setting that the court gave a definition of the notion of convention.

---

[147] Cross-reference to § 4.12.1 and 11.2.A.
[148] Andrew Heard used this expression as the subtitle of his book entitled *Canadian Constitutional Conventions - The Marriage of Law and Politics* (Toronto: Oxford University Press, 1991).

The constitutional system of Canada comprises as its control element the Constitution itself, but also consists of the "laws of the Constitution" and the "conventions of the Constitution." These conventions are the expression of the country's constitutional values and principles. They are rules of a political nature, based on precedents established by the institutions of the legislative and executive branches of government. They are necessary complements to legal rules.

The court drew clear distinctions between politically based conventions and the law of the Constitution. First, only legal rules are enforceable by the courts, while conventions are applied by the government of the day. Further, only the law of the Constitution is subject to legal sanctioning; conventions can be sanctioned by the institutions of government or by public opinion. In fact, the judgment not only implies the flexible nature of conventions, but also goes further to declare that conventions can at times be in conflict with the law. Depending on the value or principle of the Constitution that a convention is meant to safeguard, it can even be of greater importance than the law.

Finally, the court hinted at the pattern of evolution of conventional rules. They develop from the prevailing usages and practices of political life and they can crystallize into law by way of statutory adoption. Thus, the political legal system is in constant evolution.

See also *Québec (Procureur général) v. Canada (Procureur général)*, [1982] 2 S.C.R. 793 (S.C.C.) and *Reference re Language Rights Under s. 23 of Manitoba Act, 1870 & s. 133 of Constitution Act, 1867*,[149] 19 D.L.R. (4th) 1 (S.C.C.) and (1985), 26 D.L.R. (4th) 767 (note) (S.C.C.) and [1990] 3 S.C.R. 1417 (S.C.C.).

---

[149] Cross-reference to § 2.4 and 8.9.

§ 1.12.2[150]
New Brunswick Broadcasting Co. v.
Nova Scotia (Speaker of the House of Assembly)
Supreme Court of Canada; January 21, 1993
[1993] 1 S.C.R. 319

The central issue in this case was whether the Speaker of the Nova Scotia House of Assembly had, for reasons of order and decorum within the chamber of the Legislature, the authority to exclude television cameras that broadcasters wanted to place there for the purpose of reporting on the conduct of parliamentary business. The Supreme Court of Canada held that this decision was a matter of parliamentary privilege that fell into the category of the exclusion of strangers from the House, and that the Speaker was entitled to decide on the basis of that privilege, without being limited by the tenets of the *Canadian Charter of Rights and Freedoms*, in particular the section 2(b) freedom of expression.

Throughout the case, the court referred exclusively to the notion of "parliamentary privilege." It is possible, for purposes of the treatment of our subject matter to state that there is an overlap between that notion and the broader heading of "constitutional conventions." In the most serious work on the subject of conventions,[151] those of the legislature are included and that very case is mentioned.

It is generally agreed that such constitutional conventions as the privileges of Parliament and the legislatures of all the provinces were introduced into modern Canadian law and political life by the Preamble of the *Constitution Act, 1867*, and in particular by the phrase that made the Canadian constitutional system similar in principle to that of the United Kingdom. The court here traced the common origin of British and Canadian parliamentary privilege further back to the *lex et consuetudo Parliamenti*, the law and custom of Parliament.

> The Parliamentary privilege of the British Parliament at Westminster sprang originally from the authority of Parliament as a court. Over the centuries, Parliament won for itself the right to control its own affairs,

---

[150] Cross-reference to § 1.2.2, 8.2.C.2 and 8.4.
[151] Andrew Heard, *Canadian Constitutional Conventions - The Marriage of Law and Politics* (Toronto: Oxford University Press, 1991).

independent of the Crown and of the courts. The courts could determine whether a parliamentary privilege existed, but once they determined that it did, the courts had no power to regulate the exercise of that power.[152]

Based on that origin, parliamentary privilege is a convention that is an integral part of the current constitutional framework in Canada and which is indeed found to be necessary for the proper functioning of parliamentary institutions in a modern democratic system.

> In summary, it seems clear that, from an historical perspective, Canadian legislative bodies possess such inherent privileges as may be necessary to their proper functioning. These privileges are part of the fundamental law of our land, and hence are constitutional. The courts may determine if the privilege claimed is necessary to the capacity of the legislature to function, but have no power to review the rightness or wrongness of a particular decision made pursuant to the privilege.[153]

Moving from general contemplation of privileges to dealing more specifically with the one that is the subject of the current examination, the court expresses its approval of the exclusion of strangers as one of the privileges necessarily inherent to parliamentary deliberation.

> In my view, this privilege is as necessary to modern Canadian democracy as it has been to democracies here and elsewhere in past centuries. The legislative chamber is at the core of the system of representative government. It is of the highest importance that the debate in that chamber not be disturbed or inhibited in any way. Strangers can, in a variety of ways, interfere with the proper discharge of that business. It follows that the Assembly must have the right, if it is to function effectively, to exclude strangers. The rule that the legislative assembly should have the exclusive right to control the conditions in which that debate takes place is thus of great importance, not only for the autonomy of the legislative body, but to ensure its effective functioning.[154]

Finally, the court seeks to put parliamentary privilege in its proper perspective, as one of the unifying factors in the proper functioning of government.

---

[152] [1993] 1 S.C.R. 319 at 379 b-d.
[153] *Ibid.* at 384 i to 385 a.
[154] *Ibid.* at 387 e-h.

I add this. Our democratic government consists of several branches: the Crown, as represented by the Governor General and the provincial counterparts of that office; the legislative body; the executive; and the courts. It is fundamental to the working of government as a whole that all these parts play their proper role. It is equally fundamental that no one of them overstep its bounds, that each show proper deference for the legitimate sphere of activity of the other.[155]

1.13 ISSUE: GOVERNMENT

1.13.A—DEFINITION OF GOVERNMENT[156]

---

§ 1.13.A.1
Clement, Re
British Columbia Supreme Court; January 22, 1919
(1919), 44 D.L.R. 623[157]

In 1918, the British Columbia government established a royal commission to inquire into the importation and sale within the Province of intoxicating liquor. In the context of examining whether a provincial royal commission could look into breaches of federal law, the court had to interpret a provision of the provincial *Inquiries Act* pursuant to which commissions may be established "into any matter connected with the good government of the province...or the administration of justice therein."[158] The court concluded that the true meaning of the expression "good government" referred to "the exercise of the executive and ministerial functions and to the management and conduct of official business,"[159] rather than in any wider sense drawn from what was then the *British North America Act*, relating to the powers of the Dominion. The court felt that only this restrictive understanding would give the expression the meaning intended for the power assigned to the Province to legislate in respect of merely local matters. There is a limit in this judgment that the court may have thought that the concept of government was more extensive

---

[155] *Ibid.* at 389 b-d.
[156] Cross-reference to § 9.2.
[157] Reversed [1919] 3 W.W.R. 309 (B.C. C.A.).
[158] S.B.C. 1917, c. 30, s. 3, quoted at (1919), 44 D.L.R. 623 at 626.
[159] (1919), 44 D.L.R. 623 at 626.

at the federal than at the provincial level; such an interpretation would not be acceptable today.

In current understanding, the court here was equating the notion of government with its limited and constitutionally correct meaning at both federal and provincial levels, referring to the executive branch of the State, rather than to the entire apparatus of State administration.

In the end, the court held that the provincial legislation did not authorize coercive inquiry into matters under federal control and it declared the commission *ultra vires*.

---

§ 1.13.A.2
Formea Chemicals Ltd. v. Polymer Corp.
Supreme Court of Canada; June 3, 1968
[1968] S.C.R. 754

Before the *Charter*'s incorporation as the cornerstone of Canada's system of law and politics, the occasions when the courts needed to define the concept of "government" or "Government of Canada" were quite limited. Polymer held a patent; the particularity of the corporation was that most of the shares were held by the Minister of Munitions and Supplies (later known as the Minister of Defence Production and later still as the Associate Minister of National Defence). Because of this, the *Government Companies Operation Act*[160] was made applicable to the company; as of August 1, 1946 it became an agent of Her Majesty. When Formea applied for an injunction against alleged infringement of one of its own patents and damages, the courts had to interpret section 19 of the *Patent Act*,[161] which said that upon payment of compensation, the Government of Canada may use any patented invention. The Supreme Court of Canada, confirming the holdings of two lower courts, denied the claim on the grounds that Polymer had statutory authority to use the patent. The ratio was that the "Government of Canada" was synonymous with "the Crown." The court backed its decision by reference to sections 9 to 13 of the *British North America Act, 1867*.[162]

---

[160] S.C. 1946, c. 24, later R.S.C. 1952, c. 133.
[161] R.S.C. 1952, c. 203.
[162] Now entitled: *Constitution Act, 1867*, as amended.

See also *R. v. Achtem* (1979), 52 C.C.C. (2d) 240 (S.C.C.); *Quebec (Attorney General) v. Blaikie*, [1981] 1 S.C.R. 312 (S.C.C.) and *R. v. Giguère*, [1983] 2 S.C.R. 448 (S.C.C.).

---

§ 1.13.A.3
Dolphin Delivery Ltd. V. R.W.D.S.U., Local 580
Supreme Court of Canada; December 18, 1986
[1986] 2 S.C.R. 573

This case was one of the first of the generation of cases that explored the principles of the *Charter* and its limits, after the latter's incorporation into the legal system of Canada. The issue was an application for injunction to prevent secondary picketing in the context of a labour relations dispute. The key to the outcome was whether the activity involved—picketing—could be considered as speech, which was constitutionally protected by the *Charter*. The Supreme Court of Canada formulated the matter so that it included in its analysis the question whether the *Charter* applied to private litigation, seeing that section 32 of the *Charter* specified that it would apply to the legislative, executive and administrative branches of government, but not to private litigants. At the time, this question had not yet been fully determined.

The court came down strongly on the side of the argument test that the *Charter* did not apply to private litigation. It is this key that led it to unlock the door of the meaning of "government." The first part of the explanation was a distinction of the legal sense of the word from the generic meaning, as well as the distinction of government as "executive government" from the legislative branch.

> [W]here the word 'government' is used in s. 32 it refers not to government in its generic sense—meaning the whole of the governmental apparatus of the state—but to a branch of government. The word 'government', following as it does the words 'Parliament' and 'Legislature', must then, it would seem, refer to the executive or administrative branch of government. This is the sense in which one generally speaks of the Government of Canada or of a province. I am of the opinion that the word 'government' is used in s. 32 of the *Charter* in the sense of the executive government of Canada and the Provinces. This is the sense in which the words 'Government of Canada' are ordinarily employed in other sections of the *Constitution Act, 1867*. Sections 12, 16 and 132 all

refer to the Parliament and the Government of Canada as separate entities. The words 'Government of Canada', particularly where they follow a reference to the word 'Parliament', almost always refer to the executive government.[163]

The court went on to make a number of pertinent and interesting points. Having created limits for the concept of government, it explored what kind of action by government is necessary to bring the *Charter* into play. The legislative branch acts by means of legislation, while, "Action by the executive or administrative branches of government will generally depend on legislation, that is, statutory authority..."[164]

This is not a complete description, however.

> It would also seem that the *Charter* would apply to many forms of delegated legislation, regulations, orders in council, possibly municipal by-laws, and by-laws and regulations of other creatures of Parliament and the Legislatures. It is not suggested that this list is exhaustive. Where such exercise of, or reliance upon, governmental action is present and where one private party invokes or relies upon it to produce an infringement of the *Charter* rights of another, the *Charter* will be applicable.[165]

Finally, the Supreme Court queried whether the notion of government should be understood to include the judicial branch. Here also, it found the generic or popular understanding of the concept insufficiently clear to satisfy the norm of legal analysis required pursuant to the *Charter*.

> While in political science terms it is probably acceptable to treat the courts as one of the three fundamental branches of Government, that is, legislative, executive, and judicial, I cannot equate for the purposes of *Charter* application the order of a court with an element of governmental action. This is not to say that the courts are not bound by the *Charter*. The courts are, of course, bound by the *Charter* as they are bound by all law. It is their duty to apply the law, but in doing so they act as neutral arbiters, not as contending parties involved in a dispute.[166]

---

[163] [1986] 2 S.C.R. 573 at 598 e-i.
[164] *Ibid.* at 599 a.
[165] *Ibid.* at 602 i-603 a.
[166] *Ibid.* at 600 f-i.

§ 1.13.A.4
McKinney v. University of Guelph
Ontario Court of Appeal; December 10, 1987
(1987), 46 D.L.R. (4th) 193[167]

This is one of a number of cases on mandatory retirement that Canada's senior courts handled in the initial years of the *Canadian Charter of Rights and Freedoms*. From the perspective of constitutionally protected rights, this case is about equality, as protected by section 15(1) of the *Charter*. The first key to resolving this matter lay in determining whether the retirees' employer was or was not "government." It was in this process that the Ontario Court of Appeal defined the notion of "government." This definition was made in light of the *Charter*. The general application of the concept is far more extensive, however, and is of fundamental interest to those studying political law.

> The problem in this appeal is to determine if the respondent universities constitute "government" in the sense contemplated by s. 32(1) and if their activities in mandatorily retiring the appellants constitute "government action" so as to attract the reach of the Charter.

> . . .

> It is our responsibility as a court to scrutinize the tlegislative and other acts of both levels of government to ensure in specific cases that come before us that they are not inconsistent with the Charter, but the objects of this scrutiny are the two levels of government and generally not those who are subject to their authority. Those who are subject to the authority of government include those legal entities which are the creation of those governments by Acts of Parliament and the legislatures.

> . . .

> Because a government creates a corporation does not necessarily mean that the corporation is an extension of government.[168]

In order to satisfy itself as to whether the University of Guelph and the other Ontario universities involved in these proceedings were government or not, the court conducted a rather extensive checklist

---

[167] Affirmed [1990] 3 S.C.R. 229 (S.C.C.).
[168] (1987), 46 D.L.R. (4th) 193 at 205-206.

that looked primarily at the nature of the subject action. It reached the following conclusions:

- the creation of an institution by government is not enough to make it government;
- institutions created by government can perform public functions or private functions but they amount to government only if they perform public functions instead of government;
- the funding of an institution by government is not determinative;
- the exercise of statutory authority by an institution, a test developed by Professor Hogg, the even-then noted constitutionalist, is not the proper test; the statement that a corporation exercising statutory powers must stay within the ambit of those powers does not mean that in exercising these powers it does so as "government";[169]
- regulation made applicable to an institution's operations by a ministry, such as here by the Ministry of Education, makes no difference; and
- subjection to the supervision of the courts is not the proper test either.

> In support of the submission that universities are bound by the Charter, counsel argued that they form part of the administrative machinery of government because they are subject to the supervisory authority of the courts through the traditional prerogative remedies. This can hardly be the test since our courts have never been reluctant to interfere in the internal affairs of wholly private organizations where members complain of a breach of internal rules or a denial of natural justice. Whether relief is available through civil action for declaratory relief, injunctive relief, an award of damages or resort to the *Judicial Review Procedure Act*, R.S.O. 1980, c. 224, is merely a matter of choice of remedies and is not determinative of whether or not a body is an emanation of government, performing a governmental function.[170]

After all these negative analyses, the court looked at the three reasons put forward by the universities to show that they were not bound by the *Charter*. In a manner similar to the foregoing arguments, the court disposed of the "degree of control" test and the "clear nexus" test. It was only on the "nature of the action" test that the justices gave more in-depth analysis.

---

[169] *Ibid.* at 215.
[170] *Ibid.* at 216-217.

Before concluding on this subject we should say that we are aware of the oft quoted words of Dickson C.J.C. in *Operation Dismantle Inc. v. The Queen, supra,* where he said at p. 494 D.L.R., p. 459 S.C.R.:

> I would like to note that nothing in these reasons should be taken as the adoption of the view that the reference to "laws" in s. 52 of the Charter is confined to statutes, regulations and the common law. It may well be that if the supremacy of the Constitution expressed in s. 52 is to be meaningful, then all acts taken pursuant to powers granted by law will fall within s. 52.

> This remark has not been repeated by the Supreme Court of Canada but, in any event, it must be limited by the decision of that court in *Dolphin Delivery, supra,* that the "acts" must be acts of the government before they are subject to the provisions of s. 52. In our opinion, for all of the reasons set out above, we would hold that the Charter has no direct application to the respondent universities or to their contracts of employment with the appellants.[171]

All in all, the court's reasons here were not very clear; they used somewhat circuitous logic to arrive at the position that institutions constitute "government" if their acts are governmental. The merit of this case is more in eliminating criteria than in clarifying the central issue at stake.

---

§ 1.13.A.5[172]
Stoffman v. Vancouver General Hospital
British Columbia Court of Appeal; January 6, 1988
(1988), 49 D.L.R. (4th) 727[173]

The Vancouver General Hospital functioned under the *Hospital Act*[174] and under the *Vancouver General Hospital Act.*[175] In accordance with the Medical and Allied Staff Regulations made pursuant to the first of these statutes, it applied a mandatory retirement policy at age 65. Stoffman was a physician affected by this policy. He brought suit,

---

[171] *Ibid.* at 219.
[172] Cross-reference to § 1.3.A.3.
[173] Reversed (1990), [1991] 1 W.W.R. 577 (S.C.C.).
[174] R.S.B.C. 1979, c. 176, and amendments.
[175] S.B.C. 1970, c. 55, and amendments.

attacking the validity of the regulation as being contrary to section 15 of the *Canadian Charter of Rights and Freedoms*.

The first aspect of the case that the court dealt with was to determine whether the *Charter* could be applied to Stoffman's circumstances. Toward that end, it had to analyze whether the Vancouver General Hospital could be considered a governmental body in the sense that it was connected to one of the legislative, executive or administrative branches of government "in a direct and precisely defined way."[176] The court also had to look at whether the hospital's actions, consequently, constituted government actions "because they bear a direct connection to the actions of a branch of government."[177]

The court came to the general conclusion that the requisite connections did exist, on the basis of control of the hospital's activities by government: "The control exercised by the government over the operation of the hospital generally, and the formulation of its retirement policy in particular, put the question beyond doubt, in our opinion."[178]

It later stated in similar fashion that "the effective control of the hospital by the government is affirmed by the *Vancouver General Hospital Act*."[179] This holding was generally conclusive, but left the observer with the question of what is effective control and what are the elements of such control, unresolved. The interest of the case is that it provided a detailed answer to that fundamental question.

Referring to the judgment of the Supreme Court of Canada in the *Dolphin Delivery* case, the British Columbia Court of Appeal reiterated the test of governmental status as being the presence of a direct and precisely defined connection with government. The court drew on the stipulations of the *Hospital Act* to provide the details:

(a) governmental representation on the management board of the institution in question;

(b) opinion of the relevant Minister that a board and by-laws are necessary;

---

[176] (1988), 49 D.L.R. (4th) 727 at 730.
[177] *Ibid.* at 730.
[178] *Ibid.* at 730.
[179] *Ibid.* at 731.

(c) Ministerial approval of the constitution, by-laws and rules of the institution, for them to become effective;

(d) requirement that the constitution, by-laws and rules comply with conditions prescribed by the Lieutenant-Governor in Council (the Cabinet);

(e) the unassailable right of the government to appoint persons to the management board of the institution;

(f) the authority of the relevant Minister to require revision of by-laws to his or her satisfaction;

(g) the ability of the Lieutenant-Governor to make any additional regulations he or she thinks necessary;

(h) provision for additional Ministerial control where the institution receives money;

(i) authority for the government to appoint a public administrator to manage the institution and displace its board; and

(j) the potential assumption of total control of the institution by the administrator.

All of these criteria are drawn from the *Hospital Act* and, in this case, are specific to the circumstances of the Vancouver General Hospital. They can, however, be considered as a complete and comprehensive example of the bases on which to determine whether any particular institution is governmental in nature.

The court went on to invalidate the mandatory retirement regulation.

---

§ 1.13.A.6[180]
Angus v. R.
Federal Court of Appeal; July 4, 1990
(1990), 72 D.L.R. (4th) 672

The matter for determination by the court here was whether the *Environmental Assessment and Review Process Guidelines Order* (EARPGO)[181] was applicable to the Order in Council made by the Governor in Council as the instrument implementing a budgetary decision to downsize VIA Rail. In order to make the determination of the applicability of the EARPGO to the Governor in Council, the court had to examine whether the institution of the Governor in

---

[180] Cross-reference to § 1.8.B.2.
[181] SOR/84-467.

Council was synonymous and/or co-extensive with the notion of the "Government of Canada."

The court perceived that it was common ground that the phrase "the Government of Canada" was used to mean the executive branch of government. It also found, however, that the "Governor in Council" could not be identified with the executive power as such, meaning that it was not the same. It referred first to sections 9, 10, 11 and 13 of the *Constitution Act, 1867*. Significantly,

> Beyond that, the operation of the executive is shrouded in the conventions of responsible government. What is clear is that, in the words of Professor Peter W. Hogg, *Constitutional Law of Canada*, 2nd ed. (Toronto: Carswell Co. Ltd., 1985), at p. 195, "The whole Privy Council meets very rarely, and then only for ceremonial occasions", and that it is the Cabinet, in form merely a Committee of the Privy Council, which in reality constitutes the "Council" advising the Governor General at any particular time.

> The Governor in Council does not, then, in law encompass the whole of the executive power. Executive authority is vested in the Governor General under the Queen, and he or she retains reserve or personal powers, such as the choice of a prime minister. Even if one can say, with Professor Hogg, at p. 195, that "the Cabinet...is in most matters the supreme executive authority", even its *de facto* authority is not the whole of the executive power.[182]

On this basis, it was held that the Governor in Council was indeed the first emanation of executive power, but that in the sense of the precise words of the EARPGO, it was not a "board or agency of the Government of Canada."

The court also remarked, "One cannot ignore that in modern administration, decisions are not planned, made or acted upon by the Governor in Council without the assistance of specific ministers and departments."[183] Thus, while it was felt inappropriate to impact constitutional nuances into the EARPGO or the legislation pursuant to which it was made, further explanation of the concept of "government" was necessary to resolve this case.

---

[182] (1990), 72 D.L.R. (4th) 672 at 683 e-684 a.
[183] *Ibid.* at 690 a.

The practice of government, in Canada, is defined as follows by Peter W. Hogg, *Constitutional Law of Canada*, 2nd ed. (Toronto: Carswell Co. Ltd., 1985), at pp. 195-6, 203:

> When the ministers meet together as a group they constitute the cabinet...

> The cabinet, which does meet regularly and frequently, is in most matters the supreme executive authority...The cabinet formulates and carries out all executive policies, and it is responsible for the administration of all the departments of government. It constitutes the only active part of the Privy Council, and it exercises the powers of that body. The Governor General does not preside over, or even attend, the meetings of the cabinet. The Prime Minister presides. Where the Constitution or a statute requires that a decision be made by the "Governor General in Council" (and this requirement is very common indeed), there is still no meeting with the Governor General. The cabinet (or a cabinet committee to which routine Privy Council business has been delegated) will make the decision, and send an "order" or "minute" of the decision to the Governor General for his signature (which by convention is automatically given). Where a statute requires that a decision be made by a particular minister, then the cabinet will make the decision, and the relevant minister will formally authenticate the decision. Of course a cabinet will be content to delegate many matters to individual ministers, but each minister recognizes the supreme authority of the cabinet should the cabinet seek to exercise it.

> . . .

> It will now be obvious that in a system of responsible government there is no "separation of powers" between the executive and legislative branches of government. The head of the executive branch, the cabinet, draws its personnel and its power to govern from the legislative branch, the Parliament; and the cabinet controls the Parliament.[184]

In support of this explanation, reference was made to Australian constitutional law writing, which, in parallel to the Canadian system, equated the executive government with the "Crown" and the depersonalized "Queen." The government is that collection of individuals and institutions that exercise the executive functions of government; these include, according to the Australian constitutionalist Fajgenbaum, ministers, public servants, a Cabinet, the Executive Council, a Governor or Governor General, and statutory agencies. While this

---

[184] *Ibid.* at 690 c-g.

listing may be overly broad for our purposes, it can be illustrative of the core of the notion of "government" even without the hoped for pinpoint precision.

---

§ 1.13.A.7[185]
Douglas/Kwantlen Faculty Assoc. v. Douglas College
Supreme Court of Canada; December 6, 1990
(1990), 77 D.L.R. (4th) 94

In the political legal edifice largely built upon the 1982 *Canadian Charter of Rights and Freedoms*, there is an indissoluble link between the concepts of "government" and "law." In order for an instrument of governance to be considered "law" by the courts, it must emanate from a governmental institution. In the present instance, the instrument brought before the Supreme Court of Canada for adjudication was a collective agreement concluded between a college and its teachers' union. If the rules made by the collective agreement were governmental in nature—that is, if the college could be perceived to be government—the matter would fall within the *Charter* definition and constitutional adjudication could proceed.

The panel of seven justices agreed that the college indeed amounted to government, that its actions were governmental in nature, thus leading to the enshrinement of the collective agreement as law. La Forest, J. concluded rather rapidly that Douglas College was simply a delegate through which the province operated a system of post-secondary education and as such, it had Crown agency status.

Justice Wilson wrote a more methodical analysis, constructing a three-point test to determine what bodes constituted government.

> ...I would favour an approach that asks the following questions about entities that are not self-evidently part of the legislative, executive or administrative branches of government:
>
>> 1. Does the legislative, executive or administrative branch of government exercise control over the entity in question?

---

[185] Cross-reference to § 1.3.A.5.

2. Does the entity perform a traditional government function or a function which in more modern times is recognized as a responsibility of the state?

3. Is the entity one that acts pursuant to statutory authority specifically granted to it to enable it to further an objective that government seeks to promote in the broader public interest?

In my opinion, application of this three part test leads to the conclusion that the Charter applies to Douglas College.[186]

The control test consists of looking at the governing structure of the institution being examined, its policy and its funding. Here, the college was incorporated through an Act of the provincial legislature and its powers could be exercised only as an agent of the Crown. Pursuant to powers established under the Act, the Minister involved has authority to mould college policy and effectively controls the activities of its board. Moreover, the overwhelming majority of the college's funding was provided by the government. The college was also financially accountable to the government. These criteria all made it part of the apparatus of government.

With respect to the function test, the court relied on its decision in *McKinney* and concluded that the provision of education is one of the roles or functions of modern government. This was held to be particularly true of community colleges.

Justice Wilson entitled the third part of the test the public interest test. Going beyond the fact that statutory authority for the founding of the college existed, she looked broadly at how the institution so established served the benefit of the people.

> Government involvement in this area is easily justified. In brief, the availability of adequately trained technical support staff is essential to the successful growth and expansion of the economy. Technological advancement is thwarted without a sophisticated labour force ready to work in these fields. It has thus been in the public interest that educational services be provided in technical areas.[187]

On the basis that Douglas College met all the criteria set out by the court, it was found to be part of the government for the purposes of

---

[186] (1990), 77 D.L.R. (4th) 94 at 98 h-99 b.

[187] *Ibid.* at 102 e.

section 32 of the *Charter*. The greater significance of the case, however, is its drawing up of the test for determining governmental status for constitutional purposes.

See also *Canadian Jewish Congress v. Chosen People Ministries Inc.*, 231 D.L.R. (4th) 309 (Fed. C.A.).

1.13.B—BRANCHES OF GOVERNMENT AND SEPARATION OF POWERS

See *Singh v. Canada (Attorney General)*,[188] [2000] 3 F.C. 185 (Fed. C.A.), leave to appeal refused (2000), 259 N.R. 400 (note) (S.C.C.).

1.14 ISSUE: GOVERNMENTAL FUNCTION, GOVERNMENT ACTION OR DECISION

§ 1.14.1
J.E. Verreault & Fils Ltée v. Quebec (Attorney General)
Supreme Court of Canada; March 26, 1975
(1975), 57 D.L.R. (3d) 403

This is a case essentially involving the contracting practices of government. On June 7, 1960, during the campaign leading up to a general election in the Province of Québec and at a time when it was already plainly apparent that a government of a different political conviction would be elected, an order in council was issued, authorizing the Minister of Social Welfare to sign a contract for the purchase of land on which a home for the aged was to be built. The Minister immediately proceeded to enter into a contract with Verreault for the construction. Following the election of June 22, 1960, which did in fact put a new Liberal government into office, the new Minister of Social Welfare cancelled the contract in order to enable another contractor to perform the work. Verreault sued for damages.

The decision turned on whether a minister required specific statutory authorization to enter into a contract such as the one in question. The

---

[188] Cross-reference to § 9.9.B.

Supreme Court of Canada concluded that he did not, and adjudged the company an amount for loss of profit.

In dealing with the applicability of the general rules of mandate to ministers, the court was brought to analyze elements of the system of governmental decision making. It first referred to the British foundations and then applied these to the Canadian context.

> Inasmuch as the monarch of the United Kingdom can only act through privy councillors, or upon their advice, it follows that all the higher and more formal acts of administration must proceed from the authority of the sovereign in council, and their performance be directed by orders issued by the sovereign at a meeting of the Privy Council specially convened for the purpose.

> No precise rule or definition can be made to discriminate between those political acts of the crown which may be performed upon the advice of particular ministers, and those which are properly exercised only 'in council.' The distinction depends partly on usage, and partly, in certain cases, upon the wording of Acts of Parliament. It may be assumed, however, that acts of the most general operation and importance, such as the issue of new regulations for the organisation or government of the civil service, or affecting the administration of the army or navy, should be authorised in council, while prerogatives affecting individuals, such as appointments to office, or the grant of pardons, are performed upon the advice of particular ministers.

> It is quite clear that the learned author was there dealing with distinctions resting on usages and conventions, not with legal limitations, apart from limitations following from Acts of Parliament. As is well known, under the British system, which basically applies in Canada, important rules of Government are nothing more than usages, devoid of any legal sanction.[189]

These passages relate to the concept of governmental action or decision prior to the adoption of the *Canadian Charter of Rights and Freedoms*. The 1982 reforms would enshrine the concept with an entirely new meaning.

---

[189] (1975), 57 D.L.R.(3d) 403 at 408-409.

§ 1.14.2
Ferranti-Packard Ltd. v. Cushman Rentals Ltd. et al.
Ontario High Court of Justice (Divisional Court); June 6, 1980
(1980), 30 O.R. (2d) 194[190]

In the era of the *Charter*, the courts' attention has been focused on the notion of "governmental action or decision" as part of interpreting sections 32 and 24 of the *Constitution Act, 1982*. This has not, however, lessened the importance of the concept of "governmental function," which predates the *Charter* and which is examined here. This is also of interest to political law students.

This case arose out of a motor vehicle accident in which the New York State Thruway Authority (the Authority) became one of the defendants. The Authority tried to rely on a defence of sovereign immunity. The court rejected this defence and in the process, it analyzed two facets of the corporate existence of the Authority. The first was the degree of independence of the Authority from the State of New York. The question here was whether the Authority was under governmental control; in other words, did it stand on its own feet and did it act on its own initiative? As part of this examination, the court borrowed Lord Denning's phrase to see whether the body was "an alter ego or organ of the government." In the present case, the Authority was found to be independent. The second criterion was whether the Authority was carrying out a governmental function. The question here was whether the Authority was performing a responsibility inherent to governance; in other words, was it a functionary of the State, was it a public authority and, ultimately was it exercising governmental powers or conducting commercial activities. Again using the test devised by Lord Denning, the court determined the criterion of governmental function on the basis of the functions of the Authority "were, in practice, nothing more than 'the policy of the Government...itself.'"[191]

---

[190] Affirmed (1981), 31 O.R. (2d) 799 (Ont. C.A.).
[191] (1980), 30 O.R. (2d) 194 at 199, citing from *Mellenger v. New Brunswick Development Corp.*, [1971] 2 All E.R. 593 (Eng. C.A.).

§ 1.14.3[192]

McKinney v. Liberal Party of Canada

Ontario Supreme Court (High Court); September 16, 1987

(1987), 43 D.L.R. (4th) 706

During the 33rd Parliament,[193] McKinney, an elector dissatisfied with the long-standing practice of party discipline, applied to have the Liberal Party as well as the two other political parties then represented in the House of Commons[194] enjoined on an interim and permanent basis from continuing to apply this practice to their Members of Parliament. The major ground on which the cause was based was that the application of discipline by political parties was alleged to violate McKinney's freedoms guaranteed by section 2 of the *Canadian Charter of Rights and Freedoms*, in particular his freedoms of thought, belief, opinion and expression.

Prior to determining whether McKinney's *Charter* rights had been infringed, the court was called upon to examine whether the *Charter* was applicable at all. In a motion to have the case dismissed, the defendants argued that the plaintiff could not obtain relief under the *Charter*, as political parties were not emanations of government in the sense of section 32 of the *Charter*:

> **32.** (1) This Charter applies
>
> > (a) to the Parliament and government of Canada in respect of all matters within the authority of Parliament including all matters relating to the Yukon Territory and Northwest Territories; and
>
> > (b) to the legislature and government of each province in respect of all matters within the authority of the legislature of each province.

On this issue, McKinney presented an ingenious reply to the effect that Parliament is constituted of the Members elected to it and that if some of those Members coerce or restrain others, then that conduct

---

[192] Cross-reference to § 6.2.2.

[193] The 33rd Parliament lasted from September 4, 1984, until November 22, 1988.

[194] The other two parties were the New Democratic Party and the Progressive Conservative Party.

could be held to be directly related to the workings of Parliament. As such, section 32(1)(a) should be considered to govern the activity complained of.

The court emphasized that a long line of jurisprudence had established that the *Charter* applied exclusively to relations between the State and its citizens. It then went on to distinguish between acts undertaken by the components of the State relevant to the *Charter*, namely the Parliament or the Government of Canada, and those engaged in by political parties. In effect, the court refused to equate the State institutions, Parliament, with the political parties functioning within it. As it had held that the latter was unincorporated associations independent of the State, it could conclude only that section 32 should not be applied.

"The exercise of party discipline is not a governmental act, but the act of an unincorporated private association and cannot be regulated by the Charter."[195] In short, this case stands for the principle that political parties are not governmental actors and that their functions and decisions are not those of the State.

See also *Harrison v. University of British Columbia*, 49 D.L.R. (4th) 687 (B.C. C.A.), reversed (1990), 91 C.L.L.C. 17,001 (S.C.C.), leave to appeal allowed [1988] 4 W.W.R. lxxii (S.C.C.).

---

§ 1.14.4[196]
National Party of Canada v. Canadian Broadcasting Corp.
Alberta Court of Appeal; October 1, 1993
(1993), 106 D.L.R. (4th) 575[197]

In conjunction with the 1993 federal general election, several television networks with nation-wide audiences formed a broadcasters' consortium in order to organize debates among the leaders of the political parties seeking seats in Parliament. On the basis of the rules of participation devised by the consortium, the leaders of the five major parties (Progressive Conservative, Liberal, New Democratic, Reform and Bloc Québécois) would debate each other and the leaders

---

[195] (1987), 43 D.L.R. (4th) 706 at 710-711.
[196] Cross-reference to § 5.9.6.
[197] Leave to appeal refused [1994] 2 W.W.R. lxv (note) (S.C.C.).

of the other parties vying for power would face-off in a separate debate.

The National Party requested to be included with the major parties but was relegated to the secondary debate. It sued in the Alberta Court of Queen's Bench and pursued its appeal through the Alberta Court of Appeal to the Supreme Court of Canada. Considering that the arguments put forward by the party were based principally on the *Charter*, the courts of first instance and appeal concentrated on determining whether the *Charter* ought to be applied to the circumstances at hand.

The applicant contended that the Canadian Broadcasting Corporation (CBC), the only member of the broadcasters' consortium that was sued, was of a governmental character, thereby attracting the provisions of the *Charter*. As evidence of this, it pointed to the statutorily determined mandate of the CBC, which required it, among other things, to:

> "safeguard, enrich and strengthen the cultural, political, social and economic fabric of Canada, (para. ((d)(i));
>
> provide of a wide range of programming that reflects Canadian attitudes, opinions, ideas, values..." (para. ((d)(ii));
>
> "reflect the circumstances and aspirations of Canadian men, women and children, including equal rights..." (para. ((d)(iii));
>
> "be varied and comprehensive" (para. ((i)(ii)); and
>
> "provide a reasonable opportunity for the public to be exposed to the expression of differing views on matters of public concern" (para. ((i)(iv)).[198]

The party also sought to rely on statutory provisions indicating that the CBC is an agent of the Crown and that it reports to Parliament through a Minister designated for this purpose.

The court examined both the nature of the CBC as an institution and its decision-making and its role in the orchestration of the debates as

---

[198] S. 3(1), *Broadcasting Act*, S.C. 1991, c. 11, as quoted in (1993), 106 D.L.R. (4th) 568 at 571 g.

a specific set of programs for airing. It held that the standard should be determined as follows:

> The relevant inquiry is whether in all of the circumstances it can fairly be said that the decision to organize the debates and to invite certain political leaders to the exclusion of Mr. Hurtig is a decision of government. Can it fairly be said that government, mindful of the *entire* legislative framework and the evidence before me, sufficiently partook in the decision-making process so as to render the decision an act of government?[199]

The court applied this standard to the evidence of decision-making with respect to the debates. It found nothing to show that Parliament had forced the CBC to join the broadcasters' consortium or to organize the debates. Neither did it find evidence to indicate that the government had a hand in determining which party leaders were to be invited to the debates, and which not. Further, it saw no suggestion of manipulation of the electoral process by the fact that Mr. Hurtig, Leader of the National Party, would participate in the secondary party leaders' debate. Rather, the court found that the terms of the *Broadcasting Act* were designed to ensure that journalistic decisions at the CBC would be made in a manner "unfettered by government influence or interference."[200] It thus concluded that, despite the CBC's status as a Crown agency, the decisions made in respect of the debate and of the invitations thereto were not to be characterized as decisions of government.

On that basis, the National Party's application was denied. The Alberta Court of Appeal upheld the lower court ruling. The only *ratio* with which it reinforced the Queen's Bench decision was that neither the establishment of the broadcasters' consortium nor the debate qualifications were based on anything but journalistic freedom.

---

§ 1.14.5
Hill v. Church of Scientology of Toronto
Supreme Court of Canada; July 20, 1995
[1995] 2 S.C.R. 1130

This case enunciates the principles that not all actions taken by public

---

[199] (1993), 106 D.L.R. (4th) 568 at 572 c.
[200] *Ibid.* at 573 h.

servants, even within their area of professional responsibility, amount to government action. In fact, only those professional actions of public servants that are mandated by the Crown amount to government action. The effect of this case is thus to set limits to the concept of government action.

The factual background is part of a complex process of litigation. Hill's employment was formally described as being Counsel with the Crown Law Office, Criminal Division, of the Ministry of the Attorney General for the Province of Ontario. In short, he was a Crown prosecutor in Toronto. As such, he was not only a public servant but also had duties of a professional nature as a lawyer and was senior enough to be considered an agent of the Crown. Over a number of years, Hill had participated in prosecutions against the Church of Scientology. As a result of Hill's execution of his professional activities, Scientology had classified him as an "enemy" and attempted to disqualify him from the ongoing search and seizure of its documents. On September 17, 1984, Scientology launched criminal contempt proceedings against Hill, alleging that he had misled a judge and had breached orders relating to the sealing of documents pertaining to the prosecutions of Scientology. Scientology's lawyer held a press conference on the courthouse steps, accusing Hill and making its case against him known to as wide a media audience as possible. This attack was made despite the fact that Scientology and at least some of its lawyers knew that there was no evidence to support the allegations. On December 7, 1984, the application against Hill was dismissed.

On December 14, 1984, Hill launched a libel action against Scientology and Manning, the lawyer who had held the press conference. At first instance as well as on appeal, Hill was successful. The defendants appealed to the Supreme Court of Canada, which upheld the lower court judgments in regard to the fact that Hill had been libelled, as to the inapplicability of the *Charter* to this case and as to the quantum of damages.

Before the Ontario Court of Appeal and the Supreme Court of Canada, one of the issues on which the case turned was whether the action for damages for libel commenced by Hill constituted "government action" and hence whether the *Charter* applied. The importance of whether Hill's commencing the libel action amounted to government action or not was that in the affirmative, the *Charter* would apply to the proceedings and that would have a bearing on the disposition of the issue of the libel. The Court of Appeal "rejected the argument that Casey Hill's position as a public figure implicated the government in whatever action he pursued. It also dismissed the submission that the government funding of his action was relevant to this question."[201]

In the Supreme Court proceedings, the defendants reiterated their earlier position that by reason of Hill's employment with the Government of Ontario, his action in damages constitutes government action. In support of this contention, they pleaded that (a) at all material times, Hill was an agent of the Crown, acting on behalf of the Attorney General; (b) the defamatory statements were made in relation to acts undertaken by Hill in his official capacity; and (c) Hill started the action at the direction and with the financial support of the Attorney General in order to vindicate the reputation of the Ministry. From all this, the defendants tried to draw the following conclusions: "It is, therefore, contended that this action represents an effort by a government department to use the action of defamation to restrict and infringe the freedom of expression of the appellants in a manner that is contrary to the *Charter*."[202]

The Supreme Court unreservedly rejected these contentions as having no legal, evidentiary or logical basis of support. It held that the determination of Hill's constitutional status and of whether there existed State involvement should be determined not by the nature of the allegations but rather "upon the circumstances surrounding the institution of the libel proceedings."[203] In the opinion of the court, the following matters were pertinent. The reputation that was impugned was that of Hill, not the government. The action was instituted by Hill in his own capacity, not in his official function. The Ministry did not require Hill to commence the action, nor even request him to do so. The Ministry did not control the conduct of the litigation. Significantly, "the fact that Casey Hill's suit may have been funded by the Ministry of the Attorney General does not alter his constitutional status or cloak his personal action in the mantle of government action."[204]

---

[201] [1995] 2 S.C.R. 1130 at 1155, para. 54.
[202] *Ibid.* at 1160, para. 70.
[203] *Ibid.* at 1161, para. 71.
[204] *Ibid.* at 1162, para. 75.

These considerations can be deemed to constitute the test for distinguishing between government and private action. In addition, as an aspect of *Charter* litigation in respect of this specific case, the court added that the defendants had failed to provide any evidentiary basis to show that the case fell into the ambit of section 32 of the *Charter*. Such evidence is required to sustain *Charter* litigation.

The court went beyond the individual considerations of the test and made comments of a more general nature that flowed from the analysis.

> The fact that persons are employed by the government does not mean that their reputation is automatically divided into two parts, one related to their personal life and the other to their employment status. To accept the appellants' position would mean that identical defamatory comments would be subject to two different laws, one applicable to government employees, the other to the rest of society. Government employment cannot be a basis for such a distinction. Reputation is an integral and fundamentally important aspect of every individual. It exists for everyone quite apart from employment.[205]

---

§ 1.14.6
Adler v. Ontario
Supreme Court of Canada; November 21, 1996
[1996] 3 S.C.R. 609

The court defined the issue in this case as being whether the absence of funding by the Government of Ontario, through the tax system and by means of grants, for private religious-based independent schools, is consistent with the Constitution of Canada. In the educational system of Ontario, the province provides public funding for "public schools," which are in essence secular. As a result of reforms brought about in the 1980s,[206] the province also supports a "Roman Catholic Separate" schooling system. This, the court qualified as a constitutional anomaly. Other schools may be accredited by the Ministry of Education, but do not receive the province's financial support. It is the legality of this absence of funding that the court had to

---

[205] *Ibid.* at 1161, para. 72.
[206] *An Act to Amend the Education Act*, S.O. 1986, c. 21, Bill 30 of 1985; see also *Reference re Bill 30, an Act to amend the Education Act*, [1987] 1 S.C.R. 1148 (S.C.C.).

interpret here. It emphasized that it left to the legislature the decision as a matter of public policy whether the funding of other schools is desirable. The novel element in the case and the point of interest in the evolution of the concept of government action is that, in the sense of section 32 of the *Canadian Charter of Rights and Freedoms*, the Ontario Court of Appeal perceived this not as government action but rather as government inaction.

The applications in this case were presented on the grounds of section 2(a) of the *Charter*, which guarantees freedom of conscience and religion. The applicants' argument was that the scheme of the *Education Act*[207] first made school attendance mandatory and second, by the inability of public schools to accommodate the applicants' children because of the lack of Jewish religious instruction necessary to keep the Jewish community vibrant, compelled their payment of tuition fees to independent religious-based schools.

The court held it was the fact that the legislation did not compel the applicants to send their children to private, religious-based independent schools that constituted the absence of government action, rather than the actual non-funding of such schools. On this basis, the absence of funding did not contravene section 2(a) of the *Charter*.

The particular way in which the applicants' arguments were structured and that in which the court set out its reasoning unfortunately did not require that the court further explain the difference between government action and inaction by government. Thus, while the precedent was established that the court recognized not only government action *vis-à-vis* action by bodies or persons other than government, but also inaction by government, it appears from this case that the definition of inaction may be left for determination upon the facts of each set of circumstances presented to the courts.

In the present case, the Ontario Court of Appeal held that the remedy sought to counteract the inaction by government could not be available.

> There is no direct public funding to support such private schools, but there is indirect financial aid in the form of property tax exemptions for non-profit schools, and income tax deductions both for tuition attribut-

---

[207] R.S.O. 1990, c. E.2.

able to religious instruction, and for charitable donations to religious schools.

Free tuition is only one ingredient of the publicly funded school system presently in place in Ontario. Extending public school funding to private schools, which are not universally accessible and which are managed, operated and funded by private agencies, would be completely inconsistent with the objectives of the current legislation and could impair or thwart those objectives.[208]

An appeal to the Supreme Court of Canada failed to reverse this ruling.[209] The court of final resort specifically noted that failure by the State to act in such a manner as to facilitate the practice of religion cannot be considered State interference in freedom of religion. The lack of provision of funding for private education does not infringe the freedom to educate children in accordance with religious beliefs where there is no restriction on religious schooling. Economic costs incurred in sending children to religious schools do not amount to an infringement of a freedom protected by section 2(a) of the *Charter*, here the freedom of religion. The most important lesson to retain from this case for the analysis of political law is that it is now settled that State inaction does not amount to State action in terms of the *Charter*.

While the judgment of the Supreme Court of Canada put an end to the litigious phase of this controversy, the political matter at hand was, at the time of writing, still not resolved. In Ontario at least, during 2001, in response to public pressure, the provincial government was contemplating the idea of replacing the right Adler had sought to obtain through law, by the tax policy mechanism, of issuing parents tax credits in respect of the amount they would spend on their children's education in independent or religious schools. This reform was instituted in 2002 but revoked after the provincial election of 2003. The issue is still under political discussion. This is a clear example of continuing a process in the conduct of public affairs through political means where potential legal remedies have been exhausted. In modern society, law, politics and policy are but diverse aspects of the same comprehensive evolution, intensely linked and responsive to each other.

[208] (1994), 19 O.R. (3d) 1 at 27h-28b
[209] Leave to appeal allowed (1995), 21 O.R. (3d) xvi (note) (S.C.C.), affirmed [1996] 3 S.C.R. 609 (S.C.C.).

§ 1.14.7[210]
Ferrell v. Ontario (Attorney General)
Ontario Court (General Division); December 28-29, 1995,
and July 9, 1997
(1997), 149 D.L.R. (4th) 335[211]

On June 25, 1995, the people of Ontario elected a Progressive Conservative government, which came in with a platform entitled "The Common Sense Revolution." This administration held views about politics and the place of government in society that were quite radically different from those of the preceding, New Democratic, government. Whereas the earlier government of Premier Bob Rae had, in 1993, enacted the *Employment Equity Act*,[212] the government of Premier Mike Harris presented totally contrary proposals to the Legislature within the first six months of its taking office. Thus, on December 13, 1995, the *Job Quotas Repeal Act*[213] was enacted and on the following day received Royal Assent. Its principal feature was to repeal outright the *Employment Equity Act*. No later than December 15, 1995, Ferrel applied for an interlocutory injunction to suspend the operation of the repealing legislation pending determination of its constitutional validity. The motion for injunction was dismissed. Among other considerations, this decision was based on the fact that the *Job Quotas Repeal Act* was not the enactment of substantive new provisions, but amounted only to a repealing measure. Given that proving the presence of a serious constitutional issue was one of the tests Ferrel had to meet, at this preliminary stage the court found nothing in the repealing statute that could be measured against the *Charter*.

This background set the stage for consideration by the Ontario Court (General Division) of the question of whether the *Charter* could be read so as to require that once legislation to correct a perceived ill in society had been enacted, there ensued a duty to leave that legislation in place. The other way of phrasing this is to inquire whether a statute

---

210 Cross-reference to § 7.2.1.
211 Affirmed (1998), 42 O.R. (3d) 97 (Ont. C.A.), leave to appeal refused (1999), 252 N.R. 197 (note) (S.C.C.).
212 S.O. 1993, c. 35.
213 S.O. 1995, c. 4.

for the repeal of substantive legislation could be considered as amounting to government action.

> The issue in this application, however, is whether, as a result of a change of government and a resulting change in policy, the legislature may remove such a statute as the *Employment Equity Act, 1993*. The issue is not whether the repealing statute is intrinsically bad, as being in violation of the *Charter*. That is so because Bill 8 has no substantive element. It simply repeals an existing statute without making any attempt to replace it.[214]

The court noted that no precedents existed on the argument being put forward. Thus, its attention focused on the applicants' point that once a government had decided to provide constitutional protection under the *Charter*, it must not turn around and remove the protection thereby allowing discrimination.

> The issue is whether the applicants have a right under s. 15 of the *Charter* to force the present government to retain intact social legislation enacted by a previous one.

> ...That right is to have the *Employment Equity Act*, 1993 not repealed or abrogated in such a way as to remove the protective shield of the *Act* with respect to that group while continuing to maintain it for others.

> I agree.[215]

The court thus framed the problem to be resolved in the eyes of the law correctly. However, it then retreated from the opportunity the facts of the case were giving it to apply a constitutional standard to the repeal of a *Charter*-based right. It cited the availability of alternative remedial measures in the *Ontario Human Rights Code*[216] that already existed, as well as in the Employment Opportunity Program with which the government intended to replace the *Employment Equity Act*. More importantly, it then seemed to resort to judicial deference by qualifying the repeal as inaction, rather than action, on the part of the government, tying this in with the notion that the *Charter* does not impose a constitutional obligation to act. The court then went even further and equated what it perceived as legislative inac-

---

[214] (1997), 149 D.L.R. (4th) 335 at 343.
[215] *Ibid.* at 345 and 343.
[216] R.S.O. 1990, c. H-19.

tion with political action and suggested that the appropriate remedy was not in the courts, but at the polls.

> The decision to scrap what the present government saw as a quota-driven response and replace it with a voluntary program was a political one and, right or wrong in the political sense, was one which it was entitled to take. It had the right to select its own method of combatting inequality and discrimination. It may well be that the electorate will decide that it prefers some other solution; that is the electorate's privilege to exercise at election time. A new government may well decide that something similar to the *Employment Equity Act, 1993* should be revised; if so, it will have the same right to make that political decision as the present government had to scrap the *Employment Equity Act, 1993* and replace it with an alternative program.[217]

The *Employment Equity Act* disappeared and the *Job Quotas Repeal Act* was allowed to remain in force and effect.

---

§ 1.14.8
Vriend v. Alberta
Supreme Court of Canada; April 2, 1998
(1998), 156 D.L.R. (4th) 385

Several of the foregoing cases, starting with *McKinney* examined the circumstances in which the enactment of legislation and the practice of governance in consequence of such legislation amount to government action or decision. In *Ferrel*, the issue was whether the repeal of legislation, that is the undoing rather than the doing of something, could constitute government action. Here, the Supreme Court of Canada found an opportunity to develop and indeed to expound the notion of government action, by determining whether lack of legislative action could be considered in light of the *Charter* as government action.

Vriend was an employee of a private religious school. When the school authorities discovered he was homosexual, his employment was terminated. Vriend lodged a complaint under the *Individual's Rights Protection Act*[218] to the Alberta Human Rights Commission.

---

[217] *Supra* note 214 at 345-346.
[218] R.S.A. 1980, c. I-2.

This was rejected because the legislation in question did not prohibit sexual orientation as a ground of discrimination. Vriend then sought a declaratory judgment to the effect that the Act was contrary to section 15(d) of the *Canadian Charter of Rights and Freedoms*. The trial court agreed but the Alberta Court of Appeal reversed.

The Supreme Court of Canada sharply rebuked the highest court in Alberta and made new law by allowing Vriend's appeal. The pith and substance of the ruling is that deliberate legislative omission can be considered a form of governmental action. Relying on the precise words of section 32(1)(b) of the *Charter*, which talks about "matters" rather than merely "positive acts" within the authority of a legislature, and reinforcing its holding with the influence of scholarly writings, the court declared, "The application of the *Charter* is not restricted to situations where the government actively overreaches on rights."[219] It went on, however, to analyze two interconnected and significant aspects of this holding. First, while it noted the merit of judicial deference to legislative action, it set limits to that doctrine by stating that such deference to legislative choices should not be used to completely immunize legislative decisions from *Charter* scrutiny. Even more importantly, the court pronounced itself more broadly on the relationship of the Judicial Branch to the Legislative.

> It is suggested that this appeal represents a contest between the power of the democratically elected legislatures to pass the laws they see fit, and the power of the courts to disallow those laws, or to dictate that certain matters be included in those laws. To put the issue in this way is misleading and erroneous. Quite simply, it is not the courts which limit the legislatures. Rather, it is the Constitution, which must be interpreted by the courts, that limits the legislatures. This is necessarily true of all constitutional democracies. Citizens must have the right to challenge laws which they consider to be beyond the powers of the legislatures. When such a challenge is properly made, the courts must, pursuant to their constitutional duty, rule on the challenge. It is said, however, that this case is different because the challenge centres on the legislature's failure to extend the protection of a law to a particular group of people. This position assumes that it is only a positive act rather than an omission which may be scrutinized under the *Charter*. In my view, for the reasons that will follow, there is no legal basis for drawing such a distinction. In this as in other cases, the courts have a duty to determine whether the challenge is justified. It is not a question, as McClung J.A. suggested, of

---

[219] (1998), 156 D.L.R. (4th) 385 at 414.

the courts imposing their view of "ideal" legislation, but rather of determining whether the challenged legislative act or omission is constitutional or not.[220]

The Supreme Court of Canada felt, clearly, that the way in which the Alberta Court of Appeal had posited the relation of the branches of government to each other and their respective roles in dealing with the role of law in the State was wrong. More fundamentally, it perceived the Alberta view as a challenge to the courts' role under the *Charter* and it answered that view. The remedy applied by the Supreme Court was to read the permitted protection into the Alberta statute: "Both Judge Iacobucci and Judge Cory were critical of the provincial government for making several conscious decisions over the past decade to deny legislative protection to a minority that has suffered persecution for centuries."[221]

Clearly, the Ottawa and Edmonton views of democracy are different.

See also international comparison *Florida Prepaid Postsecondary Education Expense Board v. College Saving Bank*, 144 L.Ed.2d 575 (1999).

1.15 ISSUE: GOVERNMENT OFFICIAL

See *R. v. Jones*, [1965] 3 C.C.C. 263 (B.C. Co. Ct.).

1.16 ISSUE: PUBLIC SECTOR

See *Gaboriault v. Tecksol Inc.*, [1992] 3 F.C. 566 (Fed. C.A.), leave to appeal refused (1993), 149 N.R. 238 (note) (S.C.C.).

---

[220] *Ibid.* at 413.
[221] Norm Ovenden, "Provinces must protect gays against bias: Supreme Court," *Ottawa Citizen*, April 3, 1998.

---

§ 1.16.1
Assn. of Private Care (British Columbia) v. British Columbia
(Attorney General)
British Columbia Court of Appeal; March 21, 1997
(1997), 144 D.L.R. (4th) 425

During the 1990s, the Government of British Columbia commissioned
a series of reports dealing with various aspects of health care. The
first dealt in November 1991 with "Health Care and Costs." In June
1993, another report was produced on the "Public Service and Public
Sector." Finally, in May 1995, a further report on "Reshaping Health
Care Bargaining Units" was tabled. The common goal of these studies
was rationalization, efficiency and cost restraint, "while maintaining
an acceptable level of health care."[222] The government's specific policy aims were avoiding duplication and developing uniformity in the
health care field. In pursuit of these aims, the government revised the
Health Authorities Act[223] and the *Public Sector Employers Act*;[224] consequentially it designated some 250 previously private health care
facilities and agencies that operated on a "for profit" basis, as being
part of the public sector. This case is the result of the objection of
those bodies to being included in the public sector.

The Supreme Court of British Columbia denied the application to
have the designation declared *ultra vires* and the Court of Appeal
upheld the first judgment. It held that the profit-making nature of an
institution was not a bar to its being designated as part of the public
sector. Not every such institution needs to be self-evidently public in
nature. Private institutions—meaning privately owned ones—that
meet the criteria in the designation-making power in the *Public Sector
Employers Act* are indeed participants in the public sector. "If 'public'
in these enactments is understood to modify 'sector', rather than to
refer to the profit motivation of the employer, no absurdity in the
designation can be seen."[225] This is reinforced by the fact that there
is no difference in the service provided by the applicants and other
health care providers. In sum, the court interpreted the *Health Authorities Act* as authorizing "a broad restructuring of labour relations

---

[222] (1997), 144 D.L.R. (4th) 425 at 429.
[223] S.B.C. 1993, c. 47, as amended.
[224] S.B.C. 1993, c. 65.
[225] *Supra* note 222 at 430.

in health care and by necessary implication thus includes all employers, public or private, operating in the health care sector."[226] As long as the government drafted the legislation in a rational framework and the court properly applied the rules of statutory construction, the concept of "public sector" could be determined in a flexible manner.

1.17 ISSUE: PUBLIC AUTHORITY

See *Canada Post Corp. v. Post Office*, [2001] 2 F.C. 63 (Fed. T.D.).

1.18 ISSUE: PUBLIC SERVICE

See *Canada (Attorney General) v. P.S.A.C.* (1991), 80 D.L.R. (4th) 520 (S.C.C.).

1.19 ISSUE: PUBLIC PURPOSE

§ 1.19.1
Eurig Estate, Re
Supreme Court of Canada; October 22, 1998
(1998), 165 D.L.R. (4th) 1

The issue in this action was whether the executrix of an estate was required to pay probate fees in order that she be issued letters probate for the process of execution. This question led the court to examine whether a probate levy was indeed a fee, or a tax. The criteria in making this determination include the questions of whether the imposition of a levy is: (a) compulsory and enforceable by law; (b) imposed under the authority of the legislature and levied by a public body; (c) for a public purpose; and (d) subject to a *nexus* between the *quantum* charged and the cost of the service provided. The Supreme Court of Canada agreed that, as the levy was imposed by the Ontario

---

[226] *Supra* note 222 at 436.

Court (General Division), it meets the criteria of being levied by a public body. The further requirement of there being a public purpose involved was also held to have been met, as the revenue was held to be used for defraying the costs of court administration in general, not simply to offset the costs of granting probate.

The analysis of the Supreme Court was adapted and simplified by the Ontario Superior Court of Justice in the case of *Ontario Cattlemen's Assn. v. Thames Sales Yard Ltd.*[227] The pith and substance of the public purpose analysis involves primarily the determination of whether a fee is levied by a public body or a private body. The courts will also look at whether the subject fee is administered by the public through the government, or by the private body involved, through itself and for itself. Finally they also consider whether there is a *nexus* between the revenues and services provided. In this case, this question was settled by looking at whether the fees were supplemented by investment income and grants, no part of which reverted to the province.

1.20 ISSUE: POLITICAL TRUST

See *Guerin v. R.* (1984) 13 D.L.R. (4th) 321 (S.C.C.) and *Authorson (Litigation Guardian of) v. Canada (Attorney General)* (2002), 58 O.R. (3d) 417 (Ont. C.A.), additional reasons at (2002), 215 D.L.R. (4th) 544 (Ont. C.A.), leave to appeal allowed (2002), 302 N.R. 397 (note) (S.C.C.), reversed (2003) 66 O.R. (3d) 734 (note) (S.C.C.).

---

[227] (2002), [2002] O.J. No. 1473, 2002 CarswellOnt 1358 (Ont. S.C.J.), affirmed (2003), 175 O.A.C. 104 (Ont. C.A.).

1.21 ISSUE: UNCERTAINTY IN THE CHARACTERIZATION OF INSTRUMENTS: IS IT LAW, POLICY OR POLITICS ?

§ 1.21.1[228]
R. v. Canadian Broadcasting Corp.
Ontario Court (General Division); May 12, 1992
(1992), 72 C.C.C. (3d) 545[229]

This case arose out of the refusal of several broadcasting undertakings to include the leader of the Green Party of Canada in a nationally televised leaders' debate in the campaign leading up to the federal general election of 1988. The court had to examine the interaction between, on the one hand sections 303-322 of the *Canada Elections Act*[230] dealing with political broadcasting, and on the other hand, section 8 of the *Television Broadcasting Regulations*. The regulations in question are regulations in the sense of the *Statutory Instruments Act*, having legally binding force and effect. They were made by the Canadian Radio-Television and Telecommunications Commission under a regulation-making power set out in subsection 6(1)(b)(iii) of the *Broadcasting Act*.

Despite the clear evidence, which the court itself provided in the judgment, of the nature of section 8 as a legal instrument, it distinguished between the different legal provisions by referring to one as the "legal framework" and to the other as the "policy." The characterization of a legal instrument as a policy should not be understood literally. The true meaning of this qualification, as expressed elsewhere in the ruling, is that while the provisions of the *Canada Elections Act* should be construed as specific, that of the *Television Broadcasting Regulations* are more general. The rules of statutory construction required that the specific provisions oust the application of the more general one. The reader may be allowed to presume that the court did not intend to use the expression "policy" here to indicate that a

---

[228] Cross-reference to § 1.11.3 and 5.9.5.
[229] Affirmed (1993), 51 C.P.R. (3d) 192 (Ont. C.A.), leave to appeal refused (1994), 72 O.A.C. 158 (note) (S.C.C.).
[230] Currently S.C. 2000, c. 9, ss. 330-348.

regulation did not have force of law, but rather that it provided a rule of a more general or generic nature.

---

§ 1.21.2
Kohl v. Canada (Department of Agriculture)
Federal Court of Canada – Trial Division; July 8, 1994
(1994), 81 F.T.R. 35[231]

The expression "policy" is current in a number of different contexts dealing with governance, both as a noun and as a qualifying adjective. Most often, it is used without definition or even precision. For this reason, it can and does engender confusion.

In relation to semantics, the interest of the *Kohl* case is that it fulfils the very important service of helping to set the bounds between political law and administrative law. Political law is concerned with the notion of policy as one of a variety of instruments of governance; it examines the interaction among the various types and analyzes the use and the binding quality of each type of instrument in the conduct of governmental affairs. By contrast, in administrative law, the principal concern is with official decision-making, the distinction between policy decisions and other types of decision, and the supervision of the courts in reviewing the legality of such decisions.

In this instance, the subject matter of the litigation was the "policy decision" taken by the Minister of Agriculture on December 14, 1993, to destroy all cattle imported into Canada from the United Kingdom between January 1982 and 1990, in order to prevent the spread of BSE, a disease otherwise known as "mad cow disease." This decision was followed on January 11, 1994, with a Notice of Requirement to Dispose of Animals, addressed specifically to Kohl. Kohl sought judicial review. The Federal Court determined that what it had to review was not the Notice based on the Minister's decision but rather the decision itself. For reasons unconnected with the preoccupation of this study, the court quashed the Minister's decision.

Much of the judgment focused on the characteristics of the Minister's policy decision. By ascertaining what type of decision it was in ad-

---

[231] Reversed (1995), 34 Admin. L.R. (2d) 34 (Fed. C.A.).

ministrative law terms, the court determined that the decision was subject to judicial review.

The salient feature of the case for the present study is that the court also distinguished that so-called "policy decision" from a "guideline," which is one of the policy-type of instruments of governance. It indicated that the policy directive, the Minister's December 1993 decision, was a decision required to be implemented in each, meaning every case to which its criteria were applicable. Thus, it was held to be more than a "mere policy" intended to be followed in individual cases—that is, in some cases. While contributing yet more to the terminological confusion, it is safe to conclude that the court meant that the Minister's decision was a binding order or ruling, while a policy instrument in the nature of a guideline would, in its view, have been only generally indicative of a course of action to follow, binding only in some cases, and that such an instrument would not have been subject to judicial review. This categorization by the court may not be entirely accurate. It does, however, fully illustrate the problems arising out of the almost indiscriminate use of the expression "policy."

See also *Ontario NDP Application for Standing Ruling by the Walkerton Inquiry*, September 12, 2000 and international comparison *U.S. v. Munoz-Flores*, 495 U.S. 385 (1990).

2

RELATION OF, AND RELATIVE INFLUENCES AMONG, LAW, POLICY AND POLITICS

2.1 GENERAL PRINCIPLES

See Volume I, Chapter 2.

2.2 ISSUE: LAW AND POLICY

2.2.A—AUTHORITY TO CREATE POLICY INSTRUMENTS

§ 2.2.A.1
Burke v. Canada (Employment & Immigration Commission)
Federal Court of Canada – Trial Division; June 7, 1994
(1994), 79 F.T.R. 148

Burke had been an employee of the Sydney Steel Corporation and was laid off when he stopped work because of illness. He applied for benefits under the *Labour Adjustment Benefits Act*.[1] The Canada Employment and Immigration Commission, administering that legislation and the various subordinate instruments made pursuant to it, denied the claim. The present case was an application for judicial review of the Commission's decision. Burke's application was denied.

The case hinged in part on the validity of the calculation method used by the Commission in determining the normal allowance applied to

---
[1] R.S.C. 1985, c. L-1.

the applicant in the part of the country in which he lived. That allowance was calculated by the Commission on the basis of "guidelines" developed by the Nova Scotia Department of Consumer Affairs and the National Council of Welfare. The applicant argued that the guidelines were not justified in his case, but failed to substantiate how or why this was so. In dismissing the application, the Federal Court said that "it is well settled that where Parliament delegates a general discretion, without specific guidelines as to how that shall be exercised, as it did here under s. 13(4) and s. 14(2) of the *Act*, in the exercise of that discretion the Commission may adopt guidelines for purposes of objective decision-making in applying general discretion to individual cases."[2] The implication of this judicial statement is that governmental offices and agencies have authority, when the circumstances of the legal system require it, to adopt instruments of a policy nature, such as guidelines, in order to complement the legal framework pursuant to which they carry out their functions.

2.2.B—CONSTITUENCY OF POLICY INSTRUMENTS WITH CONSTITUTIONAL NORMS

<hr>

§ 2.2.B.1
C.U.P.E. v. Minister of National Revenue
Federal Court of Appeal; January 26, 1993
(1993), 93 D.T.C. 5099

<hr>

The type of instrument discussed in this case is the pension, plan which can be registered pursuant to sections 147.1 and 172 of the *Income Tax Act*.[3] The union requested that the Minister register an amendment to a pension plan so as to include same-sex couples in that plan. The Minister refused and the union sought to exercise a recourse to the Federal Court, where its plea was also denied. The court reiterated that the duty of the Minister was to administer the Act; in administering instruments under the Act, he would have to apply the requirements of the Act as they stand. The Minister was not entitled to ignore the conditions prescribed in the Act if he considered them to be unconstitutional. He was bound to administer the instrument in accordance with the constitution and the law.

<hr>

[2] (1994), 79 F.T.R. 148 at 159.
[3] S.C. 1970-71-72, c. 63.

---

§ 2.2.B.2
Bal v. Ontario (Attorney General)
Ontario Court (General Division); December 5, 1994
(1994), 21 O.R. (3d) 681[4]

In the few years preceding this case, the courts of Ontario had gone a long way toward secularizing the province's public education system and ensuring that public funding should be available to non-religious schools only. In that context, this case was part of the continuing conflict between advocates of a quasi-universal publicly funded, secular, non-denominational school system for Ontario, and proponents of a collection of diverse school systems and schools, fragmented on the basis of diverse religious identities. The government reacted to each successive decision in the former direction by wilfully complying with it. This enabled the Ontario Court (General Division) to state here that: "The matter arises in the context of judicial pronouncements and governmental response."[5]

From the point of view of political law, the significance of this case among the others is that here, the proceeding was based on testing the conformity of a policy instrument to the *Charter*.

On December 6, 1990, in response to one of the earlier cases in this line of jurisprudence, the Ontario Ministry of Education adopted *Policy/Program Memorandum 112*, entitled "Education about Religion in the Public Elementary and Secondary Schools." Consequentially, it amended the relevant sections of a regulation made pursuant to the *Education Act*.[6] The basic principles expressed in the Policy Memorandum were based on the Canadian Civil Liberties Association decision of the Ontario Court of Appeal[7] and they were clearly phrased in binding and prescriptive terms.

---

[4] Affirmed (1997), 34 O.R. (3d) 484 (Ont. C.A.), leave to appeal refused (1998), 113 O.A.C. 199 (note) (S.C.C.).
[5] (1994), 21 O.R. (3d) 681 at 685 h.
[6] Sections 28 and 29 of Regulation 298 made under the *Education Act*, R.S.O. 1990, c. E.2.
[7] *Corp. of the Canadian Civil Liberties Assn. v. Ontario (Minister of Education)* (1990), 71 O.R. (2d) 341 (Ont. C.A.).

The instrument required primarily that first, the school's approach to religion be one of instruction, not one of introduction, and secondly that primacy must not be given to any particular religious faith. The results of these mandatory instructions were that religious instruction and education became prohibited during school and that the establishment of religious schools within the public school system became prevented.

Bal, a Sikh, as well as parents of Hindu, Reformed Protestant, Muslim and Fundamental Christian faiths, challenged the Policy Memorandum on the grounds that it denied their *Charter*-protected freedom of conscience and religion (section 2(a)), freedom of expression (section 2(b)) and equality rights (section 15). They wanted access to public funding for all of the religious schools their respective children attended.

As opposing counsel could not even agree on the basis of the contention to be resolved, the court itself was forced to define the central issue of this case as follows:

> In my opinion, the issue is:
> Does the *Charter* give to the applicant parents the right to require the Minister of Education to provide and fund denominational religious schools for minority religious groups within the public school system? Is it a *Charter* infringement for the government to fail to do so?[8]

It conducted a very thorough analysis of the *Charter* issues involved. It rejected each of the grounds of alleged contravention of the *Charter* and, on the merits, arrived at the following conclusion:

> ...in this case, it is not the policy memorandum and regulations which impose obligations, penalties, restrictive conditions on the applicants, and not on others. Instead, it is the applicants' choice of education for their children. The public school system is secular, it does not present the opportunity for education in any particular denomination or faith. The objective is to provide non-denominational education. Should parents desire that their children have a religious education they must assume the cost. This does not mean that there is adverse effect discrimination. The government prohibition is just, fair and constitutional.[9]

---

[8] *Supra* note 5 at 703 h-704 a.
[9] *Ibid.* at 714 f-h.

The court reached an even more significant conclusion, which was both procedural and substantive in nature, and which is the genuine point of interest for the present study. It not only found, as was quite obvious, that in order for Policy Memorandum 112 to be allowed to remain in effect, it had to be held to be constitutionally valid. It went further, in analyzing the necessary quality of constitutionality of the policy instrument.

> Mr. Jervis argued that Policy Memorandum 112 constitutes government action thereby distinguishing the *Adler* decision which dealt with government inaction. Policy Memorandum 112 requires public schools to be secular. In my opinion, it does not constitute a form of government action which prefers one religion over another, nor does it represent majoritarian religious views. This policy seeks to abolish distinctions in the public school system which are based on religion. It dictates what must be done to secularize the public school system. There is no foundation for the argument that this policy constitutes government action which infringes a person's right to freedom of conscience and religion. Rather, it evolved from judicial pronouncement concerning compliance with the *Charter*.[10]

The general conclusion to be derived from the foregoing is that in order for a policy instrument to be valid, it must comply with constitutional standards. That is so to the same extent as if the policy were a statute.

Proper reading of this case must lead the observer of political law to draw an analogy between the educational matters discussed here and the issue of broadcasting in politics dealt with in the case of *R. v. Canadian Broadcasting Corp.*[11] This court defined secularism in the public school system as being the goal of educating, rather than indoctrinating, and as being neutral rather than coercive. This secularism, in contrast to religious education, is comparable to the distinction drawn by the same court between programs containing political content and which are informational in nature, being contrasted to political broadcasts directed at persuading or conveying partisan or ideological points of view.

---

[10] *Ibid.* at 705 h-706 b.
[11] (1992), 72 C.C.C. (3d) 545 (Ont. Gen. Div.), affirmed (1993), 51 C.P.R. (3d) 192 (Ont. C.A.), leave to appeal refused (1994), 72 O.A.C. 158 (note) (S.C.C.).

2.2.C—APPLICATION OF LEGAL NORMS TO POLICY INSTRUMENTS

---

§ 2.2.C.1

Brown v. British Columbia (Minister of Transportation and Highways)
Supreme Court of Canada; March 17, 1994
(1994), 112 D.L.R. (4th) 1
-and-
Swinamer v. Nova Scotia (Attorney General)
Supreme Court of Canada; March 17, 1994
(1994), 112 D.L.R. (4th) 18

These are parallel cases grounded in administrative law issues, which are significant because they raise a most important question of political law.

Brown was a user of provincial highway in British Columbia on November 8, 1985. Despite his exercise of caution in driving, for reasons directly attributable to the unkept condition of the icy roadway, he crashed and was injured. At the time, the provincial department had made the decision to retain the summer schedule for road clearance in that area. Brown sued for damages and lost at trial, at appeal, and before the Supreme Court of Canada. The highest court's ratio was that the province did owe a duty of care under tortious liability to the users of its roads; however, that duty can be excluded where the damage to a user of the road results from the application of statute or from a departmental decision that is of a policy nature. Here, the decision to remain on summer schedule, which was at the root of the injury, was held to have been a policy decision and the injured party therefore had no action.

The court explained its administrative law reasoning by distinguishing policy decisions from operational ones. Policy decisions by governmental or public authorities are ones that involve, or are dictated by, financial, economic, social or political factors or constraints, including personnel issues or matters of significant negotiations with government unions. In such cases, moreover, it is the nature of the decision itself that is of import, not the position of the person who makes it. By contrast, operational decisions involve the performance or the carrying out of policy; they are the product of administrative discretion, expert or professional opinion, technical standards, or general standards of reasonableness. In common parlance, policy decisions are broad and fundamental, dealing with the management of governmental programs and systems, while operational decisions are of lesser scope, relating to the mechanics of application of those programs and systems. The simile of managerial strategy and tactics could be used. The Supreme Court specified that policy decisions can be attacked only if they are made in bad faith or if they exceed the jurisdiction of the decision-maker. Operational decisions are subject to legal overview. Thus, legal norms can be applied to policy decisions in only limited circumstances, circumstances that are themselves dependent on interpretation by the courts.

The *Swinamer* case involved a comparable fact situation. The Nova Scotia Department of Transportation had undertaken to survey dead trees that could cause a hazard along its roads. On November 26, 1983, as Swinamer was driving past a tree that had not been found to be a hazard, it fell on his truck and injured him. The Supreme Court of Canada also denied his claim. On the same reasoning as in the Brown case, the court held that the decision to conduct the survey was a policy decision in a process that would eventually involve expenditures and the allocation of funds. Such decisions must be immune from the private law standards of tort liability.

In both cases, several of the justices gave divergent reasons for concurring judgments. This led one legal commentator to note, "The unpredictability of administrative law is notorious. These two decisions are remarkable in demonstrating the relative stability of the tests used to determine when public authorities will be liable for negligence."[12]

The general press reaction to these cases was also relevant to our particular perspective on these matters:

> The Supreme Court of Canada, in two related decisions this week setting out the "duty of care" that state agencies owe the public, said that governments must be permitted the latitude to make policy decisions.

---

[12] (1994), 3 R.A.L. 198 at 200.

. . .

But the court made it clear that when governments make policy decisions, they are not to be held to the same standard as individuals or
companies for damage that results.[13]

The question that these rulings engender for the study of political law
is that if legal standards arising out of tortious liability are set aside
in the face of governmental decisions that are of a policy nature, are
legal standards arising out of legal instruments also set aside in the
face of instruments of a policy nature? In other words, can the legal
consequences of governmental decisions and of instruments of governance be assimilated? The answer seems to be that the norms arising
from legal instruments exert a greater, although not universal influence on other forms of instruments of governance than do legal norms
in decision-making. This is both the subject matter of this chapter and
one of the primary distinctions between administrative law and political law.

2.2.D—CONSISTENCY OF LEGAL INSTRUMENTS WITH PUBLIC POLICY

---

§ 2.2.D.1
Canadian Pacific Ltd. v. Matsqui Indian Band
Federal Court of Canada – Trial Division; October 13, 1992
(1992), 58 F.T.R. 23[14]

Nothing illustrates better the symbiotic relationship between law and
policy that, while the focal argument of section 2.2 of this book is that
policy instruments must be in accord with the law they complement,
the law itself must be in accord with public policy as a broader concept. This is not an effort at irony; rather, it is a reminder of the
distinction between the notions of "policy" or "policy instruments"
on one hand and "public policy" on the other. The language is insufficiently clear on these issues but public policy is certainly meant to
be a broader, more encompassing phrase, perhaps one on a higher
level of ideas. The present case illustrates this.

---

[13] Sea Five, "There's a big 'but' to consider if one sues government," *Globe & Mail*,
March 19, 1994.
[14] Reversed [1993] 2 F.C. 641 (Fed. C.A.), affirmed [1995] 1 S.C.R. 3 (S.C.C.).

In 1992, certain Indian bands acquired the right to assess taxation on the lands under their control. One of these, the Matsqui Band, issued assessments on Canadian Pacific (CP). Canadian Pacific applied to the Federal Court by way of originating notice of motion under section 18 of the *Federal Court Act* to strike the assessments, alleging that the Band lacked jurisdiction to make the assessment because the lands were not within their reserve. The Band applied here to strike CP's motion. After thoroughly examining the requirements for judicial review and examining the difference between judicial review and appeal, the court granted the Band's application to strike out the CP motion. It reasoned that on the basis of discussions involving the federal, provincial and band authorities, the policy decision had been made for British Columbia to relinquish its historical power of taxation over reserve bands in favour of the bands, operating through by-laws under the *Indian Act*. These bands were, it said, cloaked with the mantle of legitimacy in running their own systems of taxation. "It leads me to conclude that for purposes of settling the issue before me, it would not be in the public interest and it would not favour public policy at this time to bypass the appeal provisions in the by-laws."[15]

See also *Brantford (Township) v. Doctor* (1995), 29 M.P.L.R. (2d) 300 (Ont. Gen. Div.).

2.2.E— SUPREMACY OF LEGAL NORMS OVER POLICY INSTRUMENTS IN MATTERS OF PUBLIC ADMINISTRATION

§ 2.2.E.1[16]
Canadian Wildlife Federation Inc. v. Canada (Minister of the Environment)
Federal Court of Canada – Trial Division; April 10, 1989
[1989] 3 F.C. 309[17]

This is one of a number of cases relating to the environmental consequences of the Rafferty-Alameda damming project in Saskatchewan. The Premier of Saskatchewan announced the project on February 12, 1986. Authorization to proceed was provided by the

---

[15] (1992), 58 F.T.R. 23 at 33.
[16] Cross-reference to § 1.3.A.4, 1.3.D.3, 2.6.1, 11.7.4 and 11.14.2.
[17] Affirmed (1989), [1990] 2 W.W.R. 69 (Fed. C.A.).

Saskatchewan Minister of the Environment on February 15, 1988. The appropriate Saskatchewan authority also applied to the Minister of the Environment of Canada for a licence. This was issued on June 17, 1988, but with no assessment and review having been conducted pursuant to the *Environmental Assessment and Review Process Guidelines Order* (EARPGO).[18] One would have been required under the *International River Improvements Act*.[19] In the present action, the Federation maintains that the federal Minister of the Environment ought to have conducted an EARPGO review. The Minister's position is that the EARPGO order applies only to proposals undertaken by a federal agency.

The court reasoned that the Souris River is an international waterway and that, on the basis of its review of the statutory and regulatory provisions, in order to construct, operate or maintain an international river improvement, a person must hold a valid licence, which, in turn, means compliance with the requirements set out in the Regulations, including EARPGO.

Further, the court considered whether the EARPGO was an instrument grounded in the legal system and therefore mandatory, or merely an instrument of an administrative or policy nature, and therefore not strictly enforceable by the courts. In determining this question, the court looked to the statutory definition of the parameters of the legal system.

>...the EARP Guidelines Order is an enactment or regulation as defined in section 2 of the *Interpretation Act*, i.e.:
>
>> 3) "enactment" means an Act or regulation or any portion of an Act or regulation;
>>
>> "regulation" includes an order, regulation, rule of court, form, tariff of costs or fees, letters patent, commission, warrant, proclamation, by-law, resolution or other instrument issued, made or established
>>
>>> (*a*) in the execution of a power conferred by or under the authority of an Act, or
>>> (*b*) by or under the authority of the Governor in Council;

---

[18] SOR/84-467.
[19] R.S.C. 1985, c. I-20.

> Therefore, EARP Guidelines Order is not a mere description of a policy or programme; it may create rights which may be enforceable by way of *mandamus*.[20]

Having discerned that the EARPGO creates legal rights and duties that are, inherently, of a mandatory nature, as opposed to being optional, the court felt that the Minister had misread the jurisdictional limits of his powers under EARPGO by seeking to limit them to federal projects only, rather than by interpreting them as including projects in which there was a federal interest or responsibility such as migratory birds, inter-provincial affairs or fisheries. The applicants were therefore entitled to the *mandamus* they sought.

The court also took note with some delicateness of the different advice tendered to the federal minister. It contrasted the advice from the minister's lawyers with that coming from the policy officials and upheld the former.

> Incidentally, some effort was made by counsel for the respondent Minister of the Environment that actions taken by federal officials met the requirements of the Guidelines or actions were taken in the spirit of the Guidelines but it was clear throughout that Department of the Environment officials were maintaining that the EARP Guidelines did not apply to this project.[21]

This decision was upheld on appeal.[22]

---

§ 2.2.E.2[23]
Yhap v. Canada (Minister of Employment & Immigration)
Federal Court of Canada – Trial Division; October 2, 1989
(1989), 29 F.T.R. 223

This case illustrates the way in which courts will interpret diverse instruments in a situation in which the body of rules applicable to a portfolio subject matter comprise both legal and policy instruments that constitute a regime where federal law is perceived to be in a state

---

[20] [1989] 3 F.C. 309 at 322 d-g.
[21] *Ibid.* at 325 i-j.
[22] (1989), 99 N.R. 72 (Fed. C.A.).
[23] Cross-reference to § 2.2.E.3.

of imprecision and flux. In this instance, the portfolio subject matter was immigration. In the period of the late 1980s, a very great number of would-be immigrants attempted, with or without justification, to get into Canada by filing claims for refugee status rather than by following more traditional avenues of immigration procedure. A considerable "backlog" of refugee application cases had developed as immigration authorities could not cope with the influx. In response, there was much rule-making activity. The statutes, however, were "not yet consolidated, nor yet fully tested as to constitutionality, legality of procedures or the fairness of their enforcement"[24] and they were accompanied by a plethora of ministerial statements and directives, together with lacunae in the regulations.

Yhap had arrived from China in July 1986 and soon thereafter had made a claim as a refugee on the ground of fear of persecution by reason of political opinion. By 1989, he was facing a final review of his application for permanent residence, or a credible basis hearing, all pursuant primarily to the procedures set out in the *Immigration Act* and in its amendments designed to cope with the backlog.[25] However, in addition to the statutes, the Minister of Immigration had issued "guidelines" and "directives" regarding the backlog clearance process for claims made prior to January 1, 1989, and concerning in particular persons in Canada from the People's Republic of China. These were contained in a pamphlet and were intended, eventually, to be consolidated into "regulations."

> It is noted in that pamphlet itself that it "should not be considered a legal document." Indeed, if the treatment visited upon the applicants be contrary to the law, then it must always be the latter which prevails, not the pamphlet. No regulations have yet been promulgated in order to give effect to this process described in the pamphlet.[26]

After the events of June 4, 1989, in China, in particular the massacre at Tienanmin Square in Beijing, the Minister announced a policy of non-removal to the People's Republic of China, and of opportunities for Chinese in Canada to apply and be landed from within Canada on humanitarian and compassionate grounds. Various other policy

---

[24] (1989), 29 F.T.R. 223 at 231.

[25] S.C. 1988, c. 35.

[26] *Supra* note 24 at 228.

pronouncements and instruments were also applicable to this situation.

At this time, Yhap presented before the Federal Court of Canada – Trial Division a motion in the nature of an interlocutory injunction, for a stay to prohibit the Minister from making any form of final determination and from potentially removing Yhap back to China until his case had been resolved on the merits. Yhap's proceeding was taken by the court as the stereotypical case of a large number of applicants in a similar position. The court allowed the application only insofar as these particular applicants were concerned. It would, it said, not issue a more general order that "would cause the whole refugee claim process to grind to a halt."[27]

The way the *ratio* of the judgment is expressed presents two points of fundamental interest in the political law context. It is based on the simultaneous consideration by the court of both legal texts and other instruments in the nature of policy, under various designations such as policies, "guidelines," "directives," "memoranda" and "ministerial statements." Even more pertinently, this comprehensive overview of all the instruments applicable to the case leads the court to conclude that the law prevails over the other instruments not only in circumstances of contradiction, but also where there is uncertainty, or where the system has not yet been consolidated, on where groups may remain in the rules about the subject matter. The facts of this particular case, as well as the judge's sense of fairness and the logic of the law required such a result.

> One may sympathize with a refugee claimant who is ordered out of Canada according to laws of known validity and lawful procedures, but the Court will decline to intervene in such circumstances. On the other hand, it would be cold comfort indeed to the applicant or any of his fellows to be removed and then to learn that the law under which he was processed had been declared to be invalid or the proceedings found to be unfair or unlawful.[28]

While the court upheld the supremacy of law over policy, its decisions nonetheless afforded the Minister's policy pronouncements some influence on its reading of the situation. Those statements raised Chinese applicants' legitimate expectations and if they were not legally

---

27 *Ibid.* at 231.
28 *Supra,* note 24.

reified—that is, carried into the law—the expectations so raised could be frustrated.

---

§ 2.2.E.3[29]
Yhap v. Canada (Minister of Employment & Immigration)
Federal Court of Canada – Trial Division; March 8, 1990
[1990] 1 F.C. 722

In the mid-1980s, there developed in Canada a backlog of refugee claims that numbered well over 100,000 individuals. In order to deal with this large number of applicants for refugee status, Parliament enacted amendments to the *Immigration Act* and the Minister of Employment and Immigration put in place mechanisms to process the claimants. The refugee backlog clearance process included, among other features, an interview with an immigration official at which the applicant was to be questioned on the humanitarian and compassionate aspects of his claim. This was later supposed to be followed by a hearing before the Refugee Determination Division of the Immigration Commission, at which the veracity of the claim was to be examined.

On August 16, 1989, Yhap underwent the interview before an immigration official in Toronto. The official followed a set of "guidelines" entitled the *Refugee Claimant Backlog Procedures*. He posed questions that sought to elicit information other than that regarding the humanitarian and compassionate aspects of Yhap's application. He then determined that there were insufficient grounds to accept Yhap's application for permanent residence in Canada. Yhap sought *certiorari* in the Trial Division of the Federal Court to quash that decision, as well as *mandamus* to compel the immigration authorities to process his application in accordance with the law and in accordance with the duty of fairness. The court granted his application. This case also served as an exemplar case for 25 other applicants. In the view of the court, no one simple case could have indicated the problem with the way in which immigration officials applied the *Backlog Clearance Policy*, but the large number of similar cases did show the consistency of the problem. This judgment therefore had far-reaching effect in respect of all the similar applicants, and even greater reach in the *ratio*

---

[29] Cross-reference to § 2.2.E.2.

it developed as to the proper interpretation and application of policy instruments.

The provision of statute that formed the basis of the proceedings in question here was section 114(2) of the *Immigration Act*, which referred to facilitation of a person's admission into Canada "for reasons of public policy or due to the existence of compassionate or humanitarian considerations." The purpose of the *Refugee Claimants Backlog Procedure* was to devise a policy instrument to complement this section and to give guidance to immigration officers in the field as to how to apply it to specific instances. The court characterized this policy instrument on several occasions as a "rule of thumb," which we can take as meaning that it should have been a subordinate aid to the application of discretion in a decision-making system based on law. As such, the central issue for the court's consideration in the matter of the use of discretion was whether the policy was applied in a flexible manner, or as a hard and fast rule. If the policy was applied rigidly, it could limit the scope of the immigration officials' discretion, thereby causing a deviation from the way the statute was intended to be applied.

> The applicants argue that the present policy guidelines applied by the Immigration Commission constitute a fetter on the statutory power of the Governor in Council to both exempt persons from the requirement of subsection 9(1) of the Act, and to authorize the landing of persons for humanitarian and compassionate reasons pursuant to subsection 114(2) of the Act. The applicants concede that policy guidelines may be established, but submit that these guidelines cannot be applied in such a manner as to fetter a statutory power of discretion.[30]

In considering this argumentation, the court turned to a leading textbook on Administrative Law in Common Law Canada to emphasize "the importance of flexibility in the adoption of policy or guidelines as a means of structuring discretion"[31] and to underline the difference between general and inflexible policy.

> On the other hand, it would be incorrect to assert that a delegate cannot adopt a general policy. Any administrator faced with a large volume of discretionary decisions is practically bound to adopt rough rules of

---

[30] [1990] 1 F.C. 722 at 726d-f.
[31] D.P. Jones & A.S. deVilliers, *Principles of Administrative Law* at 137, quoted *ibid.* at 739 a.

thumb. This practice is legally acceptable, provided each case is individually considered on its merits.[32]

The court also quoted from the Immigration Department's own manual to reinforce the manner in which the *Backlog Clearance Procedures* should have been used.

> Chapter 9 opens with the following passage, which appears under the heading "Exercise of Discretionary Powers:"
>
>> It is important...that officers realize that these guidelines are not intended as hard and fast rules. They will not answer all eventualities, nor can they be framed to do so. Officers are expected to consider carefully all aspects of cases, use their best judgement [*sic*], and make the appropriate recommendations.[33]

On the basis of evidence, the Trial Division of the Federal Court concluded that the Guidelines had not been applied in a sufficiently flexible manner, but had been used as strictly as if they had been rules of a statutory nature. In confirmation of the notion that policy rules are subordinate to legal ones, that they are less binding, and that they must be applied with less rigour, the court concluded as follows:

> Unfortunately, the guidelines adopted as "Humanitarian and Compassionate Review Criteria" in the "Refugee Claimants Backlog Procedures" directive do not, in the same way, impress me as criteria expressing general policy and "rough rules of thumb." The criteria much more strongly resemble inflexible self-imposed limitations on discretion, which clearly result in the pursuit of consistency at the expense of the merits of individual cases, I am of the opinion that this fettering of discretion constitutes a jurisdictional error which can only be redressed by providing the applicant with a full and fair interview of his humanitarian and compassionate claim in accordance with the law and the duty of fairness.[34]

---

[32] *Supra* note 30 at 739 c.

[33] *Ibid.* at 739 h.

[34] *Ibid.* at 740 i-741 a.

§ 2.2.E.4
R. v. Sparrow
Supreme Court of Canada; May 31, 1990
(1990), 70 D.L.R. (4th) 385

The core of this decision was the Supreme Court of Canada's first consideration of the genuine meaning and extent of the provision introduced into the Constitution of Canada by the 1982 amendments that recognized and affirmed existing aboriginal and treaty rights of aboriginal peoples.[35] Litigation ensued when a member of the Musqueam Band of Indians in British Columbia, who was fishing in a manner he alleged was consistent with existing aboriginal rights, was charged with having committed an offence under the *Fisheries Act*.[36]

The principal way in which this case developed the law in Canada was to determine that in giving meaning to the recognition of existing aboriginal rights, there must be a link between the question of justification of the action and the allocation of priorities. Federal power, for example here in the field of fisheries, must be reconciled with the federal duty toward aboriginals. It is in this context that the court addressed the issue in political law terms. The court looked at policy not in terms of a specific instrument of governance, but rather as a continuous practice. Even in this light, the judges concluded that the law held superiority over policy.

> ...historical policy on the part of the Crown is not only incapable of extinguishing the existing aboriginal right without clear intention, but is also incapable of, in itself, delineating that right. The nature of government regulations cannot be determinative of the content and scope of an existing aboriginal right. Government policy *can*, however, regulate the exercise of that right, but such regulation must be in keeping with s. 35(1).[37]

---

[35] *Constitution Act, 1982*, s. 35.
[36] R.S.C. 1970, c. F-14.
[37] (1990), 70 D.L.R. (4th) 385 at 403.

---

§ 2.2.E.5
W.G. Knight & Associates Inc. v. Manitoba (Securities Commission)
Manitoba Court of Queen's Bench; December 14, 1990
(1990), 47 Admin. L.R. 234

The field of securities regulation makes extensive use of policy instruments and is thus fertile ground for the development of jurisprudence rules about the proper role of such instruments. Here, the subject matter was the interest retention by broker/dealers on investors' payments of mutual fund purchases, pending the transfer of the purchase price by the broker to the distributor of the funds. The operation was subject to *National Policy 19*, adopted by the Manitoba Securities Commission and also in use in other Canadian jurisdictions. At the time this instrument was put in place, there were few independent brokers such as Knight. As more entered the market, the Commission extended the meaning of the policy to include these independents. *National Policy 19* dealt with the proper way of accounting for investors' payments received by brokers for the purchase of mutual funds, but its drafting was unclear and faulty. The court established two rules to guide the relations among instruments and therefore of bearing to political law. It said that in order to be applicable, policy rules must be drafted clearly and without technical faults. In this, they must follow the practice that dominates in the drafting of legal rules. Moreover, in the case of uncertainty, the party subjected to the policy is entitled to rely on an interpretation most favourable to itself.

---

§ 2.2.E.6[38]
Friends of the Oldman River Society v. Canada (Minister of Transport)
Supreme Court of Canada; January 23, 1992
[1992] 1 S.C.R. 3

We have encountered this decision in respect of the definition of law. It is also of great import in demonstrating the supremacy of norms provided in legal instruments over those which derive from policy instruments. The Oldman River project consisted of a dam's construction and the Society that initiated this action relied on the *Environ-*

---

[38] Cross-reference to § 1.3.A.6.

mental Assessment and Review Process Guidelines Order (EARPGO)[39] as being binding on the government departments involved, in order to attempt to have the work stopped.

Having determined the criteria for distinguishing legally and therefore judicially binding instruments from policy and therefore administratively binding ones, the court went on to set out the manner in which the two interact. It concluded first that Ministers had an implicit power to issue subordinate instruments such as "directives" in order to implement the administration of statutes for which they are responsible. It then went on to state quite clearly that among such subordinate instruments, those that do not amount to law are of a lower order and must give way to the law in order to respect the rule of law and to assure the integrity of the legal system.

> Here though we are dealing with a directive that is not merely authorized by statute, but one that is required to be formally enacted by "order," and promulgated under s. 6 of the *Department of the Environment Act*, with the approval of the Governor in Council. That is in striking contrast with the usual internal ministerial policy guidelines intended for the control of public servants under the minister's authority. To my mind this is a vital distinction. Its effect is thus described by R. Dussault and L. Borgeat in *Administrative Law* (2nd ed. 1985), vol. 1, at pp. 338-39:
>
> > When a government considers it necessary to regulate a situation through norms of behaviour, it may have a law passed or make a regulation itself, or act administratively by means of directives. In the first case, it is bound by the formalities surrounding the legislative or regulatory process; conversely, it knows that once these formalities have been observed, the new norms will come within a framework of "law" and that by virtue of the Rule of Law they will be applied by the courts. In the second case, that is, when it chooses to proceed by way of directives, whether or not they are authorized by legislation, it opts instead for a less formalized means based upon hierarchical authority, to which the courts do not have to ensure obedience. To confer upon a directive the force of a regulation is to exceed legislative intent. It is said that the Legislature does not speak without a purpose; its implicit wish to leave a situation outside the strict framework of "law" must be respected.

> The word "guidelines" cannot be construed in isolation; s. 6 must be read as a whole. When so read it becomes clear that Parliament has

---

[39] SOR/84-467.

elected to adopt a regulatory scheme that is "law," and thus amenable to enforcement through prerogative relief.[40]

---

§ 2.2.E.7

Rhéaume v. Canada

Federal Court of Appeal; December 2, 1992

(1992), 11 Admin. L.R. (2d) 124[41]

Rhéaume was involved in a grievance procedure before the Public Service Staff Relations Board (PSSRB). Her request to have the proceedings tape recorded was refused and she appealed. The Federal Court of Canada – Trial Division dismissed the case and here, the Federal Court of Appeal upheld the dismissal.

The court recognized the absence, in this instance, of any statutory provision regarding the recording of proceedings and hearings. In such a legal void, the PSSRB, or in fact any tribunal, whether a court of record or not, has complete discretion to adopt a general policy on the recording of its own proceedings. A policy adopted in these circumstances is legally unassailable, "provided that no discrimination is allowed to enter into the application of the policy."[42] The sense of this judgment is that in the absence of law, the court will intervene in the use of a policy instrument only if that instrument is applied in a discriminatory fashion; that is, only if the use of the policy results in the breaches of a legal norm.

---

§ 2.2.E.8

Nguyen v. Canada (Minister of Employment & Immigration)

Federal Court of Appeal; July 12, 1993

[1994] 1 F.C. 232[43]

This case questioned the binding and enforceable quality of policy instruments and did so by comparing them to the law itself. Nguyen was one of the people who succeeded in leaving Vietnam by boat after the fall of Saigon in 1975 and making his way as far as Hong

---

[40] [1992] 1 S.C.R. 3 at 36 a-h.

[41] Leave to appeal refused (1993), 11 Admin. L.R. (2d) 126n (S.C.C.).

[42] (1992), 11 Admin. L.R. (2d) 124 at 125.

[43] Leave to appeal refused (1994), 22 Imm. L.R. (2d) 159n (S.C.C.).

Kong. There, he was held in the Shumshui Po Detention Centre. A relative from Canada attempted to sponsor him as an immigrant to this country. Despite the fact that the *Immigration Manual* imposed on local immigration officers a duty to deliver an "Application for Landing" form to Nguyen, they did not do so. Consequently, he was screened out from eligibility as a convention refugee.

Where the courts look at a duty on public servants created by statute, they do not need to ask whether it is executable; they implicitly agree that it is. Here, however, the subject of examination was the *Immigration Manual*, a policy instrument. In the view of the majority of the court, the visa officers did have a duty to deliver the application form even though they saw the difference in the type of instrument.

> It is, of course, quite clear that the Immigration Manual by itself is nothing more than a set of administrative directives and, as such, does not have the force of law. Accordingly, failure to comply with the manual *simpliciter* does not necessarily involve a breach of duty such as could give rise to an order of *mandamus*. That is not an end of the matter, however. Not all duties imposed by law are express. An implied duty is nonetheless enforceable. At the very least, a document such as the Immigration Manual serves as evidence of what those charged with the administration of the *Immigration Act* and Regulations consider to be sound administrative practice. Nor is there any necessary discrepancy between such practice and the duty imposed by law.[44]

Thus, the public servant's opinion or assertion that execution of the duty imposed by the policy instrument is not possible is not sufficient to absolve him from such execution.

This view, which tends to assimilate a policy-based duty to legal obligation, was not unanimously held, however. The Chief Justice, in dissent, disagreed with the assumption on which Nguyen based his action, namely that internal directives could form the basis of a public duty sufficient to issue a writ of *mandamus*. Such a writ, he thought, could arise from a legal duty solely, one provided in a statutory provision. This would make policy directives such as the *Immigration Manual* unenforceable and therefore less binding and lower in the hierarchy of instruments than legal ones.

The debate on this matter is not yet concluded.

---

[44] (1993), [1994] 1 F.C. 232 at 245 d-h.

This is a practical decision. Large bureaucracies routinely issue their own internal policies and guidelines, and often publish these policies and provide them to the public. Certainly members of the public have been known to expect published policies to have some sort of legal force or at least limit the discretionary power of the bureaucracy. The majority decision in *Nguyen* is in accordance with what most people would expect of government agencies. As Chief Justice Laskin stated in *Martineau*, to permit an agency to disregard its own policies whenever it is so inclined is "much too nihilistic a view of law."[45]

---

§ 2.2.E.9
MacMillan Bloedel Ltd. v. Simpson
British Columbia Supreme Court; October 14, 1993
(1993), 12 C.E.L.R. (N.S.) 81
-and-
British Columbia Court of Appeal; March 28, 1994
(1994), 113 D.L.R. (4th) 368[46]

Many cases that reveal the manner of law's supremacy over policy arise from within legal proceedings and evoke sparse public attention. These judgments, however, are the result of a genuine public controversy in which the principles were forged in the limelight of popular and media scrutiny. The subject matter underlying the case was the issue of permits by the British Columbia government to MacMillan Bloedel, allowing it to cut timber in the Clayoquot Sound area of Vancouver Island. A number of environmentalists opposed the logging physically. They were enjoined from continuing their protest but refused to obey the order of the court. On October 5, 1993, the British Columbia Supreme Court found several of them guilty of criminal contempt of court, while some pleaded guilty.

The important element of the ruling for these purposes is that dealing with sentencing, in which the judge made a separate part of the judgment on October 14, 1993. This part of the judgment can be summed up as reaffirming the principle that in relations between the State and its citizens, actions based on the perceived benefit of a particular policy, such as the limitation of logging for reasons of

---

[45] (1993), 3 R.A.L. 3 at 5.
[46] Additional reasons at (1994), 43 B.C.A.C. 136 (B.C. C.A.), additional reasons at (1994), 1994 CarswellBC 2252 (B.C. C.A.), affirmed [1995] 4 S.C.R. 725 (S.C.C.), leave to appeal refused (1994), 179 N.R. 79 (note) (S.C.C.).

conservation, or those based on a political view or an ideology, namely environmentalism, cannot override general legal obligations such as maintaining the rule of law. This is even truer, the court felt, where other alternatives are available. Not even a moral conviction can be used as reasoning to justify breach of the law.

The categorical tone of the judgment, which may be thought to be excessive by some, belies the sound fundamental analysis it contains. The court's first pronouncement was that "democracy allows a society to govern itself by the rule of law and not by the rule of the individual,"[47] which should for these purposes be read as the rule of the individual's views and beliefs. It went on to explore the relationship of democracy and dissent.

> Some contend the democratic process did not work because the defendants were unable to persuade others as to the rightness of their cause. They say that disobedience to the law was their last and only resort. However, democracy does not fail just because a minority is unable to persuade the majority. It is the arguments of the minority that fail. When that happens, democracy expects the minority to refine their proposals and try again. Democracy does not accept their right to commit a public display of ill temper by defying a court order.

> . . .

> Standing on the side-lines and complaining about government policy is no test of character. Neither does it take much to go and sit on a road, block traffic and ask to be carried away by the police. What really shows a commitment to this country and to an idea is persistent involvement in the political process, listening to opposing points of view, fashioning reasonable replies and persuading others. That is difficult and time-consuming work. But it is what democracy is all about.[48]

Beyond the conceptual generalities, the judge scrutinized the conflict between the necessities of the rule of law and the legal system on the one hand, and the environmental policy views of the defendants on the other. It is interesting to note that he alternatively describes these policy views as political. With respect to the conduct of the trial and the defendants' desire to be tried separately, he motivates his refusal in part by indicating that if the defendants had stuck to legal issues

---

[47] (1993), 12 C.E.L.R. (N.S.) 81 at 105, para. 5.
[48] *Ibid.* at 108, paras. 17 and 20.

as compared to the political ones, the entire trial could have been concluded in no more than two weeks. He also comments, perhaps somewhat harshly, on defence counsel.

> The conduct of Mr. Moore Stewart was a great disappointment to me during this trial. He has little understanding as to his role as counsel. He allowed himself to become enmeshed in the largely irrelevant political issue that most defendants tried to pursue. In other words he lost his objectivity.[49]

In the fixing of sentences, finally, the judge finally situates the matter on the most appropriate plane and firmly refutes the defendants' attempt to use their own trial as an opportunity to examine British Columbia's forestry policy: "They appeared to think that they could try the issue of provincial government forestry policies if they wished."[50]

The flavour of this judgment was best captured by the *Globe & Mail*, when it reproduced excerpts from it under the title of, "The price of throwing 'an illegal public tantrum.'"[51]

The British Columbia Court of Appeal upheld the lower court's ruling. The substantive addition of the judgment on appeal to our understanding of the interaction of legal and political obligations is principally that the defence of necessity cannot operate to excuse conduct that has been specifically enjoined. The appeal justices also rejected the pleading that the defendant's conduct was a *Charter*-protected form of freedom of expression. If, in the end, individuals cannot decide which laws they will obey and which they will not, it is because law has precedence over actions motivated by personal views motivated by ideology, whether these are characterized as policy or political.

---

[49] *Ibid.* at 114, para. 55.
[50] *Ibid.* at 115, para. 61.
[51] October 18, 1993.

§ 2.2.E.10
Canada (Human Rights Commission) v.
Canada (Minister of Indian Affairs & Northern Development)
Federal Court of Canada – Trial Division; December 30, 1994
(1994), 89 F.T.R. 249

This case is an eloquent statement of the truth that a policy validly made pursuant to valid statutory provisions is valid and in effect, even if the statute pursuant to which it was made constitutes bad law. The precept that policy is subservient to law can thus be expanded to include the scenario that the validity of a policy does not depend on the quality or merit of the law it derives from and complements, but only on the validity of that law.

The Department of Indian Affairs and Northern Development (DIAND) adopted a policy in 1970 enabling parents of Indian children to choose the schools that their children would attend, taking religious criteria into consideration. Where the school chosen was distant, residential and transportation costs for the children would be assumed by DIAND. In 1987, the policy was changed to induce parents to send their children to local schools. We may presume that DIAND's motivation was financial savings. Faced with this change of policy, Prince, a Catholic mother of a student, lodged a complaint with the Commission, alleging that DIAND was engaging in discriminatory practices on grounds of religion, contrary to the *Canadian Human Rights Act*.[52] A Human Rights Tribunal heard the case and on January 6, 1993, dismissed the complaint on the ground that it lacked jurisdiction, as the *Indian Act*,[53] pursuant to which the 1987 policy change had been made, was shielded from the effect of the Canadian Human Rights Act by the following provision: "Nothing in this Act affects any provision of the Indian Act or any provision made under or pursuant to that Act."[54]

On an application for judicial review of the Tribunal's decision, the Federal Court – Trial Division agreed with the first ruling on the merits and also declined jurisdiction. It did so, however, in a way nothing short of spectacular. First, the court emphasized strenuously

---

[52] R.S.C. 1985, c. H-6.
[53] R.S.C. 1985, c. I-5.
[54] R.S.C. 1985, c. H-6, s. 67.

the characteristic of Canada as a secular state, one that is neither a theocracy nor an atheistic country. It then noted that confessional schooling was the one constitutional exception to the absolute secularity of the Canadian State, with a historically developed dichotomy between Catholic and Protestant/public school systems. It also observed that this dichotomy had been imparted into the *Indian Act*. On these bases, the court concluded that in withdrawing support for attendance at distant schools of a particular faith through the change of policy, the DIAND Minister had not acted illegally and was within his powers under the *Indian Act*. In essence, the new policy could not constitute religious discrimination as it was not meant to thwart provision of Catholic schooling to Prince's daughter.

The most significant analysis was that of the need for section 67 of the *Canadian Human Rights Act* in light of the true nature of the *Indian Act*.

[23] The need, if such there be, for such legislation is obvious. The *Indian Act* is racist. It countenances the segregation of people by race, into racist enclaves according to racially discriminatory laws. It makes financial dependents of those who pay no taxes as an eternal charge on those who are taxed to meet the expense of such dependency. The *Indian Act* fosters (along with the aboriginal treaties) an establishment of apartheid in Canada. If it were not for s. 67 of the *CHRA*, human rights tribunals would be obliged to tear apart the *Indian Act*, in the name and spirit of equality of human rights in Canada. They would be obliged to tear away the dependency and place Indians socially and financially shoulder to shoulder with all other Canadians, whether of the bland majority or of the visible minorities, and all Canadian taxpayers. Racial discrimination based on dependence would have to come, officially, to an end in Canada. The purpose of s. 67 is to avoid the stated values and imperatives of the constitution which would naturally put an end to the racial dependence of the *Indian Act* and the treaties, now countenanced by s. 35, Part II of the *Constitution Act, 1982*.

[24] Section 67 of the *CHRA* immunizes not only the legislative provisions of the *Indian Act*, but also that which is done by the Minister and by DIAND pursuant to the *Indian Act*, legally or illegally. Of course, s. 67 grants no immunity for illegal conduct by the Minister or DIAND. They are always subject to suit or judicial review for illegalities which are committed by government officials. But government officials who are actually administering the tax-free, financially dependent form of racism countenanced by the *Indian Act*, are immunized for so doing because of s. 67 of the *Canadian Human Rights Act*. The latter statute

simply cannot be invoked in circumstances such as those of this case, for over time if all the incorrect or illegal administration of the Indian Act were corrected by human rights tribunals that Act would be so permeated by human rights precepts that it would be ultimately destroyed.[55]

This unusually forceful definition of the *Indian Act* as being unsuited to the Canada of the 1990s had the effect of upholding the policy as having been validly made but damming its content as being necessarily consequent to the *Act*. The judgment was favourably received by progressive commentators.

> A coruscating judgement by Mr. Justice Francis Muldoon about racism in the Indian Act flashed briefly into the headlines last week.
>
> . . .
>
> The front line of the Federal Court is the trial division, where Mr. Justice Francis Muldoon has been speaking truth to the powerful for the past dozen years.
>
> . . .
>
> Never obscured by the legal citations, however, is the passion. In judgment after judgment, Muldoon returns to the "beauty" of Canada's constitutional values.
>
> . . .
>
> Nor is Muldoon afraid to criticize the powerful when these values are violated. It is one thing for a judge to illuminate Parliament's hypocrisy over racism in the *Indian Act*.[56]

See also *Gay v. Council, Township of Keppel* (November 27, 1997), (Ont. Gen. Div.), not completed.

---

[55] (1994), 89 F.T.R. 249 at 261.
[56] "Judge calls the powerful to account," Peter Calamai, *Ottawa Citizen*, January 14, 1995, p. B6.

2.2.F— SUPREMACY OF LEGAL NORMS OVER POLICY INSTRUMENTS IN CRIMINAL MATTERS

§ 2.2.F.1
R. c. Gosset
Québec Court of Appeal; May 24, 1991
[1991] R.J.Q. 1567[57]

Gosset, an officer of the Montreal Urban Community (MUC) Police, drew his gun on a person who had not paid his taxi fare; he called out a warning and as he did so, he shot the person in the temple, killing him. He was accused of manslaughter and acquitted. The Crown appealed. Among other grounds, it alleged that the trial judge erred in refusing to put into evidence the MUC Police "directives" regarding the use of firearms, thereby preventing the jury from determining properly whether there was negligence by Gosset in the use of his weapon.

Two of the three justices of the Court of Appeal reversed and sent the case back to be re-tried. Only the dissident judge analyzed the issue of the directive. While it may be argued that the strength of the argument is affected by the fact that it was made in dissent, we may also consider that the outcome of the judgment did not turn on this issue and that the dissenting judge was not contradicted on this point.

The trial judge had affirmed that the commission of an offence requires action contrary to a statute or a regulation adopted pursuant to it. Because of the variety of regulations regarding use of weapons by the police, the judge held that non-compliance could be no more than a matter for disciplinary action. Moreover, in order for the directives to be properly brought into the trial, the Crown would have had to question the accused about them. The dissenting appeal judge agreed with this reasoning. However, the important point he raised in regard to the directives was that in a criminal proceeding, they could not have the effect of altering the requirements set out in the *Criminal Code*.

---

[57] Affirmed [1993] 3 S.C.R. 76 (S.C.C.).

Je partage entièrement l'opinion du premier juge et les arguments de la
défense à ce sujet, que le simple dépôt de normes écrites propres à la
Communauté urbaine de Montréal ne peut modifier les exigencies du
Code criminel et, en soi, transformer en infraction ce qui ne le serait pas
objectivement par ailleurs, à moins que l'on établisse qu'elles se fondent
sur des normes de prudence raisonnables et justifiables. Sans explication,
il me parait que ces directives écrites ne peuvent avoir de poids ou de
pertinence dans l'appréciation de la conduite de l'intimé.[58]

2.2.G—POLICY INSTRUMENTS INCONSISTENT WITH LEGAL NORMS

§ 2.2.G.1
*Independent Contractors & Business Assn. (British Columbia) v.
British Columbia*
British Columbia Supreme Court; April 11, 1995
[1995] 7 W.W.R. 159

In British Columbia, the *Wage (Public Construction) Act*[59] determined
the wages payable to workers doing construction work for the Crown.
By way of a news release of March 30, 1992, the Minister of Labour
and Consumer Services issued an instrument entitled the *Fair Wage
and Skills Development Policy*, which purported to set out different
rules for the same area of business activity. On August 20, 1993, the
Minister extended the ambit of the Policy to include construction
projects of a lesser value as well. The Association applied for judicial
review to have the Policy declared a nullity.

The first matter considered by the court was the nature of policy
instruments. The Association said that a non-binding general expression of future intention would qualify as a policy, but that this instrument was more of a legal decree or rule promulgated by the government and attempted to be made applicable to all Ministers. The
Crown's reply on this point as that:

> Cabinet's source of authority for the Policy is not a statute or regulation,
> it is said, but, rather, its power to set and formulate government policies.
> Under basic principles of responsible government Cabinet is charged

[58] [1991] R.J.Q. 1567 at 1580.
[59] R.S.B.C. 1979, c. 426.

with the responsibility of setting government policies. It is accountable to the Legislative Assembly for the policies it chooses to pursue, and not to a court of law. Whilst implementation of a policy may be subject to judicial scrutiny, the formulation of government policy is not amenable to judicial review because of its inherently political nature.[60]

The Association's principal argument was that the Policy should be declared null because it conflicted with the statute. It ruled that the government had the power under common law and outside the provisions of a statute to establish the terms and conditions under which it would enter into construction contracts. The important point, however, was that "this power cannot be exercised in a way which is inconsistent with the provisions of the binding legislation."[61]

The Crown replied with a number of arguments. It contended that even though the instrument in question was characterized as a policy, it did not involve a power or right conferred by an enactment; essentially this meant that in the Crown's perception this was not subordinate legislation, and that judicial review therefore ought not to be available. It put forward that

> The formulation of the Policy here was a valid exercise of Cabinet's executive power to set government policy in respect of which it is accountable to the Legislature and not the Court. Cabinet's right to set policy is unaffected by legislation. Moreover, its authority to implement the Policy flows from Cabinet's ability as contractor to stipulate the conditions under which it will contract. That is a facet of the government's spending power and, whilst legislation may limit the government's exercise of its spending power, Cabinet's right to formulate and set policy with respect to the spending power is not affected by legislation and is not properly a matter for the Court to oversee.[62]

For good measure, the Crown also alleged that the policy did not conflict with the legislation.

The court determined first that the Policy was in fact a *Cabinet Directive*; that is, more than a mere policy instrument. The distinction arose from the actual formulation of the document, which included means for the enforcement of the policy. As such, the Policy ought, as the

---

[60] [1995] 7 W.W.R. 159 at 173.28.
[61] *Ibid.* at 170.17.
[62] *Ibid.* at 175.35.

Association pleaded, to have been in accordance with the legislation, but it was not. The differences related first to the geographic applicability of the various wages, and second to the procedure for determining fair wages. Once the statute existed, the subject matter dealt with in the law would have to be treated in compliance with the terms of the law or not at all.

If the Policy had been allowed to stand, the court would effectively have sanctioned two parallel regimes, one subject to statute and the other subject to the Policy. Determining which to apply would have become an extra-legal decision. Stated in another manner, the government could not amend a law through the vehicle of a policy. Moreover, the existence of two parallel regimes causes confusion and distortion in the legal system. The instrument inconsistent with legal norms had to be declared inapplicable and null.

2.2.H—ABSENCE OF LEGAL NORMS UNDERLYING POLICY INSTRUMENTS

§ 2.2.H.1
Concerned Citizens of Vinemount, Fruitland & Winona v. Canada Post Corp.
Federal Court of Canada – Trial Division; November 27, 1992
(1992), 58 F.T.R. 140

Policy goals may not be asserted by judicial means where there is no legal norm underlying these goals, or the instruments through which they are attempted to be expressed.

The communities of Vinemount, Fruitland and Winona, in southern Ontario, have been well-established and have used these geographic designations since before Confederation. In 1974, they were included within the City of Stoney Creek, itself part of the Regional Municipality of Hamilton-Wentworth. This latter entity was created by a statute of the province. The development of urban groupings allowed for limited use of traditional place names. In 1992, the plaintiffs applied to the Federal Court for prohibition or injunction to prevent Canada Post from completing a conversion plan for the entire City of Stoney Creek, leading to the use of the latter designation for postal service. The communities thereby wanted to protect their distinct identities.

The citizens relied for their case on customary usage of the place names they sought to preserve. The postal officials argued that the change was based on valid provincial legislation in the municipal field and contended that the citizens' application fail as it was grounded on no legal norm. The court dismissed the application principally on the ground that the citizens' reliance on custom alone would not justify their claim in law.

> While I can appreciate the residents of Vinemount, Winona and Fruit-land wish to maintain their "unofficial" names, I cannot see how this well intentioned desire has any basis in law upon which to assert rights against others. It appears that the closest the applicants can come to a legal basis is a right to customary usage.[63]

The court went on to declare that "the mere assertion of a legal right...that purports to create an issue for decision does not, of itself, and without some support in statute, case authority or text reference, meet this standard."[64]

From the political law perspective, the applicants' failure was that the policy or custom they advocated was made in the absence of legal grounding and could therefore not be applied by the court.

2.2.I—ABSENCE OF POLICY IMPLYING RESORT TO LAW

See *GHZ Resource Corp. v. Vancouver Stock Exchange* (1993), 1 C.C.L.S. 229 (B.C. C.A.), affirmed (1993), 1 C.C.L.S. 246 (B.C. C.A.).

---

§ 2.2.I.1
Gleason v. Lethbridge Community College
Alberta Court of Queen's Bench; December 5, 1995
(1995), 179 A.R. 130

Several complaints for sexual harassment were lodged against Glea-

---

[63] (1992), 58 F.T.R. 140 at 145.
[64] *Ibid.* at 146.

son, a student at the Lethbridge Community College. On less than one day's notice, he was called to a full meeting of the College's Sexual Harassment Committee. The rules applicable to the functioning of that Committee, to the creation of offences, and to the potential sanctions for such offences were contained in a policy instrument, which, at the time Gleason was called to the meeting and even at the start of the meeting, was still in draft form. The College's *Personal Sexual Harassment Policy* was in fact only adopted during the meeting at which Gleason's case was considered. Gleason was found to have contravened the policy and was suspended from the College for three-and-a-half years. Because of the schedule of the courses he was attending, this in effect amounted to an expulsion for four years. Gleason appealed.

The court allowed the application and set aside the decision to suspend. It held in very firm terms that an action on the basis of a policy can take place only if the policy has been adopted and is in effect, rather than being in draft form. While the court emphasized this criterion, it unfortunately failed to clarify whether the policy needed to have been adopted at the time of the charge and of the procedure based on that charge, or even earlier, at the time the offence was alleged to have taken place. The latter interpretation would appear more plausible, given the purpose of the ruling.

The court also motivated its ruling on the ground that in order for the policy to be applied, the accused would have to have known the manner of making the complaint, the procedure to follow, as well as the potential sanctions. Instead, Gleason was provided incomplete and imprecise information. The court also noted that the college did not even act in accordance with the conformity of the draft policy to the *Individuals' Rights Protection Act*,[65] which was the aim stated in the preamble of the instrument.

The court drew a simile to show how such a situation would have been reflected at the purely government level.

> Surely a draft Bill, discussion paper, or white paper put forward by an arm of government bears no authority until it is adopted in its final form by the appropriate legislative body. Does the Lethbridge Community College have some unknown ability to suspend students as a result of

[65] R.S.A. 1980, c. I-12.

policy not even approved by its governing body? I think not. The fact the policy was enacted part way through the harassment hearing cannot, in my view, cure a fatal flaw.[66]

In the absence of an existing and valid policy, the court had to resort to the law as it read it from the cases, in particular in terms of notice, procedural fairness, and general duty to act fairly.

---

§ 2.2.1.2
Trinity Western University v. College of Teachers (British Columbia)
Supreme Court of Canada; May 11, 2001
(2001), 199 D.L.R. (4th) 1

While it is recognized that policy instruments are to be within the bounds of law, there are instances where a court will carry that requirement to the extent of denying the binding nature of a policy, thereby putting its very existence into question in any capacity other than a self-generated statement of goals or intent. In such circumstances, the court can have resort to no other instrument but the law itself. The crux of such situations is the kind of circumstance, such as here, where the court purposely interpreted a policy not to be binding, apparently so that it would not be in contravention of legal norms, and so that the court could apply its own view of the law.

Trinity Western University was a religious institution of higher education based in Langley, near Vancouver. It expressed its fundamentalist world view in a policy that asked students to refrain from certain Biblical sins. The University's teacher training program consisted of four years of study on its own campus, with a fifth year spent under the *aegis* of Simon Fraser University. In 1995, Trinity applied to the B.C. Teachers' College, the provincial certification body, to be able to administer the fifth year of its program independently. Basing itself on the fact that Trinity's world view was in contradiction to the Canadian and British Columbia human rights legislation, the College rejected Trinity's application. The court was called upon to determine whether that rejection was valid. In particular, the issue at hand was whether Trinity's world view constituted discrimination against homosexuals, by policy and in contravention to the law.

---

[66] (1995), 179 A.R. 130 at 134.

A majority of the Court of Appeal of British Columbia quashed the decision of the College on the grounds that they either misapprehended or overlooked the evidence in the record. They agreed that students and faculty at Trinity were asked to signify their adherence to the precepts of the world view, but immediately turned around to indicate that the students did not have to subscribe to Trinity's statement of faith, nor did they have to adhere to it. They also noted that up to ten per cent of the student body could be non-adherents to the Christian world view. In effect, the court held that the policy was non-binding to the point of practical non-existence. They did not look at the persuasive effect of the policy. In the court's opinion, the College acted in anticipation of intolerant behaviour, thus making its decision patently unreasonable.

The decision included a strong and well-reasoned dissent, which presented the University's world view as a code of conduct; it may not have been phrased in a compulsory manner, but adherence to it was expected. The dissent was also based on the notion of the public interest in the education system, as well as on the distinction between the University's world view and the College's statement of the secular values of Canadian society, which included tolerance and recognition of the diverse nature of society. The legal view underlying the dissent was that Trinity's world view policy was a meaningful document and that consideration of its discriminatory nature was within the jurisdiction of the B.C. College of Teachers.

The College's appeal to the Supreme Court of Canada was dismissed by eight of the nine justices. They held first that the Teachers' College had jurisdiction to consider whether there were discriminatory practices at Trinity. They went on to say that the evidence in this case was speculative, involving considerations of potential future beliefs and conduct. The key to the court's finding, in which they essentially affirm the point made by the Court of Appeal in this regard, is that "although the BCCT was right to evaluate the impact of TWU's admission policy on the public school environment, they should have considered more."[67] In fact, the court clarifies that the "more" that the College ought to have considered is the *Human Rights Code*.[68] Looking at a policy with only a potential application was not enough; regard had to be had for the law.

---

[67] (2001), 199 D.L.R. (4th) 1 at 31, para. 32.
[68] R.S.B.C. 1996, c. 210.

2.3 ISSUE: LAW AND POLICY DISCRETION

See *LaSalle (Ville) c. Lavigne*, [1993] R.J.Q. 1419 (Que. S.C.) to 1431 and *Jerram v. Canada (Minister of Agriculture)*, [1994] 3 F.C. 17 (Fed. T.D.).

2.4 ISSUE: LAW AND POLITICS[69]

§ 2.4.1
Inuit Tapirisat of Canada v. Canada (Attorney General)
Supreme Court of Canada; October 7, 1980
[1980] 2 S.C.R. 735

This case is one of the most important and fundamental ones in recent Canadian history on the subject of the link between law and politics. In order to be properly understood in context, it must be read together with, and in contrast to, the *Operation Dismantle* case. On their face, these are administrative law cases. However, they both deal, with only a five-year interval between them, with the extent of the influence of legal norms on the processes of executive government. Stated more clearly in political law terminology, they illustrate the requirement to apply legal norms to essentially political processes at the highest level of governance, namely in the federal Cabinet. While they are both based on specific fact patterns and cannot be held to be of universal application, they do lay down the broadest terms of judicial opinion in this domain. The interval between these two cases was the time during which the *Canadian Charter of Rights and Freedoms* was adopted. This is the circumstance that provides the interest of their contrast.

On June 1, 1977, the Canadian Radio-Television and Telecommunications Commission (CRTC) authorized Bell Canada to increase its telephone rates in Québec, Ontario and the Northwest Territories. Following the path set out in section 64(1) of the *National Transportation Act*,[70] the Inuit Tapirisat of Canada (ITC) and the National Anti-

---

[69] Cross-reference to § 4.3, 6.6, 6.7, 10.8, 10.13 and 11.8.
[70] Then R.S.C. 1970, c. N-17, as amended.

poverty Organization petitioned the Governor in Council (Cabinet) to vary the CRTC's decision. The important facts of the case concern the manner in which the Cabinet conducted the hearing it was required to process in response to this petition. In all respects, this was a paper hearing; no witnesses were heard. The controversy related to the fact that:

- ITC's petition was put before the Cabinet through the filter of officials of the Department of Communications;
- the papers so prepared were not communicated to the parties;
- the CRTC was asked by Cabinet to offer its input and did so *ex parte*;
- the Minister of Communications made recommendations on the matter to the full Cabinet and participated in the deliberations;
- Bell was enabled to reply to ITC's case but ITC was not offered an opportunity to respond; and
- finally, that the Cabinet came to a decision on the basis of no further ITC input.

In the face of the manner in which the Cabinet reached its decision to leave the rate increase in place, ITC sought relief from the Federal Court of Canada – Trial Division and pursued the matter all the way through to the Supreme Court of Canada. Its principal contention was that the Cabinet process did not amount to a fair hearing of the case it wished to present.

> The plaintiffs submit that in the circumstances, the Governor-in-Council held no hearing in any meaningful sense of that word, and that, therefore, the decisions and Orders-in-Council made pursuant to them are nullities. Alternatively, it is submitted that if there was a hearing, the procedure employed did not result in a fair hearing, hence the decision and orders resulting are nullities.[71]

In the ITC's view, the Cabinet owed it a duty of fairness that comprised disclosure of the various submissions to the parties, the opportunity to reply, and notice by Governor-in-Council to all participants.

The Supreme Court framed the contention in administrative law terms, as follows:

---

[71] [1980] 2 S.C.R. 735 at 739-740.

The substance of the question before this Court in this appeal is this: is there a duty to observe natural justice in, or at least a lesser duty of fairness incumbent on, the Governor in Council in dealing with parties such as the respondents upon their submission of a petition under s. 64(1)?[72]

According to the specific perspective of this study, the matter is better characterized in terms of the relative influences of law, or legal norms, and political considerations on the decision that Cabinet had to make pursuant to section 64(1). To what extent was the Cabinet free to exercise its political perceptions and conversely, how much was its political will fettered by law?

The Supreme Court's view on the answer to this question must be stated carefully, because it is rather complicated. As a general rule the court seems to lay down the presumption of observance of legality: "...in my view the essence of the principle of law here operating is simply that in the exercise of a statutory power the Governor in Council, like any other person or group of persons, must keep within the law as laid down by Parliament or the Legislature."[73]

While this is clear enough, the court also relies on House of Lords precedent[74] to indicate that the rules of natural justice are not presumed to apply to bodies charged with administrative or executive functions.

In fact, this limitation on what the court sees as the requirement of Cabinet's submission to the rules of legality sets the tone for the entire judgment. The Supreme Court's decision is to deny the declaratory relief sought by ITC and consequently to leave the increased Bell rates unaffected. The core of the judgment is that the Cabinet's decision-making is not beyond judicial review merely by the fact that it is vested with a statutory power such as section 64(1). That review, however, is not one that aims to incorporate the rules of natural justice or procedural fairness into the deliberations of Cabinet members. Rather, it looks at whether Cabinet has observed the condition precedent arising out of law to its consideration of a matter. Where such a condition precedent has not been observed, the court can declare the exercise to be a nullity. In not binding the executive cabinet to the

---

[72] *Ibid.* at 745.
[73] *Ibid.* at 752.
[74] *Pearlberg v. Varty (Inspector of Taxes)*, [1972] 1 W.L.R. 534 (U.K. H.L.).

same standard of procedure as is applicable to the judiciary, the Supreme Court relied here on long-standing precedent arising from Canada.[75]

The court added much needed clarification to the way it felt Cabinet ought to render decisions that were essentially political but which nevertheless held a legal component.

> The petition does not constitute a judicial appeal or review. It merely provides a mechanism for a control by the executive branch of Government applying its perception of the public interest to the facts established before the Board, plus the additional facts before the Council. The Lieutenant-Governor in Council is not concerned with matters of law and jurisdiction which are within the ambit of judicial control. But it can do what Courts will not do, namely, it can substitute its opinion on a matter of public convenience and general policy in the public interest.
>
> . . .
>
> I prefer to regard the power as one reserved by the legislative to the executive branch of Government acting on broad lines of policy. There is no reason to fetter and restrict the scope of the power by a narrow judicial interpretation.[76]

In sum, the proper view of the influence of law before the *Charter* was that Governor in Council processes were broader and less fettered by constraints of legal principle than the work of the courts, but still subject to jurisdictional limits arising from statute.

Having provided a general position on the issue of law and politics, the court also offered pertinent indications relating to law in governmental operations. It emphasized that the executive branch could not be deprived of resort to its staff, whose role is to offer comments and advice concerning the policy issues of economic, political, commercial or other nature to ministers. It allowed that such advice could replace oral hearings by Cabinet that had taken place in earlier times. The evolution of Canadian government and society no longer rendered it possible for Cabinet to fulfil its functions in the manner of earlier decades.

---

[75] *Esquimalt & Nanaimo Railway v. Wilson* (1921), [1922] 1 A.C. 202 (British Columbia P.C.).

[76] *Supra* note 71 at 751-752.

These proceedings do no more than illustrate the change in growth of our political machinery and indeed the size of the Canadian community. It was apparently possible for the national executive in those days to conduct its affairs under the *Railway Act, supra,* through meetings or hearings in which the parties appeared before some or all of the Cabinet. The population of the country was a fraction of that today. The magnitude of government operations bears no relationship to that carried on at the federal level at present. No doubt the Governor in Council could still hold oral hearings if so disposed. Even if a court had the power and authority to so direct (which I conclude it has not) it would be a very unwise and impractical judicial principle which would convert past practice into rigid, invariable administrative procedures.[77]

The discretionary power that the court here called "complete" and subjected only to jurisdictional boundaries was, interestingly, to survive only for less than two years beyond this judgment. For reasons totally unconnected to the case, the means of conducting Canadian politics and the grip of law on Canadian political life would change forever upon the *Charter*'s incorporation into the Constitution.

---

§ 2.4.2
Thorne's Hardware Ltd. v. R.
Supreme Court of Canada; February 8, 1983
(1983), 143 D.L.R. (3d) 577

While this case is listed under the rubric of "Law and Politics," which is one of the fundamental links at the heart of political law study, the facts and arguments in issue would enable it to be more appropriately labelled as a case on the "Proper Exercise of Power" or even on "Governance." In that sense, this case flows directly from the Supreme Court's decision in the matter of *Inuit Tapirisat* and, in respect of the issue that is of greatest interest to us, it in fact relies on that precedent. The vital importance of this case is its analysis of the motives of the government in combining law and politics to govern.

Thorne's Hardware was a subsidiary of Irving Oil Ltd. and one of a number of related companies comprising the Irving conglomerate, the dominant economic power in New Brunswick. In the early 1970s, the Irving companies built harbour and related facilities near what

---

[77] *Supra* note 71 at 755.

was then the port of Saint John for the shipment of oil. They benefited from consequentially improved navigational facilities but avoided harbour tolls. In 1977, the Governor in Council, that is, the federal Cabinet, amended the *Saint John Harbour Boundaries Order*,[78] made pursuant to the *National Harbours Board Act*,[79] thereby including the Irving property within the limits of the port and enabling the port authorities to impose tolls on ships using the Irving dock. Irving Oil Ltd. instituted an action to avoid paying the tolls. In respect of the political law issue raised in this action, the outcome turned on whether the Order in Council extending the limits of the Port of Saint John was *ultra vires* the Cabinet on the basis of the motives underlying adoption of that Order in Council. Otherwise, the action also alleged that the National Harbour Board by-law imposing dues on ships using the port should not apply to Irving companies.

The company based its attack of the validity of the Order in Council on two grounds. First, it said that the instrument was made by the Cabinet for the purpose of enabling the National Harbours Board to collect harbour dues from Irving's navigation company without offering anything in return, and that this was an "improper motive." Second, it alleged that the Order in Council constituted a form of expropriation without compensation.

The most striking and important point of the case, that of the motive for the making of the Order in Council, attracted a unanimous negative response to Irving's line of argumentation by the sole judge of the Trial Division of the Federal Court of Canada, a panel of three judges of the Federal Court of Appeal, as well as a panel of five judges on the Supreme Court of Canada, including two future Chief Justices.

> In the Trial Division of the Federal Court, Dubé J. held the Order in Council *intra vires* and that, in the circumstances, the Order in Council could not be attacked on the ground of bad faith on the part of the Governor in Council...

> A unanimous Federal Court of Appeal...agreed with Mr. Justice Dubé that the Order in Council could not be successfully challenged on the ground of improper motive or discrimination...

---

[78] Order in Council P.C. 1977-2115; SOR/77-621.
[79] R.S.C. 1970, c. N-8.

I agree with the Federal Court of Appeal.[80]

The Supreme Court of Canada went on to explain its rejection of the Irving argument. It wanted to show that it was jurisdictionally competent to deal with the matter; toward that end, it affirmed its own holding of three years earlier in the *Inuit Tapirisat* case, to the effect that jurisdictional review can apply to decisions of the Cabinet where, as here, the decision in question is made on the basis of a statutory power.

> Law and jurisdiction are within the ambit of judicial control and the courts are entitled to see that statutory procedures have been properly complied with:
>
> . . .
>
> Decisions made by the Governor in Council in matters of public convenience and general policy are final and not reviewable in legal proceedings. Although, as I have indicated, the possibility of striking down an Order in Council on jurisdictional or other compelling grounds remain open, it would take an egregious case to warrant such action. This is not such a case.[81]

With respect to the allegation that the Cabinet had acted in bad faith, the court started by adopting as its own the reasoning of the Federal Court of Appeal.

> The reasons the Governor in Council may have had for exercising this authority, in addition to being unknown to us, are of little importance, since I do not see how they could affect the validity of the order. I would add that a desire to increase the revenues of a harbour appears to me to be a justifiable reason for extending the harbour's boundaries.[82]

Responding, further to the pleading that the Federal Court of Appeal had not examined adequately whether the Cabinet had exercised what Irving's lawyer called "proper motives" in making the Order in Council, the court reacted categorically: "It is neither our duty nor our right to investigate the motives which impelled the federal cabinet to pass the Order in Council."[83]

---

[80] (1983), 143 D.L.R. (3d) 577 at 580.
[81] *Ibid.* at 580-581.
[82] *Ibid.* at 581.
[83] *Ibid.* at 581.

This was still not enough, however, and the court stated its position in broader terms: "Governments do not publish reasons for their decisions; governments may be moved by any number of political, economic, social or partisan considerations."[84]

The foregoing can be taken as the general position of the judiciary on the jurisdictionally proper exercise of power by the executive branch of government. The statement is to the effect that government does not publish reasons for governing, but its real meaning is that the government does not legally need to publish reasons for undertaking the decisions it does. Provided that the government respects its legal and jurisdictional limits, the courts must, and will, leave it free to apply the proper blend of public policy and politics through which it wants to exercise power, that is, to govern. In essence, the court recognized a veil that reserved a domain for governance within the bounds of law. This position is noteworthy not only in respect of the relationship of law and politics, but also has importance in regard to the relations among the branches of government.

We must remember that this was a pre-*Charter* case. A few years later, the *Charter* would qualify the position of the judiciary both *vis-à-vis* the veil protecting the executive from scrutiny as to its motives and *vis-à-vis* the extent of the domain of law.

Having declared that it need not examine the government's motives, the Supreme Court of Canada in effect did so and in the process offered a fascinating look beyond the veil and inside the thinking of government. It applied the rules it had laid down to this particular case. Under the legislation that constituted the National Harbours Board, despite Irving's allegation that the Saint John Harbour limits could not be extended so as to increase revenues, the court felt that the extension was designed as much for rationalization of the harbour as for additional revenue generation.

> I have referred to these several pieces of evidence, not for the purpose of canvassing the considerations which may have motivated the Governor in Council in passing the Order in Council but to show that the issue of harbour extension was one of economic policy and politics; and not one of jurisdiction or jurisprudence.[85]

---

[84] *Ibid.* at 582.

[85] *Ibid.* at 584.

The merit of this citation is to show that while legal considerations used to be borne in mind, Cabinet decisions such as this one are motivated to a great degree by policy and political considerations. The law is present and it influences both what happens in politics and how it happens, but its influence on the minds of governmental decision-makers is different, in the sense of unique, from that of politics or policy.

---

§ 2.4.3[86]
Operation Dismantle Inc. v. R.
Supreme Court of Canada; May 9, 1985
(1985), 18 D.L.R. (4th) 481

This case is one of the most significant judicial statements of the current, *Charter*-era state of the relationship of law and politics in Canada. It is particularly noteworthy because it follows in the traces of the *Inuit Tapirisat* case and provides a contrast with that decision; *Inuit Tapirisat* was decided in the last years of the pre-*Charter* era, while *Operation Dismantle* came shortly after the *Charter*'s adoption fostered in this country a thorough rethinking of the law-politics link and drew the two much more closely together. In both instances, what was at stake was the legal validity of a Cabinet decision made on political grounds.

On July 15, 1983, the Canadian Government of Prime Minister Trudeau made a decision in response to a request of the American Government of President Ronald Reagan. The Cabinet permitted that cruise missiles of the United States military be tested in the airspace over Canadian territory. Operation Dismantle Inc., a grouping of organizations and unions, started an action on July 20, asking for a declaration that this decision violated the rights of Canadians under section 7 of the *Charter*, which protected the right to life and security of the person, in that it would increase the risk for Canada of nuclear war. They also sought an injunction and damages. On August 11, 1983, the Crown presented a motion to strike out the Statement of Claim as disclosing no reasonable cause of action, as being frivolous and vexatious, and as constituting an abuse of process. The litigation evolved from this motion. The Federal Court of Canada – Trial Di-

---

[86] Cross-reference to § 1.3.A.1.

vision refused it. The Federal Court of Appeal allowed an appeal thereby throwing out the case. The Supreme Court of Canada refused a further appeal, resulting in the success of the Crown motion and the striking of Operation Dismantle's Statement of Claim.

The pith and substance of the decision was that, in this case, the applicant on the merits, Operation Dismantle, was unable to make out its case because the evidence it submitted was imprecise and speculative, thereby not supportive of the conclusions it had reached.

> What can be concluded from this analysis of the statement of claim is that all of its allegations, including the ultimate assertion of an increased likelihood of nuclear war, are premised on assumptions and hypotheses about how independent and sovereign nations, operating in an international arena of radical uncertainty, and continually changing circumstances, will react to the Canadian Government's decision to permit the testing of the cruise missile.
>
> . . .
>
> In brief, it is simply not possible for a court, even with the best available evidence, to do more than speculate upon the likelihood of the federal Cabinet's decision to test the cruise missile resulting in an increased threat of nuclear war.[87]

The court also indicated what standard the applicant should have met in order to make the case.

> Thus, to succeed at trial, the appellants would have to demonstrate, *inter alia*, that the testing of the cruise missile would cause an increase in the risk of nuclear war. It is precisely this link between the Cabinet decision to permit the testing of the cruise and the increased risk of nuclear war which, in my opinion, they cannot establish.[88]

These words were rather prophetic as, since the *Operation Dismantle* case, many litigants in law and politics cases have had great difficulty in handling social science evidence before the courts in a manner suitable for judicial analysis and decision-making.

As part of the court's *ratio*, however, the Chief Justice did make a fundamental statement that drew the clear line of distinction between

---

[87] (1985), 18 D.L.R. (4th) 481 at 490.

[88] *Ibid.* at 488.

this case and *Inuit Tapirisat*. This is so important that it is worth reproducing in both ways it was phrased.

> Thus, although decisions of the federal Cabinet are reviewable by the courts under the Charter, and the government bears a general duty to act in accordance with the Charter's dictates, no duty is imposed on the Canadian Government by s. 7 of the Charter to refrain from permitting the testing of the cruise missile.[89]

...and then later...

> I agree with Madame Justice Wilson that Cabinet decisions fall under s. 32(*a*) of the Charter and are therefore reviewable in the courts and subject to judicial scrutiny for compatibility with the Constitution. I have no doubt that the executive branch of the Canadian Government is duty bound to act in accordance with the dictates of the Charter. Specifically, the Cabinet has a duty to act in a manner consistent with the right to life, liberty and security of the person and the right not to be deprived thereof except in accordance with the principles of fundamental justice.[90]

The effect of this holding is that even in its political decision-making, the Cabinet, as the highest institution of the Government of Canada, would be subject to the constitutional-legal norms established by the *Charter*. The reach and influence of law into the realm of governance and its ascendancy over politics was now far greater than in the days of *Inuit Tapirisat*, thanks to the profound change brought about by the *Charter*. In sum, this general rule set out by the court in the present case was far more important that the negative adjudication of Operation Dismantle's own application.

While the outcome of this litigation is noteworthy and the new statement of the law-politics relationship it provided is worthy of even greater retention, *Operation Dismantle* also provides a wealth of analysis on the legal doctrines underlying the law-politics link. It was Madame Justice Wilson's judgment in particular that developed this topic.

Wilson wrote on the doctrine of justiciability, as it applied in Canada. She characterized this as the ability of the courts to deal with political issues. The lower courts had relied on the argument that the case of

---

[89] *Ibid.* at 485.
[90] *Ibid.* at 491.

Operation Dismantle was either not susceptible of proof, or that it was
of a nature that the courts were incapable of evaluating. She thought
that that prejudiced the substance of the plaintiff's case in a motion
proceeding such as this one. Cases relating to political decisions and
therefore involving the true (*i.e.*, vital) interests of the country, depending on an infinity of considerations, including military, diplomatic, technical, psychological and moral one, are triable, she said.[91]
This brought Wilson to address the question of whether there is
judicial competence to look at matters of this nature brought before
the courts. Were such matters within the province of the courts to
assess? Were the evidentiary problems insurmountable?

> The real issue there, and perhaps also in the case at bar, is not the *ability*
> of judicial tribunals to make a decision on the questions presented, but
> the *appropriateness* of the use of judicial techniques for such purposes.
>
> I cannot accept the proposition that difficulties of evidence or proof
> absolve the court from making a certain kind of decision if it can be
> established on other grounds that it has a duty to do so. I think we should
> focus our attention on whether the courts *should* or *must* rather than on
> whether they *can* deal with such matters.[92]

Clearly, in Wilson's opinion, political questions were of a nature
which courts could address and the difficulties of framing evidence
in such a manner that the judiciary would be able to deal with it on
legal grounds ought not to be deemed insurmountable.

On this point, Wilson's ruling was clearly the best statement of the
position of the Supreme Court of Canada. The Chief Justice specified
his agreement with her analysis.

> I agree in substance with Madame Justice Wilson's discussion of justi-
> ciability and her conclusion that the doctrine is founded upon a concern
> with the appropriate role of the courts as the forum for the resolution of
> different types of disputes. I have no doubt that disputes of a political
> or foreign policy nature may be properly cognizable by the courts.[93]

---

[91] Wilson's opinion was based on the precedent of *Chandler v. Director of Public Prosecutions* (1962), [1962] 3 All E.R. 142, [1964] A.C. 763 (U.K. H.L.).

[92] *Supra* note 87 at 500.

[93] *Supra* note 87 at 494.

Wilson then went on to give depth to the justiciability argument by distinguishing it from the related doctrine of political questions, which had been adopted by the American courts. By contrast to the examination of the courts' ability to deal with political matters under the doctrine of justiciability, the heart of the political questions doctrine was the appropriateness for the courts of undertaking examination of such questions. The doctrine of political questions was a principle of American constitutional law that flowed from the separation of powers, which is much stronger in the United States than in countries such as Canada, with a parliamentary system. Its major tenet is that there are political disputes with which a court ought to refuse to deal.

> Prominent on the surface of any case held to involve a political question is found a textually demonstrable constitutional commitment of the issue to a coordinate political department; or a lack of judicially discoverable and manageable standards for resolving it; or the impossibility of deciding without an initial policy determination of a kind clearly for nonjudicial discretion; or the impossibility of a court's undertaking independent resolution without expressing lack of the respect due coordinate branches of government.[94]

The classic American case on this issue is *Baker v. Carr*.

Wilson continued the distinction of the two doctrines by pointing out that the United States Supreme Court had applied the political questions doctrine unevenly and had not allowed its own respect for, or deference to, the other branches of government, or the judicial unmanageability of cases, to prevent it from deciding cases in which it had felt a need to render a decision. Neither in the United States nor in the United Kingdom, she thought, did the doctrine effectively prevent the judiciary from adjudicating on political matters; that is, from extending the rule of law onto the domain of politics. In the later discussion of section 1 of the *Charter*, she noted that this provision was the uniquely Canadian mechanism to enable the courts to determine the justiciability of issues that come before them, and that it obviates the need for a political questions doctrine in this country. The implication of Wilson's opinion can only be that Canadian courts should not refrain either from following a similar pattern. The consequence is a fundamental extension of the role of law, based on legal

---

[94] *Supra* note 87 at 500-501, citing from *Baker v. Carr*, 369 U.S. 186 (1962) at 217.

reasoning, provided this is done in the proper manner. The summary of Wilson's conclusion is that:

> It seems to me that the point being made by Lord Devlin, as well as by Tigar and Henkin in their writings, is that the courts should not be too eager to relinquish their judicial review function simply because they are called upon to exercise it in relation to weighty matters of State. Equally, however, it is important to realize that judicial review is not the same thing as substitution of the court's opinion on the merits for the opinion of the person or body to whom a discretionary decision-making power has been committed. The first step is to determine who as a constitutional matter has the decision-making power; the second is to determine the scope (if any) of judicial review of the exercise of that power.
>
> . . .
>
> I do not think it is open to it to relinquish its jurisdiction either on the basis that the issue is inherently non-justiciable or that it raises a so-called "political question."[95]

With specific reference to this case, Wilson set out, finally, the limits of the court's duty in examining political matters.

> I would conclude, therefore, that if we are to look at the Constitution for the answer to the question whether it is appropriate for the courts to "second guess" the executive on matters of defence, we would conclude that it is not appropriate. However, if what we are being asked to do is to decide whether any particular act of the executive violates the rights of the citizens, then it is not only appropriate that we answer the question; it is our obligation under the Charter to do so.[96]

Thus, this case not only determined that Cabinet is subject to constitutional-legal considerations in its political decision making but also laid out the road map for Canadian courts in dealing with legal disputes based on decisions so made.

See also *Reference re Language Rights Under s. 23 of Manitoba Act, 1870 & s. 133 of Constitution Act, 1867*,[97] [1985] 1 S.C.R. 721 (S.C.C.).

---

[95] *Supra* note 87 at 503-504.
[96] *Supra* note 87 at 504.
[97] Cross-reference to § 1.12 and 8.9.

---

§ 2.4.4[98]
Dixon v. British Columbia (Attorney General)
British Columbia Supreme Court; April 18, 1989
(1989), 59 D.L.R. (4th) 247

The British Columbia Supreme Court was faced with a petition to have declared unconstitutional these provisions of the province's *Constitution Act*,[99] which established the distribution of electoral constituencies within the province. For reasons relating to the extent of deviation of constituencies from the norm of voting parity, the provisions were struck down as being contrary to section 3 of the *Canadian Charter of Rights and Freedoms*.

The court, having reached its conclusion on the merits of the case, proceeded to examine the potential remedies. As part of this process, it dealt with the submission of the Attorney General that judicial intervention regarding the composition of electoral districts was inappropriate because the matter should be left for argumentation through the political process. Dixon countered, pleading that, to the contrary, as a constitutionality argument had been raised in light of the *Charter*, the court not only had no discretion to decline to deal with the matter, but also had indeed a duty to decide. This was the first consideration of a *Charter* section 3 argument based on unequal electoral apportionment in a province by a superior court since the advent of the *Charter*; at least on the subject matter, the court was venturing onto new ground. Moreover, the case dealt both with the relationship of law and politics as aspects of governance, as well as with the relationship of power between the judicial and legislative branches of government.

The ruling relied extensively on the Supreme Court of Canada's decision in *Operation Dismantle*[100] and, as that case had done, cited from American cases dealing with the political questions doctrine. On the basis of precedents, the court came to the conclusion that the matter was justiciable; that is, that it was susceptible of judicial decision-making. Going further, in light of the *Charter*, the court saw that if it

---

[98] Cross-reference to § 3.6.1.
[99] R.S.B.C., 1979, c. 62, s. 19 and Schedule 1.
[100] (1985), 18 D.L.R. (4th) 381 (P.E.I. C.A.).

was going to uphold the supremacy of the Constitution *vis-à-vis* other laws, it had a duty to adjudicate.

> There is no question that the process of electoral districting is first and foremost the task of legislature; nor any question that the balancing of the disparate interests and considerations involved in a process that affects the root of one of our most basic political institutions renders it a task best undertaken by our elected representatives. However, the mere fact that the legislature is better suited to weight the myriad factors involved in electoral apportionment, does not remove from this court the ultimate responsibility of weighing the product of the exercise of the legislature's discretion against the rights and freedoms enshrined in the Charter and from examining the justification for any infringement that the courts are required to undertake under s. 1. This is not merely a question of the separation of powers and the authority of the legislature to act: the right to vote is entrenched in our Constitution and is of such importance that it is above the override powers in the Charter, s. 33. If in giving substance to this right to vote, the court interprets s. 3 as granting to citizens the right to a certain degree of proportionate representation, then legislative efforts must be measured against this standard and if they fall short, be declared unconstitutional.
>
> The existence of an alternate political remedy is no answer to the Court's duty to pronounce on constitutional questions.[101]

This *ratio* is important in itself, in that it was one of the milestones of securing the *Charter's* role as the arbiter of the legality of political processes. The ingenuity of the case is that it went even one step beyond this, finding that, "The existence of an alternative political remedy is no answer to the Court's duty to pronounce on constitutional questions."[102]

Thus, even where a process could be both political and legal, and where the legislature and the judiciary could share functions in respect of finding and stating the law, the courts could not abdicate their fundamental role.

---

[101] (1989), 59 D.L.R. (4th) 247 at 278.
[102] *Ibid.*

§ 2.4.5[103]
Thomson Newspapers Corp. v. Canada (Attorney General)
Supreme Court of Canada; May 29, 1998
[1998] 1 S.C.R. 877

In the course of an election campaign, when the attention of the citizenry is focused on politics more than at any other time, what information about electoral issues and about prospects of political success, which can affect the outcome of the campaign, can be laid before the electorate? By whom? In what manner? One school of thought holds that it is the duty of the State to attempt to create a playing field as level as possible in order to prevent the electorate from being influenced in an undue manner, perhaps by incomplete or false information, to which the electorate cannot obtain sufficient clarifying counterpoint. Another school voices the opinion that all information created or compiled by anyone should be placed before the electorate and that it should be left up to voters alone to determine the veracity and value of all information made available to them, no matter its origin, its timing or the purpose, political, electoral or otherwise, of its release. In Canada, this debate has raged throughout most of the last decade in respect of the use of public opinion polls as elements of information in election campaigns.

In 1993, in expectation of an oncoming general election, the Progressive Conservative Government of Prime Ministers Mulroney and later on Campbell, had Parliament enact a new provision into the *Canada Elections Act*, regarding polls.[104] This section 322.1 was rooted in the recommendations of the Lortie Royal Commission, which had reported to Parliament in November, 1991.[105] It prohibited broadcasting, publishing or disseminating the results of opinion surveys analyzing the prospects of electoral success of parties, or those regarding issues that would permit the identification of a political party or candidate, during the last weekend of a campaign, as well as on voting day.

---

[103] Cross-reference to § 5.10.
[104] S.C. 1993, c. 19, s. 125; assented to May 6, 1993; in force June 25, 1993.
[105] Final Report, Royal Commission on Electoral Reform and Party Financing (November 1991).

This measure was highly controversial while it was proceeding through the Parliamentary process. Upon its enactment, it became a lightning rod for criticism, in particular from the media. Even before the campaign for the 35th federal general election, set for October 25, 1993, was completed, the national press announced that they would combine to challenge the constitutionality of section 322.1 on grounds of "reckless interference with free expression"[106] and because the provision amounted to "keeping useful information from the voting public at the time when it is most needed."[107]

The *Charter* challenge did move ahead after the election. On May 15, 1995, the Ontario Court (General Division) upheld the validity of the legislation.[108] The Ontario Court of Appeal also upheld it on August 19, 1996.[109] By the spring of 1997, when the Supreme Court of Canada had granted leave to appeal the case to it, the political mood indicated the imminence of another general election. In order to avoid the applicability of section 322.1 to them during that election, the newspapers motioned the Supreme Court to abridge time and expedite its hearing; this was refused.

The 36th federal general election was held on June 2, 1997, with section 322.1 in place. The Supreme Court eventually issued its decision on May 29, 1998. It agreed with the plaintiffs-appellants that section 322.1 was an infringement on their freedom of expression and that it was not saved by section 1 of the *Charter*. The merits of the case in respect of the law on public opinion polling is best left to be dealt with in Chapter 5 of this study. The matter of greater interest for students of political law is what the court said in respect of the law and politics relationship.

The justices of the Supreme Court broke into two camps on this matter. A majority of five felt that the blackout on polls at the end of a campaign was a breach of the *Charter's* 2(b) protection of freedom of expression. In the necessarily consequential section 1 analysis that followed, under the pen of Justice Bastarache, they examined the contextual factors at play. They looked first at the nature of public

---

[106] "Newspapers challenge ban on polls," *Globe & Mail*, October 16, 1993.
[107] "The Hamburger Poll Act," *Globe & Mail*, October 22, 1993, p. A20.
[108] (1995), 24 O.R. (3d) 109 (Ont. Gen. Div.).
[109] (1996), 138 D.L.R. (4th) 1 (Ont. C.A).

opinion polls as political speech, or, more precisely, political information.

> In this case, the speech infringed is political information. While opinion polls may not be the same as political ideas, they are nevertheless an important part of the political discourse, as manifested by the attention such polls receive in the media and in the public at large, and by the fact that political parties themselves purchase and use such information. Indeed, the government argues that opinion polls have an excessive impact on the electoral choices made by voters. As a genre of speech, unlike hate speech or pornography, this expression is not intrinsically harmful or demeaning to certain members of society because of its direct impact, or its impact on others. It is without moral content, and yet it is widely perceived as a valuable and important part of the discourse of elections in this country. The government urges, however, that under some circumstances polls may come to have an effect which interferes with the ability of individuals to make an informed choice.[110]

The core of the government's defence of the restriction on the dissemination of the political information contained in polls was that the law should provide an end-of-campaign period of reflective rest for voters and that the law should guard against inaccurate polling. The court rejected both those objectives. What is interesting for our purposes, however, is that, beyond the strict *Charter* analysis involved, the case enabled the court to make a statement about the law-politics link and to expound on the extent to which the law should penetrate this aspect of political life, namely the organization of information for the electorate. The court's view on this matter can best be summarized as being that the law can, in general, be used to guide the use of polling information, but that this law in particular, namely section 322.1, was not properly designed to fit within *Charter* parameters. In this regard the particulars of the court are most pertinent.

The majority made two statements about the law's view on the ability of voters to discern political information.

> An examination of this purpose reveals some disturbing assumptions. First, this purpose does not rely on the inaccuracy of any opinion survey results. Rather, it suggests that Canadians will become so mesmerized by the flurry of polls appearing in the media that they will forget the issues upon which they should actually be concentrating. This reasoning

---

[110] [1998] 1 S.C.R. 877 at 943, para. 81.

cannot be countenanced. Canadian voters must be presumed to have a certain degree of maturity and intelligence. They have the right to consider the results of polls as part of a strategic exercise of their vote. It cannot be assumed that in so doing they will be so naive as to forget the issues and interests which motivate them to vote for a particular candidate. Nor can Canadians be presumed to assume that polls are absolutely accurate in predicting outcomes of elections and that they thus will overvalue poll results. Many polls are released in the course of an election campaign which belies the suggestion that any one poll could be perceived as authoritative. These opinion polls yield differing results even when conducted contemporaneously, and, perhaps more importantly, opinion poll results fluctuate dramatically over time. I cannot accept, without gravely insulting the Canadian voter, that there is any likelihood that an individual would be so enthraled by a particular poll result as to allow his or her electoral judgment to be ruled by it.

I am thus unable to perceive, and nor has the government seriously argued before us, that any pressing and substantial objective is served by the existence of a "rest period" for polls prior to the election date. I would, therefore, find that s. 322.1 is not justified under s. 1 according to this objective.[111]

Later on, the court picked up the same theme again, that the law should treat members of the electorate as political actors in such a manner that they be enabled to make political decisions autonomously on the basis of the various and possibly contradictory political information placed before them.

> The impact on freedom of expression in this case is profound. This is a complete ban on political information at a crucial time in the electoral process. The ban interferes with the rights of voters who want access to the most timely polling information available, and with the rights of the media and pollsters who want to provide it. It is an interference with the flow of information pertaining to the most important democratic duty which most Canadians will undertake in their lives: their choice as to who will govern them. Such a polling ban also sends the message that the media in their role as a reporter of information, and not as an advertiser, can be muzzled by the government. Rather than approaching the problem of inaccurate polls as a question of *too little* information, or added incentives for preventing the publication of *inaccurate polls*, the government constrains the range of evaluations that a voter is permitted to make in fulfilling their sacred democratic function as a citizen. It justifies such a measure on the basis that some indeterminate number of

---

[111] *Ibid.* at 949-950, paras. 101-102.

voters *might* be unable to spot an inaccurate poll result *and might* rely to a significant degree on the error, thus perverting their electoral choice.[112]

The final word of the majority was a rejection of the option selected by Parliament.

> ...nor can I accept here a measure which decides that information which is desired and can be rationally and properly assessed by the vast majority of the voting electorate should be withheld because of a concern that a very few voters might be so confounded that they would cast their vote for a candidate whom they would not have otherwise preferred. That is to reduce the entire Canadian public to the level of the most unobservant and naive among us. This concern is also very remote from any danger that the guarantee of effective representation will be undermined.[113]

The minority comprised the Chief Justice and Justices L'Heureux-Dubé and Gauthier, the three Québecers on the court. In their view, the outright suppression of polls would not have been permissible, but their regulation, as put forward in section 322.1, was valid as a legislative objective and caused no breach of section 2(b) of the *Charter*. While the minority realized the importance of public opinion polls and perceived their contribution to a well-informed electorate, they affirmed that its purpose was to improve the flow of information to the electorate during a campaign; it did not dictate or deal with the content of the expression.

> The *Charter* should not become an impediment to social and democratic progress. It should be made to serve substantial commercial interests in publishing opinion poll results, by defeating a reasonable attempt by Parliament to allay potential distortion of voter choice.[114]

As can be expected, the press reacted to this decision with unbridled glee. Their reaction was once again outraged, however, when, in 1999, the government introduced a new legislative proposal in the context of the Bill C-2 overhaul of the *Canada Elections Act*. This measure was given Royal Assent on May 31, 2000, as S.C. 2000, c. 9. The new provisions shorten the blackout period on polls and obliges the pub-

---

112 *Ibid.* at 971, para. 127.
113 *Ibid.* at 972, para. 128.
114 *Ibid.* at 908, para. 30.

lication of methodological data about them. It appears possible that this measure will be challenged in the courts as well.

---

§ 2.4.6[115]
Reference re Secession of Québec
Supreme Court of Canada; August 20, 1998
(1998), 161 D.L.R. (4th) 385

In no case discussed in this book, and certainly in no litigation undertaken since the Confederation of Canada in 1867, has the relationship of law and politics, and in particular the role of law in the conduct of public affairs, been more important, or more interesting, than in this one.

Through the public debate of the issue of an eventual secession by Québec from Canada, through the marshalling of the arguments by the litigators taking instructions from their political clients, real or putative in the case of the *amicus curiae*, through the judgment itself, as well as through the undiminished public, political, scholarly and media discussion thereafter, we can see that law and politics are not only inextricable in democratic governance, they are indeed complementary aspects of the same subject matter. They are indispensable to each other and unavoidable as much to the governors as to the governed.

The externalities of the law and politics issue in relation to this reference, namely whether the defence of the State, its sovereignty and unity, are better undertaken by legal or by political means, or in other words should this matter have been referred to the court, is dealt with separately in Chapter 4. In this analysis, the focus is maintained on the law-politics reasoning within the case.

The initial point to address is whether such a reference, and more directly whether this particular reference, is a matter of politics or law. It is far too easy to slip into a subjective response by merely rereading the statements of the antagonists or tallying up the editorial opinions. There was cohesion on the one side between the federalist argument that the legality of secession needed to be established before

---

[115] Cross-reference to § 1.2.3, 3.1, 4.2.2, 4.3.1, 4.6.1, 10.2.1 and 11.2.C.1.

the political process was engaged in or not, and therefore the matter needed to be referred to the courts. Symmetrically, the sovereignist side was consistent in declaring that the issue of Québec's future was for its people alone to decide by so-called "democratic" means in a referendum, and that the court would only intrude in an area in which its opinion was beyond its jurisdiction. Yet observers of political law will find these tautological arguments insufficient. An objective perspective, based on Canadian history and on the present-day character and characteristics of the Canadian federal State is more appropriate and necessary for this study.

The proper vision of the respective roles of law and politics in a democratic State is that while they are notionally autonomous of each other, the very quality of democracy in a State depends on the primacy of constitutional legal norms over political will, thus making law independent of politics and political developments dependent on the legal framework which sets out what and how the State may do, and how State officials must conduct themselves. In real life, the mortar that enables public life to evolve in this democratic fashion is that the law and the politics continually influence each other and in some sense develop together.

The opening sentences of the most knowledgeable source on Canadian constitutionalism, Dean Hogg's textbook, confirm this interpretation:

> Constitutional law is the law prescribing the exercise of power by the organs of the State. It explains which organs can exercise legislative power (making new laws), executive power (implementing the laws) and judicial power (adjudicating disputes), and what the limitations on those powers are.[116]

It is inherent and intrinsic in this constitutional regime of democracy that political change takes place upon legal grounds. In respect of all instances save an acknowledged revolution, the legal system requires adherence to this rule. In respect of all instances save an acknowledged revolution, the political system admits the requirement that it adhere to this rule. True democracy is thus not the execution of any decision favoured by the majority of the electorate on any issue,

---

[116] Peter W. Hogg, *Constitutional Law of Canada*, Loose Leaf Edition (Toronto: Carswell, 1997) at 1-1.

decided in any manner. Rather, it is the execution of the constitutionally correct and legally valid option adopted by the legally determined majority of the electorate, decided in the manner determined
by the legal framework. The alternatives to this public order based
on legal norms are dictatorship and chaos.

The answer to the question of whether the present reference constitutes politics or law, is that in the sense of aiming at the clarification
of a set of rules on how to change the system of government, if that
system is to be changed, the reference is both politics and law. In fact,
it is a necessary legal step required by the democratic nature of the
country in order for the political aspects of the matter to be susceptible
of proper determination.

The truth of this view was underscored by the rather eloquent pronouncement of the federal Minister of Justice, Allan Rock. Here, not
even his partisan role in the reference can detract from the strength
of the message.

> The separatist leaders argue that the rule of law is simply a ruse by which
> the Canadian Government intends to defeat an expression of democratic
> will by Quebecers—a trick to deny the results of a lost referendum. They
> argue that to require an orderly process within the legal framework
> would place Quebec in a straightjacket, defeating the democratic result
> of a future referendum.
>
> Such arguments are made for political effect. They are based on the
> misunderstanding that the rule of law and democratic action are some-
> how mutually exclusive. That is quite wrong. In fact, they coexist in
> harmony. The safety of both depends upon the integrity of each. The
> failure to observe either endangers the two at once.[117]

From the Supreme Court's own perspective, the core of the law and
politics debate was the issue of justiciability. It recognized the implicitly dual nature of the issue before it in the very opening lines of
its opinion.

> This Reference requires us to consider momentous questions that go to
> the heart of our system of constitutional government. The observation
> we made more than a decade ago in *Reference re Manitoba Language Rights*,

---

[117] Warren J. Newman, *The Quebec Secession Reference: The Rule of Law and the Position
of the Attorney General of Canada* (Toronto: York University Press, 1999) at 30.

[1985] 1 S.C.R. 721, 19 D.L.R. (4th) 1 *(Manitoba Language Rights Reference)*, at p. 728, applies with equal force here: as in that case, the present one "combines legal and constitutional questions of the utmost subtlety and complexity with political questions of great sensitivity." In our view, it is not possible to answer the questions that have been put to us without a consideration of a number of underlying principles. An exploration of the meaning and nature of these underlying principles is not merely of academic interest. On the contrary, such an exploration is of immense practical utility. Only once those underlying principles have been examined and delineated may a considered response to the questions we are required to answer emerge.[118]

The justiciability argument became one of the preliminary objections to which the court turned its initial attention. It took the opportunity to define the limits of justiciability and then declared that it would indeed deal with the questions put before it.

Though a reference differs from the Court's usual adjudicative function, the Court should not, even in the context of a reference, entertain questions that would be inappropriate to answer. However, given the very different nature of a reference, the question of the appropriateness of answering a question should not focus on whether the dispute is formally adversarial or whether it disposes of cognizable rights. Rather, it should consider whether the dispute is appropriately addressed by a court of law. As we stated in *Reference re Canada Assistance Plan (B.C.)*, [1991] 2 S.C.R. 525 at p. 545, 83 D.L.R. (4th) 297:

> While there may be many reasons why a question is non-justiciable, in this appeal the Attorney General of Canada submitted that to answer the questions would draw the Court into a political controversy and involve it in the legislative process. In exercising its discretion whether to determine a matter that is alleged to be non-justiciable, *the Court's primary concern is to retain its proper role within the constitutional framework of our democratic form of government*...In considering its appropriate role the Court must determine whether the question is purely political in nature and should, therefore, be determined in another forum *or whether it has a sufficient legal component to warrant the intervention of the judicial branch*. [Emphasis added.]

Thus the circumstances in which the Court may decline to answer a reference question on the basis of "non-justiciability" include:

---

[118] (1998), 161 D.L.R. (4th) 385 at 393-394, para. 1.

(i) if to do so would take the Court beyond its own assessment of its proper role in the constitutional framework of our democratic form of government or

(ii) if the Court could not give an answer that lies within its area of expertise: the interpretation of law.

As to the "proper role" of the Court, it is important to underline, contrary to the submission of the *amicus curiae*, that the questions posed in this Reference do not ask the Court to usurp any democratic decision that the people of Quebec may be called upon to make. The questions posed by the Governor in Council, as we interpret them, are strictly limited to aspects of the legal framework in which that democratic decision is to be taken. The attempted analogy to the U.S. "political questions" doctrine therefore has no application. The legal framework having been clarified, it will be for the population of Quebec, acting through the political process, to decide whether or not to pursue secession. As will be seen, the legal framework involves the rights and obligations of Canadians who live outside the province of Quebec, as well as those who live within Quebec.

As to the "legal" nature of the questions posed, if the Court is of the opinion that it is being asked a question with a significant extralegal component, it may interpret the question so as to answer only its legal aspects; if this is not possible, the Court may decline to answer the question. In the present Reference the questions may clearly be interpreted as directed to legal issues and, so interpreted, the Court is in a position to answer them.[119]

This determination of the justiciability of the matter of secession was the court's response to the carefully crafted federal position that dealing with a decision by Québec to secede would have to be done within the context of the Constitutional framework and the legal system. In an incident that can only be described as unintentional to a great degree, on the first day of the hearing of the reference by the Supreme Court, the person who by then had become Minister of Justice, Anne McLellan, seemed to undermine that entire strategy. In an interview to the *Toronto Star*, she indicated that a referendum result favourable to secession would create a set of extraordinary circumstances that could not be dealt with within the Constitution. This led to questioning of the federal government's lead counsel by the justices. He referred to the doctrine of necessity, according to which in case of

---

[119] *Ibid.* at 401-402, paras. 26, 27 and 28.

impasse, in eventual negotiations, the very constitutional principles that he was defending might be required to be set aside in favour of the rule of law. This exchange was inconclusive, except in the sense that it underscored the court's attention to pertinent political declarations.

These legal proceedings included a number of other highly political elements. Given that the Government of Québec decided not to participate or be represented, the matter of representation of what would have been the Québec position needed to be resolved. An *amicus curiae* was appointed, resulting in the unique circumstance that Ottawa was one of the parties before the court and also had a hand in selecting the person to represent the opposing view, and paying him.

It is also possible to argue, still objectively, that the nature of the Supreme Court's opinion in this case was as political as it was legal. It devised a resolution to the issues placed before it that could be appropriated by all parties and give each a sense of success through compromise. The legal questions having been resolved in the sense that neither Canadian nor international law provided a mechanism for Québec to secede, the court offered two additional thoughts which became advice to Canadian legislators and politicians on how to pursue the debate in the political sphere.

The court felt, significantly, that a decision on secession would have to be made by a clear majority on a clear question. This became the grounds upon which the Parliament of Canada was to enact, in May 2000, the so-called "Clarity Bill," *An Act to give effect to the requirement for clarity as set out in the opinion of the Supreme Court of Canada in the Québec Secession Reference.*[120]

Moreover, the court indicated to all of the parties concerned that they would be required to negotiate.

Secession is a legal act as much as a political one.

. . .

The federalism principle, in conjunction with the democratic principle,

---

[120] Bill C-20, 2nd Sess., 36th Parl., enacted as S.C. 2000, c. 26, assented to on May 29, 2000.

dictates that the clear repudiation of the existing constitutional order and the clear expression of the desire to pursue secession by the population of a province would give rise to a reciprocal obligation on all parties to Confederation to negotiate constitutional changes to respond to that desire. The amendment of the Constitution begins with a political process undertaken pursuant to the Constitution itself. In Canada, the initiative for constitutional amendment is the responsibility of democratically elected representatives of the participants in Confederation. Those representatives may, of course, take their cue from a referendum, but in legal terms, constitution-making in Canada, as in many countries, is undertaken by the democratically elected representatives of the people. The corollary of a legitimate attempt by one participant in Confederation to seek an amendment to the Constitution is an obligation on all parties to come to the negotiating table. The clear repudiation by the people of Quebec of the existing constitutional order would confer legitimacy on demands for secession, and place an obligation on the other provinces and the federal government to acknowledge and respect that expression of democratic will by entering into negotiations and conducting them in accordance with the underlying constitutional principles already discussed.[121]

No statement by a court could be a clearer prescription as to how to conduct politics in accordance with legal norms, without necessarily prescribing a particular solution. The court had fulfilled its function admirably, by dealing with the legality of the political and politicized issue before it, and not overstepping its bounds.

See also *Arsenault-Cameron v. Prince Edward Island*, [2000] 1 S.C.R. 3 (S.C.C.) and *Glacier View Lodge Society v. British Columbia (Minister of Health) Columbia*, 136 B.C.A.C. 198 (B.C. C.A.).

---

§ 2.4.7[122]
Colt and Glover v. The Bishop of Coventry and Litchfield
Chequer – Chamber; date unknown
Hob. 140, 80 E.R. 290

The relationship of linkage between law and politics and indeed the competition between them to govern the conduct of public affairs has been a constant feature of public life in the State ever since the de-

---

[121] *Supra* note 118 at 422, para. 83, and 424, para. 88.
[122] International comparison.

velopment of various modern notions of power. This tension in governance can be expressed in several ways. Shall law instruct the public actions of public figures, or shall politics be the supreme consideration in matters of statecraft? Which should accommodate the other when such accommodation is necessary? Is the legal system applicable to the leadership of the State, or as applicable to it as it is to the population? Does the executive branch defer to the judiciary or vice versa?

These questions certainly reflect a modern concern for the guiding influences on the exercise of State power. While that preoccupation is expressed above in current terminology, the contest of forces and interests underlying it has taken centuries to crystallize. Thus, while most cases in this sub-chapter are relevant to present-day issues, establishing an historical basis for this conflict is not inappropriate.

This case, commonly entitled "The Commendam Case," concerns an appointment to a church position in the English village of Clifton Camvill and the enjoyment of the benefits that flow with that appointment. On appeal from the Court of Common Pleas, the Chequer-Chamber held that a *commendam* purported to be made by the Bishop of Coventry and Litchfield was void in law and that the plaintiff was entitled to the appointment.

Much of the judgment dealt with the confrontation between ecclesiastical law on one hand and the temporal law of England on the other, which is expressed as comprising the royal prerogative, the common law, and statute. This, however, is shown only as an aspect of the struggle within England between the power of the monarch and that of the church.

The interest of the case is that the court deals with the position of one who holds a *commendam* as if it were a public office. In discussing the legal nature and the manner of creating *commenda*, it indicates that within England, the Pope can claim no legislative power and the ecclesiastical authorities can thus not exercise the temporal power of changing the law to suit their purposes. To justify this, the court relies on the maxim that politics is subordinate to the law, rather than the law to politics: "*Politiae legibus, non leges politiis adaptandae.*"[123]

---

[123] Hob. 140, 80 E.R. 290 at 303.

From this saying, there is a direct conceptual line to the preamble of the *Constitution Act, 1982*, which declares that Canada is founded upon principles that recognize the rule of law.

See also *Bush v. Gore*,[124] 148 L.Ed.2d 388 (2000).

2.5 ISSUE: LAW AND POLITICAL SCIENCE

See *Reference re Amendment to the Constitution of Canada*, [1981] 1 S.C.R. 753 at 802 (S.C.C.) and *Goddard v. Day*,[125] 200 D.L.R. (4th) 752 (Alta. Q.B.).

2.6 ISSUE: POLICY AND POLITICS

§ 2.6.1[126]
Canadian Wildlife Federation Inc. v. Canada (Minister of the Environment)
Federal Court of Appeal; December 21, 1990
(1990), 121 N.R. 385

This case is unique in that in the context of a dispute of a legal nature, the court was led to analyze the links between policy and political instruments and to form a judgment on the relative binding influence of each on a conflictual circumstance in public life. The fact situation concerned the Rafferty-Alameda project, envisaging the construction of a series of dams by the Souris Basin Development Authority (SBDA) along the Souris River, the whole in aid of agriculture and irrigation. While the farming community, the Saskatchewan Government, and the Government of Canada were in favour of the under-taking, certain riparian farmers and environmental organizations expressed their opposition through the courts.

The background facts are significant in this scenario. The project was announced on February 12, 1986. The Saskatchewan Water Corpo-

---

[124] Cross-reference to § 5.12.
[125] Cross-reference to § 6.6 and 11.8.7.
[126] Cross-reference to § 1.3.A.4, 1.3.D.2, 2.2.E.1, 11.7.4 and 11.14.2.

ration issued the requisite provincial licence to the SBDA to construct the Rafferty Dam on February 23, 1988. The federal licence equally required under the *International River Improvements Act*[127] was issued by the Minister of the Environment on June 17, 1988. As a result of a first court action, the Federal Court of Appeal quashed that federal licence on April 10, 1989.[128] The Minister of the Environment then initiated an environmental review procedure that was supposed to be in compliance with the *Environmental Assessment and Review Process Guidelines Order* (EARPGO). An Initial Environmental Evaluation (IEE) was prepared by August of 1989. At that point, rather than continue with the EARPGO process and appoint an environmental review panel, the Minister issued a second federal licence on August 31, 1989.

Two separate actions were started in the Federal Court of Canada – Trial Division to quash this second federal licence. These cases were joined and on December 28, 1989, the court handed down the judgment that would eventually form the basis for this appeal. Mr. Justice Muldoon concluded that in considering the (IEE) as the basis for the second federal licence, the Minister of the Environment had come to conclusions that were doubtful and questionable. The decision not to appoint an EARPGO panel was found to have been unlawful. More precisely, that court found that on the basis of the material before the Minister, he should not have reached the conclusions he did, but rather should have referred the matter to a panel for public review. The court therefore "ordered mandamus requiring the Minister to comply with the EARPGO Panel appointment provisions, and in exercising his discretion ordered certiorari to quash the license unless a Panel was appointed prior to a specific time."[129]

This case is obviously important in terms of administrative law and environmental law. In initiating its analysis of the case before it, the Federal Court of Appeal looked at the assertions in the IEE that dealt with mitigation of environmental impacts. It stated that the interpretation of the EARPGO was the central issue in the case and left no doubt that the determination of these matters "is of considerable importance not only to the parties and a wide group of affected people

---

127 R.S.C. 1985, c. I-20.
128 *Canadian Wildlife Federation Inc. v. Canada (Minister of the Environment)* (1989), 99 N.R. 72 (Fed. C.A.).
129 (1990), 121 N.R. 385 (Fed. C.A.) at 392 para. 20.

but also tot he scope and effect of federal environmental legislation and regulations."[130]

Even without a statement to such effect by the court, it is equally patent that this case has importance in political law because of its treatment of the instruments involved in the complex of litigation. In this regard, the only hint from the court is a rather unusual remark in the judgment about the fact that despite the importance of the case, counsel for the Minister of the Environment would take no position in the proceedings. One may be tempted to add that the Minister's instructions to his counsel could be seen as even stranger than the mention by the court; it is possible that this can also be attributed to discussions and negotiations between the governments of Canada and Saskatchewan which, at that time, were like-minded, but still representing interests of different perspectives.

The Federal Court of Appeal dealt first with a cross-appeal by the Saskatchewan Water Corporation. This respondent's position was that the EARPGO did not require that a panel be appointed and consequently, the Minister of the Environment was justified in issuing the second licence. The court dismissed this plea on the ground that the respondent had wrongly interpreted the EARPGO's provisions dealing with various gradations of impact on pollution. It stated that clearly, a public review by a panel was required.

The appellant's case, by contrast, was that the lower court should have gone farther than it did and quashed the second licence absolutely, as long as the panel was not appointed and its report had not been considered by the Minister prior to the issuance of the licence. The court could not agree with this plea either. It held that the Minister was bound to comply with the EARPGO as a legal instrument but focused on the question of just what constituted compliance. On the basis of the precise wording of the Order and relying as well on the precedent in the *Naskapi-Montagnais* case, the court found that while the Minister was bound to appoint a panel, he was not compelled to await the report before acting on the subject matter being considered. This part of the judgment was legally correct, but pointed out the weakness of the federal environmental assessment process from the public administrative point of view.

---

[130] *Ibid.* at 388, para. 3.

It is at this point in the court's analysis that the political law issue arose most clearly. The panel's report, had one been done, would not have been legally binding on the Federal Environmental Assessment and Review Office or on the Minister therefore further weakening the public administration process. The IEE, which was done, was not legally binding either. The recommendation arising from the Review Office and the IEE could be adopted, amended, or set aside. The importance of this point is that an IEE and a panel report are only policy instruments, the EARPGO text demonstrates:

> that the Panel provisions were not intended to be complied with in a literal or mandatory fashion since they could be changed by the Office. What is required is that a Panel must be appointed, and hopefully, it will report before any permanent decisions are made but there is no require-ment that any report be made and considered before any ministerial decisions are made. Hence, public review is required to inform the pub-lic, who can then participate in the debate on the environmental aspects of the proposal under review, but it is open to the Minister, if in his opinion there are good reasons for doing so, to proceed with the project during the time the review is going on.[131]

Bearing in mind that the Minister does not have to await a panel's report, and taking into account the non-compulsory nature of panel recommendations, the court considered the Minister to be legally competent to make a decision on the licensing of a project once he had merely appointed an EARPGO panel. The court made it abso-lutely clear, however, that a ministerial decision to issue a licence at this point in time—that is, before a panel had reported—would be an instrument of a political nature. The court was thus drawn to analyze the link between, and to compare the relative weight of, on the one hand the policy instrument—that is, the panel report—and on the other hand the political instrument; that is, the licence issued in the absence of a panel report.

> In that connection, as the EARPGO is intended to ensure that decision making in government is balanced by a concern for environmental con-sequences, I do not think that the Panel report provisions of the EARPGO scheme, which admittedly has much ambiguity in it, can be taken to prevail in an absolute and complete way over the normal decision mak-ing of Ministers. It is not disputed by any of the parties that the Panel report's recommendations can be ignored by Ministers subject to what-

---

[131] *Ibid.* at 401, para. 47.

ever political consequences flow therefrom. Similarly, that is the real sanction for not waiting for the Panel report as Madame Justice Reed acknowledges: the Minister responsible will be politically accountable for any decisions made. The thrust of § 21 to 32 is for public involvement but that involvement has not been elevated to curtailing or otherwise preventing ministerial decisions that presumably could be based themselves on an arguably greater public interest than waiting for the Panel report.[132]

The court concluded its analysis of this link by stating, "In short, I find the provisions of the EARPGO dealing with the submission of a report by the Panel for Ministerial review to be laudatory to but not obligatory on the Minister."[133]

This case can be taken to indicate judicial impartiality as between policy and politics.

2.7 ISSUE: LAW, POLICY AND POLITICS

§ 2.7.1
Roman Corp. v. Hudson's Bay Oil & Gas Co.
Supreme Court of Canada; May 7, 1973
[1973] S.C.R. 820

Circumstances in which public decision-making involves all three types of considerations—the legal, the policy and the political—may not be uncommon. What is rare, however, is that a senior court is afforded, in the guise of a legal dispute brought before it on appeal, an opportunity to analyze the interplay of all these considerations in the execution of public duties by the most senior of governmental officials and thereupon to make authoritative statements on the priority that is to be accorded to each of the considerations. This case is instructive not only because it links all the fundamental elements of political law, but also because it clearly establishes the supremacy of legal considerations in decision-making over both other types, even when they are present simultaneously.

---

[132] *Ibid.* at 401, para. 48.
[133] *Ibid.* at 401-402, para. 49.

On February 24, 1970, Roman entered into an oral agreement to sell shares of Denison to Hudson's Bay Oil and Gas (HBC). Denison's business was uranium mining, an activity in which Canada perceived a strategic national interest. As HBC was foreign owned, its purchase of the Denison shares would pass control of Denison to foreign holding. On March 2, 1970, the Prime Minister, Pierre E. Trudeau, made a statement in the House of Commons to the effect that the sale was a matter of concern and that the government would prevent it, if necessary by amending the *Atomic Energy Control Act*.[134] On March 19, the Prime Minister sent a telegram to Roman to confirm that the transaction would not be acceptable pursuant to the "guidelines" being announced that day. In Parliament, on the same day, the Minister of Energy, Mines and Resources, Joe Greene, stated that regulations would be made restricting foreign ownership of uranium works in Canada. The Minister further clarified the government's position in the House of Commons on September 18 by indicating that legislation to achieve its policy goal would be required.

On December 1, 1970, Roman brought an action in damages against the Prime Minister and the Minister of Energy, Mines and Resources on the ground that its deal with HBC was not completed because of their statements. Against HBC, Roman Corporation sought a declaration that their original verbal agreement was a valid contract. By December 23, Trudeau and Greene responded with a motion to strike out the statement of claim as disclosing no reasonable cause of action. They based their application on the narrow ground that the statements they made in the House of Commons were privileged and that their communications to Roman were extensions of those privileged statements.

The Supreme Court of Ontario granted the defendants' motion ostensibly on the ground of Parliamentary privilege. In fact, the court also referred to the fact that the officials were carrying out their public duties. This ruling was thus based on legality as contrasted to politics, without the court explicitly using the latter term.

> However, on a careful examination of the statement of claim, I am satisfied that the plaintiffs have no cause of action against the defendants Trudeau and Greene.

---

[134] At that time R.S.C. 1952, c. 11.

It is of the essence of our parliamentary system of government that our elected representatives should be able to perform their duties, courageously and resolutely, in what they consider to be the best interests of Canada, free from any worry of being called to account anywhere, except in Parliament. As I have pointed out earlier in this judgment, there is no allegation that the defendants Trudeau and Greene acted with malice or for personal gain; their *bona fides* is in no way attacked. Surely the actions which are alleged against them in the statement of claim are exactly what one would have expected of persons in their position, when confronted with a transaction which they believed to be detrimental to the best interests of this country.[135]

The Ontario Court of Appeal confirmed the first ruling, giving a clearer determination. It said first that allegations concerning statements made in the House of Commons were not to be considered by the courts, because they were privileged. With this reason it was heading in the direction of agreeing that Roman's case disclosed no cause of action. More fully than the lower court, however, it explained how such statements were both policy and political in nature. The statements were made in the course of their functions and in good faith in the promotion of what they perceived to be the public interest. This can be taken as a non-partisan, perhaps even objective, criterion, based on policy grounds of the public benefit of Canada. The court also took judicial notice of the fact that the foreign ownership of Canadian resources was a matter of public concern; this introduced the political element, the subjective necessary response of Parliamentarians/Cabinet Members who are also politicians to public opinion and the dictates of national politics and national interest. Whatever consideration or combination of considerations applied, the Court of Appeal found no tort in Trudeau's and Greene's pronouncements.

> The lawful justification for their alleged actions at the meeting is thus so plain as to completely sweep away any foundation whatsoever for a claim in tort based on inducement to breach of contract (if there were inducement as contrasted with mere advice), conspiracy, intimidation or otherwise.[136]

The Supreme Court of Canada upheld both lower judgments. It wanted, though, to take a broader view than that based on parliamentary privilege. It looked at the effect of the statements on the

---

[135] [1973] S.C.R. 820 at 826.
[136] *Ibid.* at 827.

minds of the prospective parties to the contract and at the actions they took or failed to take as a result of those statements.

> What has occurred here, as stated in the pleadings, is that the parties did not, after the statements made by the respondents, proceed to complete their agreement. Clearly, this was because they apprehended that legislation, by way of regulation or statute, would be enacted to prevent the control of Canadian uranium resources passing from Canadian to non-Canadian hands.

> If valid legislation for that purpose were enacted and it prevented performance of a contract for transfer of such control, there is no doubt that the parties to the agreement would have no cause of action arising out of the enactment of such legislation. A statement of policy made *bona fide* by a Minister of the Crown of the intention of Government to enact such legislation cannot, in my opinion, give rise to a claim in tort for inducing a breach of contract if the parties to the contract elect, in the light of that statement, not to proceed to perform the contract.

> . . .

> In my opinion, it cannot be said that a declaration made in good faith by a Minister of the Crown as to Government policy and the intent to implement that policy by appropriate legislation is a threat of an unlawful act. On the contrary, it is part of a Minister's duty to the public to disclose that policy from time to time.[137]

The ultimate reason for holding that Roman had no reasonable cause of action was that, notwithstanding the policy and political considerations involved, Trudeau and Greene had acted legally in enunciating government policy and planning legislation in good faith and in doing so they were acting in the performance of their public duties. This was held to be exactly the opposite consideration than that which had animated Premier Duplessis in Roncarelli's action against him.[138]

---

[137] *Ibid.* at 829-830.
[138] *Roncarelli v. Duplessis*, [1959] S.C.R. 121 (S.C.C.).

LEGAL ELEMENTS OF DEMOCRACY

3.1 GENERAL PRINCIPLES

See Volume I, Chapter 3.

3.2 ISSUE: RECOGNITION OF THE DEMOCRATIC NATURE OF CANADA

---

§ 3.2.1[1]
Reference re Electoral Divisions Statutes Amendment Act, 1993 (Alberta)
Alberta Court of Appeal; October 24, 1994
(1994), 119 D.L.R. (4th)

This is a case referred by the Government of Alberta to the province's Court of Appeal. The subject matter was the constitutional validity of the provincial electoral boundaries redistribution scheme worked out by a 1992 Select Committee of the Legislature, enacted on February 12, 1993, and intended to remain in force until the year 2001.

By tradition, the province's rural population had been over-represented and its city dwellers had been under-represented. Both the Legislature and the courts in Alberta had for several years contended with the issue of developing equitable and constitutionally valid electoral districts. In a 1991 reference, while the Court of Appeal had refused to endorse the scheme then submitted, it did acknowledge that the province had made what it termed gradual and steady pro-

---

[1] Cross-reference to § 5.3.2.

gress toward a fair and balanced system of representation of the electorate. The implication was that a better plan would have to be devised. Here, the court was being asked to attest to the conformity with the *Charter* of the redistribution scheme developed in response to the 1991 decision. In light of the fact that the fundamental right of appropriate representation had gone unresolved in Alberta for so long and that the same contention had been brought before the court in several cases, the justices cast this ruling in broad terms, referring to the concept of democracy in both its legal and political connotations.

The link between the redistribution of electoral boundaries and the concept of democracy is two-fold. There is first a textual foundation for elevating this process to such a high plain. The guarantee of the right to vote as one of the rights and freedoms of Canadians is set out in section 3 of the *Charter*, the title for which is "Democratic Rights." In addition, that aspect of the right to vote which deals with effective voting power and especially with permissible deviations from equality of voting power, was discussed in the most significant case on this issue, the *Carter* decision,[2] very much in the broad terms of democracy, freedom and equality, in both the legal and political aspects of these ideals.

This reference is based on those textual and jurisprudential links. It explained further the application of the *Charter* provision on the right to vote, and the natural consequence of that right, namely the requirement that the effect of each vote be as equal as possible to the effect of every other vote. It detailed how these principles were to be reflected in the electoral boundaries redistribution legislation and in the methodology of drawing boundaries.

The court stated plainly not only that these principles had not been observed by Alberta, but that the historical disparity of urban versus rural electors' representation had been worsening year by year. These observations led the court to reach the most significant conclusion of the case: "This cannot be permitted to continue if Alberta wishes to call itself a democracy."[3]

---

2 *Reference re Provincial Electoral Boundaries*, [1991] 2 S.C.R. 158 (S.C.C.).
3 (1994), 119 D.L.R. (4th) 1 at 17 b.

The indissoluble connection between the legal analysis of the Alberta Court of Appeal and its reference to the political absence of democracy clearly shows that in the court's perception, the *Charter* is not only a constitutional/legal text, but also the legal foundation of democracy as a political system. This pronouncement demonstrates by necessary implication that the court recognizes the democratic nature of Alberta, and hence of Canada, and is seeking to apply the provisions of the *Charter* in order to preserve that democratic characteristic of the country.

The court's response to the reference was that it could not certify the electoral boundaries redistribution scheme as being in conformity with the *Charter*. In equating a system of equitable and constitutionally valid representation of electors with democracy, given the facts of this case, the court had no other option but to conclude in tandem with its *Charter*-based legal analysis that the continuation of inequitable representation would endanger the democratic character of the province. The court reaffirmed this point by indicating that, "While we hesitate to use the term crisis, there was a serious problem for the legislature to address."[4] Such foreboding language is rarely used by the courts and is reserved for instances where it protects the most cherished legal and political characteristics of society.

---

[4] *Ibid.* at 18 d.
No footnote 5.

3.3 ISSUE: CONSENSUS ON THE POLITICAL/LEGAL REGIME

3.3.A—CANADA'S FORM OF GOVERNMENT

§ 3.3.A.1

Roach v. Canada (Minister of State for Multiculturalism & Culture)
Federal Court of Appeal; January 20, 1994
[1994] 2 F.C. 406[6]

Roach was a lawyer living in Toronto. He was a native of Trinidad and Tobago but had lived in Canada for over 34 years before he began this litigation. He alleged that as a British subject and a permanent resident of Canada, his rights had been eroded so that he could no longer vote in Canadian elections, could neither stand for public office, nor be employed in the Public Service. In order to remedy these circumstances, Roach wanted to assume Canadian citizenship. A believer in a republican, rather than a monarchical form of government for Canada, he was willing to take an oath to be a loyal Canadian citizen and to fulfil the duties of citizenship. However, he was unwilling to take the oath of allegiance to the Queen which was required by the *Citizenship Act* and the regulations thereunder.

Roach first sought to be exempted from the necessity of the oath, or of a solemn affirmation in lieu thereof, to the monarch through application to public officials. He was not successful. He then brought suit before the Federal Court.

Roach's principal contention was that he objected to making any commitment of loyalty to Her Majesty the Queen in her capacity as Queen of Canada that would be binding on his conscience, regardless of whether that commitment was to be expressed in a religious or secular manner. By expressing his republican sentiment in this manner, Roach was in fact indicating a lack of consensus on the political/ legal regime prevailing in Canada while that consensus was presumably still accepted by a sizeable proportion, if not a clear majority, of

---

[6] Leave to appeal refused (1994), 113 D.L.R. (4th) 67n (Fed. C.A.).

the population. Roach's application, although seemingly of limited and technical scope in law, offered the judicial system an opportunity to explore the legal aspects and ramifications of a disagreement with the prevailing regime so fundamental as to lead one to desire its replacement with another.

The Associate Senior Prothonotary granted a motion by the Crown to strike Roach's application as disclosing no reasonable cause of action. The Trial Division heard an appeal from the Prothonotary. That court made two relevant observations. It reiterated that "in the Canadian context, the Queen is equivalent to 'state' and 'Crown,'"[7] and that therefore, it is:

> quite proper for Parliament to require of persons wishing to become Canadian citizens that they swear or affirm their loyalty to our head of state. That the head of state should be found in the person of Her Majesty the Queen might be a matter of debate but it is nevertheless as much a part of our constitutional framework as are the provisions of the Charter.[8]

The Trial Division also indicated that in its view, the applicant could not challenge the oath of citizenship on *Charter* grounds, but should he wish to change the country's political/legal regime, his remedy would lie with Parliament, that is in the political arena. With these comments, the Trial Division upheld the striking of Roach's application.

Roach in turn appealed this decision to the Federal Court of Appeal. There, two of the three judges dismissed. However, Mr. Justice Linden, one of the most incisive legal minds in Canada, wrote a most thorough dissenting opinion which merits analysis even though it did not change the outcome of the case.

Linden considered each of the applicant's *Charter* arguments in detail to determine if they should be retained for trial, or struck out in accordance with the motion the Crown had presented before the Associate Senior Prothonotary.

---

[7] (1992), 88 D.L.R. (4th) 225 at 228 (b), as cited at [1994] 2 F.C. 406 at 419 (i), leave to appeal refused (1994), 113 D.L.R. (4th) 67n (Fed. C.A.).
[8] *Ibid.* at 228 (e).

With respect to the allegation that the oath contravened Roach's section 2(a) freedom of conscience, the real objection was held not to the
method of oath making, but rather to the contents of the oath and on
that ground the claim was struck. The claim that the oath contravened
the applicant's freedom of religion, also protected under section 2(a)
of the *Charter*, was similarly struck on the ground that in framing the
oath or affirmation, Parliament had wanted "to require a statement
of loyalty to Canada's head of state and to its institutions," rather
than "to the Queen in her capacity as Head of the Church of England."

Roach also claimed that the oath would violate his section 2(b) freedom of thought, in that by pronouncing it meaningfully, he would
be restricted in thinking and expressing beliefs about the abolition of
the monarchy. Here, Judge Linden drew a parallel between the applicant and the Members of Parliament elected in the then recent 1993
federal general election under the banner of the Bloc Québécois,
whose political commitment was to "working democratically to
achieve a monarch-less independent state,"[9] but who were willing to
take the oath to the Queen that is required of parliamentarians. He
recalled that criticism of the monarchy had at one time been regarded
as treasonous, attracting criminal law sanctions. While today, freedom to criticize the monarchy and Canadian institutions is guaranteed by the *Charter*, Linden did express some doubt as to whether the
oath had value in achieving any more than to get someone to promise
not to violate criminal law and to refrain from illegal political methods, something they are obliged to do in any event. This doubt led
him to refuse to strike out the claim for disclosing no reasonable
chance of success.

> In my view, it is arguable, at least, that the oath of allegiance has some
> meaning other than merely promising to obey the criminal law and to
> use legitimate means for political change. What is involved here is not
> the mere utterance of a few words, as my brother MacGuigan suggests,
> but the expression of a "solemn intention to adhere to the symbolic
> keystone of the Canadian Constitution as it has been and is, thus pledg-
> ing an acceptance of the whole of our Constitution and national life" as
> he also recognizes. If someone is fundamentally opposed to a significant
> aspect of that Constitution, and wishes to work toward its abolition, not
> merely its reform, it is arguable that that person may violate the oath by
> words and conduct in furtherance of that goal. It may not be unreason-

---

[9] [1994] 2 F.C. 406 at 430 (j), leave to appeal refused (1994), 113 D.L.R. (4th) 67n (Fed.
C.A.).

able for the appellant, if he truly holds the beliefs he claims to hold, to feel that, by taking this oath, he is inhibited to some extent in his anti-monarchy activities. In other words, his serious view of the oath might be taken seriously. It may be that, after a trial, it might be concluded that the appellant was being made to choose between his political principles and his enjoyment of Canadian citizenship, something the Charter is supposed to prevent. It may be that Mr. Justice MacGuigan's view would prevail. It may be that section 1 might be invoked to justify any *prima facie* violation of the Charter, or it might not. In light of the uncertainty surrounding this question, it would be advisable, before resolving this matter, to have the benefit of factual underpinnings and full legal argument based on those facts.[10]

On the grounds of freedom of expression, equally protected under section 2(b), Linden also refused to strike out the claim.

> Turning to the effect of the legislation, the burden will be on the appellant to show that the effect of the oath or affirmation is to restrict his freedom of expression and that his expression seeks to promote at least one of the principles underlying freedom of expression, namely seeking and attaining the truth, participation in social and political decision-making or individual self-fulfilment and human flourishing. Promoting republicanism likely falls within these parameters. Thus, strict adherence to the oath or affirmation of loyalty to the Queen might be felt by the appellant to prevent him from expressing his republicanism, even though it might not in law actually do so.[11]

> Before leaving this topic, it should be mentioned that one might argue that the appellant's personal feelings of inhibition regarding his belief in and expression of his republicanism are not constitutionally or legally irrelevant. An argument might be made that there is no nexus between the oath of citizenship and the appellant's freedom to believe in and to express his republicanism. It might be said that it is the appellant's republicanism, when combined with his belief that the terms of an oath must be faithfully observed, that prevents him from getting citizenship, and not the oath itself.[12]

Linden gave less weight to the section 2(c) protection of freedom of assembly, striking out this part of the claim. He held that this provision of the *Charter* protected an assembly itself, rather than the objects of the assembly. Such objects, namely freedom of thought, belief,

---

[10] *Ibid.* at 431 (f)-432 (b).
[11] *Ibid.* at 433 (f)-(i).
[12] *Ibid.* at 434 (d)-(f).

opinion or expression, or freedom of association, would be independently protected.

The section 2(d) claim under the heading of freedom of association was not struck out. In the judge's mind, the key to this part of the claim was not whether the applicant was in fact prohibited from associating with others sharing his political views but rather, whether, having taken the oath, he may feel himself restricted in so associating.

> It may be argued that it strikes at the very heart of democracy to curtail collective opposition and incentive for change by demanding loyalty to a particular political theory. Similarly, it may be said that it is wrong to build a barrier to joining associations dedicated to a different political theory. The appellant, though perhaps not legally forbidden to do this, might well feel so circumscribed, given the primitive state of the law at this time.[13]

Linden saw no merit in Roach's argument based on section 12 of the *Charter*, guaranteeing freedom from cruel and unusual punishment.

Under the rubric of *Charter* subsection 15(1), equality rights, Roach presented three related pleadings. He objected first that while Canadian citizens by birth are not required to take the oath, naturalized citizens must do so. This claim was not struck out on the basis that the Supreme Court had already held "that citizenship is an analogous ground under section 15(1) and that non-citizens constitute a disadvantaged group in Canadian society that can be characterized as a 'discrete and insular minority.'"[14] The judge's conclusion as to the application of that judgment was that while a process may be set up for new citizens, such a process ought not to be discriminatory.

Roach's second *Charter* section 15 argument related to the distinction between citizens by birth and those by naturalization in the attainment of full political rights. He also objected to what he termed the perpetual superiority of the Windsor family and the consequential prevention of people from outside Great Britain from attaining the highest office in Canada. These claims were struck out.

---

[13] *Ibid.* at 437 (g)-(i).
[14] *Ibid.* at 442 (e). This finding is based on the judgment of the Supreme Court of Canada in *Andrews v. Law Society (British Columbia)*, [1989] 1 S.C.R. 143 (S.C.C.).

Finally, Roach presented a claim based on the *Charter's* section 27, dealing with the preservation and enhancement of the multicultural heritage of Canada. He argued that the existence of an English hereditary monarchy precluded the full participation of different racial and multicultural groups in the governance of Canada. Justice Linden interpreted this as a substantive challenge to the monarchy itself but held that *Charter* section 27 is only an aid to interpretation and not a particular right or freedom in itself. This part of the claim was therefore struck.

Although several parts of Roach's claim were not struck out in this dissenting opinion, even the dissenting judge could not grant the remedy Roach sought, namely a declaration of entitlement to citizenship, as he had no such right or entitlement. Nor would a constitutional exemption be granted. The outcome of the dissent was to enable some portions of the claim to have been disposed of at a trial, but the majority of the Federal Court of Appeal prevented a trial on the substantive issues from being held. The merit of the case is thus its analysis in light of the *Charter*, of the legal elements of a fundamental disagreement with the Canadian regime.

Roach did eventually follow the advice of the Trial Division to take these matters to the political realm, by becoming the solicitor and, one presumes an adherent of, the Party of the First Republic.

In the political realm, the echoes of the position espoused by Roach are rare. One of the few senior political figures who has, in recent years, made public pronouncements in favour of republicanism in Canada is the Minister of Foreign Affairs, John Manley.

> Although known as one of the most conservative members of the Liberal Cabinet, Mr. Manley told a Vancouver newspaper this week he favours radical change to Canada's constitutional landscape. He called for the abolition of the Senate and an end to the Queen's role as head of state in Canada.
>
> Government sources said yesterday that Mr. Manley sought and received approval from the Prime Minister's Office to make public his views on the monarchy and on the Senate, suggesting the Liberals are testing the waters to see if there's an appetite for such a debate.[15]

---

[15] "Abolish monarchy, Manley says," Andrew Duffy, *Ottawa Citizen*, September 13, 1997, p. 1.

At the time of this statement, there was none.

---

§ 3.3.A.2
Speaker's Ruling on Display of the Flag in the House of Commons
Hansard, March 16, 1988, p. 4902

The flag of a country is a highly emotive political symbol, signifying loyalty, attachment, belief and patriotism. In short, it is a focus of the consensus surrounding the country itself and its government on the world stage. It is only on those occasions when political consensus breaks down that the flag becomes a symbol of controversy involving such legal issues as national sovereignty and freedom of expression.

During the 1998 Winter Olympics in Nagano, Japan, Suzanne Tremblay, an outspoken Bloc Québécois Member of the House of Commons, protested that there were too many maple leaf flags displayed in the Canadian Olympic Village. On February 26, 1998, when the same parliamentarian rose in the House to speak in the Debate on the Budget, at the behest of a Liberal MP, a number of MP's, mostly those of the Reform Party of Canada, interrupted her by singing the national anthem and placing Canadian flags on their desks. The Acting Speaker, perceiving the disruption in the debate, referred to the gesture as being not unparliamentary, but inappropriate and asked that the flags be put away. They were not. Later that same day, the House Leader of the Bloc Québécois raised a Point of Order, claiming that the flag had been used by the Members who had displayed it in order to create a demonstration causing disorder, preventing a Member from speaking and in disregard of the Speaker's Orders.

The atmosphere in the House was so intense that even during the raising of the Point of Order, the Acting Speaker was forced to remind Members of the need for civility, using the occasion to remind them of the nature of parliamentary representation in Canada.

> I remind all members of this House that we are members of Canada's Parliament. This means we were all elected by Canadians across the country.

> That is one thing about which there is no doubt.

When members of Parliament stand in this place, they stand among us as equals. It does not matter what province they come from, it does not matter what region they come from. You have elected me to see that you are respected and indeed that you respect yourselves and the rules of this House.

We have a Canadian Member of Parliament on his feet. We are going to hear what he has to say. We do not have to agree with it but he is elected like every one of us in this House. I am going to hear what my hon. colleague from Roberval has to say.[16]

On March 16, the Speaker ruled on the Point of Order, disallowing the use of flags as props by any Member within the House.

The issues that face the nation and that are debated in this House are formidable. During debate, emotions can run high and, in the heat of the moment, behaviour can sometimes stray beyond the bounds of what is acceptable. When that happens, the Chair must be vigilant in bringing the House back to order and insisting that our practices be respected.

I have looked carefully at practice here in the House of Commons and in other Canadian legislatures; in the House of Commons of the United Kingdom and in other Westminster-style Parliaments. Everywhere we have looked, we have found that the orderly conduct of business is fundamental to parliamentary practice. Here, in their own vigilant defence of orderly proceedings, my predecessors have consistently ruled out of order displays or demonstrations of any kind used by members to illustrate their remarks or emphasize their positions. Similarly, props of any kind, used as a way of making a silent comment on issues, have always been found unacceptable in the Chamber.[17]

Perhaps even more significant than the ruling itself were the reasons cited by the Speaker in explaining it. The tone of the decision was one in favour of the unfettered ability of each parliamentarian to express himself without disruption, with regard for the rules of debate. The only way to protect parliamentarianism was to uphold the law of Parliament from excessive politicization, even, or perhaps especially on so fundamental an issue.

But this ruling is not about the flag. It is not about the national anthem. It is not about patriotism. It is not about the rights of one political faction

---

[16] Hansard, February 26, 1998, p. 4510.
[17] Hansard, March 16, 1998, p. 4902.

over another. As I said earlier—and it bears repeating—the basic principles at issue here are order and decorum and the duty of the Speaker to apply the rules and practices of the House.

Our law guarantees the right of all duly elected members to speak; our practice guarantees their right to be heard. It is the duty of the Speaker to guarantee that those rights are respected by guaranteeing that the House's rules and practices are respected.

Today, my duty for which I have taken an oath as Speaker requires me to uphold the rules, precedents and traditions of this House that have served us so well during the last 130 years of parliamentary democracy in Canada. The events during question period on February 26 were clearly out of order, according to our parliamentary rules and practices. I therefore rule that such an incident must not be repeated.

However, I have been challenged to show my colours as a patriotic Canadian by allowing the unfettered display of flags in the Chamber. This would constitute an unprecedented unilateral change to the practice of the House of Commons, a change, my colleagues, that no Speaker has the authority to make. So, whatever pressure that I have to do so, I cannot and I will not arrogate such authority to myself. Unless and until the House decides otherwise, no displays will be allowed and current practice will be upheld.[18]

It is worthy of note that as part of his ruling, the Speaker also berated the hyperlative media comment that would have thrown out decorum in favour of the symbol of patriotism, calling it foolhardy. On one side and the other, verbal and written excesses indicated how politically explosive the issue had become and how little politically motivated individuals know, or took account of the applicable rules.

The very next day after the one on which the Speaker ruled on the flag issue, was one reserved for an Official Opposition-led debate. The Leader of the Opposition, Mr. Manning, used the opportunity to move,

> That this House should recognize the Canadian flag as an acceptable symbol that may be displayed at any time on the desks of Members of Parliament in the House of Commons, provided that only one flag be displayed on a Member's desk at any given time, and that the said flag

---

[18] *Ibid.*, p. 4903.

remain stationary for the purposes of decorum and be no larger than the standard recognized desk flag.[19]

This motion was defeated by 194 votes to 51.

In the course of this debate, the most interesting comment, pointing out the power and effect of symbolism in relation to the establishment of a consensus on country, democracy and rule of law, was that of the Leader of the New Democratic Party, Alexa McDonough.

> The Reform Party would try to create the impression that this is a simple, straightforward issue, that it is a simple question of whether members of the House want to display on the corner of their desks a Canadian flag. That is all it is about. That is all there is to it. Let us just vote for it and get on with it.

> I want to say that I do not think that is what this issue is really about. I do not think that is why the official opposition has put before the House today a motion which it wants Canadians to interpret as meaning that we either vote for its motion on its terms and show we are for Canada, we are for the flag, or if we vote against the motion on its terms and then we are not for the flag and we are not for Canada.

> This debate is about Reformers whose approach to politics is so simplistic that they would have Canadians believe that flags on the corner of the desks of members of Parliament will unite the country.

> There is no committed federalist in this House who is not proud of the Canadian flag. There is no committed federalist in Canada who is not proud of the Canadian flag. Let us be clear. What this is about is the Reform Party trying to create division among those who were elected to this House of Commons to stand up for Canada and to fight for a united Canada. We will not be divided by those crass, cheap political tactics.[20]

In the end, media reaction to the entire incident was not kind. However, while it concentrated on the terms of the debate, it failed to assess the more underlying difficulty that both Suzanne Tremblay's original comments and the Reform caucus' reaction to them indicated, namely the fact that political options favoured by divergent parties had become so distant from each other as to seriously jeopardize the consensus on the country and its political legal regime.

---

[19] Hansard, March 17, 1998, p. 4942.
[20] Ibid., p. 4951.

While the debate on flags in the House of Commons is ended, display of the maple leaf flag remains a matter of contention. On February 7, 2000, the National Council of the Parti Québécois, in power as the Government of Québec, adopted a resolution which would have the government prohibit any flag other than the fleur-de-lis from flying on public buildings in the province.

> There are no real winners, however. Reform may have made the three other federal parties appear soft on the Bloc. On the other hand, the other parties were somewhat successful in making Reform appear a tad too nationalistic. Ill-will now seethes below the surface in the Commons like a leaking pool of radon gas. Speaker Parent remains in office, but is weakened and under close media scrutiny.
>
> And all this because of a small piece of red and white nylon attached to a little stick of black plastic which proved to be so much more than the sum of its parts.[21]

See also *O'Donohue v. Canada* (2003), 109 C.R.R. (2d) 1 (Ont. S.C.J.).

3.3.B—CANADIAN UNITY AND SOVEREIGNTY

---

§ 3.3.B.1
Speaker's Ruling in the Matter of Oaths of Office
Speaker of the House of Commons of Canada; November 1, 1990
Hansard, November 1, 1990, p. 14969

The inclusion of rulings by the Speaker of the House of Commons in a volume on jurisprudence may initially seem surprising, as the Speaker is not generally thought of as a "court" in the common use of that term. An analytic perspective will dispel that particularity, however. Procedures of argumentation by members of parliament leading to a Speaker's ruling, such as Questions of Privilege and Points of Order, in the truest sense involve matters in which law, policy and politics are just as intertwined as court proceedings in matters of political law. The pleadings in such cases are certainly adversarial. The rulings regarding the issues raised are without question authoritative and binding. Moreover, they are without appeal. Indeed, Speaker's rulings have the force of law in the sense of devel-

---

[21] "The great Canadian flag flap," Sean Durkan, *Hill Times*, March 23-29, 1998, p. 7.

oping the law of Parliament. In many instances, such as here, with respect to the consensus on the Canadian political/legal regime, such decisions also foster the evolution of political law and such rulings ought therefore to be conceived of as having a proper place in jurisprudential texts on this subject matter.

The Preamble of the *Constitution Act, 1867* referred to the union of colonies into "One Dominion." The Preamble of the *Constitution Act, 1982* refers even more compactly to "Canada" and in its sections 3, 4 and 5 set out the rights of its citizens which it describes as "democratic rights." These are the highest expressions of a set of assumptions that Canada is both a single and a democratic country. The political/legal culture which has blossomed in this country since 1867 has, with some notable exceptions, engendered a consensus on the existence and the continuing unity of the country, on the characteristics of its political systems, on its grounding in the rule of law and on the influence of law on its political life. These factors all together are accepted as Canada's political/legal regime.

The first among the legal components of democracy is the recognition of this consensus. This recognition is best examined through the testing of its limits by dissident groups and individuals. The participation of Québec sovereignists in federal political and parliamentary life, notably through the vehicle of the Bloc Québécois, a political party formed in 1990, has caused many instances in recent Canadian public life in which the fundamental consensus of the majority of the Canadian population on that political/legal regime has, in fact, been seriously tested.

The Bloc Québécois was first comprised of dissident Progressive Conservative and Liberal members of Parliament who quit their respective parties in connection with the failure of the *Meech Lake Accord* in June, 1990. The first individual elected to the House of Commons under the Bloc's banner was Gilles Duceppe, who won the Montréal riding of Laurier–Sainte-Marie on August 13, 1990. After his election, he followed all substantive procedures and formalities required to assume his functions as an MP. Thus, on August 27, 1990, as required by section 128 of the *Constitution Act, 1867*, Duceppe made a solemn affirmation in lieu of the oath of allegiance to the Monarch. Parliament scheduled to reconvene after the summer break on September 24, and on September 23, Duceppe made a public statement expressing his loyalty to the people of Québec.

For several days thereafter, the statement was widely reported and caused much consternation among Canadians opposed to the ideological and political views of the Bloc. On October 3, 1990, a Liberal Member of Parliament from a Toronto area electoral district, Jesse Flis, raised a Question of Privilege with the Speaker of the House. He indicated that in his view, the purpose of the oath of allegiance was to illustrate that MP's work for the best interests of Canada and that those Members who do not give meaning to that oath should not sit in the Commons. He further reported that some of his constituents had urged him not to sit in the Chamber with MP's who seemed to have repudiated the oath of allegiance. On that basis, Flis demanded that Duceppe apologize and restore his oath, or be expelled by the Speaker, or in the alternative that the matter be referred to a Committee of the House for discussion.

The defence was mounted by another Bloquiste MP, Jean Lapierre from Shefford, who had originally defected from the Liberals. His line of reasoning was that no violation of the Canadian Constitution had occurred, and no law of Parliament or the *Criminal Code* had been breached. Rather, the new Member had exercised his freedom of expression in a spirit of respect for democracy. Indeed, he claimed, although this was a rather weak point, his words could be justified by reference to the concept of "no taxation without representation" and the people of Québec were taxpayers.

Lapierre also listed the historical precedents of some MPs who, at various times, had expressed disagreement with the prevailing notion of Canada: Joseph Howe, the anti-federalist Nova Scotian in 1867; Louis Riel, who was elected in 1873 and again in 1874 while advocating the formation of a Métis nation in what is now Manitoba; and Fred Rose, elected in 1940 as a Communist. They had all taken the oath and functioned as MPs, at least for some time, despite their lack of agreement with the majority view of Canada.

Lapierre's key argument was that the Members of the National Assembly in Québec, who, just like federal MPs, were found to take the oath of allegiance pursuant to the *Constitution Act, 1867*, were also required by section 15 of the *National Assembly Act* to swear loyalty to Québec.

> To be helpful, Mr. Speaker, I would like to say that the oath of allegiance, as prescribed by law and by the Constitution, was respected. A person

can swear allegiance to the Queen because she represents the people. We certainly do not place our trust in the monarchy. We place our trust in the people of Québec, the people we represent, and we do so proudly in this House, Mr. Speaker.[22]

Duceppe then spoke in defence of his own actions. By contrast to the general statement of position expressed by Lapierre, he offered the perspective of the individual MP.

> Mr. Speaker, I wish to correct the record. First, I never mocked the Canadian Parliament nor the Queen. I swore the oath of allegiance with all due regard for the democratic institution that the Canadian Parliament is. I did not later say that I was washing my hands of the oath. I did say that it was a formality, and I stand by what I said. It is a formality. I swore allegiance first and foremost to my Laurier–Sainte-Marie constituents, who knew very well, from the start, that I advocated sovereignty. The election results, must I remind you, Mr. Speaker, were conclusive: 68 percent voted for me, 19 percent for the Liberals, 8 percent for the NDP and 3.9 percent for the Conservative Party.[23]

The link between the two parts of the Bloc position was a concept fundamental not only to this line of argumentation and to the role of law in this situation, but also to the essence of the Canadian consensus: one loyalty and allegiance does not exclude the other. In this circumstance, this could serve as clever political reasoning. What gives it its strength, however, is that, having regard to the democratic nature of Canada and the fundamental freedoms expressed in the *Charter*, it can also be seen as being objectively correct in law.

The Speaker handed down his ruling on November 1, 1990, after thorough reflection and research. While using language designed to assuage the conflicting political perspectives, he clearly chose the path animated by constitutional and legal norms, rather than by political passion and ideological rhetoric.

> As the hon. member for Cape Breton-East Richmond has eloquently stated, the fact that an hon. member holds views which are vigorously opposed by other hon. members can in no sense be allowed to detract from his right to present them.[24]

---

[22] Hansard, October 3, 1990, p. 13738.

[23] *Ibid.*, p. 13739.

[24] Hansard, November 1, 1990, p. 14970.

He also adopted the phrase used by Lapierre, "l'un n'empêche pas l'autre," in concluding that Duceppe's words did not constitute breach of Parliamentary privilege as contempt.

The Speaker used his ruling to analyze the sources and elements of this conflict. He expressed his regard for the importance of the matter to the MP's involved as well as to the citizenry at large. He reflected quite appropriately that the contentious nature of the debate had been fuelled by media reports and commentary, something quite typical in such highly visible matters of political law. With respect to the validity of Duceppe's oath, the Speaker accepted the parallel of the twin oaths required of Members of the National Assembly in Québec. Regarding the significance and the sincerity of Duceppe in making the oath, he unequivocally stated that that was a matter of conscience upon which he could not make a judgment. He allowed that the House must accept the word of an MP no matter how the media construes the situation. Finally, on the facts, he asserted that Duceppe had not repudiated his official oath of allegiance by also declaring his loyalty to the people of his own Province.

It is perhaps ironic that in a case involving a dispute regarding the loyalty of a Québec sovereignist MP to the British-based monarch of Canada, recourse should also be had to British precedent. This is legally correct, however, considering that the Canadian Constitution declares that it is "similar in Principle to that of the United Kingdom."[25] In Lapierre's comments, he referred to the question of oaths taken by MP's at Westminster, despite their lack of consensus with the foundations of that political system.

> Mr. Speaker, I will not bore you with a description of the situation in other countries, but I would like to recall the situation in Great Britain. To our friends who sought refuge during the past few days in the monarchy and the Queen's prerogatives, I would like to say, especially to the hon. member for York South–Weston, that in Great Britain, members of the nationalist Welsh and Scottish parties were elected to the British House of Commons and sat in the House after swearing their oaths. Better still, members of the Labour Party, who have a certain philosophy in common with the Liberal Party, campaign against the monarchy in every election but they still sit in the British House of Commons.[26]

---

[25] *Constitution Act, 1867*, Preamble.
[26] Hansard, October 3, 1990, p. 13738.

In his ruling, the Speaker reflected on that defence approvingly.

> A historical perspective on parliament here in Canada and in Great Britain reveals ample precedent for the presence in the House of duly elected members whose ultimate goal may be at odds with, even inimical to, the constitutional *status quo*.[27]

---

§ 3.3.B.2
Speaker's Ruling on the Matter of the Official Opposition
House of Commons of Canada; February 27, 1996
Hansard, February 27, 1996, p. 16

In the general election of October 25, 1993, while the Liberal Party formed the government with 176 members of the House of Commons out of 295, the Bloc Québécois became the Official Opposition on the basis of its 54 seats. The Reform Party obtained 52 seats and became the Third Party. The fact of having a political party with a platform based on the sovereignty of Québec as the Official Opposition in the lower house of the Canadian Parliament was a major source of ideological conflict for the Reform Party, which strenuously wanted to achieve Official Opposition status. It was also a motive for political dissatisfaction to a sizeable part of the electorate. In the period between the election of the 35th Parliament and the holding of the Québec referendum of October 30, 1995, the Reform Party and the members of its Parliamentary caucus emphasized the point on a number of occasions that because of this party's loyalty to Canada only it and not the Bloc Québécois ought to be eligible to form the Official Opposition.

Events, political and otherwise, were to render this matter ripe for judicial consideration. During 1995, a Bloc MP was killed in an automobile accident. In the by-election which followed to fill the vacancy,[28] the seat was taken by the Liberals. This brought the ratio between the second and the third parties to 53-52. Then, in the aftermath of the sudden resignation of Premier Jacques Parizeau following the narrow defeat of the YES in the 1995 Québec referendum, it became clear that Lucien Bouchard, the Leader of the Bloc Québécois in the House of Commons and the Leader of Her Majesty's Loyal

---

[27] Hansard, November 1, 1990, p. 14970.
[28] By-election in Brome-Missisquoi, Québec, March 25, 1996.

Opposition, would resign his seat in the House in order to run for the leadership of the Parti Québécois in Québec, thereby becoming the next Premier of Québec and also leaving a further vacancy in the Commons. That would bring about a 52-52 parity between the Bloc and Reform parties.

Based on these circumstances, on December 14, 1995, the last day of the First Session of that Parliament, the House Leader of the Reform Party asked the Speaker of the House to consider and rule on a Point of Order to the effect that, upon the resumption of Parliament for the Second Session, the status of Official Opposition be conferred upon the Reform Party. The Reform Party based its argumentation on three aspects of the issue at hand: democracy, the role of an opposition in a parliamentary democracy and the Office of the Leader of the Opposition. Essentially, however, the fundamental issue of political law to be examined here was whether a political party with views and a platform contrary to the civic consensus on the Canadian political/legal regime could act as Official Opposition, and whether Parliament could function with such a party fulfilling that role.

The Reform Party recognized that traditionally any formation that constituted the Official Opposition was in fact the government in waiting, ready to fulfil the task of governing if the current government were to resign for any reason. It also acknowledged that in the past, the main criterion for selection of the Official Opposition had been electoral results borne out of the prevailing Canadian electoral system of "first-past-the-post," namely the number of seats obtained. Nevertheless, it urged that being the second largest party no longer be the only criterion. Reform asked that instead, the Speaker accept new and additional criterion in the determination of Official Opposition status. Among these, it cited as important factors the number of provinces in which a party had elected members (5 for Reform, 1 in the case of the Bloc); the percentage of popular vote obtained in all of Canada (18% for Reform, 13.5% in the case of the Bloc); and the range of interests espoused and expressed by each party (allegedly broader for Reform, narrower in the case of the Bloc). Applying these standards, the Reform Party not only claimed to be the largest and strongest of the parties claiming to be a government in waiting but also indicated that in its opinion, the political system could not expect a party whose raison d'être was the break-up of the Canadian Confederation to be the Official Opposition.

Mr. Ian McClelland (Edmonton Southwest, Ref.): Mr. Speaker, what is happening today is perhaps the most important consideration that will be faced by this Parliament. Make no mistake, Mr. Speaker, the point has been missed thus far in this debate. The fact is that our country is at peril, every bit as much as if we were facing an enemy from without. We have an enemy in our midst. We have given the Trojan horse in our Parliament the ability to subvert the actions of the House. The really important consideration is we are going into a life and death battle for the future of the country. The separatists, the Bloc, have a democratic right to be here. They have a democratic right to fight this on any battle-field they can get and to do so with passion.

We have the same right to use everything in our power, every resource we have, to fight them. For the last two years our fight has been one of retreat. Every opportunity the country has had to face the separatists, to stare them down, we have retreated. That is what damn near cost us the country on October 30.

The time to start facing down the separatists is now in the very centre of the country, the House of Commons. They have no right to be the official opposition. They do not represent the continuation of the country as a whole and complete entity.[29]

The Reform Party's argument may, in part, have been designed to develop the law and convention on the selection of the Official Opposition. It is equally patent though, given the self-serving selection of proposed new criterion and upon examination of the foregoing extract from the debate on the point of order, that Reform's line of reasoning was also based on political and electoralist considerations such as loyalty to Canada and belief in the Canadian consensus, ideological divergency between Reform and the Bloc, as well as partisan and Parliamentary advantage. In this regard, the precedents of Parliamentary practice cited by the Reform did not prove helpful to the case.

During the Christmas break of 1995, Mr. Bouchard actually did resign his seat in the House of Commons and by January 15, 1996, the second and third parties were at parity. It seemed likely, however, that in the by-election to be held in his electoral district of Lac-St-Jean, the Bloc would retain the seat.

---

[29] Hansard, December 14, 1995, p. 17676.

The Speaker of the House delivered his ruling on the very first day of the Second Session. His approach to the matter was factual, methodical and comprehensive, highlighting the great extent to which this matter had become politicized. The controversy on the status of Official Opposition was lively, the stakes were very high for all parties involved and the electorate was focused on the political, rather than the legal and customary aspects of the issue.

The Speaker's first response to the Reform arguments was that selection of the government and of the government-in-waiting was the prerogative of the Governor General on the advice of the Privy Council, rather than being within his own role in the political system. Any other view would have been an encroachment on the royal prerogative and a violation of long established constitutional practice.

The ruling also pointed out that designation of the Official Opposition had never been decided on the floor of the House of Commons. In this connection, the Speaker declared himself to be available as an impartial, neutral facilitator, uninvolved in partisan matters, in case any group of members wished to meet outside the Chamber of the House to deal with this type of matter. The clear and obvious, even if perhaps not completely expressed, implication of this phrasing was that the leadership of the parties involved would have to resolve the designation of the Official Opposition amongst themselves, but that if they invited the Speaker to chair their meetings or proffer advice to them, such assistance from the Speaker would have to be given on the basis of the existing binding rules of Parliamentary law, custom and precedent, no matter what the political views of the party that would emerge as the Official Opposition.

Thus, in reviewing the role of the Official Opposition and of Leader of the Opposition, the Speaker laid great emphasis in his ruling on terms and expressions such as "fundamental," "traditionally" and "firmly anchored in our parliamentary system of government through practice and the implementation of various statutes and rules of procedure."[30] Only by basing his decision, which would in any event be seen in a political context, on the rules of law and tradition, would the Speaker arrive at a result that would be equally democratic, legitimate and just.

---

[30] Hansard, February 27, 1996, p. 17.

The ruling seemed to reject all the precedents raised by the Reform and relied instead on one drawn from New Brunswick. In a ruling of December 16, 1994, the Speaker of that Province's Legislature had held that the Official Opposition must be determined by the number of seats held by a party, not by the popular vote it obtained.

Based on that precedent and on his view of the situation of the competing political parties in the 35th Parliament of Canada, the Speaker ruled as follows, enabling the Bloc to continue serving as the Official Opposition despite its disagreement with the general scheme of Canada.

> By convention the number of seats held by a party in the House has been the determining factor. I would like to address the new reality which the House faces today, and that is the issue of the equality of seats of the Bloc Québécois and the Reform Party.
>
> At the beginning of this Parliament the Bloc Québécois, the largest minority party in the House, assumed the role of the official opposition with their leader taking up the duties of the Leader of the Official Opposition. As a result of a by-election and the resignation of the hon. member from Lac-Saint-Jean on January 15, the Bloc Québécois and the Reform Party now have the same number of seats in the House.
>
> Just as Speaker Dysart of New Brunswick was required to do in 1994, I must answer the following question: is the existence of a tie sufficient to overthrow or displace the recognized official opposition? From my examination of the precedents from other Canadian jurisdictions, including the most recent precedent from New Brunswick, I must conclude, just as Speaker Dysart and other Speakers have, that in the case of a tie during the course of a Parliament incumbency should be the determining factor and the status quo should therefore be maintained.
>
> An equality of seats in the two largest opposition parties should neither deny the members of the Bloc Québécois their position today as the official opposition nor prevent them from choosing from among their members the leader of the official opposition. Thus the Bloc Québécois will currently retain its status as the official opposition until a further review of this status is warranted.[31]

See also *Senate Speaker's Ruling on Official Opposition in the Senate,* Senate Hansard, February 6, 2001, p. 63.

---

[31] *Ibid.,* p. 20.

3.3.C—INCLUSION OF ABORIGINALS IN CANADIAN STATEHOOD

§ 3.3.C.1
R. v. Ashini
Newfoundland Court of Appeal; October 19, 1989
(1989), 51 C.C.C. (3d) 329

The Innu people, formerly called the Eskimos, are one of the Aboriginal groups within what is today Canada. In recent times, some Innu have developed the political argument that they are not part of Canada. They base this contention on the historically correct reasoning that they never ceded their inherent independence. Ironically, however, the argument of a residual Innu independence is often used to establish land claims, or to obtain better social conditions within Canada. The political position so stated sometimes finds its way into legal argumentation. It is used as a defence to criminal charges, for example. The political law ramification of this line of reasoning is to determine whether the defence can be admitted by the courts as valid, and whether the level of success of that argumentation can put Canadian sovereignty over what Canada considers its people and its land in jeopardy, or at least if it can colour that sovereignty.

On September 15, 1988, over 100 Innu wilfully entered the Canadian Forces Air Base at Goose Bay, in Labrador, to protest the low level NATO training flights of Canadian, Dutch and West German air forces, which were based there. Several of the protestors were charged with mischief pursuant to section 430(1)(c) of the *Criminal Code*. Ashini and his co-accused raised the Innu sovereignty defence.

> When the members of the Innu people forced their way on to the Canadian Forces Base at Goose Bay in Labrador on September 15, 1988, they appear to have been protesting low level military flights over Labrador.

> The respondents through their counsel took the position that the land where the base is located and the land over which the flights were taking place is Innu land, that the Base had no right to be there, that the flights should not be taking place and that the Innu people have sovereignty over the land and are not bound by Canadian law.

They were charged but declined to plead to the charge. Those who testified did so, from their point of view, only for the purpose of explaining why they did what they did.[32]

At trial, this defence resulted in acquittal on the merits.

> In my opinion, Mr. Olthuis has presented a valid defence and also a successful one. We are not dealing with any land which has been the subject of divestiture through treaties, as under the *Indian Act*, R.S.C. 1970, c. I-6. Each of these four persons based their belief of ownership on an honest belief on reasonable grounds. Through their knowledge of ancestry and kinship they have showed that none of their people ever gave away rights to the land to Canada, and this is an honest belief each person holds. The provincial and federal statutes do not include as third parties or signatories any Innu people. I am satisfied that the four believe their ancestors predate any Canadian claims to ancestry on this land.[33]

On appeal, the issue of law before the court was whether the accused should have been tried separately or together. On that basis the trial was declared to have been a nullity. The majority of the Newfoundland Court of Appeal only noted the nature of the defence. The lone dissenter thought that the appeal should be dealt with on the merits, focusing on the Innu ancestral claims.

See also *Coon Come v. Commission Hydro-Électrique de Québec*, [1991] R.J.Q. 922 (Que. C.A.); *R. c. Cross*, [1992] R.J.Q. 1001 (Que. S.C.); *Québec Prosecution of Mohawks for the Events of Oka in 1990*, July 1992 and *Favreau v. Québec (Cour de Kahnawake)*, [1993] R.J.Q. 1450 (Que. S.C.), affirmed [1995] R.J.Q. 2348 (Que. C.A.).

---

§ 3.3.C.2

R. v. Jones

Supreme Court of Canada; August 22, 1996

[1996] 2 S.C.R. 821

The *Criminal Code*, a statute designed by Parliament for all Canadians and the writ of which ostensibly runs throughout the territory of the entire country, prohibits gaming at section 201(1), as well as schemes

---

[32] (1989), 51 C.C.C. (3d) 329 at 332 e-f.

[33] [1989] 2 C.N.L.R. 119 (Nfld. Prov. Ct.) at 129, quoted at (1989), 51 C.C.C. (3d) 329 at 332 b-333 a.

for determining the winners of property (such as bingo) at section 206(1)(d). It is of breaches of these provisions that Pamajewan and others were accused. Their defence, which brought the case into the realm of political law, was based on assertions of the non-applicability of the *Criminal Code* to them, arising from their status as aboriginals and their aboriginal rights which have been constitutionally protected since 1982. In one instance within this action, the claim was of self-government, while in the other, it was framed as self-regulation in spheres of economic activity. The dilemma of a political nature which this case points to is whether assertions of self-government, or other related claims, are compatible with the political and legal consensus of Canadian sovereignty.

At trial in Provincial Court, before the Ontario Court of Appeal and here, before the Supreme Court of Canada, all three levels of the Canadian legal system, relying on constitutional and legal reasoning, denied the claims.

The Chief Justice provided us here a methodology for analyzing claims of self-government.

> Aboriginal rights, including any asserted right to self-government, must be looked at in light of the specific circumstances of each case and, in particular, in light of the specific history and culture of the aboriginal group claiming the right. The factors laid out in *Van der Peet*, and applied, *supra*, allow the Court to consider the appellants' claim at the appropriate level of specificity;[34]

He was backed up in this by a concurring opinion of Madam Justice L'Heureux-Dube.

> Accordingly, aboriginal practices, traditions and customs would be recognized and affirmed under s. 35(1) of the *Constitution Act, 1982* **if they are sufficiently significant and fundamental to the culture and social organization of a particular group of aboriginal people.** Furthermore, the period of time relevant to the assessment of aboriginal activities should not involve a specific date, such as British sovereignty, which would crystallize aboriginal's distinctive culture in time. Rather, as aboriginal practices, traditions and customs change and evolve, they will be protected in s. 35(1) provided that they have formed an integral part

---

[34] [1996] 2 S.C.R. 821 at 834.

of the distinctive aboriginal culture for a substantial continuous period of time. [Emphasis added.][35]

Taken together, these citations affirm that self-government can be claimed as an aboriginal right under the umbrella of s. 35(1) of the *Constitution Act, 1982*. They also stand for the proposition that each such claim must be analyzed on its own; there is thus no concertation of claims arising from the aboriginal communities of Canada, nor any blanket response from the courts.

This case is of interest in additional ways, however. At trial, the accused tried to assert both self-government and native sovereignty as defences, although the sovereignty defence disappeared on appeal. It is clear that these notions are difficult for plaintiffs or accused persons to define and distinguish. In fact the two theories are completely different. What is most significant for us is that claims or assertions of sovereignty, of not belonging within Canada, or of the inapplicability of Canadian law to aboriginals on the bare ground that they are aboriginals, are legally not correct. In addition to that part of the above citation from Justice L'Heureux-Dube which deals with the issue of sovereignty, she went on to treat the matter as follows, citing from the applicable literature.

> The common feature of these lands is that the Canadian Parliament and, to a certain extent, provincial legislatures have a general legislative authority over the activities of aboriginal people, which is the result of the British assertion of sovereignty over Canadian territory.[36]

These judicial pronouncements lead us to conclude that the judiciary implicitly recognize that neither aboriginal rights in general, nor self-government in particular amount to sovereignty. In the eyes of the law, full sovereignty in the sense of constituting a single country from the perspective of public international law lies with Canada.

One other fundamental insight by the court is worth mentioning. In rendering judgment, the Chief Justice gave a clear sign that he understood the source and motivation of the claim of self-government, and perhaps of its confusion with sovereignty even though in law, he could not concede the point.

---

[35] *Ibid.* at 838.
[36] *Ibid.* at 839 citing from Brian Slattery, *Understanding Aboriginal Rights* (1987), 66 Can. Bar Rev. 727 at 743-44.

The appellants Gardner, Pitchenese and Gardner argued that they should not be convicted because s. 206 of the *Code* unjustifiably interfered with the Eagle Lake First Nation's s. 35(1) right to self-government. Flaherty Prov. Ct. J. rejected this argument. He held that the appellants' argument amounted, in essence, to an attempt to base the right to self-government on the economic disadvantages suffered by the Eagle Lake First Nation. Flaherty Prov. Ct. J. held that such a claim must fail:

> However one may wish to complain about one's economic disadvantage and however apparent it might be, redress needs to be found in other ways. People need to find ways of creating wealth and generating revenue that are not contrary to the Criminal law....I am not persuaded that the economic disadvantages of the Eagle Lake First Nations people as evident as they have been established to be in these proceedings and of First Nations people generally can be addressed by activity which contravenes the Criminal law nor can I strike down a section of the Criminal Code which is otherwise constitutionally valid for the reasons carefully and ably submitted in this case.[37]

See also *Timiskaming Indian Band v. Canada (Minister of Indian & Northern Affairs)* (1997), [1997] F.C.J. No. 676 (Fed. T.D.) and *Delgamuuwk v. British Columbia* (1997), 153 D.L.R. (4th) 193 (S.C.C.).

---

[37] *Ibid.* at 829-830.

---

§ 3.3.C.3[38]
Campbell v. British Columbia (Attorney General)
[1999] 3 C.N.L.R. 1 (B.C. S.C.)[39]
-and-
B.C. Fisheries Survival Coalition v. Canada (1999)
[1999] B.C.J. No. 109, 1999 CarswellBC 116 (B.C. S.C.)[40]
-and-
B.C. Citizens First Society v. British Columbia (Attorney General) (1999)
[1999] B.C.J. No. 120, 1999 CarswellBC 115 (B.C. S.C.)[41]
-and-
House of Sga'Nisim v. Canada
2000 BCSC 659 (B.C. S.C.)[42]

On April 13, 2000, royal assent was given to federal legislation implementing the *Nisga'a Final Agreement*, which was concluded in August 1998 and to which the parties were the Governments of Canada and British Columbia, with the Nisga'a people, an aboriginal nation in north-western British Columbia. The *Agreement* gave the Nisga'a people limited rights of self-government and operated adaptations of the legal system to Nisga'a culture in an area of the Nass Valley, close to the Alaska Panhandle.

> They will have powers of government: in taxation, land use, family, social and health services, police, courts, schools (which they run already), language and culture. They will own forest and mineral resources and the right to revenues from them, plus a 26% share of the salmon fishery and tax revenue from other commercial activities. They will also get C$121m to help set up their new authorities, build infrastructure, and buy fishing boats and licences; plus C$190m, over five years, in pure settlement of their claims.[43]

Despite the fact that the *Final Agreement* was the result of negotiations which had stretched over 100 years, the deal was extremely contested.

---

[38] Cross-reference to § 3.14.3.
[39] And (1999), [1999] B.C.J. No. 233, 1999 CarswellBC 188 (B.C. S.C.) and 2000 BCSC 619 (B.C. S.C.) and (2000), 189 D.L.R. (4th) 333 (B.C. S.C.), additional reasons at 2001 BCSC 1400 (B.C. S.C.).
[40] And (1999), [1999] B.C.J. No. 660, 1999 CarswellBC 572 (B.C. S.C.).
[41] And (1999), [1999] B.C.J. No. 662, 1999 CarswellBC 583 (B.C. S.C.).
[42] And 2000 BCCA 260 (B.C. C.A.).
[43] "Canada: A new deal for a first nation," *The Economist*, August 8, 1998, p. 34.

Those who lost the parliamentary debates in the British Columbia Legislative Assembly on this issue determined to continue the struggle against the *Agreement* by seeking through the courts to have it declared unconstitutional. The prime mover of the litigation was Gordon Campbell, the leader of the provincial Liberal Party. He was joined by various other parties fearing the consequences of the *Agreement* for British Columbia's political evolution.

The applications were for declaratory relief to the effect that the *Agreement* was contrary to section 3 (voting rights) and section 15 (equality provision) of the *Canadian Charter of Rights and Freedoms*. The applicants also sought to show that the *Agreement* redistributed legislative authority; in popular parlance, they were saying that a new, third order of government was being created. They also sought to prove that the *Agreement* would deny constitutionally guaranteed rights to non-Nisga'a people. This referred in particular to the fact that at some levels of local government established by the *Agreement*, only Nisga'a people could be enrolled to vote. In sum, the applicants' position was that the *Agreement* put into question the fullness of Canadian sovereignty in the lands to which it would apply and that the precedence of legal systems, Canadian and British Columbian, or Nisga'a would be brought in question.

The first judgments were only on preliminary issues. This does not detract from the importance of the question in several ways. Clearly, the litigation is the extension of parliamentary and public discussion into the judicial branch, and highly politicized. It is also an indicative example of the question whether, in the face of the amending formula set out in Part 5 of the *Constitution Act, 1982*, there are new ways, statutory but not constitutional, being devised to amend the substance of Canada's constitutional framework.

The public debate on the legal merits of the *Nisga'a Final Agreement* was further fuelled, in anticipation of the expected May 15, 2000 trial of the actions about it, by no less than a former justice of the Supreme Court of Canada. In an interview with the National Post, which was widely reproduced, former Justice Willard Estey qualified the *Agreement* as potentially unconstitutional because of the possibility that the powers created pursuant to it could in some instances supersede those of Canada or British Columbia. In response, the Chief of the Nisga'a offered assurances that the treaty absolutely does not take precedence over either the *Charter* or the rest of the Constitution.[44] Ultimately, only the courts can determine this matter of precedence, which may affect the nature of Canadian sovereignty, authoritatively. Undeniably, this is a matter of extreme importance for the country.

On July 24, 2000, the British Columbia Supreme Court issued a further decision in this case, in which it rejected Gordon Campbell's attempt to have the *Nisga'a Final Agreement* declared inconsistent with the *Constitution of Canada* and therefore of no force or effect. The court interpreted the terms of the *Agreement* as creating a *sui genesis* form of government which amounted neither to sovereignty nor to a new order of government after the federal and provincial levels. In its view, the right to self-government was not extinguished at Confederation, but only diminished. Here, what the *Nisga'a Final Agreement* did was to define and give content in a treaty to the self-government rights of the Nisga'a people.

The context into which this constitutionally valid self-government is to be inscribed is that of a decentralized country. The *Constitution Act, 1867*, recognized a form of diminished aboriginal self-government after the assertion of sovereignty by the Crown. It thus continued British imperial policy. However, this court added a fundamental re-evaluation of the 1867 scheme of attribution of jurisdictions which forms the basis of its recognition of Nisga'a rights.

> Thus, what was distributed in ss. 91 and 92 of the *British North America Act* was all of (but no more than) the powers which until June 30, 1867 had belonged to the colonies. Anything outside of the powers enjoyed by the colonies was not encompassed by § 91 and 92 and remained outside of the power of Parliament and the legislative assemblies just as it had been beyond the powers of the colonies.

> . . .

> This demonstrates that the object of the division of powers in § 91 and 92 between the federal government and the provinces was not to extinguish diversity (for aboriginal rights), but to ensure that the local and district needs of Upper and Lower Canada (Ontario and Québec) and the maritime provinces were protected in a federal system.[45]

---

[44] "Retired Supreme Court judge criticizes Nisga'a treaty but chief says he's heard it all before," Greg Joyce, *Ottawa Citizen*, March 21, 2000.

[45] 2000 BCSC 1123 (B.C. S.C.) at paras. 76 and 78.

Some two years after its original article on the matter, *The Economist* once again wrote about the Nisga'a issue and the other major land claims negotiation in British Columbia, that of the Sechelt Band.

> British Columbia's New Democratic Party government supports the treaty-making process. But it is almost certain to be voted out at an election due next year. The province's Liberal Party, the likely winner, is against the negotiation. So, too, is Stockwell Day, the new leader of the federal opposition, the Canadian Alliance Party. Unless compromises are swiftly struck, years of conflict may lie ahead.[46]

The London newsmagazine's electoral forecast was prophetic. On May 16, 2001, a Liberal government replaced the New Democrats in Victoria. Campbell, the original applicant, became premier. Federal–Provincial meetings took place and B.C. engaged in discussions with the Nisga'a to find a solution to what had at first seemed to be contradictory positions. The Liberal Party's accession to power led it to take not only less contradictory and confrontational positions, but also more responsible ones designed to accept some form of Nisga'a autonomy within the Canadian framework of governance.

> "British Columbia's Liberal government will likely 'water down' the language in a controversial referendum on treaty negotiations," says a confidential report. While the newly elected government has promised a province wide referendum on treaty negotiations within a year of taking office, the Liberals may be softening their approach, according to an assessment completed just before the provincial election.
>
> The report, submitted to the federal treaty commission, cites the Liberal approach to the Nisga'a treaty in northern British Columbia.
>
> . . .
>
> "The B.C. Liberals appear to be back-pedalling when it comes to their controversial court challenge to the Nisga'a treaty," the report says.
>
> The party has already scaled down its challenge to the historic treaty, asking the Supreme Court of Canada to give an opinion on self-government status rather than outright challenge its constitutionality.[47]

---

[46] "Canada: First nationalism," *The Economist*, August 5, 2000, p. 38.

[47] "B.C. Liberals likely to 'water down' native treaty referendum, says report," Dene Moore, *Ottawa Citizen*, August 20, 2001.

The final resolution of the Campbell action came on August 29, 2001, when the Government of British Columbia announced that it was discontinuing the litigation altogether, although it did maintain its intention of proceeding eventually with the referendum on the Nisga'a *Agreement*. While this move did not necessarily terminate the other court cases initiated by private parties, it did, for all intents and purposes, take the wind out of their sails. This is clear evidence that in litigation, as in many other spheres of governance, forming a government fundamentally changes a political party's and politicians' perspectives. The real difference can be said to be not between left and right but between those in power and those seeking it. It is a truism of political law that office and power responsibilize.

A postscript to the judgment on the merits came in the form of an application by Campbell and the "et al.," namely DeJong and Plant, for costs in this case. This was heard on September 28, 2001 and decided on October 10 of that year, both dates well after Campbell had become Premier of British Columbia and had named Plant as his Attorney General. The defendants included the Attorney General of the Province. This put Campbell in the strange position of suing his own Attorney General; Plant was in the even more curious circumstance of suing his office-holding self. Notwithstanding the other parties to the case, the genuine aim was for Campbell et al. to have their costs reimbursed by the Nisga'a Nation even though they had lost the case as plaintiffs. The fact that the court denied their motion was predictable. The reasoning, however, adds to our understanding of political law litigation, going beyond the main subject matter of the case, which is dealing with the issue Canada's form of government.

The plaintiffs here relied on the argument that they had no personal, proprietary or pecuniary interest in the outcome. Rather, they pleaded that "the action raised constitutional issues of broad importance and that the resolution of these questions is of benefit to the public at large, including the Nisga'a Nation."[48] Thus, they wanted to be held to be public interest litigants, but the court, rightly, refused.

> The plaintiffs brought their action, they stated, in their capacity as members of Her Majesty's Loyal Opposition. While it may be true that they have no personal, proprietary or pecuniary interest in the outcome of

---

[48] 2001 BCSC 1400 (B.C. S.C.), at para. 7.

the proceedings, they might have obtained a political benefit. They are not an organization which has as its object the taking of litigious initiatives to affect public policy. The principal forum in which they operate is the legislative assembly. Within that forum, they have a highly visible platform, ready access to the media, and legislative immunities which give them rights to raise issues and to challenge government initiatives in a manner denied other groups in society.

However, when in their capacity as members of the opposition they decide to act outside of the legislative process and resort to the courts, they become private citizens subject to the usual rules of court.

I also agree with Smith, J.'s observation, in para. 47, that the task of an elected government includes seeking to achieve a balance between competing interests of various segments of society. It follows that where one group purporting to defend the public interest brings an action putting forward a view that is not universally shared, it would not be wise to establish a principle that such people, even though their concern is *bona fide*, should be exempt from the normal rule of costs. To do so would be to penalize those who had no role in bringing the claim, who disagree with the position advanced, and who found they had to defend the action.

Finally, I observe that the plaintiffs had every right as individuals to bring their application before the court. No one, I would hope, would suggest they did not. However, that they also happened at the time to be members of the opposition party in the legislative assembly and expressly brought the action in that capacity is not in itself reason to treat them differently than any other litigants before the court. Nor is the fact that the issue to be determined was reportedly one of considerable public interest.[49]

See also *Scott v. Fulton*,[50] 137 B.C.A.C. 77 (B.C. C.A.); *House of Sga'nisim v. Canada*, 2000 BCCA 260 (B.C. C.A.); *Martel v. Samson Band* (2000), [2001] 1 C.N.L.R. 173 (Fed. T.D.); *Mushkegowuk First Nation v. Ontario*, 184 D.L.R. (4th) 532 (Ont. C.A.); *Mitchell v. Minister of National Revenue* (2001), 199 D.L.R. (4th) 385 (S.C.C.); *Hupacasath First Nation v. British Columbia*, British Columbia Supreme Court, March 27, 2002, unreported and 2002 BCCA 238 (B.C. C.A.) and 2002 BCSC 802 (B.C. S.C. [In Chambers]); *Bob v. British Columbia*, 2002 BCSC 733 (B.C. S.C. [In Chambers]); *Azak v. Nisga'a Nation*, 2003 BCHRT 79 (B.C. Human

---

[49] *Ibid.*, paras. 13, 14, 18 and 31.
[50] Cross-reference to § 6.6.D.

Rights Trib.) and *Idaho v. Coeur d'Alene Tribe of Idaho*,[51] 138 L.Ed.2d 438 (1997).

3.4 ISSUE: CONSTITUTIONALISM, RULE OF LAW, LEGAL SYSTEM BASED ON FUNDAMENTAL RIGHTS

§ 3.4.1

Quebec Assn. of Protestant School Boards v.
Quebec (Attorney General) (No. 2)
Supreme Court of Canada; July 26, 1984
[1984] 2 S.C.R. 66

The essence of this case is the nature of constitutionalism, which in the viewpoint of this study, consists of the supremacy of the constitution over other legal instruments even in circumstances where those other legal instruments, such as ordinary, non-constitutional statutes, were adopted by a Legislature and Government in furtherance of a particular political goal which may otherwise be believed to be valid by society at large, or by a majority of the population.

Successive governments in Québec had, since the late 1960's, adopted measures to protect the French language, including provisions aimed at directing an ever-growing proportion of the student population into the French-language school system, by gradually restricting qualifications for enrolment in English-language schools. On August 26, 1977, the *Charter of the French Language*[52] came into effect, as part of this process. Chapter VIII of this statute defined in a far more restrictive manner than had been done before the qualifications for attending English schools. Much political controversy resulted.

On April 17, 1982, the *Constitution Act, 1982*, came into effect, including the *Canadian Charter of Rights and Freedoms*. This *Charter* set out a new Canada-wide regime for minority-language education rights and it became patent that there was contradiction between the two charters. Barely a few weeks after the adoption of the federal *Charter*,

---

[51] International comparison. Cross-reference to § 1.2.4.
[52] R.S.Q. 1977, c. C-11.

the Protestant School Boards, in which the largest number of English-language students were registered and whose interest it was to continue to offer English education within Québec, applied for declaratory judgments regarding the admission of students to English-language education and the provincial funding of such education. The findings of the Québec Superior Court, the Québec Court of Appeal and the Supreme Court of Canada to the effect that the Canadian *Charter* overrode the *Charter of the French Language* were unanimous. Sections 72 and 73 of the Québec *Charter*, found in Chapter VIII thereof, were therefore declared to be of no force or effect to the extent of the inconsistency, unless they were legitimized by section 1 of the Canadian *Charter*, to the extent that section 1 could apply to the minority language educational rights regime established by section 23.

The genuine import of this case is the analysis it provided in respect of the principle of constitutionalism and the mechanics for the application of that principle through legal analysis.

The Supreme Court found that section 23 of the Canadian *Charter* was drafted with the *Québec Charter* in mind, specifically so as to override it.

> However, once again, to our knowledge no other provincial statute that was in force at the time the *Charter* was adopted and which dealt with the language of instruction has criteria as specific as those in s. 73 of *Bill 101*. These criteria are not only specific, but are also unique as a whole; it may be wondered whether the framers of the Constitution would have drafted s. 23 of the *Charter* as they did if they had not had in view the model which s. 23 was indeed in large measure meant to override. In their memorandum, the individual respondents, after referring to the Quebec statutes on the language of instruction, add, and in substance, properly so:
>
>> Indeed, Sec. 23 was modelled on those laws, except that it provided somewhat broader rights. No other Canadian legislation bases children's education on their parents' in a geographic area.[53]

Moreover, the justices concluded not only that section 23 was not intended to be saved by section 1, the catch-all clause referring to the

---

[53] [1984] 2 S.C.R. 66 at 83j-84b.

limitation of rights in a free and democratic society, but further that section 23 could not be saved by section 1.

> It goes without saying that in adopting s. 73 of *Bill 101* the Quebec legislature did not intend, and could not have intended, to create an exception to s. 23 of the *Charter* or to amend it, since that section did not then exist; but its intent is not relevant. What matters is the effective nature and scope of s. 73 in light of the provisions of the *Charter*, whenever the section was enacted. If, because of the *Charter*, s. 73 could not be validly adopted today, it is clearly rendered of no force or effect by the *Charter* and this for the same reason, namely the direct conflict between s. 73 of *Bill 101* and s. 23 of the *Charter*. The provisions of s. 73 of *Bill 101* collide directly with those of s. 23 of the *Charter*, and are not limits which can be legitimized by s. 1 of the *Charter*. Such limits cannot be exceptions to the rights and freedoms guaranteed by the *Charter* nor amount to amendments of the *Charter*. An Act of Parliament or of a legislature which, for example, purported to impose the beliefs of a State religion would be in direct conflict with s. 2(a) of the *Charter*, which guarantees freedom of conscience and religion, and would have to be ruled of no force or effect without the necessity of even considering whether such legislation could be legitimized by s. 1. The same applies to Chapter VIII of *Bill 101* in respect of s. 23 of the *Charter*.[54]

The court also determined that the *Charter of the French Language* would not have been saved by section 1 if it had been adopted after, rather than before, the Canadian *Charter*. The only constitutional provision which would have placed the Québec scheme beyond constitutional review by the judiciary would have been use of the "notwithstanding clause" of section 23 of the Canadian *Charter*. Moreover, the French language charter cannot be used as a way of amending the Constitution of Canada, because that can only be done by the methods prescribed at section 38 and following of the *Constitution Act, 1982* itself.

In sum, a Legislature cannot by ordinary statute set aside a scheme set out in the Constitution of Canada. An entrenched provision overrides one that is not. It is not the legislators' intent that is important, but the actual nature and scope of the provisions enacted.

> By incorporating into the structure of s. 23 of the *Charter* the unique set of criteria in s. 73 of *Bill 101*, the framers of the Constitution identified the type of regime they wished to correct and on which they would base

---

[54] *Ibid.* at 84c-i.

the remedy prescribed. The framers' objective appears simple, and may readily be inferred from the concrete method used by them: to adopt a general rule guaranteeing the Francophone and Anglophone minorities in Canada an important part of the rights which the Anglophone minority in Quebec had enjoyed with respect to the language of instruction before *Bill 101* was adopted.

If, as is apparent, Chapter VIII of *Bill 101* is the prototype of regime which the framers of the Constitution wished to remedy by adopting s. 23 of the *Charter*, the limits which this regime imposes on rights involving the language of instruction, so far as they are inconsistent with s. 23 of the *Charter*, cannot possibly have been regarded by the framers of the Constitution as coming within "such reasonable limits prescribed by law as can be demonstrably justified in a free and democratic society." Accordingly, the limits imposed by Chapter VIII of *Bill 101* are not legitimate limits within the meaning of s. 1 of the *Charter* to the extent that the latter applies to s. 23.[55]

This judgment provided evidence, if such was still needed, that despite the politically motivated views held by some, to the effect that the Canadian *Charter* did not apply in Québec because Québec's representatives had not agreed to it, the federal *Charter* did indeed apply.

---

§ 3.4.2
Foghanian-Arani, Re
Federal Court of Canada – Trial Division; October 31, 1991
(1991), 50 F.T.R. 1

The Federal Court of Canada overturned the decision of a Citizenship Judge, pursuant to which the applicant was rejected for citizenship on the ground that he had insufficient knowledge of Canada. This matter gave the court the opportunity to indicate, through the concept of the responsibilities of citizenship, those elements of constitutionalism which are the most significant in relation to Canada's political system and governmental institutions. The court referred first to the rights and freedoms of citizens, in particular to freedom of religion, speech and expression and to the right of security of the person. It also emphasized the secular nature of the Canadian State as part of its essential nature. It held that detailed knowledge of electoral law and procedure could be acquired sometime later. In both civil matters

---

[55] *Ibid.* at 87j-88e.

determined through elections and in religious ones, "in Canada, the norm is to be able to disagree without becoming violently disagreeable."[56] The noteworthiness of this case is that it presents the subjective perspective on constitutionalism, the importance of knowledge of it.

See also *MacLeod v. Canada (Canadian Armed Forces)* (1990), [1991] 1 F.C. 114 (Fed. T.D.); *Schachter v. Canada*,[57] [1992] 2 S.C.R. 679 (S.C.C.) and *R. v. S. (R.J.)*, [1995] 1 S.C.R. 451 (S.C.C.).

3.5 ISSUE: SEPARATION OF GOVERNMENT AND PARTY, MULTIPARTYISM

§ 3.5.1
Decision on the Lawlessness of the Communist Regime
Constitutional Court of the Czech Republic; December 21, 1993
Pl. US 19/93

Constitutionalism and the supremacy of law require that there be a genuine link between legitimacy and legality, rather than between legitimacy and the political stance of one particular party. This implies that where one party succeeds in acquiring control of society and the apparatus of the State, the claim is broken and a *de facto* lawlessness results even if the formalities of law are observed. This is the major thrust of this case, which is one of the most interesting and instructive decisions rendered on this issue.

In 1993, the Parliament of the Czech Republic enacted Act No. 198/93, a statute by which it declared that the Communist Regime which had existed in Czechoslovakia from 1948 to 1989 had been lawless. On September 15, 1993, 41 Deputies petitioned the Constitutional Court to have this law declared incompatible with the new Constitution which the Czech Republic had adopted, with the country's *Charter of Fundamental Rights and Basic Freedoms*, the *International Covenant on Civil and Political Rights* and a number of other international instruments. On December 21, the petition was rejected. The resolu-

---

[56] (1991), 50 F.T.R. 1 at 2.
[57] Cross-reference to § 8.9.2.

tion of the issues raised by the Deputies led the court inevitably into political analysis, into the exploration of the role of law in constitutionalism, into the distinction between government and party and into the collective responsibility of members and supporters of the Czechoslovak Communist Party for the absence of the rule of law during the period of the Communist regime.

The preamble and the first part of the statute assert,

> ...that the Communist Party of Czechoslovakia, its leadership, and its members are responsible for the manner of rule during the period 1948-1989...Thereafter it expresses the joint responsibility of those who supported the Communist regime for crimes committed and other arbitrary acts...and declares the regime founded on the basis of Communist ideology to be criminal, illegitimate and abominable.[58]

The Deputies' petition against this statutory declaration fails on the basis of the court's analysis of the nature of the manner in which the Communist regime used the law to acquire, hold and abuse power. Basing itself on the constitutional history of Czechoslovakia since the establishment of the country, the court looked at the nature of constitutionalism.

> Constitutions enacted on this basis are neutral with regard to values: they form the institutional and procedural framework, which is capable of being filled with very diverse political content because their criteria for constitutionality is merely the observance of the jurisdictional and procedural framework of constitutional institutions and procedures, thus criteria of a formal, rational nature.[59]

It then goes on to deal with the issue of legitimacy, indicating the fundamental contradiction between a monopoly on power and democratic legitimacy.

> In a regime, in which hardly anybody was unaware that the elections were not elections, that the parties were not parties, that democracy was not democracy, and that the law was not law [at least not in the sense of a law-based state, since the application of the law was politically schiz-

---

[58] The only translation of the judgment into English which seems to be readily available is on the Internet at http://www.concourt.cz/angl-ver/decisions/doc/ p-19-93.html, p. 3.

[59] Ibid., p. 6.

ophrenic and everywhere discarded when the interests of those governing entered into the picture], in such a regime it is even less possible to
reduce the concept of legitimacy to that of the formal legality of nor-
mative legal regulation.[60]

The court concludes that in light of this background and the nature
of the Czech Republic's post-Communist constitution, the Deputies'
formal and legal arguments must bow to the sovereignty of the people, which takes precedence even over the sovereignty of enacted
law". . .in the framework of this Constitution, the constitutive principles of a democratic society are placed beyond the legislative power
and thus *ultra vires* of the Parliament."[61] Technically, the consequence
of this reasoning is that a law which recognizes the state of fact as to
lawlessness in a previous regime cannot be unconstitutional.

The court also considered whether the limitation period on criminal
acts committed between February 25, 1948, and December 29, 1989,
could be deemed to have been suspended by the illegality of the
regime. It also dismissed this line of reasoning on the grounds that
the State, its institutions and its agents engaged in illegal and criminal
activity and the political power in control of the state guaranteed the
non-sanctionability of the offenders and ensured their immunity from
the application of criminal law. In the field of criminal law, the confusion between the legality and political power arose from the monopoly of the Communist Party over the levers of the State.

> However, these legal norms became fictional and hollow whenever the
> party recognized such to be advantageous for its political interests. Its
> monopoly on political and governmental power and the bureaucratically
> centralized organization of them were constructed upon this simple
> expedient, and they resulted, never from the division, but from the
> concentration of power and from firmly linking the political and gov-
> ernmental bodies, as well as from the lack of basic democratic relations
> in society. The anchoring of the Communist Party's leading role in so-
> ciety and state (in Article 4 of the 1960 Constitution) was not the cause,
> rather the resulting manifestation, of the realities which had much earlier
> led to the strengthening of this power monopoly.

---

[60] Op. cit., p. 7.
[61] Op. cit., p. 8.

. . .

> The authorities in charge of the protection of legality thus became in-
> struments of the central monopoly power.[62]

In this argumentation as well, the general political analysis is sustained by technical legal reasoning, but which is itself based on the
court's understanding of the political realities in the Communist era.

> An action is barred at the end of the limitation period only if at that time
> the ongoing efforts of the state to prosecute a criminal act have been in
> vain. This prerequisite cannot be met for the category of politically pro-
> tected offenses from 1948 until 1989. The condition of mass, state-pro-
> tected illegal activities was not the consequence of individual errors,
> blunders, negligence or misdeeds, which would have left open some
> possibility for criminal prosecution, rather it was the consequence of the
> purposeful and collective behaviour of the political and state authorities
> as a whole, which ruled out criminal prosecution in advance. By these
> means, the protection of offenders became as universal as the system of
> power.[63]

3.6 ISSUE: REPRESENTATIVE GOVERNMENT, FREE AND FAIR ELECTORAL SYSTEM AND ADMINISTRATION[64]

§ 3.6.1[65]
Dixon v. British Columbia (Attorney General)
British Columbia Supreme Court; April 18, 1989
(1989), 59 D.L.R. (4th) 247

Among the legal components vital to render a political system democratic in nature, the one perhaps closest to the core in popular as
well as expert opinion is the holding of genuine elections. Indeed the
expression by the people of a preferred choice among divergent political options is, both in reality and in perception, a fundamental and

---

[62] Op. cit., p. 9.
[63] Op. cit., p. 12.
[64] Cross-reference to § 5.2.
[65] Cross-reference to § 2.4.4.

necessary element in order for a regime of governance to be democratic. The manner in which that choice is expressed and the effectiveness of that expression are no longer left to the domain of political
analysis alone. In the Canadian context, the right to vote was constitutionally enshrined through section 3 of the *Charter* in 1982. Since
then, a string of very important cases has defined the characteristics
with which the electoral system must be endowed in order that it be
representative of the people's wishes through a free and fair process.
The *Dixon* case is the first of these.

In 1984, the *Constitution Act*[66] established for British Columbia's provincial political structure a system of constituencies divided among
several categories: metropolitan, suburban, urban-rural, interior,
coastal and remote. Each category of constituency was assigned a
population quota, which was based on the average population per
member of the Legislature, with Vancouver for the mainland and
Victoria-Oak Bay for Vancouver Island as the bases. Electoral boundaries were then drawn on the basis of these quotas. The consequences
of this categorization of constituencies were that extremely wide deviations arose from the norm of an average population per elected
representative, and the power of rural voter was disproportionately
enhanced. "The effect of the quota is to give relatively greater weight
to non-urban votes than to urban votes."[67] The problem was com-
pounded yet further in that some constituencies were represented by
one member and some by two.

It was against this system of representation that Dixon initiated a
petition, asking for an order declaring the relevant provisions of the
Constitution Act invalid. The court first held that the provincial legislation was in fact subject to *Charter* review.[68] It then invalidated the
electoral boundaries scheme of British Columbia and provisionally
suspended its declaration of invalidity to give the province time to
reshape its electoral constituencies.

The great interest of the Dixon case is the legal reasoning it provided
on the notion of representative government and on the requirements
of a constitutionally valid electoral system. It phrased this under the

---

[66] R.S.B.C. 1979, c. 62.

[67] (1989), 59 D.L.R. (4th) 247 at 253.

[68] In this it was upholding an earlier ruling by the same court: (1986), 31 D.L.R. (4th)
546 (B.C. S.C.).

rubric of "the right to vote," following the language of section 3 of the *Charter*. Thus, to the extent that the electoral system is at the heart of the democratic form of governance, democracy is not only a political philosophy but also a coherent set of legal norms which a political legal system must implement.

> Viewed in its textual context, the right to vote and participate in the democratic election of one's government is one of the most fundamental of the *Charter* rights. For without the right to vote in free and fair elections all other rights would be in jeopardy. The *Charter* reflects this.[69]

The court recognized that section 3 of the *Charter* embodied not only the right to vote, but also a number of ancillary rights, among them a right relating to the equality of votes. The quality of electoral boundaries distribution was the vehicle for assuring that equality. An alternative description of equality of voting power is "representation by population." Whichever way described, this rule implied a number of recognized principles relating to voting. The court thought it worthwhile to extend that list of principles.

> It cannot be denied that equality of voting power is fundamental to the Canadian concept of democracy. The claim of our forefathers to representation by populations—"rep by pop"—preceded Confederation and was confirmed by it.

> As I have earlier noted, the purpose of the s. 3 guarantee of the right to vote must be to preserve to citizens their full rights as democratic citizens. The concept of representation by population is one of the most fundamental democratic guarantees. And the notion of equality of voting power is fundamental to representation by population. The essence of democracy is that the people rule. Anything less than direct, representative democracy risks attenuating the expression of the popular will and hence risks thwarting the purpose of democracy.

> It cannot be denied that Canadian society rests in large part on the traditional liberal ideal of equal respect for the dignity and worth of each individual. Where political rights are concerned, this ideal would accord equal rights to participate freely with one's fellow citizens in the establishment of the laws and rules which govern the conduct of all. The correlative of liberty is the assurance that each citizen is equally entitled to participate in the democratic process and that each citizen carries an

---

[69] (1989), 59 D.L.R. (4th) 247 at 257.

equal voice in that process: John Rawls, A Theory of Justice (1971), p. 221.[70]

The court concluded that despite differences between Canadian and American notions of democracy, the notion of equality was inherent to the Canadian concept of voting rights.

Having equated representative government with representation by population and equality of voting rights, the court proceeded to define further the notion of equality in this sphere. It did so through a series of questions and comparisons with the most readily available possible model/contrast, that of the United States. The first glance was at the notion of absolute equality, which was the standard demanded by American courts, notably in the case of *Baker v. Carr*[71]

> Democracy in Canada is rooted in a different history. Its origins lie not in the debates of the founding fathers, but in the less absolute recesses of the British tradition. Our forefathers did not rebel against the English tradition of democratic government as did the Americans; on the contrary, they embraced it and changed it to suit their own perceptions and needs.

> What is that tradition? It was a tradition of evolutionary democracy, of increasing widening of representation through the centuries. But it was also a tradition which, even in its more modern phases, accommodates significant deviation from the ideals of equal representation. Pragmatism, rather than conformity to a philosophical ideal, has been its watchword.[72]

This difference between the Canadian and American systems of representation was not only a matter of history. The court also concluded that the *Charter* did not alter the Canadian democratic system by introducing new political rights.

Rather than adopting absolute equality of voting rights, the court settled on relative equality. This in turn required an examination of the extent of deviation from the norm, which would be permissible, and the justification for such deviations.

---

[70] *Ibid.* at 259.
[71] 7 L.Ed.2d 663 (U.S. S.C., 1962).
[72] *Supra* note 69 at 262.

In determining the amount of deviation permissible, deference must be accorded to the legislature. It is in a better position than the courts to determine whether deviation is required. However, in making that determination, the legislature must act in accordance with such legal principles as may be found to be inherent in the Charter guarantee of the right to vote.[73]

On this basis, the most important factor in drawing constituency boundaries and in providing for relative equality of voting power is population. Whether it is in respect of the legislative functions of members of the legislature or their fulfilment of the "ombudsman" function, only these deviations from the norm can be admitted which can be justified on the ground that they contribute to better government of the population as a whole. Examples of such justifications are regional issues among the electorate and geographic considerations related to the territory governed.

---

§ 3.6.2[74]
Reference re Provincial Electoral Boundaries
Supreme Court of Canada; June 6, 1991
[1991] 2 S.C.R. 158

Of all the cases which Canadian courts heard during the 1990's on the issue of representation and redistribution, this is the one in which they took the broadest perspective, analyzing the political work of legislatures in establishing electoral constituencies from the point of view of voters' constitutional rights. In examining the validity of Saskatchewan's electoral map, the Supreme Court of Canada defined here the specifically Canadian notion of representative democracy, by focusing the debate on the meaning of the right to vote enshrined in section 3 of the *Charter*.

Pursuant to the *Representation Act*,[75] an independent commission mandated by the Saskatchewan Legislature recommended in 1989 a proposed redistribution scheme in which it distinguished between urban, rural and northern electoral districts. The scheme contained a number of ridings in which the deviation from the electoral quotient

---

[73] *Ibid.* at 266.
[74] Cross-reference to § 5.3.1.
[75] S.S. 1989-90, c. R-20.2.

was greater than the 15 per cent permitted by statute and in which there was under-representation of urban areas. A reference to the Saskatchewan Court of Appeal resulted in a judgment to the effect that the redistribution plan infringed on section 3 of the *Charter*. The Supreme Court of Canada allowed an appeal and determined that the plan put forward by the commission was valid. This judgment touched on two aspects of the matter. The factors proper to a redistribution are considered at § 5.3. Here, the focus is on representative democracy.

The majority opinion was prepared for the court by Madam Justice McLachlin, who, as the author of the *Dixon* decision, already had experience with redistribution matters, as well as definite and enlightened views on the nature of Canadian democracy. She started by framing her views on the interpretation of the right to vote as being guided by the ideal of Canada as a "free and democratic society," the core concept of section 1 of the *Charter* and by interpreting the right in accordance with its purpose. This enabled her to look beyond the legalistic versions of the right and to also involve the philosophical and historical underpinning of the *Charter*.

In McLachlin's opinion, the validity of the Saskatchewan voting map should be decided by contrasting the equality of voting power of citizens with what she termed effective and fair representation.

C. The Meaning of the Right to Vote

It is my conclusion that the purpose of the right to vote enshrined in s. 3 of the Charter is not equality of voting power per se, but the right to "effective representation." Ours is a representative democracy. Each citizen is entitled to be represented in government. Representation comprehends the idea of having a voice in the deliberations of government as well as the idea of the right to bring one's grievances and concerns to the attention of one's government representative; as noted in Dixon v. B.C. (A.G.), [1989] 4 W.W.R. 393, at p. 413, elected representatives function in two roles—legislative and what has been termed the "ombudsman role."[76]

Having set out her preference for the doctrine of effective and fair representation, McLachlin defined what this consisted of. The first condition required is relative parity of voting power. The Canadian

---

[76] [1991] 2 S.C.R. 158 at 183 f-i.

form of government had accepted, since Sir John A. Macdonald's time, that voter parity could not be realized. Given that voters die, that they move, as the first Prime Minister stated, even with the aid of frequent censuses, drawing boundary lines so as to guarantee the same number of voters in each electoral district is impossible. If that was true then, in the 1860's, it would become even truer with the higher birth rates, expanded immigration and ease of mobility of the 20th and 21st centuries. The relativity of voting power which is the hallmark of Canadian electoral practice was derived from the attachment to the basic counting of population and of other considerations to be weighed in the balance, such as the need to represent interests, classes and localities. These considerations are intrinsic to the development of Canadian society and polity, with its composite population and difficult geography.

The second condition of effective representation is the achievement of a balance between as much relative parity as may be possible on the one hand, and a combination of other factors such as geography, community history, community interests and minority representation on the other. The purpose of such a balance is "to ensure that our legislative assemblies effectively represent the diversity of our social mosaic."[77] McLachlin went on to clarify that the factors enumerated here were but examples and that the list was not closed.

The conclusion which emerges from these conditions is that in order to seek the goal of effective representation, certain deviations from absolute voter parity are justifiable where they are based on the practical impossibility of providing more effective representation. This judgment should be understood to mean that effective representation could be achieved through relative voter parity, that deviations could be justified on a number of social and historical grounds, but that deviations were nevertheless to be limited.

> I adhere to the proposition asserted in Dixon...that "only those deviations should be admitted which can be justified on the ground that they contribute to better government of the populace as a whole, giving due weight to regional issues within the populace and geographic factors within the territory governed."[78]

---

[77] *Ibid.* at 184 i.
[78] *Ibid.* at 185 b.

The Canadian model of representative democracy was compared with that adopted in 1975 by the High Court of Australia.[79] The ground similarity cited was common ascendancy in the British legal system, the absence of rejection of that evolutionary model and the shared tradition of Commonwealth countries. Our system was also brought into sharp contrast with that of the United States, where the Supreme Court was said to have adopted a more radical approach based on the doctrine of "one person-one vote."[80] In sum, the watchword in the Canadian doctrine of representation is pragmatism, rather than conformity to a philosophical ideal, without, however, excusing historical anomalies.

> In the final analysis, the values and principles animating a free and democratic society are arguably best served by a definition that places effective representation at the heart of the right to vote. The concerns which Dickson C. J. in Oakes associated with a free and democratic society—respect for the inherent dignity of the human person, commitment to social justice and equality, respect for cultural and group identity, and faith in social and political institutions which enhance the participation of individuals in society—are better met by an electoral system that focuses on effective representation than by one that focuses on mathematical parity. Respect for individual dignity and social equality mandate that citizen's votes not be unduly debased or diluted. But the need to recognize cultural and group identity and to enhance the participation of individuals in the electoral process and society requires that other concerns also be accommodated.[81]

---

§ 3.6.3
Haig v. R.
Supreme Court of Canada; September 2, 1993
[1993] 2 S.C.R. 995

This case merits particular attention because it is one of the richest sources of legal principles which illuminate the core democratic element of the Canadian political system, the freedom of citizens to express their political opinions in a manner organized by statute into elections or referenda.

---

[79] *Australia (Attorney General) v. Commonwealth* (1975), 135 C.L.R. 1 (Australia H.C.).
[80] *Baker v. Carr*, 369 U.S. 186 (1962).
[81] *Supra* note 76 at 188 e-h.

In adopting the *Referendum Act*,[82] Parliament gave itself the power to organize referenda on constitutional questions in part or all of Canada. In the fall of 1992, the Government and Parliament of Canada decided to hold a referendum on the *Charlottetown Accord*, to ask the population whether it wished to agree to a large number of constitutional changes all combined into a political package. For reasons flowing from the failure to adopt the *Meech Lake Accord* in 1990 and from the consequential political promises in Québec to hold a provincial referendum on constitutional options, technically, the referendum of October 26, 1992, was organized as two parallel referenda. Within Québec, that province's own *Referendum Act*[83] applied and the polling divisions were those in force in the provincial elections. In the rest of Canada, the federal legislation applied and federal electoral districts were used as the divisions to determine the residency of voters and the counting of votes. Each statutory scheme had its own rules on residency of voters.

Haig moved from Ontario to Québec less than six months prior to the issue of the writs for the referendum. At the time of enumeration, he was no longer resident in Ontario and could not be enumerated but as he had not yet resided in Québec for six months, he could not be enumerated there either. Pursuant to the rules applicable in the scheme of the federal legislation, Haig lived in a part of the country which was not covered by the legal instruments instituting the referendum under federal rules. Consequently, he could not vote. He sought declarations that would result in enabling him to vote, as well as *mandamus* to require the Chief Electoral Officer to make reasonable provisions to enable him to vote. The Federal Court of Canada – Trial Division and the Federal Court of Appeal both dismissed the action. On October 22, 1992, four days before the holding of the referenda, the Supreme Court refused to hear the case on the merits on the basis of one day's notice. It did hear arguments on March 4, 1993, and issued its decision on October 2 of that year. Notwithstanding the fact that the substantive question had become moot, the court felt the importance of clarifying the legal issues involved which were determinative of some of the fundamentals of present and future Canadian political life. The judgment was to the effect that Haig had no case and his constitutional rights had not been infringed.

---

[82] S.C. 1992, c. 30.
[83] R.S.Q. 1977, c. C-64.1.

The court set the scene of the intensely controversial nature of the situation in 1992.

> At that specific moment in Canadian history, there was a confluence of political pressures, concerns and events. Among these was the ongoing and often politically heated constitutional dialogue. In order to seek the views of Canadians on this crucial issue of constitutional change, the federal government and the provincial governments who so desired had available a variety of options: commissions, surveys, opinion polls, referenda, etc. Quebec had legally bound itself to hold a referendum on sovereignty, while British Columbia and Alberta had articulated the possibility that they would hold provincial referenda dealing with constitutional change, and that they would consider themselves bound by the results. It was in this context that the federal government undertook to hold a referendum in those provinces where a provincial referendum would not otherwise be held. This choice was in accord with the desire and the authority of the provinces to consult their own electors as they saw fit.[84]

Setting aside the particularities of Haig's own circumstances, it is possible to distil from the general statements the *ratio* of the case no less than seven important principles relating to the legal aspects of representative democracy.

The most fundamental issue addressed by the Supreme Court was that of the true meaning of section 3, the voting right provision, of the *Canadian Charter of Rights and Freedoms*. Recognizing that the right to vote is synonymous (but not coextensive) with democracy, and mindful of the Canadian system of effective representation, the court declared that

> The purpose of s. 3 of the Charter is, then, to grant every citizen of this country the right to play a meaningful role in the selection of elected representatives who, in turn, will be responsible for making decisions embodied in legislation for which they will be accountable to their electorate.[85]

It went on, nevertheless, to draw a sharp distinction between elections and referenda, both as to the government's option to hold referenda and to the government's duty to abide by the results of such consultations. In the case of elections, there are legal obligations in respect

---

[84] (1993), 105 D.L.R. (4th) 577 at 581 g-582 a.
[85] *Ibid.* at 601 a.

of both criteria. In the case of referenda, the choices and the remedies are in the political field. The court therefore concluded that section 3 does not contemplate the right to vote in a referendum and that therefore "the citizens of this country cannot claim a constitutional right to vote in a referendum under s. 3 of the Charter."[86]

In discussing the proper interpretation of the *Referendum Act*, the court also set out the parameters of its reading of the statute. This second principle is to the effect that the right interpretation of legislation in order to determine its compliance with the constitutional factors it must meet is to encompass the wording, but also the spirit of the Act. Further, it referred to the object of the Act, in the sense of its objective. These elements, wording, spirit and objective, ought to be considered as the complete guide to the interpretation of statutes as to their constitutionality.

The third principle in this case relates to the proper way, under the law, to administer the electoral/referenda process. What is the obligation to law of the Chief Electoral Officer? The *Referendum Act* and the *Canada Elections Act* on which it is based both include provisions respecting adaptation of the legislation to the execution of its intent. This is a discretionary power which the court held needed to be exercised within the limits set by law, in the manner dictated by law and for the purposes delineated by law.

> Though the Chief Electoral Officer is given a discretionary power to adapt the legislation, this power does not extend to authorize a fundamental departure from the scheme of the Referendum Act (Canada). In exercising his discretion, he must remain within the parameters of the legislative scheme.
>
> . . .
>
> The discretionary power of the Chief Electoral Officer cannot be exercised to extend the entitlement to vote beyond the parameters established in the Order-in-Council. Were he to adapt the legislation in a manner that extended the reach of the underlying Order-in-Council, the Chief Electoral Officer would exceed the boundaries of his jurisdiction and, in my view, he would be exposed to having his decision quashed upon judicial review.[87]

---

[86] *Ibid.* at 602 a.
[87] *Ibid.* at 596 e-h.

What was asked of the Chief Electoral Officer in this instance, namely to enable a person to vote without that person being associated with a particular polling division in respect of which the writs for referendum had been issued, was clearly an attempt to stretch the use of the adopting provision beyond the authority of the Chief Electoral Officer. This was true even though the spirit of the *Referendum Act* was to encourage a very broad view of the concept of residence. Thus, in administering the mechanics of democracy, the first duty of the Chief Electoral Officer was to act in accordance with the requirements of the statute as it was given to him by Parliament.

The fourth principle of democracy enunciated by the court was to define in law the nature of a referendum. "A referendum...is basically a consultative process, a device for the gathering of opinions."[88] By contrast to elections which are required to be held at intervals by virtue of section 4 of the *Charter*, the holding of referenda is entirely optional. There is no positive duty on governments to consult the people by referendum. The only instance in which a referendum is binding is if a government and legislature voluntarily undertake to hold that type of consultation. Moreover, the results of a referendum are legally binding only if there is an undertaking in advance to so require.

Having differentiated between elections and referenda, the court analysed, as its fifth principle, the freedom of expression issue of a referendum, as derived from section 2(b) of the *Charter*. It reiterated that voting is a form of expression. However, given that no section 3 right has been found that would guarantee Canadians a constitutional right to vote in a referendum, there can be no section 2(b) right of expression built thereon.

> A referendum is a creation of legislation. Independent of the legislation giving genesis to a referendum, there is no right of participation. The right to vote in a referendum is a right accorded by statute, and the statute governs the terms and conditions of participation. The Court is being asked to find that this statutorily created platform for expression has taken on constitutional status. In my view, though a referendum is undoubtedly a platform for expression, s. 2(b) of the Charter does not impose upon a government, whether provincial or federal, any positive obligation to consult its citizens through the particular mechanism of a referendum. Nor does it confer upon all citizens the right to express their

---

88 *Ibid.* at 601 e.

opinions in a referendum. A government is under no constitutional obligation to extend this platform of expression to anyone, let alone to everyone. A referendum as a platform of expression is, in my view, a matter of legislative policy and not of constitutional law.[89]

It is interesting that on that point, Justice Iacobucci dissented. He agreed that the federal government was bound neither to hold the referendum, nor to be legally bound by its results. However, having decided to hold it, and in particular having created expectations through political pronouncements by the Prime Minister and others, it must hold the referendum in compliance with the *Charter*, that is by allowing all citizens a voice. It could not rely on the technicality of separate referenda under parallel legal schemes to avoid the conclusion that a section 2(b) right existed.

> "[C]ommunicating one's constitutional views to the public and to governments is unquestionably an expressive activity protected by paragraph 2(b)" (p. 211). I would agree. Casting a referendum ballot is an important form of expression which is worthy of constitutional protection. In my view, the appellant Haig's right to express his political views by participating in the referendum was guaranteed by s. 2(b) of the Charter. He was denied the right to participate and thus his s. 2(b) rights were violated.[90]

The sixth principle to be gleaned from the judgment relates to the consequences of the absence of a section 3 right. As if there was no legal right to vote in this consultative event, the law-politics relationship was implicitly drawn into question. What motivated the government in resorting to the holding of a referendum? This was a matter of political decision-making.

> These comments are apposite here. Section 3(1) of the Referendum Act (Canada) confers upon the Governor in Council a discretionary power to direct that a referendum be held in any number of provinces. Nowhere in the Canadian Constitution is there mention of an obligation on the Governor in Council to hold a referendum, or to see that a referendum is held in all provinces. Both the decision to hold a referendum, and the decision as to the number of provinces in which a referendum will be held are policy decisions left entirely to governments and legislatures. They involve matters of political consideration. Besides, the Governor in Council is not required to justify the reasons for any particular exercise

---

[89] *Ibid.* at 608 a.
[90] *Ibid.* at 626 e.

of his discretion. As Dickson J. said in Thorne's Hardware Ltd. v. The Queen, [1983] 1 S.C.R. 106, at pp. 112-13:

> Governments do not publish reasons for their decisions; governments may be moved by any number of political, economic, social or partisan considerations.[91]

Finally, from the pen of Justice Iacobucci, we can draw the seventh principle, which is applicable even though written by a dissenter on the ruling. This was the matter of the outcome of the referendum. In the context of looking at the freedom of expression which he perceived, Iacobucci also noted that, in the political realm, the referendum did create obligations. He agreed with the majority who said that the legal nature of the referendum was consultative only and that the government was not legally bound to adopt its results.

> Although Parliament was under no legal obligation to follow the results of the referendum, apparently a political obligation to do so had been assumed. Despite the absence of such a legal obligation, nevertheless, the referendum was exceedingly important expressive activity that is worthy of Charter protection, as was acknowledged by Minister Danis in his comments quoted above.[92]

The outcome of this case could have been different if Haig had actioned on the basis of the legal lacuna caused by the interaction of the federal and Québec referendum laws. As the case was actually framed, in aiming to obtain remedy only under Canada's *Referendum Act*, Haig made a strategic error in litigation which cost him the right to vote, but which gave the Supreme Court the opportunity to make necessary new political legal analysis.

---

§ 3.6.4
Québec (Directeur général des élections) c. Fortin
Québec Court of Appeal; December 17, 1999
1999 CarswellQue 3821 (Que. C.A.)

In order for the electoral administration of a jurisdiction to contribute to the free and fair nature of the electoral system, and hence to serve

---

[91] *Ibid.* at 611h-612 c.
[92] *Ibid.* at 626 b.

as one of the components of a truly democratic political legal regime, it must be scrupulously impartial and law-abiding. The fact that in Canadian practice, such qualities are deemed to be permanent and taken for granted make it all the more remarkable when the courts put it in doubt.

The referendum organized in Québec, on the issue of eventual sovereignty, on October 30, 1995, was very hotly contested. While the result obtained by the NO option stood at 50.58% and that garnered by the YES was at 49.42%, the most surprising part of the outcome was that a greater number of ballots were rejected than the difference between the NO and YES votes. In three electoral districts, the proportion of rejected ballots reached 11.6%, 5.5% and 3.6%; in each case this was beyond statistical error or electors' customary behaviour.

Québec's Chief Electoral Officer conducted an investigation and, as a test case, initiated a prosecution against two election officers, including Fortin. At the Québec Court and Superior Court levels, the charges against the accused were dismissed, for lack of evidence. The Chief Electoral Officer appealed.

On December 17, 1999, more than four years after the holding of the referendum, the Québec Court of Appeal issued a judgment which was useful in that it developed the underlying substantive issues of election law, but even more significantly, which cast a doubt on the impartiality of Québec's electoral administration at the time the prosecution was initially conducted, and which therefore called into question the democratic quality of the electoral administration.

With respect to the accused, the Court of Appeal unhesitatingly concluded that they had acted in a manifestly unreasonable manner in rejecting the large number of perfectly valid ballots. The court squarely laid the blame for the actions of the accused on the YES Committee training which had influenced them and tainted their judgment. It must be noted that the accused were Francophone, young, inexperienced and susceptible to being influenced, and that the three electoral districts in which these events took place held significant Anglophone populations. While none of these factors personal to the accused could excuse their behaviour, the blame for their actions must be apportioned with the YES Committee which provided training obviously so partisan and undemocratic as to render their work potentially criminal.

The court went on to characterize the defendants' actions in a manner that, in judicial practice, is unusually harsh.

> ...les résultats du dépouillement dans chacun des bureaux de vote où les intimés ont agi comme scrutateurs sont absolument aberrants, pour ne pas dire révoltants...[93]

Despite this unmistakeable finding of culpability on the part of the accused, the court then made the astonishing finding that it could not hold them guilty because at first instance, they had not been prosecuted in a proper legal manner, based on sufficient evidence and testimony. The court set out a number of elements in the prosecution's case which it expressed to have been inadequately done. The most direct conclusion that the alert observer can draw is that the court felt, and said, that the Office of the Chief Electoral Officer itself had not acted with the fairness and impartiality which were its democratic obligations.

> Il faut donc examiner la conduite des intimés pour déterminer s'ils ont agi d'une manière incompatible avec les activités honnêtes ou honorables.

> Avant de le faire, je ne peux faire autrement que de constater la faiblesse de la preuve qui a été offerte par le poursuivant en première instance et qui contraste avec la façon rigoureuse dont ses représentants ont plaidé les pourvois dont nous sommes saisis. En effet, dans la cause de Lefebvre, la poursuite n'a fait entendre aucun témoin, pas même le directeur local du scrutin. Elle s'est contentée de soumettre une preuve documentaire à laquelle elle a joint quelques admissions. Pourtant elle connaissait la défense de Lefebvre, puisqu'il avait donné sa version des évènements aux enquêteurs du DGE.

> La poursuite n'a pas fait entendre Réal Lafontaine qui a donné une "formation" aux scrutateurs et aux représentants du camp du Oui. Il aurait été pertinent de savoir si la même "formation" a été donnée dans les 125 circonscriptions de la province ou seulement dans des circonscriptions ciblées selon les tendances révélées par les sondages.

> La poursuite n'a pas fait entendre non plus le préposé à l'information et au maintien de l'ordre, le Prime, alors qu'il aurait été important de savoir qui il a contacté pour pouvoir instruire Lefebvre sur la bonne façon d'enregistrer les votes.

---

[93] (1999), 1999 CarswellQue 3821 (Que. C.A.) at para. 69.

Il aurait été important de savoir également si le DGE était au courant de la formation qui était donnée aux scrutateurs par le Comité du Oui, et s'il l'était, pourquoi il n'a pas corrigé les instructions erronées qui ont été données à ceux-ci.

Même si j'ai cru opportun de faire les remarques ci-dessus, il n'en reste pas moins que la question qui nous est soumise doit être tranchée à la lumière de la preuve faite en première instance.[94]

In the political culture which prevails in Canada and Québec, only a judicial pronouncement such as this judgment can validly contain criticism of the electoral administration on grounds of failure to observe impartiality. There is an implicit desire on the part of political actors to avoid such criticism and there is a fervent wish that the electoral administration will "do the right thing." This may explain the rather muted reaction to the court's judgment.

Tom Mulcair, Liberal MNA for Chomedey riding, said he is happy with the ruling. Although the court upheld the acquittals, the ruling makes it clear that ballots were wrongly rejected and that it was done under instructions from Yes-committee organizers, he said.

I can live with this. It proves what we suspected for four years.

Now, Mulcair said, the key is for elections officials to follow the road map drawn for them by the judgment and ensure that proper cases are presented against the remaining defendants, particularly those accused of organizing the ballot-rejection scheme.

"It's the chief electoral officer's job. Let them do it properly this time."[95]

This issue has continued to stay under the political legal spotlight. In early August 2000, the English rights group Alliance Québec announced that it would publicly display copies of some of the ballots rejected in the 1995 referendum. These copies were obtained as part of the evidence in the trial of Mathieu Lefebvre. The litigation arising out of the referendum also continued for several years. The Montréal newspaper *The Gazette* asked the courts for permission to see the ballots from those electoral districts in which the number of rejected

---

[94] *Ibid.* at paras. 61-66.
[95] "Ballot probe hotbed: judge," Elizabeth Thompson, *The Gazette*, Montréal, December 18, 1999.

ballots was unusually high. This matter went as far as the Québec Court of Appeal, which refused the application, and the Supreme Court of Canada would not grant leave to appeal.[96]

See also *Gazette (The) c. Conseil du Référendum*, [2000] R.J.Q. 1082 (Que. C.A.), leave to appeal refused (2001), 267 N.R. 400 (note) (S.C.C.); *Speech from the Throne, July 24, 2001 and Constitution (Fixed Election Dates) Amendment Act, 2001*, S.B.C. 2001, c. 36 and *Gombu v. Ontario (Assistant Information & Privacy Commissioner)* (2002), 59 O.R. (3d) 773 (Ont. Div. Ct.), additional reasons at (2002), [2002] O.J. No. 2570 (Ont. Div. Ct.), leave to appeal allowed (2002), 2002 CarswellOnt 2874 (Ont. C.A.).

3.7 ISSUE: LEADERSHIP IN GOVERNANCE THROUGH AN INTEGRAL LEGISLATIVE SYSTEM

See *Reference re Anti-Inflation Act, 1975 (Canada)*, [1976] 2 S.C.R. 373 (S.C.C.).

---

§ 3.7.1[97]
P.S.A.C. v. Canada
Supreme Court of Canada; April 9, 1987
(1987), 38 D.L.R. (4th) 249

In the 1970's, the Government of Canada had tried to defeat the scourge of inflation by legislative means and the matter had ended up before the Supreme Court of Canada. During the 1980's, the economic problems persisted and different means were attempted, but again through legislative action. This second attempt at controlling economic malaise by Parliamentary action led to the present litigation, which, again, went to the highest court in the land. The notoriety of this case is that the explanation contained in the partially dissenting ruling of the Chief Justice of Canada would, in the long term, turn out to be much more important than the immediate outcome of the case, as decided by the majority.

---

[96] *Gazette (The) c. Conseil du Référendum*, [2000] R.J.Q. 1082 (Que. C.A.), leave to appeal refused (2001), 267 N.R. 400 (note) (S.C.C.).
[97] Cross-reference to § 9.8.A.1.

Here, the Public Service Alliance of Canada (PSAC) was acting on behalf of the interests of some of the country's railway employees. It applied for a declaration that the *Public Sector Compensation Restraint Act (PSCRA)*[98] was contrary to the section 2(d) protection of freedom of association in the *Charter* and to section 1(b) of the *Canadian Bill of Rights*, which recognized the rights of individuals to equality before the law and the protection of the law. The *PSCRA* was the statute enacted on August 4, 1982, to institute the government's "6 and 5" program, whereby the rate of increase of salaries in the public sector was restrained for several years. The statute had as an effect to displace collective agreements. The PSAC argued that interference with collective agreements, with collective bargaining and with the right to strike infringed the rights of those affected.

A majority of the Supreme Court of Canada rejected the union's reasoning and agreed with earlier judgments to that effect, rendered by the Trial and Appeal Divisions of the Federal Court.

The determinative words used by Chief Justice Dixon were as follows:

> I believe that freedom of association in the labour relations context includes the freedom to participate in determining conditions of work through collective bargaining and the right to strike. The *Public Sector Compensation Restraint Act*, by automatically extending the terms and conditions of collective agreements and arbitral awards and by fixing wage increases for a two-year period, infringes the freedom of public sector employees to engage in collective bargaining.[99]

It was in section 1 of the *Charter* analysis, to analyze whether the legislative interference in the subject rights could be justified in a free and democratic society, that the significant part of Chief Justice Dixon's analysis arose. The theme he adopted was that of the symbolic leadership role which the government adopted through use of the legislative system. In response to the union's argument that the "6 and 5" legislation would affect only 5% of the Canadian labour force, he said,

> Due deference must be paid as well to the symbolic leadership role of government. Many government initiatives, especially in the economic sphere, necessarily involve a large inspirational or psychological com-

---

[98] S.C. 1980-81-82-83, c. 122.
[99] (1987), 38 D.L.R. (4th) 249 at 258.

ponent which must not be undervalued. The role of the judiciary in such situations is fairly implemented with as little interference as is reasonably possible with the rights and freedoms guaranteed by the Charter. Thus, in the present case, I am prepared to accept the respondent's submission that compensation controls, even if limited to a select class of employees, could reasonably have been expected to have a positive, albeit partial and indirect, impact on combating inflation in the economy in general. I am also prepared to accept that the temporary suspension of collective bargaining on compensation issues was a justifiable infringement of freedom of association having regard to the third limb of the proportionality test.[100]

Going beyond questions of symbolism, the Chief Justice reinforced his point of view with regard to the genuine leadership exercised by government through legislation.

I cannot accept, however, that Parliament must consider the government to be just another employer. I have referred, above, to the important leadership role of the government, and to the psychological component of that role in relation to economic matters. Rightly or wrongly, the public sector is perceived to occupy a central role in defining the parameters of negotiations between employer and employee. By enacting its "6 and 5" programme, Parliament intended to send a dramatic message conveying its resolve to fight inflation. It wished to demonstrate to the nation in an unequivocal fashion that it was prepared to take tough measures within its own sphere of employer-employee relations. During the House of Commons debate the Deputy Prime Minister and Minister of Finance emphasized the leadership role of government:

The private sector and the provinces could not be expected to accept income restraint *unless the government of Canada showed leadership* in the conduct of its own affairs. The government has therefore *decided to lead the way* by implementing the proposed strategy in the federal public sector for a period of two years... (House of Commons Debates, June 28, 1982, p. 18878.) [Emphasis added.]

The President of the Treasury Board explained that the federal public sector controls programme was designed as a "striking example" for Canadians to follow:

All realized that it was imperative for the federal government to accentuate the anti-inflationary impact of its economic policies *by taking a more determined stand* on wage rates. The federal public sector

---

[100] *Ibid.* at 261.

246 / LAW OF DEMOCRATIC GOVERNING – VOLUME II: JURISPRUDENCE

> compensation restraint program alone cannot resolve all the eco-
> nomic problems Canadians are wrestling with today. *It should be
> seen as a serious and striking example* that all Canadians, employers
> and employees, individually and collectively, must follow if they
> are the least bit concerned with maintaining their competitive po-
> sition abroad and their standard of living at home. (House of Com-
> mons Debates, July 9, 1982, at p. 19182.) [Emphasis added.]

> In my view, the leadership role of government constitutes justification
> for Parliament's legislative focus on the public sector.[101]

The Chief Justice concluded that in legislating as it had done in order
to achieve the specifically desired goals by using the Parliamentary
route rather than other means, the government's leadership was "incremental and unspectacular." This latter expression was used to
mean not out of the ordinary and therefore judicially acceptable. In
further assessing the section 1 issue, the judge referred to the "sincerity of the legislative objective" as a standard against which to
measure the success of the scheme put in place by the legislation; was
the law really designed to achieve the results it obtained? Here, he
was able to respond in the affirmative. In the end, Chief Justice Dixon
held that most of the legislation was justified under section 1.

See also *Canada v. Ahenakew*, 2003 FCT 306 (Fed. T.D.) and *R. v. Lyons;
R. v. Saunders; R. v. Parnes; R. v. Ronson*,[102] [2001] EWCA Crim 2860.

---

[101] *Ibid.* at 262-3.
[102] International comparison.

3.8 ISSUE: JUDICIARY INDEPENDENT OF POLITICAL INFLUENCES[103]

§ 3.8.1[104]

R. c. Atlantic Sugar Refineries Co.

Québec Court of Appeal; October 20, 1976

(1976), 72 D.L.R. (3d) 95

This case provides a fundamental application of that rule of democratic governance in Canada which holds that the Judicial Branch of Government is independent of the Legislative and Executive Branches and that this independence is a requirement for the judiciary to be able to function according to the dictates of constitutionalism and legality, and especially free from political interference. It is also a manifestation of the linkage between the independence of the Judicial Branch and the accountability of members of the executive government and of parliamentarians to the law. These two doctrines of constitutional practice are in fact each other's complementary counterparts.

At material times, Ouellet was Minister of Consumer and Corporate Affairs in the Liberal Government of Prime Minister Trudeau. On December 19, 1975, in reacting to a judgment of the Québec Superior Court in a combines investigation case, Ouellet made comments publicly which amounted to a questioning of the judge's sanity. That aspect of the matter which relates to the Minister's political involvement in litigation is dealt with at § 10.13.1.

As a consequence of Ouellet's unconsidered outburst, he was summoned to appear on January 8, 1976, before the judge who had rendered the decision, to answer a charge of contempt of court. The accused Minister mounted a substantive defence. He was convicted. He then appealed and this is the judgment of that appeal.

It is the actions of other ministers during the progress of Ouellet's case which lead to the importance of this matter in terms of the

---

[103] Cross-reference to § 10.2.

[104] Cross-reference to § 10.13.1.

independence of the judiciary. While the Superior Court was considering Ouellet's actions and his defence, Charles Drury, the Minister of Public Works, a fellow Montréaler and political ally of Ouellet, interceded with the Associate Chief Justice of the Superior Court on Ouellet's behalf. The judges of the Superior Court responded to the attempted interference by addressing a letter of complaint to the Minister of Justice. That letter was rendered public in a national newspaper and the matter became a scandal. Minister Drury offered to resign, but the Prime Minister only required an apology from him. Mr. Trudeau did, however, ask for Ouellet's resignation on the ground that it was he who had asked Drury to speak to the court for him in an *ex parte* manner.

The Ouellet incident was but the latest in a series of ministerial approaches to members of the judiciary. In order to clarify the proper role and behaviour of Ministers vis-à-vis judges, the Minister of Justice of the day, Ron Basford, asked the Chief Justice of the Québec Superior Court to prepare a report. This was tabled in the House of Commons on March 12, 1976. The conclusion of that report was that none of the ministerial actions were illegal and thus were not of a nature leading to prosecution by the law officers of the Crown. They did, however, contribute interference in the judicial process and as such were improper.

The same day on which the report was tabled, at the time set aside for statements by Ministers, Prime Minister Trudeau commented in the following manner on the importance of judicial independence.

> I agree with the Chief Justice that the independence of the judiciary is a cornerstone of our democratic system and must be jealously guarded against all attacks. Indeed, I would go further and say that we must do what we can to avoid affecting the principle of judicial independence with even the appearance of possible compromise.[105]

Turning from the general matter of principle to the action which the government would take to react to the difficulty raised by improper ministerial contact with judges, the Prime Minister continued.

> Indeed, it is clear that the rules on contact with judges vary somewhat not only in what they say, but in how they are customarily applied in

---

[105] Hansard, March 12, 1976, p. 11771.

the various jurisdictions of this country. Some hon. members of this House may even have different views as to what their duties to their constituents require them to do from time to time in getting in touch with judges.

But, in so far as this government is concerned, I believe that it must be clearly established that in future no member of the cabinet may communicate with members of the judiciary concerning any matter which they have before them in their judicial capacities, except through the Minister of Justice, his duly authorized officials or counsel acting for him, nor may any member of the cabinet communicate with members of quasi-judicial bodies which are constituted as courts of record concerning any matter which they have before them in their judicial capacities except through the minister responsible, his duly authorized officials, or counsel acting for him.[106]

Without reference to these parliamentary deliberations or the creation of new rules on the basis of the Prime Minister's statement, on October 20, 1976, the Québec Court of Appeal upheld Ouellet's conviction on the contempt charge.

---

§ 3.8.2
R. v. Valente (No. 2)
Supreme Court of Canada; December 19, 1985
[1985] 2 S.C.R. 673

In most cases where the independence of the judiciary becomes an issue in litigation, the issue arises in an ancillary fashion and is dealt with in that manner by the courts. Here, however, the independence of the judiciary in both senses, namely as an institution that is as the Judicial Branch of Government, and also in the sense of the judges who comprise it, is the pivotal issue of the case. This gave the Supreme Court of Canada the opportunity to address the matter in a comprehensive way and to set out a fundamental ruling.

The way the Supreme Court of Canada framed the question was to see if, pursuant to section 11(d) of the *Canadian Charter of Rights and Freedoms*, the Ontario Provincial Court (Criminal Division) was an independent tribunal. The court also looked separately at whether

---

[106] *Ibid.*

the Provincial Court was impartial. The general approach to the question was in recognition of its fundamental importance to the democratic character of a legal and political regime. The nature of the body making judicial decision as being unfettered by considerations other than legal ones or by pressures based on the interests of the Executive Branch is intrinsic to democracy. The first regard was for the distinction between the two concepts.

> Although there is obviously a close relationship between independence and impartiality, they are nevertheless separate and distinct values or requirements. Impartiality refers to a state of mind or attitude of the tribunal in relation to the issues and the parties in a particular case. The word "impartial" as Howland C.J.O. noted, connotes absence of bias, actual or perceived. The word "independent" in s. 11(d) reflects or embodies the traditional constitutional value of judicial independence. As such, it connotes not merely a state of mind or attitude in the actual exercise of judicial functions, but a status or relationship to others, particularly to the executive branch of government, that rests on objective conditions or guarantees.[107]

The court looked next at the criterion of independence, which it held to be the relationship of the judges and of the Provincial Court (Criminal Division) itself to the executive government of the province, and in particular to the Ministry of the Attorney General. On the basis of a thorough review of scholarly writings and the applicable jurisprudence, the court returned the following essential criteria on which to assess the independence of the judiciary:

a) Security of tenure, meaning that prior to the advent of retirement, judges may be removed from their functions only for cause. The Executive Branch may not interfere in their tenure, or their work in a discretionary or arbitrary manner. Citing from a report of the Canadian Bar Association, the court went on to espouse the view that:

> After referring to s. 99 of the *Constitution Act, 1867* respecting the tenure of superior court judges, the committee said: "Since the independence of the judiciary depends to a significant extent on the judges' security of tenure it is appropriate that their removal be a major undertaking, bring-

---

[107] [1985] 2 S.C.R. 673 at 685 g-j.

ing the politicians who must accomplish it under close scrutiny. The removal of a judge is not to be undertaken lightly."[108]

These words are particularly significant in that they contrast the immovability of judges vis-à-vis legislators and members of the executive, who stand for principles and practices other than law, within government. Both the nature and the duration of judicial positions and functions are more permanent and steady. The court even went on to support its thesis on grounds of governmental practice and experience.

> Tradition, reinforced by public opinion, operating as an effective restraint upon executive or legislative action, is undoubtedly a very important objective condition tending to ensure the independence in fact of a tribunal. That it is not, however, regarded by itself as a sufficient safeguard of judicial independence is indicated by the many calls for specific legislative provisions or constitutional guarantees to ensure that independence in a more ample and secure measure.[109]

b) Financial security, meaning that the right to salary and pension be established by law and not based on arbitrary or interested decision-making by the Executive. The objective of fixing remuneration by law is to render the executive incapable of interfering with judicial decision-making, preventing it from dictating or even influencing decision.

c) Institutional independence with respect to matters of administration which bear directly on the exercise of the judicial function. The internal administration of the courts is, and should be, autonomous.

See also *MacKeigan v. Hickman* (1988), 85 N.S.R. (2d) 126 (N.S. C.A.); *Ruffo c. Québec (Conseil de la magistrature)*, 130 D.L.R. (4th) 1 (S.C.C.); *R. v. Campbell*, [1997] 3 S.C.R. 3 (S.C.C.), additional reasons at 155 D.L.R. (4th) 1 (S.C.C.); *Scierie Amos inc. c. Lord* (1999), [2000] 3 C.N.L.R. 78 (Que. S.C.), leave to appeal allowed (2000), 2000 CarswellQue 38 (Que. C.A.), reversed [2000] 3 C.N.L.R. 107 (Que. C.A.), leave to appeal to the Supreme Court of Canada refused [2001] 2 C.N.L.R. iv (note) (S.C.C.); *Proposal for a Judicial Accountability Act, 2000*, First Reading, Legislative Assembly of Ontario, April 18, 2000; *Newfound-*

[108] *Ibid.* at 697 a-b.
[109] *Ibid.* at 701 f-g.

land (Treasury Board) v. N.A.P.E., 221 D.L.R. (4th) 513 (N.L. C.A.), leave to appeal allowed (2003), 105 C.R.R. (2d) 188 (note) (S.C.C.) and *City of Boerne v. Flores*,[110] 138 L.Ed.2d 624 (1997).

3.9 ISSUE: BALANCE BETWEEN THE LEGISLATIVE AND JUDICIAL BRANCHES

§ 3.9.1
Reform Party Motion to Avoid Judicial Rulings on Legislation
Speaker of the House of Commons
Hansard, June 8, 1998, p. 7677

The notion of democracy implies a sense of balance between the Legislative, Executive and Judicial branches of government. Part of that balance is the appropriate role assigned to the Legislature and to the courts in respect of legislation. Parliaments make laws and the courts interpret them. In constitutional systems with written instruments of rights and the declared supremacy of the constitution over other laws, the pivot which holds the political legal system together is the authority of the courts to review statutes as to their constitutionality. This is the regime that was put in place in Canada by the 1982 *Charter.*

Despite the general popularity of the *Charter* as a symbol, not every segment of political opinion agrees with its natural consequences. In particular, not everyone is at ease with the ability of the courts to review legislation for its adherence to constitutional norms, especially when the substantive result of such review produces political or social results contrary to their points of view.

Thus, on June 8, 1998, in response to a ruling of the Ontario Court of Appeal which involved the definition of "spouse," the Reform Party tabled the following motion in the House of Commons on an Opposition Day:

> That, in the opinion of this House, federal legislation should not be
> altered by judicial rulings, as happened in the redefinition of the term

---

[110] International comparison.

"spouse" in the Rosenberg decision, and that, accordingly, the government should immediately appeal the Rosenberg decision.[111]

The position espoused by the proponents of this motion was that Parliament being the only elective institution, its will should be supreme. The code words in support of this proposition were "representative democracy," "democratic parliamentary process," "judicial activism" and "unaccountable, unelected judges."

The Reform Member of Parliament who presented this motion went directly to the heart of the controversy.

> Am I being too strong or melodramatic when I say that increasingly judicial rulings are undermining democracy in this country? On the contrary, I know there are many who believe I am not stating the situation strongly enough.
>
> . . .
>
> To my knowledge this type of activity by some judges is relatively new but an increasingly prevalent phenomenon in Canada. Prior to 1982 there was an understanding that under the Canadian bill of rights we all had inherent rights unless they were limited by a particular legislation. In addition, certain rights would receive protection from government interference or intervention in the lives of our citizens.
>
> With the constitutionalization of the charter of rights and freedoms in 1982 some judiciary have taken greater power than warranted or authorized.[112]

While the generation which followed the *Charter* of 1982 enthusiastically adopted the supremacy of the Constitution as one form of democracy, the Reform view of this political legal philosophy to this day, albeit under a different party name, favours a return to Parliamentary supremacy, hence a more limited role for law and for judges. Systems of governance based on either variant are practicable and moreover, both are democratic. Ultimately, however, either Parliament or the Constitution must be supreme. The guiding factor in each system is different: Parliament decides on the basis of politics, public

---

[111] Hansard, June 8, 1998, p. 7677.
[112] *Ibid.*

opinion and public consensus. The Supreme Court and other courts let principles rule.

Considering this fundamental divergence of opinions, it is hardly surprising that very shortly after the debate began, its focus shifted to include the method of appointment of judges.

> We have in our party a specific position about the constitution of the Supreme Court and the appointments to the higher courts of the provinces which states:
>
> A. The Reform Party supports more stringent and more public ratification procedures for Supreme Court Justices in light of the powers our legislators are handling the courts. We believe that an elected Senate should ratify all appointments to the Supreme Court of Canada and all Courts where the judges are appointed by the federal government.
>
> B. The Reform Party supports efforts to secure adequate regional representation on the Supreme Court, and that nominations should be made by provincial legislatures, not provincial governments.
>
> C. The Reform Party supports the appointment of judges at the Supreme Court of Canada level for fixed, non-renewable terms of ten years.
>
> It is a concern about the appropriate role of the court that ultimately parliament must be supreme. If we are to get into those kinds of policy debates which the member opposite seemingly wanted to get into today, that is fine and well, but those issues must be decided by parliament and not by the courts.
>
> Now that we have a charter court, we must look very carefully at who is doing the deciding as well as what is being decided. Hopefully the court will stay appropriately within its bounds and allow parliament to do its work.[113]

These views are not those of the majority of Canadians, nor, more importantly, of Canadians with a progressive view of the role of law and of the courts in society. By contrast to them, the most eloquent expression of the forward looking view was expressed by the Justice

---

[113] *Ibid.* p. 7682.

critic of the Progressive Conservative Party, a former Crown counsel, who said:

> It appears we are debating issues that have been with us for time im-memorial. We are talking about basics here, of how the judiciary and the legislative body operate independent of one another.
>
> The hon. member for Calgary Centre in his motion appears to have overlooked some of the very basics that we learned in politics 101. What we are talking about is a demonstration of a profound understanding of the basic principles of democracy. Today we are spending valuable time discussing and perhaps reinforming the Reform Party about the basic principles of democracy. I would have preferred spending precious time in the House debating more constructive issues.
>
> Our democracy, I think we can all agree, is not perfect by any means but is one of the best democracies in the world. One of the reasons why our democracy is so well respected and so envied by the world is that it lays upon some of the very strong rules of law, that the executive, the judi-ciary and the legislative powers are separate and independent of one another.
>
> If politicians were to have significantly more power than the judiciary and be in a position to at their whim and at the drop of a hat reverse legal decisions, we would live in potential chaos. There are checks and balances intrinsic to the system if the system is to work.
>
> . . .
>
> If legislative power is there to legislate, then the judiciary is surely there to make sure the laws are going to be respected. Judges are also there to make sure laws passed by parliamentarians are respected. This is part of the highest court in the land, certainly, but the Constitution and the charter of rights also have to be respected. Sometimes it comes to being, perhaps wittingly, perhaps unwittingly, that these are infringed by leg-islation that has been passed at some time in the past or perhaps some-thing that comes out as recently as today.[114]

The Liberal Government's representative in the debate, the Secretary of State (Multiculturalism) added her agreement to this view.

> I want to speak first to the issue of how it offends the principles of democracy. The balance in a democracy between an elected body like

---

[114] *Ibid.* p. 7686.

the House of Commons and the supreme court of the land or the courts of the land is to find a way in which justice can be served through the law and the interpretation of the law. That is especially true in our country right now.[115]

This societal debate continues.

See also *Doucet-Boudreau v. Nova Scotia (Department of Education)*, 2003 SCC 62 (S.C.C.).

---

§ 3.9.2[116]
Marbury v. Madison
United States Supreme Court; February 24, 1803
5 U.S. 137 (U.S. Dist. Col., 1803)

This case, which is at the origin of the concept of judicial review in the American system of justice, has had great exemplar effect in a number of jurisdictions, including Canada. In March 1801, as one of a number of judicial appointments made on the last day of the presidency of James Adams, Marbury was named a justice of the peace for the District of Columbia, but there was insufficient time for him to receive his commission. Upon assuming office, President Jefferson disregarded the appointment and refused to deliver the commission. Marbury took action in the Supreme Court in December 1801, seeking *mandamus* to force Madison, the incoming Secretary of State, to deliver the commission. The court agreed on the ground that Marbury had a vested right to the commission. Madison ignored the preliminary writ, believing it was judicial interference in executive matters.

In February 1803, Chief Justice Marshall wrote an opinion on Marbury's application. First, he found the matter to be justiciable, on the ground that Marbury had a vested legal right. On that basis, he also found that the law could afford Marbury a remedy. The final step in the analysis was for the court to compare the powers set out for it in the United States Constitution with those contained in the *Judiciary Act* of 1789. The Constitution did not include a power to issue writs of *mandamus* to federal officials. The *Judiciary Act* purported to grant the court that authority.

---

[115] *Ibid.* p. 7693.
[116] International comparison.

The key to this case was that the Supreme Court held that in enacting the *Judiciary Act*, Congress's attempt was to extend the authority established in the Constitution, which it could not do. The relevant provision of the legislation was declared void. Marbury consequently did not obtain his position.

The Supreme Court used the case to examine some of the fundamental principles and relationships at play in the still new American republic.

> Whether or not judicial review was the logical culmination of Anglo-American constitutional development, however, the fact is that it began to emerge in recognizable form in the 1780's as a means of restraining state legislatures. The founding fathers accepted judicial review, and in the first decade after ratification the federal judiciary acted on the assumption that it could declare acts of Congress unconstitutional. Path-breaking as it was in the development of modern judicial power, therefore, John Marshall's assertion of judicial review in Marbury v. Madison rested on intellectual tendencies that began at least during the Revolution.[117]

The ruling distinguished, first, between the political and legal responsibilities of government officials. It said that when they act as agents of the executive with a constitutional or legal discretion, their acts are only politically examinable. On the other hand, when they perform a duty imposed by law and which can affect rights of individuals, they are subject to judicial scrutiny. Even more importantly, the court set out the principles that the constitution is the supreme law of the land, that any legal test or act of government that is contrary to the constitution is void to the extent of the repugnancy and finally, most importantly, that it is the courts which are the arbiters of the constitution and the law.

The idea that courts could review the validity of legislation was not of American, but rather of English origin. However, the form of government adopted by the United States, being based on a much sharper division among the legislative, executive and judicial functions, could not but lead to the development and increasing importance of judicial review. This concept has become so significant in the modern forms

---

[117] Kelly, Alfred H., Winfred A. Harbison and Herman Belz, *The American Constitution, Its Origins and Development*, 7th ed., Vol.1, Norton & Company, New York, 1991, p. 170.

of democracy that it is one of the cornerstones of the influence of the judiciary in governance and one of the pillars on which the singular importance of the role of law in governance is based. Political legal analysts have, in a number of countries, adopted various versions of constitutional/judicial review to such an extent that it is now difficult to conceive of a political regime as being democratic in nature unless it incorporates this legal element.

What interests us here in particular is the effect of judicial review on the balance of powers first between the legislative and executive branches of government on one hand and the judicial branch on the other, and secondly between the political and legal considerations in governmental decision-making.

> In the twentieth century the judiciary has monopolized constitutional interpretation, and judicial review has become a powerful instrument of policy-making. By contrast, in the early years of the republic, it was principally a means of holding the legislature in check and protecting courts against legislative encroachment. Similarly, where we now take it for granted that Supreme Court decision-making is political, in the early nineteenth century defenders of judicial review drew a distinction between law and politics, reserving the former sphere to the judiciary and the latter to the political branches. However political early instances may appear in retrospect, jurists in Marshall's era *thought* that their office obligated them to eschew politics and to confine themselves to legal considerations. It was in this intellectual context, and in the hostile climate produced by Republican efforts to make the judiciary more politically accountable, that judicial review emerged.[118]

As Chief Justice Marshall indicated, emphatically, the province and duty of the judicial department is to say what the law is. In direct succession to that concept, this case has significance in the modern world as well.

> Taken out of context, Marshall's syllogism – the courts declare the law, the Constitution is law, therefore the courts declare the meaning of the Constitution – can be read as an assertion of the modern judicial monopoly theory of judicial review, which holds that the Supreme Court can apply and interpret the Constitution as though it were ordinary law. In fact it was not what Marshall meant. Early in the opinion Marshall acknowledged a sphere of political questions arising under the Constitution exclusively reserved for executive determination. "By the consti-

---

[118] Op. Cit., p. 17.

tution," Marshall observed, "the President is vested with certain important political powers, in the exercise of which he is to use his own discretion, and is accountable only to his own country in his political character and to his own conscience." Matters entrusted to the President under his constitutional powers were political because they concerned "the nation, not individual rights," Marshall said. The decision of the executive was conclusive concerning the propriety of actions taken in this sphere.[119]

See also *R. v. Parliamentary Commissioner for Standards, ex parte Al-Fayed*, [1998] 1 All E.R. 93.

3.10 ISSUE: PARTICULAR ROLE OF THE MINISTER OF JUSTICE/ATTORNEY GENERAL WITHIN CABINET[120]

§ 3.10.1
Barreau de Montréal c. Wagner
Québec Queens Bench; June 14, 1967
(1967), [1968] B.R. 235

On October 10, 1965, Wagner, then a member of the Montréal Bar, a member of the Québec Legislative Assembly and the Province's Minister of Justice, delivered a speech in which he made remarks attacking the professional conduct of Bérubé, a judge. Bérubé lodged a complaint with the Bar, which agreed with the allegations against Wagner and imposed a sanction on him. Wagner applied to the Superior Court to have the Bar's decision quashed. That court issued a writ of summons and the present case came about as an appeal of the issuance of the writ. Wagner argued that he had been invited to speak as Minister of Justice and that in that capacity he was immune from being summoned to testify.

The Québec Court of Appeal rejected Wagner's case. It interpreted the *Bar Act*[121] as meaning that the summons issued pursuant to it

---

[119] *Ibid.*, p. 174.
[120] Cross-reference to § 1.4, 3.11, 11.12 and 11.14.
[121] Now L.R.Q. 1977, c. B-1; then S.R.Q. 1964, c. 247 and S.Q. 1966-67, c. 77.

would not affect the rights and prerogatives of the Crown even if Wagner made his remarks in his capacity as Minister. The significance of the holding in the case was not only its characterization of the work of the Minister of Justice, but also the fact that even the highest law officer of the State, the Minister of Justice, received direction from the law as to how to fulfil his functions.

> Quand le ministre de la Justice exerce les pouvoirs qui lui sont conférés par la loi, il exerce le pouvoir exécutif de la Couronne et il agit pour la Couronne.[122]

---

§ 3.10.2
Bisaillon c. Keable
Québec Court of Appeal; October 21, 1980
[1980] C.A. 316[123]

This case examines that part of the responsibilities of the chief law officer of the Crown which concerns criminal law, prosecutions and the supervision of police forces. In Québec, at the material time, these functions were carried out by the Minister of Justice. In some other Canadian jurisdictions, they were, or are, executed by a separate official called the Solicitor General, to whom the same principles apply as to the minister titled the "Minister of Justice."

On June 15, 1977, the Government of Québec established a commission of inquiry headed by Keable, charged with investigating the activities of various police bodies in relation to their handling of a number of related files in which they appeared to be suppressing Québec separatists. As part of its investigation, the Keable Commission heard testimony from Bisaillon, a police officer of the Montréal Urban Community (MUC) Police. Keable wanted Bisaillon to divulge certain sources of police information and to explain the police's confidential methods of operation. Bisaillon attempted to avoid responding by applying for a writ of evocation on November 27, 1979. The Superior Court rejected the application and the Court of Appeal upheld that refusal.

---

[122] (1967), [1968] B.R. 235 at 237.
[123] Reversed [1983] 2 S.C.R. 60 (S.C.C.).

Bisaillon's case was that as a police officer, he was not subject to political authorities but only to the supervision of the courts, according to the system of governance established in England.

> Ce qui est en cause, c'est le rôle respectif dans notre droit public du Procureur général et de l'agent de la paix ou, plus précisément, selon l'appelant, de l'agent de la paix en chef sur un territoire, de même que la nature et l'étendue du principe de la confidentialité des sources d'informations de la police et la question de savoir qui peut le soulever.

> L'appelant soumet que l'agent de la paix, dont le chef ou directeur sur un territoire est indépendant du pouvoir politque, doit fáire son devoir selon la loi et sa conscience de l'intérêt public tel qu'il le voit, sujet au seul pouvoir de contrôle et de surveillance des Tribunaux supérieurs.

> . . .

> Il prétend que ce principe tient du privilège de la Couronne, du moins est un principe de droit public que toute personne, à plus forte raison le «*chief constable*» d'un territoire, peut soulever devant un tribunal et qu'il appartient aux tribunaux et non au pouvoir exécutif de déterminer s'il s'applique dans le cas soulevé: que, de plus, seule une Cour supérieure est un tribunal compétent pour décider d'écarter le principe ainsi invoqué.[124]

The court agreed that Bisaillon correctly stated the principle as it existed in England but distinguished the matter on the ground that the circumstances in which the police functioned in England had evolved differently in Canada and particularly in Québec. It recalled that there is no Ministry of Justice in England and that in consequence, executive responsibilities relating to the administration of justice are distributed, principally between the Home Secretary, the Attorney General and the Director of Public Prosecutions. With respect to the administration of justice in particular, the Attorney General did assume certain political and quasi-judicial functions. The court went on to clarify that in light of the particular evolution of the legal system in this country, the roles and responsibilities of the Attorney General in respect of the administration of criminal law were different and more precisely defined by statute.

---

[124] [1980] C.A. 316 at 318, reversed [1983] 2 S.C.R. 60 (S.C.C.).

> Chez nous, le Procureur général exerce les fonctions de chef du ministère public (*Chief Law Enforcement Officer of the Crown*) et assume des responsabilités a l'égard des policiers que ne permettent pas de comparer l'autonomie du directeur du Service de police de la C.U.M. à celle d'un «*chief constable*» anglais.

> La *Loi sur le ministère de la justice (10)* détermine les pouvoirs et les responsabilités du ministre de la Justice qui est d'office Procureur général.

> En vertu de l'article 3 de cetter Loi, le ministre de la Justice veille à ce que les affaires publiques solent administrées conformément á la Loi et il a la surveillance de toutes les matières que concernent l'administration de la justice au Québec. En vertu de l'article 4, le Procureur général est chargé de la surveillance, de l'administration ou de l'exécution, suivant le cas, des lois relatives à la police.[125]

The court's conclusion, based on this differentiation, was that the Attorney General is the guardian of public order and the head of the prosecution service.

The immediate meaning of this holding was that in the Québec legal system, the police are subject to the Attorney General and that a police officer could not refuse to reply to the questioning of a validly constituted commission of inquiry if the Attorney General did not raise an objection of privilege to the question. There is, however, a broader and far more significant implication arising out of the case. The Court of Appeal weighed the policeman's notion of public interest against that of the Attorney General and sided with that of the latter.

> De plus, comme l'explique le premier juge, c'est le Procureur général qui, de concert avec les Tribunaux, est le gardien de l'ordre public. Je suie d'opinion que l'intérêt public invoqué par l'appelant et par son directeur de police ne peut prévaloir sur l'intérêt public que a présidé à la décision du Lieutenant-Gouverneur en Conseil d'ordonner la tenue d'une telle commission d'enquête.[126]

The aspect of this decision is of importance for political law is that in the Attorney General's capacity as the law officer responsible for criminal matters, his first allegiance is to the law and to the public

---

[125] [1980] C.A. 316 at 320, reversed [1983] 2 S.C.R. 60 (S.C.C.).
[126] *Ibid.* at 323.

interest, rather than to political power and authority. Thus, while Bisaillon did not succeed in his argument on the specific point he invoked about the police, his wider view of the function of the Attorney General as owing a primary duty to the law was not contradicted.

The primary loyalty of the Minister of Justice is to the proper administration of justice, even more than to the government or to the cabinet of which he is a member. While this may on occasion create a conflict of attitudes or even of interests which the Minister of Justice must resolve to the best of his professional conscience, the view of the legal tradition is that the Minister must resolve any such conflict in favour of his duty as chief law officer of the State and legal advisor to the Crown. This is a key aspect of the concept of the rule and primacy of law, in particular where that primacy is contrasted to politics.

See also *Air Canada v. British Columbia (Attorney General)* (1986), [1986] 2 S.C.R. 539 (S.C.C.); *Kindler v. Canada (Minister of Justice)*, [1991] 2 S.C.R. 779 (S.C.C.) and *Ng, Re*, [1991] 2 S.C.R. 858 (S.C.C.).

---

§ 3.10.3
Idziak v. Canada (Minister of Justice)
Supreme Court of Canada; November 19, 1992
[1992] 3 S.C.R. 631[127]

Idziak was an American citizen living in Canada since 1956 and a landed immigrant. In 1983, he was charged in Michigan with conspiracy to obtain funds through fraudulent representations. In 1987, he was arrested and proceedings were begun for his extradition. As part of that process, Idziak applied to the Minister of Justice to have the Minister refuse to exercise his discretionary power to surrender Idziak to the U.S. authorities. The Minister nevertheless did sign the warrant of surrender. Idziak applied to the Supreme Court of Ontario on July 5, 1989, for a writ of *habeas corpus* with *certiorari*, to set aside the warrant of surrender. The application was dismissed by that court, the Ontario Court of Appeal as well as here, by the Supreme Court of Canada.

---

[127] Reconsideration refused (1992), 9 Admin. L.R. (2d) 1n (S.C.C.).

The application of Idziak was based on an allegation of breach of his right to liberty, as guaranteed by section 7 of the *Charter*. This claim was based primarily on an allegation that the extradition process showed an institutional bias against the extraditable person. Within the framework of a judicial examination of the legality of the Minister's decision to complete the extradition of Idziak, this case amounted to a review of the role of the Minister of Justice in the extradition process, in which legal and political considerations are significantly blended. From the specific part of the judgment in which this review is conducted, we can draw conclusions about the particular nature of the Justice portfolio within Cabinet.

The Supreme Court began its analysis of the functions of the Minister of Justice by reference to the manner in which his tasks are set out in the statute creating the department and his ministerial portfolio, the *Department of Justice Act*. The most pertinent of these provisions for the purposes of this case is section 4 of the *Act*, which lists the powers, duties and functions of the Minister in his capacity as Minister (rather than as Attorney General):

> 4. The Minister is the official legal adviser of the Governor General and the legal member of the Queen's Privy Council for Canada and shall
>
> (*a*) see that the administration of public affairs is in accordance with law;
>
> (*b*) have the superintendence of all matters connected with the administration of justice in Canada, not within the jurisdiction of the governments of the provinces;
>
> (*c*) advise upon the legislative Acts and proceedings of each of the legislatures of the provinces of Canada, and generally advise the Crown on all matters of law referred to the Minister by the Crown; and
>
> (*d*) carry out such other duties as are assigned by the Governor in Council to the Minister.[128]

The court then detailed its view of the extradition process and outlined the role of the Minister of Justice in its various phases. It said

---

[128] *Department of Justice Act*, R.S.C. 1985, c. J-2, s. 4, cited in [1992] 3 S.C.R. 631 at 639-640, reconsideration refused (1992), 9 Admin. L.R. (2d) 1n (S.C.C.).

that extradition encompasses two distinct phases, the first of which is a court proceeding to determine whether the factual and legal basis exists for extraditing a person sought by a foreign government. At this stage, the Minister acts as prosecutor, seeking to have a warrant of committal issued by the court against the accused.

If the first phase is successful, a second phase, this one being characterized as ministerial, occurs. Here, the decision-making process undertaken by the Minister is policy-oriented and political in nature. "The Minister must weigh the representations of the fugitive against Canada's international treaty obligations"[129] in determining whether to issue the warrant of surrender and actually hand the person over to the authorities of the requesting State.

The first way in which the court had to look at the matter of the possibility of institutional bias was to see if this dual role of the Minister could constitute such bias. The court held that it did not, because of a clear division between the Minister's two roles in the two phases of the extradition process and also because of the separation of the Minister's personnel involved in the two phases.

The court then looked at the nature of the Minister's decision-making process in the second, the ministerial phase. It reiterated the distinctions created in administrative law between adjudicative decisions, where the important factor is the decision-maker's adherence to a standard of judicial impartiality, and legislative decisions, for which administrative bodies determine policy issues on the basis of expert knowledge presented by representatives of interested parties. Expressed in terms of these broad categories of administrative law, "the exercise by the Minister of Justice of the authority to surrender an individual committed for extradition clearly falls in the legislative end of the continuum"[130] of the decision-making spectrum.

The court felt, however, that these generalizations needed to be complemented by information of a more explicit nature on the Minister's decision-making at the second phase of the extradition process, which is essentially political in the context of this study on political law.

---

[129] [1992] 3 S.C.R. 631 at 658, reconsideration refused (1992), 9 Admin. L.R. (2d) 1n (S.C.C.).
[130] *Ibid.* at 661.

Parliament chose to give discretionary authority to the Minister of Justice. It is the Minister who must consider the good faith and honour of this country in its relations with other states. It is the Minister who has the expert knowledge of the political ramifications of an extradition decision.[131]

The court continued its analysis.

It is correct that the Minister of Justice has the responsibility to ensure the prosecution of the extradition proceedings and that to do so the Minister must appoint agents to act in the interest of the requesting state. However the decision to issue a warrant of surrender involves completely different considerations from those reached by a court in an extradition hearing. The extradition hearing is clearly judicial in its nature while the actions of the Minister of Justice in considering whether to issue a warrant of surrender are primarily political in nature. This is certainly not a case of a single official's acting as both judge and prosecutor in the same case. At the judicial phase the fugitive possesses the full panoply of procedural protection available in a court of law. At the ministerial phase, there is no longer a *lis* in existence. The fugitive has by then been judicially committed for extradition. The Act simply grants to the Minister discretion as to whether to execute the judicially approved extradition by issuing a warrant of surrender.[132]

The most important lesson to be derived from this case in relation to the *modus operandi* required of the Minister of Justice, is that even in the second phase of the extradition proceedings, which the court entitles "political" and in which the technical expertise of the Minister, and by extension of his Department of Justice lawyers, is called upon, the Minister is bound to act in a fair manner. The court did not hesitate to declare that the standards of the *Charter* apply to the extradition procedure and therefore empower it to analyze the fairness of extradition decisions. In order to evaluate whether the Minister's decisions in this regard are fair, the court will look to see if the Minister achieved a reasonable balance between the interests of the State and those of the individual.

While the *Idziak* decision deals only with the subject-matter of extradition, it enables the observer to extrapolate general rules of conduct applicable to the Minister of Justice. If the Minister of Justice is bound, even in his political decision-making, by constitutional standards of

---

[131] *Ibid.* at 659.
[132] *Ibid.* at 659-660.

fairness, then he, most stringently among his cabinet colleagues, is required to include legal criteria and to adhere to legal norms in making political decisions. The law is ever present in this Minister's work.

See also *United States v. Monsalve* (1993), [1993] O.J. No. 1180 (Ont. Gen. Div.), affirmed (May 9, 1994), Doc. CA C16354, [1994] O.J. No. 1099 (Ont. C.A.).

---

§ 3.10.4
Thatcher v. Canada (Attorney General)
Federal Court of Canada – Trial Division; October 3, 1996
(1996), 120 F.T.R. 116

This case illustrates a particular aspect of the special position of the Minister of Justice and Attorney General within Cabinet, in that he alone is responsible for the administration of the power of mercy which is related to the legal system. It also exemplifies that in particular procedures such as these, the guiding criterion on the Minister is fairness, an aspect of legality. Political considerations and partisan sentiment can play no role in decision-making even when the individual seeking mercy is a prominent member of an opposing political formation. This case thus reinforces the principle that the highest duty of the Minister of Justice is to the law and the legal system, rather than to any form of action motivated by political persuasion.

Colin Thatcher, the applicant, was the son of Ross Thatcher, who was Premier of Saskatchewan from 1964 to 1971, and a successful parliamentarian in his own right. He was first elected in 1975 as a Liberal Member of the Legislative Assembly for the electoral district of Thunder Creek, but in 1977, he switched allegiances to the provincial Progressive Conservative Party. He was re-elected in 1978 and 1982 and in that year, he became Minister of Energy and Mines in the incoming government of Premier Grant Devine. He was relieved of his portfolio in 1983.

His arrest and conviction in 1984 for the brutal murder of his ex-wife, with whom he had for several years been locked in bitter dispute, marked the first time in Canadian history that a former government minister had been convicted of such a crime.[133]

Thatcher's conviction for murder by the Saskatchewan Queen's Bench in November 5, 1984, was upheld by the province's Court of Appeal and by the Supreme Court of Canada on May 14, 1987. He started serving his term in prison but on October 11, 1989, he applied to the Minister of Justice for the "mercy of the Crown," pursuant to section 690 of the *Criminal Code*. At the time of the application, the Minister of Justice was Doug Lewis, a member of Prime Minister Mulroney's federal Progressive Conservative government. The Minister and the Department of Justice followed all the procedures required in order to apply section 690. The decision dismissing Thatcher's application was rendered on April 14, 1994. By that time, a federal general election had intervened and Prime Minister Chrétien and the Liberal Party of Canada had come to government; the Minister of Justice who rendered the decision was Allan Rock. It is from that decision, denying mercy, that Thatcher sought judicial review by the Federal Court.

The ruling dealt first with the court's jurisdiction to review mercy decisions made by a Minister of Justice. It set the stage for the primacy of law in this sphere by relying on the *Operation Dismantle* case[134] which stated that:

> I have no doubt that the executive branch of the Canadian government is duty bound to act in accordance with the dictates of the Charter.[135]

It confirmed that decisions of this nature, made under authority of the royal prerogative, are reviewable by the courts and subject to judicial scrutiny for compatibility with those provisions of the *Charter* which protect the right to life, liberty and security of the person and the right not to be deprived thereof except in accordance with the principle of fundamental justice.

The heart of the judgment was the court's ratio regarding the nature of the duty of the Minister of Justice under section 690 of the *Criminal Code*. This provision was said to be a delegation to the Minister of an

---

[133] *The Canadian Encyclopedia*, 2nd ed., 1988, Hurtig Publishers, Edmonton, Vol. IV, p. 2136.

[134] [1985] 1 S.C.R. 441 (S.C.C.).

[135] (1996), 120 F.T.R. 116 at 119.

aspect of the sovereign's discretion. In the English system, from whence the notion of mercy originated for Canada, it was said that,

> Mercy is not the subject of legal rights. It begins where legal rights end. A convicted person has no legal right even to have his case considered by the Home Secretary in connection with the exercise of the prerogative of mercy. In tendering his advice to the sovereign the Home Secretary is doing something that is often cited as the exemplar of a purely discretionary act as contrasted with the exercise of a quasi judicial function.[136]

In the Canadian adaptation of this power, the discretion must be exercised in light of the *Charter*. Therefore, the Minister's principal duty is one of fairness under the *Charter*, having regard to the fact that at the point in time at which a mercy application is presented, there is no longer a legal contention or a court proceeding between the applicant and the Crown.

The court explained the mechanics of the decision-making standard the Minister of Justice must apply in such cases. No legislative framework exists. No rules of procedure are laid down. The Minister therefore is given wide allowance to exercise his discretion. The core of the Minister's obligation is his duty to act fairly, which the court defined as follows:

> Content of the Minister's Duty
>
> [13] Having regard to the nature of proceedings under s. 690 and the consequences to the individual, I am of the view that the content of the Minister's duty of fairness under s. 690 is less than that applicable to judicial proceedings. In exercising his discretion under s. 690, the Minister must act in good faith and conduct a meaningful review, provided that the application is not frivolous or vexatious. The convicted person should have a reasonable opportunity to state his case. However, proceedings under s. 690 do not constitute an appeal on the merits.[137]

Finally, there is no limitation on the number of applications a person can present, but the Minister's decision is final and without appeal.

An implicit component of fairness in this context is that no Cabinet consideration, issue of government solidarity, or partisan thinking

---

[136] *Ibid.*
[137] *Ibid.* at 120.

can bear on the Minister's decision. Moreover, the decision is the Minister's alone and the Cabinet seems bound to accept his judgment and consent to it.

Considering that in this instance, Thatcher's application was based in large part on the allegation that the Minister did not disclose some advice and opinions, the court added that,

> There is no general right of disclosure to everything considered by the Minister or his officials...

> To the extent that the Minister's investigation discovers new relevant information, the convicted person should have adequate disclosure of that new information.[138]

Thatcher has made several further attempts to be released but remains incarcerated today.

---

§ 3.10.5
Ontario (Attorney General) v. O.T.F.
Ontario Court (General Division); November 3, 1997
(1997), 36 O.R. (3d) 367

This case is significantly instructive in respect of the professional dilemma which the Attorney General must face in his work within Cabinet. In highly contentious circumstances, where there is apparent social conflict, does his loyalty lie with the political stance of his First Minister and his Cabinet colleagues, or is his genuine master the law and the legal system, as he is the Chief Law Officer of the Crown? In addition, this case demonstrates that reference to the judgment in a court case may sometimes not be sufficient, because a judge gives greater weight to some arguments and pleadings than to others; here, for example, thorough understanding of the real issue at stake neces- sitates perusal of the parties' pleadings as well as the judgment.

As part of the Common Sense Revolution promised by the Progres- sive Conservative government of Premier Harris in the 1995 general election in Ontario, the Legislature enacted Bill 160, the *Education*

---

[138] *Ibid.*

Quality Improvement Act[139] in October 1997. This was an extensive law reform effort: it brought about changes in school governance, in the financing of elementary and secondary education, as well as in the collective bargaining regime applicable to teachers. On October 27, 1997, in response to the enactment of this new law, 126,000 teachers went out on strike. As soon as October 31, the Attorney General applied to the General Division for an interlocutory injunction to restrain the defendants, the teachers' unions and their individual leaders, from unlawfully striking, contrary to the *School Boards and Teachers Collective Negotiations Act*.[140]

The court rendered its decision rapidly by November 3. The first issue it considered was whether the application should be heard. The teachers contended that in the circumstances of the dispute, the Attorney General ought to have proceeded under a provision of the *Courts of Justice Act*[141] which dealt with labour disputes. Outside the court however, the teachers had characterized their struggle differently. They had indicated that their protest was not a labour matter but a political dispute with the government. They argued this point in some of their factums as well. In particular, the Ontario Secondary School Teachers' Federation and the Ontario English Catholic Teachers Association made the point that their protest was political in nature.

> It is submitted that this characterization applies with equal force to the teachers' political protest at issue in this case. The protest relates to significant policy issues which are attracting a high degree of public debate, namely, the system of public education program delivery, and the funding and governance of this system. The teachers are engaging in this protest in order to communicate their deep concern that the government's proposed legislation will have a harmful impact on the quality of education in Ontario.[142]

The court reacted by judging that the teachers could not have it both ways.

> The teachers' position on this issue is seriously undercut by the way they have chosen to describe their conduct. In both the public arena and in

---

[139] S.O. 1997, c. 31.
[140] R.S.O. 1990, c. S.2.
[141] R.S.O. 1990, c. C.43.
[142] Factum of the Ontario English Catholic Teachers Association, filed October 30, 1997, paragraph 63.

these court proceedings, they have termed their conduct a political protest, not a labour dispute. It is true that they acknowledge that their conduct is a strike which is, of course, a well-known component of many labour disputes. However, the teachers assert that their conduct is much more than a strike, it is also a political protest directed not against their employers, the school boards, but against the Government of Ontario with respect to the Government's policies and proposed law on various education matters.

In short, the teachers cannot have it both ways. If they want to label their conduct "political protest" and make submissions in court based on that label, they cannot limit the Attorney General's motion to the procedure which governs a labour dispute.[143]

The court therefore rejected this line of argumentation. For our purposes of analysis, however, it is interesting that this case was so close to the line of demarcation between law and politics as to enable the judge to address the issue of the category into which it belonged. One cannot resist the conclusion that it was both.

The court then applied the classic tests in adjudicating applications for injunction. It found that there was a serious matter to be resolved. However, it determined that the Attorney General had not been able to show that irreparable harm would result if the injunction were not granted, or that the balance of convenience favoured him. The deciding factor in the court's disposition of this case was that it held the application to be premature. It felt the parties should have gone to the Ontario Labour Relations Board first.

In its consideration of the principal substantive issue, namely whether to grant the interlocutory injunction, the judgment dealt in a single paragraph with the role of the Attorney General. Within that paragraph, the judge pronounced a single, rather laconic, dispositive sentence on this fundamentally important matter:

> There is no question the Attorney General has an important role to play in securing compliance with the laws of the land.[144]

He also quoted from the *Dieleman* case which dealt with the use of litigation for political purposes. No matter how circumspect the

---

[143] (1997), 36 O.R. (3d) 367 at 371 c-f.
[144] *Ibid.* at 371 h-372 a.

LEGAL ELEMENTS OF DEMOCRACY / 273

wording through which the court expressed its idea, the reader of the judgment must ask whether in the circumstances of this case, there may be a conflict that should prevent the Attorney General from taking steps to uphold the law.

What led to this one sentence in the judgment? In the motions brought by several of the defendant unions to quash the Attorney General's application for injunction, they raised the matter of the dual nature of the role of the Attorney General within Cabinet. In one sense, the function of this minister is to exercise solidarity with his fellow ministers, to work together with them to realize their common political goals and, given his domain of specialization, to represent and defend them in court proceedings. That is his political task. In his other capacity, the legal one, the Attorney General, as chief law officer of the Crown, has the duty of upholding and defending the legal system itself. This defence must include its protection from politically motivated encroachments, such as its unwarranted or unjustified use of the law to achieve the ideological or partisan goals, even by the government of which the Attorney General is a member. The issue for consideration is which consideration takes precedence in the Attorney General's actions. This is the dilemma of the Attorney General's interpretation of the public interest.

The factums submitted by the Ontario Teachers' Federation and by the Federation of Women Teachers' Associations of Ontario expressed this dilemma in a rather coy fashion, by claiming no more than that the Attorney General was not entitled to seek the orders he had requested because the Government had not satisfied the principle of equity that using the well-known phrase "those who come into equity must come with clean hands."

The Ontario Secondary School Teachers' Federation also referred to clean hands. It went further, however, in dealing with the Attorney General's dilemma as one tied to the administration of law; this was likely the formulation of the issue which led to the judge's expression of the principle.

> Where the party seeking an injunction is a public authority the court retains its discretion to refuse an equitable remedy where the public authority has acted contrary to the public interest. For instance, the court will not act to assist a public authority whose actions are tainted by corruption, where the authority has acted in a discriminatory manner,

or where to do so would constitute a veritable travesty to the administration of the law.[145]

This factum then applied the notion of "clean hands" to the specifics
of the case and bluntly stated what it perceived to be the fault in the
submission of the matter to the court by the Attorney General.

> The government, and therefore the Attorney General, is a partisan in a
> dispute with the defendants. The Attorney General's position is akin to
> that of a private litigant. That is, the Attorney General is primarily acting
> in the furtherance of the goals of one of the disputants, namely the
> government.

> In the circumstances of this case the disputant is the government of
> Ontario and its interest is the political expedience of eliminating effective
> political protest against its arbitrary actions relating to education. An
> interim injunction would simply be part of the government's larger
> arsenal which to date has included inventing a crisis, the curtailing of
> democratic debate, the enactment of arbitrary and constitutionally sus-
> picious legislation, and attempting to camouflage the removal of ap-
> proximately $667 million from the provincial education budget.

> In the present case the government of Ontario does not come before this
> Honourable Court with clean hands. Rather the government comes as
> the instigator of a scheme to create a crisis, or at least to create the
> perception of a crisis, respecting public education.

> Apart from the government engaging in wrongful and misleading con-
> duct, it attempts to flout our constitutional tradition in proposing to
> enact a statutory provision which places itself above the law and legis-
> lature.[146]

The most elaborate, explicit and legally well grounded pleadings
were submitted by the Ontario Public School Teachers' Federation
(OPSTF). While their factum also started by referring to the doctrine
of "clean hands," it spelled out in detail the argument that in its view,
the Attorney General had allowed himself to follow the political
aspect of his role, rather than the legal, and that he had unjustifiably
taken political direction from his Cabinet colleagues.

---

[145] Factum of the Defendant Ontario Secondary School Teachers' Federation (OSSTF),
filed October 30, 1997, para. 55.
[146] Ibid., paras. 56-59.

In addition, it is respectfully submitted that this Court should dismiss, stay or quash the Attorney General's motion for injunctive relief on the basis that:

the Attorney General has acted improperly and in derogation of his responsibilities by bringing the instant motion at the behest and direction of, or under improper pressure from, the Premier of Ontario, Michael Harris, and the Minister of Education and Training, David Johnson, instead of exercising his discretion independently, in accordance with established principles and criteria required by law, as codified in section 5 of the *Ministry of the Attorney General Act*, R.S.O. 1990, c. M.17, and required by the *Constitution Act, 1982*;[147]

The OPSTF went on to give explicit reasons which, it alleged, amounted to the absence of standing for the Attorney General in seeking the injunction, based on the *Ministry of the Attorney General Act*,[148] as well as on scholarly writings.

The Attorney General is the Chief Law Officer of the Crown. Historically, by constitutional convention (and now reflected in the specific terms of section 5(d) of the *Ministry of the Attorney General Act* and forming part of the rule of law recognized in the *Constitution Act, 1982*), the Attorney General has unique and special responsibilities in relation to the exercise of certain extraordinary powers. This includes the decision to initiate injunctive relief to restrain alleged wrongdoing in the public interest.

However, in recognition of these unique powers and responsibilities, the responsibility for exercising decisions in the public interest must be the Attorney General's alone. This is to ensure that, in exercising his prerogative and statutory powers, the Attorney General takes into account only the public interest, and not partisan or politically-motivated considerations. For these reasons, the Attorney General cannot be put under any pressure by his Cabinet colleagues in determining whether to exercise his unique powers and responsibilities, but must act independently and be seen to be acting independently. Thus, it is contrary to established principles and conventions for the Premier, the Minister of Education or any other minister of the government to direct or to bring political pressure to bear on the Attorney General in the exercise of the Attorney General's quasi-judicial powers. In the case at bar, the record indicates not only that the Premier and Minister of Education have di-

---

[147] *Ibid.*, para. 9 a).
[148] R.S.O. 1990, c. M.17.

rectly brought pressure to bear on the decision, but that, indeed, their decision led to the bringing of this motion by the Attorney General.

. . .

> In the instant case, it is respectfully submitted that the Attorney General has failed to comply with the fundamental constitutional and legal principles and requirements set out above. As the record demonstrates, the proceedings were brought at the direction of, or at the very least influenced by pressure from, the Premier and/or the Minister of Education. In this regard, it was the Premier and Minister of Education who publicly announced on Monday of this week that injunctive proceedings would be initiated at their direction or by them, and made repeated public statements characterizing the conduct of the Defendants as "illegal." With the Premier and the Minister of Education having publicly committed themselves to the view that the strike was "illegal," it is submitted that the Attorney General had no alternative but to proceed with this motion.[149]

In support of this view of what the proper stance the Attorney General ought to have adopted, the OPSTF cited as precedent Sir Hartley Shawcross' speech to the British House of Commons in 1951, made in relation to the Gas Strikers case, and reproduced from J.Ll.J. Edwards' study entitled "The Attorney General, Politics and the Public Interest."[150]

> "The true doctrine," said Shawcross, "is that it is the duty of the Attorney General, in deciding whether or not to authorise the prosecution, to acquaint himself with all the relevant facts, including, for instance, the effect which the prosecution, successful or unsuccessful as the case may be, would have upon public morale and order, and with any other consideration affecting public policy. In order so to inform himself, he may, although I do not think he is obliged to, consult with any of his colleagues in the government, and indeed, as Lord Simon once said, he would in some cases be a fool if he did not. On the other hand, the assistance of his colleagues is confined to inform him of particular considerations which might affect his own decision, and does not consist, and must not consist, in telling him what that decision out (sic) to be. The responsibility for the eventual decision rests with the Attorney General, and he is not to be put, and is not put, under pressure by his colleagues in the matter. Nor, or (sic) course, can the Attorney General shift his responsibility for making the decision on to the shoulders of his

---

[149] *Supra* note 145, paras. 10, 11 and 16.
[150] London, Sweet & Maxwell, 1984.

colleagues. If political considerations which in the broad sense that I have indicated affect government in the abstract arise it is the Attorney General, applying his judicial mind, who has to be the sole judge of those considerations."[151]

It is a pity for the development of political law that the court did not retain more of that line of argumentation, reproduce it as part of the argumentation, or analyze it in greater depth. Even without it, the court subtly and effectively got its point across.

See also *O.T.F. v. Ontario (Attorney General)* (1998), 39 O.R. (3d) 140 (Ont. Gen. Div.); *Alberta Teachers' Assn. v. Alberta*, 2002 ABQB 240 (Alta. Q.B.); *United States v. Burns*, 195 D.L.R. (4th) 1 (S.C.C.); *Speaker's Ruling on the Duty of the Minister of Justice to the House of Commons in respect of the Introduction of Legislation*, Hansard, March 19, 2001, p. 1839; *Fourteenth Report of the Standing Committee on Procedure and House Affairs*, May 9, 2001; *Speaker's Ruling on the Duty of the Minister of Justice to the House of Commons in respect of the Introduction of Legislation*, Hansard, October 15, 2001, pp. 6082-6085; *Proulx c. Québec (Procureur général)*, 206 D.L.R. (4th) 1 (S.C.C.); *Motion of Loss of Confidence in the Attorney General*, Vote by the British Columbia Law Society, May 22, 2002; *C.U.P.E. v. Ontario (Minister of Labour)*, 2003 SCC 29 (S.C.C.) and *Dickerson v. United States*,[152] 166 F.3d 667 (4th Cir., 1999) and 120 S. Ct. 2326 (U.S. Va., 2000).

---

§ 3.10.6[153]
McGonnell v. United Kingdom
European Court of Human Rights; February 8, 2000
(2000), 30 E.H.R.R. 289

This case originated in a situation which evolved on the Channel Island of Guernsey but could have profound effect on the political legal system which has developed in the United Kingdom over several centuries. McGonnell was refused planning permission to build a dwelling house on his own land by the Island Development Committee. His appeal to the Royal Court was presided by the Bailiff of

---

[151] *Supra* note 145, para. 12.
[152] International comparison.
[153] International comparison.

Guernsey; it was rejected. McGonnell attacked that decision before the European Commission on Human Rights, on the ground that there was a breach of Article 6 of the *European Convention on Human Rights*, which guaranteed litigants a fair hearing by an independent and impartial tribunal. In this instance, the judicial function of Bailiff was held by the same individual who was also the President of the States of Deliberation, the Guernsey legislature. The same official was also the head of the administration of the island.

It is possible to perceive this case as dealing with the independence of the judiciary. However, because of the possible effect of the European Court's holding on the United Kingdom, it is much more significant to look at it from the perspective of the role of the minister of justice. In the British system of governance, the Lord Chancellor, in effect the minister of justice, has legislative functions as a member of the House of Lords, executive functions as a member of Cabinet and cumulates these with judicial functions as a member of the Appellate Committee of the House of Lords. Despite the fact that the current incumbent, Lord Irvine of Lairg, has restricted his participation in the hearing of human rights and same other public law cases, the European Commission of Human Rights, the first level of European Union court which heard this case, did not believe that was enough.

> The commission accepted that the bailiff's other functions did not directly affect his judicial duties in Mr. McGonnell's own case, and that most of his working time is devoted to the administration of justice. Nevertheless, the commission concluded that "it is incompatible with the requisite appearances of independence and impartiality for a judge to have legislative and executive functions as substantial as those" carried out by the bailiff. Those other functions meant that "his independence and impartiality are capable of appearing open to doubt." Therefore, there was a breach of Article 6.[154]

This litigation is focused on a modern interpretation of Montesquieu's doctrine of separation of powers, which, ironically, he originally drew from analysis of the British Constitution. On one side of the argument is the notion of impartial and independent tribunals, with the appearance thereof. Facing this, the Lord Chancellor "has vigorously defended his right, and duty, to follow the example of his predeces-

---

[154] "A large shock from a little island for the Lord Chancellor," David Pannick, QC, *The Times*, London, September 21, 1999.

sors and sit in a judicial capacity, so enabling him to keep in touch with legal and judicial practice, and influence the development of the common law."[155]

The court found that Article 6 had been breached; its statement of the principles involved was much more significant. The judgment rested on the ground that the same officer of State could not, properly, hold executive functions relating to the justice portfolio, as well as judicial ones. Interestingly, the court was more inclined to assert the independence of the judicial function than to insist on the fact that the executive direction of the justice system should be held separately.

> ...the Court is faced solely with questions of whether the Bailiff had the required "appearance" of independence, or required "objective" impartiality.
>
> . . .
>
> In this connection, the Court notes that the Bailiff's functions are not limited to judicial matter, but that he is also actively involved in non-judicial functions on the island. The Court does not accept the Government's analysis that when the Bailiff acts in a non-judicial capacity he merely occupies positions rather than exercising functions: even a purely constitutional role must be classified as a "function." The Court must determine whether the Bailiff's functions in his non-judicial capacity were, or were not, compatible with the requirements of Article 6 as to independence and impartiality.
>
> . . .
>
> With particular respect to his presiding, as Deputy Bailiff, over the States of Deliberation in 1990, the Court considers that any involvement in the passage of legislation, or of executive rules, is likely to be sufficient to cast doubt on the judicial impartiality of a person subsequently called on to determine a dispute over whether reasons exist to permit a variation from the wording of the legislation or rules at issue.[156]

While this case originated in Guernsey, its broader repercussions on the overall British system of governance have not yet been fully felt. Specialized public opinion is, however, paying very close attention

---

[155] Ibid.

[156] (2000), 30 E.H.R.R. 289 at 307, paras. 51, 52 and 55.

to the reforms which may be needed. In particular, the specialists are being led to examine the implications of the case for the Judicial Committee of the Privy Council.

"For my part," Lord Steyn the law lord, has stated, "the proposition that a Cabinet minister must be the head of our judiciary in England is no longer sustainable on either constitutional or pragmatic grounds."

. . .

A further impetus for change to the role is the European Convention on Human Rights, Article 6 of which requires that both criminal cases and civil cases concerning "civil rights and obligations" be heard by an "independent and impartial tribunal established by law." Case law has established that by "independent" is meant "independent of the executive and also of the parties," and of Parliament.

. . .

The Lord Chancellor, as Speaker of the House of Lords, takes a direct role in the passage of legislation. Before his role is reformed, he is likely to fall foul of Article 6 if he hears cases involving the interpretation of legislation passed while he has been in office.[157]

In the present case, the European Court of Human Rights set out the test for separation of the various powers of officials involved in the justice system, most significantly among them the one fulfilling the function of minister of justice or Lord Chancellor.

Any direct involvement in the passage of legislation, or of executive rules, is *likely* to be sufficient to cast doubt on the judicial impartiality of a person subsequently called to determine a dispute over whether reasons exist to permit a variation from the wording of the legislation or rules at issue.[158]

It is worth deliberately noting that most commentators approach this case from the point of view of protecting the independence of judicial decision-makers from the executive, or more appropriately stated for these circumstances, protecting the independence of the judicial lobe

---

[157] "Lord Chancellor and master of the multifarious roles," Daniel Lightman, *The Times*, London, February 27, 2001.

[158] *McGonnell v. United Kingdom*, the Lord Chancellor and the Law Lords, Richard Cornes, [2000] P. L., Summer, p. 166 at 168.

of a single governmental decision-maker from the executive lobe of that same individual's mind. In this regard, the analysis of Richard Cornes is particularly instructive.

> If the level of influence a judge has in an executive or legislative capacity is relevant, then the Lord Chancellor, as a member of the United Kingdom cabinet, is on a par with the Bailiff. However, the Lord Chancellor and the Law Lords in the House of Lords, except in exceptionally close votes, are clearly a minority. There are at least two counter arguments suggesting this distinction is unhelpful. First, one of the rationales of the Lord Chancellor's presence in Cabinet is that *because* of his judicial position, his opinion on legal matters will be given greater weight.
>
>   . . .
>
> Second, in terms of considering whether, to an outsider, the Lord Chancellor or Law Lords, when sitting as judges, are impartial, what does it matter whether the views they express in cabinet or the House of Lords are determinative?[159]

In this study, the emphasis is on the reverse, in the sense of maintaining the independence of the function of the minister of justice, but the methodology can be used in either direction. This is just as significant for the rule of law as the non-interference of the legal executive in the judiciary's workings and decisions.

In light of the *McGonnell* case, and the general trend it seems to represent in the institutional analysis of European human rights authorities, it is previsible that the institutions of the United Kingdom may have to be reformed as part of both modernization and Europeanization.

> McGonnell is simply another of the pressures building on the United Kingdom for reconsideration of the structure, operation and functions of the Appellate and Judicial Committees, and the judges who may sit on them. These institutions and their judges are central to the operation of the state, especially as the *Human Rights Act 1998* comes into effect and disputes begin to arise about the implementation of the devolution Acts of 1998. Principles of "joined up government" suggest that serious consideration should be given now to the United Kingdom's top courts, and how their structure and operation may need amendment in light of

---

[159] Op. cit., p. 169.

constitutional developments (both those driven by domestic statutes and by international judicial rulings). Detailed consideration of what any reform to avoid breach of Article 6(1) might entail is however the subject of a much broader paper. As Robert Stevens said recently on this topic:

> The English like to think of their constitution as growing organically. The organic may have to give way to the planned.[160]

See also *Confirmation of John Ashcroft as Attorney General of the United States*, Hearings in the United States Senate, February, 2001.

3.11 ISSUE: APOLITICAL CRIMINAL LAW, OBJECTIVE PROSECUTORIAL AUTHORITY[161]

§ 3.11.1[162]
Tremblay c. Québec (Commission de la Fonction publique)
Québec Superior Court; May 14, 1990
[1990] R.J.Q. 1386

Tremblay was a member of the Québec public service who had spent his entire career in the Crown prosecutions office. From 1983 until 1988, he was a full-time prosecutor. In that year, with the federal general election pending, he advised his hierarchical superior, the Associate Deputy Minister of Justice for Criminal and Penal Affairs, that he wanted to be a candidate in that election. The Deputy applied section 8 of the *Act respecting Attorney General's Prosecutors*[163] and informed Tremblay that upon his declaration of candidacy, he would be fired. One day thereafter, Tremblay entered the political fray.

The Québec Superior Court held that Tremblay's firing was contrary to the applicable provisions of the *Canadian Charter of Rights and Freedoms* and ordered that he be reinstated retroactively to the date of his dismissal. This result was based on the court's judgment that the relevant provision in Québec's public service legislation was not

---

[160] *Ibid.*, p. 177.
[161] Cross-reference to § 1.4, 3.10, 11.12 and 11.13.
[162] Cross-reference to § 11.14.3.
[163] L.R.Q., c. S-35.

in compliance with the *Charter*. The real significance of the case is that it consecrates the importance for democratic governance from several perspectives, of the need for an impartial prosecutorial authority.

The judgment appealed from, that of the Public Service Commission of Québec, had already recognized that the objective of the impugned legislation was:

> la promotion "du maintien de l'autorité de la neutralité et de l'impartialité réelle et apparente, et de l'intégrité du système judiciaire en matière de justice criminelle et pénale."[164]

At this instance as well, the court could not have been more forthright in agreeing with the importance of the original goal of the *Act Respecting Attorney General's Prosecutors*, namely the impartiality of the justice system. It held that,

> L'article 8 de la Loi sur les substituts est motive, a tort ou a raison, par le danger que le procureur de la Couronne sont tributaire d'un parti politique et compromette l'objectif législatif de neutralité, d'impartialité et de transparence de la justice.[165]

The court attempted to be comprehensive in its understanding of the concept of impartiality, as including public perception of the judicial system. The court urged caution in delimiting impartiality, so as to avoid both laxism on one side and rigidity on the other. It held that the notion of appearance of the impartiality of the judicial system is fluid and ambiguous, without set standards. What the court was really expressing was that the principle must be acknowledged to exist broadly, but its application and interpretation needs to be conducted in a case-by-case basis. In the present case, the Québec authorities should have adduced more evidence to show that enabling a Crown prosecutor to stand for political office, albeit under the specifically limited procedures already applicable to the government's other lawyers, would have tainted the administration of justice irremediably. As they did not, Tremblay's democratic right under section 3 of the *Charter* was held to prevail.

The court did set the specific limits applicable to the present circumstances. While Tremblay could not simultaneously be a Crown pros-

---

[164] [1990] R.J.Q. 1386 at 1397.
[165] *Ibid.* at 1410.

ecutor and a candidate for election, he could take an unpaid leave of absence from his prosecutorial functions to run for office without damaging the impartiality of the administration of criminal justice or rendering himself incapable of returning to his professional legal tasks in case of loss.

See also *R. v. Shirose*, [1999] 1 S.C.R. 565 (S.C.C.) and *R. v. Regan*, 209 D.L.R. (4th) 41 at 115 (S.C.C.).

---

§ 3.11.2[166]
Ex parte Attorney General; Re the Constitutional Relationship between the Attorney General and the Prosecutor General
(1995), 3 L.R.C. 507 (S.C.)

After a long and troubled quasi-colonial relationship with the Republic of South Africa, the country which had earlier been known as South-West Africa gained its independence on March 21, 1990, under the name of Namibia. A new constitution had come into effect in February, 1990, within which section 8 established the position of Attorney General as a member of the executive and section 87 delineated his powers and functions as the principal legal advisor of the President. The latter was appointed the Attorney General. Section 88 of the constitution provided for a separate Prosecutor-General to be appointed on the recommendation of the Judicial Services Commission, for the purpose of prosecuting criminal proceedings. The relevant provisions read as follows:

Article 87 [Powers and Functions of the Attorney-General]

The powers and functions of the Attorney-General shall be:

a) to exercise the final responsibility for the office of the Prosecutor-General;
b) to be in principal legal adviser to the President and Government;
c) to take all action necessary for the protection and upholding of the Constitution;
d) to perform all such functions and duties as may be assigned to the Attorney-General by Act of Parliament.

---

[166] International comparison.

Article 88 [The Prosecutor-General]

1. There shall be a Prosecutor-General appointed by the President on the recommendation of the Judicial Service Commission. No person shall be eligible for appointment as Prosecutor-General unless such person:

   a) posesses legal qualifications that would entitle him or her to practice in all the Courts of Namibia;
   b) is, by virtue of his or her experience, conscientiousness and integrity a fit and proper person to be entrusted with the responsibilities of the office of Prosecutor-General.

2. The powers and functions of the Prosecutor-General shall be:

   a) to prosecute, subject to the provisions of this Constitution, in the name of the Republic of Namibia in criminal proceedings;
   b) to prosecute and defend appeals in criminal proceedings in the High Court and the Supreme Court;
   c) to perform all functions relating to the exercise of such powers;
   d) to delegate to other officials, subject to his or her control and direction, authority to conduct criminal proceedings in any Court;
   e) to perform all such other functions as may be assigned to him or her in terms of any other law.[167]

Both these sections are in the chapter of the constitution which deals with the Administration of Justice and which also includes the framework of the judicial branch, thus giving them a fundamentally law-based tone.

In August 1993, the Attorney General attempted to instruct the Prosecutor General to withdraw a prosecution, but the latter refused. The conduct of the criminal trial in question was postponed and, on a procedure that in Canada would be called a reference, the Supreme Court of Namibia was asked whether in the exercise of his powers, the Attorney General effectively had the authority to instruct the Prosecutor-General regarding prosecutions and whether the Prosecutor-General had to render account to the Attorney-General. The Attorney-General's position was that the Prosecutor-General was

---

[167] Constitution of Namibia, sections 87 and 88. This material was obtained from an Internet website entitled NambiWeb located at http://www.namibweb.com/const.htm.

subordinate to his authority and he based this primarily on the read-ing of pre-independence criminal procedure legislation, with mean-ings updated to reflect the new constitutional framework of the coun-try. In defending his independent position, the Prosecutor-General grounded his argument on the constitution itself.

The ruling of the Supreme Court was of course phrased in terms proper to the Namibian situation and it even specifically refused to rely on precedents from other Commonwealth countries, but only because of the variety of models of roles adopted by these countries for the positions of Attorney-General and Director of Public Prose-cutions. Nevertheless, the principles enunciated in this decision had a universal resonance in political law, in that they stressed the im-portance of the rule of law, the cardinal values of the constitution and the avoidance of executive domination and State despotism as the hallmarks of a properly constituted prosecutorial function in a dem-ocratic state. Most important of all, the judgment sketched the re-quired bounds for apolitical and objective prosecutorial powers and emphasized the separation of legal from political considerations in the conduct of criminal matters.

> ...on a proper construction of the Constitution of the Republic of Namibia there was nothing to make the office of the Prosecutor-General subject to the superintendence or direction of the Attorney-General. It was clear from the articles whereby the offices were constituted that the appoint-ment of the Attorney-General was political and that the Attorney-Gen-eral's functions were executive in nature whereas the Prosecutor-Gen-eral's functions were quasi-judicial. Public confidence in the criminal justice system could only be maintained where there was no abuse of prosecutorial powers. Allowing a political appointee to dictate which prosecutions might be initiated and which should be terminated or how prosecutions should be conducted would not protect the fundamental human rights and freedoms under the Constitution of the Republic of Namibia, since there was always a potential danger that such an ap-pointee would allow his political considerations to influence his deci-sions.[168]

---

[168] Commonwealth Law Bulletin, January and April 1996, p. 127. The full case is at (1995), 3 L.R.C. 507 (S.C.).

3.12 ISSUE: NON-PARTISAN PUBLIC SERVICE AND ARMED FORCES

3.12.A—CANDIDACY OF PUBLIC SERVANTS FOR POLITICAL OFFICE[169]

See *O.P.S.E.U. v. Ontario (Attorney General)* (1979), 24 O.R. (2d) 324 (Ont. H.C.), affirmed (1980), 81 C.L.L.C. 14 (Ont. C.A.), affirmed [1987] 2 S.C.R. 2 (S.C.C.); *O.P.S.E.U. v. Ontario (Attorney General)* (1980), 118 D.L.R. (3d) 661 (Ont. C.A.), affirmed [1987] 2 S.C.R. 2 (S.C.C.); *Fraser v. Nova Scotia (Attorney General)* (1986), 30 D.L.R. (4th) 340 (N.S. T.D.); *O.P.S.E.U. v. Ontario (Attorney General)*, 41 D.L.R. (4th) 1 (S.C.C.); *O.P.S.E.U. v. Ontario (Attorney General)* (1988), 52 D.L.R. (4th) 701 (Ont. H.C.), reversed (1993), 14 O.R. (3d) 476 (Ont. C.A.) and *Barke v. Calgary (City)* (1989), 98 A.R. 157 (Alta. Q.B.).

---

§ 3.12.A.1

Osborne v. Canada (Treasury Board)

Supreme Court of Canada; June 6, 1991

(1991), 82 D.L.R. (4th) 321

No compendium on jurisprudence involving the relationship of the legal system to active politics would be complete without consideration of one of the most fundamental cases now guiding this subject matter. The *Osborne* case is the most authoritative judicial pronouncement on the partisan activities of public servants in general and on their candidacy for political office in particular.

The background of the controversy arises from a longstanding tradition in the Canadian political system which has also acquired the status of a constitutional convention, namely that of a politically neutral public service. Both in appearance and even more so in reality, members of the Public Service of Canada were expected to be officials of the State, overtly and covertly unconnected with any political party. The philosophy underlying this convention was that only with the detachment which non-partisanship and depoliticization as-

---

[169] Cross-reference to § 5.5.B.

sumed could public servants carry out their duties professionally and with the political neutrality required to assure "Peace, Order and Good Government."

The challenges which were eventually united into the *Osborne* case arose from the federal electoral district with probably the highest concentration of public servants in the country, Ottawa Centre. Several public servants wanted to work for the New Democratic Party's candidate for election to Parliament, Mike Cassidy. They sued to have the statutory provision barring them from such activity, section 33 of the *Public Service Employment Act*, declared contrary to the freedom of expression [s. 2(b)] and freedom of association [s. 2(d)] provisions of the *Charter*. The Trial Division of the Federal Court dismissed the claim. Significantly, the trial judge acknowledged the existence of a convention of political neutrality in the public service. He seemed to concede that it infringed on the *Charter* but opined that as the restrictions on political activity were no more than necessary to attain the objective, they were justified under section 1.

The Federal Court of Appeal overturned and the Supreme Court of Canada retained the latter's judgment. Mr. Justice Sopinka wrote for the majority, covering the matter from all angles.

The first notable part of the judgment was that the political neutrality convention, said to be central to the principle of responsible government, was generally accepted. The question in respect of this convention was whether the statutory provision which implemented it could be considered to be inconsistent with the constitution. The key to this is the distinction between the legal and political aspects of the constitution.

> Therefore, while conventions form part of the Constitution of this country in the broader political sense, *i.e.*, the democratic principles underlying our political system and the elements which constitute the relationships between the various levels and organs of government, they are not enforceable in a court of law unless they are incorporated into legislation. Furthermore, statutes embodying constitutional conventions do not automatically become entrenched to become part of the constitutional law, but retain their status as ordinary statutes.[170]

---

[170] (1991), 82 D.L.R. (4th) 321 at 333 h.

Consequently, section 33 of the *Public Service Employment Act* could not be immune from *Charter* scrutiny.

Next, the court asked whether there was in fact a *Charter* infringement. Undoubtedly the reply must be affirmative. "By prohibiting public servants from speaking out in favour of a political party or candidate, it expressly has for its purpose the restriction of expressive activity."[171] Moreover, "while the historical origins of the concept are to be taken into account in ascertaining the scope of a *Charter* right, the 'traditional' meaning ascribed to such right is not conclusive for the purposes of the *Charter*."[172] The infringement which was found was in respect of section 2(b), on freedom of expression.

Finally, the court looked at whether the infringement could be justified under section 1. The downfall of section 33 was caused by its over-inclusive nature; it failed on the ground that it was not a reasonable limit.

With respect to the scope of the public servants to whom the restrictions of section 33 applied, the court felt that,

> The result of this broad general language is that the restrictions apply to a great number of public servants who in modern government are employed in carrying out clerical, technical or industrial duties that are completely divorced from the exercise of any discretion that could be in any manner affected by political considerations. The need for impartiality and indeed the appearance thereof does not remain constant throughout the civil service hierarchy. As stated by Dickson, C.J.C. in *Fraser, supra*: "It is implicit throughout the adjudicator's reasons that the degree of restraint which must be exercised is relative to the position and visibility of the civil servant." (p. 130). To apply the same standard to a Deputy Minister and a cafeteria worker appears to me to involve considerable overkill and does not meet the test of constituting a measure that is carefully designed to impair freedom of expression as little as reasonably possible.[173]

With respect to the nature of the various political activities in which the applicants wanted to engage, the court also drew distinctions. Dividing lines would have to be shown between attending meetings,

---

[171] *Ibid.* at 337 h-338 a.
[172] *Ibid.* at 335 g.
[173] *Ibid.* at 34 e-g.

contributing funds to parties, public expressions of support and volunteer work.

On the basis of this almost clinical, entirely textual legally-based reasoning, Sopinka, J. and the majority held that section 32 was of no force and effect, except as it applied to deputy ministers and their equivalents.

The court was not unanimous, however. In a well-grounded dissent, Mr. Justice Stevenson preferred looking at the general purpose of the restriction, rather than at its scope.

> ...in my view, the case against partisan activities at all levels is a strong one. No civil servant must owe, or be seen to owe, appointment or promotion to partisan activities. Activities tend to be overt and they are likely to be known or become known to those within and without the public service. Once allegiances are known, the principles of neutrality, impartiality and integrity are endangered. There is a danger within the service that those seeking appointments or promotions will feel some incentive to cut their cloth to the known partisan interests of those who have influence over appointments and promotions. Visible partisanship by civil servants displays a lack of neutrality, and a betrayal of that convention of neutrality. The public perception of neutrality is thus severely impaired, if not destroyed.[174]

Just as the majority brought in examples from other jurisdictions, Mr. Justice Stevenson referred to jurisprudence from the United States.

> ...that it is in the best interest of the country, indeed essential, that federal service should depend upon meritorious performance rather than political service, and that the political influence of federal employees on others and on the electoral process should be limited.[175]

It was widely expected within the ranks of the Public Service that this judgment would lead to new rules and perhaps even to a revision of the section by Parliament. In fact, the policy instruments of the Public Service Commission have simply acknowledged the Supreme Court's ruling. Moreover, the ruling seems to have cleared the issue of its controversial nature, as no other major cases have arisen on this point.

---

[174] *Ibid.* at 349 f-g.
[175] *Ibid.* at 351 e, citing from *United States Civil Service Commission v. National Assn. of Letter Carriers, AFL-CIO*, 413 U.S. 548 (U.S. Dist. Col., 1973) at 557.

3.12.B—PUBLIC EXPRESSIONS OF POLITICAL OPINION BY PUBLIC SERVANTS AND MILITARY PERSONNEL

See *Fraser v. Canada (Treasury Board, Department of National Revenue)* (1985), 23 D.L.R. (4th) 122 (S.C.C.).

---

§ 3.12.B.1
Radiomutuel Inc. c. Wlihelmy
(September 14, 1992), Doc. C.S. Québec 200-05-002998-925
(Que. S.C.)[176]

Most of the judicial pronouncements regarding the requirement of the public service to be politically neutral result from the attempts by the State to prevent public servants from espousing issues of governance publicly and in a partisan manner. The circumstances of public life can, however, on occasion produce situations in which it is the public servant involved who tries to safeguard the political neutrality of the service from being considered partisan or from becoming politicized. This is what happened in the case of Diane Wilhelmy, who was the Secretary for Canadian Intergovernmental Affairs to the Québec Cabinet at the time of the negotiations leading up to the conclusion of the *Charlottetown Accord* in the summer of 1992. In her capacity as Secretary to the Cabinet, Wilhelmy held the rank of Deputy Minister and worked in close cooperation with the Premier of the Province, Robert Bourassa, with her own Minister, Gil Rémillard, as well as their other close advisers.

In late August, 1992, Bourassa led a Québec delegation to Ottawa for discussions with federal authorities and those of the other provinces and the territories. They were trying to put together a package of constitutional reforms that would be acceptable to all parties. The question whether the package would satisfy the aspirations and demands of Québec was particularly significant for all of Canada, and even more vital for Québec. The reason why these discussions and

---

[176] And (September 22, 1992), Doc. C.A. Québec 200-09-000619-921 (Que. C.A.) and (September 24, 1992), Doc. C.S. Québec 200-05-002998-925 (Que. S.C.) and (September 30, 1992), Doc. C.S. Québec 200-05-002998-925 (Que. S.C.).

negotiations were taking place in 1992 was that the *Meech Lake Accord*, the previous constitutional deal, had failed to be adopted in 1990. That had left a great deal of political rancour in Québec. At the time of the meeting in Ottawa in August, 1992, therefore, the political and constitutional stakes were high for all participants, but especially for Québec. The collective attention of Canadians, including in particular that of the media, was focused on the proceedings.

On August 22, Premier Bourassa participated in a tentative agreement that he believed in and which he thought would satisfy Québec. As it would later be learned, there was much controversy about that pact among the members of the Québec delegation. As Wilhelmy was ill on that day and did not take part in the deliberations, it took her a few days to realize the elements of the deal. On August 28, she had a cellular phone conversation with André Tremblay, a constitutional law specialist and Bourassa's own constitutional affairs adviser. She expressed her opinion of the Premier's acceptance of the tentative accord very candidly. She was reported to have said, among other things, that "It has taken me three days to accept the fact that we have settled for so little...I keep telling myself this can't be, this can't be. I probably don't understand. There must be a strategy behind all this."[177] Wilhelmy's interlocutor, Tremblay, used even more blunt language in responding: "He didn't want one. He didn't want a referendum...on sovereignty. In any event, we caved in; that's all."[178]

Unbeknownst to Wilhelmy at the time of this telephone conversation, a third party had locked on to the signal of her phone and had recorded the conversation. In the second week of September, Radi-omutuel, a Québec-based broadcasting enterprise, announced on the air that it had the tape and that it intended to play it. The effect of the Wilhelmy story on Québec public opinion was instantaneous and electric.

Upon the rendering public of the Wilhelmy-Tremblay discussion, the story evolved into two separate sets of issues. The first concerned the role of Québec in the ongoing constitutional negotiations, the influence the Province's delegation could exert on that of the other players at the table and the influence of the opinions expressed by Wilhelmy

---

[177] Quoted in Delacourt, S., *United We Fall: The Crisis of Democracy in Canada*, Toronto, Viking Press, 1993, p. 179.

[178] "Québec judge lifts gag order," *Toronto Globe and Mail*, October 1, 1992, p. A-3.

and Tremblay on Québec public opinion. This cluster of issues was, for the time being, exclusively political. Its outcomes were reflected in the vote of the population of Québec in the constitutional referendum that took place on October 26, 1992, and at which the question to be determined was whether to accept or reject the package of constitutional reforms put forward. In Québec, the results were 56.68% for the NO and 43.32 % for the YES.

The second issue was the consequence in political law of Wilhelmy's confidential opinions, and by implication her advice, having been made public. In a move unprecedented for a senior public servant, Wilhelmy herself applied in the Québec Superior Court to have an injunction imposed on Radiomutuel and everyone associated with it, to prevent them from broadcasting her conversation or in any way further rendering it public. Her case was primarily based on the twin pleadings that public servants were independent of government and non-partisan, and that their political neutrality needed to be protected. She argued that in order to enable senior public servants to tender non-partisan advice to their political masters, they needed to protect the confidentiality of that advice, in accordance with the *Public Service Act*,[179] as well as her oath of office. To support these points, she relied on the *Québec Charter of Human Rights and Freedoms*[180] as well as on the privacy provisions of Québec's legislation on access and privacy.[181] Wilhelmy submitted further pleadings based on public order and on observance of the requirements of the *Criminal Code*.[182]

Essentially, Wilhelmy's position was that she had an obligation of political neutrality and confidentiality which could only be maintained through a practice of reserve and forbearance in the expression of opinions on government and political matters.

This turned out to be a case in which the pleadings presented to the court were much more significant and instructive than the judgments eventually based on them. On September 14, 1992, the Superior Court issued an interim injunction, valid for 10 days. The effect of this order

---

[179] R.S.Q. 1977, c. F–3.1.
[180] R.S.Q. 1977, c. C-12.
[181] *Act respecting access to documents held by public bodies and the protection of personal information*, R.S.Q. 1977, c. A-2.1.
[182] R.S.C. 1985, c. C-46, with amendments.

294 / LAW OF DEMOCRATIC GOVERNING – VOLUME II: JURISPRUDENCE

was to forbid publication of the contents of the conversation and to direct Radiomutuel to deliver the recording and its transcripts to the court so that they could be sealed. The judgment consisted only of the ordering provisions and a number of ancillary measures relating to service on the various defendants so as to ensure that the order would become immediately effective. No motive was set out. We are therefore left to surmise that the court accepted as legally valid Wilhelmy's assertions regarding the nature of senior Public Service work as being non-partisan and independent of government, as well as the need for confidentiality of advice as a means of protecting those characteristics of her work.

On September 22, 1992, the Québec Court of Appeal refused Radiomutuel's application for leave to appeal. This ruling was based solely on the civil procedure issues relating to notice to the defendants and service upon them. On September 24, 1992, at the term of the provisional injunction, the Superior Court issued an interlocutory injunction, very much along the same lines as the original one.

Two sets of facts extraneous to the actual court proceedings, but having an obvious bearing on them, need to be noted. The first is Wilhelmy's decision as to the choice of forum. She brought the action in the Québec courts; their writ ran only within the limits of the Province. During the time she was pursuing her case, the *Toronto Globe and Mail*, the *Ottawa Citizen* and various other news outlets in other parts of Canada had published stories about the conversation. By this time, everyone who wanted to know what Wilhelmy and Tremblay had said to each other could find it out. It is possible that Wilhelmy could have achieved different results by suing in Federal Court, the writ of which ran to all parts of Canada, but in the highly politically charged atmosphere of that period, that in itself may have been perceived as a contentious, partly legal, partly political, statement.

Of greater importance was the fact that while the Wilhelmy conversation had taken place on August 28, by September 28, 1992, the political situation of which the court case was but an aspect had completely changed. The terms of the *Charlottetown Accord* had been finalized and a Canada-wide referendum on it had been called on September 17, for October 26. Premier Bourassa was by now most determined to get on with the campaign for a YES vote and he therefore needed to have Wilhelmy's court action resolved. Upon his urging, the parties reached an understanding and on the basis of that court-sanctioned settlement, the Superior Court issued a final judgment on September 30, 1992.

This was an injunction which prohibited the defendants from broadcasting the recorded conversation or a copy of it, but allowed broadcasting of the text of the conversation. Both from its own awareness of the factual situation and on the basis of the agreement reached by the parties, the court could not do otherwise than to make a ruling that would recognize that the information sought to be restrained had, by other means and through other jurisdictions, been rendered public. Thus, while Wilhelmy's victory was phyrric at best as to the practical result she had intended to accomplish, the point of political law involved, namely the importance of the political neutrality of public servants, was left undamaged.

It is interesting to note that on June 23, 1993, at least in part, no doubt, under the influence of the Wilhelmy affair, Royal Assent was given to a set of amendments and additions to the *Criminal Code* and the *Radiocommunications Act*, whereby the interception of private communications by cellular phone was made an offence. These changes came into effect on August 1, 1993.

See also *R. v. Prunelle*, Court Martial Transcript Summaries, C.F.B. Valcartier; April 15, 1997, file 04/97 and *Mayor of Toronto (City) v. Ontario* (2000), 47 O.R. (3d) 177 (Ont. S.C.J.).

---

§ 3.12.B.2
Toronto Police Services Board v. Toronto Police Assn.
Ontario Superior Court of Justice; February 11, 2000
[2000] O.T.C. 327

Can the Toronto Police Association becoming politically active be compatible with the maintenance of the professionalism of the Toronto Police and the maintenance of civilian control over the police? These are the issues raised by this case.

On January 11, 2000, under the leadership of a particularly confrontational management, unbending to the law and to Canadian custom in the domain of policing, the Toronto Police Association instituted a campaign entitled "Operation True Blue." This consisted of direct fundraising, essentially for police participation in the electoral process, in support of public officials and candidates for office who agree with the union's position on criminal justice and law enforcement matters. In imitation of similar campaigns undertaken in the United States, the Association president made public pronouncements about defeating "the enemies of the police." On January 28, 2000, pursuant to the *Police Services Act*,[183] the Toronto Police Services Board adopted *By-law 130*, regulating the fundraising activities of the police for political purposes. On the same day, the Chief of Police wrote to the Association, ordering that Operation True Blue cease. By a press release dated January 31, 2000, the Association indicated it refused to comply. It appeared that democratic control of the police by the municipal authorities was faltering. There was intense media coverage and much political attention and reaction.

The Chief of Police and the Police Services Board applied for an interlocutory injunction to stop the Operation, and after the motion was served, the Association announced it was stopping these activities. Nevertheless, it applied for judicial review of the *By-law*. The position most pertinent to the issues at the core of this controversy was expressed by the intervenors in the injunction motion of the Chief of Police, namely the Urban Alliance on Race Relations and the Chinese Canadian National Council (Toronto Chapter). In their factum, these intervenors linked the principles of restriction on the political activities of the police and of accountability of the police to civilian authority, these being necessary for the subordination of the police to the law and the maintenance of the rule of law.

> Any consideration of where the limitations are on police involvement in politics, must, it is submitted involve curtailing their direct or indirect participation in the electoral process, through fundraising or otherwise. This is precisely where the current Toronto Police Association has crossed the line and where the potential for the intimidation of elected officials becomes most acute. The danger is clear, the position of power and trust held by police officers can far too easily be converted for partisan purposes which in turn would invariably skew any election process. Operation True Blue, according to the Association's own literature is intended, at least in part, for the targeting of so called "enemies" of the police. This entire exercise represents an unseemly flexing of police muscle. In the end, the very real risk is that those elected politicians who

---

[183] R.S.O. 1990, c. P.15, as amended.

are appointed to scrutinize the police will simply be intimidated from doing their job. This is inimical to democracy. This is the danger against which society must be protected.[184]

The intervenors also relied on the elevation of the principle of public service neutrality, that is abstinence from involvement in politics, to the level of a constitutional convention.

The Ontario Superior Court agreed with this line of reasoning in granting an interim interlocutory judgment. It recognized that there were serious issues for trial, indicating that "In particular, there is the issue of whether political fundraising of the nature and type of Operation True Blue is unlawful."[185] The court also perceived that there was a possibility of irreparable harm. This branch of the test for obtaining an injunction was met, in that intrusive telemarketing with no guarantees that personal identification would not be confidential, and which could create the appearance of intimidation and the conferring of preferred status in policing would not be susceptible to compensation by damages.

With respect to the balance of conveniences, the position of the court was that the Association was bound to comply with the by-law until it was declared invalid.

> It is especially important that the law be complied with where the defendants are police officers and where the evidence establishes a serious impact on members of the public and their elected representatives...What is being balanced here is the defendants' right to raise funds as compared to the public confidence in the Toronto Police Services and the justice system. One is clearly compensible in damages, while the other is not. The balance of convenience favours the plaintiffs.[186]

The court exercised the self-restraint required to adjudicate serenely on the basis of legal norms, even in the face of the extreme controversy and the heightened public attention to the matter. Attentive reading of the judgment does reveal, however, some impatience on its part with the position of the Association and perhaps a hint of its feeling as to the good faith of the Association. It said that the discontinuance

---

[184] Factum of the Intervenors, The Urban Alliance on Race Relations and the Chinese Canadian National Council (Toronto Chapter), February 8, 2000, para. 23.

[185] (2000), [2000] O.J. No. 1674, 2000 CarswellOnt 1669 (Ont. S.C.J.), para. 11.

[186] Ibid., paras. 13, 14.

of Operation True Blue was no reason to dismiss this application: the Association had asserted that its political activity was permanently discontinued and therefore the injunction was unnecessary, but offered not evidence to that effect. The court also pointed out that as Operation True Blue was discontinued only after the injunction papers were served on the Association, the discontinuance could not be characterized as either voluntary or legitimate. Finally, the court noted that the Association's reference to the discontinuance as compliance was a misnomer.

Clearly, the court believed that the entire campaign had been contrary to statute and convention and was determined to restore the apolitical stance required of the police. Law enforcement was not to be tainted by political activity.

It would appear that the decision of the court did not carry much weight with either the management of the Toronto Police or the leadership of the Toronto Police Association. Both the Chief of Police and the union president continued during 2000 to engage in partisan political activities, including support and opposition for specific candidates for Council and Mayor, participation in provincial party conventions, of course for the Progressive Conservative Party, and the expenditure of funds for the union's extensive so-called war chest. In all of these activities, they received help from Republican Party organizers from the United States.

Both the Canadian Civil Liberties Association and the Law Union of Ontario made representations against these practices. Police and police union assertions that they were doing nothing wrong did not change the reality of their ignorance of the law and their wilful disregard for the Canadian legal system and custom.

> "The political neutrality of the police is essential to protecting the rule of law," said the law union's Catherine Glaister, who maintained that the association's politicking contravened the provincial Police Services Act.[187]

The Toronto Police Services Board had to issue further orders requiring these activities to stop until the law was clarified. There is reason

---

[187] "Watchdog tells Fantino to keep union out of politics," Robert Benzie, *National Post*, September 1, 2000, p. A-18.

to doubt that civilian and especially legal control over the police is complete, in the face of such undemocratic police union behaviour.

See also *Toronto Police Association v. Toronto Police Services Board*, Divisional Court, filed February 1, 2000, file no. 58/2000, settled May 2, 2000; *Mercier c. Québec* (March 23, 1994), Doc. C.A. Québec 200-10-000062-914 (Que. C.A.); *Haydon v. R.* (2000), [2001] F.C. 82 (Fed. T.D.); *Chopra v. Canada (Treasury Board)* (2003), 2003 PSSRB 115 (Can. P.S.S.R.B.) and *Haydon v. Canada (Treasury Board)*, 2004 FC 749 (F.C.).

3.12.C—INCITEMENT OF PUBLIC SERVANTS TO TAKE POLITICAL POSITIONS

---

§ 3.12.C.1

Report of the Standing Committee on Procedure and House Affairs on the Letter to the Armed Forces by a Bloc Québécois Member of Parliament
Hansard, June 18, 1996, p. 3988

The law on the neutrality of the public service vis-à-vis the Government, supplemented by long-standing convention, favours the abstention of at least senior public servants from active engagement in political life and partisan activities. In this respect, despite the paramount nature of national unity as a constant political issue in Canada, public servants are not legally bound to refrain from overt participation in the referendum process in the sovereignty of Québec but left it to the Governor in Council to make regulations as to the use of that right.[188] However, for no category of public servants can such rules be more sensitive than members of the armed forces. Thus it is not surprising that when, in the politically volatile atmosphere of the campaign preceding the Québec referendum of October 30, 1995, on sovereignty, a Member of the Parliament of Canada belonging to the Bloc Québécois issued a letter which may be considered as inciteful, the political and legal issues involved attracted serious attention.

On October 26, 1995, Jean-Marc Jacob, the Bloc Québécois critic for national defence and MP for Charlesbourg, issued a communiqué regarding the prospective national defence policy of an independent Québec. A key element of this document was that portion of its text

---

[188] *Referendum Act*, S.C. 1992, c. 30, s. 32.

300 / LAW OF DEMOCRATIC GOVERNING – VOLUME II: JURISPRUDENCE

which indicated that after a vote in favour of secession, members of the Canadian Forces who were Québecers should be offered the chance to serve in the armed forces of the independent Québec instead. This could be understood as an inducement to favour the YES vote and to help in the establishment of the forces of the proposed independent country. While the issues of freedom of expression and parliamentary privilege were patently involved, from the popular perspective and in light of the focus of this study, the most significant element of the matter is the apparent politically motivated inducement to public servants to espouse political actions in the most drastic manner possible.

On March 12, 1996, Jim Hart, the Reform Member for Okanagan-Similkameen-Merritt, British Columbia, raised this issue as a Question of Privilege in the House of Commons. Conscious of the fact that Parliament was not a court, and could not judge the allegedly criminal or treasonous nature of the action, this member interpreted the communiqué as "encouraging members of the Canadian Armed Forces to choose sides on the secession debate"[189] and suggested that this amounted to "contempt of Parliament." The Speaker referred the matter on March 18 to the Commons Standing Committee on Procedure and House Affairs.

Following debate which might best be described as acrimonious, the Committee reported back to the House on June 18, 1996. The Committee interpreted its mandate as determining whether the Jacob communiqué was a breach of Parliamentary privilege, contempt of the House or whether the actions he had undertaken were appropriate for a Member of Parliament. The Committee's Report took an even-handed and legally correct view of the communiqué, recognizing its inflammatory nature but concluding that neither its content nor its dissemination amounted to actions punishable by law.

> Most members of the Committee disagree strongly with the ideas contained in the communiqué. When read as a whole, the communiqué is clearly partisan propaganda, designed to minimize the consequences of voting Yes in the referendum. The Committee rejects Mr. Jacob's explanations that he was merely providing information to concerned voters. It is clear that Mr. Jacob knew exactly what he was doing and intended it to have an effect on members of the military. In his testimony before

---

[189] Hansard, March 12, 1996, p. 558.

the Committee, Mr. Jacob argued that the communiqué should be viewed in the context of the Québec referendum and Québec politics; by the same token, he should have realized the effect that the communiqué, coming when it did, had on many Canadians.

Mr. Jacob acted imprudently in sending out this particular press release, and demonstrated extremely poor judgment. He contravened the traditional arm's length relationship that exists between Parliament and the Canadian Armed Forces. In short, his actions were inappropriate for a Member of Parliament.

. . .

After serious reflection, and based on all of the testimony and evidence that we heard, the Committee has concluded that the communiqué of October 26, 1995 does not constitute a contempt of the House of Commons. While Mr. Jacob's actions were ill-advised, they do not amount to contempt or a breach of parliamentary privilege. We do not countenance the actions of Mr. Jacob in sending out a communiqué in the terms it was, nor do we feel that Mr. Hart was acting in an entirely non-partisan way in raising the matter as a question of privilege when he did.[190]

The matter was so controversial that both the Bloc Québécois and the Reform Party Members issued dissenting reports as appendices to the formal report of the committee. The Blocquistes emphasized that Parliament required the freedom to express divergent opinions and felt that the real contempt involved was the effort to restrict their expression of the sovereignist position. The Reformers sought to find Jacob in contempt and to have him sanctioned; they also wanted to have it declared unacceptable and contemptuous of Parliament for any MP to engage in interference with the allegiance of members of the Canadian Forces.

In this instance, clearly, legal and conventional principles were overtaken by political and even ideologically motivated opinions, and partisanship designed for each party's electorate.

---

[190] Standing Committee on Procedure and House Affairs, Twenty Second Report, June 18, 1996, pp. 49-50.

3.12.D—POLITICAL ASPECTS OF PUBLIC SERVANTS' UNION ACTIVITIES

See *Lavigne v. O.P.S.E.U.*, [1991] 2 S.C.R. 211 (S.C.C.), reconsideration refused (1991), 4 O.R. (3d) xii (S.C.C.).

---

§ 3.12.D.1
Canada (Attorney General) v. P.S.A.C.
Federal Court of Appeal; June 15, 1993
(1993), 107 D.L.R. (4th) 178

This case arose out of the fact that in a federal government office in Bathurst, New Brunswick, the employer, then still entitled Revenue Canada, refused the requisite authorization for the union representing the employees, the Public Service Alliance of Canada (PSAC), to post several notices, on the ground that these were adverse to the interests of the employer. The notices in question contained criticism of the Goods and Services Tax (GST), which was then the subject of political and partisan discussion. They also related in part to the fact that the then Mulroney government intended to appoint additional senators in order to ensure adoption of the GST legislation by the Senate. Given the circumstances prevailing in Canada, the matter was one not only of labour relations, but also had direct political impact.

The Public Service Staff Relations Board ruled that the employer had acted wrongly in prohibiting the posting of these notices. In so doing, it established the principle that at least some expressions of opinion on political issues do not taint the apolitical and non-partisan nature of the Public Service. The Federal Court of Appeal unanimously upheld this view. It reiterated its belief in the necessity of maintaining the political neutrality of the Public Service, on which public confidence it is based. It cited approvingly several of the classical precedents affirming this principle, such as the *Fraser*,[191] *Osborne*[192] and *O.P.S.E.U.*[193] cases. However, the court pointed out that even though some of the comments on the GST contained in one document were harsh and critical of the government of the day, by their style and

---

[191] (1985), 23 D.L.R. (4th) 122 (S.C.C.).
[192] (1991), 82 D.L.R. (4th) 321 (S.C.C.).
[193] (1987), 41 D.L.R. (4th) 1 (S.C.C.).

content, or by being posted, they could not cause the employer any injury. It also felt that in another document of three pages, a three-line statement regarding the appointment of the additional "GST senators" could not cause harm to the employer within the context of the clause of the collective agreement which dealt with the posting of notices.

3.13 ISSUE: PUBLIC ACCESS TO STATE RECORDS AND PROCEEDINGS

See *Montmigny c. Québec (Commission d'accès à l'information)*, [1986] R.L. 570 (Que. C.A.); *Canada (Information Commissioner) v. Canada (Solicitor General)*, [1988] 3 F.C. 551 (Fed. T.D.); *Bland v. Canada (National Capital Commission)*, 41 F.T.R. 202 (Fed. T.D.), reversed (1992), 46 C.P.R. (3d) 21 (Fed. C.A.); *Canada (Information Commissioner) v. Canada (Prime Minister)* (1992), [1993] 1 F.C. 427 (Fed. T.D.) and *Rubin v. Canada (Clerk of the Privy Council)*, [1993] 2 F.C. 391 (Fed. T.D.), reversed [1994] F.C.J. No. 316 (Fed. C.A.), affirmed 191 N.R. 394 (S.C.C.).

---

§ 3.13.1
Tafler v. British Columbia (Commissioner of Conflict of Interest)
British Columbia Court of Appeal [In Chambers]; March 30, 1995
(1995), 5 B.C.L.R. (3d) 336

There can be little doubt that the publicity of proceedings involving public figures, such as examinations into whether they have breached provisions relating to their avoidance of conflict of interest, improves the democratic quality of governance. This position is sustained by those principles underlying section 2(b) of the *Charter* dealing with the various freedoms of the press and media.

Allegations having been made in respect of the breach by Harcourt, then Premier of British Columbia, of his professional ethics as a Parliamentarian, the province's Commissioner of Conflict of Interest was conducting interviews and a hearing process. The publisher and editor of a news magazine wanted to write about these proceedings but were prevented from doing so because the Commissioner decided to conduct them *in camera*. On behalf of the magazine, Tafler, its editor, applied to the Supreme Court for judicial review of the Commissioner's decision. He asserted that:

> ...access by the public remains a matter of right and that presence of the public during the remainder of the interview or hearing process, and public disclosure of the record to date, would have a beneficial effect on the quality of the information or evidence yet to be given before the Commissioner makes his decision.[194]

The Commissioner sought to have the petition summarily dismissed. The court refused and imposed a term requiring that during the court proceedings the Commissioner conduct his business in public.

Even though the trial had not ended, the Commissioner applied to the Court of Appeal for an immediate ruling to overturn these lower decisions. The Court of Appeal dismissed the Commissioner's application. It asked the Commissioner to explain the nature of the public interest involved that would require such an immediate ruling and mandatory continuation of the Commissioner's proceedings in private. The reasoning offered was that,

> ...any delay in completion of the hearing will result in there being a cloud of uncertainty over the Premier's conduct, which must affect the business of government and result in continuing calls for the Premier's resignation. Counsel agreed that the matter could be resolved by concluding the Commissioner's inquiry in public, but said that this would establish a precedent in a matter which ought instead to be judicially resolved.[195]

The Court of Appeal did not find this motivation sufficient, despite the politically sensitive nature of the situation which publicity may create.

> I concluded that extension of the political controversy over the complaints being considered by the Commissioner, however regrettable that may be, had not been shown before me to be a factor of such overwhelming importance as would justify interference on an emergency basis in the exercise by the Judge of his discretion in the matters in question. I came to that conclusion having in mind that political life in a democratic society is often beset by charges and counter charges and resulting public

---

[194] (1995), 5 B.C.L.R. (3d) 336 at 338.4.
[195] *Ibid.* at 339.11.

disquiet, and that resignations are not infrequently called for in political debate.[196]

See also *M-Jay Farms Enterprises Ltd. v. Canadian Wheat Board* (1997), [1998] 2 W.W.R. 48 (Man. C.A.), leave to appeal refused (1998), 126 Man. R. (2d) 154 (note), (S.C.C.), reconsideration refused (August 6, 1998), Doc. 26346 (S.C.C.); *The Globe and Mail v. Ontario Ministry of Finance,* January 1999; *Canada (Attorney General) v. Canada (Information Commissioner),*[197] [2002] 3 F.C. 606 (Fed. T.D.), affirmed 2003 CAF 285 (Fed. C.A.) and 2004 FC 431 (F.C.); *O'Connor v. Nova Scotia (Deputy Minister of the Priorities & Planning Secretariat)* (2001), 209 D.L.R. (4th) 429 (N.S. C.A.), leave to appeal refused (2002), [2001] S.C.C.A. No. 582 (S.C.C.) and *United States President's Executive Order on Presidential Papers,* November 1, 2001.

3.14 ISSUE: IMPARTIAL AND UNFETTERED NEWS MEDIA

See *MacLeod v. Canada (Canadian Armed Forces)* (1990), [1991] 1 F.C. 114 (Fed. T.D.) and *Canada (Information Commissioner) v. Canada (Minister of National Defence)* (1996), 116 F.T.R. 131 (Fed. T.D.).

---

§ 3.14.1
Adbusters Media Foundation v. Canadian Broadcasting Corp.
British Columbia Supreme Court; November 8, 1995
(1995), 13 B.C.L.R. (3d) 265[198]

In the age of information, an element that is vital to the assurance and

---

[196] *Ibid.* at 340.12.

[197] [NOTE: This complex of litigation deals with access to the agendas of ministers of the Crown. It contains a number of other files and judgments, some of which are listed below.] *Canada (Attorney General) v. Canada (Information Commissioner)* (2000), [2000] F.C.J. No. 1648 (Fed. T.D.), reversed [2001] F.C.J. No. 282 (Fed. C.A.), leave to appeal refused (2001), [2001] S.C.C.A. No. 233 (S.C.C.), reversed [2001] F.C.J. No. 283 (Fed. C.A.), leave to appeal refused (2001), [2001] S.C.C.A. No. 234 (S.C.C.); *Canada (Information Commissioner) v. Canada (Attorney General)*, [2001] F.C.J. No. 926 (Fed. T.D.) and [2001] F.C.J. No. 924 (Fed. T.D.) and *Canada (Attorney General) v. Canada (Information Commissioner)*, 2003 FCA 285 (Fed. C.A.).

[198] Affirmed (1997), 49 C.R.R. (2d) 168 (B.C. C.A.), leave to appeal refused (1998), 51 C.R.R. (2d) 188 (note) (S.C.C.).

preservation of democracy is the existence of impartial news media. The notion of impartiality here is in reference to the media's support for, or opposition to, the State and to the government. Impartiality requires the absence of control by the State, interference or influence from the State and the reliance on the standard of journalistic freedom and organizational autocracy as the norms of reporting and analyzing in the news. These are the factors assessed in the *Adbusters* case.

The Adbusters Media Foundation promoted educational and environmental causes through social marketing. As part of that activity, it placed advocacy ads on a CBC program. On the basis of complaints, the CBC realized that it had accepted the ads in error, as its advocacy advertising policy had been translated from French into English erroneously. The foundation used the CBC's refusal to run further ads in the contracted for-program slot to launch a breach of contract action. It also sought a declaration that CBC had breached the *Charter*'s provisions on freedom of expression and on equality.

The principal question before the court was whether the CBC was subject to the *Charter*. The answer lay in the analysis of whether in its dealings with the Adbusters Foundation, the CBC had acted in a governmental capacity.

The judge allowed himself to be guided by the Supreme Court of Canada in distinguishing between operational, routine or regular control, versus ultimate or extraordinary control.[199] Here, the type of control of the government over the CBC could first be seen in its framework. The national broadcaster was established by Parliament, most recently continued by the *Broadcasting Act*.[200] It also remained ultimately responsible to Parliament through a Minister. What was more to the point, however, was the CBC's activity in the area of programming.

> It is overall control of programming that lays at the base of the issue here. "Program" is a defined term under the *Broadcasting Act*, Section 2(1) as:
>
> > "Program" means sounds or visual images, or a combination of sounds and visual images, that are intended to inform, enlighten or

---

[199] *Stoffman v. Vancouver General Hospital*, [1990] 3 S.C.R. 483 (S.C.C.) at 513-514.
[200] S.C. 1991, c. 11.

entertain, but does not include visual images, whether or not combined with sounds, that consist predominantly of alphanumeric text.

The *Broadcasting Act* makes clear that the CBC in pursuing its objects and in the exercise of its powers enjoys "...freedom of expression and journalistic, creative and programming independence." [Section 46(5)].

The *Broadcasting Act* provides to both the CBC specifically and to broadcasters generally the protection of this independence through directed interpretation of the statute and strongly indicates the importance placed by Parliament upon the preservation of those freedoms from governmental influence or control.[201]

The court went on to cite several provisions of the *Broadcasting Act* as evidence of the intention of Parliament that freedom of expression and journalistic independence be enjoyed by the broadcaster. Equally significant, it showed that the CBC was, in its organization and functioning, not subject to the governmental controls of the *Financial Administration Act*.[202] The ability of the broadcaster to function without the monetary and accounting controls applicable to the substantive portfolio or line departments of government was a further layer designed to preserve its independence.

The court concluded that the specific policy applicable to the acceptance and airing of Adbusters' advertisements was in no way related to government. Rather, it was part of the CBC's "carefully protected mandate."[203] This was part of the corporation's broadcasting, and therefore private function.

The aspect of the national broadcaster that the court pointed out here was its autonomy from the State and from the government of the day. This autonomy is what enables the CBC to exercise an independent judgment and to be impartial in reporting on news, especially including legal, public administration and political matters. By extrapolation, if these principles apply to the national broadcaster, they apply equally to media that are privately established and held.

[201] (1995), 13 B.C.L.R. (3d) 265 at 273, affirmed (1997), 49 C.R.R. (2d) 168 (B.C. C.A.), leave to appeal refused (1998), 51 C.R.R. (2d) 188 (note) (S.C.C.).
[202] R.S.C. 1985, c. F-11 and its amendments.
[203] *Ibid.* at 274.

The British Columbia Court of Appeal dismissed Adbusters' attempt to get the trial judgment reversed. They noted in particular that the case could be decided on other grounds and where that is so, the policy of the court favouring restraint in constitutional cases was sound. While this court refused to rule on the *Charter* issue, it was on less certain footing than the lower court, hinting that it could, if it were minded to make a declaration, consider the CBC a governmental body and therefore subject to the *Charter*. It would only acknowledge that the CBC's only response to the *Charter* issue was that it was not a governmental actor. The appeal judges also refused to rule on whether the use of radio frequencies brought all broadcasters under the *Charter*. As the program into which Adbusters had tried to place its ads had been taken off the air, the matter was held to be moot.

---

§ 3.14.2[204]
Prime Minister's Office Complaint About CBC Reporting on APEC
Canadian Broadcasting Corporation Ombudsman
Complaint initiated October 16, 1998

The democratic form of governance can survive only if legal instruments are in place to protect the freedom of the media; that freedom implying both the independence of the media from governmental authorities and the impartiality of the media toward the power of the day. In such a system, the role of the media is to investigate and report on the news. That role includes questioning, probing and uncovering facts and interpreting them, but it does not include outright opposition to government, which can either entail, or be the result of, loss of objectivity. There is thus a fine line between exaggerated criticism of government amounting to opposition under the guise of reporting on one hand, and hindrance or silencing of journalistic criticism for the purpose of monitoring a hold on power, on the other. This is the range within which judicial-like arbitration of the impartiality of the news media must take place, as a legal aspect of democracy.

On September 9, 1998, Terry Milewski, a reporter for CBC Television News, presented a story in which he said, among other things, of the role of the Prime Minister's Office and the R.C.M.P. in relation to the November 1997 APEC Conference in Vancouver:

---

[204] Cross-reference to § 9.9.B.1.

Was there a secret deal to protect Indonesian President Suharto at the Asia Pacific Economic Conference summit in the fall of 1997? The images from outside last fall's APEC summit in Vancouver were alarming. Student demonstrators say their most basic rights were trampled and a public commission is about to hear those complaints. CBC News has learned that there was a concerted effort to keep a lid on protest at the summit by both the Prime Minister's Office and the RCMP. The aim was to save Indonesia's unpopular ruler from embarrassment.

. . .

Internal government documents from the Prime Minister's office and the RCMP show that they were determined to keep a lid on protests even if they had no legitimate security grounds to do so.[205]

By the time Milewski wrote his story, a panel of the R.C.M.P. Public Complaints Commission had been constituted in response to the complaints of a number of students at the University of British Columbia who had been pepper-sprayed by the police during their demonstration at the APEC conference, held on the campus of that university. One of the students had also initiated legal action in the Supreme Court of British Columbia. In Parliament, the Opposition was questioning the Government vigorously about the political influences brought to bear on the R.C.M.P. The matter had become extremely controversial.

The airing of Milewski's account of the way the students were handled during their demonstration resulted in a complaint which the Director of Communications of the Prime Minister's Office (PMO) lodged with the Ombudsman of the CBC, by way of an exchange of letters. The complaint ostensibly dealt with the content and tone of Milewski's report; in fact it also brought into issue the manner in which Milewski had developed the story.

In the initial complaint, the PMO qualified the reporting as one-sided and biased, complained of the use of confrontational language and argued that Milewski's claims were not substantiated. It also protested that Milewski had advised and conspired with one of the complainants before the R.C.M.P. Public Complaints Commission.

---

[205] The text of this report was reproduced at http://tv.cbc.ca/national/pgminfo/apec/index.html.

> Clearly, the issue here is not aggressive reporting. On the APEC matter, as with any other subject or issue, there can be no complaint against vigorous and probing journalism. It is essential in a democracy. Indeed, through the years this fair and vigilant approach has been a hallmark of the CBC. Moreover, we in this office and government have enjoyed and continue to enjoy cordial and professional relations with CBC journalists. Their standards are among the highest in the industry.
>
> What we are dealing with is a concerted campaign to, in the words of Mr. Milewski, "milk" the APEC issue, and promote a one-sided account, while working secretly with an interested party in the matter.[206]

Had the PMO restricted the complaint to the reporter in question, the matter would have been fairly simple, despite the circumstances. It extended its complaint to the CBC itself, however, thereby raising issues of fundamental principle involving the rules of democracy.

> I should also note, with some astonishment, that the CBC, which has publicly prided itself on its leadership in reporting APEC-related stories, has not reported on Mr. Milewski's conflict of interest since it became public almost a week ago. On The National last night only the most oblique and cryptic reference was made to Mr. Milewski's "correspondence that was part of the process in developing the story." None of the e-mail contents were exposed; rather, they were referred to as "private" correspondence. It is doubtful that if similar revelations came forward about any other public figure that the CBC would be so reticent.
>
> This is a serious and deeply disturbing matter. Canadians have a right to expect honest, fair and balanced reporting from the CBC. These revelations indicate that as far as APEC is concerned, the CBC has provided anything but. And that in its biased pursuits it may well have violated journalistic integrity and betrayed the confidence of Canadians.[207]

The Broadcaster replied to the accusations regarding both its reporter and itself. It started by making the rather key remark that the PMO had given wide distribution to the accusations and that this posed a threat to the CBC's reputation. It is interesting to note that the CBC phrased this defence on the grounds of potential damage to its reputation, without outright reference to its independence and therefore impartiality. It went on to remind the PMO that the CBC's coverage

---

[206] Letter of October 16, 1998, from Peter Donolo, Director of Communications in the Prime Minister's Office, to David Bazay, CBC Ombudsman.

[207] *Ibid.*

was no different from that of other news organizations and that journalists other than Milewski had reached conclusions similar to his.

> We are unaware, at this point, of any significant difference in the substance of our coverage from that of other leading journalistic outlets. Except to say that through the aggressive diligence of Terry Milewski, we were, more often than not, breaking new ground on the story, ground which other outlets covered as quickly as they could catch up. We are satisfied that our coverage has been equal—even superior to—that of other media on this story.

> Yet on any contentious and ongoing story, we are well aware that a reporter, no matter how successful and experienced he or she might be, can become so immersed in a situation that perspective could be a risk. Here, the role of the editorial desk becomes even more critical to ensure that all aspects of a case are taken into account and that fairness and balance are maintained. This is in no way a comment on the work of Terry Milewski in covering APEC—it is an honest acknowledgement of a reality well known in any newsroom and one which The National editors were very much conscious of in their vetting of the APEC stories. We state it here to assure you that much vigilance and care was taken to ensure that our coverage was a fair and accurate representation of the story as we knew it.[208]

The CBC also presented a number of other arguments related to the veracity of the news and comments aired, to their importance and to the absence of systematic bias. It also emphasized the need to report the news.

> We recognize, of course, that both the RCMP and the PMO have the absolute right to refuse to speak and to cite the Public Inquiry as the proper place for these answers to emerge. But that is a judgment call on your part. It is also possible to argue that there is an inherent and overriding reason to satisfy the public's need to hear from its leaders now, since the details and the rationale behind what transpired at APEC and the events leading up to it are—for whatever reason—in the public domain at this moment.[209]

---

[208] Letter of October 19, 1998, from Bob Culbert, Executive Director, TV News, Current Affairs and Newsworld; Sandy McKean, Head, TV News, and Kelly Crighton, Executive Producer, The National, to Peter Donolo, Director of Communications in the Prime Minister's Office.

[209] *Ibid.*

In further correspondence, the PMO continued its attack on the national broadcaster in a manner that could be interpreted as being politically aimed at deflating criticism. The core of the CBC's last formal response on the matter was to attempt to redirect the PMO's generalized attack toward a professional assessment of Milewski's reporting.

> What developed therefore is a perfectly acceptable and proper process in a thorough journalistic investigation—an aggressive reporter developing a strong point of view on a major controversial story. It was not a point of view he started out with, but a point of view developed through rigorous research and careful analysis of the events at APEC.

> What was that point of view? All the facts did not add up; the civil liberties of Canadians may have been restricted; it was important to find out to the best of his abilities exactly what happened; why did the RCMP act the way they did; is this how peaceful protest is normally handled in Canada; were the RCMP under special instructions; if so, was there any information available to them to justify these instructions?[210]

Milewski agreed with the CBC to be withdrawn from the story. Continual reporting was carried out by someone else. The outcome of this very public and rather unusual confrontation was somewhat clouded by side issues. Milewski was suspended on two separate occasions, the first time, for three days, as a result of having communicated with one of the complainant students in a manner that could be interpreted as being partial. The second suspension was for having written an opinion-editorial in the November 10, 1998, edition of the *Globe and Mail*, in which he referred to a campaign by the government to derail his coverage of the APEC story. This suspension lasted 15 days.

The lesson to be drawn from this case is that the democratic requirement for an impartial and unfettered fifth estate may not be written, but it is nevertheless valid and necessary. While a broadcaster should make every effort to retain its own and its reporters' objectivity, the government must exercise the self-restraint needed to enable news organizations to report within legal bounds and without political intimidation.

---

[210] Letter of November 6, 1998, Bob Culbert and Sandy McKean to Peter Donolo.

§ 3.14.3[211]
Government of British Columbia v. David Black Newspapers
Decision of the British Columbia Press Council; January 15, 1999[212]

What is the role of the media and in what manner ought media outlets use their independence vis-à-vis government in respect of issues of significant public debate? These are the questions which arose out of the public interest in the conclusion of the *Nisga'a Final Agreement* by Canada, British Columbia and the Nisga'a First Nation in 1998.

David Black, the owner of a chain of community newspapers in the province, ordered that his editors take a position of opposition to the treaty and instructed that a series of columns about the treaty and its potential effects be run by his papers. The Government of British Columbia filed a complaint with the province's Press Council, asking that the directive be retracted, alleging that it was in contradiction to the provision of the Council's *Code of Practice* which defended newspapers' "exercise of the widest possible latitude in expressing opinions."[213] The Council made a decision in which it dismissed the complaint. It contrasted the papers' right to expression of opinion with the controversiality of those opinions and their unpopularity with the government. The Council also looked at the matter from the perspective of its view of the public interest.

> With respect to the government's complaint that the directive was a breach of the duty of the David Black newspapers to act in the public interest, the Council held that by leading comment, widening the debate and presenting a range of diverse opinions on matters of public significance, newspapers demonstrate their social responsibility and, at the same time, perform a valuable public service.[214]

While the ruling relied further on the principle that in a free and democratic society newspapers were the public watchdogs of government and that Mr. Black's actions were fully consistent with the traditions of newspapers in democratic societies, it detracted from the strength of the decision by confirming the private ownership

---

[211] Cross-reference to § 3.3.C.3.
[212] http://www.bcpresscouncil.org/reports/1999.html/govtbc.
[213] British Columbia Press Council Code of Practice, s. 4.
[214] Decision of the British Columbia Press Council, January 15, 1999, para. 12.

aspect of the issue, in that the ultimate obligation and right to direct the editorial policy of a paper is the owner's.

See also *Speaker's Ruling on Disclosure of Ontario Liberal Caucus Meeting of February 25, 2004*, Hansard, March 26, 2004, p. 1712.

3.15 ISSUE: FOREIGN RELATIONS BASED ON POPULAR LEGITIMACY

§ 3.15.1[215]
Decision regarding the Referendum on Accession to NATO
Constitutional Court of Hungary; October 14, 1997
Decision No. 52/1997 (X.14)

The foreign relations of a country consist not only of its web of alliances, but also of the image which, in a global community of sovereign countries, it wants to project of itself to the outside world. The question of whether this aspect of a country's public life is reserved, as an exercise of power, for the political executive, or, as an added legal measure of democracy, it is opened to the citizenry for exercise and influence through means determined by the constitution and by statute, is fundamental. The involvement of the people in decision-making on matters of foreign relations is certainly a legitimate factor in determining both the legality and the political acceptability of such matters.

In the Hungary of the post-Communist era, which started in 1989, the most significant decision in the realm of foreign relations, the realignment of the country into membership in the North Atlantic Treaty Organization, was made subject to democratic and legal processes. A referendum on accession to the Organization was scheduled for November 16, 1997.[216] Despite the overwhelming support of the

---

[215] International comparison.
[216] The political legal rules on referenda in general and, in context, those applicable to referenda in Hungary's post-Communist system in particular are set out in a Hungarian language book entitled *Képviselet és Választás a Parlamenti Jogban* by Professor Màrta Dezso, published by Kozgazdasàgi és Jogi Konyvkiado, Budapest, 1995. See in particular pp. 121-135.

elites and the massive consensus of public opinion for accession, six deputies addressed a petition to the Constitutional Court, seeking to stop the holding of the referendum by pleading that the then current law on referenda[217] did not accord with section 2 of the Constitution which set out the fundamental political legal characteristics of Hungary and with section 28, which determined the constitutional modalities of referenda. This constitutional petition was launched while Parliament was in the last stages of enacting a new referendum law. The NATO issue also became closely tied to another proposed referendum, that one on foreign ownership of real property. The entire procedure was thus rooted in politics and intensely linked to parliamentary procedure.

The Constitutional Court overturned a 1993 precedent in which it had held that the highest form of popular sovereignty was exercised through elected representatives. It decided, rather, that direct voting by referendum is the highest form of exercise of the people's sovereignty. Although the referendum is an exceptional measure, it has precedence over the exercise of power through parliamentary representation. The court also had to decide what the relation was between the compulsory and optional types of referenda.

> In contrast to its former decision, in 1997 the Constitutional Court decided (52/1997, issued on October 14) that although the exercise of direct power is an exceptional form, it has precedence over the exercise of power though [sic] representation, if people make use of it.

> The decision of the Court stated that: "The connection between the two types of referenda, regulated in par. 28/C (2) and par. 28/C (4) respectively, is determined by the fact that the exercise of direct power as one form of exercising popular sovereignty, as determined in par. 2 (2) of the Constitution, is performed in its integrity by the obligatory referendum, as ruled in par. 28/C (2). The exercise of direct power is an exceptional form of exercising popular sovereignty, which, however, in its exceptional performance is superior to representative power. Thus, an obligatory referendum has precedence over a discretionary referendum, specified in par. 28/C (4), which contains the elements of exercising both representative and direct power."

> According to the Constitution, an initiative to call for an [...] obligatory referendum has precedence from the moment when the collected sig-

---

[217] Law XVII of 1989.

316 / LAW OF DEMOCRATIC GOVERNING – VOLUME II: JURISPRUDENCE

natures are handed over to the Speaker of the House. Afterwards, all decisions which are related to discretionary referendum initiatives (presented during the time of collecting signatures on the same subject matter) should be suspended or their implementation should be postponed until the signatures are validated. If as a result of validation the referendum must be held, this would exclude the discretionary referendum.[218]

The primary effect of this decision was to enable the referendum on NATO accession to proceed. A further outcome was to strengthen the role of the Constitutional Court as the guarantor of legality in the Hungarian democratic regime to the point where it is possible to say that among democratic systems, Hungary's Constitutional Court, and therefore its reliance on law as the primary instrument of governance, is among the most extensive.

> Consequently, it established a new scope of authority for itself, which otherwise only the parliament could do. In addition, the Court ensured a much wider authority for itself with respect to constitutional complaints regarding referendum initiatives, and to make the new legislation "perfect" it even formed the new paragraph.

> This is not simply an activist understanding of the role of the Constitutional Court but law-making in the strict sense of the word, which the Constitutional Court has never had the authority to do. As a result of this decision, the Constitutional Court did not only become a law-maker but made a political decision in the obviously political (and not constitutional, although disguised that way) debate between the government and opposition parties, and thus undertook an active role in determining a political controversy.[219]

> The immediate impact was to give the people of Hungary a voice in the determination of the direction in which the country would realign its foreign relations. After forty years of forced alliance with the Soviet Union and membership in the by-then defunct Warsaw Pact, the outcome of an overwhelming choice in favour of NATO membership was not a great surprise. The element to note in this process from the political law perspective was the convergence of public decision-making on the basis of legal norms as framed by the constitutional Court, with the development of a broad political consensus among the people and the

---

[218] *Hungarian Political Yearbook 1998*, p. 47. In the original, this work is entitled *Magyarország politikaièvkonyve 1998*, published by Demokràcia Kutatàsok Magyar Kozpontya Alapitvàny, Budapest, 1998.
[219] *Ibid*, p. 49.

political parties which spoke for them. The construction of a new foreign policy on foundations of popular legitimacy, is, without a doubt, one of the legal aspects integral to democracy.

In a broad perspective, this case provides a good example of the pivotal role played by the constitutional Court, and hence of law and legality in the democratisation of Hungary after the collapse of Communism. Perhaps in no other country on the path of democratisation has a constitutional court developed such an extensive jurisdiction as in Hungary. This regime has even been characterized by one expert as a "courtocracy."[220]

The Rule of Law

Of all constitutional principles, the rule of law played a special, symbolic role: it represented the essence of the system change, being the watershed between the nondemocratic, nonconstitutional, socialist system and the new constitutional democracy. Therefore the rule of law was the constitutional concept in the frame of which the difference in nature and characteristics of system change could find their expression. Even the traditional difference between the formal and substantial concepts of the *Rechtsstaat* (the formally legal functioning of state machinery as opposed to the protection of fundamental rights) was revived and had to be reinterpreted. There were two ways in which the system change could be adhered to: on the one hand, a rather value-neutral, formalistic approach, emphasizing procedural guarantees, legal continuity and, above all, legal certainty; and on the other hand substantive justice, allowing exceptions from formal guarantees of rights under exceptional circumstances and emphasizing the total break with previous law. Both conceptions have become embedded in wider concepts of "restoration" or a "prospective" type of transition, interdependently, again, with the particular history of the given countries. Hungary (and especially the Constitutional Court, which elaborated the concept) opted for a more neutral and formalistic understanding of the rule of law. From 1965 on, state socialism in this country was mild; steps toward a market economy had been taken in the 1980s, and suppression of freedom was not omnipresent or brutal. Paradoxically, even these facts gave the rule of law a unique importance in Hungary: here—and only here—the contrast with the old regime was absolute. The Court made both the politicians and the population conscious of the secure protection of constitutional rights (and through this, of the difference between permission and right) and aware of one of the most important characteristics of the rule of law: political intentions can only be implemented lawfully and within the

---

[220] Professor Kim Scheppele, University of Pennsylvania.

framework of the Constitution—not vice-versa, as before, when the law was conceived of as merely a political tool.[221]

3.16 ISSUE: ACKNOWLEDGEMENT OF THE DEMOCRATIC NATURE OF A FOREIGN COUNTRY

§ 3.16.1

Hlavaty v. Canada (Minister of Employment & Immigration)
Federal Court of Canada – Trial Division; October 27, 1993
(1993), 69 F.T.R. 259

The assessment by a Canadian court of the democratic nature of another country can be merely responsive to an allegation, made on the part of a non-politicized person in the course of attempting to settle in Canada, as was the case in *Yakhin*. Such an analysis is even more stark in a case such as this, where the applicant himself is not only a political actor, but is plainly anti-democratic.

Hlavaty landed at Gander off a Prague-Havana flight and made a claim for Convention refugee status on November 27, 1990. The Convention Refugee Determination Division (CRDD) of the Immigration and Refugee Board (IRB) rejected his application. He appealed to the Federal Court of Canada – Trial Division and in the present judgment, the court dismissed the appeal on the basis, primarily, of its own analysis of the nature of what by then had become the Czech Republic, as well as on the basis of its agreement with the reasoning of the CRDD.

Hlavaty was a Slovak nationalist. In November, 1989, in the midst of Czechoslovakia's velvet revolution, he attended a rally against Communist rule, which earned him a beating by police and acts of harassment. In March, 1990, by which time Czechoslovakia had become a democratic State, Hlavaty joined the Slovak National Party for the purpose of promoting a separate Slovakia. Throughout 1990, he par-

---

[221] *Constitutional Judiciary in a New Democracy: The Hungarian Constitutional Court,* Solyom, Laszlo and Georg Brunner, The University of Michigan Press, Ann Arbor, 2000.

ticipated in Slovak separatist activities. He alleged that as a consequence of this, he suffered detentions, beatings and an arrest at the
hands of the Czech police. However, by his own admission, the applicant helped to celebrate the anniversary of a former Fascist dictator
of Slovakia and took part in a demonstration against linguistic rights
for minorities within Slovakia.

On the basis of the evidence, the CRDD refuted Hlavaty's allegations
that he was persecuted or that if he returned, he would be. Rather, it
held that:

> These police tactics to silence a person's freedom of expression and of
> association belong to the context of the former totalitarian regime. There
> is no mention anywhere in the documents which date from November
> 1989 of police employing these methods to silence dissent.
>
> On the contrary, there is much in the documents about the progression
> towards developing Slovak national identity, vigorous debate about the
> language laws, the separatist policies formulated by various political
> factions and their opponents, the early calls for a referendum on the
> issue of Slovak statehood by President Havel himself...[222]

The CRDD also believed that the conduct of the Czech police and law
enforcement authorities was controlled, that the applicant would,
upon return, be free to express his beliefs and to engage in political
activities and that there had been improvements in the system of
criminal justice, as well as significant changes to the judicial process.

By the time the Federal Court rendered its judgment on October 27,
1993, not only had Communism ended in Czechoslovakia, but an
independent Slovak Republic had been founded on January 1, 1993.
The court's analysis consisted of a combination of political circumstances as well as substantive and procedural legal factors and the
application of relevant principles of immigration law.

Lifting determining factors from an American report on human rights
practices in the former Czechoslovakia that had been prepared as
long ago as 1990, the court reasoned that:

- with the disbanding of the State security apparatus, illegal practices
  and abuses of human rights had ended;

---

[222] (1993), 69 F.T.R. 259 at 261.

. . .

- legislation providing for the rights of free speech, assembly, association, and press was adopted, and the citizenry embraced these rights to create an active, pluralistic political life[223]

- persons charged with crimes had the right to be arraigned before a judge within 24 hours and this right was observed in practice;

. . .

- persons charged with criminal offences are entitled to fair and open public trials;[224] and

- there are no political prisoners.[225]

The sum of these political legal circumstances amounted to a country in which the rule of law prevailed, constituting the democratic application of criminal law, thus avoiding any fear of persecution on the part of Hlaverty for his political views and activities.

The court also took into consideration the changing nature of the political system in Czechoslovakia and relied on the doctrine of cessation in reinforcing its ruling.

> Cessation is not a decision to be taken lightly on the basics of transitory shifts in the political landscape, but should rather be reserved for situations in which there is reason to believe that the positive conversion of power structures is likely to last. This condition is in keeping with the forward-looking nature of the refugee definition, and avoids the disruption of protection in circumstances where safety may be only a temporary situation.[226]

---

[223] *Ibid.* at 264.
[224] *Ibid.*
[225] *Ibid.*
[226] *Ibid.* at 263.

§ 3.16.2
Yakhin v. Canada (Minister of Citizenship & Immigration)
Federal Court of Canada – Trial Division; September 18, 1996
(1996), 1996 CarswellNat 1932
-and-
Kadenko v. Canada (Solicitor General)
Federal Court of Canada – Trial Division; October 15, 1996;
(1996), 206 N.R. 272[227]

This judgment arose from the claims of five members of the Yakhin family for refugee status in Canada. The Yakhins were Muslim Tartars who emigrated from the Soviet Union to Israel in 1991 on the basis that Mrs. Yakhin's mother had been Jewish. Their applications to enter Canada as convention refugees were based on allegations that the entire family had undergone persecution in Israel because of their nationality and religion. The procedure of the Yakhin family was not unique. From 1992 on, a number of Israeli citizens, most of them originally immigrants from the Soviet Union who could not integrate into Israeli society, sought entry into Canada as political asylum seekers or as would-be convention refugees. Some of these applications were granted.[228] That of the Yakhins was denied, first by the Convention Refugee Determination Division of the Immigration and Refugee Board, and later by the Federal Court of Canada – Trial Division.

The interest of the *Yakhin* case in particular is that among those in this category, it is one in which the Canadian court based its finding on the unequivocal declaration that the foreign country against policies and/or practices of which allegations of persecution had been made, was generally thought of as being democratic in nature and was in fact so. The testimony of the applicants' experience was declared to lack credibility in comparison to the massive documentary evidence assembled regarding the nature of governance in Israel.

Significantly, the court's ruling on the democratic nature of Israel was not an impressionistic or unsubstantiated declaration, but rather the result of a detailed and thoroughly documented analysis. The court

---

[227] Leave to appeal refused (1997), 218 N.R. 80 (note) (S.C.C.).
[228] "Fleeing the promised land," *Maclean's Magazine*, January 13, 1997, p. 58.

relied on expert reports which set out the specific evidence of democracy as including the following elements, and it even cited many of these criteria in the judgment:

- a constitutional democracy, that is a country founded on the basis of a democratic constitution;

- a democratic form of government, including a state of law, free elections and universal suffrage;

- a charter of rights and the country's participation in international treaties on human rights;

- an independent judiciary, professionally composed;

- access to the courts and the availability of judicial recourse;

- governmental and police protection of citizens, including legal protection for identifiable groups;

- freedom of the press;

- freedom of religion; and

- the availability of recourse through non-governmental organizations.

While noting that no country is entirely free of problems of discrimination, the court concluded that that overwhelming evidence of the democratic structure of, and governmental processes within, Israel, when considered together with the programs of assistance for immigrants from the Soviet Union, could only lead it to reject the applications.

This is the judicial standard of analysis of a country's democratic nature: overwhelming evidence of democratic structure and processes.

3.17 ISSUE: THE DILEMMAS OF DEMOCRACY

3.17.A—THE INTERNAL DILEMMA: THE TRADE-OFF BETWEEN HUMAN RIGHTS FOR DOMESTIC ENEMIES OF DEMOCRACY AND NATIONAL SECURITY

See *Suresh v. Canada (Minister of Citizenship & Immigration)*, 208 D.L.R. (4th) 1 (S.C.C.).

3.17.B—THE EXTERNAL DILEMMA: THE TRADE-OFF BETWEEN THE EXPORT OF DEMOCRATIC IDEAS AND THE FORCEFUL IMPOSITION OF DEMOCRATIC INSTITUTIONS

See *New Partnership for Africa's Development*, Africa Action Plan Highlights, 2002 G-8 Meeting, Final Communiqué, June 27, 2002; *Declaration and Plan of Action to Strengthen Democracy*, Organization of American States Summit of the Americas, Final Communiqué, April 22, 2001 and *Bush Plan for Middle East Peace*, Speech by President George W. Bush in the Rose Garden, June 24, 2002.

4

SOVEREIGNTY, LEGITIMACY AND GOVERNANCE

4.1 GENERAL PRINCIPLES

See Volume I, Chapter 4.

4.2 ISSUE: CHARACTERIZATION OF "CANADA"[1]

See *Jones v. Canada* (Attorney General) (1974), [1975] 2 S.C.R. 182 (S.C.C.).

---

§ 4.2.1[2]
Reference re Legislative Authority of Parliament of Canada
Supreme Court of Canada; March 20, 1979
(1979), 102 D.L.R. (3d) 1

The subject matter to which the Government of Canada asked the Supreme Court of Canada to address its attention in this case was the ability of the federal authorities alone to reform the Senate. In conducting its analysis, the court looked primarily to the original text of the Constitution, the *British North America Act, 1867*.[3] The structure of that text, the framework of the country which it established, as well as the history of the amendments made to the *British North America Act* after 1867 all led the court to emphasize the federal nature of the Dominion and the consequential distinction between the legislative

---

[1] Cross-reference to § 1.2 and 1.3.D.
[2] Cross-reference to § 1.2.1, 8.2.A.1 and 8.2.B.1.
[3] R.S.C. 1985, Appendix II, No. 5; 30 and 31 Victoria; c. 3 (U.K.).

powers attributed to the Canadian or federal Parliament and those attributed to the legislative assemblies of the various provinces. It was against this background that the court found it necessary to examine the term of art, namely "the Constitution of Canada," used in subsection 91(1) of the *British North America Act*, added by the 1949 amendment.[4] This, in turn, required the analysis of the meaning of "Canada."

In the opinion of the Supreme Court, "the word 'Canada' as used in s. 91(1) does not refer to Canada as a geographical unit but refers to the juristic federal unit."[5] If this word does not refer to the geographical unit, we may also conclude that in this context, it does not mean the political unit either, the sovereign country of Canada. Thus, while in its generally accepted political usage "Canada" refers to the entire country, in the strict legal sense, it designates the federal level of State and governmental power. The court went on to reinforce this conclusion by adding that the "Constitution of Canada" is only that portion of the *British North America Act, 1867* which constitutes federal, as distinct from provincial, government. We may, perhaps, also draw the implication that the term "laws of Canada" means federal laws only.[6]

This use of terminology was followed in the *Canadian Charter of Rights and Freedoms*, where so indicated by the context.

---

§ 4.2.2[7]
Reference re Secession of Québec
Supreme Court of Canada; August 20, 1998
(1998), 161 D.L.R. (4th) 385

The three questions addressed by the Government of Canada to the Supreme Court in this reference were whether Québec can secede unilaterally in domestic law, whether it can do so pursuant to international law, and in case of conflict between the two, which prevails. These questions go to the very heart of the statehood of Canada. They

---

[4] *British North America Act (No. 2)*, 1949, 13 Geo. VI, c. 81 (U.K.); repealed by the *Constitution Act, 1982*.

[5] (1979), 102 D.L.R. (3d) 1 at 12.

[6] See *Canadian Pacific Ltd. v. Quebec North Shore Paper Co.* (1976), 71 D.L.R. (3d) 111 (S.C.C.). [See § 1.3.D.1.]

[7] Cross-reference to §1.2.3, 2.4.5, 3.1, 4.3.1, 4.6.2, 10.2.1 and 11.2.C.1.

call into contention the fundamental nature and characteristics of Canada as a State among the states of the international community.

The doctrines applicable to "statehood" in public international law hold that a State requires the simultaneous convergence of four factors: a territory, a people, a government and the capacity to engage in foreign relations. With Confederation in 1867, Canada acquired the first three of these. In the course of its constitutional development, the fourth criterion evolved more gradually, but has been complete for several decades. Canada is thus, undeniably, a State.

Each State is characterized by specific political legal attributes. In the case of Canada, the principal such attribute was that specified in the Preamble to the 1867 *British North America Act*: this country was designed to have a governmental system similar in principle to that of the United Kingdom. This similarity included, but was not restricted to the continuity of constitutional principles, including democratic institutions and the rule of law, as well as the continuity of the exercise of sovereign power transferred from the United Kingdom to the two levels of government within Canada. Canada's attributes were fashioned and explained further in a number of constitutional and other statutes and in the judgments of senior courts. Some of these were explicitly stated while others could be implied from these texts and from conventions and practices.

The Supreme Court of Canada saw, in the way it needed to answer the first of the three questions posed to it here, the opportunity to further define and expand on the way it perceived Canada as a political legal entity, on the way it characterized this country.

> The "Constitution of Canada" certainly includes the constitutional texts enumerated in s. 52(2) of the *Constitution Act, 1982*. Although these texts have a primary place in determining constitutional rules, they are not exhaustive. The Constitution also "embraces unwritten, as well as written rules," as we recently observed in the *Provincial Judges Reference, supra*, at para. 92. Finally, as was said in the *Patriation Reference, supra*, at p. 874, the Constitution of Canada includes the global system of rules and principles which govern the exercise of constitutional authority in the whole and in every part of the Canadian state.

> These supporting principles and rules, which include constitutional conventions and the workings of Parliament, are a necessary part of our Constitution because problems or situations may arise which are not

expressly dealt with by the text of the Constitution. In order to endure over time, a constitution must contain a comprehensive set of rules and principles which are capable of providing an exhaustive legal framework for our system of government. Such principles and rules emerge from an understanding of the constitutional text itself, the historical context, and previous judicial interpretations of constitutional meaning. In our view, there are four fundamental and organizing principles of the Constitution which are relevant to addressing the question before us (although this enumeration is by no means exhaustive): federalism; democracy; constitutionalism and the rule of law; and respect for minorities.[8]

The court went on to examine and explain each of these characteristics. In crafting the constitution of 1867 as an act of nation-building,

> Federalism was a legal response to the underlying political and cultural realities that existed at Confederation, political leaders told their respective communities that the Canadian union would be able to reconcile diversity with unity.[9]

The court went on to emphasize the common political and legal nature of federalism as that part of the national fabric which recognizes the diversity of the component parts of the country and which facilitates democratic participation by a combination of geographic and substantive jurisdictional distribution of power and powers.

While federalism was welcomed by the original Maritime partners in Confederation, Nova Scotia and New Brunswick, it had particular significance for Québec.

> The principle of federalism facilitates the pursuit of collective goals by cultural and linguistic minorities which form the majority within a particular province. This is the case in Quebec, where the majority of the population is French-speaking, and which possesses a distinct culture. This is not merely the result of chance. The social and demographic reality of Quebec explains the existence of the province of Quebec as a political unit and indeed, was one of the essential reasons for establishing a federal structure for the Canadian union in 1867. The experience of both Canada East and Canada West under the *Union Act, 1840* (3 & 4 Vict.), c. 35, had not been satisfactory. The federal structure adopted at Confederation enabled French-speaking Canadians to form a numerical

---

[8] (1998), 161 D.L.R. (4th) 385 at 403, para. 32.

[9] *Ibid.* at 407, para. 43.

majority in the province of Quebec, and so exercise the considerable provincial powers conferred by the *Constitution Act, 1867* in such a way as to promote their language and culture. It also made provision for certain guaranteed representation within the federal Parliament itself.[10]

In the sense of this judgment, democratic political institutions include freely elected representative legislative bodies at the federal and provincial levels. It is important to note that the court uses the verb "to include." It explains this choice by noting that the concept of democracy is not concerned only with the process of government. Rather, it goes on, "democracy is fundamentally connected to substantive goals, most importantly, the promotion of self-government."[11] Despite this minor departure, it is clear that the court holds that democracy is primarily the establishment and functioning of freely elected legislative bodies.

The highlight of the analysis of democracy as one of the fundamental characteristics of Canada is the drawing of the common thread of law and politics through it.

> The consent of the governed is a value that is basic to our understanding of a free and democratic society. Yet democracy in any real sense of the word cannot exist without the rule of law. It is the law that creates the framework within which the "sovereign will" is to be ascertained and implemented. To be accorded legitimacy, democratic institutions must rest, ultimately, on a legal foundation. That is, they must allow for the participation of, and accountability to, the people, through public institutions created under the Constitution. Equally, however, a system of government cannot survive through adherence to the law alone. A political system must also possess legitimacy, and in our political culture, that requires an interaction between the rule of law and the democratic principle. The system must be capable of reflecting the aspirations of the people. But there is more. Our law's claim to legitimacy also rests on an appeal to moral values, many of which are imbedded in our constitutional structure. It would be a grave mistake to equate legitimacy with the "sovereign will" or majority rule alone, to the exclusion of other constitutional values.[12]

Constitutionalism and the rule of law is also explained as one of the foundations of the Canadian State. This explanation is closely linked

---

[10] *Ibid.* at 413, para. 59.

[11] *Ibid.* at 415, para. 64.

[12] *Ibid.* at 416-417, para. 67.

to the primacy of law among the instruments of governance and the requirement for other instruments and for governmental action to be in accordance with instruments of a legal nature, arranged in that internal hierarchy, with the Constitution at the apex of the political legal system.

> The constitutionalism principle bears considerable similarity to the rule of law, although they are not identical. The essence of constitutionalism in Canada is embodied in s. 52(1) of the *Constitution Act, 1982*, which provides that "[t]he Constitution of Canada is the supreme law of Canada, and any law that is inconsistent with the provisions of the Constitution is, to the extent of the inconsistency, of no force or effect." Simply put, the constitutionalism principle requires that all government action comply with the Constitution. The rule of law principle requires that all government action must comply with the law, including the Constitution. This Court has noted on several occasions that with the adoption of the *Charter*, the Canadian system of government was transformed to a significant extent from a system of Parliamentary supremacy to one of constitutional supremacy. The Constitution binds all governments, both federal and provincial, including the executive branch (*Operation Dismantle Inc. v. The Queen*, [1985] 1 S.C.R. 441 at p. 455, 18 D.L.R. (4th) 481). They may not transgress its provisions; indeed, their sole claim to exercise lawful authority rests in the powers allocated to them under the Constitution, and can come from no other source.[13]

Finally, the court explores the protection of minorities as being a specifically Canadian characteristic. Most noticeable among the kinds of measures involved here are the protection of minority religious and educational rights, minority language rights and aboriginal and treaty rights.

The highlighting of these defining factors was no mechanical enumeration by the court. In the immediate, it served to resolve the specific set of issues put before the justices. It enabled them, and the readers of their opinion, to better see and to more clearly understand the nature of Canada. For the future, this listing of characteristics, defined as constitutional principles, has opened up new avenues of litigation, through which to continue the development of Canada as a country and as a democracy, in the broadest sense of that expression, as the main essence of its political legal system.

---

[13] *Ibid.* at 418-419, para. 72.

§ 4.2.3

Lalonde v. Ontario (Commission de restructuration des services de santé)
Ontario Court of Appeal; December 7, 2001
(2001), 208 D.L.R. (4th) 577[14]

The facts and the socio-political stresses underlying this litigation were most appropriate for the court to rise above the mere technicalities of the litigation and to make new political law.

One of the cornerstones of the program of the Progressive Conservative government which came to power in Ontario in 1995, under the leadership of Premier Mike Harris, was the reduction of government expenditures. This program was carried into the field of health care, along with a number of other sectors of governmental activity. Thus, in April, 1996, a Health Services Restructuring Commission was established. It became the province's instrument in recommending the closure of entire hospitals and the reduction of services performed by others throughout Ontario. Among other recommendations, the Commission proposed to close the Montfort Hospital in Ottawa, the only health care institution in the province operating primarily in the French language.

The Montfort closure recommendation immediately aroused extreme social and political controversy. A movement formed for the purpose of keeping the hospital open and active was headed by Lalonde, a former mayor of Vanier, a predominantly Francophone suburb of Ottawa. She was successful in uniting the local ethno-cultural community and the Francophone population of all of Ontario. Even Lucien Bouchard, the Premier of Québec, otherwise not a participant in such matters beyond the borders of his province, spoke in favour of maintaining Montfort. When all political pressure failed to influence the Ontario government, Lalonde had to resort to legal action. She applied to have the Commission's closure decision set aside on the ground that it offended section 15(1) of the *Charter*, the equality rights provision, or alternatively that it was a violation of the principle of protection of minorities, or on administrative law grounds, in that it was patently unreasonable. The court focused on the constitutional aspects of the pleadings, and in particular on the issue of protection

---

[14] Additional reasons at (2002), 2002 CarswellOnt 336 (Ont. C.A.).

of minorities, derived from the Québec Secession Reference [see § 4.2.2].

In this case, the Ontario Superior Court took the protection of minorities reasoning much further than it had been developed up to then and in fact based on this ground a political legal statement as to the character of Canada as a State. The court's view of Canada was, pointedly, not only at odds with the view prevailing among the members of the current Government of Ontario, but was infinitely more generous than the government's.

The judgment traced the highlights of the Franco-Ontarian community which, even today, comprises ten per cent of the population of the province. It recognized the particular needs of this community to have its collective existence protected. It realized that the vehicle for such protection was the language of institutions and concluded that the Montfort Hospital was a necessary institution for the provision of such linguistic protection.

> What is at stake in these proceedings is not simply a minority language issue or a minority education issue. What is at stake is a minority culture issue. The Commission's Directions bring into play considerations bearing upon the preservation and protection of not just language and not just education and, indeed, not just health services. They bring into play a combination of all of these concepts plus the factor of linguistic and cultural symbolism which, according to Dr. Bernard, makes Hopital Montfort "une institution qui incarne et evoque la culture francaise en Ontario."
>
> . . .
>
> Thus, this is not a minority language rights case. This is not a minority language education rights case. This is a case about whether the rights of the Franco-Ontarian minority have been undermined by the Directions of the Commission in a fashion which violates the "protection of minorities" principles, one of the fundamental organizing principles underlying the Canadian Constitution.
>
> . . .
>
> What the Applicants are seeking to do, he submits, is to extend the constitutionalization of minority language and minority language education rights into new areas - to French language health services and to

French language post-secondary medical education - which are not already provided for in what he labels as an "exhaustive" code of minority language rights established in sections 16 to 23 of the *Charter*.[15]

Having noted the constitutional significance of the protection of minorities and indeed having elevated this to being an element of the "Canadian-ness" of the state, the court acted in a fully consequential manner. It found that the Health Services Restructuring Commission was bound, in its decision making, to take account not only of the health care, social and economic considerations of its mandate, but to temper its recommendations with the broader view encompassing the very nature and character of Canada as a country recognizing minority protection as one of its fundamental elements.

> Given the constitutional mandate for the protection and respect of minority rights - an "independent principle underlying our constitution," a "powerful normative force" - it was not open to the Commission to proceed on a "restructured health services" mandate only, and to ignore the broader institutional role played by Hôpital Montfort as a truly francophone centre, necessary to promote and enhance the Franco-Ontarian identity as a cultural/linguistic minority in Ontario, and to protect that culture from assimilation. We find this is what the Commission did. Accordingly, its Directions cannot stand.[16]

This decision may henceforth affect not only the political legal view of Canada but also the manner of rendering public policy decisions. Given the temper of the times and the attitutde of the Government of Ontario towards its electorate, on December 13, 1999, the Attorney General announced that he would appeal.

The Ontario Court of Appeal ruled on this case on December 7, 2001, dismissing both the appeal and a cross-appeal. This decision is significant not only in its length but even more so in its fundamental re-examination of the effect of constitutional rights on the Canadian body politic. The aspect of the ruling bearing immediate effect was that, in affirming the Divisional Court's ruling to the effect that closure of the Montfort hospital would not only reduce the availability of health care services in French, but also impair Montfort's broader

---

[15] (1999), 181 D.L.R. (4th) 263 at 287-288, additional reasons at (2000), 2000 CarswellOnt 1460 (Ont. Div. Ct.), affirmed (2001), 208 D.L.R. (4th) 557 (Ont. C.A.), additional reasons at (2002), 2002 CarswellOnt 336 (Ont. C.A.).

[16] *Ibid.* at 299.

role as a linguistic, cultural and educational institution, the Court of Appeal rendered it politically impossible for the government to close this hospital.

For the longer term, the Court of Appeal set out its view of minority group language rights in the Canadian socio-political fabric.

> ...we have concluded that the Constitution's structural principle of respect for and protection of minorities is a bedrock principle that has a direct bearing on the interpretation to be accorded to the F.L.S.A. [French Laguage Services Act] and on the legality of the Commission's directions affecting Montfort.[17]

The court went on to affirm that the relevant legislation should not be interpreted on the basis of the wording of the Act alone. Rather, the constitutional principle of respect for and protection of the francophone minority in Ontario, together with the broad purposive interpretantion of language rights, should infuse political and public administration decisions such as that which the Health Services Resturcturing Commission had to make.

With the following words, the Court of Appeal opened an even greater window in the development of the principles and values of Canadian constitutionalism, thereby helping to define a more legally generous country.

> Fundamental constitutional values have normative legal force. Even if the text of the Constitution falls short of creating a specific constitutionally enforceable right, the values of the constitution must be considered in assessing the validity or legality of actions taken by government. This is a long-established principle in our law. Before the advent of the *Charter* and the constitutional entrenchment of rights and freedoms, there can be no doubt that those same rights were constitutuional values. Although they had not been crystallized in the form of entrenched and directly enforceable rights, they were regularly used by the courts to interpret legislation and to assess the legality of administrative action.[18]

See also *Gauthier c. Canada (Conseil de la Radiodiffusion & des Télécommunications)* (2001), [2000] C.S.C.R. No. 575 (S.C.C.), Federal Court of

---

[17] (2001), 208 D.L.R. (4th) 577 at 630, para. 125, additional reasons at (2002), 2002 CarswellOnt 336 (Ont. C.A.).

[18] *Ibid.* at 642, para. 174.

Appeal, file A-11-00 and *Baie d'Urfé (Ville) c. Québec (Procureur général)*, 27 M.P.L.R. (3d) 295 (S.C.C.).

4.3 ISSUE: DEFENCE OF SOVEREIGNTY BY THE STATE[19]

§ 4.3.1[20]
Reference re Secession of Quebec
Supreme Court of Canada; August 20, 1998
(1998), 161 D.L.R. (4th) 385

It is incontestable that the very existence and survival of Canada as a State united in a federal system is the most fundamental issue of the political legal life of the country. The way to resolve such an issue is not to be easily decided. During the 20th Century and indeed throughout history, many states have resorted to the force of arms to remain united. In the Canadian context, despite occasional apocalyptic writings, that is unthinkable. The viable choices are through discussion, negotiation, concession, compromise and consensus building, in short by using the vast arsenal of political means, either to frame the matter in more principled terms before an impartial and politically neutral third party capable of making authoritative decisions, in short by resorting to law and the courts, or to rely on both political and legal means. In the context of Canadian political evolution in the latter 1990's, put more simply, the question was whether or not the federal state should put the matter of Québec secession before the Supreme Court for a reference opinion as to the legalities of the matter.

The antecedents of the decision whether to involve the judiciary and the law in the State's defence of its own sovereignty are dealt with in § 4.4.2, the *Bertrand* case.

The core of this analysis is only in part the relevant point of the opinion of the Supreme Court. It is, much more pertinently, a look at the intense public debate which took place in Canada between the

---

[19] Cross-reference to § 2.4, 6.6, 6.7 and 10.8.
[20] Cross-reference to § 1.2.3, 2.4.6, 3.1, 4.2.2, 4.6.1, 10.2.1 and 11.2.C.1.

date of the announcement of Ottawa's reference to the court, on September 26, 1996, and the date of the actual hearing, on February 16-19, 1998. This period of a year and a half gave rise to a genuinely passionate debate about the appropriateness of referring the matter of secession to the Supreme Court. Statesmen, politicians, litigators and legal scholars, as well as journalists and interested members of the public offered opinions and arguments which, starting from the particulars of this case, broadened to encompass views on the role of law in democratic society, its primary or limited nature vis-à-vis politics and its utility in retaining the seamless fabric of nation-wide unity. Some of this debate was purely partisan and adversarial. Much of it, however, was a mix of intellectual and practical argumentation based on professional experience and good faith unfettered by partisanship.

The discussion was joined first by the federal Minister of Justice and Attorney General, Allan Rock, in the speech he made to the House of Commons on September 26, 1996, when he announced the reference.

> That is the reason that we became involved in the Bertrand litigation before the Supreme Court last May. It was only after the attorney general of Quebec brought a motion last spring to dismiss that litigation that we decided to involve ourselves. The attorney general of Quebec based his motion on the argument that neither the courts nor the Constitution of our country have any relevance to the process that the Quebec government intends to follow in advocating separation, but that international law alone applies.

> It was my obligation as the attorney general of Canada, and the custodian of the Constitution of our country, to respond in the courtroom. There we argued that the Constitution is indeed relevant and that the courts have jurisdiction to deal with these issues. In addition, we argued that the Quebec government would have no right under international law to a unilateral declaration of independence. We submitted that where there are some limited circumstances in which international law provides a people with the right to secede unilaterally from an existing country, none of those circumstances exist in the case of Quebec within Canada. Our conclusions in this regard are largely consistent with those of five legal experts in international law, retained in 1991 by the commission dealing with the issues relating to Quebec's sovereignty, which was established by the Government of Quebec.

> When I welcomed the decision by Mr. Justice Robert Pidgeon on August 30, I noted in particular that by deciding that the court had jurisdiction

to deal with the question before it, Judge Pidgeon had confirmed the primacy of the rule of law.

What is this "rule of law?" What is its practical meaning, its social value? Is it simply a technical nicety used to overrule democratic decisions that the federal government does not agree with?

First and foremost, the rule of law, as it has developed in Canada and in other democratic countries around the world, is not simply a legal abstraction or a technical precept; it is a living principle that is fundamental to our democratic way of life. In substance, it means that everyone in society, including ministers of government, premiers, the rich and powerful, and the ordinary citizen, is governed by the same law of the land. We are all bound by the Constitution, by the Criminal Code, by acts of Parliament and the provincial legislatures. In cases of disputes regarding the interpretation or application of the law, the courts are the final arbiter.

The great value of the rule of law is that it is democratic. Its substance is derived from our democratic institutions. It applies to everyone without qualification. It also permits democracy to flourish because it establishes a stable framework within which the democratic process can work.

The separatist leaders argue that the rule of law is simply a ruse by which the Canadian government intends to defeat an expression of democratic will by Quebecers - a trick to deny the results of a lost referendum. They argue that to require an orderly process within the legal framework would place Quebec in a strait-jacket, defeating the democratic result of a future referendum.

Such arguments are made, of course, for political effect. They are based on the pretension that the rule of law and democratic action are mutually exclusive. That is quite wrong. In fact, they co-exist in harmony. The safety of both depends upon the integrity of each and failure to observe either endangers the two at once.[21]

The most significant response to this view came from Lucien Bouchard, the Premier of Québec, on the occasion of a speech at the Faculty of Law of the Université de Montréal. Sharing with his audience a dramatically different vision of the role of law, based on a completely divergent view of the history of Confederation and of Québec within it, he said:

---

[21] Hansard, September 26, 1996, p. 4708-4709.

Le gouvernement québécois, lui, ne sera pas présent lors de ces audiences. Pas seulement parce que les juges sont nommés par le fédéral, pas seulement parce que la Cour n'a pas juridiction en droit international ou parce qu'elle n'a pas le droit moral de s'occuper de questions politiques. Alors pourquoi? Répondre à cette question, c'est aller au coeur du différend qui oppose depuis bientôt presque deux siècles la démarche québécoise à celle du Canada. La réponse, c'est la primauté de la démocratie.

L'Assemblée nationale du Québec, le gouvernement des Québécois, sont des émanations de la démocratie québécoise. Nous sommes les dépositaires des choix que font les Québécois aux élections et lors des trois référendums que trois gouvernements ont organisés. Nous respectons les décisions prises par la démocratie québécoise. Mais le droit de choisir—leur gouvernement ou leur avenir—appartient aux Québécoises et aux Québécois. Il n'appartient pas au gouvernement.

Le gouvernement du Québec ne peut donc soumettre ce droit à un tiers, à un tribunal ou à un autre gouvernement. Mettre ce droit en balance, l'exposer au jugement d'autrui, ce serait manquer à la responsabilité, au devoir que nous avons de protéger le droit de Québécois de choisir. Plaider à la Cour, ce serait cautionner, à l'avance, le jugement qui prétendrait, demain, restreindre, réduire, nier, même, le droit des Québécois.

Le consensus au Québec sur notre droit de choisir est clair, il transcende les partis. L'Assemblée nationale parle d'une seule voix. La position fédérale, elle, relève du dédoublement de personnalité. Sur la question de la souveraineté, le gouvernement fédéral déclare, d'une part, que le Canada ne peut retenir les Québécois dans la fédération contre leur gré. Mais il affirme d'autre part que, par la constitution, il détient un droit de veto sur la souveraineté du Québec, donc qu'il peut retenir les Québécois dans la fédération contre leur gré.

Ce curieux monstre à deux têtes a pris naissance le jour même de l'annonce, par Ottawa, du dépôt de son renvoi en Cour suprême, en septembre 1996. Dans un discours en Chambre, au nom du gouvernement fédéral, le ministre de la Justice—c'était Allan Rock—reconnaissait que le Québec avait parfaitement le droit de tenir un nouveau referendum sur la souveraineté et que les Québécois pouvaient, s'ils le désiraient, devenir souverains. Mais il ajoutait aussitôt qu'il faudrait d'abord «des négociations et des ententes» entre le Québec et le Canada, sur les sujets suivants—et je le cite—: «les arrangements commerciaux et économiques, les droits des citoyens de se déplacer à l'intérieur du pays, le partage de la dette et des biens publics, l'utilisation de la monnaie et une foule d'autres questions.»

. . .

Bref, le Québec a choisi de fonder la légitimité de sa question référendaire sur le débat des élus à l'Assemblée nationale. Le gouvernement fédéral, lui, a décidé de ses questions en vase clos, sans débat, unilatéralement. Il a demandé aux juges, qu'il nomme unilatéralement, de se prononcer sur la base de sa constitution, qu'il a imposée unilatéralement, et il pense qu'au terme de ce processus, il pourra torpiller, unilatéralement, la démocratie.

Il est bien sûr regrettable que le gouvernement canadien s'engage dans cette voie, qui ne lui fait pas honneur.

. . .

Qui, donc, aura le dernier mot?

Il y a deux thèses.

Selon le gouvernement fédéral, le dernier mot lui revient, à lui, en vertu d'une constitution que n'a aucun fondement démocratique et de l'interprétation qu'en ferait une Cour qu'il a lui-même nommée. M. Chrétien nous dit: l'État, c'est moi; le droit, c'est moi; le choix, c'est moi, unilatéralement. Comme au temps des Patriotes, comme au temps de l'Union forcée, comme au temps de la constitution de 1867, comme au temps du coup de force de 1982.

Selon nous, selon tous les démocrates québécois et un nombre croissant de démocrates canadiens, le dernier mot n'appartient pas à un homme, pas à un gouvernement, pas à un texte imposé d'en haut. Selon nous, le dernier mot appartient à la démocratie québécoise, au peuple québécois. Et ce mot, que sera-t-il? Ce sera le mot Oui, prononcé le jour du prochain référendum.[22]

The discussion and debate, grounded as it was on such unappeasable opposites, did not produce any genuine outcome or resolution. Each of the camps stood firm in its viewpoints. The examination of the topic was not sterile, however. It showed the extent to which each of the sets of antagonists was willing to use the law as an additional line of argumentation to achieve its political goal, or attempt to avoid the

---

[22] Speech by Québec Premier Lucien Bouchard to students at the Faculty of Law of the Université de Montréal, February 12, 1998. http://www.uni.ca/bouchard_renvoi.html

arguments of legality for fear of damaging the chance of success of its political goal. The stakes were so high that the purity of the law was not the primary consideration on anyone's mind. Both camps dealt with legal issues as handmaidens of politics. The most patent intellectual gap between them was the vision of law as an aspect of what they called "democracy," in this case meaning the will of the people, or as an impediment to it.

In the pleadings presented by the Attorney General of Canada to the Supreme Court, the federalist argument on this point was reduced to a few short paragraphs under the rubrics of "The Rule of Law" and "The Role of the Courts."

The Rule of Law

Constitutional government is predicated upon the rule of law, a concept which the Supreme Court of Canada has described as "convey[ing] [...] a sense of orderliness, of subjection to known legal rules and of executive accountability to legal authority." The rule of law assumes that adherence to a basic framework of constitutional precepts is essential to the maintenance of stability and order.

Reference Re Resolution to Amend the Constitution,
[1981] 1 S.C.R. 753 at 805-06
[hereinafter *Patriation Reference*].

. . .

The Role of the Courts

Canadian courts are the guardians of the Constitution, charged with ensuring that the rule of law prevails. This principle has been consistently affirmed, perhaps most clearly in the following passage from *Amax Potash Ltd. v. Government of Saskatchewan*:

"[...] it is the high duty of this Court to insure that the legislatures do not transgress the limits of their constitutional mandate and engage in the illegal exercise of power."

Amax Potash Ltd. v. Government of Saskatchewan,
[1977] 2 S.C.R. 576 at 590
see also: *Hunter v. Southam Inc., supra* at 155

The Queen v. Beauregard, [1986] 2 S.C.R. 56 at 71-72

Similarly, in the *Manitoba Language Reference*, the Court spoke of the "mandate of the judiciary to protect the Constitution" and of the courts' "duty of ensuring that the government complies with the Constitution" and "that the constitutional law prevails."

> *Manitoba Language Reference, supra* at 745
> see also: *Patriation Reference, supra* at 841, 877[23]

The Supreme Court could not ignore the debate raging about the legitimacy of its consideration of an issue which many in the country thought political and not legal, nor of the matter of whether it was proper for the state to defend its sovereignty and federal unity through judicial means. It could not, however, enter the debate on legal or political methods of resolution, save by legal arguments. It thus rephrased the matter for itself on the ground of whether it could undertake an advisory function pursuant to section 53 of the *Supreme Court Act*. Its answer was clear.

> There is no plausible basis on which to conclude that a court is, by its nature, inherently precluded from undertaking another legal function in tandem with its judicial duties.

> Moreover, the Canadian Constitution does not insist on a strict separation of powers. Parliament and the provincial legislatures may properly confer other legal functions on the courts, and may confer certain judicial functions on bodies that are not courts. The exception to this rule relates only to s. 96 courts. Thus, even though the rendering of advisory opinions is quite clearly done outside the framework of adversarial litigation, and such opinions are traditionally obtained by the executive from the law officers of the Crown, there is no constitutional bar to this Court's receipt of jurisdiction to undertake such an advisory role. The legislative grant of reference jurisdiction found in s. 53 of the *Supreme Court Act* is therefore constitutionally valid.[24]

Observers should not doubt that this was a masterful response to a preliminary objection which was one of the most delicate points ever presented to the court. Declining jurisdiction on this ground and throwing the substantive points into the political arena alone, without a ruling, could have assured a vastly different prospect for Canada and a degradation of the rule and the role of law in this country.

---

[23] Factum of the Attorney General of Canada, paras. 66, 69 and 70.

[24] (1998), 161 D.L.R. (4th) 385 at 397, para. 14, and 398, para. 15.

See also *Ontario (Ministry of Finance) v. Ontario (Inquiry Officer)* (1999), 118 O.A.C. 108 (Ont. C.A.), leave to appeal refused (2000), [1999] S.C.C.A. No. 134 (S.C.C.); *Therrien c. Québec (Ministre de la justice)*, 200 D.L.R. (4th) 1 (S.C.C.); *Seminole Tribe of Florida v. Florida*,[25] 116 S.Ct. 1114 (1996) and *Alden v. Maine*,[26] 144 L.Ed.2d 636 (1999).

4.4 ISSUE: DEBATE OF SOVEREIGNTY ISSUES BY CITIZENS

§ 4.4.1
Aaron v. Bouchard
(November 17, 1993); Doc. 93-CQ-44891CP (Ont. Gen. Div.)
abandoned

The federal general election of October 25, 1993, resulted in a majority government of the Liberal Party. With 54 seats out of 296 in the House of Commons, the Bloc Québécois became the Official Opposition. This political party was based solely in the Province of Québec and had a platform based primarily on achieving the sovereignty of Québec outside of Canada. The role of the Bloc in federal political life in general, and its status as the Official Opposition party in particular aroused much controversy both in Parliament and among the population at large. Within the House of Commons, the party which placed third with 52 seats, the Reform Party, contended unsuccessfully that because of the federalist stance, it should become the Official Opposition.

The electoral success of the Bloc also led citizens committed to the continuation of the federation to contest the function of this party, as well as its political program, before the courts. The case of *Aaron v. Bouchard* was the first such judicial attempt to defend Canada's federal sovereignty. Raymond Aaron, a Toronto businessman, initiated a class action suit less than a month after polling day at the election, in accordance with the *Class Proceedings Act, 1992* of Ontario. He made himself the plaintiff representing the class, which he alleged consisted of all citizens of Canada who were on the official list of electors of

---

[25] International comparison.
[26] International comparison.

either the October 25, 1993 general election, or on that of the constitutional referendum which had been held one year earlier, on October 26, 1992. In support of the class and in order to finance the action, he established a non-partisan non-profit organization entitled the "O Canada Forever Unity Organization." Aaron sought, as remedies, (a) general damages in the amount of $500 billion for loss of property values and income resulting from the unlawful activities of the defendants, "(b) a declaration that the defendants have engaged in conduct, and continue to engage in conduct, which is contrary to the Constitution of Canada and the laws of Canada including the provinces,"[27] "(c) an interim and permanent injunction restraining the defendants from pursuing any aim in breach of the Constitution of Canada and the laws of Canada including its provinces,"[28] as well as other ancillary relief. The defendants in the case were all 54 of the Members of Parliament elected under the banner of the Bloc Québécois.

While it is undeniable that since the incorporation of the *Canadian Charter of Rights and Freedoms* into the Constitution of Canada in 1982, many topics of a policy or political nature which would not have been litigated earlier were being submitted for judicial consideration, no case had yet been initiated that was so thoroughly political in nature as to examine the very continuation of Canada as a unified country. Thus, both in the sense that this case seemed to be a judicial continuation of the political battle fought on the hustings during the election campaign, and in the sense of the intensely political flavour of the case submitted for adjudication by the legal system, this case was doubly sensational.

The case of *Aaron v. Bouchard* comprised two tactical flaws which hindered its prospects for success. The first was that the quantum of the damages it sought was not only exaggerated but was also incapable of substantiation. More to the point was that in listing all 54 Bloc Members of Parliament as defendants, the plaintiff would have to serve the action on each of them, a task he would not be able to accomplish.

---

[27] Statement of Claim in *Aaron v. Bouchard* (November 17, 1993), Doc. 93-CQ-44891CP (Ont. Gen. Div.), s. 1(b)

[28] *Ibid.*, s. 1(c).

The genuine significance of the case is that it set out the general categories of pleadings, based both in law and politics, into which the arguments against the sovereignty plan of the Bloc Québécois would fall. The first of these categories related to the constitutional function which the party had achieved through the election. The Statement of Claim briefly traced the history of the Bloc and high-lighted as a ground of claim the very reason for the existence of the party, namely its aim of achieving the political sovereignty of Québec, which would necessarily involve the separation of Québec from the federal State of Canada and its institutions in all three branches of government. As the counterpart of this goal with respect to Québec, the claim stated that for citizens in the other parts of Canada, the aim of the Bloc was intimidation into appeasement in order to win con-cessions in favour of the constituents of the Bloc MP defendants, even if such concessions would hurt Canada as a whole. As an alternative, Aaron argued that since Bloc Members realized that Québecers would never choose to separate from Canada, they had in fact been elected on the basis of misrepresentations made to their own constituents and to the Canadian electorate as a whole. The conclusion of this line of reasoning was that the aim of the defendants in putting the interests of Québec ahead of those of Canada as a whole was inconsistent with their status as Members of the House of Commons, which represented the entire nation. It was also argued that a party acting in this manner could not properly be a "government in waiting" and ought therefore not to be allowed to occupy the position of "Her Majesty's Loyal Opposition." This political argument thus combined contestation of the validity of the party's goal, objection to its Members' functioning as federal parliamentarians and as the Official Opposition, and even contention of the premises of their electoral victories.

The case of Aaron's claim related to the very ideology and political goal of the Bloc, all from a legal perspective. It indicated that,

> By definition and by necessary implication, a truly sovereign Quebec is inconsistent with the sovereignty of Her Majesty the Queen in right of Canada and the sovereignty of Her Majesty the Queen in right of Quebec, and the concept of a sovereign Quebec is therefore fundamentally re-pugnant to the Constitution of Canada.[29]

---

[29] *Ibid.*, s. 17.

As reinforcement of this argument, the plaintiff relied on section 52 of the *Constitution Act, 1982*, which enshrined the twin notions that the Constitution itself is the supreme law of Canada and the ineffectiveness of any law that is inconsistent with the Constitution. In light of this reliance on the existing legal system, the argument continued, seeking authority for Québec sovereignty through the referendum to be held in Québec alone would be inconsistent with the constitutional framework of the larger federal State. In order for secession to be legally feasible, it would have to be accomplished by means of the formula for constitutional amendment inscribed into the existing Constitution, requiring the assent of both the House of Commons and the Senate, as well as that of all provincial legislatures.

The link between the political aspect of the *Aaron* case, set out above, and the constitutional legal one shown here, was made in respect of the constitutional duty of parliamentarians vis-à-vis the electorate.

> The plaintiff states that there is an implied duty arising out of custom and conduct between the electorate of Canada and all individual members of the House of Commons that each member submit to the constitution as laid down in the *Constitution Acts, 1867 to 1982* as the supreme law of the land, and relies upon the provisions of section 52 of the *Constitution Act, 1982* that "The Constitution of Canada is the supreme law of Canada," and that "Amendments to the Constitution of Canada shall be made only in accordance with the authority contained in the Constitution of Canada."[30]

An argument closely related to that of the general requirements of the Constitution and the use of the existing constitutional amendment process was the one based on citizens' rights and freedoms guaranteed in the *Charter*. The claim stated in particular that Québec's sovereignty would be inconsistent with the section 6 right of mobility throughout Canada and with the right of all Canadians, by virtue of section 15, to be treated equally.

Aaron also argued that the Bloc's plan for a sovereign Québec would be damaging on the international plane. The stability of Canada and its integrity in the family of nations were being called into question in the legal, political, economic, territorial, military and cultural fields by the Bloc's activities. Interestingly, the international argument was also applied to the field of business in particular; it was pleaded that

---

[30] *Ibid.*, s. 20.

346 / LAW OF DEMOCRATIC GOVERNING – VOLUME II: JURISPRUDENCE

Canada's competitive strength in relation to the rest of the developed world was declining for the same reasons.

Additional arguments of lesser significance were presented in respect of the impact of sovereignty on business and property values, the potential that the move toward sovereignty would generate violence, and the allegedly treasonous nature of the aim of secession.

In order to pursue the case effectively, the plaintiff needed not only to serve the court documents, but also to maintain publicity about it and in particular to finance its conduct. The reaction of the defendants to the case was to attempt to ignore it. To the extent possible, Bloc Members of Parliament would not accept service of the claim and, by strategic design, they refused to react to it. In the six months after the case was filed, Aaron thus managed to serve only 32 of the 54 sitting Bloc MPs. The Bloc's Whip, Gilles Duceppe, stated in an interview that:

> On était sûr de gagner, fini les folies. Il ne faisait aucun doute pour nous, a-t-il ajouté, que cette poursuite n'avait aucun fondement et que les motifs allégués étaient frivoles et vexatoires.[31]

After the initial flurry of media attention, interest seemed to wane quickly. At that time, the major aspect of the debate on the viability of separation was political and partisan, and the principal arenas of deliberation were Parliament and the Québec National Assembly, rather than the courts. The federalist Liberal Party in Québec was still in office, but a provincial election was approaching.

The problem of financing the case was even more difficult for Aaron. It is reported that he sought financial assistance from the federal authorities but was turned down. Appeals to the public did not generate sufficient revenue either for a long court battle such as would have been required to deal with the variety of issues raised in the case. On the other side, the management body of Parliament, the Board of Internal Economy, was asked by the Bloc Québécois to have its legal fees paid. The Board consented in the following terms:

---

[31] "Raymond Aaron renonce à sa poursuite de 500 milliards contre le Bloc," *La Presse*, Montréal, May 19, 1994, p. B6

The Board approved the reimbursement of reasonable legal fees in the event that the defence against the lawsuit was successful, on condition that legal counsel retained by the Bloc Québécois Members of the House of Commons involve General Legal Counsel of the House to ensure that questions of parliamentary law are properly represented in the proceedings.[32]

This wording leaves observers to ponder what was planned in terms of costs if Aaron's case had been successful.

The case was set down for hearing on June 13, 1994, but on May 18, Aaron abandoned the proceeding as he could no longer fund it personally. The *Aaron* case did not lead to a judgment, and in the strict sense of the term, there is no resulting jurisprudence. The action is worth noting, nonetheless, even if only through its Statement of Claim.

No concept of politics and law is more fundamental to the existence and to the continuation of a State than sovereignty. In that context, the *Aaron* case was a prime example of the extension of political discourse into the judicial arena. Essentially, every one of Aaron's pleadings, no matter how they were framed and whether they referred to a constitutional or a statutory provision or not, was simultaneously legal and political in nature. In sum, this was the continuation of the political argumentation of the 1993 election campaign in the judicial/legal environment. This case also served to emphasize both the expanded role of the judiciary in delving into political life and the public perception and acceptance of this increased role. Significantly, it is highly doubtful that such a claim could have arisen without the *Charter* being in place and without the changes in political legal culture which the *Charter* has brought about.

All of these factors, objective and subjective alike, indicate the blurring of the bounds between law and politics in respect of the vital interests of the State, such as sovereignty, and of those of the citizens committed to the survival of the State they perceive as their own. The reaction of the Bloc MPs reveals that this is true in both the plaintiff's and the defendants' camps. Finally, this case can be held as having served as a precursor for several others which were to follow in subsequent years. It was a first test in the marshalling of arguments

---

[32] Minutes of the Board of Internal Economy.

dealing with sovereignty in a manner that could be recognizable by a court and it served to crystallize an important aspect of the public legal/political debate on the prospects for Canada's future.

---

§ 4.4.2
Bertrand v. Québec (Procureur général)
Québec Superior Court; September 8, 1995
(1995), 127 D.L.R. (4th) 408
-and-
Bertrand v. Québec (Attorney General)
Québec Superior Court; August 30, 1996
(1996), 138 D.L.R. (4th) 481

This is one of the most instructive cases in the practice of Canadian political law, as well as in the effect of litigation on the development of politics.

The background leading up to the case is well worth noting. The genuine antagonists on the issue of the federal unity of Canada, as opposed to the legal ability of Québec to secede, are the federal government and the government of the Province of Québec. At the 35th federal general election held on October 25, 1993, the Liberal Party of Canada won a majority and assumed the reins of office. At the provincial election of September 12, 1994, the Parti Québécois came into power in Québec City. No two antagonists could be more diametrically opposed on the issue of the legality, or the politics, of sovereignty.

On December 6, 1994, the Government of Québec presented Bill 1, *An Act Respecting the Future of Québec*, in the National Assembly. This was seen as a step along the path that would lead to a referendum which would form the basis of Québec's secession. The referendum would be the government's authority to complete the enactment of Bill 1, to negotiate on terms of secession with the rest of Canada and eventually, to declare an independent State of Québec. In order to facilitate this process, on June 12, 1995, the Parti Québécois-led Government of Québec forged an alliance with the smaller of the two opposition parties in the National Assembly, the Action Démocratique, and with the sovereignist Official Opposition in the federal Parliament, the Bloc Québécois. The stage was set for the referendum.

On August 10, 1995, Bertrand, a former sovereignist who had recently become an ardent convert to federalism, and who practised law in Québec City, initiated a legal action designed to undermine the sovereignist alliance's plans. In itself, this was a brilliant example of the use of law and litigation to influence and impact the course of political life. The more far-reaching effect of the case was to serve as one of the catalysts for the Québec Secession Reference which the Government of Canada would eventually bring before the Supreme Court.

Bertrand brought in Québec's Attorney General, the province's Premier and its Chief Electoral Officer as defendants. For maximum effect, he also named the Leader of the Official Opposition Liberal Party of Québec, the federal Minister of Justice and the Attorneys General of all the other jurisdictions in Canada as "mis-en-cause," or impleaded party. The action was for declaratory judgment and for a permanent injunction. In essence, Bertrand argued to stop the referendum by arguments phrased and made in the most spectacular manner possible.

A)   Droit

11.   Le demandeur entend démontrer par la présente procédure que gouvernement du Québec, dans la mesure où il a l'intention d'aller de l'avant avec son avant-projet de loi sur la souveraineté du Québec et avec l'entente du 12 juin 1995, porte atteinte à ses libertés et droits garantis par la *Charte canadienne de droits et libertés*;

12.   Le demandeur entend démontrer que le gouvernement du Québec n'a pas les pouvoirs constitutionnels pour présenter, à l'Assemblée nationale du Québec un projet de loi qui vise essentiellement à sortir le Québec du reste du Canada sans utiliser la procédure de modification prévue à la *Loi constitutionnelle de 1982*;

13.   En ce faisant, le gouvernement du Québec se place hors la loi, viole la suprématie du droit, usurpe son pouvoir de dépenses et affecte des fonds public à des fins impropres et illégales;

14.   Bref, le demandeur entend démontrer que la conduite du gouvernement du Québec, de même que ses faits et gestes en regard de l'avant-projet de loi sur la souveraineté et de l'entente du 12 juin 1995, constituent un véritable coup d'État parlementaire et constitutionnel, une fraude à la Constitution canadienne et un détournement de pouvoirs qui auront

pour conséquences de violer et de nier le droits et les libertés du demandeur et ceux de tous les contribuables québécois;[33]

In the fact that this case was being made pursuant to the *Charter* and
on other rights-based arguments, in the serious and voluminous nature of the pleadings and in every other respect, this was a far more
serious attempt to use the law to defeat the political purpose and goal
of the sovereignty movement than the *Aaron* case had been. The use
of the expression "parliamentary and constitutional *coup d'État*" was,
in particular, a tool in galvanizing public and media attention.

More importantly, the filing of this action focused the attention of the
Government of Québec to the legal aspect of its political option, a
component of it to which it had so far been utterly blind. The province's response, at this stage, as later, was entirely political in nature
and based on an ideological perspective which left legal considerations in a secondary or subservient position.

> On August 24, 1995, the Attorney General of Quebec filed a motion to
> dismiss Mr. Bertrand's motion for interlocutory relief directed against
> the legality and the holding of the sovereignty referendum, arguing that
> the petitioner was seeking to have the Court interfere in the legislative
> powers, functions, and privileges of the National Assembly, and that the
> referendum and the referendum process were part of a "demarche dé-
> mocratique fondamentale qui trouve sa sanction dans le droit interna-
> tional public et dont l'opportunité n'a pas a être débattue devant les
> tribunaux." The Attorney General of Quebec added in his motion that:
> La tenue du référendum en cause a pour fondement la principe démo-
> cratique et il s'agit d'une question qui ne relève pas de la juridiction des
> tribunaux.[34]

In an initial procedural ruling, the Superior Court refused Québec's
motion to dismiss.

The more significant, substantive, judgment was handed down on
September 8, 1995.

The case presented the Superior Court a genuine dilemma in the sense
of having to deal with the legalities of a comprehensive position on

---

[33] Action pour jugement déclaratoire et injonction permanente, paras. 11-14.
[34] Newman, Warren J., *The Québec Secession Reference; The Rule of Law and the Position
of the Attorney General of Canada*, York University Press, Toronto, 1999, pp. 10-11.

the architecture of the State that was being espoused and strongly driven by the duly elected government of the day, that was intensely political, partisan, controversial and even inflammatory, and which stood the risk, if it were carried out, of being in contradiction with the established legal order. Moreover, in its analysis, the court could not simply dismiss the planned reform of the State in such a manner that its judgment would be irrelevant.

The justice chosen to hear the case was the son of a former Québec Premier who had been a federalist but a strong innovator, Jean Lesage. He broached a number of interrelated issues: Are the proposed actions of the Québec Government a form of constitutional amendment? Is this process leading to a unilateral declaration of independence? Would there be a breach of the *Charter* if the sovereignty project succeeded? Is the use of public funds for the goals set out here legal? Is there parliamentary privilege involved?

These questions, to which the court turned its mind, elicit a particularly political law-based set of issues. It is apparent that a referendum such as the one proposed here is a blending of legal and political processes, but in this context, the fundamental points to be addressed are

a) to what extent is this law and to what extent politics?

b) in what measure and in what manner does each influence the other?

c) which consideration is to prevail in the given circumstances?

d) how does a court of law deal with such an openly political matter?

Whether the issues at stake are addressed strictly from the perspective of the court itself, or from that of the observer and analyst trying to gauge the impact of divergent forces of public life on and in the judicial decision-making, the outcomes are singularly important.

Québec's first line of defence had been that the matter did not belong before the courts at all. In the government's point of view, the basis for the holding of a referendum was what it called "the democratic principle." Its pleadings seemed to give to this principle the restrictive meaning of a decision of a political nature based solely on the will of the people, separate from and seemingly outside the existing constitutional and legal order. The logical conclusion of this stance was that law and politics were at odds and that in such a case, politics could displace legality. On these grounds, Québec argued that the action breached the privileges of the National Assembly. The court rejected this line of reasoning, holding that Bill 1 was not an act of the National Assembly but a political document of the Government and therefore did not fall under the protection of parliamentary privilege.

The heart of the court's analysis was its setting out of the principles guiding its determination.

Some principles

A society's political organization is derived from the sociological and historical wellsprings of the nation. The state is a product of the political organization. Not all states necessarily exercise full sovereignty over their territory and the people that inhabit it. We have the example of the provinces in our federal system, as in any federation. International recognition is a factor in establishing a country's sovereignty.

The constitution of a sovereign country—the set of rules governing the institutions that make up its political organization—is not always written. The constitution is not a statute, in the sense that it does not emanate from the legislative authority of the country, although it may take the form of a statute. Still less may the constitution be contingent upon a statute. A statute must be consistent with the constitution, and not the converse. That is why the Constitution of Canada is characterized as the "supreme law of Canada" in the *Constitution Act, 1982* (s. 52).

The legal system is a manifestation of state sovereignty which must pass muster with the judiciary. In societies that recognize the supremacy of the law, the judiciary exists to enforce the rule of law and, pre-eminently, the laws enacted by the legislature. In a federal system, the legal system includes some rules that govern the distribution of powers between the central state and the federated states. These rules are enforceable by the courts.

The judiciary does not create the law, still less the constitution of which it is an emanation. It interprets them. It is distinguished as well from the executive authority, the government, which alone has the duty and responsibility to act on behalf of the state. The role of the judiciary is circumscribed by the existence of rules of law, which are normally contained in statutes. Now, it is recognized that some constitutional usages, referred to as conventions, are not rules enforceable by the courts: *Reference re Amendment of the Constitution of Canada (Nos. 1, 2 and 3)* (1981), 125 D.L.R. (3d) 1, [1981] 1 S.C.R. 753 *(sub nom. Re: Resolution to Amend the Constitution*, [1981] 6 W.W.R. 1 *sub nom. Attorney General of Manitoba v Attorney General of Canada)*. Contrary to a convention, a *coup d'etat* or revolution may occur, breaking the continuity of the legal order, and the courts are powerless to intervene.

A country's sovereignty is, in effect, based on the *de facto* exercise of authority over a territory and the people who inhabit it. This exercise is secured through the voluntary or involuntary acceptance of the rules, including the constitution, that govern the relationships between the state and its citizens. These rules may be altered in accordance with the procedure provided by the existing legal system, *i.e.*, by following the path of legality, but they might also be altered by a declaration by some authority that places itself over and above the existing constitution and ensures its physical control of the territory and acceptance by the population occupying that territory.

This latter course is not legal. A new legal order can arise only after the *fait accompli*.[35]

On the basis of this analysis, which could just as well have been in a political science textbook as in a constitutional law compendium as in this judgment, the court determined that Bertrand had raised a serious matter of constitutional law, given the manifest intention of the Government of Québec to reform the constitutional framework of Canada without resort to the amending formula in the text of the *Constitution Act, 1982*. Thus the preponderance of inconvenience required that, in order to serve the public interest, the court issue relief that would be practical and effective. The court refused to enjoin the holding of the referendum or to forbid the spending of public funds towards its organization. However, the court did make the declaration that

> ...a bill that reiterates the terms of the agreement ratified and executed on June 12, 1995, by Messrs. Jacques Parizeau, Lucien Bouchard and Mario Dumont, that would grant the National Assembly of Quebec the capacity or power to declare the sovereignty of Quebec without following the amending procedure provided for in the Constitution of Canada,

---

[35] (1995), 127 D.L.R. (4th) 408 at 424 f-425 f.

constitutes a serious threat to the rights or freedoms of the plaintiff guaranteed by the *Canadian Charter of Rights and Freedoms*, particularly in § 2, 3, 6, 7, 15 and 24(1).[36]

With this remedy, the die was cast. The sovereignty proposal did not, as it was proposed to be carried out, comply with existing Canadian constitutional requirements. The clearest explanation of this reality came in the starkest comments of the court.

> The legitimation or forced imposition of a new legal order can in no way be considered a contingency that a court should take into account.

> The supremacy of law is recognized by the Constitution of Canada (preamble of the *Canadian Charter of Rights and Freedoms*) and our superior courts have stated many times that the courts are the guardians of the Constitution. We know of no authority to the contrary.[37]

A further view of this judgment is helpful.

> A trial, Lesage J. concluded that it was not necessary for the court to preside over the question of whether the government plan embodied in the proposed law would actually be realized. It was sufficient that the Government's activities seriously undermined the basis of Canadian political institutions and denied Quebeckers such as Bertrand the protection of the *Charter of Rights and Freedoms*.[38]

On October 30, 1995, the referendum was held. By January 3, 1996, Bertrand filed a further amended version of his application, raising yet more reasons to enjoin any further referendum on sovereignty and asking for yet more declarations.

Given the razor thin result by which the people of Québec had voted NO to the referendum question and in light of the continuing implacably opposite views of the federal and Québec governments on the issue of sovereignty and secession, during the winter of 1995-96 and through the spring of 1996, it seemed increasingly possible that rather than merely waiting for political events to evolve at their own pace, the federal authorities might in some way join into the legal

---

[36] *Ibid.* at 432 e.
[37] *Ibid.* at 427 c-d.
[38] Sossin, Lorne, *Boundaries of Judicial Review; The Law of Justiciability in Canada*, Carswell, Toronto, 1999, p. 60.

battle brewing on this issue. When, on April 12, 1996, the Québec Government filed a motion to have the *Bertrand* case dismissed, the Attorney General of Canada who had since the start of the process been impleaded, announced on May 10, 1996, that he would respond to Québec's position.

Why is the Federal Government Participating?

The Attorney General of Quebec is making some arguments that are of concern to the federal government. These relate to the relevance and applicability of the Constitution to the issue of Quebec separation, and to the jurisdiction of Canadian courts to consider these matters. If accepted, the Quebec Government's position would deny the Canadian Constitution and Canadian courts any relevance in relation to a declaration of sovereignty.

The Attorney General of Canada has a duty to protect the integrity of the Constitution and to uphold the role of the courts as the primary guardians of the Constitution and the rule of law.

The federal government's response to the motion of the Attorney General of Quebec takes no position on the substance of Mr. Bertrand's arguments. What has prompted the federal government's involvement at this point is not the claims advanced by Mr. Bertrand but the legal position of the Attorney General of Quebec on its motion to dismiss.[39]

The Superior Court ruled on August 30, 1996, on Québec's motion to dismiss Bertrand's renewed action by dismissing it. With respect to the claim of parliamentary immunity, the court held that Québec cannot rely on it to evade the Constitution of Canada in order to accomplish a unilateral secession. On the defence that the argument was strictly political, the court felt it had no choice but to refer the matter to the judge in the main action. Nevertheless, the judgment did offer insight on this vital point.

The courts have consistently refused to interfere in political debates unless there is a significant legal issue or controversy to be resolved, which, the defendant argues, is not the case in this instance.

The plaintiff, on the other hand, argues that this exception to dismiss is unfounded. The question raised is of course basically political, but the

---

[39] Department of Justice News Release, May 10, 1996.

courts are not barred from reviewing its legality, since it includes legal questions including that of the rule of law. The court should therefore leave it to a judge hearing the case on its merits to decide, after hearing the evidence, whether the issue is so political as to be immune to judicial review. A judge hearing a motion to dismiss cannot assess the nuances.

The intervener argues that the expression "process of accession to sovereignty," legally speaking, evokes a large number of actions each of which is governed by an existing legal order and therefore subject to review by the courts. In short, each of the steps in this process corresponds to a legal reality, and it is indisputable that the courts have jurisdiction to determine the legality of the actions taken. The idea that such a process cannot be supervised by the courts has no place in a state such as ours, based on the rule of law.[40]

On the matter of the consistency of the sovereignty project with international law, the court perceived the lack of clear consensus. Arguments based on the hypothetical nature of the action were also dismissed and finally, the court held it inappropriate to deal with the fact that some documents incorporated into the *Constitution* had not been translated. In sum, the court was saying that the issues raised by Bertrand should be dealt with on the merits.

This judicial position precipitated consequences which would affect not only the development of political law but Canadian political life and, possibly, the course of the country's history as well.

On September 4, 1996, the Attorney General of Québec announced that he would no longer participate in the *Bertrand* litigation. This was the logical consequence of its position that secession was a strictly political and not legal decision. It failed twice to get the case dismissed on procedural grounds, had failed and was not willing to join battle on the merits of the case.

The federal authorities, meanwhile, were under ever increasing pressure to become more directly involved in getting the matter legally clarified. With Québec's withdrawal, in effect Ottawa had no genuine opponent. Thus, it was forced to undertake alone the steps required to get a judgment. On September 26, 1996, the federal Minister of Justice announced in the House of Commons that the Québec Secession Reference would be launched in the Supreme Court of Canada.

---

[40] (1996), 138 D.L.R. (4th) 481 at 500 h-501 d.

The spark set by Bertrand in August 1995 had its intended consequences by September of the following year.

In a strange twist of fate, by 2002, Bertrand had reverted to advocacy of Québec separation.[41]

See also *Singh v. Comité des Québécoises et Québécois pour le Non et al.*, Conseil du Référendum, October 31, 1995, not reported; *Singh v. Québec (Attorney General)*, Québec Superior Court, filed October 23, 1995, not completed and *Comité spécial pour l'unité canadienne c. Conseil du referendum* (17 décembre 1996), n° C.S. Montréal 500-05-012726-954, [1996] A.Q. No. 4240 (Que. S.C.) and (16 novembre 2000), n° C.A. Montréal 500-09-004438-974, [2000] J.Q. No. 5643 (Que. C.A.).

---

§ 4.4.3
Les Artistes pour la Souveraineté v. Axworthy
Québec Superior Court; filed May 20, 1997
file no. 500-05-032235-978; settled

The discussion and debate through legal and judicial channels of sovereignty issues is not all one-sided in the sense of defending the sovereignty and national unity of Canada. In fact, the range of argumentation of the characteristics and of the future evolution of Canadian sovereignty has expanded in a number of directions. This case shows how the debate about Canada has come to permeate all facets of public life.

As part of the mandate and mission which it adopted for its portrayal of Canada abroad, the Department of Foreign Affairs and International Trade established a Program of International Cultural Relations. This program included the availability of financial assistance for Canadian artistic expression abroad for which the objective comprised the promotion of Canadian sovereignty and national unity. The guidelines on criteria for eligibility reflected these objectives. On May 20, 1997, a number of artists' associations and individual artists based in and around Montréal applied to the Québec Superior Court to have the guidelines of the Program for International Cultural Re-

---

[41] "Quebec 'hero of federalism' converts to new cause," Chantal Hébert, *The Toronto Star*, October 14, 2002.

lations declared unconstitutional. Their argument was that the guidelines breached the section 2(b) freedom of opinion and expression, and the section 15 (equality) provisions of the *Charter*, as well as being contrary to the Preamble of the *Charter* which referred to the principle of the rule of law. In order to make their action more complete, they added that the Program contravened both those sections of the *Québec Civil Code* which prohibited contracting in a fashion contrary to public order, and the Common Law doctrine of public policy in contractual matters. The defendants were the Minister and the Department of Foreign Affairs and International Trade and the Attorneys General of Canada and Québec.

Rather than contest the action, get involved in potentially protracted litigation and possibly give greater international exposure to the debate of Canadian sovereignty before the courts, Axworthy amended the Program's eligibility criteria as of July 15, 1997, and on September 9, 1997, the case was settled. Thus, what is of interest in this matter are the characteristics and the implications of the litigation.

The most patent result from the perspective of political law is that a policy instrument that was allegedly contrary to the Constitution was, essentially without resistance, amended to comply and to be seen by the plaintiffs to comply with the democratic principles of the supreme law of Canada. Two other aspects of the case must be considered in conjunction: the international dimension of the debate on Canadian sovereignty and the commercial repercussions of that debate. The plaintiffs contended that they were ineligible for financial assistance to present their intellectual and artistic works abroad because their political views were not in accord with the objectives of Canadian foreign policy, which was itself an extension of domestic policy.

> Dans la situation actuelle, les requérants voulant véhiculer des opinions ou pensées politiques doivent créer et interpréter uniquement des oeuvres conformes à de tels objectifs de la politique étrangère canadienne s'ils venlent bénéficier d'une aide financière aux fins de développement international.[42]

The most significant point in the plaintiffs' pleading is an argumentation based on the democratic nature of dissent. They argued that the Program guidelines favour those who espouse Canadian unity

---

[42] Requête en Jugement Déclaratoire en Nullité, May 20, 1997, art. 17.

and thus amount to subsidy for the promotion of a particular political point of view. In their view, by contrast, Québec is the primary focus of the contention of Canadian unity and most pertinently, the debate about the sovereignty of Québec constitute a characteristic of Québec's national identity. The necessary implication is that the debate on Canadian unity is a characteristic of Canadian public life which should be reflected in the artistic expression abroad subsidized by the Department.

On these grounds, the plaintiffs base their reasoning that the Program lacks the quality of democracy required pursuant to the *Charter*.

> En effet, une société libre et démocratique offre la même tribune à tous ses citoyens, sans discrimination quant à leurs origines ou leurs opinions;

> Une démocratie eu santé ne peut justifier l'existence d'une culture officielle ou d'une culture étatique;

> Dignes des sociétés totalitaires, ces atteintes aux libertés de la communauté artistique ne peuvent se justifier dans une société libre et démocratique;[43]

See also *Henderson v. Villeneuve*, Québec Superior Court, filed December 10, 1997, file no. 500-05-037916-978, not completed.[44]

---

§ 4.4.4
Algonquin College Student Association v.
Cour du Québec, chambre criminelle et pénale
Québec Superior Court; April 2, 1997
(1997), 1997 CarswellQue 4006

While this is a very short case which deals only in part with the defence of Canadian sovereignty and the unity of the entire country by its citizens, its ramifications are considerable in deciding that Canadian citizens from parts of the country other than Québec may also have a voice in determining the future of that province.

---

[43] *Ibid.*, arts. 27, 28 and 29.
[44] Cross-reference to § 5.7.A.

The referendum held in Québec on October 30, 1995, was organized pursuant to provincial legislation, namely the *Special Version of the Election Act Designed for the Holding of Referenda*.[45] Just a few days before the vote, on October 27, 1995, seeking the maximum political effect that an apparently Canada-wide desire for Québec to remain in Confederation could produce, a so-called "unity rally" was held in Montréal. In order to induce individuals to attend, some employers, organizations and institutions offered free transportation to those wishing to attend. Student Association of Algonquin College, a junior college situated in Ottawa, was one such institution. The rally was well attended, yet its effect on the outcome of the referendum has never been precisely assessed.

Following the thin victory in the referendum of the NO side, that is the side advocating the retention of Québec within Canada, the Chief Electoral Officer (CEO) had his legal services investigate the matter of the transport of participants to the rally. The investigation focused in particular on whether there had been breach of section 413 of the *Election Act* as adapted for the conduct of referenda:

> 413. During a referendum period, only the official agent of a national committee, his deputy or a local agent may incur or authorize regulated expenses.[46]

The CEO concluded that prosecutions should be laid and mandated that a private lawyer outside his office take the necessary steps on his behalf. The prosecutions were first heard by the Québec Court, which held that it had jurisdiction to determine the matter. Six of the accused took an action in evocation, an administrative law remedy seeking to have the matter considered by the Superior Court of Québec, a higher level court. Their application sought to have the judgments of the Québec Court, in which they had been found guilty, overturned. As well, they asked for a declaration that the courts of the province lacked territorial jurisdiction to deal with the matter. Their argument rested on the point that the subject Québec legislation had effect within the bounds of the province only and that the acts alleged to have taken place, namely the expenditure of funds for transport, took place outside Québec.

---

[45] R.S.Q. 1977, c. E-3.3.

[46] R.S.Q. 1977, c. E-3.3, s. 413, as adapted.

Much of this judgment revolved around the issue of the CEO's authority to delegate power to conduct the prosecutions. Only the territorial jurisdiction aspect of the case is of interest in the context of political law.

The actual charge read as follows:

> Le 26 octobre 1995, pendant la période référendaire précédant la consultation populaire du 30 octobre 1995, alors qu'elle n'était pas un agent officiel d'un comité national ni son adjoint, ni un agent local, a illégalement fait une dépense réglementée au montant de S 749 représentant le prix de location d'un autobus payé à la compagnie Voyage Colonial Limited pour transporter des manifestants à Montréal le 27 octobre 1995 rassemblement organisé par le Comité national des Québécois et des Québécoises pour le NON et mieux connu sous le nom de la "Marche pour l'Unité," le tout constituant un service utilisé pour favoriser directement une option soumise à la consultation populaire contrairement à l'article 413 de la Version spéciale de la Loi électorale pour la tenue d'un référendum, édictée conformément à l'article 45 de la Loi sur la consultation populaire (L.R.Q., C. c-64.1), commettant ainsi l'infraction prévue à l'article 5 de cette version spéciale.[47]

The court reasoned first that the offence was the making or the authorization of the regulated expenditure. The use of the service purchased, in this instance the renting of the bus by the Student Association to take demonstrators from Ottawa to Montréal, had nothing to do with the infraction, except in terms of specifying and defining the expenditure objected to.

Even more importantly, the court held that the validity of the charge rested on whether it indicated, in accordance with *Québec's Code of Criminal Procedure*, the location where the offence was alleged to have been committed. Combining these two elements, the court concluded that the charge did not indicate where the Student Association had made or had authorized the expenditure. It held that this omission was fatal to the case. The court felt itself incapable of asserting that the offence was committed within Québec; in fact, it could only conclude that the site where the expenditure was made or authorized was at the Association's office in Nepean, Ontario. The Superior Court said that the Québec Court had erred in holding that Montréal, as the place where the transport had been destined, was the site of the

---

[47] (1997), 1997 CarswellQue 4006 at para. 21.

infraction. That link with Montréal was insufficient to grant the court jurisdiction.

> Il va sans dire qu'un tribunal de la province de Québec na pas la compétence de poursuivre un défendeur domicilié hors du Québec pour une infraction commise hors du Québec. Pourtant, ceci est précisément ce que le DGE a invité la Cour du Québec à faire. Elle ne peut le faire.[48]

The question of whether the possible secession of Québec from Canada is a matter in which only Québecers have a voice, or if all Canadians can contribute to the discussion, has been a contentious aspect of the sovereignty debate. This case arose out of a prosecution that is penal in nature. The application for evocation went only as far as the Superior Court. Its value as a precedent of general application is therefore somewhat limited. Nevertheless, this judgment has, by judicial means, opened at least some aspects of the sovereignty debate to legitimate input by other Canadians and in that sense has altered the rules for future political debate on this most important matter for Canada.

---

§ 4.4.5
Bertrand v. Québec (Premier ministre)
Quebec Superior Court; March 6, 1998
[1998] R.J.Q. 1203 to 1221

This case should be seen in the context of the litigation relating to the possibility of Québec secession, as it was making its progress through the courts. In 1995, Bertrand had initiated his first action. When the Government of Canada initiated its Secession Reference case, Bertrand agreed to proceed no further with his original litigation until the Supreme Court rendered its ruling. Yet it seemed important to Bertrand that citizens be involved in the debate over sovereignty and that matters other than those raised in the reference also be made subject to judicial examination.

On October 6, 1997, therefore, with the added expertise of Patrick Monahan, a professor at Osgoode Hall Law School in Toronto, and William Roberts, an American constitutional law litigator, Bertrand launched this, his second action, dealing with the financial and fiscal outcomes of a possible Québec secession. Bertrand himself character-

---

[48] *Ibid.* at para. 27.

ized the action as constituting an insurance policy for Québec tax-payers. He addressed head on the motivation for launching this action in terms intimately related to the law and political debate. Citing the many indications of the Québec authorities that they would not accept the eventual ruling of the Supreme Court of Canada in the reference case, Bertrand situated this as a rule of law proceeding.

> Primacy of the rule of law or of Premier Bouchard
>
> This grave assault on the rule of law by M. Bouchard is unprecedented in Canadian history. Governments in this country have always abided by the rulings of courts, even though judges do not maintain police forces or armies, and thus cannot directly compel politicians to comply with their decisions. It has always been understood by political leaders, and certainly by ordinary Canadians, that the protection of liberty and individual rights in a modern and democratic society is only possible where the government accepts the decisions of courts as binding.
>
> Therefore, if successful, M. Bertrand's public interest action would preempt Premier Bouchard's attempt to undermine the authority of the courts and the primacy of the rule of law. M. Bertrand is seeking a ruling that, in the event the Quebec government declares sovereignty in defiance of the Canadian constitution and the rulings of the courts, Quebec taxpayers would have the right to remit their Quebec income taxes to an independent trustee rather than to the province. By acting illegally, the Quebec government would lose the right to compel the payment of taxes from its residents.[49]

Bertrand's pivotal argument was that if Québec were to separate from Canada, it would no longer have the authority to raise taxes from Québec residents as, pursuant to section 92 of the *Constitution Act, 1867*, it would no longer be a province. Moreover, as both Québec and Canada would continue to demand payment of taxes, there could arise a situation in which Québec residents would be required to pay the same tax to two competing governments, resulting in fiscal chaos and confusion.

> The confusion that would necessarily result from a unilateral declaration of independence would not be limited to the fact that residents of Quebec would not know which of Canada or Quebec was the lawfully constituted taxing authority in the province. The confusion would be com-

---

[49] Executive Summary of the action, prepared by Me. Guy Bertrand and dated October 6, 1997, para. II, pp. 2 and 3.

364 / LAW OF DEMOCRATIC GOVERNING – VOLUME II: JURISPRUDENCE

pounded by the fact that the entire tax structure of both the federal and provincial governments in Quebec is premised upon the fact that Quebec residents are also resident in Canada. If Quebec were suddenly to be transformed into a sovereign state, the premise upon which both the federal and provincial taxing regimes rests would immediately collapse, leaving both tax systems in chaos.[50]

In order to remedy this eventual situation, Bertrand sought a declaration that in the event of secession contrary to the dispositions of the Canadian Constitution and the relevant decisions of Canadian courts, Québec residents would remain subject to federal income taxation legislation, would not be subject to taxation legislation enacted by Québec and would be required to remit taxes due to a court appointed administrator or trustee. These measures were described as the absence of duty to pay taxes to a "revolutionary" government. Bertrand also sought a number of related declarations designed to ensure that the people of Québec would continue to pay taxes to the federal authorities if a unilateral declaration of independence (UDI) were undertaken.

The success of such a legal action would be to starve an eventually independent Québec of its resources and therefore of its operating capacity. In the same spirit as the reaction of the Québec government to the launching of the reference, the authorities of the province voiced a response based on politically-motivated assertion of rights, combined with outrage. Premier Bouchard said: "It's some kind of delirium. It goes beyond common sense."[51] The view of the powers in Québec City continued to be that the entire matter of the province's future was one of political discussion, rather than for submission to the judiciary.

Notwithstanding the political pronouncements, the Québec government determined that it should defend this case. The Minister of Justice, Serge Ménard, presented a motion asking the Superior Court to dismiss the action. Québec's arguments were that the remedies were both premature and hypothetical.

A most interesting aspect of this case was the position adopted by Anne McLellan, the federal Minister of Justice. From a political per-

---

[50] *Ibid.*, para. V, p. 7.
[51] "Bertrand heads to court with plan to deny taxes to sovereign Quebec," Terrance Wills, *Ottawa Citizen*, October 7, 1997.

spective, there must have been some federal sympathy in the attempt to tie the hands of the Québec authorities. However, the entire federal position vis-à-vis the sovereignist option was that the rule of law must prevail over political desires and aspiration; and that political goals could be achieved only by means consistent with the law. Consequently, the federal Crown was bound to take a position based on prevailing legal norms. The Justice Canada litigators therefore argued against Bertrand, preferring to have the hearing of this case delayed until the decision of the Supreme Court on the reference was known.

> Quant au procureur général du Canada, mis en cause, il soumet essentiellement que le contexte factuel, à la base du présent recours, n'est pas fondé sur de simples appréhensions puisque la démarche sécessionniste du Québec constitue une menace constante. Il plaide toutefois que les questions qu'il soulève sont prématurées puisqu'elles présument du sort du renvoi actuellement soumis à la Cour suprême du Canada concernant la légalité du projet de souveraineté québécois.
>
> . . .
>
> Le procureur général du Canada soutient au contraire que les tribunaux font montre de retenue judiciaire lorsqu'ils sont en présence de questions abstraites ou hypothétiques. En effet, bien que la reconnaissance de la qualité pour agir ait pour objet d'empêcher que les actes publics soient à l'abri de contestations, le droit d'action n'est pas conféré pour faire réparer un préjudice dont on ne sait s'il se réalisera. Par conséquent, il est préférable d'attendre de trancher une question lorsqu'elle se pose dans un contexte contradictoire. En l'absence d'une difficulté réelle à laquelle le jugement déclaratoire est susceptible d'apporter une solution concrète et définitive, les tribunaux doivent s'abstenir de répondre aux questions constitutionnelles soulevées par une partie.[52]

The court agreed with Québec's motion that the case was "irrecevable," meaning that it ought not to be heard on the merits and it nullified Bertrand's action. The court felt that what it was being asked to do was to adjudicate on the legality of secession itself and it did not want to prejudice the freedom of the Supreme Court of Canada to determine that issue. It held that Bertrand's case was premature and that a remedy such as that he sought could be granted only after the alleged wrong had been committed. In this instance, there had

---

[52] See Newman, Warren J., *The Quebec Secession Reference*, York University Press, Toronto, 1999. The outcome of this case is set out at footnote 38, on p. 89.

been no provincial election, no referendum approving secession and no UDI.

Bertrand appealed to the Québec Court of Appeal and the case was even set down for hearing on September 16, 1999. In the meantime, the Supreme Court of Canada rendered its reference judgment, largely determining the underlying issues that Bertrand had hoped to address, namely the legality of secession. In August 1999, therefore, on the basis of mutual consent, the plaintiff desisted.

See also *Québec (Procureur général) c. Henderson*, [2002] R.J.Q. 2435 (Que. S.C.).

4.5 ISSUE: LIMITATION OF SOVEREIGNTY

See *Regina v. Secretary of State for Transport*, Ex parte Factortame Ltd. (No. 2), [1991] 1 A.C. 603 (U.K. H.L.); *Décision 93-308; Traité de Maastricht sur l'Union européenne*, Conseil Constitutionnel, le 9 avril 1992 and *Décision 92-312; Traité de Maastricht sur l'Union européenne*, Conseil Constitutionnel, le 2 septembre 1992.[53]

---

§ 4.5.1
*Regina v. Secretary of State for Employment,
Ex parte Equal Opportunities Commission*
House of Lords; March 3, 1994
[1995] 1 A.C. 1

The purpose of the United Kingdom's domestic legislation, the *Employment Protection (Consolidation) Act* of 1977 was to prevent the unfair dismissal of employees and to provide redundancy pay for employees working continuously for a number of years and hours a week. As the statute excluded employees working less than eight hours a week, the Equal Opportunities Commission considered it to be discriminatory against women. It wrote to the Secretary of State for Employment asking that he reconsider the legislation. The Secretary of State responded, indicating that the threshold was justifiable. The Commission applied for judicial review.

---

[53] Cross-reference to § 1.2.3, 2.4.6, 3.1, 4.2.2, 4.3.1, 10.2.1 and 11.2.C.1.

The U.K. courts dealt with several domestic aspects of the issues raised here. Notably, they looked at whether the letter of the Secretary of State was susceptible to judicial review. Ultimately, the House of Lords held that it was not a decision. This aspect was the basis upon which the courts could consider the relationship between U.K. law and Community law and the limitation on sovereignty flowing from the subordination of the domestic legal system to the regime established by the various EC treaties.

The Divisional Court's holding was that even though the letter was susceptible to judicial review, the Court could not direct the Secretary of State to introduce legislation, nor declare that the United Kingdom was in breach of its obligations under the E.E.C. Treaty. The Court of Appeal held that if the U.K. was judged to have failed to meet the E.E.C. Treaty obligations, it was for the European Commission to bring proceedings. The view of the House of Lords was that the Secretary of State's letter was not a decision but despite that, the Divisional Court did have jurisdiction to declare that the U.K.'s domestic legislation was incompatible with Community law; the Divisional Court would also be the appropriate forum in which to determine the substantive issues raised by the case.

See also *Carlsen v. Prime Minister*, Danish High Court, Eastern Division, June 27, 1997.

4.6 ISSUE: LEGITIMACY OF A NEW POLITICAL/ LEGAL REGIME

§ 4.6.1[54]
Reference re Secession of Québec
Supreme Court of Canada; August 20, 1998
(1998), 161 D.L.R. (4th) 385

The Québec Secession Reference is a veritable font of knowledge in matters of political law. Among the topics it covers regarding the relationship of law and politics is that of legitimacy. The actual ques-

---

[54] All international comparisons.

tion can be posed in the following manner: in Canadian law, what is necessary to endow a new governmental regime with the legitimacy required for it to be able to function and survive? The answer to that question lies in the realm of legitimacy.

Legitimacy is a concept that does not lend itself to easy definition. Generally, it can be taken to mean a combination of factors lending legal and political validity and popular acceptance to a governing regime. The Supreme Court's general commentary on this aspect of the issue before it is as follows.

> The consent of the governed is a value that is basic to our understanding of a free and democratic society. Yet democracy in any real sense of the word cannot exist without the rule of law. It is the law that creates the framework within which the "sovereign will" is to be ascertained and implemented. To be accorded legitimacy, democratic institutions must rest, ultimately, on a legal foundation. That is, they must allow for the participation of, and accountability to, the people, through public institutions created under the Constitution. Equally, however, a system of government cannot survive through adherence to the law alone. A political system must also possess legitimacy, and in our political culture, that requires an interaction between the rule of law and the democratic principle. The system must be capable of reflecting the aspirations of the people. But there is more. Our law's claim to legitimacy also rests on an appeal to moral values, many of which are imbedded in our constitutional structure. It would be a grave mistake to equate legitimacy with the "sovereign will" or majority rule alone, to the exclusion of other constitutional values.[55]

The lesson which observers of political law should draw from this citation is that there can be no legitimacy without a legal foundation. Politics is not enough; the popular will is not sufficient for democratic legitimacy; law must be a part of the formula of governance.

The rest of the court's thinking about legitimacy in the context of a change of governmental regimes and in the case of the establishment of a new political legal regime must flow consequentially from this basis. Should one of the participants in Confederation, in this instance, Québec, legitimately assert its rights, including the right to secede, then two legitimate majorities would face each other. These would be the representatives of the clear majority of the population

---

[55] (1998), 161 D.L.R. (4th) 385 at 416-417, para. 67.

of Québec and those of the clear majority of Canada as a whole. They would both be subject to an obligation to negotiate the terms of the secession. As the Supreme Court phrased it in one of the most significant sentences of its ruling: "The corollary of a legitimate attempt by one participant in Confederation to seek an amendment to the Constitution is an obligation on all parties to come to the negotiation table."[56]

In addition to merely coming to the negotiation table, the parties would have to conduct the negotiations in a legitimate fashion, that is in full observance of the fundamental constitutional principles which the court elsewhere showed as the characteristics of Canada.

> To the extent that a breach of the constitutional duty to negotiate in accordance with the principles described above undermines the legitimacy of a party's actions, it may have important ramifications at the international level. Thus, a failure of the duty to undertake negotiations and pursue them according to constitutional principles may undermine that government's claim to legitimacy which is generally a precondition for recognition by the international community. Conversely, violations of those principles by the federal or other provincial governments responding to the request for secession may undermine their legitimacy. Thus, a Quebec that had negotiated in conformity with constitutional principles and values in the face of unreasonable intransigence on the part of other participants at the federal or provincial level would be more likely to be recognized than a Quebec which did not itself act according to constitutional principles in the negotiation process. Both the legality of the acts of the parties to the negotiation process under Canadian law and the perceived legitimacy of such action, would be important considerations in the recognition process. In this way, the adherence of the parties to the obligation to negotiate would be evaluated in an indirect manner on the international plane.[57]

What is the genuine meaning of this analysis of a possible sequence of events? Quite simply, it is that in the process of transferring governmental power from one established authority to another, and from one ruling elite to another, that is in the process of creating a new sovereignty, the quality of legitimacy must attach to the proceedings through every stage of the process. The new political legal regime, must, in the end, be endowed with the same kind of constitutional

---

[56] *Ibid.* at 425, para. 88.
[57] *Ibid.* at 430, para. 103.

legal basis and the same acceptability as the earlier power. There must be an evolutionary transfer of authority, with respect for the rule of law and the other characteristics and guarantees of the people's rights, rather than a revolution.

In this context, we may refer to legitimacy as the transitional quality of legality in the process which Dean Hogg calls a break in legal continuity.[58]

See also *Madzimbamuto v. Lardner-Burke* (1968), [1969] 1 A.C. 645 (Southern Rhodesia P.C.); *Ex parte Chairperson of the Constitutional Assembly, in re Certification of the Constitution of the Republic of South Africa*, 1996, 1996 (4) SA 744 (CC) and *Certification of the Amended Text of the Constitution of the Republic of South Africa*, 1996, Constitutional Court, December 4, 1996, file CCT 37/96.[59]

---

§ 4.6.2
Hong Kong Special Administrative Region v.
Ma Wai Kwan, Daniel & others
Hong Kong Court of Appeal; July 29, 1997
(1997), H.K.L.R.D. 761

This case arose in the first few days after the People's Republic of China resumed sovereignty over Hong Kong. The United Kingdom and China had laid the groundwork for the handover during the several years preceding July 1, 1997, by means of a series of treaties and British, Chinese and Hong Kong domestic instruments, each of which was essentially both political and legal in nature. It was up to the courts of the former Crown Colony, now called a Special Administrative Region, to have the final say as to whether the transfer of sovereignty had been done in a manner compatible with both British and Chinese law. If their answer was affirmative, the new political legal regime in Hong Kong would have the legitimacy required to function properly, with the acceptance and the certainty of the population. The stakes revolving around this case were therefore high.

The respondents were first charged in 1995 with conspiracy to pervert the course of public justice, a common law offence. Their trial was

---

[58] Hogg, P., *Constitutional Law of Canada*, loose-leaf ed., Carswell, Toronto, 1997.
[59] All international comparisons.

scheduled to begin on June 16, 1997; it continued in such a manner that it straddled the July 1, 1997 transition. On July 3, the first court date after the transition, the accused started proceedings to have the indictments against them quashed by raising questions of a constitutional nature. These questions were reserved for the determination of the Hong Kong Court of Appeal. The principal question was as follows:

> Is the offence at common law of conspiracy to pervert the course of public justice part of the laws of the Hong Kong Special Administrative Region [HKSAR]?[60]

The first major issue to be addressed was whether the common law was still part of the law of Hong Kong after the transition. From July 1, 1997, the *Basic Law* became the constitution of the HKSAR. This was a law enacted by the National People's Congress, the Parliament of the People's Republic. At section 160, the *Basic Law* provided that laws previously in force in Hong Kong, including the common law, should be adopted. The accused/respondents argued that for adoption to take place, a positive act had to be taken by either the National People's Congress or by the legislature of the HKSAR. As no such positive act was done, they argued that common law had not survived the transition.

The Attorney General of Hong Kong presented a detailed submission to the Court of Appeal, in which he argued that no formal act of adoption of the common law previously in force was necessary or required pursuant to the *Basic Law*. He relied on section 8 of the *Basic Law* as providing the starting point for the reception of the laws previously in force.

> BL 8 provides the starting point for the reception of the laws previously in force. The English text provides:–
>
> The laws previously in force in Hong Kong, that is, the common law, rules of equity, ordinances, subordinate legislation and customary law *shall be maintained*, except for any that contravene this Law, and subject to any amendment by the legislature of the Hong Kong Special Administrative Region.[61]

---

[60] (1997), HKLRD 761 at 771 j.

[61] *Basic Law*, s. 8, as cited in HKSAR's Submissions in Criminal Case No. 1 of 1997, p. 8, para. 15.

For complete precision, the Attorney General indicated that this provision both catalogued the laws previously in force and declared that such laws shall be maintained. Moreover, the expression "shall be maintained" in the provision was use of imperative language, not use of the future tense. In other words, the intention of the legislature was that the common law be mandatory.

The court agreed with the reasoning of the Attorney General in favour of the continuity of the pre-existing legal system, thereby securing the legitimacy required for it to continue to be applicable. It held that the *Basic Law* did not have the effect of requiring that elements of the pre-transition legal system in force in Hong Kong be formally adopted. In fact, the intention was that there be no change in the legal system or in the laws, except where these contravened the *Basic Law*.

The notion of the "adoption" of English common law resonates in the Canadian context, as each of the British North American colonies had its legal system formed by such an adoption process. In this sense, the cut-off date for Hong Kong's adoption process was held to be June 30, 1997.

The Court of Appeal also determined that the Provisional Legislative Council which had been set up in December, 1996 was established "with the intention to implement the provisions of the *Basic Law* and the NPC Decisions."[62] It went on to decide that the Provisional Legislative Council was working within the ambit of the authority and powers conferred on it by the decisions of the National People's Congress. It was legally established and could therefore not be challenged.

This judgment is singularly interesting not only because of the subject matter as dealing with a significant news story of the latter 1990's and as being of potential guidance to Canadian courts in the event of the secession of a province. Its interest also stems from the fact that in order to make its determination, the court had to examine a series of intertwined legal instruments all based on political arrangements and requiring understanding of and attention to ongoing political developments, even if this aspect of the judges' perception was mostly implicit. This is the type of analysis required for judicial decision-making on matters of legitimacy.

---

[62] *Supra* note 60 at 785 j.

The unanimity of the Court of Appeal did not dampen the ardour of those who, for various reasons, disputed the post-transition nature of the Hong Kong legal system. The very next day after the ruling, the discussions about legitimacy and the forecasts of future challenges continued in the serious media.[63]

---

§ 4.6.3
Ng Ka Ling et al. v. Director of Immigration
Court of Final Appeal of the Hong Kong
Special Administrative Region;
January 29 and February 19, 1999
[1999] HKCFA 11[64]

This case is an example of a political attack on legality and the legitimacy of a new political legal regime. It also demonstrates very clearly how vitally important the independence of the judiciary is to the notion of legitimacy, in particular when that independence is threatened by government officials motivated by political ideology.

Ng Ka Ling was one of a number of applicants for permanent residency status in Hong Kong. What was particular about these applicants was that most were the children of families with only one parent who was mainland Chinese and who themselves had not yet obtained permanent residency. The court interpreted the *Hong Kong Ordinance* on matters of immigration and the right of abode in the Special Administrative Region in light of the *Sino-British Joint Declaration* which formed the basis of the colony's reunification with China and the *Basic Law*, Hong Kong's constitution. On these bases, it determined that the applicants were entitled to the right of abode. While this decision was the source of the subsequent controversy, and while the case would have wide substantive repercussions because it could affect a great number of people, the immigration aspect of the matter became incidental to the real stakes, the legal autonomy of Hong Kong and the maintenance of its own legal system.

The status of Hong Kong is based on the dovetailing of constitutional provisions in China and the Special Administrative Region. Article

---

[63] See articles entitled "Legislature left open to attack," Charlotte Parsons and "Dark day for our rights," Yash Ghoi, *South China Morning Post*, July 30, 1997.
[64] And [1999] HKCFA 19.

31 of the Constitution of the People's Republic enables the establishment of special administrative regions. The preamble to Hong Kong's *Basic Law* continues from there to state that:

> ...under the principle of one country, two systems, the socialist system and policies will not be practised in Hong Kong. The basic policies of the People's Republic of China regarding Hong Kong have been elaborated by the Chinese Government in the Sino-British Joint Declaration.[65]

The key to the application of this doctrine of "one country, two systems" is the relationship between the judiciary of the Hong Kong Special Administrative Region and the political authorities of the People's Republic of China. This relationship, which can be described as a blending of independence and accommodation, is set out in Article 158 of the *Basic Law* as follows:

> The power of interpretation of this Law shall be vested in the Standing Committee of the National People's Congress.
>
> . . .
>
> The Standing Committee of the National People's Congress shall authorize the courts of the Hong Kong Special Administrative Region to interpret on their own, in adjudicating cases, the provisions of this Law which are within the limits of the autonomy of the Region.
>
> The courts of the Hong Kong Special Administrative Region may also interpret other provisions of this law in adjudicating cases. However, if the courts of the Region, in adjudicating cases, need to interpret the provisions of this Law concerning affairs which are the responsibility of the Central People's Government, or concerning the relationship between the Central Authorities and the Region, and if such interpretation will affect the judgments on the cases, the courts of the Region shall, before making their final judgments which are not appealable, seek an interpretation of the relevant provisions from the Standing Committee of the National People's Congress through the Court of Final Appeal of the Region. When the Standing Committee makes an interpretation of the provisions concerned the courts of the Region, in applying those provisions, shall follow the interpretation of the Standing Committee. However, judgments previously rendered shall not be affected.

---

[65] Preamble of the *Basic Law*.

. . .

> The Standing Committee of the National People's Congress shall consult
> its Committee for the Basic Law of the Hong Kong Special Administra-
> tive Region before giving an interpretation of this Law.[66]

In order to determine the immigration issue here, by looking at the
constitutional validity of the Ordinance dealing with the right of
abode, the Court of Final Appeal needed to set out the extent of the
constitutional jurisdiction of Hong Kong's courts. In the earlier *Ma
Wai Kwan Daniel* case, the Court of Appeal had held that the Region's
courts had no jurisdiction to query whether acts of China's Parliament, the National People's Congress, applied or not to Hong Kong,
because they were the acts of the sovereign power. That judgment
limited the jurisdiction of the Hong Kong courts to examining the
existence of acts of the Sovereign. Here, that judgment was specifically overruled.

The constitutional competence of Hong Kong's courts focuses first
on examining whether legislation enacted within the Region or acts
of the executive authority of the Region are consistent with the *Basic
Law*. To the extent of the inconsistency, they are invalid. The court
laid great emphasis on the binding and compulsory nature of this
fundamental and intrinsic constitutional role.

> The exercise of this jurisdiction is a matter of obligation, not of discretion
> so that if inconsistency is established, the courts are bound to hold that
> a law or executive act is invalid at least to the extent of the inconsistency.
> Although this has not been questioned, it is right that we should take
> this opportunity of stating it unequivocally. In exercising this jurisdic-
> tion, the courts perform their constitutional role under the Basic Law of
> acting as a constitutional check on the executive and legislative branches
> of government to ensure that they act in accordance with the Basic Law.[67]

The foregoing citation is consistent with constitutional evolution in
common law jurisdictions and is not unfamiliar for Canadian constitutionalists. It is the subsequent point of the court's analysis of the
Hong Kong judiciary's powers, that most directly gives meaning to
the "one country, two systems" doctrine as the cornerstone of the
new political legal regime, which merits our attention. In effect, Hong

---

[66] [1999] HKCFA 11, pp. 5-6.
[67] *Ibid.*, p. 14.

Kong assumed authority to determine which part of the mainland legal system would be applicable to it.

What has been controversial is the jurisdiction of the courts of the Region to examine whether any legislative acts of the National People's Congress or its Standing Committee (which we shall refer to simply as "acts") are consistent with the Basic Law and to declare them to be invalid if found to be inconsistent. In our view, the courts of the Region do have this jurisdiction and indeed the duty to declare invalidity if inconsistency is found. It is right that we should take this opportunity of stating so unequivocally.

Under the Chinese Constitution (Articles 57 and 58), the National People's Congress is the highest organ of state power and its permanent body is the Standing Committee and they exercise the legislative powers of the state. So their acts are acts of the Sovereign. The jurisdiction of the Region's courts to examine their acts to ensure consistency with the Basic Law is derived from the Sovereign in that the National People's Congress had enacted pursuant to Article 31 of the Chinese Constitution the Basic Law for the Region. The Basic Law is a national law and is the constitution of the Region.

Like other constitutions, it distributes and delimits powers, as well as providing for fundamental rights and freedoms. As with other constitutions, laws which are inconsistent with the Basic Law are of no effect and are invalid. Under it, the courts of the Region have independent judicial power within the high degree of autonomy conferred on the Region. It is for the courts of the Region to determine questions of inconsistency and invalidity when they arise. It is therefore the courts of the Region to determine whether an act of the National People's Congress or its Standing Committee is inconsistent with the Basic Law, subject of course to the provisions of the Basic Law itself.

This proposition gains added strength from the circumstance that the Basic Law was enacted to implement China's basic policies regarding Hong Kong to remain unchanged for 50 years as declared and elaborated in the Joint Declaration. Article 159(4) of the Basic Law provides that no amendment thereto shall contravene the established basic policies. The jurisdiction to enforce and interpret the Basic Law necessarily entails the jurisdiction stated above over acts of the National People's Congress and its Standing Committee to ensure their consistency with the Basic Law.[68]

---

[68] *Ibid.*, pp. 14-15.

This judgment can be characterized as the legal and judicial expression of the political deal between the United Kingdom and the People's Republic of China for the return of Hong Kong to Chinese sovereignty. The reactions which the judgment elicited can, in counterpoint, be described as the politicization of the law. Within a very short time after the judgment, the Director of China's State Council Information Office was reported to have criticized it and suggested that it be overturned. While pro-Beijing legal experts saw this ruling as a challenge to the supremacy of the National People's Congress, Hong Kong lawyers perceived it as the application of the Special Autonomous Region's own legal system and warned that if the ruling was required to be "rectified," a constitutional crisis would ensue.[69] The line of the pro-Beijing press seemed to be that this was interference in China's internal affairs, but such comments can only be made by those who do not fully comprehend the independence of the judiciary. The British Government reacted to the criticism by warning that restrictions on Hong Kong's courts would be a matter of serious concern. The Region's chief executive attempted to explain the controversy by indicating that problems in implementing the "one country, two systems" concept would be inevitable. Perhaps the most pertinent editorial comment was that of the *South China Morning Post* which wrote that, "Anything which smacked of an attempt to get the court to modify its position for political reasons would be a grievous blow for the rule of law."[70]

Nevertheless, on February 26, 1999, on the motion of the Director of Immigration, the court issued a clarification of that part of its judgment which relates to the National People's Congress and its Standing Committee. The court agreed that the various interpretations put on its original judgment had given rise to much controversy and to an exceptional situation. While, in its original judgment, the court had indicated that its jurisdiction to enforce and interpret the *Basic Law* derived from, and was subject to the *Basic Law* itself, here it clarified that its jurisdiction was derived from authorization by the Standing Committee, under provisions of the *Basic Law*, a subtle but meaningful difference. For good measure, the court emphasized that it could not and did not question the authority of the National People's Con-

---

[69] "China tells Hong Kong it Wants Immigration Ruling Rectified," Mark Landler, *New York Times*, February 14, 1999, p. 13.
[70] Cited online, February 25, 1999, by the BBC.

gress or the Standing Committee to do any act which is in accordance with the provisions of the *Basic Law* and the procedure therein.

---

§ 4.6.4
Lau Kong Yung v. The Director of Immigration
[1999] HKCFA 78; December 3, 1999

Under the guise of an immigration case, this decision is, to date, the latest pronouncement of the highest court of Hong Kong on the development of the legitimacy of the Special Administrative Region's constitutional regime as politically united into the People's Republic of China, but with its own legal system.

The roots of this litigation are to be found in the case of Ng Ka Ling in which the issue was to determine which categories of Chinese nationals could establish themselves in Hong Kong. There, the court modified Hong Kong's immigration scheme. As a result of the judgment, and based on relevant provisions of the Chinese Constitution and Hong Kong's *Basic Law*, the court sought an interpretation of the law establishing the immigration scheme from the Standing Committee of the National People's Congress. This latter body is the highest legislative body, the Parliament, for all of the People's Republic of China and it is guided by the political power in place, the Communist Party. On June 26, 1999, the Standing Committee adopted an *Interpretation* on matters of immigration from China to Hong Kong.

In order to determine the present case, the Court of Final Appeal of Hong Kong first had to decide whether the Standing Committee of the National People's Congress had the power to make the *Interpretation*. The court held that the *Interpretation* was properly made. Indeed, it held that while in some instances under section 158 of the *Basic Law*, the Court of Final Appeal had a discretion to refer matters to the Standing Committee; in others, it was obliged to do so.

> Accordingly, the Standing Committee has the power to make the Interpretation under Article 158(1). The Interpretation is binding on the courts of the HKSAR.

> This conclusion on the power of the Standing Committee to interpret under Article 158(1) derives some support from Professor Yash Ghai in his work: "Hong Kong's New Constitutional Order" (2nd ed. 1999) p.

198. He expressed the view that the power of the Standing Committee to interpret is a general power. It is "plenary in that it covers all the provisions of the Basic Law; this power may be exercised in the absence of litigation."[71]

The court went on to explain that once made, the *Interpretation* had effect on the Hong Kong legal system.

> I am equally in no doubt that the Interpretation took effect as from 1 July 1997. In making it, the Standing Committee did not purport to act, and has never purported to act, as a Court. Nor did it purport to be amending the law. It was doing exactly what it said it was doing, namely interpreting the law. That must mean that they were explaining what the law is and has been since the Basic Law came into effect.[72]

In this regard, it is important to note that the purpose of the interpretations so allowed is to give general guidance on the regime of law, rather than to legislatively determine the outcome of particular court cases.

In perhaps the most significant explanation, the court approved the legitimacy of this element of Hong Kong's political/legal system.

> As is the case with constitutional divisions of power, a link between the courts of the Region and the institutions of the People's Republic of China is required. In a nation-wide common law system, the link would normally be between the regional courts and the national constitutional court or the national supreme court. Here, however, there are not only two different systems, but also two different legal systems. In the context of "one country, two systems," Article 158 of the Basic Law provides a very different link. That is because the Article, in conformity with Article 67(4) of the PRC Constitution, vests the general power of interpretation of the Basic Law, not in the People's Supreme Court or the national courts, but in the NPC Standing Committee.

> . . .

> This conclusion may seem strange to a common lawyer but, in my view, it follows inevitably from a consideration of the text and structure of Article 158, viewed in the light of the context of the Basic Law and its

---

[71] http://www.worldlii.org/hk/cases/HKCFA/1999/78.html at p. 16.
[72] *Ibid.* at p. 30.

380 / LAW OF DEMOCRATIC GOVERNING – VOLUME II: JURISPRUDENCE

character as the constitution for the HKSAR embodied in a national law enacted by the PRC.[73]

Observers of democracy will note that, as this court acknowledged, the traditional concept of the rule of law puts the judiciary in the position of speaking on the constitutionality and legality of the instruments arising out of legislative bodies. In the Hong Kong model, the national parliament not only legislates, but also has the power to provide interpretations which are partly legislative, partly judicial instruments in that they are binding on the courts. The relations between the two branches of government are therefore quite different than in some other jurisdictions. In fact, when one realizes that the legislature is controlled by the political power which is itself behind the executive, the form of legitimacy resulting from such a constitutional framework is radically different from that to which we are accustomed in countries such as Canada.

It will be necessary to keep watching how the Standing Committee exercises its power of interpretation and whether it becomes a method of overturning rulings of the British-styled independent judiciary.

---

§ 4.6.5
Prosecution of Prime Minister Mian Muhammad Nawaz Sharif
Anti-Terrorism Court No. 1, Karachi; April 6, 2000
SPL. Case No. 385/1999
and Sindh High Court; October 30, 2000
-and-
Illahi Bux Scomro et al. (Pakistan Muslim League) v.
General Pervez Musharraf et al.
Supreme Court of Pakistan; May 12, 2000
Constitution Petitions Nos. 62/99, 63/99, 53/99, 57/99, 3/2000,
66/99 and 64/99

On October 12, 1999, the army seized power in Pakistan, deposing the legitimately elected Prime Minister, Nawaz Sharif. As in all coups, the actual facts and the sequence of conspiracy and execution of the takeover are shrouded in confusion and secrecy. What was clear from the outset of the military regime, however, was that the strongman heading it, General Musharraf, was intent on deflecting the criticism

---

[73] *Ibid.* at pp. 32 and 33.

of public opinion in democratic countries and in particular in the Commonwealth, which threatened to suspend Pakistan from membership if it did not restore democratic rule. The means attempted to achieve this goal was that of the prosecution of the deposed Prime Minister. On November 19, 1999, Nawaz Sharif was charged with murder, hijacking, kidnapping and terrorism. Rather than using law to give itself the desired cloak of legitimacy, this prosecution only exacerbated the new regime's situation, serving as a focus of democratic criticism. As early as in its November 27, 1999 edition, *The Economist* pointed out the conflict between justice and retribution. Pakistan's place in the Commonwealth was indeed suspended. Beyond the political rhetoric and the media observation from a distance, the relationships among democracy, legitimacy, legality and domestic acceptance of the new regime involved genuine paradoxes.

> The easing of pressure on Pakistan marks Commonwealth awareness of the uncomfortable truth that its current rules on what constitutes a democracy with which the organisation can do business are inadequate. Pakistan's ousted civilian Government was elected, and therefore automatically deemed a worthy Commonwealth member. Yet it behaved in an outrageously undemocratic fashion, suppressing the very things - press freedom and judicial independence - that democratic governments are supposed to encourage. By contrast, the country's current leader, General Pervaiz Musharraf, is not elected, yet his pledges to uproot corruption, calm religious strife, and restore democratic freedoms are believed at home, making him more popular than his predecessor.[74]

Not unexpectedly, on April 6, 2000, Sharif was convicted of the hijacking and terrorism charges and sentenced to two life terms, a fine and confiscation of his property. On April 12, he appealed. The Sindh High Court dismissed his appeal on October 30, 2000. The only salutary news for Sharif was that the prosecution's application to impose the death penalty was denied.

For good measure, on May 11, 2000, another prosecution, for tax evasion and corruption, was instituted against Sharif in the Accountability Court. Also somewhat predictably, on July 22, 2000, Sharif was convicted of these charges and sentenced to another 14 years of imprisonment; he was also barred from entering political life for 21 years and fined 20 million rupees.

---

[74] "A more realistic route to popular rule in Pakistan," *The Times*, London, November 12, 1999.

More pertinent to the issue of legitimacy than these prosecutions which may simply be regarded as politically motivated measures to dispose of the predecessor, is a proceeding initiated autonomously on November 22, 1999, by the Pakistan Muslim League, in which it sought to have the country's Supreme Court declare the coup itself illegal. Judgment was issued on May 12, 2000. The court, in essence, held that General Musharraf had to seize power because the country was slipping toward chaos. This, the court thought, empowered Musharraf to amend the constitution and make other legislation for the good of the people. The court referred to "the doctrine of State necessity" to justify this finding, relying on the principle of *salus populi suprema lex*.

The exact legal train of thought of the Supreme Court is worth setting out. The thirteen justices unanimously held that where

> the representatives of the people are accused of massive corruption...there is a general perception that corruption is being practised by diversified strata including politicians, parliamentarians, public officials...where economic stability in Pakistan was highly precarious...where a situation had arisen under which the democratic institutions were not functioning in accordance with the provisions of the Constitution...[and] where Narwaz Sharif's constitutional and moral authority stood completely eroded...the extra constitutional step of taking over the affairs of the country by the Armed Forces for a transitional period to prevent any further destabilization, to create corruption free atmosphere at national level through transparent accountability and revive the economy before—restoration of democratic institutions under the Constitution, is validated, in that Constitution offered no solution to the present crisis.[75]

This essentially political analysis led the court to enable itself to justify the coup. Nevertheless, the court emphasized that the period of military rule should be transitional. Noting that its own task would be to steer a middle course so as to ensure that the Order pre-existing the coup survived this "constitutional deviation," it held that civilian rule must be restored within three years of the date of the army takeover.

In a notable twist, the court recognized that despite its justification of the coup, it still needed to account to democratic principles. It

---

[75] Constitutional Petitions Decision of the Supreme Court, p. 7.

therefore directed General Musharraf to hold a general election by the end of 2002. On May 25, 2000, the BBC reported that Musharraf indicated his intention to abide by that part of the ruling as well. In execution of that intention, on August 14, 2001, Musharraf set out a road-map for his country's return to democracy, scheduling the holding of national elections from October 1 until October 11, 2002. These dates were strategically chosen, as October 12, 2002 would be the three-year anniversary of the coup.

Observers of political law are left to wonder at the extent to which such judge-made law is an accommodation to political circumstances and to which it can be thought of as the expression of a judicial wish for return to genuine legalism and legitimacy, albeit in extremely trying circumstances. This must also be considered a singular inducement for observers to continue to follow developments in this living laboratory of law and political reality.

See also *Republic of Fiji and Attorney General v. Prasad*, [2001] 2 L.R.C. 743; *Supreme Court Bar Association v. Federation of Pakistan*, Constitutional Petition No. 1/2002, Supreme Court of Pakistan, April 27, 2002; *Pakistan Lawyers' Forum v. General Pervez Musharraf*, Constitutional Petition No. 6/2002, Supreme Court of Pakistan, April 27, 2002; *Wattan Party v. Federation of Pakistan*, Constitutional Petition No. 7/2002, Supreme Court of Pakistan, April 27, 2002; *Rai Muhammad Nawaz Karal v. Federation of Pakistan*, Constitutional Petition No. 8/2002, Supreme Court of Pakistan, April 27, 2002 and *Pakistan Bar Council v. Federation of Pakistan*, Constitutional Petition No. 12/2002, Supreme Court of Pakistan, April 27, 2002.

4.7 ISSUE: LEGITIMACY OF NEW GOVERNMENTAL INSTITUTIONS

§ 4.7.1
Ng King Luen v. Rita Fan
Supreme Court of Hong Kong; June 12, 1997
(1997), H.K.L.R.D. 757

Matters of legitimacy can never be divorced from politics, even if they are cast in legal terms. In this connection, without a doubt, one of the most unique and sensitive set of facts submitted for the consideration of a court, in one of the most politicized environments, is that relating to the legitimacy of the legislative body established for Hong Kong by the People's Republic of China, in anticipation of the return of the Crown Colony to Chinese sovereignty on July 1, 1997.

The legal regime of the British Crown Colony of Hong Kong was based on *Letters Patent* passed under the Great Seal of the United Kingdom and on the *Royal Instructions to the Governor*. The *Letters Patent* provided authority not only for the election of a Legislative Council, but also for the making of laws for the "peace, order and good government" (a term familiar in Canada) of the colony by the Governor, by and with the advice of that Legislative Council. The only other sources of law for Hong Kong were statutes of the United Kingdom Parliament and United Kingdom orders in Council.

The governments of the United Kingdom and the People's Republic of China agreed in the early 1980's that on July 1, 1997, Hong Kong would revert to Chinese sovereignty after over 150 years of colonial status. On March 23, 1996, the Preparatory Committee, the Chinese body overseeing the transfer of sovereignty announced what would become the Hong Kong Special Administrative Region, pending the election of a new legislature under the *Basic Law* that would eventually govern Hong Kong after the transfer. On December 21, 1996, the Chinese side announced the composition of the Provisional Legislature and on January 25, 1997, this body began to hold meetings at Shenzen, across the border in China. In many respects, it emulated the form and substance of the proceedings of the work of the elected Legislative Council in Hong Kong. As part of its work, it adopted bills purporting to amend existing Hong Kong Ordinances, giving these amendments force and effect as of July 1, 1997, that is, as of the day of the transfer. It also publicized its deliberations and the results of its work in Hong Kong. The most controversial such enactment of the Provisional Legislature was the *Public Order (Amendment) Bill*, which purported to amend the *Public Order Ordinance* of Hong Kong, restricting the rules on demonstrations to be held after the handover.

In the months leading up to the transfer of sovereignty, the Democratic Party, one of the political formations then represented in the Legislative Council, declared its intention to challenge the legality of the work of the Provisional Legislature. In the highly charged political environment of Hong Kong, such a challenge would constitute an attack on the legitimacy of the incoming legislative body and on its work.

On June 7, 1997, Ng, one of the senior members of the Democratic Party and a deputy in the Legislative Council, did bring the present application before the Supreme Court of Hong Kong, citing as respondent Fan, another member elected to the Legislative Council who was also a member selected for the Provisional Legislature, and its President. This case provided the vehicle for the leader of the Democratic Party, Mr. Martin Lee, Q.C., to conduct the essentially political pleadings in a judicial setting.

This was an application for leave to apply for judicial review. The applicant also sought an injunction against the usurpation by Fan of the office of Hong Kong Legislative Councillor, a declaration this usurpation was contrary to the provisions of the *Letters Patent* which establish the Legislative Council and which provide for the Governor's law making authority with the Legislative Council, as well as

> a declaration that the tabling of documents described as Bills, and deliberation and passage of such so-called Bills by the said body acting under the presidency of Mrs. Fan are of no legislative effect and are null and void.[76]

The application specified that there is no other legal means for making laws in Hong Kong than through the process mandated by the *Letters Patent*. It submitted that only members of the legally constituted Legislative Council were entitled to undertake "the deliberative part of the legislative process for Hong Kong."[77] It went on to argue that Fan's actions went "far beyond the mere preparation for the enactment of legislation by a new legislative body after the transfer of sovereignty over Hong Kong."[78] Based on these arguments, the principal conclusion of the application was that

> The existence of 2 bodies purporting to legislate for Hong Kong, one of which is lawful and the other unlawful, diminishes the rule of law and

---

[76] Notice of Application of Ng King Luen in the Supreme Court of Hong Kong for leave to appeal for judicial review; June 7, 1997, p. 2.
[77] *Ibid.*, p. 6, para. 25.
[78] *Ibid.*, para. 26.

creates public confusion and uncertainty. It is therefore a matter of urgent public importance that the relief sought by this application is granted.[79]

The judgment refused leave to apply for judicial review on a number of grounds. If the analysis to be conducted by this study dealt exclusively with legal criteria, the reader may be tempted to draw the conclusion that the court exercised a remarkable degree of judicial restraint. From the particular perspective of political law, however, this ruling must be looked at as a particularly cautious balancing act, in which the judge found every possible reason, allegedly not to entangle the court, and hence the application of legal norms, in what it perceived to be a primarily political domain. Considering the specific factual situation of the imminent return of Hong Kong to China, this case may also be considered as an example of the limits of law and legality in dealing with political acts and processes "on the ground," affecting a change in sovereignty and the consequential creation of a new legitimacy.

At the outset, the court boldly characterized this matter to be political, it felt that the application sought to involve it in a political conflict and indicated that "courts are not concerned with political matters. They are solely concerned with issues of law."[80]

Involving the courts in such an issue would threaten the independence of the judiciary. The court also held that the establishment of the Provisional Legislature and the approaching dissolution of the existing Legislative Council were consequences of a political impasse among the powers involved. Hence, it felt that whether the Provisional Legislature was necessary, or legal, was not its concern.

On the issue of standing, the court thought that Ng lacked sufficient interest to be the applicant in the case, a function that only a person adversely affected by a particular decision could properly fulfil. In an indirect remark about the fact that the application was being funded through legal aid, the court even suggested that Ng was being used as a nominative applicant for other interests. The application was said to raise important constitutional matters; consequently, the case ought to have been brought to court by the Attorney General.

---

[79] *Ibid.*, para. 32.
[80] *Ng v. Fan* Case AN No. 39 of 1997, p. 2-R.

The court went on to state that framing the case as an application for judicial review was not the proper format. There was no decision of an inferior tribunal or court to challenge.

The *ratio* most strongly expressed to support the ruling was that the court lacked territorial jurisdiction. The actions complained of by Ng were taking place in China, where the writ of the Hong Kong courts did not run. This motive was undeniably correct from a purely legal point of view. It was, however, not only the key to the outcome of the case but also the very reason for which the incoming power, China, presumably decided to hold the pre-July 1997 meetings of the Provisional Legislature on Chinese soil. In a process so deliberately prepared as the transition of Hong Kong, it is difficult to imagine that the meeting place of the Provisional Legislature was not carefully chosen, with political purposes in mind and in such a manner as not to contravene the legal framework of the British regime in Hong Kong. The result of this political process was to leave the legitimacy of the Provisional Legislature in a kind of legal grey zone, as its legality could not be successfully challenged.

There seems nothing overly unusual or controversial in the reasons expressed above by the court. However, the judgment did venture into two other areas in which some doubt may be indicated. Not only did the court refuse the relief sought on the ground of lack of jurisdiction, but it also said that there was nothing unlawful in what the members of that Provisional Legislature were doing and that even if they had done it within Hong Kong, it would not be breaking the law. It went on to indicate that it could not say that what Fan did was usurpation because that is a political matter into which the court could not get involved. Moreover, the Provisional Legislature had not done anything that should be supervised by the court. Were it otherwise, the Attorney General would have come to court.

This reasoning may lead observers to conclude that the court was so anxious to avoid becoming embroiled in politics that its overly expressed neutrality ended up becoming a political statement in itself. Moreover, in light of the clear provisions of the Letters Patent on Hong Kong's legislative process, one may doubt the part of the judgment which states that had the alleged usurpation occurred within Hong Kong, it would not be a breach of the law.

The final significant aspect of the judgment related to the legality of the amendments made by the Provisional Legislature to Ordinances of the Legislative Council. The court framed this potential problem in the following cautious terms, indicating that its opinion on this part of the matter was somewhat different from the other parts of the case.

> I accept that there may well be problems in the future - and I put it no higher than that - as to the legality of certain amendments to our ordinances which may be passed after July the 1st, for example, the Public Order Amendment Bill which was passed by the Provisional Legislature. The arrangements for public processions for persons to give notices prior to July the 1st. That of course is impossible because this would not become law until July the 1st and that has been recognised by a recent alteration to that order so that the Commissioner of Police is given power himself either to object or not to object under new arrangements.[81]

Despite the moderate use of words, with these few lines the court may have left the new masters of Hong Kong a poisoned pill by opening the door, at least pursuant to the British-based legal system, to eventual challenges to the legality of the work of the Provisional Legislature done prior to July 1, 1997. It even developed this thought by stating further that,

> If in the future this applicant, or any other citizen of Hong Kong considers that a law is unlawful matter and they are prosecuted for an unlawful law, they can raise the matter in court. Then the judge would consider whether or not that law is indeed a lawful one.[82]

Thus, while the conclusion of the case is that the attack on the legitimacy of the Provisional Legislature as an institution failed completely, the legitimacy of its work was left open to future litigation. Such an avenue could only be cut off if the post-transition political-legal regime in Chinese Hong Kong found a way of closing it.

This case elicited enormous interest and much media comment in Hong Kong. Perhaps the most telling description was provided the day after the ruling by the *South China Morning Post*, which explicitly acknowledged the linkage between the legal system and the political

---

[81] *Ibid.*, p. 5-P through 6-D.
[82] *Ibid.*, p. 7-I through L.

regime of Hong Kong, whichever one is in place, in the following terms.

> However, judicial independence cuts both ways. Mr. Justice Sears may have had strong grounds for yesterday's decision since the provisional legislature's actions have not yet affected anyone in Hong Kong. But the real test will only come when a case arises where the law requires a less politically convenient conclusion. The courts will have to show they can be impartial, not just in reaching decisions that happen to concord with Beijing's wishes, but also in those that go the other way.

> That could be put to the test very shortly. Although meetings of the provisional legislature have now been deemed to be legal, Mr. Justice Sears acknowledged that the laws they pass may fall into a different category. After July 1, anyone prosecuted under such ordinances will be able to challenge their legality with some prospect of success.

> But, with such a strong judicial team now in place, there is cause to hope that the courts of the Special Administrative Region will handle such cases according to the law, regardless of the political consequences.[83]

4.8 ISSUE: FORMATION AND COMPOSITION OF GOVERNMENTS AND OPPOSITIONS

See *Official Status for the British Columbia N.D.P. Opposition*, Speaker's Ruling, July 12, 2001.

---

§ 4.8.1
Case of Prime Minister Sergei Kiriyenko
1998; litigation not initiated

The Soviet Union was formally dissolved on December 21, 1991, by the *Declaration of Alma Ata*. To observers better versed in Western traditions of parliamentary democracy, the first years of post-Communist rule in Russia have seemed to resemble a permanent struggle for power among rival parties and factions. It is to the benefit of the implementation of democracy in Russia that a large part of this struggle has occurred within the State Duma, the Lower House of the

---

[83] *South China Morning Post*, June 13, 1997, p. 22.

Federal Assembly, the Parliament of the Russian Federation. It is hardly surprising that in the unstable political and degenerating economic circumstances of Russia in the 1990's, the role of law is rather less weighty than in other countries with a longer tradition of legality and with internal peace and stability. Nevertheless, the Russian experience does provide a fascinating example of constitutional practice in the realm of the formation of a new government, which is also a case exhibiting vital characteristics of political law.

The origins of this situation need to be traced back to the adoption of Russia's first post-Communist constitution. On December 12, 1983, at the same time as Russia held its first multi-party parliamentary elections, it held a referendum to adopt a new constitution. The style of government favoured by Russia was a presidential system in which the President was charged with nominating the Prime Minister, formally called the Chairman of the Government of the Russian Federation. The nominee for this position had to be accept by the Duma. The institutional design adopted in the Russian Constitution was that if the President's choice was rejected, he could put forward a second and even a third nominee. The exact text of the relevant provision, subsection 111(4) of the Constitution, reads in context as follows:

> **Article 111**
> (1) The Chairman of the Government of the Russian Federation shall be appointed by the President of the Russian Federation with consent of the State Duma.
> (2) The proposal on the candidacy of the Chairman of the Government of the Russian Federation shall be made no later than two weeks after the inauguration of the newly-elected President of the Russian Federation or after the resignation of the Government of the Russian Federation or within one week after the rejection of the candidate by the State Duma.
> (3) The State Duma shall consider the candidacy of the Chairman of the Government of the Russian Federation submitted by the President of the Russian Federation within one week after the nomination.
> (4) After the State Duma thrice rejects candidates for Chairman of the Government of the Russian Federation nominated by the President of the Russian Federation, the President of the Russian Federation shall appoint Chairman of the Government of the Russian Federation, dissolve the State Duma and call a new election.[84]

---

[84] This translation is found on the Internet at a site entitled "ICL-International Constitutional Law," located at http://www.oefre.unibe.ch/law/icl/rs00000_html.

It must be noted that section 111(4) does not indicate whether the President could nominate three separate candidates or the same candidate three times, or take an intermediate solution.

The first President of post-Communist Russia to whom these powers were available was Boris Yeltsin, who took office after the demise of Gorbachev. Yeltsin was later elected in a two-turn presidential election on June 16 and July 3, 1996. Later on, in the period leading up to late March, 1998, Yeltsin's Prime Minister, with the apparent confidence of the Duma, was Viktor Chernomyrdin.

The immediate events which led to the use and testing of section 111(4) started on March 23, 1998, when Yeltsin unexpectedly fired Chernomyrdin as Prime Minister, citing the latter's lack of dynamism to affect economic reforms. He then appointed as Acting Prime Minister the man who had been Minister of Energy in the Chernomyrdin government, Sergei Kiriyenko, a technocrat with a business background and relatively little experience in government. Yeltsin also indicated that he would nominate Kiriyenko to be Prime Minister, in accordance with section 111. This started a month-long governmental crisis.

The genuine stake in the conflict was control of the levers of governmental power, the economy and modernization reforms in Russia. Seen from the West, the principal antagonists seemed to be, on the one hand, President Yeltsin and the economic reformers who constituted his entourage and on the other, the shifting coalitions of Duma deputies among whom the electorally reinvigorated Communists played a prominent role, with far right nationalists appearing to increase their power as well. The most significant aspect of the entire conflict was that it was played out in the institutions and the halls of government, rather than on the streets or in the barracks.

On March 27, Yeltsin formally nominated Kiriyenko and on April 10, the Duma voted his candidacy down by 186 votes to 145; he would have needed 226 votes to be accepted. In an atmosphere of increasingly acrimonious parliamentary debates and manoeuvring, Yeltsin nominated Kiriyenko a second time and on April 17, the Duma rejected him by the even worse result of 271 against, 115 for, with 11 abstentions.

It was at about that time that the process of formation of the Kiriyenko government took a legal excursion in the midst of its so far essentially political evolution. A group of Deputies in the Duma, refusing to accept the President's interpretation of section 111(4), "challenged Yeltsin's right to nominate the same candidate more than once"[85] and sought leave to address the matter of the interpretation of this constitutional provision, and hence the validity of the President's second nomination of Kiriyenko, to the Constitutional Court of Russia.

> But the issue never made it to the Constitutional Court, whose strict schedule, it would appear, is not subject to last-minute modification to serve short-term political ends. One judge suggested it would be at least two months before the Court could consider the matter.[86]

This was alternatively set out in the following terms, which also add to our understanding of the events:

> Constitutional Court Chairman Marat Baglai confirmed on April 16 that the court is unlikely to consider that appeal before the fall.[87]

As soon as the Duma's second vote was completed, Yeltsin nominated Kiriyenko a third time. He applied a great deal of political pressure and succeeded in splitting the Communist deputies. The third vote, on April 24, 1998, was 251 in favour and 25 against. Some days later, the President's representative to the Duma intimated that the real reason for Chernomyrdin's dismissal had not been economic stagnation, but rather a move to forestall the holding of a vote of non-confidence in the government by the Duma. If that is true, Yeltsin's move was a tremendous gamble which paid a handsome political profit for the President.

Some points of interest must be noted in regard to the Kiriyenko case. The first is that while there have been several notable challenges to governments that have dealt with, or resulted in, dissolution, instances of attempts to seek judicial intervention in the formation of a government are exceedingly rare. Further, it is significant that even

---

[85] This information, as well as a complete chronology of the related events is available on the Internet at the site of the NVPI - Centre for Russian Studies, located at http://www.nupi.no/cgi-win/Russland/krono.exe.

[86] Letter dated May 12, 1998, addressed by the Canadian Embassy in Moscow to the author.

[87] Website of NUPI - Centre for Russian Studies, report dated April 17, 1998.

in a country such as Russia with a governmental tradition more thoroughly focused on power than on rules, the process of democratization should produce a desire to resort to the court for a constitutional interpretation as part of, or as an aid in a power struggle is a sign of the somewhat increasingly significant role of law in democratic governance.

Finally, observers of legality must pay close scrutiny to the reaction of the court itself in essentially refusing to deal with the case purported to be submitted to it. The question must be asked whether the court was acting in accordance with its own statute and procedures, or did it make its refusal to analyze the President's interpretation of the Constitution a political gesture of support for the power that was then in office. A look at the material readily available, the provisions of the Russian Constitution dealing with the Constitutional Court, will only give the beginning of a reply.

Article 125

...(5) The Constitutional Court of the Russian Federation on request by the President of the Russian Federation, the Federation Council, State Duma, the Government of the Russian Federation, legislative bodies of subjects of the Russian Federation shall interpret the Constitution.[88]

See also *Action by Agreement Democratic Unionist Party*, [2001] NIEHC, November 5, 2001 (Ireland); *Chaudhury v. Qarase and President of the Republic of Fiji Islands*, Fiji Court of Appeal, February 15, 2002, Miscellaneous No 1/2001 and *Prosecution of George Speight for treason*, February 18, 2002 (Fiji).

---

[88] Website of ICL - International Constitutional Law.

4.9 ISSUE: DISMISSAL AND DISSOLUTION OF GOVERNMENTS

§ 4.9.1

Bavarda v. Attorney General

Supreme Court of Fiji; August 14, 1987

[1988] L.R.C. (Const.) 13

The Dominion of Fiji had functioned under a constitution adopted in 1970 and inherited from its British colonial history. During the spring of 1987, there was conflict between the island's Fijian and Indican communities. In the elections held that year, the victors were a coalition of the mainly Indian-based National Federation Party and the Fiji Labour Party. Dr. Timoci Bavarda, an ethnic Fijian, became Prime Minister and put together a government which reflected the multi-racial character of Fiji's population. This did not satisfy the Tankei movement of indigenous Fijians who were clamouring for empowerment. On May 14, 1987, the army unlawfully seized power. The Prime Minister, the entire Cabinet and these members of the House of Representatives who had been elected into the majority were arrested and detained. On May 19, the Governor General dissolved Parliament by proclamation, purportedly made pursuant to the constitution and declared the offices of Prime Minister, Ministers (including that of the Attorney General), Leader of the Opposition and Speaker of the House of Representatives to be vacant.

These facts gave rise to a most interesting challenge using law to defeat actions based on the extra-constitutional use of political power and armed force to determine the rightful government. The Prime Minister deposed in the coup, Bavarda, commenced an action in the Supreme Court, seeking ten declarations that were aimed at having the actions taken by the army, and the measures taken by the Governor General in concert with it, found unconstitutional. The assent of the court would inevitably lead to the restoration of the country's legitimate and democratically elected government. Although no new elections had been held by the time this case was heard and consequently no new Attorney General was constitutionally in office, the actually functioning Attorney General countered Bavarda's action by applying to have all parts of the application struck out on the grounds that they disclosed no reasonable cause of action, that they were frivolous, vexatious or otherwise an abuse of the process of the court.

The court refused to strike out Bavarda's claims. This case is noteworthy for political law in several ways and its major points are worth analysis even far away from Fiji. The Bavarda judgment provides a clear example of the reliance on legal norms to overcome the unconstitutional use of political power in attempting to ensure that the legitimacy of an elected government is maintained. First, it shows the willingness of the court to grasp the fundamental nature of the conflict and to deal with the case even though considerations other than legal ones are involved. Moreover, the judgment provides reasons for its refusal to hold most of the ten applications frivolous, vexatious or abusive. Finally, it provides in legal terms a general indication of the need for political normalization, that is, an indication of the requirement to resume the conduct of political life and public affairs in accordance with constitutional and legal norms.

The court reacted extremely firmly to the Attorney General's pleading that the applicant had no reasonable cause of action. Basing itself on the test developed in English precedent, it said that it would refuse to strike out the application and that it would proceed to try the issue where the pleading raised a question of general importance or serious questions of law. Applying both sides of that test, clearly in the belief that the situation at hand involved questions of both general, that is, political, as well as legal importance, the court declared that:

> This is probably the most significant and important action ever brought before any Court in Fiji. To claim that it is frivolous, vexatious or an abuse of the process of the Court is entirely inappropriate.[89]

The most fundamental point of Bavarda's application sought a declaration that the proclamation issued by the Governor General on May 19, 1987, was unconstitutional, unlawful and invalid on the ground that the Prime Minister had not advised a dissolution and that neither of the conditions precedent to a dissolution without the advice of the Prime Minister, which were set out in section 70(1) of the Constitution, had been satisfied. In seeking to convince the court of this allegation, the plaintiff argued that while the constitution did

---

[89] [1988] L.R.C. (Cons.) 13 at 16 c.

preclude a court from considering whether the Governor General acted on advice received, it did not preclude the court from determining the question whether the Governor General did receive advice upon which he could or should have acted. The court recognized that this was the core of the issue and agreed with Bavarda in the following terms:

> Furthermore, the Supreme Court may have to determine what powers the Governor-General retained after the abduction of the plaintiff and his Cabinet and in what circumstances and for what purposes he could exercise any such powers. This is not a case in which the Supreme Court is called upon to adjudicate questions arising out of constitutional issues contemplated by the Constitution itself. The present action depends upon an extraordinary situation in which the executive and legislative institutions founded in the Constitution have been effectively subverted. It raises difficult and complicated questions of law and I decline to strike out the plaintiff's claim.[90]

The deposed Prime Minister also sought to have the court declare that he remain an elected member of the House of Representatives and that he continue to hold the office of Prime Minister. The Attorney General countered that there is no private right to the office of Prime Minister and that "the question of who should be Prime Minister and as such in control of the Government of the nation is not a matter for the court to consider."[91] While this may have been the position of the Attorney General at law, it was also clearly politically self-serving. In any event, the court refused to strike out this part of the claim, thus refuting the Attorney General's argumentation.

Bavarda further claimed that as the state of emergency had ceased with the release of the detained governmental officials, the Governor General had a duty to return executive power to the democratically elected government and to call for the House of Representatives to reconvene. Here also, the court refused the Attorney General's counter that this was not a matter for the court's consideration and it refused to strike out the claim.

There were two significant parts of Bavarda's claim which the court refused to allow to go to trial on the merits. The first of these was the application for a declaration that the session of the House of Repre-

---

[90] *Ibid.* at 19 b-d.
[91] *Ibid.* at 20 g.

sentatives which was forcibly and unlawfully interrupted on May 14 be held to stand adjourned. Mindful of the duty of the judiciary not to interfere in matters pertaining to the legislative branch of government, the court held that the decision as to if and when the House of Representatives would convene was one for the House alone to decide.

The court also refused to undertake to adjudicate on the merits the issue of the residual power of the Crown to amend Fiji's constitution. In this regard, the court held that it had jurisdiction to inquire into the existence of prerogative powers. It recognized the sovereign's pre-eminence and reaffirmed that she herself was limited by her duty to obey the law.

> The Queen may not dispense with laws. She cannot, therefore, alter or repeal the Constitution of Fiji which is the supreme law (section 2) or any part of it... "It is inconceivable that Her Majesty would under any circumstances attempt to alter the Constitution or the laws of Fiji by means other than those provided in the Constitution itself."[92]

On this basis, the court held the claim that the Crown could not amend the constitution outside of the constitution amendment provision to be unsustainable, and allowing it to proceed to trial would serve no useful purpose.

Bavarda's tenth and final claim related to the power to legislate and the power of the executive for the appropriation and expenditure of public funds other than in compliance with the constitution. In the period between the coup and the hearing of this case, the authorities in place had promulgated several measures and incurred State expenditures. The court used its analysis of this part of the action to indicate its opinion on the requirement for Fiji to return to legality.

> The absence of a House of Representatives makes it impossible for Parliament to make laws for the peace, order and good government of Fiji (section 52). More than 60 days have now passed since the date of the dissolution of Parliament and writs for a general election of members of the House of Representatives have not been issued although this is a requirement of section 69(3) of the Constitution. Thus, Fiji is without a legislature and it does not appear to be the present intention to create one in the manner provided in the Constitution. This creates a grave

---

[92] *Ibid.* at 22 g and 23 d.

situation which becomes more serious as each day passes and the need arises to obtain supply in order to continue the Government and the services which it provides.

. . .

Those measures are of a legislative character. It is not for me to say at this time to what extent these Proclamations are within the authority that His Excellency has assumed.

But there can be no doubt that the measures already taken and those which may be in contemplation raise serious and difficult issues which may have to be resolved by this Court either in this or other proceedings. I am not persuaded that the plaintiff should now be prevented from placing them before this Court for consideration and judicial determination and I decline to strike out the claim.[93]

While, in essence, the court's judgment was a direction to the instigators of the coup to restore legality, that is not how events turned out. A few weeks after the judgment, in September 1987, a second coup took place and Fiji's situation of illegality was sanctioned by its expulsion from the Commonwealth. In October of that year, Fiji became an independent republic. It was not until 1990 that a new constitution was adopted. This basic law ensures that the functions of both President and Prime Minister are fulfilled by ethnic Fijians. In the first election held under the new constitution, the coup leader, Siteveni Rabuka, became Prime Minister.

The adoption of the 1990 Constitution did not solve the political disquiet of the island nation's ethnic population. In 2000, another coup took place, which led to yet further litigation of interest for political law.

See also *Nawaz Sharif v. President of Pakistan*, P.L.D. 1993 Sup. Ct. 473; *Mohtarma Benazir Bhutto v. President of Pakistan*, P.L.D. 1996 Sup. Ct. 388 and *In re Article 55 of the Constitution*, [2003] N.R.S.C., Constitutional Reference No. 1 of 2003, Supreme Court of Nauru, January 11 and January 17, 2003.

---

[93] *Ibid.* at 23 g-24 c.

4.10 ISSUE: PARTICIPATION IN PUBLIC LIFE

§ 4.10.1[94]
Penikett v. R.
Yukon Territory Court of Appeal; December 23, 1987
(1987), 45 D.L.R. (4th) 108[95]

On April 30, 1987, the Prime Minister of Canada and the premiers of the ten Provinces met near Ottawa to devise a constitutional amendment plan to resolve the impasse that had resulted from the patriation of the Constitution from the United Kingdom to Canada without the consent of the Government of Québec. At that meeting, they concluded a political agreement which became known as the *Meech Lake Accord*. The intention of the participants was to convert the pact from a merely political one to a legal text that would be submitted to the 11 legislative bodies and would presumably be adopted as further modifications to the Canadian constitutional framework. The First Minister of the Yukon Territory, Penikett, was not invited to participate in the Meech Lake discussions and had no influence either on the content of the resulting *Accord,* or on the process that would have to be used to achieve formal adoption of the resulting legal instrument.

Penikett did not approve of the *Meech Lake Accord* and brought suit in the courts of the Yukon Territory to have it declared contrary to specific provisions of the *Canadian Charter of Rights and Freedoms*. At trial level, the court believed that the *Charter* could be held to apply to the *Meech Lake Accord*, but the Crown appealed. Before the Yukon Territory Court of Appeal, Penikett's application contained a number of petitions for declaration. Among these, Penikett sought the assent of the judiciary to the argument that he, as leader of the Yukon Government, one of the jurisdictions constituting Canada, should not have been left out of the Meech Lake deliberation.

(4) That denying the Yukon Territory a voice in constitutional matters was inconsistent with the right of every citizen to vote (s. 3 of the

---

[94] Cross-reference to § 4.13.B.1.
[95] Leave to appeal refused (1988), 88 N.R. 320n (S.C.C.).

Charter) and rendered votes to elect the Yukon Territory Government ineffective;[96]

There are two layers of irony in this argument. It was an unwritten, although obvious, aspect of this petition for declaratory relief that the very reason for the *Meech Lake Accord* was that Québec had been left out of the patriation deal, and now it was the Yukon that was being left out. Underlying the petition was another unwritten aspect of the same issue, namely the question of the relative importance and po-litical weight of diverse jurisdictions within the federation. If a full deal could not be achieved without Québec, could one be struck without the Yukon, with its territorial status of not quite being a province, its minuscule population, its tiny economic base and its out-of-the-way location vis-à-vis the centres of Canadian public life? These were of course purely political arguments that could not even be raised in the pleadings before the courts. Yet the very reason why a court challenge seemed appropriate was because these arguments were carrying no weight in the political arena either.

Very closely linked to the issue of the Yukon's absence from the forum of constitutional discussion was the likely effect of that absence and of the potential adoption of the *Accord* on the Yukon's prospects for constitutional evolution toward provincehood. Thus, additional pe-titions were framed as follows:

(5)   That the agreement surrendered the residual discretion of the fed-eral government to establish new provinces and was inconsistent with their continuing constitutional duties and obligations and vi-olated established constitutional principles;

(6)   The agreement limited the eligibility of the territories to admission as provinces and was a violation of a constitutional guarantee to territories' residents to protect their legal rights by courts of com-petent jurisdiction;

(7)   That the effect of the accord was inconsistent with a constitutional convention that the Yukon will have an increasing right of self-determination culminating in provincehood;

(8)   Provisions in the International Covenant on Civil and Political Rights and the Universal Declaration of Human Rights were vio-

---

[96]   (1987), 45 D.L.R. (4th) 108 at 111, leave to appeal refused (1988), 88 N.R. 320n (S.C.C.).

lated by the restriction of eligibility of the Yukon to admission as a province without any or adequate defining principle or criteria for a veto;

(9)   This restricted eligibility for admission was inconsistent with a constitutional right of the Yukon to be admitted as a province on the same basis as the other provinces were admitted;

(10)   The Yukon has a unique status in Canada with greater rights and privileges than non-members of the union which might seek admission as provinces and provisions of the Accord which would restrict that status were contrary to prevailing constitutional values and principles.[97]

In Canada's long history of constitutional discussions and federal-provincial conferences, the ability to a seat at the table had always been acquired on the basis of an invitation, which was itself issued as a result of consensus among the participants. Moreover, the issue of participation and the issuance of invitations had always been purely political decisions. The great interest in the *Penikett* case was its innovation in attempting to legalize and judicialize the matter of participation in the process of constitutional reform.

The Yukon Territory Court of Appeal dealt with the matter of Penikett's lack of participation in the discussions leading to the *Meech Lake Accord* as an aspect of the question of justiciability. In other words, the court perceived that it would have to decide the point by determining whether this was a subject for legal adjudication or political negotiation.

Penikett alleged that the Prime Minister breached a duty of fairness in failing to invite the Yukon's representatives to attend the conferences leading up to the *Accord* and in failing to consult its representatives before committing the Government of Canada to the terms of the legal text based on the political *Accord*. Yukon residents, he contended, had a legitimate expectation to be consulted and to be invited to any conference involving their future rights, liberties and privileges under the Constitution.

The court recognized that it had the power to impose a duty of fairness on the executive branch in the realm of quasi-judicial, administrative

---

[97]   *Ibid.*

and executive acts. However, upon its reading of the introductory words of section 41 of the *Constitution Act, 1982*, which dealt with the constitutional amendment process, the court felt that the Meech Lake process was more in the nature of a legislative act.

> In our opinion, it is implicit in s. 41 that an amendment to the Constitution of Canada which falls within the purview of that section would require prior agreement of the Prime Minister and the Premiers of each of the provinces before the necessary resolutions could be introduced. Prior agreement would be required as to the terms of the resolution and the amendments to be sought in respect of the Constitution. Coming to agreement as to the terms of the resolution and the amendments to be made to the Constitution would be the first step in invoking the procedure for amending the Constitution of Canada set out in Part V of the *Constitution Act, 1982*.[98]

The court concluded on this petition that in convening the conference of First Ministers at Meech Lake, the Prime Minister of Canada was initiating a process of legislation for the purpose of amending the Constitution of Canada. This clearly fell within the ambit of Part V of the *Constitution Act, 1982*. Thus, the Meech Lake process was legislative in nature and the matter was not justiciable. On this point, the Court of Appeal specifically overruled and reversed the ruling of the lower court. This finding of the court was significant because it extended the concept of the legislative process in constitutional matters. Indeed, it brought under the umbrella of the concept of the legislative process even that phase of constitutional development which might earlier have been thought of as the "executive" phase or the "pre-legislative" phase, which is in fact the political phase consisting of discussions among ministers in their executive capacity, rather than in their capacity as parliamentarians or legislators. In that sense, the *Penikett* decision is fundamental. This case characterized the ability to be seated at the constitutional discussion table as a legislative matter rather than as an executive one. That interpretation was necessary for the court to render itself able to reserve this essentially political decision of participation, for political decision-makers. One would therefore not be wrong in concluding that the courts perceive the entire legislative process in the constitutional arena as a political matter, not subject to their review on the ground of absence of justiciability. The *Penikett* ruling was instrumental in ensuring that seating at the table of constitutional deliberations would remain a decision

---

[98] *Ibid.* at 118.

at the discretion of the inviters. The courts could not be used to obtain a seat by right of law.

The Court of Appeal went on to examine whether the Governor in Council owed a fiduciary obligation to the people of the Yukon in relation to the *Accord*. Penikett's petition in this regard had alleged that the federal government owed, and by its actions had violated, a "political trust duty" and a "fiduciary duty" to Yukoners.

The court acknowledged that there exists a "general governmental duty to govern wisely"[99] but distinguished each of the other concepts of duty from this. A fiduciary obligation, that is the duty to govern for the benefit of the people, arose in respect of the Canadian North from both constitutional provisions and unilateral undertakings made by the federal government. The relevant constitutional provisions are the ones relating to the incorporation, in 1870, of Rupert's Land and the Northwest Territory into Canada. The Yukon was part of the lands so transferred from British to Canadian jurisdiction. In the court's view, the texts relating to the transfer created only a general governmental obligation, but no fiduciary obligation on the part of the federal government.

The relevant unilateral undertakings were ministerial speeches in the House of Commons. The court indicated that these were purely political statements, without legal weight, for which accountability lay with the electorate.

With respect to the concept of a political trust duty, the court examined the Canadian and British precedents. It concluded that this concept dealt essentially with the distribution of public funds held by a government. It did not extend to the subject-matter of the present case and this part of Penikett's argument was also set aside.

The court's overall conclusion on Penikett's affirmation of some form of political or quasi-political obligation on the part of the federal government to include the Yukon in the Meech Lake deliberations was also that the matter was not justiciable. Viewed in its entirety, the effect of this decision was to push Penikett away from his attempt to exercise recourses of a legal nature and to steer him back into the political forum. There, however, Penikett was to be no more success-

---

[99] *Ibid.* at 122.

ful in his tries to stop the *Meech Lake Accord.* That was to happen by the hands of others, in entirely different circumstances. Nevertheless, Penikett opened the way for other occasions at using the courts in bids to be seated at the constitutional table.

---

§ 4.10.2[100]
Sibbeston v. Northwest Territories (Attorney General)
Northwest Territories Court of Appeal; February 3, 1988
(1988), 48 D.L.R. (4th) 691

At the time of these proceedings, Sibbeston was the First Minister of the Northwest Territories. The petition is presented, however, on his behalf in the capacity of a private citizen. Sibbeston sought a series of declarations through which he attempted to have rendered unconstitutional the *Meech Lake Accord* of April 30, 1987, the purpose of which was to amend the *Constitution Act, 1982,* the so-called patriation package. One of the declarations Sibbeston asked the court to issue was to the effect that the *Accord* was unconstitutional, as the conference of First Ministers at which it had been reached had not included representation from the governments of the Northwest Territories (NWT) or the Yukon Territory (YT). This petition was rejected.

The *Constitution Act, 1982* had been drafted in recognition of the fact that various constitutional issues remained unsettled. The text therefore included a provision, section 37, which required that a constitutional conference be held within a year, regarding constitutional matters affecting the aboriginal peoples of Canada. This section required that government representatives from the NWT and YT be invited to participate in the discussion of issues which would directly affect their jurisdictions. At the 1983 conference, section 37 was replaced with a new section 37.1, which mandated two further such conferences. The arrangements for territorial participation were carried over from section 37 to section 37.1. On the basis of these provisions, the First Ministers of the NWT and the YT did participate in all three conferences. Thereafter, section 37.1 ceased to have effect on April 18, 1987.

---

[100] Cross-reference to § 4.13.B.2.

In a series of proceedings relating primarily to the constitutional situation of Québec, but not dealing at all with aboriginal constitutional issues, the First Ministers of Canada and the ten provinces held a constitutional conference on April 30, 1987. No representatives of the NWT were invited. At that conference, the *Meech Lake Accord* was struck.

The court held that the NWT government had no right to attend the Meech Lake meeting and that the *Accord* was not unconstitutional merely because of the NWT's non-participation.

> We are of the view that there is no obligation to invite the representatives from the Northwest Territories government to the 30th April, 1987 meeting. Section 37.1(3) creates an obligation to invite such participation only if the conference is convened under subs. (1). After 18th April, 1987, s. 37.1 no longer existed. No further conferences could be called under subs. (1) and there could be no further obligation to invite participation from the territorial governments under subs. (3). In any event, that the 30th April meeting related to the inclusion of Quebec under the Constitution Act, 1982, and the amendments that might be required to the Constitution relate to Pt. V of the Constitution Act, 1982. Nowhere in Pt. V is the participation of the government of the Northwest Territories required.[101]

The sense of the judgment was that section 37 and section 37.1 had created a constitutional obligation to invite the NWT to the three conferences specified. Once these provisions ceased to have effect, they did not engender a constitutional convention that Territorial governments be invited to every constitutional conference thereafter, nor was there an inherent right for them to be at the table of constitutional discussion.

---

[101] (1988), 48 D.L.R. (4th) 691 at 698.

§ 4.10.3
Native Women's Assn. of Canada v. R.
Federal Court of Canada – Trial Division; March 30, 1992
(1992), 90 D.L.R. (4th) 394[102]
and
Federal Court of Appeal; August 20, 1992
(1992), 95 D.L.R. (4th) 106[103]
and
Supreme Court of Canada; October 27, 1994
(1994), 119 D.L.R. (4th) 224
-and-
Native Women's Assn. of Canada v. R.
Federal Court of Canada – Trial Division; October 16, 1992
(1992), 97 D.L.R. (4th) 537[104]
and
Federal Court of Appeal; November 13, 1992
(1992), 97 D.L.R. (4th) 548

These cases address the principle of inclusiveness in political life in the era of the *Canadian Charter of Rights and Freedoms*. Can the law be used to secure inclusion into the highest levels of public processes, in particular into the process of constitutional development, on the ground that the applicant group intends to voice a point of view based on legal norms, and which it contends no other affected group is capable or desirous of voicing? The alternative is the continued use of political arguments, discussion and negotiation to affect constitutional development.

In the course of the years 1991 and 1992, the Government of Canada was orchestrating a discussion and negotiation process, informally entitled the Canada Round, to develop a constitutional package of amendments to replace the *Meech Lake Accord* which had failed in June 1990. Part of the Canada Round was the proposal to entrench rights to aboriginal self-government. In addition to the governments of the provinces, the Government of Canada extended participation to certain select aboriginal organizations, namely the Assembly of

---

[102] Reversed (1992), 95 D.L.R. (4th) 106 (Fed. C.A.), reversed (1994), 119 D.L.R. (4th) 224 (S.C.C.).
[103] Reversed (1994), 119 D.L.R. (4th) 224 (S.C.C.).
[104] Affirmed (1992), 97 D.L.R. (4th) 548 (Fed. C.A.).

First Nations, the Native Council of Canada, the Métis National Council and the Innuit Tapirisat of Canada.

In the first of these actions, the Native Women's Association of Canada sought an order of the Trial Division of the Federal Court of Canada to deny further funding to these four groups until it was also enabled to participate in the constitutional negotiations and funded to do so. The Association based its application on the allegation that it represented native women in a male-dominated community, with interests divergent from and sometimes contradictory to the male-dominated organizations seated at the discussion table, and that the Government of Canada had shown a historical preference for the views of male-dominated aboriginal groups on issues relating to women's equality. In the Association's view, the actions of the federal authorities breached the *Charter's* section 2(b) protection of their freedom of expression, section 15 equality right, as well as section 28 which dealt with gender equality and section 35(4) which related to gender equality in aboriginal and treaty rights.

The first focus of judicial deliberation was whether, by this action, the Association could become included among those participating in the constitutional development process. Was there a sufficient legal ground to determine the extent of mandated involvement in politics? The respondents opposed the Association in this respect.

> As counsel for respondent points out, reliance on freedom of expression as a basis of the right to be present at the discussion table is a claim that any individual or interest group might make, and, in discussion of proposals for constitutional amendment, to hold that freedom of expression creates a right for everyone to have a voice in these discussions would paralyze the process.[105]

> Respondent's written submission states: "...it is evident that governments have invited the four national Aboriginal organizations to participate fully in the discussion because they consider these organizations to be broadly representative of the Aboriginal peoples as a whole not of some particular constituency."[106]

---

[105] (1992), 90 D.L.R. (4th) 394 at 406 d, reversed (1992), 95 D.L.R. (4th) 106 (Fed. C.A.), reversed (1994), 119 D.L.R. (4th) 224 (S.C.C.).

[106] *Ibid.* at 407 h-408 a.

The court responded to this line of argumentation by holding first that government policy was based not on the fact that the members of the Association were women, but rather that there need not be a yet further group representing the Aboriginal community. In the view of the Government of Canada, as expressed in the correspondence of the minister in charge of the process, the Rt. Hon. Joe Clark, national aboriginal associations represent both men and women within their communities. Secondly, the court determined that the Association's freedom of expression had not been infringed. Even if they were not at the table, they could make their position known.

> I do not conclude therefore that there has been any infringement of applicants' Charter right of freedom of expression.
>
> With respect to discrimination as to sex, the disproportionate funds provided for the Native Women's Association of Canada results not from the fact that they are women but from the unwillingness of the Government to recognize that they should be considered as a separate group within the aboriginal community from the four named groups and treated accordingly. Whether this is fair or contrary to natural justice will be dealt with under another argument respecting the issue of a writ of prohibition, but it does not constitute *per se* discrimination on the basis of sex in contravention of the Charter.[107]

This case also delves into the difference which the presence of the Association at the constitutional negotiation table would entail. In particular, the Association presents the argument that it would best expound on the matter of the applicability of the *Charter* to aboriginal self-government activities.

> It is contended that by financing the four recipient groups in the constitutional renewal discussions under way the Government of Canada is assisting some of them to propagate the view that the said Charter of Rights and Freedoms should not apply to aboriginal self-government activities, whereas applicants and other aboriginal women's groups require similar funding and participation in said discussions as they consider that it is essential that the said Charter should continue to apply in order to safeguard and promote the equality of aboriginal women.[108]

Here again, the court denied the relief sought by the Association, but for different reasons.

---

[107] *Ibid.* at 406 e-g.
[108] *Ibid.* at 397 c-d.

One further issue should be dealt with, namely, that the results which applicants hope to obtain in their fear of loss of Charter protection is speculative. This would only occur if the participants in the constitutional discussion accepted the position of the Assembly of First Nations and others on this issue and if subsequently resolutions to that effect were adopted by Parliament and the legislatures. Applicants will have further opportunities to express their concerns before any such changes become law, if in fact any such changes will even be recommended.

. . .

The purpose of the impending multicultural discussions on the Constitution is to "bring the Canada Round to a successful conclusion." Success will be measured by the level of agreement reached as to the proposals for constitutional amendments to be incorporated in draft parliamentary resolutions. The discussions are therefore only part of the legislative process in which courts should not intervene.[109]

The entire history of this litigation is worth retracing and reciting because of the variety of judicial opinions on the questions raised before the courts and because of the vital importance of the matter.

With respect to section 35 of the *Constitution Act, 1982*, this court found the Association's claim without merit; the right of Aboriginal peoples to participate in the constitutional deliberations in a manner different from other Canadians derives from sections 37 and 37.1 of the *Constitution Act, 1982*, itself, not from existing aboriginal treaty rights. The remedy sought under section 15 was also denied. Not only does section 15 guarantee rights to individuals rather than collectives, but at the time of this decision, the fear of loss of equality was hypothetical and not the present denial of a right. In this regard, significantly, the court added that:

The law does not accord any individual the right to be present at the table at constitutional conferences nor the right to public funding to develop and communicate a constitutional position.[110]

This is perhaps the clearest statement that if one claims an entitlement to participate in a political process from a legal rather than a political source, that claimant must stand on solid legal, rather than political ground.

---

[109] *Ibid.* at 398 h-399 a and 399 c-d.
[110] (1992), 95 D.L.R. (4th) 106 at 118 e, reversed (1994), 119 D.L.R. (4th) 224 (S.C.C.).

Notwithstanding these reasons, the Federal Court of Appeal perceived a threat to the equality of Aboriginal women greater than the Trial Division had. In making their argument on the point of freedom of expression, the Association, significantly, referred "to the limitations on federal election spending as demonstrating the government's recognition that disparate financing of political points of view enables the ideas of some to command public attention at the expense of others."[111]

On the grounds of section 2(b) and section 28 of the *Constitution Act, 1982*, alone, the court found that the federal government had restricted the freedom of expression of aboriginal women. Considering that in the time since the Trial Division decision, the process had progressed beyond the consultative state, the court resorted to the only remedy it thought appropriate, a declaration. It refused to suspend or stop the funding of the other groups. The explanation of the merits of the ruling was linked to the genuine core of the matter at hand, namely that the court felt it necessary for someone to be at the table to espouse the view that aboriginal self-governments should also be subject to the *Charter*.

> Measured against the norms of Canadian society as a whole, it is in the interests of aboriginal women that, if, as and when they become the subjects of aboriginal self-governments, they continue to enjoy the protection of the *Canadian Charter of Rights and Freedoms* and, in particular, the rights and freedoms accorded them by sections 15 and 28, or by equivalent provisions equally entrenched in aboriginal charters, if that be legally possible. It is by no means certain that the latter alternative can or will be realized. The interests of aboriginal women, measured by the only standard this court can recognize in the absence of contrary evidence, that of Canadian society at large, are not represented in this respect by AFN, which advocates a contrary result, nor by the ambivalence of NCC and ITC.[112]

It is noteworthy that, in respect of the Constitutional amendment process, basing itself on the decision in the *CAP Reference*[113] and in

---

111 *Ibid.* at 119 e.
112 *Ibid.* at 120 f-g.
113 *Reference re Canada Assistance Plan (Canada)* (1991), 83 D.L.R. (4th) 297 (S.C.C.).

Penikett,[114] the court crystallized the following principles of law applicable to politics.

> a. the Charter, Part I of the *Constitution Act, 1982*, cannot be invoked to interfere with the process of amending the Constitution mandated by Part V;
>
> b. the process of amending the Constitution, as a legislative process, begins not later than when first ministers are convened to agree upon a constitutional resolution they will put to their legislatures; and
>
> c. the formulation of a constitutional resolution is part of the legislative process of amendment with which the courts will not interfere except, possibly, where a Charter guaranteed right may be affected.[115]

The Supreme Court of Canada took yet another view. It allowed the appeal in respect of the *Charter* section 2(b) freedom of expression issue, holding that the government's failure to provide funding to the Association did not violate section 2(b). Under the pen of Mr. Justice Sopinka, the court felt that the freedom of expression guaranteed by this provision did not extend to the guarantee of any particular means of expression, nor did it place on the Government of Canada a positive obligation to consult any person or group. In his view, the Association had not presented evidence to the effect that the four groups at the table were less representative of Aboriginal women's viewpoints than the Association itself.

> Similar to a referendum, the Government of Canada was engaging in a consultative process to secure the public opinion with respect to potential constitutional amendments. To further this goal, a parallel process of consultation was established within the Aboriginal community. It cannot be claimed that NWAC has a constitutional right to receive government funding aimed at promoting participation in the constitutional conferences. The respondents conceded as much in paragraph 91 of their factum as well as in oral argument. Furthermore, the provision of funding and the invitation to participate in constitutional discussions facilitated and enhanced the expression of Aboriginal groups. It did not stifle expression.[116]

---

[114] *Penikett v. R.* (1987), 45 D.L.R. (4th) 108, leave to appeal refused (1988), 88 N.R. 320n (S.C.C.).

[115] *Supra* note 110 at 124 h-125 a.

[116] (1994), 119 D.L.R. (4th) 224 at 244 h-245 a.

Writing in agreement with the court, Madam Justice McLachlin added that in choosing and funding their advisor on matters of policy, governments must be free and not constrained by the *Charter*.

While this first case was proceeding through the courts, after the Federal Court of Appeal had issued its ruling and after the writs had been issued for the Canada-wide referendum on the *Charlottetown Accord*, but before the voting was held, on September 15, 1992, the Association initiated a second action before the Trial Division of the Federal Court of Canada. The basis on which the second action was framed was that the plaintiffs, individually and as members of the class of native women, contended they were doubly disadvantaged by reason of both race and sex. In this and in the other elements of their analysis, the plaintiffs relied extensively on the findings of the Federal Court of Appeal in the first case. They then went on to apply their legal reasoning to the *Consensus Report on the Constitution*, which the First Ministers and those Aboriginal groups who had been participating in the process had concluded on August 28, 1992.

> 21. Paragraph 41 of the Consensus Report provides that:
>
> The Constitution should be amended to recognize that the Aboriginal peoples of Canada have the inherent right of self-government within Canada. This right should be placed in a new section of the *Constitution Act, 1982* section 35.1(1).
>
> 22. There is no provision in the Report for the application to the inherent right of self-government of the principle of equality between men and women. Paragraph 52 of the Report provides that the existing section 35(4) of the *Constitution Act, 1982* should be maintained; that section merely guarantees equally to men and women "existing Aboriginal and treaty rights." Paragraphs 52 and 53 of the Consensus Report stipulate that the issue of gender equality will not be dealt with until at least 1996, and possibly later, at future First Ministers' Conferences on Aboriginal constitutional matters. Nothing in the Report provides that NWAC shall be invited to those meetings; as the Court of Appeal noted, NWAC was not permitted direct participation, in its own right, in the First Ministers Conferences on Aboriginal matters required to be held by the *Constitution Act, 1982*.[117]

---

[117] Amended Statement of Claim, filed September 17, 1992, paras. 21 and 22.

The plaintiffs claimed that their exclusion from this part of the constitutional process violated their section 2(b) and section 28 rights, that they suffered damages in the amount of $5 million, which would have been the amount of constitutional funding they would have been entitled to if equitable principles would have been applied, and that as Prime Minister Mulroney and the Minister Responsible for Constitutional Matters, Joe Clark, had behaved toward them in a contemptuous, lawless and high-handed fashion, they were entitled to punitive damages as well.

In respect of these matters, in addition to the damages, the Association claimed for

(c) an injunction prohibiting the continuation of discussions between the defendants, or any of them, on the one hand, and the AFN, ITC, NCC or MNC, or any of them, on the other hand, on subjects dealt with in the Consensus Report of August 28 or any Political Accord or legal text related thereto unless and until the Native Women's Association of Canada is accorded a right to participate in the constitutional review process on equal terms;

(d) an injunction prohibiting the defendants, or any of them, from continuing with the Referendum scheduled for October 26, 1992 or other Referendum "based on" or otherwise invoking the Consensus Report of August 28, 1992 or related documents;[118]

The core of the Association's argument was that the continuation of its exclusion from the discussions would mean that it would have no part in shaping the institutions of government under which they would live, and that the package of constitutional amendment which had by then been developed would deny equality to Aboriginal women. This raised the interesting and rather fundamental question of whether democracy as a form of government implied a political right to participate in the development of institutions and rights which would frame one's life, and whether that political right, if it existed, could be expressed in terms of legal rights of the citizens involved and obligations incumbent on the State.

In his Memorandum of Fact and Law, the Deputy Attorney General of Canada took note of the political developments but reasoned on grounds of law as if the case were any other injunction matter. He

---

[118] *Ibid.*, para. 37(c) and (d).

pleaded that there was no issue, let alone a serious issue, in the case, that the court should not interfere in the legislative process, that because of the uncertainty of the outcome of the constitutional amendment process, the plaintiff's allegation of irreparable harm was speculative, and that the public interest weighs overwhelmingly in favour of allowing the legislative process to continue. He also disputed the court's jurisdiction to hear this matter.

On October 16, 1992, ten days before the scheduled referendum, the Trial Division dismissed the Association's application. It held that the request to enjoin the meetings of government leaders and the holding of the referendum disclosed no reasonable cause of action and was an abuse of process.

Drawing its reasoning from the Supreme Court decision in the *CAP Reference*, the court determined that the question as to when federal and provincial governments ought to meet with and consult during the development of constitutional amendments is not a justiciable one. Thus, there was no legal right for the Association to secure a seat at the table.

> Indeed, however one may define the "legislative process"—and in my view it is very difficult in an evolutionary process by which ideas for constitutional change eventually find their way into constitutional amendments, to fix a date when that process becomes "legislative"—the fundamental problem is that certain issues are not justiciable. Among those are questions as to whom federal and provincial governments ought to meet with and consult during the development of constitutional amendments. That issue is not justiciable unless there are legal or constitutional rules which a court can apply for their determination. See, e.g., *Reference re: Canada Assistance Plan* case, *supra*, note 9, at pp. 545-546. What principles are the courts to apply in making up an invitation list for a constitutional conference? Assuming that, for example, section 15 or 28 of the Charter require that there be a gender balance in the interests represented at the constitutional table, how is one to define those interests? To what extent should they be regarded as legitimate freestanding interests, of compelling importance in disregard of competing interests and requiring separate representation? How is a judge to determine who genuinely represents those interests and who does not? These are surely political questions for which there are no legal or

constitutional principles to guide a court in its decision. I cannot think that such decisions are the proper function of judges.[119]

More generally, the court also concluded that the *Charter* does not apply to the activities of governments when they are preparing or making amendments pursuant to Part V of the *Constitution Act, 1982*. The Association's efforts to enjoin the holding of the referendum was specifically denied. The referendum was being conducted pursuant to the *Referendum Act*.[120] Neither the Prime Minister nor the Minister responsible for Constitutional Affairs had authority to stop it.

The Federal Court of Appeal did not consider the case until after the holding of the referendum. It dismissed. By November 13, 1992, the date of the judgment, the *Charlottetown Accord* had been voted down by the people of Canada and had become dead letter.

As a result of all of the Association's litigation, there is still no legal right to participate in constitutional negotiations, even where the proponent of such a right hopes to influence a process relevant to its own future legal status and evolution. This is a matter for political deliberation alone.

See also *Hupacasath First Nation v. British Columbia*, 2002 BCCA 238 (B.C. C.A. [In Chambers]) and 2002 BCSC 802 (B.C. S.C. [In Chambers]) and *Bob v. British Columbia*, 2002 BCSC 733 (B.C. S.C. [In Chambers]).

---

[119] (1992), 97 D.L.R. (4th) 537 at 545 g-546 c, affirmed (1992), 97 D.L.R. (4th) 548 (Fed. C.A.).

[120] S.C. 1992, c. 30.

4.11 ISSUE: LEGAL EXPRESSION OF THE EXPANSION OF THE CANADIAN POLITY

4.11.A—TERMS OF UNION WITH BRITISH COLUMBIA IN 1871

---

§ 4.11.A.1

Vancouver Island Railway, An Act Respecting, Re

Supreme Court of Canada; May 5, 1994

(1994), 114 D.L.R. (4th) 193

This is the first of a string of modern cases analyzing the obligations of a constitutional nature relating to the governance of Canada which derive from various Terms of Union by which other British North American colonies united with Canada. These cases are of interest and have significance not only because they illustrate the legal quality of the conduct of government in today's Canada, but also because they unravel the historical roots of our government in both legal and political terms. This particular case deals with the maintenance of rail service on Vancouver Island.

> The issue arises out of the beginnings of British Columbia's history as part of Canada and, despite the modest size and importance of this line of railway, arises directly out of the Terms of Union entered into between British Columbia and Canada in 1870 which led ultimately to the creation of the transcontinental line of the C.P.R., a crucial element in the history of this country...They are part of our written constitution.[121]

By an Order in Council dated October 27, 1989, made pursuant to the *National Transportation Act, 1987*,[122] the Government of Canada authorized the discontinuance of rail service on Vancouver Island. The Attorney General of British Columbia thereupon petitioned for a declaration that Canada has a perpetual obligation to maintain that rail service because that is what the province alleged Canada had agreed to at the time of and as one of the conditions of Union.

---

[121] (1989), 65 D.L.R. (4th) 494 at 497 h-498 a, reversed (1991), 84 D.L.R. (4th) 385 (B.C. C.A.), reversed (1994), 114 D.L.R. (4th) 193 (S.C.C.).

[122] S.C. 1987, c. 34.

The province's position is that maintenance of this rail service is a federal obligation of a constitutional nature. By the Terms of Union concluded in 1871,[123] the parties agreed that the railway linking British Columbia to the other parts of the country would be begun within two years and completed within ten. The Dominion was the party charged with executing that obligation and it was clear from the start that the Vancouver Island portion was included in the original intention. Neither of these deadlines was met.

A second agreement on the specific point of railway construction was reached on August 20, 1883. This was confirmed in both federal and provincial legislation. The actual obligation subject of this litigation arose out of schedule 1 to the federal statute,[124] which reproduced in its entirety the contract between the Dominion and the railway consortium. The expression used there was "construct, complete, maintain and work continuously." In 1905, Parliament enacted further legislation[125] by which the Vancouver Island portion of the rail line was made a work for the general advantage of Canada. Throughout this history, the province relied on federal promises substantiated by legally binding instruments.

> Now the Province is saying, to paraphrase the words of the Minister of Justice in 1917, that in the proper execution of Canada's powers and the obligation of honour and good faith assumed by it in 1883, Canada cannot exercise its powers over the railway to authorize it not to operate, and thus diminish further the slender consideration received by the province under the accord of 1883.[126]

Canada's position was that it was under no obligation to maintain the service. In a curiously weak and contrived argument, it submitted that the qualifier "continuously" did not mean perpetuity of service but the physical uninterruption of the track. This line of reasoning was dismissed and the declaratory judgment sought by British Columbia was granted.

The court relied heavily on a similar case interpreting Canada's *Terms of Union with Prince Edward Island*, in which a promise of continuous

---

[123] R.S.C. 1985, App. II, No. 10.
[124] S.C. 1884, c. 6.
[125] S.C. 1905, c. 90.
[126] (1989), 65 D.L.R. (4th) 494 at 517 b-c, reversed (1991), 84 D.L.R. (4th) 385 (B.C. C.A.), reversed (1994), 114 D.L.R. (4th) 193 (S.C.C.).

operation of the ferry service was held to imply perpetuity in favour of the province. More significantly, this court borrowed from the Supreme Court of Canada's earlier analysis of another aspect of the B.C. *Terms of Union.*

> *This is not to be looked upon as a transaction between the crown and a private individual,* or to be governed by principles applicable to transfers between private parties. *This was a statutory arrangement between the government of the Dominion and the government of British Columbia, in settlement of a constitutional question between the two governments, or rather, giving effect to, and carrying out, the constitutional compact under which British Columbia became part and parcel of the Dominion of Canada.*[127] [Emphasis in original.]

The arguments to which the court gave the greatest weight in holding for the province were the constitutional and free nature of the 1883 Agreement and the province's reliance on the Dominion to enforce the obligation it had agreed to undertake and carry out.

> Given all the circumstances existing in 1883, including the relatively local nature of the island railway and the structure of the transaction, I infer that the province relied upon the undertaking to operate continuously given to the Dominion as a benefit which the Dominion impliedly offered to maintain for the benefit of the province.
>
> . . .
>
> I also conclude that the province is correct in maintaining that the effect of the events of 1905, which gave the Dominion regulatory powers as well as contractual rights against the railway company, strengthened the claim of the province to be able to require the Dominion to enforce the company's obligation. It follows that, in my view, it is not open to Canada to unilaterally exercise its regulatory powers to bring about a cessation of service, as it has purported to do by the order in council of 27th October, 1989 quoted above.[128]

The British Columbia Court of Appeal upheld Canada's continuing obligation to ensure operation of the rail service. However, the Supreme Court of Canada took the contrary view, indicating that the

---

[127] *Ibid.* at 511 d-e, quoting from the "Precious Metals case" cited as *British Columbia (Attorney General) v. Canada (Attorney General)* (1887), 14 S.C.R. 345 (S.C.C.), reversed (1889), LR 14 App. Cas. 295 (Canada P.C.).

[128] *Ibid.* at 515 b-d.

duty imposed by Term 11 of the 1871 Terms of Union between British Columbia and Canada related to the construction of a rail link, not its operation. Through the operation of the statutes regarding the railway, the Esquimalt and Nanaimo Company never became obliged to ensure continuous operation of the line on Vancouver Island. Moreover to effect termination of the rail line, "it is not necessary for Parliament to enact special legislation."[129]

The interest of the case, ultimately, is not in its outcome for the railway, but rather in its historical analysis and reasoning as applied to modern politics. This judgment offered the Supreme Court the opportunity to delve into the political and legal history of the arrangement whereby the colony of British Columbia entered the Dominion of Canada.

> Although constitutional terms must be capable of growth, constitutional interpretation must nonetheless begin with the language of the constitutional law or provision in question.[130]
>
> . . .
>
> Although Lord Watson held that Term 11 "merely embodies the terms of a commercial transaction," I do not believe he meant to assert that those terms were not, in themselves, of constitutional stature. Rather, I believe that Lord Watson intended to circumscribe the reasons of Gwynne, J. Read expansively, Gwynne J.'s reasons might suggest that Term 11 authorizes treaty-making *not confined by* the language of Term 11 itself. I believe Lord Watson's statement is grounded in s. 146 of the *Constitution Act, 1867*, which states in part that the Terms of Union could only be "subject to the Provisions of this Act." In other words, a meaning for Term 11 could not have been negotiated by Canada and British Columbia in contravention of the *Constitution Act, 1867* itself, so as to extend unjustifyably the reach of the Terms of Union.[131]

See also *New Democratic Party of British Columbia v. Southam Inc.*, British Columbia Supreme Court, Vancouver registry, No. C984790 filed September 21, 1988, dismissed November 18, 1999.

---

[129] (1994), 114 D.L.R. (4th) 193 at 261 c.
[130] *Ibid.* at 231 f.
[131] *Ibid.* at 238 d to g.

420 / LAW OF DEMOCRATIC GOVERNING – VOLUME II: JURISPRUDENCE

4.11.B—TERMS OF UNION WITH PRINCE EDWARD ISLAND IN 1873

§ 4.11.B.1[132]
R. v. Prince Edward Island
Federal Court of Appeal; December 5, 1977
(1977), 83 D.L.R. (3d) 492

When Prince Edward Island (P.E.I.) united with Canada, effective July 1, 1873, the Imperial Order-in-Council which set out the terms of union included an obligation upon the Dominion Government to maintain and finance a maritime link between the island and the mainland, so that there be continuous communication between the island's and the Dominion's railways. This measure was in further-ance of section 146 of the then *British North America Act*, which dealt with the accession of other British colonies to Canadian provincial status. Already at the time of union but especially later on with the growth of commerce and tourism, this maritime link was the vital lifeline of P.E.I. On two occasions in the late summer of 1973, the link, which by then had become a ferry service operated by the Canadian National Railway, was shut down by strikes. Thereafter, the province sued Canada for compensation. The questions which this action raised related first to the definition of the duty of the Dominion Government to assure the continuity of P.E.I.'s communication with the mainland and also to the nature, legal or political, of that duty.

> Basically what the statement of claim alleges is a statutory duty on the Dominion Government to assume and defray the cost of efficient and continuous communication for the conveyance of mails and passengers between the Island and the mainland, a breach of that duty culminating in a claim for damages in an unspecified amount for that breach.[133]

The Trial Division of the Federal Court identified two significant factors in the case. The first was that there had been earlier interrup-tions in the continuity of service to P.E.I. which had been settled by political rather than judicial action. The second was that the manner in which the Dominion Government had undertaken the ferry service

---

[132] Cross-reference to § 7.7.1.
[133] (1976), 66 D.L.R. (3d) 465 at 472, reversed (1977), 83 D.L.R. (3d) 492 (Fed. C.A.).

was a clear indication of the way in which it construed and discharged its obligations under the terms of union.

The most thorough element of legal analysis was about the actual obligation created by the terms of union. The Order-in-Council was silent about the locus of the responsibility for the service. The court found that this was to be a new service and that it must have been contemplated to fall into the jurisdiction of the Dominion; it also noted that this interpretation was reinforced by the acquiesence of the parties through practice. Moreover, the obligation to establish and maintain the service comprised the duty to finance it. In sum, this was termed a general public duty for the residents of all of Canada.

The court then asked whether the Dominion had breached its obligation because of the strikes. This obligation was held to be one of required results. With the strike, the remaining private sector ferry service which continued to function was inadequate for the need. The purpose of the ferry service was to maintain service of a continuous nature and prevent the isolation of the island.

> In view of the mandatory nature of the language of the Order in Council it is not an answer to the obligation imposed on the Dominion Government thereby to say that the obligation has been discharged by taking all reasonable steps to do so. The obligation is to establish and maintain an efficient service between the Island and the mainland thereby placing the Island in continuous communication. As I have found, if the service provided is not adequate for the end to be achieved it is not efficient and if a service is interrupted it lacks continuity...[134]

There remained the province's demand for damages to consider. The doctrine of the indivisibility of the Crown caused the court some concern.

> The Queen in the right of Prince Edward Island is the same Queen as the Queen in the right of Canada. Here the liability is that of the Queen in the right of Canada. The action to enforce that liability by way of compensation in damages is by the Queen in the right of the Province who is the same Royal Person, although advised by different ministers, but it is the Queen suing Herself which is incongruous.[135]

---

[134] Ibid. at 480.
[135] Ibid. at 485.

For this reason the Trial Division concluded that the breach of duty by the Dominion toward P.E.I. did not give rise to an action for damages. It further developed this line of reasoning by stating that the federal and provincial Crowns could be considered separate entities only for determining the legal rights and obligations of each. The very nature of the Constitution, as outlined in the *British North America Act*, also prevented contemplation of a judgment for monetary damages. Most pertinently, the judgment did not stop there, but went on to indicate what other alternative remedies could have been provided, if they had been sought. Basing itself on the notion that the ferry service was a general public duty of the Dominion, it determined that both legal and political remedies existed and, as historical precedent showed, could have been used.

> ...in this case the duty to provide and pay for a ferry service, does not give rise to a civil action in damages against the Crown in the right of Canada. There are other remedies, the first of which would be an action for declaratory relief under section 19 of the *Federal Court Act*, or, secondly, by political action to which the Province has resorted on the two previous occasions mentioned in the agreed statement of facts with respect to this very ferry service and on each occasion a measure of relief was obtained.[136]

The Deputy Attorney General appealed on the issue of the breach, by Canada, of the Term of Union which required continuous communication between the Island and the mainland. The Court of Appeal considered that the lower court had made a finding of fact which was not wrong and agreed with its conclusions, thus dismissing the appeal.

> The essential argument on the appeal, as I understood it, was that Canada has an obligation to provide a service of a certain general character but not an obligation to operate such a service without interruption. There is a sense in which a service may be generally efficient despite occasional stoppages or interruptions. But "efficient" in the Terms of Union does not simply mean a service that is so organized as to be capable of maintaining continuous communication between the Island and the mainland. It must in fact produce that result. The efficiency of the service is to be judged with regard to its operation. Whether a particular stoppage or interruption of the service is such that the service cannot for that period of time be considered to be an efficient one within

---

[136] *Ibid.* at 483.

the meaning of the Terms of Union is a question of fact—a matter of degree.[137]

The Province cross-appealed with regard to the issue of damages. The Court of Appeal allowed this and referred the matter back to the Trial Division for further proceedings. Here, the court engaged in extremely interesting interpretation of the nature of Canada's sovereignty. Chief Justice Jackett qualified the legal personality of Her Majesty as being murky because of the fact that our Constitution "adopts, for a country with divided sovereignty, a sovereign whose legal characteristics have been developed for a unitary state."[138]

The court also made an important statement about the legal nature of the governments comprising the Canadian federation:

> By 1867, it would seem that, while provinces and colonies such as the ones in question here were subject to the sovereignty of the British Crown, each of them had, as a political matter, achieved a political identity of its own within the British Empire not unlike the political identity of sovereign States in the international sphere. While such a political identity was not, at that time at least, in the eyes of the ordinary municipal law, a "person" capable of having rights and liabilities and suing and being sued, it was a political reality in the sense that the people of a particular "self-governing" region had to be accepted and dealt with as a unity having desires and interests in common, as is demonstrated by the fact that they were, by *The British North America Act, 1867*, so dealt with.[139]

Placing the matter within the sphere of statutory interpretation, the court concluded that:

> In each case, as I view it, the "obligor," while it was described as the "Dominion Government" or the "Government and Parliament of Canada," was the newly created political entity called "Canada" and the obligee was a province or provinces. Neither the obligor nor obligee was an entity having status...in any British or international court of law. Nevertheless, the United Kingdom Parliament, by imposing duties on one in favour of another, made them parties to statutory rights or duties, no matter how unorthodox it may be to create legal rights without legal remedies. It is important to emphasize that what we are discussing is "a

---

[137] (1977), 83 D.L.R. (3d) 492 at 535.
[138] *Ibid.* at 503.
[139] *Ibid.* at 510.

general statutory arrangement" and not a contract or "independent treaty between two governments."[140]

On these bases, there was a statutory right to have something done with no express sanction for breach. *Prima facie*, this resulted in an implied right to be compensated for a breach of such a right.

---

§ 4.11.B.2
Prince Edward Island (Minister of Transportation & Public Works) v. Canadian National Railway
Federal Court of Appeal; June 20, 1990
(1990), 71 D.L.R. (4th) 596

This case continued the disposition through legal interpretation of the historical bargains relating to the tying of Prince Edward Island to Canada in both the physical and political senses. Moreover, it deals with the modernization of the country through the substitution of contemporary meanings of legislation for earlier ones, thus enabling the use of more modern technologies.

In this instance, the National Transportation Agency (N.T.A.) authorized the abandonment of railway lines which, taken together, constituted the entire rail system of the island province. Such decisions were taken by the Agency at the request of the railway company for economic reasons; most people had abandoned rail transport in favour of automobiles. The Province's Minister of Transportation and Public Works appealed to the Federal Court. His principal argument was that the *Terms of Union* were a constitutional instrument and that pursuant to section 52(1) of the *Constitution Act, 1982*, a law inconsistent with these *Terms* was therefore of no effect. He also tried to argue that the *Terms* contained implied guarantees of the continuation of rail service on the island and from the island to the mainland. The court disagreed.

The relevant legal element resulting from the *Terms of Union*, which was a product of the political negotiation regarding the province's joining Confederation, was "a continuous communication obligation."[141] In that instance, the word "continuous" had a seasonal or

---

[140] *Ibid.* at 511.
[141] (1990), 71 D.L.R. (4th) 596 at 602 c.

temporal meaning relating to the problem of crossing the Northumberland Strait toward the rest of Canada in all seasons, giving islanders access to what was then the Intercolonial Railway. The court concluded that neither the continuous communication obligation nor the clause in the *Terms* vesting property in the rail lines with Canada entailed an obligation on Canada to operate the railway in perpetuity. Consequently, the N.T.A.'s decision was not in breach of the *Terms of Union.* The sense of this ruling was that in inducing Prince Edward Island to join it, Canada had agreed by the *Terms* to maintain the steamship service with rather than rail service on the island. The court compared these *Terms of Union* with those relating to British Columbia and reached a different conclusion from that of the British Columbia Supreme Court on the basis of the different wording in the two documents.

See also *Friends of the Island Inc. v. Canada (Minister of Public Works),* [1993] 2 F.C. 229 (Fed. T.D.), reversed (1995) 191 N.R. 241 (Fed. C.A.), leave to appeal refused (1996), [1996] S.C.C.A. No. 80 (S.C.C.).

4.11.C—TERMS OF UNION WITH NEWFOUNDLAND IN 1949

§ 4.11.C.1[142]
Currie v. MacDonald
Newfoundland Court of Appeal; January 22, 1949
(1949), 29 Nfld. & P.E.I.R. 294, 82 A.P.R. 294

Newfoundland is the latest, and perhaps last British North American colony to have joined Canada by means of Terms of Union. It is also the only jurisdiction which did so on the basis of consultation of the electorate by referendum. It is against that factual backdrop that Currie and a number of other former Newfoundland legislators attempted by litigation to stop the union of the colony into Canada and its conversion into a province.

As a result of the world economic crisis, as of 1933, Newfoundland was no longer self-sufficient. It asked the Imperial powers in the United Kingdom to suspend its Responsible Government. Starting

---

[142] Cross-reference to § 10.8.1.

on January 30, 1934, Newfoundland was governed by an appointed Governor and a Commission of Government with both legislative and executive powers.[143] This form of governance was to last until the people resolved whether the colony could once again become self-supporting and whether they wanted a return of responsible government. Along the path toward return of self-governance, on the basis of the 1946 *National Convention Act*,[144] a convention was held in 1946 to deliberate the colony's prospects. In 1948, a *Referendum Act*[145] was passed, rendering possible the holding of two referenda which considered, among other options, whether Newfoundland should unite with Canada. The matter was highly controversial.

In this action, the plaintiffs sought to achieve the restoration of Newfoundland to its pre-1934 status, as a separate and self-governing colony, rather than have her become a Canadian province. Toward that end, they applied to the Supreme Court of Newfoundland for declarations that the *National Convention Act* and the *Referendum Act* were *ultra vires*, that they were repugnant to the *Newfoundland Act* and to have the court state that the option of joining Canada should not have been included in the referenda.

The principal force behind the judgment was Justice Dunfield, who, surprisingly, wrote the Supreme Court ruling and also participated in the Court of Appeal panel hearing the case. In his view, the claim is based on the ideas that at the time Responsible Government was suspended, Parliament made an implicit promise that it would eventually be restored, and that the plaintiffs are the group entitled to call for the performance of that promise and to prevent the development of Newfoundland's political future in any other direction. The court utterly destroyed this line of reasoning.

> But even allowing them their premise (which I do not in law) as the best they could claim, the position is that the people of Newfoundland were the body entitled to claim the performance of that alleged promise; and that the people, with the only voice they have, the voice of a majority, have dispensed with that promise, and have said that they do not wish to have it carried out, but would prefer to have something different, namely Confederation with Canada on the terms put before them.[146]

---

[143] *Newfoundland Act, 1933* (Imperial) and Letters Patent of January 30, 1934.
[144] S. Nfld. 1946, c. 16.
[145] S. Nfld. 1949, c. 9.
[146] (1949), 29 Nfld. & P.E.I.R. 294, 82 A.P.R. 294 at 303-304.

In light of the fact that the question of joining Canada had already been put to the people by way of referendum and had garnered considerable approval, the court characterized the plaintiffs' position as amounting to a statement that the will of the people could not be validly ascertained by referendum. The answer to that was: "But what better way could there be?"[147]

The court's *ratio* in response to Currie's application was, ultimately, based on two grounds. The first was primarily legal, in that in response to the allegation that the inclusion of the Confederation option among the choices on the Referendum was illegal, the court held that this amounted to arguing that it is illegal to take the opinion of the people by plebiscite or referendum. On this point, the court replied that no support for such a pleading of illegality had been submitted and with good reason, it said, because such a contention could not be maintained. The second deciding factor was primarily political in the sense of giving due weight to the democratic expression of the people of Newfoundland.

> And the only right of the individual citizen that I can see is the right to put in his little contribution, his one vote, towards the general decision. He cannot have a right to stand in the way of the majority and prevent them from having their will, or to get a court to prevent them, even if it could. There is no magic formula which will enable a minority to defeat a majority.
>
> . . .
>
> I cannot see how, consistent with democratic theory, any other voice can be attributed to the people than that of the majority; in that way lies chaos.[148]

These findings of the court led it to the even more fundamental analysis which it made regarding the litigation of political and partisan issues.

See also *Hogan v. Newfoundland (School Boards for Ten Districts)* (1997), 149 D.L.R. (4th) 468 (Nfld. T.D.)[149] and *Hogan v. Newfoundland (Attorney General)* (1998), 156 D.L.R. (4th) 139 (Nfld. T.D.).

---

[147] *Ibid.* at 304.
[148] *Ibid.* at 304-305.
[149] Cross-reference to § 5.8.4 and 8.8.3.

§ 4.11.C.2[150]
Hogan v. Newfoundland (Attorney General)
Newfoundland Court of Appeal; February 28, 2000
(2000), 183 D.L.R. (4th) 225[151]

In the years 1997 and 1998, the Government of Newfoundland sought to modernize the province's education system by amalgamation of its denominational school systems. The legal views expressed by the Roman Catholic community in opposition to this change included the argument that the restructuring was contrary to Term 17 of the *Terms of Union of Newfoundland with Canada*.[152] In this, the third consecutive case on this issue, one of the pleadings put forward by Hogan, as the representative plaintiff of the Catholics was that of estoppel, founded on the political history of Newfoundland. At the time of Newfoundland's entry into Confederation, they said, in order to induce the Catholic community to support union they were promised the right to publicly funded denominational schools for as long as they wished to keep these schools separate. Having made that promise, they argued, Canada could not go back on it. The Trial Division of the Newfoundland Supreme Court rejected the argument of the perpetual nature of Term 17.

> Times change, circumstances change and public attitudes change. At the time of Confederation the denominations had a secure hold on the schools of this province. Over the past 50 years that control has slipped away. There has been more and more government involvement. There have been elected school boards and the financial obligation for schools and education has been taken over by government. From the evidence presented to me it seems clear that the plaintiffs' position is untenable with respect to their claim for estoppel.[153]

As collateral evidence for this view, the court even cited the fact that all electoral districts in Newfoundland except one voted in favour of the reform. In sum, Hogan's application to quash the proclamation declaring a plebiscite was denied, his request for a declaration that

---

[150] Cross-reference to § 5.8.4 and 8.8.3.
[151] Leave to appeal refused (2000), 264 N.R. 395 (note) (S.C.C.).
[152] R.S.C. 1985, Appendix II, No. 32.
[153] (1999), 173 Nfld. & P.E.I.R. 148, 530 A.P.R. 148 at 165-166, para. 71, reversed (2000), 183 D.L.R. (4th) 225 (Nfld. C.A.), leave to appeal refused (2000), 264 N.R. 395 (note) (S.C.C.).

the Referendum was invalid was also denied, but his application for recovery of the disbursements expended in the NO campaign were allowed.

The Newfoundland Court of Appeal denied Hogan's appeal and allowed Newfoundland's cross-appeal on the issue of the expenditures on campaigning. In its view, the real question in issue was whether Term 17 created rights or duties for third parties which may be enforced by them and if it did, was the consent of those third parties necessary for any amendment to Term 17? The court was inimical to such an interpretation.

> The quintessence of a federation is such that in arriving at a consensus respecting the character of the country and the form and content of its Constitution there are inevitably negotiations between representatives of the different entities making up the federation. Further, there will be compromises respecting different interests which will ultimately be reflected in the constitutional documents.
>
> . . .
>
> the idea of a restraint on the ability of a legislative body to perform its function is unacceptable, except to the extent mandated by the Constitution itself.[154]

The court also rejected the arguments advanced by Hogan in favour of estoppel. Moreover, it held that an amendment of Term 17 would not constitute a change to the *Charter* under another guise.

This court also made a significant statement about the law – politics aspect of this debate, based on the finding of the Supreme Court of Canada in the Québec Secession Reference that where there was an obligation to negotiate, the topics of the negotiation were of a political nature, subject only to political evaluation. In the present instance, those topics would be Newfoundland's policy on educational reform, the quality of the political debate on the proposed amendments, the analysis of the results of the vote, the balancing of political interests regarding the amendment of Term 17, and the specific motivations of members of the Legislative Assembly.

---

[154] 2000 NFCA 12 at paras. 54 and 60, leave to appeal refused (2000), 264 N.R. 395 (note) (S.C.C.).

...the appellants look to the "political' statements to support their submission that while the referendum may not have been constitutionally
required, it was instrumental in the voting by the members of the legislative bodies.

The Court has no role in examining the motivation of the members of
the Legislature or the Houses of Parliament in casting their votes. The
interpretation of and weight to be given to the results of the referendum
is a political matter.[155]

See also *Canadian National Railway v. Moffatt* (2001), 207 D.L.R. (4th)
118 (Fed. C.A.) and *Newfoundland Threat of Separation Over Fisheries*,
Proceedings of the House of Assembly, Vol. XLIV, No. 18, May 7,
2003, http://www.gov.nf.ca/hoa/business/hansard/44th,%205th/
h03-05-07.htm.

4.12 ISSUE: PRINCIPLES OF CONSTITUTIONAL DEVELOPMENT

§ 4.12.1[156]
Reference re Amendment to the Constitution of Canada
Supreme Court of Canada; September 28, 1981
(1981), 125 D.L.R. (3d) 1

In 1980 and 1981, the public debate relating to the patriation of the
Constitution, which had been proposed by Prime Minister Trudeau,
was raging throughout Canada. Several, if not most of the provincial
premiers were opposed to the patriation package as it had been put
to them, for fear that their autonomy within the federation would be
curtailed and their power-base shrunk. The premiers were unable to
convince the federal authorities of the rightness of their arguments
through political discussion. The British Government, a necessary
participant in the patriation process, refused to entertain appeals from
provinces but would deal with Ottawa only. In order therefore to
force the hand of the federal authorities to the extent they could,

---

[155] *Ibid.* at paras. 108-109.
[156] Cross-reference to § 1.12.1 and 11.2.A.

The premiers resolved to approach the matter indirectly by way of application for declaratory judgment by the respective provincial courts of appeal ... The Supreme Court of Canada might take the matter on appeal from the various provincial courts of appeal; or the federal government, facing one or more adverse court of appeal decisions, might then move to resolve the political embarrassment by seeking a final, definitive ruling from the Supreme Court on appeal.

The court strategy was to launch common actions, accompanied by multiple, mutually supportive interventions, choosing only those courts thought to be favourable to the dissident premiers' viewpoint. Harassment could backfire in the event of court rejections of the provinces' arguments. The courts selected as being most sympathetic were Manitoba, Newfoundland, and Quebec—a representative sample in regional, cultural and linguistic, and legal (civil law, common law) terms, though not inevitably pro-provincial.[157]

This was one of the great instances of Canadian history in which the use of law was the last and best mechanism to resolve a political deadlock. It is both significant and symbolic that the provinces in which the references were initiated, including Québec, believed they could rely on the judges to resolve essentially political dilemmas through legal reasoning. At the time of this decision, the political situation in Canada had not yet developed to the stage in which appeals were suspect because provinces perceived federal, and in particular, Supreme Court of Canada judges as being inherently centralizing. The phrase "their judges" had not yet gained currency.

The major outcome of the case was the cautious response of the Supreme Court of Canada with respect to the central political legal matter which confronted it: was provincial consent to fundamental constitutional reordering necessary, and if so, what degree of such consent was necessary? Without delving into arithmetic specifics, the court articulated a principle of constitutional development which was entirely legal and entirely political in nature. According to the majority led by Dickson J., the then, and Lamer, the future Chief Justice, a substantive degree of provincial consent was required for the Constitution of Canada to be amended according to the plan which had been formulated by the government. Moreover, the degree of consent needed was left to the determination of the politicians. In the days

---

[157] McWhinney, Edward, *Canada and the Constitution 1979-1982*, Toronto, University of Toronto Press, 1982, p. 74.

prior to the existence of a specific amendment formula, this decision was a key to the development of Canada and had the patriation package, including the 1982 amending mechanisms, not been adopted, this judgment would doubtless have had an even greater impact on eventual developments in Canada. As it is, this principle enabled the patriation process to move forward. Today, the principle can be thought of not only as the inchoate expression which led to the 1982 amending formulae but also as a living principle on which the 7-50 part of the formula rests.

> One might normally have expected the majority to rule that the issue of conventionally was not a legal issue and therefore not one on which the Supreme Court could, or should, deign to rule. The doctrine of "political questions," as outlined earlier by Chief Justice Freedman, provided a perfect justification for judicial self-restraint and for returning the issue of whether or not there was a convention to the ordinary political processes (general elections and the like) for decision. Instead, the six-man majority opinion on conventionality ventured into what must be characterized as an extended *obiter dictum* on general constitutional morality.[158]

See also *R. v. Langlois*, Superior Court of Québec, filed April 21, 1988, pending and *Potter c. Québec (Procureur général)*, [2001] R.J.Q. 2823 (Que. C.A.), leave to appeal refused (2002), 2002 CarswellQue 2259 (S.C.C.).

---

[158] Op. cit., p. 84.

4.13 ISSUE: LATEST ATTEMPTS AT CONSTITUTIONAL REFORM

4.13.A—PATRIATION

§ 4.13.A.1
Larouche c. Gouvernement du Québec
Québec Superior Court; November 20, 1997
(1997), 1997 CarswellQue 1362

Prima facie, this case is about the methodology of constitutional re-form. In 1997, the Québec National Assembly and the Parliament of Canada co-operated in enacting a constitutional amendment for the purpose of reorganizing the system of school boards in Québec. Whereas earlier they were based along religious lines, as provided for in section 93 of the *Constitution Act, 1867*, henceforth, with the amendment, they would be structured along linguistic lines. This constitutional amendment was in fact eventually made. While the constitutional amendment proposal was moving through the special legislative process required by section 43 of the *Constitution Act, 1982*, for such amendments, involving a single province and the federal authorities, Larouche applied for an interlocutory injunction to prevent completion of the process.

On the basis of the legal rules applicable to injunctions, the Superior Court rejected the application. As an additional reason, it held that the applicants could not sue the National Assembly because the latter lacked the requisite legal personality.

For the study of political law, the elements of interest in this case are: another line of argumentation developed by the applicant, that based on the inapplicability to Québec, of the *Constitution Act, 1982*, and the court's response thereto. Larouche argued that Québec did not have the right to adopt a motion proposing the subject constitutional amendment essentially because it contemplates an amendment to the *Constitution Act, 1982*, which, in turn, Québec does not recognize or apply. Larouche therefore concludes that the National Assembly's motion is a legal nullity because it is addressed to the Governor

General; that the 1982 *Constitution* provides for the cessation of United Kingdom legislative power in Canada and therefore, as Québec does not recognize the 1982 *Constitution*, only the United Kingdom Parliament can legislate for Québec. Based on all this, the National Assembly ought to have petitioned the monarch to amend the *Constitution Act, 1867*, in order to carry the school reform through.

The application carries on with a particular and even peculiar view of the state of law in Québec, founded on a politically motivated perspective.

> Lors de leur plaidoirie, les requérants soumettent donc que comme le Québec a refusé de ratifier la modification constitutionnelle de 1982, et persiste à vouloir se dire «séparé du Canada» il ne reconnaît donc pas la *«rule of law.»* Depuis 1982, plaide-t-on, «le Québec est en fait séparé du Canada, puisque la constitution ne le concerne plus.» «On cache la vérité à la population, les ministères de la Justice sont complices», soumet-on. «C'est seulement le Parlement du Royaume-Uni qui peut légiférer.»

> Selon les requérants, «on est en train d'établir une dictature au Québec.» «Le Québec viole la procédure en ne la reconnaissant pas.»[159]

In addition to these general comments, the application also contains criticism of the co-operation of the Québec and federal Attorneys General, claiming that they stand for the same philosophy, same doctrine, same political orientation with respect to the (Québec) nation.

The court acknowledged the good faith of the applicant but determinedly refuted these arguments. First, it explained in open court that judges must be guided by law and not by sentiments or sympathies.

The court, moreover, could not be clearer in its conclusion as to the politically motivated argument of Larouche.

> La légalité et l'applicabilité de la *Loi constitutionnelle de 1982* est incontestable.

---

[159] (1997), 1997 CarswellQue 1362 at paras. 13 and 14.

. . .

Il n'y a donc *aucun fondement de droit* à l'affirmation des requérants à l'effet que du fait que l'Assemblée Nationale du Québec n'ait pas reconnu la *Loi constitutionnelle de 1982* elle ne saurait légalement participer, selon l'article 43, au processus de modification constitutionnelle quant à l'article 93 de la *Loi constitutionnelle de 1867*.[160]

This conclusion at law was deemed not to be sufficient, however. The court felt it necessary to add that the applicant was fooled by the contents of his own political discourse.

On doit le dire. *Les requérants confondent l'applicabilité en droit de la Loi constitutionnelle de 1982 et le discours politique.*[161]

While the application for interlocutory injunction was thus rejected, the case is proceeding on the merits. The Federal Department of Justice is attentive not only because this is one of a number of cases involving the political aspects of the Canadian constitutional framework, but also because an adverse judgment on the merits could subject the constitutional amendment process to judicial review, changing the delicate balance among the branches of government with respect to the modernization of the *Constitution of Canada*.

---

§ 4.13.A.2
Bédard et al. v. Québec (Procureur Général) et Canada (Procureur Général)
Québec Superior Court
filed February 24, 1998; file no. 500-05-039679-988; abandoned

---

This case continues the examination of the constitutional amendment formula adopted in 1982, that was begun in the *Larouche* case. The background here is also the 1997 constitutional amendment by which Québec changed its school system from one based on confessional lines of division to one based on linguistic grounds. Whereas in *Larouche*, the argument was that Québec did not have the right to use the amendment formula, here the plaintiffs' plea was that in order to amend the application of section 93 of the *Constitution Act, 1867*, to Québec, the bilateral mechanism, involving only Québec and the

---

[160] *Ibid.* at paras. 30 and 34.
[161] *Ibid.* at para. 36.

federal authorities, was not the appropriate vehicle. In that sense, the argumentation started on the grounds agreed in the patriation and extended to the very nature of the political compact through which Canada had been formed.

Bédard argued that the purpose of the incorporation of section 93 in Canada's original constitutional deal was to provide for equal treatment of religious groupings on all constitutional parts of Canada, that is Québec, Ontario, Nova Scotia and New Brunswick, rather than each of these jurisdictions individually. Consequently, in order for Québec to change its confessional school system, the other provinces would also have to agree.

> Ainsi, tel que la Cour suprême l'a affirme dans *P.G. Québec c. Blaikie* [1979] 2 R.C.S. 1016, dans la mesure où une disposition constitutionnelle est le fruit d'un arrangement politique comportant des contreparties obligationnelles pour les parties prenantes à tel arrangement, il devient impossible de modifier l'une de ses composantes sans affecter l'ensemble du compromis;

> Dans la présente affaire, la modification et/ou l'abrogation de l'article 93 dans son application au Québec affecte ou altère de façon irrémédiable le pacte confédératif de sorte que la modification d'une telle disposition ne peut etre operée que du consentement de toutes les parties au compromis historique;[162]

The federal Crown's defence was the allegation that section 43 of the constitutional amendment formula agreed to in 1982 was indeed applicable, as only Québec was involved in the reform and modernization of its own school system. The amendment was set out in what would be section 93A of the *Constitution Act, 1867*. Considering that the amendment would impact only one province, other provincial jurisdictions were not involved in the process. Hence, the bilateral, Québec and federal, part of the amendment formula was the one to use. This defence was also based on the reasoning that the court should adopt a logical and a reasonable reading of the constitutional text, rather than one leading to the absurd result of requiring other provinces, in particular Ontario, to agree to a change that affected Québec only. At Confederation, and at the union of additional British North American colonies with Canada, the school systems of the

---

[162] Plaintiffs' statement of claim; Action directe en nullité selon l'article 33 du Code de Procédure civile du Québec; paras. 35 and 36, February 24, 1998.

various jurisdictions had been distinct and diverse. The purpose of section 93 was to create guarantees of religious equality where there had been minority systems, not to create a cross-country regime of equality. The essence of the Canadian compact was maintenance of diversity.

> Les obligations confessionnelles en matière scolaire n'ont jamais été réciproques ni même identiques entre le Québec et l'Ontario. Elles sont indépendantes les unes des autres car elles étaient prévues dans des lois préconfédératives distinctes. Ces obligations de même nature, mais non identiques dans les deux provinces ont ensuite continué de s'appliquer après 1867 en vertu du mécanisme de constitutionnalisation prévu aux paragraphes (1) à (4) de l'article 93.[163]

The constitutional amendment regarding Québec's school system has been adopted and put into effect.[164] In due course, this action was abandoned.

4.13.B—MEECH LAKE ACCORD

---

§ 4.13.B.1[165]
Penikett v. R.
Yukon Territory Court of Appeal; December 23, 1987
(1987), 45 D.L.R. (4th) 108[166]

It is rare for a court to begin a judgment purporting to resolve a concrete and present legal matter placed before it by tracing the origins of the dispute back into Canada's constitutional history of five years earlier. Yet, quite rightly, that is the way in which the Yukon Court of Appeal addressed Penikett's case. The matter at hand was an attack on the constitutional validity of the *Meech Lake Accord* of 1987, but the source of the problem to be adjudicated was to be found in the patriation of 1982.

In 1982, the Constitution of Canada was patriated from the United Kingdom to Canada. Unusually venturing into the field of political

---

[163] Défense filed on behalf of the Attorney General of Canada on July 17, 1998; para. 69.

[164] Constitution Amendment, 1997 (Quebec), SI/97-141, December 22, 1997.

[165] Cross-reference to § 4.10.1.

[166] Leave to appeal refused (1988), 88 N.R. 320n (S.C.C.).

commentary but making a patently true statement, the court called this a phyrric victory, as Québec did not agree to the result of the process. The constitutional wound left on the Canadian body politic by Québec's disagreement was a most powerful one, causing endless polemic. It is noteworthy that this polemic involved two schools of thought. The first held that the reason Québec rejected the patriation deal was because at the time it was led by a Parti Québécois sovereignist government and that that government would have rejected any deal, given its secessionist intention. Proponents of the other school were of the opinion that the governments of the other Canadian jurisdictions deliberately excluded Québec from the constitutional compromise that was reached. There are perhaps grains of truth in both interpretations.

Despite the argumentation, and perhaps in part because of it, it was clear to informed observers that sooner or later, Québec's assent would have to be obtained. The first serious attempt at "bringing Québec into the Constitution," as the phrase ran in popular parlance, occurred in the spring of 1987. The Prime Minister of Canada convened the Premiers of the Provinces to Meech Lake, near Ottawa, in order to work out a constitutional deal that would meet the then current "minimum demands" of Québec and that would, hopefully, be sufficient to induce Québec to adopt the 1982 amendments and additions to the Constitution of Canada, after the fact. By this time, the Québec government was again formed by the Provincial Liberal Party, a federalist formation, but one still intent on securing a special place for that Province within Canada, and one still very much pushed by a considerable "nationalist" faction of public opinion, of the electorate and of the political elite to ensure Québec's specificity.

Unexpectedly, the Meech Lake meeting produced an *Accord* among the first ministers assembled. This *Accord* consisted of proposed constitutional changes on five issues, all of fundamental interest to Québec:

- recognition of Québec as a distinct society,
- role for the provinces in the selection of senators,
- federal-provincial linkages on immigration,
- entrenchment of the Supreme Court of Canada, and
- limitation of the federal spending power in fields of provincial jurisdiction.

At the time of the *Accord*, Penikett was the Chief Minister in the Government of the Yukon Territory. This Territory did not have the status of a Province and its administration was therefore autonomous but in part reliant on the federal government. As the leader of a Territorial, rather than a Provincial, government Penikett was not invited to participate in the Meech Lake deliberations and had no political way publicly known to make his views on the *Accord* available to his counterparts. In fact, he disagreed with the substance of the *Accord* on grounds of principle and also because, in his opinion, adoption of the *Accord* would delay or perhaps frustrate the constitutional evolution process whereby the Yukon hoped to achieve provincehood, rather than remaining a Territory. Thus, very early after the publication of the *Accord*, Penikett applied to the Yukon Territory Supreme Court for a series of declarations to the effect that the *Meech Lake Accord* would violate section 7 (legal rights) and section 15 (equality) of the *Canadian Charter of Rights and Freedoms*. To the question whether the *Charter* could apply to that part of the Constitution which dealt with the constitutional amendment process, the court answered in the affirmative. On the issue of justiciability, the Supreme Court held that the *Accord* was not itself an act of the Government of Canada, that it had no effect in law and that as the action was therefore premature, the matter was not justiciable. The court also decided that Penikett had standing.

The Government of Canada could not countenance that its principal, not to say vital, constitutional initiative be derailed by that part of the judgment which rendered the constitutional amendment process subject to the *Charter*. It thus brought the matter before the Yukon Territory Court of Appeal. That court reversed the first ruling and brought this challenge to the *Meech Lake Accord* to an end.

The Court of Appeal recited all the grounds of complaint in Penikett's petition. For our purposes of dealing with the political law aspects of the case, the most important ones are the following:

(1)   That the Accord was inconsistent with the rights of Yukoners to equal protection and benefit of the law (s. 15 of the *Charter*) because of the restriction of Supreme Court appointments from the provincial bars; the appointment of senators on the recommendations of provincial governments; the requirement that unanimous consent of all eleven governments would be required to establish any new provinces; the failure to include the consent of the Yukon in the

440 / LAW OF DEMOCRATIC GOVERNING - VOLUME II: JURISPRUDENCE

proposed amending process; and not including an elected representative of the Yukon at the annual First Ministers' Conference;

(2)   That all of the above areas were also inconsistent with the right of Yukoners under s. 7 of the *Charter* to life, liberty and security of the person;

(3)   That it was inconsistent with conventional democratic principles in that the determination of the eligibility of the Yukon for provincehood was in the authority of provincial legislatures in which the Yukon has no representation and lacks any franchise to respond to the provincial exercise of power;[167]

In response to these applications for declaratory relief, the court looked first, as the lower court had, at the issue of whether the constitutional guarantees set out in the *Charter* could be applied to the constitutional amendment process outlined in other provisions within the same Constitution. This significant point of the case was determined at this level in the negative. The decision merits attention because it was the first time that an appellate court ventured into this issue. Within the four corners of the ruling, the Yukon Territory Court of Appeal made new constitutional law. The political law significance of the case results to a greater extent from the impact of the case on the constitution building process, in that opponents of constitutional reform later than patriation found they could not rely on the *Charter* to stop the process.

The court held that all the Constitution Acts from 1867 through 1982 must be read together to arrive at the complete written constitutional framework of Canada. Within that unified body of law, it is section 32 of the *Charter* which determines the "matters" to which the *Charter* applies.

In our view "all matters" cannot apply to procedures under the amending formulas. The word "matters" in s. 32(1) of the Charter parallels its use in ss. 91 and 92 of the *Constitution Act, 1867*. Constitutional powers in Canada have always been divided between Parliament and the provincial legislative assemblies by these sections. The Parliament of the United Kingdom possessed the power to amend the Constitution of Canada until 1982. This power, as embodied in Part V of the *Constitution*

---

[167] (1987), 45 D.L.R. (4th) 108 at 111, leave to appeal refused (1988), 88 N.R. 320n (S.C.C.).

Act, 1982, is now possessed jointly by Parliament and the provincial legislative assemblies. A constitutional amendment is not a "matter" within the authority of either Parliament or the provinces. The amending power is vested in a joint decision of both federal and provincial authority.[168]

Several important consequences flow from this interpretation. Primarily, of course, this means that section 32 of the *Charter* cannot apply to an amendment that is properly enacted pursuant to Part V of the *Constitution Act, 1982*, the part that deals with amendments. The major legal consequence of this finding is that no part or no provision of the Constitution of Canada is paramount to any other. This principle observes the spirit of section 52 of the *Constitution Act, 1982*, which describes the "Constitution of Canada," in effect meaning that the entire Constitution of the country is "the supreme law of the land."

The inapplicability of the *Charter* to the process of constitutional amendment also has an important implication for the relationship of the legal to the political aspect of constitutionalism.

> In a democracy such as Canada, the elected representatives must be able to make such amendments as are required. Indeed, the Charter exists because it was created by the elected representatives of Canada, as Lamer J. commented in *Reference re s. 94(2) of the Motor Vehicle Act* (1985), 24 D.L.R. (4th) 536 at p. 545, [1985] 2 S.C.R. 486 at p. 497, 23 C.C.C. (3d) 289:
>
>> It ought not to be forgotten that the historic decision to entrench the Charter in our Constitution was taken not by the courts but by the elected representatives of the people of Canada.[169]

The court stated its overall conclusion of this entire line of reasoning in the most direct terms possible, its decision exercising an effect on Canadian political life no less than on the development of Canadian law:

> The Charter cannot be used to prevent constitutional amendments.[170]

---

[168] *Ibid.* at 113-114.
[169] *Ibid.* at 114-115.
[170] *Ibid.* at 115.

§ 4.13.B.2[171]
Sibbeston v. Northwest Territories (Attorney General)
Northwest Territories Court of Appeal; February 3, 1988
(1988), 48 D.L.R. (4th) 691

This case constituted a challenge by Sibbeston, then First Minister of the Northwest Territories, to the constitutional validity of a set of proposals to reform the Constitution of Canada, entitled the *Meech Lake Accord*. At the time of this challenge in 1988, the *Accord* was only a political agreement among the Prime Minister of Canada and the Premiers of the 10 provinces, arrived at on April 30, 1987. In order for the *Accord* to become law, it would still have to be approved by every jurisdiction, in accordance with those provisions of the *Constitution Act, 1982*, namely Part V thereof, which dealt with the procedure for amending the Constitution of Canada. Ultimately, some two and a half years after this judgment, the *Accord* would fail to be adopted.

The case was framed in terms of an application for a number of declarations regarding the unconstitutionality of the *Accord* itself, as well as the unconstitutionality of certain provisions of the constitutional amendment process itself. The application can be divided into several categories. There were challenges to specific provisions of the *Accord* based on section 7 (legal rights) and section 15 (equality rights) of the *Canadian Charter of Rights and Freedoms*. Other challenges focused on the fact that the *Accord* was alleged to be in breach of constitutional conventions. Yet other challenges were launched on the basis of the legislative process used to devise the *Accord*. Finally, one challenge to the *Accord* was based on the argument that it violated principles of international law; unfortunately for our understanding of the matter, the court did not deal with this point, so nothing further can be written about it.

The court characterized the fundamental issue of the case as being whether the *Charter*, and therefore judicial scrutiny, has any role to play in the evolution of the process of amending the Constitution of Canada under Part V.

---

[171] Cross-reference to § 4.10.12.

It read section 52 of the *Constitution Act, 1982* which is, in effect, a statutory definition of the "Constitution of Canada" and concluded strongly in the unity of the Constitution as a single instrument in which all components, meaning the text originating in 1867 together with its amendments, the *Charter*, as well as the other elements of the 1982 patriation package, are all on an equal footing.

The court also held that no case can be made to show that the *Charter* applies specifically to the amending process here because the reach of section 32, dealing with the extent of application of the *Charter*, does not itself extend beyond the validity of executive and legislative action by the entities named in that section, the Parliament and government of Canada and the legislature and government of each province. By contrast, the constitutional amendment process is a joint exercise involving the Governor General, the Senate, the House of Commons and the provincial legislative assemblies, as required by the amending formula, rather than one involving the sole exercise of either representative or governmental bodies.

Most significantly, the court held that there could be no judicial review of the Constitution itself. The *Constitution Act, 1982*, it indicated, is unassailable and within it, Part V is a complete code, which it qualified as being immune to extraneous challenge.

> The respondent's amended petition cannot be pursued under principles of Canadian constitutional practice that must now be regarded as established. They include the political reality that it is the people of Canada, expressing their political will through the joint constitutional authority of the Parliament of Canada and the elected legislative assemblies of the provinces, who are sovereign in the delineation of federal-provincial power sharing under the Constitution of Canada. Beyond that, no segment of the Constitution of Canada, including the Canadian Charter of Rights and Freedoms, is paramount to other segments, or indeed the balance, of the Constitution. The Constitution "as a whole" is Canada's supreme law.[172]

In so holding, the court even gave Sibbeston a mild rebuke, reminding him that this issue had already been decided by the Yukon Territory Court of Appeal in the *Penikett* case in which Sibbeston had been an intervenor.

---

[172] (1988), 48 D.L.R. (4th) 691 at 695-6.

With respect to the argument on the conflict between the *Accord* and the constitutional convention regarding the establishment of new provinces, the court found that section 42(1)(f) of the *Constitution Act, 1982*, the written constitutional provision on this matter, had taken the topic out of the realm of convention and codified it, thus effectively abolishing the convention. The *Accord* could not conflict with a convention by then defunct.

That part of the challenge involving the legislative process leading to the *Accord*, which was not based on the *Charter*, also failed, on the ground that it was non-justiciable.

> Insofar as the declarations sought in the amended petition seek to attack the legislative process, they must fail. The political exchange which became the Meech Lake Accord was a matter preparatory to amending constitutional legislation. It may find its final expression in a proclamation authorized jointly by resolution of the Senate, the House of Commons and the legislative assemblies of the existing provinces. However they may be couched, on non-Charter declarations sought by the amended petition fall under this objection. The complaints in the amended petition are directed against an agreement of purely and quintessentially political consequence. It has no immediate legal impact, nor is it self-executing. The complaints are, in our view, and beyond doubt, not justiciable.[173]

At the conclusion of the case, the court used a U.S. precedent, convenient for its character of being foreign to the then-raging Canadian constitutional debate surrounding the *Meech Lake Accord*, to indicate that what it had to look at was the legality of the issue placed before it by the litigants, not the judge's own agreement with the substance, suitability, goal or general conception of the legal test. At its plain meaning, this statement is correct. Because of the way it is expressed, however, it would seem to show more. While judges interpret the law and refrain from overt political comment, they can nevertheless find subtle ways, such as this can be thought to be, to express their own position on issues of current political debate.

---

[173] *Ibid.* at 699.

§ 4.13.B.3
Cdn. Coalition on the Constitution Inc. v. R.
Federal Court of Canada – Trial Division; September 27, 1988
(1988), 1988 CarswellNat 1264

On April 30, 1987, amid extreme controversy, the first ministers of Canada, assembled at Meech Lake, adopted an *Accord* containing proposals for constitutional change. This *Accord* was formalized in legal language and signed by them on June 5, 1987. It may generally be stated that the thrust of the *Accord* was in the direction of decentralization of the Canadian federation. In order to incorporate the amendments proposed in the *Accord* into the Constitution, the ratification of each of the federal and provincial legislative bodies would be required in the three years following its signature. Nevertheless, in some respects, the Government of Canada started behaving as if the *Accord* had already been ratified. For example, on December 30, 1987, it elevated to the Senate Gerald Ottenheimer of Newfoundland in accordance with the provisions of the *Accord*, that is by a process intimately involving provincial authorities in the process of selection of Senators. Several other Senators were to be elevated in this fashion.

Using the Senate appointments as a catalyst, on May 2, 1988, the Canadian Coalition on the Constitution (the Coalition), a group of citizens opposed to the *Meech Lake Accord*, brought suit in the Trial Division of the Federal Court. The Coalition claimed that governmental behaviour in accordance with the *Accord*, and in particular the Senatorial appointments made in that manner were contrary to law. It sought on that basis to obtain declarations to the effect that:

a) the Government of Canada lacked authority to transfer its fundamental jurisdiction and power to the provinces, as would be provided in the *Accord*;

b) it lacked jurisdiction to relinquish its exclusive authority to appoint Senators and justices of the Supreme Court of Canada;

c) it lacked jurisdiction to adopt an amending formula that irrevocably entrenched a transfer of power to the provincial level;

    d) the *Accord* was null and void because it was so imprecise, ambiguous and broad as to destroy the integrity of the division of powers which had been established since 1867; and

    e) certain select clauses of the *Accord* could derogate from the *Charter*.

In sum, this was a challenge through the courts to a deal reached in a political forum and then set out in legal terms. It amounted to the continuation by judicial means of the political and legal controversy then swirling around the *Accord*. It had become, however, no more possible to distinguish the political from the legal aspects of the *Accord* than it proved feasible to draw a boundary between the political and legal components of the discussion and debate around it. What was being contemplated were competing visions of Canada, which necessarily involved considerations of both law and politics.

The Crown's response to the challenge was an application to the court to strike out the statement of claim as not disclosing a reasonable cause of action and as being frivolous and vexatious. On September 27, 1988, in a judgment so short and devoid of reasoning that its full text has never been reported, the court ordered the claim to be struck. Basing itself on criteria borrowed from the *Inuit Tapirisat* case,[174] it held that the action was premature and not justiciable. It went on to explain briefly that the *Meech Lake Accord* had not yet been passed and that no action to amend the Constitution could occur unless and until the agreement would be completed. With respect to the appointment of Senator Ottenheimer, the court thought that the behaviour of the Prime Minister of Canada and the Premier of Newfoundland in acting as if the *Accord* were in place ought not to be remedied because the proper procedures and necessary legal steps had in fact been followed. In this regard, the court took the rare step of appearing to signify its disdain for the plaintiff's case by associating its tenor with an unpleasant reminder of Canadian political history.

---

[174] *Inuit Tapirisat of Canada v. Canada (Attorney General)* (1980), 115 D.L.R. (3d) 1 (S.C.C.) [See § 2.4.1.]

In the past we have had no indication about the process former Prime Ministers have used to select members of the Senate. (Did Prime Minister King use his crystal ball?)[175]

After the ruling, this case proceeded no further, but in June 1990, less than two years later, the *Accord* itself failed on the shoals of changed political circumstances.

In this matter, the pleadings were lengthy and intricate and the judgment rather disappointingly inexpressive. In traditional treatises of law, a case with such a sparse judgment would, at best, merit a footnote as part of Canada's legal history. From the perspective of political law, however, we must ask whether further analysis is warranted in the category of "Constitutional development." Let us look at the vital arguments.

1) The pleadings and the argumentation presented by the Coalition are of legal interest in themselves.
2) The claim offers a historical snapshot of the state of the public debate about the *Meech Lake Accord* in Canada at that time.
3) The decision was not reported and it is important that the pleadings not be lost in terms of public legal memory.
4) The fate of this case justifies the query whether what was then Rule 419 of the *Rules of the Federal Court* is an appropriate and adequate tool to deal with issues in which law and politics are blended and which may even be premature, but which raise serious matters for judicial reflection nonetheless.
5) There is always a possibility that some other such "politicized" case could succeed, based on how it is framed, how it is pleaded and the willingness of the court to entertain mixed arguments of law and politics.
6) The fact that the mixed political-legal discussion was attempted to be resolved by legal means rather than by further political negotiation is most indicative of the heightened role of the courts in the country's public life and is at the heart of the nature of political law.

---

[175] *Cdn. Coalition on the Constitution Inc. v. R.* (1988), 1988 CarswellNat 1264 (Fed. T.D.), p. 2; not reported.

448 / LAW OF DEMOCRATIC GOVERNING – VOLUME II: JURISPRUDENCE

The Coalition's major pleading concerned an exceeding of jurisdiction on the part of the Government of Canada in signing and ratifying the *Accord* "in that they have undertaken to irrevocably transfer to the provinces, powers indispensable to their capacity to exercise their authority as a national government."[176] In support of this contention, the Coalition relied on the principle that powers in section 91 of the *Constitution Act, 1867* could not be delegated to the provinces by virtue of the doctrine of *delegatus non potest delegare*.

Applying this reasoning to the Senate, the Coalition argued that the terms of the *Accord* would provide for an activist provincial body exercising substantive powers in areas over which the national government had exclusive jurisdiction. The unanimity requirement for future reforms of the Senate would, additionally, entrench veto power in a provincially selected body over a federally selected one in areas of exclusive federal jurisdiction.

> (xii) The effect of the aforesaid is a Senate that will evolve into a "house of the provinces" with members owing their allegiances to provincial interests and thus fundamentally impeding the national government's ability to exercise its exclusive jurisdiction under section 91 of the *Constitution Act, 1867*.[177]

Similar opposition to the decentralizing tendencies of the *Accord* were expressed with regard to the Supreme Court of Canada. Under Meech Lake, the Government of Canada would have to relinquish the exclusive jurisdiction to select and appoint Supreme Court justices. This was seen as essentially undermining the scheme established by section 101 of the *Constitution Act, 1867*.

The Coalition also attacked the *Accord* on the grounds that it was "so imprecise, ambiguous and broad as to destroy the integrity of the division of powers between the federal and provincial governments."[178] This criterion was applied to the proposed reform of the spending power, in particular as it related to the criterion of "national objectives" which provincial programs would have to meet.

Another and very significant part of the Coalition's brief was its attack on the concept of "Distinct Society" for Québec. It criticized this

---

[176] Statement of claim, p. 4, para. 10.

[177] *Ibid.*, p. 8, para. (xii).

[178] *Ibid.*, p. 13, para. 11.

motion as being imprecise and vague. It also pleaded that the impact of the motion on the *Charter* was in dispute. The Coalition argued that this undefined notion of distinct society would expand the powers of Québec's National Assembly, limit the rights of Anglophone Québecers and colour the interpretation of the *Charter*. In its eyes, this amounted to a seizure of greater powers by Québec and, by the admission of the Québec Premier, was to be exploited on the basis of ambiguity, leading to further decentralization.

Of all the arguments relating to Québec and distinct society, those involving the *Charter* were the most fundamental.

> 16.   The plaintiff states that clause 1 of the Accord (section 2 of the *Constitution Act, 1867*) provides, *inter alia*, that the guaranteed rights and freedoms set out in the *Charter* are now to be read subject to the Province of Quebec's legislative and governmental mandate to preserve and promote the distinct identity of Quebec.[179]

In support of this perceived need to safeguard the *Charter* from encroachment, the Coalition recited supportive comments by public figures from political parties and academia who had voiced similar reservations.

The Coalition also attacked all other elements of the *Accord*, including the spending power provisions.

The statement of claim, and later on the Coalition's factum in response to the application to have the claim struck, raised before the court mixed issues of law and politics. The factum added valuable arguments of a nature relevant to political law to this case, namely ones dealing with justiciability. This was the core issue as to whether the matter belonged in the court or not. The effect of these arguments was designed to try to get the Crown to address the substance of the points raised by the Coalition.

---

[179] *Ibid.*, p. 20, para. 16.

Justiciable Issues

21. It is submitted that the statement of claim raises serious justiciable issues appropriate for determination by this Honourable Court. In *Reference Re Amendment of the Constitution of Canada (Nos. 1, 2 & 3)* counsel for the federal government objected to the Court's consideration of the second question in the reference, to wit: Whether constitutional conventions were legally enforceable. It was contended by the Government that the question was "a purely political one." The Supreme Court of Canada held the led was "unclear and a matter for debate." The Court further held that the federal government's characterization of the issues as being "purely political" overstates the case.

Reference: *Reference Re Amendment of The Constitution of Canada (Nos. 1, 2 & 3)*, op. cit. at p 87.

22. The Supreme Court of Canada further held that it was inevitable that issues of constitutional law would have a strong "political element," however that does not remove the "constitutional feature" of the issue. Accordingly the court held that the issue raised had a constitutional character and "would legitimately call for our reply."

Reference: *Reference Re Amendment of The Constitution of Canada (Nos. 1, 2 & 3)*, op. cit. at p 87 & 88.

23. The fact that the court subsequently ruled that constitutional conventions were not legally enforceable was not cause to find that the issue before it was not justiciable.

Reference: *Reference Re Amendment of The Constitution of Canada (Nos. 1, 2 & 3)*, op. cit.

24. Finally, in response to the federal government's objection that the issues raised by Manitoba, Newfoundland and Quebec were "purely political," the Supreme Court of Canada held that traditionally the courts have not shrunk from adjudicating "on account of the political aspects of conventions, nor because of their supposed vagueness, uncertainty or flexibility."

Reference: *Reference Re Amendment of The Constitution of Canada (Nos. 1, 2 & 3)*, op. cit. at p. 89.

25. In *Thorson v. A.-G. Can. et al*, Laskin, J. (as he then was) stated that "the question of the constitutionality of legislation has in this country always been a justiciable question."

Reference: *Thorson v. A.-G. Can. et al* (1974), 43 D.L.R. (3d) 1 at 11.[180]

These arguments did not sway the court's mind. One can imagine no case possibly more closely associated with the political legal fabric of Canada and in which a serious and substantive judicial opinion would have added to the debate and expanded its range and depth. There are legal mechanisms available in democratic countries in which courts, and in particular constitutional courts, have the ability to give advance opinions on the legality and on the legal implications of matters for which the process of enactment is not yet complete. In circumstances such as those of this case, that type of hearing could prove most useful for the full ventilation of fundamental legal issues in Canada.

4.13.C—CHARLOTTETOWN ACCORD

---

§ 4.13.C.1
British Columbia (Attorney General) v. Mount Currie Indian Band
British Columbia Court of Appeal; October 1, 1992
(1992), 18 B.C.A.C. 301[181]

Rather than providing an opportunity for the courts to make good law by authoritative pronouncements on matters of partly legal, partly political, controversy, this case demonstrates only the extent to which the *Charlottetown Accord* of 1992 became what, in the vernacular, is known as a political football and the subject of bad litigation leading to a ruling which can be considered interesting but of no great jurisprudential value.

In 1990, some native youths obstructed a public highway in British Columbia known as the Lilloet Lake Road. The British Columbia Supreme Court ordered by injunction that the blockage stop and later added that breach of the injunction be treated as criminal contempt. On April 15, 1991, that court found several youths guilty of criminal contempt *ex facie curiae*. The Attorney General of Canada appealed on the ground that contempt matters relating to youths were outside the jurisdiction of the British Columbia Supreme Court. On behalf of

---

[180] *Ibid.*, p. 12, para. 21 to p. 14, para. 25.
[181] Leave to appeal refused (1992), 10 C.P.C. (3d) 366n (S.C.C.).

some of the original defendants, counsel made a submission to the effect that the British Columbia Court of Appeal lacked territorial jurisdiction.

On September 21, 1992, the same counsel also gave the case a political law colouration by applying for an interlocutory injunction to prevent the holding of the constitutional referendum on the *Charlottetown Accord* in British Columbia pending disposition of the matter of the court's territorial jurisdiction. That referendum was scheduled to be held on October 26, 1992. In support of the application, counsel cited the political principles embodied in the *Consensus Report on the Constitution*, agreed to at Charlottetown on August 28, 1992, in particular these points in that Report which dealt with native issues and self-government. He argued that those principles were based

> upon 3 fraudulently misleading and *prima facie* rebuttable assumptions of law, namely that:
>
> (a) non-native courts *prima facie* have jurisdiction beyond the treaty frontier;
>
> (b) federal and provincial legislatures *prima facie* have jurisdiction there; and
>
> (c) land beyond the treaty frontier *prima facie* is within the gift of the crown.[182]

The applicants intended to submit that the *Referendum Act* did not provide the proper legal standard as to the manner and form of constitutional change. However, in addition to involving the *Charlottetown Accord*'s provisions in native self-government and the referendum intended to approve that *Accord* in a case on the jurisdiction of the British Columbia Supreme Court, where Charlottetown was an extraneous argument, the applicants' counsel made a mistake fatal to his case. He believed that in British Columbia, the referendum would be organized pursuant to provincial legislation,[183] whereas in fact it was to be run according to the federal act.[184] Under this mistaken apprehension, the applicants pleaded that the legislative intent would be "frustrated if the public is involved to vote upon the basis

---

[182] Memorandum of Argument on behalf of the Applicants, September 19, 1992, p. 2.
[183] *Referendum Act*, S.B.C. 1990, c. 68.
[184] *Referendum Act*, S.C. 1992, c. 30.

of fraudulent misrepresentations regarding the nature and character of the existing law to which amendment is proposed."[185]

The applicants built their entire case on the argument that all B.C. courts lacked jurisdiction to hear the case. When the Court of Appeal dismissed that line of pleading it consequentially dismissed, without explicit reasoning, the attempt to enjoin the referendum.

---

§ 4.13.C.2
Coyne v. R.
Federal Court of Canada – Trial Division; July 30, 1993
file T-381-93; not reported

The attempts by the Canadian polity to deal with the consequences, both legal and political, of the 1982 constitutional reform, have caused profound cleavages both in the country as a whole and within its various organized political communities. Perhaps in no domain of Canadian public life has this been more true than in the field of the relationships between the two "founding" linguistic groups and in the attempts to define their equality of status. In Québec, the controversy has been about whether to grant political acceptance or not to the 1982 amendments which are legally in force in any event in that province as validly as in the rest of the country. By contrast, in neighbouring New Brunswick, where the demographic distinction between Anglophones and Francophones is the closest to even, the debate has focused on incorporation into the constitutional framework of an expression of the equality of the two groups, how that should be done and what the consequences would be.

The first effort at constitutional revision after 1982 was the process throughout 1987-1990 resulting in the *Meech Lake Accord*. The *Meech Lake Accord* was first struck in the spring of 1987 and Frank McKenna's Liberals were elected on October 13, 1987. The New Brunswick authorities then adopted a "Companion Clause" to the *Accord*, which would have had the effect of amending the Constitution to provide for equality of status of and legal rights and privileges to, the English and French linguistic communities of the province, as well as of giving a role to the legislature and government of New Brunswick to pre-

---

[185] *Supra* note 182, p. 4.

serve and provide these rights and this status. This clause was also directed at amending a part of the Constitution's amending formula so as to render the subject of linguistic equality in New Brunswick subject to the approval of Canada and New Brunswick authorities only, but to give the other jurisdictions no voice in the matter. The Companion Clause died with the entire Meech package.

In the subsequent Charlottetown exercise, which lasted from 1990 to 1992, the *Accord* also included provisions for the addition of a section 16.1 to the *Charter*, the purpose of which was to render the linguistic communities of New Brunswick equal, and which would similarly have been subject to bilateral, that is Canada and New Brunswick, control. When the constitutional referendum of October 26, 1992 failed, this proposal also died.

Notwithstanding these two failed attempts, on December 4, 1992, the New Brunswick legislature adopted a measure designed to accomplish for the province that part alone of the Charlottetown reform that would have referred to New Brunswick, so as to ensure the equality of the two linguistic communities. This proposed constitutional amendment regarding New Brunswick was also adopted by the Senate on December 13, 1993, and by the House of Commons on February 1, 1993. In the normal course of events, at this point the matter having been substantially agreed upon, a number of formalities were to occur and the Governor General was to make a *Constitutional Amendment Proclamation* which would eventually be registered as a statutory instrument and be published in the *Canada Gazette*.

All along the legislative path, however, the proposal to adopt this amendment in respect of New Brunswick had encountered divergent views and even caused ruptures among members of the federal and provincial Liberal Parties. Throughout most of the Meech process and all of the Charlottetown processes, as well as at the time of the enactment of the New Brunswick resolution, the provincial Liberals were in office, led by Premier Frank McKenna. He, of course, was in favour of the resolution even if it would have a bearing on the *Canadian Charter of Rights and Freedoms* incorporated into the Constitution in 1982. Former federal Prime Minister Pierre Elliott Trudeau, who was no longer in public life but who continued to exercise considerable intellectual sway throughout the Liberal Party and in the entire country, held the view that the supremacy of the *Charter* should be unaltered.

When those holding Trudeau's vision could not convince the New Brunswick Liberals of the merits of their arguments, one of Trudeau's followers, Coyne, a co-founder of the Canada for All Canadians No Committee at the time of the 1982 referendum, resorted to legal proceedings. On January 4, 1993, she wrote to the Attorneys General of all provinces, seeking to have them institute a reference so as to determine the proper scope and application of the bilateral amendment formula set out in section 43 of the *Constitution Act, 1982*, and to have determined whether it is appropriate to use the formula in respect of the New Brunswick constitutional amendment. None of the Attorneys General took action on Coyne's letter, so she brought suit herself, on February 15, 1993, in the Federal Court of Canada.

Coyne sought to obtain a declaratory judgment that the Governor General had no jurisdiction, power or authority to issue the proclamation to amend the Constitution by adding the N.B. amendment to it. Her legal argumentation amounted to a comprehensive expression of the competing philosophical views about the place of the *Charter* in Canada's constitutional framework.

The plaintiff asserted that the proposed amendment to the Constitution could not be made by way of the bilateral, that is Canada-New Brunswick, amendment formula of section 43, which "should be limited to modifications or adjustments to discrete, self-contained constitutional provisions not applying to all provinces, which do not involve the creation of new elements and basic structures in the Canadian constitutional order, such as the introduction of collective rights into the *Charter*."[186] The pleading reiterated the point with even greater emphasis.

> 22. The bilateral amending formula in section 43 of the Constitution Act, 1982, can only be used in limited circumstances for amendments "in relation to any provision that applies to one or more, but not all, provinces," including amendments relating to "the use of the English or French language within a province." For example, a province could declare itself officially bilingual within the meaning of the Charter language provisions pursuant to section 43. In order for the bilateral amending formula in section 43 to apply, the amendment must be characterizable, in form, substance, purpose and effect, as an amendment to an

---

186 Statement of claim in *Coyne v. R.*, February 15, 1993, para. 35.

existing constitutional provision that is explicitly limited in application to one or more, but not to all provinces.[187]

Thus, instead of the section 43 limited amending formula, the general formula of section 38(1) ought to have been used according to Coyne.

This attempt to ensure that the proper vehicle of constitutional amendment was used was also attempted to be justified by comparison of the New Brunswick matter to that of the controversy over the notion of "Distinct Society" for Québec.

> 31. The New Brunswick Amendment, if permitted to be made pursuant to the bilateral amending formula, will set a powerful precedent for future bilateral amendments such as Quebec's Distinct Society Clause, something which was always considered to have required the general amending formula in section 38(1) of the Constitution Act, 1982.[188]

The heart of Coyne's argument lay in the reasons for her assertion that section 43 should not be used. The proposed amendment, she contended, would effectively alter, in respect of New Brunswick alone, section 23 of the *Charter*, that provision dealing with minority language education rights all across Canada and would alter the coherence and comprehensiveness of section 23, thereby changing its very core. The amendment, Coyne also alleged, would create a special legislative status for the New Brunswick Legislative Assembly in respect of the preservation and promotion of the equality of status and equal rights and privileges of the two linguistic communities in New Brunswick and in so doing, it would diminish federal power in several areas, particularly language, culture, broadcasting and communications. Coyne's next argument was the greatest anathema of defenders the purity of the *Charter*; she contended that the amendment would introduce collective rights, namely that of New Brunswick's linguistic communities, into the *Charter*, which was based on the protection of individual rights alone.

Few statements of claim in the evolution of Canadian public law have contained legal arguments so fundamentally and thoroughly steeped in philosophical perspectives about the nature of the country and in the controversy of topical and current political discussion. Even in

---

[187] *Ibid.*, para. 22.
[188] *Ibid.*, para. 31.

this legal perspective, the action was a reflection of the political conflict internal to the Liberal Party. It was, in fact, an attempt by the *Charter*-purists to avoid piecemeal reforms motivated by political accommodations, so as to protect the universality of principles which had not yet been universally applied. This was an attempt to safeguard the positions acquired through the reforms of 1982.

Beyond the legally-based argumentation, the case relied on primarily political reasoning as well. In order to determine the appropriate procedure through which the New Brunswick amendment ought to have been made, as well as to assess the substantive aspects of the changes the amendment would bring about, Coyne emphasized the criterion of "the intent of the framers of the *Charter*."

> 23. While of limited significance with respect to Charter rights of a universal nature such as the Fundamental Rights and Freedoms, the purpose of the framers is of considerable weight in determining the meaning of those provisions of the Constitution that derive directly from a political bargain or compromise.
>
> . . .
>
> 34. Section 43 should be interpreted strictly. The core of the political compromise which informed the amending formula provisions in the *Constitution Act, 1982* was the requirement of a high degree of provincial consent wherever an amendment affects the structural and symbolic functions of the constitution as a fundamental framework for government and society.[189]

This best demonstrates the degree to which the judicial argument presented by Coyne both comprised and was an outgrowth of the public debate about constitutional reform that was still active at the time, despite the media's insistence on constitutional fatigue.

Despite the initiation of this action, the Governor General did proclaim the New Brunswick constitutional amendment. Its text, which is now section 16.1 of the *Constitution Act, 1982*, as amended, read as follows in SI/93-54, dated April 7, 1993:

> 1. The "Constitution Act, 1982" is amended by adding thereto, immediately after section 16 thereof, the following section:

---

[189] *Ibid.*, paras. 23 and 34.

16.1(1) The English linguistic community and the French linguistic community in New Brunswick have equality of status and equal rights and privileges, including the right to distinct educational institutions and such distinct cultural institutions as are necessary for the preservation and promotion of those communities.

(2) The role of the legislature and government of New Brunswick to preserve and promote the status, rights and privileges referred to in subsection (1) is affirmed."

2. This Amendment may be cited as the "Constitution Amendment, 1993 (New Brunswick)."[190]

Coyne did not follow up on the statement of claim. On March 3, 1993, however the Attorney General of Canada presented a motion based on the rules of the Federal Court, to have the statement of claim struck. The grounds cited by the Attorney General were the ones traditionally used in cases where the plaintiff's arguments are based at least in part on political reasonings: namely that the case discloses no reasonable cause of action, and that the statement of claim is an abuse of the process of the court. In this instance, the Attorney General added that the plaintiff lacked standing. On July 14, Coyne signified her consent to the motion and thereby agreed to the striking of the case. On July 30, 1993, the Federal Court ordered that it be struck, on the ground that the court had no jurisdiction to entertain the action. Coyne contemplated bringing the matter forward in the courts of New Brunswick[191] but took no further action. It is perhaps unfortunate that no court heard arguments on the merits, but the case is instructive nonetheless.

4.13.D—SENATE REFORM

§ 4.13.D.1
Brown v. Alberta
Alberta Court of Appeal; August 31, 1999
[1999] 12 W.W.R. 330

In the *Constitution Act* adopted by Canada in 1867 along the British

---

[190] *Canada Gazette*, Part II, Vol. 127, No. 7, p. 1588.
[191] Joan Bryden, "N.B. Constitutional amendment challenge dropped," *The Montreal Gazette*, July 6, 1993, p. A-8.

model, sections 17 and 21 established the Senate and section 24 set out the manner in which Senators were to be named: they are appointed. For all intents, this means senators are chosen by the incumbent Prime Minister. Since that time, despite the progress of representative democracy, the Senate has remained an appointed body. It has become increasingly anachronistic in an age of democracy but it has managed to survive relatively unchanged despite numerous proposals for modernization. Immediately after the 1982 patriation, it was thought that Senate reform would be the next item on the constitutional development agenda, but the scarcity of time left in the mandate of the Trudeau government did not render the reform possible. Neither the Meech Lake nor the Charlottetown rounds succeeded in revitalizing the Senate. This institutional immobilism left many citizens perplexed and cynical. In the Western Provinces however, it fuelled the sense of local alienation from the federal capital. Groups such as the Canada West Foundation and the Canadian Committee for a Triple-E Senate (CCTES) conducted vociferous lobbying for the constitutional changes required to set right this perceived wrong. The expression "triple-E" of course means elected, effective and equal. The most visible result of these efforts was the enactment by the Alberta legislature of the *Senatorial Selection Act*,[192] which was brought into force and effect on with Royal Assent on August 18, 1989.

The enactment of this statute was not a guarantee of its use. In fact, the federal government of Prime Minister Chrétien, elected in 1993 and re-elected in 1997, decided not to abide by the results that could be produced by use of the mechanisms provided in the Act.

On November 19, 1997, most likely with a view to inducing greater attention on the part of the federal authorities to the *Senatorial Selection Act*, Brown, the Chairman of the CCTES, filed an action in the Alberta Court of Queen's Bench. The application simply sought

> an Order declaring that the provisions of the Canadian constitution providing for the appointment of senators by the Governor General-in-Council are contrary to democratic principles, and that to conform with the principles of democracy in Alberta, senators must be selected in a

---

[192] S.A. 1989, c. S-11.5.

> manner consistent with the processes of the Senatorial Selection Act,
> Chapter S-11.5 of the Statutes of Alberta, 1989.[193]

This action was approved of by the Reform Party at the federal level and by the Progressive Conservative government of Alberta. It also received wide support in the press. In addition to the favourable comment which might have been expected from the *Calgary Herald*, the *Montreal Gazette* and the *Financial Post* carried supportive editorials. Most significantly, the idea of Senate reform received the active backing of the *Globe and Mail*, which styles itself as Canada's national newspaper. Indeed, the great part of Brown's affidavit in support of his action consisted of the transcript of September 20, 1997, by William Thorsell, the *Globe and Mail's* editor, to the Vancouver Institute. Among other matters, this speech touched in very general terms on the ailments of the Senate as currently constituted, structured and empowered. The other documentary evidence advanced by Brown consisted of a letter jointly signed by two political science professors from the University of Lethbridge, in which the requirements and the urgency of Senate reform were set out in the context of the further democratization of the Canadian body politic.

At about the same time, several vacancies in the Senate were due to be filled. The Alberta government, as well as the media, urged that Prime Minister Chrétien avail himself of the process rendered possible by the *Senate Selection Act* to designate at least those who would represent Alberta in the Upper Chamber. On November 26, 1997, contrary to this advice, the Prime Minister appointed new senators in the traditional fashion, using section 24 of the *Constitution Act, 1867*, including one from Alberta.

The federal Crown's response to Brown's action, moreover, was an application to have it struck out, pursuant to the Alberta *Rules of Court*. The argument presented was essentially that Brown's case disclosed no legal issue and that under the *Judicature Act*,[194] legal remedies were available only in respect of legal claims. On July 28, 1998, the court granted the motion and struck out the case on the basis of the following disposition:

---

[193] Originating Notice of Motion, p. 1.

[194] R.S.A. 1980, c. J-1, in particular ss. 8 and 11.

[46] Brown admits there is no legal right or interest here. He does not allege the violation or threatened violation of any legal right. He does not challenge the constitutionality of the *Senatorial Selection Act* nor of s. 24 of the *Constitution Act, 1867*. He does not allege any violations of the *Charter of Rights and Freedoms*.

[47] There is no legal issue in the originating notice, as modified by the particulars. The court has no jurisdiction to grant the declaration Brown seeks. The Federal Crown's application to strike out the originating notice is granted as against all respondents, since it is "plain and obvious" that the originating notice cannot succeed, as it discloses no cause of action.

[48] That the court has no role in the issue as framed should have no bearing on the current debate on Senate selection and reform. Informed, open and vigorous debate is vital to a democratic society. However, the same democratic principles that encourage and protect debate also demand that a court remain uninvolved unless proper legal issues are placed before it.[195]

Brown's strategy in addressing this matter to the court and in doing so at this time deserve close scrutiny. The principal argument advanced was that the Senate is a major constitutional issue in Canada. This is one of the two last countries in the world with an appointed chamber as part of its legislative structure. In the view of Brown, the Senate should be the regionally representative body it was originally meant to be.

While these points may have validity as topics to be advanced in the course of a speech or at a class in political science, a legal issue of a litigious nature seems to be missing and this is what doomed the action. The action may have had merit in the sense of raising the profile of the Senate reform issue, but without a genuine litigious cause, Brown's chances of obtaining a declaratory order seemed rather slim from the outset. This case amounted to a request for a court to make a legal pronouncement in the absence of a legal issue, almost as if a private citizen wished to initiate a reference and to ask for an opinion which, at that, would be an expression of a political position by the court. To avoid this type of misuse, the court reiterated

---

[195] Report of the Chief Electoral Officer of Alberta on the Senate Nominee Election held on October 19, 1998; June 15, 1999.

that the entire purpose of a court of law is to adjudicate on matters of law, not otherwise.

Consequently, this court was correct in holding that it has no authority to award a remedy where there is no legal issue before it. The judgment leads the political law observer to two conclusions. A mixed issue of law and politics can be put before the courts and a matter that is contemporaneously the subject of public debate can be submitted for adjudication, but the legal component must be an issue, comprising adversarial positions, for the court to grapple with the substance of the case. In addition, the manner in which a political question is framed for presentation to the court affects whether the court can indeed discern the presence of a legal issue.

Brown argued that a court may make a declaratory order even if there is no legal issue before it, or a justiciable issue, as long as there is another "useful purpose." Here, that purpose would have been the importance of the Senate to Canadians, the influence of the eventual court order on the Governor General in making future Senate appointments, as well as the public attention and the pressure to use the *Senatorial Selection Act*. The court refuted that argument, determining that a legal interest is required to be at stake before it can issue declaratory relief.

In the court's further view, Brown's application amounted to an attempt to limit the powers of the Governor General in exercising the section 24 senatorial appointment process. The Constitution gave it no such power.

One final point in this judgment also merits attention. In listing the arguments Brown failed to make, the court may have brought into future litigants' view a line of reasoning which may render them more successful. It said that "Brown is not claiming that democratic principles are part of the Constitution, such that the appointment power in section 24 must be read subject to such principles."[196] We are not told what those democratic principles are, nor how they are to influence the reading of the Constitution, but the door opened by this line in the judgment is worthy of closer examination by other would-be reformers of Canadian institutions such as the Senate.

---

[196] 1998 ABQB 665 at para. 6, affirmed 1999 ABCA 256 (Alta. C.A.).

Notwithstanding this litigation, and despite the fact that by the time the matter was adjudicated, no Senate seats from Alberta remained to be filled, the Alberta authorities proceeded on October 19, 1998 to hold a vote pursuant to the *Senatorial Selection Act*. A total of 891,583 electors cast ballots for one of four candidates. Brown received a plurality, with 332,766 votes, representing 37.3%.

Brown's appeal was based on the argument that the Québec Secession Reference decision of the Supreme Court of Canada had modified the test for determining what is a "legal issue." He reasoned that in light of that changed test, a judicial declaration to the effect that the present method of appointment to the Senate is not consistent with democratic principles would be persuasive, even though without legal effect. The Court of Appeal disagreed. "Absent a legal issue, it is not within the competence of the court to make statements whose sole purpose is political persuasion or social comment."[197] Moreover, even though the Supreme Court referred to the democratic principle among the interpretive canons underlying the constitution, a court cannot be an arbiter of the democratic character of senatorial appointments. In order for a court to make such a statement, it must have jurisdiction, which arises only where there is a legal issue. The democratic principle, *per se*, devoid of legal issues, is not sufficient. "The Quebec Secession Reference does not change the law on the scope of the court's jurisdiction to grant declaratory relief, nor does it overrule existing authorities to set out what constitutes a 'legal issue.'"[198]

The search for a revitalized Senate, commensurate with a 21st Century democracy, goes on in the political realm.

---

§ 4.13.D.2
Samson v. Canada (Attorney General)
Federal Court of Canada – Trial Division; September 1, 1998
(1998), 165 D.L.R. (4th) 342

The failure of the *Brown* case and the evolution of circumstances through the summer of 1998 ensured that the subject matter of Senate reform would remain highly visible in the political law agenda in

---

[197] 1999 ABCA 256 at para. 18.
[198] *Ibid.* at para. 26.

Canada. With the present case, the argumentation of a legal nature became more profound and refined while the stakes for political factions were raised and the consequential interest among the public, particularly in the West, increased significantly. The *Samson* case essentially addressed the argument of Senate reform from two perspectives. It looked, first, at the issue of whether the Senate was an exclusively federal institution in regard to which federal political officials had a free hand, or whether the Canadian concept of democracy in both its political and legal manifestations, and federal-provincial co-ordination, had sufficiently evolved for there to be a need for the assent of the people affected by Senate appointments. On another level, this case delved into the resolution of perceived conflict between the written part of the Constitution and the country's political evolution, and whether that evolution could be alleged, ostensibly for partisan advantage, to have created a convention that had changed the written Constitution.

Even though the *Meech Lake Accord* of 1987 had not eventually been adopted as a set of amendments to the Constitution and thus produced no legal obligations, those pressing for reforms along the lines agreed to at Meech continued to rely on it. Thus, in correspondence conducted in 1998 between Premier Klein of Alberta and Prime Minister Chrétien, the former urged that the method of appointing Senators written into the *Accord*, namely federal selection off provincially devised lists, be adopted. The Prime Minister's response was negative. Nevertheless, in line with the *Senatorial Selection Act*,[199] when Alberta scheduled its municipal elections for the fall of 1998, on June 19, 1998, it also issued writs for the selection of what were then thought to be Senators-in-waiting. On August 28, Senator Jean Forest, a member of Alberta's deputation to the Senate, resigned prematurely and this gave the entire matter a sense of urgency.

Samson and other officials of the Reform Party of Canada and the Reform Party of Alberta applied immediately to the Trial Division of the Federal Court with a motion for interlocutory injunction to prevent the summoning of a Senator from Alberta other than a person democratically elected pursuant to the *Senatorial Selection Act*. This litigation was the legal argument of the pursuit of the policy goal of Senate reform genuinely desired by westerners and Albertans in particular, carried on at both political and legal levels. It was no less a

---

[199] S.A. 1989, c. S-11.5.

politically partisan manoeuvre by the Reform Party which had a near stranglehold on Alberta politics and which would benefit from such a process in terms of publicity. Moreover, it was a timely move which the Reform Party could use to divert attention from its internal leadership problems.

The plaintiff's principal argument was that their objective was to improve the democratic nature of the Senate, as one of Canada's two legislative houses. In support of this position, they argued that adoption of the process developed in Meech would in no way violate the *Constitution Act, 1867*, nor require constitutional changes to be effected to that text. They also relied extensively on arguments based on constitutional principles, many of which were drawn into their pleadings in the manner in which they had been stated by the Supreme Court only days before, in its judgment on the Québec Secession Reference. In particular, they emphasized that:

> The Constitution of Canada is based on such principles as democracy and federalism, respect for democratic processes and institutions and the rule of law. These underlying constitutional principles give rise to substantive legal obligations, which constitute substantive limitations upon government action. The unilateral Senate appointment process employed by the present federal government is unconstitutional.[200]

The technical arguments in favour of the injunction were that its refusal would cause irreparable harm to the applicants as a Senator once named could not be unseated; that damages could not be adequate to redress the situation, regardless of the outcome; and that the balance of convenience weighed heavily in favour of the applicants.

In a first hearing as soon as August 28, 1998, the very day of Senator Forest's resignation, the Federal Court refused to hear the matter *ex parte*. In a substantive ruling handed down on September 1, 1998, the court dismissed the motion. It agreed that there was a serious issue to be tried, but in reading the relevant provisions of the *Constitution Act, 1867*, sections 24 and 32, it determined that the Governor General's power to appoint Senators is discretionary and that this discretion could not be ignored. The court perceived the plaintiff's case as a desire to limit the appointment discretion and concluded that such a limitation could be achieved only by an amendment of the written

---

[200] Notice of Motion, page 5, para. 12, August 31, 1998.

part of the Constitution, a process which the court could not impose to be done.

The court drew a very useful distinction between a simply political decision and a convention. It noted that in one case, in 1990, a Senator had been named by the process Samson wanted to have used here. In its view, however, one previous occasion did not constitute a convention which would alter the express wording of the written Constitution. This instance had been no more than "a political decision made by the Government of the day at a particular time in our nation's history."[201] This reinforced the substance of conventions as being derived from repeated practice over time.

This court was fully aware of the politicized nature of the legal situation with which it was presented and of the partisan implications of the issue. In that sense, the most important aspect of its ruling was not the rejection of the injunction, but its cautionary advice to both lawyers and politicians seeking to reform the Senate.

> The Governor General's constitutional power to appoint qualified persons to the Senate is also purely political in nature. In practice, the Governor General exercises his power of appointment on the advice and recommendation of the Governor-in-Council. In the event that the Governor-in-Council makes a recommendation which ignores the pending election to be held in Alberta under the provisions of the provincial *Senatorial Selection Act*, it proceeds at its own political peril. However, that is a purely political decision to be made by politicians, without the interference or intervention of the Court.
>
> . . .
>
> In my opinion, the applicants' claim in this matter is political, and not legal, in nature. As a result, the relief which the applicants seek in their application may only be attained in the political arena by means of a constitutional amendment. I have therefore concluded that the applicants have failed to establish that the case raises a serious issue to be tried. In the circumstances, it is unnecessary for me to address the other two branches of the test.[202]

See also *Lord Mayhew of Twysden's Motion*, [2002] 1 A.C. 109 and *Lord Gray's Motion*, [2002] 1 A.C. 124.

---

[201] (1998), 165 D.L.R. (4th) 342 at 346, para. 8.

[202] *Ibid.* at 345, paras. 6 and 9.

5

ELECTIONS

5.1 GENERAL PRINCIPLES

See Volume I, Chapter 5.

5.2 ISSUE: ELECTORAL SYSTEMS, THE MEANING OF "ELECTION" AND POLITICAL REPRESENTATION[1]

§ 5.2.1
British Columbia Civil Liberties Assn. v. British Columbia
(Attorney General)
British Columbia Supreme Court; filed March 16, 1998
file No. 980711, Vancouver Registry
adjourned *sine die* June 6, 1998

In a country such as Canada with a political legal system similar in principle to that of the United Kingdom, there is an objective understanding that the consequence of an election is that in each constituency the person elected is, by the fact of that election, enabled to represent the local population and to act as a parliamentarian for the entire duration of the legislative body to which he was elected.[2]

---

[1] Cross reference to § 3.6.

[2] This case is based on the Canadian electoral system, in which the standards are a first past the post voting method leading to single-member constituencies. For an interesting discussion on the right to vote as a fundamental political right across dissimilar jurisdictions, see the Hungarian book entitled *Képviselet és Vàlasztàs a Parlamenti Jogban* by Professor Màrta Dezsö, published by Közgazdasàgi és Jogi Könyvkiadó, Budapest, 1995, especially pp. 24-29. It is unfortunate for the transnational study of political law that books such as this have not yet been translated into English.

Moreover, voters are entitled to their subjective legitimate expectation that, short of resignation or death, each legislator is to serve out the full term for which he was elected. That is the traditional understanding of the meaning of "election." In this scenario, legislators balance competing interests and act in the general public interest.

In British Columbia, where, during the 1990's, politics were severely polarized, this consensus about the meaning of election was not universally shared. Following a referendum on this matter held in conjunction with the provincial election of October 17, 1991, the province's Legislative Assembly adopted a *Recall and Initiative Act*,[3] which received Royal Assent on July 8, 1994. The essence of the recall provisions in this legislation was that upon fulfilling certain requirements as to form, a registered voter for an electoral district could apply for a petition to recall his Member of the Legislative Assembly. On the basis of such a petition, a recall process, one akin to reversal of the electoral result in the constituency, could take place. In February 1998, recalls were attempted in this manner against the provincial Minister of Education, Skills and Training, Paul Ramsay, and another Member, Helmut Geisbrecht, both New Democrats.

In response to these attempts and to their near success, the British Columbia Civil Liberties Association initiated an action in the Supreme Court to have the *Initiative and Recall Act* declared unconstitutional pursuant to section 52 of the *Constitution Act, 1982*. That section formed the basis of the list of statutes of a constitutional nature. The effect of invoking it was to attempt to show that, because the *Initiative and Recall Act* was of a constitutional nature but not listed in the schedule to section 52, it was unconstitutional. The Association qualified the recall campaigns as divisive, disruptive, polarizing and abusive. More specifically, it argued that the recall provisions in the legislation were in violation of section 41 of the *Constitution Act, 1982*, because they alter the Office of the Lieutenant Governor. With specific reference to the nature of Canada's political system, the Association argued that:

> The Recall Provisions are also *ultra vires* the Legislature of British Columbia because they offend against the Preamble to the *Constitution Act, 1867* which guarantees a "Constitution similar in Principle to that of the United Kingdom." The Recall Provisions introduce political institutions

---

3 Now R.S.B.C. 1996, c. 398.

foreign to and incompatible with the Canadian system of parliamentary democracy. In particular, but without limiting the generality of the foregoing, the Recall Provisions:

    a. weaken the fabric and practice of responsible and representative government;

    b. entrench a theory of government which sees Members as merely the delegate or "mouthpiece" of their constituency rather than their representatives in the Legislative Assembly;

    c. interferes with the tenure of the Members even though they have committed no crime or otherwise engaged in corruption or other serious misconduct;

    d. undermines the established systems of party discipline and determination of confidence in the government;

    e. undermines the effectiveness of Cabinet and renders the Ministers of the Crown particularly vulnerable to special interests and pressure groups (including those that are not constituents) who are critical of governmental policy and legislative decisions, interferes with the enactment of laws and other public policies that are in the public interest, for example:

        (i) members may become advocates of their electoral districts to the exclusion of Province-wide or societal interests;

        (ii) policy solutions that require a compromise between different communities may be disadvantaged;

        (iii) the interests of the organized, wealthy and dominant in the society may be favoured to the disadvantage of minorities, the poor and the less well organized;

        (iv) members may become overly concerned with keeping their seats and thereby refrain from action in the public interests in order to avoid conflict or controversy.

    f. undermine government stability, particularly when the government is elected with only a small majority;

    g. are demagogic and anti-democratic;

    h. will result in recall campaigns that might be divisive, disruptive, polarizing and abusive.[4]

Further, specifically regarding the constitutionally protected rights of citizens to vote, the Association presented the following pleading:

> Furthermore, the Recall Provisions infringe the citizen's right to vote as guaranteed by section 3 of the *Canadian Charter of Rights and Freedoms* for reasons which include the following:
>
>   a. they infringe the citizen's right to representative democracy;

---

[4] Statement of claim, para. 11.

b. they infringe the citizen's right to effective representation in the Legislative Assembly;

c. they frustrate and undermine the votes of those citizens who voted for a Member even though the Member committed no crime or otherwise engaged in serious misconduct;

d. there is no secret ballot;

e. the votes of those not signing the petition are not counted;

f. the result is not determined by a plurality of votes;

g. the citizens are not presented with a choice of candidates;

h. the citizens are not provided with sufficient information about public policies to permit an informed decision;

i. the citizens of the electoral district in which recall petitions are successful are denied representation in the Legislative Assembly until a by-election and, by virtue of section 27 of the Act, may be denied representation until a general election in the case of a second recall petition.[5]

The Provincial Government put in a vigorous statement of defence, based in part on legal principles and in part on its explanation of the evolution of the province's political system and its capacity to incorporate the *Initiative and Recall Act*, even though it was the only Canadian jurisdiction to have such a law giving dissatisfied citizens the potential capacity to undo election results.

The defence started by pointing out that over 80% of those voting in the 1991 referendum had approved the introduction of the recall legislation. It went on to state that:

> The impugned legislation has been enacted by a democratically elected legislature, in circumstances showing it to have been (and to continue to be) overwhelmingly supported by the public. It enhances rather than detracts from a system of responsible and representative government, and is highly democratic in nature. The Plaintiffs' claims that the legislation is "demagogic and anti-democratic," "weakens the fabric and practice of responsible and representative government," and "infringes the citizen's right to representative democracy" are either demonstrably false or rely on perversions of the meaning of such terms as "democracy," "responsible government" and "representative government" to such an extent as to render the issues non-justiciable.

. . .

Further, the Constitution of Canada has proven itself capable of accom-

---

[5] *Ibid.*, para. 13.

modating significant changes to electoral practices. At the time the *British Columbia Terms of Union* were negotiated, British Columbia did not have a wholly elected Legislative Council, and Responsible Government was not mandated, though it was contemplated.[6]

The entire defence of the legislation could have been read as a textbook in political science, dealing with the fundamental characteristics of democracy and the electoral system, just as easily as a court document. Its most significant and encompassing statement was that,

> To the extent that the impugned legislation results in any evolution of Parliamentary traditions, such changes are exceedingly minor compared to those which have been accommodated by the introduction of elected government, the rise of political parties as the primary forces in Canadian politics and by the enfranchisement of large portions of the public. Incremental change in electoral practices, such as that occurring as a result of the impugned Legislation, is within the scope of the preamble and other portions of the *Constitution Act, 1867*.[7]

In essence, these pleadings represented not only divergent positions on points of law, but dramatically different perspectives on British Columbia political society. Had the case proceeded to court, beyond the initial exchange of written pleadings, this case could have become the focal point of a much broader debate on the nature of the province's electoral system and indeed, the fundamentals of its democracy. Sadly for this study, neither party pursued the matter and the focus of the ideological conflict over representation in the B.C. Legislature shifted to the subject matter of political promises, dealt with in the case of *Friesen v. Hammell.*

This case did, nonetheless, resonate two other issues. It raised prominently the question of whether the modification of the institutions of representative democracy is feasible outside the limits of the schedule of constitutionalized statutes pursuant to section 52, thus raising the issue of the need for constitutional amendment to resolve such conflicts, but not settling it.

Finally, this case opened yet again the discussion of whether matters of this type, relating to the political system, were best resolved by political means, in the legislative forum, or through legal principles,

---

[6] Statement of defence, paras. 14 and 18.
[7] *Ibid.*, para. 19.

by the courts. The Leader of B.C.'s Official Opposition wrote thought-fully on this.

> In a startling move last week, the B.C. Civil Liberties Association asked the Supreme Court of this province to declare that British Columbia's recall law is unconstitutional. The BCCLA has been against recall in the past, but surely a court is not the right place to work out the proper institutions of democracy, a profoundly political question. And what a painful irony it is that an organization founded to defend citizens from governments is now trying to defend a government from its citizens.

> . . .

> It all comes down to two things: discretion and accountability. Who is to have the discretion in determining which political practices and ground rules are appropriate in our democracy? The Constitution no-where mentions cabinet government or the party system, and says noth-ing about electoral systems except that everyone will have a vote. Should decisions on those questions be made by unelected judges and frozen in the Constitution, or by politicians elected from time to time, modifying practices from time to time? And do we really want to imprison ourselves in the practice of the Britain of 1867?

> As to accountability, there is a clear principle: The voters can hire poli-ticians and fire them. That is the bottom line. The only issue is when. Some contracts are longer, some are shorter. A U.S. congressman's ten-ure is only two years. Under B.C. law, the recall process cannot even be started for 18 months. Good or bad? Judges are not accountable them-selves and should not be deciding these things.[8]

See also *Russow & The Green Party of Canada v. Canada (Attorney General)* (May 1, 2001), Doc. 01-CV-210088 (Ont. S.C.J.); *B.C. and Canadian bills to fix the date of elections* and *Litigation by the Association for the Revendication of Political Rights,* filed in Québec Superior Court, March 17, 2004.

---

[8] "B.C.'s recall debate doesn't belong in the courts," Gordon Gibson, *Globe and Mail*, Toronto; March 24, 1998.

§ 5.2.2
Foster v. Love
United States Supreme Court; December 2, 1997
139 L.Ed.2d 369 (1997)

This is a case in appearance primarily concerned with the federalism issue of conflict between an electoral scheme enshrined in a Louisiana statute and the requirements of American federal law based on the United States Constitution. Despite this appearance as well as the succinctness of the judgment, the case is of importance to political law as it both provides a judicial definition of what is an election and reinforces the principle of uniformity of timing of an election held over the geographic extent of an entire country.

In the United States Constitution, responsibility was assigned to the States for legislation on the mechanics of congressional elections, that is for dealing with the times, places and the manner of holding elections. This power, however, was subject to the pre-emptive power of Congress to legislate instead of the individual States.[9] Pursuant to the Constitution, Congress established specific times for senatorial and congressional elections, namely the Tuesday next after the first Monday in November in even numbered years. The goal of this legislation was to determine a uniform federal election day.[10] This regime had functioned unchanged for a long time when, in 1975, Louisiana enacted a system of conducting what it entitled "open primaries" for its senatorial and congressional offices.[11] Two elements of this system must be mentioned in particular. First, it enabled all voters to vote, regardless of their party affiliation and it showed all candidates on the same ballot, equally without distinction as to party. This clearly distinguished the plan from what is ordinarily described as a "primary" in American electoral practice. Second, the so-called open primary was scheduled for October, the month before the "general election." There was an even more contentious aspect of the Louisiana plan, which related to the consequences of the vote for candidates.

---

[9] Constitution of the United States, Article I, § 4, clause 1.
[10] 2 U.S.C., § 1 and 7.
[11] La. Rev. Stat. Ann. § 18:511(A) (West Supp. 1997).

> If no candidate for a given office receives a majority, the State holds a run-off (dubbed a "general election") between the top two vote-getters the following month on federal election day. § 18:481 (West 1979). But if one such candidate does get a majority in October, that candidate "is elected," § 18:511(A) (West Supp. 1997), and no further act is done on federal election day to fill the office in question.[12]

Several voters in the State of Louisiana brought suit against Foster, the Governor, and the State's Secretary of State, challenging the validity of the open primary system as being a violation of federal law. The United States Supreme Court held that the open primary system was an ostensible election which runs afoul of the relevant federal statute and is void to the extent of the conflict.

In order to render this judgment, the court needed to address the matter of what is an election and it characterized the concept in the following manner:

> When the federal statutes speak of "the election" of a Senator or Representative, they plainly refer to the combined actions of voters and officials meant to make a final selection of an officeholder (subject only to the possibility of a later runoff, see 2 USC § 8 [2 USCS § 8]. See N. Webster, An American Dictionary of the English Language 433 (C. Goodrich & N. Porter eds. 1869) (defining "election" as "[t]he act of choosing a person to fill an office").[13]

The key element in the concept of election is thus finality or definitiveness of the choice of the electorate.

Even more important than the matter of timing which the court also considered, what the court objected to in the Louisiana scheme was a combination of the acts posed, their effect and their definitive nature in placing individuals into elective offices. In sum, it said that a system in which a contested election of candidates for a congressional office that could be concluded as a matter of law before the federal election day, with no further act in law or in fact being required on the federally appointed election day was contrary to the federally legislated election system. In justifying this negative view of the State's position, the court cited from the Louisiana statute itself in order to conclude

---

[12] 139 L.Ed.2d 369 (1997) at 374.
[13] *Ibid.* at 374-5.

that the nature of the voters' voice in the open primary could be definitive.

> Because the candidate said to be "elected" has been selected by the voters from among all eligible office-seekers, there is no reason to suspect that the Louisiana Legislature intended some eccentric meaning for the phrase "is elected."[14]

Significantly, the court went on to affirm that voting at variable times distorts the voting process because an early election in one State can influence later voting in other States. Should this be allowed, some States would have undue advantage, which is wrong. Historically, the United States has resisted States' attempts to introduce such elements of distortion and undue influence.

See also *Adams v. Clinton; Alexander v. Daley*, 90 F. Supp. 2d 27 (D.C.C., 2000) and *The New Jersey Democratic Party et al.v. Hon. David Samson et al.*, 175 N.J. 178, October 2, 2002.1[15]

5.3 ISSUE: DRAWING ELECTORAL BOUNDARIES

§ 5.3.1[16]
Reference re Provincial Electoral Boundaries
Supreme Court of Canada; June 6, 1991
[1991] 2 S.C.R. 158

The confection of electoral maps is an extremely delicate political operation. If a legislature is to be representative of the people for whom it enacts laws and whose interests it espouses and promotes, then democracy requires the citizens have a relatively equal voice in electing their legislators. This implies that equitable rules regarding the equality of electorates on a constituency-by-constituency basis be adopted and applied. It also means that the political party in power at the time boundaries are drawn not fix either the rules of redistribution, or the results, in its own favour. Since the advent of the *Charter*,

---

[14] *Ibid.* at 375.
[15] Both international comparisons.
[16] Cross-reference to § 3.6.2.

the conception and application of rules for redistribution have been the subject of a great deal of litigation. This is an area of political life where the law has made a great impact. The present case is the clearest recent statement of the constitutional and legal principles which legislators and public administrators must take into account in drawing electoral districts.

This reference was based on an electoral map prepared for Saskatchewan in 1989. The province's Court of Appeal of the province declared it to be in breach of section 3 of the *Charter*, the right to vote provision. Here, the Supreme Court of Canada overturned that ruling and upheld the validity of the scheme.

The first matter regarding the drawing of electoral boundaries which the court looked at was the applicability of the *Charter*. Despite the contentions of the Minister of Justice of the Northwest Territories that the method and process of creation of electoral boundaries are within the domain of constitutional convention and therefore impervious to judicial review, the court did not hesitate to assert that the provincial exercise of legislative authority on this topic is subject to the *Charter*. While the court thus saw a role for itself and therefore for legal analysis of the political decision-making involved, it qualified that power by indicating that it should be used with caution.

> This Court has repeatedly affirmed that the courts must be cautious in interfering unduly in decisions that involve the balancing of conflicting policy considerations:
>
> . . .
>
> These considerations led me to suggest in *Dixon*, supra, at p. 419, that "the courts ought not to interfere with the legislature's electoral map under s. 3 of the *Charter* unless it appears that reasonable persons applying the appropriate principles...could not have set the electoral boundaries as they exist."[17]

The core of the judgment was the Supreme Court's advice to politicians and public administrators as to how to design constituencies. In this regard, the court was presented with a number of positions. At one end of the spectrum, a non-governmental organization called "Equal Justice for All" had advocated strict observance of equality,

---

[17] [1991] 2 S.C.R. 158 at 189 d and f-g.

save for justified aid to disadvantaged groups. Astonishingly, the Attorney General of Alberta denied that equality of voting power was a fundamental value in assessing the right to vote. The court found a genuinely Canadian middle ground, indicating that the appropriate approach was to aim for effective representation of electors based on their relative parity of voting power. Thus, in devising constituencies the numerical calculation of population based on an electoral quotient, could be tempered by justified deviations based on social considerations such as community history, community interests and minority representation as well as geographic factors. It is also very important to note that the court left the door open for the eventual use of further criteria justifying deviations.

The court also ventured into the socio-technical aspects of constituency design. It recognized the validity of differentiations between urban, rural and northern electoral districts. There was no dispute about northern, large distant and sparsely populated districts which needed a wider margin of deviation from the electoral quotient in order to achieve effective representation. The urban-rural split, on the other hand, was a most contentious issue here and has dogged constituency designers in several provinces ever since the judgment.

> Before examining the electoral boundaries to determine if they are justified, it may be useful to mention some of the factors other than equality of voting power which figure in the analysis. One of the most important is the fact that it is more difficult to represent rural ridings than urban. The material before us suggests that not only are rural ridings harder to serve because of difficulty in transport and communications, but that rural voters make greater demands on their elected representatives, whether because of the absence of alternative resources to be found in urban centres or for other reasons. Thus the goal of effective representation may justify somewhat lower voter populations in rural areas. Another factor which figured prominently in the argument before us is geographic boundaries; rivers and municipal boundaries form natural community dividing lines and hence natural electoral boundaries. Yet another factor is growth projections. Given that the boundaries will govern for a number of years—the boundaries set in 1989, for example, may be in place until 1996—projected population changes within that period may justify a deviation from strict equality at the time the boundaries are drawn.[18]

---

[18] *Ibid.* at 194 j – 195 d.

The court admitted that the trend was for urban seats to be more populous than rural ones. It decided that in this case, the margin between under-representation of urban areas and the consequential over-representation of rural ones on the basis of the respective urban and rural populations within the province was not wide enough to warrant a finding of breach of section 3 of the *Charter*.

In a most delicate fashion, fitting the contentious nature of the political-legal argument itself, the court breached the matter of the partisan foundations of the issue. In concluding its remarks about the urban-rural split, the court stated that: "It is thus seen that the effect of the allocation of seats to urban and rural ridings in the 1989 legislation was mainly to increase the number of urban seats to reflect population increases in urban areas."[19] This is a mere factual explanation. However, the court then goes on to indicate why this explanation was necessary by saying that, "This belies the suggestion that the 1989 Act was an unjustified attempt to adjust boundaries to benefit the governing party."[20] With this one sentence out of the entire judgment, the court gives voice to the entire line of argumentation that the government's desire to perpetuate the urban-rural split in favour of the latter was to retain its hold on power by increasing the electoral weight of its natural political base. Being an institution for the statement of law, the court would venture no further into the obviously political debate, but this was enough to acknowledge that partisan politics was involved. Commensurately, by limiting its comments on the political aspect to this one sentence, the court was determined to channel the debate into a constitutional and legal framework, thereby disarming those who would continue the political debate. One result of this judgment has been that in subsequent years, while a number of other redistribution debates have occurred, many of which focused on the urban-rural split, the participants in them have had resort to the legal *fora* for such debates, the courts.

---

[19] *Ibid.* at 193 b.
[20] *Ibid.*

§ 5.3.2[21]
Reference re Electoral Divisions Statutes Amendment Act, 1993 (Alberta)
Alberta Court of Appeal; October 24, 1994
(1994), 119 D.L.R. (4th) 1

The population of Alberta had its roots in farming and ranching and until very recently, the province's electoral map reflected the influence of this agricultural community in society, to the detriment of the dwellers of Alberta's recently-grown cities, Edmonton and Calgary. Until 1989, urban voters were under-represented and rural voters over-represented in the Legislative Assembly. In the years since then, the redistribution of electoral boundaries along more equitable lines and in a manner more in keeping with the principles flowing from the *Canadian Charter of Rights and Freedoms*, has been attempted on several occasions. The design of a constitutionally valid and politically acceptable electoral map has also been a subject of persistent public policy debate and much litigation.

The Alberta Court of Appeal was first asked to agree to an electoral boundaries scheme in 1991. Its judgment in that case[22] was somewhat inconclusive in that the court would not declare that the province's 1989 electoral boundaries legislation offended the *Charter*. The court used the expression that the scheme showed gradual but steady change toward a valid approach. This was tantamount to an invitation to the legislature to try again, and so it did. In November 1992, a Select Committee of the Legislative Assembly devised a new map and this was incorporated into the *Electoral Divisions Statutes Amendment Act, 1993*. The present reference is based on the request of the Alberta Government to have the Court of Appeal declare whether this latest scheme is in conformity with the *Charter* and if not, how so.

The court interpreted the government's reference as an opportunity to focus its analysis on the matter of what constitutes undue dilution of the political force of one's vote.

---

[21] Cross-reference to § 3.2.1.
[22] *Reference re Electoral Boundaries Commission Act (Alberta)* (1991), 86 D.L.R. (4th) 447 (Alta. C.A.).

Before providing an extensive reply to the question it was asked to address, the court characterized the process of drawing electoral boundaries as an "artful balancing"[23] of a variety of factors among which it cited population requirements, geographic and demographic features, as well as community interests. Basing itself on the decision of the Supreme Court of Canada in the *Carter* case,[24] by then the most authoritative judicial pronouncement on the confection of electoral boundaries, as well as on its own 1991 reference decision, the court felt it should interfere in such cases only if the redistribution decision adopted by the legislature was "palpably wrong or manifestly unreasonable."[25]

Having so cautioned itself, the court proceeded to deliver a searing rebuke to the process followed and to results achieved by Alberta, all couched in exceedingly polite and self-restrained terms.

On the heart of the matter, representation for non-urban electors, the judgment restated that the principle of fair representation was based on equality of voting power, thus requiring that deviations from the norm in establishing constituencies must be justified on a case-by-case basis. While the Constitution of Canada could be flexible enough to admit variations in the size of electorates in constituencies based on specific and specified criteria, such variations needed to be justified by reference to the factual evidence. Here, the court rejected both the distance of a constituency from the provincial capital, the strong rural tradition of the province and the demands on legislators as such factual evidence. It agreed that variations may be common, but disputed that that commonality would render deviations permissible by themselves.

With respect to the process used to arrive at the electoral map being proposed, the court simply balked at the absence of reasoning and declared that without the explanations necessary to complement the lines on the map, it could not answer the major question put to it, namely that of the constitutional validity of the scheme. The court noted that explanations were promised by the 1992 Select Committee, but none were tendered. What would in fact have been required was riding-by-riding justification. In their absence, the court could no

---

23 (1994), 119 D.L.R. (4th) 1 at 11e.
24 *Reference re Provincial Electoral Boundaries,* [1991] 2 S.C.R. 158 (S.C.C.).
25 (1994), 119 D.L.R. (4th) 1 at 12a.

more deal with the interventions of third parties than with the government's position.

The need for judicial restraint was also mentioned, but only in the face of errors committed in the redistributing process. Judicial restraint ought not to be, the court felt, a consideration that would inspire a boundary-writer. In this sense, while the 1989 redistribution had made progress toward a scheme in accord with the *Charter*, the 1992 version was not felt to contain the gradual but steady evolution in the proper direction.

In place of what the Select Committee offered, the court considered three alternatives which would address the constitutional problem at hand. The creation of mixed urban and rural constituencies was discussed and dismissed as being politically unacceptable. The increase in the number of seats in the legislature was also set aside as not being favoured by the people. The only other option was to keep the number and separate urban and rural characteristics of the constituencies, but to assign more of them to the cities. In this regard, the court even mentioned that one of the least populous rural seats was that of the highest ranking members of the Select Committee. It was acknowledged that such a reorganization of electoral boundaries would require massive surgery. Nonetheless, if other options were not to be adopted, popular opposition to this means of achieving effective representation could not be a valid reason. The fact that some electors would undergo a sudden reduction in the level of representation they had enjoyed was not a valid reason to deprive other electors from achieving adequate representation.

This judgment concluded not only with the court expressing its inability to affirm or deny whether the plan put forward by the 1992 Select Committee met the standard for redistribution under the *Charter*. It also indicated clearly "that a new and proper review is essential before the constitutional mandate of the present government expires, and, we hope, before the next general election. We reject any suggestion that the present divisions may rest until after the 2001 census."[26] In other words, the court told the government that while it could not reply to its question as to the validity of the plan directly, the government should redraw the map along constitutionally acceptable lines and with constitutionally valid reasons, and that it should do so

---

[26] *Ibid.* at 18h.

immediately. Moreover, the court also gave a clear indication that the result it was being asked to examine was the way it was because those who were its authors were "not insulated from partisan influence."[27] On this basis, while it could not rely on the *Charter* to recommend that further redistribution be performed by a commission independent of the legislature, it did propose that only an independent review of redistribution schemes could do justice to the principles of the *Charter*.

There could be no clearer instance in which the function of the court was not only to balance competing considerations within the law, but also to weigh the relative merits of legal versus political considerations. Despite the restrained tone, it is clear that the court felt politics had intruded here into the domain of law, and unjustifiably so.

The court's wish to have a further redistribution exercise take place was in fact carried out. On June 21, 1996, the 1995/96 Alberta Electoral Boundaries Commission which had specifically been constituted for this purpose delivered its Final report to the Speaker of the Legislative Assembly of the province. This Report made specific reference to the law, as set out in recent decisions of the Alberta Court of Appeal and the Supreme Court of Canada. Moreover, it set out in clear terms the perspective and approach which the Commission had taken and indicated that these were in line with the current state of the law on electoral boundaries redistribution. The Commission was cautious in explicating its methodology and the reasons for its proposals. The Report gained public acceptance and was not challenged in the courts. It established the electoral map on which the next provincial election was fought, on March 3, 1997.

---

§ 5.3.3
Plant v. British Columbia (Attorney General)
Supreme Court of British Columbia
filed April 3, 1997; file No. 97 1582, Victoria Registry
discontinued; July 31, 1997

Governments must abide by the rule of law, including the meeting of statutory deadlines in the accomplishment of public processes.

---

[27] *Ibid.* at 19b.

Where the subject matter involved is political, such as redistribution, and is highly controversial, respect for the requirements of law, including deadlines, is even more important. In case the law is breached, the government's political adversaries will not hesitate to resort to legal means to ensure that the public goals provided for in the statute are met. The question which this raises is whether such actions are legal or political; the best answer is that they reflect, inextricably, the two aspects of the same reality.

The British Columbia *Electoral Boundaries Commission Act*[28] provided that an Electoral Boundaries Commission shall be appointed during the first session of the Legislature following the second general election after the provision comes into force. Considering that this provision came into effect on July 7, 1989, that the second general election thereafter was held on May 26, 1996, and that the first session of the province's Legislative Assembly after that ended on March 24, 1997, that date would have been the last on which the Commission could have been appointed. However, no Commission was constituted.

By a petition addressed to the Supreme Court on April 3, 1997, the Justice Critic of the Opposition Liberal Party, Geoffrey Plant, sought a declaratory judgment to the effect that any appointment of an Electoral Boundaries Commission after March 24, 1997, would be unlawful and of no force and effect. He also alleged that the Speaker of the Legislative Assembly had taken steps subsequent to the deadline which demonstrated his intention to name a Commission.

Plant's public commentary on the issue demonstrates perfectly the fact that the action he took was legal and political simultaneously.

> Liberal justice critic Geoff Plant said he was going to court because the government was operating as though it still had the authority to set up such a body even though the deadline has passed.
>
> "This is a government that is either so incompetent or so disrespectful of the law that it doesn't care what happens when statutes are violated," he said.
>
> . . .
>
> "We need an electoral boundaries commission," he said, "because there

---

28 S.B.C. 1989, c. 65, s. 5; now R.S.B.C. 1996, c. 107.

is a long history in British Columbia of gerrymandering electoral distribution in ridings."[29]

Similarly, the government presented a public defence based in both
legal and political norms, acknowledging through the Attorney General its evident embarrassment. Rather than fight the motion in court,
the government amended the legislation so as to remedy its fault. Bill
13 of 1997, an amendment to the *Electoral Boundaries Commission Act*,
was passed by the Legislative Assembly on July 16, 1997. It changed
the provision regarding the timing of the appointment of the first
commission so as to oblige that appointment to take place during the
second session of the 36th Parliament. The government did meet this
remedied deadline.

This case not only exemplifies the obvious interaction between statutes and litigation, but also indicates the use of litigation to force
government to abide by the rule of law.

In the Liberal government that came into office in British Columbia
in May, 2001, Plant became Attorney General.

---

§ 5.3.4
Société des Acadiens & des Acadiennes du Nouveau-Brunswick c.
Nouveau-Brunswick (Gouverneur en Conseil)
New Brunswick Court of Queen's Bench – Trial Division
April 29, 1997
(1997), 188 N.B.R. (2d) 330
-and-
Raîche v. R.
Federal Court of Canada – Trial Division; filed September 12, 2003
file T-1730-03

This case is in the direct intellectual furrow traced by the Saskatchewan Reference. In purely legal terms, it is a struggle between competing rights and competing visions of rights. Nevertheless, it was
highly politicized because its timing overlapped with the campaign
heading up to the 36th federal general election of June 2, 1997, and
because its outcome had both immediate and, prospectively, long-

---

[29] "Threat of lawsuit spurs B.C. N.D.P. to change law," Craig McInnes, *Globe and Mail*,
Toronto, April 4, 1997.

term influences on the way the people of New Brunswick were represented in the Canadian House of Commons.

The Société des Acadiens had been unhappy with the outcome of the 1990's federal redistribution ever since it was completed.[30] The effect of that redistribution was to reduce by one the number of seats within New Brunswick's House of Commons deputation of ten in which there would be a majority of francophone Acadians. The new ridings were to be used in any federal election called after January 9, 1997. By early April of that year, it was becoming clear that an election would be held shortly. On April 14, therefore, the Société filed an application in the New Brunswick Queen's Bench and also sought an interlocutory injunction. The arguments it put forward were essentially based on the reasoning of the Supreme Court of Canada in the Saskatchewan Reference, with the striking addition that they sought to add the ground of ethnic composition and homogeneity of population to the list of criteria which that earlier decision had started to develop. The Société advanced that the *Electoral Boundaries Redistribution Act* had been applied in a manner contrary to section 3 [right to vote] and section 15(1) [equality] of the *Charter* and that this amounted to discrimination in that it deprived the Acadians of effective representation. It sought to have the right to vote considered in a historical and social context. It qualified Acadians as a minority identifiable by ethnic origin and language and reiterated that they constituted one of the two linguistic communities of New Brunswick recognized by the *Charter*. The evidence submitted was precisely on the point of ethnic composition of ridings.

> Le démantèlement des circonscriptions de Madawaska-Victoria et de Restigouche-Chaleur au profit des nouvelles circonscriptions de Tobique-Mactaquac et de Madawaska-Restigouche, et dans une moindre mesure, les changements a l'actuelle circonscription d'Acadie-Bathurst, auront pour effet de priver le nord de la province d'un siège au Parlement.
>
> . . .
>
> ...le résultat des changements proposés est la dilution du vote acadien dans la circonscription de Beauséjour, d'une part, et la perte nette d'une

---

[30] Proclamation Declaring the Representation Order to be in Force Effective on the First Dissolution of the Parliament that Occurs after January 9, 1997, SI/96-9, *Canada Gazette*, 1996.II.687.

circonscription dans le nord de la province là ou se trouve la plus forte concentration d'Acadiens et d'Acadiennes, d'autre part. Pour en arriver à ce deuxième résultate, la population francophone des localités de Grand-Sault (ville et paroisse), Drummond (village et paroisse) et Saint-André se voit engloutie dans la nouvelle circonscription majoritairement anglophone de Tobique-Mactaquac.[31]

The object of the action was no less spectacular than the novelty of its argumentation. The Société sought an injunction to prevent the application of the 1990's redistribution to New Brunswick, or in the alternative, a declaration that the Proclamation of the new boundaries as well as the Report of the New Brunswick Federal Redistribution Commission was contrary to the *Charter* and therefore unconstitutional. As well, it wanted a new Redistribution Commission to be established. The practical result of this would have been that the 36th federal general election would have been fought on the 1996 boundaries in all of the other parts of Canada, but on the 1987 boundaries in New Brunswick.

The media interest in the case was intense in the province. It even caught all the key phrases of "identity," "historical links," "people of similar history," "language" and "community of interests."

> [Mr. Bilodeau] and his clients say that the francophone vote across New Brunswick has been diluted:
>
> ○ Because one majority-francophone riding in the north, Madawaska-Victoria, has effectively been killed; and
>
> ○ Because francophones who once lived in ridings that were mostly French-speaking, are being forced to vote inside mostly anglophone ones.
>
> Mr. Bilodeau says these changes violate the charter, because "this Acadian and francophone community of New Brunswick is not being treated equally."
>
> The changes also violate federal law, he says, because they ignore people's identity, historical links, and language - all factors the government must consider when it re-jigs federal ridings.

---

[31] Affidavit of Ronald Brun, President of the Société des Acadiens, filed April 14, 1997, paragraphs 47, 45.

"If you look at the federal law, when a commission is changing bound-aries it has to take into effect not just the numbers of people, but also the community of interests," says Mr. Bilodeau.

"They have to try and shape ridings which include as much as possible people of similar history, background, identity and all this type of busi-ness."[32]

The request for injunction was heard and decided on April 29, 1997, two days after the writs for election had been issued. The court ruled in full appreciation of the caution issued by the Supreme Court of Canada as to suspending the application of regularly adopted statutes prior to the determination of their constitutional validity and the barriers this could put in the way of governance and the application of a democratic legal system. With respect to the issue of irreparable harm, the court thought that the use of the 1987 boundaries would cause confusion, while it saw less danger of the loss of individuals' right to vote if the 1996 boundaries were kept. Significantly, it noted that the struggle here was between a precise right and the application of a general constitutional principle. On the balance of inconvenience, the court also favoured leaving the newly proclaimed boundaries in place. It concluded that even if the election had not been called at the time the application was made, it was already imminent, the prepa-rations for it were well under way and its motives were valid in refusing the injunction.

In due course, this case was abandoned because the plaintiffs realized that yet a further redistribution, that of 2002-2003, was starting and would render their argumentation out of date.

The *Raîche* action is, in respect of the redistribution exercise completed in 2003 and presumbably to be first applied in the general election of 2004, a judicial expression of the same dissatisfaction of certain Aca-dians as was true in the earlier case. The sentiment prevailing in the Acadian community of New-Brunswick is that, pursuant to the prov-ince's constitutional principle of official bilingualism, they should be able to consider a certain number of federal constituencies as belong-ing to the Francophone linguistic community. In relation to this most recent redistribution, this sentiment was translated into political legal

---

[32] "Much riding on Acadian challenge," Richard Foot, *Saint John Telegraph Journal*, April 16, 1997, p. 1.

terms in the community's refusal to accept that certain portions of gloucester county where there is a majority Acadian population be transferred from Acadie-Bathurst electoral district to that of Miramichi. The proclamation to bring the *Representation Order, 2003* into effect was dated August 29, 2003. In this action, Raîche sought to invalidate that part of the proclamation which relates to the proposed electoral district of Acadie-Bathurst.

The trial of this action took place on May 4 and 5, 2004; judgment was rendered on May 11, literally days before the issue of the writs for the anticipated 38th federal general election.

With respect to section 3 of the *Charter*, the court held that no breach had been committed by the *EBRA* Commission. Nevertheless, it added that if such a breach had occurred, the Commission's report would not have been saved by section 1 of the *Charter*. With respect to the *Electoral Boundaries Redistribution Act* itself, the court found that the Commission had not properly applied section 15 and it therefore set aside the Commission's Report. In the court's view, the legislation allows commissions to draw maps with reasonable derogation from their province's electoral quotient. The court thought that in this process, commissions should give greater weight to communities of interest or to geographic particularities than to parity of voting power calculated solely on the number of voters. In the case of Acadie-Bathurst, the New Brunswick Commission had not done that because it had not maintained the pre-existing community of interest which had been demonstrated to exist. Moreover, by transferring some Acadian voters from Acadie-Bathurst to Miramichi, it did not make Acadians' representation in the latter constituency more effective. The Commission erred particularly in the manner in which it had interpreted its own discretion.

> Last, and realizing just how difficult the Commission's task was, the Court believes that forming communities of interest and increasing a community's political power depend on a large number of factors, and they do not occur simply because a community achieves a critical mass. Adding other members of the community to the electoral district, in the hope that effective representation will follow, is something of a gamble. That position is not consistent with the spirit of the Readjustment Act.[33]

---

[33] 2004 FC 679, para. 81.

A further aspect of the importance of the *Raîche* case is that the Commissioner of Official Languages became an intervenant in it, a move that is unprecedented in judicial consideration of electoral boundaries disputes. The Commissioner's position was that the *Official Languages Act* binds all federal institutions which carry out the objectives of the federal government, while the Crown retorted that the *OLA* was aimed at institutions of the federal government alone. Moreover, the Commissioner argued that there was no issue of precedence between the *EBRA* and the *OLA*, as there was incompatibility between them. To this, the Attorney General replied that the *EBRA* applies as the single statute dealing with the specific subject matter, to the exclusion of the *OLA* as a general statute. On both grounds, the court preferred the Commissioner's view to that of the government. Basing itself on the Ontario Court of Appeal's decision in the *Montfort Hospital* case, the court wrote:

> The Court also agrees with that argument. The Readjustment Act imposes an obligation on the Commission to consider the community of interest, including a community of interest that is defined by the French language, and the OLA requires that government institutions enhance "the vitality of the...French linguistic minority communities in Canada". In fact, the two Acts have similar goals.[34]

The court held that the New Brunswick *EBRA* Commission had tried to apply Part VII of the *OLA* but had failed, although we may surmise that such a finding would have caused the Commission surprise. On this basis also, the court invalidated the Commission's decision.

On the matter of remedies, the court conceded not only that it could not substitute its own decision for that of the *EBRA* Commission, but also that it could not invalidate a severed part of the Proclamation making the *Representation Order 2003*, nor re-establish the *Representation Order 1996*. Consequently, the court order invalidated the New Brunswick *EBRA* Commission's Report but did not touch the Order in Council making the *Representation Order 2003* or the Proclamation giving it force of law. In order to afford the appropriate authorities an opportunity to take requisite corrective measures, the court suspended its own Order for a maximum of one year.

---

[34] *Ibid.*, para. 88.

The Member of Parliament who had exercised most active interest in this issue all along was Yvon Godin (NDP, Acadie-Bathurst, NB). The very day after the court judgment was delivered, he rose in question period to ask whether the Minister of Justice could "...make a commitment today to introduce a bill immediately—before the imminent election call—to implement the Federal Court ruling and ensure justice is done to the people of Acadie-Bathurst, who were overlooked by the commission."[35] The Leader of the Government in the House of Commons and Minister responsible for Democratic Reform offered the following cautious reply: "...this decision raises questions that go far beyond simply establishing the electoral map for two electoral districts. It questions the very independence of the commission, which was established under the laws of our Parliament specifically to be separate from political interference. The hon. member's request for a bill would compromise the commission's independence. We must consider all this before we decide what to do."[36]

We may speculate concerning the government's eventual reaction to this judgment. If the Attorney General leaves the Federal Court's findings in place, and takes the requisite steps to correct New Brunswick's political map along the lines the court suggests, the government will implicitly have accepted not only the reinterpretation of section 15, in the sense that the linguistic and ethnic composition of regions within provinces should also matter in the design of political mapping, but as well that the *EBRA* should be applied in accordance with the spirit, if not the letter, of the *OLA*. This would give legal sanction to a new and vast set of considerations in political mapping. It would also further emphasize the role of law in politics and would underscore the increasing influence of the judiciary in the balance among the three branches of government. On the other hand, a successful appeal could restore the autonomy of the *EBRA* vis-à-vis the *OLA*. The stakes are significant. It is reasonable to believe that this case is headed toward the Supreme Court of Canada. Any course of action the government undertakes will also entail political, and indeed electoral, consequences in the long run.

---

[35] Hansard, May 12, 2004, p. 3077.
[36] *Ibid.*

§ 5.3.5
Friends of Democracy v. Northwest Territories (Commissioner)
Supreme Court of the Northwest Territories; March 5, 1999
(1999), 171 D.L.R. (4th) 551[37]

Effective April 1, 1999, the Northwest Territories (NWT) were divided, with the Eastern Arctic being elevated to the status of a separate Territory called Nunavut. In line with the wishes of the inhabitants of the area, the political goals of this separation included the
creation within Canada of a jurisdiction in which the Inuit people
would constitute a majority of the people and in which the political
and legal traditions of the Inuit, as influenced by Canadian-style
democracy, would prevail. Even before Nunavut acquired the status
of a Territory, the influence and outcomes of its separation and of the
special nature of the new Territory began to be felt in the public life
of what would remain of the NWT.

In order to provide for an electoral system in the remaining NWT
after division, a readjustment of electoral boundaries was necessary;
this was carried out in 1998 by an independent Electoral Boundaries
Commission. This body recommended that, although only 14 seats
would remain in the NWT's geography, the new NWT Assembly
comprise of 16 seats, with the addition of two seats to the representation of the City of Yellowknife, the capital. This was rejected in mid-
November 1998, by the Assembly. Their decision was to have the
membership remain at 14. The importance of the matter arose from
the fact that in the pre-division NWT Legislature, there had been a
majority of Aboriginal members, representing a population that had
been comprised of a majority of Aboriginals. There was a strong
sentiment that the NWT Assembly should be a forum for Aboriginal
representation. If the post-division Legislature held 14 seats, that
characteristic would be maintained, while with 16 seats it would be
lost to a European-based majority.

On November 25, 1998, the Friends of Democracy, the Mayor of
Yellowknife and other citizens filed the present application, seeking
a declaration that the instruments creating the revised electoral map
of the NWT were contrary to the right to vote guarantee contained in

---

[37] Leave to appeal refused (1999), 176 D.L.R. (4th) 661 (N.W.T. C.A.).

section 3 of the *Charter*. The court considered the applicants' arguments on the numbers involved. The City of Yellowknife had for a long time been under-represented by between 6% and 9%. With the proposed new map, it would have 44% of the NWT's population, with only 29% of the seats, implying a shortfall in representation of 15%. Despite the fact that there is in any legislative assembly a firm and finite number of seats, the court took the view that while over-representation of rural and distant communities could be justified, the under-representation of others was inadmissible.

The court's treatment of the basic issue of variations of electoral population from the norm, of the resulting breach of *Charter* section 3, as well as of the consequential injustice which needed to be remedied, was in line with the reasoning based on *Dixon* and the *Saskatchewan Electoral Boundaries* case.This case also involved new arguments and analysis, however, which infuse it with a specific political law flavour.

In response to the argumentation based on the equality of each citizen's right to vote, as demonstrated through the relatively equal population of constituencies, the respondents found new grounds on which to urge that the court allow the *status quo* of unequal weight of voters to remain in place. In particular, they proposed that the court interpret section 3 of the *Charter* as being qualified by sections 25 and 35 of the *Constitution Act, 1982*, which recognized Aboriginal rights.

> As I understand the position of the Intervenors, nothing should be done to affect the *status quo* in the distribution of seats in the Legislative Assembly until such time in the future as shall see the resolution of their on-going aboriginal land claims and aboriginal self-government negotiations with the governments of Canada and of the Northwest Territories. The Intervenors do not suggest that there is any existing aboriginal or treaty right on which they can rely in making this submission, other than the process rights implicit in section 25 of the Charter and section 35 of the *Constitution Act, 1982* as well as in existing aboriginal land claims agreements and related negotiations.[38]

Given that the Aboriginal right which the respondents were invoking as qualifying the section 3 right to vote was the land claims agreement process, the court was able to deem that this was a suspensive mech-

---

[38] (1999), 171 D.L.R. (4th) 551 at 561-562, leave to appeal refused (1999), 176 D.L.R. (4th) 661 (N.W.T. C.A.).

anism rather than a substantive right and could not go along with the respondent's position.

> As the foregoing is intended to show, I remain unpersuaded that section 3 of the Charter is in any sense to be understood as qualified by section 25 of the *Charter* or section 35 of the *Constitution Act, 1982*, at least in the present instance, given the evidence before the court in this application. It is entirely unacceptable that such a fundamental right of citizenship as that recognized and guaranteed in section 3 of the Charter (and thus in the Constitution of Canada) should be held in suspense, and thus be withheld, during government negotiations over the future self-government of aboriginal or other groups which might yet take decades to bring to a conclusion.[39]

The argument that the expected resolution of land claims negotiations was an Aboriginal right was in itself one of a highly politicized nature, even though the court did not so indicate outright. The court did recognize, though, the true nature of the respondents' arguments as being on the one hand ethnic and sectarian in tone and on the other hand being based on matters of power and politics. The ethnic element was the subtle conflict between the Aboriginal and European segments of the NWT population. The court alluded to this indirectly, when it referred to the fact that in times past, some residents of the NWT had been denied the right to vote, but that these denials of right have long been corrected by legislation. In fact, it was only in 1960 that the Inuit were enfranchised. In this regard, mention was also made that the under-represented constituencies in Yellowknife also held Aboriginal populations.

The reason for which the Aboriginal-European dichotomy in the population mentioned was that each community sought to achieve political power within the remainder of the NWT. The court addressed squarely the political nature of the discussion which the parties had put before it.

> To the extent that the underlying issue is, as suggested by the Respondent and Intervenors, one of where the political power in the Legislative Assembly is or should be, so that the court should respond to the present application only with the greatest restraint (and preferably by declining to grant any remedy at all to the applicants), it therefore appears that removing the basis for the existing gross numerical under-representation

---

[39] *Ibid.*

in the Assembly of citizens at Yellowknife need not in any really significant way alter the existing balance of political power in the Assembly as it directly concerns the Intervenors and the aboriginal population of the Northwest Territories.[40]

In discussing this political aspect of the case, the court noted the particularities of the NWT's system of governance, namely the absence of political parties and the "consensus government" which took their place, as well as the ombudsman function of the Assembly members and the greater ease of fulfilling that role at in the case of Yellowknife's members.

Having taken all these matters into consideration, in order to maintain the essence of the free and democratic society of the NWT, the court determined that the applicants were entitled to a partial remedy. Thus, rather than invalidate the entire electoral map, the court declared as being in breach of section 3 only the three most seriously under-represented constituencies. With the ruling being issued on March 5, 1999, the court suspended its application until April 1, 1999, to enable the NWT authorities to sort out the consequences of the ruling. These, of course, would cascade onto at least these constituencies which abutted the three with unconstitutional boundaries. The deadline was later extended into September of that year.

The political element of this case which is most worthy of retention is the lingering issue of ethnic divisions among constituencies.

> It has fundamentally changed the rules of the political ball game in the Northwest Territories. Aboriginal rights do not override the rights of everyone else to have a vote/voice.
>
> Stephen Kakfwi, the territory's Minister of Resources, Wildlife and Economic Development, said the ruling will be difficult for many of the territory's aboriginals to accept, since it will likely lead to non-aboriginals eventually holding the balance of power in the territory.[41]

Following this decision, during the summer of 1999, the NWT electoral map was redrawn and by the time the following general election was held on December 6, 1999, the remainder of the Territories com-

---

[40] *Ibid.* at 563.
[41] "Parts of NWT electoral law declared unconstitutional," Mark MacKinnon, *Globe and Mail*, March 8, 1998, p. A-4.

prised 19 constituencies which, although they continued to be politically controversial, met the standard demanded under section 3 of
the *Charter* at least to the extent that they did not give rise to further
litigation. Seven of those ridings were in the City of Yellowknife.

On June 16, 1999, the Territorial Court of Appeal denied an application for leave to appeal presented by the Métis Nation, an intervenor
at trial.[42] In July, the Assembly voted to add one seat in Yellowknife
and another in Inuvik. The next general election was set for December
6, 1999. In the campaign for that election, the media qualified the
political circumstances prevailing in the NWT as "challenging times,"
with the redrawing of electoral boundaries to reflect the split between
the capital and the outlying areas, as well as between Aboriginal and
European communities, as one of the NWT's principal challenges.

See also *Application by West Toronto Junction Historical Society*, Ontario
Municipal Board, November 26, 1999, file no. PL990500; *Ottawa (City)
v. Ontario (Minister of Municipal Affairs & Housing)* (2002), 62 O.R. (3d)
503 (Ont. Div. Ct.) and (2003), 63 O.R. (3d) 785 (Ont. Div. Ct.) and
Davis v. Bandemer,[43] 106 S.Ct. 2797 (1986).

---

§ 5.3.6[44]
*Department of Commerce et al. v.
United States House of Representatives et al.*
United States Supreme Court; January 25, 1999
142 L.Ed.2d 797 (1999)

The basic component element in the establishment of electoral constituencies is population. In the United States as in Canada there is
legal mandate for a decennial census which is the foundation on
which the entire process of redistribution is based. Until 1999, the
Executive Branch advocated in interpretation of the *Census Act*[45]
which, for purposes of apportionment, opposed statistical sampling
of segments of the population, by contrast to the "actual Enumera-

---

[42] (1999), 176 D.L.R. (4th) 661 (N.W.T. C.A.). The Supreme Court ruling in this case is
analysed here because it is much more explicit than the decision of the Court of
Appeal.
[43] International comparison.
[44] International comparison.
[45] 13 U.S.C. § 1 *et seq.*

tion" directed by the Constitution. In response to evidence, however, that the traditional method of census-taking consistently resulted in an undercount of identifiable groups whose members would be more likely to vote Democratic, two lawsuits were filed to prevent the Clinton Administration's plan to use statistical sampling of population in the 2000 census. The plaintiff in the first lawsuit was President Clinton himself.[46] In that connection, it is interesting to note that this judgment was issued while the Senate, with the Chief Justice of the United States presiding, was conducting the impeachment of the President.

The Supreme Court, split along strict ideological lines, decided by 5-4 that the authority of the Secretary of Commerce to conduct the census in the form and content he may determine must be read together with another provision prohibiting the use of statistical sampling for the determination of population for purposes of Congressional apportionment of seats among the States.[47] The majority reached this conclusion on the basis of the rules of statutory interpretation and did not deal with the constitutional issue of equal representation. The minority looked at statistical sampling as a methodological improvement meant to ease the administrative burden, the of which would yield absurd results.

Notwithstanding that the court relied on the less controversial argumentation and the press qualified the judgment as being devoid of rhetoric, the issue of census sampling is acknowledged to be a gritty political issue, involving not only voting patterns and the success of parties, but also the levels of appropriations needed for diverse types of census operations.

> Far from putting the issue of census sampling to rest, today's Supreme Court decision is virtually certain to lead to fierce battles in Congress, state legislatures and courts nationwide over what census figures should be used to draw district lines and to distribute Federal money, electoral officials and census experts said.[48]

See also *Virginia v. Reno*, 117 F. Supp.2d 46 (D.D.C., 2000) and *Vieth v. Jubilier*, United States Supreme Court, file 02-1580, in progress.

---

[46] *Clinton, President of the United States, et al v. Glavin et al;* case No. 98-564.

[47] See *Census Act*, 13 U.S.C. § 195.

[48] "Split Decision Sets Stage for State and Local Battles," James Dao, *New York Times*, January 26, 1999, p. A-20.

5.4 ISSUE: VALUATION OF THE RIGHT TO VOTE

§ 5.4.1
Shewfelt v. Canada
British Columbia Court of Appeal; March 5, 1998
(1998), 1998 CarswellBC 2894[49]

In constitutional law terms generally, this case deals with the definition of the category of rare cases in which a plaintiff is entitled to damages in compensation for breach of a constitutional right. More specifically in regard to the matter of elections, it deals with the availability of damages for denial to an individual of his right to vote by an agent of the State and with the quantifying of such damages.

On October 14, 1994, Shewfelt issued a Writ of Summons and on November 28, 1994, he filed a Statement of Claim, in both of which he alleged that he was entitled to declaratory relief (this ground was later abandoned), as well as to general and punitive damages on the following grounds. Between October 1987 and December 1988, he was incarcerated at a federal institution in Victoria, British Columbia. In September and October, 1988, during the campaign leading up to the 34th federal general election, Shewfelt applied to the warden of his prison to be able to vote. His request asserted that he had a constitutionally entrenched right to vote. Indeed, the *Canadian Charter of Rights and Freedoms* did contain a provision stating that every citizen had the right to vote. In this scenario however, the key facts were that what was then section 14(4)(e) (later to become section 51(e)) of the *Canada Elections Act* stated that inmates were not qualified to vote; and that the constitutional validity of this provision had not yet been successfully challenged before the courts. Given that the state of the law at the time of Shewfelt's request did not allow inmates to vote, the warden denied the request. Shewfelt followed no other legal course of action. The election was held on November 21, 1988, and Shewfelt did not vote. His action stated that the denial caused him to suffer damages *per se* for the infringement of this constitutional right.

---

[49] Leave to appeal refused (1998), 234 N.R. 195 (note) (S.C.C.).

498 / LAW OF DEMOCRATIC GOVERNING – VOLUME II: JURISPRUDENCE

The Crown responded with a motion to dismiss the case. Its defence was that the warden had acted in accordance with the law in force at the relevant time and that the applicable enactment, the *Canada Elections Act*, is presumed to be constitutionally valid until a court finds it in violation of the *Charter*. The Crown also pleaded that no finding of unconstitutionality could be retroactive or retrospective. This argument was necessary as in the interval between the warden's denial and the commencement of this action, section 51(e) had undergone several judicial examinations, and consequential changes. Considering that the warden's refusal to enable Shewfelt to vote was in accordance with the law, the substantive issue for determination became focused on the availability and the quantum of damages for the loss of the constitutionally protected right to vote. On this, the defence stated that:

> There is no monetary entitlement, economic loss, financial damage, loss of income earning livelihood, or loss of liberty interest, or any other quantifiable consequence or damage flowing to the Plaintiff as a result of the Defendants' actions. There has been no tort committed by the Defendants in refusing the Plaintiff's request to vote which would entitle the Plaintiff to any damages in tort. There is no damage award available to the Plaintiff under any legal head of damage. Therefore, in the absence of the possibility of a damage award, there is no necessary reason to bring this claim. Nothing would be served by proceeding with this action because no damages are available to the Plaintiff and because the issue the Plaintiff seeks to litigate is moot.[50]

The British Columbia Supreme Court agreed, on July 26, 1995, that the case be dismissed.[51] The Court of Appeal believed that the Crown had not been able to establish an absolute barrier to prevent Shewfelt's action from proceeding on the merits.[52] The case therefore went back to the Supreme Court for consideration of the merits.

The decision issued on February 27, 1997, by the Supreme Court was affirmed without written reasons on March 3, 1998, by the Court of Appeal and is therefore the definitive pronouncement on this matter.

---

[50] *Shewfelt v. Canada* (1997), 28 B.C.L.R. (3d) 340 (B.C. S.C. [In Chambers]), affirmed (1998), 1998 CarswellBC 2894, leave to appeal refused (1998), 234 N.R. 195 (note) (S.C.C.); Applicants' (Defendants') Argument, March 9, 1995, p. 27, para. 58.

[51] B.C. Supreme Court, June 30, 1995.

[52] (1996), 77 B.C.A.C. 308, 126 W.A.C. 308 (B.C. C.A.), additional reasons at (1999), 1999 CarswellBC 2583 (B.C. C.A.).

The court agreed that the central issue of the action was whether Shewfelt was entitled to damages "because he was a member of the class of persons not qualified to vote in the November 21, 1988, federal election through the operation of s. 14(4)(e) of the *Canada Elections Act* then in force."[53]

The court gave two substantive responses to the principal argument raised by Shewfelt. First, with respect to the availability of damages and the valuation of the right to vote, it said:

> Mr. Shewfelt made no judicial challenge to the legislation existing at the time of his incarceration. There is no evidence he suffered any loss or damage different from any other inmate of a federal institution as a result of s. 14(4)(e) of the *Canada Elections Act* barring him from voting in the November 1988 federal election.
>
> . . .
>
> None of the several authorities the plaintiff cites where damages were awarded for lost voting rights concerns the loss of a voting opportunity as a result of legislative effect.[54]

It went further, though, in determining that in the absence of damages, which type of remedy could have been available to Shewfelt.

> The plaintiff's position is that as nothing can restore his lost ability to vote in the 1988 election, an award of damages is an appropriate and just remedy; indeed, the only available remedy. He thereby seeks to individualize the "wrong" caused by the legislation which was later found to have breached section 3 of the *Charter* and thereby affected a segment of our society – those serving a prison sentence at an election time.
>
> . . .
>
> It was the existence of the legislation itself that denied Mr. Shewfelt the vote. The fact he requested ability to vote is immaterial. No person prevented his voting. He was restrained by the effect of statute during his incarceration.[55]

---

[53] (1997), 28 B.C.L.R. (3d) 340 at 435, affirmed (1998), 1998 CarswellBC 2894 (B.C. C.A.), leave to appeal refused (1998), 234 N.R. 195 (note) (S.C.C.).

[54] *Ibid.* at 345, 348.

[55] *Ibid.* at 347, 346.

While this case guides plaintiffs as to their choice of remedies to seek in response to breach of constitutional rights, the most significant contribution to political law is its holding that no damage action may lie for loss of the right to vote and that no monetary value can be assigned to that right.

This holding of the British Columbia Supreme Court was affirmed on March 3, 1998 by the B.C. Court of Appeal and on September 24, 1998, the Supreme Court of Canada denied Shewfelt's application for leave to appeal.

See also *Audziss v. Santa* (2003), 223 D.L.R. (4th) 257 (Ont. C.A.), additional reasons at (2003), 2003 CarswellOnt 497 (Ont. C.A.).

5.5 ISSUE: INCLUSION FOR PARTICIPATION IN THE ELECTORAL PROCESS

5.5.A—VOTING

§ 5.5.A.1
Canadian Disability Rights Council v. Canada
Federal Court of Canada – Trial Division; October 17, 1988
[1988] 3 F.C. 622

In the first few years following the adoption of the *Canadian Charter of Rights and Freedoms* in 1982, most federal statutes which predated the *Charter* were systematically brought into line with the norms of the new constitutional framework. The *Canada Elections Act*[56] was one of the rare exceptions. That is why this Act needed to be reformed through *Charter* litigation. Many of these cases constituted both an affirmation of rights and the continuation of lobbying by legal means. This is one of those cases. In the course of the campaign leading up to the 34th federal general election of November 21, 1988, several groups acting on behalf of persons with mental disabilities, and several individuals, applied to have the provision of the *Canada Elections Act* which declared as not qualified to vote those persons restrained

---

[56] At that time R.S.C. 1970, c. 14 (1st supp.).

of liberty of movement or management of their property by reason of mental disease,[57] declared unconstitutional. One of the applicants was a Minister in the Québec Government, who later became a federal Minister, Lucienne Robillard. In a judgment rendered quickly enough to have effect on that very election, the court agreed.

The Federal Court of Canada – Trial Division believed that mental competence and judgmental capacity are required to vote. It held, however, that the subject provision of the *Canada Elections Act* was too broadly worded and that it did not address itself only to those criteria; the limitation was therefore arbitrary. Moreover, "empirical research indicates that the voting pattern of psychiatric patients parallels that of the general population."[58] The use of a *Charter* challenge to accomplish a socio-political goal demonstrates the conjunction of legal development and political evolution.

---

§ 5.5.A.2
Muldoon v. Canada
Federal Court of Canada – Trial Division; November 3, 1988
[1988] 3 F.C. 628

This is the case which determined whether members of the federally appointed judiciary, and by implication all judges, could become involved in the electoral system solely to the extent of acquiring the right to vote. Besides the substantive outcome of the matter, the additional interest of the judicial discussion in this ruling is whether the inclusion of judges among those eligible to vote should be accomplished by the Legislative Branch through an amendment of the *Canada Elections Act*,[59] or by the Judicial Branch itself through a judgment.

Until this case arose, section 14(4)(d) of the *Canada Elections Act*,[60] disqualified judges from voting in federal elections. In expectation of the federal general election of November, 1988, one of Canada's most outspoken and knowledgeable judges, Justice Muldoon of the Federal Court – Trial Division, initiated with his colleague Teitelbaum an

---

[57] s. 14(4)(f).
[58] [1988] 3 F.C. 622 at 625.
[59] R.S.C. 1985, c. E-2, as amended. At the time of this decision, R.S.C. 1970, c. 14 (1st Supp.), as amended.
[60] In the R.S.C. 1985 this was s. 51(d).

application for declaratory judgment to the effect that the provision was contrary to section 3 of the *Charter*, which recognized the right of citizens to vote in the Constitution. Their case was pleaded by Mrs. Teitelbaum and was heard by one of their fellow judges of the same court. After the interpretation of the *Charter* in 1982, the Department of Justice had prepared several extensive Bills to bring pre-*Charter* legislation into line with the *Charter*, but the *Canada Elections Act* had not been affected by the modernizations so made. Parliament did not seem pressed to amend this, one of the most fundamental statutes of the Canadian democratic framework.

Muldoon contended that while some limits to the right to vote ought to remain, the disqualification of all judges appointed by the Governor in Council could not be demonstrably justified. He took pains to limit the extent of the change he sought. In normal circumstances, the right to vote implied the right to run for elective office. Here, the plaintiffs disclaimed any qualification for membership either in the House of Commons or any other public elective position. They were also aware of the potential political repercussions of obtaining the right to vote.

> They further concede they have no claim to participate as public political partisans in any such election or at all, and in order to maintain the politically non-partisan and objective requirements of their judicial offices they rely on the secrecy of the ballot box.[61]

As part of the judges' argumentation, they also indicated that in a number of democratic jurisdictions, most notably in Ontario, their counterparts had been given the right to vote.

In response to Muldoon's action, the Crown filed a statement of defence which, while it was not a confession of judgment under the Rules of the Federal Court, was in fact an admission of all the arguments raised. It is interesting that in later years, Muldoon would criticize from the bench other instances in which the Crown would choose not to mount a substantive defence in matters of public law. In this regard, this court already expressed its anxiety about agreements between the parties which could lead to inadequate discussion of the issues involved. It indicated that if there had been full contestation, the case may have been decided either way. However, as there

---

[61] [1988] 3 F.C. 628 at 630 g.

was agreement, the court should deny it only where the conclusion could be denied by the facts or where the agreement would result in a miscarriage of justice. Most importantly, the court felt that it should not deal with issues such as this, which were best left for Parliament to handle, as this practice could eliminate the need for legislation.

On the substantive issue, the court granted the application. It discussed two specific aspects of the matters, along the lines of the arguments raised by Muldoon. First, despite granting judges the right to vote, it saw merit in protecting them from the perception that they held partisan political views.

> I am certainly not suggesting that judges lack the discretion to be careful in not indicating any political views. Many judges have had political affiliations before their appointment, but it has never been suggested that, once appointed, they have ever allowed these views to affect their judgments. They must not only be politically neutral, as plaintiffs concede, but must be perceived to be so by the public. For this reason I am of the view that even if permitted to vote many judges would not wish to do so and refuse to be enumerated and appear on voters roles and thereby be subject to approaches by political canvassers. The removal of the restriction of paragraph 14(4)(d) of the Elections Act will have the effect of leaving this decision to the individual consciences of the judges. While there is nothing wrong with this and certainly they are entitled to have personal opinions on political issues, as all citizens are it at least might have been arguable that there is a valid objective in restricting their right to vote which might be a reasonable limit prescribed by law, in order to protect them from any possible criticism of not being completely apolitical.[62]

The other issue noted by the court was the list of democratic societies in which superior court judges are enable to vote; the court would, in a contested case, have liked to see more discussion and evidence.

> While it has been decided that a court should not decide such an issue without some evidence on which to base the decision, a contestation might of course have introduced evidence of other free and democratic societies in which the vote is not given to judges, or have pointed out differences in the societies referred to, such as the fact that United States judges are in most instances elected and therefore not non-partisan.[63]

---

[62] *Ibid.* at 632 h-633 c.
[63] *Ibid.* at 633 f-g.

In sum, through both issues, the court was determined to ensure that the extension of the franchise to judges would enable them to remain politically neutral and separated from the fray of partisan activities and perceptions. The link between this requirement and keeping the Judicial Branch independent of political influences is patent.

---

§ 5.5.A.3
Reid v. Canada
Federal Court of Canada – Trial Division; January 27, 1994
(1994), 73 F.T.R. 290

The timing of this action, started on September 22, 1992, was most appropriate, as at that time the campaign for the constitutional referendum scheduled for October 26, 1992, had already begun. The plaintiffs were a number of infants and their parents acting both as next friends and in their personal capacities. The purpose of the litigation was, among others, to extend the meaning of section 3 (voting rights) of the *Charter* to secure for infants the right to vote in both elections and referenda. In particular, the plaintiffs proposed a system in which children of the age of twelve would be able to vote by themselves, while parents would cast votes on behalf of infants from birth until age 12. The court's ratio in rejecting this scheme was that the remedy sought was beyond the scope of the protection afforded by section 3. It accepted that limiting the right to vote to those of the age of majority was a rational dimension of the right, part of the reasonable restrictions and obvious exclusions that needed to be attached to the right. While the court acknowledged that this limit needed to be justified under section 1, it found the limitation so reasonable that it required no evidence on the question. In the end, the defendant's motion to strike the case as frivolous and vexatious was granted.

Along the way, the plaintiffs had moved to postpone the referendum until after a trial of the substantive matter; this motion was set aside.

See also *Sauvé v. Canada (Chief Electoral Officer)* (1999), 180 D.L.R. (4th) 385 (Fed. C.A.), leave to appeal allowed (2000), 2000 CarswellNat 1724 (S.C.C.), reversed [2002] S.C.J. No. 66 (S.C.C.).

5.5.B—CANDIDACY FOR OFFICE[64]

§ 5.5.B.1
Delisle c. Canada (Procureure général)
Québec Superior Court; September 2, 1998
[1998] R.J.Q. 2751 to 2767

There is an inherent conflict between the policy goal of demanding that the members of a profession whose vocation is to uphold the law in an apolitical fashion be restrained from becoming candidates for elective office, and the legal rule that all citizens are constitutionally equal. No matter how long-standing and seemingly valid and appropriate the policy is, it must give way to a more fundamental right which stems from the most fundamental legal source of all, the constitutional *Canadian Charter of Rights and Freedoms.*

Delisle joined the R.C.M.P. in 1969 and by 1995 had achieved the rank of Staff Sergeant. On November 5, 1995, while on active duty, he was elected mayor of the village of St.-Blaise-sur-Richelieu in Québec. His assumption of this function was contrary to section 57 of the Royal Canadian Mounted Police Regulations, 1988.[65] After a number of internal administrative procedures, the R.C.M.P. ordered Delisle to leave the mayoral office and on June 2, 1997, he resigned. He then applied to the Québec Superior Court for a declaration that section 57 was contrary to section 2(b) [freedom of expression], section 2(d) [freedom of association], section 3 [right to vote and eligibility to hold office] and section 15(1) [equality] guaranteed by the *Canadian Charter of Rights and Freedoms.* Delisle's action was also abased on the arguments that section 57 was *ultra vires* and that it was applied in an abusive and discriminatory fashion. He also alleged that the provision was contrary to the Québec *Charter* and to the province's legislation on electoral matters. To a great extent, the application relied on a plan then being contemplated to revise section 57 so as to allow participation in political life by members of the R.C.M.P., that would have brought them more in line with the rules applicable to civilian public servants.

---

[64] Cross-reference to § 3.12.A.
[65] SOR/88-361.

The court ruled first that section 57 was not *ultra vires* because it fell within the parameters of the *Royal Canadian Mounted Police Act.*[66] The federal Crown admitted that section 57 restricted Delisle's rights under section 2(b) and (d) and section 3 of the *Charter*. The case therefore essentially focused on whether the alleged infringement of Delisle's equality right under section 15 of the *Charter* could be justified under section 1, as a valid limitation in a free and democratic society.

The court looked first at the objective of section 57, the insurance that the R.C.M.P., the only police force with jurisdiction throughout Canada, would remain untainted by political influences. It focused on the nature of police power and authority as being answerable to no authority of the State, but to the law alone.

> The independence theory has it that police officers exercise an original, not a delegated, authority *(I.T. Oliver, Police, Government and Accountability (Great Britain: MacMillan Basingstoke 1987)*, 16-17). That is, it is a police officer's duty to enforce the law of the land. In doing so, the responsibility for law enforcement is upon the officer: the officer "is answerable to the law and to the law alone." *(R. v. Commissioner of Police of the Metropolis, Ex parte Blackburn, [1968] 2 Q.B. 118 at 135, per Lord Denning)*. Thus, the independence theory has three parts to it: (1) that the function of a police officer is to enforce the law of the state; (2) that this duty is owed to the public, no (sic) to the executive of government; and, therefore, (3) that in order to be able to comply freely with that function and that duty, independence from political masters is necessary. As noted by the Law Reform Commission of Canada, this theory was adopted in Canada over a hundred years ago. *(Law Reform Commission of Canada, Controlling Criminal Prosecutions: The Attorney General and the Crown Prosecutor (Working Paper 62) (Ottawa: Law Reform Commission of Canada 1990)*, 29). While it has been recognized that police may be subject to some statutory regulation, *(Reiner, Politics, 17)* conferral of independence by statute is not necessary. It would simply be declaratory of a long-established constitutional position.[67]

The judge then went on to consider the proportionality of the provision being attacked to the objective sought to be achieved by it. Was there a rational link? Was the restraint exercise minimal in extent? It was this latter question that particularly preoccupied the court. The independence and objectivity of those applying the law is essential. Does the preservation of these criteria require an absolute ban on

---

[66] R.S.C. 1985, c. R-10.
[67] [1998] R.J.Q. 2751 à 2767 at 2759.

running for elective office? In order to find the right reply to that, the parties had examined the *Osborne* decision. More specifically applicable to police forces, both Québec and Ontario had adopted schemes which permitted certain political activities to members of their provincial forces. Assisted by these comparisons, the court found that the impairment of rights was not minimal.

> Le Tribunal ne peut en convenir. Les interdits de l'article 57 portent atteinte très souvent de façon absolue aux droits démocratiques de plus de 15,000 canadiens. Ce qui est en cause, ce n'est pas tant la presénce d'interdits lorsque l'individu accomplit son travail de policier que l'absence d'alternatives lorsque ce même individu veut se prévaloir de droits démocratiques enchâssés dans la constitution.

> On n'y fait place à aucun aménagement permettant de concilier des droits démocratiques avec la fonction exigeante et importante d'un policier. En ce sens, cette disposition réglementaire ne constitue pas une atteinte minimale. Elle va au-delà de ce qui est nécessaire pour atteindre l'objective législatif.[68]

The lesson of this ruling is that while there is a recognized need for the cloistering of police work from political influences, the legislator must find ways of accomplishing that goal that are less severe than a total ban on eligibility of police officers from seeking elective office.

It is interesting to note that for the sake of maintaining the independence and political neutrality of the police while the rules arising out of section 57 were being rewritten, the court, following the precedent in *Schacter*, suspended its declaration of the invalidity of the provision until January 1, 1999. The rules were changed in time to meet this deadline.

> Soon, RCMP officers will be able to join political parties, run for office and campaign for candidates.

> If they do, however, they must take an unpaid leave of absence for the duration of any campaign and must resign from the force if elected, under proposed regulations made public this week.

---

[68] *Ibid.* at 2765 – 2766.

The regulations are in response to a Quebec court ruling last month that said the force's current rules are unconstitutional.[69]

The political conflict between the independence and impartiality of the R.C.M.P. and the right of police officers on the force to run for public office has continued to be of interest in the political legal system. In April 2002, a committee of the House of Commons proposed that R.C.M.P. officers' right to participate in politics be enshrined in law. The government refused.[70]

---

§ 5.5.B.2[71]
Nunziata v. Toronto (City)
Ontario Court of Appeal; September 15, 2000
(2000), 189 D.L.R. (4th) 627[72]

In an era when the *Canadian Charter of Rights and Freedoms* guarantees the right of citizens to run for federal and provincial legislative bodies, is it a valid limitation on citizens' ability to run for municipal office to require that they resign from the House of Commons? Worded in a different manner, are legislated incompatibilities for candidate to political office constitutionally valid? In some instances such an issue might have been decided by a court almost in obscurity. Here however, the applicant, a Member of the House of Commons since 1984, was not only a prominent fixture on the Toronto political scene, but also something of a nationally known maverick in federal politics. There was consequently much publicity, undoubtedly some of it generated by the applicant himself.

On March 24, 2000, Nunziata tried to file papers to be nominated for candidacy to the mayoral position in the civic election of November 13. His nomination was rejected by the City Clerk in early April; the immediate result was his inability to seek campaign funds, an operation that would have tested Nunziata's electability at the municipal level or led him to retain his Commons seat. The core of Nunziata's

---

[69] "Political restrictions on Mounties to be eased," Paul Waldie, *Globe and Mail*, Toronto, November 4, 1998.

[70] "RCMP's political rules do not need to be law, Ottawa says," *National Post*, April 16, 2002, p. A-9.

[71] Cross-reference to § 10.4.3.

[72] Additional reasons at (2000), 137 O.A.C. 70 (Ont. C.A.).

reasoning was that the combined provisions of the *Municipal Act*[73] and the *Municipal Elections Act, 1996*[74] result in the exclusion of Members of the House of Commons from becoming candidates for municipal office because of their exercise of the rights enshrined in section 3 of the *Charter*. The court agreed that this was so but in denying the application it concluded that that was exactly the purpose of the legislative scheme.

> This is undoubtedly true. However, this does not necessarily infringe his rights to be qualified for membership in the House of Commons, which is his *Charter*-protected right. If Mr. Nunziata had never filed his nomination papers, he would have remained qualified for membership in the House of Commons; having filed his nomination papers, and the Clerk having refused to receive them, Mr. Nunziata remains qualified for membership in the House of Commons. Nothing has changed.[75]

The majority of the court then went on to clarify its position.

> I mean no disrespect to the office of the Mayor of Toronto when I conclude that Mr. Nunziata's ineligibility for that office, (if the ineligibility can be said to be an indirect, coercive burden,) is trivial and insubstantial in relation to Mr. Nunziata's right to be qualified for membership in the House of Commons. The duties and responsibilities of a member of the House, and of the Mayor of Toronto, are onerous. Neither function is trivial and insubstantial. However, the ineligibility to be nominated or elected as Mayor, while sitting as a Member, I find to be trivial and insubstantial in relation to Mr. Nunziata's right to be qualified for membership in the House of Commons.[76]

One of the three justices constituting the panel of the Divisional Court wrote a serious and well-reasoned dissent. In his view, the effect of the legislated incompatibility is to take away from Members of the House of Commons rights to be elected or to hold office at the municipal level. This raises the issue of the extent to which a provincial legislature can strip MP's of their rights without violating the *Charter*. Clearly, the intent of the legislation was to separate the various layers of political functions within Canada, but can this political goal be

---

[73] R.S.O. 1990, c. M.45, s. 37(1).
[74] S.O. 1996, c. 32, Sched., s. 29(1).
[75] (2000), [2000] O.J. No. 2272, 2000 CarswellOnt 2106 (Ont. Div. Ct.), para. 16, affirmed (2000), 189 D.L.R.(4th) 627, additional reasons at (2000), 137 O.A.C. 70 (Ont. C.A.).
[76] *Ibid.*, para. 20.

legally justified? The disagreement of this judge with his brethren is stark.

> Municipal councils may not be as important as the House of Commons of Canada or a legislative assembly, but they are an important part of our democratic government. The right to seek election to a municipal council and to sit as a member of council, in my opinion, is not trivial or insubstantial. It is an important right, and the denial of that right to members of the House of Commons of Canada is a significant entrenchment on the rights of members of the House of Commons.

> . . .

> In my opinion, s. 3 protects members of the House of Commons from any laws which take from them, because of their membership in the House of Commons, material rights enjoyed by other citizens. In my opinion, the impugned provisions in s. 37(1), clause 3 of the MA constitute such legislation. In the result, I hold that the words in clause 3 "or House of Commons of Canada" violate the rights of the applicant under s. 3 of the Charter. The impugned words in clause 3 will be struck out.[77]

The practical element of the dissent is that it shows an alternative solution to avoid the mischief of holding two offices currently. Individuals in this situation could, under cover of section 3 of the *Charter*, be required to resign from the House of Commons upon their election to the mayoralty.

The Ontario Court of Appeal heard an appeal of the first judgment, on the *Charter* issue; in a very short ruling which seemed to reflect the consensus among the justices, on September 15, 2000, it dismissed on the ground that the *Charter* does not guarantee the right to run for, or hold, municipal, as opposed to federal or provincial, office.

> The basic difficulty the appellant has is that while he has a constitutionally protected right to remain in Parliament until the next election, the "right" to *run* for municipal office, which the impugned legislation prevents, is not a constitutionally protected right, and therefor an infringement of that right does not raise a constitutional issue. The wording of s. 3 of the *Charter* is clear: it protects only the right to vote in an election of members of the House of Commons or of a legislative assembly and to be qualified for membership therein. There is nothing in the provisions of the *Municipal Act* and the *Municipal Elections Act* which in any way

---

[77] *Ibid.*, paras. 38 and 40.

intrude on the appellant's right to continue to sit in the House of Commons. The wording of s. 3 of the Charter restricts the right to those that concern the federal and provincial legislatures.[78]

Nunziata was politically knowledgeable enough not to resign his seat in the House of Commons for the sake of his potential City of Toronto candidacy. Thus, as a result of these judgments, he was not able to present himself at the municipal level. He did run again, however, in the 37th federal general election of November 27, 2000, as a "non-affiliated" candidate in the electoral district of York South – Weston. This time, he received 41.3% of the votes and was narrowly defeated by Tonks, a Liberal who, having become well-known in Metro Toronto government, received 45%.

At the time of writing, there was renewed speculation of a Nunziata candidacy for the Toronto mayoralty in 2003, when he may be facing one of his erstwhile caucus mates, Sergio Marchi.[79]

5.5.C—INCURRING ELECTION EXPENSES

§ 5.5.C.1
R. v. Roach
Ontario County Court; June 12, 1978
(1978), 25 O.R. (2d) 767

The incurring of expenditures for the purpose of electing or defeating a political party or a candidate, designated in the *Canada Elections Act* as an election expense, is at the heart of the electoral process and one of the most persistently controversial elements of the regulation of electioneering. The incurring of such expenses by public servants or, as here, by a Public Service Union, is not only an aspect of the rules relating to participation in the electoral process; it has a patent impact on the requirement for a non-partisan Public Service, which is one of the legal elements of democracy. From either perspective, what is at stake is the legality of the freedom of expression of a group involved in public administration on matters of current political interest.

---

[78] (2000), 189 D.L.R. (4th) 627 at 631, para. 10, additional reasons at (2000), 137 O.A.C. 70 (Ont. C.A.).
[79] "Sergio Marchi eyes run for mayor of T.O." *Hill Times*, August 13, 2001, p. 1.

On the occasion of a by-election in the federal constituency of Ottawa-Carleton, due to be held on October 18, 1976, Roach, acting on behalf of a local of the Ontario Housing Corporation Employees Union, leased a plane to fly over Ottawa, dragging a banner which said "O.H.C. Employees 767 C.U.P.E vote but not Liberal." The message was intended to convey the Union's opposition to the anti-inflation legislation which also capped salary increases that the federal Liberal government had brought in. The expenses related to this publicity were in contravention of a provision of the *Canada Elections Act* prohibiting others than candidates or parties from incurring election expenses, "for the purpose of promoting or opposing, a particular registered party or the election of a particular candidate."[80] The Crown charged Roach but both at trial and on appeal he was acquitted. It is important to remember that this case was decided prior to the advent of the *Charter*.

The County Court held that on the facts, the flying of the banner could not be said to have been direct support or opposition. It went on to more significant reasons for acquittal, namely that the accused could rely on the statutorily sanctioned defence that he was expressing views on an issue of public policy and that in so doing, he had acted in good faith. The court recognized, as Parliament had done earlier by its wording of the legislation that there was a difference between politically partisan support or opposition of a party or candidate on one hand, and public expression of views on a current and perhaps even politically controversial issue of public policy on the other. The intent of this judgment was, under the guise of looking at election expenses legislation, to affirm that the general public debate of issues relating to the conduct of public affairs should be inclusive. That inclusion would even extend to Public Service Unions, notwithstanding their duty to remain non-partisan. Interpreting the election expenses rules restrictively was the way to achieve this.

The court's final reason for judgment was that if Parliament had intended to prohibit such acts as that of the defendant, it would have used clearer language.

> This Court is not oblivious to the history of the legislation. While this Court cannot construe an Act of Parliament by the motives which influ-

---

[80] *Canada Elections Act*, R.S.C. 1970, c. 14 (1st Supp.), s. 70.1(3); enacted by S.C. 1973-74, c. 51, s. 12.

enced the House of Commons yet when legislation tells the Court what the object of the legislation was, the Court must see whether the terms of the section are such as fairly to carry out that object and no other, and read the sections with a view to finding out what they mean and not with a view to extending the meaning to something that was not intended: see *Holme v. Guy* (1877), 5 Ch. D. 901.

Likewise, this Court cannot encroach on the legislative function of Parliament by reading in some limitation which it thinks was intended but which cannot be inferred from the words of the Act: see *A.-G. Northern Ireland v. Gallagher,* [1963] A.C. 349.[81]

§ 5.5.C.2
National Citizens' Coalition Inc./Coalition nationale des citoyens Inc. v. Canada (Attorney General)
Alberta Court of Queen's Bench; June 25, 1984
(1984), 11 D.L.R. (4th) 481

What is the extent to which non-political individuals and organizations, that is actors in the electoral system other than candidates and political parties, may participate in the electoral process and exercise an influence on that process through the uncontrolled expenditure of funds? A more blunt way of posing the same question is to ask whether the State may take legislative measures to avoid circumstances in which special interests can spend their way to their own electoral successes. In such cases, does it make a difference whether those special interests are independent of political parties or if they are acting in concert with one of them? The general issue underlying these immediate questions is the extent to which the citizenry can freely participate in elections. A corollary to that question, as posed in this specific case, is the matter whether there is evidence of the influence of election expenditures on the outcome of elections.

Canada has had a modern history of legislative attempts to control election expenses since the mid-1960's. There has been recognition of the increasing cost of electioneering, in particular after the beginning of the use of television, an extremely expensive medium, in campaigning. The first efforts were directed at limiting campaign expenditures, so that electors would not be restricted to the wealthy. The

[81] (1978), 25 O.R. (2d) 767 at 772-773.

companion measures that were adopted later were limited State subsidization of candidates' and parties' election expenses and provisions to assure access of all voices to electoral broadcasting. The common goal of all these measures to adapt election legislation to the requirements of the late 20th century was the provision of equal chances to all candidates and political parties.

In 1983, the Parliament of Canada took what seemed to be the next step along the same path. By an amendment to the *Canada Elections Act*,[82] it inserted a new section into the statute, then section 70.1, so as to provide that only candidates or their registered agents, or registered political parties acting through their registered agents could incur election expenses during the period of an election campaign. In effect, this reserved the electoral field for formal participants in elections and excluded any participation by others such as citizens or citizens' groupings, that would involve the expenditure of funds "for the purpose of promoting or opposing, directly and during an election, a particular registered party, or the election of a particular candidate."[83]

The National Citizens' Coalition (NCC) initiated an action against this amendment to the election law, in expectation of the fact that in 1984 there would be a federal general election and in the hope of being able to participate in it legally. The action was based on the claim that the limitation of election related spending to candidates and parties was contrary to section 2(b) [freedom of thought, belief, opinion and expression] and to section 3 [democratic right to vote] of the *Canadian Charter of Rights and Freedoms*. The NCC was a right wing organization which wanted not only to convince the electorate to espouse conservative viewpoints on a number of public issues, but was also determined to assist in the election of candidates favourable to its point of view. In common parlance, it was a lobby group.

The action by the NCC brought to the fore fundamental philosophical differences between those who favoured unfettered freedom of expression in election campaigns, which in the era of media-driven campaigning also meant unlimited expenditures, versus those who hoped to give all points of view in the campaign an equal chance of

---

[82] *An Act to amend the Canada Elections Act (No. 3)*, S.C. 1980-81-82-83, c. 164.
[83] These words are drawn from the definition of "election expenses" in s. 2 of the *Canada Elections Act* as it was then, R.S.C. 1970, c. 14 (1st Supp.).

expression, or rather a chance of expression equalized by the limitation of unbridled expenditures.

The NCC based its argument on the premise that,

> the freedom to express oneself freely...is said by many to be one of the most significant of freedoms in a democratic society since the political structure depends on free debate of ideas and opinions. This is said to be of particular importance at election time. It is further suggested that freedom of expression concerning activities of government should be protected from limitations since this is essential to the functioning of a democracy.[84]

In favour of this position, it brought up as an example the judgment of the United States Supreme Court in *Buckley v. Valeo*,[85] in which limitations on campaign expenditures and contributions had been struck down as being contrary to the protection of freedom of speech guaranteed by the *First Amendment of the U.S. Constitution*. The Alberta Court of Queen's Bench took note of that precedent in terms of subject-matter, but, quite cautiously, reminded that it must be understood in the light of the differences between the two countries.

The Attorney-General's defence was based, first, on the evolution of the *Canada Elections Act* toward this form of limitation. His principal argument, however, was based on the desired equitable nature of the electoral process in affording fairness to all parties.

> It is submitted on behalf of the defendant that one must consider the importance of the Canadian electoral system as it has developed in our society and the value of the existing legislation which permits every Canadian citizen to make an informed electoral choice in electing Members of Parliament. This requires a consideration to be made of the law pertaining to election expenses and the benefits gained from past experiences both in this country and in other countries that operate under a similar system. It requires an appraisal to be made of the reasons provided for an ostensible breach of a Charter guarantee.[86]

The nature of this electoral system, according to the Attorney General, implies that if candidates and parties were subject to limitation of

---

[84] (1984), 11 D.L.R. (4th) 481 at 492.

[85] 424 U.S. 1 (U.S. S.C., 1976).

[86] *Supra* note 84 at 487.

election expenses, the absence of such limits on others would give them an unfair advantage. This would be especially true in the case of those who could have access to large campaign funds. The example of "political action committees" in the United States was brought up as a development to avoid.

One of the Attorney General's chief witnesses was a notable professor of political science from the University of Saskatchewan, John Courtney, a specialist in electoral systems. He bolstered the government's case in respect of the damages both to the legal and to the political systems if candidates and parties were treated one way, and other groups interested in contributing their say into the election campaign another way.

> Were special interest groups or individuals free to participate in the electoral process totally without constraints, they would enjoy advantages not otherwise available to the political parties. The fact is that the respective roles and responsibilities of political parties and special interest groups are different. Political parties are electorally accountable for their acts, which is one of the ways in which the term "responsible government" is given meaning in a parliamentary system. Generally every three or four years political parties are held to account by the electorate. They have more narrowly-defined interests, goals and memberships than political parties and, in the final analysis, they are not electorally responsible for their activities.[87]

The Attorney General contended, finally, that if the limitations inscribed in the Act were to assure equality of participation by all participants in elections, that benefit would be lost if it did not apply to so-called third parties. If the rule designed to achieve this purpose of equality resulted in the limitation of rights, such a limitation should be held to be reasonable and justified in a free and democratic society.

The court perceived that its determination had to be between the purpose of the statute on the one hand and the value that the constitutionally guaranteed freedom of participation in elections was intended to serve on the other. It reasoned at the outset that the attacked provision was limitative of rights on its face, so most of the judicial analysis was based on whether the limitation could be justified. The court concluded that it was not. In a somewhat theoretical response to the very concrete question before it, the court opted in favour of

---

[87] *Ibid.* at 496.

the value of freedom of expression and determined that the limitation of that freedom could not be justified. It based its ruling on the freedom of expression clause of the *Charter* only, and did not deal with the arguments relating to the right to vote.

> In my opinion the limitation must be considered for the protection of a real value to society and not simply to reduce or restrain criticism no matter how unfair such criticism may be. It has been said that the true test of free expression to a society is whether it can tolerate criticism of its fundamental values and institutions. A limitation to the fundamental freedom of expression should be assessed on the basis that if it is not permitted then harm will be caused to other values in society. This requires, as has been said, a balancing of the respective interests of society and of the individual.[88]

This judgment was handed down on June 25, 1984. Although, at that time, the expected federal election had not yet been called, there was a general sentiment that it would be imminent. The government therefore decided not to appeal the case and to give the law a degree of certainty. As a decision of an Alberta court, this judgment had effect within the province only. However, in order to have a uniform legal regime all across Canada, the government also decided not to enforce section 70.1 anywhere in the country. In the election that was eventually held on September 4, 1984, the NCC spent freely, as did others. The full impact of the change brought about by this decision was not felt until the next general election, that of 1988, in which the main issue was Canada-U.S. free trade. During the last two weeks of that campaign, the pro-free trade lobby, favouring the platform of the Progressive Conservative Party, spent zealously to get its point of view across. It may be validly argued that that participation and spending had a significant impact on the outcome of the election.

See also *McConnell v. Federal Election Commission*, 000 U.S. 02-1674 (2003).[89]

---

[88] *Ibid.*
[89] International comparison.

5.6 ISSUE: RESTRAINTS ON PARTICIPATION IN THE ELECTORAL PROCESS

See *Communist Party of the United States v. Subversive Activities Control Board No. 12*, 367 U.S. 1 (1961); *U.S. Term Limits Inc. v. Thornton*, 131 L.Ed.2d 881 (1995); *Bates v. Jones*, 131 F.3d 843 (9th Cir., 1997); *Kilosbayan Inc., Santiago et al.v. Commission on Elections et al.*, Supreme Court of the Philippines, October 16, 1997, case no. GR128054; *Buckley v. American Constitutional Law Foundation*, 142 L.Ed.2d 599 (1999) and *Cook v. Gralike*, 149 L.Ed.2d 44 (2001).[90]

5.7 ISSUE: EXCLUSIONS FROM PARTICIPATION IN THE ELECTORAL PROCESS

5.7.A—EXCLUSION OF PARTIES, PARTY LEADERS AND CANDIDATES

See *Communist Party of Canada v. Canada (Attorney General)*, Ontario Court (General Division), October 1, 1993, not reported; *Figueroa v. Canada (Attorney General)*[91] (1997), 147 D.L.R. (4th) 765 (Ont. Gen. Div.), varied (2000), [2000] O.J. No. 3007 (Ont. C.A.), leave to appeal allowed (2001) [2000] S.C.C.A. No. 511 (S.C.C.), reversed 227 D.L.R. (4th) 1 (S.C.C.); *Henderson v. Villeneuve & Mouvement de Libération Nationale du Québec*,[92] Superior Court of Québec, filed December 10, 1997; *R.C.M.P. Investigation of Canadian Alliance Payment to Jim Hart, M.P.* and international comparisons *Australian Communist Party v. The Commonwealth* (1951), 83 C.L.R. 1; *Petition on the Legality of the Communist Party*, Russian Constitutional Court, June 26, 1992; *The Matter of Megawati Sukarnoputri*, Litigation in 1996-1998, limited information available; *Goh Chok Tong v. Joshua Benjamin Jeyaretnam* (1998), 3 S.L.R. 337; *Ability of President Color de Mello to be a candidate*, Supreme Court of Brazil, December 3, 1997; *United Communist Party of Turkey v. Turkey* (1998), 26 E.H.R.R. 121; *The Socialist Party and Others v. Turkey* (1998), 27 E.H.R.R. 51; *Banning of the Islamic Welfare Party*, Constititutional Court of Turkey, February 22, 1998; *Banning of the*

---

[90] All international comparisons.
[91] Cross-reference to § 6.2.
[92] Cross-reference to § 4.4.

Islamic Virtue Party, Constitutional Court of Turkey, June 22, 2001; *Refah Partisi (Welfare Party) v. Turkey* (2002), 35 E.H.R.R. 3; *Özdep v. Turkey* (2001), 31 E.H.R.R. 27 and *Banning of Suharto's Golkar Party*.

5.7.B—EXCLUSION OF THIRD PARTIES

See *Canada (Attorney General) v. Somerville*, 184 A.R. 241 (Alta. C.A.); *Foret v. British Columbia (Attorney General)* (1996), 48 C.P.C. (3d) 165 (B.C. C.A.) and *Pacific Press v. British Columbia (Attorney General)* (1997), 45 B.C.L.R. (3d) 235 (B.C. S.C.) and [2000] B.C.J. No. 308 (B.C. S.C.).

---

§ 5.7.B.1
Cit-Can Foundation v. Québec (Attorney General)
Québec Superior Court; filed August 6, 1997
file no. 500-05-034521-979; adjourned *sine die*

The ability of third parties to play an active role in the electoral process, that is to establish and communicate positions publicly, to spend on electoral activities and to broadcast and publicize their points of view on issues related to the conduct of public affairs, is touched on in previous cases dealing with federal election law and Québec referendum law. Here, the same issue was addressed again by a non-profit foundation for the promotion and appreciation of the multi-cultural and multi-ethnic composition of Canada.

Cit-Can was asking the court to declare that a number of provisions in the *Election Act* which provided for a legislative scheme by which only candidates and registered parties may spend money to communicate their positions to the public were contrary to the *Canadian Charter of Rights and Freedoms*, section 2(b) freedoms of thought, belief, opinion and expression, including freedom of the press and other media of communication; to the section 2(d) freedom of association; and to section 3, the right to vote in an election of members of the Québec National Assembly. The plaintiffs, Cit-Can and a professor of psychology at McGill University, Don Donderi, sought declaratory relief to the effect that the subject provisions of the *Election Act* were inoperative and of no force and effect. They attacked that part of the legal régime which set out that:

No prosecution for breach of the impugned sections can be undertaken except during or after the election and thus there will be no opportunity to challenge the constitutionality of the sections in the context of a prosecution until after the election;[93]

The significance of this litigation, conducted in parallel to the earlier cases, is that it is bound up with the movement within Québec to protect the Anglophone community's rights. In that sense, the case is politicized and it touches not only on the subject matter of elections, but on the development of Canadian constitutionalism and the protection of constitutionally and politically recognized components of the population as well.

It is worthy to note that Cit-Can's action also sought to affirm the unconstitutionality of those provisions of the Québec *Election Act* that restrict the timing of political broadcasting at the beginning and end of election campaigns.

The conduct of this litigation was strategically linked to the developments in the *Libman* case. For the time being, the proceedings in this case are adjourned *sine die*. Cit-Can's legal counsel may revive the case at an appropriate time.

---

§ 5.7.B.2
Harper v. Canada (Attorney General)
Supreme Court of Canada; May 18, 2004
2004 SCC 33

The finding of an appropriate balance between the section 3 *Charter* right of voters to an informed vote and the section 2(b) right of political actors other than parties (commonly called third parties) has proved difficult, if not elusive for Canadian courts. The *Harper* case is the latest in the series of legal actions began with the National Citizens' Coalition action in 1983-84. From a constitutional law perspective, this matter deals with the reconciliation of conflicting constitutional rights. In a political law perspective, we also need to look at whether the state of Canada's election law enables those with deep pockets, and therefore greater influence, to distort electoral results in their own favour.

---

[93] Motion for Declaratory Judgment, s. 15.

On May 31, 2000, the *Canada Elections Act* was fundamentally revised.[94] This version of the statute included a set of amendments limiting the advertising expenditures of each third party to a total amount of not more than $150,000.00 during an election period.[95] Within this overall limit, each third party was authorized to spend no more than $3,000.00 to promote or oppose the election of one or more candidates in a given electoral district.[96] Various other rules and limitations were also enacted.

The ink had barely dried on the revised *Act*, when on June 7, 2000, Harper, then still President of the National Citizens' Coalition, initiated a challenge to its constitutional validity, on the grounds that it infringed the freedoms of expression and association protected by the *Charter*. The trial of the action was held in the Alberta Court of Queen's Bench on October 1 to 13, 2000. On October 22, the writs were issued for the 37th federal general election.

Harper applied for an injunction to suspend the application of the relevant provisions of the legislation until the Queen's Bench ruled on the merits of the action. The Queen's Bench granted the application and the Alberta Court of Appeal upheld that judgment, leading the Chief Electoral Officer of Canada to announce that he would not enforce the third part expenditure provisions anywhere in Canada. However, the Crown sought a motion for stay of the Court of Appeal's ruling in the Supreme Court of Canada and on November 10, that Court granted the stay. The Chief Electoral Officer thereupon announced that he would indeed enforce the new *Act*. Thus, in respect of this issue, the 37th general election was fought under different rules at different times.

In addition to the saga of the injunction litigated in connection with the 2000 general election, this case presents several politically notable facts. While at the outset, Harper had been the President of a third party lobby group, during 2001, he became Leader of the Canadian Alliance political party. At the 2000 general election, the Alliance had become the second party in the House of Commons, so Harper's assumption of its leadership also made of him Leader of the Opposition. Thus, he was particularly interested when the Alberta Queen's

---

[94] S.C. 2000, c. 9, previously Bill C-2.
[95] S.C. 2000, c. 9, s. 350(1).
[96] S.C. 2000, c. 9, s. 350(2).

Bench declared the third party expenditure provision unconstitutional on June 29, 2001,[97] and even more so when the Alberta Court of Appeal upheld that decision on December 16, 2002.[98]

The Supreme Court of Canada granted the Attorney General leave to appeal on September 4, 2003. The hearing of that appeal took place in February 2004. The judgment of the Supreme Court was delivered on May 18, 2004, a mere five calendar days before the issue of the writs for the general election. For the first time since 1984, Canada would have rules in respect of the participation of third parties in the election that would be final and definitive, decided at the highest level. The Supreme Court reversed the rulings of the Alberta Queen's Bench and of the Alberta Court of Appeal and held that the impugned provisions of the Act were constitutional. The effect of this judgment was also to repudiate the 1984 findings of the Alberta Queen's Bench in the NCC case, as well as to overrule the 1996 decision of the Alberta Court of Appeal in the *Somerville* case.

In the court's view, not only did the constituent parts of the third party electoral advertising regime stand on their own, but the entire regime was also held to be internally coherent. The heart of the judgment was that the majority of justices accepted the egalitarian model of elections, that is one offering equal opportunity for all third parties to be heard, not on the basis of their treasury, but rather on the basis of a level playing field. This, they held, is the mechanism required to enable voters to be better informed. The courts' philosophy in the decision was based on the notion of electoral fairness. The harm it sought to avoid was electoral unfairness.

In adopting this view, the court gave a thorough analysis of its motives.

> In my view, the findings of the Lortie Report can be relied upon in this appeal to determine whether the third party advertising limits are justified. Indeed, this Court has already provided significant guidance in its past jurisprudence on their importance of the following objectives based on the Lortie Report; see *Harvey, supra; Libman, supra;* and *Figueroa, supra*.

---

[97] 2001 ABQB 558.
[98] 2002 ABCA 301.

ELECTIONS / 523

(i)   To Promote Equality in the Political Discourse

As discussed, the central component of the egalitarian model is equality
in the political discourse; see *Libman, supra,* at para. 61. Equality in the
political discourse promotes full political debate and is important in
maintaining both the integrity of the electoral process and the fairness
of election outcomes; see *Libman, supra,* at para. 38.

(ii)   To Protect the Integrity of the Financing Regime Applicable to
Candidates and Parties

The primary mechanism by which the state promotes equality in the
political discourse is through the electoral financing regime. The Court
emphasized the importance of this regime in *Figueroa, supra,* at para. 72:

The systems and regulations that govern the process by which governments are formed should not be easily compromised. Electoral financing
is an integral component of that process, and thus it is of great importance
that the integrity of the electoral financing regime be preserved.

Accordingly, protecting the integrity of spending limits applicable to
candidates and parties is a pressing and substantial objective.

(iii)   To maintain Confidence in the Electoral Process

Maintaining confidence in the electoral process is essential to preserve
the integrity of the electoral system which is the cornerstone of Canadian
democracy. In *R. v. Oakes, [1986] 1 S.C.R. 103,* at p. 136, Dickson C.J.
concluded that faith in social and political institutions, which enhance
the participation of individuals and groups in society, is of central importance in a free and democratic society. If Canadians lack confidence
in the electoral system, they will be discouraged from participating in a
meaningful way in the electoral process. More importantly, they will
lack faith in their elected representatives. Confidence in the electoral
process is, therefore, a pressing and substantial objective.[99]

Stated in pure constitutional terms, the expenditure limits set out in
section 350 of the *Canada Elections Act* infringed on the section 2 (b)
freedom of political expression guaranteed by the *Charter,* but that
infringement was justified under section 1 of the *Charter.* Protecting
the integrity of spending limits was a pressing and substantial objec-

[99] *Harper v. Canada (Attorney General),* 2004 SCC 33, paras. 100-103.

tive. The limits were rationally connected with preservation of the integrity of the regime and they caused minimal impairment.

In addition, the court held that section 350 did not infringe section 3 of the *Charter*, the constitutional safeguard of the right to vote. In this regard, it held that the right of meaningful participation should not be confused with the exercise of freedom of expression. It stressed the importance of having voters well informed, with citizens being able to weigh the relative strengths and weaknesses of each candidate and political party.

> The question, then, is what promotes an informed voter? For voters to be able to hear all points of view, the information disseminated by third parties, candidates and political parties cannot be unlimited. In the absence of spending limits, it is possible for the affluent or a number of persons or groups pooling their resources and acting in concert to dominate the political discourse. The respondent's factum illustrates that political advertising is a costly endeavour. If a few groups are able to flood the electoral discourse with their message, it is possible, indeed likely, that the voices of some will be drowned out; see *Libman, supra; Figueroa, supra,* at para. 49. Where those having access to the most resources monopolize the election discourse, their opponents will be deprived of a reasonable opportunity to speak and be heard. This unequal dissemination of points of view undermines the voter's ability to be adequately informed of all views. In this way, equality in the political discourse is necessary for meaningful participation in the electoral process and ultimately enhances the right to vote. Therefore, contrary to the respondent's submission, s. 3 does not guarantee a right to unlimited information or to unlimited participation.
>
> Spending limits, however, must be carefully tailored to ensure that candidates, political parties and third parties are able to convey their information to voters. Spending limits which are overly restrictive may undermine the informational component of the right to vote. To constitute an infringement of the right to vote, these spending limits would have to restrict information in such a way as to undermine the right of citizens to meaningfully participate in the political process and to be effectively represented.
>
> The question, then, is whether the spending limits set out in s. 350 interfere with the right of each citizen to play a meaningful role in the electoral process. In my view, they do not.[100]

---

[100] *Ibid.*, paras. 72, 73 and 74.

The Supreme Court's own summary of its views can be stated as follows:

> The deleterious effect of s. 350 is that the spending limits do not allow third parties to engage in unlimited political expression. That is, third parties are permitted to engage in informational but not necessarily persuasive campaigns, especially when acting alone. Then weighed against the salutary effects of the legislation, the limits must be upheld. As the Court explained in *Libman, supra*, at para. 84:
>
> > [P]rotecting the fairness of referendum campaigns is a laudable objective that will necessarily involve certain restrictions on freedom of expression. *Freedom of political expression, so dear to our democratic tradition, would lose much value if it could only be exercised in a context in which the economic power of the most affluent members of society constituted the ultimate guidepost of our political choices.* Nor would it be much better served by a system that undermined the confidence of citizens in the referendum process. [First emphasis in original; second emphasis added].
>
> Accordingly, s. 350 should be upheld as a demonstrably justified limit in a free and democratic society.[101]

It would be most difficult to overstate the underlying importance of this decision for the originality of the Canadian system of political law or for the Canadian version of democracy. Indeed, the decision was the subject of extensive reporting by the general media.[102] It also made the headline of the specialized legal press.[103] As could be expected, it was excoriated by an unconvinced NCC as a stab at the heart of democracy.

In an unprecedented and most interesting fashion, the Supreme Court agreed to hear not only from the parties to the action, but to also allow an intervention from a sitting Liberal Member of Parliament, John Bryden, who represented the electoral district of Ancaster-Dundas-Flamborough-Aldershot, Ontario. This MP put forward evidence which indicated the Courts had always lacked, namely the most direct

---

[101] *Ibid.*, para. 121.

[102] "Supreme Court upholds election spending law," CBC news, May 18, 2004; "Limits upheld on lobbyists' election spending," Tonda MacCharles, *Toronto Star*, May 19, 2004 and "Keeping a level playing field," Chantal Hébert, *Toronto Star*, May 19, 2004

[103] "Election Act's limits on 3rd-party spending upheld by SCC, 6-3," Cristin Schmitz, *The Lawyers Weekly*, May 28, 2004, p. 1.

experience and the most informed opinion, derived from the practice of a parliamentarian on the impact of third part advertising on a campaign.

During the election campaign, speaking on behalf of the Conservative Party, Stephen Harper proposed to overturn the Supreme Court's decision by repealing third party election advertising limits from the Act and supported such a reform with the notwithstanding clause. However, the election result will afford the Conservatives no opportunity to do this.

The outcome of this action will be significant, but perhaps not final. The ability of third parties to participate in political life through expenditures is an extensively debated topic, in which the holders of divergent views do not seem to be amenable to convincing. Moreover, those opposed to limits seem to be well financed for continuing court battles and are intense practitioners of rhetorical flourish. Ultimately, what is at stake is the ability of private groups to secure electoral results they desire simply by spending sufficiently, without contributing to the genuine substantive political debates of the action.

5.8 ISSUE: POLITICAL BROADCASTING AND ADVERTISING[104]

See *Turmel v. Canada (Canadian Radio-Television & Telecommunications Commission)* (1980), 117 D.L.R. (3d) 697 (S.C.C.).

---

§ 5.8.1
Federal Liberal Agency of Canada v. CTV Television Network Ltd.
Federal Court of Canada – Trial Division; November 8 and 10, 1988
[1989] 1 F.C. 319[105]

These cases had the effect of infusing meaning into the provisions of the *Canada Elections Act* which declare the right of parties to broadcast

---

[104] Cross-reference to § 6.6 and 6.7.
[105] Affirmed (1988), 24 C.P.R. (3d) 466 at 470 (Fed. C.A.), leave to appeal refused (1989), 24 C.P.R. (3d) 466n (S.C.C.) and (1988), [1989] 1 F.C. 324, affirmed (1988), 99 N.R. 74 (Fed. C.A.).

their political messages. The first dealt with the jurisdictional aspect of the matter, while the second was about the merits of an application for interlocutory injunction. The timing of the cases was crucial, given that they were pleaded during the campaign leading up to the 34th federal general election of November 22, 1988.

On October 25, 1988, the leaders of the then three major political parties, Progressive Conservative, Liberal and New Democratic, participated in a televised debate. The Liberal Party then sought to use a 30-second clip from the debate as a paid political advertisement and a 120-second extract as a free-time political broadcast. The two major networks, CBC and CTV, refused. The Liberal Party's advertising arm took the matter to court.

In the initial ruling, the Federal Court of Canada - Trial Division recognized its own jurisdiction on the ground that there are twin obligations arising out of the *Canada Elections Act*, namely for the networks to make time available to the parties and to broadcast the partisan material presented to them.

> If the broadcasters or networks have a statutory obligation to provide broadcasting time it follows, in my view, that it is just as much a statutory obligation that they must, unless they can demonstrate a very clear legal reason for not doing so, broadcast the material with which they are presented by those respective parties.[106]

Here, the court also stated that neither the Broadcasting Arbitrator nor the Canadian Radio-Television and Telecommunications Commission can have a say on the contents of the ads, or censor them.

The second ruling reinforced these points in more fundamental terms. The networks contended that the constitutional freedom of the press gave them the liberty to refuse to broadcast any political advertisement which they might not wish to, for any reason. In effect, they were attempting to argue that the *Charter* could be used to supersede the political broadcasting provisions of the *Canada Elections Act*. The court wisely concluded that the freedom of the press argument did not apply here, except where the plaintiffs would argue that the networks should carry their political programming in the manner

---

[106] (1988), [1989] 1 F.C. 319 at 322 h, affirmed (1988), 24 C.P.R. (3d) 466 at 470 (Fed. C.A.), leave to appeal refused (1989), 24 C.P.R. (3d) 466n (S.C.C.).

provided by the *Canada Elections Act*. The Act was thus held to be a vehicle for the execution of the *Charter*, rather than an impediment to it.

> Sections 99.13 and 99.21 of the *Canada Elections Act* create legal obligations on the part of the defendants to provide free and paid broadcasting time for the broadcast of partisan political programming. I know of no reason why that obligation cannot be enforced by order of this Court if the defendants wrongfully refuse to broadcast the material presented to them by the plaintiffs.[107]

The Federal Court of Appeal upheld both judgments, showing that the networks' attempt backfired completely. The effect of these judgments was to reinforce the right of political parties to the airwaves, within the bounds of law.

---

§ 5.8.2
Libertarian Party v. Dalfen
Federal Court of Appeal; September 3, 1992
file A-916-88; not reported

As mandated by the *Canada Elections Act*, in preparation for the 34th federal general election which was held in 1988, on August 18, 1988, the Broadcasting Arbitrator made an allocation of paid political broadcasting time to the various registered political parties. On the basis of the formula set out at section 310 of the Act, the Arbitrator allocated 195 minutes to the Progressive Conservative Party, but only 5 minutes to the Libertarian Party. The Libertarian Party applied for judicial review to have the decision of the Arbitrator set aside and shortly thereafter sought an adjournment. Four years later, the application had still not been heard on the merits. When, in an effort to clear the rolls of cases unlikely to proceed, the Chief Justice ordered that the case be set down for hearing, the Libertarian Party withdrew the application.

The interest of this attempt at litigation is that it highlights the politically controversial aspect of the broadcasting provisions in the *Canada Elections Act* and shows how they are a constant source of friction, not between parties of the left and right, nor even between those in

---

[107] *Ibid.* at 328 j-329 a.

office and those in opposition, but specifically between large, traditional, well-established parties and the smaller entities seeking to
enlarge their influence in the political spectrum. In the subject allocation, the Broadcasting Arbitrator applied the criteria listed in the
statute strictly. These essentially reward past electoral success; they
involve the percentage of seats in the House of Commons obtained
at the last general election, the percentage of the popular vote and
the number of candidates endorsed by each party as a percentage of
all candidates endorsed by all parties. A further provision gives the
Arbitrator discretion to vary the results of the formula, so as to achieve
a more equitable allocation. On this occasion, the Arbitrator chose
not to exercise that discretion.

The Libertarian Party's application referred to the *Canadian Charter of
Rights and Freedoms*. More pertinently, it relied on a public notice
issued by the Canadian Radio-Television and Telecommunications
Commission (CRTC) dated September 2, 1988, in which the Commission had adopted a policy expressing

> ...obligation on the part of the broadcaster to provide equitable—fair and
> just—treatment of issues, candidates and parties which flows from the
> " ...public's right to be informed of the issues...so that it has sufficient
> knowledge to make an informed choice from among the various parties
> and candidates."[108]

Basing itself on this ground and on its interpretation of the purposes
of the broadcasting provisions of the *Canada Elections Act*, the Libertarian Party sought to show that the decision complained of precluded its meaningful access to broadcast media during the campaign, permitted the development of a historical disadvantage based
on the Party's political association and beliefs, hindered the Party's
chances of success, created an undue advantage for previously successful parties and a tremendous disadvantage for previously unsuccessful parties.

While the fact the applicants did not pursue this case prevented the
court from considering the merits of its case, the line of argumentation
set out by the Libertarian Party has been used by small and devel-

---

[108] Memorandum of Points of Argumentation filed by the Applicants; January 18,
1989; para. 15.

oping political parties in Canada vis-à-vis the well established ones ever since.

See also *Reform Party of Canada v. Canada (Attorney General)*, 165 A.R. 161 (Alta. C.A.), additional reasons at 32 Alta. L.R. (3d) 430 (Alta. C.A.).

---

§ 5.8.3
R. v. Peterson
Ontario Court (Provincial Division); October 1, 1997
file CE 87921-1; not reported

It is clear that the objective of the *Canada Elections Act*, including that of its provisions relating to political broadcasting and advertising and prohibiting behaviour in respect thereof, is to ensure that campaigns are conducted fairly for all, rather than to determine results. Such provisions were legislated even though the activities they regulate may or may not produce results in the minds of the electorate. This principle was illustrated in the prosecution of Andrew Peterson, brother of a former Liberal Premier of Ontario and of the Liberal candidate in the federal general election of June 2, 1997, in the electoral district of Willowdale, in Toronto. On June 1, 1997, Andrew Peterson was caught on videotape removing campaign posters of his brother's Reform Party opponent. He was charged under the relevant provision of the *Canada Elections Act* and on October 1, 1997, he pleaded guilty and was fined. The prosecution was fit punishment and hopefully served as a deterrent to future offenders, in particular because of its extensive reportage. However, it is questionable whether either the subject posters or their removal had much effect on convincing electors. "It's unlikely the sign scandal had much effect on the election results, Mr. Cobbold conceded. Jim Peterson won the riding with 27,283 votes. A Progressive Conservative candidate came in second with 9,968 votes. And Mr. Cobbold, representing Reform for the second election running, finished third with 6,004."[109]

---

[109] "Caught in the act," Mike Shahin, *Ottawa Citizen*, October 16, 1997, p. 1.

§ 5.8.4[110]
Hogan v. Newfoundland (Attorney General)
Supreme Court of Newfoundland – Trial Division; February 28, 2000
(2000), 183 D.L.R. (4th) 225[111]

In the process engaged by the Government of Newfoundland to modernize the province's school system by integration of its religious components, the principal opposition came from the religious communities which had for a long time controlled the school systems. They mounted a political campaign, part of which consisted of lawsuits grounded partly on constitutional and legal, partly on politically-motivated arguments. This was the third such case.

On July 31, 1997, the government announced that a plebiscite or referendum would be held and on September 2, 1997, it was. On a simple question dealing with the establishment of a unified school system, 71% of electors voted YES. Based on this vote, the House of Assembly approved the constitutional amendment to Term 17 of the *Terms of Union of Newfoundland with Canada*, which was necessary to realize the government's scheme. The matter was sent to Parliament, where the House of Commons and the Senate also passed the amendment. Royal Assent was given on January 8, 1998.

In this case, leaders and adherents of the Roman Catholic community sought a number of declarations, among them one which would state that the province's failure to provide funding for the NO campaign was an infringement of their rights under sections 2(b) [freedom of expression] and 15 [equality] of the *Canadian Charter of Rights and Freedoms*. They also claimed as damages the amount of money the NO side spent on political advertising in the plebiscite campaign.

The court assessed that the YES side campaign cost the government probably close to $400,000, while the NO side expended around $135,000. It analyzed this discrepancy from several points of view. It found, first, that there was no spending limit on either side, but that there should have been. This finding holds true according to the court even if it is taken into consideration that part of the funds spent by the government was for informational advertising and part was for

---

[110] Cross-reference to § 4.11.C.2 and 8.9.3.
[111] Leave to appeal refused (2000), 264 N.R. 395 (note) (S.C.C.).

advertising to promote the YES side in the campaign. In the court's opinion, the government should have separated the cost of its information advertising concerning the announcement and wording of the referendum from the amounts spent on the YES campaign.

The innovative element in the judgment is that the court favoured a doctrine of fairness in respect of the two sides in the referendum, calculated in terms of the partisan advertising spending. Notwithstanding that the court admitted that results in electoral events were not necessarily tied to the level of spending by the proponent of any particular view, it held that if the government funded the YES side, it should also have funded the NO side. It thus awarded the applicants, as damages, the total amount they had spent on their political advertising.

See also *Francis v. Mohawk Council of Kanesatake*, 2003 FCT 115 (Fed. T.D.) and *CBS Inc. v. Federal Communications Commission*,[112] 453 U.S. 367 (1980).

---

§ 5.8.5[113]
Australian Capital Television v. Commonwealth of Australia
New South Wales v. Commonwealth of Australia
High Court of Australia; January 15, 1992
(1991), 104 A.L.R. 389
-and-
Australian Capital Television Property Ltd. v. Commonwealth (No. 2)
High Court of Australia; September 30, 1992
(1992), 108 A.L.R. 577

The issue of how best to regulate the broadcasting of political advertising during election campaigns preoccupied not only Canada, but also Australia. In 1991, Parliament added a Part III D to the *Broadcasting Act 1942* by means of the *Political Broadcasts and Political Disclosures Act 1991 (Cth.)*. These new provisions prohibited radio and television broadcasting of political material in the period leading up to elections and referenda at all levels of government and compelled broadcasters to provide free election broadcasting time during election periods. In January 1992, at a time when a by-election was under

---

[112] International comparison.
[113] International comparison. Cross-reference to § 1.11.7.

way for a constituency in the New South Wales Legislative Assembly and general elections were under way for the Tasmania House of Assembly and for the Legislative Assembly of the Australian Capital Territory, Australian Capital Television applied for interlocutory injunctions pending claims for declarations that Part III D was constitutionally invalid.

The broadcaster alleged that the new provisions constituted expropriation, that they amounted to a breach of freedom of communications as protected by section 92 of the Constitution of Australia, that they denied an implied right of access to, and criticism of, federal institutions in relation to political and electoral processes, and that they breached an implied right arising from the concept of the common citizenship of the Australian people. After holding that there was a serious question to be determined but insufficient time for the court to form a view, the court refused the injunction, primarily on the following ground.

> What the plaintiffs really seek is an injunction in the terms sought which would give them an immunity against any executive action by way of enforcement of the law pending this court's decision on the question of validity. To grant relief on this footing would, in my view, fail to recognise sufficiently the fact that the statute is in operation and that, assuming its validity, it is currently a source of legal rights and obligations producing legal consequences.
>
> It seems to me that the plaintiff licensees must decide for themselves whether they are justified, on the basis of the legal advice they have received, in refusing to comply with the statutory provisions. If they refuse to comply, then it may be that the tribunal will seek to exercise its powers under the Act.[114]

The court agreed that the matter should be heard on an expedited basis, but was to do so at a date later than the electoral contests then being waged.

On the merits, a majority of the High Court held that the entire scheme of Part III D was invalid. In a voluminous judgment, the court's analysis of the nature of the Australian political system was at least as noteworthy as the outcome of the case. Chief Justice Mason started by examining the nature of representative government and represen-

---

[114] (1991), 104 A.L.R. 389 at 394; 11-24.

tative democracy in Australia. A highlight of these passages is the description of the effect on Australian sovereignty and legislative capacity of the *Australia Act, 1986* (U.K.), an enactment very much akin to the United Kingdom Parliament's *Canada Act, 1982*.[115]

With respect to the core of the issue of political broadcasting, relying heavily on Canadian precedents, the court determined that inherent to the Constitution, there existed an implied right of freedom of communication in relation to political matters.

> Freedom of communication in relation to public affairs and political discussion cannot be confined to communications between elected representatives and candidates for election on the one hand and the electorate on the other. The efficacy of representative government depends also upon free communication on such matters between all persons, groups and other bodies in the community. That is because individual judgment, whether that of the elector, the representative or the candidate, on so many issues turns upon free public discussion in the media of the views of all interested persons, groups and bodies and on public participation in, and access to, that discussion (6). In truth, in a representative democracy, public participation in political discussion is a central element of the political process.[116]

In the view of the majority, this implied freedom was based on the structure of the Constitution as a whole and the structure of the institutions it established, but not on any specific provision within the Constitution. This method of reading indicated both that other such implied rights might be found, but also that the court would not be unrestricted in its capacity to find such rights.

The twin tests used by the court to determine whether Part III D was valid was to balance the public interest in free communication against the competing public interest which the restrictions set out in the Part were designed to serve, as well as to determine whether the restrictions were reasonably necessary to achieve that competing public interest. The court assumed that the purpose of the legislation was to safeguard the interests of the political process by reducing pressure on parties and candidates to raise substantial sums of money. Nevertheless, in applying the standards, it would not accept at face value claims by the legislative and executive branches that unless a curtail-

---

[115] 1982, c. 11 (U.K.).
[116] (1992), 108 A.L.R. 577 at 594-22 to 595-6.

ment of freedom of communication was exercised, corruption and distortion of the political process would result. The court felt that the scheme discriminated against new and independent candidates by denying them meaningful access. It also objected to the fact that the operation of the regime was dependent upon the making of regulations at the discretion of the executive. It felt that the ban would operate too frequently, covering the election periods of the Commonwealth, the States, the Territory and local governments. Finally, the court based its judgment on the view that freedom of communication in relation to public affairs and political discussions was indivisible.

See also *R. v. BBC (Ex parte Prolife Alliance)*, [2003] UKHL 23.

5.9 ISSUE: PARTY LEADERS' AND CANDIDATES' DEBATES

See *Turmel v. Canada (Canadian Radio-Television & Telecommunications Commission)* (1983), 48 N.R. 80n (S.C.C.) and *R. v. Gauvin* (1984), 2 O.A.C. 309 (Ont. C.A.), leave to appeal refused (1984), 57 N.R. 159n (S.C.C.).

§ 5.9.1
Turmel v. Canada (Radio-Television & Telecommunications Commission)
Federal Court of Canada – Trial Division; April 24, 1985
(1985), 16 C.R.R. 9

In respect of the participation of candidates in televised debates, the heart of the issue from the campaign perspective is access to the electorate, while in legal terms it is the notion of "equitable time" set out in the statutes and regulations of the Canadian Radio-Television and Telecommunications Commission (CRTC). On April 24, 1985, the CBC organized a debate among candidates representing the big three parties (Progressive Conservative, Liberal, NDP) in a by-election to be held in Ottawa-Centre, but failed to invite Turmel, a perennial independent candidate. On the very day of the debate, Turmel sought a writ of *mandamus* to force the CRTC to make time available in the debate to all candidates on an equitable basis. The Federal Court of Canada's Trial Division followed precedent in holding that "equitable time" does not mean "equal time" and denied the motion. It gave a strong indication that the law on this point needs clarification and that policy instruments were needed to complement the law. Without these, the applicant would continue to be frustrated in that his prediction that the CRTC would only regulate after the fact would become self-fulfilling. Turmel also raised one argument based on the section 15 equality provision of the *Charter* only a few days after that provision had come to life. While the court pondered whether section 15 could be of greater help to him, it would not adjudicate on this art of the motion for procedural reasons.

---

§ 5.9.2
Turmel v. Cdn. Radio-Television & Telecommunications Comm.
Federal Court of Canada – Trial Division; September 10, 1987
(1987), 14 F.T.R. 22

During the Ontario provincial general election campaign of September 10, 1987, Turmel applied for an order of *mandamus* to compel the CRTC to order Global and other television networks to invite the participation of political parties other than the three major parties into a planned debate. The court dismissed the application on the ground that Turmel could not show "a clear legal right to have a duty performed which is actually due and obligatory,"[117] in other words, that he had not met the administrative law requirement to obtain the type of order applied for.

The court recognized that Turmel, who was active in political life, had cast this application in an ingenious manner. He applied as a private citizen, arguing that the airwaves were a public trust and that the limited format of the debate set out by the broadcasters would preclude him from finding out the policies of the other parties, as well as their proposed solutions to the issues facing the electorate. Despite this recognition, the court felt that the resolution of this essentially political dilemma was not within its strictly legal mandate. "I am not suggesting that there is no merit in the applicant's quest for what he considers a better deal for minor parties. His case, however, does not raise legal issues. It raises policy issues which this Court cannot entertain."[118] The court's confusion of policy with po-

---

[117] (1987), 14 F.T.R. 22 at 23, at para. 6.
[118] *Ibid.*, para. 7.

litical issues here does not detract from the clarity of its view of its law-based role in regard to the matter of party leaders' debates.

---

§ 5.9.3
Trieger v. Canadian Broadcasting Corp.
Ontario High Court of Justice; October 21, 1988
(1988), 54 D.L.R. (4th) 143

This judgment was the first of a series of significant cases in Canada which addressed seriously the issue of the extent to which the courts would use the law to guide the essentially political process of staging debates among the leaders of political parties vying with each other to be elected to high office. The *Trieger* case set the pattern in several respects: such cases are considered in an atmosphere of urgency, not giving the court time for sufficient reflection; the pleadings often resemble each other; and the results seem to be consistently discouraging for smaller or weaker political parties. Parties in various jurisdictions continue to attempt to resort to the courts in the belief that the greater publicity resulting from exposure through participation in leaders' debates cannot but lead to greater electoral success. The courts have been unwilling to interpret the factual evidence or the legal principles applicable to reach this political conclusion.

In the federal campaign for the general election of November 21, 1988, the Canadian Broadcasting Corporation (CBC) scheduled nationally televised debates for October 24 and 25. The leaders of the Progressive Conservative, Liberal and New Democratic parties alone were invited as participants. These were then the major political formations in Canada. Seymour Trieger, then leader of the Green Party, applied for an injunction or a mandatory order to be included. Trieger expressed the belief that he had a constitutional right to be one of the debaters. In the alternative, he asked that either the debate should not proceed or that another debate be organized in which he could appear on an equal footing with the major party leaders.

Trieger's argument was founded on the four grounds that would, in various combinations, be used in later similar cases: a) the principle of equitable treatment of partisan political issues and parties, as set out in the regulations of the Canadian Radio-Television and Telecommunications Commission, b) the freedom of expression guaranteed in section 2 of the *Charter*, c) the freedom of association guaranteed by section 2(d) of the *Charter*, and finally d) the right to equal protection and benefit of the law provided for in section 15 of the *Charter*.

The court looked first at the question whether the *Charter* applied at all and concluded that it did not. The trigger rendering the *Charter* applicable was the notion of governmental action, but here, the CBC was acting in an independent capacity.

Despite this first finding, the court went on to look into the merits of the case and despite the urgency, it conducted a remarkably thorough examination of the issues. The court analyzed its own position as guarantor of the law in the circumstances presented to it.

> What the applicants are really asking this court to do is to dictate the content and the agenda of the political debate in the forthcoming federal general election. It is for the leaders of the various political parties to decide of their own free will and accord, without any coercion from this court, whom they want to debate and when and on what terms such debates should take place. It is not for this court to dictate the agenda of political debate. It is not for this court, certainly on an interlocutory application of this nature without full opportunity as at trial to canvas the facts and the legal issues, to interfere with the freedom of speech and expression of the various party leaders by dictating the debate format, content, or participants. Neither is it up to this court to dictate in any way to broadcast editors what is news and what is not news, subject of course to non-publication orders in criminal cases and a few other exceptional cases. It is up to broadcasters and editors to decide what they wish to publish.[119]

This passage was such a fundamental judicial pronouncement on the matter that it has been quoted verbatim.

The court then proceeded to respond to the argument based on section 15 of the *Charter*, the equality provision. This passage is most noteworthy as, given both the evidence and the court's own familiarity with Canadian political life, it conducted an essentially political analysis of the facts and made comments on the evidence that are as political as legal.

---

[119] (1988), 54 D.L.R. (4th) 143 at 148.

As to s. 15 of the *Charter of Rights and Freedoms* I will say little except that I seriously doubt whether the applicants are similarly situated with the major parties. That is an essential element in the test for the application of the equality rights provision of s. 15 of the *Charter*. In the first place the media obviously from the material here, do not consider the pronouncements of the applicants to have the same news significance to the public as the pronouncements of the leaders of the major political parties. It has been stated that it is the view of the media that one of the leaders in the three major political parties will end up after the election as the Prime Minister of Canada and the media therefore consider those three leaders more newsworthy than the applicants. In the second place I doubt that the applicants are similarly situated with the major leaders because the leaders of the major parties have not agreed to debate with the leader of the Green Party. We have on the one hand consensual participants in a scheduled debate, and on the other hand someone who wants to participate in that debate without the consent or the agreement of the other parties.[120]

Part of this analysis comprises the consent of the court to the conjecture of the broadcaster as to which candidates stand a chance of having sufficient electoral success to be able to form a government. This is an eminently political decision both on the broadcaster's part and on that of the court. At this stage in the development of the law, no specific label is attached to this notion. Only later, in the *Perot* case, decided in the United States in 1996, was this notion to be elevated to a more explicit level as the concept of "winability."

Overall, the court declared itself not to be satisfied with the legal elements of the applicant's position in order to grant the relief sought without a full trial. It perceived that there were serious issues of what it called public policy to be addressed but it refused to do so on the basis of insufficient legal argumentation by the applicant. The court's dismissal of *Trieger* was also based, finally, on the public interest argument, namely that depriving the public of the opportunity to hear the debate as it had been planned would not serve its interest.

The Green Party would not abandon its desire to seek redress in other ways.

---

[120] *Ibid.* at 149.

§ 5.9.4
Green Party Political Assn. of British Columbia v.
Canadian Broadcasting Corp.
British Columbia Supreme Court; October 8, 1991
(October 8, 1991), Collver J. (B.C. S.C.)

In the British Columbia election campaign of October 17, 1991, the Green Party's leader was left out of a scheduled television debate. The party sued for an injunction either to have its leader included or to have the debate cancelled. The application failed. With respect to the requirements for obtaining an injunction, the court felt that the balance of convenience was not satisfied by the applicant, the granting of either alternative sought would have resulted in substantial disruption that would not be in the public interest. By contrast to the other cases on this issue, the court accepted that the party could be considered as a "major" one, but thought that that should not entail its inclusion in the debate on grounds of equity. The CBC had editorial discretion in the matter and exercised it properly.

§ 5.9.5[121]
R. v. Canadian Broadcasting Corp.
Ontario Court (General Division); May 12, 1992
(1992), 72 C.C.C. (3d) 545[122]

Canada's 34th federal general election was held on November 21, 1988. In preparation for that event, nationally televised debates of the leaders of the three traditionally major political parties were held on October 24, 1988, in French and October 25 in English. A member of another formation, the Green Party of Canada, brought a private prosecution against the Canadian Broadcasting Corporation, the Canadian Television Network and Global Communications Ltd., alleging that their refusal to include the leader of the party in the debate constituted an infringement of section 8 of the *Television Broadcasting Regulations, 1987.*

---

[121] Cross-reference to § 1.11.3 and 1.21.1.
[122] Affirmed (1993), 51 C.P.R. (3d) 192 (Ont. C.A.), leave to appeal refused (1994), 72 O.A.C. 158 (note) (S.C.C.).

The broadcasters involved contended that section 8 should be interpreted as applying to paid time and free time political broadcasts regulated pursuant to the *Canada Elections Act*, but that it had no application to programs containing political content, such as a leaders' debate. The Ontario Court (General Division) dismissed the charge on the ground that while a debate among leaders of political parties competing in an election was an informational program, it was not a program of a politically partisan character within the meaning of section 8.

The court drew upon the experience of past federal election campaigns to set out the recognized characteristics of leaders' debates. It held that such programs:

a) are initiated by the networks,
b) are organized by the networks,
c) are the product of negotiations between the networks and the political parties,
d) are conducted in a format determined by the networks,

Generally speaking, a panel of journalists asks questions of the leaders and each leader is given the opportunity to provide his or her views in respect to each question. Depending on the format, each leader may have a short period of time to make a general statement in respect to the policies of his or her party.[123]

e) have participation by invitation of the networks, and
f) have voluntary participation by party leaders.

The court considered that as the *Broadcasting Act* and the *Television Broadcasting Regulations* were silent on the issue of leadership debates, Parliament cannot be considered to have delegated authority to the regulator of broadcasting matters, the Canadian Radio-Television and Telecommunications Commission, to organize leaders debates. Moreover, as the *Canada Elections Act* did not refer expressly to such debates within the scope of political broadcasts governed by that Act, the production of debates, as well as the rules for selecting participants and the guidelines in respect of the format of each debate was left up to broadcasters and network operators.

---

[123] (1992), 72 C.C.C. (3d) 545 at 571 e, affirmed (1993), 51 C.P.R. (3d) 192 (Ont. C.A.), leave to appeal refused (1994), 72 O.A.C. 158 (note) (S.C.C.).

§ 5.9.6[124]
National Party of Canada v. Canadian Broadcasting Corp.
Alberta Court of Appeal; October 1, 1993
(1993), 106 D.L.R. (4th) 575[125]

This case arose against the backdrop of the campaign leading up to Canada's federal general election of October 25, 1993. The National Party was a political formation established in November 1992 by a well-known publisher with nationalistic tendencies and aspirations based in Edmonton, Mr. Mel Hurtig. It fielded candidates in many of the 295 electoral districts in 1993. It was one of a large number of political parties contesting that election.

Throughout the summer of that year, the country's largest television networks, the Canadian Broadcasting Corporation (CBC) and its French twin, Société Radio-Canada, the Canadian Television Network and the Global Television Network, were planning for the party leaders' debates they expected to organize during the campaign. For this purpose, they also formed a broadcasters' consortium and determined their own rules on participation in the various debates.

> The Broadcasters' Consortium decided to include in the debates those party leaders whose parties met all the following criteria...
> a. having at least one representative sitting as a Member of Parliament;
> b. showing itself consistently over recent years to have had an impact on the Canadian Public inasmuch as each has scored more than 5% popularity in various public opinion polls;
> c. its leader [having] been involved in a very publicly visible manner in the constitutional and economic debates in Canada over recent years.[126]

Using these criteria, the broadcasters' consortium decided that it would organize an English and a French language debate involving the leaders of the Progressive Conservative, Liberal, New Democratic, Reform and Bloc Québécois parties. The leaders of parties which did not qualify under the broadcasters' criteria, including Mel

---

[124] Cross-reference to § 1.14.4.
[125] Leave to appeal refused [1994] 2 W.W.R. lxv (note) (S.C.C.).
[126] (1993), 106 D.L.R. (4th) 568 at 569, affirmed (1993), 106 D.L.R. (4th) 575 (Alta. C.A.), leave to appeal refused [1994] 2 W.W.R. lxv (note) (S.C.C.).

Hurtig on behalf of the National Party, would be invited to debate each other on another occasion. Each debate would be nationally televised, live, in prime time. All the debates were scheduled to take place early in October.

On September 8, 1993, the National Party and Hurtig applied to the Alberta Court of Queen's Bench, claiming a declaration that the CBC had infringed their rights, an order to declare that the CBC was required to provide equitable treatment to the National Party and in particular to include Mr. Hurtig in the debate of the major parties, as well as other relief. Despite the expertise of the party's counsel, the action was initiated against the CBC alone, among consortium members; it relied to a great extent on arguments founded on the *Canadian Charter of Rights and Freedoms*. The appeal processes were carried on until the last possible moment before the time of the debate which it sought to influence.

The National Party's Statement of Claim in this case is noteworthy in several respects. First, it is a court document which so thoroughly blends legal and political argumentation that the two become indistinguishable. More importantly still, the statement of claim sets out a complete marshalling of arguments on behalf of an emerging political party seeking to achieve political visibility, notoriety and acceptance through the use of the judicial system.

The general introductory pleading is that inclusion of the National Party in the debate of major parties will afford it greater exposure and enable it to receive equitable treatment from the CBC. In support of its request, the party thus relies on the statutory mandate and the obligations

> of the CBC under the Broadcasting Act "to safeguard, enrich and strengthen the cultural, political, social and economic fabric of Canada" (section 3(1)(d)(i)) and to "provide a reasonable opportunity for the public to be exposed to the expression of differing views on matters of public concern" (section 3(1)(i)(iv)), as well as its obligation under section 8 of the Television Broadcasting Regulations, 1987, SOR/87-49 to provide for "equitable treatment to all accredited political parties and rival candidates represented in an election."[127]

---

[127] Statement of claim, section 6, dated and filed September 8, 1993; *National Party v. Canadian Broadcasting Corp.*; Court of Queen's Bench of Alberta.

The precisions were contained in the affidavit of the party's chief agent which accompanied the statement of claim. The first specific argument was that of the singular importance of televised debates. In the election campaign, it stated, the leaders' debate would be one of the most crucial events, as it would draw the greatest audience of interested voters.

The natural consequence of the importance of this event led to the argument based on the public interest. Exposure to various political views was said to be in the interest of the public and Hurtig's absence from the debates would deny Canadians information necessary to make informed decisions in the election.

The National Party's uniqueness was also an argument. It was said that none of the leaders of the other parties represent the beliefs or support the policies of this Party. In particular, the National Party was shown to have views and a platform different from that of any of the parties invited to the major debates. As an aspect of this argument, the major planks of the National Party platform, a political manifesto of sorts, were listed in the court documents. While several of these planks had a legal aspect in the sense of requiring legislation to bring them into effect, they were presented as essentially political in nature, constituting the basis on which the National Party wanted to form the Government of Canada. A layer of semantic complication was added by the use of the expression that these were the party's "policy initiatives."

The next argument was that of access to the voters. It was pleaded that exclusion of Hurtig from the major debates would deprive him and his party of an opportunity to deliver the National message. As a vehicle for communication with the electorate, the debates were said to be unique and compelling, with even the ability to change the course of the election.

The next point addressed was that of potential political damage resulting from exclusion. The party, the leader and each of the candidates was said to potentially suffer irreparable damage if Hurtig were not allowed to join the major party leaders. The deleterious effect would be felt in diminution of the chances of National Party candidates in being elected to Parliament or in receiving a significant proportion of votes.

Lastly, the court documents referred to the editorial attention which the staging of the televised debates and the participation in them had received in the written media. In support of this contention, the affidavit had a voluminous annex of newspaper clippings, which were generally favourable to Hurtig's inclusion in the debates.

On the basis of the heads of argumentation listed here the claim also alleged that the CBC's refusal to invite Hurtig would constitute breaches of the *Charter's* guarantees of freedom of expression, effective exercise of political rights, equality, and would be contrary to the freedom of speech provision of the *Canadian Bill of Rights*.

This case was considered by the Alberta Court of Queen's Bench, the Alberta Court of Appeal and the Supreme Court of Canada. The first of these judgments is the most substantive one, and the best reasoned. The court only noted in passing that the rules on participation were established by the broadcasters' consortium but that only the CBC was a defendant. It did, however, conclude that failure to serve the other members of the consortium was fatal to the National Party's case. The court focused on the fact that the relief sought was based on *Charter* arguments and thus concentrated its analysis on whether the public broadcaster was in this instance acting as an arm of government and could therefore be subject to the requirements of the *Charter*. With respect to the substantive political arguments raised, the court only commented as follows.

> The statutory scheme, I find, has as its object to safeguard the journalistic integrity and programming independence of the C.B.C. Absent cogent evidence of mischief calculated to subvert the democratic process and absent evidence of statutory breach, this Court should not enter the broadcasting arena and usurp the functions of the broadcast media. The political agenda is best left to politicians and the electorate; television programming is best left to the independent judgment of broadcast journalists and producers.[128]

In its very brief judgment, the Alberta Court of Appeal dismissed the National Party's appeal of the dismissal of its application. The appeal judges examined solely the issue of the applicability of the *Charter* and added nothing to the argumentation on leaders' debates. The debate of the major party leaders was scheduled for the evening of

---

[128] *Supra* note 126 at 574.

October 4, 1993. On that very day, the Supreme Court of Canada heard the National Party's application to abridge the time within which its application for leave to appeal to that court would be heard and denied it. The debates went ahead as planned by the broadcasters' consortium and Hurtig appeared in a subsequent, separate debate with leaders of other parties which did not meet the broadcasters' criteria as being major. On February 3, 1994, the Supreme Court ended these proceedings by denying the application for leave to appeal. Throughout the time of this litigation, the National Party was the subject of much media attention as a result of its court action.

---

§ 5.9.7
Natural Law Party of Canada v. Canadian Broadcasting Corp.
Federal Court of Canada – Trial Division; October 1, 1993
[1994] 1 F.C. 580

The facts which gave rise to this case in the context of the campaign for the federal general election of October 25, 1993, are the same as those which prompted the action of the National Party. The Canadian Broadcasting Corporation (CBC) and other broadcast networks formed a consortium to organize debates among the leaders of the political parties seeking election to Parliament. Given the large number of parties, the consortium decided on the basis of specifically designed criteria to invite the leaders of the five parties they judged to be most serious and prospectively successful to debate each other. The other leaders, including Neil Patterson on behalf of the Natural Law Party (NLP), were invited to address a "town hall" meeting, to be held separately and later. The NLP's legal strategy was to seek to have its leader included in the debate of those of the major parties.

The NLP initiated its first action some two weeks after the National Party had applied to the Alberta Court of Queen's Bench for an order to have Mel Hurtig included in the major leaders' debate, but two days before that court handed down its dismissal of the application. This first action by the NLP was a statement of claim, also in the Alberta Court of Queen's Bench, but not against the CBC or the consortium of broadcasters. It was an application against the Attorney General of Canada, seeking declarations that sections 303 through 320 of the *Canada Elections Act*, all of which regulate political broadcasting through allocated paid time and free time advertisements, were, variously, in infringement of the *Canadian Charter of Rights and Freedoms*, in infringement of the *Canadian Bill of Rights*, and *ultra vires* the Parliament of Canada.

The co-plaintiffs in this action were the NLP and its treasurer, Frank Haika. The factual basis was that in an order issued pursuant to subsection 314(1) of the *Canada Elections Act*[129] on August 3, 1993, the Broadcasting Arbitrator had allocated only five minutes of paid air time and three minutes of free air time on each broadcast undertaking throughout Canada for the NLP to broadcast its messages to the electorate during the campaign. Moreover, section 319(c) of the *Act* prohibited broadcasters from making more time available to political parties than that which had been allocated. The NLP decried the fact that this regime would not enable it to communicate its campaign platform adequately to the voters.

> 12. The rules governing political broadcasts set forth in the impugned sections have the effect of discouraging the participation of legitimate but new political parties in the Canadian democratic process. New parties, no matter how broad their public support, can be given a handicap of up to 195 to 1. In the absence of the unanimous agreement among registered political parties, sections 307 through 310 of the Act require the Broadcasting Arbitrator to allocate 390 minutes of broadcasting time during prime time among parties on the basis of success in the previous general election, with no party receiving an allocation of more than fifty percent (195 minutes).[130]

Haika crystallized the NLP's position in respect of its desire for more air time in a press interview, when he asked:

> Why give time to the old parties who have created Canada's existing problems?...Why not give an equal chance to the new parties with fresh ideas?[131]

---

[129] 314. (1) In each of the calendar years following the calendar year in which an allocation of broadcasting time has been made under section 309 and 310 or a political party has requested and is entitled to broadcasting time under section 311, the Broadcasting Arbitrator shall convene and chair a meeting of the representatives of all registered parties to review the allocation or entitlement.

[130] Statement of claim, para. 12, dated and filed September 21, 1993, *Natural Law Party of Canada v. Canada (Attorney General)*, Court of Queen's Bench of Alberta.

[131] "Party Wants More Air Time," *Calgary Sun*, September 25, 1993, p. 22.

The judicial challenge of the exclusion of a party leader from the debate of major party leaders by this means, that is by an attack on the constitutional validity of the broadcasting provisions of the *Canada Elections Act*, was a clever strategy. Not long earlier, on November 30, 1992, the Alberta Court of Queen's Bench had already held invalid section 310 of the *Canada Elections Act* in a case initiated by the Reform Party.[132] That judgment had been appealed to the Alberta Court of Appeal, the case had been heard and the court had even decided to re-hear it, but the appeal ruling had not yet been issued. The NLP probably believed it could use the Queen's Bench decision on the Reform Party's case and build on it to further unravel the broadcasting provisions in the *Canada Elections Act* so as to give new and emerging parties less fettered and therefore greater access to the airwaves.

Two days after the NLP filed its statement of claim in the Alberta Queen's Bench, that court decided in the case of the National Party, rejecting its claim to have Hurtig participate in the debate of the leaders of the major parties. This ruling caused the NLP to change its strategy. The action before the Queen's Bench was abandoned. Instead, a completely new action was started by the party, with Donald Jackson, one of its candidates in Toronto as co-plaintiff, in the Federal Court of Canada - Trial Division, sitting in Edmonton. This time, the action was directed at the CBC, as the National Party had done before.

The Statement of Claim in this action, filed on September 27, 1993, reflected to a remarkable extent, the claim which the National Party had filed on September 8, 1993, in the Alberta Court of Queen's Bench.[133] The nature of the document, blending legal and political arguments, was the same. Indeed, many of the NLP's arguments were cast in very similar terms as those earlier made by the National Party and in some cases, the points of law were repeated verbatim. It is interesting to note, however, that while the National Party's brief had listed the major points of that party's platform, the NLP's political

---

[132] *Reform Party of Canada v. Canada (Attorney General)* (1992), [1993] 3 W.W.R. 139 (Alta. Q.B.), additional reasons at (1993), 7 Alta. L.R. (3d) 34 (Alta. Q.B.), reversed [1995] 4 W.W.R. 609 (Alta. C.A.), additional reasons at [1995] 10 W.W.R. 764 (Alta. C.A.).

[133] This similarity may be explained at least in part by the fact that the same law firm represented the Natural Law Party in these proceedings as had acted on behalf of the National Party.

agenda was expressed less specifically, perhaps reflected the difference in the agendas of the two groupings.

> The Natural Law Party offers the voters of Canada a new perspective
> on politics, proposing to implement, if elected, a number of creative and
> scientifically proven programs for the solution of a wide range of social,
> medical, legal and economic problems. It proposes, for example, the
> establishment of an all-party government, composed of the best talents
> from all fields and all political allegiances.[134]

This second action by the NLP was generally based, as the National
Party's case had been, on the party's desire for greater exposure and
equitable treatment. There was a difference in emphasis, however, in
that this action incorporated many of the arguments the NLP had
submitted before the Alberta Queen's Bench and it relied to a greater
extent on what the NLP alleged was the restrictive nature of the
provisions of the *Canada Elections Act* in terms of political broadcasting. It pointed out the perceived inequity in a scheme which enabled
the Progressive Conservative Party to receive an allocation of free
time that was over twenty times greater than what the Broadcasting
Arbitrator had assigned to the NLP. Thus, it claimed a series of declarations that the CBC's refusal of Mr. Patterson's participation in the
major debate was inconsistent with the *Charter* or the *Bill of Rights*, or
that it was *ultra vires* the Parliament of Canada, along with an order
requiring the CBC to include Mr. Patterson.

The Federal Court of Canada proved no more receptive to the NLP
than the Alberta Queen's Bench had been to the National Party. Its
first ground of refusal was pursuant to the *Broadcasting Act*, the Canadian Radio-Television and Telecommunications Commission
(CRTC) had jurisdiction, rather than the Federal Court. It then went
on to state that even if it did have jurisdiction, it would deny the
party's application for a number of reasons. This court brought little
that was new to the reasoning of such cases, preferring to rely extensively on the decision of the Ontario High Court of Justice in the
Trieger case.[135]

---

[134] Statement of claim, para. 5, dated and filed September 27, 1993, *Natural Law Party
of Canada v. Canadian Broadcasting Corp.*, Federal Court of Canada – Trial Division,
T-2319-93.
[135] *Trieger v. Canadian Broadcasting Corp.* (1988) 54 D.L.R. (4th) 143 (Ont. H.C.).

With respect to the *Charter* arguments, the Federal Court of Canada held that the CBC was acting here as a broadcaster, not as an agent of the government and that in these circumstances the *Charter* did not apply to its actions. On the subject of the criteria of selection of which party leaders would be invited to the major debate, the court felt, interestingly, that

> There is nothing on the face of the criteria chosen which is so unreason-able as to require the intervention of the court. The criteria are not arbitrary, unfair or based on irrational considerations on their face.[136]

The most noteworthy ratio of the case is its consideration of broad-casting policy. In a quote from the *Trieger* decision, the court affirmed its belief that the correlation of the impairment of a citizen's right to vote with the failure of a party to obtain the media attention which it requires had not been clearly demonstrated. On this basis as well the court thought it best to avoid interfering with the political debate going on in the election campaign by forcing a particular format on the leaders' formal debates.

This judgment comprises a comparative aspect which bears mention. In discussing the CBC's independence from government and the fact that no legislation exists in Canada to prevent broadcasters from participating in leaders' debates, the court remarks that in this re-spect, the American jurisprudence is of no assistance to it. Yet, in further analysis of the same topic, it cites a passage from the *Trieger* judgment which refers to the American cases on point. There is then, perhaps, some merit in examining such issues in a transnational man-ner.

The Federal Court – Trial Division rendered this ruling on October 1, 1993, the same day on which the Alberta Court of Appeal turned down the National Party's appeal of its own dismissal by the Queen's Bench. The debates of the leaders of the major parties went ahead on the evenings of October 3 and 5, 1993, without either Patterson or Hurtig.

---

[136] (1993), [1994] 1 F.C. 580 at 587 a.

§ 5.9.8
Dumont c. Johnson
Québec Court of Appeal; August 24, 1994
[1994] A.Q. No. 604

A variation on the scenario of party leaders' debates was played out in the context of the campaign for the Québec general election of September 12, 1994, in which the Parti Québécois, the province's sovereignist political formation, would come back into office after having spent some nine years in opposition. In preparation for this election, a consortium consisting of Société Radio-Canada, TVA (Télé-Métropole) and Radio-Québec organized a debate to involve the incumbent Liberal Premier, Daniel Johnson, the Leader of the Opposition, Jacques Parizeau, without the leader of the Action démocratique du Québec, Mario Dumont. This debate was to be held on August 29, 1994.

Dumont applied to the Québec Superior Court for an interlocutory injunction to order the broadcasters to include him in the debate, to provide equitable air time to the leaders of parties represented in the National Assembly, including him, and to order the other leaders to cede portions of their air time in the debate so as to enable him to participate in an equitable manner. Dumont relied in large part on his interpretation of section 423 of the Québec *Election Act*,[137] which purported to ensure qualitatively and quantitatively equitable free air time for the advertisements of the leaders and candidates of political parties. He alleged that the consortium's refusal to admit him into the debate violated the spirit and the letter of the *Election Act* and would result in depriving the population of complete information.

The networks' response was that a debate was not subject to section 423, but was rather a public affairs broadcast in which the guiding

---

[137] 423. During an election period, a radio, television or cable broadcaster and the owner of a newspaper, periodical or other publication may make air time on the radio or television or space in the newspaper, periodical or other publication available free of charge to the leaders of the parties and to candidates, provided he offers such service equitably as to quality and quantity to all the candidates of the same electoral division or to all the leaders of the parties represented in the National Assembly or which obtained at least 3% of the valid votes at the last general election.

criteria was their journalistic discretion. They also acknowledged that they would apply section 423 in its proper context and enable party leaders and candidates to advertise equitably. Québec's Chief Electoral Officer, Côté, presented a noteworthy intervention, contending not only does section 423 not apply, but that the issue under discussion was within his, rather than the court's jurisdiction. The court chose not to comment on this submission.

In an unreported judgment,[138] the Superior Court denied the application. It said first that if it were to grant the remedy sought, it would also have to issue a catalogue of directives on how to use its order, on alternative solutions and on production plans. It felt it could not order the consortium of broadcasters to admit the applicant without interfering both in the content and the format of the program, none of which was its role. The judgment was also motivated on grounds of the law of injunctions: the applicant had shown no colour of right[139] and moreover, the court did not want to bind the hands of the judge who may hear the case on the merits. The extreme urgency of the application also became a factor: the court said it could not consider the evidence, nor deliberate, adequately. Going beyond these reasons, which resemble these in other similar cases, one particular comment stands out in this judgment:

> Le requérant subit le préjudice de tous ceux qui font oeuvre de prioriser dans un domaine particulièrement exigeant.[140]

This can be taken as referring to the difficulty of making a case for an interlocutory injunction, but it can also be interpreted as an indirect reference to the jurisprudence on applications to join leaders' debates. While the ruling did not refer to precedent, the press reports on the case indicated that the judge had thoroughly prepared for the hearing, despite the short notice. He also arrived in court with the judgment ready.[141]

Dumont applied to the Québec Court of Appeal for leave to appeal but was refused on this proceeding as well. The relevant part of this judgment is that the lower court's view on the inapplicability of

---

138 [1994] R.D.J. 406 (Que. S.C.).
139 The expression used in French was "apparence de droit."
140 *Supra* note 138.
141 "Le débat: Mario Dumont est débouté en Cour Supérieure," *La Presse*, August 20, 1994, p. F-16.

section 423 of the *Election Act* to leaders' debates was upheld. While expressing disappointment that the debate would not bring out issues which the people really wanted to hear, Dumont was said to have accepted his fate stoically after this second reversal.

---

§ 5.9.9[142]
Scottish National Party et al. v. Scottish Television et al.
Scottish Court of Session; April 15, 1997
limited information available

On March 21, 1997, Her Majesty Queen Elizabeth II prorogued the United Kingdom Parliament and authorized a Parliamentary General Election to be held on May 1, 1997.[143] The principal contenders for Parliament were the Labour Party, the Conservative Party and the Liberal Democrats. In Scotland, another serious contender was the Scottish National Party (SNP). Using several criteria, the SNP described itself as the second largest party in Scotland. They were well represented at the local level, they were seriously represented in the European Parliament and they showed some measure of success in public opinion polling. The principal plank in the SNP's program was its advocacy of independence for Scotland, but they had developed positions on a number of other matters of political controversy besides constitutional affairs, among them taxation, defence and housing. The SNP presented candidates for all 72 seats in Scotland.

During the early part of the election campaign, there was discussion of the prospect for a televised debate among several of the leaders of the political parties vying for office. The rules under which such a debate would be governed were set out in the *Broadcasting Act 1990*, and in the licences issued to Scottish Television, respectively, by the Independent Television Commission (ITC). The principles of broadcasting and the criteria applicable to political programmes which could be gleaned from these instruments were primarily "accuracy" and "impartiality." The *ITC Programme Code* added to these the notions of "fairness" and "respect for the truth."

Pending a final decision on the holding of such a proposed debate, the preliminary arrangements involved the leaders of the Labour and

---

[142] International comparison.
[143] The total number of seats in the U.K. Parliament was 659.

Conservative parties, as well as perhaps the leader of the Liberal Democrats. The Scottish National Party expressed reservations that the possible holding and televising of a party leaders' debate that would not involve their leader would not only fail to abide by the principles set out for political broadcasts, but would, further, be politically biased. For this motive, the SNP submitted a petition to the Court of Session, asking for *interdict* and *interdict ad interim*, the Scots Law versions of injunction and interim injunction, seeking to restrain the respondent broadcasters from broadcasting prior to the general election of May 1, 1997, any political programme relative to a debate among the leaders of the Labour, Conservative and Liberal Democrats parties, which would not involve the leader of the SNP on an equal basis with the other leaders.

The SNP's central argument was set out in its petition in the following terms:

> In the circumstances, the petitioners are reasonably apprehensive that the controversial political subjects upon which they express views including, for example, those relative to Scotland's constitutional future, taxation, defence and housing will not be treated with due accuracy and impartiality. There will be a strong political bias against the petitioners and in favour of their political opponents. This will, for example, involve a bias towards the political viewpoint which advocates the preservation of the United Kingdom. They are also reasonably apprehensive that such a political broadcast, made shortly before a General Election, without the petitioners having an opportunity to reply, in a broadcast of comparable format and content, will be unduly and unfairly influential on the electorate in Scotland.[144]

The petitioner seemed to be particularly anxious that a debate involving the SNP leader reach the populations of what it called central and northern Scotland. This was ostensibly related to the reach of the two broadcasters involved; it could also have been a factor of the location of the ridings in which the SNP believed it had the best chance of winning.

In making out its case, the SNP relied essentially on the five key elements which have become the standard line of reasoning in such applications to the courts:

---

[144] Petition of the Scottish National Party, para. 6.

a) controversial subjects of political discussion;
b) need for impartiality and accuracy on the part of broadcast-
    ers;
c) desire of the petitioning party to avoid political bias by the
    fact of its exclusion from the proceedings;
d) assertion that the broadcast would be influential on the elec-
    torate; and
e) if excluded, lack of opportunity for the party to reply in time
    to those which had participated in the debate.

In all these respects, the SNP's petition was remarkably similar to the
recourses attempted in similar circumstances by Canadian political
parties.

The court refused the petition and in its reasons also, making allowance for the differences between U.K. and Canadian law, echoes of
Canadian judgments can be found. The court held first that the petition was hypothetical. It considered in this regard that at the time of
the petition, no final agreement had yet been reached, nor as to the
length, format or characteristics of an eventual debate, nor as to
whether the respondents or the BBC would broadcast it.

The court conceded that political broadcasting must be impartial. It
interpreted the concept of impartiality as applying not to each individual program, but rather to a broadcasting service, that is over a
period of time and over a range of broadcasting output relative to the
particular field or topic.

> For that very practical reason also it is in my view plain that in judging
> whether a licensee is observing due impartiality, particularly in the con-
> text of political broadcasting in an election campaign, it is the generality
> or entirety of the broadcasting output in the relevant field to which one
> must look, rather than a single programme in isolation.[145]

In the tradition of the independence of broadcasters from the State,
great weight was also ascribed to their discretion and judgment in
determining the content, format and other characteristics of the political program that would constitute the party leaders' debate.

---

[145] Opinion of Lord Eassie, April 15, 1997, p. 4.

It may possibly be that if a debate were to take place and if it were available to the respondents as a network programme its format, duration and likely public impact could present the respondents with a decision of greater difficulty that than (sic) presented by other network programmes in the field of politics and current affairs. They would no doubt have to assess carefully whether the impact of such a programme, if transmitted by them in Scotland, would present in the context of politics in Scotland a partiality which could not be overcome having regard to the complete range and type of programmes relating to the election which they were proposing to broadcast. But in my view that is primarily a matter for their judgment.[146]

Finally, the court also applied a criterion of administrative law to its assessment of the petition. The ITC Programme Code calls for the exercise of a "due degree of impartiality" on the part of the broadcasters. This was held to constitute a discretionary power in the hands of the latter. The proper test to determine whether they exercised their discretion of judgment correctly is that set out by U.K. jurisprudence regarding the judicial review of discretionary powers.[147] The court concluded that this petition being premature, the SNP did not assert that in applying that test, the broadcasters' assessment of their own due impartiality was unreasonable.

In terms of comparing how different legal systems address similar issues of political law, the key notions to retain here are the independence of broadcasters in exercising their judgments on programming and the unwillingness of the courts to interfere with such decisions.

As events unfolded, the leaders' debate that had been discussed was not held. In the general election of May 1, 1997, the SNP won 6 seats, three more than its 1992 results.

---

[146] *Ibid.*, p. 5.
[147] *Grieve v. Sir Alec Douglas Hume*, 1965 S.C. 315 at 318.

§ 5.9.10[148]
Perot et al. v. Federal Election Commission
United States Court of Appeals, District of Columbia Circuit
October 11, 1996
97 F.3d 553 (D.C. Cir., 1996)

Advanced democracies often face similar issues and controversies in the cause of governance. It is therefore perhaps not coincidental that similar resolutions are developed, while noting the local particularities of different legal systems. Thus, the matter of whether third party candidates in the United States presidential election of 1996 possessed sufficient capacity to win and should therefore be included in the campaign debates of the most serious candidates, from among whom a head of government was likely to emerge, was dealt with in a fashion rather similar to that of inclusion of second string candidates for the office of Prime Minister in the Canadian general election of 1993.

In the 1996 American election campaign, Bill Clinton stood for the Democratic Party and Bob Dole for the Republican Party. These candidates were invited by the Commission on Presidential Debates (CPD) to engage in a series of televised debates, to start on October 6, 1996. Ross Perot, the candidate of the Reform Party, who had participated in the 1992 debate between George Bush and Bill Clinton, was not included. He and Dr. John Hagelin, the candidate of the Natural Law Party, both applied first to the Federal Election Commission (FEC) and then on September 23 and 13 respectively to the U.S. District Court for the District of Columbia. They sought an injunction to prevent the FEC and the CPD from excluding them from the debates. The Green Party filed an *amicus curiae* brief and the Rainbow Coalition sought to intervene but was not allowed to.

This court, as was true in several of the Canadian cases dating from 1993, referred to the exigencies of the case and in particular to the brevity of time between the institution of the actions and the start of the debates. This was the primary reason why the District Court

---

[148] International comparison.

issued a bench opinion, which, although no more than a transcription of the judge's words, was well reasoned and complete.[149]

The ruling applied all the criteria required for the issue of a preliminary injunction: likelihood of success on the merits, irreparable injury, balance of equities and the public interest. It weighed these factors on the determination of debate selection criteria to be applied by the CPD and found that both the Ross and Hagelin applications for injunction were to be denied and the FEC and CPD motions to dismiss were to be granted.

The court's historical perspective and realization of the significance of television in presidential campaigning was most perceptive.

> While recognizing that the debate medium through the TV and the exposure is not only important but probably vital and essential in today's world of electronic communication, vastly different than referred to earlier in the Lincoln-Douglas debates, where it was a room perhaps of this size that the debates occurred in or outdoors with a group of people, today to really meaningfully communicate, it is, I would believe most will agree, essential that the candidates have access to TV.[150]

The court laid emphasis on the ground that in a trial on the merits, the applicants had substantial barriers to the likelihood of success. Nevertheless, it did seem to express some sympathy with their position.

> The Court recognizes the frustration and perhaps this, I think, admitted by the defendants perhaps unfairness in the process that does not allow all those who consider themselves legitimate candidates for our most important office in the country to fully participate, but I believe the complaint should be with Congress and the statutory framework established for the FEC to operate and that this carefully crafted statute and the regulations promulgated by the FEC under their authority and expertise are not easily challenged.[151]

The court even concluded its judgment by speculating that perhaps in the future, a different debate system may be established so that

---

[149] *Hagelin et al v. Federal Election Commission et al*; Civil Action 96-2132 and *Perot et al v. Federal Election Commission et al*; Civil Action 96-2196. Bench ruling of the Hon. Thomas F. Hogan, United States District Judge; October 1, 1996; not reported.

[150] Judgment of the District Court, pp. 7-8.

[151] *Ibid.*, p. 9

debates may become more open and accessible to those who should be heard by the American public in a debate circumstance. Clearly, while the court felt bound to apply the legal norms required, its sympathy was for a more inclusive or egalitarian regime of debates. In attempting to explain this view, the court drew a somewhat clumsy and rather inaccurate analogy to what it thought was the British system, and possibly, by extrapolation, the Canadian one.

The appeal was heard by the D.C. Circuit Court of Appeal only two days after the lower court judgment and it was decided on October 4. Realizing the importance of the matter in terms of the influence of the judgment on the debates, the campaign and on American political life, this court was meticulous in its analysis, taking until October 11 to issue its decision in writing.

The foundation upon which the legal recognition of presidential debates was established was a 1976 regulation issued by the FEC, which expressed the Commission's

> ...view that "nonpartisan debates are designed to educate and inform voters rather than to influence the nomination or election of a particular candidate."[152]

The core of the matter was to determine who was to organize these debates and what criteria was that organizing body to use in issuing invitations to participate. Until 1987, debates had been sponsored and structured by the League of Women Voters. In preparation for the 1988 presidential election, the CPD took over the function with a mandate from the FEC.

> The CPD, relying on its pronounced criteria, and the recommendation of an advisory committee consisting primarily of political scientists, based its decision to exclude other candidates on the grounds that no other candidates have a "realistic chance of winning" the 1996 election.
>
> . . .
>
> The CPD had concluded that the historical prominence of Democratic and Republican nominees warranted an invitation to the respective nominees of the two major parties in 1996. With respect to "non-major party candidates," the CPD announced criteria by which it could identify those

---

[152] 97 F.3d 553 at 556 (D.C. Cir., 1996).

who had "a realistic (i.e., more than theoretical) chance of being elected." These criteria included evidence of national organization (such as placement on the ballot in enough states to have a mathematical chance of obtaining an electoral college majority), signs of national newsworthiness (as evidenced, for example, by the professional opinions of the Washington bureau chiefs of major newspapers, news magazines, and broadcast networks), and indicators of public enthusiasm (as, for instance, reflected in public opinion polls). On September 17, 1996, the CPD issued a press release indicating its conclusion that no candidate other than President Clinton or Senator Dole had a realistic chance of being elected, and that, therefore, only those candidates and their vice-presidential running mates, would be invited to participate in the debates.[153]

The addition of this case to the collective wisdom of political law on electoral debates is the best definition of the concept of "realistic chance of winning" or winability for short. The court also accepted the argument that the criteria the CPD had developed to appraise various candidates' winability was objective, rather than subjective.

It was on the basis that the CPD had applied the concept of winability to Perot and Hagelin that the case turned. Hagelin's appeal was dismissed on grounds of jurisdiction. Perot's argument was more subtle: he pleaded that in making the CPD responsible for the debates, the FEC had subdelegated a power which Congress had vested with the agency in order to administer a statute, here the *Federal Election Campaign Act*.[154] The court rejected that argument and remanded the case to the District Court for dismissal without prejudice to Perot's claim.

> In the case before me, however, the FEC has not delegated any authority to the CPD. It has issued a regulation permitting eligible non-profit organizations to stage candidate debates, provided that they employ "pre-established objective criteria" to determine who may participate. Rather than mandating a single set of "objective criteria" all staging organizations must follow, the FEC gave the individual organizations leeway to decide what specific criteria to use. 60 Fed. Reg. 64,262 (1995). One might view this as a "delegation," because the organization must use their discretion to formulate objective criteria they think will conform with the agency's definition of that term. But in that respect, virtually any regulation of a private party could be described as a "delegation"

---

[153] *Ibid.* at 556-557.
[154] 2 U.S.C. § 431 *et seq.* (1994).

of authority, since the party must normally exercise some discretion in interpreting what actions it must take to comply.[155]

---

§ 5.9.11[156]
Arkansas Educational Television Commission v. Forbes
United States Supreme Court; May 18, 1998
140 L.Ed.2d 875 (1998)

The U.S. Supreme Court added depth to the debate on whether there exists a right for candidates to participate in broadcast debates leading up to an election, by splitting a decision on a 6-3 basis. The majority decided that no such right can be claimed, but the case provides further insight into the matter because the minority opinion was based on well-principled reasons and most credible factual grounds.

In the 1992 general election, Forbes, who had been a "perennial candidate" in previous electoral contests, was an independent candidate for the 3rd Congressional District of Arkansas. The Arkansas Educational Television Commission (AETC) organized a candidates' debate for that district, for broadcasting, but it denied Forbes permission to participate. On October 19, 1992, before the date of the election in which he was eventually to lose, Forbes sued the AETC, seeking an injunction, declaratory relief and damages. The U.S. District Court denied the claims on the ground that Forbes' exclusion was not influenced by political pressure on the AETC's disagreement with his views. The Court of Appeals for the Eighth Circuit reversed, holding that the televised debate on a publicly mandated and funded network was a public forum to which all candidates had a right of access, and that political viability was not a valid ground on which the broadcaster could exclude a candidate.

The ruling of the Supreme Court comprised a division about the manner in which decisions relating to participation in such debates should and could be made, which revealed a deep ideological cleavage on the role of principled decision-making in politics. The court started off with a fully realistic appraisal of the importance televised debates have come to play in election campaigns.

---

[155] *Supra* note 152 at 559-560 (D.C. Cir., 1996).
[156] International comparison.

...in our tradition, candidate debates are of exceptional significance in the electoral process. "[I]t is of particular importance that candidates have the opportunity to make their views known so that the electorate may intelligently evaluate the candidates' personal qualities and their positions on vital public issues before choosing among them on election day." *CBS, Inc. v. FCC*, 453 U.S. 367, 396 (1981) (internal quotation marks omitted). Deliberation on the positions and qualifications of candidates is integral to our system of government, and electoral speech may have its most profound and widespread impact when it is disseminated through televised debates. A majority of the population cites television as its primary source of election information, and debates are regarded as the "only occasion during a campaign when the attention of a large portion of the American public is focused on the election, as well as the only campaign information format which potentially offers sufficient time to explore issues and policies in depth in a neutral forum." Congressional Research Service, Campaign Debates in Presidential General Elections, summ. (June 15, 1993).[157]

The majority view was based primarily on an analysis of the application of the *First Amendment to the United States Constitution* [freedom of speech] to the modern practice of broadcasting candidates' debates and it concluded that Forbes' exclusion was consistent with that Amendment. The reasoning underlying this conclusion was that while the importance of debates could not be contested, when they are held in state-mandated broadcasting undertakings, they do not constitute a public forum but, rather, one subject to the proprietary rights of the broadcaster. It was in this context that the AETC had lawfully reserved eligibility and made individual determinations as to who could participate in the program, which the court characterized as a vehicle for the expression of political views. In a seemingly overreaching attempt to justify this argument, the court went so far as to state that opening the airwaves to all candidates would lessen the free speech protection afforded them because of the logistical problems and the consequential reduction in the time available to each candidate.

Without much factual analysis, the court accepted the plea that Forbes' exclusion was motivated by journalistic, not political, factors and consented to designating the decision as being based on objective criteria.

---

[157] 140 L.Ed.2d 875 at 885 (1998).

In this case, the jury found Forbes' exclusion was not based on "objections or opposition to his views."

...Forbes was excluded because (1) "the Arkansas voters did not consider him a serious candidate," (2) "the news organizations also did not consider him a serious candidate;" (3) "the Associated Press and a national election result reporting service did not plan to run his name in results on election night;" (4) Forbes "apparently had little, if any, financial support, failing to report campaign finances to the Secretary of State's office or to the Federal Election Commission;" and (5) "there [was] no 'Forbes for Congress' campaign headquarters other than his house."

. . .

There is no substance to Forbes' suggestion that he was excluded because his views were unpopular or out of the mainstream. His own objective lack of support, not his platform, was the criterion.[158]

The majority's overall justification was that the decision to exclude Forbes was a reasonable viewpoint-oriented exercise of journalistic discretion, made in good faith. There is reason to doubt the wisdom of this ruling and the minority on the bench did just that most eloquently.

The dissent was motivated principally by the argument that the AETC's decision to exclude Forbes from the debate was of a standardless character. The AETC failed to define the contours of the debate forum and its decision, in the eyes of the minority, was therefore entirely subjective and *ad hoc*. There were no written criteria, nor in fact, defined criteria of any kind, apart from vague impressions and opinions, to guide the discretion of the AETC's staff. Their judgment about Forbes' viability or newsworthiness was therefore subjective.

The importance of avoiding arbitrary or viewpoint-based exclusions from political debates militates strongly in favor of requiring the controlling state agency to use (and adhere to) pre-established, objective criteria to determine who among qualified candidates may participate. When the demand for speaking facilities exceeds supply, the State must "ration or allocate the scarce resources on some acceptable neutral principle." *Rosenberger*, 515 U.S., at 835. A constitutional duty to use objective standards -*i.e.*, "neutral principles"–for determining whether and when

[158] *Ibid.* at 890.

to adjust a debate format would impose only a modest requirement that would fall far short of a duty to grant every multiple-party request.[159]

Beyond the fact that the dissenting justices considered the AETC's decision inappropriately motivated, they objected, on the facts, to the reality that the broadcaster's decision that Forbes was not serious may have been wrong. Indeed, the analysis of the results of the voting in Forbes' earlier attempts at being elected and at the 1992 results showed that the AETC's decision to exclude Forbes "from the debate may have determined the outcome of the election in the Third District."[160]

It is interesting that not even the dissenters directly confront the merit of the concept of "political viability," nor its use by broadcasters. They restrict themselves to the misuse of the concept in this particular instance. Citing from one of the earlier judgments in the case, they say that:

> ...the staff's appraisal of "political viability" was "so subjective, so arguable, so susceptible of variation in individual opinion, as to provide no secure basis for the exercise of governmental power consistent with the *First Amendment*." Forbes v. Arkansas Educational Television Communication Network Foundation, 93 F.3d 497, 505 (CA8 1996).[161]

Given the extremely high political stakes involved, namely the potential for such a decision to make or break a campaign, the litigation issues relating to debates, and other uses of television in campaigning, is sure to continue.

See also *Becker v. Federal Election Commission*, 230 F.3d 381 (1st Cir., 2000) and *Buchanan v. Federal Election Commission*, 112 F. Supp.2d 58 (D.D.C., 2000).

---

[159] *Ibid.* at 897.
[160] *Ibid.* at 891-2.
[161] *Ibid.* at 892.

5.10 ISSUE: PUBLIC OPINION POLLING

See *Thomson Newspapers Co. v. Canada (Attorney General)*,[162] [1998] 1 S.C.R. 877 (S.C.C.).

---

§ 5.10.1
Polling and the Indian General Election of 1999
Supreme Court of India; September 8 and 14, 1999
limited information available

In preparation for the 12th all-India general election to be held in February 1998, the Electoral Commission of India issued an Order on January 20, 1998, supplemented on February 19, 1998.[163] By this instrument, it forbade publication, publicization or dissemination, in any manner and by any print or electronic media, of any opinion poll conducted at any time from the first day of polling at the general elections until the closing of polls in all States and Union Territories. A ban of similar nature and extent was imposed on exit polls for the same period. In respect of allowed opinion polls and exit polls, the organizations conducting them were required to indicate the sample size, the details of methodology followed, as well as other pertinent information. The Order also indicated that these guidelines were to apply *mutatis mutandis* to all future elections to Parliament and State Legislatures.

The winner of the 1998 general election was the Hindu Nationalist BJP Party under the leadership of Prime Minister Atal Bihari Vajpayee. On April 17, 1999, the BJP was defeated on a matter of confidence by one vote. As the Congress Party failed to get the majority necessary to form a government, the 13th general elections were decreed for the period of September 5 - October 3, 1999. The 1998 Order came into effect for this election also, to last from September 3 to October 3.[164]

---

[162] Cross-reference to § 2.4.5.
[163] Order No. ECI/MCS/98/01.
[164] Order No. ECI/MCS/OP-EP/99, dated August 20, 1999.

In a decision reported by the BBC on September 8, 1999,[165] the Supreme Court of India upheld the ban against a broadcaster entitled Jain TV. In a separate action, the Electoral Commission of India sought the Supreme Court's approval of the ban. Seemingly based on a consensus among the political parties, the Commission argued in favour of a 48 hour period at the end of the campaign, during which voters should not be disturbed in the process of weighing the merits and demerits of political parties and contesting candidates in the election fray. It also reasoned that last minute polls were likely to influence voters and influence the results of an election. What the Commission was trying to protect was the unbiased exercise of the franchise by electors, in particular in a system where polling was staggered over a period, with different regions voting at different times.

The Commission felt the need to take this action because the *Times of India* newspaper had been publishing opinion papers almost daily, arguing that a statute enacted by Parliament and banning polls within 48 hours of voting was binding, but an Order from the Electoral Commission was not. Other media outlets had also defied parts of the ban and the matter had gone to a local court in Madras. The Supreme Court refused the Electoral Commission's petition. It said that:

> It is absolutely wrong on the part of the Electoral Commission to come to the court seeking execution of the guidelines issued by it...Even if we direct the government, how is the government going to enforce it?...In our view, the petition has no merit.[166]

The Supreme Court based its brief ruling, apparently, on the Election Commission's inability to enforce an instrument that was merely cast as a "guideline." It did note, however, that there was a larger issue of whether poll-related guidelines would violate the fundamental rights of freedom of speech and expression. The court also remarked on the Election Commission's admission that any domestic guideline could not be binding on foreign media, such as the BBC or CNN.

---

[165] http://news.bbc.co.uk/1/hi/world/south_asia/442077.stm, last consulted July 27, 2004.
[166] http://news.bbc.co.uk/1/hi/world/south_asia/446824.stm, last consulted July 27, 2004.

Based on its desire to abide by the law, on September 14, 1998, the Commission issued a new Order, withdrawing the ban on opinion and exit polls. This judgment resulted in what was termed an opening of the floodgates of polling. Even serious Canadian newspapers reported the results of exit polls showing the BJP with a slight lead over Congress.[167]

Subsequently, the Chief Commissioner made public comments in the direction that it would be beneficial for the Supreme Court to discuss this matter again, dispassionately. To date, that reconsideration has not occurred.

5.11 ISSUE: INTEGRITY OF VOTING

See *R. v. Bryan*, 2003 BCPC 39 (B.C. Prov. Ct.) and 233 D.L.R. (4th) 745 (B.C. S.C.), leave to appeal allowed 2004 BCCA 140 (B.C. C.A. [In Chambers]) and *Leat v. Thunder Bay (City)* (2004), [2004] O.J. No. 108 (Ont. S.C.J.).

5.12 ISSUE: SUSPENDING ELECTIONS

§ 5.12.1
Francis v. Mohawk Council of Akwesasne
Federal Court of Canada – Trial Division; April 22, 1993
(1993), 62 F.T.R. 314

Considering that in democratic regimes, elections are the public events which are the most intensely political in nature and which produce clearly political results, extremely rare circumstances amounting to a risk of illegality and even lack of legitimacy must arise in order for the courts to interfere with their being held at appointed times.

Akwesasne is a Mohawk community near Cornwall, Ontario, which is singular in the sense that it straddles the jurisdictional boundaries

---

[167] "Exit polls in India show BJP coalition winning," Rahul Bed, *The Gazette*, September 16, 1999, p. B-42.

of Québec, Ontario and New York. For several years prior to this litigation, the community's governance had been deadlocked by disagreements between an almost evenly split majority and minority on the Council. The Council had passed a number of resolutions in attempts to enable itself to deal with the substantial problems of the community, but to no avail. On March 4, 1993, it decided to hold an election on April 24, 1993. In the intervening period, the minority faction presented to the Federal Court of Canada - Trial Division a motion for an interim order prohibiting the holding of the election scheduled for April 24.

It was the approach of the court, in dealing with the motion with the same methodology as if it were an application for injunction, that enabled it to delve into not only the legal argumentation but also into the political circumstances of the case and to render its decision on the basis of both types of considerations. The court held, first, that there was before it a serious issue as to whether the resolution at the root of the dispute was proper authority for the holding of the proposed election. Even more to the point, the court looked at the balance of convenience and the prospects of irreparable harm to either side in the dispute. In this process, it determined that the public interest, that is the needs and best interests of the Akwesasne community, were paramount. The state of the Council, already chaotic, should not be exacerbated.

The court perceived the danger of its interference in a validly called election, but given the patent chaos on the Council, it leaned toward preservation of the status quo until the propriety of that election was determined.

> It seems to me that while the present state of affairs is obviously less than desirable, the one which would result if elections were held and were subsequently declared invalid, would be immeasurably worse.[168]

Further, the disruption resulting from voiding democratically, that is politically, valid elections would be greater than the prevention of these elections until their legality was confirmed.

It was on those two bases, namely the existing political chaos in the community as well as the desire to avoid further inflaming the situ-

---

[168] (1993), 62 F.T.R. 314 at 317.

ation, even at the price of preventing the immediate resolution of the impasse, that the court granted the interim order until the matter of the legitimacy of the election was determined. The use by the court of the expression "legitimacy" rather than "legality" in the dispositive sentence clearly indicated that in its view, the underlying conditions for the holding of the elections were that there be both a legal basis and political order.

§ 5.12.2[169]
Queremos Eligir et al v. Consejo Nacional Electoral
Supreme Court of Justice of Venezuela; May 25, 2000
limited information available

In circumstances of political instability, administrative and legal problems can reinforce each other to the extent that, in some extraordinary cases, events of a determinative nature in political law, such as a suspension and postponement of nation-wide electoral events, can occur. In February 1999, in Venezuela, Colonel Hugo Chavez, the paratroop officer who had led an unsuccessful coup d'état in 1992, came into office as President. What followed his election was a political upheaval which also bordered on legal chaos.

In December 1999, a new Constitution was adopted which required that many public positions be "re-legitimized." For this purpose, "mega-elections," that is a single event to elect public officials for some 6,200 positions throughout the country, were scheduled for May 28, 2000. There were 36,000 candidates for these offices. A computerized voting system had been set up for the National Election Council by an American company called Election Systems and Software. Because of the volume of data required to run the event, the system broke down. The American consultants attempted to retool the system but some Venezuelans, including President Chavez, levelled accusations of wilful destabilization against them. The murky topic of Venezuelan-American relations were thus in the background. Comparisons were also drawn between Venezuela and Peru, where the rule of law was also in difficulty, with presidential elections also scheduled to take place on May 28, but where the opposition candidate had withdrawn, leaving Alberto Fujimori as the sole contender.

---

[169] International comparison.

Thus, while in Venezuela the present litigants were urging for the vote to proceed, in Peru, the opposition was militating for a postponement of the election as being tainted.

Several Venezuelan citizens, acting personally and as officers of an organization entitled "We Want to Vote," and a "Committee of Relatives of the Victims of the Events of February-March 1989" (the yet previous civil disturbance, in which Col. Chavez had had a role), brought a petition to the Constitutional Chamber of the Supreme Court of Justice. On the basis of the evidence given by the Director of Automation of the National Electoral Council, the court determined that the conditions which would guarantee on absolute terms the viability and transparency of the election of May 28, 2000, did not exist. There was insufficient information in the system about all the candidates seeking to be elected. Consequently, there was a risk of violating the rights inscribed in the Constitution for an informed vote. On these findings, the court suspended the vote set for May 28; it sent the matter back to the National Legislative Commission, the interim legislature, for it to fix a new date for voting; it ordered that all campaigning be stopped and it ordered that an investigation be started to see if criminal responsibility was involved.

President Chavez was not unduly perturbed, likening the situation to a rained-out baseball game. It was thought that the delay might favour his opponent, Francisco Aria Cardenas. The elections were rescheduled for June 25. Chavez's party, the Patriotic Pole, won 59% of the vote at the national level. Foreign observers thought the balloting to have been honest, even though domestically, a large number of complaints of irregularities were made. Chavez's term of office is for six years.

5.13 ISSUE: POLITICAL INTERFERENCE IN ELECTION RESULTS

§ 5.13.1
Report of the (Monnin) Commission of Inquiry into Allegations of Infractions of the Election Act and the Election Finances Act during the 1995 Manitoba General Election
March 29, 1999

On March 21, 1995, writs were issued for an election and on April 25, 1995, the resulting general election was held in the Province of Manitoba. The incumbent, Progressive Conservative Premier Gary Filmon, was returned to office for a third term. In the period following this election, in response to the rumours that the Progressive Conservative Party (PC) had engaged in activity designed to split the vote of its major opponent, the New Democratic Party (NDP), the Office of the Chief Electoral Officer investigated the matter. The rumours nevertheless persisted and in October 1998, Mr. Justice Alfred Monnin of the Manitoba Court of Appeal was appointed as sole commissioner of an inquiry into the role played by the Manitoba Progressive Conservative Party and by various individuals associated with it to engage in political or partisan interference with the electoral system to influence the outcome of the vote. While the report of such an inquiry is, in legal terms, different from the judgment of a court, in the method of analysis of political law, it can be assimilated to a judgment, it is conclusive and not susceptible to challenge, it produces clear and definitive results. It is therefore, in its own way, binding and creative of rules.

Judge Monnin's findings were not light hearted. He set the tone by qualifying the evidence put before him.

> As a trial judge I conducted a number of trials. As an appellate court judge I read many thousands of pages of transcript in a variety of cases: criminal, civil, family, etc. In all my years on the Bench I never encountered as many liars in one proceeding as I did during this inquiry. Many witnesses admitted to me that they had lied to the investigator from Elections Manitoba and/or to my two investigators, and/or to Commis-

sion counsel. Additionally, there were witnesses whose evidence before me I cannot accept.[170]

These were the comments made most notorious by media reporting. They gave the report a condemnatory tone vis-à-vis the individuals investigated.

The core of Monnin's finding is that there existed

> ...a scheme and its purpose was to siphon votes away from the NDP candidates in [the] three ridings in order to help the PC candidates, but the plot did not succeed. Some call it vote-rigging, vote splitting or fracturing the vote. Whatever you choose to call it—in my opinion, it is improper.[171]

In his opinion, this scheme was in contravention of those provisions of *The Elections Act* which relate to inducing candidacies or reframing them.[172] The technique used to induce vote-splitting candidacy was the offer of cash and of the use of a car. The scheme to politically interfere in the election process and thereby in the election results was then followed by a cover-up, which Monnin held to be in violation of several provisions of *The Elections Finances Act*.

The report was categorical in absolving the PC Party itself of any infraction or of vicarious liability. It emphasized that the Party is a collective body in which only some individuals were in breach of the law. Given the secrecy exercised by the individuals who concocted the scheme, it even said that the Party had been harmed by their actions. Premier Filmon was insulated from blame and suffered neither legal nor political blame.

The report is most instructive in its analysis of the arrogant nature of extreme political partisanship animated by what it calls an "I know better" attitude. It provided examples of several party officials who exhibited such political attitudes toward both their opponents and the media and who, having based their actions and words on such uncompromising states of mind, were forced to make restrictions of statements. Perhaps the Commissioner's most telling comment in this regard about the supremacy of law and legal norms over politics and

---

[170] Report, pp. 16-17.
[171] *Ibid.* pp. 36-37.
[172] *The Elections Act*, R.S.M. 1987, c. E-30, s. 145(1)(2).

partisanship was that "In the British style parliamentary democracy under which we operate more restraint and respect should be shown."[173] It was primarily on this ground that Monnin made what we should take to be his most important recommendation, namely that all registered political parties prepare a Code of Ethics, which they should then adhere to. Should they not adopt such codes by December 31, 2001, he recommended that a standard code be made compulsory by legislation.

Even in a democracy, or perhaps particularly in a democratic environment, public authorities must be ever vigilant to safeguard the rule of law and the proper role of law in the maintenance of the integrity of the electoral system. The alternative is not acceptable, as

> A vote-rigging plot constitutes an unconscionable debasement of the citizen's right to vote. To reduce the voting rights of individuals is a violation of our democratic system.[174]

Monnin very appropriately linked this legal basis of the democratic principle of free and unfettered choice to public morality:

> Political mores have reached a dangerous low when one party member can actively support his party, but sees nothing objectionable in helping to finance and organize the candidate of a second party in order to harm a third party.[175]

See also *Socialist Party of Serbia v. Belgrade Election Commission*,[176] First Municipal Court in Belgrade, November 23, 1996; *Bush v. Gore*, 148 L.Ed.2d 388 (2001); *Bush v. Palm Beach County Canv. Bd.*, 148 L.Ed.2d 366 (2001); *Report of the National Commission on Federal Election Reform*,[177] July 31, 2001.

---

[173] *Supra* note 170, pp. 55-56.
[174] *Ibid.*, p. 13.
[175] *Ibid.*, p. 11.
[176] International comparison.
[177] Cross-reference to § 2.4.

PARTIES, CAMPAIGNING AND POLITICAL PROMISES

6.1 GENERAL PRINCIPLES

See Volume I, Chapter 6.

6.2 ISSUE: LEGAL PERSONALITY, STATUS AND POWERS OF POLITICAL PARTIES

§ 6.2.1
Young & Rubicam Ltd. v. Progressive Conservative Party of Canada
Québec Superior Court; March 22, 1971
not reported; file 803-933

In the political system which has evolved in Canada over the last two centuries, the primary vehicle for the organized and collective expression of political opinion, belief and vision is the political party. It is also thus in all other democratic countries around the world. Indeed, parties have become indispensable to the proper functioning of the democratic process and governance. In order to be able to carry out their tasks and mandates in the public environment, parties must be organized not only in the political sense. They must also, in some way, be recognized by the legal system. They must acquire a legal capacity to function. It is a matter of great interest to political law to determine what is the legal aspect, that is the legal personality of political parties. That legal personality will be crucial in determining the parties' capacity, what they may or may not do, and what their obligations and rights are. In short, the legal personality of parties will determine the extent of their capacity to play a role in the conduct of public affairs.

The view of Québec law on the issue of the legal personality of political parties was determined in a civil action for repayment of a debt. In relation to the federal general election of June 25, 1968, the Progressive Conservative Party of Canada ordered about $230,000 worth of publicity and advertising for the Québec portion of its campaign from the advertising agency of Young & Rubicam. Over the course of the following two years, the Party paid only $159,000, leaving roughly $70,000 unpaid. The agency sued to recover this amount. In a motion to have the action dismissed, the Party's principal argument was that it had no civil personality within the meaning of the *Québec Civil Code*[1] and therefore "no legal capacity to defend or to institute any action at law."[2] Subsidiarily, it also alleged that it had no assets. Given the Progressive Conservatives' lack of electoral success at that time, especially in Québec, this part of the defence was plausible.

The court agreed with the Party's defence, stating unequivocally that a political party does not have civil personality. The sense of the judgment was that political parties did not have legal personality pursuant to the *Civil Code*, which embodied the general private law of Québec.

Given the systems of private law co-existing within Canada, such as that based in the *Québec Civil Code*, did not recognize a legal personality in political parties, what then is the legal framework applicable to them? The formation of political parties is subject only to the terms of the *Canadian Charter of Rights and Freedoms*, in particular to the protection of freedom of association guaranteed pursuant to subsection 2(d) of the *Charter*. Thus, any group of individuals may associate and assemble peacefully to express their political beliefs and opinions. Beyond that, parties may gain the legal recognition required to operate in the political arena on the basis of specific public law statutes dealing with them as components of the electoral system.

As the federal level, in order for a party to fully participate in the electoral process and to benefit from the advantages of recognition,

---

[1] At the time of this action, the formal title of the code was the *Civil Code of Lower Canada*, as it was first enacted in 1856, prior to Confederation.

[2] Motion of Defendant/Petitioner, February 17, 1971, p. 1.

fiscal assistance and priority in ability to have its message broadcast, a party must acquire "registered status."[3] In Québec, the designation is different but the process is essentially similar. Parties must be "authorized" by the Chief Electoral Officer in order to function with full recognition of the law.[4] At both levels, the sanctioning of parties' full participation in the public life of the jurisdiction is based solely on the submission of required items of information to the respective authorities and the demonstration by each party of its ability to function seriously in the political sphere. This seriousness is judged on the basis of the ability of each party to field a minimum number of candidates.

The recognized status which is provided pursuant to various election laws contrasts sharply with the corporate legal personality engendered by incorporation under companies legislation. While a company endowed with legal personality may, in most instances, carry on any type of business and may engage in or defend actions at law, political parties are limited in the range of their activities to the cluster of activities related to the competition for office and power.

---

§ 6.2.2[5]
McKinney v. Liberal Party of Canada
Ontario High Court of Justice; September 16, 1987
(1987), 43 D.L.R. (4th) 706

By the course of the third year after the federal general election of 1984, McKinney, an elector living in the electoral district of St.-Catherines, Ontario, seemed to be displeased with the way Canadian politics was being conducted. He attributed his dissatisfaction to the system of discipline to which political parties adhered in Parliament, particularly in respect of requiring their parliamentary caucus members to vote along party lines. To resolve what he perceived as an impediment to better conduct of public affairs, he presented an application for interim and permanent injunctions to restrain political parties "from exercising party discipline over their members in Parliament to the extent that the exercise of that discipline might prevent the members from voting according to their consciences or the wishes

---

[3] *Canada Elections Act*, R.S.C. 1985, c. E-2, as amended, s. 24 *et seq.*
[4] *Election Act*, R.S.Q. 1977, c. E-3.3 as amended, s. 47 *et seq.*
[5] Cross-reference to § 1.14.3.

of their constituents."[6] The sole defendant named in the law report is the Liberal Party of Canada. Considering, however, that at the time of this case, the only other parties represented in the House of Commons were the New Democratic Party and the Progressive Conservative Party, it is safe to surmise that these were the other defendants. Together, the three parties defended the case by making a motion to strike out the action.

This case was not only a direct follow-up to that of Young & Rubicam. It cited the earlier case as the only precedent in which the issue of the legal personality of political parties had been examined to date. Two differences render comparison of the cases worthwhile. While the Young & Rubicam judgment gave the perspective of Québec Civil Law on the matter, this one provided the response of Anglo-Canadian Common Law on the same point. Moreover, whereas the earlier decision was made prior to the adoption of the *Canadian Charter of Rights and Freedoms* in 1982, this ruling was made in the *Charter* era; yet the outcome is essentially the same.

Thankfully for the development of political law, the judge in this instance did not resort to a reasoning involving justiciability. He did not just state that the matter was political and therefore out of the realm of the law. He analyzed the procedural and substantive matters pleaded before him and gave a well reasoned decision.

Despite the court's patent interest in the matter being argued, the action was dismissed on several grounds. Following the reasoning in Young & Rubicam, and converting it into Common Law concepts, the court declared that political parties had no legal existence in Common Law, but that they were unincorporated associations. A comparison was made to trade unions. The court was aware of the reference to political parties in the *Canada Elections Act* and accorded that unincorporated associations may be affected by being named in legislation. It held, however, that the *Canada Elections Act* was essentially regulatory. Thus, that Act could render a political party a person only for the purposes of prosecution under the legislation.

This part of the finding was primarily significant in that it recognized in respect of political parties the same absence of legal personality in the view of both Canada's legal systems and therefore achieved for

---

6 (1987), 43 D.L.R. (4th) 706 at 707-708.

them the same status in all parts of the country. The immediate result of this part of the judgment was that political parties could have no legal capacity to be sued, as McKinney had attempted.

Notwithstanding the absence of legal personality, parties are recognized not only in the *Canada Elections Act*, but also pursuant to the *Parliament of Canada Act* and certain legal instruments relating to broadcasting. In its 1992 report, the (Lortie) Royal Commission on Electoral Reform and Party Financing recommended a number of improvements in the registration process for parties but did not suggest attributing to them any greater legal personality.[7]

The application in this case was also based, in part, on the *Charter*. McKinney claimed,

> that his right to freedom of thought, belief, opinion and expression is violated by the defendants in that by exercising party discipline they prevent the plaintiff's elected representative from voting in Parliament according to his conscience or the wishes of his constituents.[8]

The court rejected this argument on the basis of the absence of demonstrated links between the applicant in his capacity as an elector and the parties being sued. It found no evidence either that McKinney had voted for the Member of Parliament representing him or that McKinney's choice in the previous election had been based on the expectation that there would be free voting in the House of Commons. Moreover, the court also saw no evidence that the applicant's Member of Parliament "pressed by one of the defendants, has voted in any way that would prejudice the plaintiff's right to freedom of thought, belief, opinion or expression."[9]

The court then engaged in some historical retrospective. While it did not use the expression "constitutional convention" in describing party discipline, the ruling can be said to assimilate party discipline to that category of rules binding on the political legal system.

> Party discipline has a long tradition in our Westminster style parliamentary system, a system recognized in the preamble to the *British North*

---

[7] Royal Commission on Electoral Reform and Party Finance, Report, February, 1992; Volume I, pp. 238-245.

[8] *Supra* note 6 at 711.

[9] *Ibid.*

America Act, 1867 (now the *Constitution Act,* 1867 (U.K., 30 & 31 Vict.), c. 3). It is unlikely that the system can be upset on the basis of the facts pleaded here.[10]

See also *Parti Union Nationale c. Côté,* [1989] R.J.Q. 2502 (Que. S.C.) at 2505-250.

---

§ 6.2.3
R. v. Andrews
Supreme Court of Canada; December 13, 1990
[1990] 3 S.C.R. 870

This case was a prosecution under subsection 319(2) of the *Criminal Code,* which deals with the wilful promotion of hatred. The significant element of the case is that the two accused, Andrews and Smith, were respectively the leader and the secretary of the Nationalist Party of Canada, a white nationalist political organization but a party not registered pursuant to the *Canada Elections Act.* Both were also members of the party's central committee, its directing organization. The focus of discussion by the courts in this case was whether the charging provision in the *Criminal Code* infringed the section 2(b) freedom of expression and section 11(d) presumption of innocence rights of the accused under the *Charter.* The Ontario Court of Appeal held that the *Criminal Code* provision was not contrary to the *Charter.* On a panel of seven justices of the Supreme Court of Canada, four justices, for whom the Chief Justice held the pen, concluded that section 319(2) did infringe section 2(b) of the *Charter* but also that it was saved by section 1.

From the perspective of political law, the principal issues were the manner of prosecuting the officials of a party for serious *Criminal Code* offences, and the rationale for carrying out the prosecution against the officials rather than against the party itself. Andrews and Smith had undertaken their activities in their capacities as members of the Nationalist Party's leadership. They had published and distributed their hate propaganda through the "Nationalist Reporter," a party publication. There was no doubt that these were criminal activities and that they were carried out by the officials in the name of the party and in furtherance of the party's political aims. The dilemma arises

---

10 *Ibid.*

from the fact that these political activities of a criminal nature must entail legal consequences even though political parties do not have legal personality. Thus, in this instance, the criminal proceedings were undertaken against the party leaders concerned, rather than against the political party on behalf of which the offences were committed, because only the individuals were held to be able to form the intent required to commit the criminal acts. The interest of the Crown in such cases is to stop the criminal activity and punish the perpetrators. As it was impossible to indict the political party in order to stop the party officials, the practice of the Crown in such cases is to indict the officials. The lesson of this case is that the absence of legal personality attaching to political parties will not deter the Crown from stopping political activity that is criminal in nature. Stated in another way, propagators of hate messages will not be able to hide behind the facade of a political party to avoid conviction.

---

§ 6.2.4
R. v. Barrow
Supreme Court of Canada; December 17, 1987
[1987] 2 S.C.R. 694

This case adds a dimension to the notion of the personality of political parties, in that it looks at the matter from the perspective of the *Criminal Code*. Barrow was the chairman of a finance committee constituted in 1968 for the purpose of raising funds for the Nova Scotia Liberal Association. From October 1970 until 1978, while the Liberal Party formed the Government of Nova Scotia, many of the sums collected by this finance committee were, according to the prosecution, not legitimate political contributions, but rather payments made by businesses to ensure their continuous relationship with the Government. The charge consequently brought against Barrow and two others was that of criminal conspiracy or, in common parlance, influence peddling.

In the course of the proceedings, one of the questions of law which arose was whether the Nova Scotia Liberal Association was a "person" in the sense of section 110(1)(d) of the *Criminal Code*, upon which the indictment was based. On the panel of the Supreme Court of Canada, only a dissenting justice considered this issue, but the Chief

Justice, writing for the majority, specifically indicated that he agreed with the dissenters on this point.

The Supreme Court upheld the ruling of the Nova Scotia Court of Appeal on this point and determined the matter by examining the definition of "person" in section 2 of the *Criminal Code*. That definition included societies, a concept which clearly encompassed the existence and activities of the party. Even more significant than the strict statutory interpretation of this point was what the court interpreted, quite correctly, as the purpose of the legislation. The goal of the *Criminal Code* was to not exempt political parties from conspiratorial activities and here, the Liberal Party was clearly the recipient of the benefits of the criminal activity.

> There was evidence that the Nova Scotia Liberal Association was an active organization, hiring staff, renting premises, receiving and disbursing funds and carrying on general political activities. To hold that the association was not a "person", and therefore not within the purview of s. 110(1)(*d*) of the Criminal Code, would lead to an absurd result and frustrate the obvious purpose of the enactment. I would reject this ground of appeal.[11]

---

§ 6.2.5
Canada (Human Rights Commission) v. Taylor
Supreme Court of Canada; December 13, 1990
(1990), 75 D.L.R. (4th) 577

The specific principle arising from this case which is of interest in political law is that political parties are subject to legal norms and standards, even when the political opinions they hold or the goals they wish to propagate are in conflict with or contradictory to the legal norms. Conversely, an individual cannot hide under the cover of a political party to engage in illegal activity that would not be allowed for him alone.

Taylor was the leader of the Western Guard Party, an anti-Semitic group whose goals were clearly inconsistent with the goals of the Canadian legal system and with the focus of political thought in this country. The party had made available in the Toronto area hate mes-

---

[11] [1987] 2 S.C.R. 694 at 740.

sages disseminated by telephone. Having been ordered by the Canadian Human Rights Commission to withdraw these messages, the party continued them. Thereupon, the Commission applied to the Federal Court to find both Taylor and the party in contempt. The entire case, comprising the issue of freedom of expression under the *Charter* and the contempt order, went to the Supreme Court of Canada.

The majority of that court not only affirmed vigorously the duty of a political party to obey the law, but did so by repeating verbatim the relevant portions of the Federal Court of Appeal ruling on the point, signalling its determination on the matter.

> The narrow *ratio* of Mahoney J.'s reasons, however, hinged on the fact that the appellants had not sought to challenge the legitimacy of the Tribunal order directly, but rather had simply treated the order as void and attacked it collaterally in a contempt proceeding. Adopting the rationale of O'Leary J. in *Canada Metal Co. v. Canadian Broadcasting Corp. (No. 2)* (1974), 48 D.L.R. (3d) 641 at p. 669, 19 C.C.C. (2d) 218, 4. O.R. (2d) 585 (H.C.), he stated (at p. 582):
>
> > The duty of a person bound by an order of a court is to obey that order while it remains in force regardless of how flawed he may consider it or how flawed it may, in fact, be. Public order demands that it be negated by due process of the law, not by disobedience.
> >
> > . . .
>
> I am in complete accord with the reasoning of Mahoney J. in the Federal Court of Appeal, and therefore conclude that the appellants' submission regarding a reasonable apprehension of bias is without merit.[12]

Clearly, the status of a party as a participant in the political arena, or the activity of promoting a political point of view, does not allow derogation from the primacy of law. Even though in the execution of their public activities political parties hold political goals to be paramount, legal principles and instruments are not only binding on them but take precedence over the political principles, such as party platforms, which they set for themselves.

In this case, the Supreme Court provided another extremely useful service in showing how freedom of expression and in particular the

---

[12] (1990), 75 D.L.R. (4th) 577 at 611 d-g.

limits to that *Charter* guarantee apply to the political discourse of parties.

> ...it is important that something be said regarding both the values supporting the free expression guarantee and the nature of the expression at stake in this appeal. In the abstract, it is unarguable that freedom of expression is held especially dear in a free and democratic society, this *Charter* guarantee providing the bedrock for the discovery of truth and consensus in all facets of human life, though perhaps most especially in the political arena. Additionally, this freedom allows individuals to direct and shape their personal development, thereby promoting the respect for individual dignity and autonomy that is crucial to (among other things) a meaningful operation of the democratic process.

> ...in balancing interests within s. 1 one cannot ignore the setting in which the s. 2(*b*) freedom is raised. It is not enough to simply balance or reconcile those interests promoted by a government objective with abstract panegyrics to the value of open expression. Rather a contextual approach to s. 1 demands an appreciation of the extent to which a restriction of the activity at issue on the facts of the particular case debilitates or compromises the principles underlying the broad guarantee of freedom of expression.[13]

See also *Figueroa v. Canada (Attorney General)*,[14] 227 D.L.R. (4th) 1 (S.C.C.); *Canadian Reform Conservative Alliance Party Portage-Lisgar Constituency Assn. v. Harms* (2003), 231 D.L.R. (4th) 214 (Man. C.A.) and *Bowman v. United Kingdom*[15] (1998), 26 E.H.R.R. 1.

---

§ 6.2.6[16]
Sharples v. O'Shea and Anor.
Supreme Court of Queensland; August 18, 1998
(1999), Q.S.C. 190

This case arose out of the procedures which the One Nation political party engaged in, during the run-up to the state elections of June 13, 1998, in Queensland. Notwithstanding local circumstances, the prin-

---

[13] *Ibid.* at 595 g-596 b.
[14] Cross-reference to § 5.7.A.
[15] International comparison.
[16] International comparison.

ciples illustrated here are just as applicable at the federal and provincial levels throughout Canada, as they are in other democracies.

Beyond their internal formation and constitution as a basis of existence to which the law accords legal personality, there is a more formal status for political parties which are registered. In this case,

> A "registrable political party" is an organisation whose object or activity, or one of whose objects or activities, is the promotion of the election to the Legislative Assembly of a candidate or candidates endorsed by it or by a body or organisation of which it forms a part, that either is a parliamentary party or has at least 500 members who are electors and is established on the basis of a written constitution (however described) that sets out the aims of the party.[17]

More generally, registration is an elevated status under the election law of the applicable jurisdiction, a conferring of legislative recognition beyond the ambit of a mere voluntary association, as this court phrased it. Registration results in some additional responsibilities in respect of reporting and publicity and it entails many advantages in the fields of tax relief, recognition on the ballot and political broadcasting.

The essence of this case is the fulfilment of the requirements necessary for registration and the fact that non-fulfilment of those requirements in a fraudulent manner, through misrepresentation, leads to deregistration.

One Nation came to prominence at the federal level in Australia, on a platform of restricting immigration, in particular from Asia, ending aid to the Aboriginal communities, and providing support to the domestic manufacturing, small business and rural sectors. It was one of a number of radical right parties which flowered in the 1990's. Sharples was recruited to be one of its candidates in the 1998 Queensland elections where the party took nearly a quarter of the votes. On the evening before the vote, Sharples was told by party officials that contrary to earlier agreements, the party would not be refunding any of his election expenses.

---

[17] (1999), Q.S.C. 190 at p. 10.

In its first phase, this action was to recover those expenses. It became, however, an application to review the One Nation party's registration. In the course of trial, it was discovered that the One Nation comprised not only the party itself but also an incorporated movement to support the party leader, Pauline Hanson, which was masquerading as the party and the related corporate entities. Prior to the election, in order to obtain registered status the party would have had to have at least 500 members. Party officials knowingly misled election officials to register the party, while it was the support movement that had the requisite membership. There were also complicated financial transactions among the entities collectively known as One Nation.

While the court held that the results of its decision would not retroactively affect the outcome of the 1998 election, as that could only have been done by petition to the Court of Disputed Returns, it did cancel One Nation's registered status. Its motive was based on equating registered status with truthful disclosure of party structure and organization to the electorate.

> There is a public interest that the registration of political parties should not be obtained on the basis of such crucial information known by those providing it to be incorrect. The integrity of the electoral process would otherwise be undermined and any inconvenience of the result is not a reason in this case for withholding relief.[18]

Beyond the grounds set out above, on which One Nation was in fact deregistered, this case comprises another interesting issue bearing on the purposes of establishing a political party and on the political promises it makes in consequence of those purposes. Queensland's *Election Act* requires that one of the aims of a political party be the promotion of the election of its candidates to the Legislative Assembly of that State. The plaintiff raised as one of the grounds of the application the motive that One Nation did not fulfil this requirement. The court related extensive evidence on this matter, to the effect that the party's documents for registration were based on seeking the election of candidates to federal office and when notified of this inconsistency, the constitution of the Queensland One Nation party was apparently changed at the whim of the leader, without following the proper constitutional amendment procedure. This was held not to be a de-

---

[18] *Ibid.,* p. 41 at para 139.

ciding factor in the case, but the judge left no doubt of his suspicion that in this regard, as with membership, One Nation acted fraudulently vis-à-vis the electorate and deserved to lose its registered status.

This matter surfaced again in 2002, when Pauline Hanson was prosecuted in Brisbane, on charges of fraudulently registering One Nation in Queensland and fraudulently claiming $330,000 in electoral funding in the 1997 election campaign.[19] She was convicted and sentenced to three years' imprisonment. After eleven weeks, she was freed when her conviction was overturned by the Queensland Court of Appeal.

6.3 ISSUE: PUBLIC AND PROPRIETARY RIGHTS IN A POLITICAL DESIGNATION

§ 6.3.1
Polsinelli v. Marzilli
Ontario High Court of Justice; August 20, 1987
(1987), 60 O.R. (2d) 713[20]

As part of its campaign for the Ontario provincial election of September 10, 1987, the Ontario Liberal Party nominated Polsinelli as its official candidate in the electoral district of Yorkview, in Metropolitan Toronto. Marzilli, who had earlier been expelled from the same party, declared himself a candidate in the same riding under the appropriate provision of the *Election Act*. In the absence of a nomination from a political party, Marzilli was in fact an independent candidate. For political purposes, however, he entitled himself "A Trudeau Liberal." Polsinelli sought an injunction to prevent Marzilli from using this designation on his signs and in his other campaign material on the ground that this could confuse voters as to who was the candidate officially endorsed by the Liberal Party.

The court acknowledged that in the electoral district, there was evidence of significant confusion as to which candidate was the one put

---

[19] http://news.bbc.co.uk/hi/english/world/asia-pacific/newsid_1943000/1943329.stm, last consulted July 27, 2004.
[20] Affirmed (1987), 61 O.R. (2d) 799 (Ont. Div. Ct.).

forward by the party. Nevertheless, it refused to issue the requested injunction for several reasons.

Most importantly, the court held that a claim based on the tort of passing off could not succeed, as that notion applied only in the fields of commercial trade or property.

> There is, in this context, no property in a political name. No person and no organization owns or has any monopoly on any political idea, or any designation of political belief. This is particularly so when the designation, which is impugned, is intended to convey information about the political beliefs of the person using the designation. The respondent, by referring to himself as "A Trudeau Liberal", obviously seeks to identify himself with a particular political tradition and with particular issues, and to indicate that he ascribes to and stands for particular issues and particular types of political beliefs.[21]

The court used the expression "the market-place of political ideas,"[22] thereby perhaps unadvisedly blending commercial and political notions. However, it was unequivocal in the distinction it made between property rights and commercial disputes on one hand, areas in which names that amounted to labels could receive protection, and the world of politics in the other, where politicians used names, designations and symbols of political belief and as descriptions of their respective political persuasion at election time. In this latter sphere, it emphasized that designations could receive no protection.

Similarly, the court refused relief on the basis of its reading of the applicable statutes. It found that while the legislature had prohibited the use of confusing names in regard to financial registration, it could have done the same with respect to posters and other campaign literature, but chose not to.

Lastly, the court refused the injunction on the basis of the judiciary's traditional aversion to inject itself into an election campaign. It thus left Marzilli to describe "his personal political credo in whatever words and in whatever manner he chooses."[23] Consequently, Polsinelli's claim for damages was also denied because despite the con-

---

[21] (1987), 60 O.R. (2d) 713 at 717 a, b, affirmed (1987), 61 O.R. (2d) 799 (Ont. Div. Ct.).
[22] *Ibid.* at 715 b.
[23] *Ibid.* at 717 f.

fusion, Marzilli was not holding himself out as the official Liberal candidate.

---

§ 6.3.2
Reform Party of Canada v. Reform Party of Manitoba
Manitoba Court of Appeal; October 18, 1991
(1991), 39 C.P.R. (3d) 440

This case resulted indirectly from the decision of the Reform Party of Canada, a federal political formation, to concentrate its activities in the federal political arena only. In the Province of Manitoba, the party did not take sufficient steps to prevent the use of its name by any other political party. Thus, in the spring of 1991, the Confederation of Regions (COR) Party of Manitoba applied to the Chief Electoral Officer of the province to allow it to take on the name of Reform Party of Manitoba, doubtless in the hope of greater electoral success. Pursuant to the provisions of the *Elections Finances Act*, the Chief Electoral Officer authorized the name change.

The Reform Party of Canada applied to have the name change set aside. It argued that the existence of two distinct political parties bearing similar names, the first or legal entity under federal legislation and the second registered under provincial legislation, these parties working toward different purposes, could result in confusion to the public. The court rejected this argument without explanation. It also denied the federal Reform Party's application for a declaration that the provincial Reform Party was liable of the common law tort of "passing off," as well as the federal party's application for a permanent injunction prohibiting use of the phrase "Reform Party" in the name of the provincial party. In so doing, the only clue the court gave for its refusal was to indicate that the application was based upon "an inadequate factual foundation."[24]

This decision allows us to draw two lessons. Within a federation such as Canada, a political party must take adequate measures to protect its designation from encroachment in any forum other than that in which it operates. The Reform Party of Canada seems to have realized this, as in the Province of Ontario, it took the necessary steps to reserve

---

[24] (1991), 39 C.P.R. (3d) 440 at 442.

the "Reform" name with the Election Finances Commission.[25] At the federal level alone, the *Canada Elections Act* prevents adoption by any political party seeking registration of a name that is likely to be confused with that of any other political party.[26] The ruling also allows us to believe that if an applicant does provide the court with an adequate factual foundation, that is if a party presents solid evidence of confusion caused in the electorate by the use of similar party names, that of the first party may be protected.

---

§ 6.3.3
Mangat v. Canada (Attorney General)
British Columbia Supreme Court
filed September 30, 1993; file no. A933715, Vancouver Registry
abandoned

Section 81 of the *Canada Elections Act* sets out the requirements candidates must fulfil in the process of being nominated, in the course of an election campaign. One of these requirements is that relating to the manner in which the candidate is to be labelled on the ballot. If the candidate is endorsed by a party, the name of that party may appear under the candidate's name; otherwise, the candidate can be listed as an "independent," or without a designation. This rule entails a conflict between unfettered freedom of political expression and measures designed to avoid confusion in the electoral system. The measure also shows, however, the statutory protection granted to political designations and the support of the State for the identification of recognized political parties.

In the course of the campaign for Canada's 35th federal general election, Mangat sought to be designed on the ballot for the electoral district of Vancouver South as an "Independent Liberal." One of the parties competing for that seat was the Liberal Party of Canada, which endorsed another individual as its candidate. When the Chief Electoral Officer of Canada refused to accept the designation Mangat would have wished and the returning officer in the electoral district corrected the nomination paper by striking out the qualifier "Liberal," Mangat took legal action.

---

[25] "Ontario Party can't use Reform name, panel rules," *Globe and Mail*, July 28, 1994, p. A-5.
[26] *Canada Elections Act*, R.S.C. 1985, c. E-2, s. 24(4).

This case is interesting in the purely political law sense because in seeking a declaration that the relevant portion of section 81 was contrary to section 2(b) [freedom of expression] of the *Charter*, and in applying for an order directing that the Vancouver South ballot refer to him as an "Independent Liberal," Mangat based his argumentation on the indication of his political philosophy and its proper expression.

> The description "Independent Liberal" best expresses my political philosophy and best conveys to voters the principles underlying my candidacy. Compelling me to employ either the description "Independent" or no description at all deprives me of the ability enjoyed by candidates endorsed by registered parties to convey to voters my political philosophy at the most critical phase of the election process—the ballot. The description "Independent" lumps my candidacy together with those of other candidates who hold varying political philosophies, all different from my own.[27]

In his Petitioner's Outline of Argument before the Supreme Court of British Columbia, Mangat elaborated.

> Expressing a candidate's political interest or affiliation on an election ballot constitutes an attempt to convey meaning, and is both compatible with an election ballot's principal function and promotive of one of the most cherished purposes underlying the constitutional guarantee of free expression: participation in political decision-making. The restriction contained in s. 81(1)(i) thus amounts to a violation of s. 2(b) of the *Charter*.[28]

Another merit of this case is that the Petitioner relied on a very thorough and detailed line of constitutional law argumentation, attacking the subject provision in the light of section 2 of the *Charter* and attempting to show how it was not saved by section 1. Mangat even referred to provincial and territorial statutes which, allegedly, would have allowed the description he sought.

In response, the Attorney General made a motion to strike the petition for all the usual reasons in that type of case, namely that it disclosed no reasonable cause of action, that it was unnecessary and vexatious and that it constituted an abuse of the process of the court. The Crown had some practical arguments relating to the fact that the action was

[27] Affidavit of Jaswant Singh Mangat, filed September 30, 1993, para. 5.
[28] Petitioner's Outline of Argument, filed October 8, 1993, para. 4.

filed in the course of the election campaign and that the cost of print-ing ballots was in issue. Its major reasoning, however, was expert evidence to be delivered by one of Canada's foremost political sci-entists with expertise in election matters, Professor Janet Hiebert. She was proposing to testify on the primacy of political parties in the Canadian electoral and parliamentary systems and even more to the point, on the fact that enactments such as the *Canada Elections Act* permit political parties to determine their sole delegate in each elec-toral district. The necessary consequence of this is the legislated pro-tection of political party designations and the reluctance of the State to allow their unauthorized use, even if that could amount to a limi-tation on freedom of the expression of one's political philosophy.

The court was seized of the arguments but never got the opportunity to determine their validity, whether on the grounds of freedom of expression, conveying one's political affiliation and philosophy, or participation in social and political decision-making. Once the elec-tion was held on October 25, 1993, Mangat allowed the case to stay dormant, effectively abandoning it.

---

§ 6.3.4
Desrosiers v. Gough
Alberta Court of Queen's Bench; September 30, 1998
(1998), 235 A.R. 127[29]

Desrosiers was a genuinely independent candidate in the election organized by the Government of Alberta for 1998, to designate Sen-ators-in-Waiting, in accordance with the *Senatorial Selection Act*.[30] Gough, a long-time member of the Reform Party, sought the nomi-nation of his party to be one of two Reform candidates for the same election. He obtained the required signatures for an eventual candi-dacy at a Reform Party convention. He came third among these seek-ing the party's backing and when he was not made a Reform candi-date, he registered with Alberta's Chief Electoral Officer as an "Independent" candidate. A Reform Party representative paid the required deposit for him. The party's motive in this scenario was to

---

[29] Additional reasons at (1998), 235 A.R. 127 at 130 (Alta. Q.B.).
[30] S.A. 1989, c. S-11.5.

ensure that an election be held for the two Senator-in-Waiting positions, rather than a less politically viable acclamation.

On the basis of these facts, Desrosiers applied for an order to have Gough disqualified from running as an Independent, or alternatively to have him identified on the ballot as a candidate of the Reform Party of Alberta. Desrosiers quite rightly pointed out that the ballot, as prepared, was misleading. He alleged that, in fact, Gough was being promoted by the Reform Party and was a candidate for that party in all but designation. The court acknowledged the facts submitted to it and yet denied the application.

> It seems clear that Gough was a Reformer when he filed nomination papers as an Independent and for the sake of argument I will assume that he still is a Reformer and will remain so right up to the time of the election.

> Nevertheless, I find no legal impediment to his candidacy as an Independent by virtue of that fact.[31]

The court based its startling conclusions on several questionable grounds. It found that Gough was not an "official candidate" of the Reform Party even though it admitted that the *Senatorial Selection Act* did not speak of such a category of candidates. It also reasoned that there was no legislative requirement on the Chief Electoral Officer to look behind the declarations in the nomination papers in search of a candidate's *bona fides*, nor any that would justify that course. Most importantly, the court put in the balance the right of an individual to present a candidacy in contrast to the right of electors to be informed and not to be misled. It gave greater weight to the former; in a bizarre phrasing, the court presented this as being in accord with the applicant's own argumentation.

A solid case can be made for the proposition that the court misinterpreted the law in this matter. Moreover, this judgment is dangerous because it enables candidates and parties to circumvent the intent of the legislation that candidacies be properly and honestly labelled. It is not an exaggeration to state that this is a rare example of the legal system appearing powerless in the face of partisan political trickery.

---

[31] (1998), 235 A.R. 127 at 130, paras. 16, 17, additional reasons at (1998), 235 A.R. 127 at 130 (Alta. Q.B.).

Progressive Conservative Party of Canada v. Canadian Reform Conservative Alliance and Reform Party of Canada, Federal Court of Canada – Trial Division, filed May 2, 2000, file T-795-00, discontinued; *Progressive Conservative Party of Canada v. Canadian Reform Conservative Alliance and Canada Alliance Fund*, Federal Court of Canada – Trial Division, filed May 23, 2000, file T-911-00, discontinued and *Registration of "Bloc Québécois" Name.*

6.4 ISSUE: SELECTION OF PARTY LEADERSHIP AND CANDIDATES

6.4.A—PARTY LEADERSHIP

---

§ 6.4.A.1
Rowley et al. v. Hewison et al.
Ontario Court (General Division); filed November 6, 1991
file no. 3872991U; settled

In examining the relationship between law and politics, one of the hallmarks is the reliance of political figures on legal methods and instruments to resolve disputes which are based on differences of political outlook. Such reliance is an implicit acknowledgement of the role of law as an independent and neutral arbiter of even political disputes; even further, it is an acceptance of the reality that in a democratic system the pursuit of politics can only be carried on within a legal framework. Such admissions can become most interesting when the point at issue in both political and legal terms is control of a political party and hence the setting of its direction.

Within Canada, the dismantling of the Communist regimes in Central and Eastern Europe and the decline of the Communist Party of the Soviet Union contributed to a fairly rapid and thorough reorientation of the policies of the Communist Party of Canada (CPC). The Party's Central Convention met in October 1990, less than a year after the fall of the Berlin Wall, and adopted the following new policies:

(a) support for the New Democratic Party at both the provincial and federal levels and emphasizing the Party's extraparliamentary role;

(b) the Policy of "left unity" in which the Party decided to foster improved ties with other socialists, trade union organizations and social movements in working for change instead of continuing to have the party pursue the role of political "vanguard;" and

(c) the decision to transform the role of the Canadian Tribune, the Party newspaper, so that it could be used specifically as a bridge to foster improved ties with others in the socialist movement.[32]

This change of direction may have reflected what the party leaders saw as a turning point in the history of Communism and may also have been influenced by the CPC's lack of electoral success.

Rowley, a member of the Ontario Executive of the CPC and of the Party's Central Committee, opposed these changes, was voted down, but refused to accept the Party's new stance. On August 28, 1991, under disputed circumstances, she was expelled from both her executive functions and her party membership. On October 18, 1991, the Central Committee confirmed the expulsion. Rowley had obtained a court order enabling her to make representations on the issue concerning her; she was not successful.

By this action, taken shortly thereafter, Rowley claimed $9,700,000 in damages as well as injunctions to prevent the dispersion of the Party's funds and the alienation of its real estate holdings, to have herself and other expelled members of the Ontario Executive reinstituted, and to restore the status quo ante the decisions of the Central Committee meeting of October 18, 1991, by which the Ontario Executive was dissolved. This action was never adjudicated as the factions of the CPC eventually settled their dispute and the Party has, ever since, continued to struggle to survive in what has become a political wilderness for it.

The noteworthy aspect of this case from the perspective of political law is the nature of the argumentation and the incorporation of political and ideological doctrines into the competing legal rationales.

Rowley's case was based on the motive that the expulsions were intended "to expel from the CPC those who differ with them in a scheme to fundamentally alter the name, objects and purposes of the

---

[32] *Rowley v. Hewison*; Statement of Defence dated December 17, 1991, para. 12.

organization, contrary to the Constitution."[33] In response, Hewison, the General Secretary of the Party, relied on a legal transposition of Leninist ideology.

> 10. By the Constitution of the CPC all Party members agree to carry out the Party policies and follow the directions and leadership of the Central Committee and the Central Executive Committee between Conventions. This principle "democratic centralism" has always been strictly enforced within the CPC. Its purpose is to allow full debate of difficult issues at the Central Convention and, after policies have been adopted, to allow the party leadership and all members the ability to campaign (sic) politically for the party goals without the embarrassment of factionalism or party dissension.[34]

The pleadings present further interest in their blending of legal and political instruments. Rowley alleges that all CPC members are bound by the Party Constitution, and even extends that reasoning to claim that the Constitution forms a contractual relationship between the members. She also bases her plea on a combination of the *Election Act 1984*, the *Election Finances Act* of 1986, the Constitution of the CPC, the Programme of the CPC and the resolutions of the Party's 28th Convention; the latter three are strictly political documents to which legal character is attempted to be ascribed. Rowley seeks to frame her case on lack of due process in applying all these instruments together. One part of this argumentation which may have been important but the full impact of which will never be known in the absence of a judgment is Rowley's allusion to the fact that leading members of the Communist Party of Québec were present at the October 18, 1991, meeting, despite the formal disassociation of that Party from the CPC.

Hewison's defence to these allegations is a general assertion that the expulsions were done both lawfully and in conformity with the Party Constitution; here we see the same blending of legal and political instruments. With respect to justification of the CPC's actions, Hewison contends that those expelled showed "an openly hostile attitude toward the Party"[35] and indeed that they conspired to breach the Constitution, all of which "constitute a calculated disregard of the rights of the members of the CPC under the Constitution to have the

---

[33] Statement of Claim, para. 19.
[34] Statement of Defence, para. 10.
[35] *Ibid.*, para. 11.

Central Committee carry out policy and organize Party activities in accordance with Central Convention policy."[36]

Perusal of these pleadings illustrates the extent to which legal rights and ideological positions are intertwined in subjective perceptions of disputes involving different types of rules.

---

§ 6.4.A.2
Cameron v. Boyle
Ontario Court (General Division); April 15, 1994
1994 CarswellOnt 2820
-and-
National Party of Canada v. Stephenson (1996)
Federal Court of Canada – Trial Division; December 4, 1996
124 F.T.R. 108[37]

Political position and status is highly coveted, even in circumstances where success may mean no more than leadership of a formation entirely rejected by the electorate. In certain extreme cases, such as here, vying factions feel the need to resort to the courts, that is to the use of law, rather than politics, to achieve their desired position. This kind of exercise can only reinforce the role of law as the impartial arbiter of political conflicts.

The National Party was founded in November 1992 as the renewed embodiment of the previously well established tradition of English Canadian nationalism. Its principal proponent was the publisher of the *Canadian Encyclopedia*, Mel Hurtig, who had flirted with politics before. In the 1993 federal general election, the National Party ran 171 candidates but was not successful in any electoral district. Nonetheless, it hoped to continue functioning and planned a convention for June 1994 to end the interim phase of its activity related to the 35th general election. The first of these cases arose out of procedural difficulties surrounding the composition of the party's National Board of Directors. At a meeting held on February 19, 1994, the Board chose to meet in private and to exclude some officers who believed on the basis of having been elected in the regions that they ought to have been allowed to participate in the deliberations. One of those

---

[36] Statement of Defence and Counterclaim, para. 37.
[37] Affirmed (1998), 154 F.T.R. 160 (note) (Fed. C.A.).

excluded took action. The Ontario Court (General Division) stated the case most vividly:

> The National Party of Canada is being rent by two factions, to use Lord Durham's phrase, "warring in the bosom of a single" party.
>
> As a result the party is blessed with two leaders, two presidents and two boards of directors. Politics may be the art of the possible. Nevertheless, such a bifurcated party must be a daunting challenge to the most dedicated of members.[38]

Besides this characterizing of the circumstances, however, this court's only contribution was to state vigorously that it would leave the determination of the party's actual leadership for the party to settle; it was concerned only with natural justice and procedure. It held that the expulsion of some executive members was not valid because of the absence of notice regarding their ability to participate, and that took the directors' actions out of the realm of natural justice. The court did not, however, vitiate the positions of those otherwise validly at the helm of the party.

Shortly thereafter, Hurtig resigned as leader, the party became irretrievably beset by internal dissent and the factions continued to fight by using the courts and the law. Their fight over control of the party and its remaining funds came to be phrased in terms of the party registration provisions of the *Canada Elections Act*. On December 14, 1995, the Chief Electoral Officer registered Reid as interim leader of the National Party, thereby refusing the similar application of Whetung. The latter applied to the Federal Court for judicial review.

The Trial Division dismissed the application. It noted approvingly that the Chief Electoral Officer had acted in strict conformity with section 26 of the *Canada Elections Act*, which deals with variations in registration resulting from a change in the leadership of a registered party. The key to the decision was that in taking the documents provided to him and using the information from them, the Chief Electoral Officer was said to have declined to become involved in the internal affairs of the party.

---

[38] *Cameron v. Boyle*; Reasons for Judgment; p. 1.

The *Canada Elections Act* does not give Elections Canada a mandate to regulate the activities of political parties beyond the collection of information to maintain the Registry of Political Parties up to date.[39]

Thus, whether Whetung had acted in conformity to the party constitution in dismissing certain members of the party's governing council, or not, was immaterial to the Chief Electoral Officer's appreciation of the documents sent to him to advise of the change in party leadership. The function of the electoral administration was not to favour one candidate or the other but merely to take the evidence and verify it and give each faction a reasonable opportunity to be heard. The Federal Court of Appeal confirmed this ruling.[40]

The holdings by the Federal Court were, by themselves, a clear indication of the legalities of the National Party's leadership struggle. Despite that, the struggle over this issue resulted in a number of other court cases in various provincial jurisdictions.[41]

---

§ 6.4.A.3
Cavilla v. Canada (Chief Electoral Officer)
Federal Court of Canada – Trial Division; September 21, 1993
(1993), 76 F.T.R. 77

Cavilla was the Leader of the Christian Heritage Party of Canada when, at one of its meetings, that party chose a new leader. On the basis of the report submitted by the new leader, the Chief Electoral Officer registered the change of leadership. Cavilla sued, claiming that the outgoing leader, rather than the incoming one, should have signed the report. The court denied judicial review. Its proper interpretation of the relevant provision of the *Canada Elections Act*[42] was that the need for the report arose out of the change of leadership and

---

[39] (1996), 124 F.T.R. 108 at 110, affirmed (1998), 154 F.T.R. 160 (note) (Fed. C.A.).

[40] (1998), 154 F.T.R. 160 (note) (Fed. C.A.). The judgment is so short that it is unlikely to be reported.

[41] *Whetung v. Boyle et al*, British Columbia Supreme Court, Victoria Registry, Court file 94-4041; *Ranta et al v. Alain et al*, British Columbia Supreme Court, Vancouver Registry, Court file C950096; *Godlewski v. McGurk and Whetung*, Ontario Court (General Division) Toronto Registry, court file 95-CO-81; *National Party of Canada v. Stephenson* (1996), 124 F.T.R. 108 (Fed. T.D.), affirmed (1998), 154 F.T.R. 160 (note) (Fed. C.A.). All these cases were pending at the time of writing.

[42] R.S.C. 1985, c. E-2, s. 26, as amended.

that at the material time, as the new leader was the only leader, only he could submit the report. The court also relied on the further reason that to decide otherwise would be contrary to what it termed sensible administrative practice. Beyond the correct application of the rules of statutory interpretation, the conclusion to be drawn from this case in terms of political law is that even in the midst of a conflict between factions of a political party, the court will inquire only into the legalities of the selection of a new leader but will not intervene into the party's internal political affairs.

---

§ 6.4.A.4

Baldasaro v. Candidate Liaison Committee of the Progressive Conservative Party of Canada

Federal Court of Canada – Trial Division; January 27, 2000

file T-1566-98; not reported

Baldasaro applied for judicial review of a decision of the Progressive Conservative Party's Candidate Liaison Committee in connection with the process followed in the party's selection of Joe Clark as leader in 1998. Baldasaro would have liked to be a candidate but, pursuant to the party's rules, the Committee required genuine candidates to make a $30,000 deposit. The applicant cleverly argued that the Committee amounted to a "tribunal" in the sense of s. 18 of the *Federal Court Act* and tried to show that its dismissal of his complaint about the deposit was both contrary to the Constitution of the Progressive Conservative Party and to the *Charter*. This application was dismissed on the grounds that there was no governmental activity involved and that the actions of the party or its Committee were not authorized or exercised pursuant to a federal statute. This reaffirms the rule that the internal politics of parties are just that, and not matters of law susceptible of *Charter* review.

See also *Reform Party of the United States et al. v. Gargan et al.*, 89 F. Supp.2d 751 (W.D. Va., 2000); *Reform Party of the United States et al. v. Verney et al.*, U.S. District Court, Western District of Virginia, March 27, 2000, Case no. 6, 00CV00014/50012 and *Reform Party of the United States of America v. Hagelin et al.*, California Superior Court, County of Los Angeles, South District, September 15, 2000, Case no. NC 028469.[43]

6.4.B— CANDIDATES

§ 6.4.B.1
Li Preti v. Chrétien
Ontario Court (General Division); September 21, 1993
1993 CarswellOnt 4306
and Ontario Court (General Division); September 23, 1993
unreported; file no. 93-CQ-36709
-and-
Johnston v. Li Preti
Ontario Court (General Division); October 8 and 12, 1993
unreported; file no. 93-CQ-43281
-and-
Munro v. Canada (Attorney General)
Ontario Court (General Division); October 13, 1993
[1993] O.J. No. 2370[44]
-and-
Kelly v. Liberal Party of Canada
Ontario Court (General Division); November 28, 1994
(1994), 120 D.L.R. (4th) 746

The preparation for the 1993 federal general election within the Liberal Party of Canada gave rise to a flurry of litigation which tested the powers of the leader of a party to designate candidates for elective office and which showed whether the internal processes of political parties were required to be conducted in accordance with legal norms.

The first of this cluster of cases is that of *Li Preti v. Chrétien*, concerning the electoral district of York Centre in Metropolitan Toronto. Li Preti wanted the opportunity to contest the Liberal Party's nomination for the riding, but as early as October 1992, before then Prime Minister Mulroney took any steps toward his resignation and the lead-up to the election, Jean Chrétien, by then Leader of the Liberal Party, designated a Toronto municipal political figure, Art Eggleton, to be the

---

[43] All international comparisons.
[44] Additional reasons at (1994), 1994 CarswellOnt 3254 (Ont. Gen. Div.).

party's candidate in York Centre. First, Li Preti sought an interlocutory injunction to prevent Eggleton from being the candidate endorsed by the party. In the first of several judgments, on September
21, 1993, during the campaign, the Ontario Court (General Division)
refused to grant injunctive relief. If the relief sought was given, Eggleton would be seriously prejudiced and the Liberal Party would
not be able to run a candidate in the riding. The court did not want
to grant an injunction where it would affect not only the parties to
the case, but would also affect the public interest or the electoral
process.

On the merits, Li Preti argued that the 1992 *Constitution of the Liberal
Party* had been invalidly approved, that in consequence Ontario candidate selection rules were also invalid and that therefore Chrétien
had exceeded his authority in appointing Eggleton. He also sought
damages of $1.5 million on the ground that Chrétien had engaged in
the tort of conspiracy. The application was denied on procedural
grounds on September 23, but not entirely thrown out; the court
stayed further proceedings until the Liberal Party of Canada, the
Liberal Party of Canada (Ontario) and the riding association were
joined as parties. This never happened but Li Preti's attempts to be
given the opportunity to contest a nomination did not close.

Undaunted by his inability to force the Liberal Party by means of
court motion to enable him to contest the York Centre nomination,
Li Preti started campaigning in the electoral district as if he were the
Liberal candidate. This led to what effectively became a countersuit.
Don Johnston, then national president of the Liberal Party of Canada,
made application on September 3, 1993, for an interlocutory injunction to prevent Li Preti from representing himself as running for or
on behalf of the Liberal Party. The Party thought of Li Preti as a
member of the New Democratic Party, a late arrival in the fold, attempting to cause confusion among voters. It argued that

> 31. Following the oral judgment of Mr. Justice Borins on September 21,
> 1993 dismissing Li Preti's injunction motion, Li Preti and his campaign
> workers have increased their mischievous attempts to disrupt Eggleton's
> campaign by trying to confuse the voters of York Centre as to who is the
> official candidate of the Liberal Party of Canada. In particular, and
> among other things:

. . .

32. Li Preti's campaign materials and the statements made by Li Preti and his campaign workers are causing confusion among electors as to whether Eggleton or Li Preti is the official candidate of the Liberal Party of Canada in York Centre.[45]

The Liberal Party's pleading was that these actions amounted to "injurious falsehood and passing off."

On October 8, 1993, the court ordered Li Preti to cover up the word "Liberal" on his campaign signs and on October 12, it issued the interlocutory injunction which the Party had applied for, restraining Li Preti from representing that he is the endorsed candidate of the Liberal Party of Canada and representing that he is either a "Liberal" or a "Liberal candidate." He was also required to remove from public display or cancel the portions of all campaign signs that include the words "Liberal Ind.," meaning Liberal Independent.

It is an interesting point of law, although not strictly relevant to the outcome, that in order to address this application for injunction to the court on behalf of the Liberal Party, Johnston had to seek a Representation Order pursuant to the *Rules of Civil Procedure of Ontario* which deal with the representation of a class of persons such as an unincorporated association.

The third case, entitled *Munro v. Canada*, bears interest not only because of the political issue of addresses, but also due to the litigants' references to democracy in their pleadings, to their serious attempt to extend the meaning of law through this case and the consequential legalization of politics. The Munro here is the former Member of Parliament from Hamilton, Ontario, and Minister of Indian and Northern Affairs in the Government of Prime Minister Trudeau. At the time of these proceedings, he was considered a political liability to the Liberal Party because of the fact that he was being prosecuted for allegedly having committed fraud in relation to the 1984 leadership campaign within the party. Together with the Li Preti of the previous case and another would-be candidate, Albert Kergl, Munro brought suit when he was unable to receive the Liberal Party's endorsement.

---

[45] Factum of the plaintiffs (moving parties), paras. 31 and 32.

> Liberal Leader Jean Chretien says several "bad apples" with dubious backgrounds were rejected from his 1993 team of candidates.
>
> "It's the standard of a leader to want to have the respect of the Canadian people, because integrity is a very important element," Mr. Chretien explained. "You know, it's not very pleasant when we see on the national news that members of Parliament are in front of the court for abuse of public trust. And we have had great numbers since 1984. No wonder why the people distrust politicians."
>
> The quality of "Team Liberal" is one of the major themes that the Liberals are stressing as they make their pre-election pitch before the expected fall vote.[46]

On March 26, 1993, the nomination meeting to select the Liberal candidate for the electoral district of Lincoln, Ontario, was held. Munro's position was that on that occasion, irregularities occurred which effectively prevented him from being nominated. On July 27, 1993, Munro, Li Preti and Kergl filed a Notice of Application and Notice of Constitutional Question in the Ontario Court (General Division), based on an extremely cleverly crafted set of arguments. They argued that the Liberal Party had violated sections 3 [voting rights] and 15 [equality] of the *Canadian Charter of Rights and Freedoms*. In their view, the Liberal Party was part of the democratic process and the absence of an internal review mechanism within it was contrary to democracy.

> The Liberal Party of Canada has adopted rules for the selection of candidates which permit the Party Leader to appoint candidates to stand for election to the House of Commons and which permit no internal or judicial review of such decisions, which permit the campaign chair for Ontario to call nomination meetings with a retroactive cut off date for memberships and which permit no internal review or judicial review of instances where abuse of power or discretion is alleged. Such powers have been exercised in a manner which is contrary to democratic practices as understood in Canada and in a manner which is not demonstrably justifiable in a free and democratic society.
>
> The above mentioned powers granted to the Party Leader and in the Province of Ontario to the Campaign Chair are broad powers with no enumerated guidelines for their exercise. As such they are subject to

---

[46] "Bad apples can't run, Chretien says," Susan Delacourt and Craig McInnes, *Globe and Mail*, Toronto, July 29, 1993.

being misused and the Applicants claim they have been used in a number of instances in a manner which is contrary to democratic principles and practices. There are no internal mechanisms within the Party whereby the exercise of such broad powers may be evaluated to determine if they conform with democratic norms or whereby abuse of powers by officials in the Party hierarchy can be challenged and corrected.[47]

The applicants went on to invoke the *Canada Elections Act* and its failure to ensure that parties apply democratic principles in their internal processes.

> The *Canada Elections Act*, while it controls many aspects of election process, fails to ensure that the political parties, whose representatives are seeking to be qualified for membership in the House of Commons, comply with democratic principles and practices in relation to such elections.[48]

The application concludes, more generally, that the absence of legislative insurance of democratic practices supports their case.

> There is no internal mechanism which permits the party to internally review practices which are abusive, undemocratic or unfair. Further there is no review available to the Courts. There are no legislative provisions in place which ensure compliance with democratic practices and processes by political parties in relation to federal elections. This contravenes section 3 and 24(1) of the Charter.[49]

The Liberal Party brought a motion to strike out the application and the Attorney General of Canada moved that it be dismissed against him. On October 13, when the deadline for nominating candidates had already passed but still before the election, the court agreed to the motions and dismissed the application. This ruling was based first on the status at law of the Liberal Party as a voluntary association of individuals, that is, an unincorporated association. The only instruments regulating them were held to be the party constitution, by-laws and rules, but no legislation. The party could therefore not be sued in its own name.

---

[47] Notice of application and notice of constitutional question, paras. 3 and 4, pp. 3 and 4.

[48] *Ibid.*, paragraph mistakenly shown as 4 but which should have been 5, p. 4.

[49] *Ibid.*, para. 3(c), p. 5.

With respect to the *Canada Elections Act*, the court noted that it was mentioned but that the applicants had failed to seek a declaration of invalidity regarding any of its provisions. Counsel explained this as a drafting deficiency but the judge's conclusion was that the candidate selection process was simply not covered by the Act.

The court handled the invocation of the *Charter* most adroitly, rendering the decision in such a manner as to leave the heart of the matter for future litigation.

> I agree, therefore, with Ms. Jackman that making allowance for drafting deficiencies it cannot be said that it is plain and obvious that the application will fail on the ground that the selection by the LPC of its candidates for a federal election does not constitute government action within the meaning of s. 32 of the *Charter*.

> In my view, the appropriate course to follow is to dismiss the application against the LPC because it is an unincorporated association which cannot be sued in its own name and to dismiss it against the Attorney General of Canada because no relief is claimed against the Attorney General or against any entity for which he or Her Majesty is responsible. However, for the reasons which I have discussed the dismissal of the application is without prejudice to the applicants reconstituting the application in regard to the proper parties and clearly stipulating the remedies which they seek, or commencing a fresh application.[50]

The applicants reconstituted their argument later but they did meet the respondents in court early again, on the issue of costs. They argued that no costs should be awarded against them as they had advanced noble legal and public interest issues. On May 3, 1994, the Ontario Court (General Division) held against them again. Not only had the case not been properly constituted and the issue not been argued on the merits. The court also faulted them for having attempted to litigate the case in the news media by calling a press conference prior to their service of the claim. While that may have been a factor in the purely legal procedure leading to the award of costs, publicity was one of the necessary, if costly, tactics in this kind of politicized case.

---

[50] *Munro v. Canada (Attorney General)* (1993), 1993 CarswellOnt 2785 (Ont. Gen. Div.), additional reasons at (1994), 1994 CarswellOnt 3254 (Ont. Gen. Div.), pp. 7-8.

On September 22, 1993, before the court had had an opportunity to issue its judgment in the case discussed in the previous paragraphs, Munro embarked on the reconstituted case which the earlier proceedings had induced him to undertake. Here, he was together with Kelly, who had hoped to be the Liberal Party's standard bearer in the Toronto riding of Beaches-Woodbine, and Kergl. This was an application for declaratory judgment, seeking to show that the Party was in breach of section 3 [voting rights] of the *Charter*. The application was drafted more in the style of a political science treatise focusing on the role of political parties in the development of Canadian democracy, and dealing with the particular role of the Liberal Party and its close link to the Canadian State, than a traditional statement of claim. It attacked in particular the candidate selection process which the Party had resorted to in Beaches-Woodbine and in *Lincoln*.

The plaintiffs sought to have declared as contrary to the *Charter* those rules of the Liberal Party of Canada and Liberal Party of Canada (Ontario) for the selection of candidates which granted the party leader the power to appoint a candidate without any limitation that this power would be exercised in a demonstrably justifiable manner in a free and democratic society, as well as those which gave the Ontario Campaign Chair of the Party sole and unfettered discretion to fix a date for a meeting to choose a candidate. Alternatively, they asked to have declared as contrary to section 3 of the *Charter* those provisions of the *Canada Elections Act* which fail to prevent the Party from violating their rights as candidates. They also attacked the constitutional validity of section 82(1)(h) of the Act, which vested in the leader the power to determine if the name of the party shall appear beside a candidate's name.

The plaintiffs' last two alternative remedies were the boldest and most intriguing. They tried to show that the *Canada Elections Act* favoured political parties above independent candidates, thus breaching sections 3 and 15 of the *Charter*. Finally, they asked for

> An injunction, under section 24(1) of the Charter, enjoining the federal government from holding any further federal election, including by-election, until the *Canada Elections Act* is amended by Parliament or other such appropriate legislation relating to federal elections in Canada is

passed and proclaimed by Parliament to remedy the lack of effective protection of the Plaintiff's rights under section 3 of the *Charter*.[51]

The Ontario Court (General Division) decided this case on November 28, 1994, more than a year after the election, on the basis of a defence motion to stay, considering that the order for costs in the earlier action was still outstanding. Unfortunately for the settling of the substantive issues at stake and for the development of political law, the ruling was made on the issue of costs from the earlier action. The action was stayed in its entirety.

This is where the matter ended. Munro was never to be a parliamentarian again, but he was eventually exonerated of the fraud charges and, much later, compensated by the Government of Canada. The candidate selection process is still a matter internal to political parties, untouched by legal norms.

---

§ 6.4.B.2
Lortie-Hinse v. Pageau & St. Laurent
Québec Superior Court; September 7, 1993
file no. 500-05-011895-933; not reported

Canadian courts have traditionally been reticent to involve themselves in the internal functioning of political parties. This may be due to the fact that the law classifies parties as unincorporated associations and it may result from the existence for each party of a constitution which attributes duties to specified officials and provides for procedural mechanisms to achieve political goals, such as the nomination of candidates for election.

In the course of preparation for the federal general election of October 25, 1993, the Outremont riding association of the Progressive Conservative Party, in Montréal, set the date of September 9 to hold its candidate selection meeting. Lortie-Hinse filed papers with the association, seeking to become its candidate. According to the party's constitution, she should have been sent a list of the members of the association by a set deadline prior to the meeting, so that she may engage in campaigning. There was a disagreement as to the length of

---

[51] Statement of claim, para. 1(e).

the advance notice required for such a transmission and Lortie-Hinse applied to the Superior Court for an injunction to have the meeting set for a later date and for a declaration that at that meeting, the voting should be carried on according to the requirements of the party's constitution.

The court refused every part of the application. It said that it should interfere in the internal functioning of a political party only in exceptional circumstances, but did not indicate what those might be. It also stated that if there were contradictions between the party constitution and rules of procedure on the one hand, and the constitution of a riding association on the other, such discord should be resolved by the mechanisms set out in the instruments governing the party's functioning, all the more so as these allow for an internal right of appeal. In the end, Lortie-Hinse did not become the party's candidate and the party did not win the Outremont seat.

See also *Corriero v. Liberal Party of Ontario* (August 31, 2001), Doc. 01-CV-216594-CM (Ont. S.C.J.), not reported; *Galati v. McGuinty* (1999), [1999] O.J. No. 2171 (Ont. S.C.J.), affirmed (1999), 127 O.A.C. 161 (Ont. C.A.), leave to appeal refused (2001), 275 N.R. 391 (note) (S.C.C.); *Pick v. Conservative Party of Canada* (February 26, 2004), Doc. Q.B. No. 32 of 2004 (Sask. Q.B.), not reported; *VanKoughnet v. Conservative Party of Canada* (February 20, 2004), Doc. 04-CV-026769 (Ont. S.C.J.), not reported and *Hoeppner v. Manning et al.*, Manitoba Court of Queen's Bench, file No. CI 04-01-36726, in progress.

---

§ 6.4.B.3[52]
Jepson and Dyas-Elliott v. The Labour Party
Leeds Industrial Tribunal; January 8, 1996
[1996] I.R.L.R. 116

In the entire post-World War II period, the Labour Party in the United Kingdom has faced a gender gap in its attempts to be elected to government. Women have had a greater tendency to vote for the Conservatives than for Labour. In addition,

---

[52] International comparison.

Older voters tend to be more Tory; and among the old, there are more women than men. So there are proportionately more women than men among Tory voters.[53]

To circumvent this double disadvantage, in 1993, at a time when Labour had been out of government for about a decade and a half, the party introduced a positive discrimination arrangement (in Canadian terminology: affirmative action) in favour of prospective women candidates. This was meant, first, to increase the proportion of women among all of Labour's candidates. In the longer term, with Labour then preparing for the next general election, it hoped to use this as a means of redressing the chronic under-representation of women in the House of Commons, whereby, with women constituting slightly more than 50% of the population, they comprised less than 10% of the Members of Parliament.

The party's scheme was to present all women short lists for the selection of their official Parliamentary candidates in 50% of those constituencies in which a sitting Labour MP would not stand in the next general election, in those which the party thought to be the most winnable but where the sitting MP was not Labour, and in new constituencies. By applying these rules, the Labour Party effectively prevented Mr. Dyas-Elliott from being considered to carry its colours in the riding of Keighley. It similarly turned away Mr. Jepson in the riding of Regents Park and Kensington North, and in Brentford and Iselworth. Both refusals were because the applicants were men.

The two disappointed prospective candidates sued the Labour Party at the national level and the Labour Party of the three affected constituencies (in Canadian terminology: the constituency associations) before the Industrial Tribunal, asking for declarations that they had been unlawfully discriminated against on the grounds of their sex. The tribunal held their complaints to be well-founded and made the declarations sought for each of the three parallel cases. No damages were requested or awarded.

The Industrial Tribunal started by asserting that even despite its position as an inferior court, it saw its jurisdiction as attributed by Parliament as including sex discrimination matters, when these touched on the rights of individuals in an area of considerable public

___

[53] *Labour Sexual Politics* in *The Economist*, January 13, 1996, p. 54.

interest. One presumes that the expression "public interest" was used here as the term of art, referring to the welfare and benefit of the people, rather than as a synonym for their collective attention. The tribunal also emphasized that it realized the importance of the matter before it, declaring that it had been asked to determine an issue having potentially profound constitutional implications. With these preliminaries out of the way, the judgment focused, perhaps in a rather technical manner, on the application of the *Sex Discrimination Act 1975* (the Act) and on its interpretation of various provisions of that Act.

The crux of the Labour Party's defence was based on the argument that Part II of the Act, which dealt with "Discrimination in the employment field" did not apply because being an MP is not "employment," but rather "holding office." It indicated in this sense that adopting an individual as one of the party's prospective candidates amounts to a commitment to the provision of facilities and services to that candidate by the central party and by its constituency wing.

The party also submitted that

> ...neither the appointment of a prospective Parliamentary candidate nor election as an MP is engagement in a particular profession or trade. The candidate is not paid. The MP is not an employee. The definition of a profession in section 82 does not refer to the well known category of office holder and he submits in no way can be described as covering prospective Parliamentary candidates or MPs.[54]

The tribunal's principal reason for allowing the complaint was its view that, notwithstanding Labour's ingenious defence, the Act should be held to apply. It read the heading of Part II of the Act not as "discrimination in employment," but more broadly as "discrimination in the employment field." Moreover, with respect to section 13 of the Act, which rendered it unlawful for an authority to discriminate on the ground of sex in conferring an authorization or qualification necessary for engagement in a profession or trade, the tribunal held the following:

> As the section now stands it covers and in our view was widely drafted as being clearly intended to cover, all kinds of professions, vocations,

---

[54] [1996] IRLR 116 at 118, para. 17.

occupations and trades in which persons may engage whether paid or unpaid and whether they be employment as defined in section 82 or not (for example doctors, lawyers and judges) including thereby persons who hold public offices. We find no significance in the absence of reference to "public office" since that is already covered in the wide definition of profession i.e. to include any vocation or occupation.[55]

Labour's defence also relied on an exception written into the *Equal Treatment Directive*[56] emanating from the European Commission as justifying the party's positive discrimination arrangement of having women-only short lists. The tribunal read the terms of the Directive, which forbids derogation by member States of the European Communities from equal treatment "for access to all jobs or posts whatever the sector or branch of activity, and to all levels of the occupational hierarchy."[57] The tribunal saw no difficulty in bringing MPs within that wide coverage. It accepted that even though MPs are not in employment, "they are engaged in an occupation which involves public service and for which they receive remuneration from public funds."[58]

Thus, on the basis of both domestic British law, and supranational European law, the tribunal struck down the Labour Party's experiment with all women short lists for candidacies. Sensing the possible approach of the general election toward which these candidacies were aimed, neither party appealed. The Labour Party in particular wanted to avoid leaving some seats without candidates. That election was eventually held on May 1, 1997, at a time when appeals would likely not yet have been decided. *The Economist* reported that the new Labour leader, Tony Blair, had called the policy "not ideal" and it thought that scrapping the policy would seem sensible.

This judgment did hold one other significant point of interest not only for those seeking to elaborate the political law on the selection of candidates but also for students of the British electoral system. In commenting on the European Directive, the tribunal analyzed the possibility for candidates to present themselves as independents, thus bypassing the need to be put on any party list. It did not hold that

---

[55] *Ibid.*, para. 20.
[56] Directive 76/207.
[57] *Equal Treatment Directive*, Article 3, quoted in [1996] IRLR 116 at 118, para. 21.
[58] *Supra* note 54, para. 22.

alternative to be a serious possibility, given the entrenchment of parties in British political life.

> It is no answer to say that the applicants could still stand for Parliament without endorsement by a major political party. We would be putting our heads in the sand if we did not recognise, as Mr. Jepson submits, that the only realistic way by which any person aspiring to be a Member of Parliament in the United Kingdom can achieve their ambition is first to be selected as an official candidate by one of the principal parties.[59]

6.5 ISSUE: CAMPAIGNING BY POLITICAL PARTIES, CANDIDATES AND REFERENDUM COMMITTEES

See *Ramsden v. Peterborough (City)*, [1993] 2 S.C.R. 1084 (S.C.C.) and *Beaumier v. Brampton (City)* (1998), 46 M.P.L.R. (2d) 32 (Ont. Gen. Div.), affirmed (1999), 7 M.P.L.R. (3d) 219 (Ont. C.A.).

---

§ 6.5.1
Comité Provisoire pour Le NON c. Ministre des Transports du Québec
Québec Superior Court; September 21, 1995
file no. 500-05-010066-957; not reported

The legislation on elections, or referenda, set out the rules on the organization of electoral events, but they do not constitute complete codes on campaigning. This case reinforces the principle that parties and candidates in elections and option committees in referenda must conduct their political campaigns in accordance with all legal requirements applicable to the activities they undertake.

Section 304 of the *Highway Safety Code*[60] authorizes the putting up of campaign signs along the highways of Québec, provided this is done once the campaign has been launched in law. Against that backdrop, on the weekend of September 16-17, 1995, the NO Committee placed a very large number of signs along the roads. It was only on September 20 that the National Assembly adopted the text of the question for a referendum on the secession of the province to sovereignty. The writ was issued on October 1, for the vote to be held on October 30.

---

[59] *Ibid.*, para. 23.
[60] S.Q. 1981, c. 7.

The NO Committee had acted allegedly in the belief that a Ministry of Transport official had given them permission. When they discovered that the official in question did not have the right to issue the permission, they applied to the Superior Court for a temporary injunction to restrain the Minister of Transport and his Deputy Minister from having the offending signs removed. The court held that the application should be refused as the NO Committee had not made out a case at all. The officials responsible for the Committee decided not to appeal and declared they would abide by the ruling, despite the very intense political and partisan atmosphere of the time. The final word in the matter was that of the Deputy Minister of Transport, who stated that,

> On vent que la campagne référendaire se fasse dans l'ordre, selon une procédure précise. Et cela vont pour le OUI et pour le NON.[61]

---

§ 6.5.2
Sexton v. Holden
Manitoba Court of Appeal; February 19, 2001
[2001] 6 W.W.R. 116

The issue addressed by this case is whether it is proper to conduct a political activity, namely in this instance an election campaign, in such a manner as to circumvent and defeat both the bounds and the purposes of the applicable law.

On October 28, 1998, municipal elections were held throughout Manitoba, including in the Rural Municipality of Winchester. In order to qualify as a voter, one had to be either a resident or a landowner. Sexton and Holden both contested the position of councillor for ward 4 of the municipality. After Holden won 67 votes to Sexton's 53 out of the 120 votes cast, it was discovered that Holden had personally and through a farming company he presided, sold parcels of land to 23 individuals, thereby enabling them to become voters although they were non-residents. Each parcel sold was a small portion and each sale was for $1.00. Sexton petitioned to have the election voided.

At trial, the judge phrased the issue this way: "When does the size of the interest (in land) become so small that it's legitimate to carry a

---

[61] "La guerre des pancartes," Louise Lemieux, *Le Soleil*, Québec, September 21, 1995.

vote?"[62] The judgment held that the normal purpose of real property purchases is to become registered owner of the land in question.

> It is the acquisition of the registered interest to the real property from which the qualification to become an elector arises. The transfer of the property is in fact the transaction and the entitlement to vote is ancillary thereto.[63]

The evidence disclosed that the purpose of the transaction, its essence, was to gather the right to qualify as an elector and a new election was ordered. The purchasers' interest was therefore colourable and the election was declared to be void. As Holden stated that he genuinely believed that such transfers were legally permitted, he was only fined $1.00. However, the entire scheme was conducted at Holden's initiative and, whatever his belief, he did breach the principle of election law by attempting to place his political interest above the rules of the statute. The court consequently made him ineligible to be elected or to hold office in Winchester for three years.

This litigation arose around the time of the Monnin Inquiry. In the environment of political caution which the Report of that Inquiry forced upon the Manitoba Progressive Conservative Party, one of the individuals who bought land from Holden lost the opportunity to be nominated to carry that party's colours in the Manitoba general election of September 21, 1999.

The Manitoba Court of Appeal upheld the trial judgment. It emphasized that one of the purposes of the *Local Authorities Election Act* was "to assure that voters are not influenced by promises, threats, favours or dishonest manipulation."[64] Campaigning cannot be conducted in such a manner as to destroy the integrity of the electoral system. In plain English, democracy allows no room for dirty tricks.

---

[62] "Vote list 'stacked' by sale of land," Bill Redekop, *Winnipeg Free Press*, July 29, 1999, p. A-6.

[63] (1999), 141 Man. R. (2d) 239 at 244, para. 20, affirmed [2001] 6 W.W.R. 116 (Man. C.A.).

[64] [2001] 6 W.W.R. 116 at 121, para. 22.

6.6 ISSUE: POLITICAL DISCOURSE AND RHETORIC[65]

6.6.A—CHARACTERIZATION OF POLITICAL SPEECH

See *Klein v. Law Society of Upper Canada* (1985), 16 D.L.R. (4th) 489 (Ont. Div. Ct.).

6.6.B—POLITICAL SPEECH ABOUT PUBLIC SERVANTS

See *Bangoura v. Washington Post* (2004), [2004] O.J. No. 284 (Ont. S.C.J.), additional reasons at (2004), 2004 CarswellOnt 675 (Ont. S.C.J.) and *Young v. Toronto Star Newspapers Ltd.* (2003), 66 O.R. (3d) 170 (Ont. S.C.J.).

6.6.C—POLITICAL SPEECH ABOUT POLITICAL FIGURES

See *Bhaduria v. Standard Broadcasting Inc.* (August 16, 1996), Doc. CP-12321-95, [1996] O.J. No. 2853 (Ont. Gen. Div.).

---

§ 6.6.C.1
Allegation of Unfair Cartooning by the Reform Party of Canada
1997; litigation not initiated

In the campaign leading up to Canada's 36th federal general election in 1997, the Reform Party undertook great efforts to form the Official Opposition, thereby displacing the Bloc Québécois, and for this it needed to capture at least some of the seats in Ontario. Reform represented the centre right to the radical right of the political spectrum. Despite its attempts to appear mainstream, the popular conception of its political views was further yet to the right. The use by the party of campaign slogans such as "No More Prime Ministers from Quebec" contributed to this impression.

In the central Ontario riding of Simcoe North, on Saturday, May 31, 1997, that is two days before the polling, the only daily newspaper, the Orillia Packet and Times, published a cartoon. It showed the

---

[65] Cross-reference to § 2.4, 4.3, 5.8, 6.7, 10.8, 10.9 and 11.9.

leader of the Reform Party, Manning, wearing the headgear of an Ayatollah and holding the image of a newspaper with a purported headline to the effect that "Black Turban Key to Iranian President's Victory." In the cartoon, Manning is seen saying, "I'll worry about how I get into the Legion later" and the caption states: "Preston hits upon foolproof way to form majority government." Besides the confusion of Iranian with Indian headdress, the cartoon was understood to be meant as being derogatory toward Reform, and probably was. The reference to the Legion derived from the exclusion from some premises, by the Royal Canadian Legion, a few years earlier, of persons covering their heads; this had been perceived as a racist slight to Sikh veterans.

The Simcoe North Reform Constituency Association raised a number of objections to the cartoon. It did not want to have Canadian elections compared to those of undemocratic countries, or to have its leader singled out among party leaders as being frivolous or desperate about being elected. It felt that the cartoon attacked Reform's credibility as a party and Manning's personal integrity as leader, each of which would hinder the party's electoral success. It also decried the attempt to link Reform to the controversy surrounding the Legion. Significantly, another of the constituency association's sources of dissatisfaction was the timing of the cartoon's publication, on the second day before polling day and the day after Manning made his campaign concluding stop in Orillia. The crux of this argument was that Reform would not have time to reply. This last line of reasoning is noteworthy because it is the same one raised by the Attorney General of Canada in its unsuccessful defence of section 322.1 of the *Canada Elections Act* before the Supreme Court of Canada. That provision, dealing with the ban on the publication of new public opinion polls in the last days of a campaign, was the subject matter of the case of *Thomson Newspapers Co. v. Canada (Attorney General).*[66] It is interesting to note that on that issue, the position adopted by the Reform Party's critic on issues of democratic reform, was for freedom of speech and against "gag-laws." The readers, he said, would be smart enough to judge for themselves.[67]

---

[66] [1998] 1 S.C.R. 877 (S.C.C.). [See § 5.10.1.]
[67] This information was gleaned from a telephone interview of the author with the critic, Ted White, MP for Vancouver North, on July 24, 1998. The Reform Party itself was said to have no official position on the *Thomson Newspapers* litigation.

The constituency association lamented the absence of a mechanism for what it called "immediate redress" of the situation. After the vote on June 2, 1997, it briefly considered initiating legal action. It was deterred from doing so, however, by the prospect of expenditures and the time that would have been needed by the candidate and his official agent to pursue the issue. Reflection upon Reform's electoral result in the riding also indicated no likelihood of political gain from the action. The Reform candidate came second, with the margin being 8,412 votes.[68] It is unlikely that that number of people could have been affected by the cartoon alone.

Reform's national office saw the matter as a local concern and would have been prepared to provide technical support, but not financing, for litigation. Thus, it was decided not to bring suit and Reform's local officials attempted to resolve the controversy by lodging a complaint with the newspaper, and in discussing with its publisher and editor what they considered to be an imbalance in the content and nature of the cartoon, which they attributed to the political leanings of the cartoonist and the paper's city editor. Participants in this matter also decided that prior to the next federal election, they would hold a meeting with the media directors for all candidates, to discuss guidelines for coverage and procedures that could be followed if such concerns arise again.

This incident illustrates primarily that in politically motivated disputes infused with legal reasoning, parties can often take divergent legal stances on related issues if they believe in each case that it will advance their electoral ambitions. In such circumstances as election campaigns, partisan advantage can sweep consistency of legal reasoning aside. The case also merits attention from the perspective that methods of dispute resolution alternative to law, such as here, all-party-negotiation, or party-media discussion, can resolve partly political, partly legal disputes.[69]

---

[68] The Liberal, Paul De Villiers, obtained 22,775 votes; the Reform candidate, Peter Stock, received 14,363.

[69] Much of the material for this analysis originated in a letter of July 12, 1998, addressed to the author by Mr. John Forrest, a Reform Party local official in Simcoe North.

§ 6.6.C.2
Allegations of Illegal Signage Against the Alliance for the Preservation of English in Canada
1997; prosecution not initiated

The most fundamental rule of a legal nature applicable to political speech is that guaranteed by section 2(b) of the *Canadian Charter of Rights and Freedoms*, namely freedom of expression, including freedom of the various media of communications. In a democratic society, however, in particular based on the tolerant cohabitation of social, linguistic and cultural groups, that freedom of political expression ought to be exercised within the bounds of political ethics and within the four corners of statutes designed to prevent abuses of the freedom.

In the course of the campaign leading up to the federal general election of June 2, 1997, an organization called the Alliance for the Preservation of English in Canada (APEC) placed signs in public places in the electoral district of Barrie-Simcoe-Bradford, Ontario, with the messages "No More Prime Ministers from Quebec" and "Vote No to a Distinct Society." In the Canadian context, these messages were well known to be both anti-Québec and anti-French Canadian in nature. The posting of the signs as well as the messages on them were supported by the local candidate of the Reform Party. In these circumstances, the allegations of the President of APEC to the effect that "The signs are not illegal, we're not a political group..." and "We can express any opinion any time we like"[70] sound hollow and lacks the civic self-restraint necessary for democratic political life.

Objections based on legal grounds could be raised to these messages on the basis of the *Criminal Code* provision against inciting hatred, the prohibition contained in the *Canadian Human Rights Act* against publishing discriminatory notices or even the obligation set out in the *Canada Elections Act* to sign posters of a political nature.

On May 26, 1997, the New Democratic Party's candidate in the electoral district lodged a complaint in respect of these signs with the Canadian Human Rights Commission. On the ground that other ways of settling the matter also existed, the Commission carried out

---

[70] "Signs stay, APEC vows," by Margaret Bruineman, *Barrie Examiner*, May 24, 1997, p. 1.

no investigation. None of the other federal or provincial bodies which could have taken investigatory or prosecutorial action did so either.

See also *Possibility of Litigation by Senator Pat Carney*, 1997, litigation not initiated; *Hervieux-Payette c. Société St-Jean Baptiste de Montréal* (1997), [1998] R.J.Q. 131 to 153 (Que. S.C.), reversed [2002] J.Q. No. 1607 (Que. C.A.) and *Threat of Litigation by Candidate Lou Sekora*, 1998, litigation not initiated.

---

§ 6.6.C.3
Copps v. Hustler Magazine Inc. and Riverain
1999; litigation not initiated

The specific aspect of political discourse raised by this case is whether legal liability can arise out of the use of pornography as part of the commentary on matters of current public interest and concern. The context in which the relevant events unfolded was the shepherding through the House of Commons, starting on October 8, 1988, of Bill C-55 of 1998, *An Act respecting advertising services supplied by foreign periodical publishers*,[71] by Copps who at the time was Minister of Canadian Heritage. This proposal was extremely controversial. If enacted, it would create the offence for foreign periodical publishers of supplying advertising services directed at the Canadian market to Canadian advertisers. In essence, this was an attempt to render it illegal for Canadian companies to advertise in the Canadian editions of split-run magazines. Its purpose was to foster greater advertising revenues for genuinely Canadian magazines. *Hustler* magazine would be one of the publications affected. The American authorities protested this measure vehemently and in various ways.

While Parliament and the Government were considering whether this method of promoting the Canadian magazine industry was feasible or appropriate, the February 1999 Canadian edition of *Hustler* magazine, a pornographic publication directed by Riverain, featured Copps as part of a pornographic spoof context in which it asked readers why they would like to have sex with her. The publication led Copps to threaten legal action; the way the Minister reacted was personal, not relating the magazine's description of her to the debate

---

[71] Bill C-55, First Session, Thirty-sixth Parliament; First reading, October 8, 1988.

about the legislation she was trying to have enacted and that would have a potential effect on the profitability of *Hustler's* Canadian edition. "I've never felt so personally violated as I did when I saw that article," said Copps. "It's absolutely gross. I've been called a lot of names over the years...I just felt after I saw it that I couldn't allow it to just roll off the book."[72]

Copps did retain legal counsel but the dispute was settled with the condition that the terms of settlement remain confidential to the parties. It is unfortunate that this issue was not determined through a judgment that would have resulted from litigation. Informed observers can conclude that the terms of a libel action such as that intended to be conducted by Copps would have been based on objections to the alleged offensiveness of the article, to the resulting ridicule for the Minister in her public life and to her loss of face in the community in which she exercised her professional life, that is in politics. Imaginative lines of argumentation could have been to the action to the political issue of advertising in magazines, to the timing of the article, coming as it did in the midst of a Parliamentary and political debate relating to magazine advertising and publishing, to the consequential damage to Canada vis-à-vis the United States authorities which represented the major opposition to the proposed public measures, or even to the fact that *Hustler* itself was in a potentially conflictual position with Copps, as its revenues could be affected by the measures Copps envisaged. It is also likely that Hustler's defence would have been based on the ground of freedom of expression.

We may surmise that Copps' lawyer was familiar with the decision of the United States Supreme Court in *Hustler Magazine v. Falwell*,[73] a remarkably similar case in which the publication had spoofed Falwell, a well-known figure on the American political scene. In its November 1983 issue, a year before the next presidential election, *Hustler* prepared a parody of a political advertisement made to look like a campaign ad. This parody claimed that Falwell, a minister (in the Christian religious sense) and a leader of the Moral Majority/ Christian Coalition, was a hypocrite who had an incestuous relationship with his mother. Falwell's resulting libel action was based on a claim of intentional infliction of emotional distress. The defence was

---

72 "Sheila Copps' lawsuit against Hustler magazine is obscene," Claire Hoy, *Hill Times*, March 22, 1999.
73 485 U.S. 46 (U.S. S.C., 1988).

the caricature's outrageous nature. The court grounded its ruling on the U.S. Constitution's *First Amendment* ensuring freedom of speech. While the court found that Falwell was indeed a public figure, it felt that the parody could not be understood as describing actual facts and was therefore not reasonably believable. It concluded,

> that public figures and public officials may not recover for the tort of intentional infliction of emotional distress by reason of publications such as the one here at issue without showing in addition that the publication contains a false statement of fact which was made with "actual malice," i.e., with knowledge that the statement was false or with reckless disregard as to whether or not it was true.[74]

In particular on the outrageous nature of the published text, the court commented thus:

> "Outrageousness" in the area of political and social discourse has an inherent subjectiveness about it which would allow a jury to impose liability on the basis of the jurors' tastes or views, or perhaps on the basis of their dislike of a particular expression, and cannot, consistently with the First Amendment, form a basis for the award of damages for conduct such as that involved here.[75]

Despite the differences in the way the *First Amendment* affects American libel law from the way the *Canadian Charter of Rights and Freedoms* affects Canadian libel law, by not going to court, Copps may have wished to prevent the Canadian courts from following the line of reasoning of the U.S. Supreme Court in case she lost. More likely however, she preferred to come to a quick settlement that prevented the protracted public repetition of the offending publication and the continuation of the public embarrassment to her. This would have been a largely politically indicated decision on her part.

Bill C-55 was adopted by the House of Commons on March 15, 1999, was passed by the Senate on June 8, 1999, and was given Royal Assent on June 17, 1999.

---

[74] *Ibid.* at 56.
[75] *Ibid.* at 55.

§ 6.6.C.4
Ripley v. Bastin
Nova Scotia Supreme Court; August 5 and November 24, 1999
not reported

Deep-seated political rivalries give rise to attempts to enlist the courts in the continuation of such vendettas, resulting in the legal action itself becoming political rhetoric, rather than just the rendering of a judgment in law about political speech.

Gerald Regan was the Liberal Premier of Nova Scotia from October 28, 1970, until October 5, 1978. Ripley, a fundraiser for the province's Progressive Conservative Party, provided information to the R.C.M.P., which led to an investigation of Regan for sexual crimes, and ultimately to his being prosecuted. In December 1998, the charges were set aside; part of the judgment was that the prosecution constituted an abuse of process by Crown lawyers who had lost their perspective, meaning that the charges were politically motivated. In 1999, the case against Regan was continued in the Nova Scotia Court of Appeal. In the meantime, Kimber wrote a book entitled "Not Guilty: The Trial of Gerald Regan," published by Stoddart, of which Bastin was an executive.

On July 19, 1999, Ripley applied to the Nova Scotia Supreme Court for an injunction to stop further distribution and sale of the book, alleging that it defamed him. He relied on the following arguments.

> Stephen Kimber has written falsely in part and without correction of detail or balanced facts, about me in the book *Not Guilty*.

> The book is, when pertaining to me, lies.

> The account is incomplete.

> . . .

> Public Policy:

> Public policy and the law encourages people to report crimes to the police. If everyone who does so suffers the tirades of dishonest reporters,

the reporting of crimes will be discouraged. I reported a crime; I have been harassed ever since.[76]

Ripley's entire case was based on unsubstantiated or unclarified allegations.

The defendants argued that the application be struck out as it disclosed no reasonable cause of action. They also pointed out that Ripley did not specify which parts of the book allegedly defamed him. "The courts of justice in Nova Scotia are not a forum where irrelevant and unfounded scandalous allegations can be put forward with impunity."[77]

In order not to disadvantage Ripley, who was not a lawyer but represented himself, the court offered him an opportunity on August 5, 1999, to perfect the action as to form. He failed to do so and on November 24, 1999, by consent, the application was struck. This ruling shows not only that legal discourse must be more precise and supported by evidence than political speech; it also demonstrates that the process of law cannot be improperly appropriated to resolve conflicts of a purely political nature.

See also *R. c. Robert* (2000), [2000] J.Q. No. 2919 (Que. Mun. Ct.) and *R. c. Foisy* (May 17, 2000), Doc. Montréal 199 092 891, [2000] J.Q. No. 2990 (Que. Mun. Ct.).

---

§ 6.6.C.5
Parizeau v. Lafferty, Harwood & Partners Ltd.
Québec Court of Appeal; October 24, 2003
[2003] R.R.A. 1145[78]

While freedom of expression, including of course that in the realm of politics, is one of the hallmarks of democratic governance, it is best exercised with a measure of dignified self-restraint and composure. No participant in public life ought to engage in wildly outrageous and willfully injurious discourse, without any limitations, merely on

---

[76] Application for Interlocutory Injunction, Memorandum of Law filed by the Plaintiff file S.K. 86 3C, filed July 28, 1999.

[77] Memorandum of Law filed by the Defendants, filed July 27, 1999, para. 29.

[78] Leave to appeal allowed (2004), 2004 CarswellQue 1073 (S.C.C.).

the ground of claiming that it is his right to do so. This is the sense of the action initiated by the then Leader of the Opposition in Québec and the Leader of the Bloc Québécois Party at the federal level, both of whom were ardent believers in the scission of Québec from Canada and were therefore figures of extreme controversiality in Canadian political life.

In a private financial newsletter, Lafferty wrote the following about the plaintiffs in January 1993.

> Jacques Parizeau, the leader of the Parti Québécois at the provincial level, and Lucien Bouchard, the leader of the Bloc Québécois at the federal level, aim their appeal entirely at nationalism. It is a classic form of demoguery and is no different from what Hitler did although Hitler at the time was operating in a greater political vacuum than that which presently prevails in Québec or Canada, although with the financial pressures developing both constituencies are coming into a political inoperative environment.[79]

While this text was privately distributed, it came to public knowledge through an article in the Montréal newspaper *Le Devoir* on February 9, 1993. In the February 1993 edition of the newsletter, there was further use of language such as that cited.

Parizeau and Bouchard sued Lafferty, claiming $150,000 each for libel. They founded their action in their own and their movement's attachment to democratic principles.

> Tout au cours de leurs prestigieuses carrières, les demandeurs JACQUES PARIZEAU et LUCIEN BOUCHARD ont toujours prôné les valeurs démocratiques qui sont chères à l'ensemble du peuple québécois et c'est sur cette base qu'ils préconisent les changements politiques importants dont font la promotion leurs partis politiques;

> Il va sans dire que la crédibilité personnelle et la réputation des deux (2) demandeurs quant à leur attachement aux valeurs démocratiques constituent des facteurs d'une importance crucials pour aux que la population dans son ensemble prendra nécessairement en considération avanat de leur accorder sa confiance dans la poursuite da leur projet de sociéte;[80]

---

[79] Statement of claim, para. 21(a).
[80] *Ibid.*, para. 19 and 20.

They qualified the language of the article alternatively as incendiary, injurious and as lying and hateful defamation. They particularly emphasized their revulsion at the association with the leader of a notoriously odious movement which was associated with the genocide of an entire people (nation). This form of discourse, they contended, went beyond the bounds of justifiable speech in a free and democratic society.

On March 16, 2000, the Superior Court issued a judgment which essentially agreed with the position espoused by the plaintiffs and which granted them a total of $40,000 in damages. The main thrust of the ruling was that while criticism of public figures was acceptable in political life, language that was so invective, hurtful and ungrounded in the facts was beyond the acceptable; critics of political figures would have to exercise a certain self-restraint.

> MM. Parizeau et Bouchard ont tous deux reconnu qu'ils avaient souvent été attaqués, insultés. On les a souvent traités de dictateurs, de traîtres et de démagogues. Pour aller en politique, il faut accepter, selon eux, d'être sujets à la critique et pouvoir y résister. Mais il y a une limite à respecter et celle-ci a, selon, eux, été franchie.
>
> Le Tribunal est d'accord. Lorsque l'article libelleux a été écrit, tant MM. Parizeau que Bouchard étaient dans l'opposition. Ils n'avaient jamais été premiers ministres et pourtant, on les comparaît à Hitler qui avait gouverné l'Allemagne nazie pendant de nombreuses années et qui, en tant que chef d'Etat, avait commandé les pires atrocités.[81]

The court rejected both Lafferty's contention of fair comment, considering that he had neither studied the writings of Hitler nor read the program of the Parti Québecois, and the defence that he was not attacking the public figures but their political options. It held that this was one and the same. The court also specifically accepted the plaintiffs' contentions that they had always striven to act democratically. In sum, political opponents cannot scandalize each other over differences in views and political preferences, with no knowledge of the facts.

---

[81] (2000), [2000] J.Q. No. 682, 2000 CarswellQue 472 (Que. S.C.), para. 52 and 53, affirmed [2003] R.R.A. 1145 (Que. C.A.), leave to appeal allowed (2004), 2004 CarswellQue 1073 (S.C.C.).

As the testimony of the B'nai B'rith League for Human Rights, which the court adopted, showed:

> Poor research, a poor understanding of nationalism and history and a brutally inappropriate conclusion.
>
> . . .
>
> To draw an analogy between the policies of Jacques Parizeau and those of Hitler is scurrilous and just plain wrong.[82]

On October 24, 2003, the Québec Court of Appeal confirmed the judgment of the Superior Court, but increased the award to the plaintiffs to $100,000 each. Of these amounts, $75,000 was for moral damages and $25,000 for exemplary damages. As to the reasonable nature, or otherwise, of Lafferty's comments, Justice Letarte adopted a standard based on reason, knowledge of the facts and democratic self-restraint.

> Les appelants comparent un homme que l'histoire a méprisé parce qu'il était un tyran sanguinaire, raciste et antisémite, à deux hommes politiques, chefs d'État en puissance, dont la preuve révèle que le combat a été marqué au coin du respect des principes de la démocratie. La plus simple évocation des faits réputés de connaissance judiciaire sur la vie de Hitler démontre le caractère déraisonnable de toute comparaison avec le sintimés.[83]

In this, they clearly distinguished the present case from that of *Hervieux-Payette c. Société St-Jean-Baptiste de Montréal*,[84] in which the rhetoric litigated about arose in the heated context of the patriation of the Canadian Constitution. As to the quantum of damages, the judge held the damages of $40,000 diminished the significance of a serious libel and was therefore insufficient. Justice Nuss wrote about the political and democratic aspects of the false analysis made by Lafferty.

> On the political level, power in Germany was exercised through violence and fear and replaced even the pretence of decisions made through a democratic or fair process.

---

[82] *Ibid.*, para. 60.
[83] *Ibid.*, para. 40.
[84] (1997), [1998] R.J.Q. 131 (Que. S.C.) at 153, reversed [2002] R.J.Q. 1669 (Que. C.A.).

. . .

Appellants invoked Hitler as a comparison to the Respondents and, without stating that they excluded the evil acts associated with Hitler, now seem to imply that it is the reader who, on his own, should make abstraction of the abominable horrors for which Hitler is responsible. The force of the comparison Appellants made is that Respondents are taking us down the same path as the one taken by Hitler. That path leads to a totalitarian dictatorship, deprivation of our freedoms and liberties, punishment of opponents, the elimination of the rule of law, government by fear and violence, dehumanization of the individual, racial hatred and genocide.

. . .

Apellants committed a fault, and it is rather futile on their part, to point to characteristics which are not the ones central to and at the crux of Hitler's infamy, and contend that the comparison with that evil person is not a comparison of the evil advocated and carried out by that person, but rather of characteristics found also in others who are not despicable and which do not necessarily expose a person to contempt, hatred and scorn. Placing Respondents in the category of Hitler with respect to nationalism demagoguery, and his promotion of fear by the administration of punishment, inevitably resulted in grouping Respondents with Hitler, not because of nationalism and demagoguery, but because of the crimes and atrocities for which he is notorious and infamous. The images evoked by the impugned article could not help but cast Respondents in the mold of a hated tyrant and expose them to contempt, hatred and scorn. This is all the more so in the eyes of those readers and/or electors who participated in the Second World War in the fight against Hitler and those who survived his brutality, as well as their families.[85]

The judge's conclusion on this point was the only one which could reasonably by reached.

Freedom of expression is one of the most important freedoms in Canada but it is not absolute; there are boundaries which, when transgressed, result in sanctions provided by the criminal or civil law (including administrative law).[86]

---

[85] *Supra* note 82, paras. 90, 93 and 95.
[86] *Ibid.*, para. 100.

See also *Allegation against the Canadian Alliance of Spying on the Government*, April 7, 2001; *R. v. Brown*,[87] 2001 PESCTD 6 (P.E.I. T.D.); *Landry c. Diffusion Métromédia C.M.R. Inc. and The Gazette*, REJB 1999-12769; settled January 4, 2002; *Johnson c. Arcand*, [2002] R.J.Q. 2802 (Que. S.C.), varied (2004), 2004 CarswellQue 117 (Que. C.A.); *Parrish v. Cosgrove and National Post*, Ontario Superior Court of Justice, filed April 23, 2003 and international comparisons *Columbia Broadcasting System v. Democratic National Commission*, 412 U.S. 94 (1973); *Miami Herald Publishing Co. v. Tornillo*, 418 U.S. 241 (U.S. Fla., 1974) and *Prebble v. Television New Zealand*, [1994] 3 N.Z.L.R. 1.

6.6.D—POLITICAL SPEECH BY POLITICAL FIGURES ABOUT EACH OTHER

See *Stopforth v. Goyer* (1979), 23 O.R. (2d) 696 (Ont. C.A.).

---

§ 6.6.D.1
Rizzuto c. Rocheleau
Québec Superior Court; February 20, 1996
[1996] R.R.A. 448

At the time of the campaign leading up to the federal general election of October 25, 1993, plaintiff Rizzuto was a Liberal Senator and chair of the Electoral Commission of the Liberal Party. Defendant Rocheleau, a former Mayor of Hull and a former Liberal Member of Parliament, was a candidate for the opposing Bloc Québécois in the electoral district of Hull-Aylmer. At his nomination meeting on September 13, Rocheleau made a number of *ad hominem* personal attacks against Rizzuto. He made ethnic slurs regarding Rizzuto's Italian background, then made unsubstantiated and erroneous allegations linking the Senator to organized crime. More specifically, Rocheleau accused Rizzuto of political machinations in regard to the way the Liberal candidate for Parliament in Hull-Aylmer had been designated by the party hierarchy, rather than having been selected at the constituency level. In fact, the decision not to have a Liberal nomination meeting in Hull-Aylmer had only been communicated to the opponent front-runner by Rizzuto; he had not been involved in the decision.

---

[87] Cross-reference to § 8.4.

After an initial half-hearted apology, Rocheleau went on for several days to defame Rizzuto publicly, accusing him of undemocratic behaviour for having denied the people of Hull-Aylmer the right to select their own Liberal candidate. Media coverage, locally and nationally, was extensive and the incident was even reported in the international francophone and italophone news services. This issue in fact became the central focus of the campaign in the riding. Rocheleau's own party leader disassociated himself from the comments.

Rizzuto had refused Rocheleau's temporary apology and after the election sued for defamation. The judgment focused to some measure on the usual issues in such cases, in particular the competing values of freedom of expression and the protection of reputation. On the basis both of the facts and of what it called Rocheleau's combative and vindictive testimony, however, the court rejected the defence arguments that his actions were designed to protect the public interest of the people of the riding. It also found unbelievable the defence that his statements were taken out of context.

In several respects, the court considered the particular circumstances of the case, in that it involved long-time active figures in political life and, at the material time, were involved in the heat of election campaigning. Most significantly, the court drew a clear distinction between campaign political rhetoric that is within the bounds of law and that which is legally not appropriate or acceptable. The judgment refers approvingly to the central point of Rizzuto's testimony:

> Il souffre de ces accusations car elles portent atteinte à son intégrité. En politique, il fait accepter d'être contesté, nous ce sont les idées qui sont en cause.[88]

In sharp contrast, the court pointed out the reckless and unruly nature of Rocheleau's actions and speech during the campaign, based on rough tactics, the creation of suspicion and the spreading of innuendo. Parts of Rocheleau's testimony are quoted, "il met des gants de boxe...c'est la guéguère dans Hull-Aylmer....On se battait du mieux qu'on pouvait."[89]

---

[88] [1996] R.R.A. 448 at 457.
[89] *Ibid.* at 459.

By setting out so clearly the types of political speech which are legal and these which do not meet the standard of law, the court is not so much developing the private law of defamation as applying it to the public political arena. This is clear judicial guidance to candidates for elective office, directing them to express their political views and visions, rather than merely attacking their opponents.

This judgment is also pertinent in its analysis of the political damage done by Rocheleau's rhetorical excesses to Rizzuto. It states that while public figures are more open to criticism and even to maligning than others, they retain the fundamental right to their reputation, honour and dignity. Here, the Senator was said to have had his political reputation tarnished. He encountered difficulty in fulfilling his subsequent functions as a Senator and as a widely-known public figure even more than in his private life. Even though he testified that he did not lose his positions in the Senate or in the party, doubts about his integrity persisted well beyond the end of the campaign and his effectiveness in political life was diminished. In respect of these outcomes, the court awarded general damages of $150,000 as well as exemplary damages of $20,000. In the month following the judgment, the parties concluded a confidential agreement on the payment of the award and the defendant desisted from appealing.

See also *Allegations of Racism against the Reform Party*, Hansard, February 4, 1997, pp. 7645-6 and February 5, 1997, pp. 7716-7; *Pratt v. Meredith* (January 29, 1997), Doc. 99756/96 (Ont. Gen. Div.), settled June 23, 1998; *Meredith v. Pratt* (1999), [1999] F.C.J. No. 15 (Fed. T.D.) and *Stinson v. Cannis*.

---

§ 6.6.D.2
Ghitter v. Anders, Levant and Anderson
Alberta Court of Queen's Bench
filed October 20, 1998; file no. 9801-14126; settled

This case examines the use of language that can be considered excessive in political life, not merely as general comment, but where publication is collateral to achieving particular gains in a current political process. The interest of the matter is twofold: translating a political debate into legal analysis of content and use of the courts to continue the publicity of the contentious statements.

Ghitter is a Progressive Conservative Senator; Anders is a Reform Party Member of Parliament, while Levant and Anderson are officials of the Reform Party. In September 1998, in conjunction with the campaign of the Reform Party to have Senators elected rather than appointed, the defendants prepared and distributed to a broad audience of Alberta residents a letter for the purpose of fund raising. In addition to requesting contributions, they wrote personal and professional insults regarding the plaintiff and made accusations against him. Their avowed goal was to shame Senator Ghitter out of office. In an attached document, they attacked "Ottawa courts" as having "a history of siding with Ottawa politicians against Albertans;"[90] they went on to describe the Senate election campaign and the court action related to it, in which the Reform Party was also active, as a two-front war. Ironically, this use of confrontational language was reminiscent of that of the Bloc Québécois. The language was so acrimonious that it elicited negative comment from within the Reform Party and in the Edmonton media. Ghitter sought a retraction and an apology; he did not even receive a reply.

On October 20, 1998, Ghitter initiated an action for defamation and claimed $1,000,000 general damages and $500,000 punitive and exemplary damages. The basic issue at stake is to determine where the boundary lies between fair comment in politics and defamation. Ghitter alleged that the statements made about him and the tone used were unjustifiable.

> The words contained in the Fundraising Letter, the Calgary Herald, the Edmonton Journal and on the Reform website, in their natural and ordinary meaning, or in the alternative by way of innuendo, were meant and understood to mean that the Plaintiff is lazy and neglectful of his Senatorial duties, that he is greedy and had personally brought about a pay raise for himself, that he is both disrespectful and contemptuous of Albertans in general and that he is dishonest, unworthy of trust and public confidence and not worthy to hold office.
>
> . . .
>
> As a result of the statements of the Defendant, as aforesaid, the Plaintiff has been lowered in the estimation of right-thinking members of society generally and has been seriously injured in his character, creditability and reputation in the community and in his office, and has been held up

---

[90] Statement of Claim, para. 13, p. 8.

to public scandal, odium and contempt. The Defendants' conduct has further caused the Plaintiff to suffer distress, embarrassment, loss of reputation and humiliation.[91]

Ghitter also added that the defendants had specialized knowledge of the matters and knew their own statements to be false, and that the statements were timed to garner widespread attention.

The defendants' principal reply was, as could be expected, that they were justified by having acted in good faith.

> In further answer to paragraph 24 of the Statement of Claim the Defendants say that the facts and opinions that were published in the fundraising letter, in the statements to the press and on the Reform Website were all made during a political campaign, namely the Alberta Senatorial election, and were made honestly and without malice in support of an elected Senate and as such are protected by qualified privilege and/or fair comment. The Defendants further deny that the facts upon which they based their political comment and expressed their opinions were false but say that those facts are substantially true.[92]

The legal argumentation also brought out a number of interesting points of contention. The defendants claimed and Ghitter disputed, that his public and community service and his representation of the people of Alberta were matters of opinion or fact. The defendants' arguments were, further, based perhaps comprehensively on several sections of the *Charter* and on section 52 of the *Constitution Act, 1867*. Ghitter replied that the *Charter* could not be invoked as there was no governmental act involved. The defendants went on to claim qualified privilege, arising from the fact that Anders was an MP making political comment about a public official, all of which was a matter of common interest for the Alberta electorate debating the Senatorial election process. Ghitter countered that no privilege, qualified or absolute, attached to the statements published. Another of Ghitter's arguments was that the text complained of was not imputable to political comment at all, but was simply an attack on his reputation.

An element of the case that is worth noting is the defence's tactic of attempting to use the court documents to further publicize the text being litigated. The entire fundraising letter had been reproduced in

---

[91] *Ibid.*, paras. 18 and 21.
[92] Statement of Defence, para. 14.

the Statement of Claim; that was necessary for evidentiary purposes. There seems no need to reproduce it again as part of the defence, except to extend its reach.

At the time the action was started, Senator Ghitter offered the following political explanation to his parliamentarian colleagues. Considering that this case was arising at the time when the impeachment of President Clinton in the United States was generating much comment about political libel and the use of judicial means to achieve political objectives, the plaintiff's comments are not necessarily self-serving.

> **Hon. Ron Ghitter:** Honourable senators, today in Calgary my lawyers filed a statement of claim alleging that I was defamed by a Reform member of Parliament and an employee in Preston Manning's office, along with the Reform Fund of Canada.
>
> . . .
>
> I have taken such action because it is the only recourse available, and because to do nothing would be tantamount to accepting the correctness of the allegations contained in the letter, and to encourage a course of political tactics that are repugnant and unacceptable in Canadian political life.
>
> . . .
>
> This Americanization of our political way of life will only serve to demean and undermine the ability of our democratic institutions to function. It fuels the coals of cynicism, negativism and disrespect for our Parliament, our courts and their servants. It will only serve to discourage talented, educated and wise Canadians from entering public life—a serious problem, in my view, and confirmable by anyone in this place who has endeavoured to encourage someone to seek public office.[93]

The matter seemed to be resolved on April 10, 2000, when Senator John Lynch-Staunton read into the Senate Hansard an apology authored by Rob Anders, MP and Ezra Levant, which they were proposing to also have published in several Calgary and Edmonton newspapers. The signatories acknowledged that their attack was unfounded and defamatory. They admitted that some of their state-

---

[93] Senate Debates, October 20, 1998, pp. 2008-9.

ments were based on false facts and on their interpretations out of context.

---

§ 6.6.D.3
Ammeter v. Perrier
Manitoba Court of Queen's Bench; July 7, 1999
[1999] 10 W.W.R. 725[94]

Ammeter, supported by witnesses and some evidence, alleged that in the campaign leading up to the local election for the Rural Municipality of Tache, in Manitoba, Perrier included in his campaign a number of *ad hominem* attacks, such as allegations that Ammeter was "a crook," that he had stolen from the municipality and that he had been involved in "back room deals" during his earlier term of office. Pursuant to the *Local Authorities Election Act*,[95] publication of a false statement in relation to the personal character or conduct of a candidate during an election renders the perpetrator liable to a fine. Where the perpetrator is a candidate or his agent, the election of that candidate may be voided. In this instance, the court concluded that the remarks attributed to Perrier were not statements of opinion but were statements of a factual nature and were intended by the statute. "They are false statements of fact in relation to Mr. Ammeter's personal character and they were made for the purposes of electing Mr. Perrier."[96] However, it dismissed Ammeter's election petition because it applied a standard of proof of beyond a reasonable doubt rather than a simple balance of probabilities, and the applicant's evidence was not strong enough.

The aspect of the case that is of particular interest involves the judge's analysis of the provision of the Act which punishes defamation. He traced its origin to an 1895 British statute[97] which received its most appropriate interpretation in jurisprudence dating from 1911:

> A politician for his public conduct may be criticised, held up to obloquy: for that the statute gives no redress; but when the man beneath the

---

[94] Affirmed (2000), [2001] 6 W.W.R. 226 (Man. C.A.).
[95] C.C.S.M., c. L180.
[96] [1999] 10 W.W.R. 725 at 736, para. 53, affirmed (2000), [2001] 6 W.W.R. 226 (Man. C.A.).
[97] *Corrupt and Illegal Practices Prevention Act*, 1895, (U.K.), 58 and 59 Vict., c. 40, s. 3.

politician has his honour, veracity and purity assailed, he is entitled to demand that his constituents shall not be poisoned against him by false statements containing such unfounded imputations.[98]

The emphasis here was on distinguishing the intent of the legislature in not dealing with opponents' criticism of a political figure's publicly espoused positions. Allegations regarding the personal character or conduct of a politician are a different matter; this is what the legislature wanted to prevent.

In the Canadian context also, the aim of this provision was to prevent "unsubstantiated statements of a factual nature, attacking the personal character or conduct of the candidate."[99] An accusation of being a thief is an attack on personal character, whether the theft occurred in the course of one's duties as a politician or in his personal life.

---

§ 6.6.D.4
Bonneville v. Frazier
British Columbia Supreme Court; March 7, 2000
(2000), 12 M.P.L.R. (3d) 236

In instances where legislation exists to protect electors from being misled by candidates for public office, the courts will protect the good faith and integrity of the electoral system from political discourse which is made or distributed by a candidate who knows it to be false. In British Columbia, the *Municipal Act* forbids the persuasion of voters by means of abduction, duress or fraudulent means.[100] In the last two days of a campaign for the election of a mayor in the Village of McBride, the respondent spread electoral documentation of an accusatorial nature about the applicant, which he knew to contain false information. Later, he indicated to some voters that the information was wrong, but the document continued to spread. The court relied on the principles recently set out in *Friesen v. Hammell*[101] and drawn from the *Election Act* relating to the province, to the effect that

---

[98] *The North Louth Case* (1910), 6 O'M. & H. 3; cited at [1999] 10 W.W.R. 725, 735, para. 47, affirmed (2000), [2001] 6 W.W.R. 226 (Man. C.A.).

[99] *Supra* note 96, para. 49.

[100] R.S.B.C. 1996, c. 233, s. 152.

[101] (1999), 57 B.C.L.R. (3d) 276 (B.C. C.A.), leave to appeal refused (2000), 252 N.R. 397 (note) (S.C.C.).

Within these principles, it is, in my view, neither unwarranted nor unreasonable to expect of those who would seek the support of the electorate in a bid for public office a level of accuracy, honesty and candour which meets these criteria.[102]

In other words, a candidate who wins an election on the basis of knowingly lying is susceptible of having his victory judicially overturned. Moreover, the court added, in order to achieve such a result, it is neither desirable nor necessary to go behind the secrecy of the ballot to compel voters to testify as to their actual vote and how it would have been different, but for the conduct in question. Notwithstanding this court judgment, on May 13, 2000, the electors of McBride elected Frazier to be their mayor with a landslide victory. In this instance, the justice system and the electoral system each played its role. It is the option expressed by the population which leaves observers of political justice somewhat perplexed.

See also *Scott v. Fulton*,[103] 137 B.C.A.C. 77 (B.C. C.A.); *Clement v. McGuinty*, [2000] O.T.C. 438 (Ont. S.C.J.), additional reasons at (2000), [2000] O.J. No. 2730 (Ont. S.C.J.), reversed (2001), 143 O.A.C. 328 (Ont. C.A.); *Hoeppner v. Hermanson*, December, 2000 and (2001) Ontario Court of Appeal, April 19, 2001; *Canadian Alliance Accusation of Partiality against Mr. Justice Silcoff*, April 9, 2001 and *Complaint of Conflict of Interest by Peter Jenkins, M.L.A. against Hon. Pat Duncan, First Minister of the Yukon*, Decision of the Commissioner under the Conflict of Interest Act; November 29, 2001.

---

§ 6.6.D.5[104]
*State of Washington ex rel. Public Disclosure Commission v.
119 Vote No! Committee*
Supreme Court of Washington; August 14, 1998
957 P.2d 691 (Wash., 1998)

Should political discourse that can be held to be knowingly false be subject to constitutional guarantees of free speech or should it, for the sake of equity in the context of electoral contests, be circumscribed by statute based on that policy goal? The difference is between a

---

[102] (2000), 12 M.P.L.R. (3d) 236 at 248, para. 60
[103] Cross-reference to § 3.3.C.3.
[104] International comparison.

regime of unfettered political discourse in which the ultimate judge is the citizenry and one in which the law becomes a tool in attempting to ensure thoughtful and truthful argumentation. This illustrates the dichotomy between the use of constitutional standards to prevent the spread of false or unethically motivated statements and the use of the law of libel.

In the State of Washington, a statute was enacted to prescribe sponsoring, with malice, political advertisements containing false statements of material fact. Notwithstanding this law, the 119 Vote No! Committee published an appallingly simplistic, false, misleading and malicious ad in the context of a public debate leading to a State referendum on an initiative that was to be entitled the "Death with Dignity Act."

Initiative 119: Vote No

IT WOULD LET DOCTORS END PATIENTS' LIVES WITHOUT BENEFIT OF SAFEGUARDS

---

* No special qualifications—
  your eye doctor could kill you.
* No rules against coercion—
  Nothing to prevent "selling" the idea to the aged, the poor, the homeless.
* No reporting requirements—
  No records kept.
* No notification requirements—
  Nobody need tell family members beforehand.
* No protection for the depressed—
  No waiting period, no chance to change your mind.

INITIATIVE 119...IS A DANGEROUS LAW

VOTE NO ON INITIATIVE 119[105]

The Public Disclosure Commission alleged that the ad violated the law by publishing false political advertising and sought damages.

---

[105] 957 P.2d 691 (Wash., 1998) at 693.

The State asserts it may prohibit false statements of fact contained in political advertisements. This claim presupposes the State possesses an independent right to determine truth and falsity in political debate.[106]

The American Civil Liberties Union intervened to have the Washington statute declared unconstitutional.

The trial court found that there was no violation of the statute and concluded that the statute was constitutionally valid. The Supreme Court of Washington, by contrast, found the statute to be in contravention of the *First Amendment of the U.S. Constitution*, which guarantees freedom of speech. Consequently, it did not have to decide whether the Committee's ad was in contravention of the law. This judgment was based on the reasoning that freedom of speech should not be restricted but that the matter should be left for the decision of the electorate. In order to reach this conclusion, the following legal analysis was subscribed:

> The constitutional guarantee of free speech has its "fullest and most urgent application" in political campaigns.
>
> . . .
>
> Therefore, the State bears a "well-nigh insurmountable" burden to justify...restriction on political speech.
>
> . . .
>
> This burden requires the court to apply "exacting scrutiny."
>
> . . .
>
> Exacting scrutiny will invalidate the statute unless the State demonstrates a compelling interest that is both narrowly tailored and necessary.
>
> . . .
>
> Such burdens are rarely met.

---

[106] *Ibid.* at 695.

. . .

...the First Amendment operates to insure the public decides what is true and false with respect to governance.[107]

This court's conclusion demonstrates the American judicial instinct toward completely unfettered free speech in the political arena, which other democracies may consider exaggerated. The fundamental question underlying this dilemma, namely whether such ads as the one in question here are beneficial to, or destructive of genuine and instructive political discourse is left unanswered by the majority of the court.

The debate on whether political discourse should remain entirely unregulated in order to satisfy a purist constitutional wish is, however, thriving not only in the American polity at large, but even among the justices of the Washington Supreme Court. Several of them believed that the court had gone too far. Justice Talmadge, dissenting on this point, best formulated the minority position as follows:

> Today the Washington State Supreme Court becomes the first court in the history of the Republic to declare First Amendment protection for calculated lies. In so doing, the majority opinion flouts numerous United States Supreme Court pronouncements to the contrary. The majority determines RCW 42.17.530, a statute providing penalties for dissemination of false political advertising, is facially violative of the First Amendment because the State has no compelling interest in preventing lies in the course of an initiative or referendum campaign, no matter how egregious the lies may be.

> The sweep of the majority's rhetoric is so encompassing that no statute designed to ensure statements of fact in political campaigns are truthful would survive a First Amendment challenge. Moreover, the breadth of the majority's rhetoric has untold impacts on existing law regarding political campaigns for candidates and ballot measures.

> The majority is also shockingly oblivious to the increasing nastiness of modern American political campaigns. This trend is highlighted by a "win at any cost" attitude involving vilification of opponents and their ideas. This new type of campaign neither illuminates nor exemplifies

---

[107] *Ibid.* at 694-695.

the best of our democratic tradition, and has caused too many of our fellow citizens to turn away from participation in the political process.[108]

The gap between the philosophical stances of the majority and the minority could not be bridged, but another of the justices, Madsen, did offer a practical solution.

> In my view, there is merit to the contention that the Legislature may constitutionally penalize sponsorship of political advertising of such a nature by enacting a narrower statute than RCW 42.17.530.[109]

See also *Nebot v. Bucaram*, Supreme Court of Ecuador, August 13, 1998, limited information available and *Regina (Sivakuram) v. Secretary of State for the Home Department*, [2001] EWCA Civ 1196, July 24, 2001 and November 11, 2001.

6.6.E— POLITICAL SPEECH BY POLITICAL FIGURES ABOUT THIRD PARTIES

See *Jones v. Bennett* (1967), 59 W.W.R. 449 (B.C. S.C.), reversed (1968), 63 W.W.R. 1 (B.C. C.A.), reversed (1968), [1969] S.C.R. 277 (S.C.C.); *Aiken v. Ontario (Premier)* (1999), 177 D.L.R. (4th) 489 (Ont. S.C.J.); *Hollinger Inc. and Black v. Nystrom*, Ontario Superior Court of Justice, issued February 7 2000, file no. 00-CV-184764, discontinued and *Goddard v. Day*[110] (2000), 194 D.L.R. (4th) 559 (Alta. Q.B.).

6.6.F— POLITICAL SPEECH OF A CRIMINAL NATURE

See *Mugesera c. Canada (Ministre de la Citoyenneté & de l'Immigration)* (2003), 232 D.L.R. (4th) 75 (Fed. C.A.), leave to appeal allowed (2004), 2004 CarswellNat 377 (S.C.C.), additional reasons at 2004 CAF 157 (F.C.A.).

---

[108] *Ibid.* at 701.
[109] *Ibid.* at 699.
[110] Cross-reference to § 2.5 and 11.8.7.

6.7 ISSUE: POLITICAL PROMISES[111]

6.7.A—ELECTION CAMPAIGN PROMISES

§ 6.7.A.1
Ruffolo v. Mulroney
Ontario Provincial Court – Toronto Small Claims Court; June 28, 1988
Doc. York 363/88, [1988] O.J. No. 2670 (Ont. Prov. Ct.)

While the decision of a small claims court does not often set precedent, this ruling merits attention for two reasons. First, at the time the decision was rendered, very few courts had ventured into examination of the legal merit of campaign promises. In this case, also, the judge dealt most thoroughly with the points raised by the parties and gave a well motivated judgment.

Ruffolo, an elector in Kitchener, Ontario, sued Mulroney, then Prime Minister of Canada, and the Progressive Conservative Party, seeking $90 in damages. The action was based on the fact that as a candidate for election and as leader of the party at the federal general election of 1984, Mulroney had made promises and representations to Ruffolo regarding the improvement of postal services and the plan not to conclude a free trade deal with the United States. There were oral promises made by Mulroney in person, as well as written material transmitted from the headquarters of the party. Ruffolo alleged that he relied on these promises and representations in deciding how to vote. During the mandate that followed the 1984 election, postal services could be interpreted as having deteriorated and Mulroney led the Government of Canada in negotiating a free trade agreement with the U.S. Ruffolo argued that Mulroney was negligent in representing such commitments and policies, that he breached the promises and the concomitant duties and that he thereby caused the plaintiff damage. This judgment was based on the defence's motion to dismiss the case on the grounds that it disclosed no reasonable cause of action either in contract or in tort.

---

[111] Cross-reference to § 2.4, 5.8, 6.6, 10.8 and 11.9.

The court first made reference to the statutory aspect of the matter, namely section 327 of the *Canada Elections Act* (now section 550), which read as follows:

Signed Pledges by Candidates Prohibited

> 327. It is an illegal practice and an offence for any candidate for election as a member to sign any written document presented to him by way of demand or claim made on him by any person, persons or associations of persons, between the date of the issue of the writ of election and the date of polling, if the document requires the candidate to follow any course of action that will prevent him from exercising freedom of action in Parliament, if elected, or to resign as a member if called on to do so by any person, persons or associations of persons.

In the opinion of the court, this provision which had been adopted to preserve the freedom and integrity of a candidate, once elected to Parliament, was a bar to the existence of a contract between a candidate and an elector in respect of campaign promises. The public law aspect of this absence of a contractual relation was based on the unenforceable nature of this type of oral pledge. "...to allow an action in contract based on promises made during an election would be contrary to public policy and to the concept of representative democracy as we understand it."[112]

The court based a further rationale for the inability of the parties to form a contract on grounds of the private law elements of contracting, within the context of an election. "Secondly, there is no contract in law between a voter and a candidate. There cannot be a contract where there is no consideration and, clearly, no intention to create legal relations between the parties. There is no privity. To imply a contractual relationship within the context of an election campaign would be to ignore the realities of such a situation."[113]

In the purely legal parameters of the court's jurisdiction, that is in the process of searching whether a contract had been concluded between a party leader as a candidate for office and an elector, the breach of which could give rise to damages, the foregoing analysis of the court was entirely defensible. However, it went on and tried to draw an unfortunate parallel between an electoral promise and a statement of

---

[112] (June 28, 1988), Doc. York 363/88, [1988] O.J. No. 2670 (Ont. Prov. Ct.), p. 5.
[113] *Ibid.*, p. 6.

government policy. It said that while a statement of government policy did not amount to an offer to contract, this principle would apply even more forcefully to the electoral promise of a candidate. This comparison would seem not to add to the clarity of the judgment.

In determining whether the plaintiff had a cause of action, the court similarly attached no legal value to campaign promises. Borrowing from the law of torts, it reasoned that a person possessing special skills and ability has a duty of care toward someone seeking information, when knowing that that person would rely on his skill and judgment. However, it said that Mulroney and the Progressive Conservative Party were in the business of attempting to be elected, not in that of running the post office or negotiating free trade. Interestingly, it went on: "It cannot be said, in the context of an election campaign, that a 'politician' is a trade or profession possessing special skills."[114] While this may be true, the court omitted to consider that the candidate and the party were seeking office and power specifically for, among other reasons, the control of the post office and the decision-making ability on free trade.

To an even greater extent than the analysis on the availability of any remedy, the core of the judgment is the court's consideration of the nature of campaign promises in law. It characterized such promises as not dealing with objective facts but rather as statements of intention or opinion, or predictions. Another label used by the court was to designate campaign promises "representations as to future occurrences."[115]

Most significantly, the court held that a person had no right to rely on statements of this nature because reliance on them was not reasonable, given the electoral context in which they were made. It explained this by indicating that electoral promises reflected an intention and a determination to take action, but within the concepts of the parliamentary system and the limits of party discipline. The primary element within the parliamentary system that prevented an election campaign promise from achieving legally binding status was that neither the candidate nor the party could ever exercise complete control. Thus, electoral statements of intention could even be mere puffery.

---

[114] *Ibid.*, p. 9.
[115] *Ibid.*, p. 11.

Given that in the eyes of the law, it was not reasonable to rely on electoral promises, and considering the consequential lack of causal connection between the promise and the voting, the casting of a vote could not become a head of tortious loss. The waste of a vote and the disillusion of the voter could not be compensated. The plaintiff's remedy was therefore to change his vote. On all these grounds, Ruffolo's claim for damages was denied.

Effectively, the court drew a line of demarcation, declaring that the subject-matter of the case, namely the campaign promise, was political rather than legal in nature. It was thus only logical to instruct the plaintiff that the remedy to be sought should also be political rather than one based on law. In this case, the court expressed the traditional Common Law position on the legal value of campaign promises. It may be queried whether the outcome of the case would have been different if the relief sought had been a declaratory judgment.

---

§ 6.7.A.2
Various Federal Liberal Promises relating to the Goods and Services Tax
Hansard, April 23, 1996, p. 1803

The manner in which the Liberal Party of Canada and subsequently the Government of Canada led by that party dealt with the issue of the Goods and Services Tax (GST) in the period from 1990 until 1996 is indicative of the legal merit and enforceability of political campaign promises.

It was the Progressive Conservative Government of Prime Minister Brian Mulroney which introduced the GST into the Canadian taxation system in 1990, by means of amendments to the *Excise Tax Act*. The GST, the Canadian variation of the value added form of taxation widely used in European countries, was a substantial modernization of the previously applicable Manufacturers' Sales Tax. It was imposed on a far greater range of goods and services than the previous tax had been and it produced far greater revenues for the State. The introduction of the GST, combined with the forceful parliamentary tactics used to enact it, made it politically unpopular. Seizing on this unpopularity, during the campaign leading up to the 35th federal general election of 1993, the Liberal Party of Canada included in its collection of campaign promises, the "Red Book," a promise phrased as follows:

> A Liberal government will replace the GST with a system that generates equivalent revenues, is fairer to consumers and to small business, minimizes disruptions to small business and promotes federal-provincial fiscal co-operation and harmonization.[116]

The written promise was supplemented with speeches by the then Leader of the Opposition, Jean Chrétien, who stated in unequivocal terms that a Liberal government would replace the GST by a different scheme of taxation.

On October 25, 1993, the Liberal Party won an overwhelming victory in the general elections and left the outgoing Progressive Conservative Party with only two seats in the House of Commons. It is likely that the Liberal promise to do away with the GST contributed to the reversal of political fortunes in Canada. However, the degree to which this promise among many others influenced members of the electorate, many of whom were also otherwise disposed to a change of government, is impossible to assess. Thus, it is even more difficult to attempt analysis of whether the promise engendered an expectation among voters that during the term of the mandate which started in 1993, the incoming government would actually carry out this promise.

Aside from the subjective factors of influence and expectation on the part of the electorate, it is more appropriate to examine the objective aspect of the process. The questions which need to be addressed are: At the time the GST promise was made, was there a genuine intention to realize it? After having been in office for two and a half years and having developed first-hand experience in the administration of the GST and the level of revenues it was capable of raising, was the government still intending to fulfil its promise to replace it, especially in light of the GST's significant contribution to the government's most pressing fiscal policy, namely the elimination of the annual deficit? Given that replacement of the GST had been promised, was the government legally bound to carry out the promise, or politically bound to do so? Whether it was in fact bound by legal or political norms, did the government feel itself bound? Did a method exist to enforce the promise? Should the promise still be enforced on the government

---

[116] 1993 Campaign Liberal Party Red Book quoted by the Hon. Paul Martin, Minister of Finance, in Hansard, April 23, 1996, p. 1803.

if it was found that retention of the GST could or would be in fact more beneficial than its replacement?

The alternative scenario might also be posited. Was this promise made with the intention of attracting voters, either without fore-knowledge of the influence of the GST on the government's prospective overall performance, or with the intention of not fulfilling the promise after it had helped to get the Liberal Party elected into office?

Whichever scenario is the correct one, by the spring of 1996, the Government of Canada had not replaced the GST and appearances had led the majority of people to conclude that it would not be likely to replace it. The matter thus became the subject of intense political discourse.

Instead, on April 23, 1996, the Minister of Finance announced in the Commons that agreements had been reached between Canada and Newfoundland, Nova Scotia and New Brunswick for the integration and harmonization of the systems of sales taxes in these provinces. The Minister acknowledged that the promise to do away with the GST had been made. He addressed head on the issue of whether the promise was being kept or not and whether it would be kept or not. In terms of the fiscal system alone, he indicated that the search for alternatives had not produced suitable options.

> During the election campaign we were right to criticize the GST. It created overlap and duplication among governments. It was costing small business time, energy and money; the price paid for having to keep two sets of books, to track two sets of transactions and to deal with two tax collectors. We were right to say that all that was wrong. It still is. However, we were mistaken to have believed that once it was anchored in place a completely different alternative would be within reach, responsibly. It has not been.

> The honest truth is that for two and a half years we looked at virtually every conceivable alternative. Some were not possible or desirable because of their economic impact, others because of the nature of our federation.[117]

---

[117] Hansard, April 23, 1996, p. 1803.

This was a clear, technical, policy-based explanation. The Minister continued, however, in using the policy-based reply as a justification of a political nature for non-fulfilment of the campaign promise.

> What we have arrived at is not the best alternative conceivable; it is the best alternative possible and it is in keeping with our red book commit-ment.[118]

Finally, Minister Martin justified his decision in a context broader than that of the internal mechanics of the tax system by saying that this was a matter not only of responsible tax policy, but a broader question of responsible government.

The press commentary about the explanations the Minister had pro-vided were neither gentle nor trusting. Under the title "The height of political gall lies behind a veil of crocodile tears," Canada's national newspaper indicated that it felt the people of Canada had been know-ingly and wilfully deceived.

> The Liberals knew—oh, they knew very well—what the alternatives were. But they also knew, as did party leader Jean Chretien, that by quite deliberately deceiving the Canadian public they could reap political gain. That cynicism—not the so-called "honest error" Mr. Martin ac-knowledged yesterday—ignited a search that lasted 2 1/2 years for some politically expedient way of explaining how it was that the honest, truth-seeking, right-minded Liberal Party was itself duped, rather than the chumps who voted for it.
>
> To hear Mr. Martin tell it yesterday behind a veil of crocodile tears, the Liberals honestly believed alternatives existed, knew nothing about them before the election and searched relentlessly for them thereafter, only to conclude, sadly and after much anguish, that indeed "none made good policy sense." Hypocrisy, once unleashed, knew no limits. Said the Liberal minister: "Some options might have made cynical, short-term political sense." So the cynics now demand credit for not being cynical.
>
> . . .
>
> By the Liberals' admission about three years too late, not only are the principles underpinning the GST (the principles first articulated by the previous government) completely sound, but so is the goal the Conser-

---

[118] *Ibid.*

vatives advanced of co-ordinating, or "harmonizing," the GST with provincial sales taxes. The Conservatives in their time were right and paid the price; the Liberals were wrong and reaped the benefit.

In the annals of Canadian political gall, little can top this from the Liberals yesterday: "We could have cynically claimed that this announcement was the panacea. That as of today, the GST was dead, buried and scrapped. We know not being able to say this today means that many Canadians will be disappointed. We understand that disappointment. We share it."

Spare us your pain.[119]

The explanations provided by the Minister of Finance seem to lead to two possible conclusions. If they are to be believed, they indicate that a promise made in good faith but later found to be impracticable ought not to be carried out and in the interests of good government is not legally enforceable. If they are doubted, they portray a political ploy which, having been successful in that it resulted in electoral success, cannot be undone and either need not or cannot be legally enforced.

The matter did not end there, however. Inevitably, given the significance of the issue in the public domain, the Prime Minister was drawn into the discussion. His conclusion was that sanctified by political practice, namely that governments must respond to the evolution of public life and to the needs of the country, no matter what promises have been made.

The lesson of the Liberals' GST drama, says Prime Minister Jean Chretien, is that politicians can't be expected to keep all their promises.

"Sometimes, in the course of a mandate, you're faced with a situation where you cannot deliver," Mr. Chretien told reporters yesterday. "You have to have some flexibility...because acts of God come in the administration. And no politician can see everything happening."

. . .

Mr. Chretien's lesson, as he laid it out yesterday, does not go far beyond a mere reinforcement of an old maxim: politics is the art of the possible.

---

[119] Jeffrey Simpson in the Toronto *Globe and Mail*, April 24, 1996.

And by extension, Mr. Chretien appeared to be saying that the Liberals' big mistake was in allowing themselves to be pinned down too precisely by the electorate.[120]

In this perspective, political promises certainly do not produce legally binding or enforceable obligations.

The controversy over the GST most directly affected two other members of the government, if only in political and conventional ways, but not legal ones. The independent-minded Member of Parliament John Nunziata refused to vote for Finance Minister Martin's 1996 budget and was expelled from the Liberal Caucus. The most noteworthy consequence of the controversy, however, was the fate of Deputy Prime Minister Sheila Copps. During the 1993 campaign, she had indicated to the voters of her riding in Hamilton that if the GST was not replaced, she would resign her seat in the Commons, making a rather bold backing for the promise. On April 25, 1996, she attempted to follow the lead of the Finance Minister by qualifying her promise to resign. Her promise, however, had been so direct and unequivocal that she became unable to avoid its consequences. By May 1, 1996, she felt no other option but to resign her seat of Hamilton East, Ontario. It was clear that the government and the Liberal Party supported Ms. Copps politically; the best evidence of this was the fact that, contrary to the usual practice, the writ for the by-election which was required to fill the Commons seat she vacated was announced on the very day of her resignation. Polling was conducted on June 17, 1996. Whether the people of Sheila Copps' riding thought she had taken a principled stand on the basis of her promise, or whether they believed she had been politically induced or forced to resign, they voted her back into office with a reduced, but still substantial margin. At the 1993 general election, she had obtained 67.30% of the votes in a field of 9 candidates. In the 1996 by-election, among 13 candidates, she classed first with 46.09% of the votes.

---

[120] "We can't keep all pledges: Chrétien" by Susan Delacourt, Toronto *Globe and Mail*, May 3, 1996.

§ 6.7.A.3
Ontario Liberal Response to Progressive Conservative Tax Cuts
Statement by the Leader of the Ontario Liberal Party
December 18, 1996

The link between election campaign promises and comprehensive platforms by political parties vying for office has been strengthened during the 1990s by the emergence of campaign books at both federal and provincial levels. In every instance where party platforms have been so structured and publicized, the first line of questioning has been about their contents: Are the facts correct? Are the plans feasible? A second, and perhaps even more intense line of questioning has revolved around the combined issue of truthfulness of the party's intentions, and accountability: Will the plans actually be carried out? What sanction applies if they are not?

In the campaign leading up to the general election held on June 5, 1995, in Ontario, both the Liberal Party and the Progressive Conservative Party used platform books to attempt to sway voters, as the federal Liberal Party had done very effectively in the October 25, 1993, general election. On this occasion, however, whether because the novelty of the tactic had worn off or because the party leaders elicited less public confidence, the plans were much less well received.

> At the end of the day, though, did politicians soothe voter cynicism by releasing The Plans? Not really. No matter how many times McLeod waved her red book or Rae repeated his record, voters seemed reluctant to latch onto the "balanced" approach offered by McLeod or the "Trust me" message from Rae. Even Harris didn't catch on until he started to campaign during the election, despite the fact his plan had been out and about for months.

> No, in the end, the voters are taking the plans with a huge grain of salt. And that may be why Harris experienced a surge of popularity mid-campaign.

> That's because some voters have an interesting read on the campaign. Harris may go too far with his workfare (for welfare recipients) and boot camp (for bad kids) platform, but in the dispirited world of populist political analysis, the thinking is that no politician will do everything he or she promises in any plan. So if Harris does just one-fifth of what he's

talking about, that's more change than voters are likely to get from Liberals or NDPers. At least that's what some folks are saying.

Cynicism can do strange things to a provincial election.[121]

One political promise made by the Progressive Conservative Party under the leadership of Mike Harris, who eventually became Premier of Ontario as a result of the 1995 election, is worth mentioning. Harris mentioned often during the campaign, but more importantly he publicized in writing that,

> We will cut our provincial income tax rates by 30% in three years. Half of the cuts will come up front - in one year.[122]

Once in office as the Government of Ontario, the Progressive Conservative Party actually did in its first year begin to implement the tax cut plan. They executed the promise which was very much in line with their ideology.

In November 1996, the Liberal Party elected as its leader Dalton McGuinty, the Member of the Provincial Parliament for Ottawa South, to replace Lyn McLeod with whom they had lost the 1995 election. It was a statement McGuinty made on December 18, 1996, which brought into sharp focus the dichotomy between the value of political promises on one hand and partisan political positions on the other, under which this new leader was functioning. He advocated publicly that the government breach its promise.

> Dalton McGuinty said yesterday the $5 billion cut to provincial income tax rates is too costly and should be abandoned—even if it means a broken election promise.
>
> "I think that they should kill the tax cut and I undertake here and now not to criticize (Premier) Mike Harris if he kills the tax cut," Mr. McGuinty said in an interview.

---

[121] "Taking political promises with a huge grain of salt," Paula Todd, *Law Times*, June 5-June 11, 1995, p. 7.

[122] Ontario PC - The Common Sense Revolution; Authorized by the CFO of the Progressive Conservative Party of Ontario and all of its candidates, 1995, p. 5.

"I will applaud him if he does not proceed with the tax cut and I will not criticize him for reneging on the promise."[123]

The proposal was doubtless made on the basis of the notion that the change of policy would be better for the province and more in tune with the Liberal vision of Ontario. Nevertheless, the forthright admission by a party leader that he placed greater weight on a political approach to a matter of public debate than on the continued validity of abiding by a campaign promise is highly indicative of the level of significance and lack of permanence of such promises in politicians' own views.

---

§ 6.7.A.4
Friesen v. Hammell
British Columbia Supreme Court; February 27, 1997
(1997), 28 B.C.L.R. (3d) 354
-and-
British Columbia Supreme Court; November 4, 1997
(1997), 47 B.C.L.R. (3d) 308[124]
-and-
British Columbia Supreme Court; December 18, 1997
(1997), 45 B.C.L.R. (3d) 319[125]
-and-
British Columbia Court of Appeal; January 20, 1999
(1999), 57 B.C.L.R. (3d) 276[126]
-and-
British Columbia Supreme Court; August 3, 2000
(2000), 190 D.L.R. (4th) 210[127]

A provincial general election was scheduled for May 28, 1996. The previous Leader of the governing New Democratic Party (NDP), Premier Mike Harcourt, had been forced to resign as a consequence

---

[123] "Tories should scrap planned tax cut, Liberal leader says," *Canadian Press*, December 19, 1996.
[124] Additional reasons at (1997), 45 B.C.L.R. (3d) 319 (B.C. S.C.), affirmed (1999), 57 B.C.L.R. (3d) 276 (B.C. C.A.), leave to appeal refused (2000), 252 N.R. 397 (note) (S.C.C.).
[125] Affirmed (1999), 57 B.C.L.R. (3d) 276 (B.C. C.A.), leave to appeal refused (2000), 252 N.R. 397 (note) (S.C.C.).
[126] Leave to appeal refused (2000), 252 N.R. 397 (note) (S.C.C.).
[127] Additional reasons at 2002 BCSC 1103 (B.C. S.C.).

of a scandal relating to the financing of lottery schemes and the use of their proceeds. During the campaign, the NDP was led by Glen Clark. He made statements to the effect that the British Columbia budget for the 1995-96 fiscal year was in surplus. He made these statements in the course of campaigning, intending to influence voters' minds and for the purpose of influencing their electoral decisions. The state of the province's finances was an issue in campaigning and the allegation as to their status was thus an election promise.

As it turned out, after winning the election, the new NDP government was forced to announce that the provincial budget was in a deficit and that its politics, expenditures and programs would have to be conducted in a manner different from that which had been promised during the campaign.

At both provincial and federal levels, British Columbian political life is rather polarized. Elections are toughly contested and among a significant segment of the population, there is a militant aversion to the NDP. Some of those who were both disappointed by the results of the 1996 election and outraged by the state of the provincial finances contended that the NDP's victory had been obtained by fraudulent means and as early as the summer of 1997, they were publicly voicing the possibility of referring the matter to the courts, something that had never been done before. They constituted an organization entitled HELP BC, short for Help Eliminate Lying Politicians, and were assisted by the National Citizens Coalition.

On August 27, 1996, Friesen and several others filed a joint application to be recognized as representatives of a class of persons induced to vote for the NDP by the misrepresentations of NDP candidates. They named as respondents every NDP Member who had been elected to the B.C. Legislature on May 28, 1996. The petitioners alleged as follows:

> During the election campaign preceding the election May 28, 1996 up to and including the election day the N.D.P. through its leader Clark, its agents and its endorsed candidates and the agents of the endorsed candidates, by diverse methods and on diverse occasions misrepresented a number of material facts in order to induce potential voters, including the Petitioners, to vote for the Respondent Hammell, as well as other candidates endorsed by the Respondent, New Democratic Party.

. . .

The statements particularized in the preceding paragraph were false and known to be false at the time they were made.

. . .

The nature of the information contained in the misrepresentations is of such a kind that the N.D.P. and the candidates endorsed by it knew that some or all of the misrepresentations were false and further, the said parties disseminated such false information for the purpose of inducing the members of the electorate to vote for the candidates endorsed by the N.D.P., knowing that such misrepresentations were central to the concerns of the members of the Class. Such a scheme constitutes inducing or causing an individual to vote, by fraudulent means within the meaning of section 256(2) of the Election Act, to elect the candidates endorsed by the N.D.P., including the Respondent, Hammell.

In the alternative to paragraph 48 above, if the N.D.P., and its endorsed candidates, did not actually know whether the misrepresentations were true or false, then they were wilfully blind to or indifferent to the truth of the misrepresentations as alleged and the statements were merely manufactured without belief in or concern for the truth of the misrepresentations, for the purpose of inducing members of the Class to vote for the candidates endorsed by the N.D.P., including Hammell.[128]

Despite the recourse to the courts and the invocation of law, the readers should not be misled into thinking that the petitioners were trying to correct a legal wrong done to them in the sense of having been misled. The relief sought was a declaration that the election of each of the 38 respondents was invalid, pursuant to section 256 of the *British Columbia Election Act*. This was in all senses a political and partisan undertaking, designed to reverse the NDP's victory at the polls. These petitioners would not, it is safe to say, have taken a similar writ if they had been deceived in similar fashion by any of the right-wing parties in contention, nor would they have received the help of the National Citizens Coalition.

Whatever the motivation, the significance of this case cannot be underrated. Prior to this litigation, the legality of election campaign promises had been tested in Canadian courts only at the lowest pos-

---

[128] Petition under the *Class Proceedings Act*; August 27, 1996, paras. 46, 48, 49 and 50.

sible level. This case was brought to a superior court of record, it was a novel and inventive line of argumentation and it was well enough structured and financed to be able to be pursued all the way through. Whatever the outcome, this case would set precedent in Canadian political and legal practice.

For almost four years, this case has been the focus of political controversy and intense media scrutiny. On February 27, 1997, the B.C. Supreme Court dismissed a motion by the respondents to strike the case, brought on the ground that they did not know the particulars of the case against them, as they were entitled to where fraud is alleged. The court based its decision on the fact that in our judicial system, there is a right of access to the courts. Marginally, the obvious issues relating to the mechanics of the electoral system and the secrecy of the vote were raised.

In respect of:

* the prohibition on asking voters how they voted;

* the fact that voters must give oral evidence;

* that no election be declared invalid by reason only of an irregularity if the court is satisfied that the election was conducted in good faith and did not materially affect the result;

* whether the voters may be out of time in any event for voting in the Advance Poll.[129]

The court felt those matters could provide obstacles to the petitioners but did not want to deprive them of the opportunity of establishing a case.

On November 4, 1997, the B.C. Supreme Court dealt with the petitioners' claim to constitute a class and refused to certify the class because they lacked standing, but allowed the three petitioners to continue the proceedings in their own names against their three Members of the Legislative Assembly. The most interesting point of this judgment was that which dealt with the pleadings of the NDP's counsel as to whether fraud on the electorate creates a new criminal offence.

---

[129] (1997), 28 B.C.L.R. (3d) 354 at 370-371, para. 63.

In summary, this argument says that if an election candidate in British Columbia, or an agent or political party of that candidate, knowingly makes a false statement which might affect the outcome of the election such false statement does not come within the definition of "fraudulent means" for historical reasons dating back to the *Corrupt and Illegal Practices Prevention Act* but even if it did, then such an interpretation would place the wording beyond the legislative competence of the province meaning that the allegations in the Petition could never succeed and so the claim should be dismissed.

. . .

This approach says that the Courts should so interpret the language in modern statutes (fraudulent means) in the context of fact patterns from centuries past. This "frozen meaning" approach to statutory interpretation is not one which I would adopt any more than the Courts have adopted the frozen rights theory in Aboriginal cases. I am not unmindful of the cautious approach in reference to the *Election Act* because of an infringement on Parliamentary privilege, but I would certainly reject this argument in concept.[130]

A third successive ruling was handed down by the B.C. Supreme Court on December 17, 1997, stating that the action could not move forward against the NDP itself.

The voters who were leading this action appealed the dismissal of their petition against the premier and the party before the B.C. Court of Appeal. On January 20, 1999, that court upheld the lower court decision. On making its determination, the Court of Appeal retraced the history of the province's *Corrupt Practices Act, 1871*, and the *Trial of Controverted Elections Act* and thoroughly looked at jurisprudence from other jurisdictions, notably Australia. Despite the fact that this was still a procedural aspect of the litigation, the court came close to resolving the substantive issues involved.

In our view, the primary object of provisions such as s. 256 of the *Election Act* is to maintain and enhance the integrity of the electoral process. In that regard, it is reasonable to conclude that, in enacting s. 256 and its predecessors, the Legislature intended to safeguard the public from fraudulent conduct on the part of, or on behalf of, a candidate or a

---

[130] (1997), 47 B.C.L.R. (3d) 308 at 317, para. 29 and 318, para 34, additional reasons at (1997), 45 B.C.L.R. (3d) 319 (B.C. S.C.), affirmed (1999), 57 B.C.L.R. (3d) 276 (B.C. C.A.), leave to appeal refused (2000), 252 N.R. 397 (note) (S.C.C.).

political party, which was of sufficient import that it influenced the judgment of potential voters by causing them to vote other than they would have but for the fraudulent conduct. We are unable to find any sound justification for interpreting the legislation so narrowly as to permit electoral candidates or political parties to fraudulently mislead the public with respect to material issues which could reasonably be expected to affect their decision for whom to vote.

. . .

That is not to say that every misrepresentation, no matter how trivial, would give rise to an offence under s. 256 of the Act. In our view, the type of misrepresentations which would fall under "fraudulent means" within the meaning of s. 256(2)(c) would be misrepresentations of material fact which were intended to, and did, lead voters to vote for a candidate or party for whom the voter would not otherwise have voted, and which were made by or on behalf of a candidate or political party knowing that they were false, or without regard to their truth or falsity.

Statements of intention or belief, and statements which any reasonable person would attribute to mere puffery would not constitute fraudulent means within the meaning of this section.

In response to the argument that such an interpretation of s. 256 would have a chilling effect on freedom of political speech, or that it would otherwise be inimical to *Charter* values, we would adopt the statement of Lander J. in *Cameron* quoted at para. 71 of these reasons. Freedom of speech is a cherished value in our society, but we are unable to conclude that this value is diminished by an interpretation of s. 256 which penalizes fraudulent misrepresentations concerning material facts which go to the heart of the voter's decision for whom to vote. As noted in the Australian decisions to which we have referred, freedom of speech, even political speech, knows some limits.[131]

One of the petitioners sought leave to appeal to the Supreme Court of Canada but on January 27, 2000, that application was dismissed. This decision finally cleared the way for the merits of the case to be considered by the courts.

The expectations of the trial were very high. On April 2, 2000, for example, *The Calgary Sun* titled its editorial "B.C. Case could change

---

[131] (1999), 57 B.C.L.R. (3d) 276 at 297, para. 74, to 298, para. 77, leave to appeal refused (2000), 252 N.R. 397 (note) (S.C.C.).

politics; Government might fall if judge rules NDP purposely misled voters." The hearing started on April 10 in Vancouver. The unusual nature of the case was reaffirmed by the uncertain manner in which the judge dealt with it at the beginning.

> Lawyers for the NDP "dumptrucked" more preliminary legal arguments Monday as a case challenging the party's right to govern became bogged down as soon as it finally began.

> Lawyers for the three NDP members of the legislature who are named in the fraud lawsuits and lawyers for the citizens' group that launched it couldn't even agree on whether they were in the right place for the hearing.

> Justice Mary Humphries of the B.C. Supreme Court conceded some confusion.

> "I'm not certain of what manner of proceeding this is before me," the judge said. "I can't rule off the top of my head."

> Last week, lawyers for the three MLAs filed a motion challenging the jurisdiction of the court and its right to compel witnesses to testify.

> "This petition has been dumptrucked on the court," complained lawyer David Lunny, who represents the citizens' group Help B.C. "This is a delaying tactic."[132]

Another particularity of the case was that Glen Clark, who by then was the former Premier of British Columbia, having been forced to resign as a result of yet another scandal, was subpoenaed to testify. The former Minister of Finance, Elizabeth Cull, also received one. Throughout the trial, until July 5, 2000, the parties waged media battles for the opinions of the electorate and the large circulation newspapers paid close attention.

> Niccolo Machiavelli would not have approved of the "fudge-it" fraud trial now unrolling in British Columbia. Machiavelli opined in The Prince that "a wise ruler cannot and should not keep his word when doing so is to his disadvantage,

---

[132] "Judge unsure nature of case," Greg Joyce, *Windsor Star*, April 11, 2000, p. C-12

. . .

In general, trials dealing with frauds on the public are salutary for a democracy. Politics shouldn't exist above the truth. At the same time, certain hurdles must be set that recognize when traditional electioneering has stretched into wrongdoing. The fraud should be based on a conscious misstatement of fact, and not a promise that for one reason or another a political party was not able to meet. Subsequent elections punish politicians for not keeping their prospective word.[133]

The British Columbia Supreme Court ruled on August 3, 2000. Given that the petitioners had conceded that the respondents had not, in the 1996 general election, generally contravened section 256 of the *Election Act*,[134] and considering that no breach of the provision by either Elizabeth Cull, the Finance Minister, or Glen Clark, the Premier, acting on behalf of the NDP, was proven, the petition was dismissed. While this was the principal element of the decision, it is highly instructive to note the entire text of the paragraph which immediately follows.

In view of the conclusion I have reached, there is no need to consider the interesting arguments advanced under s. 151 of the Act as to whether the breach materially affected the election and who would bear the onus on that issue.[135]

Section 151 provides the mechanism for challenging the validity of an election. By including the foregoing paragraph in her ruling, and especially by pointing out that the argumentation based on section 151 was "interesting," Madam Justice Humphries was clearly signalling her belief in both the intellectual merit and the social relevance of the mechanism and the standard which underlies it, of honesty in politics and in making electoral promises. Her sentence is almost regretful at not having been able to confront the reasoning of section 151 and thus developing the legal arguments and standards applicable to political promises.

The first substantive component which the court discussed was the standard of proof required. The petitioners urged reliance on the standard developed in *Bonneville v. Frazier*. The court held that a

---

[133] "Fraud on the people," *Globe and Mail*, April 14, 2000, p. A-14.
[134] R.S.B.C. 1996, c. 106.
[135] 2000 BCSC 1185, para. 93, additional reasons at 2002 BCSC 1103 (B.C. S.C.).

standard based on the balance of probabilities was not sufficiently rigorous, thus recognizing the extreme seriousness of the allegations and the process they were initiating.

> Extensive argument has been addressed to me on this point. The case before me concerns the integrity of a provincial election, not a municipal election governed by the *Municipal Act*. Allegations of fraudulent conduct are made against the then Premier and the Minister of Finance going to the very root of their fitness to hold public office. The consequences to the Respondents are that they may lose their jobs and to the voters in the three ridings that their expressed choice at the polls may be set aside. This is not a task to be undertaken on an evaluation of probabilities. Having considered all the cases in the context of the legislation and the issues before me, I am of the view that the standard of proof must be "beyond a reasonable doubt." However, I should note that the conclusions I have reached would not have been different even if the lesser standard of proof were used.[136]

In respect of the campaign statements, the court found that neither Ms Cull nor Mr. Clark were proven to be agents of the NDP. It did conclude, however, that no matter how confusingly the petitioners' pleadings were drafted,

> The impugned representations about the budget were repeated during the election campaign by Mr. Clark, who admitted he spoke on behalf of the NDP.[137]

The court was certain of the political expectations of the petitioners.

> Therefore, I proceed on the basis that each Petitioner heard Mr. Clark say, during the election campaign, that the NDP had balanced the budget and expected the upcoming budget to be balanced. Each Petitioner testified that they voted for the NDP candidate in their riding on the strength of that, and would not have voted for them otherwise.[138]

In determining whether these expectations had been wilfully breached, the decision comprised what can be characterized as an explanatory manual of the province's budgetary process. The key in this was the level of care taken by Ms. Cull in assembling the facts for presentation to the Premier and delivery to the public.

---

[136] *Ibid.*, para. 14.
[137] *Ibid.*, para. 30.
[138] *Ibid.*, para. 35.

The uncontradicted and unchallenged evidence of Ms. Cull was that the B.C. economy is very difficult to predict, particularly those aspects based on commodities such as forestry which are very volatile at year end. Ms. Eaton also agreed that forestry revenues can swing by hundreds of millions of dollars at year end. Ms. Cull's staff had been instructed by her to be conservative in their forecasts so that any risk to be borne would be by her alone, and her experience with the staff forecasts had shown her instructions were borne out.

Ms. Cull testified that "revenue optimism" was a shorthand phrase used by her staff, which she came to understand and use herself, to denote the complex concept of ranges of comfort associated with revenue projections. Both Ms. Cull and Ms. Eaton testified that the $ 275 million worth of "optimism" put into Budget 95 by Ms. Cull in March of 1995 did in fact materialize.

. . .

With respect to the "options briefing note," the only evidence before the court is that various assumptions were used, figures were arrived at, and Ms. Cull made her choices. There is no evidence that Ms. Cull instructed anyone on her staff to manipulate or jiggle figures.[139]

The petitioners tried to rely on a hand-written note from one of the Treasury Board officials to show that Ms. Cull had pre-determined a required surplus figure and forced her staff to use totally unrealistic figures to achieve it. They called this note "totally damning." The evidence showed, however, not only that neither Ms. Cull nor her deputy, the Secretary of the Treasury Board, had seen this note at the material time, but also that by the time they did see it, the Budget had been sent to be printed. If anything, the evidence showed the difficulty and unpredictability of the budget and financing process, particularly with the largest economic sector being that of forestry, which was volatile.

The court came to emphasize the complexity of the budgetary process and thus, as it stated, the fundamental difficulty of this case was that the petitioners believed that the Budget was a simple concept understood by everyone. This misunderstanding of the significance of the budgetary documents by the petitioners led to the evisceration of

---

[139] *Ibid.*, paras. 47, 48 and 57.

their principal arguments, which had evidently been based on their anti-NDP beliefs and positions.

> This simplistic approach has its appeal but it is not appropriate when the decision to be made is whether the Petitioners have proven that the Respondents or someone on their behalf acted fraudulently within the meaning of section 256 of the *Act*. The best that can be done, even in an election year, is that the Minister of Finance, in this case Ms. Cull, make her decision honestly and reasonably. I found Ms. Cull to be an honest, careful, articulate and well-informed witness. I accept that she believed that her assumptions were reasonable and that she was honest in her belief that the 1995-96 budget was balanced. She was ultimately wrong but she was not fraudulent.[140]

On this basis, the court went on to explain the actions of Premier Clark and to exonerate his role in the proceedings.

> I have found that Ms. Cull's beliefs were honest and reasonable. On the evidence before me, Mr. Clark had no other source of information available to him and accepted her statements. He then made the public statement that the 1995-96 budget was balanced. The statement was not known to be false nor was it made without regard to its truth or falsity. In all of these circumstances I am unable to find that the representation that the budget for 1995-96 was balanced constitutes "fraudulent means" within the meaning of section 256 of the *Act*.[141]

The court also looked into the relationship between the Premier and the Minister of Finance.

> Ms. Cull testified that Mr. Clark never instructed her that they had to have a balanced budget but there was a clear expectation from both Mr. Harcourt and Mr. Clark that it was her job to balance both the 1995-96 budget and future budgets. No one ever told her she had to bring in a surplus budget regardless of the facts. Mr. Clark said he may have told Ms. Cull he wanted a balanced budget, although he did not think he had. He agreed that he did want one as it was good public policy.[142]

As the final point in the evidentiary puzzle, the court also accepted that among competing sets of figures. Ms. Cull had the political and legal authority to select those she did because, among other reasons,

---

[140] *Ibid.*, para. 62.
[141] *Ibid.*, para. 64.
[142] *Ibid.*, para. 76.

she alone in the Ministry of Finance was politically accountable, not her staff. Moreover, she had no involvement either in the postpone-ment of the date for delivery of the budget, or in the selection of the date for the issue of the writs.

In the final part of its judgment, the court looked at whether fraud-ulent means were used by the respondents to attract votes to the NDP.

> If the Petitioners could actually prove that there was a conspiracy be-tween Mr. Clark and/or his advisors and/or Ms. Cull to insert grossly exaggerated numbers into this budget, ones which they knew could never materialize, they might overcome the hurdle placed in their way by the Court of Appeal—that is, that statements of intention or belief cannot constitute "fraudulent means."

> In order to come to the conclusion that Ms. Cull was forced by Mr. Clark to put forward a fraudulent budget, I would have to ignore the evidence, assume both Mr. Clark and Ms. Cull lied throughout the entire process and reject everything they said on principle. Then, without any evidence to support the Petitioners' theory, I would nevertheless have to make the findings of fact they wish me to make based on the simple proposition that if Mr. Clark or Ms. Cull testified to something, the opposite must be true. This would not be an appropriate exercise of my function.

> I am unable to conclude, based on the evidence, that there was any such conspiracy and that Ms. Cull's beliefs in the projections contained in Budget 96 were anything other than her best judgment in the circum-stances. The decisions were hers alone to make; the assumptions she used and projections she reached were available to the public. The ex-istence of the contingency plan, on the evidence before me, shows caution rather than deceit. As with Budget 95, the fact that Ms. Cull's forecast was ultimately shown to be wrong does not make her statements fraud-ulent.[143]

These paragraphs in particular are highly instructive into the genuine nature of politics as an art, and especially into that aspect of the art which deals with the financing of government and of society.

By the time this ruling was handed down, Ujjal Dosanj, also of the New Democratic Party, was Premier. He characterized the proceed-ings quite accurately.

---

[143] *Ibid.*, paras. 87, 88 and 89.

Years of legal wrangling took the case, which was bankrolled by the right-wing National Citizens Coalition, all the way to the Supreme Court of Canada.

B.C. Premier Ujjal Dosanj said the court ruling was what the government expected.

"We were confident that no legal violations occurred," said Dosanj.

Dosanj criticized the atmosphere of the suit, launched by Help B.C. founder David Stockell, which he said helped perpetuate the public's view of politics as blood sport.

"What Mr. Stockell did and what his supporters did wasn't a legal case, it was a political case," Dosanj said from Chetwynd, B.C., where he was looking at environmental damage from a massive pipeline oil spill on the Pine River.[144]

The most interesting rule-creation exercise that can be directly attributed to this case was that even before the final, substantive judgment of the British Columbia Supreme Court was handed down, Bill 2 of 2000, the *Budget Transparency and Accountability Act*, was introduced in the province's Legislative Assembly. Under the governance of Glen Clark's successor, Ujjal Dosanj, the Minister of Finance introduced this Bill in response to the Final Report of the Budget Process Review Panel.

The Bill proposes:

• to broaden the government reporting entity for budgeting and other purposes;

• to disclose all material economic and policy assumptions in the budget and other documents;

• to require a senior government official to confirm that the required disclosure is complete;

• to require the government to provide and report on its strategic plan;

---

[144] "Court tosses out election fraud case against B.C.'s NDP government," *Ottawa Citizen*, August 4, 2000.

- to require ministries and Crown entities to provide and report on performance plans;

- to provide financial and other information on all major capital projects.[145]

We can draw definite conclusions from the case. The law, as here, develops from political circumstances; obviously this is most true of political law. It can also be said that law takes much longer to evolve than the pace of political events. This kind of law is, to a large part, formed on the basis of legal arguments drafted by political opponents, merely transferring their adversarial argumentation from the political plane to the legal one. Moreover, law so constructed has little effect on those who were in power at the time the case was initiated, but such cases do have the effect of adding a layer of rules on the way politics will have to be conducted in future. Finally, law can be used in this manner because it is perceived of as just another weapon in the political and partisan struggle. In the more long-term, however, it should be seen as giving rise to rules of political life based not on partisanship but on justice, on rights, on principles, and it therefore increases the legitimacy of the process.

Notwithstanding the judicial vindication of the defendants, on July 25, 2002, the British Columbia Supreme Court ordered each party to pay its own legal fees and costs. The case was characterized as being public interest litigation.[146]

See also *Promises of Premier Bernard Lord for his First 200 Days in Office and plan for an MLA Responsibility Act*, 1993 Federal Liberal Promise regarding the Ethics Counsellor, Hansard, February 8 and 13, 2001; *Canadian Reform Conservative Alliance v. Western Union Insurance Co.*, 2001 BCCA 274 (B.C. C.A.) and *Ontario Debt After the 2003 General Election.*

---

[145] Explanatory Note to the *Budget Transparency and Accountability Act* http://www.legis.gov.bc.ca/2000/1st_read/gov02-1.htm.

[146] BC NDP must pay $1 million in legal fees to fight electoral fraud case http://www.canada.com/news/story.asp?id=[:fl6EBADA61-402B-44E9-9B69-BED7A89FO.

§ 6.7.A.5[147]
Fitzgerald v. Muldoon
New Zealand Supreme Court; June 11, 1976
[1976] 2 N.Z.L.R. 615

In some instances, litigants complain that promises made during election campaigns are not kept. In others, such as here, complaints arise out of the fact that a promise made by a party is actually carried out once that party is voted into office. The legality of the manner in which campaign promises are delivered may also be in contention.

Prior to New Zealand's general election of December 12, 1975, the National Party, under the leadership of Mr. Muldoon, had been in opposition. In the campaign leading up to that election, the National Party had indicated that if it formed the government, it would abolish a superannuation scheme established by the *New Zealand Superannuation Act* of 1974, in particular the compulsory participation provided for in the Act, and that it would refund contributions that had been made by employees and employers since the inception of the plan.

Immediately upon his election, on December 12, Mr. Muldoon, by then Prime Minister, wrote to the Chairman of the Superannuation Board, indicating the government's intention in relation to the scheme and inviting comment on a draft press announcement regarding the termination of the scheme. On December 15, the Prime Minister, in his capacity as Minister of Finance, issued a first press statement specifically referring to the intent of the government to carry out the National Party's election policy to abolish the scheme and refund contributions made. The significant part of this statement, which induced this litigation, was that it provided for immediate cessation of the requirement for employee deductions and compulsory employer contributions. It indicated that the legislation that would eventually have to be introduced "would also provide that all persons who have relied on [Mr. Muldoon's] statement, and acted in accordance with it, would be excused from any penal provisions of the New Zealand *Superannuation Act*. A similar provision would be made

---

[147] International comparison.

to protect officers of the Superannuation Corporation."[148] This first announcement was reinforced by a second one issued on December 23, which clarified that "the compulsory effect of the law would be removed with retrospective effect."[149]

On the basis of the incoming government's initial actions to carry out its election promise, as well as on the ground of the manner in which the government proposed to go about this, the present action was instituted. Fitzgerald, a public servant in the Education Department, took the rather bold step for a functionary of suing several of the most senior officials of his own government. The action was addressed at the Prime Minister, the Chairman of the Superannuation Board, the Attorney General, as well as the Controller and Auditor General. The principal remedy sought was a declaration that the press statement of December 15, 1975, was illegal, as it was made without lawful authority, justification or excuse. Fitzgerald contended that the announcement constituted an exercise of a pretended power of suspension of laws, contrary to section 1 of the English *Bill of Rights* (1688). The court perceived that the *Bill of Rights* had been received as part of the law of New Zealand even though it had been enacted half a world away for extremely different purposes and almost a century before the English settlement of New Zealand. The provision read as follows:

> That the pretended power of suspending of laws or the execution of laws by regal authority without consent of Parliament is illegal.[150]

It also noted that despite the rarity of this type of litigation and the custom of governments in following established constitutional procedure, it was prepared to consider a litigant relying on the *Bill of Rights*.

The court looked first at the Prime Minister's communication to the Board and judged it to be a request, rather than an instruction. It then examined the press statements of December 15 and 23 to determine whether Fitzgerald could obtain the declaration he sought. It concluded that while the statement began with nothing more than an indication of the government's legislative intent, further parts of the

---

[148] [1976] 2 N.Z.L.R. 615 at 617:20
[149] *Ibid.* at 616:49
[150] *Ibid.* at 622:1; quoted from 6 Halsbury's Statutes of England (3rd ed.) 490.

statement contained what it qualified as an unequivocal pronouncement that the compulsory requirement for employee deductions and
employer contributions were to cease as of the date of the announcement, rather than after the adoption of new legislation by Parliament.

> The Act of Parliament in force required that these deductions and con-
> tributions must be made, yet here was the Prime Minister announcing
> that they need not be made. I am bound to hold that in so doing he was
> purporting to suspend the law without consent of Parliament. Parlia-
> ment had made the law. Therefore the law could be amended or sus-
> pended only by Parliament or with the authority of Parliament.[151]

On this ground, the court concluded that the prime ministerial announcement of December 15 was illegal for breach of section 1 of the
Bill of Rights and it issued a declaration to that effect. In this context,
the court did not deem that the suspension of the *Superannuation Act*
of 1974 needed to be explicitly stated in the press announcement. It
was implicit in the Prime Minister's text, with the authority of his
office leading to the presumption that it was done lawfully. The
significance of this case is not simply in relation to the legislative
process, in that only Parliament can amend the laws it has enacted.
It is, more pertinently, that this is true even if the government's action
being scrutinized by the court is one that has been taken in execution
of an election campaign promise. In this context, the fact the government intended to adopt the subject legislation in order to fulfill a
campaign promise is immaterial. The legislative rule of Parliament,
that is, the fundamental role of law, cannot be circumvented.

The other aspect of this case that merits attention is that of the relations
between the Executive and Legislative Branches of government. The
Executive, the government, cannot override the Legislative, parliament. In section 1 of the *Bill of Rights* the prohibition against "the
pretended power of suspending" was against what was attempted
to be done "by regal authority." The court applied the concept of
"regal authority" to the modern structure of the State and concluded
that that phrase should today be addressed to the Prime Minister.

> ...The Prime Minister and the position occupied by him, which are of
> fundamental importance in our system of government. He is the Prime
> Minister, the leader of the government elected to office, the chief of the
> executive government. He had lately received his commission by royal

---

[151] *Ibid.* at 622:28-34.

authority, taken the oaths of office, and entered on his duties. In my opinion his public announcement of 15 December, made as it was in the course of his official duties as Prime Minister, must therefore be regarded as made "by regal authority" within the meaning of s. 1.[152]

The plaintiff's other petitions, asking for injunctive relief against the Prime Minister and *mandamus* against the Superannuation Board were denied. The court accepted the government's intention to introduce amending legislation and recognized that with the government's majority, it would doubtless be enacted. It would thus be unwarranted to have the scheme start up again under judicial mandate, only to be abolished after a short time at the behest of Parliament.

See also *Secretary of State for Education & Science v. Tameside Metropolitan Borough Council* (1976), [1977] A.C. 1014 (Eng. C.A.), affirmed (1976), [1977] A.C. 1014 at 1036 (U.K. H.L.); *Bromley London Borough Council v. Greater London Council*, [1983] A.C. 768 and *Haider v. Pelinka*.

6.7.B—POLITICAL PROMISES MADE OTHERWISE THAN IN A CAMPAIGN

---

§ 6.7.B.1
De Cosmos v. R.
British Columbia Supreme Court; September 19, 1883
(1883), 1 B.C.R. (Pt. 2) 26

The courts' regard at the binding quality of promises made by government in the course of public administration and outside an election campaign began shortly after Confederation and has been remarkably consistent; the early cases appear as pertinent to the current state of the law as the more recent ones. Here, DeCosmos was the Member of the Federal Parliament for Victoria, British Columbia. In that capacity, the provincial government appointed him as its Special Agent at Ottawa to press the Dominion to complete that part of the Canadian Pacific Railway which was to be built on Vancouver Island. British Columbia also appointed him for the period extending from October 18, 1880, until May 8, 1882, as its Special Agent in England to support or petition from the provincial legislature to the Queen. DeCosmos'

---

[152] *Ibid.* at 622:43-50.

expenses were paid but he received no honorarium and he sued under the *Petition of Right and Crown Procedure Act, 1873*.

The claim was denied but the reasoning was as interesting as it is appropriate to today's circumstances. The court defined the issue as being whether DeCosmos could legally enforce his moral entitlement to compensation. It looked at this matter from two perspectives. The first distinction it drew was between promises of a commercial nature implying a pecuniary obligation and a contract; the second was between a promise in the sense of a unilateral governmental intention to do something and a *quid pro quo* arrangement evidenced by the writing of a governmental authority. The court's conclusion was that a government becomes legally bound only if there is a contract in place, evidenced by its constitutional head. The mere promise of a member of the government is not legally binding.

> ...It cannot be too strongly impressed that (apart from departmental contracts or acts authorized by statute, or necessarily pertaining to the object for which a department is created) the acts or agreements of a Government can only be evidenced in one way, that is by the action of its constitutional head. The mere promise or opinion of an individual member of a Government, however influential he may be, is in no way legally binding on the Government. The country is entitled to the collective wisdom of all the members constituting the Government. They are simply the advisers of the Lieutenant-Governor, and he it is who, under their advice, makes the contract. Promises, therefore, made by, or understandings had with, individual members of a Government are of no *legal value* in Government contracts, unless the Government had deputed a particular member to take action in the particular instance, and has subsequently confirmed and adopted his act by Order in Council as sanctioned by the Lieutenant-Governor. A country might be ruined if each individual member of its Government could legally bind it by pecuniary obligations. There is a great difference between political consequences and legal consequences. A Court of Law can only recognize the latter. The country at large passes judgment on the former.[153]

Beyond that clarification of the legal and political implications of governmental promises, the court made specific mention of payment by government on the basis of promises not set out in contract.

> The usage of the Government of British Columbia has been to pay, or not to pay, as the political aspect of the Legislature may dictate.

---

[153] (1883), 1 B.C.R. (Pt. 2) 26 at 29-30.

. . .

> The lives of great public men show us that these inducements [power, triumph, achievement] are more powerful than money, and may perhaps have tended in the administration of public affairs to introduce the system that rewards such services should be gratuitous and honorary.[154]

---

§ 6.7.B.2
Reclamation Systems Inc. v. Ontario
Ontario Court (General Division); January 19, 1996
(1996), 27 O.R. (3d) 419

What, in the context of the modern practice of governance, is the meaning and extent of a political promise made outside an election campaign? What, if anything, becomes legally enforceable as a result of such a promise? To what is a government bound on the basis of such a promise? These are the issues addressed here. This case is particularly of interest in dealing with government because of the fine points of distinction it entails.

Reclamation Systems Inc. (RSI) undertook over several years' efforts to place a non-hazardous solid waste disposal site in a quarry in the Regional Municipality of Halton within the Niagara Escarpment Plan Area, an environmentally protected area. Upon the accession to office of Rae as Premier of Ontario at the helm of a New Democratic Party Government in October 1990, RSI sought to protect its interests vis-à-vis the incoming administration's strong environmentally conscious stance. On November 9, 1990, it addressed a letter to Rae, seeking "assurances that your government supports the right of RSI to have a fair public hearing and to have a decision rendered based on the merits of its application."[155] Premier Rae replied on December 19, 1990, indicating that "I can assure you that our government will respect the environmental assessment process, a process which is independent of our actions and assumes the parties concerned a fair hearing."[156]

---

[154] *Ibid.* at 32.
[155] (1996), 27 O.R. (3d) 419 at 424 d.
[156] *Ibid.* at 424 e.

This litigation evolved essentially for the purpose of determining the meaning, extent and legally binding quality of the cited passage of the Premier's reply. The matter became contentious because on June 10, 1992, a Private Member's Public Bill was introduced in the Legislature,[157] amending the *Environmental Protection Act*[158] and banning new or expanded waste disposal sites in the Niagara Escarpment Plan Area. This Bill was enacted and given Royal Assent on June 23, 1994.

RSI's position was that Bill 62 effectively ended its chances of opening the waste disposal facility. It sued Rae and the Government of Ontario on the basis that the Premier's quoted letter constituted negligent misrepresentation. It sought $8 million in damages relating to expenditures previously incurred and $480 million in respect of lost profits. In response, Rae applied for motions to the effect that the action was barred by the immunity from proceeding clause included in Bill 62, and that the action be struck out as disclosing no reasonable cause of action. It is the latter argument of defence that dealt in particular with the legal merit of the promise contained in the Premier's letter and which therefore concerns us.

> The defendants argue that there is no possible cause of action arising out of the exchange of correspondence between RSI and the Premier. The defendants assert that it is absurd to argue that letters of a mere political nature or in the nature of a courtesy reply by the Premier could give rise to a legal cause of action.
>
> . . .
>
> Moreover, if the passage of Bill 62 is the operative cause of the plaintiff's difficulties then, the defendants submit, it was beyond the right and the power of the Premier to limit himself or any other member of the Legislature as to how votes would be cast or what would ensue in the course of the Bill proceeding through the legislative process.
>
> The Legislature is sovereign provided it is acting within the ambit of its authority under the Constitution of Canada. The Legislature can and does change the law as it deems appropriate. The defendants argue that it is the independent Legislature which is the cause of any complaint of the plaintiff and not the Premier and his Government.[159]

---

[157] Bill 62 of 1992.
[158] R.S.O. 1990, c. E.19, as amended.
[159] *Supra* note 156 at 427 a and d-f.

In sum, this defence amounted to saying that Rae's letter was not a promise, that the Premier could not bind the Legislature and that it could not be known if RSI's application would ever have been approved.

The court's first finding was that the clause in Bill 62 which sought to immunize the Crown in right of Ontario, the Government of Ontario, any member of the Executive Council (Cabinet) or any public servant from action in respect of the effect of the amendment brought to the *Environmental Protection Act* by the Bill had no application to the plaintiff's action and the first part of the defendant's motion was therefore dismissed.

With respect to the issue of whether the Rae letter instituted an actionable promise, the court's first task was to distinguish the concept of "promise." Based on both previously decided cases and scholarly writings, it held that a representation is a statement of facts relating to the past or the present. By contrast, a promise is an undertaking as to future conduct, future events or states of affairs.

> In my view, the words of Premier Rae in December 1990 are properly characterized as both a "representation" as to a present statement of fact or condition (that it is not the Government's present intention to interfere in the regulatory approvals process) and also as a "promise" (the Government will not interfere in the regulatory approvals process in the future).[160]

Having defined what the Premier wrote, the court went on to construe what his words really meant. Was his letter an untrue, inaccurate or misleading representation? The answer was no: the representation was that the government was to respect the regulatory approval process. That representation was in fact honoured and therefore not untrue. This is the heart of the decision.

> The Premier's representation, reasonably construed, meant only that the Executive Branch of government would not interfere in the regulatory approvals process. Thus, the representation was not untrue, inaccurate or misleading.

> The Premier's representation did not say or imply that, at the end of the approvals process, the Cabinet's unfettered discretion to decide as it saw

---

[160] *Ibid.* at 445 b-c.

fit on the merits was in any way bound by the findings determined by the approvals process.

The Premier also was not representing that the present and future policy of the NDP Government was to guarantee that the Ontario Legislature would not pass legislation which would have the effect of nullifying the efficacy of the approvals process by making it unlawful to have any new waste disposal site within the Niagara Escarpment Plan Area.

At most, the Premier's representation could reasonably be understood to mean that there would not be any interference by the Government in the regulatory approvals process if and to the extent that process took place. The NDP Government did not interfere in the regulatory approvals process. Government members of the Legislature did support the Legislature's decision to enact Bill C-62 which, in effect, as a consequence, negated the regulatory approvals process. However, this action by legislators was outside any reasonable interpretation as to the meaning of the Premier's words. They cannot reasonably be construed as meaning that the Government's policy for the indefinite future was to prevent the passage of a Private Members' Bill that would nullify the regulatory approvals process and hence the plaintiff's proposal.[161]

Realizing the great sensitivity of the matter, the court went on to clarify yet further the proper manner in which the Premier's letter was to be interpreted. The plain reading of the text suggested that Rae had indicated that the executive government would not interfere in the regulatory process. Moreover, the court's reasonable reading showed that the letter was not meant to indicate that the government would fetter its own future public policy initiatives which might result in changes in legislation.

The introduction, enactment and assenting to of the legislation deserves particular attention here. RSI had understood Rae's letter to mean that the law enabling it to seek regulatory authorization to open the waste disposal site would not be changed. It was surprised when Bill 62 was introduced by a Private Member of the Legislature. It claimed to have received government assurances that the Bill would not be enacted and later, that it would not be assented, before further consultation. The court held these beliefs on RSI's part to be totally unreasonable and unfounded.

---

[161] *Ibid.* at 446 b-g.

The Premier could not (and did not purport in his statement so to do) fetter the elected members of the Legislature from voting as they saw fit in the public interest.[162]

But what of the alleged indications given by others in the government?

These various statements made in 1994, at most, were opinions expressed by individuals that did not purport to and could not fetter the discretion of the members of the Legislature.[163]

Based on all of the foregoing, the court formulated two interlocking sets of conclusions, the first specific to this case and the second of a more general application.

Even taking judicial notice of the probable fact and political reality that Bill 62 could not have been enacted if the Premier (with a majority of the members in the legislature being NDP members) had actively opposed the legislation, this would not change my view as to the limited meaning of his words.

There is no vested right to continuance of the law as it stood in the past. The Legislature must have the freedom to devise policy and enact legislation that meets changing social needs. That norm is fundamental to a liberal democracy. More significantly, there could not be any reasonable inference from Premier Rae's statement that this norm was to be varied.[164]

In dealing with RSI's last ground for the action, the court determined that an action could not be based on a non-bargain contract, one in which there is no consideration received by the promisor but there is a detrimental reliance by the promisee, because there was no pre-existing contractual relation between the parties. Thus, the statement of claim was struck out as disclosing no reasonable cause of action.

From the perspective of political law, we may analyze this as an attempt by RSI unreasonably to bind the government and to reduce its range of public policy options and scope of action by ascribing an intent to the statements of the Premier and government officials that

---

[162] *Ibid.* at 448 e.
[163] *Ibid.* at 447 f.
[164] *Ibid.* at 448 e-g.

was unjustifiably broad in light of both the facts and the law pertaining to the circumstances. This case was plainly seen by the court as resulting in part from the unfortunate lack of understanding of the legal framework of the State and of the processes of governance by the plaintiff. It said as much when it stated that:

> The Legislature has the inherent right to do what it chooses in its perception of the public interest within its constitutional ambit.

> The plaintiff would know, or should have known, that the Premier would not, and could not, make any representation as to fettering the inherent powers of the Legislature.[165]

In a broader context of the state of political life in Ontario at the time, this case may even be seen as part of the exaggerated hostility of the business class to the elected government of a different colouration than its own, all under a legal cover.

---

§ 6.7.B.3[166]
Tito v. Waddell
Chancery Division; July 29, 1977
[1977] 3 All E.R. 129

This case is an example of the maxim that research can lead to the far corners of the globe to uncover fascinating points of law. The present litigation concerns the development of the Banaban people, the inhabitants of Ocean Island in the Gilbert and Ellis Islands, in the Western Pacific; it deals in particular with the effect and the enforceability of promises made to them by or on behalf of the British Crown.

In 1900, the P.I. Co. Ltd. started mining phosphate on Ocean Island. After the company went bankrupt, its activities were taken over by the British Phosphate Commissioners. At the beginning of this period, Ocean Island was a protectorate and it later became a colony. A resident commissioner represented the British government, a High Commissioner was involved and the Colonial Office in London essentially was the highest governmental authority. The Gilbert and Ellis Islands Colony also had its own government, under British co-

---

165 *Ibid.* at 449 d.
166 International comparison.

lonial tutelage. Between 1900 and 1971, when the resident commissioner was replaced by a Governor, there were a number of agreements with the Banaban people and landowners on one side and British corporate, and later, governmental authorities on the other. The essence of these agreements was to set aside royalties from the phosphate mining and to constitute a trust fund for the benefit of the Banaban people. In this action, the Banaban people claim the existence of a fiduciary relationship with the Crown and ask for specific performance of two of the agreements or damages on the ground that the Crown had acted in breach of that relationship through conflict of duty and interest.

The import of the case is that in refusing to acknowledge the existence of the fiduciary relationship, the court held that a relationship of a different kind, namely a "governmental obligation" existed. It also went some way in distinguishing the concept of governmental obligation and distinguishing it from the trust relationship in equity.

> It seems to me that the surrounding circumstances, as well as the terms of the documents, do very little to support the concept of any true trust. Instead, they do much to support the view that, subject to the limited rights created by the annuity scheme, the Banaban Fund was a fund which was subject not to any true trust but to a trust "in the highest sense," or a governmental obligation, to use it for the general benefit of the Banaban community. It was money which the Banabans were told would be expended by the government in their interests; and no doubt this acted as an inducement to the Banabans to sign the 1913 agreement.
>
> . . .
>
> The Gilbert and Ellis Islands Colony government had peculiar governmental obligations to a relatively primitive people which were not owed by the United Kingdom government to citizens in England; and the concept of trusts, quite apart from its many complex and detailed provisions, was as common-place in England as it must have been ill-comprehended on Ocean Island.[167]

The claim having been based on the equitable principles of trust, the principal task of the court in rendering its judgment was to distinguish the true meaning of governmental obligation. The main difference is that the court held such obligations not to be enforceable by

---

[167] [1977] 3 All E.R. 129 at 226c and 227 c.

the courts; it referred, rather, to other means of persuading the Crown to honour them, without enumerating these means. We may therefore be left to understand that the means of persuasion must at least include political and electoral means.

> Another way of putting much the same point is to emphasise the possible explanations that there are for a transaction. In the case of an individual, there will often be only two feasible explanations, either that he holds on a true trust, or else that he holds on no trust at all, but at most subject to a mere moral obligation. In the case of the Crown, there is a third possible explanation, namely, that there is a truest in the higher sense, or governmental obligation. Though this latter type of obligation is not enforceable in the courts, many other means are available of persuading the Crown to honour its governmental obligations, should it fail to do so ex mero motu. This is accordingly no mere moral obligation; and it can provide a satisfactory and probable explanation of a transaction which had been conducted with formalities which suggest that more than a mere moral obligation was intended. Without putting matters on the basis of any "burden of proof," the existence of this alternative explanation when the alleged trustee is the Crown means that the courts will be ready to adopt it unless there is a sufficient indication that instead a true trust was intended.[168]

In sum, British law characterizes governmental obligations as a form of "higher trust," but considers them non-justiciable.

---

[168] *Ibid.* at 222 b-d.

6.8 ISSUE: VARIATIONS OF POLITICAL ALLEGIANCE

6.8.A—CHANGES OF INDIVIDUALS' PARTY ALLEGIANCE

§ 6.8.A.1

Hoeppner v. Shaker, personally and on behalf of all other Executive Councillors of the Reform Party of Canada who voted on October 15, 1999, in favour of a resolution to revoke the applicant's membership in the Reform Party of Canada

Manitoba Queen's Bench; file C1 99-01-15378

filed November 8, 1999; abandoned December 3, 1999

Instances of expulsion of a caucus member by a political party are more common than those of the voluntary change of party allegiance by an election Member of Parliament. Such expulsions can indicate the relationship between party discipline as a political instrument of governance and law. During most of 1999, Preston Manning, the Leader of the Reform Party of Canada, favoured merging his party with the Progressive Conservative Party of Canada, so as to form a United Alternative of the Right, which could be more likely to do well in future elections against the Liberal Party. A few members of the Reform caucus, among them Jake Hoeppner, then MP for Portage-Lisgar, Manitoba, openly opposed Manning on this fundamental issue. In order to enforce party discipline, Hoeppner was at first suspended from the caucus and on August 13, 1999, he was permanently expelled. Hoeppner contemplated bringing a legal action regarding an internal party memorandum which questioned his loyalty and effectiveness. The Reform Party also urged restraint on its officials, not wishing to make Mr. Hoeppner a martyr in political life. Hoeppner also thought about filing a complaint with the Speaker of the House of Commons but eventually decided not to do so.

Hoeppner seems either to have not received advice to the effect that the justiciability of his status within the Party was questionable, or to have disregarded such advice. Preferring the litigious approach, with legal representation, on November 8, 1999, he made an application for an order to determine his rights under the Constitution of the

Reform Party of Canada and asking for an ancillary declaration that he remained a member in good standing of the party. He also sought to enjoin the respondents from removing him from the membership list of the party or compelling that he be reinastated, as well as an order quashing a decision of the party's Executive Council purporting to revoke his party membership. The principal grounds on which the application was based were Hoeppner's allegation that he had not received a "full and fair hearing" before the Executive Council and his complaint of not having been told what consultation had taken place within his riding executive. The key to the application is that it disclosed the genuine political stakes behind the application.

> (i) The applicant presently intends to run again as a Party candidate in the next Federal election. He believes his re-election and future livelihood depend on remaining a member of the Party.

> (j) In addition, the applicant has announced his candidacy for the leadership of the Party. The Party's annual convention is to be held on January 29 and 30, 2000, in Ottawa. The applicant's leadership campaign will be jeopardized if he is unable to attend the convention as a member.[169]

The legal manoevering was abandoned after about a month but in any event, it proved of no use in accomplishing the political goals which may have been behind it. By the time this action was initiated, there was too much political disagreement between Hoeppner and the Reform Party of Canada to be bridged. At the 37th federal general election on November 27, 2000, Hoeppner could not receive the endorsement of the Canadian Alliance, the successor to the Reform Party, and ran in the electoral district of Portage-Lisgar as an Independent.

This case, and therefore the notion of settling matters of change in party loyalty, proved to be more enduring than its initial phase indicated at first. During the summer of 2001, at the time when the Canadian Alliance was losing members of its Parliamentary caucus to the revolt against the leadership of Stockwell Day, the prospect of revival of Hoeppner's legal action re-emerged.

---

[169] Application, s. 1 (i), (j).

> Canadian Alliance brass are worried ex-Reform MP Jake Hoeppner will revive a lawsuit against the party if eight dissident MP's aren't stripped of their memberships.

> If the former rural Manitoba MP takes action, it will devastate the party more than the fallout suffered by the $792,000 defamation lawsuit against Leader Stockwell Day, national councillor Gee Tsang predicted yesterday.[170]

See also *Bears and Grassroots for Day v. Grey*, Alberta Queen's Bench, filed June 8, 2001, file no. 0101-11358, discontinued November 9, 2001; *Speaker's Ruling on Deborah Grey's Question of Privilege regarding seizure of computer files*, Hansard, October 15, 2001, p. 6081; *Schelin v. Grey*, limited information available; *Speaker's Ruling on the Application of the Progressive Conservative Democratic Representative Coalition for Recognition in the House of Commons*, Hansard, September 24, 2001, p. 5489; *Bill C-218 of 2001* and *Legislative Proposal on Crossing the Floor of the House of Commons*.

---

§ 6.8.A.2[171]

Timmons et al. v. Twin Cities Area New Party

United States Supreme Court; April 28, 1997

137 L.Ed.2d 589 (1997)

This was a test of the constitutionality of the laws of Minnesota which prohibited the fusion of candidacies across party lines. It was also the latest of several attempts to distinguish between election-related regulation and unconstitutional infringements on the activities of political parties by the courts of the United States.

In April 1994, a candidate for a position as a State Representative in Minnesota who ran unopposed in the primary of a major political party was also nominated as a candidate for the November 1994 general election by the New Party, a minor political entity. The State's election officials refused the filing of the candidacy by the New Party because by that time, the candidate had already been nominated by the major party. The New Party sued, claiming that the officials' action violated its rights under the First Amendment (right of asso-

---

[170] "Alliance brass fear new lawsuit," Maria McClintock, *Ottawa Sun*, May 21, 2001.

[171] International comparison.

ciation) and the Fourteenth Amendment (due process) of the *United States Constitution*.

The United States Supreme Court allowed the Minnesota law to stand. More importantly, it set out the legal criteria to be considered in matters of fusion. The interests of the State were declared to be the integrity of the ballot and the stability of the political system. Within these parameters, laws on variations of political allegiance through fusion ought not restrict the ability of party members to support anyone they like or limit the Party's access to being placed on the ballot. They should not interfere with the internal structure of a party, its governance or its policy making. On the other hand, parties must not use ballots as billboards for their political advertising. In sharp contrast to Canadian practice, the court admitted that the State could take limited measures to favour the traditional two-party system, thus enabling it to not treat all parties equally. As part of this reasoning, laws that prevented small parties from bootstrapping their way to major party status would not necessarily be unconstitutional.

6.8.B—MERGER OF PARTIES

§ 6.8.B.1
Ahenakew v. MacKay
Ontario Court Court of Appeal; June 3, 2004
(2003), [2003] O.J. No. 4821[172]
-and-
*Stevens v. Canada (Attorney General) and
Conservative Party of Canada*
Federal Court of Canada – Trial Division; file no. T-2465-03
in progress

The essence of these cases is to see whether legality or partisan political interests play the primordial role in the evolution of Canada's political life, and in particular with respect to the realignment of parties as the most powerful actors in that life.

---

[172] Additional reasons at (2004), 2004 CarswellOnt 1641 (Ont. S.C.J.), affirmed (2004), 2004 CarswellOnt 2246 (Ont. C.A.).

The roots of the situation are in the need for Canada's parties of the right to unite if they hope to present a serious challenge to the Liberal Party of Canada. When the Reform Party became the Canadian Reform Conservative Alliance in 2000, the Progressive Conservative Party of Canada launched two legal actions to protect its name and in particular the designation of "Conservative." Upon the resignation of Joe Clark as Leader of the Progressive Conservatives and the assumption of that post by Peter MacKay in the spring of 2003, the legal actions relating to party names were discontinued. In any event, by then, the name of the Alliance had become commonly used among the electorate and the citizenry.

On October 15, 2003, based on the initiative of the leaders of the two parties in question, these parties struck an Agreement-in-Principle on the establishment of the Conservative Party of Canada, by means of the merging of the two pre-existing parties. This merger was based on sections 400 and following of the *Canada Elections Act*.[173] On December 8, 2003, the Chief Electoral Officer of Canada amended the registry of political parties to reflect the merger.[174] A significant aspect of the way in which this merger was conducted was its impact in law. It was clear that as of the amendment of the registry pursuant to the *Canada Elections Act*, the pre-existing parties ceased to exist for electoral purposes and in the view of election legislation. Nevertheless, for parliamentary purposes and in the view of the *Parliament of Canada Act*, the Canadian Alliance and the Progressive Conservative parties maintained that they continued to exist as separate entities. There was very little public attention to this, as Parliament was then not in session. However, even between sessions, until the start of the 3rd Session of the 37th Parliament on February 2, 2004, the two parties continued to maintain separate existences in respect of their parliamentary functioning. The mutual impact of the *Canada Elections Act* and the *Parliament of Canada Act* on each other was thus left unresolved.

While the merger was perceived by the leaders of the two merging parties as beneficial, there was a sizeable faction within the Progressive Conservative Party which resisted the trend. Members of this faction questioned whether the Progressive Conservative Party could

---

[173] S.C. 2000, c. 9, as amended by S.C. 2003, c. 19.
[174] http://www.elections.ca/content.asp?section=med&document=dec0803&dir=pre&lang=e

enter the merger without an amendment to the party constitution. The initial steps taken by this group included obtention of a legal opinion which addressed, among other issues, whether the Agreement-in-Principle could be implemented by any other method than a properly constituted national meeting, and what legal process must the party use to implement the Agreement-in-Principle? It is of particular interest that on this last point, the opinion indicated that:

> Any amendment to the PC Constitution requires a two-thirds majority vote by those entitled to vote at a properly constituted national meeting. As the PC Constitution does not presently explicitly provide for the dissolution of the PC Party, it is likely a two-stage process would be required at that meeting.[175]

At generally the same time as the legal opinion, a group within the Progressive Conservative Party that was opposed to the merger enacted a resolution to nullify the proposed deal, in the following terms.

> Whereas the PC Party membership at a delegated Annual General Meeting in 1999 in Toronto overwhelmingly voted to run 301 PC Party candidates in every Federal election and affirmed this desire in the section 2.2.3 in our constitution at another Annual General Meeting in Edmonton in 2002, and

> whereas our National Council meeting in Richmond, September 2001, overwhelmingly defeated a motion calling for the party to work toward the formation of "a principled and unified conservative government," by amending it to read "Progressive Conservative government," and

> . . .

> whereas Peter MacKay having abdicated his first and foremost constitutional responsibility which according to 11.2 of the party's constitution is "to promote the Party and its Aims and Principles" and having breached sections 2.2.3 and 2.3 of our constitution which state respectively that our party exists to "[p]rovide an organizational framework within which Members of the Progressive Conservative Party of Canada can effect change, gather public support for its policies and influence government policy through the nomination of Progressive Conservative Members of Parliament, for the betterment of Canada" (2.2.3) and "[T]he

---

[175] Legal opinion dated October 23, 2003, by Gardiner Roberts LLP, entitled: Memo Regarding the Proposed agreement between the Conservative Party of Canada and the Canadian Alliance to Establish the Conservative Party of Canada, p. 2.

Party will operate in a manner accountable and responsive to its Members" (2.3), has endangered the very survival of the Progressive Conservative Party of Canada working actively to dismantle our party and devastate its electoral chances

BE IT THEREFORE RESOLVED that the proposed "deal" between the Progressive Conservative Party and the Canadian Alliance, which has not been mandated by the party, is null and void and will herewith not be proceeded with.[176]

The political and electoral imperative being invoked by the Party Leader, Peter MacKay, was responsive neither to the legal opinion nor to the resolution of the anti-merger faction within the party. Those opposed to the merger thus seemed to have no other option but to resort to legal action. Under the inducement of David Orchard, who, in the spring of 2003 had vied with MacKay for the leadership of the party, a number of plaintiffs thus initiated proceedings in the Ontario Superior Court of Justice on November 20, 2003.

They sought declarations to the effect that the PC Party Constitution does not permit either dissolution or merger of the party without the unanimous consent of all the members, a declaration that the party constitution prohibits the Leader of the Progressive Conservative Party from agreeing with the Leader of another party that the Progressive Conservative Party will not nominate candidates in every federal constituency in Canada, a declaration that by participating in the merger scheme, Peter MacKay was in breach of his written agreement with David Orchard not to engage in the merger, as well as other related remedies.

The hearing took place on December 4, 2003, a mere two days before the Progressive Conservative Party meeting at which the merger was to be voted on. The Court issued its ruling on December 5, dismissing the application in its entirety. The Court was satisfied that the situation was sufficiently developed to give use to an actual dispute between the parties. It considered that the dispute had arisen in extraordinary circumstances not contemplated by the Party Constitution. It also took note of the political aspect of the litigation but was not deterred from adjudicating by it.

---

[176] Resolution to Nullify the Proposed Merger, made in the Progressive Conservative Party.

I was not persuaded by the respondents' argument that Mr. Orchard might be motivated by political consideration. He is but one of the applicants. In any event, in this dispute, it would be hard to expect people not to be motivated by political consideration given the inherent nature of the dispute. My task is to focus narrowly on the real and important legal issues raised, and to remain strictly impervious to all political considerations.[177]

The Court's view was that while the party was an unincorporated association, the *Canada Elections Act* did bestow upon it some legal personality and legal capacity. It was, notably, satisfied that the party could itself be named as a respondent to this application. The Court also pronounced significantly on the issues of registration and its effects.

Thus, it can be seen that one consequence of registration is that the assets of the party may be said to acquire a public dimension. The assets are augmented by indirect and direct public funding. On the other hand, the assets may in some circumstances be paid over to the Receiver General.

I conclude that regulation of political parties under the *Canada Elections Act* is not confined to mere registration but extends to matters of essential substance.[178]

With respect to the central issue of the case, that of the merger of parties, the court held that a party's resolutions only approve "proposed mergers" and do not in themselves, accomplish the merger. That is achieved by recognition as a merged party, under the *Canada Elections Act*. It is thus that, pursuant to the *Act*, a merger "takes effect" when the Chief Electoral amends the registry of parties. In that context, the court stated that the obvious goal of the *Act* was to maintain and make available to the public accurate and up-to-date information about political parties.

A significant point raised by the applicants was that the transfer of the Progressive Conservative Party's funds to the merged Conservative Party of Canada should be declared illegal and therefore enjoined. This was also refused. The Court stated the overall ratio in the following terms.

---

[177] *Ahenakew v. MacKay* (2003), [2003] O.J. No. 4821, 2003 CarswellOnt 4930 (Ont. S.C.J.), para. 15, additional reasons at (2004), 2004 CarswellOnt 1641 (Ont. S.C.J.), affirmed (2004), 2004 CarswellOnt 2246 (Ont. C.A.).

[178] *Ibid.*, paras. 31 and 32.

It is my view that ss. 400 to 403 of the *Act* regulate the merger of registered political parties. Registered political parties may apply to merge into a single registered party. Upon the regulatory requirements being satisfied, the statute makes the merger effective. In these cases, the common law principles regarding unregulated voluntary associations upon which the applicants rely would not apply.

In expressing this view, I should not be taken to be declaring the law. In this proceeding I was asked to make declarations that the Progressive Conservative Party cannot merge, transfer its assets, or dissolve without the unanimous consent of every one of its individual members. I have decided, based on the view I take of the law, that it is not appropriate to make such declarations.[179]

The judgment of the Ontario Superior Court of Justice seemed definitive in that it enabled the PC Party Conference of December 6, 2003 to vote affirmatively on the merger. However, it did not deter continued litigation. Sinclair Stevens, one of former Prime Minister Mulroney's ministers, applied on December 30, 2003 for judicial review of the Chief Electoral Officer's decision to amend the registry. Steven sought an Order pushing the registration of the Conservative Party of Canada and restoring the Progressive Conservative Party to the registry or, alternatively, an Order setting aside the Chief Electoral Officer's decision, as well as an Order pushing transfer of the Progressive Conservative Party's funds to the Conservative Party of Canada.

The Attorney General of Canada moved on January 15, 2004 to be struck as a respondent in this action, noting the essentially political nature of the dispute.

This Application relates to an ongoing political dispute between members of the former Progressive Conservative Party of Canada, and the merger of that party with another political party, the Canadian Reform Conservative Alliance. If the AGC were to be obliged to respond to this Application, the AGC could be perceived as having an interest in what is inherently a private political dispute. It is only if the constitutionality of provisions of the *Canada Elections Act*, S.C. 2000, c. 9 that authorized the CEO's decision are challenged that the public interest is "directly affected" and the AGC called upon to represent that interest.[180]

---

[179] *Ibid.*, paras. 39 and 40.
[180] *Ahenakew v. MacKay*, Ontario Court of Appeal, Docket C41105, June 3, 2004, para. 32, not yet reported.

At the time of writing, this matter had not yet been adjudicated by the Courts.

In the meantime, the Conservative Party of Canada held the founding meeting on March 19-20, 2004 and elected Stephen Harper to be its Leader, in preparation for the 38th federal general election.

On June 3, 2004, that is not only six months after the congress unifying the Progressive Conservative Party and the Canadian Alliance into the Conservative Party of Canada, but also after the writs for the 38th federal general election were issued, the Ontario Court of Appeal handed down its ruling on the appeal of the *Ahenakew* case. It dismissed both the appeal by Ahenakew and the cross-appeal by MacKay.

The court dealt first with MacKay's argumentation to the effect that the merger was now a *fait accompli* and that the plaintiff's appeal was therefore legally moot. It dismissed this, indicating that the plaintiff could be successful and if it were, it would have to seek a remedial order undoing what had happened, rather than an order preventing it from happening. This point is extremely important in the sense that the court established its ability to order the scission of a merged political party, based on legal facts and norms, the political circumstances notwithstanding. In the long term, this part of the ruling may be the most significant contribution of the case to Canadian political law.

Next, the court turned its attention to Ahenakew's pleadings, based on the requirement that in order for the PC-Alliance merger to become valid, there would have had to be unanimous consent of all members of the PC Party. The court rejected this argument. Not only was the requirement of unanimity no longer a necessity in the common law of unincorporated associations, but the situation of political parties was also affected by the fact of their subjection to the statutory regime of the *Canada Elections Act*.

> In short, the Act is a sophisticated statutory regime under which registered political parties are recognized as entities with significant rights and obligations. Following the reasoning in Berry, I think registered political parties are legal entities at least for the purposes of fulfilling their roles in the election process. To do so they must control and regulate their internal affairs. It is as inappropriate to conceive of them as com-

prised simply of a web of contracts between members as it is to do so for trade unions.[181]

In essence, by enacting the relevant provisions of the Act, Parliament may have displaced any common law requirement that might otherwise have applied in this context.

> There is no suggestion in this detailed regulatory scheme that Parliament considered it necessary to require the unanimous consent of all of the members of a merging party. The legislation contains no such requirement. The obligation resting on a party is simply to pass the resolution approving the proposed merger. Parliament did not deem it necessary that this resolution achieve any special level of support amongst those voting, let alone the support of all of the members of the party. Rather, the legislation treats registered political parties as having reached a sufficient level of organizational maturity that they can determine for themselves whether more than majority support of those voting is needed for a resolution approving a proposed merger.[182]

The court made one other statement which is worth noting. It reinforced the fact that once the merger had taken effect, the merged party became the successor to each merging party and each of the merging parties was dissolved. This was definitely within the court's *ratio*. We may therefore be allowed to contrast this finding with the assertion made on behalf of both pre-merger parties in the period between December 2003 and February 2004, that the merger applied only for purposes of the *Canada Elections Act*, but not in respect of their existence, positions and functions within Parliament. The court's ruling might enable some to argue that a party is a party is a party, irrespective of whether for electoral or parliamentary purposes. This matter is not mere idle speculation. Between the December 2003 congress at which the merge took place and February 2004 opening of the 3rd Session of the 37th Parliament, the Alliance and PC parties continued to function in the parliamentary sphere as if they were still distinct parties.

---

[181] *Ibid.*, para. 38.
[182] International comparison.

6.9 ISSUE: POLITICAL BOOKS, DOCUMENTS AND MEMOIRS

See *Ashdown v. Telegraph Group Ltd.*,[183] [2001] EWCA Civ 1142; July 18, 2001.

---

[183] *Stevens v. Canada (Attorney General) and Conservative Party*, Federal Court of Canada – Trial Division, file no. T-2465-03; Written Representations of the Respondent, The Attorney General of Canada, para. 12.

CHOICE OF THE APPRORIATE INSTRUMENT FOR GOVERNANCE

7.1 GENERAL PRINCIPLES

See Volume I, Chapter 7.

7.2 ISSUE: CONSTITUTIONAL REQUIREMENT TO LEGISLATE

§ 7.2.1[1]
Ferrell v. Ontario (Attorney General)
Ontario Court of Appeal; December 7, 1998
(1998), 42 O.R. (3d) 97[2]

This case arose out of the controversy raging in Ontario in the early 1990's relating to the way in which to provide for equity in the employment market. In 1993, the New Democratic government of the province had enacted legislation called the *Employment Equity Act*[3] to ensure that what they perceived as disadvantaged groups in society could occupy an appropriate place in the economy. In 1995, after the Progressive Conservative government came into office, the point of view of the government became a radically different one. The *Employment Equity Act* was repealed by the *Job Quotas Repeal Act*,[4] effec-

---

[1] Cross-reference to § 1.14.7.
[2] Leave to appeal refused (1999), 252 N.R. 197 (note) (S.C.C.).
[3] S.O. 1993, c. 35.
[4] S.O. 1995, c. 4.

tive December 14, 1995. The new government proposed to supervise the labour force market by means of a non-legislated program to be called the Employment Equity Program, which introduced a voluntary equal opportunity plan. Ferrell immediately applied for an injunction to suspend the operation of the *Job Quotas Repeal Act* and also challenged the constitutional validity of the legislation, alleging that it was contrary to the section 15 equality provision of the *Charter*.

At the stage of the injunction hearing, the first threshold Ferrell was required to meet was that of proving that a serious constitutional issue had to be determined. This led the court not only into the question of measuring the *Job Quotas Repeal Act* against the standard of the *Charter* but, more deeply, into the issue of whether the *Charter* required that government remedy inequality and discrimination through corrective legislation. The court's initial response was negative.

> The problem with the Applicants' position is that Bill 8 is a repealing statute. It repeals a statute, and several provisions that can be measured against the *Charter*, including s. 15. The purpose of the *Charter* is to ensure that governments comply with the *Charter* when they make laws. The *Charter* does not go further and require that governments enact laws to remedy societal problems, including problems of inequality and discrimination. One can hope that governments will regard this as part of their mission; however, the *Charter* does not impose this mission at the high level of constitutional obligation - Section 32 of the *Charter* states that the *Charter* applies to governments. Governments speak through laws, regulations and practices.[5]

The General Division judgment on the merits of the case analysed the same point in greater detail. The main thrust of the application was that with a liberal and purposive interpretation, the *Charter* meant government had a positive duty to legislate in order to give full effect to section 15 of the *Charter*. In consequence, according to this reasoning, a posture of governmental restraint would not suffice in order to protect disadvantaged citizens.

The court focused its analysis of the application on the link between the alleged duty of the State to legislate and the notion of the rule of law, the founding principle of the *Charter*. The initial state of individ-

---

[5] Endorsement of MacPherson, J., (December 29, 1995), Doc. RE/6078/95 (Ont. Gen. Div.).

ual citizenship was based on self-help. With the advent of the social contract, citizens yielded the right to protect them to the State. From this partnership of the individual and the collectivity emerged the rule of law. The *Charter*, founded on the basis of the rule of law, added the guarantee of rights. By this level of development, the question was whether the *Charter* should be read in the sense of offering only negative, or more boldly, positive protection of rights. The next logical step in the applicants' view would be to adopt the positive approach and to compel the State to give substance to the preservation of the enumerated rights. In the opinion of the court, the precedents cited by Ferrell would not allow it to go that far.

> In my view, these arguments must all fail. Although it may be highly desirable for a government, from a social or political standpoint, to enact laws in a certain area, there is no constitutional duty on it to do so.

> The application of the *Charter* must be confined to government action as opposed to inaction. Given societal systematic discrimination, such inequality is not of the government's creation; it is a societal problem, one which the government may well address but which it is under no obligation under the *Charter* to do so. As Iacobucci J. stated in *Symes v. R.* [1993] 4 S.C.R. 695 (S.C.C.) at 764-765, "we must take care to distinguish between effects which are wholly caused, or are contributed to, by an impugned provision, and those societal circumstances which exist independently of such a provision." In *Andrews* McIntyre J. put it this way at p. 18: "To begin with, discrimination in s. 15(1) is limited to discrimination caused by the application or operation of law...."[6]

After further analysis of the related but not entirely on-point jurisprudence, the court firmly closed the door to Ferrell's argument and left the evolution of the law at its current level, namely that no positive duty to legislate exists.

> In my view, the overwhelming weight of authority negates the existence of any duty under the *Charter* to legislate.[7]

Ferrell appealed, but the Ontario Court of Appeal dismissed both lines of reasoning which he argued. With respect to section 15 of the *Charter*, Ferrell pleaded that the *Job Quotas Repeal Act* was discrimi-

---

[6] (1997), 149 D.L.R. (4th) 335 at 340, affirmed (1998), 42 O.R. (3d) 97 (Ont. C.A.), leave to appeal refused (1999), 252 N.R. 197 (note) (S.C.C.).

[7] *Ibid.* at 342.

natory because it did away with statutory measures designed to diminish discrimination in employment. In response, the court held that it is debatable whether, as the Abella Report[8] stated, systemic discrimination requires systemic remedies. Moreover, the court saw no constitutional obligation to enact the *Employment Equity Act* and said that the legislature was therefore free to return the state of the statute book to what it was prior to the 1993 legislation.

The Court of Appeal could have seized the opportunity to analyze whether the 1995 legislation, as a repealing statute, was justifiable. Rather, it looked only at whether section 15 of the *Charter* obliged governments to formulate new laws and it answered this question in the negative. However, it said that even if the answer were affirmative, the nature and scope of the obligation is not justiciable and a court is not competent to answer.

> Courts, acting under the *Charter*, have no guidance in making their determinations of what the *Charter* requires of legislatures.[9]

7.3 ISSUE: REQUIREMENT TO USE LEGISLATION AS THE PROPER INSTRUMENT

§ 7.3.1[10]
Sinclair c. Québec (Procureur général)
Supreme Court of Canada; February 27, 1992
[1992] 1 S.C.R. 579

In the mid 1980's, it was the intention of the Government of Québec to amalgamate into one municipality the two contiguous cities of Rouyn and Noranda which, for all intents and purposes, constituted a single community. Toward that end, the National Assembly enacted a Bill which became *An Act respecting the cities of Rouyn and Noranda* and which came into force on June 20, 1985. This statute provided for

---

8 Report of the Commission on Equality in Employment, 1984 (R.S. Abella, Commissioner) Rosalie Abella has since the writing of that Report become a member of the Ontario Court of Appeal.
9 (1998), 42 O.R. (3d) 97 at 116 b, leave to appeal refused (1999), 252 N.R. 197 (note) (S.C.C.).
10 Cross-reference to § 1.3.A.7 and 8.9.1.

a number of steps that would lead to the creation of the new, combined city by May 1, 1986. The two pre-existing municipalities were
to arrive at a draft agreement containing the terms and conditions of
their amalgamation. If they could not agree, the Minister of Municipal
Affairs would impose an agreement by order. It was provided that
the residents could then approve the proposed terms in a referendum.
If that produced a vote favourable to union, the government would
issue an order for the making of letters patent for the new city, those
letters patent would be made, and then published. The new city
would come into existence on the date of that publication.

As the cities could not agree on the terms of their amalgamation, the
Minister of Municipal Affairs had to issue a draft agreement by order
on January 20, 1986. This was done in French only. Preparations were
begun for the referendum to be held on March 23, 1986. At that point,
on February 27, 1986, Sinclair and several citizens of Noranda who
opposed the prospect of union started a court challenge to the constitutional validity of the legislation on grounds that it contravened
a number of provisions of the Québec *Charter of Human Rights and
Freedoms* and of the Canadian *Charter of Rights and Freedoms*. They
later extended their claim, applying for an injunction to restrain the
holding of the referendum. One of their contentions was that the
Minister's order of January 20, 1986 was invalid because, despite the
fact that as an order it was a legislative instrument, published in
French alone, contrary to section 133 of the *Constitution Act, 1867*,
which reads as follows:

> 133. Either the English or the French Language may be used by any
> Person in the Debates of the Houses of the Parliament of Canada and of
> the Houses of the Legislature of Quebec; and both those Languages shall
> be used in the respective Records and Journals of those Houses; and
> either of those Languages may be used by any Person or in any Pleading
> or Process in or issuing from any Court of Canada established under this
> Act, and in or from all or any of the Courts of Quebec.
>
> The Acts of the Parliament of Canada and of the Legislature of Quebec
> shall be printed and published in both those Languages. [11]

On March 23, 1986, the referendum on amalgamation was actually
held and subsequently, the Minister of Municipal Affairs and the
Government of Québec took all the steps set out in the legislative

---

[11] S.Q. 1985, c. 48.

arrangement leading toward amalgamation. The instruments along that path that were published were done so in the French language only.

On July 4, 1986, the Québec Superior Court dismissed Sinclair's action. As part of its judgment, it held that the order issued by the Minister on January 20, 1986, in lieu of a draft agreement between Rouyn and Noranda for the terms and conditions of amalgamation was valid, because it was not an instrument of a legislative nature. This judgment altered the focus of the litigation from one based on the compliance of the statute aiming to create the combined city with the several charters, to one focused on the linguistic requirements pertaining to the legislative process and hence on the legislative process itself.

It was from the perspective that the matter was considered by the Québec Court of Appeal which, in reversing the Superior Court, found that the various instruments made and issued in the course of the amalgamation process were legislative in nature, should have complied with section 133 and that as they had not, were of no force and effect.

The Supreme Court of Canada considered the case twice. In the first judgment,[12] it disposed in the most summary manner possible of all issues relating to the charters by rejecting the pleas of Sinclair. In this, a separate and further judgment, the court dealt with the section 133 argument alone. It is worthy of note that the litigating parties were not the only ones involved in this matter. Given their interest in matters of language, the Attorneys General of Canada and of Manitoba intervened, as did Alliance Québec, an English language lobby, and the Alliance for Language Communities in Québec.

The Supreme Court treated this case primarily as one dealing with the legislative process, its definition, extent and characteristics. In that connection, it held that "if the net effect of a series of discrete acts has a legislative character, then each of those component acts will also be imbued with the same character."[13] The apparent consequence of this reasoning is that the requirement is not that legislation must be used to accomplish a governmental goal, but only that if

---

[12] [1991] 3 S.C.R. 134.
[13] [1992] 1 S.C.R. 579 at 588d.

instruments of a legislative rather than executive nature are used, the entire process must be recognized as being legislative in nature. However, a more careful reading of this line of argumentation will allow the reader to draw further conclusions. The court expressed its views regarding instances where legislation is required to achieve a governmental goal, where the use of legislation is mandatory, rather than merely appropriate.

The question of genuine importance in Sinclair is whether this ruling can be interpreted further, to indicate that in order to accomplish a particular governmental goal, instruments of a legislative nature must be used. Traditionally, the courts may be held to interpret the requirements of the Constitution and of the legal system and in doing so, they are authorized to recognize the nature of governmental actions undertaken by the legislature and the executive. It has, however, been accepted that they cannot dictate directly to the other branches of government by what means, or through what types of instruments these must govern. In this instance, the traditional view is being eroded by the court's use of its ability to interpret the legal system.

In order to determine whether each of the instruments used toward accomplishing the amalgamation of Rouyn and Noranda was legislative and therefore subject to the section 133 requirement, or not, the court looked at those instruments individually. Its most significant ratio was written with respect to the actual letters patent of April 23, 1986, by which the new city was to be established. The way the court examined the matter was to ask whether the new city could have been created by an executive instrument, that is by something other than an instrument of a legislative character. First, the Supreme Court adopted the reasoning of the Québec Court of Appeal, which had held that:

> Ordinary letters patent creating municipal corporations are regulatory in nature; *a fortiori* those issued on an exceptional basis, without the consent of the municipal corporations of Rouyn and Noranda.[14]

The court went on to clarify the way it perceived the actions of the Québec authorities in this process. They had, it said,

---

[14] *Ibid.* at 590g.

...created a new judicial framework within which new municipal institutions would function *determining* the rights and liabilities of citizens.

. . .

An instrument which creates new local governmental institutions cannot escape the operation of s. 133 of the *Constitution Act, 1867* simply by a circuitous path of enactment. Had the National Assembly chosen to amalgamate Rouyn and Noranda on terms imposed by statute, this statute, and these terms, would have been required to be published in the French and English languages. This requirement cannot be circumvented by following the procedure that the Government of Quebec saw fit to adopt.[15]

The overall effect of this statement of the law is that in instances where public authorities have as their goal: a) the creation of a new judicial framework, and b) the determination of the rights and liabilities of citizens,[16] they must accomplish these goals by legislative means, rather than through instruments of other types.

On the ground of non-compliance with section 133, the Supreme Court's decision in law was to invalidate the instruments which were the subject of this litigation. Ultimately, though, the two cities were amalgamated. The greater significance of this ruling for political law is that it provides public administrators needed guidance regarding the mandatory use of legislation.

---

[15] *Ibid.* at 590d and h-j.

[16] The actual words of the judgment on this point at p. 590d, are more precise in French than in English. The English version may be understood to mean that the rights and liabilities of citizens may be determined by the letters patent or by the new municipal institutions they create. In the French version, the presence of a comma indicates clearly that the court meant that the rights and liabilities would be created by the letters patent, the instrument.

7.4 ISSUE: APPROPRIATE INSTANCES FOR THE USE OF LEGISLATION AS THE PROPER INSTRUMENT

§ 7.4.1
O.T.F. v. Ontario (Attorney General)
Ontario Court (General Division); February 16, 1998
(1998), 39 O.R. (3d) 140

The purpose of this category within the study of political law is to examine the jurisprudence on whether legislation is the proper instrument to be used to resolve a particular legal and political situation, as opposed to the use of another type of instrument. This case addresses that issue, but it also shows how that question is inseparable from the broader matter of whether, in the view of the applicants, use of any instrument of governance should have been undertaken. Here, the two questions arise together.

In 1997, in application of the platform of carrying out a "Common Sense Revolution," the Government of Ontario wanted to reform the education sector. One of the aspects of this reform was a discussion of whether school principals and vice-principals should remain included in, or should be excluded from, teachers' bargaining units. The topic had been under discussion from 1995 until 1997. An education-related bill was introduced in the Legislature on September 22, 1997. On October 27, a strike involving most of the teachers in the province started. The principals also struck. On October 30, the government introduced amendments to the Bill to exclude the principals from the union. Then it started an action to obtain an injunction to force the teachers back to work. The clear implication of this litigation was that, at a minimum, legislation was the wrong instrument to use to achieve the government's desired purpose, and that it was badly timed, in conjunction with the principal's decision to join the strike. The broader contextual implication was that the government should not have taken the action at all, through any means of instrumentation. Underlying all this is the political aspect of the case, namely that the principals were disputing the use to which the Progressive Conservative government was putting its majority position in the Legislature. They were questioning whether the use of voting power, seemingly unfettered by the opposition parties' minority position in the Legislature was democratic. There can be no doubt regarding the politicized and indeed partisan nature of the situation which had developed in conjunction with the proceedings of a legal nature.

> The major changes introduced by the current Government in the educational sector have been the subject of much heated debate and action in the political arena.
>
> . . .
>
> On October 30th—on the eve of interlocutory proceedings in which the Attorney General was seeking to enjoin what the Government characterizes as "an illegal strike" and what the teachers and their supporters maintain is a "political protest against the Government"—the Government introduced certain amendments to Bill 160.[17]

In response to the tabling of the amendments to Bill 160, the *Education Quality Improvement Act, 1997*, the Ontario Teachers' Federation applied for declaratory relief to show that the amendments to the Bill infringed their section 2(b) [freedom of expression], section 2(d) [freedom of association], section 7 [legal rights] and section 5 [equality rights] under the *Charter*. Even more on point in respect of the present study, they alleged that the amendments

> amount to "reprisal legislation" designed not for legitimate legislative purposes, but simply to punish the principals and vice-principals for having exercised their basic democratic rights to protest against the Government.[18]

The government's response to these allegations was that its decisions were based on objectives of public policy, as articulated by the Minister of Education. The clear implication of this litigation was, as a minimum, that legislation was the wrong instrument to use to achieve the government's desired purpose and that it was badly timed, in conjunction with the principals' decision to join the strike. The broader contextual implication was that the government should not have taken the action at all, through any instrument. Underlying all this is the political aspect of the case, namely that the principals were disputing the use to which the Progressive Conservative government

---

17 (1998), 39 O.R. (3d) 140 at 143c and f-g.
18 *Ibid.* at 143h.

was putting its majority position in the Legislature. They were questioning whether the use of voting power, seemingly unfettered by the opposition parties' minority position in the Legislature was democratic.

It was in the course of these proceedings that the principals sought to summon the Minister of Education and the Director of Policy in the Office of the Premier for examination, and to have them bring with them a number of documents. The government applied to have the summonses quashed and the Ontario Court (General Division) agreed to quash them.

The court realized that the principals' desire was to examine these officials' actions and role both in regard to the legislation and its amendment, but also as it related to the political dynamics between the teachers and the government.

> In so far as the Applicants believe that the decision was motivated by improper purposes (i.e., as a reprisal or retaliation), they contend that the testimony of these individuals is relevant to the issue of the constitutional validity of the amendments to the legislation—including the reasons for proposing and enacting it.

> On behalf of the Attorney-General, Ms. Minor argues that the summons to the Minister should be set aside on the following grounds:

> c) that it constitutes an abuse of process;

> d) that the testimony of an individual member of the Legislature is irrelevant and inadmissible to the constitutional validity of legislation; and,

> e) that mandating members of the Legislature to testify about their statements in the house or their reasons for voting violates the constitutional principle of parliamentary privilege.[19]

Nevertheless, while the court acknowledged that pursuant to the *Charter* and challenges to the constitutional validity of legislation, it could admit extrinsic evidence, it was not willing to go so far as to force ministers or their civil service or political advisers to testify as

---

[19] *Ibid.* at 145b-d.

to their motives for the introduction of legislation. The court refused to become what it called an "extension of the legislative floor."

In our system of government, distinctions must be drawn between the functions of different bodies assigned various governmental tasks. Within the legislative branch itself, there is a distinction between the intent of the Legislature and that of specific Legislators. Ultimately, legislation cannot stand or fall on the testimony of ministers or on the public servants or political advisors who are their "lesser lights." The testimony would not be forced.

7.5 ISSUE: APPROPRIATE INSTANCES FOR THE USE OF POLICY AS THE PROPER INSTRUMENT

§ 7.5.1
R. v. Secretary of State for the Home Department
House of Lords; April 5, 1995
[1995] 2 A.C. 513

Where no measure exists for the carrying out of a specific governmental purpose in the course of the conduct of public affairs, decision-makers may be free, subject to constitutional direction, to implement such a measure or not. If they decide affirmatively, they may be similarly free to select whether to address the issue through law, policy or political instruments. However, where a particular type of scheme already does exist for the purpose of benefiting society and the body politic, the option as to which type of instrument is valid is itself guided by norms arising out of the legal system.

In 1964, the Government of the United Kingdom introduced a Criminal Injuries Compensation Scheme. This was made as part of the prerogative powers of the Crown; in essence, it was a measure of a policy nature, applicable at the discretion of government officials, ultimately responsible to their Minister. In 1988, the Scheme was converted into a legal instrument by means of its incorporation into the *Criminal Justice Act* of that year. The statute was so drafted that the provisions containing the legislated version of the Scheme needed to be brought into force by the Secretary of State for the Home Office (the Minister) at the time he appointed. For several years, the Minister did not make the appointment and in 1993, he declared that the subject provisions would not be brought into force. In their place, the Minister decided to use another policy instrument. The following year, Parliament voted appropriations for the scheme as set up.

The Fire Brigades Union was comprised of individuals most likely to rely on the Scheme. They took action to obtain declarations that the Minister had acted unlawfully in refusing to bring the 1988 statutory provisions into force, and that by implementing the tariff scheme, he had abused his prerogative powers. This case can be seen as indicating whether a Minister must bring into effect provisions which he has the power to bring into effect, focusing on the administrative law aspect. It is also related to the analysis of the legislative process. For present purposes, however, the case stands for the proposition that there are instances where a policy instrument is appropriate and others in which a legal one may be required. The House of Lords sided with the applicant Union. It held that the decision to use the policy based instrument in the form of the tariff scheme was unlawful in that the Minister had a duty to consider bringing the legislated provisions into force and could not decide not to bring them into force, flying in the face of Parliament.

> Surely, it cannot have been the intention of Parliament to leave it in the entire discretion of the Secretary of State whether or not to effect such important changes to the criminal law. In the absence of express provisions to the contrary in the Act, the plain intention of Parliament in conferring on the Secretary of State the power to bring certain sections into force is that such power is to be exercised so as to bring those sections into force when it is appropriate and unless there is a subsequent change of circumstances which would render it inappropriate to do so.

> If, as I think, that is the clear purpose for which the power in section 71(1) was conferred on the Secretary of State, two things follow. First, the Secretary of State comes under a clear duty to keep under consideration from time to time the question whether or not to bring the sections (and therefore the statutory scheme) into force. In my judgment he cannot lawfully surrender or release the power contained in section 171(1) so as to purport to exclude its future exercise either by himself or by his successors. In the course of argument, the Lord Advocate accepted that this was the correct view of the legal position. It follows that the decision of the Secretary of State to give effect to the statement in paragraph 38

of the White Paper (Cm. 2434) that "the provisions in the Act of 1988 will not now be implemented" was unlawful.[20]

The conclusion of pure law we may draw from this is that where Parliament enacts legislation but leaves the timing to its entry into force to a Minister, the legislators' intent is that at some point, the enacted provisions be made part of the active law of the land. More particularly in respect of the appropriateness of the use of various types of instruments, this case tells us that policy may be the proper choice:

a) where no legislation exists;
b) where a minister has the power to decide when to bring statutory provisions into force, he has not yet thought it timely to bring those provisions into force and is still considering the matter; or
c) where Parliament has enacted legislation making it clear that a matter of public governance may be operated in part through legislation and in part through policy means.

No example of the use of category c) comes to mind. In sum, the overall conclusion can be that the use of legislation displaces the use of policy as a type of instrument of governance.

7.6 ISSUE: APPROPRIATE INSTANCES FOR THE USE OF A PROGRAM AS THE PROPER INSTRUMENT

§ 7.6.1
Speaker's Rulings on the Use of Estimates to Establish Programs
Hansard, March 25, 1981, p. 8600
and Hansard, November 25, 1997, p. 2208

While many proceedings in Parliament are designed by one political party to gain partisan advantage over its rivals, they also have the effect of developing the substantive and procedural rules of democratic governance, including of course those determining the proper use of the various instruments for governance.

---

[20] [1995] 2 A.C. 513 at 551.

The selection of instruments in Parliamentary processes is greatly influenced by the pressure of time constraints. The Parliamentary calendar is short, the legislative and other related workload is great. It is primarily for this reason that governments, such as that of Prime Minister Trudeau in 1981, have been led to attempt to include in the use of some instruments items which may not have properly belonged there but which should rather have been realized by other, perhaps more time-consuming techniques. Thus, in the Supplementary Estimates (c) for 1981-82, the government of the day introduced several lines by which the cancellation of debts was accomplished, as well as the provision of funds for the purchase of Petrofina by Petro-Canada. This latter item was part of the National Energy Program, a highly controversial initiative emanating from the government's previous budget. A Progressive Conservative MP, a member of the Official Opposition, raised a point of order in the House of Commons on March 24, 1981, complaining that the use of the Estimates for the creation of programs such as the Petrofina purchase could not be justified in an instrument intended for the appropriation of funds by Parliament to the government. The foundation of his argument was that where a "legislative principle" was involved, a program could be created only by means of legislation, here meaning substantive legislation rather than an Appropriation Act. He also alleged that this practice violated subsection 18(1) of the *Financial Administration Act*, by in effect amending that provision implicitly. That provision established the process for deletion of uncollectible debts from the accounts of the government, on the recommendation of the Treasury Board.[21]

The Speaker of the time, Hon. Jeanne Sauvé, ruled that the items attempted to be introduced into the Estimates for the purpose of cancelling debts were of a legislative nature and had legislative content. As their enactment by way of the Estimates was improper, they were deleted. Regarding the Petrofina purchase, the Speaker remained unconvinced that that infringed on the traditional use of the Estimates.

This ruling was reinforced, in part, in the more recent decision made by Speaker Gilbert Parent. In response to the point of order raised on November 24, 1997, by a Reform Party MP alleging that certain items in the Estimates were attempts to by-pass the legislative process be-

---

[21] R.S.C. 1970, c. F-13, s. 18. This section was subsequently amended by S.C. 1980-81-82-83, c. 170, s. 5.

cause the bills related to them had either died on the Order Paper of the previous (the 35th) Parliament, or were still before the current (the 36th) Parliament, the Speaker again laid down the rule that supply procedure must not be used to bypass the normal legislative process. He also indicated that the Estimates must not amend existing legislation or obtain authority which ought to be obtained through proper legislation. In this instance, the Speaker held that the items complained of did not contravene this rule.

7.7 ISSUE: APPROPRIATE INSTANCES FOR THE USE OF POLITICS AS THE PROPER INSTRUMENT

§ 7.7.1[22]
Canada v. Prince Edward Island
Federal Court of Canada – Trial Division; January 28, 1976
(1976), 66 D.L.R. (3d) 465[23]

There are instances where the courts are asked to resolve situations relating to the conduct of public affairs which are both legal and political in nature. They afford opportunities to apply and develop the doctrine of justiciability: the courts appraise the facts and determine whether there is sufficient legal aspect in the matter for the court to resolve it. Where there is, they render decisions based in law, on the legal component of the issue. Where they determine that the issue is primarily political, they can reason that the matter is best dealt with by the legislature or by the executive, or they deny the relief sought simply on the ground that it is not within their jurisdiction, *rationae materiae*. Alternatively, they can reject the claim as frivolous and vexatious. It is only in the rarest of instances that a court will not only indicate that the nature of a claim is such that it is capable of resolution in a forum of another of the branches of government, but, going further, that the litigants ought to resolve their dispute by political means. This is one of those cases.

The obligation for the Government of Canada to ensure continuous ferry service between Prince Edward Island (PEI) and the mainland

---

[22] Cross-remence to § 4.11.B.1.
[23] Reversed (1977), [1978] 1 F.C. 533 (Fed. C.A.).

was set out in the 1873 Order-in-Council which united the Island to Canada. In 1973, there were two strikes which caused interruptions in the service. The Federal Court agreed with PEI that the obligation existed and that it had been breached. However, in the course of rejecting the province's claim for damages, it determined that the proper legal claim would have been for declaratory judgment and then went on to emphasize that the dispute could have been resolved by political means so forcefully that we can only conclude that the court was prompting the parties in that direction. The legal under-pinning of this is that the appropriate remedy for the breach of a general public duty is not a civil action in damages but to undertake political action. While the court touched on the availability of declar-atory relief, it placed far greater stress on the appropriateness of a politically based remedy. It reminded the parties that there had been interruptions of service on two previous occasions and that in those instances, the matter had been resolved through politics.

The judgment that breaches general public duties is best dealt with by political means rather than legal ones, goes to the very heart of the judicial view of the difference between law and politics. This is a well-grounded legal reason for determining when politics is the ap-propriate instrument for one seeking redress. In support of the prop-osition, the court cited a case arising out of one of the numerous interruptions of postal service in Canada.[24] A plaintiff claimed dam-ages arising out of the stoppage of service resulting from a strike. The Crown's motion to strike out the statement of claim was granted.

> ...the claim for non-performance of the statutory duty on the Government of Canada to provide a postal service to the public does not give rise to a cause of action in an individual injuriously affected thereby.
>
> . . .
>
> In the result where there is an obligation created by the statute for the general public good and where there is a breach of that obligation, there is no right of action in a particular person injured by the breach. That has been held to be the case in a breach by the Dominion to provide uninterrupted postal service. There is no fundamental difference be-tween a strike affecting the postal service and a strike affecting a ferry service.[25]

---

[24] *Canadian Federation of Independent Business v. R.* (1974), 49 D.L.R. (3d) 718 (Fed. T.D.).
[25] (1976), 66 D.L.R. (3d) 465 at 484, reversed (1977), [1978] 1 F.C. 533 (Fed. C.A.).

It is worthwhile noting that this case was decided prior to the advent of the *Canadian Charter of Rights and Freedoms*, which may have changed the underlying point of law, but not the court's conclusion as to the advisability of politics as the instrument of choice in such matters.

An appeal by the Government of Canada was dismissed but a cross-appeal by the province was allowed. On the panel of the Federal Court of Appeal, Justice Jackett and LeDain struggled to find the proper characterization of the obligation linking Canada and Prince Edward Island. Jackett referred to the political identity of Canada and of Prince Edward Island within the British Empire at the time the province joined Confederation and indicated that in the ordinary municipal law of the time, PEI was not a "person" capable of having rights and liabilities, suing and being sued. In is opinion, Canada was not, either, an entity having status as a person in British or international courts. He therefore called the basis of the dispute "a general statutory arrangement" rather than a contract or an independent treaty between governments. LeDain referred to the matter as a governmental responsibility. He did not believe either that there was a right of action.

These views expressed on appeal, intimate, without spelling out clearly, that politics, rather than law, was the proper vehicle for the resolution of this type of dispute. On this point, however, we must conclude that the Trial Division's *ratio* was of greater clarity.

8

INTEGRITY OF THE LEGISLATIVE SYSTEM

8.1 GENERAL PRINCIPLES

See Volume I, Chapter 8.

8.2 ISSUE: LEGAL PERSONALITY, STATUS AND PERSONALITY OF PARLIAMENT

8.2.A—PARLIAMENT AS A WHOLE

§ 8.2.A.1[1]
Reference re Legislative Authority of Parliament of Canada
Supreme Court of Canada; December 21, 1979
(1979), 102 D.L.R. (3d) 1

On November 23, 1978, the Governor in Council used the power provided to it pursuant to the *Supreme Court Act*[2] to refer to the Supreme Court of Canada a series of questions seeking to determine in effect whether the Senate could be either abolished or so thoroughly altered as to amount to a new and different constituent element of the Parliament of Canada. The questions were framed in terms of constitutional law and the court considered them as being primarily legal in nature. However, these questions arose out of the context of the attempt by the federal government to modernize what was perceived as the institution of federal governance least reformed since

---

[1] Cross-reference to § 1.2.1, 4.2.1 and 8.2.B.1.
[2] R.S.C. 1970, c. S-19, s. 55.

its establishment in 1867. The court was mindful of this circumstantial background and was not unaware of the political consequences of its ruling. Despite the controversiality of the environment, its analysis was primarily legal in nature.

The question being whether a part of Parliament as an institution and of the legislative process as a process of governance could be done away with, the court was led to a consideration of the legal status of Parliament as a whole. It grounded its analysis firmly on section 17 of what was then still styled the *British North America Act, 1867*. This provision created the Parliament of Canada and indicated that it would consist of the Queen, an upper house known as the Senate and a lower house known as the House of Commons. Section 17 is thus important in two respects. First, it established the institution as the legislative body at the federal level, for Canada. Second, in the court's own expression, it "particularized the participants in the law-making process"[3] as being the monarch, the upper house and the lower house, each of them being necessary and required as component elements of the institution and of its work. For purposes of this particular reference, this consideration was part of the court's reasoning for holding that the Senate could not be abolished. From the perspective of political law, the court's opinion was authoritative in defining the legal status of Parliament.

The court also determined what was the legislative authority of Parliament, its sphere of legislative work.

> Section 91 confers the authority to legislate in respect of matters within that section upon the Queen, with the advice and consent of the Senate and the House of Commons. [4]

> . . .

> The opening words of s. 91, the all-important section defining federal legislative powers, have already been quoted. Power to "make laws for the Peace, Order and Good Government of Canada in relation to all Matters not coming within the Classes of Subjects of this Act assigned exclusively to the Legislatures of the Provinces" was conferred by the

---

[3] (1979), 102 D.L.R. (3d) 1 at 15.
[4] *Ibid.*

British Parliament upon "the Queen, by and with the Advice and Consent of the Senate and the House of Commons."[5]

8.2.B—SENATE

§ 8.2.B.1[6]

Reference re Legislative Authority of Parliament of Canada
Supreme Court of Canada; December 21, 1979
(1979), 102 D.L.R. (3d) 1

There are few cases in the evolution of Canadian public life which are more closely tied to contemporaneous political developments than this one. The statement of law which the Supreme Court thus made in this instance is thoroughly permeated with politics and has a profound effect on the political, as well as the constitutional and legal future of the country.

It was in the summer of 1978 that Prime Minister Trudeau presented the *Constitutional Amendment Bill, 1978*[7] before Parliament. This proposal would have fundamentally revised the *British North America Act* and given Canada a model of government very different from that adopted in 1867, and very much more modern.

> The real thrust of the Constitutional Amendment Bill, 1978, is contained in the institutional proposals. Most notable are the proposed changes in the Supreme Court of Canada and its composition and organization, and the proposals involving the replacement of the Senate by a new House of the Federation.

> . . .

> The proposed new House of the Federation (sections 62-70) would be the most important constitutional change. The new house would have the right to confirm or reject federal appointments to the Supreme Court of Canada (section 107) and to federal administrative bodies, federal Crown corporations and the like (section 70). The new house would have a virtual suspensive veto of up to two months over all bills enacted by the House of Commons, including revenue and tax bills (section 67). A

---

[5] *Ibid.* at 10.
[6] Cross-reference to § 1.2.1, 4.2.1 and 8.2.A.1.
[7] Bill C-60, 3rd Session, 30th Parliament.

suspensive veto is certainly less than the powers of the present Senate. However, the present Senate's powers have, for most practical purposes, today lapsed into desuetude or disappeared through long-time custom and convention. The new House of the Federation, with an electoral mandate of some sort, would no doubt expect to exercise to the full its right to criticize and delay House of Commons measures.[8]

The proposals contained in the Bill were so controversial that the government was forced to agree not to proceed with them until further study and discussion. In respect of the reform of the Senate, the Attorney General of Canada, Marc MacGuigan, initiated a reference to the Supreme Court. That is how the court was provided an opportunity to restate the legal status and personality of the upper house. It is important in this regard to remember that this is a decision rendered prior to the advent of the *Canadian Charter of Rights and Freedoms*, and that it is a ruling from a time when the guiding philosophy of the court was far less modernizing than it has since become.

The Supreme Court interpreted the first and principal question of the reference as, in essence, whether the Parliament of Canada had legislative authority to abolish the Senate. Its entire analysis of the Senate is thus cast in terms of the reform of that institution through abolition, while those of Ontario, Nova Scotia, New Brunswick, Prince Edward Island, Saskatchewan, Alberta and Newfoundland pleaded against.

The court recalled that it was sections 21 through 36 of the *British North America Act* which dealt with the constitution of the Senate, the number of Senators, the representation of four divisions in the Senate, the qualifications for appointment and other related matters of detail. In analyzing the Senate, however, the court concentrated on section 91, and arising from the fact that the statute contained no amendment formula, the manner in which the amending process had actually evolved. The general principles of constitutional amendment were that:

- the United Kingdom Parliament would amend the Act only upon formal request from Canada;
- the sanction of the Canadian Parliament was required for a request for an amendment;

---

[8] McWhinney, Edward, *Quebec and the Constitution 1960-1978*, Toronto, University of Toronto Press, 1979, pp. 122, 124-5.

- no amendment was made merely upon the request of a province; and
- the Canadian Parliament would not request an amendment affecting federal-provincial relations without prior consultation and agreement with the provinces.

In addition, since 1949, when section 91 was amended in regard to federal legislative authority, the Parliament of Canada could make amendments alone, but only in matters that could be qualified as federal housekeeping.

The key to this ruling is that the court judged that abolition or reform of the Senate was not a matter of federal housekeeping and could therefore not be effected by the Parliament of Canada alone.

> The legislation contemplated in the first question is of an entirely different character. While it does not directly affect federal-provincial relationships in the sense of changing federal and provincial legislative powers, it does envision the elimination of one of the two Houses of Parliament, and so would alter the structure of the federal Parliament to which the federal power to legislate is entrusted under s. 91 of the Act.[9]

This finding led the Supreme Court to qualify the Senate as being an institution which was performing a vital, that is indispensable, role in the federal system of Canada. That vitality, in the court's opinion, stemmed from the similarity of the Canadian Constitution to that of the United Kingdom in principle, from the fact that the Canadian Union was to be conducive to the welfare of the provinces, and that the *British North America Act* was to provide for the Constitution of the Legislative Authority in the Dominion as well as declare the nature of the Executive Government therein. The logic of the court's opinion was that in the structure so ordained in 1867, it was not feasible for Parliament merely to extract one of the fundamental components because of its characteristic as fulfilling a vital role.

The court substantiated its findings of general principle by precise reasons. First, it explained the requirement for the Senate as part of the legislative process.

> Section 91(1) is a particularization of the general legislative power of the Parliament of Canada. That general power can be exercised only by the

---

[9] *Supra* note 3 at 8-9.

Queen by and with the advice and consent of the Senate and the House of Commons. Section 91(1) cannot be construed to confer power to supplant the whole of the rest of the section. It cannot be construed as permitting the transfer of the legislative powers enumerated in s. 91 to some body or bodies other than those specifically designated in it.[10]

The court went on to reiterate that the powers exercised by the Senate could not merely be transferred to the House of the Federation which was being proposed in Bill C-60.

The elimination of the Senate would go much further [than delegation between Parliament and a provincial legislature] in that it would involve a transfer by Parliament of all its legislative powers to a new legislative body of which the Senate would not be a member.[11]

In sum, the powers available to Parliament to amend the Constitution of Canada were not intended to include the elimination of the Senate.

In its response to the other questions addressed to it, the Supreme Court went on to state that the Senate had an essential feature of regional representation that could not be done away with and that the then prevailing constitutional framework would not permit a partially appointed, partially elected Senate. This method of analyzing the legal personality of the Senate was not very satisfactory either in terms of definition of the law, nor in terms of political outcomes. It was one of the factors which induced elected officials to continue negotiations.

It is a very static view to regard British constitutionalism as wedded to the principle of purely nominated or hereditary upper houses (compare Australia's directly elected Senate). In truth, the British House of Lords and the Canadian Senate are the exceptions—the constitutional aberrations, if you wish—in Commonwealth constitutionalism, where the clear trend is either to abolish upper houses or to legitimate them by election. The "radical change" so deplored by the Supreme Court would in fact accord with the best trends in modern liberal democratic constitutionalism.

The Supreme Court implies that direct election would impair the function of the Senate as a "thoroughly independent body which could can-

---

[10] Ibid. at 13.
[11] Ibid. at 13-14.

vass dispassionately the measures of the House of Commons"(18). Could it be seriously contended that the Senate, filled by political patronage on an appointive basis, does that? The Court would seem not merely to have departed from its own ordinary canons of strict and literal interpretation, but to posit its conclusions upon conceptions of the function and purpose of an upper house which the constitutional historian and the political scientist alike know to be unfounded. The Court would seem to have done its best to create further clogs upon constitutional change in Canada.[12]

Consideration of the matter of reform of the Senate is still ongoing.

§ 8.2.B.2
Southam Inc. v. Canada (Attorney General)
Federal Court of Appeal; August 23, 1990
[1990] 3 F.C. 465

This case, which rendered it possible for the judiciary to define the Senate and its role in the constitutional framework of Canada, arose from a dispute involving the access of the press to the meetings of a Senate committee. In June 1980, the Senate Standing Committee on Internal Economy, Budgets and Administration, conducted an investigation regarding allegations about the use by Senator Hazen Argue of Senate funds for the campaign to secure for his wife a nomination to the House of Commons for the federal electoral district of Nepean. A reporter for the *Ottawa Citizen* was not allowed to attend. He then applied for *certiorari* and injunctive relief and in motions, the Law Clerk of the Senate and the Attorney General sought to have the Senate, the Senate Committee and Her Majesty the Queen struck as defendants. The Federal Court – Trial Division ruled that it had jurisdiction to entertain the action.

The appeal focused on the matter of jurisdiction and the Court of Appeal held that this matter was not within the jurisdiction of the Federal Court either pursuant to the *Charter*, nor, more pertinently, under the *Federal Court Act*.[13] The essence of the ruling was that the

---

[12] McWhinney, Edward, *Canada and the Constitution 1979-1982*, Toronto, University of Toronto Press, 1982, p. 21.
[13] R.S.C. 1985, c. F-7, as amended.

Senate did not fit within the confines of section 18 of the *Federal Court Act* as being a "federal board, commission or tribunal."

> The Senate, as one of the Houses of Parliament provided for in section 17 of the *Constitution Act, 1867,* is a body that, with the House of Commons, is an essential part of the process that gives birth to federal boards, commissions or tribunals, and as such the Senate simply is not on the same level as those entities.[14]

In support of this position, the court added the view expressed by the same court in the *House of Commons v. Canada Labour Relations Board* case in which the point was made that the House of Commons is far more than merely a creature of the Constitution; it is central to the Constitution. This was said to apply to the Senate as well and to hold otherwise would belittle the Senate. To treat the Senate on the same level as an ordinary board, commission or tribunal would annihilate the ordinary meaning of those terms.

[T]he court further defined the Senate by indicating that its privileges, immunities and powers were conferred by the Constitution and that those were part of the "general and public law of Canada." This phrase is borrowed from section 5 of the *Parliament of Canada Act*[15] and its sense is different from and broader than that of the expression "laws of Canada" used in section 101 of the *Constitution Act, 1867.* The effect of the *Parliament of Canada Act* was to define and elaborate upon those privileges, immunities and powers.

In its discussion of jurisdiction, the court also dealt with the existence of the Senate's institutional accountability.

> [T]he review of parliamentary proceedings is not a matter to be taken lightly given the history of curial deference to Parliament and respect for the legislative branch of government generally. I hasten to add that this does not mean that no accountability, legal or otherwise, should exist. On the contrary, courts must be quick to respond to uphold the rule of law no matter how mighty or privileged the party before the tribunal or how unpopular the decision that has to be rendered.[16]

---

[14] [1990] 3 F.C. 465 at 480 d-e.

[15] R.S.C. 1985, c. P-1.

[16] *Supra* note 14 at 478 c-e.

In the Trial Division, the matter of whether the Senate and its committees could be sued was also an issue. Unfortunately, the Court of Appeal failed to deal with this ground.

8.2.C—HOUSE OF COMMONS

§ 8.2.C.1[17]
P.S.A.C. v. Canada (House of Commons)
Federal Court of Appeal; April 12, 1986
(1986), 27 D.L.R. (4th) 481

From the time of Confederation until the mid-1980's, that is for about 120 years, the employees of the House of Commons were not unionized vis-à-vis their employer. Then, as part of an effort to protect them from the labour relations point of view, a union attempted to organize them in accordance with the *Canada Labour Code*.[18] The Canada Labour Relations Board (C.L.R.B.) certified the union to represent the bargaining unit. The House of Commons sought judicial review of that decision by the Federal Court of Appeal. A three-judge panel unanimously granted the appeal. The merit and interest of the judgment is that the two judges who wrote complementary decisions, while agreeing in the result, arrived at their conclusions through different reasoning. Justice Huguessen looked at the matter of the status of Parliament.

This ruling was based on the perspective of whether the House of Commons itself could be defined for purposes of the *Canada Labour Code* as an employer. In order to arrive at a positive response, the court would have had to agree that, based on the wording of section 107(1) of the *Code*, the House of Commons was a person. The court refused to agree to this.

> By no process of reasoning or of imagination can I conceive of the House as being a person. It is an assembly of persons, albeit, no doubt, the most important one in the country. Nothing in the *Constitution Act, 1867*, nor in the law, custom and convention of the Constitution as I understand it, gives to the House corporate status or personality. Indeed everything points the other way. It is of the essence of a corporation that it shall be

---

[17] Cross-reference to § 8.6.3.
[18] R.S.C. 1985, c. L-2.

perpetual. But the House of Commons is by its nature an ephemeral thing, having by constitutional prescription a maximum life span of five years. When the House is dissolved it ceases to exist. It is presumably for this reason that it was thought necessary to have a special statutory provision (section 18 of the *House of Commons Act*, R.S.C. 1970, c. H-9, as amended by 1985, c. 39, s. 1), for the Board of Internal Economy, the body charged with "...all matters of financial and administrative policy affecting the House of Commons, its offices and its staff" to continue to operate following dissolution. There is no similar provision with regard to the House itself.[19]

This same issue had earlier been addressed by the Québec Superior Court with regard to the province's National Assembly and the same conclusion had been reached.[20] Given the agreement of the courts on this point, the matter that in Canadian practice the legislative body does not have legal personality became well settled. However, the point still needed to be settled that if the legislature was not endowed with that personality, having been established by the *Constitution Act, 1867*, what was it and how could it be characterized? This part of the judgment did provide an answer to that question as well, indicating that the House was a *sui generis* institution.

> While, in a sense, the House of Commons may be said to be a creature of the *Constitution Act, 1867*, such a qualification, in my view, belittles both the House and the Constitution. The House is far more than a creature of the Constitution: it is central to it and the single most important institution of our free and democratic system of government. The Constitution, for its part, is far more than a statute: it is the fundamental law of the land.[21]

We may be allowed to presume that if the federal House of Commons was held to be an institution on the basis of its creation by the *Constitution Act, 1867*, the provincial legislatures can similarly be held to be institutions on the basis of the respective institutions which created each of them.

It was on the basis of this institutional nature of the House that Justice Huguessen held that its staff were employees of the Crown, in similar fashion to the employees of the judiciary. In neither case, he thought,

---

[19] (1986), 27 D.L.R. (4th) 481 at 492.
[20] *Gabais v. Assemblée législative du Québec* (May 3, 1965), Doc. 138-195 (Que. S.C.).
[21] *Supra* note 19 at 494.

would having the staff so classified in law impinge upon the independence of the institution from the Crown.

---

§ 8.2.C.2[22]
New Brunswick Broadcasting Co. v.
Nova Scotia (Speaker of the House of Assembly)
Supreme Court of Canada; January 21, 1993
[1993] 1 S.C.R. 319

This consideration by the Supreme Court of Canada of the status and personality of legislative bodies arose out of the refusal of the Speaker of the House of Assembly of Nova Scotia to allow filming of the proceedings of that legislature for television purposes. The applicant, New Brunswick Broadcasting, obtained an order from the Nova Scotia Supreme Court – Trial Division to authorize the filming in a manner worked out in co-operation with the Speaker. The Nova Scotia Court of Appeal affirmed the lower court ruling on March 21, 1991. The Speaker was then granted leave to appeal to the Supreme Court of Canada and was joined by the Speakers of the Senate, the House of Commons, eight provincial and two territorial legislatures. In the period pending the Supreme Court decision, the proceedings of the House of Assembly were actually televised.

The issue before the Supreme Court of Canada was phrased in terms of whether the section 2(b) freedom of expression, including freedom of the press, was applicable to the House of Assembly as a legislative body. One way in which the court sought to answer the question was to see whether the Assembly was a governmental actor. In this way, the court was brought to define the Legislative Assembly of the province, in the knowledge that its analysis would be applicable to all other legislative bodies in Canada, not only because the ruling emanated from the highest court but also because the interventions of the other Speakers would involve their institutions as parties.

The starting point of the majority opinion was section 32 of the *Charter*, which included among government actors for *Charter* purposes "the legislatures of each province." The core of the matter as to the status and personality of a legislative body is that in a constitutional

---

[22] Cross-reference to § 1.2.2, 1.12.2 and 8.4.

sense, the "legislature" includes the legislative assembly and the Lieutenant Governor of the province. For our purposes, the federal transposition of this concept is that "Parliament" includes the House of Commons, the Senate and the Monarch (or the Governor General).

On the basis of its reading of section 5 of the *Charter*, which it held to be more applicable to this case than definitions derived from the *Constitution Act, 1867*, the court concluded that "the word 'legislature' cannot be narrowly defined to cover only those actions for which the legislative body and the Queen's representative are jointly responsible."[23] In other words, put simply, the legislature can be taken to mean the Legislative Assembly alone. The court did not decide whether the legislature was a government actor for all purposes. It qualified it, rather, as a public body.

Having determined what is the legislature, the court still had to find whether that legislature was subject to the *Charter*. It found that curial deference did not extend to all actions of the legislature but only to certain of its activities, namely the privileges of such bodies. Thus, the *Charter* did apply to legislatures in their capacity as government actors when they made legislation, but it did not apply to legislatures when, in their residual capacity as public bodies under the *Constitution*, they dealt with matters relating to their own privileges.

Given that the exclusion of television was a matter related to the privileges of the legislature, this issue was not subject to the *Charter* and the decision of the Nova Scotia Court of Appeal was overturned.

See also *Lawpost v. New Brunswick* (1999), 214 N.B.R. (2d) 297 (N.B. Q.B.), affirmed (1999), 182 D.L.R. (4th) 167 (N.B. C.A.), leave to appeal refused (2000), 260 N.R. 400 (note) (S.C.C.).

---

§ 8.2.C.3[24]
Peltier v. Henman
United States Court of Appeals for the Eighth Circuit; July 7, 1993
997 F.2d 461 (8th Cir., 1993)

It is rare that knowledge about the legal status of the Parliament of

---

[23] [1993] 1 S.C.R. 319 at 370 g.
[24] International comparison.

Canada be supplemented by jurisprudence arising from a foreign jurisdiction and it is just that rarity which gives this case its interest. The matter is even more worthwhile in the sense that the acts which gave rise to the judgment are a complete blend of the legal and the political.

Peltier was implicated in the murder of two FBI agents at the Pine Ridge Indian Reservation in South Dakota in 1975; this was the infamous battle at "Wounded Knee." He escaped to Canada, was extradited, tried and sentenced to two consecutive life terms. This was Peltier's second application to set aside the conviction. The U.S. District Court denied the relief sought of the Warden of the Leavenworth Penitentiary where Peltier was incarcerated, Henman. Here, the 8th Circuit Court of Appeal affirmed the lower court ruling.

The particularity of the case is that, having raised a great deal of interest among the population of Canada, an attempt to take up Peltier's fate was made in Parliament. An *ad hoc* group of parliamentarians of all political persuasions took the unprecedented measure of formulating an *amicus curiae* brief to aid Peltier. In the motion to file the brief, the Members of Parliament indicated their interest in the following manner:

> The undersigned Members of the Parliament of Canada are a non-partisan *ad hoc* group who do not represent any particular committee of Parliament and who do not speak for any particular political party. The undersigned members represent all sections of Canada, and various political parties including members of the Liberal Party of Canada, the party in power at the time of the execution. They represent all parts of Canada.[25]

The essence of the brief was to challenge the legality of Peltier's 1976 extradition from Canada to the United States for the purpose of facing trial. The allegation of the parliamentarians was that the extradition had been induced through the misconduct of officials of the United States government and obtained by the fraudulent affidavit of a witness. The brief even referred to "outrageous conduct" on the part of officials. On these bases, the brief asked that Peltier's conviction be set aside and that he be returned to Canada for a proper extradition hearing.

---

[25] Motion for Leave to File Brief of *Amicus Curiae* on Behalf of Certain Members of Parliament of Canada.

The response of the American judiciary to this proceeding is interesting in that it sheds light on the nature of Parliament, and in particular on the understanding of Parliament by a foreign legal system. The motion to file the brief of the parliamentarians was granted despite the appellee's objection. On the merits, however, the court declined to consider the brief for various reasons; most prominently, it held that extradition was a matter to be handled between governments, not private parties, and in that context, the *ad hoc* group of parliamentarians were not speaking on behalf of the government, not even for Parliament.

> As far as we are aware, the Canadian government has not protested to the government of the United States the handling by the United States of Peltier's extradition from Canada. Although the amici are members of the Canadian Parliament, they do not purport to participate here on behalf of the Canadian government. They do not state that their amicus participation in this appeal is pursuant to authorization by the Canadian Parliament.

> As far as we can tell, the amici are here solely as individual members of the Canadian Parliament to protest what they believe to have been improper conduct by the United States in connection with Peltier's extradition. In that capacity, they do not speak for the Canadian government. *See President of the United States ex rel Caputo v. Kelly*, 92 F.2d 6703, 605 (2d Cir. 1937) ("[e]xtradition proceedings must be prosecuted by the foreign government in the public interest, and may not be used by a private party for private vengeance or personal purposes"), *cert. denied*, 303 U.S. 635, 58 S.Ct. 521, 82 L.Ed. 1096 (1938).[26]

It is likely that the *ad hoc* group filed their brief for a combination of legal and political motives, in the hope that it might have some bearing on the outcome of the case. It is difficult to know exactly which type of consideration prevailed, as the group included a number of seasoned lawyers and as they were represented by an expert law professor. While they case may not have helped Peltier, its lasting outcome in terms of political law was the court's judgment on the matter of the brief.

---

[26] 997 F.2d 461 (8th Cir., 1993) at 475.

8.3 ISSUE: PROTECTION OF LEGISLATIVE INSTITUTIONS AND LEGISLATORS

§ 8.3.1
R. v. McGarry and Saniforth
Ontario District Court, 1978; unreported
limited information available

The legal system will protect the ability of the political institutions to function from even the most bizarre attempts to criminally disrupt it, whether for political motives or for mere financial gain. In 1978, then opposition Member of Parliament, Elmer McKay, suspected that his office had had a listening device implanted in it by the R.C.M.P. He called on the services of a company from Toronto, Centurion Investigations, to search for bugs. McGarry and Saniforth reported finding a listening device but as it turned out, they had planted it themselves. An investigation by the Ottawa Police led to a prosecution. The fact that the accused pleaded guilty to charges of public mischief and possession of an interception device prevented the court from basing what could have been an instructive judgment on legal principles. McGarry was sentenced to two years less a day, while Saniforth to 18 months.

§ 8.3.2
R. c. Lortie
Québec Court of Appeal; September 18, 1986
[1986] R.J.Q. 2787 to 2797
-and-
Lortie c. R.
Québec Court of Appeal; June 7, 1985
[1985] C.A. 451

Of the cases dealing with the protection afforded by the State to parliamentarians in the course of their work, this is the starkest, in the sense of the circumstances posing the greatest threat to legislators, but also in terms of the outcome which showed that the law protects them to the same degree as it defends other citizens.

Lortie was a corporal in the Canadian Forces, thus having easy access to weapons. On May 8, 1984, after staging a diversionary shooting at the Citadel in Québec City, he entered the building of the National Assembly and, by force of arms, took control of the Assembly Chamber. In the process, he killed three individuals and wounded nine others. Part of Lortie's preparation for this rampage had been to prepare several audio-cassettes in which he expressed his allegedly political motivation for his actions. One of these was sent to the announcer of CJRP radio station in Québec, André Arthur.

> La cassette remise à M. Arthur avait un contenu plus général et plus politique; en effet, le caporal Lortie annonce que, dans un geste unique au Canada, il détruira le Gouvernement du Québec; il s'exprime sur plusieurs questions politiques et, en particulier, sur le sort de la langue française au pays; il se déclare normal, précise que rien, ni personne ne peuvent l'arrêter et demande qu'on ne le juge pas «parce que ce n'est pas moi.»[27]

Lortie was convicted of the three murders by the Superior Court in a judgment of February 13, 1985. He appealed and the appeal proceedings focused on his state of mind at the time of the commission of the offences; was he insane or not? The point to be retained from this case is that in the trial and the appeal of charges under the *Criminal Code*, the fact that the shootings occurred within a legislature, that the intended victims may have been and probably were legislators and the fact that the shootings disrupted the work of the National Assembly, were neither mitigating nor aggravating factors. The same was true of Lortie's political motivation. The courts dealt with the matter without reference to its political context.

The second case was ancillary to the principal criminal trial. While Lortie was in the Chamber of the National Assembly, his actions and words were recorded by the Assembly's closed circuit television system, normally used to record the legislative proceedings. Here Radio-Canada and the Montréal television station CFCF sought the court's authorization to transmit the contents of the videotape and the Crown and the President (Speaker) of the National Assembly were opposing their motion. In effect, despite the apparently criminal designation of the case, this was in effect a civil matter relating to access to the trial

---

[27] [1986] R.J.Q. 2787 to 2797, at 2788-2789.

material and evidence. The Crown's argument was based on the possibility that publication of the videotape could prejudice Lortie's chances for a fair trial. The broadcasters were seeking to inform their audiences, but in the process, were each vying judicially to scoop their competition.

By a 2 to 1 majority, the Court of Appeal of Québec decided that even though the matter, in its perception was of interest and was even fascinating, it was not the appropriate forum for a final ruling on this civil aspect of the criminal trial. For the duration of the criminal proceedings, for the sole purpose of safeguarding the rights of the accused to a fair trial, the court prohibited publication. It was clear from the manner in which the court crafted its decision that it was sensitive to the public and indeed the political interest of the matter before it. Yet, it came to its conclusions purely on the basis of legal criteria and reasoning. We may thus conclude that in both substantive terms and their ancillary aspects, criminal law protects parliamentarians in their work in the same fashion as it does other professions not pertaining to the State.

The matter of Lortie's attack on the work of the legislature did not result in new legislation. It did entail changes, however, in the security policy and practices applied in the parliamentary precincts in both Québec City and Ottawa.

---

§ 8.3.3[28]
R. v. Van Hee
Ontario Court (Provincial Division); June 21, 1991
file no. Ottawa 91-11045; unreported

In this case, Van Hee, a Catholic priest, was charged with the obstruction of a peace officer when, in the process of demonstrating on Parliament Hill in Ottawa, he was told to move behind a barricade with his placard and did not. The most significant aspect of the decision was not that this particular demonstrator was acquitted, but rather what the court said about public speech on the Parliamentary precinct and therefore within sight of parliamentarians.

---

[28] Cross-reference to § 10.11.4.

Parliament is arguably the most public place in this country and nowhere should the lawful exercise of Canadian citizens' rights and freedoms be more scrupulously respected. Is there a tribune better suited for ordinary Canadians upon which to fearlessly voice their opinions and to circulate freely?[29]

On the matter of the arresting officer's conduct, the court felt the use of the powers associated with his duty was unjustifiable. The court defined the elements of that duty as being comprised of five elements: 1) appropriately interpreting the concept of "demonstration," as holding a placard, being in the company of other demonstrators, using inflammatory expression or presenting a potential threat to anyone on the grounds or in the buildings; 2) knowing the accused and his pattern of public expression; 3) considering the ostensible purpose for the erection of the barricade; 4) relating the actions of the accused to the current state of enforcement of the regulations restricting protestors on Parliament Hill; and 5) sizing up the crowd and determining whether the protestors were acting in concert.

On the basis of all these considerations, the court felt the arresting constable to have acted arbitrarily, in a manner unnecessary and unjustified in the circumstances prevailing at the time of the arrest. It also indicated, however, that it was critical of the policy the constable was attempting to enforce and had been specifically ordered to enforce.

---

§ 8.3.4[30]
Kealey v. R.
Federal Court of Canada – Trial Division; May 2, 1991
(1991), [1992] 1 F.C. 195[31]

Kealey was a businessman from the Ottawa region. He alleged that he had been cheated in a commercial enterprise by the Canadian government and held the Prime Minister of the time, Brian Mulroney, personally responsible. In order to draw attention to the matter, Kealey regularly demonstrated before that entrance of Parliament which Mulroney used to enter the House of Commons and in front

---

[29] Reasons for judgment, p. 4.
[30] Cross-reference to § 1.3.D.3.
[31] Leave to appeal allowed (1991), 139 N.R. 189 (Fed. C.A.).

of which onlookers regularly gathered. On March 1, 1990, the Public Works Nuisance Regulations, the instrument applicable to such public manifestations of expression on Parliament Hill, were amended. Thenceforth, demonstrations and loud disruptive noises were prohibited within a radius of 50 metres from any entrance to any of the buildings of Parliament on weekdays. Kealey nevertheless continued his action.

On March 19, 1990, Kealey was arrested and he was detained for four days. After his release on March 23, proceedings against him by the Crown were stayed. On June 27 of the same year, Kealey started an action in damages and for a declaration. The principal focus of the court was to show that the changes to the Public Works Nuisance Regulations were made for the improper purpose of silencing him, to specifically exclude him from demonstrating in a peaceful manner on Parliament Hill and to specifically infringe his *Charter* rights, but he also sought to show that his arrest and detention had been malicious. The defendants brought motions to strike the statement of claim.

The court referred approvingly to its own ruling in the *Weisfeld* case. On the present motions, it held that the statement of claim was to be amended so as to allow only the claims for false arrest, false imprisonment and malicious prosecution to proceed and for the Crown to be the only defendant to remain in the case.

> Because I have decided that the Federal Court does not have jurisdiction over the defendants, with the exception of Her Majesty the Queen, I must now only decide if the statement of claim discloses a reasonable cause of action as it relates to Her Majesty the Queen. The plaintiff may well be able to succeed on his claim for wrongful or false arrest and/or false imprisonment. I am satisfied that the statement of claim, which allegations for these purposes are deemed to be true, establishes that Kealey was in fact arrested and/or imprisoned, that the arrest and/or the imprisonment was caused by the defendant, and that plaintiff now states that he suffered special damages, which damages plaintiff will have to prove at a trial. [32]

---

[32] (1991), [1992] 1 F.C. 195 at 217 c-e, leave to appeal allowed (1991), 139 N.R. 189 (Fed. C.A.).

In so ruling, the court voided the direct challenge to the instrument by which Kealey's attempt to protest sufficiently close to the country's legislators to be seen and heard was regulated.

The plaintiff sought the leave of the Federal Court of Appeal to appeal this judgment and it was granted.[33] The lower court judgment was obtained on an interlocutory application but it was held to have determined the substantive rights claimed by Kealey and in that sense, it had the effect of being a final judgment. From then on, the matter must have been settled by different means, because there is no reported Federal Court of Appeal ruling on the merits.

---

§ 8.3.5
Weisfeld v. R.
Federal Court of Appeal; June 30, 1994
(1994), [1995] 1 F.C. 68

This is the case which gives the notion of the protection of the legis-lative function by the State its greatest depth in terms of the *Charter*. It was on April 18, 1983, that Weisfeld and others first established a "Peace Camp" on the lawn of Parliament Hill. The Camp consisted of a number of tents in which protestors lived, a banner to signify their presence and a table for the distribution of literature. The pur-pose of the protesters was to rally opinion against the testing of American cruise missiles in Canadian airspace. This camp was in place until April 22, 1985, when it was removed by the Department of Public Works and the R.C.M.P. On April 23, the federal Cabinet amended the Public Works Nuisance Regulations to prevent the erec-tion of a camping structure on a public work without ministerial permission. The measure was designed to clear Parliament Hill and the precincts of Parliament of protesters. Despite the fact that Weis-feld was arrested on several occasions for Peace Camp activities, he tried in the fall of 1988, during the 34th federal general election cam-paign, to erect the camp again but was prevented from doing so by the R.C.M.P. In fact, from November 11, 1988, until November 22, 1988, Weisfeld was jailed.

---

[33] (1991), 139 N.R. 189 (Fed. C.A.).

As a result of these events, Weisfeld applied for a declaration that the removal of the camp had constituted a breach of his freedom of expression under s. 2(b) of the *Charter*. He also sought to have the Public Works Nuisance Regulations pursuant to which the camp had been removed declared unconstitutional. He also sought damages. The Federal Court – Trial Division found that the territory of Parliament Hill was vested in the Crown in right of Canada and that it was under the care of the Minister of Public Works. It also held that the actions taken to dislodge the Peace Camp were not an unconstitutional hindrance to Weisfeld's freedom of expression. The message conveyed by Weisfeld was political; the tents and other structures were not conveying a message and therefore did not convey a message; the communications between Weisfeld and passers-by did convey a message but were not prohibited. The 1985 amendments to the Regulations were not directed at the message but only to the reasonable regulation of the time, place and manner of its propagation.

Weisfeld appealed to the Federal Court of Appeal. The first issue which the court considered was whether the Peace Camp really did amount to a form of expression susceptible of constitutional protection under paragraph 2(b) of the *Charter*. Following the *Irwin Toys* decision,[34] the court found that not only words, but also activity can constitute expression in the sense of section 2(b). Indeed, it felt that expression goes beyond words. Thus, the court had no difficulty that the establishment and maintenance of the Peace Camp constituted expression.

> With respect, I disagree with this conclusion. It may be that a person walking by the Peace Camp would not immediately have realized that the appellant's specific message was "we don't want the Canadian government to accede to U.S. requests to test cruise missiles in northern Alberta." This does not mean, however, that the placing of the structure on Parliament Hill did not convey or attempt to convey a message. The act of private citizens building a very visible structure on the grounds of Parliament Hill, as well as maintaining a vigil there for more than two years, certainly conveys some kind of meaning. Similar peace camp protests were used in other countries at that time. This camp was meant to link up with other similar protests. The structure itself, therefore, helped to dramatize the message the appellant was seeking to communicate. It also manifested the protestors' commitment to the cause.[35]

---

[34] *Irwin Toy Ltd. c. Québec (Procureur général)*, [1989] 1 S.C.R. 927 (S.C.C.).
[35] (1994), [1995] 1 F.C. 68 at 84 j-85 c.

In addition, the important element in this activity, which attracts constitutional protection, is the conveying of the expression, not its reception. In this case, moreover, the "public forum" doctrine did not restrict the protection to which Weisfeld was entitled.

The court then went on to see whether the government's actions constituted a breach of Weisfeld's constitutional rights. Here the Crown's purpose was not to silence the protest but, in a more limited fashion, to control the activities constituting the expression. It wanted to protect the legislative function by preserving the pristine character of Parliament Hill. The effect, however, was restrictive with respect to Weisfeld. Seeing that Weisfeld's political protest in this case promoted the principle of participation in decision-making, what the police and Public Works staff did was indubitably an infringement of rights.

In the final phase of analysis, the court looked at whether the government could justify its infringement on the grounds of section 1 of the *Charter*. It was only in this part of the judgment that the court examined the policy motivations of the government in dealing the way it did with the Peace Camp. The considerations included fire hazard, health hazard, proper maintenance of Parliament Hill, damage to the lawns, security burden, as well as the aesthetic beauty of Parliament Hill and its value as a tourist attraction. Most important of all, the court referred to "the symbolic importance of Parliament Hill,"[36] a clear allusion to the protection of parliamentarians in their functions. The justices' pens flowed easily into the political considerations as well.

> One of the Government's legitimate objectives in this case was to keep the Hill in a clean and aesthetically pleasing condition, so that it could be enjoyed by Canadians and visitors alike. It is easy to understand the desire of the Government to remove what was described in letters of protest to it as an "eyesore," a "blemish," a "blot" and a "mess." [37]

The court then proceeded to deal explicitly with the role of the government in protecting Parliament Hill in its capacity as the home of parliamentary democracy.

---

[36] *Ibid.* at 99 a.
[37] *Ibid.* at 98 i-j.

Madam Justice McLachlin, in *Commonwealth of Canada, supra,* pointed out that the objective underlying government regulation over the use of public property may, properly, extend beyond concerns with the purely physical consequences to that forum, to include theoretical considerations such as dignity or decorum, damage to which could affect the long-term functioning of that forum:

> For example, political placards might be barred from a courtroom, not because they would be likely to disrupt or influence the judge, but rather because they interfere with the dignity and decorum of the courtroom. In reducing the aura of impartiality which is sought to be maintained in the courtroom, they may in a larger sense detract from its purpose and impact on its function.

> Parliament Hill is a powerful symbol of Canada, representing our democratic tradition both to its citizens and residents, as well as to the millions of visitors who come to this country each year. As the seat of our federal system of government, the Parliament Buildings and the grounds upon which they are situate deserve respect and admiration from all Canadians. The care and management of these, the most important institutions of our democratic society, is vested in the Government and the Department of Public Works. Their objective is to maintain these symbols in a manner which accords with their importance as political institutions and in a condition to be enjoyed by all Canadians.[38]

On this basis, the court held that the government had pressing and substantial objectives which met the various parts of the *Oakes* test. The government's actions were thus deemed to be justified and the appeal was therefore denied.

The court felt obliged to deal with a final aspect of the case, namely the actions of the R.C.M.P. in removing the protest material of Weisfeld on those occasions when Weisfeld simply set up a table, rather than a full camp, at the approaches to Parliament. It held that the Public Works Nuisance Regulations could not be used to shut down a protest solely based on a display table on the Hill.

> I am able to say, however, that, in an appropriate case, it may well be beyond the respondent's right to remove a table or a soap box or other prop from Parliament Hill as that may violate someone's constitutional rights, although it may also be permissible for the respondent to regulate these matters as to time, place and manner. In other words, tables or

---

[38] *Ibid.* at 99 a-g.

other supporting articles might have to be allowed, but the duration of their use, their location on the property and the way in which they are employed may be reasonably controlled.[39]

---

§ 8.3.6
Ontario (Speaker of the Legislative Assembly) v. Casselman
Ontario Court (General Division); March 18, 1996
(March 18, 1996), Winkler J., [1996] O.J. No. 5343 (Ont. Gen. Div.)

On February 26, 1996, in response to the policies of the Progressive Conservative Government led by Premier Mike Harris, the Ontario Public Service Employees' Union (O.P.S.E.U.), initiated a strike by the public servants of the province against the province's government. On March 18, the first day of the Spring session of the provincial Legislative Assembly, the union organized a demonstration and picketing activity around Queen's Park, the legislative building, and the Whitney Block where some offices of the Legislature are also located. The goal of the protestors was to block access to, and egress from, these buildings by legislators and their assistants, as well as by the staff of the Legislature itself.

In his capacity as Speaker of the Legislative Assembly, The Honourable Allan Mclean applied to the Ontario Court (General Division) for interim, interlocutory and permanent injunctions, not to stop the demonstrating and picketing, but so as to allow unobstructed passage to and from the precincts where Ontario's parliamentarians conducted their work. The first ground on which the Speaker's notice of application was founded was a legal characterization of the Legislative Assembly.

> The Legislative Assembly is the seat of legislative authority in Ontario. As such, it constitutes one of the central institutions of our democratic system of governance, independent and distinct from the other branches, including the executive branch, which is more commonly referred to as the "Government."[40]

---

[39] Ibid. at 102 f-h.

[40] Ontario (Speaker of the Legislative Assembly) v. Casselman Notice of Application, March 18, 1996, para. 13(a).

The application then cited the historical rights and privileges of the Legislative Assembly, the rights of Members to be free from intimidation in the course of discharging their parliamentary duties, the fact that the union activists' actions constitute unlawful obstruction and, remarkably, that police assistance had been and would continue to be unsuccessful in preventing obstruction and interference. The Speaker asserted that it was one of his functions to guard the rights and privileges of the Assembly and of its Members. The application also emphasized that the Assembly and its Office were independent of the Government and that the latter had no authority over it. Among a variety of statutory provisions, the application referred to section 69 of the *Constitution Act, 1867*[41] and the Preamble of the *Constitution Act, 1982.*[42]

The court framed its decision in the language of the law of injunctions but seemed very sensitive to the highly politicized and delicate nature of the conflict and of the balancing of rights it was being asked to undertake. It held that an interlocutory injunction was the issue. While the application had greatly focused on the inviolability of the legislative precinct, the court seemed much more dedicated to protecting the Parliamentary function of legislators.

The first *ratio* the court adopted was that obstruction of the Members' access to the Legislative Assembly constituted a breach of their Parliamentary privilege. It relied on statutory and jurisprudential grounds, as well as on scholarly authors to acknowledge the existence of parliamentary privilege and to emphasize that access by parliamentarians to their workplace formed an integral part of that body of privilege. To reinforce this opinion, the court adopted the characterization of this privilege as absolute and constitutionally valid.[43]

Further, the court declared that obstruction of the legislative function is *per se* unlawful and "causes irreparable harm which cannot be remedied in damages."[44] Finally, with respect to the balance of con-

---

[41] "69. There shall be a Legislature for Ontario consisting of the Lieutenant Governor and of One House, styled the Legislative Assembly of Ontario."

[42] "Whereas Canada is founded upon principles that recognize the supremacy of God and the rule of law."

[43] *New Brunswick Broadcasting Co. v. Nova Scotia (Speaker of the House of Assembly),* [1993] 1 S.C.R. 319 (S.C.C.) at 378-379; quoted in the judgment of the Ontario Court (General Division) in the Mclean case, at p. 8.

[44] (March 18, 1996), Winkler J., [1996] O.J. No. 5343 (Ont. Gen. Div.) at para. 22.

venience among the Speaker, union and the public, the court held that the public's convenience must prevail. "Delay and obstruction of entry and egress of Members and essential staff of the Legislative Assembly strikes a blow at the very heart of our society and is unacceptable."[45]

In this instance, the decision of the court did not completely dispose of the matter. The Speaker's application was dated March 18, 1996, it was heard that day and the ruling was also issued on the same date. However, some hours before the injunction was issued and could be enforced, the union members' protests developed into a severe "confrontation between fearsomely garbed police and apparently unarmed demonstrators."[46] In fact, during that morning, the Ontario Provincial Police and the Metro Toronto Police were deployed among the various legislative buildings. These forces clashed with the demonstrators and several individuals were injured.

The confrontation around Queen's Park aroused much public sentiment and resulted in the establishment of a Commission of Inquiry into the events of March 18, 1996, headed by Mr. Justice Willard Estey, formerly of the Supreme Court of Canada. This Commission reported to the Attorney General of Ontario on October 22, 1996. The report included as an annex the judgment under discussion. Mr. Justice Estey found that among the combination of circumstances which led to the occurrences of that day was "the change of legislation with respect to politically charged and sensitive labour issues coupled with the largest strike in the history of the province."[47]

The Commission of Inquiry had more time and fewer fetters of trial procedure than the court to deal with the central issue of this matter, the protection of the function of legislators by means of ensuring their access to the Legislature. Its assessment of the facts of the case and of the principles involved was also much more directly stated than had been by the court.

> The Commission wishes to state one fundamental truth as plainly and as forcefully as possible at the very outset of this report. No one has the

---

[45] *Ibid.* at para. 23.
[46] Report of the Commission of Inquiry into Events of March 18, 1996, at Queen's Park, Willard Z. Estey, Q.C., Commissioner, Queen's Printer for Ontario, October 22, 1996, p. 9, para. 6.
[47] *Ibid.*, p. 5, para. 27(a).

right to impede the access of an MPP seeking to enter the Legislature to represent his or her constituency, be it by picket line, demonstration or otherwise. It is simply wrong to do so and breaches an important principle highly valued in our democratic system. The attempt to do this was the original sin from which all other transgressions that occurred in this matter flowed. The fact that this Commission is critical of the actions of a number of other parties does not mean and should not be taken as meaning that the Commission condones this wrong. Whether it was the result of original intent (which the Commission does not consider to be the case), or a foreseeable risk taken heedless of the outcome does not alter the wrong or its gravity. The fact is that here the blockage did occur as a result of the actions taken by the picketers which were wrong.[48]

---

§ 8.3.7
Zündel v. Liberal Party of Canada
Ontario Court of Appeal; November 10, 1999
(1999), 46 O.R. (3d) 410[49]

The question which this case is designed to address is whether, in order to protect the work of parliamentarians and the precincts of Parliament from being tainted by association with persons who are morally, legally and politically abhorrent to Canadian society, Parliament is justified in banning such persons from the parliamentary precinct.

Despite the entirely misleading characterization of himself as a "German-Canadian publisher, writer, broadcaster and human rights activist,"[50] Zündel is patently nothing more than an anti-Semitic Holocaust denier. While being an accused before a Canadian Human Rights Tribunal, under a charge of exposing Jews to hatred, pursuant to subsection 13(1) of the *Canadian Human Rights Act*,[51] he made arrangements to hold, on June 5, 1988, a press conference in a particular press conference room in the Centre Block of the Parliament Buildings. His intention was allegedly to discuss the case as an issue of national interest and to disseminate to Canadians his view of the rulings of the Tribunal and of their implications.

---

[48] Op. cit., p. 3, para. 12.
[49] Leave to appeal refused (2000), 259 N.R. 399 (note) (S.C.C.).
[50] Statement of claim, para. 2.
[51] R.S.C. 1985, c. H-6, as amended.

When Zündel's intentions became known to the Canadian Jewish Congress and to parliamentarians, the latter undertook to have the Parliamentary Press Gallery, which administers the press conference room in question, cancel the event. Upon the Press Gallery's refusal, the House Leader of the Government proposed in the Commons the following motion which was unanimously adopted.

> That this House order that Ernst Zündel be denied admittance to the precincts of the House of Commons during and for the remainder of the present session.[52]

As a consequence of his inability to use the room he had reserved for the press conference, Zündel talked to some reporters on the sidewalk in front of Parliament.

By a statement of claim filed on October 30, 1998, Zündel brought in as defendants the five parties represented in the House of Commons, the Canadian Jewish Congress and its president, the Prime Minister, the Minister of Public Works and Government Services, the Minister of State (Multiculturalism), the leaders of all opposition parties as well as a number of Members of Parliament. He claimed that their actions constituted a wrongful and malicious conspiracy to ban him from the precincts of Parliament, thereby denying him access to the House of Commons, the Senate, the Library of Parliament and the office of his own Member of Parliament, for the purpose of denying him freedom of speech. From each defendant, Zündel claimed $250,000 general damages for breach of his *Charter* right to freedom of speech under section 2(b), $250,000 general damages for conspiracy to injure him and a further $500,000 in punitive damages.

In addition to the principal issue of the case, the court will have to inquire into the other matters arising from this case, namely whether parliamentary privilege applies, whether the use of premises within the Parliamentary precincts by a litigant to discuss a case against him is appropriate and whether political parties have the legal personality required to be defendants in a *Charter*-based action.

Given Zündel's background, it is quite clear that he is using this litigation for the political purpose of exposure in substitution for the press conference he was not able to hold.

---

52 Hansard, June 4, 1988, p. 7617.

The General Division, quite rightly, looked at the matters in issue from a legal perspective only. Its principal conclusion was that in light of the fact that political parties did not have legal personality, they could not be sued. On that basis, it dismissed the action. The court reached this conclusion on the basis of the applicable jurisprudence;[53] notwithstanding that the *Canada Elections Act* infuses into parties some elements akin to personality.

> The fact that the *Elections Act of Canada* provides for the Chief Agents to conduct affairs on behalf of the political parties does not vest the political parties with the capacity to sue or be sued. The Canada Elections Act does not go that far to provide them with that right and responsibility. It is common ground by counsel for all of the political parties that the political parties have no assets, hold no real estate, employ no people, and as such are not a legal entity. I agree with their position and on that basis I would dismiss the claim as against the political parties.[54]

The court also considered that aspect of the controversy which related to the privileges of Parliament. It said that Zündel could not be considered to be interfering with Parliament by booking a room in the House of Commons; he was a stranger to the House. However, in restricting the use of its own precincts, the House of Commons was exercising its privilege and therefore the court should not interfere with the decision of Parliament. The reason behind the decision was to preserve the dignity and integrity of Parliament; in a subtle manner, the court agreed with this motivation.

The press commentary on this ruling was most pertinent from the political law point of view.

> "If one is guided by law one would probably [be better] ot (sic) to appeal the ruling on political parties," said Mr. Montenegrino. "But if you're in for a penny, in for a pound, why not argue against it? You're already there, and you're spending the money anyway."[55]

Bearing in mind that the entire exercise was a search for publicity and political advantage on Zündel's part, he did appeal but fared no

---

[53] *McKinney v. Liberal Party of Canada* (1987), 43 D.L.R. (4th) 706 (Ont. H.C.).

[54] (1999), 60 C.R.R. (2d) 189 (Ont. Gen. Div.) at 195, affirmed (1999), 46 O.R. (3d) 410 at 415, leave to appeal refused (2000), 259 N.R. 399 (note) (S.C.C.).

[55] "Political parties and legal entities, can't be sued judge rules," Kady O'Malley, *Hill Times*, February 1, 1999, p. 9.

better in the Ontario Court of Appeal. This court relied on parliamentary privilege to conclude that the trial judge had properly adverted to the correct test.

> In my view, it should be self-evident that control over the premises occupied by the House of Commons for the purpose of performing the Members' parliamentary work is a necessary adjunct to the proper functioning of Parliament. Surely, someone must be in control of the premises. Who better than the Speaker, who historically has exercised this control for the House? In my view, the courts would be overstepping legitimate constitutional bounds if they sought to interfere with the power of the House to control access to its own premises.[56]

See also *R. v. Behrens* (2001), [2001] O.J. No. 245 (Ont. C.J.); *R. v. Curtis*, Provincial Court of New Brunswick; case no. 07624605, sentencing January 6, 2004 and *Thomas et al. v. British Columbia and Canada (Attorney General)*.

---

§ 8.3.8[57]
Gravel v. United States
United States Supreme Court; June 29, 1972
408 U.S. 606 (1972)

Protection of the legislative function involves not only the range of measures designed to guarantee that legislators work in a manner unencumbered by physical disruption, whether in or surrounding the precinct in which the legislature meets. It also involves the emplacement of a special legal shield around the expression of views and opinions, as well as around actions taken by legislators in order to express those views and opinions in the course of their work as legislators. In no circumstances can such a shield be more important than in a situation of great public controversy, and when there is conflict between the legislative and executive arms of the State.

Controversy and conflict were the principal circumstances at play in relation to the public release of the Pentagon Papers in the United

---

[56] (1999), 46 O.R. (3d) 410 at 415, leave to appeal refused (2000), 259 N.R. 399 (note) (S.C.C.).
[57] International comparison.

States in 1971, at the height of the Vietnam War.[58] Senator Mike Gravel of Alaska hired a certain Leonard Rodberg as an assistant for the purpose of working on the Pentagon Papers and on June 21, 1971, the Senator read from the Papers at a meeting of a Senate Sub-Committee. He then made the entire study, consisting of 47 volumes, public. Gravel later had a hand in arranging for the Pentagon Papers to be edited in book form for general availability. In conjunction with a grand jury investigation as to whether the publication of the Pentagon Papers constituted criminal activity in the sense of publication of classified material, Rodberg was subpoenaed as a witness, as was Webber, the Director of the press which had published the book. Gravel intervened and filed motions to quash the subpoenas. He relied on Article I, § 6, clause 1 of the *United States Constitution*, the "Speech or Debate Clause."

> The Senators and Representatives shall receive a Compensation for their Services, to be ascertained by Law, and paid out of the Treasury of the United States. They shall in all Cases, except Treason, Felony and Breach of the Peace, be privileged from Arrest during their Attendance at the Session of their respective Houses, and in going to and returning from the same; and for any Speech or Debate in either House, they shall not be questioned in any other Place.[59]

The Federal District Court in Massachusetts held that this clause protected all legislative acts and was a proper shield from inquiry into anything the Senator did at the subject meeting or in preparation for it. The privilege enjoyed by the Senator equally protected his agents or assistants in things done which would have been legislative acts.[60] The U.S. Court of Appeal for the First Circuit agreed with this aspect of the protection of the legislative function. However, in this case, neither the District Court nor the Court of Appeal were willing to extend the protection of the clause to private publication.[61] The Court of Appeal also found that a Common Law privilege attached to legislative aides "akin to the judicially created immunity of executive officers from liability for libel contained in a news release issued in the course of their normal duties."[62]

---

[58] The full title of the work was the History of the United States Decision-Making Process in Viet Nam Policy.

[59] *Constitution of the United States*, Article I, § 6, cl. 1.

[60] *U.S. v. Doe*, 332 F. Supp. 930 (Mass., 1971) at 935.

[61] *U.S. v. Doe*, 455 F.2d 753 (1st Cir., 1972).

[62] 408 U.S. 606 (1972) at 612.

Before the U.S. Supreme Court, Senator Gravel claimed that the Speech or Debate Clause protected him from criminal or civil liability with respect to his legislative work or from questioning about that work. The court found this claim to be incontrovertible.

> The Speech or Debate Clause was designed to assure a co-equal branch of the government wide freedom of speech, debate, and deliberation without intimidation or threats from the Executive Branch. It thus protects Members against prosecutions that directly impinge upon or threaten the legislative process. We have no doubt that Senator Gravel may not be made to answer—either in terms of questions or in terms of defending himself from prosecution—for the events that occurred at the subcommittee meeting. [63]

The Supreme Court also held that Senator Gravel's privilege extended to Rodberg in the latter's capacity as Gravel's assistant. The legislator and his aide were to be treated as one. This needed explanation.

> Both courts recognized that the Senate of the United States urgently presses here: that it is literally impossible, in view of the complexities of the modern legislative process, with Congress almost constantly in session and matters of legislative concern constantly proliferating, for Members of Congress to perform their legislative tasks without the help of aides and assistants; that the day-to-day work of such aides is so critical to the Members' performance that they must be treated as the latter's alter egos; and that if they are not so recognized, the central role of the Speech or Debate Clause—to prevent intimidation of legislators by the Executive and accountability before a possibly hostile judiciary, *United States v. Johnson*, 383 U.S. 169, 181 (1966)—will inevitably be diminished and frustrated. [64]

This reasoning can be applied to a number of other parliamentary bodies.

The part of the ruling which had the most fundamental effect is the definition, for such purposes, of the concept of legislative acts. What part of the legislative function does the constitutional provision in question protect; that is the central question here.

> Legislative acts are not all-encompassing. The heart of the Clause is speech or debate in either House. Insofar as the Clause is construed to

---

[63] *Ibid.* at 616.
[64] *Ibid.* at 616-617.

reach other matters, they must be an integral part of the deliberative and communicative processes by which Members participate in committee and House proceedings with respect to the consideration and passage or rejection of proposed legislation or with respect to other matters which the Constitution places within the jurisdiction of either House. As the Court of Appeals put it, the courts have extended the privilege to matters beyond pure speech or debate in either House, but "only when necessary to prevent indirect impairment of such deliberations." *United States v. Doe*, 455 F. 2d, at 760. [65]

The court's other holding was that Senator Gravel's publication arrangement for the Pentagon Papers did not fall within the ambit of the constitutional protection being invoked.

This decision is significant, first, in the sense of defining another fundamental aspect of the protection of the legislative function, beyond that dealt with in the foregoing cases. It is also noteworthy in its wise application of legal standards in an environment of great political upheaval within the United States.

This case is included in the present study because it is one of the most resounding demonstrations of legal protection for legislative work. Students of political law should note, however, that similar, although perhaps not exactly the same privileges for parliamentarians exist throughout Canada and in other countries with longstanding democratic parliamentary traditions.

8.4 ISSUE: PRIVILEGE: THE REGIME OF RULES APPLICABLE TO PARLIAMENTARY BODIES AND PARLIAMENTARIANS[66]

See *New Brunswick Broadcasting Co. v. Nova Scotia (Speaker of the House of Assembly)*, [1993] 1 S.C.R. 319 (S.C.C.);[67] *Harvey v. New Brunswick (Attorney General)*, [1996] 2 S.C.R. 876 (S.C.C.);[68] *R. v. Brown*, 2001 PESCTD 6 (P.E.I. T.D.);[69] *Ontario (Speaker of the Legislative Assembly) v. Ontario (Human Rights Commission)* (2001), 201 D.L.R. (4th) 698 (Ont.

---

[65] *Ibid.* at 625.
[66] Cross-reference to § 11.5.
[67] Cross-reference to § 1.2.2, 1.12.2 and 8.2.C.2.
[68] Cross-reference to § 8.5.5.
[69] Cross-reference to § 6.6.

C.A.); *Speaker's Ruling on the Nature of Parliamentary Privilege*, Hansard, May 26, 3003, p. 6413 and *Telezone Inc. v. Canada (Attorney General) and Manley* (2004), [2004] O.J. No. 5 (Ont. C.A.).

8.5 ISSUE: MEMBERSHIP IN PARLIAMENTARY BODIES

See *R. v Clark*, [1943] O.R. 501 (Ont. C.A.), leave to appeal refused (1943), [1944] S.C.R. 69 (S.C.C.).

---

§ 8.5.1[70]
MacLean v. Nova Scotia (Attorney General)
Nova Scotia Supreme Court – Trial Division; January 5, 1987
(1987), 35 D.L.R. (4th) 306

The first key issue in dealing with membership in a parliamentary body is the ability of such bodies to link the capacity for electability to that of compliance with legality. Similarly important is the determination of whether, in the era of the *Charter*, parliamentary decisions in this regard are subject to constitutional rules and review. Considering, however, that legislatures are institutions dedicated as much to politics as they are to law-making, the courts know full well that legal qualifications for membership are indelibly tinged with political considerations. A clear example of the courts' handling of this combination of factors is the *MacLean* case.

MacLean was elected to the Nova Scotia House of Assembly in 1981 and re-elected in 1984. In the Progressive Conservative administration of Premier John Buchanan, he was even elevated to the portfolios of Minister of Culture, Recreation and Fitness and Minister in charge of administering the *Lotteries Act*. In 1986, MacLean was charged with several counts of the *Criminal Code* offence of knowingly having used forged documents. In essence, he defrauded the House in relation to his living and travel expenses. On October 3, 1986, MacLean pleaded guilty to the charges and on October 30 he was expelled from the House. The expulsion was accomplished by means of the enactment of *An Act Respecting Reasonable Limits for Membership in the House of*

---

[70] Cross-reference to § 11.5.1.

Assembly (the Act).[71] This statute contained a very explicit preamble attempting to ensure its accommodation to the standards of the *Charter*; it added provisions to the *House of Assembly Act* to provide that a Member convicted of a serious offence cannot be nominated or elected, and it made these provisions retroactive. The Act also contained a provision aimed at making MacLean's expulsion automatic.

MacLean thereupon sued, claiming that this legislation was in breach of section 3 [democratic rights], section 7 [legal rights], section 11 [proceedings in criminal trials] and section 15 [equality] of the *Charter*. If he were able to convince the court, he would not only save his own career as a parliamentarian but also have a greater effect on the rules governing membership in legislative bodies.

The court addressed its mind to three aspects of the matter. In the first instance, as the claim was made that the rules on membership in the House were part of the Constitution of Nova Scotia, the court had to determine whether the Act was reviewable by it. The court held that provincial laws which are part of the Constitution of the province but which are not part of the Constitution of Canada as referred to in section 52(2) of the *Charter*, such as laws purporting to deal with the eligibility of individuals for membership in provincial assemblies "must be capable of being tested and the challenge must take place in the courts."[72] The test which such enactments must meet is that of section 3 of the *Charter*, dealing with democratic rights.

Having set the general parameters, the court looked more specifically at whether the House of Assembly had the power to expel one of its Members. In MacLean's view, the power of expulsion was historically part of the prerogatives of the legislature, but these prerogatives themselves ought now to be considered as being qualified by the *Charter*. Here, the court seemed somewhat uncertain. It reasoned first that

> . . .the power to expel a person by resolution of the Assembly remains a valid function of the Assembly, and if by resolution, would normally not be reviewable by the Court. In my opinion s. 3 of the Charter on its plain meaning does not encompass s. 2 of the Act which I find is severable and could stand on its own. [73]

---

[71] S.N.S. 1986, c. 104.
[72] (1987), 35 D.L.R. (4th) 306 at 313.
[73] *Ibid.* at 315.

It then went on to say that if it was wrong in this conclusion, then the Act must be looked at under section 3. It did so and found no breach of section 3 in the provision of the Act affecting the expulsion.

Lastly and most importantly, the court considered the constitutional validity of the House's attempt to impose restrictions on future membership. This was the part of the impugned legislation that was both the most controversial and in which the court recognized the inherent symbiosis of legal and political elements. According to the legal standard which was the basis of the court's consideration, the attempt to apply a forward-looking 5-year ban on nomination and election of a Member expelled upon a criminal conviction was unconstitutional because of the element of retroactivity written into the Act.

> On the plain meaning of the words in s. 3 of the Charter, I find that an attempt to put limits on membership qualification violates Mr. Mac-Lean's right as a citizen to be qualified for membership in the House of Assembly of Nova Scotia.

> Clearly the effect of the legislation is unconstitutional. It attempts to retroactively set standards for future members, which are over and above the requirements of s. 3 of the Charter.[74]

Given the court's conclusion that in regard to the future, the legal sanction attempted to be applied to MacLean could not be imposed upon him, the judgment recognized that a political solution deliverable by the electorate was still to be considered.

> The content of s. 1 of the Act affects the rights of Mr. MacLean and others to run and be elected. It also impinges on the rights of voters to elect a member of their choice by a majority vote. Surely the citizens of this province should be given credit for having the sense to determine who is a proper member. The voters now know the facts about Mr. MacLean and should he choose to run, it should be the voters who decide whether he is the person they want to represent them in the House. The legislation is paternalistic and excessive and under the proportionality test is unnecessary to protect society. The prohibition has turned from protection to punitive.[75]

---

[74] *Ibid.* at 316.
[75] *Ibid.* at 318.

The judgment ended, wisely, with the indication that the purpose of the entire proceeding was to ensure that public trust be maintained in the membership of the House. The thrust of the ruling is that in order to re-establish that public trust as the social bond of the political legal system, co-operation was necessary between the courts as interpreters of the law and the electorate as the guardians of political morality.

§ 8.5.2[76]

Reference re ss. 26, 27 & 28 of Constitution Act, 1867
British Columbia Court of Appeal; February 6, 1991
(1991), 78 D.L.R. (4th) 245

The matter of the appointment of additional senators pursuant to section 26 of the *Constitution Act, 1867* was explored in another manner in the Court of Appeal of British Columbia. The principal question put to that court by reference was whether the section was still operative in light of the constitutional development of the country since Confederation and in particular given the adoption of the 1982 amendments to the constitution.

The Attorney General of British Columbia, acting on behalf of the Social Credit government of Premier Vander Zalm, argued that section 26 had been rendered inoperative. Originally, advice on use of the provision was meant to come from British advisors. With the constitutional development of Canada toward legal independence and the severance of the constitutional legal tie to the United Kingdom in 1982, such advice could no longer come from those who would formerly have proffered it. The Attorney General of Ontario advanced that the section was analogous to an emergency power. In response, the Attorney General of Canada relied on the plain meaning of section 26 under the rules of statutory construction. The provision, he said, had been neither repealed nor amended. Its only requirement was advice to the Queen by the Governor General of Canada.

The court held that section 26, as a matter of law, was indeed still operative. Also as a matter of law, there are no limitations on the power of the Queen to appoint additional senators beyond the words

---

[76] Cross-reference to § 8.6.5.

of section 26. The court also determined that the modalities of the application of the provision were a matter of convention rather than law, an area into which it refused to venture.

> It is submitted that it is the nature of conventions that they mature and evolve so that the rigid legal powers contained in the Constitution are exercised in accordance with the prevailing political and constitutional norms. It is then said to be in accordance with the constitutional evolution and independence of Canada that the convention of the Queen acting on the advice of the Imperial Privy Council be replaced with one which has Her acting on the advice of Her Canadian Privy Council.[77]

In response to this, the justices simply held that their function was not to go beyond legal determinations. They were thus able to conclude that the Queen's distinction in making section 26 appointments was not fettered as had been advocated by the British Columbia Attorney General.

Another of the pleadings is worth noting. The Canadian Union of Public Employees had contended that the qualifications for appointment to the Senate, set out in section 23 of the *Constitution Act, 1867*, were contrary to the equality provision contained in section 15 of the *Constitution Act, 1982*. Similarly, the Aboriginal Council of British Columbia had alleged that section 26 was in contradiction to sections 38 and 42 of the *Constitution Act, 1982*, which deal with the methods of constitutional amendment, in that it alters the proportional representation of the provinces in the Senate. On this point, the court retained approvingly the response of the Attorney General of Canada to the effect that "one provision of the *Constitution* cannot be said to be in violation of another, and...section 26 contains an existing power whose exercise neither directly nor indirectly amends the *Constitution*."[78]

The entire purpose of this case was to obtain a determination in law of a matter that was to a great extent a political conflict. In this regard, our attention should be directed to the third question the Government of British Columbia referred to the court.

---

[77] (1991), 78 D.L.R. (4th) 245 at 258 f.
[78] *Ibid.* at 259 e.

If the Queen or the Governor General retains legal authority to direct that members be added to the Senate pursuant to s. 26 is either obliged to follow the advice of the Queen's Privy Council for Canada?[79]

The court answered this with "No," thereby leaving open the possibility for the public debate to continue on the political level, concentrating on the appropriateness of the Queen accepting the advice tendered to her.

§ 8.5.3
Leblanc v. Canada
Ontario Court of Appeal; May 10, 1991
(1991), 80 D.L.R. (4th) 641

By the fall of 1990, in the middle of its second consecutive majority term, the Mulroney government was deeply unpopular. The method it had undertaken to ensure that legislation putting in place the new Goods and Service Tax (GST), that is the stacking of the Senate by appointment of eight additional Senators, raised even higher the level of the government's controversiality. In British Columbia, the provincial government had resorted to a reference. In Ontario, a private citizen, Singh, and a number of Liberal Senators, led by LeBlanc, initiated their own lawsuits to attempt to stop the GST by attacking the validity of the appointment of those specifically called upon to enact it. This exercise in the use of judicial means to achieve political and partisan goals failed in that it did not stop the adoption of the GST legislation. It succeeded, however, in that it shed additional light both on hitherto unexplored areas of constitutional law and on that aspect of political law which deals with membership in Parliament.

The *Singh* and *LeBlanc* cases consisted of applications for declarations to the effect primarily that the appointments of the additional Senators were invalid; that section 26 of the *Constitution Act, 1867*, which provided for the appointments, was itself invalid; and that section 26 had been repealed by implication. The cases were both denied by the Ontario Court (General Division). Before the Ontario Court of Appeal, they were heard together and decided on in a single judgment.

---

[79] *Ibid.* at 247 g.

The first ground of appeal was that section 26 of the *Constitution Act, 1867*, was a "Confederation compromise which had developed into a convention that required that in making the appointment of additional Senators, the Queen take advice from her British Ministers, independently of her Canadian Ministers." This was framed as an attempt to withdraw the issue of section 26 from the field of Canadian politics.

> In other words, the decision to augment the membership of the Senate under s. 26 was required to be made by a person independent of Canadian politics. The argument concluded that, because of Canada's constitutional evolution, the Queen is no longer independent of her Canadian Ministers and thus could no longer be the independent arbiter required by the convention as a precondition of the invocation of s. 26.[80]

The court examined the drafts which had led in 1867 to the definitive version of section 26. The fact that the requirement for the monarch to rely on British advice, which had figured in one draft, was left out of the final text was taken to mean that the Queen was bound by no such legal requirement. Even more to the point, if, as put forward, this requirement had evolved into a convention, the court felt, basing itself on clear precedent,[81] that it was not legally enforceable.

> Section 26 does not limit the Queen's exercise of the power it confers by forbidding the Queen from taking the advice of her Canadian ministers. This court cannot impose a limit which is not contained in the constitution.[82]

The appellants also contended that section 26 had been rendered invalid by repeal by implication. To this the reply of the Court of Appeal was agreement with the trial judge, who had qualified section 26 as a "viable enactment."

It was further alleged in appeal that the effect of the 1947 *Letters Patent to the Governor General* had been a transfer to the sovereign's power to use section 26, to the Governor General. The court disagreed, finding that section 26 requires both the Queen and the Governor General

---

[80] (1991), 80 D.L.R. (4th) 641 at 646b.
[81] *Reference re Amendment to the Constitution of Canada* (1981), 125 D.L.R. (3d) 1 (S.C.C.) at 85-86.
[82] *Supra* note 80 at 647 a.

to play roles in the process and holding that the 1947 instrument had not delegated the Queen's authority in this regard.

The most closely politicized of the legal arguments put forward by the appellants was that use of section 26 was appropriate only in the case of a deadlock in the legislative process, when the government would otherwise be incapable of functioning. The court preferred to relegate this argument to the political plane by concluding that "the question whether such a deadlock existed is not appropriately a jus-ticiable question."[83] This, however, most interestingly, was not a sufficient disposition of the pleading and the justices pursued the matter, relying on the precedent in the *Thorne's Hardware* case. This in turn led to a remarkable characterization of political questions.

> Assuming the necessity for some form of deadlock, the recommendation of the Governor-General to the Queen, the direction by the Queen, and the subsequent summonses by the Governor General pursuant to s. 26 relate to matters of public convenience and general policy within the contemplation of the quoted passage [from *Thorne's Hardware*] and do not constitute appropriate objects for curial review.[84]

The court was also asked to address the apparent inconsistency of section 26 with section 51A, in light of the fact that with the appoint-ment of the additional Senators, New Brunswick would have more Senators than MPs. The court interpreted section 51A, the "Senate Floor Rule," as being related not to section 26, but to section 22, the one dealing with the general composition of the Senate. It held the application of section 26 to be temporary. Nonetheless, it felt that even if section 51A were engaged by the exercise of section 26, that would not invalidate the appointment of New Brunswick's 11th Sen-ator.

With respect to membership in Parliament, the applicants made a final allegation against the fitness and qualification of one of the additional Senators. They said that the allegations of misconduct against him as the former holder of a public office rendered him unfit. The court would not deal with unproven allegations and in any event, it doubted whether this was a proper matter for judicial resolution.

---

[83] *Ibid.* at 648 g.
[84] *Ibid.* at 649 c.

§ 8.5.4
Weir v. Canada (Attorney General)
New Brunswick Court of Appeal; September 11, 1991
(1991), 84 D.L.R. (4th) 39

This case underscores the merit of litigating the same set of facts from the perspective of different provinces and therefore the benefits of federalism for the development of political law. Here, as in the *LeBlanc* case the matter that gave rise to the controversy was the appointment, on September 27, 1990, of eight additional Senators. These appointments were made at the behest of the government of Prime Minister Mulroney for the purpose of securing the enactment of several items of controversial legislation, in particular that dealing with the Goods and Services Tax (GST).

Weir was the leader of the New Democratic Party in the Legislative Assembly. She applied to the New Brunswick Court of Queen's Bench for a declaration to the effect that the appointment of the GST Senators was unconstitutional in that it violated section 51A of the *Constitution Act, 1867*. That provision stated that the representation of a province in the House of Commons shall not be less than that province's representation in the Senate. In fact, with the appointment of a GST Senator from New Brunswick, the province had 10 MPs and 11 Senators. In the alternative, Weir contended that an additional seat should be created in the House of Commons for New Brunswick.

The Queen's Bench concluded that the additional appointments to the Senate were not invalid. However, it also set the stage for making new law by finding that the resulting situation called for the establishment of an 11th House of Commons seat for New Brunswick. The Attorney General of Canada appealed on this issue, while Weir cross-appealed on the matter of the constitutionality of the appointments to the Senate. Her principal contention was that the trial judge had not given sufficient consideration to the relationship between section 51A and section 26, which is the provision that rendered the appointment of the additional Senators possible. "In short, she submits that compliance with s. 51A is a condition precedent to invoking s. 26."[85]

---

[85] (1991), 84 D.L.R. (4th) 39 at 45 c.

In the New Brunswick Court of Appeal, a majority of two of the three justices followed the lead of their Ontario colleagues in holding that while section 51A dealt with membership in the House of Commons, section 26 looked at membership in the Senate. They also felt that in the matter of the relation between membership in the two Houses of Parliament, the criterion of s. 51A were meant to have a bearing on s. 22, the provision determining the basic representation in the Senate, rather than on section 26 which deals exclusively with the additional Senators. The purpose of including section 51A in the Constitution had been to provide a guaranteed floor of representation for Prince Edward Island, the least populous province.

> It was worded so as to extend the same guarantee to any other province whose population might decline or grow so slowly that its Common's representation would, on a population basis, fall below its normal Senate representation.[86]

Moreover, the majority was not convinced that merely because New Brunswick may, according to the wording of section 51A, become "entitled" to an additional Commons seat, that would render the appointment of the 11th Senator invalid.

In analyzing this case, we must also bear in mind the effect of unavoidable, and unexpected, circumstances on the development of political law. The principal issue which the court dealt with was the constitutionality of the appointment of the additional Senators. However, it had also been asked to deal with the need to appoint an 11th MP. Between the time the appeal and cross-appeal were lodged and the time they were heard, one of New Brunswick's Senators died. The court thus held that the Attorney General's appeal on the issue of the need to appoint an 11th MP had become moot. That death in effect prevented the Court of Appeal from adjudicating on what would have been the matter of greatest interest for political law, as well as the matter of greatest controversy.

The dissenting justice made out a strange case to the effect that the appointment of New Brunswick's additional Senator was constitutionally invalid and that it would have been valid only if, as a result, New Brunswick would also have been represented by 11, rather than

---

[86] *Ibid.* at 46 b.

10 MPs. Relying on the application of the rules of statutory interpretation to section 51A, he said:

> If the words "shall always be entitled to" are to have any significance, they must be taken to mean more than an abstract or potential entitlement. The entitlement must be one in fact or at least, the legal mechanism for the election of an additional member or more if needed, must be in place although the member may not yet be elected.[87]

The purpose of the enactment in his view was the protection of the representation of smaller provinces.

---

§ 8.5.5[88]

Harvey v. New Brunswick (Attorney General)
Supreme Court of Canada; August 22, 1996
[1996] 2 S.C.R. 876

There can be no clearer statement than this case to show that the domain of law in a truly democratic society includes the application of legal norms to that most political of procedures, the electoral process. If, in the conduct of an election campaign, a candidate for office knowingly breaches the law with respect to even a single elector, it is a legal and not merely a political price that he has to pay. In that sense, this case applies the principle that was laid down in the *MacLean* case in an even more definitive fashion.

Harvey was a candidate in the electoral district of Carleton North in the general election to the Legislative Assembly of the Province of New Brunswick, held on September 23, 1991. In the course of that campaign, he induced a 16-year-old to cast a vote, fully knowing that the individual was not eligible to vote. This individual's vote would not have been necessary, because Harvey won the seat comfortably. Later, Harvey was charged with and convicted of the offence of having induced the person to vote, contrary to specified provisions of the New Brunswick *Elections Act*.[89] As a consequence of the conviction, Harvey's seat in the Legislature was declared to be vacant and

---

[87] *Ibid.* at 48 f
[88] Cross-reference to § 8.4.
[89] R.S.N.B. 1973, c. E-3, ss. 111(1), 118(2) and 119(a), (b), (c).

he became ineligible to be elected for five years from the date of the conviction.

On January 13, 1993, Harvey instituted proceedings to challenge the constitutionality of the provision in the *Elections Act* which caused him to lose his seat and which would prevent him from trying to regain it. The entire proceeding thereafter focused on the effect of section 119 of the *Election Act* on the election process as an aspect of democracy. The question became framed in terms of the reasonableness of the provision. The heart of the judicial debate was thus under the aegis of section 1 of the *Canadian Charter of Rights and Freedoms*: was section 119 validated by being a reasonable limitation on political activity? The New Brunswick Court of Queen's Bench thought that section 119 violated Harvey's rights and was not saved by section 1 of the *Charter*. The New Brunswick Court of Appeal was prepared to give greater weight to law as a control on electoral politics and held that while section 119 was indeed a violation, it was appropriate in light of section 1 considerations. The Supreme Court of Canada agreed, but a more detailed exposition of the diverse reasoning is called for.

The most exhaustive analysis was penned by Justice LaForest. He set aside the notion of Harvey's actions having been an innocent mistake; he took the conviction at face value and said that Harvey's enthusiastic electioneering "amounted to an attack on the integrity of the electoral process which is at the heart of a free and democratic society and constituted a breach of trust deserving of censure."[90] Despite this, LaForest found that section 119 was at odds with section 3 of the *Charter*, which is the guarantee of the right to vote and of election to and membership in a legislative body. The heart of the ruling is the section 1 discussion.

> In the present case the right in issue is the very embodiment of democracy—the right of citizens to elect their government and the right of each individual to attempt to become part of that government. The value at the heart of s. 119(c) is in many ways an extension of this right, the expectation of citizens to have a fair electoral process so that the right found in s. 3 does not become a hollow and empty one, devoid of meaning or substance.[91]

---

[90] [1996] 2 S.C.R. 876 at 892.
[91] *Ibid.* at 901.

Accepting arguments relating to the integrity of the electoral process, LaForest saw the pressing and substantial concern embodied in section 119. He strongly backed the rational connection between the enactment of the provision and the objective which section 119 sought to achieve. Giving genuine teeth to the application of legality, he went on to affirm that,

> To argue, as the appellant does, that one less vote would not have changed the outcome of the election is to misunderstand the concept of integrity.[92]

In addition, LaForest was of the opinion that section 119 met the minimal impairment test. The penalty of expulsion has been the historical response to activity that he qualified as ultimately inimical to the goal of effective representation. Finally, he held that the effects of section 119 are proportional to the objective of preserving the electoral system.

In a separate but concurring opinion, Justices McLachlin and L'Heureux-Dube came to the same conclusion on the basis of different grounds. In their view, the determination of membership in a legislative body is a matter that falls into the domain of the historical privileges of legislatures. Consequently, judicial review should not even be applied. This opinion laid much greater emphasis on the right of Parliamentary bodies to regulate their own affairs on the basis of the preamble to the *Constitution Act, 1867*. It also relied, perhaps too much, on the notion of the separation of powers and the resulting requirement of each branch of government to refrain from interfering with the work of the others. In order to compensate for this stricter view of the division of powers, McLachlin advocates reconciling the notion of parliamentary privilege with section 3 of the *Charter* by interpreting section 3 in a purposive way, the purpose being the preservation of democratic values inherent in the *Constitution*.

In essence, this case should serve as a signpost to would-be parliamentarians that, for whichever reason, application of section 3 of the *Charter* or reliance on a history of parliamentary privilege, the courts will uphold legal values as supreme in adjudicating the activities of

---

[92] *Ibid.* at 903.

those seeking legislative office and membership in parliamentary bodies.

[T]he individual elected to the legislative assembly holds a position of great trust and responsibility and it is important that such representatives and those seeking such high office be in no doubt that their participation in the proscribed conduct attracts precise and grave consequences.[93]

See also *Bhaduria v. The Liberal Party of Canada and Chrétien*, Ontario Court (General Division), filed October 1, 1996, file no 103091/96, discontinued; *Powell v. McCormack, Speaker of the House of Representatives et al.*, 395 U.S. 486 (1969).[94]

---

§ 8.5.6[95]
Hesford v. General Council of the Bar
United Kingdom High Court; July 22, 1999
[1999] T.N.L.R. No. 617

Hesford was a barrister who had accepted a brief for which a trial date had been set for May 18, 1997. He was also a Member of Parliament who, on May 15, received a three-line whip to attend and vote on the Queen's Speech in the House of Commons, the British equivalent of the Speech from the Throne. He attended the House and missed the trial. The client on whose behalf he was to appear complained and the disciplinary committee of the Bar suspended Hesford for three months. On appeal, the court applied the 1990 *Code of Conduct of the Bar of England and Wales* which forbade barristers from returning a brief so as to attend, among other things, "a non-professional engagement." This phrase was held to refer to matters other than a person's practice as a barrister. Hesford's argument that voting in Parliament was not the kind of non-professional engagement to which the *Code* applied was not accepted. In the court's view, the duty of the barrister was paramount even to that of the MP. "Mr. Hesford's conduct in voting in Parliament was non-professional notwithstanding whether or not such an engagement was originally

---

[93] *Ibid.* at 902.
[94] International comparison.
[95] International comparison.

intended to be caught by these words."[96] The suspension was replaced with a reprimand.

See also *R. v. Archer* [2002] EWCA Crim 1996, July 22, 2002.

8.6 ISSUE: WORK OF THE LEGISLATIVE BRANCH

§ 8.6.1
Coorsh v. Decker
Québec Queens Bench; July 13, 1955
(1955), [1956] Que. Q.B. 78

In the Province of Québec in the mid-1950's, given the influence of
the ultramontaine Catholic hierarchy even on matters of State, the
only way to obtain a divorce was by petition to the Senate of Canada.
That body had constituted a Committee on Divorce specifically to
receive such petitions and hear evidence in regard to them. Its recommendations were then forwarded to the full Senate which, in case
of a positive recommendation, adopted a private bill to grant the
divorce. In this instance, Coorsh made allegations of adultery against
his wife, Decker; the Senate Committee held them to be untrue and
rejected the petition. In the context of those proceedings, the present
judgment is based on a procedural motion for permission to file a
supplementary plea. The Québec Superior Court had to decide
whether the rejection of the divorce petition by the Senate Committee
constituted *res judicata*, binding on it.

This case has two related aspects of interest. The first touches on the
distinction between the work of parliamentary and judicial institutions. The court delved into whether the Senate Committee on Divorce, and indeed the Senate itself, could be considered a court. Pursuant to article 1241 of the *Civil Code of Lower Canada*, the Committee
decision could constitute *res judicata* only if that committee was a
court. While, on the basis of scholarly texts on the law of Parliament,
this decision left reason for doubt as to whether Parliament as a whole
can be considered a court, the holding on this matter, that the Senate
Committee on Divorce was not a court, was found on the fact that

---

[96] *The Times*, London, August 20, 1999.

the committee was not one of the federal courts organized under the *Constitution*. Moreover, the hearing of petitions by the committee did not amount to "judicial proceedings." The recommendation of the committee could therefore not be an order of a court constituting *res judicata*.

The second point of interest is the Supreme Court's characterization of the actual work of Parliament.

> ...the truth is that Parliament is the supreme power in the field of legis-
> lation and that the duly constituted Courts are the supreme power in
> the field of the interpretation and of the application of the laws passed
> by Parliament; while Parliament may make laws, within the frame of
> the Constitution, superseding and on occasions rendering without effect
> decisions of the Courts, such laws do not constitute judgments, but the
> expression by Parliament of the exercise of its supreme power in the
> field of legislation. [97]

This decision was upheld by the Québec Court of Appeal.[98]

See also *R. v. Bruneau* (1963), [1964] 1 O.R. 263 (Ont. C.A.).

---

§ 8.6.2
Waddell v. British Columbia (Governor in Council)
British Columbia Supreme Court; July 17, 1981
(1981), 126 D.L.R. (3d) 431[99]

Ian Waddell, the Member of Parliament for Vancouver-Kingsway, British Columbia, took this action against the Governor General exemplifying the Governor General in Council. He alleged that certain Orders in Council, permitting the transmission of Canadian natural gas from Alberta to the United States, are *ultra vires* the *Northern Pipeline Act*, the purpose of which had been to create a scheme establishing a pipeline for the transmission of American gas from Alaska to the Canada-U.S. border. Waddell argued that the Orders in Council amounted to an unauthorized attempt to by-pass the parliamentary

---

[97] (1955), [1956] Que. P.R. 200 (Que. S.C.) at 206, affirmed (1955), [1956] Que. Q.B. 78 (Que. Q.B.).

[98] *Decker v. Coorsh* (1955), [1956] B.R. 78 (Que. Q.B.).

[99] Affirmed (1982), [1983] 1 W.W.R. 762 (B.C. C.A.), leave to appeal refused (1982), 46 N.R. 261 (S.C.C.).

process. He also reasoned that being a Member of Parliament, he was an elected representative of the people and that the government's use of Orders in Council deprived him of his right to vote on a law before it became law. The executive branch was legislating and infringing on his exclusive right to do so. The defence was based on the argument that Members of Parliament have no special status not enjoyed by members of the public, and that Waddell should voice his complaints about the Orders in Council in Parliament, not in the courts.

In this court's view, the plaintiff's pleadings as a Member of Parliament were sufficient to accord him standing to maintain the action. It also decided that the plaintiff had indeed raised a justifiable constitutional issue. The plaintiff was directly affected by the Orders in Council both as a member of the public and as a Member of Parliament and the action could proceed.

See also *Québec (Procureur général) c. Collier*, 23 D.L.R. (4th) 339 (Que. C.A.), affirmed 66 D.L.R. (4th) 575 (S.C.C.) and *Québec (Procureur général) c. Collier*, [1990] 1 S.C.R. 260 (S.C.C.).

---

§ 8.6.3[100]
P.S.A.C. v. Canada (House of Commons)
Federal Court of Appeal; April 23, 1986
(1986), 27 D.L.R. (4th) 481

This is essentially a labour relations case dealing with whether the employees of the House of Commons were susceptible to being unionized under the *Canada Labour Code*.[101] The Canada Labour Relations Board (C.L.R.B.) had issued a ruling certifying a union to represent certain employees of the House and the House had appealed the matter to the Federal Court of Appeal. The appeal was allowed and the certification was overturned.

One of the members of the unanimous panel of three judges, Justice Pratte, analyzed the issue from the perspective of whether Parliament had enacted the *Canada Labour Code* so as to render that legislation applicable to employees of the House. First he retraced the origins of

---

[100] Cross-reference to § 8.2.C.1.
[101] R.S.C. 1985, c. L-2.

the House itself to the *Constitution Act, 1867*. He looked at the establishment of the senior positions in the House's hierarchy and then examined whether the staff of the House were ordinary public servants. His conclusion was that neither the *Public Service Employment Act*[102] nor the *Public Service Staff Relations Act*[103] applied to those here sought to be unionized.

With respect to the applicability of the *Canada Labour Code* itself, the key to the matter lay in whether the House of Commons could fit into the definition of those employers to which the *Code* applied pursuant to section 2, namely whether it was a "federal work, undertaking or business." To assess this, Justice Pratte judicially defined what the House of Commons does.

> Indeed, what the House does is to perform its constitutional task of participating in the making of laws. That is not, in my view, the operation of a work, undertaking or business. Parliament does not operate a federal undertaking or business; the House, which is nothing but an element of Parliament, does not either.[104]

And he went on to say:

> The operations of the House are of another nature: they are all ancillary to the performance of its sole task of participating in the making of laws and, for that reason, unlike most operations of a municipal corporation, cannot be assimilated to operations of private employers.[105]

Based on this analysis, the court concluded that the work of the House could not be embraced in the sanctified phrase of "federal work, undertaking or business." Consequently, the *Canada Labour Code* was not applicable.

This decision left the Government of Canada in a difficult position with respect to employees of the House. They were not subject to the *Canada Labour Code* and could not be thought of as being under the umbrella of the labour relations regime of Ontario, where the House of Commons happened to be situated because their activities certainly were not of a provincial or local nature. Moreover, they were not

---

[102] R.S.C. 1985, c. P-33.
[103] R.S.C. 1985, c. P-35.
[104] (1986), 27 D.L.R. (4th) 481 at 485.
[105] *Ibid.* at 487.

subject to the *Public Service Staff Relations Act*, the separate labour relations code applicable to federal public servants. Effectively, House staff were subject to no regime of labour relations. In response to this ruling, the government enacted very promptly and had Parliament enact a completely new framework for the labour relations of the House staff. This became the *Parliamentary Employment and Staff Relations Act*,[106] which received royal assent a mere three months after the judgment.

---

§ 8.6.4[107]

Sethi v. Canada (Minister of Employment & Immigration)
Federal Court of Appeal; June 20, 1988
(1988), 52 D.L.R. (4th) 681[108]

The addition of this case to our understanding of the work of the legislative branch is that it establishes the distinction between the factual and the speculative aspects of the legislative process.

Sethi sought to be admitted to Canada as a Convention refugee. The Minister of Employment and Immigration rejected the application and Sethi sought redetermination by the Immigration Appeal Board (IAB). Contemporaneously, Parliament was considering a bill to abolish the IAB and to replace it with the Immigration and Refugee Board.[109] Sethi sought to have the IAB decline jurisdiction. In respect of that application, this case was about reasonable apprehension of bias; it was alleged that the tribunal members could be influenced in their decision-making by their desire to be selected for positions on the new tribunal and would therefore seek to satisfy the same authorities, which had adopted a position contrary to Sethi's application. The IAB refused to decline jurisdiction on those grounds. The Federal Court – Trial Division perceived a potential bias and quashed the Board's ruling. The Federal Court of Appeal allowed an appeal by the Minister and definitively determined that no potential of bias could be perceived.

---

[106] S.C. 1986, c. 41, Royal Assent on June 27, 1986; R.S.C. 1985, c. 33 (2nd Supp.).

[107] Cross-reference to § 9.3.A.1.

[108] Leave to appeal refused (1988), 92 N.R. 325 (note) (S.C.C.).

[109] Bill C-55, 2nd Session, 33rd Parliament, 1986-87, *An Act to Amend the Immigration Act, 1976 and to amend other Acts in consequence thereof.*

The key to the Trial Division and the Court of Appeal decisions was whether the impression made on the minds of the judges by the progress of Bill C-55 through the legislative process should be taken into consideration as a factor in their determination of potential apprehension of bias among members of the IAB. This is what led them to analyze the work of the legislature from several perspectives.

The first finding of the Court of Appeal was that the introduction of a bill in Parliament by a government "is indicative of the government's intention that it become law as introduced. That is a fact and will remain a fact until the Bill does become law, it 'dies on the Order Paper' as a result of Parliament proroguing without passing it, or the government announces a different intention."[110] This is the general rule, and it is emphasized as the factual element of the legislative process. Based on familiarity with the specificities of Canadian legislative practice, the court accepted that the occasional introduction of a bill as a substitute for a "White Paper" was an exception to this general rule. Moreover, it said that only those amendments to a bill previously introduced, which are proposed in Parliament by a Minister of the Crown or the responsible parliamentary secretary, are indicative of the government's intention.

The court then expressed the judicial perspective on the progress of bills through the legislative process. It also distinguished the analysis of this progress from the introduction of legislation by qualifying it as the speculative element as opposed to the factual. The components of this analysis can be listed as follows:

- the stages of progress of a bill are not relevant to judicial consideration;

- the assumption that any bill will proceed to enactment is sheer speculation; and

> That is so regardless of the majorities which the governing party may enjoy in either or both of the Houses of Parliament, the potential longevity of the particular Parliament and other factors which might be thought to militate in favour of the certain passage of government bills to law. The forces at work within a government and a Parliament that influence

---

[110] (1988), 52 D.L.R. (4th) 681 at 687-688, leave to appeal refused (1988), 92 N.R. 325 (note) (S.C.C.).

the progress of a bill to law are not very different in terms of predictability than those Dickson, J., as he then was, in *Operation Dismantle Inc. v. The Queen* (1985), 18 D.L.R. (4th) 481 at p. 490, [1985] 1 S.C.R. 441 at p. 454, 13 C.R.R. 287 (S.C.C.), noted as "operating in an international arena of radical uncertainty, and continually changing circumstances." That the arena is national does not appreciably enhance its certainty.[111]

This part of the judgment can in fact be summarized by stating that the legislative process after introduction is uncertain and unpredictable until its very end. The corollary of this, for the courts, is of course that they are to consider as rules of law only those Bills which have actually been enacted into statutes. Seen in this light, the judicial advice that the progress of Bills along the legislative path is to be ignored is eminently sensible.

This judgment comprises one other observation which deserves mention. The court notes that among the factors which can persuade the government to alter its intentions with respect to the enactment of legislation after introduction into Parliament are the general public, as opposed to Parliamentary, debate on the Bill and, even more significantly, litigation about the Bill, such as this case was.

---

§ 8.6.5[112]
Reference re ss. 26, 27 & 28 of Constitution Act, 1867
British Columbia Court of Appeal; February 6, 1991
(1991), 78 D.L.R. (4th) 245

The principal issue which gave rise to this case was the desire for judicial determination of the constitutional validity of section 26 of the *Constitution Act, 1867*, dealing with the appointment of additional senators. In the contest of examining the work of the legislature rather than the composition of that branch of government, however, this is one of the rare cases which delves into the scenario of discord between the two Houses of Parliament and the struggle between the Commons and the Senate for the determinative voice on political legislative issues.

---

[111] *Ibid.* at 687.
[112] Cross-reference to § 8.5.2.

At the time the matter of the appointment of additional senators arose, the government was of Progressive Conservative colouration, meaning that that party had a majority of Members in the House of Commons. In the Senate, however, up until the appointment of the additional senators, there remained a majority of Liberals who had been appointed by the government of Prime Minister Trudeau. The government of the day in 1990, having been elected, sought to ensure enactment of Bill C-21, an *Unemployment Insurance Act* amendment, Bill 28, an *Income Tax Act* amendment and most particularly Bill C-62, the *Excise Tax Act* amendment which would put the Goods and Services Tax (GST) regime in place. The duly appointed, but not democratically based, Senate had delayed but not rejected passage of all three legislative items. We may presume that their opposition was based on the view that these amendments constituted bad policy, but also on grounds of partisan advantage. In terms of the work of the legislative branch, the question of law and politics here was which of the two Houses would prevail. From this perspective, the interest of section 26 is not whether it is still operative, but that it was intended as a mechanism to break a deadlock between the Commons and the Senate.

This aspect of section 25 was addressed directly only by the Attorney General of Canada:

> ...the Attorney General of Canada submits that had it not been for the appointment of the additional senators, the GST legislation would have been defeated in the Senate.[113]

Even though this argument is somewhat speculative, it was not rebuffed by any of the parties holding contrary views. The Attorney General of British Columbia came closest in his allegation that under section 26, it had been intended that the monarch be advised by the Imperial Privy Council rather than the Canadian cabinet. Such an argument could only be justified on the basis of 19th century concepts of limited democracy and the preservation of the power of an appointed body vis-à-vis an elected one.

In its determination of the question whether section 26 remains operative, the court referred also to the matter of ensuring that the work

---

[113] (1991), 78 D.L.R. (4th) 245 at 253 e.

of the legislature could continue by breaking deadlocks between the two Houses.

> This provision did not form a part of the proposal for the constitution of the Senate agreed at the Quebec Conference. Its inclusion was pressed upon the Canadian delegates in London by the British government. The Colonial Secretary, Lord Carnarvon, argued that there was no mechanism to escape from a serious deadlock between the two Houses. The accepted method of dealing with a situation of this kind in the United Kingdom was the creation of additional peers by the Sovereign. But the appointment of additional Senators could wreck the delicately balanced composition of the Senate, finally achieved after patient negotiation at the Quebec Conference. Macdonald set to work to devise a formula for appointing additional Senators without, at the same time, violating the agreement on balanced representation. As a result, the permitted number of extra appointments is so few that it is difficult to see what circumstances would be clarified by such appointments.[114]

See also *MacDonell v. Québec (Commission d'accès à l'information)*, [2002] 3 S.C.R. 661 (S.C.C.); *Petravic v. Cullen*, Superior Court of Justice, Small Claims Division, filed March 13, 2002; *Authorson (Litigation Guardian of) v. Canada (Attorney General)*, 227 D.L.R. (4th) 385 (S.C.C.).

---

§ 8.6.6
2003 Ontario Extra-Parliamentary Budget Process
Legal Opinions Submitted to the Government House Leader and to the Speaker of the Legislative Assembly
-and-
Speaker's Ruling on a Question of Privilege, May 8, 2003
-and-
Martin v. Ontario, Ontario Superior Court of Justice; January 20, 2004

The question raised by this case is whether parliamentary privilege, and more generally the law and custom of parliament, dictate that the major parliamentary functions such as the delivery of the government's budget actually take place in the legislature itself.

---

[114] *Ibid.* at 261 h-262 b, citing from *The Structure of Canadian Government*, rev. ed. (1977) by Professor J. R. Mallory.

In the first few months of 2003, the Province of Ontario was living in an interregnum. Premier Mike Harris, who had led the Progressive Conservative Party for two consecutive majority governments, had retired from active politics, to be replaced by Ernie Eves. While it was palpable that a general election was close, the direction in which the electorate was headed could not yet be firmly determined. Both the incumbent Progressive Conservatives and their main challengers, the Liberals, were seeking every possible advantage of a political and policy nature. In that environment, the government decided that, as a matter of novelty, it would hold the 2003 budget speech and deliver the budget on March 27, in the private facility of an automobile parts manufacturer, rather than in the Legislative Assembly. Neither the Premier nor the Minister of Finance was able to offer any reason for such an unprecedented break with the way in which the government had consistently conducted its work, except to insist on its allegedly innovative nature. The plan also raised serious questions as to the relationship between the executive and legislative branches, which the government treated dismissively. There arose a great controversy, which was clouded by partisan rhetoric on all sides.

This political issue could not escape legal analysis. In the week leading up to the delivery of the budget, the Government House Leader sought and obtained no less than four letters of opinion from reputable Toronto law firms. These were made public but were not tabled in the Legislature. The Speaker of the House requested an opinion letter of his own. All these documents focused on the constitutional convention at stake, the political convention, the matter of contempt of the House and on the doctrine of responsible government. In sum, what was at stake was the legal element of democracy in the work of the Legislature.

Perhaps not surprisingly, the opinions requested by the Government House Leader all agreed that the procedure contemplated was neither unconstitutional, nor illegal, nor in breach of convention if a convention requiring delivery of the budget in the Legislature existed at all. The opinion delivered to the Speaker was in the contrary direction.

> The Ontario Government and Legislative Assembly have thus established a strong precedential record of presenting the Budget by means of documents and a speech to the Assembly. While the precise procedures for presenting the budget have developed, with the consent of the Assembly, over time, one constant has remained: the first place in which

the Government publicly announces the Budget has always been within the Legislative Assembly.[115]

This opinion went on to indicate the source of the Government's conventional duty to the Legislature and linked the matter to democracy.

> The legislative control of the appropriation of public monies thus begins as a legal constitutional matter. If, for instance, the Government were seeking to pass a supply bill without the consent of the Legislative Assembly, or indeed to originate it in a Committee rather than the Assembly itself, there would clearly be a violation of the written Constitution.
>
> . . .
>
> While strictly speaking the Budget Speech itself is not part of the "origination" of a money bill as described in section 53 of the Constitution, the process of delivering a Budget Speech to the Legislative Assembly is nonetheless intimately related to this process. It is a focal point of the democratic political process.[116]

Finally, in carefully couched language, the opinion of the Speaker indicated that the Government's plan was contrary to democratic principles and intimated at the political motivation involved.

> The Government's current proposal, refusing to recall the Legislative Assembly for the purpose of presenting the Budget Speech and instead making its presentation to a silent group of individual citizens thus conflicts with the constitutional convention that the democratically-elected Assembly is to be given the first opportunity to consider and debate Budget statements and their corresponding financial legislation.
>
> Even if a Budget whose presentation bypassed the House were subsequently presented to the Legislative Assembly for debate, the process would undermine democratic principles. The public elects its legislators not only for the purpose of forming a Government, but also to hold that Government accountable. Once the Budget is presented, the public wants to ensure that the Government is held to account for that Budget.

---

[115] Opinion letter dated March 24, 2003 from Neil Finkelstein to the Honourable Gary Carr, Speaker of the Legislative Assembly of Ontario, p. 8.

[116] Op. lit., pages 19 and 20.

The manner of doing so, according to the dictates of responsible government, is to have the matter debated in the Assembly.[117]

The extra-parliamentary budget proposal engendered not only voluminous comments, but also serious press criticism. Newspapers of a seemingly liberal bent carried articles attacking the Government's position. Those with a more conservative flavour presented stories more favourable to the Government's perspective, although that intention did not always bear fruit. For example, the *National Post* of March 19, 2003, indicated that the Premier seemed to have lost confidence in the Speaker,[118] hardly a story that could uphold the Government's viewpoint. The most significant media comment related to the 2003 budget process related the evident displeasure of the people at the plan, expressed by Baroness Boothroyd of Sandwell, a former Speaker of the United Kingdom Parliament who was held in general esteem.[119]

The Ontario Government nevertheless proceeded with the plan it had announced. On March 27, 2003, at a time the Legislative Assembly was not sitting, the budget was delivered in a privately industrial location owned by an obviously partisan friend of the party in power. While the potential damage to democracy had been done, the legality of the matter could not be settled on the basis of conflicting opinions alone. After the resumption of the session, Shawn Convey, a Liberal Member of the Legislative Assembly representing Renfrew-Nipissing-Pembroke, raised a question of privilege, alleging that the way the budget had been presented constituted an offence against the authority and dignity of the House. The Speaker ruled on the question on May 8. He indicated that while there have been other occasions when a budget or a budget type speech had been presented elsewhere than in the House, he found that in this instance, a *prima facie* case of contempt had been established. He left it up to the House to determine what to do. The Speaker was not as reticent in his ruling to allude to the obvious political motivation of the Government as had been the lawyer who authored the opinion earlier addressed to him.

---

[117] *Ibid.*, p. 22 and 23.
[118] "Premier lambastes 'biased' Speaker," Robert Benzie, *National Post*, March 19, 2003, page A-16.
[119] "Eves blasted for lack of Parliamentary respect," Arthur Milnes, *Hill Times*, March 29, 2003, page 1.

Having reflected on these authorities, I will apply them to the case before me now. It is hard to recall a time in recent memory when a matter of parliamentary process has so incensed people inside and outside this province. Many Ontarians from all walks of life have complained in an overwhelmingly negative way—to my office, to members directly, through various media, and to the government itself—that the government's approach to communicating the 2003 budget to Ontarians has undermined parliamentary institutions and processes.

. . .

To the extent that they imply that parliamentary institutions and processes in Ontario tend to interfere with the government's message to the public, such statements tend to reflect adversely on those institutions and processes. If the government has a problem with those institutions and processes, or if it wants to improve them, why did it not ask the House sometime during the last session to reflect on the problem and to consider appropriate changes? Traditional ways to do just that would be to introduce a bill, table a notice of motion, enter into discussions at the level of the House leaders, or ask the standing committee on the Legislative Assembly to study and report on the problem. Given the public's reaction to the government's decision to stage a budget presentation outside the House, I think Ontarians are rather fond of their traditional parliamentary institutions and parliamentary processes, and they want greater deference to be shown towards the traditional parliamentary forum in which public policies are proposed, debated and voted on.

When the government or nay member claims that a budget presentation is needed outside the House well before it happens inside the House in order to communicate directly with the people or because of a perceived flaw in the parliamentary institution, there is a danger that the representative role of each and every member of this House is undermined, that respect for the institution is diminished, and that Parliament is rendered irrelevant. Parliamentary democracy is not vindicated by the government conducting a generally one-sided public relations event on the budget well in advance of members having an opportunity to hold the government to account for the budget in this chamber.

I can well appreciate that parliamentary proceedings can be animated and often emotional, and they can be cumbersome. It may not be the most efficient of political systems, but it is a process that reflects the reality that members, like the people of Ontario, may not be of one mind on matters of public policy. A mature parliamentary democracy is not a docile, esoteric or one-way communications vehicle; it is a dynamic, interactive and representative institution that allows the government of the day to propose and defend its policies – financial and otherwise. It also allows the opposition to scrutinize and hold the government to account for those policies. It is an open, working and relevant system of scrutiny and accountability. If any members of this House have a problem with the concept of parliamentary democracy, then they have some serious explaining to do.[120]

Based on the Speaker's ruling, Mr. Conway moved on May 8 "that this House declares that it is the undoubted right of the Legislative Assembly, in Parliament assembled, to be the first recipient of the budget of Ontario." On May 21, this motion was defeated by a vote of 53 to 42.

The essential quality of the issue for democratic governance was illustrated by the fact that neither the battle of legal opinions, nor the question of privilege, was able to resolve the controversy. On June 3, 2003, Peter Martin, a citizen, filed a Notice of Application for declaratory judgment based on constitutional law and constitutional convention. Most importantly, he sought to have the Ontario Superior Court of Justice declare that under any circumstances whatsoever, the reading of the budget by a Minister of the Crown, outside the Legislative Chamber is unconstitutional. The respondents moved to strike out the application on the ground that Mr. Martin had no standing, that the issues raised were by then moot, and that the conduct complained of did not give rise to any legal effect which may properly be the subject of judicial proceedings. Separately, the Speaker also moved to strike the Application, on the ground that the court lacked jurisdiction to adjudicate on the issues raised.

With respect to the Speaker's motion the court concluded that the matter before it was one of parliamentary privilege, therefore erasing the court's jurisdiction. Sole and exclusive authority to deal with it therefore lay with the Speaker and the Legislature. The court also agreed with the Crown's motion to the effect that the issue was moot. There was no matter susceptible of judicial determination. It also dismissed those points in the application that were based on *quo warranto*, relating to the fact that the extra-parliamentary budget would render government expenditures illegal. The principal meaning of the ruling is that the issue of whether the budget needed to be

---

[120] Official Report of Debates, (Hansard), Thursday, 8 May, 2003, pp. 233-234.

delivered in the Legislature or could be read outside it, was a matter for the Speaker and the Legislature itself to resolve. This was a parliamentary, not a judicial matter. While this court ruling was legally correct, it did not amount to a reply to the substantive question which the episode had raised in terms of democracy. The controversy eventually died down, save in the minds of political law specialists. In respect of the population at large, the subsequent general election, at which the Liberal Party was given a clear majority in the Legislature, was the resolution. It is likely that the extra-parliamentary budget and its patent abuse of parliamentary tradition based on constitutional accountability, contributed to the demise of the Progressive Conservative Party.

It is indicative of the nature of the budget episode a further chapter of the matter was written in the political sphere. In the Speech From the Throne which was delivered after the general election by the incoming Liberal Premier, Dalton McGuinty, on November 20, 2003, he referred back to the previous government's experiment.

> The spring Budget will be held in this chamber. Every budget will. And every budget will reflect what Ontarians have told this government they want done.[121]

In a final irony, the Speaker of the Ontario Legislature who had opposed his own government on the issue of the budget, Gary Carr, and who had at the relevant time been a Progressive Conservative, won the Liberal nomination for the 38th federal general election in the electoral district of Halton on March 26, 2004. He won convincingly.

---

[121] Speech From the Throne: *Strengthening The Foundations for Change*, November 20, 2003, http://www.premier.gov.on.ca/english/Library/ThroneSpeech112003_ts.asp. Last consulted August 16, 2004.

§ 8.6.7[122]
Raines v. Byrd
United States Supreme Court; June 26, 1997
138 L.Ed.2d 849 (1997)
-and-
Clinton v. City of New York
United States Supreme Court; June 25, 1998
141 L.Ed.2d 393 (1998)

In the system of governance of the United States, the work of legislating is very much affected by the doctrine and practice of the separation of powers. According to the *United States Constitution*, all legislative powers are vested in Congress, but in order for laws voted by Congress to come into effect, they must be presented to the President for approval. For a long time, presidents have sought authority to be able to veto certain portions of bills adopted by Congress, so as to prevent what they considered excessive spending. This selective assent has become known as the "line-item veto" and it has been the subject of intense political debate over the past two decades. After the mid-term Congressional elections of 1994, two years into the presidency of William Clinton, the Republican Party obtained a majority in the House of Representatives and put forward the so-called "contract with America," a political program involving a number of right-wing reforms. The only element in that program which was endorsed by the President was the line-item veto, which was then characterized as a means of lowering the American Government's massive budget deficit.

This was the background against which the *Line Item Veto Act* was introduced in the Senate on January 4, 1995, by Senator Bob Dole, Clinton's eventual opponent in the 1996 campaign. This legislation, which was to amend the *Congressional Budget and Impoundment Control Act*, was signed into law by Clinton on April 9, 1996.[123] The purpose of the provision was described as being:

> ...to authorize the President to cancel in whole any dollar amount of discretionary budget authority, any item of new direct spending, or any

---

[122] International comparison.
[123] Pub. Law No. 104-130, 110 Stat. 1200 (1996), codified as 2 U.S.C., Sec. 681, note, 691 *et seq.*

limited tax benefit signed into law, if the President: (1) determines that such cancellation will reduce the Federal budget deficit and will not impair essential Government functions or harm the national interest; and (2) notifies the Congress of any such cancellation within five calendar days after enactment of the law providing such amount, item, or benefit. Requires the President, in identifying cancellations, to consider legislative histories and information referenced in law.[124]

The line item veto had no sooner come into effect on January 1, 1997, when, as a continuation of the political disputes it had engendered during its enactment phase, six then active and former Senators and Congressmen filed suit to have it declared unconstitutional. It is interesting to note that this was a political debate relating to the legislative process rather than to party interests. Just as the co-sponsors of the bill had been of both party allegiances, the plaintiffs included both Democrats and Republicans. "The suit, filed in Federal District Court here (New York), says the President's new power circumvents what the Supreme Court has described as a 'single, finely wrought and exhaustively considered procedure' for making law."[125] This was the first of the two cases cited in the heading, *Byrd v. Raines*.

On April 10, 1997, the District Court accepted the arguments presented to it by the plaintiffs and declared the line-item veto to be in breach of the constitutional scheme intended by the founders of the republic.

> Under the Act, however, as plaintiffs describe it, the Member's same vote operates only to present the President with a "menu" of **items** from which he can select those worthy of his approval, not a legislative *fait accompli* that he must accept or reject in whole, as in the past. As one Senator characterizes it, his vote for an "A-B-C" bill might lead to the *post hoc* creation of an "A-B" law, or a "B-C" law, depending on the President's use of his newly conferred cancellation authority, for which neither he nor his colleagues would have voted so reconfigured.
>
> . . .
>
> Under the Act the dynamic of lawmaking is fundamentally altered.

---

124 Westlaw United States Bill Tracking Database; 1995 US S.B.4 (SN).
125 Suit Challenges Line-Item Vetoes, Robert Pear, *New York Times*, January 3, 1997, p. 1.

. . .

The Line Item Veto Act, in contrast, hands off to the President authority over fundamental legislative choices. Indeed, that is its reason for being. It spares Congress the burden of making those vexing choices of which programs to preserve and which to cut. Thus, by placing on itself the "onus" of overriding the President's cancellations, Congress has turned the constitutional (sic) division of responsibilities for legislating on its head.

The Court therefore agrees with plaintiffs.[126]

This first decision was on the merits of the issue. On June 27, 1997, however, the Supreme Court allowed an appeal on the issue of standing by a 7-2 margin. It ruled that the law could be challenged by anyone affected by a line-item veto once the President has exercised that authority, but in the meantime, the parliamentarians who sued had no standing as they had not alleged sufficiently concrete injury.

The real test of the line-item veto came after the President actually used it to cancel section 4722(c) of the *Balanced Budget Act* of 1997. The effect of this was to waive the statutory right of the Federal Government to recoup up to $2.6 billion in taxes which the State of New York had levied against providers of Medicaid services. In response, the City of New York and others sued, alleging that the use of the line-item veto contravened the *Presentment Clause* of the *U.S. Constitution*,[127] which set out the various courses of action authorized to the President after a bill had been voted by Congress and was "presented" to the President for signature. Opponents of the line-item veto also started another action based on the same legal grounds in relation to the cancellation of a provision of the *Taxpayer Relief Act of 1997*. The U.S. District Court for the District of Columbia consolidated the cases and held that, on the merits, the line-item veto was unconstitutional.[128]

The matter went before the Supreme Court of the United States, which, on June 25, 1998, determined that the line-item veto was indeed unconstitutional, thus ending the debate definitively and removing from the hands of the President what the press had called a

---

[126] 956 F. Supp. 25 (1997) pp. 5 and 10.

[127] Art. I, § 7, c. 2.

[128] 985 F. Supp. 168 (1998).

powerful political tool. On the issue of standing, the court held that the matter was justiciable and assented to the plaintiffs' contention that they had a personal stake in the outcome, rather than an institutional injury which the court held to be more abstract and widely dispersed.

The court saw the line-item veto as a direct contradiction of the intent of the framers of the Constitution. Its use to cancel specific provisions in legislation voted by Congress prevented those provisions from having legal force or effect. In both legal and practical effect, the President has amended two Acts of Congress by repealing a portion of each. Repeal of statutes, no less than enactment, must conform with Art. I of the *United States Constitution*.

> There is no provision in the *Constitution* that authorizes the President to enact, to amend or to repeal statutes. Both Article I and Article II assign responsibilities to the President that directly relate to the lawmaking process, but neither addresses the issue presented by these cases.[129]

The court went on to clarify the role of the President in the legislative process. Once Congress had voted a bill, the President could, according to the *Constitution*, sign it or veto it whole. The veto, or in constitutional language, return, takes place before the bill becomes law. The purported statutory cancellation envisaged in the line-item veto takes place after the bill becomes law and relates only to a part of it. In the view of the court, the constitutional silence on this point was the equivalent of an express prohibition.

> Our first President understood the text of the Presentment Clause as requiring that he either "approve all the parts of a Bill, or reject it in toto." What has emerged in these cases from the President's exercise of his statutory cancellation powers, however, are truncated versions of two bills that passed both Houses of Congress. They are not the product of the "finely wrought" procedure that the Framers designed.[130]

By way of acknowledging the intensity of the political debate about the line-item veto and the profound consequences of its ruling, the court ventured away from the purely legal aspects of the issue to voice additional, political commentary. First, it indicated that despite the support of many members of both major political parties who had

---

[129] 141 L.Ed.2d 393 (1998) at 414.
[130] *Ibid.* at 415.

served in the Legislative and Executive Branches, and despite the great debate and deliberation of the line-item bill in Congress and its signature by the President, it would "express no opinion about the wisdom of the procedures [so] authorized."[131] If anything, this was a strong hint to the other Branches of the court's disapproval. Next, the court felt it needed to reaffirm that it had addressed only the legal aspect of the overall political debate, looking only at "finely wrought" procedures commanded by the *Constitution*. Finally, the justices thought it necessary to reassure that their judgment was based on the narrow ground that the *Line Item Veto Act* was not authorized by the *United States Constitution*.

> If the Line Item Veto Act were valid, it would authorize the President to create a different law—one whose text was not voted on by either House of Congress or presented to the President for signature. Something that might be known as "Public Law 105-33 as modified by the President" may or may not be desirable, but it is surely not a document that may "become a law" pursuant to the procedures designed by the Framers of Article I, § 7, of the Constitution. [132]

In the political circumstances, namely where the Legislative and the Executive Branches seemed to have agreed on a purpose-driven new method of legislating, the Judicial Branch wanted to avoid being the legal bulwark against political progress. It thus needed to be cautious in reminding the other two branches that if they wanted to achieve renewal, in the work of legislating, they would have to use the existing constitutional framework.

> If there is to be a new procedure in which the President will play a different role in determining the final text of what may "become a law," such change must come not by legislation but through the amendment procedures set forth in Article V of the Constitution. Cf. *U. S. Term Limits, Inc. v. Thornton*, 514 US 779, 837, 131 L Ed 2d 881, 115 S Ct 1842 (1995).[133]

Short of this kind of constitutional reform, existing constitutional and legal processes would have to prevail over the will for politically motivated compromises for reform.

---

[131] *Ibid.* at 419.
[132] *Ibid.* at 420.
[133] *Ibid.*

8.7 ISSUE: UNFETTERED NATURE OF THE LEGISLATIVE PROCESS FROM POLICY AND POLITICS

§ 8.7.1

Iscar Ltd. v. Karl Heitel GmbH

Federal Court of Canada – Trial Division; January 29, 1988

(1988), 19 C.P.R. (3d) 385

In the course of an action regarding a copyright matter, the defendant applied for a stay of proceedings on the grounds that a bill comprising amendments to the *Copyright Act* was then before Parliament and that if it were enacted without change, the *Copyright Act*, so amended, would deny the plaintiff the right to the relief claimed. The prothonotary of the Trial Division of the Federal Court refused the application for stay. On appeal, the court upheld the denial.

The court emphasized the unpredictable nature of the legislative process and by inference, the fact that neither the decision of a court nor other factors could be deemed to have a fettering influence on the course of action to be adopted by Parliament, in advance of its legislative decision-making. Among specific factors cited in making it "impossible to predict whether any measure will become law, let alone when,"[134] was the possibility of a hostile reaction by the Senate to a legislative initiative undertaken by the House of Commons. The court also referred to the "ever-present possibility of a crisis leading to an election or a general election without such a crisis."[135] At the time of this decision, the court must have been clearly conscious of the balance of forces among the political parties in Parliament, as the then overwhelming Progressive Conservative majority in the House of Commons was facing a Liberal dominated Senate.[136] In fact, it was only ten months later in the same year, 1988, that the government

---

[134] (1988), 19 C.P.R. (3d) 385 at 387.

[135] *Ibid.*

[136] At the time of this decision, the standing in the House of Commons was: Progressive Conservatives 207, Liberals 39, New Democrats 32, with 3 Independents. In the Senate, there were 61 Liberals, 32 Progressive Conservatives, 5 Independents and 6 vacant seats.

went to the people in a general election on the clear issue of free trade with the United States, in an atmosphere of controversy, albeit not of crisis. In the context of the relations between the two Houses of Parliament and its unpredictable effect on the legislative process, a parliamentary crisis of the kind contemplated in this judgment did arise in September 1990, when the returned Progressive Conservative government needed to appoint so-called "additional" Senators pursuant to the never before used procedure of section 26 of the *Constitution Act, 1867*, in order to ensure that it be able to enact legislation on the Goods and Services Tax.

As a further and specific ground for upholding the dismissal of the application for stay, the court recognized that if the legislation sought by the government to be enacted were retroactive in nature, it would increase the prospect of amendments during the legislative process. If enacted in that manner, the validity of the legislation would also be more likely to be litigated.

The judge's most lasting characterization of the legislative process to arise from this case was to the effect that "I cannot imagine anything less predictable than the course of legislation through Parliament. Indeed, the only thing that is certain about life in Parliament is that nothing is certain."[137] This judge was in a perfect position to write these lines, having previously been Speaker of the House of Commons.[138]

See also *O.T.F. v. Ontario (Attorney General)* (2000), 49 O.R. (3d) 257 (Ont. C.A.), leave to appeal refused (2001), 80 C.R.R. (2d) 187 (note) (S.C.C.); *Aviation Portneuf Ltée c. Canada (Procureur général)*, 2001 FCT 1299 (Fed. T.D.); *Ainsworth Lumber Co. v. Canada (Attorney General)*, 85 B.C.L.R. (3d) 62 (B.C. C.A.), reversing 2000 BCSC 1399 (B.C. S.C. [In Chambers]); *Shade v. Canada* (Attorney General), 2003 FCT 327 (Fed. T.D.).

---

[137] *Supra* note 134 at 386-7.

[138] James Jerome was Speaker of the House of Commons from September 30, 1974, until April 14, 1980, the only person so far to hold the position under two administrations led by different parties.

§ 8.7.2[139]
Morrissey v. State of Colorado and U.S. Term Limits Inc.
-and-
Goggin v. State of Colorado
Colorado Supreme Court; January 20, 1998
951 P.2d 911 (Colo., 1998)

The events leading up to this case, as well as the judgment itself, are in direct consequence of the decision of the United States Supreme Court in *United States Term Limits v. Thornton*.[140] When that ruling determined that States could not set term limits for their Congressional representatives by way of voter indicated amendments to State Constitutions, the authorities in Colorado attempted to achieve the same results by other means which they hoped would be sustainable in law. On December 26, 1996, an amendment to the *Colorado Constitution* was proclaimed, setting forth the exact language of a proposed *Term Limits Amendment* (TLA) to the *United States Constitution*. This Colorado amendment also contained four controversial elements. It directed state legislators to apply for a convention to amend the *U.S. Constitution* so as to limit terms of office and directed them to ratify the TLA in such a convention. It directed Colorado's Congressional representatives to approve the TLA. Further, it instructed new candidates for Colorado state office and for Colorado's Congressional offices to sign a pledge to use their legislative powers to enact the TLA and if elected, to vote for the TLA. Finally, as a measure of compliance, the amendment required that Colorado's state and federal ballots indicate whether candidates had made the pro-TLA pledge or had voted on this issue in accordance with voter instructions.

In two separate cases which were joined, Morrissey and Goggin sought to have the amendment to the *Colorado Constitution* declared unconstitutional on the ground that it violated the terms of Article V of the *U.S. Constitution*, which declared that the *U.S. Constitution* could be amended only upon proposal by two-thirds of both Houses of Congress or upon application to Congress by two-thirds of the State legislatures to call a constitutional convention. This scheme did

---

[139] International comparison.
[140] 514 U.S. 779 (1995).

not render possible voter initiated procedures. Several judgments had already held various plans involving voter participation unconstitutional.

The Colorado Supreme Court held the amendment to the State's Constitution to be unconstitutional, determining that it was not only designed to circumvent the requirements of *Article V* of the *U.S. Constitution,* but also that it undermined representative government and disturbed the balance of the representative system. Most importantly, it held that this was an intrusion into the legislative realm.

The judgment was supported by a number of mutually complementary reasons. The court held first that Colorado's amendment abrogated the representative form of government because it took away from elected officials the right to exercise their own judgment and to vote the best interests of their constituents as they perceived them. It gave explicit details of this rule against fettering.

> Our system of election contemplates free and full discourse concerning a candidate's positions on a variety of issues before an election. The electorate explores not only the ideological bent of a particular candidate, but also the candidate's integrity, honesty and record. Voters choose the people whom they believe will best represent their own beliefs, preferences, and interests. At the next election, citizens speak their approval or disapproval of a legislator's record with their votes.[141]

The court reinforced this view with that of a California precedent.[142]

> Article V...envisions legislators free to vote their best judgment, responsible to their constituents through the electoral process, not puppet legislators coerced or compelled by loss of salary or otherwise to vote in favour of a proposal they may believe unwise.[143]

Later, the court returned to this reason under a different title, reinforcing the notion that elected representatives could not be deprived of legislative discretion. "In our system, the people set policy by choice, not control, of their elected representatives."[144]

---

[141] 951 P.2d 911 (Colo., 1998) at 917.
[142] *AFL-CIO v. March Fong Eu,* 686 P.2d 609 at 622 (Cal., 1984) as cited at 951 P.2d 911 (Colo., 1998) at 915.
[143] *Supra* note 141 at 915.
[144] *Supra* note 141.

Another major objection raised by the court was that in its view, the American system of government does not require an elected representative to proceed in any particular or foreordained manner on any issue. It said that voters cannot dictate a course of action to elected officials, thereby controlling the hand and voice of those officials.

The court also held that if the amendment remained, it would impose a majoritarian view and effectively silence minority viewpoints.

Lastly, the court delved into the electoral outcomes aspect of the matter, arising out of the requirement in the amendment to label candidates on the ballots.

> Contrary to such passive and informational designations, Amendment 12's ballot designations are negative and instructional, apprising voters of particular candidates who have disregarded or declined to follow the people's will and are therefore unworthy of holding public office. The usual and expected consequence of these state sanctioned labels, which incite voters at precisely the moment when they are most susceptible to persuasion, is more votes cast in favor of other, more cooperative, candidates... Without any effective means to combat these ballot designations, lawmakers are essentially forced to choose between wholesale adherence to Amendment 12's instructions and political death.[145]

---

§ 8.7.3[146]
Report of the Parliamentary Commissioner for Standards; July 1997
-and-
Hamilton v. Al-Fayed
House of Lords; March 23, 2000
[2001] 1 A.C. 395
and
Court of Appeal (Civil Division); December 21, 2000
[2000] E.W.J. No. 6960

In respect of political law, the significant conclusion of this series of proceedings, involving a veritable rogue's gallery of individuals who used their roles and duties in public life to sabotage the public interest, is that the work of parliamentarians is to be based on constitutional

---

[145] *Supra* note 141 at 916.
[146] International comparison.

and legal duties and ethical behaviour alone. This is as true in respect of the legislative process as it is in dealing with other aspects of parliamentary work. Legislators' tasks are not for sale.

In a television program aired in January 1997, Al-Fayed, a business-man, alleged that Hamilton, then a Member of the British Parliament, had accepted cash for asking questions on his behalf in the House of Commons in 1985, in relation to Al-Fayed's takeover of a company which controlled Harrod's, a famous London department store. Ham-ilton was also alleged to have received various other gratuities in return for performing favours in the course of his parliamentary work.

At the general election held on May 1, 1997, Hamilton lost his seat to a former BBC correspondent who ran against him on an anti-corrup-tion ticket.

The most important ruling in this matter was that of the Parliamen-tary Commissioner for Standards who, in July 1997, found that Ham-ilton had indeed accepted cash from Al-Fayed for lobbying services. This report was approved by a resolution of the House of Commons in November 1997.

Nevertheless, Hamilton denied any wrongdoing and went so far as to initiate proceedings for defamation against Al-Fayed. This gave rise to a thoroughly complex round of litigation, involving various interrelated issues touching on the public trust and on the appropriate venue for dealing with abuse of the functions of parliamentarians.

In a procedural phase of the litigation, Al-Fayed sought to have Ham-ilton's action struck on the ground that it was abuse of process, or alternatively to have it stayed because parliamentary privilege pre-cluded the challenging of evidence given to a parliamentary inquiry. This application was dismissed by the trial judge and by the Court of Appeal.[147] The House of Lords also denied Al-Fayed's application, on grounds that parliamentary privilege vested the jurisdiction of the courts to hear evidence as to what was testified to a parliamentary body, such as the Commissioner for Standards.

---

[147] [1999] 3 All E.R. 317.

It is my judgment firmly established that courts are precluded from entertaining in any proceeding (whatever the issue may be at stake in those proceedings) evidence, questioning or submissions designed to show that a witness in a parliamentary proceeding deliberately misled Parliament. To mislead Parliament is itself a breach of the code of parliamentary behaviour and liable to be disciplined by Parliament: see *Church of Scientology v. Johnson-Smith* [1972] 1 QB 522 and *Pickin v. British Railways Board* [1974] AC 765, 800, per Lord Simon of Glaisdale. For the courts to entertain a question whether Parliament had been deliberately misled would be for the courts to trespass within the area in which Parliament has exclusive jurisdiction.[148]

The action could thus proceed on the merits.

In 1999, the trial was held in High Court and despite the murky circumstances and evidence by Al-Fayed, which the court characterized as confused, inconsistent and varying in detail, a jury essentially came to the conclusion that Hamilton had behaved in a corrupt fashion.

The jury were required to address two basic issues of fact:

(i) did Mr. Al-Fayed pay Mr. Hamilton for asking parliamentary questions?

(ii) did Mr. Hamilton seek payment from Mobil for moving a parliamentary amendment?

These issues were crystallised in the single question put by Morland, J. to the jury:

"Are you satisfied on the balance of probabilities that Mr. Al-Fayed has established on highly convincing evidence that Mr. Hamilton was corrupt in his capacity as a member of Parliament?"

The jury answered "Yes" and found accordingly for Mr. Al-Fayed.[149]

On December 21, 2000, the court of Appeal rendered its decision, denying an appeal by Hamilton.

---

148 [2001] 1 A.C. 395 at 403.
149 [2000] E.W.J. No. 6960 at p. 10.

Mr. Hamilton sued Mr. Al-Fayed for libellously alleging in a 1997 television broadcast that Mr. Hamilton had solicited and accepted from him cash payments in return for tabling Parliamentary questions in Mr. Al-Fayed's interests. Similar allegations had been published by the guardian newspaper in 1994, but the libel action brought in respect of these by Mr. Hamilton and the lobbyist Mr. Ian Greer was abandoned on the eve of the trial. Mr. Al-Fayed's defence was that his allegations, relating to the period from early 1987 to the end of 1989, were true. Because the allegations amounted to an assertion that Mr. Hamilton was guilty of corrupt practice as a Member of Parliament, Mr. Al-Fayed was given permission shortly before the hearing to add to his defence an assertion, based upon documents lately produced by the Cabinet Office, that Mr. Hamilton had in 1989 solicited from Mobil Oil a fee for having moved on its behalf or in its interests an amendment to a Finance Bill. This, it was said, served both as corroboration by similar facts of the first defence and as independent justification of the sting of the libel.[150]

Hamilton's blatant disregard for parliamentary legality in prostituting his parliamentary function and then actioning for defamation when his actions became public knowledge were bruisingly rewarded. In addition to losing his seat in Parliament as well as the litigation, Hamilton's political prospects disappeared and he was seriously indebted to other Conservative parliamentarians who had contributed to his legal fund.

8.8 ISSUE: VALIDITY OF THE LEGISLATIVE PROCESS

§ 8.8.1
Gallant v. R.
Prince Edward Island Court of Appeal; December 20, 1948
(1948), [1949] 2 D.L.R. 425

During the 1940's, Prince Edward Island was still subject to prohibition, as it had been since 1900. In that context, the subject matter of this case was two appeals from convictions for possession of intoxicating liquor. Until 1945, provincial legislation prohibited the possession of liquor not obtained from a licensed vendor. In that year,

---

[150] *Ibid.* at p. 2.

the *Prohibition Act*[151] was amended by the adoption of the *Cullen Amendment*, which permitted the sale of liquor for medicinal purposes. On July 6, 1948, the entire legislation was repealed.

In order to adjudicate on the appeals, the court conducted an extensive examination of the applicable federal and provincial legislation relating to the prohibition, trade, sale and consumption of liquor. It came to the conclusion that in order to determine the innocence or guilt of the accused, it would have to examine whether the *Cullen Amendment* had been validly adopted. The court expressed its procedure in rather elegant, theatrical terms. It felt that in some matters, in order to reveal the fundamental issue behind the scene of a particular case, it was "constrained to penetrate the cellophane curtain"[152] of the legislative process.

When the provincial legislature had enacted the *Cullen Amendment*, it had presented it to the Lieutenant Governor for royal assent, but this was withheld. Later during the same year the succeeding Lieutenant Governor purported to give royal assent to the *Amendment*, on the advice of Cabinet. Looking at this sequence of events, the court set out the steps necessary for a bill to become law and listed the various outcomes of the Lieutenant Governor's actions upon presentation of a Bill to him for royal assent. In the Canadian constitutional framework, a Bill may be granted royal assent or that assent may be withheld. There are also proceedings for disallowance or reservation which are still written in the *Constitution* today, but which have fallen into disuse. There was, however, no provision for the granting of royal assent once it had been withheld.

> The total result is that a Lieutenant-Governor may assent to a Bill in the Sovereign's name, or he may withhold the Sovereign's assent, or he may reserve the Bill for the Signification of the Governor-General's pleasure. A Bill which has received the Royal Assent may later be disallowed; or a Bill which has been "reserved" may later receive assent; but there is no provision for reconsideration of a "withheld" assent. Even in the case of a "reserved" Bill, it is the Governor-General who may grant subsequent assent.[153]

---

151 R.S.C.P.E.I. 1937, c. 27.
152 (1948), [1949] 2 D.L.R. 425 at 429.
153 *Ibid.* at 430.

The further and just as fundamental point made by the court is that the Lieutenant Governor, as the representative of the Sovereign within the Province, is part of the Legislature and, by implication, an indispensable part of the legislative process. Consequently, where the Lieutenant Governor's assent to a Bill is withheld, as happened in the case of the *Cullen Amendment*, the Lieutenant Governor is *functus*. The court even ventured that after withholding of royal assent, the only solution may be to represent the same Bill, that is to re-enact it and then present it for royal assent anew.

Given the circumstances, the *Cullen Amendment* was held by the court never to have become law and the convictions stood.

See also *Turner v. R.*, 93 D.L.R. (4th) 628 (Fed. C.A.), leave to appeal refused (1993), 148 N.R. 238n (S.C.C.).

---

§ 8.8.2
Bedford (Town) v. Nova Scotia (Law Amendments Committee)
Nova Scotia Court of Appeal; April 22, 1993
(1993), 123 N.S.R. (2d) 355

Notwithstanding the expertise of policy advisors, legislative drafters and legislators themselves, instances do occur where a legislative body enacts a statute comprising a defect. When such a faulty statute may entail political consequences in addition to the injustice resulting from the legal problem, the urgency of correcting the mistake, as well as its controversiality, are even greater.

Nova Scotia conducted an electoral boundaries readjustment process in the early 1990's. The Boundary Revision Commission recommended to the Law Amendments Committee of the House of Assembly that the entire Town of Bedford form part of the new riding of Bedford-Falls River. Based on subsequent hearings, it was decided that the part of the town situated west of Highway 102 became part of the riding of Sackville-Beaverbank. In preparing the necessary legislation,[154] the Law Amendments Committee deleted the portion of Bedford that lay to the west of the highway from Bedford-Falls River, but omitted to add it to Sackville-Beaverbank. When the Com-

---

[154] *An Act to Amend the House of Assembly Act*, S.N.S. 1992, c. 1.

mittee became aware of its own mistake, it acted under the *Statute Revision Act*[155] to correct the inadequately drafted *House of Assembly Act.*[156]

On behalf of the residents of the affected area, the Town sued in Supreme Court, asking for a declaration to the effect that the Law Amendment Committee had acted *ultra vires* by using the *Statute Revision Act* to repair its own mistaken drafting. That action was dismissed, the Town appealed and the appeal was set down for hearing for October 6, 1993. Fearing that a provincial general election would be instituted in the intervening period, the Town brought the present interlocutory motion to a single Court of Appeal judge in chambers. It sought to have stayed the fixing of a date for the writ for the election in the two affected ridings as well as the issue of the writ for those two ridings by the Chief Electoral Officer, pending resolution of the appeal on the merits.

After the motion was made but before it could be heard, on May 16, 1993, writs were issued for the general election for May 25. On May 23, the judge in chambers dismissed the motion.

The judgment had two effects. Principally from the perspective of the validity of the legislative process, the redistribution scheme provided by the *House of Assembly Act*, as corrected in respect of Bedford by the *Statute Revision Act*, was left in place. Subsidiarily, on the electoral substance of the matter, the Town of Bedford remained split between two ridings. For voting purposes, the residents of the area to the west of the highway were isolated, despite the allegation of community of interest.

The reasoning of the court in refusing the remedy sought was essentially that it was faced with a number of impossibilities. It could not stay the fixing of the date, nor the issue of the writs, as those had already occurred. It could not judge that the Law Amendment Committee had acted *ultra vires* because the House of Assembly had been dissolved and the Committee therefore no longer existed. As a corollary, if the Committee were judged to have acted *ultra vires*, the residents of the affected areas would end up being disenfranchised.

---

[155] R.S.N.S. 1989, c. 443.
[156] R.S.N.S. 1989, c. 210.

In the court's view, the corrective procedure used by the Committee also raised the *Charter* issue of the community of interest among the residents of the westerly part of Bedford with the inhabitants of the other parts of the Town.

> The issue before the trial court, and the issue on appeal, is the narrow one of whether the Law Amendments Committee was justified in adding Bedford West to Sackville-Beaverbank by way of a statutory revision. If that appeal succeeds constitutional arguments may well be made later in the course of arriving at a solution. However, I accept the argument of counsel for the respondent and the Attorney General that the constitutional matter is not properly before me on this application. Therefore a *Charter* remedy is not available.[157]

Finally, the court held that the benefits envisaged by the Town for the remedy it sought would have a real effect only if the appeal on the merits were to be allowed and the election would have to be invalidated as a result. It would not envisage this, as it felt that the election may not necessarily be overturned even if the appeal were successful.

> While uncertainty with respect to an election is undesirable, it is not unknown, and there are statutory remedies when an election is overturned. Given that the election will not necessarily be overturned even in the event of a successful appeal, I must find against the applicants on the balance of convenience.[158]

See also *Cencourse Project Inc. v. Ontario* (1995), [1995] O.J. No. 3445 (Ont. Gen. Div.).

---

§ 8.8.3[159]
Hogan v. Newfoundland (Attorney General)
Newfoundland Supreme Court; January 8, 1998
(1998), 156 D.L.R. (4th) 139

This case is rather singular in Canadian jurisprudence on matters dealing with the legislative process because it calls into question the nature of the function exercised by the Governor General in giving

---

[157] (1993), 123 N.S.R. (2d) 355, 340 A.P.R. 355 at 358.14.
[158] *Ibid.* at 359.19.
[159] Cross-reference to § 4.11.C.2 and 5.8.4.

royal assent to legislation and in issuing the proclamation required to breathe life into a constitutional amendment. This litigation and the judicial pronouncement which resolved it are political in two related respects. First, recognizing that the constitution itself is inherently both a legal instrument and a political document, the same must be held true of constitutional amendments. In addition, the legal argumentation presented here is but the last phase of an intense and highly controversial political debate which emanated Newfoundland in the late 1990's. The twin nature of the issue is recognized by the court itself.

> The second point is that, in considering the arguments made, the court is concerned only with interpreting and applying the law. Issues and concerns that are of a political nature, individual beliefs in the need, or otherwise, for reform of the education system, and sympathy for what some suggest is an exercise of majority rule at the expense of a previously protected minority, cannot and should not influence the outcome. If the law affords the plaintiffs protection, and if the relief requested can and should otherwise be granted, the relief will be given; conversely, the plaintiffs will fail if the relief requested cannot or should not be granted.[160]

This case also represents a point of interest in that not only did the court perceive the political context of the legal debate, but it also came close to stating outright that the plaintiffs' action was tantamount to a rearguard procedure in which they attempted to force through the courts and by the use, or misuse, of law a delay in a political process which they had perceptibly lost.

> The legality of the proposed amendment will be decided on the basis of the law and not on the basis of positions previously advanced by the plaintiffs. But in the context of exercising a discretion to grant pre-trial equitable injunctive relief, I would not be disposed to grant such relief in the face of such conduct by the plaintiffs. In the circumstances with identical legal characteristics, to obtain one injunction based on certain fundamental assertions and then in short order, and during the currency of that injunction, seek a further injunction based on directly contrary assertions, is very close to an abuse of the court's process.[161]

---

[160] (1998), 156 D.L.R. (4th) 139 at 144, para. 10.
[161] *Ibid.* at 173, para. 12b.

In 1949, when, through the *Terms of Union of Newfoundland with Canada*,[162] the tenth province joined Confederation, Term 17 of those *Terms of Union* assured for it a system of education in which the Catholic and Pentecostal communities would each retain their denominational school systems. By the latter part of the century, given the cost of education, the financial and fiscal status of Newfoundland and the relatively limited population base of the province, this denomination division among schools was becoming difficult to justify and maintain. In October 31, 1995, the House of Assembly passed a resolution to amend Term 17 to reduce the role of the churches in public education. The Catholic and Pentecostal churches together challenged the validity of that amendment and on July 8, 1997, the Newfoundland Supreme Court issued an interlocutory injunction pending trial, to restrain the implementation of the legislation. The province thereupon organized a referendum to sanction a more thorough reform of the school system to render it secular. On September 5, 1997, the House of Assembly unanimously voted a complete overhaul of Term 17.

The procedure to be followed in order to achieve the reform was the bilateral constitutional amendment process, involving one province and the federal authorities, pursuant to section 43 of the *Constitution Act, 1982*. Thus, on December 9, 1997, the House of Commons voted the amendment sought by Newfoundland and on December 18, 1997, the Senate did likewise. The sole remaining step was for the Governor General to make the necessary proclamation to bring the amendment into force.

At this point, the plaintiffs, allegedly representing the interests of the Catholic community, applied to the Newfoundland Supreme Court for an injunction to stop the Governor General from affixing his signature and issuing the proclamation. This procedure in terms of constitutional amendments was the equivalent of royal assent in the ordinary legislative process. The court refused the application, holding that it did not have jurisdiction to enjoin the Governor General, in his capacity as representative of the Sovereign, from completing the legislative process and issuing the proclamation which was to amend Term 17.

---

[162] *Newfoundland Act*, R.S.C. 1985, App. II. No. 32.

The court's ratio in this matter is most instructive. It reiterated that the legislative process consisted of the enactment of legislation by the two Houses and its sanction by the Sovereign, all points being required. Once the Commons and the Senate had done their work, current constitutional convention requires that assent be given.

> Thus it is a constitutional requirement that every enactment, whether federal or provincial, receive royal assent as part of the legislative process. No bill becomes law until assented to by the Sovereign. It is the act of the Sovereign—through the Governor General or a Lieutenant-Governor—that breathes life into the law; it does not change the constitutional position that, by convention, the Sovereign acts only on the advice of the legislative bodies. Neither does it affect the constitutional position that an Act may, by its terms, not come into force until a date to be proclaimed by the Governor or Lieutenant-Governor in Council. Royal assent is required in every case.[163]

Moving from the general legislative process to the more specific category of amendments to constitutional instruments in particular, the court looked at section 48 of the *Constitution Act, 1982*, which provides that upon adoption of the resolutions required for an amendment to be made by proclamation, the Privy Council shall advise the Governor General to issue that proclamation. It recognized that the authorizing resolutions constituted the precondition to the issuance of the proclamation and determined that it is the proclamation which effects the constitutional amendment in the same way as the royal assent completes the legislative process.

> Royal assent is and remains an absolute requirement of all legislation passed in Canada, whether that legislation is federal, provincial, or an amendment to the Constitution of Canada.

> Thus, in issuing the proclamation under s. 48 to amend Term 17, the Governor General is acting as the Crown. Indeed it would be more difficult to contemplate a circumstance in which the Governor General was more clearly acting as the Sovereign in Canada.

> . . .

> I have concluded that, in issuing the s. 48 proclamation, the Governor General is acting in his legislative capacity. He is as much a part of this

---

[163] *Supra* note 160 at 151, para. 40.

particular legislative process, and as necessary to it, as are the House of Assembly for the Province of Newfoundland, the House of Commons, and the Senate of Canada. The law is quite clear that the courts cannot intervene in the legislative process; they enjoy a supervisory jurisdiction once a law has been enacted, but until that time, a court cannot interfere in the process of enacting legislation. To conclude otherwise would be to obliterate the boundaries that properly separate the functions and roles of the legislatures and the courts.[164]

The holding set out in the foregoing paragraph, to the effect that the courts ought not to intervene in the legislative process and hence will not stop the issuance of the proclamation by the Governor General is the determinative element of the ruling.

In extensive *obiter*, the court rejected every one of the plaintiffs' other arguments. It refuted the argument that Term 17 is not part of the *Constitution of Canada* or that it is not an instrument of a legal nature. It also denied the validity of the argument that Term 17 was ineffective or unconstitutional because it did not comply with a constitutional convention. It saw no merit in the argument that changing Term 17 would modify the *Charter*. Finally, it rejected the notion of a link between Term 17 and section 93 of the *Constitution Act, 1867*, which deals with legislative authority for educational matters.

In dealing with the plaintiffs' assertions aimed at proving that they were submitting a serious issue to the court, the judgment expressed surprise at the concession made by the Attorney General of Canada to that effect. This brief but noticeable admonition was a sign that the federal authorities ought perhaps to take a tougher stand in defending the constitutional system.

The ultimate indication arising from this case which merits the attention of scholars of political law is the court's borrowing of terminology from Peter Hogg in describing the Constitution:

> ...it is the supreme overarching law of Canada and serves to "recognize and protect the values of a nation."[165]

---

[164] *Ibid.* at 154, para. 58, to 155, para. 60.
[165] *Ibid.* at 151, para. 44.

Here the value of the validity of the legislative process in the constitutional domain was greater than that asserted but not proven by the proponents of confessional schools.

---

§ 8.8.4

Tunda v. Canada (Ministre de la Citoyenneté & de l'Immigration)
Federal Court of Canada – Trial Division; June 11, 1999
[1999] F.C.J. No. 902[166]

Royal assent is as much a requirement of the legislative process as the adoption of the subject Bill by the House of Commons and its enactment by the Senate. It is also true that the royal assent given to convert an adopted Bill into a Statute must be validly granted and that part of that validity implies that the official giving the assent must have the authority to do so. In that context, this case stands for the proposition that Justices of the Supreme Court of Canada who stand in for the Governor General in the latter's absence and perform tasks of administering the government of Canada, in particular the giving of royal assent, do so validly.

This ruling arose out of the attempt by Kassongo Tunda, an illegal entrant into Canada from Zaire, to quash an expulsion order. He argued, among other points, that the *Immigration Act* amendments enacted in 1995 were *ultra vires* because they had been assented to by Mr. Justice Sopinka, then a Puisne Judge of the Supreme Court of Canada, in his capacity as Administrator of the Government of Canada. The court rejected all of the arguments sustaining this allegation. It held that the *Letters Patent* of 1947[167] did in fact authorize the Governor General to name a Supreme Court judge as a deputy for himself; that the fact of a Supreme Court judge acting for the Governor General did not breach the requirement of the *Judges Act*[168] that judges perform only judicial tasks; and, that the action of a judge standing in for the Governor General in no way affected the independence of the judiciary. For all these motives, the court held that the *Immigration Act* amendments had been validly adopted.

---

[166] Additional reasons at (1999), 177 F.T.R. 274 (Fed. T.D.), affirmed (2001), 214 F.T.R. 159 (note) (Fed. C.A.).
[167] *Constitution Act, 1982*, Appendix II, No. 31.
[168] R.S.C. 1985, c. J-1.

The pleadings of the plaintiff's counsel included the same grounds as those recited above in an attempt to show that the *Constitution Act, 1985,* which was in fact the *Representation Act, 1985,* a change to the composition of the House of Commons, had been invalidly assented to because it was done by then Chief Justice Brian Dixon. This argument was also refuted. The consequence of agreeing to counsel's argument would have been that the House of Commons would thereafter have been improperly constituted and all laws passed by it would have been unconstitutional. The court roundly rejected this scenario, concluding,

> Accordingly, in keeping with the rules underlying the Canadian Constitution, restated by the Supreme Court of Canada, I conclude that to avoid the creation of a legal vacuum it is impossible to declare the entire body of Canadian legislation invalid. Thus, the plaintiff's argument that all Canadian legislation is unconstitutional because it was adopted by a Parliament which was itself unconstitutionally constituted is purely academic since in fact the said legislation will continue to be applied.[169]

The case went to the Federal Court of Appeal on other grounds.

See also *P.S.A.C. v. R.* (2000), 192 F.T.R. 23 (Fed. T.D.).

8.9 ISSUE: MAINTAINING INVALID LEGISLATION FOR PUBLIC POLICY PURPOSES[170]

See *Reference re Language Rights Under s. 23 of Manitoba Act, 1870 & s. 133 of Constitution Act, 1867,* [1985] 1 S.C.R. 721 (S.C.C.).[171]

---

[169] (1999), [1999] F.C.J. No. 902, 1999 CarswellNat 3160 (Fed. T.D.), p. 32, additional reasons at (1999), 177 F.T.R. 274 (Fed. T.D.), affirmed (2001), 214 F.T.R. 159 (note) (Fed. C.A.).

[170] Cross-reference to § 11.14.

[171] Cross-reference to § 1.12 and 2.4.

§ 8.9.1
Sinclair c. Québec (Procureur général)
Supreme Court of Canada; February 27, 1992
[1992] 1 S.C.R. 579[172]

This case arose out of the means used by the Government of Québec to achieve the amalgamation of the cities of Rouyn and Noranda. The National Assembly enacted a special statute to enable the process to take place. Pursuant to that Act, the new city was to be brought into existence through letters patent which the Minister of Municipal Affairs was to issue and was to have published. Various other instruments would also have to be issued during this process.

Sinclair attempted by this legal action to have the legislation authorizing the amalgamation cancelled, as well as to obtain declaratory judgment that the letters patent and the other published instruments were invalid because, as instruments of a legislative nature, they ought to have been published in both official languages, as prescribed by section 133 of the *Constitution Act, 1867*. *An Act respecting the cities of Rouyn and Noranda*[173] was given assent and came into force on June 20, 1985. This action was first launched on February 27, 1986. The first judgment in the case was rendered by the Québec Superior Court on July 4, 1986. It dismissed the action and on that basis rendered it possible for the province to move forward with its plan. On the very next day, July 5, 1986, the letters patent were published in the *Gazette officielle du Québec* and they came into force on that date. Thus, as of July 5, 1986, the new city of Rouyn-Noranda came into existence.

Notwithstanding the initial judicial setback, Sinclair appealed. The Québec Court of Appeal reversed the Superior Court on January 5, 1990, and gave reason to Sinclair's contention that the instruments used to achieve the amalgamation were constitutionally invalid. The Attorney General of Québec thence appealed to the Supreme Court of Canada. It was not until February 27, 1992, that the highest court rendered its ultimate judgment in this case, agreeing with the Québec Court of Appeal on the major issue of the case, namely that the letters patent and the other instruments ought to have been published in

---

[172] Cross-reference to § 1.3.A.7 and 7.3.1.
[173] S.Q. 1985, c. 48.

both official languages. The consequence in law of this judgment was that from the date of its establishment on July 5, 1986, as a united city, until the date of the judgment on February 27, 1992, that is for a period of over five and a half years, Rouyn-Noranda was founded on an invalid constitutional basis, grounded on instruments that were "nullities and of no legal force and effect."[174]

This finding of the lack of legal qualification of the municipality did not change the fact that the public administrative and political life of Rouyn-Noranda had been established, had actually been functioning and had evolved. While law could be the only basis of the founding and operation of a governmental entity such as a municipal government, the court recognized that its clarification of the true state of the legal characteristic of this municipality later than the city's establishment should not be the basis for a retroactive invalidation or even disintegration of the public administration and political aspects of the city and of its community.

> One cannot ignore, however, that *de facto*, a new city of Rouyn-Noranda has been in existence since 1986, operating on the faith of purported letters patent establishing its constitution. This purported municipal constitution, and consequently all acts performed pursuant to it are, and have been, illegal and of no force and effect.

> It would be wrong to throw the affairs of the citizens of Rouyn and Noranda into a state of chaos on account of the procedure chosen by the National Assembly of Quebec to effect their purported amalgamation into the new city of Rouyn-Noranda.[175]

With the court's observation of the fundamental discrepancy between the legal status of Rouyn-Noranda on the one hand and its functioning public administrative and political life on the other, what realistic options were available to it to reconcile the divergent elements of the situation? As a court of law, it could not declare inapplicable its own judgment and thereby merely give sanction to the existing illegality in order to abide by the *de facto* state of affairs. Neither would it be practicable for the court to create a void in the public life of the municipality by retroactively declaring null and void everything that had happened in municipal administration and politics, for the sake of conformity to the law.

---

[174] [1992] 1 S.C.R. 579 at 593 e.

[175] *Ibid.* at 593 e-h.

The remedy which the Supreme Court of Canada chose was both legal and politically astute. It exercised its suspensive power. That is, it did declare that the instruments which had been the subject of the litigation were invalid as being contrary to section 133, the linguistic equality clause of the *Constitution Act, 1867*. It also held, however, that those same instruments should continue in force for a period of one year from the date of this judgment. During that interval, the National Assembly would have to undertake the steps required to remedy the constitutional defects. Only thus could the existence and the functioning of Rouyn-Noranda on a viable legal basis be confirmed.

In order to comply with this ruling, the Minister of Municipal Affairs of Québec did re-issue the letters patent of Rouyn-Noranda in the two languages.[176] Taking full account of the judgment, the National Assembly went beyond this single case and enacted a statute by which it corrected the same constitutional deficiency in respect of a number of other municipalities.[177]

See also *Schachter v. Canada*, [1992] 2 S.C.R. 679 (S.C.C.).[178]

8.10 ISSUE: LEGAL SUPPORT FOR THE WORK OF LEGISLATORS[179]

---

§ 8.10.1
Speaker's Ruling on the Role of Legislative Counsel
Speaker of the House of Commons; October 23, 1997
Hansard, October 23, 1997, p. 1003

Members of Parliament (MPs) fulfil several functions in the political system. Their principal role is to be legislators, that is the makers of

---

[176] *Gazette Officielle du Québec*, Partie II, No. 7, p. 1063 (F) and 817 (E), February 17, 1993.

[177] *Loi concernant des jugements rendus par la Cour suprême du Canada sur la langue des lois et d'autres actes denature législative*, L.R.Q., c. J-1.1, as amended by L.Q. 1992, c. 37

[178] Cross-reference to § 3.4.3.

[179] Cross-reference to § 11.4.

laws, a task involving the design of legislative schemes and the crafting of legislative texts. Individual MPs exercise this legislative function both in the process of enacting government legislation, public bills, and in the course of initiating their own contributions to the legal system, private members' public bills. For all MPs and in particular for those who are not legally trained, specialized legal advice, counsel and assistance with legislative drafting is of paramount importance for the effective accomplishment of this role. It is in this context that the work of the legislative counsellors to the House of Commons has been the subject of parliamentary consideration on several occasions.

On October 2, 1997, Jay Hill, Reform Party Official Opposition MP for Prince George-Peace River, British Columbia, raised a question of privilege in the House in this regard. He had submitted a private member's public bill for drafting to the legislative counsel's office after the general election of June 2, 1997, and before the House was first convened on September 22, 1997. This Bill was not eligible for the first draw of MPs' Business for the 1st Session of the 36th Parliament because over some two and a half months, it was not drafted. Hill pointed out that there were only two legislative drafters for the 301 MPs and that approximately 150 of the 170 bills requested to be drafted were stuck in a backlog. He thus based his question of privilege on the assertion that

> The inadequate resources devoted to private members' bills especially at peak periods adversely affects the ability of all members of this House to perform their parliamentary duties... I would request that the House immediately allocate additional resources so this backlog of Private Members' Business can be cleared up as quickly as possible.[180]

On October 7, 1997, a Liberal government back bencher, Roger Galloway from Sarnia-Lambton, Ontario, presented another question of privilege in the same vein. He argued that with the number of MPs increased through redistribution and the legislative staff decreased by attrition, the office and position of legislative counsel had effectively ceased to exist. He added that the substitution of legislative clerks having minimal training for House of Commons lawyers acting as legislative counsel, as had been done at Westminster, was inadequate. This situation resulted in the absence of independent legal

---

[180] Hansard, October 2, 1997, p. 414

advice to MPs, in their inability to get amendments to legislative proposals drafted, and in the necessity for MPs to fulfil their roles as legislators without legal counsel. Galloway characterized these factors taken together as constituting an impediment in his, and in other MPs' performance of parliamentary work.

The question of privilege led this MP to attempt to table a motion that the matter of the lack of legislative counsel to assist members be referred to the Commons Standing Committee on Procedure and House Affairs. In support of this motion, his main argument was that this was a non-partisan issue which should be addressed in the proper forum within Parliament.

> What I am asking of you is to uphold my rights as a member of this House and not my interests as a member of a particular political party which we know is reflected in the composition of the Board of Internal Economy. When the Board of Internal Economy meets, its members present the positions of their parties and members but do not speak or represent each and every member of the House. Only you, Mr. Speaker, as guardian of privileges can act in such a manner.[181]

The point raised by Galloway was affirmed by a member of each of the parties represented in the Commons. The most cogent of these arguments was put forward by an MP for the Bloc Québécois, who said:

> The fact I would like to add is that having only two permanent law clerks for 301 members is the result of a number of years of systematic erosion of the resources available to us to perform our duties as members.[182]

Further attempts to raise the issue were made by a Reform Party member on October 21 and 22, 1997.[183]

The Speaker handed down his ruling on October 23, 1997. Rather than deal with the merits of the case, he judged that this was not a question of privilege but rather an administrative issue concerning the services of the House. In so deciding, the current Speaker was following the precedent set on December 12, 1982, by one of his

---

[181] *Ibid.*, p. 617.
[182] Paul Crête, Bloc Québécois MP for Kamouraska-Rivière-du-Loup-Temiscanata-Les Basques, Québec. Hansard, October 7, 1997, p. 618.
[183] Gary Breitkreuz, Reform Party MP for Yorkton-Melville, Saskatchewan.

predecessors, Speaker Sauvé, in response to the raising of the same question by one of the members of the 32nd Parliament.

The ruling was also based on section 52.3 of the *Parliament of Canada Act*, pursuant to which the Board of Internal Economy is the body "entrusted with specific administrative oversight functions such as the delivery of legislative counsel services to members."[184] The Speaker went on to indicate that the Board already had a subcommittee struck to deal with the proper functions of legislative counsel and the proper level of resourcing needed for these functions, and that that body would conduct a review of these issues.

The questions of privilege which are from time to time raised by MPs in defence of the office of legislative counsel serve to highlight the intrinsically legal nature of the position of a Member of Parliament, as well as the absolutely indispensable nature of legal support, indeed of adequate legal support for the legislative work of MPs, which is the focal point of their range of tasks. It is patent both to MPs and to informed observers that parliamentarians as legislators must be supported by an adequate legal and legislative infrastructure.

By contrast, the Speaker's ruling denotes the inherent tension and conflict between the cost-cutting exercises seen to be required for good management on one hand and the managerial tools and support required to assure the supremacy of law on the other hand. In this sense, there is room to doubt the wisdom of this line of Speakers' rulings. Entrusting the availability of legislative counsel to the Board of Internal Economy could become counterproductive, as that is the very body which, over the years, has mandated the reduction of legislative staff to its current level and which has devised the plan to transfer responsibilities from legislative counsel to legislative clerks. Of all the activities and expenditures in support of legislators, from the perspective of political law, this one more than others should have been adjudged on the basis of constitutional, Parliamentary and legal standards, needs and benefits, rather than on the basis of its value in the eyes of managers.

Yet another aspect of this issue, its political context, was raised in a newspaper article relating to this matter, published the very day following the ruling. There, Galloway was said to be "using the whole

---

[184] Hansard, October 23, 1997, p. 1003.

business of legal counsel as a surrogate for the larger issue of more power for MPs."[185] After limited media attention,[186] the matter ceased being in issue.

See also *Retention of outside counsel by the House of Commons*, Hill Times, September 22, 1997; *Speaker's Ruling on the Privacy Commissioner's Comments regarding the Information Commissioner Canada*, Hansard, May 28, 2001, pp. 4276-4277.

8.11 ISSUE: EMPLOYEES OF PARLIAMENT

See *Canada (Canadian Human Rights Commission) v. Lane*, [1990] 2 F.C. 327 (Fed. C.A.).

---

[185] "Restless Grits show shades of Reform," Hugh Winsor, *Globe and Mail*, Toronto, Friday, October 24, 1997.
[186] "Students drafting bills a slight, MP says," Scott Feschuk, *Toronto Globe and Mail*, November 19, 1997.

9

LEGALITY IN GOVERNMENTAL MANAGEMENT

9.1 GENERAL PRINCIPLES

See Volume I, Chapter 9.

9.2 ISSUE: LEGAL PERSONALITY, STATUS AND POWERS OF GOVERNMENT DEPARTMENTS[1]

§ 9.2.1[2]

Westlake v. Ontario
Supreme Court of Canada; March 2, 1973
(1973), 33 D.L.R. (3d) 256
-and-
Duggan v. Newfoundland
Newfoundland Supreme Court – Trial Division; April 22, 1992
(1992), 99 Nfld. & P.E.I.R. 56

The legal personality and status of entities created by governmental power for the performance of public functions and duties can most directly be determined by reference to a statutory declaration of the entity's corporate existence. In Canadian practice, it is by way of creation by statute that the principal departments of government are created. Other criteria must also be examined, however, to determine a governmental body's legal personality in terms of characteristics and extent. Among these are the reviewability of the body's proceed-

---

[1] Cross-reference to § 1.13.
[2] Cross-reference to § 9.7.1.

ings by way of extraordinary remedies of prohibition, *certiorari* and *mandamus*, the body's ability to sue and be sued, its capacity to enter into contracts and its ability to acquire and hold property.

The general rule in this regard was laid down in the *Westlake* case,[3] which arose out of the bankruptcy of the Prudential Finance Corporation in 1966. Westlake and other holders of securities in Prudential alleged that the Ontario Securities Commission failed to perform its duties in respect of Prudential's prospectus and related documentation. The province brought an application to strike out the statement of claim on the ground that the Commission was not an entity which could be sued for damages. This motion was granted and the decision was upheld on appeals all the way to the Supreme Court of Canada.

The element of the case that is worthy of retention is the following classification of governmental bodies devised by the High Court of Justice:

1) There are bodies corporate which are not expressly declared to be suable. As a result of section 26 of the *Interpretation Act*, bodies corporate created by statute may sue and be sued unless the incorporating statute otherwise provides.

2) There are bodies corporate which are expressly declared to be suable.

3) There are bodies corporate which are expressly declared not to be suable.

4) There are non-corporate bodies which are, by the terms of the statute creating them, expressly liable to suit.

5) There are non-corporate bodies which are not by the terms of the statute incorporating them expressly liable to suit but which are by necessary implication liable to be sued in an action for damages.

6) There are non-corporate bodies which are not by the terms of the statute incorporating them or by necessary implication liable to

---

[3] *Westlake v. R.*, [1971] 3 O.R. 533, affirmed [1972] 2 O.R. 605 (Ont. C.A.), affirmed (1973), 33 D.L.R. (3d) 256 (S.C.C.).

be sued in an action for damages, but which are legal entities in that their actions may be reviewed in proceedings brought against them by way of the extraordinary remedies of *certiorari*, *mandamus* and prohibition.

It was in this last category that the court placed the Ontario Securities Commission.

The *Duggan* case indicates that some two decades after *Westlake*, the criteria set out in that judgment are still applicable and reliable. Duggan ran a boarding house which she wanted to sell. Newfoundland's Welfare Institutions Licensing and Inspection Authority (the Authority) had, through its Chairman, made affirmative representations to her and she had relied on them. The Authority later refused to allow Duggan to transfer the license to operate the home together with the sale of the building. She sued the Authority and its individual members. The Crown made an interlocutory application to determine, among other things, whether the Authority was a legal entity capable of being sued. If the court determined that it was not, the Crown wanted Duggan's case quashed on the ground that there was no reasonable cause of action. The Newfoundland Supreme Court's analysis consisted of a review of the applicable jurisprudence. On the basis of the criteria set out in *Westlake*, it held that the Authority could not be sued but as it added that actions may be against the members of the Authority, it refused to quash the case.

---

§ 9.2.2
Turner v. Canada
Federal Court of Canada – Trial Division; April 26, 1990
(1990), 21 A.C.W.S. (3d) 799

This case shows that even though the departments of government have legal personality and status for some purposes, neither they, in their own right, nor their ministers in their capacities as ministers in charge of departments can be sued. Turner brought an action in respect of amendments to the *Yukon Quartz Mining Act*, which, he alleged, put him alone in a disadvantaged position. He sued the Departments of Justice, Indian Affairs and Northern Development, and Energy, Mines and Resources. The list of defendants also included the Queen, the Prime Minister and Ministers Hnatyshyn,

McKnight and Masse respectively. Among his allegations was that the Departments had engaged in a hidden duplicitous campaign. The federal Crown motioned to strike out the statement of claim. At the hearing, the plaintiff was brought to agree that the departments named as defendants could not be sued. The implication, both in terms of substance and procedure, is that if government authorities are the intended targets of an action, a plaintiff must sue the entity legally capable of being sued, Canada.

See also *Forget c. Québec (Commission des valuers movilières)*, [1993] R.J.Q. 2145 to 2170 (Que. S.C.).

---

§ 9.2.3
Ontario (Chicken Producers' Marketing Board) v.
Canadian Chicken Marketing Agency
Federal Court of Canada – Trial Division; October 14, 1992
(1992), [1993] 1 F.C. 116

This case reinforces the principle that a body established by government may exercise only those powers which are assigned to it by the legal instruments governing its existence and functioning. The Ontario Board was established pursuant to provincial legislation. The Canadian agency was established by proclamation pursuant to federal legislation. In 1974, they both participated in a federal-provincial agreement to create a comprehensive chicken marketing program in Canada. In 1984, by an amendment to the intergovernmental agreement, a system of yearly production allocations was set up. Jurisdictions which exceeded their allocation would be required to pay liquidated damages. In 1991, Ontario exceeded the allocation and paid the assessment; it then applied for judicial review of the assessment decision. Canada applied to have the Ontario application quashed.

In order to decide the case, the court was called upon to determine whether the federal-provincial agreement was an exercise of powers granted to the Canadian Agency by the legislation which had established it. It determined that the legislation did not authorize the Canadian agency to do what it had purported to do by entering the agreement and instituting a system of liquidated damages.

The Canadian Agency, which by its very nature is a creature of statute and proclamation, may only exercise those powers specifically accorded to it by the Act or Proclamation.[4]

The federal-provincial agreement was an expansion of the powers that Parliament had mandated to the agency. This decision should be seen not only in its obvious administrative law context, regarding the powers legitimately possessed by public authorities. The litigation also called for the court to determine the nature of intergovernmental agreements. Such agreements may be set out in legal instruments, but they are essentially based on political deals among governments. The court held that,

> An agreement negotiated between federal and provincial governments pursuant to the provisions of a statute is not an ordinary, private contract, but rather an agreement between governments.[5]

From the perspective of this study, therefore, the appropriate conclusion is that branches and agencies of government may exercise only those powers authorized by law and may not rely on politically based instruments to expand their powers.

---

§ 9.2.4
Canadian Egg Marketing Agency v. Richardson
Supreme Court of Canada; November 5, 1998
(1998), 166 D.L.R. (4th) 1

The principal matter at issue in this litigation was the constitutional validity of the legislative framework by which Canadian authorities established an orderly market for the distribution of eggs throughout the country. The scheme administered by the Canadian Egg Marketing Agency (CEMA) did not comprise the Northwest Territories, from which Richardson's company marketed eggs interprovincially. In 1992, CEMA sued Richardson. The core of the defence was that the federal legislation pursuant to which CEMA was operating was unconstitutional, as being contrary to section 2(d) [freedom of association], section 6(2)(b) [right to gain a livelihood in any province] and section 15 [equality] of the *Charter*.

---

[4] (1992), [1993] 1 F.C. 116 at 129 b.
[5] *Ibid.* at 129 g.

Both the trial court and the Northwest Territories Court of Appeal had held that Richardson had public interest standing. This aspect of the case was also argued before the Supreme Court of Canada. That court held that Richardson did not need to seek public interest standing because he had standing as of right.

> They do not come before the court voluntarily. They have been put in jeopardy by a state organ bringing them before the court by an application for an injunction calling in aid a regulatory regime.[6]

Moreover, the public importance of the question involved and the national importance of the subject scheme were among the arguments used by the court to bolster its holding on the issue of standing.

> The constitutionality of the federal egg marketing scheme is clearly an issue of national importance, as are the more specific issues raised with regard to whether ss. 2(d) and 6 of the *Charter* apply to corporations. These issues were addressed in the courts below and could have been dealt with by this Court based on this residuary discretion.[7]

In this reasoning, the key expression of interest in the political law frame of reference is "state organ." The Supreme Court did not, and perhaps need not, explain this phrase specifically. The characteristics such an entity has are that it is: a) a body corporate; b) established by executing a policy or program of, or in some other way related to the State; c) other than an ordinary department, but d) involved in a question of public importance. It is also patent from the context that a "state organ," as that expression is used here, has the capacity to sue and therefore to be sued.

In the immediate instance, this is a state organ of the commercial type. There may be other types, such as cultural ones or yet others dedicated to research or development. The court did not establish the limits of the categorization. It may now be legally valid to use the label of "state organ" with respect to some or all institutions linked to public governance that are not departments in the traditional sense and do not belong to other well defined categories of public institutions like the courts or parliamentary agencies.

---

[6] (1998), 166 D.L.R. (4th) 1 at 22.
[7] *Ibid.* at 20.

Without explaining whether it was using the phrase as a synonym for "state organ," the Supreme Court also used the term "state agency" in this case.

See also *Canada (Attorney General) v. Canada (Information Commissioner)*, [2001] F.C.J. No. 282 (Fed. C.A.), leave to appeal refused (2001), [2001] S.C.C.A. No. 233 (S.C.C.) and *United Parcel Service of America, Inc. v. Government of Canada*, filed April 19, 2001, http://www.dfait-maeci.gc.ca/tna-nac/parcel-en.asp.

9.3 ISSUE: IMPLEMENTATION OF GOVERNMENT POLICY WITHIN LAW[8]

9.3.A—LEGALLY VALID MANAGEMENT

§ 9.3.A.1[9]
Sethi v. Canada (Minister of Employment & Immigration)
Federal Court of Appeal; June 20, 1988
(1988), 52 D.L.R. (4th) 681[10]

This is a case involving an apprehension of bias on the part of members of the Immigration Appeal Board, based on the fact that at the time of the litigation, Parliament was in the process of enacting a Bill[11] to reform that Board into the new Immigration and Refugee Board. The court looked at whether Board members could be influenced in their decision-making in a case where the Minister of Employment and Immigration had adopted a position, by the fact that the same Minister was shepherding the reform legislation through Parliament. Would they wish to please the Minister through their rulings in order to be invited to membership on the new Board?

The Federal Court of Appeal replied to this query emphatically in the negative.

---

[8] Cross-reference to § 11.3.
[9] Cross-reference to § 8.6.4.
[10] Leave to appeal refused (1988), 92 N.R. 325 (note) (S.C.C.).
[11] Bill C-55, 2nd Session, 33rd Parliament, 1986-87, *An Act to Amend the Immigration Act, 1976, and to amend other Acts in consequence thereof.*

> While the Minister is the party adverse in interest to them in proceedings before the board, the Minister is also the person ultimately responsible for the administration of the Act in a manner that accords with the law. If the Minister opposes an application or appeal, it is because there is a genuine disagreement to be resolved by the board, not because the Minister, or the government, has an interest personal to the individual concerned.[12]

Observers of political law should note that in the court's view, the principal duty of the Minister in relation to the [Immigration] Act is that it be accomplished in a manner that accords with the law. Thus, to the extent that the Act is the expression of governmental policy, taken here in the sense of a legislated expression of governmental intent, that policy is to be carried out in a lawful and legal manner. This is a general matter of principle and it includes the consideration that if the Minister opposes an application or an appeal, such as Sethi's, the motivating factor is taken to be the Minister's opinion that a genuine disagreement is to be resolved and not a personal interest relating to the applicant. Law is both principled and impersonal.

---

§ 9.3.A.2
Arthur (Village) v. Ontario
Ontario Court (General Division); October 4, 1991
(1991), 1991 CarswellOnt 2343

On May 7, 1991, the Ontario Ministry of Consumer and Commercial Relations announced that as a measure of consolidation, it would close land registry offices in the Village of Arthur and in the Town of Durham. Subsection 4(2) of the *Registry Act* authorized the Lieutenant Governor in Council to combine registry divisions within certain limitations, which were not exceeded in this instance. In documents issued separately, the minister did not refer to the Act but indicated that the closure decision was based on the government's principles, in particular to help segments of the population affected by the recession of the early 1990's. In line with these principles, it would be more appropriate to divert the funds previously used in operating the registry offices to other initiatives under the Anti-Recession Fund in the affected areas, such as the provision of affordable housing.

---

[12] (1988), 52 D.L.R. (4th) 681 at 688, leave to appeal refused (1988), 92 N.R. 325 (note) (S.C.C.).

The legal question submitted to the court's determination was whether the Cabinet's discretion under section 4(2) of the *Registry Act* is to be interpreted as being fettered by the requirement of a causal relationship between the proposed closing and the Act or the regulations made thereunder. Phrased more broadly, the issue of governance is whether a government acting within the legal framework established for a procedure such as centralization is free to allocate or reallocate financial resources to program activities undertaken in line with the policy goals it had adopted and proclaimed. The importance of this case is that in upholding the government's margin of manoeuvre in governing within the legal framework, the court adopted reasons from two precedents. First, it confirmed that in making regulations under the *Registry Act*, the government must, as opposed to merely being able to, take financial and budgetary matters into account.[13] It went even further in upholding the link between governmental expenditures and policy goals by affirming that:

> The government has the right to order its priorities and direct its fiscal resources towards those initiatives or programs which are most compatible with the policy conclusions guiding that particular government's action. This was simply a statement of funding policy and priorities and not the exercise of a statutory power of decision attracting judicial review.[14]

Finally, the court acknowledged the primacy of the executive branch in determining the linkage of expenditures to the policy initiatives of the government.

> ...I am forced to the conclusion that it is not for any court to oversee a Minister of the Crown in policy decisions or in the exercise of his or her discretion in the expenditure of public funds entrusted to his or her department by the legislature.[15]

See also *Pulp, Paper & Woodworkers of Canada, Local 8 v. Canada (Minister of Agriculture)* (1994), 174 N.R. 37 (Fed. C.A.).

---

[13] *Durham (Town) v. Ontario (Attorney General)* (1978), 23 O.R. (2d) 279 (Ont. H.C.) at 287.

[14] *Hamilton-Wentworth (Regional Municipality) v. Ontario (Minister of Transportation)* (1991), 2 O.R. (3d) 716 (Ont. Div. Ct.) at 731 g, leave to appeal refused (1991), 4 Admin. L.R. (2d) 226 (Ont. C.A.)

[15] *Ibid.* at 733 g.

---

§ 9.3.A.3
Position of the Premier of Québec on Bilingual Signage
Press conference by The Rt. Hon. Lucien Bouchard
October 1, 1998

In the Province of Québec, constitutionally guaranteed rights, legislation and public policy regarding the linguistic relations between the Francophone and Anglophone communities include the matter of the language of business and commerce. Within this category, the most visible and most controversial aspect has, for decades, been the language of signs. At the material time, the state of the law was that bilingual signs on the outside of a business establishment were allowed, as long as the French version of the sign was more prominent. The widely developed practice, however, was that most stores posted signs in French only. This practice had gained the grudging acceptance of those among the Francophone community who had hoped to end the right to post signs in languages other than French, and it had been resigned to by those among Anglophones who had wanted to use the rights they had according to law.

After the election in 1998 of William Johnson as President of Alliance Québec, an Anglophone rights group, there was some picketing by Anglophones of department stores in Montréal for the purpose of convincing them to post signs in English also. This move drew a very negative reaction from the Premier of Québec.

> "I don't understand why they would break such an equilibrium, so they have to know that it is completely unacceptable, and it is a kind of conversation of that kind that I would like to have with them," Bouchard said.[16]

On October 1, 1998, the Premier, the Deputy Premier and the Minister responsible for the French language convened the representatives of the Québec Retail Council to a meeting at which they planned to discuss the department store managers' reactions to the pressure brought to bear by Alliance Québec for greater use of English signage. The press conference given by Premier Bouchard after that meeting was a clear demonstration of the irony of linguistic legislation in

---

[16] "Signs alarm Quebec: Premier urges retailers not to post English ones," Elizabeth Thompson and Kate Swager, *The Gazette*, Montréal, October 1, 1998.

Québec and showed how in some circumstances the difficulty of governing with, and within the bounds of law is great, in particular when there is a gap between the legislation adopted by one government and the policy espoused by its successor.

Premier Bouchard's statement at the press conference was, effectively, an explicit recognition that the law provided a right to English language signage. Immediately thereafter, however, Bouchard went on to admonish the owners of the stores in question not to use the rights they had because that would destroy what he termed the linguistic equilibrium which had developed in Québec.

> Cette rencontre qui avait été convoquée par le gouvernement a débuté par une intervention que j'ai faite pour rappeler la séquence des événements depuis quelques jours et expliquer pourquoi je les avais convoqués. Et je leur ai dit que le gouvernement éprouvait des appréhensions à la suite des discussions que ont eu lieu lundi dernier - Mme Beaudoin - les appréhensions que portent sur les menaces qui pèsent sur l'équilibre linguistique que s'est établi au Québec depuis quelques années. J'ai rappelé que cet équilibre s'est installé à l'intérieur d'un cadre juridique qu'il ne remplit pas complètement, mais qui s'est défini à partir d'une sorte de consensus implicite que oui ces pouvoirs additionnels avaient été concédés par le gouvernement libéral du temps, oui, ces pouvoirs n'ont pas été retirés par le gouvernement que je dirige, mais *sur la foi de ce consensus implicite* que avait été méme considéré et exprimé même de façon expresse par Monsieur Ryan au moment où la loi a été adopté. Et je me suis employé à leur décrire rapidement le parcours de notre société pour arriver à cet équilibre - les nombreux débais, ... les dialogues, les concessions qui ont été faits de part et d'autre pour *arriver à cette espèce de patrimoine*, je dirais, d'un minimum de *sérénité linguistique qui* était en train de se cristalliser et de s'affermir chez nous dans l'intérêt de la stabilité de notre société. "Et je leur ai dit que les propos qui ont été soulevés lundi dernier en réaction aux manoeuvres d'intimidation de Monsieur Johnson et de certains autres, nous inquiétaient pour l'équilibre linguistique ci, en conséquence, *je leur demandais instamment de ne rien faire qui puisse perturber cet équilibre.*"[17]

From the perspective of a lawyer, particularly one specializing in constitutionally protected rights, it would seem astounding to hear the Head of a Government in a democracy address a segment of his jurisdiction's population to tell them they have a right, but that they

---

[17] Press conference of Lucien Bouchard after meeting representatives of the Québec Retail Council, October 1, 1998, unofficial transcript.

should not exercise it. The point of view of a political figure, however, especially one such as Premier Bouchard, who was then days away from launching an election campaign, is completely at odds with the view based on law. The Premier's interest was in attempting to govern, to maintain what he perceived as an established consensus and to restrain the highly inflammatory issue of linguistic rights from becoming an election issue.

The observer is justified in inquiring whether government policy is being implemented without legal norms in circumstances where a legal right exists but the potential users are dissuaded from using them. In this instance, the matter went even further when, in the course of the questions and answers after the Premier's comments at the press conference, discussion turned to possible amendment of the existing language legislation to restrict the right to English language signage and to the possible use by the Government of Québec of the "notwithstanding clause" of the *Canadian Charter of Rights and Freedoms* to extract the language law from constitutional interpretation by the courts.

The Alliance Québec demonstrations led to threats of counter-boycotts of the stores by labour unions if English signage were posted. By October 4, 1998, the demonstrations ended but the polemic continued for a few more days among those in the Anglophone community who would have preferred to continue. In a press conference of his own held on October 8, 1998, William Johnson suggested that Alliance Québec test the constitutional validity of the commercial sign regulations through litigation. In a further irony, the government's response was to indicate that it would defend in court the very law which provided the rights it did not want the Anglophone community to use.

See also *R. v. Saplys*, 60 C.R.R. (2d) 287 (Ont. Gen. Div.) and *Report of the Westray Mine Public Inquiry*, Justice K. Peter Richard, Commissioner, November, 1997.

§ 9.3.A.4
Canadian Council of Christian Charities v. Canada (Minister of Finance)
Federal Court of Canada – Trial Division; May 19, 1999
(1999), 168 F.T.R. 49[18]

Prima facie, this is an access to information case. The Council applied to force the Minister of Finance to disclose government documents which relate to the government's interpretation of the notion of "religious orders" within the meaning of section 18(1)(c) of the *Income Tax Act*, all this in dealing with the entitlement to the "clergy residence" deduction. The court accepted the Minister's reasoning that most of the documents were exempt from disclosure and ordered that the others be disclosed.

However, what the court stated about the nature of governance in much broader terms is not only more pertinent to this study, but also of far wider importance. At first, the court seemed to be chastising the heads of government institutions for equating the public interest with reasons for not disclosing information and interpreting the *Access to Information Act*[19] in a manner so as to protect the information in their possession from disclosure. This tendency was clearly misdirected, for "A central purpose of the *Access to Information Act* is, after all, to enhance the democratic foundations of government, and accountability."[20] From this criticism, it is clear that the court is encouraging deputy ministers to manage within the letter and the spirit of the law.

The question is how the spirit of the law is to be applied so that, in respecting the law, the government can fulfil the functions assigned to it. This conundrum can only be resolved by a legally sensitive and practical balancing of interests. The court indicates the way, showing its intimate knowledge of the policy development system.

> Despite the importance of governmental openness as a safeguard against the abuse of power, and as a necessary condition for democratic accountability, it is equally clear that governments must be allowed a measure

---

[18] Additional reasons at (1999), 99 D.T.C. 5408 (Fed. T.D.).
[19] R.S.C. 1985, c. A-1.
[20] (1999), 168 F.T.R. 49 at 59, para. 36, additional reasons at (1999), 99 D.T.C. 5408 (Fed. T.D.).

of confidentiality in the policy-making process. To permit or to require the disclosure of advice given by officials, either to other officials or to Ministers, and the disclosure of confidential deliberations within the public service on policy options, would erode government's ability to formulate and to justify its policies.

It would be an intolerable burden to force Ministers and their advisors to disclose to public scrutiny the internal evolution of the policies ultimately adopted. Disclosure of such material would often reveal that the policy-making process included false starts, blind alleys, wrong turns, changes of mind, the solicitation and rejection of advice, and the re-evaluation of priorities and the re-weighing of the relative importance of the relevant factors as a problem is studied more closely. In the hands of journalists or political opponents this is combustible material liable to fuel a fire that could quickly destroy governmental credibility and effectiveness.

On the other hand, of course, democratic principles require that the public, and this often means the representatives of sectional interests, are enabled to participate as widely as possible in influencing policy development. Without a degree of openness on the part of government about its thinking on public policy issues, and without access to relevant information in the possession of government, the effectiveness of public participation will inevitably be curbed.[21]

It is most significant that the court set out not only the process, that is the balancing of interests internal to the procedure of governance within legal bounds, but states a goal and a standard which these procedures are directed to, namely effectiveness.

The Act thus leaves to the heads of government institutions, subject to review and recommendations by the Information Commissioner, the discretion to decide which of the broad range of documents that fall within these paragraphs can be disclosed without damage to the effectiveness of government. There is very little role for the Court in overseeing the exercise of this discretion.[22]

See also *Marshall v. Canada*, [1999] 3 S.C.R. 456 (S.C.C.), reconsideration refused [1999] 3 S.C.R. 533 (S.C.C.); *Reference re Firearms Act (Canada)*, [2000] 1 S.C.R. 783 (S.C.C.); *Blencoe v. British Columbia (Human Rights Commission)*, [2000] 2 S.C.R. 307 (S.C.C.); *Little Sisters Book*

---

[21] *Ibid.*, paras. 30, 31 and 32.
[22] *Ibid.*, para. 40.

& *Art Emporium v. Canada (Minister of Justice)* (2000), [2000] 2 S.C.R. 1120 (S.C.C.); *Haydon v. R.* (2000), [2001] 2 F.C. 82 (Fed. T.D.); *Proper Handling of Harassment in the Canadian Forces*, Report of the Military Ombudsman, August 14, 2001; *Final Report of the Walkerton Inquiry*, Hon. Dennis O'Connor, issued January 18, 2002 and *Porter v. Magill*[23] (2001), [2002] 2 A.C. 357 (U.K. H.L.).

9.3.B—MALADMINISTRATION/MALFEASANCE/ MISFEASANCE; ABUSE OF POWER; BREACH OF TRUST BY PUBLIC OFFICIALS

See *R. v. Campbell*, [1967] 2 O.R. 1 (Ont. C.A.), affirmed (1967), 2 C.R.N.S. 403 (S.C.C.); *Canada v. Evans* (1983), 1 D.L.R. (4th) 328 (Fed. C.A.); *R. v. Dubas*, [1992] B.C.J. No. 2935 (B.C. S.C.), affirmed (1995), 60 B.C.A.C. 202 (B.C. C.A.); *Gerrard v. Manitoba* (1992), 98 D.L.R. (4th) 167 (Man. C.A.); *First National Properties Ltd. v. Highlands (District)*, 198 D.L.R. (4th) 443 (B.C. C.A.), leave to appeal refused (2001), [2001] S.C.C.A. No. 365 (S.C.C.); *Goose Bay Outfitters Ltd. v. Newfoundland (Minister of Tourism, Culture & Recreation)* (2002), 214 Nfld. & P.E.I.R. 326 (Nfld. T.D.); *Investigations of the Management of the Office of the Privacy Commissioner, Annual Report of the Privacy Commissioner to Parliament for 2002-2003; Matters Relating to the Office of the Privacy Commissioner; Fifth Report of the Standing Committee on Government Operations and Estimates, June 2003; Statement of Resignation of the Privacy Commissioner, June 23, 2003; Public Service Commission Audit of the Office of the Privacy Commissioner, September 2003; Auditor General's Report on the Office of the Privacy Commissioner of Canada, September, 2003; Matters Related to the Review of the Office of the Privacy Commissioner, Ninth Report of the Standing Committee on Government Operations and Estimates, November 2003; Lamarche v. Canada (Attorney General)*, Federal Court of Canada – Trial Division, case no. T-299-04; *Odhavji Estate v. Woodhouse*, 233 D.L.R. (4th) 193 (S.C.C.) and *Weir v. Secretary of State for Transport*,[24] High Court of Justice, Chancery Division.

---

[23] International comparison.
[24] International comparison.

9.4 ISSUE: LEGALITY IN THE MANAGEMENT OF THE MACHINERY OF GOVERNMENT[25]

§ 9.4.1

Canada (Auditor General) v.
Canada (Minster of Energy, Mines & Resources)
Supreme Court of Canada; August 10, 1989
(1989), 61 D.L.R. (4th) 604

As the Chief Justice of Canada noted in the opening statement of this judgment, this case concerns the proper role of the courts and their constitutional relationship to the other branches of government. Stated in a different way, the matter at stake is the type of remedy, political or legal, exercisable by the Auditor General of Canada, in fulfilling his obligations pursuant to the statute which created his office, and more specifically section 7(1)(b) thereof, which concerns his ability to access information. The Chief Justice also took pains to emphasize that this was not a *Charter* case. It involved, essentially, the contrast of legal and political means within the machinery of government.

The factual background relates to the purchase of Petrofina Canada Inc. by Petro-Canada in early 1981. This was one of the transactions designed to bolster Petro-Canada's position as a key player in the Canadian energy market. The involvement of the Minister of Energy, Mines and Resources arises from the fact that he was the member of Cabinet responsible for Petro-Canada. In order to audit the purchase, the Auditor General requested information from Petro-Canada and from the Government of Canada. He also wrote to the Prime Minister. The information requested was denied on the grounds that it contained confidences of the Privy Council. Thereupon, he brought suit to force disclosure by declaratory judgment. The Supreme Court of Canada dismissed the Auditor General's case.

The first aspect of the issue considered by the court was its justiciability.

---

[25] Cross-reference to § 9.6.

There is an issue which arises prior to those identified in the courts below, namely, whether the Auditor General's remedies for the claimed s. 13(1) entitlement are limited to those explicitly contained in the *Auditor General Act*. That is to say, does the Auditor General have recourse to the courts, as an alternative remedy, in the event of the denial by Parliament, responsible Ministers, and the Governor in Council to make available to him all of the documentation he may seek in what he regards as the discharge of his responsibilities in auditing the accounts of Canada?[26]

In fact, a large part of the Supreme Court's analysis was cast in terms of justiciability reasoning. Given the lengthy and detailed examination of the issues and of the applicable jurisprudence, the decision was an implicit agreement that the matter was in need of legal clarification. However in denying the remedy sought, the court indicated that the political remedy made possible by the legislation was the appropriate and sufficient one.

In this case, it is reasonable to interpret s. 7(1)(*b*) as the Auditor General's only remedy for claimed denials of s. 13(1) entitlements not only because the text is conducive to such an interpretation but also because, in the circumstances, a political remedy of this nature is an adequate alternative remedy. The Auditor General is acting on Parliament's behalf carrying out a quintessentially Parliamentary function, namely, oversight of executive spending pursuant to Parliamentary appropriations. Where the exercise of this auditing function involves the Auditor General in a dispute with the Crown, this is in essence a dispute between the legislative and executive branches of the federal government. Section 7(1)(*b*) would seem to be the means by which Parliament itself retains control over the position it wishes to take in such a dispute.[27]

Given the court's acknowledgement that in the *Operation Dismantle* case it had adjudicated that political disputes or matters of foreign policy could be cognizable by the courts, it felt the need to explain the distinction it was drawing here. It restricted the hearing of this case to the interpretation of a single statute and held that its analysis should not detract "from the fundamental principle the courts should not readily decline to grant remedies for rights recognized by the laws of Canada."[28]

---

[26] (1989), 61 D.L.R. (4th) 604 at 629.

[27] *Ibid.* at 643-4.

[28] *Ibid.* at 649.

Having limited the hearing of this decision, what is its true meaning? According to the Chief Justice, the rights of access here was limited to the provisions set out for that purpose in the *Auditor General Act*.[29] Once those remedies have been exhausted, the Auditor General's only recourse is to inform Parliament of difficulties in obtaining the information and explanations required. In enacting this political re- porting provision, Parliament intended to retain control over any position it may wish to take in a dispute with the government. In such a dispute, it would not be appropriate for the courts to intervene. In sum, there is a role for judicial remedies and one for political remedies; they are to be distinguished by reference to the statute, which of course is itself legal in nature.

---

§ 9.4.2
Rural Dignity of Canada v. Canada Post Corp.
Federal Court of Canada – Trial Division; January 22, 1991
(1991), 78 D.L.R. (4th) 211[30]

This case amounted to an effort by litigants to establish that there was a conflict between the legal duties and the policy choices adopted by a governmental corporation, but the court disagreed. The outcome reinforced the principle that a decision in the sphere of the adminis- tration of the machinery of government can be successfully chal- lenged only if there are legal grounds to do so, rather than mere dissatisfaction with a program executed in pursuit of a policy.

The Canada Post Corporation was established in 1981, replacing the previous government department that had carried out the same func- tion. In 1987, it started carrying out a program for the closure of rural post offices, in conformity with policies of cost-cutting and modern- ization of its business practices. During the years 1989 and 1990, the Corporation made decisions in respect of four rural post offices in Saskatchewan, New Brunswick and Nova Scotia which were to result in the substitution of retail outlets for post offices. Rural Dignity and several individuals applied for *certiorari* against the decisions to close the post offices and for *mandamus* to require the Minister responsible for the Corporation to direct the Corporation to reopen the post of-

---

[29] R.S.C. 1985, c. A-17.
[30] Affirmed (1992), 54 F.T.R. 80 (note) (Fed. C.A.), leave to appeal refused (1992), 141 N.R. 399 (note) (S.C.C.).

fices. The Federal Court – Trial Division rejected every ground raised by the applicants.

The focus of the court's decision was the application for judicial review. In this context, the court held, first, that the Canada Post Corporation was part of the government decision-making machinery and was within the ambit of section 2 of the *Federal Court Act*. The court accepted the allegation that the decisions regarding the specific post offices were examples of the exercise by the Corporation of its general management powers under the legislation which created it. The most important conclusion reached by the court was that such management decisions were, pursuant to the ruling of the Supreme Court of Canada in the *Operation Dismantle* case, subject to the *Charter*.

> That passage leads me to conclude that the closure decisions, whether taken under s. 16 of the Act or under the Corporation's s. 19 regulatory authority, would be reviewable for compliance with the *Charter*. The Chief Justice does not appear to concern himself with the particular statutory authority for the decision but with the decision itself which should not be taken in a discriminatory way so as to contravene the requirements of s. 15 of the *Charter*.[31]

Having determined that the closure decision needed to be analyzed for its conformity to the *Charter*, the court found that no breach of the principles of the *Charter* had occurred, as there was no unequal treatment under section 15(1). The closure policy was applied equally to all; the Corporation was not treating rural post offices worse than urban ones.

The applicants had also argued that the Corporation was acting in breach of its duties under section 5 of its Act, to provide specified services. In support of that contention, they advanced a speech by the Minister who had been responsible for piloting the legislation through Parliament in 1980, André Ouellet.

> And this sentence, Mr. Speaker, is essential to make hon. members of the House and particularly the Canadian public understand that the creation of a Crown corporation does not mean a reduction of services usually assured to the public. We wanted to write down this guarantee in the act so that Canadians, particularly in remote areas of the country

---

[31] (1991), 78 D.L.R. (4th) 211 at 225 d-e, affirmed (1992), 54 F.T.R. 80 (note) (Fed. C.A.), leave to appeal refused (1992), 141 N.R. 399 (note) (S.C.C.).

and rural sectors which are often affected by decisions made by large Canadian corporations, would not be penalized by the creation of a Canada Post corporation which would operate in the Canadian capital and that would become insensitive to the aspirations of those Canadians, particularly in the rural and remote areas of the country. So I say that clause 5 guarantees that the same level of essential services will be maintained and this is one of the objectives of the legislation for which the new corporation will be responsible.[32]

Counsel for the applicants contended that the relevant statutory provision ought to be interpreted in light of this statement. The court found that while the speech undoubtedly represented the Minister's view of how that section was to be interpreted in the political context, the section was not capable of that judicial interpretation.

The Corporation was under no duty to provide local post offices even if that conflicted with the Minister's statement.

---

§ 9.4.3
S.G.E.U. v. McKenzie
Saskatchewan Court of Queen's Bench; October 4, 1991
(1991), 96 Sask. R. 22

This was an attempt, through the use of law, to counteract a politically motivated governmental measure relating to the machinery of government. What made it even more interesting and what raised the stakes for all parties was that the action was taken in the midst of an election campaign. The applicant discovered that it not only had to base its attack in legal terms, but that it also had to make out its case based on legally, as opposed to politically valid criteria in order to win in the legal forum. This it could not do. The litigation nevertheless did result in political effects in the form of publicity and profile for the argumentation. It can also be taken to have contributed to the political decision, taken by the incoming government after the election, to end the controversial program.

On March 4, 1991, Premier Grant Devine, who had led the Progressive Conservative government of Saskatchewan since May 1982, announced a program of decentralization of a number of public service

---

[32] *Ibid.* at 229 c-e.

positions from Regina to smaller locations. The government justified the program as a measure for economic recovery and budgetary restraint.

In order to stop this "Fair Share Saskatchewan" program, the Saskatchewan Government Employees' Union (S.G.E.U.) applied to the Court of Queen's Bench for an order prohibiting the execution of the program. It cited as grounds for its application that the program breached section 7 of the *Charter*, which protected the life, liberty and security of the person; it also alleged that the program usurped the authority and jurisdiction of the Public Service Commission in regard to transfers and conditions of employment.

The S.G.E.U.'s principal argument, however, was that the program breached a duty of fairness in that there were no consultations or hearings on the transfers. It went on to state that it had a legitimate expectation for such consultations. The first facet of this plea was the public policy dimension: the union agreed that the decision to implement Fair Share Saskatchewan was a purely ministerial one. Clearly, though, the matter had and was alleged to have a political dimension as well.

> "Fair Share Saskatchewan" is a political undertaking to relocate public servants for the purpose of directly enhancing the political standing of the Premier and the political party he represents in rural Saskatchewan, contrary to s. 50(1)(a) of *The Public Service Act* which reads as follows:
>
> > 50. (1) No person in the public service shall:
> >
> > > (a) be in any manner compelled to take part in any political undertaking, or to make any contribution to any political party, or be in any manner threatened or discriminated against for refusing to take part in any political undertaking.[33]

The Government of Saskatchewan vehemently denied this allegation.

> The Government of Saskatchewan says that it has the responsibility and authority to determine where its various offices will be located and that the announcements described in the Statement of Claim were made on

---

[33] Statement of claim, dated June 25, 1991, para. 26.

> behalf of the Government of Saskatchewan acting within that authority.[34]

> The Defendants deny that the acts complained of in the Statement of Claim, or any of them, compel any of the Plaintiffs to take part in a political undertaking within the meaning of clause 50(1)(a) of *The Public Service Act* and the Defendants say that the purpose of the Fair Share Saskatchewan Program is to protect the Saskatchewan way of life by stabilizing the economies of cities and towns in every region of the province as part of the Government of Saskatchewan strategy for economic recovery, other elements of which include the farm safety net program and community bonds.[35]

The court seemed extremely reticent to enter into the political aspect of the pleadings. It in fact addressed that issue only in the most circumspect fashion.

> The applicants have conceded that an examination of the efficacy of the Fair Share Saskatchewan program is beyond the jurisdiction of this court.[36]

In the course of the proceedings, the applicant retreated from a number of its original grounds of pleading and the case it made for breach of legitimate expectations was quite weak. It was essentially for that reason that the union was unsuccessful. It would have needed to base its legitimate expectation on established practice which, in this matter, was not shown.

In the meantime, the fact that this matter had been brought into the judicial arena itself became more newsworthy than the Fair Share Saskatchewan program had been.

On October 17, 1991, the Saskatchewan Court of Appeal suspended the application of the program pending hearing and determination of an appeal on the merits. This never occurred, though, because in the provincial general election held on October 21, 1991, the New Democratic Party came to power under Premier Roy Romanow and on November 6, 1991, the new government halted the program de-

---

[34] Statement of defence, undated, para. 12.

[35] *Ibid.*, para. 20.

[36] (1991), 96 Sask. R. 22 at 27, para. 18.

finitively. On November 19, 1991, the government solicitor wrote to the S.G.E.U.'s lawyer to dispose of all pertinent litigation.

§ 9.4.4
Hébert et al. v. Canada (Attorney General) and Baird
Federal Court of Canada – Trial Division
filed December 6, 1991; file T-3035-91; settled

This case analysis is based primarily on a statement of claim, rather than on the consequential decision of the court to which that claim was addressed. In this instance, that is even more beneficial than if a judgment had been rendered and the matter complained of been treated from its legal perspective alone. This case is most instructive in that it shows clearly how, in operating the machinery of government, the legal and public administration considerations must be harmoniously meshed. The law applicable to these proceedings is the *Inquiries Act* and the Orders in Council made thereunder. The public administration considerations are the policies and practices adopted in the name of the Royal Commission in question and said to be based upon its constitutive instruments. The case also demonstrates that the spirit in which public administration procedures are carried out must conform to the general understanding and intent of the legislation on which that administration is based, as developed through precedents. If these criteria are not fulfilled, administrative chaos, and possibly litigation, can result.

By an Order in Council dated October 25, 1989[37] made pursuant to the *Inquiries Act*,[38] the Government of Canada established a seven-member Royal Commission on New Reproductive Technologies. Its mandate was to inquire into and report upon current and potential medical and scientific developments in this area and to consider their social, ethical, health, research, legal and economic implications and the public interest. The government's decision to establish a multi-membered royal commission recognized the sensitivity of the issue to be explored, as well as its complex and controversial nature for Canadian society. The Royal Commission's discussions were to be conducted in the broadest possible form.

---

[37] P.C. 1989-2150.
[38] R.S.C. 1985, c. I-13.

Two characteristics of the Royal Commission are to be noted in particular. Its composition was intended to be multidisciplinary in nature, comprising specialists from a number of fields. Its final report and recommendations were, also, to amount to an honest work of collegiality. Indeed, the concept of collegiality was essential to the proper functioning of a royal commission consisting of several members.

From the outset, however, the element of collegiality was absent from the internal workings of the Commission. Moreover, it would seem that the Commission did not pursue its organization, administration and financing in the light of precedents established under the *Inquiries Act*. In particular, several commissioners indicated that there were no democratic rules concerning the conduct of meetings, such as quorum, agenda, proposals, amendments, votes or minutes. In the view of these commissioners, Baird, the chair of the commission, had assumed exclusive authority to make each and every procedural and substantive decision and was exercising sole responsibility for the commission's work. This, they said, was a breach of the law on inquiries and the government's intent in framing the mandate and work of the Royal Commission and the preparation of its report. As a result, four of the commissioners alleged that they were prevented from participating in the decision-making process and claimed that this rendered them unable to fulfil their legal mandates or their responsibility to the public.

The four commissioners expressed their views to the government through the Clerk of the Privy Council. As a result, the government issued a second Order in Council on August 28, 1990.[39] This instrument increased the number of commissioners from seven to nine and effectively transferred to the chair responsibility for all administrative matters relating to the Royal Commission's work. However, it left in place the commissioners' public accountability for expenditures and legally obligated them to the preparation of the report. The institutional difficulties continued.

By the close of 1991, four of the now nine commissioners felt they had no other option to resolve their inability to make progress within the framework than to attempt to resolve the situation through judicial action. They thus brought the present action before the Federal Court

---

[39] P.C. 1990-1801.

– Trial Division on December 6, 1991. Their general complaint was expressed as follows:

> Unfortunately, from the very first meeting, the collegiality hoped for has not materialized. Instead any attempts at collegiality have been continually undermined and over time it became apparent to the plaintiffs that all substantive decisions about every aspect of the Commission's work were being made under the authority of one person, namely the Chairperson, Patricia Baird.[40]

It is very difficult to establish the reason for this internal conflict within the Royal Commission. Among other possible reasons, we may cite the close rapport of the government of the day and the pharamaceutical industry, which was keen on directing the work of the commission toward its own profitability and which greatly believed in secrecy and the proprietary nature of research. Another factor which can not be excluded was the fact that another of the dissenting commissioners was Maureen McTeer, the wife of Prime Minister Mulroney's predecessor as Leader of the Progressive Conservative Party, Joe Clark, who still had a following within the party and could be seen as a potential rival.

In addition to the general complaint, the plaintiffs made more specific pleas relating to the personalization of authority over the Royal Commission's work by its Chair and her bad faith in administering its work. The Chair had accused the plaintiffs of breach of confidentiality in their outside communication and indicated she was relying on a legal opinion to state that position but refused to produce the alleged opinion, so that the commissioners against whom the allegation was made could not respond to it. Baird unilaterally imposed new and arbitrary rules of conflict of interest, thereby preventing commissioners from exercising their professional activities. The Chair singlehandedly controlled the Royal Commission's expenditures and refused even to explain her decisions. She alone determined the research program and gave the other commissioners no role in designing it, participating in it or effectively commenting on it. Indeed, there were occasions when commissioners needed to resort to the *Access to Information Act* to see documents on the research work of their own commission. Baird alone also asked the government for an extension in the Royal Commission's term and obtained it. The Chair,

---

[40] Statement of claim, para. 13.

finally, made public representations and statements that were either not based on the consensus of commissioners or in contradiction to the opinions of commissioners.

Two further sources of the Statement of Claim deserve to be specified as being of particular interest for political law. The first was the plaintiffs' point that a breach of proper legal and public administration criteria occurred in that the Chair failed to involve these commissioners who were lawyers in addressing the constitutional and legal ramifications of the Royal Commission's work.

Second, in relation to the control of expenditures, the Statement of Claim contained the significant allegation of the confusion of the notion of "the public interest," which was drawn from the Royal Commission's original Order in Council and which had not been amended, with the concept of measured "public opinion."

> With respect to the plaintiffs' investigative responsibilities, they state they were denied the powers outlined specifically in sections 4 and 5 of Part 1 of the *Inquiries Act*; and confronted with decisions already taken, for instance, to carry out public opinion polls and to later make some of their results public, in spite of commitments from the Chair, that these were for internal use only, annexed hereto as Schedule 12. These decisions incurred incredible costs to the Commission for work whose importance and pertinence were never shown; and which, indeed, were premised on a mistaken reading of the mandate itself, which confused "public interest" and "public opinion."[41]

If for no other reason than relating to these two issues, it is indeed unfortunate that the court did not get the opportunity to adjudicate this case.

The overall conclusion reached by the four plaintiff commissioners was that the result of the Chair's actions was to change the entire character of the royal commission and its work. To remedy that, they asked the Federal Court to grant declaratory relief to recognize that:

- the second Order in Council was inconsistent with the *Inquiries Act* and therefore of no force and effect;

---

[41] *Ibid.*, para. 39.

- the plaintiffs were entitled to the various resources needed to enable them to prepare and submit their report; and

- the Chair had conducted the Royal Commission on New Reproductive Technologies in a manner contrary to the *Inquiries Act* and to the provisions of the original Order in Council.

The case never went to trial. Through documents filed on March 11, 1992, the suit was discontinued. While there is no public indication as to what transpired to bring about this result, we are justified in presuming that the Clerk of the Privy Council brokered a settlement of the Royal Commission's internal disputes. Even though this case did not produce a judgment, it is indicative of the profound need for both collegiality and adherence to law and precedent in conducting the operations of governmental institutions.

The Royal Commission handed down its final report on November 15, 1993. By that time, however, the four commissioners who had been plaintiffs in the action were no longer on the case. In an unprecedented move, a very short time after the action was begun, the Government of Canada fired them from their positions as commissioners.

Canadian legislation on reproductive technology was first enacted by Parliament in March 2004.[42]

See also *Flieger v. New Brunswick*, [1993] 2 S.C.R. 651 (S.C.C.).

---

§ 9.4.5

A.U.P.E. v. Alberta

Alberta Court of Queen's Bench; November 27, 1996

(1996), 46 Alta. L.R. (3d) 44

The Progressive Conservative administration in office in Alberta since 1982 and headed by Premier Ralph Klein had engaged in substantially reducing the expenditures of government. Part of this exercise was the reduction of the public sector workforce. In this context,

---

[42] *An Act respecting assisted human reproduction and related research,* Bill C-6, 3d Sess., 37th Parl. enacted as S.C. 2004, c. 2.

in January 1996, Alberta announced that it would downsize some services in the Department of Transportation from 203 offices to 85. In July of the same year, the Province decided to restructure a branch of the Department of Labour from 30 to 10 officials.

The applicable provisions of law were the *Public Service Act*, as well as the various collective agreements made thereunder. The scheme established by these instruments provided that in instances where positions are abolished, the employees displaced have preferential rights to be redeployed into other public service provisions. In the present instances, rather than applying the statutory and collective bargaining rules which set up this system of preferential treatment, the government filled the newly established positions first and only then eliminated the positions it had decided to declare redundant. This way of proceeding left the incumbents no option but termination of career and enabled the government to restructure the departments involved in a manner to suit its political program, while evading its legal obligations.

The Alberta Union of Public Employees (A.U.P.E.), brought suit to obtain an interim injunction to stay the restructuring decisions, as well as for judicial review, declare that Alberta had contravened the relevant provisions of the *Public Service Act*. The union also sought an order of *certiorari* to have the restructuring decisions quashed.

In a decision dealing at first only with the issue of the injunction, the court acknowledged that the manner in which the government had acted, namely by holding less than department-wide competitions in each case, was in violation of the *Public Service Act* and that none of the affected employees were able to access the preferential status rights granted them under that Act. Nevertheless, the application for injunction was denied. The court justified this by accepting the government's contention that section 17 of the *Proceedings Against the Crown Act*, which prohibited that granting of injunctions against the Crown, constituted an absolute bar to the relief sought.

First, neither counsel was able to show Alberta precedent to the effect that this provision did not apply in the case of an application for judicial review. Further, the court went on to give clear indication of its preference not to interfere with the government's scheme. Counsel for the union did find one instance in which an Alberta court had refused to follow the prescription of the *Proceedings Against the Crown*

Act. The court refused to follow that case, but without any meaningful explanation. The union's lawyer also pointed to a case from the neighbouring Province of Saskatchewan, in which some judges had been willing to circumvent an equivalent provision, presumably in order to reach an equitable result. The Alberta Queen's Bench refused that precedent on the ground that it was not an appellate ruling.

---

§ 9.4.6
Hopkinson v. Canada (Commissioner of Patents)
Federal Court of Canada – Trial Division; June 13, 1997
(1997), 74 C.P.R. (3d) 332[43]

This was an application for declaratory relief instituted by a number of officials who fulfilled the functions of patent examiners. One of the issues raised in the case brought into question whether the branch of Canada's federal administration entrusted with the issuing of patents existed at all, or was properly constituted. The court phrased the question as "Does the Patent Office as described herein meet the requirements of section 3 of the *Patents Act?*"[44]

During the time when this action was proceeding, several rounds of reform took place in Canada's departmental structure. In the 1980's, the Patent Office had become part of the Directorate of Intellectual Property within the Department of Consumer and Corporate Affairs. On December 21, 1992, that directorate was renamed the Canadian Intellectual Property Office (CIPO) to bring it into line with the newly constituted World Intellectual Property Organization. In June 1993, the Department of Consumer and Corporate Affairs was itself merged into what was the Department of Industry, Science and Technology. Finally, on March 29, 1995, with the coming into force of the *Department of Industry Act,*[45] the Department of Industry was established. The branch dealing with the issuing of patents has, since then, been part of the Department of Industry and is now functioning as a Special Operating Agency. The specialty resides in the relative independence of the CIPO within the public sector, so as to function in a manner to provide quasi-business-like service to its clientele. As a

---

[43] Reversed (2000), 5 C.P.R. (4th) 414 (Fed. C.A.).
[44] (1997), [1997] F.C.J. No. 848, 1997 CarswellNat 1207 (Fed. T.D.), para. 7, reversed (2000), 5 C.P.R. (4th) 414 (Fed. C.A.).
[45] S.C. 1995, c. 1.

result of these various organizational changes, the present version of the text of law constitutive of the patent issuing function of government states that,

> 3. There shall be attached to the Department of Industry, or such other department of the Government of Canada as may be determined by the Governor in Council, an office called the Patent Office.[46]

As part of the plaintiffs' case, they relied on this section to question whether a "Patent Office" presently exists, on the ground that no entity bearing such a name was included in recent governmental organizational charts. The court reaffirmed the existence of the Patent Office as part of Canada's machinery of government in several ways.

The most significant holding was that, on the basis of the evidence, "the Patent Office meets the requirements of section 3 of the *Patent Act*."[47] The genuine meaning of this finding is that in the Canadian framework of government, the fulfilment of governmental functions and the establishment of institutions to fulfil those functions must be grounded in law. No Patent Office can exist as part of the apparatus of the state without statutory authority. Moreover, if a branch of the Public Service operates for the purpose of fulfilling the patent-issuing function, the Patent Office exists and the institutional requirements contained in the law is met. This is notwithstanding so that the function may be carried out by a grouping operating under a different title, such as in the case of the CIPO. Furthermore, the presence or absence of the grouping on an organizational chart is immaterial.

The court also had to examine whether the actual functioning body satisfied that part of the requirements of section 3 that the Patent Office be "attached" to the Department of Industry. It held that in the sense intended here by Parliament, being "attached" meant "to form part of." The wording in section 2 of the *Public Service Staff Relations Act*, which dealt with portions of the Public Service being "in or under" "a department was held as being merely descriptive and in no way contradictory to the requirements of the *Patent Act*. The court assimilated the meanings of the terms.

---

[46] *Patent Act*, R.S.C. 195, c. P-4, s. 3, as most recently amended by S.C. 1995, c. 1, s. 63(1)(e).

[47] *Supra* note 44, para. 48.

Lastly, the court reaffirmed the unavoidability of legislation in this sphere of governmental activity and this judgment clearly establishes the general principle that machinery of government is based on statutory, thus legal, authority.

> The Patent Office has been established by legislation; no one is called upon to establish it. It exists by virtue of the statute and is not a physical location. What matters is that the functions mandated by legislation to be performed by the Patent Office be carried out. I am satisfied that these functions are being carried out under the direction of the Commissioner regardless of whether the agency is described as the Patent Office, the Bureau of Intellectual Property, the Intellectual Property Directorate, the Patent Branch or the Canadian Intellectual Property Office (CIPO). Section 2 of the Patent Rules states that "Patent Office" means the Patent Office established by section 3 of the Act.[48]

This decision was eventually overturned on appeal. Its interest is not so much in the final outcome of the dispute as in the political legal argumentation.

See also *Dixon v. Canada (Somalia Inquiry Commission)*, [1997] 2 F.C. 391 (Fed. T.D.), reversed 149 D.L.R. (4th) 269 (Fed. C.A.), leave to appeal refused (1998), [1997] S.C.C.A. No. 505 (S.C.C.); *Dixon v. Canada (Somalia Inquiry Commission)*, [1997] 3 F.C. 169 (Fed. C.A.), leave to appeal refused (1998), [1997] S.C.C.A. No. 505 (S.C.C.) and *Beno v. Canada (Somalia Inquiry Commission)*, 149 D.L.R. (4th) 118 (Fed. T.D.).

---

§ 9.4.7
Simpson v. Ontario
Ontario Court of Appeal; March 30, 1999
[1999] O.J. No. 895

This case brought into focus the issues of legality and that the relationship between instruments of a legal and of a policy nature in regard to the topic of executive compensation in the Public Service of Ontario.

In the period from the fall of 1989 until mid-1991, the Government of Ontario modernized the work classification of its executives and sen-

---

[48] *Ibid.*, para. 22.

ior managers through the creation of the Senior Management Group (SMG) category. It also redesigned the salary scheme applicable to this new group by establishing the SMG Compensation Plan, which was based on a 1991 base salary with possible increases based on the performance of each member of the category. The pay cycle of the SMG category was to be conducted in lock step with the fiscal cycle of the government, as described in the testimony of the Assistant Deputy Minister of the Management Board of Cabinet.

> The creation of the pay grid was a contemporaneous act with the preparation of the budget. The essence of budget making is the taking into account of current economic and political factors and these factors applied equally and coincidentally to the issue of salary increases. The question for government, in simple terms, was what, if any, salary increase can we afford politically and economically this year. Such a decision was a decision made for the upcoming fiscal year; there was nothing about the exercise which required the government to predict what it could afford a year later. Moreover, those members of the SMG who were once members of the ECP Plan knew that the pay grid which triggered increases was always struck annually and following the completion of the performance cycle. Striking a pay grid far in advance of its implementation did not accord with the well known fiscal routine of government.[49]

On October 2, 1991, before the completion of the first full-year cycle, the Minister Chair of the Management Board of Cabinet announced in the Legislature that due to fiscal pressures, the recession and the federal government's cap on transfer payments to the province, salaries for the SMG group, among others, would be frozen as of January 1, 1992. This freeze lasted until January 1, 1997. On July 21, 1992, Simpson, acting as the appointed representative of a class of plaintiffs, all members of the SMG group employed as managers in the Ministry of Correctional Services, applied for judicial review of the decision to freeze and for damages. The plaintiffs' position was that the SMG manual, a policy instrument, constituted a contractual undertaking to pay annual increases. They also claimed that the imposition of the freeze was ineffective as it was based on no legislative authority.

The court made several noteworthy findings. First, it looked at the instruments creating the SMG category and at those which defined

---

[49] *Simpson v. Ontario*, Ontario Court (General Division), July 4, 1997, unreported, pp. 6-7.

the compensation scheme for the category. It concluded that these instruments could not be interpreted as creating a legal duty to pay increases. Rights and liabilities, it said, could arise only from legislation or from contracts. Here, even the order in council which established the SMG category contained no more than a signal of the government's intention to rely on performance rating as the basis of compensation. Moreover, the Crown having reserved to itself "the right to determine what, if any, salary increase would be awarded to the SMG,"[50] the instruments could at best have a contractual flavour. They created only a conditional promise to pay which could give rise to no estoppel against the Crown. In sum, the actions of the Chair of Management Board were backed by the legislative authority which is extended to the Chair under the *Management Board of Cabinet Act*.[51] Given the powers flowing from that Act, the imposition of the freeze was a valid exercise of ministerial power in the conduct of the business operations of government. The conduct of such operations in relation to its employment agreements was found by the court to be managerial, internal or operational, but not the performance of a public duty under the Act.

Simpson appealed but lost. The Ontario Court of Appeal held that he and the other plaintiffs failed to establish a breach of contract in relation to receiving yearly raises of salary.

See also *Alliance for Public Accountability et al. v. R.C.M.P. and Canada (Attorney General)*, Federal Court of Canada – Trial Division, filed February 28, 2001, abandoned and *Closure of British Columbia Human Rights Commission*, 2002.

9.5 ISSUE: POLITICAL INTERFERENCE IN STATE APPOINTMENTS

See *Jones v. Bennett* (1968), [1969] S.C.R. 277 (S.C.C.) and *Walker v. Toronto (City)* (1993), 14 O.R. (3d) 91 (Ont. Gen. Div.).

---

[50] (1997), [1997] O.J. No. 3082, 1997 CarswellOnt 3083 (Ont. Gen. Div.), para. 21.
[51] R.S.O. 1990, c. M.1.

§ 9.5.1
Petryshyn v. R.
Federal Court of Canada – Trial Division; May 31, 1993
[1993] 3 F.C. 640

This is the first of several cases which arose out of circumstances in which individuals appointed to fulfil state functions by one government were dismissed by a succeeding government of a different political colouration earlier than the term of their appointments. The officials who found themselves in this position were aware that the premature termination of this mandate could be attributable to matters of political persuasion and association. This, however, was not a legally probable criterion in court. Political compatibility between governments and most of their order in council appointees is a fact of political life in Canada but it is not a matter of a legal nature which the courts feel at ease in considering directly as a *ratio* in adjudication. Nevertheless, in every such case, whether the destituted appointees argued for payment of lost income, restitution of position, or damages, the courts have found ways to ensure that politically neutral justice is served. In some cases, such as here, the finding of such solutions has also entailed payment by the government that caused the dismissal of a political legal price imposed by the judiciary in a manner that made it understood by the executive that while it may have acted with legality, the politically motivated actions were unjust.

Petrychyn, along with four other plaintiffs whose cases were heard jointly, had been appointed to the Immigration Appeal Board (IAB). This body was originally constituted in 1967[52] and was reorganized in 1976.[53] At the time of each appointment, the government in office was that of the Liberal Party of Canada. After the election to government of the Progressive Conservative Party of Canada in 1984, it was decided to reorganize the IAB once again. In 1987, a Bill[54] was introduced to reform the handling of immigration matters and it included reorganization of the IAB into an Immigration and Refugee Board. The proposed legislation specified the destitution of members of the IAB as of the date the new Act would come into force, as well as the

---

[52] S.C. 1966-67, c. 90.
[53] S.C. 1976-77, c. 52.
[54] Bill C-55, *An Act to amend the Immigration Act, 1976 and to amend other Acts in consequence thereof.*

denial of members of the former board to compensation or damages. Despite the attempt of the Senate to delete from the Bill the provision denying compensation and to treat the incumbents equitably and according to accepted legal principles, the Commons forged ahead and enacted the entire Bill. The IAB positions were thus abolished as of January 1, 1989.

The plaintiffs sought to recover income they would have had as members of the IAB had that Board not been abolished. The essential argument was not that Parliament lacked authority to abolish their offices without compensation. Rather, they contended that "Parliament should not be taken to have deprived them of a right to compensation when it abolished their offices, in the absence of a clear statement of intention to do so."[55] In the court's opinion, the plaintiffs had reasonable expectations of serving the full terms for which they were appointed. According to the terms of their appointments, they could be dismissed for cause and there was here no cause for dismissal.

The precedents submitted by the parties led the court to examine the issue of the nature of public offices. Basing itself on *Reilly v. The King*,[56] a Judicial Committee decision, the court held that the abolition of a statutory office by Parliament is an expression of the intention to repeal the authorization of compensation for anyone filling that position. In taking this position, the court rejected the notion that appointment to an office is akin to a grant of property.

> I doubt however that it is now appropriate to speak of the "property" in an office. It is true that in medieval common law many offices, including those of certain court officials, were considered to be property. They were sold or granted by the sovereign or other feudal lord and could be resold or transmitted by inheritance. This concept depended on feudal institutions and probably reflected the paucity of doctrines of contract or administrative law. The evils of this system of sale of offices included a rigidity caused by those with vested rights opposing the introduction of any administrative reform that might interfere with their monopoly of fee-earning services to the public. It was not until the 19th century that the sale of most offices was abolished. There is nothing in the modern history of Canada to support the concept of public offices as property and, notwithstanding the treatment of the plaintiffs in the present case,

---

[55] [1993] 3 F.C. 640 at 653 b.
[56] (1933), [1934] 1 D.L.R. 434 (Canada P.C.).

there appears to be no legal justification for doing so now. It is true that in the passage from the *Beauregard* case quoted above Thurlow C. J. said [at page 1024] that the grant of an office entitled the appointee to the accompanying salary...**in much the same way** as a grant of money or land vests title to the money or the land in the grantee. [Emphasis added.]

But in saying this he appears to be stating that an office is not property although much the same.[57]

Despite rejecting the principal legal argumentation of the plaintiffs, the Federal Court took particular note of the evidence led by them concerning activity in, or relation to, the Liberal Party. It was perhaps in irony that their counsels "confirmed that they were not suggesting that partisan politics played a part in the loss of their positions."[58] If this fact had really not played a part in the plaintiffs' case, it would not have been mentioned by their lawyers. Given the way the argument was presented and the fact that this reasoning was extraneous to the legal argumentation required to be presented to a court, this court could not rely on partisanship as a ground in its decision-making, but it did react with the same subtlety shown by the plaintiffs. It did find ways of indicating it understood perfectly well the genuine motive behind the dismissals.

The court recalled that as part of the conversion from the Immigration Appeal Board to the Immigration and Refugee Board, the plaintiffs had been offered appointments to the new body; these appointments were shorter than their original mandates would have been and were offered conditionally, on the plaintiffs' abandonment of any claim they may have exercised against the government or its representatives for loss of income. It was in examining this aspect of the case that the court found a way to indicate its true judgment in regard to the matter. It concluded that the plaintiffs had not been treated fairly. Later, it took the unusual step of emphasizing that in denying compensation for lost income, it was doing so reluctantly, thus sending a clear signal of its discontent. It may even have engaged in some irony of its own by stating that "no one questions the good faith of the Minister or advisers in offering new positions to members of the old Board."[59]

---

[57] *Supra* note 55 at 657 i-658 e.
[58] *Ibid.* at 647 g.
[59] *Ibid.* at 659 g.

Having ostensibly exonerated political masters of the situation and their political advisers, it nonetheless held accountable the Public Service institution which was involved in the appointments process, the Privy Council Office, effectively the Prime Minister's Department. Their approach in mixing the two issues of offering new positions and dealing with compensation matters in respect of the earlier positions, the court said, was not only unfair and coercive, "It was also in my view an abuse of power in effect amounting to the sale of public offices."[60] It went on with its criticism:

> In effect these plaintiffs were being asked to pay for their new order in council appointment by surrendering any claim they might have against the government or its officials. It is obvious both the plaintiffs and the Privy Council Office considered such a claim to have potential value; otherwise the latter would not have demanded the former would not have refused, the execution of a release. Therefore the plaintiffs were being asked to pay something thought to be of value in order to get an appointment. I cannot think that this is a proper condition for the Governor in Council to impose in making appointments to quasi-judicial bodies; it is indeed surprising that the Governor in Council would be advised to proceed in this manner.[61]

The finesse of this judgment was that even though it could not accede to the legal point raised by the plaintiffs, it was able to use legal reasoning as a substitute for saying that it could not adjudicate in respect of a political vendetta.

---

§ 9.5.2
Lederman and Morley v. MacLellan and Dingwall
Nova Scotia Supreme Court, Trial Division
filed August 14, 1994; file S.T. no. 05608; abandoned

Within the category of cases dealing with political interference in appointments to, and dismissals from, state positions, the focus on those positions in which the legal representation of the state is involved is of particular significance in this study. While the Department of Justice of Canada does have an extensive network of departmental and regional offices across Canada, its own litigators cannot

---

[60] *Ibid.* at 660 a.
[61] *Ibid.* at 660 e-h.

handle the entire volume of legal work required to be done. This had led to the evolution of a large number of "legal agent" positions: in many communities, local members of the Bar are appointed standing agents of the Department and carry the government's briefs to court. The points of contention which arise in this system are the criteria of selection of the agents so appointed and the reasons for which agents are replaced after changes in government. Do political considerations enter into the decision-making process in either instance? This matter became all the more pertinent after the federal general election of October 25, 1993, won by the Liberal Party under Jean Chrétien. The previous Progressive Conservative administration had an image tarnished by allegations of too much political partisanship and the Liberals had campaigned on a platform of cleaning up patronage.

Lederman was a lawyer practising in Truro, Nova Scotia, while Morley did the same in Amherst, Nova Scotia. Each had been made an agent for the Attorney General of Canada in his community and had conducted prosecutions, notably under the *Narcotic Control Act*. In May 1994 each of their appointments was terminated by the Department of Justice without notice or explanation. The matter might have been left at that, except for the fact that on June 3, 1994, the *Halifax Chronicle Herald* published an interview with the two defendants. At the time, MacLellan was Parliamentary Secretary to the Minister of Justice and Dingwall was Minister of Public Works.[62] Both represented Nova Scotia constituencies in Parliament. The flavour of the article was to search out whether patronage had been a factor in the dismissal of Lederman and Morley.

MacLellan was reported to have stated that Lederman "may have gotten it (the position) because he was a Tory, but he didn't lose it because he was a Tory."[63] Dingwall's interview in preparation for the article was along the same lines. He said, "competence was the only yardstick used to measure who would get the government work...whether they have political persuasions or not I don't think is the consideration here."[64]

These quotes, which denied political interference and had the effect of impugning the plaintiffs' professionalism, gave them the oppor-

---

[62] A the time of writing, Dingwall was the Master of the Royal Canadian Mint.
[63] Statement of Claim, para. 5.
[64] *Ibid.*, para. 6

tunity to allege libel and to demand damages. The action was fraught with damages for Lederman and Morley; if they won, they would succeed in pointing out that their appointments were based on political considerations; if they lost, they could be made to appear incompetent. The benefit of the case was its broader potential consequence, of pointing out the nature of the system of selection and appointment of agents.

Dingwall's defence went to the heart of the issue.

> The Defendant states that if it were indicated to Brian Underhill, that "competence was the only yardstick used to measure who would get the government work" these words meant and were only intended to mean, that as a matter of public policy, as understood by the Defendant as a Member of the Privy Council, persons, generally, obtaining future contracts for legal services would be selected on the basis of perceived competence as determined by the client.

> . . .

> The Defendant states that the words attributed to him...represent a general comment on public policy and further states that the words "whether they have political persuasions or not I don't think is the consideration here" represent a fair comment on a matter of public interest and an expression of opinion by a Member of the Privy Council not involved in processes managed by the Minister of Justice of Canada.[65]

By so phrasing his defence, Dingwall not only depersonalized the attack upon him but rendered it impossible for the plaintiffs to make their case. For good measure, he added that the content of his interview was fair comment made in good faith and without malice on a matter of public interest, and indicated that standing agents operated at the pleasure of the Crown.

Had the issue gone to trial, the court could have heard testimony about the role of politics in the appointment and replacement of legal agents. After being in abeyance for several years, however, the case was abandoned.

---

[65] Statement of Defence of David Dingwall, paras. 7 and 8.

§ 9.5.3
Weatherill v. Canada (Attorney General)
Federal Court of Canada – Trial Division; January 23, 1998
(1998), 143 F.T.R. 302

Weatherill was appointed on May 1, 1989, to a ten-year term as Chair of the Canada Labour Relations Board (CLRB). In April 1997, press stories surfaced about his extravagant lifestyle at taxpayers' expense. On the basis of an investigation by the Auditor General, the Minister of Labour announced in the House of Commons that Weatherill would be removed. The steps necessary for that process were undertaken by the Deputy Clerk of the Privy Council. On January 7, 1998, Weatherill applied to the Federal Court for an injunction, alleging that in order to protect the independence and impartiality of the CLRB, a quasi-judicial body, he could be removed only by way of an inquiry conducted by the Canadian Judicial Council. He alleged that the procedure being followed in the Privy Council Office was therefore *ultra vires*. The court found that the application was not frivolous or vexatious, but denied it on the grounds that Weatherill would suffer no irreparable harm.

> Having already traversed the well-prepared and ably-presented arguments of counsel, I need only observe that the characteristics of the proceedings which have been instituted are neither prosaic nor commonplace. Indeed rare are the occasions when either by Crown prerogative or by statute, the executive branch, namely the Governor in Council, is called upon to exercise its authority to inquire into and determine if the holder of a Crown office should or should not be removed. So rare, in fact, that there is little jurisprudence to guide the courts, each case referred to being substantially one of a kind.
>
> This means, in effect, that an issue of "behaviour" on the part of Order in Council appointments is determinable on a case by case basis, the Crown, through the Governor in Council, preserving for itself the ultimate judicial prerogative to determine when "behaviour" is or is not compatible with a particular office.[66]

The principal reasoning adopted by the court was that in assessing the balance of convenience, that of the Governor in Council, that is the public interest, should not be prevented from exercising its stat-

---

[66] (1998), 143 F.T.R. 302 at 308.

utory and prerogative powers. On January 31, 1998, Weatherill was dismissed.

The political interference aspect of this case, the matter in it that is of interest for political law, grew out of a statement made during the court proceedings by the judge hearing the case. On the day the Minister of Labour announced in the Commons that Weatherill would be dismissed, many parliamentarians, including the Prime Minister, had vociferously shown their approval. Judge Joyal responded:

> "I'm concerned as a citizen," Judge Joyal said from the bench, "that with immunity, a minister of the Crown can get up in the House - on the basis of I don't know what - and say, "I'm going to fire this guy," and everybody is up and cheering. I was thinking of these people around the guillotine. I don't know if I have a right to intervene. But it left a bad taste in my mouth.[67]

These rather unusual and perhaps ungrounded remarks led to an open dispute between the legislative and judicial branches of government, no longer about the dismissal itself, but about the ability of one branch or other to make the determining decision without interference from the other. The Reform Party in particular expressed outrage at what it qualified as the imperious attitude of a judge in a pampered position toward Parliament. They portrayed this case rather excessively as part of the struggle between Parliament and the unaccountable, unelected and unknown judiciary to run the country. Some Members of Parliament would even have liked the Commons to find Judge Joyal in contempt of Parliament and to censure him.

> The independence of the judiciary doesn't allow the judiciary to meddle in the affairs of Parliament. This is not a blank cheque for the judiciary to suggest, as he did, that MPs were no better than a member of a rabble during the French Revolution lusting for blood. I don't believe that judges on the bench are permitted to say whatever they like in any context.[68]

The matter was resolved by other means. On its own initiative, the Canadian Judicial Council's judicial conduct committee investigated

---

[67] "Judge slams Weatherill firing," Richard Foot, *Ottawa Citizen*, January 21, 1998.
[68] "Judge regrets 'guillotine' remark," Stephen Bindman, *Ottawa Citizen*, February 4, 1998.

the incident. It rebuked Judge Joyal for what it called "gratuitous and insulting" comments from the bench.

In the first judgment, the Trial Division of the Federal Court of Canada dismissed Weatherill's application for a stay of the proceedings against him because, in his view, in order to remove him, the government would have had to proceed according to section 69 of the *Judges Act*. That provision sets out the reasons for removal from office of superior court judges and those officials in similar positions. This application was denied. The merits of the case were decided by the Trial Division in the second judgment. There the court framed the question of the legality of Weatherill's dismissal in terms of the degree of tenure of members of the Canada Labour Relations Board. It held that the Board was not a court.

> It is not clear to me whether the constitutional validity of decisions of the Canada Labour Relations Board requires the same degree of security of tenure for its members. Counsel for the applicant urges that the Canada Labour Relations Board is a quasi-judicial body with a broad jurisdiction. It is entrusted with very important decisions that are not subject to judicial scrutiny except in the most limited circumstances. I agree with that. But at the same time, respondents' counsel says, correctly, that the Canada Labour Relations Board is not a court. There is no scope for the application of section 11(d) of the Charter in matters heard by the Canada Labour Relations Board.[69]

Given this analysis of the institution, the rules on tenure which protect the independence of judges from government interference did not apply and Weatherill's dismissal was held to be valid, in the manner in which it was done.

> From these comments, it appears to me that the requirement of security of tenure was met in this case by the combination of three elements. The first was the statutory requirement of "cause" as the ground for removal. The second was the obligation of the Governor in Council to observe the principles of natural justice when making a removal decision. The third was the potential for an independent inquiry under section 69 of the *Judges Act*, despite the fact that section 69 could not be engaged except at the discretion of the Minister of Justice.[70]

---

[69] [1999] 4 F.C. 107 at 133, para. 77.
[70] *Ibid.*, para. 80.

§ 9.5.4
Dewar v. Ontario
Ontario Court of Appeal; February 27, 1998
(1998), 156 D.L.R. (4th) 202

The applicant, Marion Dewar, was a former Mayor of Ottawa, a federal Member of Parliament for the New Democratic Party (NDP) and a former national President of the NDP. By an Order in Council of March 29, 1995, the Ontario NDP government appointed her to be Chair of the Public Service Board of the Regional Municipality of Ottawa-Carleton. As a result of the provincial general election of June 8, 1995, the Progressive Conservative Party formed a new government in Ontario, with a significantly different political agenda from that of its predecessor. Among the new government's initiatives was the replacement of NDP appointees. Thus, on December 13, 1995, Dewar was advised that her appointment had been terminated effective immediately, without notice or hearing. This is an application for judicial review of that termination. The case also concerns the dismissal of another similar appointee.

The General Division first addressed the specific legal issue flowing from the Orders in Council of appointment and termination. While the instrument of appointment could have been made to be "during pleasure," in this instance it contained a very clear recital to the effect that Dewar was appointed "for a term of two years." Given this wording, she could have been dismissed earlier than the end of her term for cause, such as incompetent performance of duty, but here there was no such cause.

The judgment also examined the political circumstances relating to appointments to such governmental boards. It recognized that "in addition to the permanent, non-political, professional staff of the civil service elected representatives frequently must rely upon a small group of persons who share their political views and who in a broad way wish to mould our society in a particular fashion."[71] In the court's description, not only is there nothing sinister about such appointments, but it even agreed that there are "good reasons of public

---

[71] (1996), 137 D.L.R. (4th) 273 (Ont. Div. Ct.) at 278, leave to appeal allowed (1996), 1996 CarswellOnt 4018 (Ont. C.A.), affirmed (1998), 156 D.L.R. (4th) 202 (Ont. C.A.), quoting *Neil v. Saskatchewan* (April 13, 1984), McLean J. (Sask. Q.B.), at p. 11.

policy"[72] why such appointees could hold office at pleasure. However, such officials could be validly dismissed only if their appointment was made at pleasure. The real focus of the ruling is that notwithstanding the patent utility for an incoming government of making political appointments, an election leading to a change in government could not validly affect the legality of earlier political appointments or the legal rights of the holders of such state appointments.

The political law issue underlying this case is whether an appointment made by a government of a different political colouration can be terminated on politically motivated, rather than on legal grounds. In determining whether a government is to apply the legal criterion and retain in office the appointee of its predecessor, or apply a political measure and put its own adherents into positions of authority, it must conduct a cost-benefit analysis based on legality. What is more beneficial to a government: observing the law and maintaining the rights of appointees who may be ideologically opposed, or satisfying the electoral wishes and career designs of its partisan constituency? What is more costly to a government: suffering a potential finding of the illegality of its actions by a court and the possible consequential assumption of a financial burden arising from a politically wilful breach of the law, or the political frustration of its adherents?

Here, the view of the court was that the termination of Dewar was done without legal justification. Declarations were issued rendering the revocation of the appointment invalid and entitling the applicant to serve the remainder of the two-year term of appointment. The Government of Ontario took this decision on appeal.[73]

The Court of Appeal dismissed the Government's case, relying on its own decision in the *Hewat* case.

---

[72] *Ibid.* at 279, quoting *Melsness v. Alberta (Minister of Social Services & Community Health)* (1982), 132 D.L.R. (3d) 715 (Alta. C.A.) at 721-2.

[73] The consequences of the Court of Appeal's disposition of the case is that for students of political law, the General Division decision, reported at (1996) 137 D.L.R. (4th) 273 (Ont. Div. Ct.), leave to appeal allowed (1996), 1996 CarswellOnt 4018 (Ont. C.A.), affirmed (1998), 156 D.L.R. (4th) 202 (Ont. C.A.), is much more explicative.

§ 9.5.5
Hewat v. Ontario
Ontario Court of Appeal; February 27, 1998
(1998), 37 O.R. (3d) 161

This case was conducted on the same basis as, and simultaneously with *Dewar v. Ontario*. Hewat, Kovacs and Stoykewych were appointed by Order in Council to the Ontario Labour Relations Board (OLRB). The first two commenced their terms during the time when the government was led by the New Democratic Party, the third appointment was made after the Progressive Conservative government was elected to office on June 8, 1995. On October 2, 1996, by a new Order in Council, the Government of Ontario revoked each of the three appointments. The Divisional Court held that the termination of employment was null and void and awarded damages.[74] The former members of the OLRB appealed to obtain reinstatement and the Crown cross-appealed to justify the terminations.

The Ontario Court of Appeal varied the lower court ruling to the extent that it made as the sole order of the court a declaration that the Order in Council of dismissal was null and void at its inception; it left the parties to resolve the ways of acting on this order. The court also dismissed the cross-appeal.

The judgment was based in part on the rules of statutory interpretation. More to the point, it laid great emphasis on the need for the independence and impartiality of members of tribunals, particularly of those tribunals which stand beside the courts and which perform quasi-judicial functions in specialized areas of dispute and regulation. The genuine significance of the case however, is the manner in which the court tried to balance the independence of the quasi-judiciary with the political management of the government in the process of reviewing the membership of such boards. The court rejected the argument that the issues before it brought into play constitutional safeguards against the conduct of government. It even specifically recognized "that elected governments must have room to make political decisions and to conduct themselves in a manner to assure that

---

[74] (1997), 32 O.R. (3d) 622 (Ont. Div. Ct.), leave to appeal allowed (1997), 1997 CarswellOnt 2471 (Ont. C.A.), varied (1998), 37 O.R. (3d) 161 (Ont. C.A.).

their political policies are implemented."[75] However, it clearly asserted that the public perception of the independence of quasi-judicial functions from government must be maintained. The appearance of their integrity to those who appear before such tribunals must also be upheld and for this, what the court called "some degree of independence" must exist. Based on this approach the *ratio* of the court was succinct and unmistakeable.

> The image of independence is undermined when government commitments to fixed appointments are breached. The court should not, by its orders, encourage repetition of this conduct.[76]

---

§ 9.5.6
Wells v. Newfoundland
Supreme Court of Canada; September 15, 1999
(1999), 177 D.L.R. (4th) 73

This is the first of the recent cases dealing with political interference in the tenure of public appointees to reach the Supreme Court of Canada and is worth mentioning on that ground alone. It is also of note in that it settles the judicial position on such interference by addressing the legal nature of the employment of these appointees, rather than by looking at the matter from the perspective of partisan considerations; such an approach is more in keeping with the role of the courts as arbiters of the law.

On September 19, 1981, Wells was appointed to the position of Consumer Representative on the Public Utilities Board of Newfoundland, with the rank of Commissioner. On the basis of negotiations, his appointment was framed in terms of lasting until age 70. Not long thereafter, the Board lost some of its jurisdiction as a result of new jurisprudence.[77] The province undertook a reassessment of the Board's functions and on February 16, 1990, the House of Assembly enacted a new *Public Utilities Act* reducing the Board's membership from six to three. Wells was fired without compensation or pension. The significant fact not mentioned in the judgment is that in the year

---

[75] (1998), 37 O.R. (3d) 161 at 169.
[76] *Ibid.*
[77] See *Alberta Government Telephones v. Canada (Radio-Television & Telecommunications Commission)*, [1989] 2 S.C.R. 225 (S.C.C.).

prior to Wells' firing, there was an election in Newfoundland; while Wells had been appointed under the Premiership of the Progressive Conservative Premier, Brian Peckford, the incoming Premier in 1989 was the Liberal Clyde Wells (unrelated) and Commissioner Wells was in conflict with the new government. He sued for damages resulting from his dismissal. The Newfoundland Court of Appeal held in favour of Wells, following the *Petryshyn* case.

The Supreme Court of Canada dismissed Newfoundland's appeal and awarded damages to Wells. The first element of its analysis regarded the status of public servants and the nature of their employment. Without distinguishing between public servants appointed pursuant to the merit principle and those named by Order in Council, the court took the common sense view that work for the government is in the nature of a contract. As an employer, the Crown was bound to act according to the rule of law and with respect for the rules of natural justice.

> In my opinion, it is time to remove uncertainty and confirm that the law regarding senior civil servants accords with the contemporary understanding of the state's role and obligations in its dealings with employees. Employment in the civil service is not feudal servitude. The respondent's position was not a form of monarchical patronage. He was employed to carry out an important function on behalf of the citizens of Newfoundland. The government offered him the position, terms were negotiated, and an agreement reached. It was a contract.[78]

The court emphasized the security of tenure which flowed from Wells' appointment. He could be dismissed for bad behaviour or as a result of his age only. While security did not vest in the position itself, it did apply to Wells' personal situation under the contract. In sum, it said, a contract of employment with the Crown remained binding unless and until it was explicitly displaced by statute, which was not the case here.

The next issue the court looked at was whether the Crown was entitled to abrogate the contract. While no mention was made of the change of government, the court could not entirely avoid the politicized circumstance of the dispute between Wells and the government. It referred to what it called the "eye-catching" suggestion of a senior

---

[78] (1999), 177 D.L.R. (4th) 73 at 83.

Newfoundland parliamentarian to the effect that the revised *Public Utilities Act* was designed to get rid of Wells. In line with the contractual nature of Wells' relationship to the government, this could not be done. The court made this point rather forcefully.

> In a nation governed by the rule of law, we assume that the government will honour its obligations unless it explicitly exercises its power not to. In the absence of a clear express intent to abrogate rights and obligations—rights of the highest importance to the individual—those rights remain in force. To argue the opposite is to say that the government is bound only by its whim, not its word. In Canada this is unacceptable, and does not accord with the nation's understanding of the relationship between the state and its citizens.[79]

The court then added another line of reasoning, based on the separation of powers argument. It held this to be an essential feature of our constitution, but the government could not rely on it to avoid the consequences of its own actions. In the first part of this reason, the court's argument was strong. It held that, "The separation of powers is not a rigid and absolute structure. The Court should not be blind to the reality of Canadian governance that, except in certain rare cases, the executive frequently and *de facto* controls the legislature."[80] It then went on to state that the same "directing minds," namely the executive, were responsible for both the respondent's appointment and termination. This is true only in the sense that the Government of Newfoundland appointed and terminated Wells; it ignores, however, that in the meantime, the party in charge of the government changed and the incoming government was not of the same political colouration as Wells, leading to differences of professional opinion. The court may have felt that it should address the legal aspects of the matter only, but it could not ignore the circumstances.

In fact, rather than place the matter on the political plane, the justices chose to portray the matter as one of public policy.

> The respondent's termination was the consequence of external events which had overtaken the Board on which he served, and the public policy choices taken by the Government of Newfoundland in response to changing public needs. This was not a situation where personal animus led those in government to use their authority unlawfully against an

---

[79] *Ibid.* at 88.
[80] *Ibid.* at 90.

individual over whom they had power, as was the case in *Roncarelli v. Duplessis*, [1959] S.C.R. 121, at p. 140.[81]

This enabled the court to refute Wells' argument of bad faith on the part of the government.

The approach used here by the Supreme Court is innovative in the manner it approaches a political problem. In fact, it returns the matter from the political sphere to the legal one, and depoliticizes it. The consequence is not only legal, it is just: where the state makes a promise of employment, it is wrong for that promise to be breached merely for partisan considerations.

---

§ 9.5.7[82]
MacKay v. Attorney General of Nova Scotia
Nova Scotia Supreme Court; filed October 27, 1997
file S.H. No. 145553 C; settled September 20, 2001

Federal legislation in Canada provides that if a public servant wishes to run for elective office, he obtain clearance within the Public Service; this can involve his suspension for the duration of the campaign and resignation from the non-partisan position in case of election to Parliament.[83] Many of the provinces follow the federal lead,[84] but there are cases where circumstances can bring about allegations of partisan reaction on the part of the government and even litigation based on unconstitutional behaviour by officials.

Peter MacKay was a member of the Crown Prosecution Service in Nova Scotia and the scion of a leading conservative family in the province; his father had held the portfolio of Solicitor General under Prime Minister Brian Mulroney. At the relevant time, in 1997, the provincial government of Nova Scotia was of Liberal colouration. In expectation of the upcoming federal general election, MacKay advised his superiors he intended to run under the Progressive Conservative banner. He proposed six options to avoid any conflict resulting from his political advocacy. None was accepted. On February 15,

---

[81] *Ibid.* at 91.
[82] Cross-reference to § 11.14.10.
[83] *Public Service Employment Act*, R.S.C. 1985, c. P-33, s. 33.
[84] Nova Scotia *Civil Service Act*, c. 70.

1997, MacKay was nominated and on March 20, he was dismissed from his prosecutor's function. He initiated legal action for wrongful dismissal and for breach of his freedom of association, based on section 2(d) of the *Canadian Charter of Rights and Freedoms*.

> The larger question is whether or not a civil servant should face any punishment for deciding to exercise a fundamental democratic right and enter the political arena. After all, a sound democracy depends on the awareness and participation of its citizens. The expense of a campaign and the loss of privacy already hold back many people from taking the plunge without adding on the threat of a loss of employment.[85]

This case was pending for over four years. During this time, the procedure was taken as far as having examinations for discovery. It opened up for observers the question of whether the position of a prosecutor is so sensitive, among public service positions, as to allow no political association at all, or whether the prohibition of any such association is an arbitrary and itself politically motivated interference. The dates of October 9 to 18, 2001 were set down for trial. Just prior to the commencement of that trial, on September 20, 2001, the parties reached a settlement.

By contrast to most cases in which there is a settlement, the terms agreed to here were rendered public. They are notable in that MacKay used the opportunity not only to obtain redress of his own grievance, but also to change the political legal system and to improve the manner in which prosecutors aspiring to elective office would be dealt with, reducing the influence of political considerations in this function of public service. Apart from the usual financial terms relating to legal fees and the costs of expert reports, MacKay's settlement included a promise by the Nova Scotia Department of Public Prosecutions to review the relevant civil service legislation so as to make it more palatable to the *Charter*. Finally, it also included a letter to be directed by the Crown Prosecution Service to MacKay, apologizing to him, indicating that it was never the intention of the Service to harm his reputation or to intimate that MacKay's actions had jeopardized the impartiality of his office. In essence, this settlement had a more far-reaching impact than if MacKay had proceeded with his action and won.[86]

---

[85] *Hill Times*, Ottawa, April 13, 1988, p. 4.

[86] At the time of writing, MacKay was Deputy Leader of the Conservative Party, the Official Opposition in the 38th Parliament.

A Tory MP who was fired as a Crown attorney because he ran for office says an out-of-court settlement of his wrongful dismissal case will help other public servants enter politics. The Nova Scotia government has apologized to Peter MacKay for his 1997 firing, and promised to review its Civil Service Act.

. . .

In his lawsuit, MacKay argued the Civil Service Act is unconstitutional because it restricts a person's democratic rights to freedom of political association, assembly and expression. MacKay was seeking a declaration that the relevant section of the act is void and of no force and effect, pursuant to the Charter of Rights and Freedoms, and a declaration that he was not a "politically restricted employee" under the act.[87]

See also *Mercier c. Québec (ministre du Conseil exécutif)*, REJB 1999-10883; *Condon v. Prince Edward Island*, 2002 PESCTD 41 (P.E.I. T.D. [In Chambers]).

9.6 ISSUE: POLITICAL INTERFERENCE IN PUBLIC SERVICES[88]

§ 9.6.1
Friends of the Athabaska Environmental Assn. v. Alberta (Director of Standards & Approvals)
Alberta Court of Appeal; June 17, 1992
(1992), 131 A.R. 129[89]

From one perspective, this case can be characterized as dealing with the proper role of the Executive Committee of the government (the Cabinet) in the execution of statutory duties; from another and more direct perspective, it relates to judicial assessment of political interference in the administration. Indeed, despite its brevity, the case attempts to set a modern standard for determining what actions con-

---

[87] "N.S. apologizes to Tory MP for firing him as Crown lawyer; Province says it will review Civil Service Act," *The Moncton Times* and transcript, September 27, 2001, p. A-9.

[88] Cross-reference to § 9.4.

[89] Leave to appeal refused (1993), 9 Admin. L.R. (2d) 100 (note) (S.C.C.).

stitute political interference. In common language, the case looks at "who decided?" and "on what basis was the decision made?"

In 1988, a company named Al-Pac proposed the construction of a pulp and paper mill o the Athabaska River. Pursuant to the *Clean Air Act*[90] and the *Clean Water Act*,[91] the project needed permits for construction and operation. The Director and the company performed all tasks required toward authorization of the proposal and issuance of the permits. In particular, through the Director's requests and the company's responses, a file was compiled which showed that the Director did not back off any of the conditions. It was during this process that the Alberta Minister of the Environment acted in a manner which led to this litigation.

> On July 21, 1990, the Minister of the Environment said in a news release that, in some circumstances, "Cabinet would decide the project's fate." A Cabinet "task force" was established to deal with the project. On November 23, the Minister is reported to have said in an interview, "... the decision is going to be a government decision ... I mean that's what governments are there for..." Departmental memoranda from the period in November speak of issuance of a permit "should the Government approve the company to proceed to the permitting stage." On December 20, the Premier announced that, the previous day, Cabinet had "approved the development of the ... project." The Minister for the Environment said "... It was the responsibility of the Government to take all the information gathered over two years and decide ... and that was done."[92]

Following this, the required permits were issued on December 14, 1990, and January 3, 1991, respectively.

In order to prevent the environmental damage the Friends of the Athabaska feared, they applied for judicial review of the Director's decisions to grant the permits and for a declaratory judgment. Their case was that the Cabinet had usurped the Director's role by instructing him to accept the Al-Pac proposal. The defence was an acknowledgement of the fact that had usurpation occurred, that would have been illegal, but the respondents contended that no usurpation hap-

---

90 R.S.A. 1980, c. C-12.
91 R.S.A. 1980, c. C-13.
92 (1992), 131 A.R. 129, 25 W.A.C. 129 at 131, para. 8, leave to appeal refused (1993), 9 Admin. L.R. (2d) 100 (note) (S.C.C.).

pened. The Queen's Bench found no evidence that the Director's decisions were fettered or that he was dictated to. However, the Court left the door open for an appeal by finding that there was, in Cabinet, a process "parallel" to that of the Director.

The appeal did arise and here, the Court of Appeal for Alberta dismissed it. The applicants contended that there was no room under the law for a "parallel" review by Cabinet. The defence argued that the Minister did have a collateral decision-making power.

The decision was made on two grounds that are important for political law. The first is the matter of the standard which must be applied to the question of what actions of politicians amount to political interference. In essence, the court stated that political "interest" in a matter to be decided according to statutory criteria is not enough. There must be a combination of "improper interference" on the part of the politicians and a response to the attempt at control on the part of the public official charged with administering the statutory process. Here, the court found insufficient evidence of such improper influence and response to it. In the absence of a judicial definition, we must presume that in order for influence to be improper, it must be based on or related to criteria other than those rooted in the subject statute or in the procedures mandated by the principles of administrative law.

> It is not enough to show that the Executive Council, or one of its members, claimed some veto power over the project. Even if that is proved, it does not necessarily follow that the Director approved because the Cabinet failed to reject. Nor is it enough to show that the Executive Council wanted the project to proceed. What must be shown is that the Director understood that his decision had been taken from him. Indeed, even if the Executive Council expected the Director to follow orders, the evidence must show that the Director submitted to that control. The evidence in support of that drastic proposition is, at best, equivocal. It is at least equally consistent with the idea that, notwithstanding any presumed pressure, he made his own decision.

> . . .

> The undeniable and undenied fact is that the Executive Council took an interest in the matter. Even if it was unusual or unwarranted by any statute, how can one criticize it for that? The only valid criticism must be that, having taken an interest, it then improperly influenced events

and officials intended by law to be free of its influence. It does not follow that this improper influence will occur just because an interest is taken. And, even if one infers the worst, the critical and determinative question remains whether the Director responded to the attempt at control.[93]

The second ratio motivating this judgment was that the judges specifically distinguished this case from the classic precedent of political interference, *Roncarelli v. Duplessis*.[94] The strength of this reasoning is diminished, however, by the fact that it is based on procedural arguments. Finally, it is worthy of note for the outcome that the court here exercised a patent and perhaps somewhat exaggerated deference to the executive.

---

§ 9.6.2
Thibodeau v. Prince Edward Island (Human Rights Commission)
Prince Edward Island Supreme Court; December 21, 1993
(1993), 114 Nfld. & P.E.I.R. 119[95]

The legal system of Prince Edward Island offers protection for the human rights of individuals not only on the grounds that have become traditional, such as race, religion and colour, but also, notably, in respect of political belief. The province's *Human Rights Act* is quite explicit in its definition of the concept of political belief.

"political belief" means belief in the tenets of a political party that is at the relevant time registered under section 24 of the *Election Act*, R.S.P.E.I. 1988, Cap. E-1 as evidenced by

i) membership of or contribution to that party, or

ii) open and active participation in the affairs of that party.[96]

The Act then protects individuals' employment from discrimination on the ground that their political belief is different from that of the employer by stipulating that:

---

[93] *Ibid.* at 131, paras. 12 and 13.
[94] [1959] S.C.R. 121 (S.C.C.).
[95] Additional reasons at (1994), 23 Admin. L.R. (2d) 244 (P.E.I. T.D.).
[96] R.S.P.E.I. 1988, c. H-12, s. 1(1)(m).

> No person shall refuse to employ or to continue to employ any individual,
>
> a) on a discriminatory basis including discrimination in any term or condition of employment;[97]

In the context of this statutory framework, the present case concerns government action taken after the provincial general election of April 21, 1986, as a result of which a Liberal administration was elected to replace a Progressive Conservative one. By June of that year, Thibodeau and other seasonal employees lodged complaints with the provincial Human Rights Commission (HRC) that the Ministry of Transport and Public Works, and the Ministry of Tourism and Parks respectively had refused to continue them in employment or to renew their employment. They alleged that this action was taken in each case on the basis of discrimination based on political belief.

The HRC investigated the complaints and, in February 1991, in agreement with Thibodeau, it reported to the Minister responsible for Human Rights (the Minister). This report concluded that the evidence supported the allegations of political discrimination, that the employer Ministers had failed to offer settlement as the procedure for handling such cases provided, that boards of inquiry should be convened and that, notwithstanding various delays, each case be handled as soon as possible. "The Minister responsible for Human Rights did not act on this recommendation."[98]

In August 1991, the Appeal Division of the Prince Edward Island Supreme Court, the highest court in the province, handed down a decision in the case of *Burge v. Prince Edward Island (Human Rights Commission)*.[99] As far as the HRC was concerned, the essence of that ruling was that in substituting allegations of political discrimination, complainants would have to meet a higher standard than the HRC had earlier understood to be the case. Following up on that decision, on November 26, 1991, the HRC made a second report to the Minister. It changed its earlier recommendation and now expressed the opinion that Thibodeau had insufficient evidence to warrant the convening of a board of inquiry. This is the decision of the HRC against which

---

[97] R.S.P.E.I. 1988, c. H-12, s. 6(1)(a).
[98] (1993) 114 Nfld. & P.E.I.R. 119, 356 A.P.R. 119 at 124, para. 13, additional reasons at (1994), 23 Admin. L.R. (2d) 244 (P.E.I. T.D.).
[99] (1991), 97 Nfld. & P.E.I.R. 70 (P.E.I. C.A.)

Thibodeau launched the present application for judicial review, seeking to have the decision quashed.

The Supreme Court decided that the HRC did not exercise its authority in accordance with the *Human Rights Act*. The court issued an order to nullify the act the HRC complained of and to direct the HRC to act in accordance with its authority. The effect of this judgment was not to provide a substantive remedy to the applicants, but rather to ensure that the complaints of discrimination grounded on political belief would be properly addressed and proceeded with.

> It is expected that this will result in the Commission carrying out its previous recommendation to the Minister responsible for Human Rights that a separate board of inquiry be convened for the hearing of each complaint.[100]

More importantly, the impact of the ruling was a clear signal to a political system accustomed to dispensing patronage appointments at most changes of government that the law and the safeguard from discrimination on the basis of political belief that it offered should be taken seriously and applied. The court in effect said it was up to the executive to amend its political practice so as to conform to the legal norms established by the Legislature.

The court's general conclusion was that the government's submission that discrimination could not be found in the first instance was contradicted by the record. It then went on to provide several specific motives for its decision. In its opinion, the HRC had, first, made a significant error of law in interpreting the *Burge* case in a manner that was patently unreasonable.

> In *Burge*, the direction of the court was that political discrimination cases are dealt with the same way as other cases. *Burge* did not really change anything. Normally, he who asserts must prove. The Commission made an error of law by determining that s. 1(3) of the Act created an increased standard regarding the nature and extent of the onus. It then proceeded based on that error to terminate, or effectively terminate, the process for the applicants' complaints.[101]

---

[100] *Supra* note 98 at 123, para. 10.
[101] *Ibid.* at 127, para. 27.

Were this otherwise, the court would have had to acknowledge that the HRC had acted in error between 1986 and 1991.

The court also found that the HRC had a duty of procedural fairness to the applicants and that it failed to fulfil that duty. This failure lay in the HRC's lack of communication with the applicants regarding its change of direction after the *Burge* decision. The applicants only found out about the HRC's decision from its letter of November 26, 1991, which was in effect an *ex post facto* communication. "The Commission change of direction was, for the applicants, surprising and confusing, in light of their previous information and expectations."[102]

Lastly, the court concluded that the HRC exceeded its jurisdiction by weighing the evidence at the investigation stage and deciding in advance that the complaint would not be successful at a board of inquiry. The role the HRC should have seen for itself was to investigate, evaluate and report, but not to adjudicate. Moreover, the HRC's letter to the Minister was also such that it contained insufficient information to enable an informed and reasonable decision.

Strangely, the HRC chose not to be represented by counsel before this court and not to make submissions. Thus, the court could only surmise the source of the HRC's error as being its reliance on two precedents, of which *Burge* was one. The court seems clearly to have been displeased by the HRC's lack of explanation of its notices in dealing so wrongly with Thibodeau.

By way of remedy, the court concluded that the HRC's earlier recommendation dated February 25, 1991, be reissued and that the employer Ministers be asked to decide the political belief complaints as soon as possible. It then offered very pointed advice to those Ministers, reminding them of the importance of legality in this domain.

> The court entrusts that the employer Ministers will treat this matter with the seriousness and dispatch that adherence to the law of human rights deserves. This takes on added urgency in light of the elapsed time since initial filing of the complaints in 1986; and more particularly, since the initial unanswered offers for settlement made by the Commission to the Ministers in August, 1980.[103]

---

[102] *Ibid.* at 129, para. 33.
[103] *Ibid.* at 135, para. 62.

§ 9.6.3
Burge v. Prince Edward Island (Liquor Control Commission)
Prince Edward Island Supreme Court; August 16, 1994
(1994), 123 Nfld. & P.E.I.R. 143[104]

While this case does not establish fundamental principles relating to interference into the delivery of public services based on partisan political grounds, it is a good illustration of the difficulties that may arise in the course of disposing of such matters. Burge, the scion of a well-known P.E.I. family and the son of a member of the Legislative Assembly, functioned as a supporter of the Progressive Conservative (PC) Party and one of its riding campaign chairs for the general election of April 23, 1979. The PCs won that election with a majority. On June 12, 1979, Burge was advised that he had been awarded a contract to haul beer for the P.E.I. Liquor Control Commission (LCC). At about the same time, all contracts of this type but one were replaced in similar fashion. On the second general election following thereafter, on April 21, 1986, the Liberal Party came back into office with a majority. On May 15, 1986, Burge's contract was ended and on May 20, 1986, he lodged a complaint before the provincial Human Rights Commission (HRC) on the ground that the termination of his contract was based on political belief, contrary to section 6 of the *Human Rights Act*.[105] The HRC concluded that the evidence demonstrated a *prima facie* case of discrimination and appointed a Board of Inquiry. That Board rendered its decision on February 19, 1993, awarding Burge sums for monetary loss and for injured feelings. "The Board also recommended that the Commission (the LCC) discontinue its then hiring practice for beer truckers and adopt the same or similar practice in place in New Brunswick where the breweries hire the truckers by a tendering process."[106] It is the recommendation as to remedy and quantum of damages that was the subject of this application for judicial review. After lengthy analysis of the issues involved, the P.E.I. Supreme Court referred the matter to a newly constituted Board of Inquiry.

For purposes of the present study, the real interest of this case is the manner in which the evidence of political interference was handled.

---

[104] Reversed (1995), 135 Nfld. & P.E.I.R. 245 (P.E.I. C.A.).
[105] R.S.P.E.I. 1988, c. H-12.
[106] *Supra* note 98 at 146, para. 12.

Before the Board of Inquiry even commenced its hearing, the LCC admitted the substance of Burge's complaint on the merits relating to the political motive of the termination of his contract, even though this was couched in terms drafted to mitigate the LCC's liability.

> One of the reasons, but by no means, the only or paramount reason, for the discontinuance, was the political belief of the "complainant Burge" as defined in the *Human Rights Act*.[107]

At the hearing before the Supreme Court, the Minister responsible for the LCC testified on the political process whereby Burge was engaged as a beer hauler. His testimony was to the effect that "politics played a major role in the appointment of beer haulers and specifically in the appointment of Burge."[108] In fact, according to another witness who had been a member of the government of P.E.I., after 1979, the awarding of such contracts was not only of passing political interest, this was a matter discussed at no less a level than in Cabinet, indicating the extent to which political considerations were prominent in processes that should normally have been decided on legal and commercial criteria.

A number of other parliamentarians from the years of the PC administration also testified to the effect that Burge was approached with the offer for the contract on the ground that he had worked for the party, that an elected official had recommended Burge be engaged after the 1979 election victory, that the expectation in such appointments was that the contract would be long-term, that such appointments were in fact indefinite and that the details of tenure were to be worked out within the Public Service. Evidence was also led that the appointment being political, would stay in effect until the government changed. This was confirmed by other testimony relating to complaints about problems with Burge's service and the belief among those working with him that, given Burge's political affiliation with the government of the day, "Burge had sufficient political backing so that if a complaint was made, it would not be dealt with."

This case clearly exemplifies the disadvantages of politically imposed public services and of political interference in the Public Service. The lesson to be derived from this evidence is that where partisan affili-

---

[107] *Ibid.* at 146, para. 10.
[108] *Ibid.* at 153, para. 30.

ation carries greater weight than either the results of law-based tendering or ability to perform, dependability and quality of service, the clientele and the public at large are invariably short changed.

See also *S.E.I.U., Local 204 v. Ontario Realty Corp.* (1997), 35 O.R. (3d) 345 (Ont. Gen. Div.); *Political Interference in the Human Resources Development Canada (HRDC) Transitional Jobs Fund*, Report of the Auditor General of Canada, October 2000, Chapter 11; *Fiske v. Nova Scotia (Attorney General)*, 2001 NSSC 99 (N.S. S.C.); *Ottawa (City) v. Ottawa (Chief Building Official)* (2003), [2003] O.J. No. 1945 (Ont. S.C.J.) and *Beaudoin c. Banque de développement du Canada* (2004), 2004 CarswellQue 208 (Que. S.C.).

9.7 ISSUE: LEGALITY IN THE MANAGEMENT OF SOCIAL POLICY

§ 9.7.1[109]
Duggan v. Newfoundland
Newfoundland Supreme Court – Trial Division; March 22, 1993
(1993), 107 Nfld. & P.E.I.R. 33

Duggan operated a house for former psychiatric patients. When she tried to sell it, the Welfare Institutions Licensing and Inspection Authority (the Authority) refused to approve the transfer. In the same case, earlier, the Newfoundland Supreme Court analyzed the status of the Authority as a department of government and its capability of being sued. Here, the same court dealt with the legally enforceable nature of representations and undertakings made by the Authority in the course of public administration. This case is thus also linked to the issue of political promises made otherwise than in an election, discussed at § 6.7.B. This matter is made more interesting by the fact that Duggan was known to be a personal friend of the Minister to whose department the Authority reported and was believed, although erroneously, to have been dealt with favourably. The members of the Authority denied that this information influenced them.

---

[109] Cross-reference to § 9.2.1.

In its analysis, the court dealt with three pertinent elements of the case. First, it looked at whether the Crown was liable for negligent misrepresentation because Duggan had been told that a personally qualified purchaser would be licensed to purchase her boarding home. On the matter of negligent misrepresentation in general, this court reminded us of the fact that the Supreme Court of Canada was following the common law authority on this issue, *Hedley Byrne Co. Ltd. v. Heller & Partners Ltd.*[110] On the facts of this case, no such tort liability arose. Duggan did have a discussion with the then chair of the Authority. When the latter stated that there would be no problem in getting a purchaser licensed, if that purchaser complied with the applicable regulations, he "was merely indicating to Duggan what his approach to the matter would be."[111] The chair's statement was neither a promise as to the outcome, nor even that the other members of the Authority would take the same position.

The court also noted the issue of the Crown's liability for breach of an undertaking that it would not require existing homes to close because of more onerous standards brought in under new building code regulations. The Minister alleged he had engaged in that undertaking. Given the facts, the Minister's undertaking and the subsequently made regulations in effect constituted a contract between the government and Duggan. "Does the Crown then become liable when the Authority subsequently breaches this guarantee?"[112] The decision was affirmative. The undertaking had created a binding obligation which would have continued to be met if Duggan had not sold. The benefit should also have been applied to the purchaser.

It was on the foregoing basis, namely the failure to comply with new policies that the Crown was held liable. The reasoning which led the court to this conclusion also involved the court in touching summarily on the tort liability of public officials, in the sense of the evolving concept of a tort of maladministration by public officials which, in the *Comeau* case[113] was referred to as "erratic public administration."[114]

---

[110] [1964] A.C. 465.

[111] (1993), 107 Nfld. & P.E.I.R. 33, 336 A.P.R. 33 at 48.

[112] *Ibid.*

[113] *Comeau's Sea Foods v. Canada (Minister of Fisheries & Oceans)* (1997), 142 D.L.R. (4th) 193 (S.C.C.).

[114] This reference was made in the first level decision of the *Comeau* case, by the Federal Court – Trial Division (1992), 54 F.T.R. 20 (Fed. T.D.), reversed [1995] 2 F.C. 467

Beyond the basic implications of this case that in the management of social policy, the government must have regard for legality, the court ventured into a fascinating new area, investigating whether the Crown became liable also because of the negligence of its officers in not clearly establishing for new members of the Authority the policies to be applied in the regulation of welfare institutions. In other words, does the Crown have a duty to teach those it appoints how to observe the law in the administration of their public duties? The outcome of the case did not turn on this, but the court did hold that two successive chairs of the Authority were independently briefed concerning the relevant policy of the government. This leads us toward the two implicit obligations on government to publicize its policies and to train its decision makers properly in matters of law, policy and administration.

See also *Large v. Stratford (City) Police Department*, 14 C.C.E.L. (2d) 177 (S.C.C.), reconsideration refused (January 25, 1996), Doc. 2400 (S.C.C.); *Masse v. Ontario (Minister of Community & Social Services)* (1996), 134 D.L.R. (4th) 20 (Ont. Div. Ct.), leave to appeal refused (1996), [1996] O.J. No. 1526 (Ont. C.A.), leave to appeal refused (1996), [1996] S.C.C.A. No. 373 (S.C.C.); *Decock v. Alberta*, 2000 ABCA 122 (Alta. C.A.), leave to appeal allowed (2000), 266 N.R. 200 (note) (S.C.C.); *Chaouilli c. Québec (Procureur général)* (2002), [2002] J.Q. No. 759 (Que. C.A.), leave to appeal allowed (2003), 2003 CarswellQue 850 (S.C.C.) and (2002), [2002] J.Q. No. 763 (Que. C.A.), leave to appeal allowed (2003), 2003 CarswellQue 850 (S.C.C.); *Gosselin c. Québec (Procureur général)*, [2002] 4 S.C.R. 429 (S.C.C.); *Mitchell Estate v. Ontario* (2003), [2003] O.J. No. 3313 (Ont. Div. Ct.) and *Reference re Proposal for an Act Respecting Certain Aspects of Legal Capacity for Marriage for Civil Purposes*, Supreme Court of Canada, case in progress.

(Fed. C.A.), affirmed (1997), 142 D.L.R. (4th) 193 (S.C.C.), leave to appeal allowed (1995), 198 N.R. 80 (note) (S.C.C.).

9.8 ISSUE: LEGALITY IN THE MANAGEMENT OF ECONOMIC POLICY

9.8.A—MAJOR ECONOMIC ISSUES

See *Bedford Service Commission v. Nova Scotia (Attorney General)* (1976), 72 D.L.R. (3d) 639 (N.S. C.A.), reversed [1977] 2 S.C.R. 269 (S.C.C.).

§ 9.8.A.1[115]
P.S.A.C. v. Canada
Supreme Court of Canada; April 9, 1987
(1987), 38 D.L.R. (4th) 249

The task of the Supreme Court of Canada in this instance was to determine whether the legislation designed to enact the "6 and 5" anti-inflation mechanisms, the *Public Sector Compensation Restraint Act*,[116] was contrary to specified provisions of the *Charter* and the *Bill of Rights*. The greatest part of the court's commentary was done on the issue of the legislation, its goals and degree of success. In one instance, however, Chief Justice Dixon wrote about the role of law and the role of judicial analysis of economic issues.

In my opinion, courts must exercise considerable caution when confronted with difficult questions of economic policy. It is not our judicial role to assess the effectiveness or wisdom of various government strategies for solving pressing economic problems. The question how best to combat inflation has perplexed economists for several generations. It would be highly undesirable for the courts to attempt to pronounce on the relative importance of various suggested causes of inflation, such as the expansion of the money supply, fiscal deficits, foreign inflation, or the built-in inflationary expectations of individual economic actors. A high degree of deference ought properly to be accorded to the government's choice of strategy in combatting this complex problem.[117]

---

[115] Cross-reference to § 3.7.1.
[116] S.C. 1980-81-82-83, c. 122.
[117] (1987), 38 D.L.R. (4th) 249 at 261.

See also *Oversight of Financial Institutions by the Alberta Minister of Consumer and Corporate Affairs*, Public Inquiry by the Alberta Court of Queen's Bench, 1989.

---

§ 9.8.A.2
Hamilton-Wentworth (Regional Municipality) v.
Ontario (Ministry of Transportation)
Ontario Divisional Court; March 25, 1991
(1991), 2 O.R. (3d) 716[118]

This case examines whether, and to what extent, a court can order a government's policy and expenditure priorities in a field of economic policy such as transportation, where, by making a change in those priorities, the government is not acting in breach of the law. This example is particularly sensitive in the sense that it involves a reordering of priorities resulting from a change of government.

Planning for an expressway in the Red Hill Creek area of Hamilton, Ontario, first started in the early 1950's. In 1984, the Province gave a commitment to the Region of Hamilton-Wentworth to subsidize the project. There were various agreements and on the basis of these numerous co-operative contracts, the Region had acted in reliance on the commitments in incurring expenditures and undertaking works of its own. In April 1990, construction actually started. On September 6, 1990, the provincial general election produced an unexpected result and a New Democratic Party Government took over the province. On December 17 of that year the Hon. Mr. Philip, Minister of Transportation announced that provincial financial support would be withdrawn. In the Legislative Assembly, he stated,

> We made the decision. It was a cabinet decision. *It was a proposal that I brought to the cabinet that we not fund that portion of the expressway. I felt that it was based on what we have said in an election;* namely, our commitment to have a marriage between Environment and Transportation and between Environment and other ministries. We were consistent with what we said in the election and we are consistent with our strong commitment to protecting the environment.[119]

---

[118] Leave to appeal refused (1991), 4 Admin. L.R. (2d) 226 (Ont. C.A.).

[119] (1991), 2 O.R. (3d) 716 at 727d, leave to appeal refused (1991), 4 Admin. L.R. (2d) 226 (Ont. C.A.).

The Region thereupon applied for *certiorari* to set aside the Minister's decision. It relied on the legitimate expectations created by the earlier undertakings of the Province and it argued that environmental considerations were not a proper purpose in exercising powers under a statute dealing with transportation.[120] The province retorted that no decision had been made that was subject to review by the courts.

The court's key finding in administrative law terms was that the Minister's decision was not made pursuant to the legislation governing highway improvements. Rather, the decision had only the allocation of funds as to pith and substance and was made in reversal of an earlier government decision separate from the normal allocation for construction and maintenance of roads. Thus, the decision, although evidently based on environmental grounds, was not subject to judicial review.

> The evidence leads to the conclusion that the decision was one announced by the Minister after approval of the Cabinet and in substance constitutes an expression of the intention of the government not to provide any further funding for construction of the project. The government has the right to order its priorities and direct its fiscal resources towards those initiatives or programs which are most compatible with the policy conclusions guiding that particular government's action. This was simply a statement of funding policy and priorities and not the exercise of a statutory power of decision attracting judicial review.

> . . .

> It has been a constitutional principle of our parliamentary system for at least three centuries that such disbursement is within the authority of the legislature alone. The appropriation, allocation or disbursement of such funds by a court is offensive to principle.[121]

This *ratio* was supported by reference to English jurisprudence to the effect that once funds had been appropriated by Parliament, the Executive Branch was responsible before the House for the manner in which it was spent, but was not accountable to the courts.[122] The court took this to mean that a Minister of the Crown could not be required to make a particular expenditure.

---

[120] *Public Transportation and Highway Improvement Act*, R.S.O. 1980, c. 421.

[121] *Supra* note 119 at 731f-g, and 731 h-732 a.

[122] *R. v. Lords Commissioners of the Treasury* (1872), L.R. 7 Q.B. 387 (Eng. Q.B.).

In the instant case the Minister responsible on behalf of the Cabinet has clearly indicated Cabinet's priorities for spending. While the matter has not been put before the Legislative Assembly, I am prepared to accept as inevitable that the result of such a decision will be the non-allocation of funds. Were this court to use its authority to direct the government to appropriate funds for the completion of this project by way of declaration or any other order, it would be trenching on the exclusive control [of] the revenue of a sovereign Legislative Assembly in relation to fiscal matters.

. . .

The decision in issue represents an exercise of the government's right to allocate its funds as it sees proper. Such a conclusion is essential to the parliamentary system of democracy.[123]

In further concluding that the doctrine of legitimate expectations could not impose a positive duty and that estoppel and waiver could not operate at the level of government policy, the court accepted that the problem submitted to it was for political rather than judicial resolution.

---

§ 9.8.A.3
Monks v. Canada (Attorney General)
Federal Court of Canada – Trial Division; September 1, 1992
(1992), 58 F.T.R. 196

On June 18, 1992, some 80 out of 2560 salmon commercial fishery licensees applied for interlocutory injunctions to prevent the closure for that year's season of the commercial fishery and the opening of the recreational fishery. The application was denied as it raised no serious issue. The grounds for seeking the injunction were that the subject orders were made without regard for natural justice as prescribed by the *Charter* and the *Bill of Rights*. The court held first that the closure of the commercial fishery did not amount to cancellation of the holders' licences; its real purpose was the protection of the fishery. The most significant part of the ruling was that

....both variation orders were of a legislative nature not related to the rights or interests of any specific individual but were part of the general

---

[123] *Supra* note 119 at 732 e-g and 732 h.

public management of the salmon fishery. For this reason the requirements of procedural fairness do not apply.[124]

This means that where a decision is "managerial" in the public administration sense and in the way that expression is used in administrative law, the courts will not apply standards of procedural fairness. Notwithstanding that it was not bound to do so, the court noted
that extensive public consultation had taken place, infusing the orders
with the element of fairness the applicants were claiming was absent.
Finally, it was held that granting the injunction would be a threat to
a substantial public interest. In sum, the decision did not need to be
fairly made because it was a choice by management, but was made
that way nevertheless.

---

§ 9.8.A.4
Distribution Canada Inc. v. Minister of National Revenue
Federal Court of Appeal; January 8, 1993
[1993] 2 F.C. 26[125]

This case calls into question the validity of a policy, determined by a
Minister for reasons of economic efficiency, in respect of the manner
in which the Minister administers a statute, in circumstances where
the statute in question comprises a provision obligating the Minister
to enforce the Act. The question should be addressed in political law
terms. Where a statute creates a ministerial duty to enforce, does the
systemic and macroeconomic view of the duty, which implies some
non-enforcement at the micro level, constitute a conflict between the
law and the policy?

The statute in question is the *Customs Tariff*.[126] The applicant is a non-
profit association of grocery stores, a lobbying organization. Its contention is that while the *Customs Tariff* states that the Minister "shall"
enforce the legislation, a ministerial policy not to collect duty on
certain purchases by Canadians in the United States is contrary to the
Tariff and the cause of direct harm to the applicant. It therefore sought
mandamus in Federal Court – Trial Division to force the Minister to

---

124 (1992), 58 F.T.R. 196 at 197.
125 Leave to appeal refused (1993), 12 Admin. L.R. (2d) 280n (S.C.C.).
126 R.S.C. 1985, c. C-54.

enforce the Tariff in all cases. The Trial Division rejected the application and the Court of Appeal rejected the appeal.

The essence of the policy was described in the following manner in a letter by the Minister of National Revenue, Otto Jelinek:

> At the outset, I should explain that it is my department's policy that Customs inspectors not refer travellers for duty payment on their goods when the amount owing is $1.00 or less. In addition, higher amounts may be waived when other priorities dictate. In cases where the volume of traffic results in unacceptable delays, for example, or when interdiction activities are under way, it is recognized that Customs inspectors might waive assessments of $2.00, $3.00 and $4.00 or more, depending upon conditions at the time and their ability to efficiently process traffic. ... "Interdiction activities," as that term is used in the policy, have been explained as including: a) search and seizure of vehicles and goods, b) inspection and seizure of contraband, c) search and seizure of narcotics and illegal drugs, d) detection of illegal immigrants and the other persons who are attempting to enter Canada illegally, e) detection and apprehension of terrorists, f) detection and detention of pornography, all of which activities demand considerable staff and time to deal with and process. [A.B., at p. 13][127]

The court discussed the matter of the appellant's standing; that is of interest to that study only to the extent that in the course of dealing with that issue, the court said that even though the *Customs Tariff* is intended for the benefit of Canadian producers, not distributors, the appellant does raise a strong public interest. Closely tied to this point was the destination of the Minister's duty. The trial judge had found that the Minister owed the duty to enforce the legislation to the Crown, rather than to the public or to certain members of it. The Court of Appeal did not contradict this.

The focus of the appellant's claim was that the Minister was not doing everything he could to enforce the *Customs Tariff*; that the policy with respect to non-collection amounted to a policy of doing nothing, contrary to section 19 of the Tariff. The court's view on this was that:

> It must be said at the outset that one of the purposes of the *Customs Tariff* is the collection of revenue. If the respondent finds that the cost of

---

[127] [1993] 2 F.C. 26 at 31b-d and footnote 4 thereto, leave to appeal refused (1993), 12 Admin. L.R. (2d) 280n (S.C.C.).

collecting duty and taxes from persons returning to Canada exceeds the amount collected, the Minister ought to have discretion so as to appropriately tailor the means to the end. If the enforcement of the Act leads to a depletion of revenues, the respondent cannot be said to be acting in conformity with the Act. In such cases, no more can reasonably be expected of him.[128]

In addition to leaving the Minister with discretion which the court felt was required to determine how to enforce the Act, the court also felt that the assessment of the reasonableness of the policy considerations would involve it in the manner in which the law ought to be enforced, as opposed to the manner in which it was being enforced, and was therefore outside its domain.

The appellant's other pleading was phrased in terms of the maintenance of the integrity of the revenue collection system. Here also the court believed that the method of operation of the Department of National Revenue was best left to the Minister rather than for judicial supervision.

> The respondent is limited in his operations by such elements as budget constraints, limited facilities, personnel requirements, etc. ... To compel him to proceed the way the appellant is asking this Court to direct him would be to enter into an area where the respondent, by necessity, must be the only one to manoeuvre.
>
> . . .
>
> Only he who is charged with such public duty can determine how to utilize his resources.[129]

Thus, in this instance, the court found that the law and the policy were not in conflict.

---

[128] *Ibid.* at 40d.
[129] *Ibid.* at 40i-41a and 41c.

§ 9.8.A.5
Volker Stevin N.W.T. ('92) Ltd. v. Northwest Territories (Commissioner)
Northwest Territories Court of Appeal; February 11, 1994
[1994] 4 W.W.R. 236

Legality in the management of economic policy by government may, as in this case, involve the establishment and administration of a scheme based on policy alone, without a foundation in law. In this scenario, the most important determinations in terms of political law are whether, and to what extent, legal norms must be applied to a scheme so constructed.

Volker Stevin was a construction company incorporated in the Northwest Territories (NWT) and based in Yellowknife. On June 24, 1992, the Government of the Northwest Territories (GNWT) put in place a scheme for the purpose of enabling northern businesses to provide goods and services to the GNWT and to strengthen the northern economy through the reinvestment of corporate earnings in the North. Two instruments were at the core of the scheme: a Business Incentive Policy (BIP) setting out the plan and a Business Incentive Directive, being an order internal to the GNWT to have all relevant departments apply the BIP. It is important to note that neither instrument was based on the text of a statute or on any statutory authority. The policy set out a number of criteria against which businesses were to be measured in determining whether they could qualify as northern businesses. In addition to the criteria, another way of assessment was to see if applicants complied with the "spirit and intent" of the policy. Obtaining the status of northern business resulted in various advantages in terms of contracting. The entire scheme was administered by a Preference Advisory Committee and an appeal body, the Senior Management Preference Committee.

Volker Stevin obtained the designation of northern business in 1993. Later on, a challenge was lodged against the company's status on the ground of the lack of permanence of its operation in the North. The company replied, it asked for a hearing, but when its preferential status was revoked without one on April 23, 1993, it turned to the courts. It sought judicial review of the decision in order to be reinstated. At issue was the manner in which the complaint had been dealt with and whether judicial review was available only where a public authority exercised a statutory authority, or where it exercised authority based on other grounds as well, such as a stand-alone policy. A chambers judge refused the judicial review sought, on the following grounds.

> The adoption of the policy and its administration were not an exercise of statutory authority but were merely directives to civil servants in the carrying out the government's procurement of goods and services. Being commercial decisions, these were not subject to review.[130]

The NWT Court of Appeal reversed that ruling. It recognized the binding nature of the BIP, indicating that the policy and the structures set up to administer it were "part of the machinery of government decision-making."[131] In its view, even though the source of the instrument was policy-based rather than statutory in nature, the BIP was "recognized in the Government Contract Regulations and must be applied by all government departments in assessing tenders submitted to the Government."[132]

The court granted that purely commercial decisions relating to procurement were not subject to judicial review, but it distinguished this case on the basis that the decision as to Volker Stevin went beyond mere procurement, on several grounds.

First, the administration set up to manage the policy was exercising a public duty of general application vis-à-vis all those who wished to contract with the GNWT. Second, decisions relating to the BIP had an effect on the ability of businesses to compete and their ability to obtain financial assistance through government departments. This aspect brought the notions of public duty and procedural fairness into the relationship of the parties. Third, the public, that is the citizenry of the NWT, had motives of interest in ensuring that the BIP was properly and fairly administered, namely that the public policy funds be used in the public interest, and that the northern business sector actually be strengthened and developed.

Based on these public interest aspects of the BIP, the court held that even where the instrument in place was policy but not law, that is

---

[130] [1994] 4 W.W.R. 236 at 242, para. 18.
[131] *Ibid.* at 246, para. 28.
[132] *Ibid.*

even where the grounding of the instrument of governance involved was in prerogative powers, the public body administering the BIP had a duty of procedural fairness.

> On the whole, the nature of the decision, the relationship between the parties, and the impact on the appellant, lead to the conclusion that there was a general duty to act fairly on the part of the respondent in the circumstances of this case. This general duty was not modified by statute or agreement. The decision is subject to judicial review.[133]

---

§ 9.8.A.6
Inshore Fishermen's Bonafide Defense Fund Assn. v. Canada
Nova Scotia Court of Appeal; July 19, 1994
(1994), 132 N.S.R. (2d) 370

This case attempted to go to the heart of government management of the economy, through the law. While the action itself failed in the sense that the courts did not grant the remedy sought by the fishermen, albeit for technical reasons not related to the thrust of their action, it is worthy of note for the extremely pertinent substantive arguments it raised, which can actually be taken up by others.

The essence of the fishermen's argument is that from 1979 through 1993, the government was reckless in its future to assess the fish stocks in an adequate manner and that this amounted to negligent mismanagement. More specifically, they present the following points. Pursuant to the *Constitution Act, 1867*, section 91(12), the Government of Canada has constitutional responsibility for fisheries, including for proper and effective management and conservation of this resource. The Government of Canada has assumed exclusive responsibility for proper and effective management of the resource through legislation and policies promulgated by the Minister of Fisheries and Oceans. The Government of Canada has recklessly and/or negligently failed or refused to discharge its responsibilities for proper and effective management of the resource. The particulars of this alleged recklessness or negligence include:

- failure to adequately measure or assess stock and/or failure to make appropriate recommendations;

---

[133] *Ibid.* at 248, para. 36.

- failure to regulate and manage the resource in accordance with scientific advice;

- failure to enforce the laws and regulations, including effective monitoring and inspection;

- improper allocation of entitlements to harvest the resource; and

- encouragement of practices inconsistent with prudent conservation.

The fishermen allege that it is as a consequence of these actions that the resource has declined. They therefore seek declaratory judgment and damages.

In a further part of their action, the fishermen raise the issue of unlawful policy initiatives. The specifics they complain of in this regard relate to the issue of limited entry fishery licences to non-fishermen; the cancellation of certain inshore fishermen's licences, which they qualify as capricious, arbitrary, irrational and/or high-handed; the administrative imposition of licence sanctions; and the creation of an Atlantic Coast Fisheries Board, which they qualify as unlawful.[134]

The action initiated here raises two fundamental points which are central to the political law form of analysis. First, this case raises the question whether there exists a duty of "proper and effective management" which, if breached, is legally actionable and enforceable in a civil court; in other words is there a tort of improper or ineffective management and yet otherwise posed, is proper management legally definable and cognizable by the courts. Considering that the fishermen put this in terms of a constitutional and statutory duty, even if a tort of mismanagement does not exist, can a constitutional and/or statutory duty to manage in a particular manner, so as to produce results, be enforced? Second, the case raises the question of whether a legal quality can be attached to the substance of policy initiatives, beyond the matter of jurisdiction. These questions are to be addressed in a governmental environment in which management is conceived of more as an art than a science, in particular in an area with multiple nature-based variables such as fisheries. It is also useful to remember

---

[134] The entire statement of claim is worth reading. It is dated April 29, 1993, in file S.H. No. 93-1803.

that there is no general legal instrument which deals with the substantive and methodological aspects of management.

The Supreme Court of Nova Scotia looked first at the plaintiff's standing to bring the case forward as a matter of public interest. It determined that the plaintiff had no status to bring the action and that the case was not appropriate for a representative action, the Nova Scotia designation for "class action." Despite the fact that the fishermen's action was struck on this issue rather than on the actual merits, the judge did make the following limited pronouncements on the principles involved.

> Part I of the Statement of Claim does not raise any public issue. It is merely an action for damages alleging negligence in the management of the inshore fishery over a period of 14 years. It may very well be that some of the remaining issues are public issues as they involve administrative action and policy application. There is no issue, public or serious raised in Part III D of the Statement of Claim as the legislation creating the Fisheries Board and outlining its power has not been passed and may never be.[135]

The court also opined that this was more properly an action for damages, meaning that there was nothing "public" about the group of claims. Moreover, it held that while the group could be interested in the inshore fishery, it was not directly affected by the legislation or the administrative acts involved.

The Nova Scotia Court of Appeal dismissed an appeal from this judgment, also on the issue of standing. In addition to agreeing with the lower court ruling that the plaintiffs lacked standing, the appeal justices also indicated that,

> The appellant has more or less conceded this issue but argues that the court should nevertheless issue a declaratory judgment that the fishery has been mismanaged if that has been proven. In my opinion the complexity of this issue and the time it would take to try is such that limited judicial resources should not be consumed for the purpose of granting a declaratory judgment of this nature when nothing would be accomplished by the granting of such a judgment without a damage award.

---

[135] (1994), 130 N.S.R. (2d) 121, 367 A.P.R. 121 (N.S. S.C. [In Chambers]) at 126 [A.P.R.], para. 27, affirmed (1994), 132 N.S.R. (2d) 370 (N.S. C.A.).

Mr. Justice Nunn's discretion should not be interfered with on this issue.[136]

The court also looked at the matter of whether this case could be a representative action and concluded against it not only because the class could not be defined, but also because of what it perceived as insurmountable technical difficulties.

> Secondly, the scope of the claim in Part I is totally unmanageable particularly the matter of assessing damages. Each case would have to be looked at individually and we are talking of some 30,000 or 50,000 fishermen. The court would have to determine with respect to each claim whether the loss, if any, was attributable to mismanagement of the fishery or to other factors. How one would measure the particular loss of any fisherman would be a matter of looking at his particular circumstance. The respondent would not have the benefit of discovery, production of documents or the other normal processes available to a defendant with respect to these thousands of claims. Furthermore, there is the issue of costs; the respondent is being asked to respond to possible claims from 30,000 to 50,000 fishermen, none of whom are a party to the proceeding.[137]

On this occasion, no new law was made. The issue, however, was raised for another court to deal with in due course.

---

§ 9.8.A.7
Atlantic Coast Scallop Fishermen's Assn. v.
Canada (Minister of Fisheries & Ocean)
Federal Court of Canada – Trial Division; July 5, 1996
(1996), 116 F.T.R. 81

It is commonplace to state that in countries with both a democratic political-legal system and a capitalist economic system, there is extensive co-operation between the public and private sectors in the management of the economy. In these circumstances, it is necessary to address the question of the extent to which the members of a sector of economic activity can use legal principles to force government-industry consultation on the future evolution of that sector so as to

---

[136] *Ibid.* at 377 [A.P.R.], para. 26.
[137] *Ibid.* at 378 [A.P.R.], para. 32.

attempt to exercise greater policy influence on governmental decision-making.

Throughout the 1980's successive Ministers of Fisheries and Oceans
engaged in consultations with individuals and companies involved
in the scallop fishery in the Bay of Fundy. These discussions concentrated on the separation of the various fleets involved, inshore and
offshore, as well as the reduction in the number of fishing licences.
As a result of one meeting held on October 8, 1986, members of the
fishery believed they had an agreement with the Minister and the
department and in subsequent dealings, reference was repeatedly
made to the outcome of that meeting as an agreement. In fact, no
genuine agreement, but merely a press release existed in the sense of
an instrument of understanding. When, in subsequent years, the Minister did not act according to what the members of the fishery believed
was the agreement, they applied to have decisions of the Minister set
aside by judicial review and to obtain declaratory judgment, relying
on the doctrine of legitimate expectations.

The Federal Court denied the applications principally on the ground
that, pursuant to the *Fisheries Act*, decisions regarding policy and
plans were the ultimate responsibility of the Minister and that he had
a discretionary power to exercise. From a political law perspective,
the case can be taken to mean that the allegation of a policy agreement
on development of an economic sector cannot stand as a bar to the
exercise of a legal power by the Minister. The fishermen were unsuccessful in attempting to adduce evidence of an undertaking by the
Minister or by departmental officials that they would be consulted.

> ...in my opinion, the agreement here relied on by the applicants, an
> agreement allegedly made with the offshore group, even if it were es-
> tablished, would not in itself provide a basis for the relief here sought.

> Even if the applicants were correct and the agreement concluded in 1986
> clearly provided for future discussions, that agreement with the offshore
> representatives would not bind the Minister to undertake consultations,
> unless his approval of the agreed proposals were construed as, or he
> otherwise undertook, a promise to consult at a future date before ap-
> proving a plan for 1989 for the offshore industry.[138]

---

[138] (1996), 116 F.T.R. 81 at 98, paras. 60 and 61.

See also *Comeau's Sea Foods Ltd. v. Canada (Minister of Fisheries & Oceans)*, 142 D.L.R. (4th) 193 (S.C.C.); *Labrador Inuit Assn. v. Newfoundland (Minister of Environment & Labour)* (1997), 25 C.E.L.R. (N.S.) 232 (Nfld. C.A.); *Friends of the Oldman River Society v. Canada (Minister of Fisheries & Oceans)* (1998), 29 C.E.L.R. (N.S.) 315 (Fed. T.D.); *Keating v. Canada (Minister of Fisheries & Oceans)*, 2002 FCT 1174 (Fed. T.D.) and *Rowling v. Takaro Properties Ltd.* (in receivership),[139] [1988] 1 All E.R. 163.

9.8.B— GOVERNMENT CONTRACTING

See *Peter Kiewit Sons Co. v. Richmond (City)* (1992), 1 C.L.R. (2d) 5 (B.C. S.C.).

---

§ 9.8.B.1
Ward v. Clark
British Columbia Court of Appeal; December 19, 2001
2001 BCCA 724[140]

Governmental conduct of economic issues, including government contracting, must be conducted according to legal norms which emphasize equal and fair treatment of those persons who and entities which contract with a government. As a result of this decision, words of a derogatory nature, uttered by a political figure in the context of a contracting process and about one of the bidders, can amount to libel. From the political law perspective, it can also be unjustified political interference into a domain where law alone should prevail.

On February 6, 1996, in a scrum outside the legislative chamber in the British Columbia Legislature, Glen Clark, then Minister responsible for the B.C. Ferries Corporation, stated in response to Ward's criticism of the province's fast-ferry project that Ward was a "disgruntled bidder on this project who is constantly feeding misinformation on this issue."[141] Upon Ward's action for libel, the British Columbia Supreme Court held that the words were libellous in that they tended to lower the plaintiff in the estimation of others by im-

---

[139] International comparison.
[140] Leave to appeal refused (2002), 295 N.R. 199 (note) (S.C.C.).
[141] 2000 BCSC 979 (B.C. S.C.) at para. 8, reversed 2001 BCCA 724 (B.C. C.A.), leave to appeal refused (2002), 295 N.R. 199 (note) (S.C.C.).

puting dishonourable conduct to him. The court specifically added that Clark must bear the responsibility for the defamatory consequences flowing from the publication of these words in the *Vancouver Sun*. Clark's attempt at claiming qualified privilege was unsuccessful, because of the way the statement was made.

> I am persuaded that the occasion would have been within the qualified privilege defence had the defendant said words to the effect that he understood from his advisors that the criticisms levelled by Mr. Ward were untrue... However, that is not at all what the defendant said. He said something that was disproportionate, something that was much more than that, something that brought him outside the privilege, namely, that the plaintiff was a disgruntled bidder in the sense of having sought and failed to obtain business and, because of this, was constantly feeding misinformation on the fast-ferry project.[142]

A defence of justification was also rejected. Clark, who by this time was the former Premier, was ordered to pay $150,000. Clark appealed and Ward cross-appealed. The B.C. Civil Liberties Association applied to intervene on the issue of whether qualified privilege applied to the scrum in which Minister Clark took part. Madam Justice Newbury of the British Columbia Court of Appeal denied this application in Chambers on January 30, 2001, although she stated that "this case does have an obvious public dimension and will be of public interest."[143] The Association appealed to a full panel of the Court of Appeal, but the three justices concurred with the ruling of their colleague. Their reasoning, based on precedent, was that the focus of the appeal not be permitted to be changed. In order to protect the integrity of the contracting process, the public service advisors the court referred to, should use this judgment to urge their political masters to refrain from interfering in contracting through such unguarded and disproportionate comments.

On the merits, the British Columbia Court of Appeal reversed, basing itself on the finding that Clark had made his comments without malice and had voted in good faith. The fact that Clark's language may have been disproportionate did not destroy the qualified privilege which protected it. Interestingly, the court was focussed solely on the alleged libel. It held that the facts underlying the action were

---

[142] *Ibid.*, at para. 55.
[143] 2001 BCCA 56 (B.C. C.A. [In Chambers]) at para 2, affirmed 2001 BCCA 264 (B.C. C.A.).

irrelevant to its consideration. The Supreme Court of Canada rejected Ward's application for leave to appeal.

See also *Amertek Inc. v. Canadian Commercial Corp.*, (2003), 229 D.L.R. (4th) 419 (Ont. S.C.J.), additional reasons at (2003), 39 B.L.R. (3d) 287 (Ont. S.C.J.), additional reasons at (2003), [2003] O.J. No. 5246 (Ont. S.C.J.).

9.9 ISSUE: LEGALITY IN THE MANAGEMENT OF FOREIGN POLICY, DEFENCE AND SECURITY

9.9.A—NATIONAL BOUNDARIES AND THE NATIONAL INTEREST

See *Jose Pereira E Hijos S.A. v. Canada (Attorney General)*, 2002 FCA 470 (Fed. C.A.); *Schreiber v. Canada (Attorney General)*[144] (2000), [2000] O.J. No. 1813 (Ont. S.C.J.), additional reasons at (2000), 2000 CarswellOnt 2118 (Ont. S.C.J.), leave to appeal allowed (2000), 2000 CarswellOnt 4972 (Ont. Div. Ct.), affirmed (2001), 152 C.C.C. (3d) 205 (Ont. C.A.), leave to appeal allowed (2001), [2001] S.C.C.A. No. 201 (S.C.C.), affirmed [2002] S.C.J. No. 63 (S.C.C.), reversed (2001), 206 D.L.R. (4th) 577 (Ont. C.A.), leave to appeal refused (2002), 301 N.R. 392 (note) (S.C.C.) and *Controversy Involving the Purchase of CIPRO by the Minister of Health*, October – November, 2001.

---

§ 9.9.A.1[145]
British Columbia et al. v. United States et al.
U.S. District Court for the Western District of Washington
January 30, 1998
not reported; file no. C97 – 1464C

After 15 years of negotiations, Canada and the United States concluded, on January 28, 1985, a *Pacific Salmon Treaty* (PST). The purpose of the agreement was to create agreed fishing regimes, that is in effect to jointly manage migratory stocks of fish along the northern Pacific

---

[144] Cross-reference to § 10.9 and 11.10.
[145] International comparison.

seaboard of the two countries, from Oregon through to Alaska. The goal of the parties was to put "the equity principle" in place over time. On September 11, 1995, they entered into a further agreement on mediation procedure. Responding to pressure from its underemployed fishing capacity, British Columbia brought an action against the United States and the States of Washington and Alaska, with which it shares common borders. It sought declaratory and injunctive relief in order to force the United States Secretary of State, the Secretary of Commerce and other officials involved in implementing the PST to actually implement it, to negotiate in good faith and to agree to fishing limits. The defendants "move on the grounds that the Court lacks subject matter jurisdiction over the matter, that the matter is a political question, that the PST does not provide for a private right of action, that the suit is barred by sovereign immunity, and because plaintiffs lack standing to bring this action."[146]

The court granted the defendants' motion and dismissed British Columbia's application on the ground that that was a political question and that there was no justiciable controversy before it. Citing from recent Supreme Court consideration of the political question doctrine in another fisheries matter, the court felt that:

"The political question doctrine excludes from judicial review those controversies which revolve around policy choices and value determinations constitutionally committed for resolution to the halls of Congress or the confines of the Executive Branch." *Id*. at 2866. Courts simply do not have the expertise to evaluate these types of decisions. *Id*. Nonetheless, not every case that involves foreign policy is a political question. *Id*. It is plainly a court's duty to interpret legal issues, which include statutory construction. *Id*. Consequently, in *Japan Whaling*, the Court determined that it was the duty of the Court to determine "the nature and the scope of the duty imposed on the Secretary [of Commerce] by the Amendments, a decision which calls for applying no more than the traditional rules of statutory construction, and then applying this analysis to the particular set of facts presented below."[147]

---

[146] *British Columbia et al v. United States et al*, United States District Court for the Western District of Washington; order of January 30, 1998, p. 1.

[147] Order, p. 6, citing from *Japan Whaling Assoc. v. American Cetacean Society*, 106 S.Ct. 2860 (1986).

In addition, the court held that neither the PST nor the later agreement on mediation procedure were binding on either party. Rather, they were agreements to agree and thus not enforceable.

The structure of rules set out in the international treaty, the PST, and the consequential domestic legislation in the United States, the *Salmon Treaty Act*[148] and the *Maguson Act*[149] merely set up pathways for decision-making on the American side in implementing the treaty.

> Plaintiffs contend that the Court should apply the equity principle to determine that the individual defendants are in violation of the PST. However, that principle has not been fully defined, as is evidenced by the Memorandum of Understanding, and the 1995 Treaty. Because the governments had agreed that it would take some time before the equity principle could be given full effect, and indeed are still attempting to agree to its definition, the Executive Branch has necessarily kept the issue from judicial review. The Court cannot apply principles of statutory construction to a statue that has not been finished yet. To do so would impose a foreign policy decision on the executive branch. More importantly, even if the equity principle were fully defined, it still would not require the U.S. government to accept a recommendation by the Commission.
>
> . . .
>
> Consequently, the Executive Branch has seen fit not to accept certain recommendations properly put to it by the mechanisms created by the PST, as enacted by the Salmon Treaty Act. The Court has no basis for evaluating, or questioning those policy decisions, and those claims must be dismissed.[150]

Here, the actions which British Columbia sought to have the court force on executive officials were deemed to revolve around policy choices and value determinations which the court could not force. The *United States Constitution* attributed these choices to the Executive Branch, and the Judiciary did not feel it had the required subject matter expertise.

---

[148] Pub. L. No. 105-41, 99 Stat. 7 (1985), codified as 16 U.S.C.A. § § 3631-3644 (West 1985 and Supp. 1997).

[149] 16 U.S.C.A. § § 1801-1882 (West 1985 and Supp. 1997).

[150] Order, pp. 7 and 8.

This matter is currently under appeal, reflecting the intense need for the British Columbia authorities to deal as best it can with the drastic decrease in fish stocks. Canadian students of political law should also bear in mind that this type of case, by a province against a foreign government, is linked to federal provincial aspects of the dispute. In preparation for the present case, Premier Glen Clark has stated on several occasions that he was dissatisfied with Ottawa's representation of the province's fisheries interests.

On March 2, 2000, after Ujjal Dosanj replaced Glen Clark as Premier of British Columbia, the appeal was dropped.[151]

9.9.B—FOREIGN POLICY

See *Shell Canada Products Ltd. v. Vancouver (City)*, [1994] 1 S.C.R. 231 (S.C.C.).

---

§ 9.9.B.1[152]
Jones v. Canada (Attorney General)
British Columbia Supreme Court
filed December 8, 1997; case no. C976571, Vancouver Registry
discontinued
-and-
Jones v. Chrétien and Axworthy
British Columbia Supreme Court
filed September 29, 1998; case no. C984928, Vancouver Registry
-and-
Commission for Public Complaints Against the R.C.M.P.
Interim Report; July 31, 2001; file no. PC-6910-199801
-and-
Commission for Public Complaints Against the R.C.M.P.
Final Report; March 25, 2002; file no. PC-6910-199801

This note is an analysis of a collection of related cases and proceedings which arose out of the actions of the Government of Canada in relation to its hosting, in November 1997 in Vancouver of a summit of the heads of state and government of the Asia-Pacific Economic Co-

---

[151] At the time of writing, Dosanj was the Federal Minister of Health. He was elected to Parliament on June 28, 2004.
[152] Cross-reference to § 3.14.2.

operation (APEC). Those actions and their consequences have raised the most fundamental and the most interesting questions of political law about the prevalence of legality in Canada's management of its foreign policy. At the time of writing, the APEC incidents had raised a number of issues which straddled the domestic law-foreign policy divide. These matters have aroused much controversy and have produced many partial results along the way, as well as leaving numerous unresolved problems. The fundamental underlying point, namely whether Canadian authorities acted within the bounds of legality, has not yet been resolved.

The APEC summit was scheduled for and took place on November 25, 1997. The obvious interest of the Government of Canada was to secure the attendance of as many heads of state and government as possible. One of these, President Suharto of Indonesia, presented a problem in that his officials required guarantees in advance that he would not be embarrassed by demonstrators protesting his abuse of his own population's human rights. This demand on the part of the Indonesian authorities gave rise to the central dilemma of political law which arose out of the events surrounding the conference. On the margins of the APEC summit, Canadian protestors were not allowed by the R.C.M.P. to retain in place the banners they had put up, in favour of democracy, free speech and human rights. Moreover, several individuals involved in the organization of the demonstrators were preventively detained by the police and, in the most notorious incident, when some demonstrators would not or could not clear a roadway with speed sufficient for the R.C.M.P., they and the television crews filming them were sprayed with pepper, and shoved aside with what seemed like excessive force.

The principal questions which arose from these events are whether the Prime Minister of Canada made promises or undertakings to a foreign head of state regarding the restraint of Canadian demonstrators, notwithstanding the rights of free speech, association, and possibly other rights guaranteed by the *Canadian Charter of Rights and Freedoms*, whether the Prime Minister and other public authorities of Canada acted in relation to the demonstrators at APEC in the execution of such promises or undertakings, and whether, in order to convert the promises to action, the Prime Minister and/or his political staff gave orders to the R.C.M.P. which were of questionable legality.[153]

The first legal recourse sought by a Canadian individual affected by APEC was the case of *Jones v. Canada (Attorney General)*, filed as early as December 8, 1997, in the British Columbia Supreme Court. Ironically, Jones was a law student at the University of British Columbia, the venue of the summit, and a specialist in civil liberties. He was forced on several occasions to remove signs he had put up, favouring democracy. He was arrested and detained for some 36 hours, and never charged. In response, Jones' action claimed damages on the following grounds:

> The conduct of all of the Defendants, and each of them, constitute a wanton, flagrant, intentional, or alternatively, reckless disregard for Jones' constitutional and legally protected rights including:
>
> (a) Jones' constitutional right to peacefully and publicly express his thoughts, views, opinions and beliefs as guaranteed by s. 2(b) of the *Canadian Charter of Rights and Freedoms*;
>
> (b) Jones' constitutional right to engage in peaceful assembly as guaranteed by s. 2(c) of the *Canadian Charter of Rights and Freedoms*;
>
> (c) Jones' constitutional right to liberty and security of the person as guaranteed by s. 7 of the *Canadian Charter of Rights and Freedoms*;
>
> (d) Jones' constitutional right not to be arbitrarily detained or imprisoned as guaranteed by s. 9 of the *Canadian Charter of Rights and Freedoms*;
>
> (e) Jones' common law rights to be protected from assault, battery, false and wrongful arrest and false and wrongful imprisonment.
>
> Further the RCMP's, May's, Thompsette's and Dingwall's blatant and callous disregard for the Plaintiff's constitutionally protected rights and freedoms was malicious, vindictive and designed to punish Jones. It was also designed to and had the effect of preventing him and deterring others from exercising their constitutionally protected rights and freedoms to engage in a peaceful protest of the APEC proceedings; as such

---

[153] An interesting account and analysis of the events of APEC are provided in Pue, W. Wesley, *Pepper in Our Eyes: The APEC Affair*, University of British Columbia Press, Vancouver, 2000.

the conduct of the RCMP and these Defendants is deserving of punitive damages.

Jones filed the foregoing case as a way of bringing the APEC matter into the legal arena and in order to ensure that governmental authorities would be forced to address his arguments. When the first RCMP Public Complaints Commission panel was constituted, he suspended that proceeding. Later on, when this first panel disintegrated, Jones initiated a further action.[154]

This second action, initiated on September 29, 1998, was commonly referred to in the media as a class action suit. Here, the defendants included the Prime Minister and the Minister of Foreign Affairs, a number of the senior police officers in charge of APEC security, as well as others. Notably, the Attorneys General of Canada and British Columbia were also among the defendants. This action alleged that the defendants had engaged in a conspiracy to infringe the constitutional rights of Jones. It went on to allege that the political authorities had directed the police authorities involved to act in the manner in which they had. Most importantly, the case went on to argue that these actions constituted misfeasance in public office.

MISFEASANCE IN PUBLIC OFFICE

Each of the First Set of Defendants acting alone or together abused their public office and powers by acting with malice toward the Plaintiff and the Class in directing, causing or contributing to the actions of the R.C.M.P. and persons unknown as set out in subparagraph 15(c), with an intention to injure the Plaintiff and the Class and did in fact cause injury to the Plaintiff and the Class in that the Plaintiff and the Class were denied their rights and freedoms under sections 2(b), 2(c) and 2(d) of the *Charter* without justification under section 1 of the *Charter*, and in that the Plaintiff and the Class suffered physical injury to their persons and property.

In directing, causing or contributing to the actions of the R.C.M.P. and persons unknown set out in subparagraph 15(c) above, each of the First Set of Defendants abused their public office and powers in that they knowingly acted without legal authority, causing foreseeable harm to the Plaintiff and the Class in that the Plaintiff and the Class were denied their rights and freedoms under sections 2(a), 2(b) and 2(d) of the *Charter* without justification under section 1 of the *Charter*, and in that the Plain-

---

[154] Statement of claim, paras. 23 and 24.

tiff and the Class suffered physical injury to their persons and property.[155]

In this case also, Jones claimed damages, as well as *Charter* remedies.

The Prime Minister's initial reaction to the APEC incident was dis-
missive. However, under the glare of persistent media attention and
the effect of the lawsuits, he found it impossible to ignore the matter
completely. Thus, in September 1998, a panel of the R.C.M.P. Public
Complaints Commission was mandated with conducting an investigation into the conduct of the police.

The first few months of the investigation were taken up with procedural and substantive legal problems, all of which detracted from the
main aim of the inquiry. On November 11, 1998, the Solicitor General,
the minister who was the political master of the R.C.M.P., was forced
to resign from Cabinet for having discussed the case in a public setting
and within earshot of an Opposition Member of Parliament. Allegations of bias then resulted in the resignation of the Chairman of the
Panel on December 4, 1998. The matter of public funding of the protestors' legal fees was litigated separately and even the reporting of
the APEC proceedings became the subject of public controversy between the Prime Minister's Office and the Canadian Broadcasting
Corporation, with legal overtones.

In the second year of the inquiry, once it came under the sole chair-
manship of a retired British Columbia judge, Mr. Justice Ted Hughes,
the main legal point became the one on which the inquiry needed to
focus, namely whether the actions of the police were justified or not
and whether they had been ordered to behave in the manner in which
they did, all thus for the benefit of the Prime Minister's successful
management of foreign policy.

A fascinating sideshow in this process was the political and legal
struggle aimed at determining whether the Prime Minister himself
would have to testify before the inquiry. For months, a debate raged
between lawyers who urged the Commission to subpoena the Prime
Minister to testify and those who contended that the Commission did
not have the power to do so. Prime Minister Chrétien himself partic-

---

[155] Writ of summons, paras. 21 and 22.

ipated in this controversy with a statement made in Parliament during question period.

Mr. Preston Manning (Leader of the Opposition, Ref.): Mr. Speaker, the Prime Minister has repeatedly said he was not personally involved in the security arrangements for the APEC conference. Now there is concrete evidence before the RCMP complaints inquiry quoting RCMP Superintendent Wayne May as saying "The Prime Minister of our country is directly involved." Yesterday the Prime Minister's human shield, the Deputy Prime Minister, was completely unable to answer this contradiction.

Why is the Prime Minister's story in direct contradiction to evidence presented to the RCMP complaints inquiry?

Right Hon. Jean Chrétien (Prime Minister, Lib.): Mr. Speaker, the inquiry has been going on for more than a year. There have been thousands of pages of documents and a lot of witnesses. The inquiry is ongoing. Let the inquiry do its job. It is as simple as that.

. . .

Mr. Preston Manning (Leader of the Opposition, Ref.): The Prime Minister says that he has all of this faith in the RCMP complaints inquiry. If he is so sure of his story, will he repeat it under oath in front of that inquiry?

Right Hon. Jean Chrétien (Prime Minister, Lib.): Mr. Speaker, when a member of parliament, when a minister and when a prime minister is in the House of Commons talking to the people of Canada, all the electorate of Canada, it is as good as having the Bible here.

. . .

I repeat in front of the nation and in front of God, if you want, because my name is Chrétien and I have no problem with that, that I never discussed security with anybody with the RCMP.[156]

In the end, on February 25, 2000, the Commission found that the "Indonesian issue" and the "Law school fence " issue did not justify its issuing a summons for the Prime Minister to testify. It did, how-

---

[156] Hansard, October 26, 1999, p. 693.

ever, "invite" the Prime Minister to testify. A few days, later, Mr. Chrétien declined to attend.

For more than a year thereafter, the Commission continued its gathering of evidence and its deliberations. Commissioner Hughes handed down his much awaited Interim Report on July 31, 2001; the document was made public on August 6. This Report addressed no less than 52 complaints which had been filed with the Commission. It was, according to the interpretation of most observers, a remarkably thoroughly reasoned and balanced analysis of, and conclusion for, the events which took place. This Report is massive and much more of it would merit reproduction than can actually be included here.

In a nutshell, however, the Report acknowledges the importance, for the Government of Canada, of attendance by APEC heads of State and government and it justifies many of Prime Minister Chrétien's efforts in that direction.

> Firstly, the efforts by Prime Minister Chrétien, Mr. Axworthy, Mr. Bartelman and the two ambassadors to ally President Suharto's security concerns wer proper, acceptable and to be expected of the host of a significant international event such as the APEC conference. As explained by Ambassador Edwards, it was particularly important to Canada that President Suharto attend the APEC conference. It is unrealistic to expect that, as the host of the APEC conference, the Prime Minister's Office would take no interest whatsoever in the security concerns of a foreign leader, particularly where failing to provide appropriate assurances might result in a boycott, to the detriment of the conference in general and Canada's economic aspirations in particular.

> . . .

> Without question, the Canadian government was eager to have leaders of all 18 APEC economies, including President Suharto, attend the conference. To that end, far more time and effort went into encouraging the attendance of President Suharto than was directed to any other leader. That is not objectionable. In my view, the federal government acted appropriately in all its contacts and approaches to the many Indonesian officials with whom they dealt on this issue. The Canadian government did not signal to the RCMP, either overtly or subtly, that they ought to perform as they did in order to curtail demonstrations and stamp out visible dissent.[157]

---

[157] Commission Interim Report, p. 52, section 9.3 and p. 80, section 9.7.

In response to these political imperatives, the Canadian authorities took a number of "muscled initiatives." Justice Hughes separates these clearly into ones that were justified, with some others that were not.

30.3 Police Conduct that was Justified and Necessary

There were, of course, instances of public confrontation between police and protesters where police actions were justified and necessary to preserve or restore the peace.

Examples include:

- the pepper spraying and arrests at the time of the collapse of the fence at the noon rally;
- the pepper spraying and arrest of Mr. Malmo-Levine at the flagpole climbing incident;
- the arrest of Mr. Oppenheimer; and
- the second arrest of Mr. Singh.

The police had a duty and responsibility to initiate the latter arrest given the contemptuous disregard for the rule of law by Mr. Singh, who took refuge behind that same rule of law when he complained to this Commission, successfully as it turns out, that his initial arrest earlier the same day had been inappropriate.

30.4 Improper Federal Government Involvement

The federal government's role in the removal of the tenters from the grounds of the Museum of Anthropology on November 22 was one of two instances of its improper involvement in the RCMP security operation. I am satisfied that it was because of the government's intervention that the tenters were removed that evening. Were it not for that involvement, the contrary view of Site Commander Thompsett would have prevailed. As it happened, his view did not carry the day because of the acquiescence of other RCMP personnel, principally Supt. May, who had succumbed to government influence and intrusion in an area where such influence and intrusion were inappropriate.

The other instance of improper and inappropriate federal government involvement in the RCMP's provision of security services was with respect to the size of the demonstration area adjacent to the law school. In that case, the government's efforts did not prevail due to the intervention of others, including Site Commander Thompsett, on behalf of the protesters. Had those intervenors not prevailed, the security challenges the RCMP faced on November 25 may well have been increased.[158]

Going beyond determining what the authorities did right or wrong, the Commissioner squarely addressed the allegations of improper political interference. He noted that there was such interference. He singled out the Prime Minister's Director of Operations for blame in this regard. On this point, the Interim Report does leave some possibility of interpretation, as it may not sufficiently address the source or motivation for the actions of the Director of Operations. Given, however, that the Prime Minister declined Commissioner Hughes' invitation to testify, it seems likely that the Report could not be otherwise worded.

The most significant part of the Commissioner's analysis was that of the balance between the independence and the accountability of the R.C.M.P.

10.3 Independence vs. Accountability

In my view, there are compelling public policy reasons not to extend the concept of police independence beyond that set out in *Campbell*. [R. v. Campbell, [1999] 1 S.C.R. 565] The issue is one of balance. It is clearly unacceptable for the federal government to have the authority to direct the RCMP's law enforcement activities, telling it who to investigate, arrest and prosecute, whether for partisan or other purposes. At the same time, it is equally unacceptable for the RCMP to be completely independent and unaccountable, to become a law onto themselves.

This is precisely the position taken by the McDonald Commission in its report on the activities of the RCMP vis-à-vis the Quebec separatist movement in the 1970s: *Commission of Inquiry Concerning Certain Activities of the Royal Canadian Mounted Police* (Ottawa: Canadian Government Printing Centre, 1981).

. . .

10.4 Some Principles

I have carefully considered certain propositions set out in the reply submissions of Commission Counsel after their review of the McDonald

---

[158] *Ibid.*, pp. 437-438, Closing Observations, paras. 30.3 and 30.4.

Report and the decision in *Campbell*. With that assistance, I have formulated the following principles which I believe describe the current relationship between the federal government and the RCMP:

- When the RCMP are performing law enforcement functions (investigation, arrest and prosecution) they are entirely independent of the federal government and answerable only to the law.
- When the RCMP are performing their other functions, they are not entirely independent but are accountable to the federal government through the Solicitor General of Canada or such other branch of government as Parliament may authorize.
- In all situations, the RCMP are accountable to the law and the courts. Even when performing functions that are subject to government direction, officers are required by the *RCMP Act* to respect and uphold the law at all times.
- The RCMP are solely responsible for weighing security requirements against the *Charter* rights of citizens. Their conduct will violate the *Charter* if they give inadequate weight to *Charter* rights. The fact that they may have been following the directions of political masters will be no defence if they fail to do that.
- An RCMP member acts inappropriately if he or she submits to government direction that is contrary to law. Not even the Solicitor General may direct the RCMP to unjustifiably infringe *Charter* rights, as such directions would be unlawful.[159]

Given these principles as directive of the role of the police, the Report found that the *Charter* rights of protesters had, in some respects, been infringed in order to enable the APEC Conference to be a political and diplomatic success. Significantly, the police requirement that protesters remain more than 100 meters from a venue of the conference was held to be unconstitutional as inconsistent with sections 2 (b) and 11(e) of the *Charter*, as well as inappropriate. This was also true of the police requirement that protesters within such perimeters agree to depart. Moreover, a further police requirement that protesters refrain from demonstrating was held to constitute a "blanket prohibition on political protest" and as such, contrary to sections 2 (b), (c) and (d) and 11(e) of the *Charter* and not appropriate.

The approach of the Commissioner in dealing with these matter was to weigh the balance between what he called compelling State interests and application of the *Charter*, so as to arrive at a standard of conduct that would ensure avoidance of the unnecessary erosion of

---

[159] *Ibid.*, pp. 83-84, section 10.3 and p. 86, section 10.4.

rights. In the view of the students pepper-sprayed and detained in connection with the APEC Conference, the weakness of the Report was that it did not directly link the police requirements with instructions which they had all along presumed to have come from the political level.

From the perspective of students of political law, a highlight of the Report was its recommendation that police action be undertaken on the basis of legal advice. Nothing could be more true in respect of the conduct of governance in accordance with legality and in respect of the principles of democracy.

15.9   Undertakings Should be Prepared with Legal Advice

Often there will be "compelling state interest" in taking steps to prevent those who have shown a willingness to break the law from being allowed close to Internationally Protected Persons, as they might act unlawfully again. The difficulty facing the police when they control the release of an accused is determining the proper nature and extent of any restrictions they may choose to impose. This is a complex task, as it requires the police to assess the factors listed in *Collins*; namely, the "nature of the offence, the accused's criminal record or other information tending the violence or anti-social behaviour of a dangerous nature on his behalf, and all the surrounding circumstances." They must also ensure that restrictions further a "compelling state interest," are "precisely drawn without unnecessary erosion of rights" and are not imposed on a "speculative concern of danger."

As a general rule, for example, a person charged with obstructing a police officer in the course of civil disobedience during a passive political protest should not be burdened by the same restrictions as might be placed on a protester who commits a deliberate and serious assault. Clearly, the protester who commits such an assault presents a greater risk to Internationally Protected Persons than does a passive protester and, therefore, stricter conditions may well be justified. From a practical point of view, however, can the RCMP be expected, on the spot, to tailor each undertaking document to the degree of risk presented by each accused person and account for all the surrounding circumstances without unnecessarily eroding *Charter* rights, all without the benefit of prior legal advice?

In the present case, the reality is that, given the magnitude of the anticipated protests, the RCMP quite rightly expected that people would be arrested and would be released on conditions. Therefore, they attempted to draw-up a "catch-all" document, which prisoners were ultimately, and indiscriminately, required to sign. It was not vetted in advance by Crown Counsel and it was never intended to be used by an Officer in Charge.

If a police officer prepares an undertaking document before the fact, without knowledge of the specific offence in question and the background of the accused, and without the benefit of legal advice, it will be a rare case indeed where the undertaking will properly account for the considerations referred to in *Collins*. Therefore, my view is that the RCMP should, wherever possible, ensure that their undertaking documents have been prepared, or at least vetted, by Crown Counsel or a Department of Justice lawyer. Even this measure will not guarantee that the restrictions will suit the specific circumstances of each prisoner. Unfortunately, that practice was not followed in this case and, as a result, accused persons were required to sign a document which unreasonably restricted their freedoms.[160]

The Report contained a large number of other recommendations aimed at clarifying and improving the work of the police and the democratic treatment of protesters.

The Government of Canada's reaction to the Interim report was a complete stonewalling. Its lawyer rejected the view that the Report constituted criticism of the Government, emphasizing the absence of a finding of wrongdoing by the Prime Minister. The opposition parties' call for the PM to testify on the Report before a Parliamentary committee was dismissed. On September 7, 2001, the R.C.M.P. issued its own, much more forthcoming reaction. The force's Commissioner Zaccardelli admitted that the R.C.M.P. had made mistakes, and indicated that they were learning from those mistakes. He also referred to improvements in policy and equipment.

Zaccardelli said he agreed with Hughes' recommendations that the RCMP develop a national policy on dealing with protests and that the force ensure opportunities for peaceful protesters to see and be seen.[161]

Jones, the original plaintiff, has indicated that if the response of the panel is not sufficiently determinative of the issues, he may revive one of his legal actions, most likely the original one. Thus, it is possible

---

[160] *Ibid.*, pp. 171-172, section 15.9.
[161] "RCMP commissioner accepts most recommendations in APEC report," *Ottawa Citizen*, September 7, 2001.

that the political law effects of the 1997 APEC summit may continue to be felt for several years.

Whatever the consequences of the eventual Final Report of the R.C.M.P. Public Complaints Commission and of Jones' cases, there are others to be watched, arising out of the treatment meted out by the police to students on the lawn of Green College at the University of British Columbia.

This incident has provided a rich bounty of decisions involving political rights.

See also *Singh v. Canada (Attorney General)*,[162] [2000] 3 F.C. 185 (Fed. C.A.), leave to appeal refused (2000), 259 N.R. 400 (note) (S.C.C.); *Doern v. British Columbia (Police Complaint Commissioner)*, 203 D.L.R. (4th) 295 (B.C. C.A.), leave to appeal allowed (2002), [2001] S.C.C.A. No. 504 (S.C.C.), set aside/quashed (2003), 2003 CarswellBC 1068 (S.C.C.); *Commission for Public Complaints Against the R.C.M.P.*, Chair's Interim Report on Events at the Summit of the Americas, Québec, April 20-22, 2001, October 29, 2003; *Chair's Final Report After Commissioner's Notice*, February 18, 2004; *R. v. Secretary of State for Foreign and Commonwealth Affairs*,[163] ex parte Rees-Mogg, [1994] 2 Q.B. 552.

---

§ 9.9.B.2[164]
Flatow v. Islamic Republic of Iran
United States District Court, District of Columbia; March 12, 1998
999 F. Supp.2d (D.D.C., 1998)

This case is a study of the role of law and of legal proceedings in the intricate machinations of American foreign policy. Alisa Flatow was an American student in Israel who, on April 5, 1995, was killed in a terrorist attack perpetrated by a group called Palestinian Islamic Jihad, which drew its finances from the Government of Iran. The United States law applicable to attempts to obtain compensation for Flatow's wrongful death was the *Foreign Sovereign Immunities Act*, a statute which barred individuals from suing foreign governments in U.S. courts. In 1996, Congress enacted the Anti-terrorism and Effec-

---

[162] Cross-reference to § 1.13.B.
[163] International comparison.
[164] International comparison.

tive Death Penalty, which created an exception to allow such suits in respect of "terrorist" states, among them Iran. Flatow's father sued Iran and won judgment for $247,513,200, including punitive damages of M$225, which represented three times the Iranian government's budget for terrorism. This is singular in itself.

The even more interesting political law issue related to domestic American proceedings regarding Flatow's enforcement of the judgment. In suing, being awarded judgment and enforcing it, Flatow is acting pursuant to legislation. When, however, the enforcement process began through the attachment of Iranian properties in the United States, the Justice Department and the Department of State, acting as parts of the Executive Branch, took counter steps to frustrate Flatow's lawful attempts. The judgment was perceived as interference with American foreign policy based on reason of State. The Justice Department argued motions to have the judgments allowing attachments quashed. "The basis of these motions is overtly political."[165] In order to help Flatow, in 1997 Congress clarified and enhanced the exemption it had voted, in the 1996 Act amending the *Foreign Sovereign Immunities Act*.

The legal press in the United States qualified the difference between the Executive and Legislative Branches in regard to this matter as a "political firestorm," with the diplomatic attempts to normalize American relations with Iran competing against the right to compensation for political crimes. We may be allowed to presume that neither side is seeking altruistic results, but what makes this domestic power struggle over foreign policy worthy of attention is that the tools of this struggle are statutes and the judgments which result from their use.[166]

See also *Price v. Socialist People's Lybian Arab Jamahiriya*, 110 F. Supp.2d 10 (D.D.C., 2000); *Elahi v. Islamic Republic of Iran*, 124 F. Supp.2d 97 (D.D.C., 2000).

---

[165] "D.C. Sales Team Up Against Terrorism," Michael M. Bowden, *Lawyers Weekly USA*, January 11, 1999, 99 L.W. U.S.A. 35.

[166] In order to more fully understand the context of this case, it is worth the reader's while to also see *Price v. Socialist People's Lybian Arab Jamahirija*, 110 F. Supp.2d 10 (D.D.C., 2000) and *Elahi v. Islamic Republic of Iran*, 124 F. Supp.2d 97 (D.D.C., 2000).

9.9.C—NATIONAL DEFENCE, PEACE-KEEPING AND WAR

---

§ 9.9.C.1

Hammond et al. v. The Queen
Federal Court of Canada – Trial Division; April 22, 1991
file T-210-91; not reported

On August 2, 1990, Iraq invaded Kuwait. This occurred in the midst of the collapse of the Communist domination of Central Europe, while the United States was emerging as the single remaining world power. The US saw its vital interests being threatened by the invasion and was determined to reserve its result. It generated a great deal of diplomatic activity through the United Nations and forged a military/political alliance comprising many countries, including Canada.

As early as September 15, 1990, the Governor in Council issued an Order authorizing the Canadian Forces to enter into active service.[167] This instrument was made pursuant to paragraph 31(1)(b) of the *National Defence Act* and it referred to several of the Resolutions adopted earlier by the Security Council of the United Nations. The subject provision of the *National Defence Act* reads as follows:

Active Service

Placing forces on active service

31. (1) The Governor in Council may place the Canadian Forces or any component, unit or other element therefor or any officer or non-commissioned member thereof on active service anywhere in or beyond Canada at any time when it appears advisable to do so.

. . .

(b) in consequence of any action undertaken by Canada under the United Nations Charter, the North Atlantic Treaty or any other similar instrument for collective defence that may be entered into by Canada.[168]

---

[167] SI/90-111, (1990) 124 Can. Gaz. II, 4199.
[168] *National Defence Act*, R.S.C. 1985, c. N-5, s. 3(1)(b), with amendments.

As the crisis engendered by the invasion progressed, on November 29, 1990, the UN Security Council voted Resolution 678, which became the key instrument in legitimizing and legalizing the possible eventual use of force against Iraq. This resolution essentially gave the Iraqis six weeks to withdraw from Kuwait, until January 14, 1991, and authorized States which were said to be co-operating with Kuwait to use all means necessary to have the Security Council's earlier Resolutions respected and to have peace and international security re-established in the year.

By January 16, 1991, as Iraq was still occupying Kuwait, an aerial bombardment campaign began against Iraq. It seemed that the engagement of land forces would inevitably follow. While the prospect of Canadian participation in military action against Iraq met with the approval of most of Canadian public opinion, that sentiment was not unanimous. On January 30, 1991, three law professors of the University of Ottawa filed a statement of claim in Federal Court, trying to prevent the entry of Canada into the continuing hostilities. Their line of argumentation was to the effect that Security Council Resolution 678 was contrary to section 27 of the *Charter of the United Nations*, that the military operations undertaken pursuant to that Resolution were therefore not being undertaken under the aegis of the *Charter of the UN* and consequently that Canadian participation in these operations was contrary to paragraph 31(1)(b) of the *National Defence Act*.

The key to the entire argument was the allegation of incompatibility between the subject resolution and section 24 of the *Charter*. The plaintiffs contended that the *Charter* gave permanent members of the Security Council a veto. Resolution 678, they indicated, purported to have the Security Council authorize all Member States to define individually, which means were necessary to re-establish peace and security in the area. This, they contended, offered the Member States too wide a latitude to take any measure they deemed appropriate to defeat Iraq, including occupation or the use of nuclear weapons. With this latitude, the Security Council would not be able to determine its bounds, or to set the limit of the application of Resolution 678. The overall effect was that the Security Council was abdicating its principal responsibility for the maintenance of international peace and security to Member States and the system of collective security for the common interest, intended by the *Charter*, was thus being allowed to break down.

To remedy these perceived ills, the plaintiffs sought declarations to the effect that the participation of Canada in the operations undertaken by virtue of Resolution 678 was not authorized under paragraph 31(1)(b) of the *National Defence Act* and was therefore illegal, and that Canadian forces be required to abstain from participation in these operations.

It is noteworthy that Hammond's statement of claim also focused extensively on the plaintiffs' standing to bring this action. They alleged that in case of conscription, they were all, as individuals between the ages of 25 and 30 years, subject to enrolment in the Canadian Forces. They also stated that as the starting of such an action by someone on active duty in the Gulf could constitute an offence under the *National Defence Act* and was therefore not a viable option, there was no other reasonable and effective way to test the legality of the operation but for them to start this action.

The entire Gulf War, including the portion of it which consisted of the engagement of land forces, concluded before the court had an opportunity to deal with the issue. The matter having become moot, the application was first abandoned, then dismissed on April 22, 1991.

While the Canadian contribution to the joint effort in resisting Iraqi aggression was commensurate to this country's level of power, a realistic assessment is that Canada was but one of the many players in the Gulf War, light in comparison to the leader of the alliance, the United States. In that country too, however, this military operation was the subject of litigation, although from the rather different constitutional and legal perspective of the doctrine of separation of powers inherent in the American system of political law and from the American practice of compartmentalization of the branches of government.

In the case of *Dellums v. Bush*,[169] a Member of the House of Representatives applied on November 19, 1990, for a preliminary injunction against the President. He reasoned that a military action was imminent and that it would be unlawful without a declaration of war which was within the purview of Congress alone to make.

---

[169] 752 F. Supp. 1141 (1990) United States District Court, District of Columbia.

The principal defence of the U.S. Department of Justice, on behalf of the President, was what in American law is entitled "the political question" and what Canadian jurisprudence describes as justiciability. The argument for the President's authority to conduct the operation was that the war-declaring power reserved by the *United States Constitution* for Congress should not be considered in isolation, but rather together with other war and military-related provisions, and that the harmonization of these various provisions is a political, rather than a legal question. This argument failed.

The link between the *Hammond* and *Dellums* cases can be drawn from the pleadings on the issue of standing. The American court accepted the Congressman's argument that he had standing and in the course of ruling on this issue, it stated as follows:

> With close to 400,000 United States troops stationed in Saudi Arabia, with all troop rotation and leave provisions suspended, and with the President having acted vigorously on his own as well as through the Secretary of State to obtain from the United Nations Security Council a resolution authorizing the use of all available means to remove Iraqi forces from Kuwait, including the use of force, it is disingenuous for the Department to characterize plaintiffs' applications as to the imminence of the threat of offensive military action for standing purposes as "remote and conjectural" for standing purposes. For these reasons, the Court concludes that the plaintiffs have adequately alleged a threat of injury in fact necessary to support standing.[170]

From the perspective of the *Hammond* case, what is significant here is that the judgment of the United States District Court seemed ready to accept as valid the same United Nations Security Council Resolution which Hammond and the other plaintiffs were later on to contest. While the *Dellums* judgment would, of course, not have the force of precedent before the Federal Court in Canada, if it had been used by the Crown as part of its defence, Hammond could have faced an additional burden in proving his case.

The ruling in *Dellums* was made on the third issue perceived by the court, that of ripeness. The plaintiff's motion for injunction was de-

---

[170] Quote from *Dellums v. Bush*, 752 F. Supp. 1141 (1990) drawn from *Constitutional Law: Structure and Rights in Our Federal System*, Third Edition, Braveman, Daan, William C. Banks and Rodney A. Smolla, Matthew Bender, New York, 1996, p. 150.

nied on the ground that the situation forecast did not, or at least not yet, prevail.[171]

See also *Liebmann v. Canada (Minister of National Defence)* (1993), [1994] 2 F.C. 3 (Fed. T.D.) and (1996), 110 F.T.R. 284 (Fed. T.D.) and (1998), [1999] 1 F.C. 20 (Fed. T.D.), reversed (2001), 203 D.L.R. (4th) 642 (Fed. C.A.) and *Vancouver Island Peace Society v. Canada* (1993), [1994] 1 F.C. 102 (Fed. T.D.), affirmed (1995), 16 C.E.L.R. (N.S.) 24 (Fed. C.A.), leave to appeal refused (1995), [1995] S.C.C.A. No. 103 (S.C.C.).

---

§ 9.9.C.2
Canada (Attorney General) v. British Columbia
British Columbia Supreme Court
filed August 14, 1997; file C974423; not completed

The web of co-operation between Canada and the United States includes many domains of governmental activity. While the ties that bind the military establishments of the two countries are very close, in other fields such as fisheries, there is not only co-operation but also competition. Instances in which the co-operative and competitive aspects of the international relationship reflect divergent national and sectoral interests sometimes lead to litigation which is so closely akin to politics as to be indistinguishable from it.

On September 5, 1989, British Columbia granted Canada a licence to enter the seabed at Nanoose Bay, on the eastern short of Vancouver Island. The Canadian Forces established there a Maritime Experimental Test Range and, by agreement between the Governments of Canada and the United States, the US Navy used the site for testing torpedoes.

In the mid-1990's, the Government of British Columbia became increasingly dissatisfied with the failure to convince the United States or the states of Washington or Alaska of its position with respect to the *Pacific Salmon Treaty*. Thus, on May 23, 1997, Premier Glen Clark wrote to Prime Minister Chrétien, purporting to cancel the province's licence originally granted to the federal authorities. On August 21,

---

[171] There was another American case relating to the Gulf War: *Ange v. Bush*, 752 F. Supp. 509 (1990), in which a soldier claimed that the President exceeded his authority in deploying the plaintiff to the Persian Gulf theatre.

1997, the British Columbia Minister of the Environment sent a further similar notice to the Minister of National Defence. The cancellation was, and was clearly expressed to be, a tactic of linkage of the naval testing issue to the fisheries negotiation then going on with the United States. This was, on British Columbia's part, a diplomatic tactic rather than pure litigation; in essence, therefore this case could just as easily figure in that part of this study which deals with the use of litigation for political motives.

The position of British Columbia was expressed as follows by Premier Clark:

> The failure of the United States to meet its obligations under the Pacific Salmon Treaty is a clear failure on the part of the U.S. government to honour the good neighbour policy which we have pursued to this point. It is no longer tolerable to have the U.S. government enjoy the benefits of the use of Nanoose Bay, at the same time as it denies Canada the benefits and protection owing to Canadian salmon under the Pacific Salmon Treaty. Action must be taken to protect British Columbia salmon stocks and the jobs and communities that depend on the resources, and to pressure the United States to recognize Canada's rights to Canadian fish.
>
> Cancelling the agreement will demonstrate that there are consequences when the U.S. ignores its international obligations, including treaty commitments to Canada. We are determined to do whatever is required to protect salmon stocks on the West Coast and we fully expect you will take this opportunity to send a clear message to the United States. In this regard, it is vital that the federal government take strong, direct action to show clear resolve on this issue. I am therefore urging you to take immediate steps to cause the Pacific Salmon Treaty to be fully implemented.[172]

The Attorney General of Canada took the position that in acting as it had, the province had not been in good faith and that it was interfering with domains of exclusive federal jurisdiction, including fisheries, foreign affairs and national defence.

> The Notice of Cancellation was issued of an implied term of the Licence that the parties would exercise their contractual rights and perform their

---

[172] Facsimile transmission from the Premier of British Columbia to the Prime Minister of Canada, dated May 23, 1997, reproduced in the statement of claim of the Attorney General of Canada, August 14, 1997, at para. 13.

contractual obligations reasonably and in good faith, and with due regard to the respective governmental duties, responsibilities and commitments of the parties, which term precluded cancellation of the Licence
for the sole or primary purpose of frustrating the exercise and discharge
by the Plaintiff of its powers, duties and responsibilities in relation to
matters falling within the Plaintiff's exclusive constitutional jurisdiction;
and no party in the position of the Defendant, acting reasonably and in
good faith, could have concluded that cancellation of the Licence would
serve the public interest, having regard to all the circumstances of the
case.[173]

Canada sought to have the declaration of cancellation of the licence
declared invalid. Interestingly, the federal authorities also took a
broad view of the case and of its prospective impacts. Among the
heads of damage, the Attorney General cited the potential loss of
appropriations of approximately US $100 million by the United States
Congress to provide Canada with financial assistance in its efforts to
conduct environmental clean-ups of former American military sites
in Canada. In this case, both parties engaged in linkage.

In its defence and counterclaim, the province took the rather drastic
position that Canada's occupation of the Nanoose Bay seabed
amounted to trespass.

This case never went to trial. The federal-provincial leasing arrangement expired on September 4, 1999. Shortly thereafter, the federal
authorities completed the expropriation of the site for purposes of
national defence and testing of naval equipment resumed.

The proper view of this case is that it formed part of a broader context
of British Columbia politics. Not only did the province and the federal
authorities use legal means to attempt to assert their political and
diplomatic positions, but so did citizens' groups. On the one hand, a
group of workers employed at the Test Range attempted by court
action to block British Columbia's cancellation of the licence. On the
other hand, an alliance of church groups, anti-nuclear activists and
human rights groups sought to obtain an injunction to prevent the
federal expropriation, arguing the absence of federal constitutional
authority to expropriate provincial lands for military purposes in
peacetime.

---

[173] Statement of claim, para. 15(b) and (c).

LEGALITY IN GOVERNMENTAL MANAGEMENT / 905

See also *Human Rights Institute of Canada v. Goldie* (1999), [2000] 1 F.C. 475 (Fed. T.D.); *Nanoose Conversion Campaign v. Canada (Minister of Environment)* (2000), 257 N.R. 287 (Fed. C.A.); *Society Promoting Environmental Conservation v. Canada (Attorney General)*, 2002 FCT 236 (Fed. T.D.), reversed [2003] F.C.J. No. 861 (Fed. C.A.); *Aleksic v. Canada (Attorney General)* (2002), 215 D.L.R. (4th) 720 (Ont. Div. Ct.); *Blanco v. R.*, 2003 FCT 263 (Fed. T.D.); *Turp c. Canada*, 2003 FCT 301 (Fed. T.D.); *Massachussetts v. Laird*,[174] 451 F.2d 26 (1st Cir., 1971) and *Conyers v. Reagan*, 765 F.2d 1124 (C.A. D.C., 1985).

---

§ 9.9.C.3
Legality of the Use of Force (Yugoslavia v. Canada)
International Court of Justice; June 2, 1999
I.C.J. Reports 1999[175]

In his masterpiece entitled *On War*,[176] the Prussian military theorist Karl von Clausewitz referred to war as the continuation of politics by other means. The judicial aspect of the Yugoslav campaign in Kosovo in the Spring of 1999 brings to mind the phrase that this case can be characterized as the continuation of war by legal means. Yugoslavia's action against Canada in the International Court of Justice is in fact but one of ten parallel cases which the authorities of Belgrade instituted against a number of NATO countries.[177]

As a response to Yugoslavia's practice of "ethnic cleansing" in Kosovo and in reaction to its refusal to sign onto a political resolution worked out at Rambouillet, on March 24, 1999, the military forces of NATO started bombing Yugoslavia. On April 29, the Government of Yugoslavia initiated proceedings against Canada before the International Court of Justice. The principal element of its claim was that

---

[174] International comparison.
[175] See http://www.icj.cji-org/icjwww/idocket/yca/iycaorders//yca_iorder_19990602.htm
[176] First published in 1832.
[177] The other defendants were Belgium, France, Germany, Italy, the Netherlands, Portugal, Spain, the United Kingdom and the United States.

...by taking part in the bombing of the territory of the Federal Republic of Yugoslavia, Canada has acted against the Federal Republic of Yugoslavia in breach of its obligations not to use force against another State;[178]

At the same time, Yugoslavia made ancillary Request for the Indication of Provisional Measures. In the practice of the International Court of Justice, this was the equivalent of seeking an injunction, so as to achieve an immediate cessation of the bombing.

The Court made its order on the provisional measures request on June 2, 1999, rejecting it. It also reserved the subsequent procedure for further decision, meaning that it could eventually hear the substantive issue raised by Yugoslavia, on the merits.

From the perspective of political law, there is some interest in the reasons given by the court for the order. The element of greatest significance is the position expressed before the court by Canada. The lens through which this is best analyzed is to see how the legal argumentation of the Canadian defence accommodated the country's national interest.

Canada did not want the court to rule on the request for provisional measures. It therefore raised the legal argument that the court lacked jurisdiction to hear the request, thereby hoping to keep the matter of the bombing in the political/military sphere. Two reasons for this line of argumentation are plausible. Had Canada not used an argument designed to avoid a ruling, or had Canada been unsuccessful in using that argumentation, the court could have issued an order to cease the use of force and as a staunch supporter of the court, Canada may have had no choice but to stop bombing. Moreover, Canada had, as a member of NATO and a participant in the alliance's military campaign, to keep its military participation in the alliance workable and therefore unobstructed by legal constraints arising out of Yugoslavia's application.

In realistic contemplation of the importance of the national and alliance-based interest, whether the defence in law argued by Canada

---

[178] Application instituting proceedings, filed in the Registry of the Court on April 25, 1999, http://www.icj-cij.org.

was based on genuine legal considerations, or if they had an underlying political motivation, the consequence of the judgment was that the matter was retained in the political/military sphere. Whatever its ultimate, deep, foundation, the legal argument produced the desired results in law and in politics.

The International Court of Justice indicated that it needed *prima facie* jurisdiction to deal with interim measures. Because of the success of the Canadian argument that Yugoslavia in its current form was not a member of the United Nations and that its acceptance of the compulsory jurisdiction of the court was a "transparent nullity," the court concluded that it lacked that *prima facie* jurisdiction. It also accepted the Canadian reasoning that the bombing could not be qualified as genocide, because the element of intention was absent; the concept of genocide could not be equated with the use of force nor even with aggression. Finally, the court deemed it "necessary to emphasize that all parties appearing before it must act in conformity with their obligations under the *United Nations Charter* and other rules of international law, including humanitarian law."[179] There can be no clearer indication of the court's perception that Yugoslavia itself was in clear breach of international law by its political practice of ethnic cleansing.

See also *Campbell v. Clinton*, 203 F.3d 19 (D.C. Cir., 2000); *Marchiori v. Environmental Agency*, [2002] EWCA Civ. 03, February 25, 2002; *Campaign for Nuclear Disarmament v. Prime Minister*, [2002] EWHC 2712 Admin, December 5, 2002 and [2002] EWHC 2759 (Q.B.); *Report of the Hutton Inquiry*; *Doe et al. v. Bush and Rumsfeld*, 323 F.3d 133 (CA 1, March 13, 2003) and 322 F.3d 109 (CA 1; March 18, 2003) and *Horgan v. Taoiseach*, [2003 No. 3739P], (Transcript), April 28, 2003.

9.9.D—PUBLIC SECURITY

See *Robinson v. Canada (Attorney General)* (August 8, 2001), Doc. 01-CV-215525SR (Ont. S.C.J.); *Ruby v. Canada (Solicitor General)*, [2002] 4 S.C.R. 3 (S.C.C.); *Application Under s. 83.28 of the Criminal Code, Re*, 2003 BCSC 1172 (B.C. S.C.), affirmed 2004 CarswellBC 1378 (S.C.C.); *Letelier v. Republic of Chile*,[180] 488 F. Supp. 665 (1980); *Prosecution of*

---

[179] Order, para. 18.
[180] International comparison.

José Barrionuevo,[181] Supreme Court of Spain, July 29, 1998 and *U.S. Treatment of Al-Qaeda Prisoners,*[182] Report of the American Bar Association Task Force; January 4, 2002.

9.10 ISSUE: LEGALITY IN THE MANAGEMENT OF INTERNATIONAL TRADE

9.10.A —BILATERAL AND MULTILATERAL TRADE

§ 9.10.A.1
Fogal v. Canada
Federal Court of Canada – Trial Division; January 6, 1999
(1999), 161 F.T.R. 121[183]

This is a typical case of the current application of political laws, in which a citizen and a lobby group seek to achieve a public policy and political goal by means of litigation, rather than political action. The subject matter of the instant case is the Multilateral Agreement on Investments (MAI), a trade instrument which Canada seriously contemplated adhering to and which certain nationalists fiercely opposed. We may be allowed to conjecture that the reasons for resort to legal and judicial means included the applicants' greater faith in the binding nature of legal remedies, their inability to succeed by political means, as well as their positive belief that this was the best course of action.

The MAI negotiations were initiated in 1995 by the OECD, the Organization for Economic Co-operation and Development. There is some question as to whether the WTO, the World Trade Organization, has also become involved. Fogal and the Defence of Canadian Liberty Committee sought by judicial review to challenge the jurisdiction of

---

[181] International comparison.
[182] International comparison.
[183] Also Federal Court of Canada – Trial Division; January 21, 1999 (1999), 30 C.P.C. (4th) 13, affirmed (2000), 184 F.T.R. 160 (note) (Fed. C.A.), leave to appeal refused (2001), 273 N.R. 400 (note) (S.C.C.) and Federal Court of Canada – Trial Division; April 28, 1999 (1999), 167 F.T.R. 266, affirmed (2000), 184 F.T.R. 160 (note) (Fed. C.A.), leave to appeal refused (2001), 273 N.R. 400 (note) (S.C.C.).

the federal Crown to become a party to an eventual MAI treaty. They also sought declarations and injunction to prevent signature, ratification and/or implementation of the MAI by Canada. They argue that it is *ultra vires* of the *Constitution Act, 1867* and *1982* and, most significantly from the perspective of this study, that the "treaty would not be in the best interests of Canadian citizens."[184]

In a first ruling on January 6, 1999, the Crown successfully applied to file a supplementary affidavit. Part of the evidence it wanted to submit would indicate that the MAI discussions had ceased as of October 23, 1998, so far as Canada is concerned. On this basis, the Crown argued that the court should not proceed to judicial review on the mistaken assumption that Canada is continuing negotiations.

On April 28, 1999, the Crown moved for an order to dismiss Fogal's application on the ground that it had become moot. The court agreed. It recited the history of the MAI negotiations from inception to conclusion. It acknowledged that Canadian policy favoured a revival of the MAI talks within the WTO, but it concluded that no such talks were on at the time of judgment. The applicants disputed that the talks had ended.

> I agreed that there are some legal issues in the case before me which are not moot, such as the present scope of crown prerogative and whether the executive can use the crown prerogative without parliamentary sanction as a basis to enter treaties under the *Constitution, 1982*. The issue of whether the respondents have or had the jurisdiction to negotiate a treaty similar to MAI under a constitutional framework is not moot. However the subject matter of the originating notice of application is moot.[185]

As to whether the court should entertain an interlocutory motion to dismiss, it held that it had jurisdiction, where the action had no possibility of success. On the question of whether there was a live controversy, the court felt there was none, given the published words of the Minister of International Trade to the effect that the negotiations had stopped. The court also looked at whether, if the application is moot, it should hear the application for judicial review anyway. There is a vigorous adversarial relationship. Judicial economy directed the

---

[184] Reasons for Order, (1999), 161 F.T.R. 121 (Fed. T.D.), para. 2.
[185] Reasons for Order, (1999), 167 F.T.R. 266 (Fed. T.D.), para. 9, affirmed (2000), 184 F.T.R. 160 (note) (Fed. C.A.), leave to appeal refused (2001), 273 N.R. 400 (note) (S.C.C.).

court's attention to the potential for new MAI-related legal issues in the future, but none at present. "There is no reason to believe that a treaty will be negotiated, concluded and signed before the applicants have an opportunity to bring the matter before the Court."[186]

Given the applicants' allegations, the court characterized their proceeding as a search for a legal opinion, as a private reference. The future form and content of a MAI treaty could only be speculated about. The court therefore declined its discretion to decide on the merits and it dismissed the application for judicial review.

Canada (Attorney General) v. S.D. Myers Inc., 2001 FCT 317 (Fed. T.D.), affirmed 2002 FCA 39 (Fed. C.A.), leave to appeal refused (2002), 302 N.R. 398 (note) (S.C.C.); *Canada (Attorney General) v. S.D. Myers Inc.*, 2002 FCA 39 (Fed. C.A.), leave to appeal refused (2002), 302 N.R. 398 (note) (S.C.C.); *Public Citizen v. United States Trade Representative*,[187] 782 F. Supp. 139 (D.D.C., 1992) and 970 F.2d 916 (D.C. Cir., 1992) and 822 F. Supp. 21 (D.D.C., 1993) and 5 F.3d 549 (D.C. Cir., 1993); *American Coalition for Competitive Trade v. Clinton*,[188] 128 F.3d 761 (D.C. Cir., 1997) and *Made in the USA Foundation and United Steelworkers of America v. United States of America*,[189] 56 F. Supp.2d 1226 (N.D. Ala., 1999) and 242 F.3d 1300 (11th Cir., 2001).

9.10.B —INTERNATIONAL ASSISTANCE AND ASSISTED EXPORT

See *Sierra Club of Canada v. Canada (Minister of Finance)*, 211 D.L.R. (4th) 193 (S.C.C.).

---

[186] Reasons for Order of McKeown, J, (1999), 167 F.T.R. 266 (Fed. T.D.), para. 18, affirmed (2000), 184 F.T.R. 160 (note) (Fed. C.A.), leave to appeal refused (2001), 273 N.R. 400 (note) (S.C.C.).
[187] International comparison.
[188] International comparison.
[189] International comparison.

9.11 ISSUE: LEGALITY IN THE MANAGEMENT OF THE FINANCING OF GOVERNMENT

See *Prior v. R.*, 88 D.T.C. 6207 (Fed. T.D.), affirmed 89 D.T.C. 5503 (Fed. C.A.), leave to appeal refused (1990), 44 C.R.R. 110 (note) (S.C.C.), reconsideration refused (September 20, 1990), Doc. 21709 (S.C.C.) and *Finlay v. Canada (Minister of Finance)* (1986), [1986] 2 S.C.R. 607 (S.C.C.).

---

§ 9.11.1
Winterhaven Stables Ltd. v. Canada (Attorney General)
Alberta Court of Appeal; October 17, 1988
(1988), 53 D.L.R. (4th) 413[190]

The management of the financing of government should be seen both as an ancillary aspect of the management of substantive domains of government activity, such as social policy, and as a self-standing topic of management. From both perspectives, the assurance of legality in this area is important and necessary. In fact, there can be no public sector activity without public finances conducted according to the ordered precepts of law. This entire topic takes on an added dimension, moreover, within a federal system such as that of Canada.

Against this background, the purpose of Winterhaven Stables' action was to obtain declaratory judgment to the effect that the *Income Tax Act*[191] was *ultra vires*, that is, beyond the legislative capacity of the Parliament of Canada, because some of the funds raised were transferred to the provinces pursuant to shared-cost programmes. Such programmes were prevalent notably in the portfolio of health, welfare and post-secondary education.

On the surface, the claim of the applicant, that Parliament could not spend in those domains which are within provincial legislative jurisdiction, was based on the dichotomy of sections 91 and 92 of the *Constitution Act, 1867*, the provisions which set out federal and pro-

---

[190] Leave to appeal refused (1989), 95 A.R. 236 (note) (S.C.C.).
[191] R.S.C. 1952, c. 148, as amended by S.C. 1970-71-72, c. 63.

vincial legislative jurisdiction. The court addressed the basis of the claim as follows:

> The gist of the appellants' argument on this aspect is that Canada, through the power of the purse, can invade areas of jurisdiction reserved to the provinces and coerce the provinces to adopt schemes and programmes devised by Canada. The appellant argues that in consequence, Canada through its funding, effectually usurps jurisdiction reserved exclusively to the provinces by s. 92 of the *Constitution Act, 1867*.[192]

The Attorney General dealt with this line of argumentation.

> The respondent replies that while the statutes may ultimately have an effect on matters within exclusive provincial competence they are not legislation in relation to it. They are statutes authorizing the allocation of federal funds to assist the provinces in providing services.[193]

In reality, this case can only be understood in the political context, which was the struggle relating to the concept of "national standards" pertaining to shared-cost programs, flowing from the national debate over the *Meech Lake Accord*, raging at the time this case was being litigated. Proponents of the *Accord* twisted it as a legal tool based on the reality of Canadian politics, enabling the exercise of diversity and flexibility among provincial health, welfare and education systems, all of which would be united only by the undefined legal formula or political slogan of national standards. Those countering the *Accord* saw in national standards too great a dilution of federal fiscal and financial power without the commensurate guarantees of minimal uniformity and portability of social benefit regimes.

> The Act, as a whole, contemplates Canada providing financial assistance to the provinces. The argument is, essentially, that Parliament cannot attach "strings" to that assistance in the form of national standards. A province could, presumably, take federal assistance and use it unwisely, arbitrarily, irrationally, so long as it was used for a provincial purpose. To hold that conditions cannot be imposed would be an invitation to discontinue federal assistance to any region or province, destroying an important feature of Canadian federalism.[194]

---

[192] (1988), 53 D.L.R. (4th) 413 at 432, leave to appeal refused (1989), 95 A.R. 236 (note) (S.C.C.).
[193] *Ibid.* at 433.
[194] *Ibid.*

In this context, the exact motive of the applicant in litigating is open to some interpretation. Was it simply a politically motivated attack on the tax system by a taxpayer wanting to avoid its share? Was it an expression of ideological views on provincial power aimed at reducing the perceived centralization of the federation and the contributory tax burden of the wealthier provinces? Could it have been directly related to the *Meech Lake* debate by a party favouring greater federalism and wanting to point out the weakness of national standards as an undefined concept; or more likely hoping to use the judgment to do away even with this limited unifying factor?

Whatever the motive, the Alberta Court of Appeal, as the Queen's Bench had before it, refuted Winterhaven Stables' arguments completely. It held that shared-cost programmes had been recognized in the Constitutional reform of 1982.[195] Significantly, even though the *Meech Lake Accord* was at that time no more than a political deal with an insufficient number of ratifications to give it force of law, the court cited it as sustaining the Canadian system of shared-cost programmes. Beyond these texts, the court found backing for the validity of the *Income Tax Act* and its web of shared-cost programmes based on national standards in convention.

> With the background of a long-standing convention whereby Canada and the provinces have negotiated for the establishment of national shared-cost projects, can it be suggested that the "spending statutes" here in issue are *ultra vires*? In my view, such an argument cannot be sustained.[196]

In a ruling of April 13, 1989,[197] the Supreme Court of Canada refused the applicants' motion for leave to appeal. Later still, the *Meech Lake Accord* failed but shared cost programmes are still very much in use in Canada and the concept of national standards is still in use and being debated.

See also *Reference re Canada Assistance Plan (Canada)*, [1991] 2 S.C.R. 525 (S.C.C.) and *Reference re Excise Tax Act*, [1992] 2 S.C.R. 445 (S.C.C.).

---

[195] *Constitution Act, 1982*, s. 36(1).
[196] *Supra* note 192 at 434.
[197] (1989), 95 A.R. 236 (note) (S.C.C.).

---

§ 9.11.2
Reid (Next Friend of) v. Canada
Federal Court of Canada – Trial Division; January 27, 1994
(1994), 73 F.T.R. 290

Reid's action, taken in the context of the campaign for the constitutional referendum of October 26, 1992, dealt in combination with voting rights for infants and the plaintiffs' opposition to deficit financing of government. "In fact, the entire amended statement of claim rests on the assertion that the obligation of Her Majesty to not deficit finance to the detriment of the minority should be enforceable in the courts."[198]

The action consisted of a) an application for declaration that unless there is an emergency, in order for a government to spend more than its revenues, it needs the people's approval by referendum; b) an application for injunction to bar Canada from budgeting greater expenditures than anticipated receipts in any one year, and from spending in excess of revenues, except by judicial authorization; and c) an application for damages in an amount to enable the plaintiffs to pay the portion of their future taxes which is referable to the deficit incurred prior to the time of their enfranchisement. The motives stated for this action were allegations that there existed a constitutional convention preventing borrowing, that deficit financing was discriminatory and the plaintiffs' search for relief from economic oppression. In the course of proceedings, the ground of constitution convention was amended to be stated as a fundamental principle of constitutional law enforceable by the courts.

Although the court accepted the Crown's motion to have the case struck as being frivolous and vexatious, it did engage in some substantive analysis of the claims. It referred first to the appropriate heads of legislative power under section 91 of the *Constitution Act, 1867*: 1A, Public Debt and Property; 3, Money and Taxation; and 4, the Public Credit.

> On the contrary, it is plain and obvious that Parliament has the constitutional power to borrow money in order to finance government operations. The deficit financing measures that are the subject of the Plaintiff's

---

[198] (1994), 73 F.T.R. 290 at 294.

claim are the product of the constitutional actions of a freely and democratically elected Parliament.

. . .

It follows that deficit financing measures are clearly within the powers
of Parliament and Parliament's decision to resort to borrowing in order
to finance government expenditures cannot give rise to a cause of action.

It is also apparent that the judicial supervision of federal budgeting
contemplated by paragraph 7 of the prayer for relief would contravene
... the *Constitution Act, 1867*...[199]

With respect to the claim that deficit financing benefited adults to the
detriment of minors and was therefore a violation of section 15, the
equality provision of the *Charter*, the court used the label of "pure
speculation." The plaintiffs had also tied the issue of voting rights to
deficit financing by attempting a *Charter* section 3 argument that
under the existing franchise, children were not represented and thus
their interests in government financing would be ignored. The court
called this a bold assertion, not to be taken as true and devoid of
evidentiary foundation.

See also *Croteau v. Canada* (1995), 92 F.T.R. 288 (Fed. T.D.) and *Harris
v. R.* (1998), [1999] 2 F.C. 392 (Fed. T.D.), affirmed [2000] F.C.J. No.
729 (Fed. C.A.), leave to appeal refused (2000), 264 N.R. 391 (S.C.C.).

---

§ 9.11.3
Longley v. Minister of National Revenue
British Columbia Court of Appeal; April 10, 2000
2000 BCCA 241[200]

The subject matter of this case from the political law perspective is
the analysis of the political contribution tax credit written into the
Income Tax Act in 1973.[201] Within the overall scheme of the *Income Tax
Act*, designed to raise revenues for the management of the State, is

---

[199] *Ibid.* at 295-296.
[200] Leave to appeal refused (2000), 264 N.R. 398 (note) (S.C.C.).
[201] *An Act to Amend the Canada Elections Act*, Bill C-203, 1st Session, 29th Parliament,
1st Reading, June 22, 1973; enacted as S.C. 1974, c. 51.

the use of the political contribution tax credit[202] for a purpose that could be interpreted as private and non-political a corruption of the legislation?

In 1984, Longley devised a scheme entitled the Contributor's Choice Concept (CCC). Using section 127 of the *Income Tax Act*, contributors could make political contributions to registered political parties, in accordance with the necessary methodology of the *Canada Elections Act*. The particularity of this kind of contribution was that the donor could direct the manner in which the funds were to be spent. Longley's contributions, as those of the very few other individuals who made similar contributions, were directed to be spent for their own benefits. In particular, the contributions were directed to be spent on bursaries for studies, with the alleged political purpose being support for post-secondary education. At first, Longley used this scheme on behalf of the Rhinoceros Party. Later on, he established his own Student Party through which to funnel the contributions. Throughout the period of 1985 to 1990, Longley tried to obtain the approval of Revenue Canada for the CCC scheme. It was refused.

In 1991 Longley brought suit, asking that the courts decide whether the CCC scheme violated section 127 of the *Income Tax Act*. He also sought to show that Revenue Canada had committed misfeasance in public office and that this had abridged his *Charter* rights.

The court engaged in detailed analysis of the correspondence between Longley and various Revenue Canada officials. It looked at the competing views of what type of contribution is needed to be made to constitute a political contribution that would qualify under the relevant provisions of the *Income Tax Act*. In particular, it looked at the notions of "political activity" and "political expression." Longley's view was that this was the use of one's money to support the things one believes in. The Department's position was founded on the notion of the arm's length nature of the contribution, rather than mere increase of a taxpayer's tax savings. It argued that a political purpose is achieved where a party has had control of the funds contributed and where it has defined the purpose of the expenditure undertaken.

---

[202] *Income Tax Act*, R.S.C. 1985, c. 1 (5th Supp.), s. 127.

The defendant's position that the money given pursuant to the CCC is not a contribution is premised on the traditional political party organization and focus. It does not acknowledge that there can be alternative ways of providing for political expression through registered political parties.[203]

The court's decision turned on the interpretation of the texts of the *Income Tax Act* and the *Canada Elections Act*. Both of these were silent as to the purpose of the contribution, thus leaving latitude to the contributors. Moreover, the court relied on the testimony of the minister, who, in 1973, had presented the Bill to Parliament.

> In 1973, the president of the Privy Council, the Honourable Allan MacEachen, appeared before the Standing Committee on Privileges and Elections regarding Bill C-203, the Bill which introduced the federal political tax credit. Mr. MacEachen's comments are reproduced in Issue 17 of the Minutes of Proceedings and Evidence from Tuesday, November 13, 1973, as follows:
>
> > ....I take the view that the disposition of the contribution to a registered party, say the chief agent of the registered party, the disposition of those funds is a matter for the chief agent. There is no provision in the bill that would obligate the chief agent to do as anyone asked him, but certainly if a party operated that way and wished to operate that way, there is nothing in this bill to prevent it.[204]

Thus, on the basis of the rules of statutory interpretation, the court held that at the time of Longley's efforts, the CCC was not in violation of section 127 of the *Income Tax Act*. In fact, it even found that the Department tried to mislead Longley and awarded damages of $55,000.00.

This decision is so controversial that the Crown decided very quickly to take it on appeal. Inexplicably, however, despite the fact that the Minister of National Revenue's misleading statement had been found to amount to misfeasance in public office, the Crown abandoned its appeal of the judgment. Longley cross-appealed, asking for damages of $99 billion. The British Columbia Court of Appeal was thus left with a difficult case. In essence, it chose to uphold the trial judgment

---

[203] (1999), 176 D.L.R. (4th) 445 at 460, para. 57, affirmed 2000 BCCA 241 (B.C. C.A.), leave to appeal refused (2000), 264 N.R. 398 (note) (S.C.C.).

[204] *Ibid.* at 457, para. 47.

and to dismiss the cross-appeal on the ground that Longley's proposed quantification of punitive damages was fanciful in the extreme.
The amount adjudicated below was held to be sufficient to mark the
court's disapproval of Revenue Canada's conduct.

The findings on appeal that relate to the issue of legality in the financing of government were most interesting. Longley's argument
that he had a right to issue tax receipts for political contributions, and
that that right was protected by section 7 of the *Charter*, were rejected.
His other *Charter*-based claims of freedom of expression and freedom
of association were also rejected. With respect to the constitutional
validity of the general anti-avoidance rule in the *Income Tax Act*, the
court would not indicate its opinion clearly.

See also *Québec (Attorney General) v. Canada (Attorney General)*, action
commenced December 23, 1996, contact Justice HRDC; *P.H.L.F. Family Holdings Ltd. v. R.*, [1994] G.S.T.C. 41 (T.C.C.); *Bowsher v. Synar*,[205]
92 L.Ed.2d 583 (1986) and *Attorney General of Canada v. R.J. Reynolds
Tobacco Holdings, Inc.*,[206] 103 F. Supp.2d 134 (N.D.N.Y., 2000) and
U.S.C.A. 2nd Cir., October 12, 2001.

---

[205] International comparison.
[206] International comparison.

10

LITIGATION OF POLITICAL LAW ISSUES

10.1 GENERAL PRINCIPLES

See Volume I, Chapter 10.

10.2 ISSUE: THE POLITICALLY NEUTRAL NATURE OF JUDICIAL FUNCTIONS[1]

§ 10.2.1[2]
Reference re Secession of Quebec
Supreme Court of Canada, August 20, 1998
(1998), 161 D.L.R. (4th) 385

In the argumentation presented by the *amicus curiae* acting in lieu of the legal advisors who ought to have represented Québec before the Supreme Court in the matter of Québec's right to secede unilaterally, the first set or pleadings related to the jurisdiction of the court to hear the case. While the line of reasoning was initially bound up with the issue of justiciability, in which the matter for examination was whether the substantive question for the Supreme Court's consideration was political and therefore not susceptible of judicial resolution, the *amicus'* brief also examined specifically the nature of the court itself, and of its functions.

At first, the court disposed of the question of whether a court of appeal can exercise original jurisdiction. Under the constitutional framework

---

[1] Cross-reference to § 3.8.
[2] Cross-reference to § 1.2.3, 2.4.6, 3.1, 4.2.2, 4.3.1, 4.6.1 and 11.2.C.1.

for the judiciary established by section 101 of the *Constitution Act, 1867*, this was answered in the affirmative. This is also true, by comparison, in the United States and in the United Kingdom. It is an exceptional jurisdiction but a valid one nevertheless, and one that does not interfere with provincial superior courts.

Of far greater importance was the question raised by the *amicus* as to whether the Supreme Court could issue advisory opinions, that is opinions in cases in which there is no genuine *lis pendens* or adversarial legal controversy, but only a request by reference for a judicial opinion. In alleging that no such power existed in the Canadian constitutional framework, the *amicus* relied on a ruling of the United States Supreme Court. The court refuted this argument squarely, indicating that the American result was derived from the express limitation set out in Art. III, § 2 of the *U.S. Constitution* against such advisory opinions, restricting federal court jurisdiction to actual "cases" or "controversies." Moreover, the Supreme Court of Canada noted that advisory jurisdiction exists in two State judicial systems within the United States, as well as in various European countries with systems similar to Canada's.

> There is no plausible basis on which to conclude that a court is, by its nature, inherently precluded from undertaking another legal function in tandem with its judicial duties.
>
> . . .
>
> Thus, even though the rendering of advisory opinions is quite clearly done outside the framework of adversarial litigation, and such opinions are traditionally obtained by the executive from the law officers of the Crown, there is no constitutional bar to this Court's receipt of jurisdiction to undertake such an advisory role. The legislative grant of reference jurisdiction found in s. 53 of the *Supreme Court Act* is therefore constitutionally valid.[3]

The motive of the *amicus* in making this argument was quite subtle. His putative client's principal contention was that the entire matter was political rather than legal in nature and should not be considered by the judiciary. The principal preliminary jurisdictional argument was in fact that of justiciability. This was a subordinate argument. If the case had turned on this reason, it would have prevented the court,

---

[3] (1998), 161 D.L.R. (4th) 385 at 397-398.

based on its assessment of its inability to receive references, from issuing an opinion on the substantive merits of the case. With the opinion on this point, the Supreme Court not only reaffirmed the legality of the provision which enabled it to receive references, namely section 53 of the *Supreme Court Act*.[4] Much more importantly, it enabled the Court to consider issues that are both legal and political in nature and to advise the government on the legal aspects thereof. In so doing, the court reaffirmed its role as a player in the political legal system of Canada in the era of the *Charter*.

See also *Lawpost v. New Brunswick*[5] (1999), 182 D.L.R. (4th) 167 (N.B. C.A.), leave to appeal refused (2000), 260 N.R. 400 (note) (S.C.C.); *Chavali v. Canada*, 2001 FCT 268 (Fed. T.D.), affirmed 2002 FCA 209 (Fed. C.A.); *OPSEU v. Ontario (Attorney General)*, Ontario Court of Appeal, March 26, 2002; *Crowe v. R.*, 2003 FCA 191 (Fed. C.A.) and *Saskatchewan (Provincial Court Chief Judge) v. Saskatchewan (Human Rights Commission)* (2003), 230 D.L.R. (4th) 493 (Sask. Q.B.).

---

§ 10.2.2[6]
Chisom v. Roemer; United States v. Roemer
United States Supreme Court; June 20, 1991
115 L.Ed.2d 348 (1991)

This case arises out of the system established in the United States for the election, rather than the selection and appointment of judges. In this context, the decision comprises two points of interest to political lawyers, which transcend the difference in the composition of the judiciary between the two countries.

The first issue at stake is whether a particular provision of the *Voting Rights Act*[7] can apply to the election of judges. The provision, section 2, was intended to prohibit voting procedures which result in the abridgement of the right to vote, on the grounds of the role of the voters. It also seeks to protect the participation in the political process of designated classes in their election of the representatives of their choice. The court stretched the meaning of the *Voting Rights Act* to

---

[4] R.S.C. 1985, c. S-26.
[5] Cross-reference to § 8.2.C.
[6] International comparison.
[7] 42 U.S.C., § 1973.

include judicial elections, resulting in the fundamental dilemma whether, in its American conception, judicial functions are political in nature. The majority held on this point that "the fundamental tension between the ideal character of the judicial office and the real world of electoral politics cannot be resolved by crediting judges with total indifference to the popular will while simultaneously requiring them to run for elected office."[8]

The related issue before the court was whether judges are "representatives" in the sense of the *Voting Rights Act*. While the majority held only that the term better describes the winner of popular elections, the definition provided by the dissenters is clearer. They thought that,

> Judges are not included in the ordinary meaning of the word "representative," which connotes one who not only is elected by the people, but also acts on their behalf, as judges do not do in the ordinary sense.[9]

While the concerns of State officials making judicial appointments in Canada specifically exclude the matter of representativity in the sense of espousal of political and social opinions, the influence of popular will or "community standards" and of judges' responsiveness to trends of popular opinion is probably not ignored in any system of governance.

See also *Republican Party of Minnesota et al. v. Kelly et al.*, 996 F. Supp. 875 (1998) and U.S.C.A. (8th) Circ.; November 2, 1998 and 63 F. Supp.2d 967 (1999) on appeal to the United States Supreme Court; Cert. December 3, 2001; *Starrs v. Procurator Fiscal, Linlithgow*, [1999] Scot HC 242; November 11, 1999 and *Victorian Council for Civil Liberties Incorporated v. Minister for Immigration & Multiculturalism Affairs & Ors.*, 2001 FCA 1297 (Fed. C.A.), (11 September 2001).

10.3 ISSUE: THE NATURE OF LITIGATION

See *Reese v. Alberta* (1992), [1993] 1 W.W.R. 450 (Alta. Q.B.) and *Metropolitan Separate School Board v. Taylor* (1994), 21 C.C.L.T. (2d) 316 (Ont. Gen. Div.).

---

[8] 115 L.Ed.2d 348 at 348 (1991).
[9] *Ibid.* at 350 (1991).

10.4 ISSUE: THE DECISION WHETHER TO INITIATE LITIGATION IN POLITICAL MATTERS

§ 10.4.1[10]

Premier of Ontario's Threat of Legal Challenge to NAFTA
October 13, 1993; litigation not initiated

Can the decision to litigate, as differentiated from litigation itself, be a weapon in the arsenal of political players, rather than a measure to right perceived wrongs? Can the mere threat of litigation, as differentiated from the decision to litigate, be used as a political strategy, even where evidence cannot be found to prove whether the threat was ever intended to be carried out? These are the questions raised by the events related to a speech pronounced by Premier Bob Rae in the Legislative Assembly of Ontario on October 13, 1993.

The legislation to enable Canada to participate in the North American Free Trade Agreement (NAFTA) was given Royal Assent on June 23, 1993,[11] during the short term of Kim Campbell as Prime Minister of Canada. By Labour Day of that year, the Prime Minister had resolved to obtain her own mandate and the campaign for the 35th federal general election was begun. Polling was scheduled for Monday, October 25.

From the beginning, the governing Progressive Conservative (PC) Party was faltering, but it was difficult during the seven-week campaign to predict how vertiginous their fall from majority government would be. The establishment of NAFTA and the continuing liberalization of Canada's international trade relationships was one of the planks in the PC platform. The increasingly clear front-runner of the campaign was the Liberal Party under the leadership of Jean Chrétien. That party's views on NAFTA were that it was acceptable but that it needed companion agreements in regard to environmental safeguards and other matters. The measure of electoral success of the New Democratic Party (NDP), where opposition to NAFTA was clear, was uncertain. This party was the federal counterpart of Pre-

---

[10] Cross-reference to § 9.10.
[11] S.C. 1993, c. 44.

mier Rae's Ontario NDP, with whom, seemingly, it shared a common opinion on NAFTA.

One of the cannons of the Canadian practice of federalism is that federal and provincial heads of government do not interfere in election campaigns on each others' level. Yet this cannon is more honoured in the breach than in its observation. In the interest of being able to continue to govern effectively and to pursue federal-provincial relations without undue disruption, such incursions as are made are calculated so as not to damage links with the eventual electoral victor at the other level of government completely, whichever party will form the government.

Against this background, on Wednesday, October 13, 1993, less than two weeks before the federal vote, Premier Rae made a statement in the Ontario Legislature on the subject matter of international trade. The essence of the message was that "Our government opposes NAFTA because we believe it will only add to the harm done to Ontario by the original free trade agreement."[12] He went on to announce a number of legislative and administrative measures designed to protect his province from what the Premier saw as damage caused and to be caused by the new trade deal. Of particular interest was the Premier's threat to challenge the constitutional validity of NAFTA by a reference to the Ontario Court of Appeal.

> The Ontario government has decided to challenge NAFTA through a legal reference to the Ontario Court of Appeal. Ontario's decision to challenge NAFTA in court is based on a careful review of the issues. This government believes that NAFTA violates the division of powers in the Canadian Constitution. The federal government is exceeding its jurisdiction. It is using a trade negotiation to intrude directly into important areas of provincial jurisdiction. The court challenge seeks to preserve the powers of provincial governments to act in the interests of their citizens.[13]

This threat of legal action was the most contentious part of the speech and it is the part that induced the next day's headlines and editorial comments in the press.

---

[12] Ontario Hansard, October 13, 1993, p. 3418.
[13] Ibid., p. 3419.

The court challenge to begin in Ontario's Court of Appeal is just one part of a five-pronged attack against the deal which has been accepted by Ottawa but which must still be ratified by the U.S. Congress. Under NAFTA, Ottawa has promised to enforce provincial compliance with the deal, something the NDP premier said the court could rule is unconstitutional.[14]

Premier Rae's Liberal opposition objected to the threat on its substance, arguing that this would be a waste of $300,000 because, given that trade is in the federal sphere of jurisdiction, nothing would be accomplished. The federal PCs, by the voice of the Minister of International Trade, attributed the Premier's intention to political motives. He called the expression of intent to sue a futile and petty transparent ploy designed to help the federal NDP in the election campaign.

The Liberals won the general election. The threatened legal action was never initiated.

No documentary evidence as to the preparations for a reference to the Court of Appeal has surfaced. Direct testimony from participants in these events is hampered by former officials' observance of the customary rules protecting the confidences of former governments. We must, consequently, draw our conclusions from informed observation and speculation.

Was this genuine preparation to bring a legal challenge—in other words, was this a legal move with clever timing which may later on have been abandoned in the face of legal advice giving the action little chance of success? Was the Premier's desire to limit the NAFTA-induced damage to Ontario in fact resolved by the way the Agreement was eventually implemented after the election, that is with the companion deals? Was there ever an intention to bring suit in the first place? Was this an exclusively political statement in attempted aid of the Premier's federal ideological counterparts—in other words, a cleverly disguised and appropriately aimed interference into the federal election campaign, which failed to produce the desired results? Would a lawsuit in fact have benefited the people of Ontario? Would a lawsuit have benefited the federal NDP?

---

[14] "Rae to Challenge NAFTA, Premier vows to launch court action against 'intrusive' deal," Geoffrey Scotton, *Financial Post*, October 14, 1993, p. 3.

Given all the circumstances, there are grounds to believe that Premier Rae's threat was primarily, if not exclusively, a move on the political chessboard. He was both a highly qualified lawyer with experience in the bounds between federal and provincial areas of jurisdiction, as well as a subtle politician. He had at his disposal both expert legal advisors and talented political operatives. Bearing these factors in mind, as well as the fact that the proposed challenge to NAFTA was never carried forward, it is most likely that this threat was that of a politician looking for a useful political argument, which in this case happened to have not so much a legal characteristic but merely a legal appearance.

---

§ 10.4.2
Claim of False Advertising Regarding Unemployment Insurance Reforms
1996; litigation not initiated

The distinction which is to be observed from the background of this situation is the enormous difference between the threat of litigation and the actual initiation of a court case relating to matters of governance. In many instances, such as here, the publicity given the threat is a key element in the prospective plaintiff's strategy, seeking to determine whether there is any element of public support, and if so how extensive, to going ahead with a case that may prove difficult and certainly costly.

During the first mandate of the Liberal administration of Prime Minister Chrétien (1993-1997), the Unemployment Insurance Program was substantially modified and restyled as the "Employment Insurance Plan" to indicate its new purpose and character. As part of this process, the *Employment Insurance Act*[15] was enacted to replace the *Unemployment Insurance Act*. To publicize some of the changes, the Department of Human Resources issued a pamphlet entitled "A 21st Century Employment System for Canada."[16] One page of this document related specifically to Atlantic Canada where there has traditionally been a high number of seasonal workers and explained, among other things, how benefits would henceforth be calculated on the number of hours worked, instead of the number of weeks.

---

[15] S.C. 1996, c. 23, assented to June 20, 1996.
[16] Minister of Supply and Services Canada 1995, Cat. No. LU2-150/1995-1, ISBN 0-662-62130-1.

New Hours-Based System

Under EI every hour will count toward qualifying for income benefits. The move to an hours-based system as opposed to the current weeks based system will be beneficial to seasonal workers in several ways.

- A total of 45,000 seasonal workers across Canada who are ineligible under the current system will qualify under Employment Insurance.

- Because of the long weeks which many seasonal workers put in, many will qualify sooner.

- About 270,000 across Canada will also get about two more weeks of benefits.

- Those with high weekly earnings will be able to insure more of their earnings because there is no weekly maximum.

Counting hours of work was a key recommendation of the Working Group on Seasonal Work and UI, which consulted extensively with workers and employers involved in seasonal work throughout the country.

In response to this announcement and to the distribution of the explanatory documentation, on January 25, 1996, John Murphy, Executive Secretary of the New Brunswick Federation of Labour issued a public statement which became the subject of a Canadian Press line story. The matter was picked up by more newspapers in the Maritimes region,[17] but more importantly by the CBC national radio news and was broadcast across Canada.

Murphy alleged primarily that the pamphlet was misleading because "the UI changes meant double the qualification period for workers with the switch to hours instead of the number of weeks worked. Part-time workers with 15 hours or fewer a week could end up never having enough hours to collect."[18] He went on to dispute the truth of the contents of the pamphlet, qualifying it as being "like selling a new car with no motor, yet claiming it runs." On these grounds, Murphy stated publicly that he was planning to file a false advertising suit against the federal government for its unemployment insurance reforms.

---

[17] For example the *Truro Daily News*, January 26, 1996, p. 11 (N.S.).
[18] CP wire story F18A2255, January 25, 1996.

Assuming the face value of the threat to sue, the vital questions to be addressed are i) the purpose for which the threat was made, and ii) the reason why it was made publicly. These are the determining criteria in analyzing the decision of whether or not to initiate litigation.

It is clear that the New Brunswick Federation of Labour was opposed to that substantive aspect of the reforms which related to the method of calculating time worked toward eligibility for Employment Insurance, as a possible disadvantage to those of its members who were seasonal workers. By its threat of a lawsuit, it sought to influence the course of public policy away from this change. The choice of argumentation, namely making a claim for false advertising, is interesting. It could lead the observer to surmise that the Federation had already made representations to the government on this matter, which may have elicited explanations or even promises that eligibility requirements would not be increased. Further, the issue was being described in the pamphlet in a manner different from that in which the Federation had perceived it earlier, leading it to raise the problem to the attention of its members. In selecting the line of argumentation of false advertising, akin to breach of a political promise in a matter of public administration, the Federation chose a highly visible but difficult course of action. Whatever the grounds, it was hoping to use the threat of the suit to prevent that aspect of the reform from being realized. We may safely assume that by suing, the Federation was hoping to accomplish thorough judicial and binding means what it has been unable to achieve through negotiation.

The key to the Federation's strategy leading up to the possible filing of documents in court was the publicity of its threat. There was little or no cost associated with the making of Murphy's public statement. The reaction to it, by members of the New Brunswick Federation of Labour as well as by other unions, would enable the Federation to gauge whether there existed a level of public support for the attempt to discredit the pamphlet and perhaps have the public policy behind it changed as a result, through litigation against the Crown, all of which could prove costly. After the public statement of January 25, 1996, this matter does not seem to have been raised again and the threatened lawsuit was never initiated. The reforms toward Employment Insurance proceeded as planned by the government.

The threat of the lawsuit cannot be qualified as a futile gesture in this instance. The matter may well have turned out differently if Murphy's statement to the media had raised a ground swell of opposition and would have endowed the Federation with funds sufficient to finance the challenge. In issues involving the conduct of public affairs, publicity and the financial consequences it can engender are significant and even necessary elements in determining whether litigation is feasible or advisable. These factors can also play a role in determining whether the grounds selected for possible litigation are the most appropriate ones.

---

§ 10.4.3[19]
Expulsion of John Nunziata, MP from the Caucus of the Liberal Party of Canada
1996; litigation not initiated

There exist clear limits to the legalization of politics and to the ability of participants in political life to use arguments recognizable by a court in obtaining redress of perceived political wrongs. An example of this limitation is the case of John Nunziata, the Member of Parliament first elected as a Liberal in 1984 in the Metro Toronto riding of York South-Weston. During the latter part of the 35th Parliament (1993-1997), Nunziata had a number of disagreements with his own party over issues of policy. Among other things, he contended that the measures enacted by the government formed by the Liberal Party were significantly different from the promises which that party had made in the course of the 1993 election campaign in order to be elected. Thus, he voted against his own government in respect of the 1995 budget, because it did not abolish the *Goods and Services Act*. The party responded with insistence on caucus discipline and with the demand that Nunziata not vote against the party, nor that he abstain from voting in the House of Commons, on matters of confidence such as the annual budget. Nunziata put his own principles ahead of party discipline and the rift became unbridgeable.

In the fall of 1996, the Liberal Party of Canada (Ontario) disbanded the riding association executive who were supportive of Nunziata and substituted its own appointees. One of the motives invoked for

---

[19] Cross-reference to § 5.5.B.2.

this was that the executive had failed to support the party's political principles. Nunziata was also expelled from the Liberal caucus in Parliament.

The political law question Nunziata, himself an experienced lawyer, forced in this situation was whether he could have recourse to law to be readmitted to the caucus. It was reported that he sought the advice of Clayton Ruby, a prominent Toronto lawyer, on this issue.[20] Together, they must have concluded that membership in a party caucus in Parliament, the requirements of discipline within a party and the imposition of sanctions for breach of that discipline, as well as the control by a government of the manner in which its own backbenchers vote in the House of Commons, are, in a Parliamentary system, not subject to the reach of law. In response to an inquiry about possible recourse to the courts for the purpose of readmission into caucus, Nunziata responded: "at the time I was removed from the Liberal caucus, it was suggested that there might exist grounds for legal action. I have not pursued that option."[21]

While legal arguments were apparently not available to Nunziata, he did seek political remedy by running for office again in the June 2, 1997, general election in the riding he had held as a Liberal for 13 years. This time, he was elected as an independent.

---

§ 10.4.4
Lougheed v. Canadian Broadcasting Corporation
Alberta Supreme Court; filed September 27, 1977
abandoned

In situations involving prominent public figures and in circumstances relating to contentious political events, the decision whether to initiate litigation can be more than merely the safeguarding of legal rights and privileges. In such cases, figures in public life may include in the determination of whether to sue or not additional criteria, such as the calculation of political advantage or potential electoral benefit to be derived from being seen as a determined plaintiff and from the publicity generated by the legal action itself. With such political consid-

---

[20] "Liberal Brass Toss Out Maverick MP's Riding Executive," Mike Scandiffio and Campbell Morrison, *Hill Times*, December 2, 1996, p. 4.

[21] Letter of September 29, 1997, from John Nunziata.

erations in mind, the use of the law may be not only as a restorative mechanism, but also as a weapon in one's political arsenal. A further consideration in such politicized use of legal procedures is the quantum of damages sought. The observer of such procedures must also ask whether, objectively, there is a link between the action complained of on the one hand and on the other, the harm allegedly suffered and the public outrage of the supposed victim. Another related question that must be addressed is whether there is a reasonable expectation of determining the amount of compensation applied for, or if the inflated quantum itself is an aspect of the desired publicity.

Such are the considerations to be borne in mind in analyzing the decision of Lougheed, Premier of Alberta from September 1971 until November 1985, to sue the Canadian Broadcasting Corporation (CBC) in September 1977, in respect of a program aired on September 12, 1977, by that broadcaster.

The "CBC Special" in question was entitled "Tar Sands" and it was a dramatization of the negotiations and agreements leading up to the establishment of an energy project in Alberta, called Syncrude. Through advance publicity, the CBC had garnered a nation-wide viewing audience interested in the controversial nature of the issue. In the program, an actor purported to portray the words, thoughts, actions and motives of Lougheed in the conduct of his functions as Premier in relation to the Syncrude Project. According to Lougheed, the program not only showed him as being weak and irresolute, but also gave the impression of him ignoring "the advice of his civil service in reference to the assets under his official administration"[22] and relying "on a senior civil servant of dissolute behaviour but supposedly of much higher character and concern for principle than that of the Plaintiff."[23] Lougheed's complaint concluded by indicating that the program showed him as generally committing breach of trust of the office he held relating to the natural resources under his administration. In respect of this alleged defamation, Lougheed claimed $750,000 in general and $2,000,000 in punitive damages.

The Statement of Claim in this case was issued on September 27, 1977, some two weeks after the program went to air. That is the only

---

[22] Statement of claim, September 27, 1977, para. 10(b).
[23] Ibid., para. 10(c).

document indicative of the case, as the CBC entered into a settlement, the terms of which have been kept confidential. It is notable, though, that the "Tar Sands" program was never shown again.

Several circumstantial factors may be highlighted in relation to Lougheed's decision to bring suit. Some are of a policy nature, others political. At the time of the program, the energy industry was the engine of the Alberta economy and the greatest source of the province's tax income. The success of the energy industry in that period of successive "oil shocks" caused an economic boom in Alberta. In that context, the bringing on line of Syncrude was perceived as a necessary evolution to keep Alberta prosperous. Lougheed and his party, the Progressive Conservatives, did their best to associate themselves in the collective consciousness of the electorate as the protectors of the energy boom and of the provincial defiance vis-à-vis the federal authorities. These were the political ramifications of the province's economic development policy. Thus, while Lougheed may perhaps have felt offended by the CBC program on a personal level, it could only have been also publicly and politically beneficial for him before the population of his province to resist an image of bad policy-making in the energy field, or disadvantageous political consequences of energy development. Moreover, accusing the CBC, a federal institution based outside Alberta, of defamation, could produce sound results within the province in the area of federal-provincial politics.

Overall, initiating the lawsuit may have helped Lougheed in projecting to his electorate a continued image of strength and leadership as he prepared for the next provincial general election, which was held on March 14, 1979. In that campaign, Lougheed's motto was "79 in '79," meaning that the Progressive Conservatives wanted to capture all 79 seats in the legislature in that year. Whereas at the time of the CBC program, they had 69 seats out of 75, in the 1979 election, they obtained 74 out of 79 seats. We may question whether the image presented by Lougheed in this litigation contributed to that electoral score.

See also *Allegations of Racism Against the Reform Party*, 1997, litigation not initiated and *Québec–Labrador Boundary Dispute*, 1999, litigation not initiated.

§ 10.4.5
"Bridging the Gap: From Oblivion to the Rule of Law," Development and Vitality of the Francophone and Acadian Communities; A Fundamental Obligation for Canada
Report by Senator Jean-Maurice Simard; November 16, 1999

The decision to avail oneself of the legal and judicial system to assert rights or to defend positions is not necessarily a private one made in an adversarial context. Such a decision can also be a practice or a tool of public administration designed to foster the qualities of a society which one espouses as the best and the most progressive. Moreover, there is an inevitable political component, practically indistinguishable from the purely legal element of litigation, where one uses, or promotes the use of litigation broadly to improve society and the state.

This is the spirit in which analysts of political law should see the recommendations pertinent to the present study, which were made by Senator Jean-Maurice Simard in the course of protecting and promoting the bilingual nature of Canada. Just over a decade after the adoption of the second *Official Languages Act*,[24] this Report took stock of the state of Canada's linguistic duality, its evolution, and the prospects for the communities. Among a variety of recommendations, Senator Simard addresses the issue of "Respect for and Advancement of Language Rights and the Road to Equality." He uses the Supreme Court of Canada's *Québec Secession Reference* ruling and the even more recent *Beaulac* decision[25] as a baseline and urges the purposive interpretation of language rights so as to preserve and develop Canada's official languages communities.

In pursuit of this goal, the report includes three key recommendations:

- use of the Court Challenge Program to develop test cases in the area of constitutional language rights and their extension;[26]

---

[24] R.S.C. 1985, c. 31 (4th Supp.); Consolidations c. O-3.01.
[25] *R. v. Beaulac*, [1999] 1 S.C.R. 768 (S.C.C.).
[26] Simard Report Recommendation No. 38.

- comprehensive analysis of cases in which the Federal Court can provide remedies, and the institution of proceedings for the correction of problem cases and restitution;[27] and

- broadening of the Court Challenge Program to include provincial language policies.[28]

The Report was particularly interesting in its evaluation of the criteria which must be borne in mind in respect of such litigation, the inadequacy or inexistence of government services, the cost of litigation, the duration of cases, the resulting negative social pressure, the need to avoid settlements, the value of judgments as precedent, the complexity of language rights litigation and the partial manner in which rights are implemented. In sum, the Report concluded that the Court Challenge Program was a tool of choice to develop rights in society, meaning that litigation was a positive factor which had to be developed.

As can be expected, reaction to this Report varied among Parliamentarians according to political persuasions. Notably, Senator Gérald-A. Beaudoin, one of Canada's leading constitutionalists, has contributed his voice to the advocacy of the of the use of the courts to develop bilingualism.[29]

10.5 ISSUE: THE DECISION WHETHER TO DEFEND LITIGATION IN POLITICAL MATTERS

See T1T2 Ltd. Partnership v. Canada (1994), 23 O.R. (3d) 66 (Ont. Gen. Div.) and (1995), 23 O.R. (3d) 81 (Ont. Gen. Div.), additional reasons at (1995), 38 C.P.C. (3d) 167 at 180 (Ont. Gen. Div.), affirmed (1995), 38 C.P.C. (3d) 183 (Ont. C.A.) and (1996), 48 C.P.C. (3d) 84 (Ont. Gen. Div.) and (1997), 8 C.P.C. (4th) 193 (Ont. Gen. Div.).

---

[27] Simard Report Recommendation No. 39.
[28] Simard Report Recommendation No. 40.
[29] "Bilinguisme: il faut aller en cour quand c'est nécessaire, affirme Beaudoin," Marilène Bolduc-Jacob, Le Droit, January 10, 2002.

§ 10.5.1
DeBané v. Canadian Broadcasting Corporation
Ontario Court (General Division); filed May 31, 1995
file 91722/95; not completed

The sparse evidence available in this area would tend to show that in cases where legal action of a civil nature is launched by a politically prominent person in respect of a politicized subject matter, such as here in a matter of alleged defamation, the considerations leading to a decision as to whether to defend the case or not is guided to a greater extend by the legal rules of civil procedure than by policy or political considerations. This also seems to be true in respect of cases where a defendant wishes to settle rather than plead a defence. How could it be otherwise, as once a lawsuit is launched, if it is not defended, the plaintiff may obtain judgment by default. Thus, a defendant engaged in legal proceedings by means of a politically motivated lawsuit has the following principal choices:

- settle, whether the defendant admits the substantive veracity of the claim or not;

- defend through a procedural motion based on the argument that the suit is either frivolous and vexatious, or that it is political in content rather than legal, discloses no legal argument and is therefore not justiciable; or

- defend on the legal merits.

In all of these eventualities, the choice of a course of action for the defence would seem to be dictated by legal reasons and reasoning.

An appropriate illustration of these strategies is set out in the libel action which DeBané, a Member of the Senate of Canada since June 29, 1984, and a former Cabinet minister, initiated against the Canadian Broadcasting Corporation (CBC) in 1995. On March 3 of that year, the national broadcaster ran a news story to the effect that in connection with the construction of a new headquarters building for the Canada Post Corporation in 1991, the developer paid an amount of $20,000 to DeBané. As the story indicated, this sum was in addition to a regular consulting fee paid by that developer to the Senator. The report called this payment a kickback and accused DeBané of influence peddling and improprieties. The story was repeated on a number of the broadcaster's outlets. DeBané sued for libel, alleging that the CBC had irresponsibly and oppressively abused the position of great power which it holds in the country, claiming that the allegations and innuendo were serious and criminal, and asking for general damages in the amount of $75,000 as well as punitive damages of $25,000.

The CBC may not have adequately checked the facts because, as the statement of claim indicated, it eventually made an effort to mitigate the harm caused to DeBané's reputation by broadcasting a retraction and an apology.

The national broadcaster opted in this instance to settle the case. Despite the political nature of the circumstances and despite the fact that the plaintiff was a political figure of at least past prominence, the CBC decided to respond most promptly to the lawsuit and in doing so, it was guided by the civil procedure, and therefore legal, considerations inherent to the lawsuit. It is reasonable to believe that the defendant acted in this politicized case the same way it would have responded to a lawsuit launched against it by one not involved in the political system. The only question outstanding from this matter is that of the confidentiality of the settlement. If the plaintiff relies in the action on his public and political status and on the potential impact of the defendant's actions on his continuing political career, does that not bring the entire matter into the political domain and should not the Canadian public and the electorate know the terms of the settlement?

10.6 ISSUE: JUDICIAL NOTICE OF POLITICAL FACTS, PARLIAMENTARY SPEECHES AND PUBLIC ADMINISTRATION

See *Boucher v. Canada (Immigration Appeal Board)* (1989), 105 N.R. 66 (Fed. C.A.); *Quebec (Attorney General) v. Eastmain Band*, [1992] 3 F.C. 800 (Fed. C.A.); *Canadian Free Speech League v. R.* (1992), [1992] F.C.J. No. 966 (Fed. T.D.) and *R. v. Pryce*, Ontario Court (Provincial Division), April 27, 1998, not reported, limited information available.

10.7 ISSUE: USE OF LITIGATION FOR POLITICAL AND PARTISAN MOTIVES

§ 10.7.1
Ontario (Attorney General) v. Dieleman
Ontario Court (General Division); November 3, 1993
(1993), 16 O.R. (3d) 39[30]

This case addresses the twin issues of the politics of governmental legislation. The first is whether, *per se*, litigation, which is a governmental action of a legal nature, can be or sometimes is initiated for political motivations. The second is whether the courts examine the motivation of the Crown in litigating and if they do, the manner in which they conduct that examination.

The foundation of the present decision was an application by the Attorney General of Ontario against a number of defendants including Dieleman, for interlocutory and permanent injunctions to prevent them from protesting at locations where abortions were performed as well as at the homes of health care workers providing such services. In her application, the Attorney General alleged that the action was designed to enforce public rights and was initiated in the public interest. The defendants challenged the action on the *Charter* grounds that the injunction would deprive them of their freedoms of expres-

---

[30] Leave to appeal refused (1993), 16 O.R. (3d) 39 at 46 (Ont. Gen. Div.).

938 / LAW OF DEMOCRATIC GOVERNING – VOLUME II: JURISPRUDENCE

sion and of peaceful assembly. A hearing to consider the merits of the injunction application was set down.

In preparation for the hearing on the merits, the defendants resorted to the ideologically motivated tactic often used by the pro-life movement, that is to try to impugn the good faith of those disagreeing with them. In this instance, Dieleman made a motion to have the Attorney General testify in person about the background and motivation of the application for injunction, so as to have her testimony available for the substantive hearing. The argumentation of the case was to determine whether the minister could be compelled to testify. However, it intrinsically also involved consideration of the Attorney General's motives in conducting the litigation.

Dieleman contended that the defendants were being actioned because of their political stance and their opposition to the government's policies and actions in matters related to abortion.

> The defendants also state that certain of them have been selected, not because of their very limited picketing activity, but because of their relatively high public and political profiles in the pro-life movement and because they are opposed to the current government's policies on abortion and the provision of abortion services. These defendants therefore assert the motivation for the injunction appears, in part, to be "political" as well as originating from a government task force recommendation which task force, the defendants allege, was composed of only individuals sympathetic to the government's views.[31]

In order to make out this case, Dieleman proposed to question the Attorney General primarily about the government's objective in seeking the injunction and intended to show that the evidence of that objective would be relevant to the defence she could make at the hearing on the merits. In addition, she wanted to have the Attorney General explain the factors used in selecting the specified defendants.

The government's position, by contrast, was that the proposed testimony by the Attorney General, and therefore by implication the minister's motivation in litigating, were irrelevant to the issues and that the motion to compel her to testify was itself an abuse of the judicial process.

---

[31] (1993), 16 O.R. (3d) 39 at 42 c-e, leave to appeal refused (1993), 16 O.R. (3d) 39 at 46 (Ont. Gen. Div.).

...It is emphasized that the Attorney General is the legal representative of Her Majesty and is thereby empowered to bring an action for an injunction where the rights of the public are involved...It is submitted this authority to bring an action to enjoin a public nuisance is discretionary and not reviewable. Accordingly, because the defendants are seeking information related to the decision-making process of the Minister in the exercise of her unfettered discretion, it is submitted the application amounts to an attempt to review the Minister's decision indirectly and thereby constitutes an abuse of process. In aid of this submission, it was argued that no "government action" capable of *Charter* scrutiny can arise until a court concludes a public nuisance exists and in respect of which an injunction should issue were it not for the *Charter*.[32]

Setting aside the notion that Dieleman's tactic was to defend the action by putting the government, as applicant in the case, on trial to respond to allegations of politicization, the case does indeed raise a number of pertinent and interrelated issues which deserve consideration:

- What is the government's objective in seeking the injunction?

- Can a minister's motivation in litigating be brought into issue?

- Is this action in fact legally or politically motivated?

- Is politically-motivated litigation invalid because it is to be considered in bad faith or an abuse of the legal system?

- If the answer to the foregoing question is affirmative, must the case fail?

The court did not resolve all of these dilemmas, primarily because in its eyes, the particular matter to be determined was whether the Attorney General ought to be forced to testify or not. Its decision was to grant Dieleman's motion to have the minister testify. It based this conclusion on linking the minister's decision to litigate to the eventual determination of the existence of the public nuisance which the minister was setting out to prove in the injunction action.

> The objectives of the Attorney General, as the representative of government in these proceedings, are clearly relevant to the defendants' *Charter*

---

[32] *Ibid.* at 43 e-h.

defence and the questions they wish to put to her, in my view, bear a sufficient relationship to such *Charter* issues for the motion to succeed.[33]

The court went no further than this in analyzing the possibility that political considerations induced the Minister, and the consequences of such influence. From the point of view of political law, the central question of this matter thus remained only partially answered.

The Attorney General urgently applied for leave to appeal this judgment. On November 25, 1993, the leave was denied on technical grounds. The November 3, 1993, decision was held not to conflict with any other decision by another Ontario judge; the Attorney General was not being asked to answer questions which are conclusions at law; the earlier decision was held to be correct.

---

§ 10.7.2
Trinh v. Chan
British Columbia Supreme Court; November 12, 1997
(1997), 34 C.C.E.L. (2d) 293[34]

Chan was first elected to Parliament on October 25, 1993, as the Member for Richmond, B.C. From November 1993 until September 1994, Trinh was employed as a Parliamentary Assistant by Chan, who had in the meantime become Secretary of State for Asia Pacific in the Cabinet of Prime Minister Jean Chrétien. The plaintiff soon applied for a promotion to a position as Departmental Assistant, as she came to realize that three years of work as a political assistant in a departmental position would have provided her greater job security through a right of entry into the Public Service. She was passed over in favour of another member of the Minister's entourage. Later, she arranged to be let go in a reorganization of the Minister's office and she returned to Vancouver.

Starting in the summer of 1995, Trinh campaigned for the provincial Liberal nomination in Richmond. She sought the Minister's help in that process but did not obtain it and ultimately was not nominated as a candidate, losing by a narrow margin. Subsequently, Trinh brought the present suit for sexual harassment constituting construc-

---

[33] *Ibid.* at 45 e.
[34] Additional reasons at (1998), 20 C.P.C. (4th) 142 (B.C. S.C.).

tive dismissal against Chan. She alleged that during the time she had worked in the Minister's office, Chan had on occasion acted in a manner that had demeaned her and that he had expressed unsolicited sexual attention, that she had received advice in that regard at the time of the actions but had taken no steps in order to avoid political embarrassment for the Minister.

The court dismissed Trinh's claim, finding that her allegations were untrue. This part of the judgment seemed to indicate that her motive for initiating the action was linked to the fact that she had not been offered the departmental position, as well as to her unhappiness at not receiving the Minister's political support in the nomination process, while Chan had assisted incumbents in his area. This led the judge close to concluding that Trinh had tried to use the action as a means of political vengeance; he accepted the defendant's claim that the action had been harmful to him.

The plaintiff's motive in suing actually did become part of the matter to be considered by the court because Chan counterclaimed, asking for damages for abuse of process. His plea was that the suit was filed "because the defendant refused to support the plaintiff for the provincial Liberal nomination and that after she lost she decided to 'get even' by filing this action."[35] The counterclaim offered the court the opportunity to set the test for abuse of process in such cases with political undertones. The doctrine was stated as follows.

> As stated in *Fleming on Torts*, 4th ed. (1971) pp 547-8, this cause of action arises "where a legal process, not itself devoid of foundation, has been perverted to accomplish some extraneous purpose, such as extortion or oppression. Here an action will lie at the suit of the injured party for what has come to be called abuse of process." The essence of the tort is not the launching of the process, but rather "the misuse of process, no matter how properly obtained, for any purpose other than that which it was designed to serve."[36]

The court separated its disbelief of the facts alleged in the claim from its analysis of the plaintiff's motives involved in the counterclaim and concluded that Chan had not met the test. It justified this by referring to testimony about the plaintiff's discussions regarding the defen-

---

[35] (1997), 34 C.C.E.L. (2d) 293 at 307, para. 67, additional reasons at (1998), 20 C.P.C. (4th) 142 (B.C. S.C.).

[36] *Ibid.* at 306, para. 62.

dant's conduct with one of the defendant's friends, after she had returned to Vancouver.

The court stated that in its opinion, rather than trying to mislead the court, Trinh held an honest, although mistaken belief that she had been wronged. The wording of the judgment in reaction to the counterclaim may disclose more subtle reasons as well. It said that it could go no further than to dismiss the plaintiff's action. This can be taken as indicative of the judiciary's restraint and its reluctance to becoming embroiled in a dispute which it had come as close as possible to characterizing as a politically motivated legal struggle. This equitable annulment of both sides' arguments can be seen as the only way for the court to avoid entering an area it did not deem to be its own and in which it would see recourse to the law as misuse.

---

§ 10.7.3
University of New Brunswick Student Union (1996) Inc. v.
New Brunswick (Municipal Electoral Officer)
New Brunswick Court of Queen's Bench; September 21, 1999
(1999), 217 N.B.R. (2d) 322

In ordinary circumstances of litigation, a judge before whom a legal dispute is placed for resolution analyzes the legal elements thereof and expresses conclusions with the reserve appropriate to members of the judiciary. However, where litigants entirely fail to understand that court proceedings involve matters of law and are not vehicles for the propagation of political views, judges are strained in retaining that necessary reserve. In this instance, the student unions of two universities in Fredericton presented to the court arguments designed to increase their political power in municipal elections which were so blatantly political that the judge felt obliged to start his judgment in the following manner:

> The students want the political respect that comes with an effective right to vote; they want to be seen and heard. They are not asking for political perfection, although some of them might agree with the words of the late Alden Nowlan of Fredericton:

The perfect parliament would include delegates from the living, the unborn and the dead. (Scratchings 5, from *I'm a stranger here myself* by Alden Nowlan, Clarke Irwin, Toronto, 1974, page 74.)[37]

In fact the students were attempting to state their political concerns in favour of amendments to the *New Brunswick Municipal Elections Act*[38] so as to exercise the franchise with greater ease, and they cast these political concerns as technical legal issues for decision by the court. In preparation for a Fredericton municipal by-election held on October 4, 1999, the student unions sought to have the court order the Municipal Election Officer to prepare a new voters' list perfected according to their preferences, in particular based on loose residency requirements. The court held that they had established no legal reason why the general rule as to the election officer's use of discretion, which she had declined to exercise, should apply. In its conclusions, the court explained its decision and emphasized the legal, as opposed to the political nature of litigation and the consequential need to present facts to the court, rather than merely using the court as a platform.

> This decision is not a rejection of students; it is an effort to explain to them that the court can only decide concrete legal disputes and the court does not make policy statements on hypothetical or abstract questions. The award of costs is not a punishment; it is a reminder that a legal proceeding is very serious and should not be taken lightly.

> This unsuccessful legal case should not in any way discourage interested students from encouraging registration of voters or otherwise involving themselves in the political process.[39]

---

§ 10.7.4[40]
Impeachment of President William Clinton
United States Congress; February 12, 1999

The facts of this case are so well known to consistent observers of the political scene in the United States, and they became so unavoidable to citizens of other countries such as Canada, that they bear to be only briefly summarized. In the course of preparing the case for the plain-

---

[37] (1999), 217 N.B.R. (2d) 322, 555 A.P.R. 322 at p. 1.
[38] S.N.B. 1979, c. M-21.01.
[39] *Supra* note 37 at p. 7.
[40] International comparison. Cross-reference to § 11.9.A.3 and 11.10.5.

tiff in the *Jones v. Clinton* sexual harassment litigation, investigators and lawyers seeking to uncover a pattern of behaviour on the part of President Clinton, and the Independent Counsel who had for several years been looking into the so-called Whitewater scandal, Ken Starr, were provided information concerning an alleged sexual relationship between the president and a White House intern, Monica Lewinsky. On January 16, 1998, Lewinsky was interviewed by prosecutors from the Office of Independent Counsel and made revelations about the relationship. The matter was leaked to the press. On January 26, 1998, President Clinton emphatically denied having had the sexual rela- tionship in a television appearance that has become rather memora- ble.

Thereafter, from January 26, 1998, until February 12, 1999, the entire presidency was focused on, and in some respects paralyzed by, the political legal outcome of Clinton's public lie about a purely private matter not associated with his governance or with any substantive issue of public affairs. The investigation of the Independent Counsel turned into an attempt to impeach the President. That attempt failed on February 12, 1999, when the Senate, sitting as a court, failed to vote either of the two remaining articles of impeachment from the original four which had been debated in the House of Representa- tives.

The facts of the Clinton impeachment are only the necessary back- ground for the more important aspect of this case and indeed for the more significant developments in American public life, namely the extreme politicization of the legal and judicial process and the ex- treme legalization of politics. These combined tendencies and the consequential blurring of the boundary between law and politics were themselves attributable to societal factors such as the rise of unbridled partisanship in political life, the lack of any self-restraint on the part of opponents and detractors of government and of the Clinton administration in particular, coming mostly from that part of the right-wing which was so fanatical as to be mindless, the in- creasing influence of fundamentalist religious zealotry in political life and the absence on the part of the media of a sense for the dignity and privacy of public officials. The result was a hijacking of legal rules, norms and forms by the political and partisan opponents of the Clinton Administration in their search for destruction of the Demo- cratic Party and American liberalism.

As early as the spring of 1997, a publication no less serious than *The Economist* decried "the rise of scandals, the rising use of law as a weapon of attack, the uniting of these two trends in lawsuits based on scandalous allegations."[41] A year later, in the same "Lexington" column, the magazine expressed serious misgivings about the Independent Counsel's worrying zeal at discovering the truth about Clinton. What caused this rather conservative publication anxiety was that in his evangelical zeal for truth as the primary goal of the justice system, Starr had completely lost perspective as to the lack of importance or impact on government of Clinton's lie, no matter how unjustifiable the lie was in itself; he had developed, without either legal foundation or political backing, a constitutional standard of political behaviour which the text of the *Constitution* itself had not envisaged in the expression "high crimes and misdemeanors"[42] which was the ground for impeachment. Starr had surrendered his office to the radical right, which despite the vocal nature, was a minority of the population.

The partisan attacks on Clinton, under the guise of legal writ, were even more strictly portrayed and analyzed by the Paris newspaper *Le Monde*:

> La charge du procureur Starr relève certes d'une inquisition dont on ne répètera jamais assez qu'elle menace les valeurs démocratiques d'un ordre moral aux relents totalitaires, effaçant la frontière essentielle et protectrice entre vies privée et publique. Mais Bill Clinton n'a pas su la contrer, refusant d'abord de l'affronter sur ce terrain-même—valeurs contre valeurs—puis choisissant d'entraîner les siens dans une stratégie du mensonge finalement intenable, avant d'échouer à convaincre non seulement les Américains, mais ses propres amis démocrates de son repentir.[43]

Pursuant to the *United States Constitution*, the first step in an impeachment process is the voting of an impeachment resolution continuing specific articles of impeachment, by the House of Representatives. On December 15, 1998, Representative Hyde submitted a resolution containing four Articles of Impeachment.[44] These dealt, respectively, with the President lying under oath before a grand jury, the President

---

[41] "The Paula Jones ratchet," *The Economist*, May 31, 1997, p. 31.
[42] *United States Constitution*, Art. II, § 4.
[43] "Le retour de l'Histoire," *Le Monde*, September 12, 1998, pp. 1 and 15.
[44] 105th Congress, 2nd Session, H. Res. 611, December 15, 1998.

committing perjury in giving false and misleading testimony as part of a federal civil rights action brought against him, the President causing obstruction and impeding the administration of justice, and with the President engaging in misuse and abuse of high office through perjury before the impeachment inquiry. On December 19, the House voted Articles I and III. Those votes had the effect of an indictment, which the Senate would then have to try.

The Senate impeachment trial began on January 7, 1999, under the presidency of the Chief Justice of the Supreme Court. The process was fraught with partisanship from beginning to end.

> An impeachment process against a president is inevitably political; but it does not have to be like this. The articles of impeachment against Richard Nixon were voted almost unanimously. The feeling was one of immense pride that the constitution worked, and could efficiently remove a bad apple from the presidency. By contrast, the impeachment procedures against Mr. Clinton have been so partisan that they have had the opposite effect. They do not prove that the system works; they seem merely to prove that it can be abused by zealots on both the Republican and Democratic sides.
>
> . . .
>
> Americans are no longer sure where either party, but especially the Republican one, stands on the issues that concern them: reform of entitlements, education, health care, the role of government. They have been treated to a brand of partisanship that is mostly destructive. As they see it, the impeachment process is a nasty game being played in Washington, which has nothing to do with them and makes little difference to the smooth running of the country.[45]

On February 12, 1999, the 1st Session of the 106th Senate held two roll call votes. On the first Article, the vote was 55 not guilty, 45 guilty. With respect to the second of the Articles retained, the vote was 50-50. As neither Article obtained the 2/3 required for impeachment, the President was cleared. At that time, there were 55 Republicans in the Senate and 45 Democrats. Under the pressure of history and public opinion, 10 Republicans voted not guilty in the first vote, while 5 did so in the second.

---

[45] "Bill Clinton's flawed judges," *The Economist*, January 16, 1999, pp. 20-21.

Although the President was not impeached, the remainder of his term in office was rather unremarkable, due in some measure to the caution in public life which he needed to exercise in order to avoid further potential difficulties.

In order to understand the politicization and the abuse of law which the Clinton impeachment represented, it is necessary to look first at the strictly legal components of the underlying litigation, the Paula Jones case, as well as at those of the impeachment process itself. The original provision of law which made the political legal attack on President Clinton possible was a charge in the Federal Rules of Evidence which, ironically, Clinton himself agreed to as part of a political deal so that a criminal law bill he wanted enacted would receive wider support in Congress.

> As is so often the case, however, the legal cure may have been worse than the disease. In Congress, Susan Molinari, then a Republican representative from New York, introduced changes to the federal rules of evidence to allow juries in civil and criminal sexual misconduct cases to consider evidence that the accused had engaged in such misconduct in the past. But Molinari proposed such a broad definition of "sexual assault"—which included any attempted contact, "without consent, between any part of the defendant's body or an object and the genitals or anus of another person"—that it would apply to mere fanny-pinching as well as rape. But the criminal defence lobby was no match for the women's groups on this issue. When Clinton's crime bill stalled in the House, in 1994, the president called Molinari to see what he could do to win her vote. She agreed to vote for the bill if Clinton would accept her amendments on admitting the evidence of previous offenses in sex trials. "He told me that he was shocked that it wasn't part of the bill, and he supported it," Molinari recalled to Jeffrey Rosen of *The New Yorker*. "Clinton basically assisted me in passing that legislation."
>
> The Molinari law referred to sexual relations "without consent," but as far as the questioning of defendants was concerned, many judges simply read those words out of the statute.[46]

It was this reform in the law which legitimized the questioning of Clinton's sex life and thus opened the floodgates.

Armed with the testimony so gathered, and fortified with the obvious lie which Clinton publicly announced about his relationship with

---

[46] Toobin, Jeffrey, *A Vast Conspiracy*, Random House, New York, 1999, p. 175.

Lewinsky, those in opposition to him were able not only to turn the civil matter of a sexual harassment complaint into a criminal prosecution, but were also able to coalesce, thinking they had found the legal means to drive their political enemy from office.

No matter what observers may think of Clinton as an individual and despite how they may condemn him for the way he conducts his private life, the attempt to impeach him was a manifestation of the enmity against him in his governmental capacity, as President. In that sense, the most appropriate characterization of the campaign against Clinton was that given by Hilary Clinton in a television interview on January 27, 1998.

> "But it's the whole operation," she replied. "It's not just one person. It's an entire operation...I do believe that this is a battle. I mean, look at the very people who are involved in this, they have popped up in other settings. This is the great story here, for anybody who is willing to find it and write about it and explain it, is this vast right-wing conspiracy that has been conspiring against my husband since the day he announced for president. A few journalists have kind of caught on to it and explained it, but it has not yet been fully revealed to the American public. And, actually, you know, in a bizarre sort of way, this may do it."[47]

In fact, Toobin, the most thorough analyst of the impeachment, concludes that while the Paula Jones case was an abuse of legal process influenced by politically obsessed individuals seeking financial gain, the impeachment was the product of radical and intolerant religious and moralistic influences, fuelling a partisan vendetta that showed lack of proportionality and wilful distortion of legal norms. In some respects, it may even be argued that the Clinton impeachment was the Republicans' revenge for the impeachment of President Nixon a generation earlier.

The Clinton impeachment should also be put in the broader context of the role of law and legalism in American political society. In his appreciation of Mrs. Clinton's allegation of a conspiracy, Toobin argues that law had been used as a political tool by participants in the American political system for quite some time and that before it was adopted by the right, it had been used by the left in order to advance its causes. While there may be some element of truth in this, particularly in the sense of the general blurring of the boundary between

---

[47] Op. cit., p. 256.

law and politics, the litigiousness prevalent in American society and the fundamental nature of the perception of "rights" as opposed to "obligations" or social cohesion, one must be attentive to differences of purpose and degree. In the 1960's and 1970's, the public policy use of litigation by the left was for the purpose of securing entitlements and in aid of the dispossessed in society, rather than to intentionally harm a sitting head of state for reasons essentially unrelated to governance.

To some extent, Toobin may nevertheless be correct in his systemic analysis.

> Still, Mrs. Clinton's view neglected an important, and troubling, point. Her outrage about the conspiracy presupposed a belief that there was something extraordinary about the use of the legal system to achieve political aims. In a world where, thanks largely to Democrats like the Clintons, the legal system had taken over the political system, the existence of this conspiracy was business as usual. At a time when lawsuits were replacing elections as weapons of political change, it was not surprising that Clinton's enemies chose to attack him the way they did. All they were doing was using the tools of the contemporary political trade.[48]

An even clearer picture of the use and the role of law in American politics emerges, however, in the Ginsberg and Shefter study.[49] These authors capture the full flavour of the current situation, in which not only have legal actions replaced elections as the principal battleground of political life, but in which political questions and social issues are resolved through the appointment of judges holding and expressing specific political opinions, and in which the judiciary is exercising an ever growing influence in politics through its use of what, in many other democracies, one thought of as purely, or at least primarily, legal matters: standing, recusation, class action suits, libel suits and judicial advocacy.

What then, is the legacy of the Clinton impeachment?

In the immediate, the litigation deriving from the Paula Jones case and the impeachment itself are still cascading. Maryland authorities

---

[48] *Ibid.*, p. 257.
[49] Ginsberg, Benjamin and Shefter, Martin, *Politics by Other Means*, W. W. Norton and Company, New York and London, 1999.

attempted to prosecute Linda Tripp for unauthorized recording of her phone conversations with Lewinsky. Legal actions have been contemplated against some of Starr's prosecutors for leaking information to the press. More importantly, the Arkansas Bar has undertaken to end Bill Clinton's membership in it by referring the matter to court.

More fundamental and long-term issues are also at stake, however. The questions whether the Office of Independent Counsel is the proper body to conduct an investigation of senior governmental figures which it may not be appropriate for the Attorney General to do, and whether that Office is properly constituted and staffed to carry out the function established for it after the Watergate scandal, were widely discussed. For now, these matters have been resolved by Congress allowing the law creating the Office to lapse.

The matters of the independence and impartiality of the Attorney General, and of that office holder to investigate the President and other high officials of the government of which she is a member have also been raised.

Most fundamentally of all, the United States has not yet engaged in a profound examination of the appropriate role that law does or should play in its political system. This is perhaps not surprising in a country where the strict division of power among branches of government leads to incremental, rather than comprehensive, analysis and reform. In the immediate aftermath of the Senate votes defeating the impeachment initiative, several of the key players paid for that result with their political careers. Among the population, there was also a general fatigue with the matter, following the great political intensity of 1998. In the long run, however, the matter of the best legitimate use of law in public life is unavoidable.

See also *Impeachment of President Raul Cubas*, Congress of the Republic of Paraguay, March, 1999.

§ 10.7.5
Impeachment of President Boris Yeltsin
Duma of the Russian Federation; May 15, 1999

After the dissolution of the USSR on December 21, 1991, and the consequential establishment of the Confederation of Independent States (CIS) the former constituent republics were free to adopt new and separate constitutions. The main component of the former USSR, the Russian Federated Soviet Socialist Republic, thus became the Russian Federation, an independent state within the CIS. On December 12, 1993, the Russian Federation adopted a new constitution. Some of the elements of this basic law seemed to be inspired by the *Constitution of the United States*; among these was the provisions regarding the impeachment of the president, article 93.

Article 93

(1) The President of the Russian Federation may be impeached by the Federation Council only on the basis of charges put forward against him of high treason or some other grave crime, confirmed by a ruling of the Supreme Court of the Russian Federation on the presence of indicia of crime in the President's actions and by a ruling of the Constitutional Court of the Russian Federation confirming that the procedure of bringing charges has been observed.

(2) The ruling of the State Duma on putting forward charges and the decision of the Federation Council on impeachment of the President shall be passed by the votes of two-thirds of the total number in each of the chambers at the initiative of at least one-third of the deputies of the State Duma and in the presence of the opinion of a special commission formed by the State Duma.

(3) The decision of the Federation Council on impeaching the President of the Russian Federation shall be passed within three months of the charges being brought against the President by the State Duma. The charges against the President shall be considered to be rejected if the decision of the Federation Council shall not be passed.[50]

In effect, this article put in place a four-stage procedure for impeachment, involving both legislative and judicial institutions. It also crys-

---

[50] http://www.fipc.ru/fipc/constit/ch4.html.

tallized the notion of "indicia of crime" in the actions of the President, without specifying the nature of the crime alluded to, its extent or gravity. The drafters of the provision, knowingly or with absence of foresight, created a procedure that would inherently involve a political reading of the constitution and of legal norms, and that could, in times of political division and crisis, provide a powerful weapon to the opponents of the President.

In the spring of 1999, while Boris Yeltsin was in what would turn out to be the last year of his presidency, the Duma held a majority of Communist deputies opposing Yeltsin from the left. The atmosphere at that time was one of intense partisan rivalry. Moreover, the example of the attempted impeachment of President Clinton in the United States was freshly in mind, perhaps not as a way of destituting the chief executive, but at least of paralyzing his administration. Thus, on April 12 of that year, a panel of the Duma brought charges of impeachable offences against President Yeltsin.

Five charges were brought against Yeltsin:

- treason, in respect of the 1991 agreements to terminate the existence of the USSR;

- the dissolution of the Duma in 1993 and the bombing of the Parliament Building;

- the destruction of the Russian military;

- the conduct of the war on Chechnya in 1994-1996; and

- genocide against the Russian people through their impoverishment and the reduction of life expectancy.

The extraordinary element underlying these charges was that their blatantly political nature meant that the phrase "indicia of crime in the President's actions" in section 93 of the *Russian Constitution* was as broad and difficult to interpret as the expression "high crimes and misdemeanours" in the impeachment provision of the American one.

After some delays, the debate on the charges began on May 13, 1999, and lasted two days. The Duma being comprised of 450 deputies, the required majority needed for impeachment on any charge was 300.

On the days when the debate was conducted, however, as few as 348 delegates were present; none of the charges was voted. Only in respect of the conduct of the war in Chechnya was the vote even close, with 283 deputes opting for impeachment.

President Yeltsin went on to preside over the fate of the Russian Federation for the remainder of the year, resigning unexpectedly on December 31, 1999.

The Yeltsin impeachment procedure directs our attention to two sets of conclusions. First, in looking at the domestic political legal scene within the Russian Federation, the focus on the elements and on the legitimacy of the debate. By its actions, the Duma assumed functions which, at least in appearance were judicial. In fact, what was happening was that under the authority of section 93 of the *Constitution*, the Duma, or more specifically certain factions within it hijacked the *Constitution* for political purposes. Divergent segments of the Russian political elite were engaged in a power struggle which clearly demonstrated their widely differing conceptions of the rule of law as opposed to the rule of persons in power. The procedure of section 93 must have been seen, even by the Communists, as too ponderous to succeed; they therefore used it as an opportunity for shrill expressions of political virtue and nationalistic moral values.

In the Russian context, the Yeltsin impeachment raised, but left unanswered, the most fundamental of questions: can debatable policies constitute grounds for impeachment? How far can the rule of law define politics?

In addition to the internal implications of this case, the comparative aspect, notably with the United States, must not be overlooked. In both the Yeltsin and Clinton impeachment attempts, the presence of an almost messianic flavour could be noted; the objective of the die-hard opponents was to drive an infidel out of office. In both cases, questionable legal judgments were exercised. Finally, in both exercises, the attempt was made to use constitutional legal procedures to achieve adversarial political results, unsuccessfully. It would seem that in the end, it was the constitutions themselves which succeeded by surviving in order that the processes written into them be used for more appropriate causes. Clearly, the similarity in the attempt by partisan forces to divert legal mechanisms for political motives justify not only interdisciplinary but also comparative study.

See also *Suharto v. Time Asia Inc.*, litigation initiated July 5, 1999, Central District Court, Jakarta, decision June 9, 2000, limited information available.

10.8 ISSUE: LITIGATION OF PRIMARILY POLITICAL AND PARTISAN ISSUES[51]

§ 10.8.1[52]
Currie v. MacDonald
Newfoundland Court of Appeal; January 22, 1949
(1949), 29 Nfld. & P.E.I.R. 294

One of the most fundamental matters at stake in political law is whether and to what extent a court can consider an issue that is primarily political and/or partisan in nature, but which has been brought before it by being stated in legal terms. Perhaps no case in the jurisprudence we now call Canadian addressed this question in a more authoritative and thorough manner than this one, rendered by the courts of Newfoundland in the last few months of that jurisdiction's status as a separate British colony.

From January 1934 on, Newfoundland was governed by a Governor and a Commission appointed by the United Kingdom at Newfoundland's own request. In the years from 1946 until 1949, a lively and indeed passionate debate took place as to the form of governance which the colony should adopt as it regained its ability to be self-sufficient. The focal point of that debate was the holding of two consecutive referenda in which the population was asked whether, among other options, Newfoundland should unite with Canada. It was in the midst of this process that Currie and other former members of the pre-1934 Legislature of Newfoundland brought this action. The clear motive of the plaintiffs was the political one of intending to stop the union. They were trying to accomplish through legal means and resort to the courts the goals in public life which they had not been able to achieve through political means, by convincing a sufficient segment of the population to vote according to their preference or to

---
[51] Cross-reference to § 2.4, 4.3, 6.6, 6.7 and 10.13.
[52] Cross-reference to § 4.11.C.1.

get the officials responsible for governance to espouse their views. This became the classic case of the continuation of politics by legal means.

In order to enable the court to become seized of the case, the plaintiffs could not frame their arguments in the same fashion as they had on the public podium or on the referendum platforms. They were required to cost their arguments in terms of legal concepts and principles. Thus, they addressed to the court an application for a series of declarations that would show that inclusion of the option of union with Canada among the referendum options was illegal; that Newfoundland's own *National Convention Act* of 1946 and *Referendum Act* of 1948 were *ultra vires* and invalid; and finally that the procedure undertaken in Newfoundland in moving toward union with Canada was repugnant to the *Newfoundland Act*, which the British Parliament had enacted in 1933.

There were several potential benefits for the plaintiffs in following this course of action. If they were successful, the result they would reach of preventing union with Canada would be the same by means of law as by way of politics. Second, if they won through the courts of law rather than through political campaigning, the victory would have been achieved on a basis of principles, rather than interest and power; there could be a benefit in depoliticization of the matter in terms of the abatement of discord among the population because the battle would have been fought on more proper grounds. The contrary view was that matters relating to the constitutional and political organization of the country were properly in the realm of political life, subject to popular debate, plurality of opinion, partisan belief and not scholarly or doctrinaire in nature. These discussions were noticeably prescient of the argumentation around the question of the method of deciding Québec's future, whether by referendum or by court action, almost 50 years later.

The first court to consider Currie's case was the Supreme Court of Newfoundland.[53] In its view, the grievance was that the alternative of union with Canada was offered to the people. From this, it concluded that the pleadings disclosed no reasonable cause of action and that the action should be dismissed as frivolous or vexatious. Today,

---

[53] (1948), 29 Nfld. & P.E.I.R. 314, 84 A.P.R. 314, affirmed (1949), 29 Nfld. & P.E.I.R. 294 (Nfld. C.A.).

many courts reach similar conclusions when presented with such "political" cases and offer no detailed explanation. This court however, gave explanations for its views. On the factual, political level, it thought that the referendum complained about was concluded and the action was therefore belated.

It is on the nature of the case itself that the court's pronouncements are most worthwhile noting. Justice Dunfield approached the relationship of law and politics from several perspectives and determined which elements were subject to his decision-making capacity. The selection of the options to be put before the people of Newfoundland was said to fall into the ambit of "overriding Acts of State, done by paramount power which is the sole judge of its own actions, and done with the assent of a majority of our own people."[54] This was the essence of political decision-making.

Having determined that the matter raised by the plaintiffs was political in nature, Dunfield held that it was beyond the realm of the courts.

> This court is the King's Court. It enforces the law of the realm, and restrains those who would break the law, refuse their obligations or illegally oppress their fellows. But it takes the law from the legal sources of law. The courts are regulative, not originative. The Crown in Council and the Crown in Parliament are the ultimate centres of Governmental power. Once we know that it is their will which is being done, the matter is beyond us.[55]

Not content with this explanation, the court went on to ground its decision on the motive that in a unitary jurisdiction with no formal written constitution, the principal doctrine at work was that of the supremacy of Parliament and that the latter could adopt any statute it thought opportune. This was held to be applicable to Newfoundland as well. Thus, in response to Currie's pleading that the Imperial Parliament had no power to make a law for the Confederation of Newfoundland and Canada, except at the request of a Parliament elected by the people of Newfoundland, the court responded rather categorically that:

> Every lawyer known (sic), or should know, (a) that there is no such thing as a constitutional law superior to the will of Parliament; (b) that Parlia-

---

[54] *Ibid.* at 329 (81).
[55] *Ibid.* at 317 (47).

ment could make the law suggested regardless entirely of the wishes of all of us if it were so disposed; (c) that there is no such thing as a universal right to parliamentary representation known to the law; at present we have none, and can gain none save by the will of the Crown with the assent of the Imperial Parliament; and many other parts of the Empire have none.[56]

The Newfoundland Court of Appeal was even more explicit in its reasons, and therefore more authoritative. In their respective ways, each of the judges dealt with the central issue of whether the court could adjudicate on political matter in which the legal aspect was, in their opinion, secondary if present at all. Chief Justice Emerson felt that only the Attorney General could take action to enforce rights common to all or a great number of the people. He added that a judge should not exercise his jurisdiction if evidence of an extrinsic nature had to be sought or if the argumentation entailed historical research into law. Dunfield, who had rendered the lower ruling, limited himself to the argument that the results of the referendum should be considered to be consistent with democratic theory.

The major ruling was written by Winter, J. He first indicated that the importance of the matter was political and in no sense loyal, and that the plaintiffs had confused the two. He felt that as a judge he needed good reason for stepping beyond the line which clearly separated law and politics and he would use this case to show just where that line lies.

Winter's first line of reasoning was based on the argument of politics as being law in the making. He perceived the case as being an attack on the validity of the *National Convention Act* of 1946 and the *Referendum Act* of 1948. These statutes, he said, did not create rights. They were adopted for the purpose of putting information into the hands of the Imperial Government about the state of public affairs in Newfoundland; information upon which that government might or might not take action. In turn, the Imperial Parliament may or may not implement the wishes of the government.

> I might add that, in pure theory—and that is what really matters in this sort of case—the Imperial Parliament might or might not implement the wishes of the Imperial Government itself, and indeed might ignore those of the people of Newfoundland altogether. Now, in all this we are in the

---

[56] *Ibid.* at 328 (77).

field of practical politics, not of law. The matters involved concern law in the making; the courts have to do only with law, that is to say, statute law, when made. The information obtained as the result of these two Acts could conceivably have been got through the efforts of public-spirited citizens, through some movement initiated outside of government altogether; and indeed that is how many statutory reforms are in fact brought about. I find it therefore difficult to see how it can be argued that it was, or could be, ultra vires the Commission of Government to enact these measures.[57]

Winter reiterated and reinforced this reasoning in his conclusions by emphasizing the freedom of action of Parliament and the political nature of its deliberations prior to the completion of the legislative process.

In pure legal theory—and I have to repeat that that is all this court must consider—that body is free, and cannot be trammelled, to act as it pleases.

. . .

It follows from this that the matter is still in the domain of practical politics, not of law.[58]

The second and even stronger line of reasoning adopted by Winter was based on the true meaning of "constitutional law." Currie had argued that the *National Convention Act* and the *Referendum Act* were repugnant to the *Newfoundland Act* of 1933 and therefore unconstitutional. On this point, Winter distinguished three meanings of the concept of constitutionality. The first use was as a classification or description of a large body of law and legal principle. The second use was related to countries with a written constitution and referred to the requirement that there be no repugnancy of an enactment of the legislature to the written constitution. In the United Kingdom and in Newfoundland, there was no limit in legal theory to the power of Parliament and there was no written British Constitution. Thus, the question of unconstitutionality could not arise in this sense in Newfoundland. Statutes of Newfoundland "must be valid and effective or invalid and of no effect,"[59] depending only whether they could be

---

[57] *Ibid.* at 307 (31).
[58] *Ibid.* at 312 (38).
[59] *Ibid.* at 309 (34).

held repugnant to an Imperial Statute by a British colonial court or the Privy Council.

It was the third usage which the court held to have been used in this case, mistakenly. This relates to rules which are only conventions and usages of a constitutional nature. Violating them is also termed "unconstitutional." These rules pertain more to political life than to legality. Here, the court made some fundamental observations. As to the binding characteristic of such rules, it said that

> in their own way and with different sanctions behind them they are just as binding as genuine rules of law.[60]

Further, as to the role of the courts in respect of such political rules, it said:

> Not merely has a court of law no power to redress directly a violation of a genuinely constitutional rule, but it is, I should think, the last place in which redress should be sought.[61]

The court held that this third usage was the one applicable to the plaintiff's case. It saw that the motive of the action was to have the prospect of union with Canada discussed from the Newfoundland side through the medium of a duly elected and responsible Newfoundland government. It refused to pronounce itself on the merits of the proposition as that was in the realm of politics and statesmanship. That discussion was held to be outside the province of the court and Justice Winter could only imagine that there might be strong arguments for and against it.

---

§ 10.8.2
Clark v. Canada (Attorney General)
Ontario High Court of Justice; November 9, 1977
(1977), 81 D.L.R. (3d) 33

While in *Currie v. MacDonald* we saw that significant political issues were thrust for determination before the courts at various times throughout Canadian history, the interest of this case is more im-

---

[60] *Ibid.* at 309 (34).
[61] *Ibid.* at 309 (34).

mediate in that it deals with such a topic in the course of the last few years before the adoption of the *Canadian Charter of Rights and Freedoms* as part of the legal and political landscape. It thus enables us to see how the courts dealt with political matters in recent times, but without yet having the *Charter* as a vehicle for such considerations.

The applicants here are Clark, the leader of the Progressive Conservative Official Opposition in the House of Commons, and several other parliamentarians of the same political persuasion. On the face of it, this case is almost indistinguishable from other disputes of a principally legal nature. Its particularity lies, however, in the circumstances under which it was brought before the court. This was the continuation, by judicial means, of a domestic political struggle relating to atomic energy in which the Official Opposition seemingly felt it could not succeed in other ways. The case also had international implications related to U.S. anti-trust legislation dealing with the role of uranium, a substance that is as politically sensitive as it is chemically. An astute observer can detect, even if only from the words of the judgment, but certainly from the circumstances of the issue at the time, that the applicants were not interested in obtaining redress of legal wrongs allegedly done to them, but rather in attempting to influence the flow and outcome of public debate on the matter, in determining the course of Parliamentary consideration and governmental action, and in achieving political and partisan success vis-à-vis the governing Liberal Party and its Leader, Prime Minister Trudeau. The value of this case derives from our conclusions about the approach used by the court, as a judicial body, to deal with this political dilemma.

The applicants sought judicial review of the Uranium Information Security Regulations[62] (the Regulations), the purpose of which was to prohibit the release of information about uranium, except in certain specified and limited circumstances. Prior to addressing the question on its merits, the court felt it had to determine whether it had jurisdiction in the matter. This aspect of the case was determined along legal arguments exclusively. The legal subject matter of the case being an attack on the validity of a federal instrument, there was some question as to whether an Ontario court, using the *Judicial Review Procedure Act*,[63] should be dealing with this matter or whether it

---

[62] SOR/76-644.
[63] S.O. 1971, c. 48.

should leave it for the Federal Court of Canada, using sections 17 and 18 of the *Federal Court Act*. Not being convinced that the *Federal Court Act* was designed to cover the situation, this court assumed jurisdiction. Presumably on the basis of the pleadings presented to it, however, it did not confront head on the matter whether the issue for decision was legal or political, at this stage.

The court also skirted the law-politics dilemma in respect of the application of the Canadian Civil Liberties Association for intervenor status as an *amicus curiae*. While it did not use the expression "politics," the court did however make it understood in a subtle manner that this was public interest litigation by clarifying that *amicus* interventions should be allowed only where the court is in need of assistance because of the failure to present the issues. Such interventions were, it said, unnecessary where they "would only serve to widen the *lis* between the parties or introduce a new cause of action."[64]

The court faced the crux of the issue of law and politics being combined within a litigious action in a yet further preliminary observation and on the merits of the application. The opposition parliamentarians asked that the court exercise its judicial review by issuing a number of declarations, especially those to the effect that the Regulations do not prohibit them from releasing communications facilitating the conduct of legal proceedings, and from releasing or disclosing any such documents in the course and in furtherance of Parliamentary debate.

To a great extent, the court perceived this as a premature attempt to achieve a political first strike.

> There is one aspect of this application which does concern me. In their alternative submissions, they seek a declaration that a Member of Parliament cannot be prevented from using the information in Parliament. Moreover, they seek a declaration that the Regulations do not abridge the solicitor-client privilege. In this respect, they are seeking "absolution before sinning." In my view, they should advance these two arguments as a defence if they are charged. Practically speaking, they may not be charged, in which case this part of the application is simply an academic exercise.[65]

---

[64] (1977), 81 D.L.R. (3d) 33 at 38.
[65] *Ibid.* at 43.

The court indeed repeated its expression: "absolution before sinning" in other places and emphasized that it would deal with the merits of the case with great caution. It then concluded this phase of its consideration by indicating, as a warning of the political nature of the dispute, "Once again, I am concerned that these proceedings are inappropriate."[66]

The principal "political question" of this case was whether the applicants, as Parliamentarians, would be prevented by the Regulations from releasing or disclosing documents relating to uranium in the course of, or in furtherance of Parliamentary debate. This medium of discussion of public affairs, namely Parliamentary debate, is the most intrinsic blend of law and politics possible. In order to be able to consider this properly in a pre-*Charter* environment, the court had to address the dispute in terms of Parliamentary privilege. The question then became whether the Regulations constituted an infringement of that privilege.

Here also, the court looked first at whether it had jurisdiction to deal with the matter of Parliamentary privilege. It based its affirmative response on the *Roman Corp.* case. It then went on to consider the interaction between proceeding and disclosures made in Parliament by Members of the House of Commons and statutory provisions requiring secrecy, such as the *Official Secrets Act*. It then came to the conclusion:

> Following the authorities set out above, I have come to the conclusion that a Member of Parliament may utilize information proscribed by SOR/76-644 in Parliament and may release that information to the media. However, I hold that the privilege of the Member cannot be extended to protect the media if they choose to release the information to the public. Nor do I consider that the "real" and "essential" functions of a Member include a duty or right to release information to constituents. The cases indicate that the privilege is finite and I would not be justified in extending the privilege to cover information released to constituents.
>
> . . .
>
> My reading of the authorities does not convince me that the Regulations

---

[66] *Ibid.*

can prevent the applicants from disclosing the information to their so-licitors for the purpose of obtaining legal advice.[67]

This case is unusual both because it is in some respects an advisory opinion, as no offence had yet been alleged, and because it covered a number of related but distinguishable issues. Despite these difficul-ties, we may draw several conclusions from it. First, counsel were able to cast political conflicts in legal terms and the court proved willing to be seized of the matter even though it realized that the foundation of the dispute was more political than legal. Moreover, the court was most astute in writing a Solomon-like judgment, finding that the Regulations did not prevent Parliamentary debate but also finding that most of the regulatory text was *ultra vires*. In doing so, it enabled politics to be continued in the proper forum for Parliament, while respecting the domain of law. It also declared that only Parlia-ment was entitled to judge what steps must be taken in the national interest. The court was thus expressing respect for the role reserved to each branch of government.

---

§ 10.8.3
R. v. Halpert
Ontario County Court; October 15, 1984
(1984), 15 C.C.C. (3d) 292

In the late 1970's and early 1980's, Canada took the decision to change its system of weights and measures from the Imperial system to the Metric. A small but vocal part of the citizenry resisted this evolution, on the basis of its inherent conservatism, an emotional attachment to things British and, ostensibly, on the grounds of the cost to business. The conflict became politicized and, in this case among some others, the political debate was attempted to be continued through judicial means, in the hope that the binding nature of the court rulings would lend weight to the losing side in the political discourse. The recalci-trant were not successful in stopping the march of progress, but the real interest of the matter is the way in which the court adjudicated on what had essentially become a partisan political issue.

---

[67] *Ibid.* at 58-59.

The Weights and Measures Regulations,[68] made pursuant to the *Weights and Measures Act*,[69] provided for a transition period in the process of metrification. Following an end-date for use of the gallon as the unit of measurement in the retail sale of gasoline, from January 1, 1979, until December 31, 1980, both the gallon and the litre could be used. As of January 1, 1981, the litre alone became the legal measure. In early January 1983, Halpert's gas station in Toronto offered sale by the litre at 3 pumps and by the gallon at 9 others, apparently in response to consumer demand. On January 14, 1983, the offending pumps were sealed by inspectors. With what the court called all due attendant publicity, Halpert removed the seals and resumed business as usual. He was charged with offences relating to both the sale and the removal of the seals. A Provincial Court judge patently sympathetic to Halpert's cause and perhaps somewhat too anxious to see the legal merits of his defence quashed the information. The Crown appealed and the County Court allowed the appeal, in the process demolishing every element of the lower judge's ruling.

The court started off by recognizing the openly political nature of the case, when it said that "This is a 'high profile' case which has attracted much publicity. I am reasonably confident that it will keep going as far as the obtaining of such leave as may be necessary will permit."[70] It reinforced this by showing how the volume of the file was out of all proportion to the seriousness of the issue in dispute. It was indeed unusual at this low level of court to have a nine-volume transcript.

The court then looked methodically at every one of Halpert's arguments. On the matter of the *vires of* the Regulations and, through it, of the entire metrification scheme, it pointed to the devious federal jurisdiction under section 91(17) of the *Constitution Act, 1867*, which might impinge on property and civil rights, but only incidentally. The court's approval of jurisdiction to effect metrification was definitive:

> I cannot view the legislative provision for a uniform system of measurement throughout Canada as anything other than the valid exercise of Parliament's legislative jurisdiction over weights and measures and the

---

[68] C.R.C. 1978, c. 1605.
[69] S.C. 1970-71-72, c. 36.
[70] (1984), 15 C.C.C. (3d) 292 at 295.

prohibition of commercial use through offering, advertising or display-
ing as other than essential to the achievement of that legitimate goal.[71]

The core of the judgment is the court's reaction to the contention by
Halpert that the Regulations were contrary to his freedom of expression guaranteed by section 2(b) of the *Charter*. In blunt terms, the
court said that the Provincial Court judge had become mesmerized
by this argument.

> I do find that the prohibition against the offering, advertising or dis-
> playing for retail trade of gasoline in units other than litres has a rational
> basis as part of the over-all scheme of metrification. I do not consider it
> this court's role to try to second guess the duly-elected representatives
> of the people in Parliament assembled. Parliament has decided that
> metrification is a "good thing" for Canada. I cannot imagine how that
> policy could be implemented without the ultimate goal of universality.
> To permit unbridled freedom of choice would be to Balkanize the coun-
> try and encourage the dinosaur mentality. If the restrictions contained
> in s. 336 of the Regulations constitute a restriction on freedom of expres-
> sion, such restriction is within the reasonable limits justified in a free
> and democratic society.[72]

In essence this court was saying not only that the metrification scheme
was legally valid, but also that it should apply curial deference to
enable Parliament, the political decision-maker, to determine what is
a "good thing" for Canada. The additional references to "unbridled
freedom," "Balkanization" and "dinosaur mentality" can be interpreted either as indications to Parliament not to change the scheme
in response to such judicialized political rear-guard actions, or to the
accused to accept the rational and modernizing will of the majority
of society.

The other legal arguments were similarly rejected. In a final swipe at
the bad ruling of the lower court, the judgment emphasized that that
judge lacked jurisdiction to award the exaggerated sum of $42,000 as
costs to the accused in such a summary conviction case.

The matter went no further.

---

[71] *Ibid.* at 297.
[72] *Ibid.* at 298.

See also *Tremblay c. Québec (Procureur général)*, [2001] R.J.Q. 1293 (Que. S.C.), leave to appeal refused (2001), 275 N.R. 389 (note) (S.C.C.).

---

§ 10.8.4
Black v. Canada (Prime Minister)
Ontario Court of Appeal; May 18, 2001
(2001), 199 D.L.R. (4th) 228

Conflicts of a political and partisan nature are, presumably, to be resolved in the political arena. Where political action results in what is effectively a standoff, one of the parties may transfer the conflict into the legal sphere either in the hope of resolving the matter through legally binding means or with the unexpressed purpose of protracting the conflict and publicizing it, no matter what the result, or both. In such cases, the observer can look first at the legal and judicial resolution of conflicts based on ideology, personality, conviction, enmity or all of the foregoing in various combinations, and see if the result advances either the political matter or the legal principles involved. We can ask whether there are alternative means left to decide the point, or alternative venues in which to continue to debate them. We can look at the legal effect of the resolution of the dispute by the courts and we can determine whether the legal phrasing of the claim or the defence raised new valid points about the effect and the effectiveness of law.

In the summer of 1999, the clash of world views between Prime Minister Chrétien and Canadian newspaper publisher Conrad Black reached this point of apparent standoff. In February of that year, the Leader of the Conservative Opposition in the United Kingdom, William Hague, recommended Black for a peerage. Canadian authorities apparently informed Black that they would not object if Black became a citizen of the U.K. and if he did not use the title in Canada. Black took the required steps but days before he was due to be enabled to join the House of Lords, Prime Minister Blair told him that Prime Minister Chrétien had interceded with the Queen to deny Black the honour. Black and Chrétien allegedly discussed this, but the Government of Canada would not change its position. The monarch deferred on this issue to her Canadian Prime Minister's advice.

Black alleged that Chrétien attributed his action to dissatisfaction with the way Black's newspaper, the *National Post*, had treated Chrétien negatively in general, and specifically the persistent way it had investigated job creation schemes in the riding of the Prime Minister.

Whatever Black's motivation, he transferred the matter from the royal court to the court of law. On August 5, 1998, in a singular move, and one much trumpeted by his own newspapers, Black started a legal action against the Prime Minister in Toronto for abuse of power, negligent misrepresentation and misfeasance in public office. The key elements of the claim were was follows:

> Prime Minister Chrétien asserted that he had the right to block the plaintiff's nomination, even though the plaintiff was then a dual British-Canadian citizen, because of a resolution passed by the Canadian House of Commons in 1919 ("Nickle Resolution") which required the then King to refrain from conferring any title of honour or titular distinction upon any of his subjects domiciled or ordinarily resident in Canada.

> Prime Minister Chrétien knew or ought to have known that the Nickle Resolution had no legal effect. It was not a law. In particular, Prime Minister Chrétien knew or ought to have known that the Nickle Resolution had no legal effect on the prerogatives of Her Majesty the Queen in right of the United Kingdom. Furthermore, without the status of a statute passed by both houses of Parliament and royal assent it could not affect in any way the prerogatives of Her Majesty the Queen in right of Canada. Accordingly, Prime Minister Chrétien's action in intervening with the Queen to oppose the plaintiff's appointment as a peer was wholly without legal basis.

> . . .

> Prime Minister Chrétien's conduct was wholly without legal basis. The Prime Minister has subsequently attempted to justify his actions by reference to regulations promulgated in 1968, and a policy issued in 1988, which address the receipt of foreign honours by Canadian citizens. Neither of these documents on its face applies to the plaintiff. Neither of them binds the present government and reliance on them constitutes only an *ex post facto* attempt to justify the Prime Minister's unlawful actions.[73]

---

[73] Statement of claim, paras. 13, 14 and 18.

The forceful character of this claim was diminished only by the fact that at one place it indicated that Black's peerage was suspended, while at another, it was stated to have been denied.

The Office of the Prime Minister must have anticipated the launching of this litigation as within a day, it issued a formal statement which was backed by a number of instruments on which the Prime Minister grounded this justification of his action before the public and the media. The legal defence was launched on September 10, 1999; the Prime Minister's formal response was that "the facts alleged are immune from liability for negligence because the actions and decisions alleged were 'policy' decisions and not 'operational' decisions and, as such, cannot be the basis for tortious liability."[74]

The sensational nature of the case led to extensive coverage and commentary, richly fueled by both parties. The self righteous tone of Black's own *National Post* was to be expected when it indicated that Chrétien may be called to testify at the trial: "He'll have to attend...He might be the prime minister but he's also a person like anyone else in the eyes of the law."[75] The more independent *Toronto Star* countered with a little deflating reply:

> British peerage expert Harold Brecks-Baker said peerages have traditionally been conferred on those who've made significant contributions to British society, not just on persons who contributed "substantial sums of money" to political parties.[76]

After a few days, the commentary became more sober and analytical. One commentator, noting the British political ramifications of the story, thought the entire matter internal to the U.K., with Prime Minister Blair using the opportunity of the debate between two Canadian antagonists to discredit his own Opposition Leader, Hague, by saving the Queen the need to choose between himself and Mr. Chrétien, her two Prime Ministers.[77] Even more pertinent was the legal comment on the case. It was being rumoured that Black, an admiring biogra-

---

[74] Notice of motion; para. 3.
[75] "Conrad Black sues Prime Minister over lost peerage," Charlie Gillis, *National Post*, August 6, 1999.
[76] "Black takes PM to court in title fight," William Walker, *Toronto Star*, August 6, 1999.
[77] "The whole thing is Tony Blair's fault," William Christian, *Globe and Mail*, Toronto, August 10, 1999.

pher of Québec Premier Duplessis, was intending to rely on the precedent of *Roncarelli v. Duplessis*, a case dealing with abuse of power.
The son of Roncarelli's lawyer noted the distinctions between the two
cases: Duplessis had had no legal justification for the illegal action he
took, while Chrétien had a legal rationale; Duplessis had admitted
giving the illegal instructions based on his opposition to Roncarelli's
actions, while Chrétien was denying the link of his actions to the
negative *National Post* stories.[78]

The Prime Minister made a motion to strike the statement of claim as
against him. If this were successful, the controversiality of the litigation would be dramatically reduced and perhaps, much of its political
content might disappear. The hearing was held on November 8, 1999,
and the ruling was handed down on March 15, 2000.

With respect to the claim of negligent misrepresentation, Chrétien
conceded that the claim could proceed. On the application for declaratory relief, the Prime Minister argued that jurisdiction vested in
the Federal Court, or alternatively that there was no reasonable cause
of action in respect of negligence or abuse of power. The court accepted as established the facts alleged in the amended statement of
claim.

At the outset, the court noted that despite the existence of other lesser
instruments, the Prime Minister was not acting in this case pursuant
to an Act, because none existed. Thus, his "advice" to the Monarch
may have been an intervention, but it was not an order. Thus, in
determining whether section 18 of the *Federal Court Act* applied to the
jurisdiction of the Ontario Superior Court, there was no opportunity
to determine whether the Prime Minister constituted a "federal board,
commission or tribunal."

> Since the PM's action was not exercised pursuant to an Act of Parliament
> nor was it an order, the claim does not come clearly or exclusively within
> the jurisdiction of the Federal Court (Trial Division). Because the juris-
> diction of the Federal Court is not exclusive, this superior court has
> jurisdiction to entertain the claim as against the PM.[79]

---

[78] "He won't find a foothold in the Roncarelli case," Michael Stein, *Globe and Mail*,
Toronto, August 10, 1999.
[79] (2000), 47 O.R. (3d) 532 (Ont. S.C.J.) at 539, para. 17, affirmed (2001), 199 D.L.R. (4th)
228 (Ont. C.A.).

The same principles were held to apply to the government. Thus, the court asserted jurisdiction.

Next, the court looked at what, from a legal perspective, is the core of the matter: justiciability.

> In this case the issue is the justiciability of the PM's actions. The outcome of this case depends entirely on the legal character of the actions of the PM alleged in the Amended Statement of Claim. If they reflected an exercise of crown prerogative in relation to the granting or withholding of honours, or in relation to advice given to another country, those actions are political matters beyond the reach of the court.[80]

From the point of view of adjudication, the choice was quite stark: either crown prerogative and therefore beyond justiciability, or the exercise of statutory power and therefore subject to the oversight of the court. The decision on this point was unequivocal.

> If Black acknowledges that the Queen was exercising her royal prerogative in deciding to suspend the appointment, then it is evident that the PM is exercising crown prerogative in discussing the matter with her.[81]

It is significant that in making this decision, the court indicated that it saw the political, partisan and domestically controversy-generating nature of Black's motivation in litigating. It said that Black's own pleading acknowledged that the Queen had acted within her prerogative in making her decision and that this "is indicative of why this matter is not being litigated in the United Kingdom."[82]

The court also affirmed that the conduct of foreign affairs in general and the bestowing or withholding of honours in particular are within the political arena, thus rendering the Prime Minister subject to accountability before Parliament and the electorate, but not subject to the review of the courts. It found nothing in the *Department of Foreign Affairs and International Trade Act*[83] that would expressly or implicitly trench on the PM's prerogatives in this domain.

---

[80] *Ibid*. at 540, para. 22.
[81] *Ibid*. at 541, para. 24.
[82] *Ibid*.
[83] R.S.C. 1985, c. E-22.

The court struck the claim for negligence but allowed that for negligent misrepresentation to proceed. The claim for abuse of power was also struck out. For emphasis, the court summarized its position, letting the applicant see its views that these matters were best dealt with in other *fora* of a non-legal variety.

> It is not for the court to inquire into the wisdom of the decisions made by the PM in relation to the grant or withholding of honours or his advice to the government of the United Kingdom in relation to Black. Those are political questions. Whatever the reasons for the path taken by the PM, they do not change the essentially political and prerogative nature of his decisions and actions. It is his prerogative, non-reviewable in court, to give advice and express opinions on honours and foreign affairs. Under the current state of our law his actions and his reasons for giving that advice or expressing those opinions are not justiciable.[84]

Litigious by nature, Black instructed his lawyers to immediately state publicly that an appeal would be launched, and so it was. Black appealed on the issue of justiciability and Chrétien cross-appealed regarding the jurisdiction of the Ontario Superior Court to grant declaratory relief.

The Ontario Court of Appeal ruled on May 18, 2001, dismissing the appeal as well as Chrétien's cross-appeal. This judgment, crafted under the pen of Mr. Justice Laskin, was a classic text regarding litigation of a primarily political set of issues in an environment both highly charged, in that it pitted very powerful individuals in public life, and made politically confrontational by the drastically opposite partisan views of the antagonists.

This court first looked at whether the question raised by Black was justiciable. It broke this down into two issues:

> The broad question raised by Mr. Black's pleading is whether it discloses a justiciable cause of action against the Prime Minister. As I stated earlier, this broad question divides into two issues: Is it plain and obvious that in advising the Queen about the conferral of an honour on a Canadian citizen the Prime Minister was exercising a prerogative power? If so, is the exercise of this prerogative power reviewable by the courts?[85]

---

[84] *Supra* note 79 at 543-4, para. 35.
[85] (2001), 199 D.L.R. (4th) 228 at 237, para. 22.

Black's position was based on several arguments. First, he indicated that the Superior Court was not entitled to find that the Prime Minister had exercised a prerogative power, as he had not pleaded this. The Court of Appeal disagreed, holding that whether the PM exercised a prerogative power was a question of law which it was the court's responsibility to determine. The court also strenuously rejected Black's contention that only the Governor General, but not the Prime Minister, could exercise a prerogative power in Canada, finding no support for this position in theory or in practice.

Black also submitted that even if the Prime Minister can exercise prerogative powers relating to the granting of honours or the conduct of foreign affairs, in this instance, he was doing neither, but rather intervening personally with the Queen to give unsolicited and wrong legal advice. The court treated this petty argumentation with a blistering analytical rebuke.

> Mr. Black's argument appears to rest on the notion that Prime Minister Chrétien's communication with the Queen was grounded not in the prerogative but was a "personal intervention" motivated by a "personal vendetta." He argues that the exercise of a prerogative power is confined to the powers and privileges unique to the Crown; powers and privileges equally enjoyed with private persons are not part of the prerogative. There are two answers to Mr. Black's argument. One answer is that the Prime Minister's authority is always derived from a federal statute or the prerogative; it is never personal in nature. See Dicey, *supra*, at p. 424 and Schreiber v. Canada (Attorney General), [2000] 1 F.C. 427 (T.D.) at 444. Here, Prime Minister Chrétien did not act under a statute; he therefore acted under the authority of a Crown prerogative.

> The other answer is that even if the Prime Minister does at times act as a private citizen of Canada, he could hardly be said to have been acting as one in this case. Private citizens cannot ordinarily communicate private advice to the Queen. Thus, even accepting Mr. Black's pleading, Prime Minister Chrétien's intervention with the Queen was not personal. Whatever his motivation, he was acting as the leader of this country, giving advice or communicating Canada's policy on honours to a foreign head of state.

> For these reasons, I conclude that it is plain and obvious the Prime minister was exercising the Crown prerogative relating to the granting of honours. Because I am satisfied that the Prime Minister was exercising prerogative power relating to the granting of honours, it is unnecessary

to consider the alternative basis for the motion judge's decision, the foreign affairs prerogative, or Mr. Black's submissions on it.[86]

The court then went on to examine whether the prerogative powers exercised by the Prime Minister was reviewable by the courts. This was in effect a look at the interaction of law and politics through the lens of the ability of the judiciary to oversee the legality of the actions of the Executive Branch in the domain of prerogative powers. This was held to be the main question at issue in the appeal.

The lower court had concluded that the matter was not justiciable.

> I agree with Mr. Black that the source of the power – statute or prerogative – should not determine whether the action complained of is reviewable. However, in my view, the action complained of in this case – giving advice to the Queen or communicating to her Canada's policy on the conferral of an honour on a Canadian citizen – is not justiciable. Even if the advice was wrong or given carelessly or negligently, it is not reviewable in the courts. I therefore agree with the motions judge's conclusion.[87]

From here, the court went on to analyze the history in Canada, and the modern status, of the doctrine of justiciability. What prerogative-based actions could the courts review?

The judgment looked first at the situation in respect of the *Charter*. The Crown prerogative lies within the authority of Parliament, and by section 32 (1)(a) of the *Charter*, the *Charter* applies to the Parliament and Government of Canada. Consequently, where one's claim is that the exercise of a prerogative power violates the *Charter*, the court has a duty to decide the claim.

Where, as here, the complaint is that governmental action damaged a citizen's rights apart from the *Charter*, the courts would no longer rely on the distinction between prerogative and statutory powers to avoid judicial review. The proper test for these instances is that of the subject-matter.

> Under the law that existed at least into the 1960s, the court's power to judicially review the prerogative was very limited. The court could de-

---

[86] *Ibid.* at 243, paras. 39, 40 and 41.
[87] *Ibid.* at 244, para. 44.

termine whether a prerogative power existed and, if so, what its scope was, and whether it had been superseded by statute. However, once a court established the existence and scope of a prerogative power, it could not review how that power was exercised.

. . .

By s. 32(1)(a), the *Charter* applies to Parliament and the Government of Canada in respect of all matters within the authority of Parliament. Therefore, if an individual claims that the exercise of a prerogative power violates that individual's Charter rights, the court has a duty to decide the claim. See Operation Dismantle, supra. However, Mr. Black does not assert any Charter claim."[88]

Applying this test, the court found that an exercise of a prerogative power will be justiciable if the subject-matter affects the rights or legitimate expectations of an individual. In order to apply the test, the court had to characterize the Prime Minister's actions properly.

Prime Minister Chrétien was not giving legal advice or making an administrative decision. Focusing on wrong legal advice or the improper interpretation of a policy misses what this case is all about. As I see it the action of Prime Minister Chrétien complained of by Mr. Black is his giving advice to the Queen about the conferral of an honour on a Canadian citizen. The Prime Minister communicated Canada's policy on honours to the Queen and advised her against conferring an honour on Mr. Black.

So characterized, it is plain and obvious that the Prime Minister's exercise of the honours prerogative is not judicially reviewable.

. . .

Here, no important individual interests are at stake. Mr. Black's rights were not affected, however broadly "rights" are construed. No Canadian citizen has a right to an honour.

And no Canadian citizen can have a legitimate expectation of receiving an honour.

. . .

The conferral of the honour at issue in this case, a British peerage, is a

---

[88] *Ibid.* at 244, para. 45 and 245, para. 46.

discretionary favour bestowed by the Queen. It engages no liberty, no property, no economic interest. It enjoys no procedural protection. It does not have a sufficient legal component to warrant the court's intervention. Instead, it involves "moral and political considerations which it is not within the province of the court to assess. See *Operations Dismantle, supra,* per Dickson, J. at p.465.[89]

The ruling concluded that once the exercise of the honours prerogative itself was found to be beyond review by the courts, the manner in which the power was exercised was also beyond review.

Shortly after this Court of Appeal ruling, in a fit of public pique, Black announced that he would relinquish his Canadian citizenship in favour of the U.K. citizenship he had acquired in anticipation of ascending to the House of Lords. He left it to his editorialists on the *National Post* to restate his position and his disgust at what he perceived as not having been rendered justice.

> Mr. Black sued Mr. Chrétien, claiming the PM had abused his power in furtherance of a vendetta. The Ontario Court of Appeal dismissed the suit two weeks ago. The decision did not touch on the merits of Mr. Black's complaint, but rather, concluded the Prime Minister's "prerogative power relating to the granting of honours" is immune from judicial review. In anticipation of this decision, after the court had deliberated for six months on a point of law, Mr. Black decided to renounce his Canadian citizenship. As Mr. Black said in his statement announcing this decision, "neither the trial nor the appeal courts referred [to his] status as a U.K. citizen. Nor did the court of appeal judgment deal with the essence of the argument [his] counsel presented." The substance of Mr. Black's case against Mr. Chrétien was ignored.

> It is now being ignored again, by opposing newspapers and commentators who would rather indulge their prejudices than consider the instructive and important core of Mr. Black's case.

> . . .

> They are utterly uninterested that Mr. Chrétien's actions were nakedly self-serving and authoritarian; that he used the discretionary powers of his office to harass a prominent Canadian media owner for the simple reason that he felt threatened and affronted by this newspaper's legitimate investigations; that he abused Mr. Black's status as a dual citizen

---

[89] *Ibid.* at 249, paras. 57, 58 and 250, paras. 60, 61 and 62.

to meddle in and diminish his civil rights as a citizen of the United Kingdom.[90]

Mr. Black gave one final example of his lack of understanding of the force and effect of law in governance on August 24, 2001, while he was announcing his divestiture of holdings in the *National Post*. In discussing his renunciation of Canadian citizenship, he intimated that he would keep his Canadian passport and when Mr. Chrétien was no longer Prime Minister, he would take back Canadian citizenship. Officials of Employment and Immigration Canada were quick to point out that non-citizens were not entitled to Canadian passports and that citizenship, once surrendered, could be resumed only on application.[91] Mr. Black was sworn into the House of Lords on October 31, 2001. That day, the *National Post* ran an article complaining that the litigation had cost taxpayers nearly $ 172,000, conveniently forgetting that it was its owner at the time, Mr. Black himself, who had initiated it.[92] When asked for his opinion, Prime Minister Chrétien said that he would not comment on British affairs.

Undeniably, this case offers insight into both politics and the extent of law's review of political actions.

---

§ 10.8.5[93]
Baker v. Carr
United States Supreme Court; March 26, 1962
369 U.S. 186 (1962)

The basis of this case was an attack on the constitutionality of a 1901 Tennessee statute dealing with reapportionment of electoral boundaries for the State's General Assembly, and on the failure to reapportion for some 60 years, despite the growth and redistribution of the State's population. Due to the lack of reapportionment over such a long period, the Supreme Court was able to characterize the apportionment picture in Tennessee as "a topsy-turvical of gigantic pro-

---

[90] "Dishonourable Conduct," Editorial, *National Post*, June 2, 2001, p. A-15.
[91] "Blaming Chrétien, Black opts out of Canada," Jacquie McNish, *Globe and Mail*, August 25, 2001, p. 1.
[92] "PM's battle with Black a costly one," by Nahlah Ayed, *National Post*, October 31, 2001.
[93] International comparisons.

portions"[94] and to state that "its division into electoral districts is neither consistent nor rational."[95]

The suit actually asked the court to declare the apportionment plan unconstitutional. Rather than deal with the core of the issue, the Supreme Court looked at whether the U.S. District Court for the Central District of Tennessee had jurisdiction, and at whether the plaintiffs had standing. Most important of all, it undertook to examine the justiciability of the matter presented before it; the landmark characteristic of the judgment arose from this analysis, discussed as a preliminary issue, of whether this was a matter at all for the courts to decide. On this point, the court was extremely thorough, given that on previous occasions it had accepted some cases and rejected others.

Was reapportionment a matter of politics alone, or did it have sufficient legal content for the judiciary to consider a dispute arising out of it?

The court's first statement was that "Of course the mere fact that the suit seeks protection of a political right does not mean it presents a political question."[96] It then went on to define and restate the political question doctrine of American law in a fashion that has been followed ever since then. The doctrine relates to the judiciary's own vision of its competence to hear cases, to take judicial cognizance of them, where the circumstances would lead the court to delve into the realm of politics. This doctrine, moreover, relates to the relationship of the judiciary to the coordinate branches of the federal government, rather than to the federal judiciary's relation to the States. The doctrine is thus an aspect of the separation of power philosophy which underlies the American system of government.

The court took pains to emphasize that the political question doctrine does not encompass blanket rules as to which cases a court will accept and which others refuse to hear. Application of the doctrine requires that the courts search for the analytical threads that make it up.

> It is apparent that several formulations which vary slightly according to the settings in which the questions arise may describe a political ques-

---

[94] 369 U.S. 186 (1962) at 254.
[95] *Ibid.* at 256.
[96] *Ibid.* at 209.

tion, although each has one or more elements which identify it as essentially a function of the separation of powers. Prominent on the surface of any case held to involve a political question is found a textually demonstrable constitutional commitment of the issue to a coordinate political department; or a lack of judicially discoverable and manageable standards for resolving it; or the impossibility of deciding without an initial policy determination of a kind clearly for nonjudicial discretion; or the impossibility of a court's undertaking independent resolution without expressing lack of the respect due coordinate branches of government; or an unusual need for unquestioning adherence to a political decision already made; or the potentiality of embarrassment from multifarious pronouncements by various departments on one question.

Unless one of these formulations is inextricable from the case at bar, there should be no dismissal for non-justiciability on the ground of a political question's presence. The doctrine of which we treat is one of "political questions," not one of "political cases." The courts cannot reject as "no law suit" a bona fide controversy as to whether some action denominated "political" exceeds constitutional authority. The cases we have reviewed show the necessity for discriminating inquiry into the precise facts and posture of the particular case, and the impossibility of resolution by any semantic cataloguing.[97]

The court also distinguished the political question doctrine from matters arising under the so-called "Guaranty Clause," namely Act IV, section 4 of the *United States Constitution*, which guarantees a republican form of government.

We shall discover the Guaranty Clause claims involve those elements which define a "political question," and for that reason and no other, they are nonjusticiable. In particular, we shall discover that the nonjusticiability of such claims has nothing to do with their touching upon matters of state governmental organization.[98]

Having laid down these fundamental rules, the Supreme Court went on to find that the inaction of the Tennessee authorities was in fact justiciable. There was no question to be decided by a political branch of government unequal with the court. Moreover, there was no lack of judicially manageable standards. Thus, on the basis of the Fourteenth Amendment, the Equal Protection Clause, the Supreme Court held that the matter did not fall within the political question category.

---

[97] *Ibid.* at 217.
[98] *Ibid.* at 218.

Concurring with the majority, Justice Clark issued a most interesting separate opinion. While the majority, having held the matter justiciable, sent the case back to the District Court for determination, he would have preferred that the Supreme Court decide on the merits as well.

> Finally, we must consider if there are any appropriate modes of effective judicial relief. The federal courts are of course not forums for political debate, nor should they resolve themselves into state constitutional conventions or legislative assemblies. Nor should their jurisdiction be exercised in the hope that such a declaration as is made today may have the direct effect of bringing on legislative action and relieving the courts of the problems of fashioning relief. To my mind this would be nothing less than blackjacking the Assembly into reapportioning the State. If judicial competence were lacking to fashion an effective decree, I would dismiss this appeal. However, like the Solicitor General of the United States, I see no such difficulty in the position of this case. One plan might be to start with the existing assembly districts, consolidate some of them, and award the seats thus released to those counties suffering the most egregious discrimination. Other possibilities are present and might be more effective. But the plan here suggested would at least release the strangle hold now on the Assembly and permit it to redistrict itself.[99]

The Canadian practice in this respect is not as comprehensively or as systematically set out. For that reason, an interpretation of the American doctrine into this country's legal system is most useful.

> Two rival approaches to the "political questions" doctrine developed in the U.S. Under the first approach, the doctrine is seen as a necessary corollary to the separation of powers. Declining to decide cases on these grounds is not viewed as a matter for judicial discretion but rather for judicial interpretation of the Constitution. If the Constitution is interpreted to have assigned authority over certain disputes involving government actors to the executive or legislative branch, then a challenge to those actions could not be justiciable in a court. The second approach contends that the judiciary has the authority and the responsibility to make prudential judgments in deciding which branch of government is best suited to resolving a dispute. In addition to these two schools of thought, there remain some observers who view the doctrine as incoherent in its formulations and application and contend there is no reason for its existence.

---

[99] *Ibid.* at 259-260.

. . .

The American "political questions" doctrine, which rarely invoked, continues to embody several key principles of judicial review. It stands for the proposition that a court should not decide cases which require an initial policy determination of a kind clearly for political discretion. It emphasizes that a court cannot properly adjudicate a matter where there exist no judicially discoverable standards to apply. Finally, it affirms that a court should not interfere with another branch of government's dispute resolution functions, where these have been constitutionally mandated. While the American "political questions" doctrine is clearly rooted in the unique balance of powers in the U.S. Constitution, the principles upon which it rests are of universal application for courts in democratic societies.[100]

See also *In re Fayed*,[101] 91 F. Supp.2d 137 (D.D.C., 2000).

10.9 ISSUE: REPORTING ON EVENTS AND FIGURES IN POLITICAL LIFE[102]

§ 10.9.1
Vander Zalm v. Times Publishers
British Columbia Supreme Court; January 16, 1979
(1979), 96 D.L.R. (3d) 172[103]

At the relevant time, Vander Zalm was, since December 1975, a member of the Legislature of British Columbia and Minister of Human Resources.[104] In a cartoon which appeared in the *Victoria Times* newspaper of June 22, 1978, the defendants published a drawing of Vander Zalm in the act of pulling wings from flies, but did not provide any explanation of the meaning or intent of the representation of the Minister and did not subscribe a caption to the drawing. The Minister

---

[100] Sossin, Lorne M., *Boundaries of Judicial Review: The Law of Justiciability in Canada*, Toronto, Carswell, 1999, pp. 136-137 and 138-139.
[101] Cross-reference to § 8.7.3.
[102] Reversed [1980] 4 W.W.R. 259 (B.C. C.A.). It is the British Columbia Supreme Court analysis that is of interest, regardless of the later outcome of the case.
[103] Cross-reference to § 6.6.
[104] William Vander Zalm eventually became Premier of the Province of British Columbia. He held that office from August 6, 1986, until April 2, 1991.

sued the newspaper as well as the cartoonist, the editor and the publisher, for defamation. Before the hearing, he offered to settle if the defendants would apologize, pay a modest sum to a charity and settle his legal costs. They refused.

The court held the defendants jointly and severally liable. The significance of the case is that it dealt specifically with the matter of defamation as it applied to one active in political life. The court agreed that comment and criticism by cartooning may be exercised on the positions espoused by political figures, or on their performance of public office. The defendants, however, submitted that cartoons of a political nature in particular "ought not to be and would not be interpreted by the viewing public as a sketch to be taken too seriously but rather as a symbolic drawing that would interest or amuse the reader through ridicule by showing the plaintiff in an exaggerated way and would not tend to lower the reputation and standing of the plaintiff in the estimation of right-thinking members of society generally, viewed in the light of the state of public knowledge at the time."[105] The court did not agree with interpretation either in general, or in relation to the particular character of a politician-plaintiff amounting to personal insult or vilification, as was this cartoon, were neither acceptable nor fair comment. In respect of politicians, this distinction between the public function and the personal character is important.

The Supreme Court of British Columbia went further, in holding that in the law of defamation, no special standards can be applied to criticism of political figures.

> Because the plaintiff occupies a public position, engaged upon matters of public interest he is liable to proper criticism, but the freedom of the press and of political cartoonists is a freedom governed by law and is not a freedom to make untrue defamatory statements. The publisher of a newspaper or a political cartoonist has no special immunity from the application of general laws, and in the matter of comment they are in no better or worse position than any other citizen.[106]

These comments are addressed to the defendants, members of the media. By necessary implication, however, they show that no special

---

[105] (1979), 96 D.L.R. (3d) 172 at 174, reversed [1980] 4 W.W.R. 259 (B.C. C.A.).
[106] *Ibid.*

standards apply to protect political figures from criticism when properly portrayed, of their official functions.

See also *Munro v. Toronto Sun Publishing Corp.* (1982), 39 O.R. (2d) 100 (Ont. H.C.).

---

§ 10.9.2
Pindling v. National Broadcasting Corp.
Ontario High Court of Justice; December 19, 1984
(1984), 14 D.L.R. (4th) 391

The plaintiff was Sir Lynden Pindling, then Prime Minister of the Commonwealth of the Bahamas. On the dates of September 5, 7, 12 and 22, 1983, and February 6 and 22, 1984, the defendant, one of the major television broadcasting networks in the United States, aired reports in which it alleged that while in office, the Prime Minister had engaged in dishonest, corrupt and criminal activity in relation to the drug smuggling going on in his country. Pindling first brought suit in the Bahamas but as NBC was not willing to recognize the jurisdiction of the courts there, it did not appear. Pindling then sued in the Province of Ontario, in much of which the NBC programs were also seen and heard.

This judgment arose out of a motion by NBC to set aside the service of the proceedings out of Ontario. The court held that the service was valid and that the case could proceed on the merits. The element of the ruling that is significant from the perspective of the litigation of political law issues is that of the broadcasting of political commentary into Canada from abroad. The judge based his conclusion on a 1952 decision[107] of then Chief Justice of Ontario, James McRuer, in which a somewhat similar fact pattern for broadcasting from the U.S. into Canada had occurred. It was clearly established then that broadcasts were aired for the purpose of being heard and that the intent of a broadcaster is that its programs be heard by the greatest possible audience. Most specifically, where such a broadcast is initiated south of the border, contains defamatory material and is heard and understood within Canada, the slander is deemed to have been published

---

[107] *Jenner v. Sun Oil Co.*, [1952] O.R. 240 at 249-250, [1952] 2 D.L.R. 526 at 537, leave to appeal allowed [1952] O.W.N. 370 (Ont. H.C.); quoted at (1984), 14 D.L.R. (4th) 391 at 396.

within Canada (in this case, Ontario). The court went even further in adding that the means of publication of the offending words is irrelevant; publication can take place through the written word, sound waves or airwaves. "The tort consists in making the third person understand actionable defamatory material."[108]

Among the other reasons for this conclusion the court also held that if the motion were granted and the plaintiff were forced to bring his suit in the United States, he would be barred by the Act of State doctrine of American law and would therefore be deprived of legitimate judicial advantage.[109]

Apart from its direct implications on litigation and on the foreign reporting of political issues where such reports can be heard or read within Canada, this case will also have a collateral effect on foreign, especially U.S.-origin commentary on Canadian election campaigns, through its application to the interpretation of subsection 303(1) of the *Canada Elections Act*, which deals with political broadcasts from outside the country.[110]

---

§ 10.9.3
Peat Marwick Thorne v. Canadian Broadcasting Corp.
Ontario Court (General Division); October 11, 1991
(1991), 5 O.R. (3d) 747[111]

In reporting on current events and matters of public life, the interest of the media is on urgency and on the topical nature of the reportage they present to the public. The principle illustrated by this case is that

---

[108] [1952] O.R. 240 at 251, leave to appeal allowed [1952] O.W.N. 370 (Ont. H.C.).

[109] The act of state doctrine, first formally recognized in 1897, holds that the courts of the United States may not question the "validity of the public acts a recognized foreign sovereign power commit[s] within its own territory." The citation is from *Banco Nacioinal de Cuba v. Sabbatino*, 376 U.S. 398 (1964). Lieberman, Jethro K., The Evolving Constitution, Random House, New York, 1992, p. 31.

[110] *Political Broadcasts* "303. (1) Every person who, with intent to influence persons to give or refrain from giving their votes at an election, uses, aids, abets, counsels or procures the use of any broadcasting station outside Canada, during an election, for the broadcasting of any matter having reference to an election, is guilty of an illegal practice and of an offence." Section 303 of R.S.C. 1985, c. E-2 was re-enacted as S.C. 2000, c. 9, s. 330.

[111] And Ontario Court (General Division), October 30, 1991, (1991), 5 O.R. (3d) 759.

even in instances where the public has a recognized interest in being made aware of the facts, reporting will not be damaged if it is subjected to a reasonably short delay in order to respect the legal rights of those who not only observe the events but who participate in them.

At Christmas time in 1990, as part of the democratization of Central Europe and the Balkans, the regime of Nicolai Ceaucescu was overthrown in Romania. The new Romanian government retained Peat Marwick to conduct forensic accounting in Canada to uncover whether funds had been spirited away in this country by the Ceaucescu family. On October 8, 1991, the Canadian Broadcasting Corporation's (CBC) Fifth Estate program was scheduled to run an episode on this search, which was to include material in which Peat Marwick had contributed. The parties had agreed beforehand that no confidential information would be aired. The day before the broadcast, Peat Marwick made an application for an interlocutory injunction to restrain the CBC from airing certain portions of the program containing allegations of financial improprieties by the Ceaucescu family and the efforts of Romania's successor government to recover the funds.

On the basis of the technical evidence, the court came to agree with the CBC that the program could not be separated into parts by editing it. The issue then became whether to allow all of it to air, or to postpone it. The court granted the application and determined that the program should not be aired before October 30, 1991, pending a hearing on the merits.

Much of the case revolved around the general criteria for the granting of injunctions. However, the court recognized the specificity of the CBC's arguments concerning the right of public disclosure of matters related to politics; it did not always agree with the broadcaster's point of view. The CBC based its reasoning on freedom of the press. In the particular circumstances of the case, though, it was required to abide by the terms of an agreement it had made with Peat Marwick in preparation of the program. Consequently, in the court's view, this was not a matter of freedom of the press, nor of censorship because by its agreement with Peat Marwick, the CBC had agreed to censor itself. The court then went on to the more general matter of principle involved in allowing the program to be aired on October 8 or in delaying it.

Should the standard of the media be less than what the public would expect of non-media entities? Having regard to the function of the media in a free and democratic society, to ask the question is to answer it. Confidence of the public in institutions which play a major role in a free and democratic society is the very bulwark upon which such society exists. It is important to the public that such confidence be protected and maintained. But it is said that the end (the right of the public to know) justifies the means (the manner in which the information is obtained, *viz.*, the alleged breach of agreement). In my view, such a principle is self-defeating and does more harm than good in a democratic society. It dries up sources of information. A wrong message is sent by an influential and opinion-moulding body (the press) to the public. It raises the question of how such a body would be able to criticize other bodies which follow such a principle and which play a major role in such society. It breeds cynicism. It erodes confidence.[112]

In the second of these hearings, adjudicated on October 30, 1991, Peat Marwick applied to have the injunction continued until the trial. This application was based on the position that the information provided to the CBC in interviews was to be background only and that certain excerpts of that information would breach the confidentiality of Peat Marwick itself, but more to the point, that of its client, the new Romanian government. The comments specifically objected to by the applicant dealt essentially with political realities and circumstances in Romania.

> We found that one system emerged at the key point in time, grew, developed and operated in such a way that he would not be identified as the recipient of the profits from that. it had to have top levels inside Romania direction and it could not have operated in the way it did without the personal intervention of Nicolai Ceaucescu.
>
> . . .
>
> Politics are there, I do know that times are more difficult today than they were yesterday. They were a happy lot of people in the spring of 90. The sense of freedom, it was tremendous. Today it's different.[113]

The court did not agree that such statements would breach Peat Marwick's confidentiality obligation or its ability to conduct further

---

[112] (1991), 5 O.R. (3d) 747 at 757 g-758 b.
[113] (1991), 5 O.R. (3d) 759 at 762 b and g.

work on behalf of the new Romanian government. We may correctly assume that it simply saw this as continuation, by Peat Marwick's client, of the obsession of the previous government for State secrecy. That was not a good enough reason and this second application was rejected.

---

§ 10.9.4

Hawkes v. The Toronto Sun Publishing Corporation
Alberta Court of Queen's Bench
commenced February 2, 1994; file 9401-01702; settled

This case shows that much controversy arises not only out of the words exchanged among opposing political figures, but also between the authors of public policies and their critics in the media. Moreover, while the legal actions arising as a result of such opposing discourse may be framed as actions for libel partly on the grounds of *ad hominem* attacks included in the debate, they often also constitute attempts to continue through judicial means the struggles over substantive issues of political life.

Hawkes was a Member of Parliament for Calgary West from 1979 until 1993 and in the last years of the Mulroney administration, he was the Chief Whip of the Progressive Conservative Party. From February 1992 on, he was also Chair of the House of Commons Special Committee on Electoral Reform, which had as part of its mandate to put into legislation some of the recommendations of the Lortie Royal Commission on Electoral Reform and Party Financing. One of the items brought forward by this Committee was a proposal to restrict to $1,000 the advertising expenditures which could be incurred by anyone other than a political party or a candidate during an election campaign. This provision was included in Bill C-114 of 1993 and was enacted as part of the 1993 amendments to the *Canada Elections Act*.[114] Even before this measure was given royal assent, the National Citizens' Coalition (NCC), a lobby group, applied to have it declared contrary to the *Charter*. On June 5, 1993, the Alberta Court of Queen's

---

[114] S.C. 1993, c. 19; given Royal assent on May 6, 1993. The subject provisions became ss. 259-259.5 of the *Canada Elections Act* (now S.C. 2000, c. 9).

Bench did hold the relevant sections unconstitutional.[115] On July 15, the Crown appealed.

Throughout August, September and October 1993, the *Calgary Sun* newspaper, an affiliate of the Defendant, ran a series of articles severely criticizing the $1,000 limit and the government's appeal of the ruling holding it contrary to the *Charter's* guarantees of freedom of expression, freedom of association and the democratic right to vote. The comments were in part personal attacks on Hawkes. They focused on the fact that he had steered the legislation through Parliament, that he had spoken in favour of it and that he had allegedly been instrumental in inducing the government to appeal the first court judgment invalidating it. To a far more significant extent, however, the law itself was attacked as being undemocratic. There was extensive comment, from the viewpoint that it would restrict free speech. Extremely unfavourable comparisons were made to totalitarian regimes. The method in which the law had been enacted, allegedly in secret, was criticized. The critique also included references to the imminence of the next election and contended that the government had attempted to pressure the Office of the Chief Electoral Officer to apply the provisions even while the appeal regarding them was pending.

In the federal general election of October 25, 1993, Hawkes was defeated. On February 4, 1994, he filed a Statement of Claim initiating this action, seeking $1,500,000 in punitive, aggravated and exemplary damages. The claim did seek reparation of the perceived harm to Hawkes' reputation, but more to the point, it focused on the *Calgary Sun's* efforts to discredit the legislation in question. It contended that the articles were written as part of an alliance between the newspaper and the NCC, which was lobbying against both the legislation and Hawkes' re-election, and that their purpose was to raise funds for the NCC so as to enable it to conduct its campaign.

The drafting of the key paragraph of the statement of claim sought to show that the goal of the *Sun's* articles had been to attack Hawkes' work as a legislator and his strenuous efforts to have the legislation of the government of which he was a member enacted by Parliament.

---

[115] *Somerville v. Canada (Attorney General);* Alberta Court of Queen's Bench, June 25, 1993, unreported, file 9301-05393.

> The said words in their natural and ordinary meaning, or in the alter-
> native by way of innuendo, were meant and understood to mean that
> the Plaintiff in bad faith and for improper and dishonourable purposes
> and with the intention of stymieing freedom of speech in Canada mas-
> terminded and connived through secret means and sessions to pass
> legislation that to his knowledge thwarted democracy in Canada; that
> when the said legislation was declared at trial to be unconstitutional, he
> stubbornly and arrogantly instigated and supported an appeal of the
> Judgment and attempted to have the said legislation enforced pending
> the outcome of the appeal and that he is a person unworthy of trust and
> public confidence and not fit for elected office in a democratic country.[116]

The *Sun's* response to the suit was that it had made fair comment on
a matter of public interest. After some time, the case was settled
without going to trial. This lawsuit was thus indeed more of a continuation of the debate on the merits and on the political wisdom of the
$1,000 limit than on Hawkes' character. This is particularly true as by
the time the case was started, Hawkes was no longer a public figure,
but the appeal of the case on the constitutional validity of the $1,000
limit was still proceeding through the courts.

---

§ 10.9.5
Bouchard and Best v. Arthur, Radiomedia Inc. et al.
Québec Superior Court
filed July 20, 1995; file no 500-05-007814-955; settled

At the time of the events in question here, plaintiff Bouchard was the
federal Member of Parliament for Lac-St-Jean and leader of the Official Opposition party, the Bloc Québécois. Plaintiff Best was his wife.
Arthur, the principal defendant, hosted programs entitled
"L'informateur" and "L'heure de vérité" on CHRC radio in Québec
City and CKVL radio in Montréal. On June 27, 1995, and again on
July 5, Arthur made sensationalist comments on the air about the
plaintiffs. He stated as fact that they were having marital difficulties
and that Best had rejoined Bouchard only as a matter of image at the
time of his life-threatening illness in late 1994. He further alleged that
Bouchard was regularly seeing Corinne Côté, the widow of René
Lévesque, a former premier of Québec. Arthur also evoked as pow-

---

[116] Statement of claim in *Hawkes v. The Toronto Sun Publishing Corporation*, February 2,
1994, para. 18.

erful political symbolism that Bouchard was planning to oust the then premier, Jacques Parizeau, and that after Québec's independence, he would appear publicly with Corinne Côté before the crowds on the balcony of City Hall.

Relying on the *Québec Charter of Human Rights*,[117] the federal *Broadcasting Act*[118] and the *Québec Civil Code*[119] Bouchard and Best sued Arthur for libel on July 20, 1995, and added the companies owing the radio stations and their managers as co-defendants. They also impleaded the Canadian Radio-Television and Telecommunications Commission (CRTC), Canada's broadcasting regulator. The declaration was to the effect that Arthur's on-air comments were untrue and malicious, and that Best's discreet behaviour could be explained by her deliberate attitude of reserve vis-à-vis the media. It made reference to no less than 36 earlier libel actions against Arthur and even quoted from several of the CRTC's decisions in which he was criticized for failure to maintain the Commission's requirement of high quality in his broadcasts. Plaintiffs sought a total of $1.4 million in damages and a permanent injunction from repetition of the libelous words. Before the matter could be heard by the Superior Court, the parties settled on January 31, 1996, but the remedies remained undisclosed.

Despite the fact that this matter was resolved without a formal judgment, this case is highly instructive regarding the linkage of law and political life in several respects.

This action demonstrates, first, that unsubstantiated and sensational media reports are common currency in political life, whatever their outcome in law. The most significant conclusion to be drawn from this action is that, while libel and slander actions are frequently taken in respect of public figures in various lines of professional activity, press and media reports that are blatantly false or unverifiable are thought to be more harmful in politics and to the chances of political success of the subject of the comment than to those in other fields of public endeavour. The plaintiffs expressed this clearly and rather eloquently in the declaration.

---

[117] S.Q. 1975, c. 6.

[118] S.C. 1991, c. 11, formerly R.S.C. 1985, c. B-9.01.

[119] S.Q. 1991, c. 64, especially article 317 regarding the liability of corporate officers.

990 / LAW OF DEMOCRATIC GOVERNING – VOLUME II: JURISPRUDENCE

> Le caractère public des activités du demandeur est de nature à accroître
> la propagation des affirmations et insinuations mensongères diffusées
> par le défendeur Arthur et à susciter des interrogations, voire des doutes,
> chez un grand nombre de personnes;
>
> Ce n'est pas parce que le demandeur assume des responsabilités pub-
> liques que le défendeur Arthur est autorisé à considérer sa vie privée et
> sa réputation (ainsi que celles de sa conjointe) comme livrées en pâture
> aux intrusions illicites et aux attaques diffamatoires;
>
> Les propos reprochés au défendeur Arthur produisent un effet d'autant
> plus néfaste qu'ils visent à dénigrer le demandeur et à compromettre
> ainsi sa crédibilité dans une période de sa vie publique où il s'apprête à
> proposer à la population un projet collectif qui constitue la raison d'être
> de son engagement politique;
>
> Les attaques diffamatoires et outrageantes et les atteintes à la vie privée
> dont les demandeurs sont victimes ne se justifient en aucune faccon dans
> une société libre et démocratique.[120]

The corollary of this assertion is that libellous allegations about those
involved in politics are to be compensated by a higher quantum of
damages than that applicable to even those on the periphery of political life. Thus, the claims for general damages and for exemplary
damages were in each case higher in respect of Bouchard than for
Best, and the explanation for this difference was said to be based on
political impact.

> Les montants réclamés au nom du demandeur, en ce qui concerne les
> dommages exemplaires et ceux résultant de la diffamation, sont plus
> élevés que ceux réclamés au nom de la demanderesse, en raison du fait
> que le demandeur est directement engagé dans la vie publique et que,
> dans son cas, ces dommages s'accroissent à proportion de leur impact
> politique.[121]

This case also showed that the regulatory system, here the CRTC,
proved inadequate to forestall libel and that the only effective way
to resolve such situations was by way of individual legal action,
which amounted to private defence of a public right. Given the fact
that the CRTC had to observe a balance between freedom of expres-

---

[120] *Bouchard and Best v. Arthur, Radiomedia et al.*, Superior Court of Québec, case no.
BC 2587, declaration filed July 20, 1995, paras. 69 to 72.

[121] *Ibid.*, para. 80.

sion on the airwaves and observance of the conditions that formed part of the licences it granted, the most it could achieve was to issue warnings and to renew licences for shortened terms.

For those engaged in political life, there seems to be a very particular method of using law to respond to libellous allegations. They deem it worthwhile to institute lawsuits to limit political damage from harmful media reports or commentary. Later in the sequence of legal procedure, they deem it equally worthwhile to settle such lawsuits rather than undergo the protracted presentation of testimony, evidence and assessment of damages, specifically for the purpose of avoiding distracting the relevant political clientele and the electorate from their political preoccupations and from the affected politician's opportunity to achieve success. The fact that the press is willing to settle and to cloak the terms of settlement in secrecy can be held to constitute on their part an acknowledgement of the irresponsibility of some of their reportage and of their lack of accountability in the political sphere.

---

§ 10.9.6[122]
Moores v. Canadian Broadcasting Corporation
Ontario Court (General Division)
filed on February 13, 1996; file no. 96-CU-98875; not completed

---

So far, this case contributes to our understanding of political law by serving as an example of the resort political figures tend to have to the courts in response to contentious reports they feel aggrieve them, rather than as a demonstration of new points of law. Its interest lies also in the fact that it is part of the series of cases that arose out of the Airbus scandal.

Moores was Progressive Conservative Premier of Newfoundland from January 1972 until March 1979. He then went into business, heading up the successful lobbying firm called Government Consultants Incorporated. In the 1983 race for the leadership of the federal Progressive Conservative Party, he was active on behalf of Brian Mulroney, who eventually became Prime Minister of Canada. On four occasions throughout November and December 1995, the Ca-

---

[122] Cross-reference to § 11.10.2.

nadian Broadcasting Corporation (CBC) broadcast on its English language television network a story in which it alleged that secret and
illegal commissions had been paid by Airbus Industrie as a result of
the purchase of aircraft bought from Airbus by Air Canada. The story
portrayed Moores as the conduit between the companies and busi-
nessmen involved in the scheme and Brian Mulroney. The airing of
this reportage led Moores to bring an action against the CBC, alleging
false and malicious defamation and claiming $25,000,000 in general
damages, $5,000,000 in aggravated damages and $5,000,000 in punitive damages, as well as a permanent injunction from re-broadcasting
the alleged libellous program and an order requiring the CBC to
broadcast a corrected program acknowledging the libel. In particular,
Moores' complaint concerned the aspects of the program which

- showed him participating in a criminal influence peddling scheme;
- working as a lobbyist on behalf of Airbus;
- resigning from the Board of Directors of Air Canada because of
  allegations of conflict of interest;
- opening secret bank accounts in Switzerland for himself and "a
  certain Canadian politician" who was most likely Brian Mulroney;
- receiving secret illicit commissions;
- benefiting from alleged influence peddling scheme; and
- portraying him as dishonest in his denials.

For viewers, the most interesting linkage of the political circumstances of the case into the legal forms of the participants' relationships was the following allegation in the program:

> Airbus insisted the deal be kept secret to avoid embarrassment. The
> company was paying Schreiber for his political connections, and his
> main connection in Canada was Frank Moores. Interestingly, the con-
> tracts between IAL and Airbus contained this clause: it was to be can-
> celled in the event of a major political change in Canada.[123]

The conclusion claimed by Moores on the basis of the entire content
of the four airings was that:

> The sting of the libels depends in part upon the compendious meaning
> of the words of the November 14 [and the November 18] Broadcast as a

---

[123] Words from the CBC program broadcast on November 28, 1995, quoted in the
statement of claim as p. 12, para. 18(11).

whole, together with the use of the defendants of juxtapositions of sounds and images to convey defamatory meaning.[124]

To the time of writing, the matter has not come to trial. The progress of this case, if any, is to be followed with interest.

§ 10.9.7
Bloc Québécois v. National Post Company et al.
Québec Superior Court
filed January 27, 2000; file no. 500-05-055603-003; in progress

Political parties have a vital interest in presenting before the electorate and the population at large an image of legal, democratically viable behaviour. They will thus tend to react to allegations to the contrary by resort to rapid legal means. On January 21, 2000, the *National Post*, an admittedly right-leaning newspaper, carried a front page article accusing the Bloc, a political party that is both on the progressive side of the spectrum and based on the prospect of separating Québec from Canada, of having diverted some of the funds it collected to its polling company.

The article, the newspaper's refusal to retract it and its further pursuit of the story point to a first necessary conclusion. In some cases, such as here, the press assumes a function not only of reporting but of participating on the political stage in an adversarial fashion. It is in fact a political actor. A further and reinforcing observation can be made, that such potentially libellous stories are the reflection of internal party struggles. Here, the allegations arose in the midst of the Bloc's attempt to change the sources of party funding so as to accept not only individual but also corporate donations. Whatever the political aspects of the struggle, whatever the Byzantine machinations, all participants in such controversies continue the political struggle through legal means and look to the law for definitive solutions and the restoration of truth and reputation.

In the application the Bloc filed on January 27, 2000, in Superior Court, it started by affirming, as a sign of good faith and good behaviour, that it had never been involved in a political scandal. It then denied

---

[124] Statement of claim, p. 11, para. 12, and p. 18, para. 19.

all of the elements of the *Post's* story and implied that the paper wanted to undermine the Bloc, which was at the time subject to rumours of the retirement of its leader, Lucien Bouchard.

> Essentiellement, l'ensemble des informations contenues dans ces articles se sont révélées inexactes, erronées et dans certains cas totalement fausses, de telle sorte que le requérant estime à bon droit que les intimés s'acharnent délibérément sur cette formation politique pour miner sa crédibilité et déstabiliser le leadership de ses dirigeants.[125]

The most interesting aspect of the case to date is the Bloc's listing of the heads of damage it alleges to have suffered as a result of the story, including destruction of the intangible positive characteristics and image of the party in public life.

> La parution de l'article, pièce R-1, a causé au Bloc Québécois un préjudice irréparable en ce que les propose fermes de cet article ont eu pour effet de:
>
> a) créer un doute permanent à l'égard de la probité et de l'intégrité du Bloc Québécois dans l'opinion publique;
>
> b) porter atteinte à l'estime, la confiance et al considération du public envers le Bloc Québécois;
>
> c) associer injustement le Bloc Québécois et ses dirigeants à des actes illégaux sans avoir pris la peine d'effectuer les vérifications rigoureuses qui s'imposaient en de telles circonstances;
>
> d) créer de l'incertitude chez les membres du Bloc Québécois quelques jours avant la tenue de son congrès national de la fin du mois de janvier 2000;
>
> e) occulter les véritables enjeux du congrès national du Bloc Québécois, réduisant par le fait même le bénéfice des démarches de préparation et de réflexion amorcées par le parti depuis son conseil général d'avril 1999, démarches auxquelles plus de 5000 personnes ont participé;
>
> f) miner la confiance des membres du Bloc Québécois envers la direction de cette formation politique;

---

[125] Requête, para. 33.

g) affecter le rendement de la campagne de financement du Bloc Québécois présentement en cours;

h) affecter les performances du Bloc Québécois dans le résultat d'éventuels sondages auprès de l'opinion publique;

i) miner la crédibilité de l'opinion public a l'égard du Bloc Québécois;

j) miner injustement la crédibilité d'un parti politique qui s'inscrit dans le fonctionnement démocratique des institutions tant sur la scène canadienne que québécoise alimentant ainsi le cynisme des citoyens face aux affaires politiques.[126]

In reparation of these damages, the Bloc sought compensation of $1,000,000. Rising to the challenge of the *Post's* adversarial political attack, the Bloc indicated that $750,000 of the sum, that is 75 per cent, would be funnelled into the *Fonds Lauzière pour la souveraineté* a result that the *Post* would find particularly distasteful.

It is also of note that the Bloc included in the list of remedies it sought a "Mulroney clause," asking that a retraction and a public apology be published within seven days of the judgment in Québec's ten most significant newspapers, some French and some English.

On March 29, 2000, the Superior Court rejected a motion made by the Bloc to impose a ban on the publication of the polls that would become the subject of the litigation. Embarrassment of the plaintiff would not cause sufficient harm to justify such a ban. At the same time, the court eliminated the *Fonds Lauzière* as the potential recipient of damages, indicating that it was not involved in this litigation.

At the time of writing, this case was still proceeding. Discoveries had taken place and a trial on the merits was expected to be held sometime in the future.

---

[126] *Ibid.*, para. 327.

§ 10.9.8
Earle v. Coltsfoot Publishing Co.
Nova Scotia Supreme Court; February 10, 2000
not reported; file no. 129049

Coltsfoot Publishing Co. is the publisher of *Frank Magazine*, a satirical weekly specializing in unconventional reporting about the Canadian political scene. In 1996, it ran a story about Gordon Earle, then Deputy Minister of Housing and Consumer Affairs in the Government of Nova Scotia. The article alleged that Earle was discredited within the bureaucracy and a disappointment to his political masters. As Earle was black, *Frank Magazine* also said that he was promoted to the deputy's position as an affirmative action measure. Earle sued and obtained a judgment to the effect that the story was malicious libel; damages of $60,000 were assessed and *Frank Magazine* was ordered to pay Earle's legal expenses. The particular interest of the case is that *Frank Magazine* had defended itself with the plea that the article set out its opinion, based on the editor's personal experience and evaluation. The sense of the ruling, given this defence, is that in political reporting, caution must be taken to avoid the border between publicizing an opinion and an insult. In the 36th federal general election of June 2, 1997, Earle went on to win the seat of Halifax West for the New Democratic Party.

See also *Lee v. Globe & Mail* (2001), 52 O.R. (3d) 652 (Ont. S.C.J.) and (2002), [2002] O.J. No. 16 (Ont. S.C.J.); *National Capital News Canada v. Canada (Speaker of the House of Commons)*, 2002 Comp. Trib. 38 (Competition Trib.) and 2002 Comp. Trib. 41 (Competition Trib.), affirmed [2004] F.C.J. No. 83 (F.C.A.); *Schreiber v. C.B.C.* (Ontario); *Schreiber v. C.B.C.* (Alberta) and *Schreiber v. Lavoie*[127] (2002), 59 O.R. (3d) 130 (Ont. S.C.J.), additional reasons at (2002), 2002 CarswellOnt 3695 (Ont. S.C.J.).

---

[127] Cross-reference to § 9.9.A and 11.10.

§ 10.9.9[128]
Lange v. Australian Broadcasting Corp.
High Court of Australia; July 8, 1997
(1997), 145 A.L.R. 96

This case amounts to a restatement by the High Court of Australia of that country's law on defamation, in particular as it applies to freedom of expression in the course of discussion of government and political matters. While much of the court's *ratio* is specific to the circumstances of Australian policy, principles of a broader nature and applicable to commentary about governmental and political events and persons in democratic regimes in general can be gleaned from the case.

The plaintiff was David Lange, a former Prime Minister of New Zealand and a parliamentarian active in the country's public life. He started a defamation action in the Supreme Court of New South Wales in respect of comments made in the Australian media about subjects of social interest and political, social and economic matters which had occurred in New Zealand. The defendant broadcaster presented as its first defence the plea that the matter complained of was published pursuant to the freedom of speech guaranteed by the Australian *Constitution*. Lange moved to strike this defence as being bad in law and the question was stated for the High Court of Australia. This court held that the Australian Broadcasting Corporation's defence on the constitutional ground was bad in law and the matter was sent back to the Supreme Court of New South Wales for elaboration of the defence.

The High Court's most significant conclusion of general interest was that freedom of communication between electors on the one hand and candidates for office and the government on the other, on matters of government and politics, is a central component of the system of representative government.

> Freedom of communication on matters of government and politics is an indispensable incident of that system of representative government which the Constitution creates by directing that the members of the

---

[128] International comparison.

> House of Representatives and the Senate shall be "directly chosen by the people" of the Commonwealth and the States, respectively.[129]

Comparative constitutionalists will note the similarity of this reasoning with the notion of "informed voter" expressed by the Supreme Court of Canada in the case of *Thomson Newspapers*[130] and by the Alberta Court of Appeal in the case of the *Reform Party*.[131]

The court then went on to indicate how this right to be informed about politics was put into function.

> Furthermore, because the choice given by § 7 and 24 must be a true choice with "an opportunity to gain an appreciation of the available alternatives," as Dawson J. pointed out in *Australian Capital Television Pty Ltd v. Commonwealth*, legislative power cannot support an absolute denial of access by the people to relevant information about the functioning of government in Australia and about the policies of political parties and candidates for election.

> That being so, § 7 and 24 and the related sections of the Constitution necessarily protect that freedom of communication between the people concerning political or government matters which enables the people to exercise a free and informed choice as electors. Those sections do not confer personal rights on individuals. Rather they preclude the curtailment of the protected freedom by the exercise of legislative or executive power.[132]

Next, the court made clear that the electors' right to be informed applied not only in respect of elections, but also to referenda. This was worth mentioning separately as in Australian practice, referenda on constitutional issues are much more frequent than in Canada.

A further definition of the right was the statement of its permanent nature; the institution of an electoral event is not necessary to activate the right.

> If the freedom is to effectively serve the purpose of § 7 and 24 and related sections, it cannot be confined to the election period. Most of the matters

---

129 (1997), 145 A.L.R. 96 at 106-10.
130 *Ibid.* at 106-36 to 107-4.
131 *Thomson Newspapers Co. v. Canada (Attorney General)*, [1998] 1 S.C.R. 877 (S.C.C.).
132 *Reform Party of Canada v. Canada (Attorney General)* (1995), 165 A.R. 161, 89 W.A.C. 161 (Alta. C.A.), additional reasons at [1995] 10 W.W.R. 764 (Alta. C.A.).

necessary to enable "the people" to make an informed choice will occur during the period between the holding of one, and the calling of the next, election. If the freedom to receive and disseminate information were confined to election periods, the electors would be deprived of the greater part of the information necessary to make an effective choice at the election.[133]

In going yet further, the court prescribed that the people's right to be informed was not confined to information about the executive branch as that has traditionally been conceived of, namely including ministers and the public service. The court gave it a broader ambit, including matters relating to the affairs of statutory authorities and public utilities which report either directly or through a minister to the legislature. In the Canadian context, this would include most Crown Corporations and bodies listed in the various schedules of the *Financial Administration Act*.

In analyzing the Australian Broadcasting Corporation's second defence, that of a qualified privilege, the court dealt at length with the interaction between the constitutional right of freedom of speech and the common law of defamation. Its most noteworthy comment on this relationship was as follows.

> The factors which affect the development of the common law equally affect the scope of the freedom which is constitutionally required. "[T]he common convenience and welfare of society" is the criterion of the protection given to communications by the common law of qualified privilege. Similarly, the content of the freedom to discuss government and political matters must be ascertained according to what is for the common convenience and welfare of society. That requires an examination of changing circumstances and the need to strike a balance in those circumstances between absolute freedom of discussion of government and politics and the reasonable protection of the persons who may be involved, directly or incidentally, in the activities of government or politics.[134]

The court concluded with an assessment of how these factors applied to the citizenry. Transposing the concepts to other jurisdictions, this *ratio* can have a bearing on other constitutional democracies as well.

---

[133] (1997), 145 A.L.R. 96 at 107-15.
[134] *Ibid.* at 111-5.

Accordingly, this court should now declare that each member of the Australian community has an interest in disseminating and receiving information, opinions and arguments concerning government and political matters that affect the people of Australia. The duty to disseminate such information is simply the correlative of the interest in receiving it. The common convenience and welfare of Australian society are advanced by discussion—the giving and receiving of information—about government and political matters. The interest that each member of the Australian community has in such a discussion extends the categories of qualified privilege. Consequently, those categories now must be recognised as protecting a communication made to the public on a government or political matter.[135]

See also *Reynolds v. Times Newspapers Ltd.*, [1999] 4 All E.R. 609 (U.K. H.L.); *Berezovsky v. Michaels and others; Glouchkov v. Michaels and others*, [2000] 2 All E.R. 986 and *McCartan Turkington Breen v. Times Newspapers*, [2000] 2 A.C. 277.

10.10 ISSUE: POLITICAL TRIALS: CRIMINAL TRIALS BASED ON POLITICALLY MOTIVATED OFFENCES

§ 10.10.1
United States v. Houslander
Ontario Court (General Division); March 26, 1993
(1993), 13 O.R. (3d) 44

A complete overview of the topic of litigation of political law issues requires an examination of the question whether, in a country such as Canada, with a non-political criminal code, there is such a thing as a "political offence." The one area of law in which this phrase and this concept have common currency is that of extradition. Both the *Extradition Act*[136] and the jurisprudence under it recognize that some offences are political in the sense that they are "of a political character." This case does not state but implies that the political element in cases to which this designation can be applied is the motivation of the alleged offender. The particular interest of this case is that it ties

---

[135] *Ibid.* at 115-34.
[136] R.S.C. 1985, c. E-23, in particular s. 15.

the handling of political cases by the Minister of Justice and the nature of the Minister's duties. Once a court has determined whether there is sufficient evidence to warrant committing the fugitive for surrender to the requesting nation, the Minister of Justice engages in an executive function, namely to decide whether to actually surrender the fugitive. Whether the alleged offence is of a political character or not, the Minister's decision is subject to *Charter* review.

> It is not to be assumed that the Minister of Justice and Attorney General of Canada will routinely ignore her duty to take cognizance and obey the supreme law of Canada and willy nilly surrender a Canadian citizen to a foreign jurisdiction under circumstances where so to do would be fundamentally unjust or in plain contravention of a right or freedom guaranteed under the *Charter*.[137]

---

§ 10.10.2
Gil v. Canada (Minister of Employment & Immigration)
Federal Court of Appeal; October 21, 1994
(1994), [1995] 1 F.C. 508

Gil attempted to obtain the status of a refugee in Canada but his claim was refused by the Immigration and Refugee Board. His appeal to the Federal Court of Appeal resulted in a clear definition of the concept of "political crime" and its limited applicability in Canadian law. The judgment began with a characterization of the concept and its anchoring in Canadian political and legal history.

> The very expression 'political crime' rings curiously and indeed offensively to Canadian ears. We do not think of crimes as being 'political' except in the broadest sense of that word in that they cause injury not only to individuals but also to the public peace and therefore to the polity in which we live. Politicians who commit crimes are hounded from office as well as punished. Political motivation or political purpose are for us quite simply irrelevant to the determination of whether a given action is criminal and should be punished. The murders of D'Arcy McGee and Pierre Laporte were viewed by Canadian law as simply murders, no more and no less.

---

[137] (1993), 13 O.R. (3d) 44 at 52d, citing *United States v. Iaquinto* (March 26, 1991), Watt J. (Ont. Gen. Div.).

It may come therefore as some surprise to most Canadians to learn that in two respects at least the laws of Canada recognize that the consequences of an otherwise criminal act may vary if that act can be characterized as political. In both instances the reference is to actions committed outside Canada but the standard to be applied is one which is mandated by Canadian law and administered by Canadian courts.

The two exceptions in question are found in the law of refugee status and in extradition law.[138]

It is true that many actions of a criminal nature are committed within a political context. In the eyes of the law, however, the contextual connection or the political motivation of the alleged offender is not sufficient to absolve him from criminal liability. In order for the political nature of the motivation for a crime to have an effect on the outcome of a trial, two circumstances have to be met. The first is that the action must have taken place in the course of, and be incidental to a violent political disturbance such as war, revolution or rebellion. The second is that there must be a nexus between the crime and the alleged political objective; the action must be directed at changing the political organization of the State. The political element should outweigh the common law element of the offence, such as personal pain or revenge. In short, Canadian law qualifies as "political" only those offences which are committed in furtherance of a change of government, regime or State and that take place in an environment of public disorder. Here, Gil did not fit into that category and the appeal was dismissed.

---

§ 10.10.3
R. v. Marchese
Ontario Court (General Division); January 23, 1997
not reported; limited information available

In the Canadian political legal culture, adherence to legal principles is of greater weight than the political motivation of public actions, no matter how well intentioned. Thus, where one who is accused of a criminal offence bases his defence on the fact that his actions were motivated by his political nature, political involvement or political aspirations and there is what in fact amounts to an admission with

---

[138] (1994), [1995] 1 F.C. 508 at 512 i-j.

politics as an attempted excuse, the law will be applied without leniency.

Marchese was a candidate in the Toronto school board elections held in November 1994. In a subsequent prosecution, he was charged with forgery of documents for the purpose of getting extra votes, uttering forged documents and attempted fraud while falsely registering voters. The accused was found guilty and on sentencing he asked for redemption and a public denunciation of what he had done. The essence of his plea was that he was "a political animal." His request for 200-300 days of community service as a sentence was rejected and he was given 90 days' jail, to be served on weekends. He was also made ineligible to be nominated, elected or appointed to any public office until November 2001.

See also *Zrig c. Canada (Ministre de la Citoyenneté & de l'Immigration)*, 229 D.L.R. (4th) 235 (Fed. C.A.); *Attorney General of Trinidad and Tobago and Another v. Phillip and Another*,[139] [1995] 1 A.C. 396; *Anderson v. Islamic Republic of Iran*,[140] 90 F. Supp.2d 107 (D.D.C., 2000) and *U.S. v. Pitawanakwat*,[141] 120 F. Supp.2d 921 (D. Or., 2000).

---

§ 10.10.4
Her Majesty's Advocate v. Megrahi and Fhimah
High Court of Justiciary at Camp Zeist; January 31, 2001
Case No. 1475/99 and Appeal No. C104/01, March 13, 2002.

On December 21, 1988, a Pan American flight headed from Frankfurt and London to New York through London exploded over the Scottish village of Lockerbie. Everyone on board the plane, that is 259 passengers, died, as did a number of the residents of Lockerbie. Several civil aviation agencies, police forces and espionage services conducted investigations.

There was strong suspicion that the explosion was the result of politically motivated sabotage. Suspicion fell on two employees of Libyan Airlines based in Malta, Abdellaset Ali Mohammed Al Megrahi and

---

[139] International comparison.
[140] International comparison.
[141] International comparison.

Al Amin Khalifa Fhimah. They were also alleged to be Libyan secret agents. None of the presumptions have yet been proven.

For a decade, attempts were made to extradite the accused either to the United States, whose airliner was involved, or to the United Kingdom, over whose territory the incident occurred. Libya refused to extradite and shielded the suspects. A deadlock seemed to develop. The crime was apparently politically motivated, state sanctioned terrorism. The charges were held by the would-be defendants' government to be politically motivated. The allegations of innocence were held by the would-be prosecutors to be politically motivated.

In order to enable some form of hopefully non-political justice to be rendered, a political deal was brokered to conduct a prosecution. The dealers included the Secretary General of the United Nations, President Mandela of South Africa and the Saudi ambassador to the United States. The political arrangement consisted of the temporary cession by the Netherlands of a part of an unused NATO air base at Zeist and the establishment there of a Scottish court. The accused were extradited to this air base and incarcerated there. They were charged with conspiracy to murder, murder and destruction of an aircraft. The law of Scotland was made applicable but with special circumstances; instead of the usual 15-member jury, three judges were to hear the case.

On December 7, 1999, the court started functioning. The actual trial opened on May 3, 2000 and judgment was handed down on January 31, 2001. Megrahi was convicted and Fhima was acquitted.

With the sensitive nature of the case, the court was extremely cautious to analyze the evidence and to structure its ruling on the facts and within the four corners of the applicable law. A significant part of the evidence which the court took into consideration was the motive of the bomber(s) and their backers. There were clear signs pointing to a politically-based conspiracy.

> We turn next to the evidence in relation to members of the Popular Front for the Liberation of Palestine – General Command ("PFLP-GC"). No member of that organization gave evidence but it was clear from other evidence that we heard, in particular from officers of the German police force, the BKA, that a cell of the PFLP-GC was operating in what was then West Germany at least up until October 1988. The evidence which

we accept showed that at least at that time the cell had both the means and the intention to manufacture bombs which could be used to destroy civil aircraft.[142]

The accused shared the political objectives of various Palestinian-based terrorist organizations, namely what they characterized as the complete liberation of Palestine, which would imply the destruction of the State of Israel. Given that they saw the United States as Israel's most steadfast ally, they were aiming to harm American political, security and economic interests in order to punish the U.S. for its pro-Israel foreign policy. All this had to be done with backers of similar political persuasion, which in this case was Libya.

No prosecution could be more involved in political considerations. The accused justified their criminal actions by their ideological convictions, which formed the basis of their polical defence.

> ...As we have also said, the absence of an explanation as to how the suitcase was taken into the system at Luqa is a major difficulty for the Crown case but after taking full account of that difficulty, we remain of the view that the primary suitcase began its journey at Luqa. The clear inference which we draw from this inference is that the conception, planning and execution of the plot which led to the planting of the explosive device was of Libyan origin. While no doubt organisations such as the PFLP-GC and the PPSF (Palestinian Popular Struggle Front) were also engaged in terrorist activities during the same period, we are satisfied that there was no evidence from which we could infer that they were involved in this particular act of terrorism, and the evidence relating to their activities does not create a reasonable doubt in our minds about the Libyan origin of this crime.[143]

In sum, political views motivated the actions of the accused. This frame of mind did not, however, seem to exercise on the court any effect of exculpating or excusing the actions of the accused. Megrahi's sentence was imprisonment for life, with a recommendation that he serve at least 20 years in jail in Scotland.

The political motivation behind the Lockerbie bombing and the implicitly political nature of the defence is the first significant point of this matter. The second, which in the long-term is perhaps even more

[142] Judgment, page 68, para. 73.
[143] *Ibid.* page 75, para. 82-3.

noteworthy, no matter how painful the entire case for the survivors of the many deceased, is the political arrangement which enabled the trial to take place, as it did.

> The major, and enduring, lesson must surely be that a terrorist trial under "normal" domestic law and procedure can be mounted and brought to a successful conclusion.
>
> This gives the lie to the simplistic belief in some kind of international criminal tribunal to try terrorists. Such a tribunal would face some of the problems that confronted the Scottish court in the Netherlands, such as the unavailability of witnesses and documents. In any event, the International Criminal Court, in the process of being established, would not have jurisdiction over crimes under the Montreal Convention of 1971, involving the bombing of a civil airliner.
>
> Of course, the question arises as to how "normal" the Lockerbie trial was.
>
> . . .
>
> It is worth bearing in mind that the country with the primary interest in trying international terrorists is the country in which their crimes are committed. It is understandable and legitimate, then, that the Scottish authorities should wish to prosecute the two Libyans under Scottish law and procedure. It is equally understandable that the US, as the state of registration of the Maid of the Seas and the state of nationality of most of the victims, should also wish to prosecute.
>
> One of the many unique features of this case is that Libya either could not legally extradite al-Megrahi and Fhimah, as it has asserted, or that it would not surrender the two accused, as the UK and US Governments contended and the Security Council demanded. That being so, the compromise of a trial in a neutral venue before a panel of judges utilising Scottish law and procedure was proposed and accepted. So, as a precedent for future terrorist trials, the Lockerbie model has to be confined to its own facts and circumstances.
>
> That said, the determination to bring terrorists to justice need not, in future, be stuck in the traditional legal mould, involving a touching yet inexplicable faith in juries, normal venues and normal procedures. The Lockerbie model, an adaptation of a normal Scottish trial, is itself adaptable.[144]

---

[144] "Camp Zeist breaks the mould," *The Times*, London, February 6, 2001.

The political circumstances of the crime, the context of global power conflicts, the terrorist aspect, as well as the politically negotiated nature of this prosecution all combine to make the case unique. At the basest consideration, it is significant that the parties wanted to have resort to a legal forum, rather than to more expeditious ways of attributing criminal responsibility for the bombing of the Pan Am plane. That having been decided, whether for genuine State interests or for political posturing, the parties negotiated on matters of judicial arrangements until they came to an agreement, indicating their common, if grudging, desire to see justice done.

On August 23, 2001, Megrahi sought and obtained leave to appeal. The appeal was eventually heard before five justices starting on January 23, 2002, and a judgment, confirming the trial ruling was rendered on March 14, 2002.

The appeal judgment was exhaustive. The court noted that the evidence about the PFLP-GC and the PPSF had been considered and concluded that no issue arose as to the trial court's treatment of that evidence. Further on, the court acknowledged that in the prosecution's view, the trial court's conclusion that the plot was promoted by the Libyan secret service, and that this finding was unaffected by the additional evidence, was correct. The appeal court also upheld the specific paragraph of the trial judgment that set aside the possibility that the crime was of an origin other than Libyan. With respect to certain particulars, the appeal panel left in place those points of the trial judgment which dealt with Al Megrahi's function as a procurer of military equipment, including timers, his use of a coded passport and alternative explanations for his visit of December 20-21, 1988 to Malta. On these bases, the court disposed of all matters relating to the case that could be deemed political in nature, by leaving the relevant elements of the trial judgment in place.

Upon the handing down of the appeal opinion, the Scottish Court in the Netherlands ceased to function. Al Megrahi was quickly transferred from the Netherlands to Barlinnie Prison in Glasgow to serve a life sentence. Within days, Camp Zeist, where the entire judicial process had taken place, reverted to Dutch control.

Megrahi's original life sentence included a minimum of twenty years' incarceration. In November 2003, he was informed that he would be required to serve 27 years before being eligible for parole. Megrahi thereupon lodged a further appeal against his sentence.[145]

In this respect, as well as in relation to the general political controversy relating to the guilt and/or liability of the Government of Libya in the matter of Lockerbie, the file will not easily be closed. Despite its repeated assertions of innocence in relation to the bombing, the Government of Libya was, in 2002-2003, involved in negotiations with officials of the Western powers regarding a compensation package for the families of the victims. According to reliable news reports, Colonel Gadaffi was willing to pay as much as US $3.5 billion. This initiative has nothing to do either with any acknowledgment of legal liability or with what in our legal system would be called an *ex gratia* payment without acceptance of responsibility. It is a politically motivated offer aimed at securing the lifting of UN economic sanctions against Libya, which the U.K. and the U.S. have supported over the years. Whatever benefit some victims' families may eventually accept from such a payment would thus, in the Libyan world-view, be legally incidental but politically beneficial to it. The conclusion we must draw is that in some regimes, officials of the State are, regrettably, incapable or unwilling to distinguish between legal norms and political values and of coordinating the two as the proper role of law requires, by subordinating the political to the legal. The most telling proof of this is that in the final analysis, the seeming co-operation of the Libyan authorities in resolving the Lockerbie file became linked to Libya's desire, after the 2003 war in Iraq, to avoid possible U.S. military action. That is why, in the dying days of the year, diplomatic agreement developed on both the dismantling of Libya's program of weapons of mass destruction and on the compensation of Lockerbie victims' families.

---

[145] Appeal over Lockerbie sentence, http://news.bbc.co.uk/2/hi/uk_news/scotland/3330567.stm (last consulted August 30, 2004).

10.11 ISSUE: POLITICAL TRIALS: CRIMINAL TRIALS BASED ON POLITICALLY MOTIVATED DEFENCES

§ 10.11.1

R. v. Kevork
Ontario High Court of Justice; March 3, 1986
(1986), 27 C.C.C. (3d) 271
-and-
R. v. Kevork
Ontario High Court of Justice; March 25, 1986
(1986), 27 C.C.C. (3d) 523
-and-
R. v. Kevork
Ontario Court of Appeal; October 25, 1988
(1988), 29 O.A.C. 387

This is a series of cases that offers much insight both into the attempt by the accused to base a defence on political grounds and into the reaffirmation by the courts of the apolitical nature of the criminal justice system, and indeed of the blindness of Canadian criminal justice to political, partisan and ideological considerations.

The conflict which for decades had opposed the Turkish State and its Armenian citizens, as well as people of Armenian heritage overseas, spilled over into Canada in the 1980's. On April 8, 1982, a Turkish diplomate posted to Ottawa, Kani Gurgor, was the object of an attempted assassination. The accused, Kevork, Babian and Gharakhanian, were alleged to have links to an organization known as the Armenian Secret Army for the Liberation of Armenia (ASALA). They were charged with conspiracy and attempted murder. Several years of litigation ensued from the incident.

In the first of the cases cited here, the accused sought to have the indictment against them quashed by relying on sections 7, 9 and 15 of the *Charter*. The Ontario High Court of Justice looked to the Supreme Court of Canada's Operation Dismantle decision for guidance in determining that decisions of the Attorney-General on matters relating to the conduct of criminal prosecutions were in fact reviewable because they were justiciable. The court specifically stated that the Canadian legal system does not recognize what in Armenian law is called the doctrine of political questions, which would exempt the Attorney-General from the court's power of review. Moreover, there is no lack of judicial competence to review.

> On the basis of that [the Operation Dismantle] reasoning it is not apparent how the Attorney-General as chief prosecutor ought to enjoy a position of privilege vis-a-vis the Charter. If he is answerable to the Executive or to his colleagues in the Cabinet and ultimately to the electorate, he ought not to be exempt from the position posited by the Chief Justice in relation to defence matters [in Operation Dismantle]. The administration of justice is perhaps as weighty as a matter of protection and security of the nation and of its relations with other countries.[146]

Having asserted its right to review the decisions of the Attorney-General, the court went on to specify that those decisions cannot be based on political grounds. While the decision does not clearly state this, we must surmise that the accused had pleaded that the Attorney-General had grounded the indictments on political considerations. That defence proved pointless for these accused, but it did enable the court to reaffirm the principle.

> The Attorney-General cannot be blatantly political and he must forever be free of oblique motives. In such matters supervision of the court will obtain and will suffice. It is not necessary to emasculate his office to the point that the essential nature of that office would be threatened. There is nothing in any of the sections of the Charter that even remotely suggest what counsel for the accused are in effect advocating, namely, the abolition of the office.[147]

This reference to "oblique motives" is used as a synonym for political considerations. In the absence of such unacceptable considerations in prosecuting accused, no matter what they are called, the Attorney-General is free to determine the manner in which he conducts cases and "the trial process will protect the rights of the accused."[148]

---

[146] (1986), 27 C.C.C. (3d) 271 at 277.
[147] *Ibid.* at 279.
[148] *Ibid.* at 282.

The second case concerns an application by the accused for the production of documents by the Canadian Security Intelligence Service (CSIS) on the ground that those documents may be of assistance to their defence. CSIS objected on the basis of national security. The court conducted a thorough analysis of the national security implications of the case and recognized that that element was thoroughly political and raised very particular public policy considerations. It acknowledged, while setting out the defence position,

> I repeat also that innocent persons must not be sacrificed at the altar of national security for one could then legitimately wonder about the kind of society an organization such as CSIS was trying to save.

> Also equally belonging to the category of the self-evident is the proposition that there cannot exist a system of law that will allow the staying of virtually all prosecutions once there is established the existence of some evidence material, in the judgment of the defence, in the hands of the State that cannot be divulged for reasons of national security.[149]

Nevertheless, it concluded that the burden lay on the applicants, the accused, to show that they could not make out their case without the evidence which CSIS was holding. They did not meet that burden and the application was dismissed.

Ultimately, all the accused changed their pleas to guilty and Kevork was sentenced to nine years, Babian to six and Gharakhanian to two years less a day. The Crown appealed on the matter of the sentences of the latter two. This gave the Ontario Court of Appeal the opportunity to address the question which is the key to this area of political law, namely whether the political motivation of a criminal act can be a mitigating or an aggravating factor. The court responded to this important point directly, but in an unexpected way. First, it set out the parameters of Kevork's political motivation.

> Kevork did not appeal the sentence imposed on him. There is of course a long standing history of perceived grievances on the part of persons of Armenian ancestry against the Turkish Government for alleged attempted genocide against them and seizure of their lands in Turkey. It is not necessary in these proceedings to delve into the historic details of the events which gave rise to the grievances. It is sufficient to note that the conspiracy to murder a Turkish diplomat resulted i=from such griev-

---

[149] *Ibid.* at 542.

ances and formed part of an international conspiracy on the part of members of certain groups to kill Turkish diplomats in various countries to call world attention to the alleged injustices suffered by Armenians at the hands of the Turkish government, in an effort to rectify such injustices. In essence the conspiracy involved politically motivated violence and was part of a conspiracy which was international in scope.[150]

Based on this recital, the court went on to treat political motivation as an aggravation of the offence, justifying a heavy sentence.

> The maximum penalty which may be imposed for an offence is usually reserved for a person who is considered to be the worst type of offender committing the worst type of such offence. In our opinion a conspiracy to commit murder as part of terrorist activity on an international scale to further political aims clearly falls within the ambit of the worst type of such offence.[151]

The court then added some subtle nuances to its determination. Aggravation being the general rule in cases of political motivation, where that motivation was focused on the sincere rectification of an injustice, the offender may not be the worst kind of offender. Nevertheless, where the offence was committed in a jurisdiction essentially unconnected with the injustice there is a need for strong deterrence.

> Kevork, who received the heaviest sentence may not be the worst type of offender in so far as he may have been motivated by a sincere belief that he was acting to remedy terrible injustices suffered by innocent persons of his racial background, whether such injustices were perceived or real. It may be that in some circumstances a person who is motivated to commit a criminal act by a sincere desire to remedy a past injustice real or imagined or to prevent a future perceived injustice should receive some amelioration of his sentence for that reason. Where, however, the offence committed involves a violent act of international terrorism performed in a country unconnected with the place in which the alleged injustices have been perpetrated, the need for an unusually strong general deterrent prevails and that outweighs any substantial credit which a person who is not the worst offender might otherwise receive.[152]

---

[150] (1988), 29 O.A.C. 387 at 389.
[151] *Ibid.*
[152] *Ibid.*

In sum, the court felt that the harsh punishment of Kevork was jus-tified. In addition to determining that political motivation is an ag-gravating factor in sentencing, the conclusion of this case is that the law frowns on attempts in Canada to resolve foreign political prob-lems through criminal activity committed in this country.

The other points to note from this judgment are that the court ac-cepted the Crown's argument that sentences should reflect the ab-horrence of the community for politically motivated violence, and that it also relied on the increase by Parliament of the maximum sentences for the particular form of political crime, namely terrorist acts.

---

§ 10.11.2

R. v. Yacoub

Ontario Court (General Division); April 30, 1990

file no. S.C.O. 269/89; not reported

Canadian readers may be somewhat surprised at the use of the ex-pression "political trials" in connection with the judgments of courts in this country. In fact, this is not meant to indicate that the reasoning of the court was political in nature, rather than legal. Nor is it an attempt to equate some decisions rendered in Canada with others emanating from dictatorial regimes in which the judiciary may be at the service of the executive. The expression "political trials" is used, rather, to denote judicial proceedings in which the alleged offence is in some way tainted by political considerations, or those in which the judgment amounts to the judicial assessment of a primarily or purely political situation. In such cases, the political element is more than mere judicial notice or formal acknowledgement of extrinsic political facts, as it is in § 9.6. It becomes part of the *ratio* in judicial decision making.

During 1989, Yacoub, a resident of the Montréal area and originally an immigrant from Lebanon, hijacked a bus bound from Montréal to New York, to Ottawa, where it was brought to a stop on the lawn in front of Parliament. He was charged with a number of offences under the *Criminal Code*. Both in the pre-trial proceedings and at the trial itself, Yacoub refused to acknowledge the criminal nature of his acts, insisting that he merely wanted to alert public opinion to the plight of his former homeland, where a civil war was raging at the time. He thought that instead of being tried, he ought to be awarded a Nobel Prize for Peace.

The court's principal reason in imposing a six year sentence of incarceration was Yacoub's refusal to admit the severity of his crimes. In a democracy, the judge said, there exist peaceful means to alert public opinion, without having resort to violence and without sequestering individuals under threat of death. The purpose of imposing the prison sentence was said to be to discourage others from adopting such illegal means to achieve their (political) goals. The court specifically held that the accused's politically motivated attitude could lead to recidivism and that normal protection for society from him was required.

---

§ 10.11.3
R. v. Reyat
British Columbia Supreme Court; May 10, 1991
(1991), 1991 CarswellBC 1245[153]

The essential question which recurs in political trials is whether a democratic form of government, such as exists in Canada, is compatible with violent dissent amounting to criminal activity. The view of the courts is consistently that it is not. Once that issue is settled, the secondary question which arises is whether a political motivation for the commission of a crime is a mitigating factor or an aggravating one.

Reyat, a Sikh living in Canada, was charged with a number of criminal offences including two counts of manslaughter after a bomb which he allegedly built or helped to build exploded on June 23, 1985, at Narita Airport in Tokyo, killing two baggage handlers. There was also suspicion that Reyat may have been involved in the bombing of an Air India flight heading, on the same day, from Toronto to Bombay. After a painstaking review of the circumstantial evidence, the court felt that the only reasonable inference to be drawn was that Reyat was involved in the fabrication of the Narita bomb. Rayat's actions had included statements confided to others about making

---

[153] Affirmed (1993), 20 C.R. (4th) 149 (B.C. C.A.), leave to appeal refused (1993), 25 C.R. (4th) 125 (note) (S.C.C.).

explosives to help his countrymen and remarks made in anger at the Indian government and Prime Minister Indira Ghandi in particular because of her involvement in the storming of the Sikh Golden Temple in Amritsar.

In a criminal trial relating only to the Narita explosion, in the course of which Reyat was convicted, the court dovetailed Reyat's motives with his actions in concluding that the evidence fits perfectly into an overall pattern.

> From the testimony of various witnesses it is apparent that he was keenly interested in political questions related to Sikhs in India...His expressed purpose for his attempt to get dynamite...related to violent activity of some kind directed at India. To one witness...he expressed willingness to fight and if necessary to die for his cause...[154]

Rather than being a mitigating factor, this was considered by the court to be an aggravating factor, particularly because of the loss of human life. The court held that the end does not justify violent means in a democratic society, no matter how idealistic or naive the offender.

By 2001, the various police forces involved had gathered sufficient evidence to lay charges against several individuals, including Reyat, for the Air India bombing. Just prior to the end of Reyat's incarceration, the B.C. Ministry of the Attorney General asked British authorities for permission to charge him again. This was necessary as Reyat had been extradicted for the first trial on the Narita charges only. It is foreseeable that the court handling the second trial will express itself on the political motivation of Reyat for his actions in regard to the Air India bombing as well.

This case offers but a small window on the criminal and security investigations, as well as on the complex prosecutions that have been conducted in Canada ever since the Air India disaster. The entire process involves an intricate, indeed unfathomable, combination of politics and defences in judicial preceedings that are based on political motivation. At the time of writing, the judicial phase of these processes was still ongoing.

---

[154] Supreme Court of British Columbia, full text of the judgment, pp. 24-25.

§ 10.11.4[155]
R. v. Van Hee
Ontario Court (Provincial Division); June 21, 1991
file no. Ottawa 91-11045; not reported; limited information available

The issue at stake here is whether the allegation by an accused in a criminal trial that the laying of the charge against him was politically motivated is either sufficient to make it so, or to acquit him. The answer to both parts of the question would seem to be no. On March 7, 1991, at a time when the special measures designed to protect public buildings in Ottawa in connection with the Gulf War were being eased, Van Hee, a Catholic priest, demonstrated in front of the Parliament Buildings with a placard critical of the government's policy on abortion. He was arrested and tried on a charge of obstructing a peace officer. Van Hee's defence was based in part on the allegation that the police actions were politically motivated, directed to his harassment and silencing, and to improve the prospect for success of government expression on the subject of abortion. The court rejected these allegations and confirmed that the criteria motivating the prosecution were more likely prosecutorial discretion and expediency. These considerations played no role in Van Hee's acquittal.

See also *R. v. Asgari*, Ontario Court (Provincial Division), September 1998, not reported, limited information available; *United States v. Usama bin Laden et al.*,[156] 160 F. Supp.2d 670 (S.D.N.Y., 2001) and *United States v. Zacarias Moussaoui*,[157] 205 F.R.D. 183 (E.D. Virg., 2002).

---

[155] Cross-reference to § 8.3.3.
[156] International comparison.
[157] International comparison.

10.12 ISSUE: POLITICAL INVOLVEMENT IN THE PROSECUTION OF CRIMINAL OFFENCES

§ 10.12.1[158]
Ouellet c. R.
Québec Court of Appeal; October 20, 1976
(1976), 72 D.L.R. (3d) 95

The principle established by this case is that comments by members of the Executive Branch on decisions of the Judicial Branch must be directed to the issues rather than being made in an *ad hominem* fashion, and furthermore that such comments must be made in a reserved manner. Comments other than those which respect these rules constitute political interference.

On December 19, 1975, Judge MacKay of the Superior Court rendered a judgment in a case dealing with combines investigation. That same day, Ouellet, then Minister of Consumer and Corporate Affairs and the Minister responsible for the subject matter, made a statement in the hall outside the House of Commons indicating that the judgment was "silly" and questioning the judge's sanity. On January 8, 1976, Ouellet was called to the bench to defend a contempt citation. The Associate Chief Justice of the Superior Court passed judgment holding Ouellet in contempt and imposed on him the sentence of a $500 fine and an apology to the court and to the people of Canada. Ouellet appealed on the grounds that the summary procedure was unjustified, that his statement, if made, was privileged, and that he was misquoted.

The Court of Appeal did not hesitate in setting aside the appeal and in holding that Ouellet was in contempt.

> When a Minister of the Crown finds that he cannot understand how a sane Judge could give a silly decision, such a Minister is not qualified to render justice and is not qualified to state that a Judge rendering such a decision is likely to hamper him in the exercise of their functions. Certainly, the decisions of Judges are subject to criticism as are the decisions

---

[158] Cross-reference to § 3.8.1.

all other public men. But criticism of a decision is not stat the person who gave it is an imbecile, which is contempt of Court "by scandalizing the Court" and this kind of contempt of Court is always prohibited.[159]

In fact, the court went further to express its frustration with the Minister quite openly.

....the present case has convinced me that it is idle to hope for help from the Executive Branch of Government, particularly in that most serious class of cases where the offender is himself a Member of the Executive.[160]

The court showed its awareness of the impact of the kind of statement made by Ouellet and of its ability to damage the constitutional legal fabric of the political system. It reproached to the Minister that he made the statement knowing it was likely to enjoy credit among the public, to be perceived as authoritative and to be given wide publicity. In these circumstances, it could only harm the administration of justice.

The Court of Appeal held that the trial judge was correct in the deliberate speed he exercised in calling the Minister to account and in using the summary procedure. It felt the statement was not privileged; he was not speaking on behalf of the government and the proceedings did not take place in Parliament. Finally, on the issue of the sentence, the Court of Appeal decided not to force the apology because it would not improve the administration of justice in Canada.

...but appellant has amply demonstrated that he is a man incapable of admitting that he may have been wrong...The offending words...display a lack of restraint and judgment deplorable in a Minister of the Crown, but we are all human, and there are few of us who have not at some time uttered in haste words that we have afterwards had caused to regret.[161]

---

[159] (1976), 72 D.L.R. (3d) 95 to 97.
[160] Ibid. at 102.
[161] Ibid. at 103.

§ 10.12.2
R. v. Vermette
Supreme Court of Canada; May 26, 1988
(1988), 50 D.L.R. (4th) 385

This is in several ways an exceptional case. Vermette was an inspector with the R.C.M.P. He participated in break-ins and in the theft of the computer lists of the membership of the Parti Québecois, a political party advocating the secession of Québec from Canada. In the course of time, the activities of Vermette and a number of his fellow officers came to public knowledge and they were accused of several offences, as well as of conspiracy, pursuant to the relevant provisions of the *Criminal Code.*

At the trial which began on April 13, 1982, one of the co-conspirators was brought forward as a defence witness for the purpose of showing that Vermette had acted in good faith as an R.C.M.P. officer. In the course of the testimony, the witness made accusations against the Parti Québécois and its leadership. At this time, the Parti Québécois was the governing party in the Province of Québec. The testimony in court had the effect of throwing the case into the political arena and it produced an immediate effect.

> On the day this evidence was given, during question period at the National Assembly of the province of Québec, the then leader of the opposition asked the Premier to deny or to confirm these accusations. Despite the fact that the Speaker had warned the House that these remarks tended to create serious prejudice to the rights of the respondent, the Premier denounced not only the actions of the witness, whose credibility he attacked in colourful and abusive language, but also those of the defence lawyers, the federal government and the R.C.M.P. He even accused members of the R.C.M.P. of having committed several crimes. This diatribe lasted some 20 minutes.[162]

There could only be one explanation for this. The Premier, René Lévesque, must have known the likely effect of his statements. He must be assumed to have calculated that the airing of his and his party's position on the events leading up to the trial, within the National Assembly, was more important than the continuation or the

---

[162] (1988), 50 D.L.R. (4th) 385 at 388.

success of the prosecution. Whatever the motive of the Premier, he did not exercise the restraint from comment which would have been customarily expected of members of the Executive Branch in circumstances where a matter was *sub judice*.

The publicity and exposure given the Premier's comments was eventually qualified by the Supreme Court of Canada as exceptional. Vermette's trial was halted. A new prosecution was initiated but before the matter came to trial, Vermette moved to quash the information against him and to stay the proceedings. The Superior Court considered five fundamental principles to be applicable to this situation. It held them to be principles relating to that particular criminal trial but in a broader perspective, they are also fundamental principles of political law:

- the separation of powers;
- the rule of law;
- the integrity of the judicial process;
- the independence of the judiciary; and
- the scheme of the *Charter*.

Basing itself on these grounds, the court

> came to the conclusion that the remarks made by the Premier in the National Assembly of Quebec, as well as the exceptional publicity that had surrounded them, infringed the rights of the respondent to a full and complete defence and to a fair trial guaranteed by ss. 7 and 11(*d*) of the Charter. This infringement, in the judge's view, amounted to a denial of the rights of the respondent, and the court therefore had a duty to provide a remedy.[163]

The Superior Court also considered the motion to quash the information in the light of the doctrine of abuse of process. It concluded that the quality of exceptionality was present in this case, meaning that continuation of the trial would be so oppressive and vexatious to the accused that it would constitute an abuse of process. In the court's view, the only way to safeguard the rights of the accused was to stop the proceedings and it therefore stopped the proceedings. The Court of Appeal of Québec agreed.

---

[163] *Ibid.* at 388-389.

The Supreme Court of Canada allowed the appeal. It shared the underlying concern of the trial judge that the important element was the assurance of a fair trial for the accused, but it came to the opposite conclusion as to how best to achieve that. First, it presumed that a jury should be allowed to perform its work. Moreover, it said that judicial abdication could not be the proper remedy in this case. It set out a significant judicial position for circumstances in which cases become embroiled in political considerations.

> That is all the more important in a case like the present which concerns serious accusations not only against the R.C.M.P. but also against the leaders of the federal and provincial governments. It is in the public interest that such accusations be scrutinized by the judiciary. I cannot accept that the reckless remarks of politicians can thus frustrate the whole judicial process.[164]

The court ordered a new trial for Vermette, rather than staying the case against him without resolution. The broader impact of the case, however, is that the court perceived its role as showing the way to depoliticize a matter apparently tainted by political comment. Adopting the criminal law counterpart of privity, the court emphasized that the politicians who had commented were, in the judicial sense, not involved in the process. Thus, not even the fact that the Premier was the one who had commented, nor the vehemence of his remarks, could stop the course of justice.

---

§ 10.12.3
R. v. Appleby
Ontario Provincial Court; July 16, 1990
(1990), 78 C.R. (3d) 282

This case appropriately illuminates the great caution exercised by the courts in dealing with allegations of political involvement on the prosecution side in litigation. From the purely legal aspect, there can be a serious evidentiary problem attributable to the discreet ways in which political influence is thought to be exerted. From the point of view of political law, the courts have a somewhat difficult task in such cases, considering that as their role is to state the law alone, they fear to venture beyond what they see as their competence, in order

---

[164] *Ibid.* at 393.

to assess the political components of trials or to balance the legal and political sides of matters which, if conducted properly, should be exclusively legal.

In April 1989, as then Finance Minister Michael Wilson was preparing to deliver the yearly Budget Speech in the House of Commons, two copies of an explanatory document entitled "Budget in Brief" were stolen. One of them made its way to an insurance company and the other was made available to Small, a television reporter who proceeded, on April 26, 1989, to broadcast its highlights. Due to those unexpected circumstances, the Budget Speech originally scheduled for April 27 was hastily brought forward to the evening of April 26. These events took place despite the Canadian government's long standing custom of secrecy prior to the tabling of federal budgets and in contravention of the many security measures designed to enforce that custom.

As an outcome of this leak, three of the individuals involved, including the reporter, were charged with theft and possession of stolen goods of a value not exceeding $1,000. Before the trial proceeded on the merits, the defence presented the following motion to have the charges stayed:

1. This proceeding is an abuse of the process of this court in that:

    (a) the charges against all of the accused have an improper motive in that the charge was laid and the proceedings continued in an attempt by the Executive to achieve political ends unrelated to the valid exercise of the criminal law power; and

    (b) the charge against Douglas Small has an improper and discriminatory motive in that it was laid and continued in an attempt to punish Mr. Small, not for the possession of the document allegedly stolen, but for the legitimate exercise of his right to freedom of expression as guaranteed by Section 2(b) of the Canadian Charter of Rights and Freedoms.[165]

Thereafter, the entire hearing was on this motion. It took on the flavour of a public examination, with the judge admittedly being attentive to what he called "the public good." In the end, the motion

---

[165] (1990), 78 C.R. (3d) 282 at 285.

was granted and the charges were dismissed. The court's route to that result is both delicate and fascinating.

The R.C.M.P., which was in charge of the investigation, concluded discovery of the facts by early May 1989. The investigating officers felt that charges under the *Criminal Code*, based either on property concepts or on matters of confidentiality, could not be sustained against any of the suspects. Despite these conclusions, during the remainder of May, a number of meetings took place involving the R.C.M.P. and provincial Crown prosecutors to discuss the evidence and the possible laying of charges. The court found that in these discussions, the principal investigating officer, Jordan, continued to act properly in his law enforcement capacity and made an assessment of the case in that function, rather than acting as a legal counsel. Both Jordan and his immediate supervisor refused to lay any information. Jordan's testimony was reproduced as follows:

> I did not lay these charges because I had formed the opinion that they were intended to please elected officials. It was my view that the evidence was so weak that the probability of conviction was slight. Based upon my experience as a police officer, I felt in absence of the political atmosphere no charges would be considered by the police, much less the Crown. On balance, I was unable to resolve the apparent unfairness, given the rationale for the charges, for the fact some persons involved were charged and others were not.
>
> In the final analysis, I felt support for the charges was a fragile construction to bring about the prosecution of Mr. Small. I found this to be repugnant and I could not participate further.[166]

The court noted that Jordan's observations with respect to political interference were based on impressions, not facts. Nevertheless, as a result of Jordan's refusal to lay the information, he was relieved of responsibility for this case and another, more junior, officer was found to comply with the instructions of the R.C.M.P. management. The view voiced by one senior officer in the R.C.M.P. was that everyone involved should be charged and that journalists involved should be taught a lesson.

The political interference which Jordan suspected and which the court dwelt upon in great detail was the possible involvement of the Chief

---

[166] *Ibid.* at 297.

of Staff of Prime Minister Mulroney and that of the President of the Treasury Board. While the latter admitted that two calls were made early on from his office to the Deputy Commissioner of the R.C.M.P. to obtain information to advise the President of the Treasury Board and qualified this as normal, routine and proper day-to-day functioning of government, neither political official admitted that any information flowed downward from ministerial offices to the police. They equally did not admit, and this is the key item of the testimony, that any pressure was applied by the political class to the police about laying charges, against whom they should be laid, nor according to what timetable they might be laid.

It was on the basis of this seemingly uncontradicted, but unverifiable testimony that the court made its ruling on the allegation of political interference in the prosecution.

> If a case is to be made out for either direct political interference or conduct which creates an unholy perception of political interference, then such interference must come, as Mr. Segal has aptly described it, "from the top down". Since such evidence is completely lacking in this case, I must necessarily find that there was no direct political interference and no justifiable perceptions of political interference.[167]

The court patently felt that the description and the characterization of political interference in the criminal justice process, constitutionally independent of the executive, needed to be explained in greater depth.

> Whether or not a perception of political interference (in the absence of evidence of direct political interference) can constitute grounds for a successful abuse of process motion must necessarily remain something of a moot point. The reason is somewhat obvious, in that any perception of political interference in the criminal process such as might outrage the conscience of the community would necessarily come about only as a result of the issue being explored in open court. In order to accomplish that end, someone must be placed in jeopardy, either by the laying of the charge, such as has occurred in this case, or by some other originating proceeding. In the absence of such a proceeding, the perception may not be disclosed or even come to light.[168]

---

[167] *Ibid.* at 300.
[168] *Ibid.* at 298.

The court's perceived absence of political interference led it to refute that argument in the defence motion. It also rejected the line of defence according to which there was unfair prosecutorial selection. However, this judgment leaves the alert reader with the clear impression that the court was thoroughly uncomfortable with the entire prosecution, given its basis on the laying of charges by the only police officer junior and impressionable enough to agree to do so.

> The zeal of superior law enforcement police officers in pushing ahead with the laying of charges, these charges, despite both the state of the evidence and the law, which would indicate otherwise, suggests an objective unfairness and vexatiousness, particularly with regard to the accused Douglas Small, which is indeed appropriate to criminal proceedings.[169]

The ruling was thus in effect based not directly on the elusive and unprovable political interference but rather on the direct outcome of that interference, had it been susceptible of proof, namely the laying of informations and their being laid on a selective basis, particularly against Small, the reporter. In effect, the court reached the appropriate result both in terms of criminal law, in terms of political law, as well as on an ethical basis. It needed to do so in the only way open to it without entailing a conflict between the judicial and executive branches.

The court's final comments on the role of Small in this matter are also worthy of note.

> A society that recognizes the importance to the democratic process of the free dissemination of news should not be offended if that dissemination takes place with the measure of dramatic flair demonstrated by Mr. Small.
>
> . . .
>
> If budget confidentiality continues to be a matter of quasi-constitutional concern in this electronic, technological age, then it is for Parliament to address the issue promptly with appropriate specific statutory provisions.[170]

---

[169] *Ibid.* at 307.
[170] *Ibid.* at 307-308.

10.13 ISSUE: USE OF PROSECUTION FOR POLITICAL AND PARTISAN MOTIVES[171]

§ 10.13.1
R. v. Kormos
Ontario Court (Provincial Division); November 28, 1997
(1997), 154 D.L.R. (4th) 551

This case reflects the confrontational nature of political life in Ontario following the victory of the Progressive Conservative Party and the defeat of the New Democratic Party in the election of June 1995, as well as the acrimonious tone of debate in the Legislative Assembly. Kormos had at one time been Attorney General in the NDP government. On November 7, 1996, he and Martel, another former minister, entered an office of the Ministry of the Attorney General in Downsview where Family Support Services had been rendered. They took videotape of the state of the office in an effort to prevent the closure of the office and the cessation of the service. Later on, they showed the videotape publicly. The same day, the new Attorney General Harnick, made a statement in the Legislative Assembly about the incident and said that a police investigation had been started. In the ensuing discussion which became rather heated, the Attorney General used the expression "break-in," then tried to extricate himself from having created an impression of guilt on the part of Kormos, or from having interfered in the administration of justice. Kormos was charged with assault on a security guard in the course of the visit to the office; he pleaded not guilty. Kormos then filed the application on the basis of which this judgment was rendered. What he sought was an order staying the prosecution on the ground that the Attorney General's statement in the Legislature was an abuse of process.

An uninvolved observer may have regarded Kormos' actions as an attempt to seek publicity and to shame the government. In a similar frame of mind, the Attorney General's response could have been seen as overreaction by a government sensitive to protect its reforms. In the circumstances then prevailing in Ontario, Kormos' application opened the way for the court to consider which actions by an Attorney

---

[171] Cross-reference to § 2.4 and 10.8.

General in office would amount to use of the courts for political purposes. Here, the term of art "abuse of the court's process" is a legal designation for politicization of a case, a synonym for use of the courts to achieve politically motivated goals, or in other words, the use of legal means for political victory over a government's ideological adversaries.

The central issue in this case is to determine the effect of the accusatory words by the Chief Law Officer of the Province. Kormos based his application for stay first on the argument that the Attorney General ought not to have stated his opinion about the guilt or innocence of an accused prior to the conclusion of even an investigation. He then also framed his application with regard for its specific political and parliamentary context.

> (b) The Attorney General's conduct marked these proceedings with the taint of partisan political motivation.
>
> (c) The Attorney took the unprecedented step of announcing in the Legislative Assembly that he had initiated a police investigation of a crime which he had already determined was committed.[172]

Kormos alleged that the breach by the Attorney General of these proscriptions seriously undermined the public's confidence in the administration of justice.

In his consideration of the matter, the judge placed greatest emphasis on two fundamental and related characteristics of the function of Attorney General, namely his independence and the non-partisan nature of his prosecutorial decisions. In reinforcing the argument of the Attorney General's independence from other ministers within Cabinet and from considerations other than legal ones in administering the justice system, the court cited from scholarly writings of several previous Attorneys General, in particular from a paper delivered by Ian Scott to the Canadian Bar Association, in which he indicated that

> ...issues of whether to institute a prosecution are not matters of government policy...*These decisions rest solely with the Attorney General, who must*

---

[172] (1998), 154 D.L.R. (4th) 551 at 565.

> *be regarded for these purposes as an independent officer, exercising a function that in many ways resembles the functions of a judge."* [Judge's emphasis.][173]

In this instance, this doctrinal background needed to be applied to the argument raised by Kormos justifying the stay. The court relied for this on the "clearest of cases" test developed by the Supreme Court of Canada. In order to succeed, Kormos would not only have to show a factual basis for his application, but also convince the court that the Attorney General's actions amounted to conduct that would shock the conscience of the community and be so detrimental to the proper administration of justice as to warrant judicial intervention.[174] Here, Kormos did not meet that standard.

Despite the difficulties in deciphering Hansard, which, because of the tumult, may not have completely reflected everything that was said, the court found that the Attorney General did talk in the Legislature about "a potentially serious incident...that may have involved unauthorized access to certain files."[175] However, it applied its discretion to the assessment of these facts and words and held that a dispassionate and objective review of the events should not lead to a conclusion that the judicial process was compromised to an extent that a story would be warranted. With respect to the words actually uttered by the Attorney General, the court thought,

> I would expect that most people would not find this information tainted by political malice or motive.

...and later...

> I do not find that such a course of action is *prima facie* politically motivated.[176]

The judgment did not end there, however. Even if this was not the clearest of cases, as the facts could not warrant the conclusion that, in fulfilling his role as Chief Legal Officer of the Province, the Attorney General was not conscious enough of the restraint required of him in his capacity as a parliamentarian with a known political alle-

---

[173] *Ibid.* at 566.
[174] This test was developed by Madame Justice L'Heureux-Dubé in *R. v. Power* (1994), 89 C.C.C. (3d) 1 (S.C.C.).
[175] *Supra* note 172 at 572.
[176] *Ibid.* at 572 and 573.

giance, and even if his behaviour did not lead to sanction by the court, he was held to lack caution to the degree required that the prosecution would not seem to be politically motivated.

> Although, the court recognizes that the Attorney General was involved in a heated debate, he would have been well advised to heed the practice of not commenting on the potential guilt of anyone with respect to any offence that is under investigation by the authorities or before the courts. This caution applies to all elected officials but particularly to those persons occupying the sensitive and important position of Attorney General. It would seem to me that Mr. Harnick might have exercised more control as it related to his interjections in the House in connection with potential criminal charges. As Attorney General, he must always appear to be above the fray.[177]

While denying Kormos' application and authorizing the prosecution to proceed on the assault charges, the court adopted a Solomon-like approach by stating that it had no sense that an assault had taken place and that it had no charge of break and enter before it. The judge's message to the Attorney General, namely to avoid even the appearance of using the power of prosecution for political purposes, was as clear as the one he addressed to Kormos, namely that defences to such prosecutions would be judged on their legal merits alone.

In fact, Kormos was tried early in 1998. He was acquitted.

See also *Prosecutions of former President Kenneth Kaunda of Zambia*, High Court of Zambia, December, 1997 – March, 1999; *Prosecution of Deputy Prime Minister Anwar Ibrahim*, High Court of Malaysia, September, 1998 – August, 2000, limited information available; *Threatened Prosecution of American Infantrymen*, no prosecution initiated, Yugoslavia, April – May, 1999; *Prosecution of Minister of the Interior Abdollah Nouri*, Clerical court in Teheran, November 26, 1999, limited information available and *Martinez v. Republic of Cuba*, General Jurisdiction Division, Florida, 11th Judicial District, March 9, 2001, Case no. 99-18208 CA 20.[178]

---

[177] *Ibid.* at 573.
[178] All international comparisons.

10.14 ISSUE: TESTIMONY BY POLITICAL FIGURES IN LITIGATION AND IN TRIALS[179]

See *Ontario Federation of Anglers & Hunters v. Ontario (Ministry of Natural Resources)*[180] (2002), 211 D.L.R. (4th) 741 (Ont. C.A.), leave to appeal refused (2003), 313 N.R. 198 (note) (S.C.C.).

---

[179] Cross-reference to § 8.4.
[180] Cross-reference to § 1.11.

11

LEGAL ACCOUNTABILITY TO DEMOCRACY

11.1 GENERAL PRINCIPLES

See Volume I, Chapter 11.

11.2 ISSUE: THE DOCTRINE OF LEGAL ACCOUNTABILITY TO DEMOCRACY

11.2.A— THE GENERAL CONCEPT OF ACCOUNTABILITY TO LAW

See *Reference re Amendment to the Constitution of Canada*,[1] 125 D.L.R. (3d) (S.C.C.); *Canadian Wildlife Federation Inc. v. Canada (Minister of the Environment)*[2] (1990), 121 N.R. 385 at 401 (Fed. C.A.); *Ward v. Maracle* (1995), 24 O.R. (3d) 148 (Ont. Gen. Div.); *Dagg v. Canada (Minister of Finance)*, [1997] 2 S.C.R. 403 (S.C.C.); *Bacon v. Saskatchewan Crop Insurance Corp.*, [1999] 11 W.W.R. 51 (Sask. C.A.), leave to appeal refused (2000), [1999] S.C.C.A. No. 437 (S.C.C.); *R. v. Powley*, 47 O.R. (3d) 30 (Ont. S.C.J.), leave to appeal allowed (2000), [2000] O.J. No. 1063 (Ont. C.A. [In Chambers]), affirmed [2001] O.J. No. 607 (Ont. C.A.), leave to appeal allowed, 86 C.R.R. (2d) 187 (note) (S.C.C.), leave to appeal allowed (2002), 301 N.R. 388 (S.C.C.), affirmed [2003] S.C.J. No. 43 (S.C.C.) and *Dunmore v. Ontario (Attorney General)*, 207 D.L.R. (4th) 193 (S.C.C.)

---

[1] Cross-reference to § 1.12.1 and 4.12.1.
[2] Cross-reference to § 1.3.A.4, 1.3.D.2, 2.2.E.1, 2.6.1, 11.7.4 and 11.14.3.

11.2.B— WILLINGNESS TO ABIDE BY THE LAW

§ 11.2.B.1
In the Matter of Complaints under the Human Rights Act
Saskatchewan Board of Inquiry Decision; July 23, 1999

The subject matter of this case was the controversy surrounding the manner in which the public school authorities in Saskatchewan wanted to continue the practice of having students recite prayer in school and conduct Bible readings. The parents of some students alleged that this amounted to discrimination under the Saskatchewan *Human Rights Code*,[3] the Board of Education of Saskatoon School Division No. 13 resisted adamantly. While similar cases in Ontario, Manitoba and British Columbia had all held that discriminatory use of the Lord's prayer in public schools was illegal, the legal system of Saskatchewan established on the foundations laid while this province was still part of the Northwest Territories prior to 1905, was sufficiently different to warrant separate judicial examination and conclusions.

A Board of Inquiry appointed by the Saskatchewan Attorney General held that while the relevant provision of the province's laws allowed the Board of Education to "direct" the practice to be followed, the fact that the Board had not followed that practice but rather delegated its responsibility "to the discretion of teachers by a policy statement using [these] weasel words"[4] was a fundamental flaw in its current practice. This practice amounted to a breach of section 17 of the *Saskatchewan Act*,[5] the constitutional statute that established the province, which itself incorporated the effect of The School Ordinance of 1901.[6] The immediate problem upon which the Inquiry found the illegality was that the Board's practice of delegating opened the way for the whims of teachers and their personal biases as unelected staff.

The significant element of the Inquiry's findings is derived from its more general comments. Religious instruction, the Board held, "can-

---

[3] S.S. 1979, c. 5-24.1.
[4] Decision, p. 24.
[5] R.S.C. 1985, App. II, No. 21.
[6] O.N.W.T. 1901, c. 28, s. 137.

not be used as a ruse for Bible readings...That simply warps s. 137 beyond reasonable intent."[7] The clear meaning of this phrase is that a public authority cannot use law for a purpose clearly beyond its intended application, beyond its reasonable intent. Whether such use reflects the majority opinion of interested citizens, such as here the parents, or general community standards, is immaterial. The attempt by parents to define this practice based on a distortion of the intent of the legislation as being "democratic" because of majority opinion is totally ignored by the Inquiry, and quite properly so.

In comparing the way this issue had been handled by the school authorities of Saskatchewan with what had been done in Alberta and Ontario, the Inquiry gave the most pinpointed characterization possible of the issue of accountability to law at play in these circumstances. It said, "A willing Board of Education could craft similar policies."[8] The key component in this scenario by which the Board of Education wanted to avoid its accountability to law was its lack of willingness to accept the meaning which legislators had intended for the law and the true meaning which the courts had ascribed to it. In the same vein, the Inquiry continued.

> The Board of Inquiry recommends for several reasons, that the Legislature of Saskatchewan repeal s. 182(3) of the *Education Act* (and probably its Fransaskois twin s. 183(2)). Firstly, the subsection is inconsistent with constitutionally entrenched ss. 137 and 137(2) of the 1901 *Ordinance*. More importantly, repeal would convey the message that religious discrimination in public schools is not condoned. Without s. 182(3) the Board of Education would be obliged to rely on antiquated ss. 137 and 137(2) to support antiquated thinking.

> The Board of Inquiry recommends as well, that the Board of Education shed its image as a backwater of religious tolerance by declining to direct under s. 137(2) of the 1901 *Ordinance* that the Lord's prayer be recited in public schools.

> The Board of Inquiry recommends that the Board of Education move rapidly with its plan to develop a multicultural religious proposal. However, the plan should not include use of any prayer or readings from any form of bible. If amendments are requested to the *Education Act* to achieve this objective, the Legislature should cooperate.[9]

---

[7] *Supra* note 4, pp. 27-28.
[8] *Ibid.*, p. 30.
[9] *Ibid.*, pp. 31-32.

See also *Benoit v. Canada*, 2002 FCT 243 (Fed. T.D.), reversed [2003] F.C.J. No. 923 (Fed. C.A.), leave to appeal refused (2004), 2004 CarswellNat 1209 (S.C.C.).

11.2.C— WILFUL DESIRE TO RESPECT AND APPLY THE LAW

§ 11.2.C.1[10]
Reference re Secession of Québec
Supreme Court of Canada; August 20, 1998
(1998), 161 D.L.R. (4th) 385

The Supreme Court of Canada has been quite consistent in noting the democratic nature of Canada and its profound attachment to what has traditionally been described as the rule of law in its constitutional jurisprudence. In a number of such cases, it has relied on the Preamble of the *Constitution Act, 1867*, as the most apt characterization of the political legal regime in force in Canada. It was in the *Patriation Reference*[11] that the court took this analysis furthest in the direction of the accountability of public institutions and officials to law. It stated, effectively, that on the basis of the Preamble, Canada had embraced "the rule of law" as a guiding principle. It then went on to specify that the rule of law included as one of its centrepieces "executive accountability" to legal authority.

> What is stressed is the desire of the named provinces "to be federally united...with a Constitution similar in Principle to that of the United Kingdom." The preamble speaks also of union into "One Dominion" and of the establishment of the Union "by Authority of Parliament," that is the United Kingdom Parliament. What, then, is to be drawn from the preamble as a matter of law? A preamble, needless to say, has no enacting force but, certainly, it can be called in aid to illuminate provisions of the statute in which it appears. Federal union "with a Constitution similar in Principle to that of the United Kingdom" may well embrace responsible government and some common law aspects of the United Kingdom's unitary constitutionalism, such as the rule of law and Crown prerogatives and immunities. The "rule of law" is a highly textured

---

[10] Cross-reference to § 1.2.3, 2.4.6, 3.1, 4.2.2, 4.3.1, 4.6.1 and 10.2.1.
[11] *Reference re Amendment to the Constitution of Canada*, 125 D.L.R. (3d) 1, [1981] 1 S.C.R. 753 (S.C.C.).

expression, importing many things which are beyond the need of these reasons to explore but conveying, for example, a sense of orderliness, of subjection to known legal rules and of executive accountability to legal authority.[12]

The principle of accountability to law was therefore not novel or untested by the time the Supreme Court was asked to advise on the Québec question in 1986.

In its consideration of the first question of this reference, that which dealt with the ability of the National Assembly, legislature or government of Québec to secede unilaterally from Canada under the *Constitution* of Canada, the court offered an extensive analysis of the fundamental characteristics of the Canadian State. It mentioned federalism, democracy and the protection of minorities. The centrepiece of its reasoning, however, was the characteristic of constitutionalism and the rule of law, the criterion which made Canada a country based on law and legality. In the initial expression of the functioning of this characteristic, the court reaffirmed its adherence to the analysis which it had developed in 1981 in the *Patriation Reference*.

> The principles of constitutionalism and the rule of law lie at the root of our system of government. The rule of law, as observed in *Roncarelli v. Duplessis*, [1959] S.C.R. 121, at p. 142, is "a fundamental postulate of our constitutional structure." As we noted in the *Patriation Reference, supra,* at pp. 805-6, "[t]he 'rule of law' is a highly textured expression, importing many things which are beyond the need of these reasons to explore but conveying, for example, a sense of orderliness, of subjection to known legal rules and of executive accountability to legal authority."[13]

From this acknowledgement, it is without doubt that one of the components of the rule of law is accountability to law. For the purposes of this study, in which we are concerned more with the role of law than the rule of law, the adoption of this principle is both necessary and appropriate.

The key to the meaning of the phrase and to the application of the principle also flows from the precise wording of the court's advice:

---

[12] [1981] 1 S.C.R. 753 (S.C.C.) at 805-806.
[13] (1998), 161 D.L.R. (4th) 385 at 417, para. 70.

At its most basic level, the rule of law vouchsafes to the citizens and residents of the country a stable, predictable and ordered society in which to conduct their affairs. It provides a shield for individuals from arbitrary state action.[14]

The justices are, with these words, guiding the institutions and officials of the State not only to engage passively in obedience of legal prescription, but further, to consider themselves under a positive obligation to govern in a stable, predictable and ordered manner, in a non-arbitrary fashion, thus wilfully respecting legal norms and positively applying legal, as opposed to arbitrary, standards of State conduct.

See also *Rowswell & Associates Engineers Inc. v. Brandt* (2001), 13 C.L.R. (3d) 114 (Ont. S.C.J.), additional reasons at (2002), 2002 CarswellOnt 285 (Ont. S.C.J.).

11.3 ISSUE: OBLIGATION OF PUBLIC SERVANTS TO OBSERVE LEGAL NORMS[15]

11.3.A— SUBJECTION OF PUBLIC SERVANTS TO DOMESTIC LEGAL NORMS

§ 11.3.A.1
Bown v. Newfoundland (Minister of Social Services)
Newfoundland Court of Appeal; April 3, 1985
(1985), 54 Nfld. & P.E.I.R. 258

The duty of public servants to observe legal norms and to give greater weight to those norms than to policy considerations is one of the essential elements of professionalism in the Public Service. That duty, as the *Bown* case shows, is also a fundamental aspect of the master-servant relationship between the State and its public servants.

Bown was a district manager in Labrador for the Department of Social Services. His duties included interpreting the *Social Assistance Act* and

[14] *Ibid.* at 418, para. 70.
[15] Cross-reference to § 9.3.

its Regulations, in respect, among other things, to deductions from social assistance payments to recipients having people living in their homes, who themselves had earnings. Bown disagreed with the Department's interpretation of the law and, on the basis of his own policy views, refused to apply the Regulations to Innu persons on the basis that the concept of "board and lodging" was unknown to them. After disciplinary proceedings aimed at getting Bown to apply the law as the Department interpreted it, he was first suspended and subsequently dismissed.

Bown applied to the Trial Division of the Supreme Court of Newfoundland for writs of prohibition and *certiorari* to have his dismissal quashed and to prevent the Minister of Social Services from interfering with his exercise of statutory discretion. That court upheld the dismissal and indicated without equivocation that Bown's refusal to enforce the Regulations and to make the required assessment pursuant to it was a breach of his duty. The Newfoundland Court of Appeal specifically pointed out its agreement that a breach of duty had occurred. The twin aspects of this issue, namely that public servants are obligated to observe the law and are indeed accountable to it, with their careers if need be, and furthermore that no policy-guided interpretation, or rather misinterpretation of the law may be allowed to supplant the formal application of the law by the State, are concepts fundamental to the very notion of public service. The tone of the cumulative opinions of the Trial Division and of the Court of Appeal was that the duty of observing the law springs from the nature of public service as being the profession entrusted with applying the law of the land. The unmistakeable implication of the judgments was that that duty also stems from the inherently binding nature of law as a form of instrument of governance.

To the notion of breach of duty by improper interpretation, the Court of Appeal also added an emphasis on the fact that Bown's behaviour had amounted to a fundamental breach of the master-servant relationship.

> While the appellant was given certain discretionary powers by the Social Assistance Act to determine the amounts of assistance to be paid individual persons, that did not give him the unquestioned and exclusive right to make that determination or to interpret the Rules and Regulations as he saw fit. Nor did those powers (if such they can be called) give him the right to question and defy departmental policy and the instruc-

tions of his superiors in that department, who, under the Act, had the responsibility for its enforcement and the right to prescribe the appellant's functions and duties. No Government department, or private company, could operate under such an arrangement. In our view, the appellant's action was a totally unacceptable breach of his obligation to the Department, and the Lieutenant Governor in Council had every right to terminate his employment in the circumstances.

We would add that, in our view, whether or not the appellant's interpretation of the Regulation in question was a correct one is basically irrelevant.[16]

This case may thus be taken as precedent for the notions that public servants' accountability to law is a factor of their professional tasks and of their position in a hierarchy designed to carry out the functions of the State according to law.

---

§ 11.3.A.2
Canada (Information Commissioner) v.
Canada
(Minister of External Affairs)
Federal Court of Canada – Trial Division; August 28, 1990
[1990] 3 F.C. 514

It is well established in general that, in the performance of their profession, public servants are obligated to observe legal norms and that they are more fundamentally bound to legal norms than to the standards of policy or of accepted practice. Within that overall context, this case addresses the particular circumstances in which there is a deliberate change in the law. Here, we are dealing with the *Access to Information Act (ATIA)*,[17] enacted in 1982 and in force as of July 1, 1983. Where a new law such as this is incorporated into the State's political-legal regime and specifically imposes new duties on government departments and public officials which are contradictory to long-standing practice, the duty to amend public administration so as to bring it in conformity with the new legislation is even more genuine. Negligent or deliberate obfuscation of the new legal norm so created will result at least in contrary awards by the courts. In this

---

[16] (1985), 54 Nfld. & P.E.I.R. 258, 160 A.P.R. 258 at 260.
[17] Originally S.C. 1980-81-82-83, c. 111 (Schedule 1), now R.S.C. 1985, c. A-1.

case, it also entailed the naming of high public service officials by the court, as being personally involved, and in the inclusion in the ruling of a severe rebuke to the delinquent institution.

In the period between September and December 1985, three requests were presented independently of each other to the Department of External Affairs, for access to some of its records relating to the negotiations between Canada and the United States in view of the conclusion of the *Free Trade Agreement (FTA)*. The *Access to Information Act* required that records so requested be issued within 30 days, or that a delay be requested. The vetting of the records was undertaken, but they were not made available for such a long period that the requestors could claim that the delay constituted deemed refusal. In line with the procedures set out in the Act, they turned to the Information Commissioner, who eventually brought this action in the Federal Court – Trial Division. As of then, the original requestors fell somewhat into the background and participation in the litigation was undertaken by high profile public officials who were, on one side one of the most valuable jurists of Canada and on the other, one of the most powerful ministers, backed by very experienced senior public servants. While the latter could not be accused of wanting to subvert the *Access to Information Act*, they were utterly dedicated to the completion of the *Free Trade Agreement* and seemed even ready to avoid any hindrance in achieving the *FTA*, then the major goal of the government. Sitting in judgment on these parties was one of the country's most forthright judges and one of its most erudite judgment writers, Mr. Justice Francis Muldoon.

It was only after the Information Commissioner started this action that the Minister of External Affairs responded to the original requests. By then, however, the actions laying the ground for this case had been taken.

It must be noted that in order to observe the requirements as to form in such litigation, the named respondent was the Minister of External Affairs. In fact, however, the persons whose actions were called into question were the public service officials acting in this matter on the minister's behalf. The applicant's major allegation was the tardiness of the high departmental managers in complying with the requests and the fact that his undue delay amounted to deemed refuals to disclose. Counsel for one of the requesters phrased the position of all of them on the character of the delay as follows:

"the Department of External Affairs acted unreasonably and outside the spirit of the Act by obfuscating the reasons for the delays in responding to the access requests during the course of the Information Commissioner's investigation," the applicant does not assert malice, only very great negligence. It is just as well that counsel made that concession, for the words surely do seem to convey, if not malice, then very bad faith. On this, the respondent is adamant that there was no deliberate strategy by the respondent's high officials to delay, or to obfuscate.[18]

On the main issue of the case, whether the delay in providing access was justified under the *ATIA* or not, the court had no difficulty in granting the Information Commissioner's application and, based on the position expressed above for the requesters, it held that:

> The Department acted negligently and ignorantly outside of the spirit of the Act by obfuscating (without malice) the reasons for the delays in responding to the access requests during the course of the Information Commissioner's investigation.[19]

The most significant elements of this judgment for the notion of public servants' accountability to law were even more important than the outcome of this particular set of circumstances. First, the court was aware that this was among its first opportunities to interpret the Information Commissioner's powers under the *ATIA* to "exact compliance with the law" on the part of heads of government institutions, and it seized the opportunity. It laid out a panoply of additional approaches the Commissioner could take. Among these, it cited identifying and denouncing recalcitrance, bloody-mindedness or negligence, as well as commenting or complaining to Parliament in various reports. In the conception of the court, this idea of "exacting compliance" indicated that it would tolerate no deviation, and that this attitude was based on the fact that once Parliament had spoken, the duty to obey became both compulsory and inherent.

The court then picked up on this strain of commentary and gave its own authoritative statement on the requirement by the public service to observe new legal norms directed to it by Parliament. This judge left absolutely no doubt as to his opinion of the effect, and of the influence of law.

---

[18] [1990] 3 F.C. 514 at 518 a-b.
[19] *Ibid.* at 526 a-b.

These are not cases for declining to exercise the salutary powers of review conferred on the Court by Parliament. Confession that such requests ought to be processed as expeditiously as possible may be good for an individual's soul, but it has no didactic energy in gaining the attention of government departments. It has no effect in actually providing legally that less than expeditious processing of requests for information is breaking the law, as it surely is. The purpose of the reciew is not just to make the particular respondent acknowledge unreasonable tardiness. It is, also, to let all the other potential respondents know where they stand in these matters. The Court is quite conscious that responding to such requests is truly "extra work" which is extraneous to the line responsibilities and very *raison d'etre* of government departments and other information-holding organizations of government. But when, as in the *Access to Information Act*, Parliament lays down these pertinent additional responsibilities, then one must comply.

After much consideration, the Court concludes that the findings and declarations sought by the Commissioner are amply supported by the evidence, and are all justified, except for any possible inference of deliberately "obfuscating the reasons for the delays in responding to the access requests during the course of the Information Commissioner's investigation." The evidence, rather, suggests confusion, ignorance and negligence which are at least not ignoble, but constitute no reason to award laurels, either. It cannot be doubted that one principal purpose of the Act is to force a change of public servants' habitual, ingrained reluctance to give out the government's information, even apart from the obvious, stated limitations on access.[20]

See also *Colvin, Re*, [1993] 2 F.C. 351 (Fed. T.D.), affirmed 25 Admin. L.R. (2d) 174 (Fed. C.A.); *Riot at the Kingston Prison for Women*, Report by a Commission of Inquiry, April 1, 1996 and *Complaint of Brill-Edwards to the Privacy Commissioner*, letter-decision, June 22, 1998.

---

§ 11.3.A.3
Guenette v. Canada (Attorney General)
Ontario Court of Appeal; August 8, 2002
[2002] O.J. No. 3062

A particular and delicate aspect of the obligation of public servants to observe legal norms is the treatment afforded to these public servants who, out of a sense of legality and of loyalty to professional

---

[20] *Ibid.* at 524 h to 525 e.

duty, reveal publicly that the institutions they work for tolerates non-accountability to law on the part of other public servants. The common designation for this is whistle blowing. In many cases, the institutional response to whistle blowing is defensive of non-accountable conduct, thereby creating a compounding of the problem. At various times in the years leading up to the start of this action, proposals had been made to adopt legislation to protect whistle blowers. By the time of writing, no bill of this type had been laid before Parliament. In the absence of legislation, the outcome of whistle blowing was put before the courts. As whistle blowers have no apparent personal gain from this activity, the controversy is clearly one between accountability to law and institutional loyalty.

Here, the plaintiffs were real property administrators in the Department of Foreign Affairs and International Trade (DFAIT). Their work was mandated by the *Financial Administration Act*,[21] the *Federal Real Property Act*[22] and several sets of subordinate instruments.[23] This work consisted in managing the very substantial real property portfolio of the Government of Canada in other countries, in support of Canada's diplomatic program. The mandate of the Bureau within DFAIT which administered the subject holdings was based on principles which included "economic justification," "cost-effectiveness," "efficiency" and ethics.

Guenette and the second plaintiff, Gualtieri alleged that in conducting their work, they attempted to adhere to the statutory functions and duties of their positions and to conduct cost-effective management in accordance with the applicable rules. They go on to state that they were prevented from carrying out this work by the careerism, opportunism and protection by their superior of their privileged lifestyle. More particularly,

> Guenette and Gualtieri state, and the fact is, that the culture and environment of the Department did not permit them as public servants to properly execute their duties with integrity. In fact, it promotes loyalty to the department over and above all else.[24]

---

[21] R.S.C. 1985, c. F-11.
[22] S.C. 1991, c. 50; R.S.C. 1985, c. F-8.4.
[23] Notably the Federal Real Property Regulations and the Treasury Board Real Property Policy.
[24] Statement of claim, p. 12, para. 30.

The statement of claim also referred to

> a systematic disregard of the rules and regulations governing the han-
> dling of real estate by Federal Public Servants, and more particularly the
> disregard of the financial impact of such decisions.[25]

Finally, the plaintiffs contended that

> the Bureau management displayed a cavalier attitude with respect to
> the disregard for policy and legislative spirit and ignored their man-
> date.[26]

The plaintiffs did not render public their divergence of opinion with
DFAIT as to how, in their view, their functions were to be fulfilled.
In response to their differences, however, they indicate in the suit
that they were harassed to the point of being psychologically disa-
bled. Their tasks were reduced and their performance of duty was
rendered impossible.

> Gualtieri claims that this abuse stemmed from her devotion to her duties
> and respect for and accountability to the taxpayers of Canada which
> collided with the careerism and personal motivations of senior manage-
> ment and which constituted a threat to the system and the bureaucratic
> machine including the opulent and lavish lifestyles of the foreign ser-
> vice.[27]

It is this harassment that led to the legal action. On June 10, 1998,
Guenette and Gualtieri filed in the Ontario Court (General Division),
in the meantime renamed the Superior Court of Justice, asking for
general damages of three million dollars. The significant part of the
claim is that they also sought a sum of thirty million dollars as punitive damages and proposed to use this extraordinary amount

> to establish a non-profit advocacy organisation with a mandate to rep-
> resent and protect the rights of all government employees; this will
> include lobbying for statutory and policy changes regarding employ-
> ment practices of the Federal Government, particularly as they relate to
> issues of abuse of power, harassment, principles of integrity, etc. Another
> key role will be to advocate, through the Court system if necessary,

---

[25] *Ibid.*, p. 13, para. 35.
[26] *Ibid.*, p. 13, para. 38.
[27] *Ibid.*, p. 17 para. 55.

matters which are not properly provided for by the current law, e.g. personal harassment.[28]

This case was at first thought likely to engage the court most directly in consideration of the law on what constitutes the harassment by government institutions of their public service employees. It could be almost inevitable, though, that the court be brought into examination of whether DFAIT actually breached the statutory and regulatory provisions applicable to its obligations in the realm of property management. This would, in turn, have lead the court to look at the legal validity of whistle blowing as a mechanism for ensuring public sector institutional compliance with binding rules and thus, accountability to law. A question of singular importance is the attitude the public service unions will take on the matter.

The matter was, despite all the prospects for the development of this aspect of political law, not analyzed on the merits. The defendants applied for summary judgment dismissing the actions against them. As the court found no genuine issue on the material facts, requiring trial, their motion was granted. The court held that the exaggerated or novel claim for damages was not sufficient reason to take this matter outside the purview of the collective agreement covering the plaintiffs.

The court held that notwithstanding the broad scope of the plaintiffs' claims, including their allegations of abuse of public office, breach of fiduciary duty and conspiracy, the complaints related to workplace issues between the employees and their supervisors. The plaintiffs ought, in the court's view, have used the methods available to them under their collective agreement and the applicable Public Service legislation. They refused to compromise. In seeking redress from this court, they took the matter to a body which had no jurisdiction.

This case comprises a sideshow that may be even more interesting than the somewhat predictable outcome of the main contest. The Minister of Foreign Affairs, the Hon. Lloyd Axworthy, was one of the defendants. At the hearing, he was represented by separate counsel. Axworthy assumed the portfolio after the harassing actions complained of allegedly took place. Nevertheless, the plaintiffs sought to rely on the fact that they had given notice of their alleged plight to

---

[28] *Ibid.*, p. 4, para. 2(a).

him directly. The court found no evidence of any personal liability on Axworthy's part and dismissed the action against him separately from the ground used in respect of the other defendants, the lack of jurisdiction.

In so doing, the court brought in a pertinent observation of a more directly political nature.

> But unless he has actually been party to the tortuous conduct, no such recourse lies against the Minister whose responsibility for matters embraced by the legislation is political under the theory of responsible government.
>
> . . .
>
> ...the Minister...may be personally liable for acts done in excess of his authority which could include bad faith, malfeasance or collateral purpose; he may also be personally liable for negligence in the exercise of his powers if it can be shown that in so acting he owed a duty of care to the plaintiffs...[29]

This case could have made better law in general and could certainly have clarified the political law as to the subjection of public service institutions and officials to legal norms if these particular plaintiffs had not overplayed their hand.

The plaintiffs appealed and on August 8, 2002, the Ontario Court of Appeal ruled that the case could proceed on the merits. On the same day, the Attorney General of Canada announced that he would not seek leave to appeal to the Supreme Court of Canada. At the time of writing, this litigation was still in progress.

See also *Police Raid on British Columbia Legislature Offices*, December 12, 2003.

---

[29] (2000), [2000] O.J. No. 3604, 2000 CarswellOnt 3914 (Ont. S.C.J.), para. 62, additional reasons at (2001), 2001 CarswellOnt 205 (Ont. S.C.J.), reversed (2002), 60 O.R. (3d) 601 (Ont. C.A.), citing from *Crown Trust Co. v. Ontario* (1988), 64 O.R. (2d) 774 (Ont. H.C.) at 783.

11.3.B— SUBJECTION OF PUBLIC SERVANTS TO FOREIGN LEGAL NORMS

---

§ 11.3.B.1

R. v. Bonadie

Ontario Court (Provincial Division); June 20, 1996

(1996), 109 C.C.C. (3d) 356

The accountability of public servants in the service of one government and posted and accredited to another government, to the legal system of the host country is, by exception to the rules generally applicable to public servants, subject to a number of international conventions on diplomatic and consular activity. Bonadie was in this category, a consular representative of the Government of St. Vincent and the Grenadines in Canada, with jurisdiction in Metropolitan Toronto. He was accused of perjury in relation to testimony he gave at the bail hearing of a migrant farm worker from his home country who was charged in Canada with a criminal offence. He also helped the worker escape from Canada to St. Vincent, on instructions from his government. In his defence, Bonadie applied for a stay of proceedings on the ground of immunity from prosecution pursuant to the *Foreign Missions and International Organizations Act.*[30] The *Vienna Convention on Consular Relations* was a Schedule to that Act.

The court stayed the proceedings on the basis of evidence that the duty imposed on consuls to respect the laws of the receiving State was created by the *Convention*, but that the section was only hortatory. Thus, if a consul did not comply with the domestic law of the receiving State, the proper remedy was through diplomatic, rather than judicial channels.

The court added a most noteworthy mention of a political law character on the subject of interference by foreign officials in the domestic political affairs of the receiving State.

> Moreover the reference to not interfering in the internal affairs of the receiving State is geared more to taking part in political activities against

---

[30] S.C. 1991, c. 41.

the security of the State which may or may not involve a breach of the domestic law. Thus if a consul or diplomat of the sending State were to advocate publicly the separation of a Province from the rest of Canada, he would certainly be interfering in the internal affairs of Canada even though he may not be in breach of the domestic law. If he were to espouse the overthrow of the Government of Canada or of a Province or to preach sedition, he would be interfering in the internal affairs of Canada as well as committing a breach of the domestic law.[31]

§ 11.3.B.2
Copello v. Canada (Minister of Foreign Affairs)
Federal Court of Canada – Trial Division; September 11, 1998
(1998), 152 F.T.R. 110[32]

This case is a clear manifestation that the judiciary is venturing into areas where it did not reach until the advent of the *Charter* and of the jurisprudence which has interpreted and enlarged the powers of the courts under it.

During the summer of 1998, Copello, an Italian diplomat posted to Ottawa, was involved in two incidents in which he seemed to be in breach of Canadian law, that is, for him a foreign legal system. The Minister of Foreign Affairs addressed several diplomatic notes about Copello to the ambassador of Italy and Copello was declared *persona non grata*, with a requirement that he leave Canada by September 15. He applied, on his own, to the Federal Court – Trial Division, for interim relief from the expulsion order, by asking for judicial review of the second diplomatic note. He alleged that the Minister had acted on wrong information and had breached the rules of natural justice.

The court, knowing full well that it was being presented with an unprecedented claim, granted the application with some trepidation. The judgment indicated that there would eventually be a serious question to be tried on the merits, rather than a frivolous or vexatious one. On this branch of the test for interim relief, the court acknowledged that the case was fraught with difficulties because "There are

---

[31] (1996), 109 C.C.C. (3d) 356 at 378 e.
[32] And Federal Court of Appeal, October 11, 2000; (2000), [2000] F.C.J. No. 1641, 2000 CarswellNat 2349 and Federal Court of Canada – Trial Division; December 10, 2001; (2001), [2001] F.C.J. No. 1835, 2001 CarswellNat 3592, affirmed 2003 FCA 295 (Fed. C.A.).

questions that arise from the interplay of domestic and international law, questions relating to diplomatic status, to prerogative rights, and, of course, relating to the jurisdiction of this Court."[33] It agreed with the applicant that the expulsion may harm him irreparably, in a manner not compensable by damages. The strongest reasoning invoked by the court, however, was its blunt rejection of the minister's assertion that if the application were granted, the minister would be constrained in his ability to conduct the foreign affairs of Canada. Upon analysis, the Minister did seem to have stated his case in an exaggerated manner, contributing to the result that proved to be counterproductive for him.

On October 11, 2000, a three-member panel of the Federal Court of Appeal dismissed Copello's appeal, indicating that the motions judge made no reversible error that would warrant intervention. Copello had failed to demonstrate any "special circumstances" pursuant to Rule 316 of the Federal Court Rules which would allow him to call the Chief of Protocol of the Department of Foreign Affairs and International Trade as a witness.

The issue was decided again by the Federal Court's Trial Division on December 21, 2001, on Copello's application for judicial review of the decision of the Minister of Foreign Affairs. The court held that the exclusion of foreign diplomats is a matter of Crown prerogative in the conduct of the foreign affairs of Canada and immune from judicial review. "In my opinion, a declaration of *persona non grata* is not a legal issue and remains in the political arena. The decision is not justiciable."[34] Although part of the Vienna Convention on Diplomatic Relations was given the force of law in Canada, the specific subject matter of such designations was not, because the implementing statute was silent on the point. Moreover, a diplomatic note was held not to be a decision. Overall, Copello's application was dismissed. The issue he raised was subject to prerogative powers, rather than law, but the matter was still to be determined by the Canadian political legal system.

See also *Chipkar v. Xinchun*, Ontario Superior Court of Justice, file no. 03-CV-253110CM1, endorsement February 3, 2004.

---

[33] (1998), 152 F.T.R. 110 at (p. 2).
[34] 2001 FCT 1350 at para 71, affirmed 2003 FCA 295 (Fed. C.A.).

11.3.C— SUBJECTION OF PUBLIC SERVANTS TO NORMS OF INTERNATIONAL LAW

See *United States v. Alvarez Machain*,[35] 504 U.S. 655 (1992).

11.4 ISSUE: PROFESSIONAL ETHICS OF PUBLIC SERVANTS

§ 11.4.1
Northwest Territories (Commissioner) v. Doyle
Supreme Court of the Northwest Territories; June 1, 1992
[1992] N.W.T.R. 279[36]

Most cases of fraud committed by public servants against their own governments can be characterized simply as failures to observe the obligatory nature of legal norms and standards. Here, by contrast, the presence of an intergovernmental aspect to the case, as well as the behaviour of the defendant, lent to the case an additional aspect of ethics in the governmental process.

Doyle was the Yellowknife regional superintendent of the Northwest Territories Department of Social Services. In this capacity, she defrauded the NWT Government of over $270,000 by depositing in her own accounts cheques made out to fictitious, deceased and other payees. When confronted with evidence of her actions, she made a written admission and resigned her position. However, in response to a statement of claim for repayment, Doyle defended with a general denial. She also alleged that, given the method of financing of the Social Services scheme of the NWT, the monies allegedly misappropriated were federal and not territorial. From this she argued that only the federal government and not that of the NWT had a right to maintain the action for recovery, and that the proper forum would have been the Federal Court, not the NWT Supreme Court.

---

[35] International comparison.
[36] Additional reasons at (1992), 8 C.P.C. (3d) 209 (N.W.T. S.C.).

The court analyzed the *Canada Assistance Plan*,[37] pursuant to which the funds were made available. It concluded that the funds were provided by Canada to the NWT, that the Territories were, for these purposes, treated as if it were a province, and most importantly that the legislation was to be provincially and territorially administered for the benefit of needy persons. Thus the first phase of the financial transfers were to the provincial and territorial governments, rather than directly to the needy individuals in question. "Nothing about these cheques or transactions suggests any transaction by or on behalf of the Government of Canada except insofar as the Government of the Northwest Territories is a statutory emanation of the federal power pursuant to the *Northwest Territories Act*, and, more fundamentally, s. 146 of the *Constitution Act, 1867*."[38] On this basis, it was directly and only to the NWT that the defendant had owed a fiduciary duty and it was by the NWT's action that recovery could be made.

The basis of Doyle's defense was that she owed a duty to Canada, rather than to the NWT By this defense she sought to introduce an ethical element into the case, implying that in the intergovernmental relationship her duty was to the original source of the funding. As she had no legal relationship with the Government of Canada, that duty would have been more ethical than legal. This reasoning was so perverse that the court saw through it as an obfuscatory tactic and rejected it. In fact, whether through federal or territorial legislation, public servants owe a legal duty to account for public funds entrusted to their administration.

The plaintiff sought summary judgment and, given the court's conclusion that she had presented no substantive defence, obtained it.

See also *R. v. Hinchey*, [1996] 3 S.C.R. 1128 (S.C.C.).

---

[37] R.S.C. 1985, c. C-1.
[38] [1992] N.W.T.R. 279 at 287, additional reasons at (1992), 8 C.P.C. (3d) 209 (N.W.T. S.C.).

11.5 ISSUE: OBLIGATION OF PARLIAMENTARIANS TO OBSERVE LEGAL NORMS[39]

See *Frobisher Bay Municipal Election, Re*, [1986] N.W.T.R. 183 (N.W.T. S.C.) and *R. v. Rizzotto* (1986), [1987] N.W.T.R. 63 (N.W.T. S.C.).

§ 11.5.1[40]
MacLean v. Nova Scotia (Attorney General)
Nova Scotia Supreme Court – Trial Division; January 5, 1987
(1987), 35 D.L.R. (4th) 306

The perspective in which observers of political law should look at this case is that of the accountability of parliamentarians to legal norms in their capacity as parliamentarians. Democratic governance requires that those elected to public office conduct their professional activities in accordance with the principles and precepts set out in the laws specifically dealing with their conduct of public affairs. Moreover, the distinguishing feature of this case is that it also shows that where the enactment of new legislation is deemed required to enforce the accountability of parliamentarians, legislative bodies will be held justified in taking that measure.

MacLean was twice elected to the Nova Scotia House of Assembly, in 1981 and again in 1984. During his second mandate, it was discovered that he had acted in a manner contrary to the *Criminal Code* and had defrauded the Legislature in respect of several categories of expenses relating to his function as a parliamentarian. After MacLean pleaded guilty to the charges against him in a trial, the House of Assembly went to the length of using valuable parliamentary time to enact *An Act Respecting Reasonable Limits for Membership in the House of Assembly* (the Act).[41] This legislation was designed particularly to expel MacLean and to ensure that he would not be eligible to be nominated or elected for a set period. In future, of course, this statute could be used against any other Member convicted of a criminal offence.

---

[39] Cross-reference to § 8.4.
[40] Cross-reference to § 8.5.1.
[41] S.N.S. 1986, c. 104.

MacLean thereupon initiated a challenge in court, claiming that his rights under the *Charter*, in particular those arising from section 3 [democratic rights], section 7 [legal rights], section 11 [proceedings in criminal trials] and section 15 [equality], were breached by the Act. His attempt was to prevent his expulsion from the House.

The argument of the Attorney General went directly to the heart of MacLean's obligation as a parliamentarian to abide by the legal norms applicable to him in that function.

> The defendant suggests the legislation is both protective and discipli-nary. If it is disciplinary, expulsion would accomplish that and anything more would be excessive and not demonstrably justified in a free and democratic society. Expulsion will protect the integrity of the House. The offences in which Mr. MacLean was involved were offences directly related to his role as a member of the House.

> . . .

> What the House did in expelling him, met their stated purpose of pro-tecting the integrity of the House and was demonstrably justified in a free and democratic society.[42]

Although the court concluded that that part of the Act which pur-ported to prevent MacLean from being a candidate for a certain pe-riod after his conviction was contrary to the *Charter*, it did uphold his expulsion from the House of Assembly. This is the most important finding in the decision and it must be looked at in conjunction with the very deliberate reasoning given by the court. The expression used by the Attorney General in his defence of the Act from the *Charter* challenge was that "protecting the integrity of the House" justified MacLean's expulsion. The court's response was to elevate this matter of principle to a higher plane.

> To ensure public trust is maintained in the membership of the House, expulsion is demonstrably justified in a free and democratic society.[43]

Thus, the standard of accountability to law which parliamentarians must meet is that of "the public trust." This phrase can be understood in both its meanings. In order to work within the parameters of

---

[42] (1987), 35 D.L.R. (4th) 306 at 316 and 317.
[43] *Ibid.* at 319.

legality, parliamentarians must be trusted by their electorate to act legally. They must also behave in a way that ensures that they carry out the public function and duty entrusted to them, that is to work on behalf of the benefit of the electorate and of society, not their own. No relationship can be a greater blend of legal and political aspects than the public trust.

---

§ 11.5.2
Charlottetown (City) v. Prince Edward Island
Prince Edward Island Supreme Court – Appeal Division
December 11, 1998
(1998), 169 Nfld. & P.E.I.R. 188[44]

The obligation of parliamentarians, that is of elected officials, to observe legal norms incorporates within it the duty to take greater regard for and hence to act in accordance with principles, norms and standards arising from law and of a legal nature, than political convenience meant to assure electoral success. One of the domains in which this duty can be most sharply distinguished is in the redistribution of electoral boundaries, where the political stakes can be so great. In response to those political stakes, the vigilance of the courts for the supremacy of law over politics, should be equally great. In some cases, however, such as here, the majority of an appeal court is rather too eagerly accommodating to political convenience and the minority opinion is the safeguard of the legal principles involved.

After the general election of March 29, 1993, an electoral map was prepared for the province. It was adopted by the Legislature by way of Private Member's Bill and came into effect on October 21, 1996. In the meantime, Charlottetown, the provincial capital, started an action against the province, alleging that the deviation from the electoral quotient, that is the variation in population size from a mathematical standard, set at + / - 25% was too high and therefore in breach of the voting provision in the *Canadian Charter of Rights and Freedoms*, section 3.

On the substance of the matter, the court ably captured the essence of the issue.

---

[44] Leave to appeal refused (1999), 251 N.R. 399 (note) (S.C.C.).

> This appeal and cross-appeal involves an old chestnut which has been aptly described by scholars as being how to accommodate the urbanization of society and the concept of representation by population while at the same time providing an adequate voice and service to rural representatives by their elected representatives.[45]

This introduction set the scene for a discussion of various aspects of redistribution, in which the issue which specifically interests scholars of political law is characterized here as the appropriate level of judicial deference to the legislature. In fact, this label covers the struggle between the application of legal norms or political convenience within the judgment and collaterally relates to the relations of the two implicated branches of government as well.

The majority of the province's Court of Appeal held the belief that the legislative process had to be allowed to operate without undue judicial interference. It did not clearly justify this belief. However, it approved of the respondent's argument, linked to this issue of deference, by which it sought not only to restrict the role of the courts, but to place the topic of redistribution within the sphere of politics, away from the reach of law.

> The respondent submits the present redistribution is a political compromise that accommodates, in a relatively measured way, all the competing interests involved and, as such, should not be interfered with by the courts. It submits the electoral map need not be the optimal plan that is capable of achievement in order to be constitutional. It also submits that since redistribution is a legislative function, rather than a judicial function, there must be room for legislative negotiation and compromise on practical problems.[46]

In this case, the better resolution to the legal conflict before the court, and the reaffirmation of the duty of parliamentarians to ensure that they exercise their political interests in accordance with the law, rather than the other way around, was left for the minority to state. That statement was made in very strong terms, which bear repetition in their entirety.

---

[45] (1998), 169 Nfld. & P.E.I.R. 188, 521 A.P.R. 188 at p. 1, leave to appeal refused (1999), 251 N.R. 399 (note) (S.C.C.).
[46] *Ibid.* p. 15, para. 45.

The respondent argues the current electoral map should be upheld as a reasonable and necessary political compromise. It says the need for this compromise arose because it was apparent that the recommendations of the *Election Act* and Electoral Boundaries Commission established pursuant to EC451/93 did not have sufficient support among legislators to become law. I agree with those who say that political compromise cannot and should not be divorced from the legislative process. However, the perceived need to find a compromise does not provide justification for infringement of a Charter right. Legislatures are limited in what they can do by the constitution. The *Constitution* is the supreme law of Canada, and any law that is inconsistent with it is of no force or effect. Legislators are not free to make compromises that infringe Charter rights. Accordingly, no politician or legislature has the right to compromise even a single citizen's right top to effective representation as guaranteed by s. 3 of the Charter. If legislation, whether achieved through political compromise or otherwise, violates a Charter right, there is no room for judicial deference unless it passes the test of s. 1. On the other hand, if an electoral map is the product of the reasonable application of the correct principle (equality of voting power subject only to such limits as are required for good government; per McLachlin J. at p. 271 of *Dixon*, supra, and at p. 36 of the *Carter* case, supra.) a court should not interfere even if the boundaries are not as it would have drawn them. Unfortunately the legislative solution arrived at in this case does not meet the threshold for deference.[47]

It is curious, perhaps even troubling in the democratic context, that this same defence of the democratic principle of the obligation of parliamentarians to abide by legal norms must be repeated in the face of such frequent attacks.

---

[47] *Ibid.* p. 27, para. 92.

11.6 ISSUE: PROFESSIONAL ETHICS OF PARLIAMENTARIANS

§ 11.6.1

R. v. Arseneau

Supreme Court of Canada; March 20, 1979

[1979] 2 S.C.R. 136

Legal prescriptions are necessary to support and promote honesty and public ethics in government. Such texts of law are meant to influence the behaviour of holders of public office, and by implication of public trust; looking beyond the specifications in the law, they are addressed to those exercising an official capacity in governance and if there is a convergence between the roles they play in public life, the prescriptions are to be interpreted in a purposive manner, taking into account the realities of the parliamentary system of government.

Arseneau was a lawyer practising in the New Brunswick town of Campbellton. His partner, Van Horne, was elected to the provincial legislature and became Minister of Tourism. In the course of his work, Van Horne set aside land for the establishment of a provincial park. Arseneau conspired with others to offer a bribe to Van Horne to enable those others to open a motel within the park. He was indicted on several counts, one of which was pursuant to that provision of the *Criminal Code of Canada* which dealt with offering money corruptly to a member of the legislature.[48] He was convicted in the New Brunswick Supreme Court – Trial Division and his appeal to the Court of Appeal was unsuccessful.

Before the highest court, Arsenault relied on the defence that in making the decisions relevant to the case, Van Horne had acted in his capacity as Minister administering the department over which he was temporarily presiding, but not as a Member of the Legislature.

The Supreme Court of Canada's judgment on the matter turned on the concept of "official capacity." Out of a panel of nine, two justices

---

[48] *Criminal Code*, s. 108(1)(b).

believed that Van Horne had been bribed in his capacity as Minister of Tourism but had been charged as having been bribed as a Member of the Legislature. In their opinion, this constituted a fatal defect in the proceedings because the offence of which Arseneau had been convicted did not exist and the trial was a nullity. The majority, however, took a broader view. They viewed the bribe as having been offered to Van Horne in furtherance of the motel construction plan, that is to a member of the Legislature who had also become Minister of Tourism and who therefore acted in both capacities. The court then went on to teach the accused a lesson on the parliamentary form of politics and the consequential link between the legislative and executive capacities of those parliamentarians who are also cabinet ministers.

> In the absence of evidence to the contrary, I am prepared to proceed on the basis that it was as a member of the Legislature that Van Horne was appointed to be Minister of Tourism. This would be in accord with the generally accepted practice in this country whereby ministers are accountable to the elected representatives of the people in Parliament or the Legislature as the case may be, and it is in his capacity as a member of the Legislature that a cabinet minister participates in the process of securing legislative authority for the implementation of the policies which he proposed. In the final analysis, it is as a member and not as a minister that he approves the expenditures which he may have recommended as a minister. In view of the above, I am unable to accept the contention of the appellant that Van Horne's capacity as a member of the Legislature can be so severed from the functions which he performs as Minister of Tourism as to make it an offence under s. 108 to corruptly pay money to him as a member of the Legislature and no offence to corruptly pay money to the same man in his capacity as minister.[49]

While Arseneau's defence was a clever attempt at reliance on the technicalities of the law as he perceived them, the court preferred to ground its decision on legal principles and ethical precepts in order to guide the political behaviour of those public office holders who are parliamentarians and who also happen to be in the executive government.

See also *R. c. Cogger*, [1997] 2 S.C.R. 845 (S.C.C.) and (1998), 1998 CarswellQue 657 (C.Q.).

---

[49] [1979] 2 S.C.R. 136 at 149.

11.7 ISSUE: OBLIGATION OF MEMBERS OF THE EXECUTIVE GOVERNMENT TO OBSERVE LEGAL NORMS

§ 11.7.1

Clark v. R.

British Columbia Supreme Court; March 16, 1979

(1979), 99 D.L.R. (3d) 454

Although the law reports portray this as nothing more than a simple contract case which stands for the principle that the rules of agency apply to government contracts, from the political law perspective, it is in fact much more significant and it will help us pinpoint the accountability to law of Ministers in several portfolios and of several political colourations. Most significantly, it will deal with the obligation of the Attorney General not to act in such a manner that implies disregard for the law. This case also has obvious machinery of government implications.

Clark was a broadcaster in British Columbia. On April 8, 1974, the Attorney General of the province, a member of the then New Democratic Party government, offered Clark a government position as rentlesman, pursuant to the *Landlord Tenant Act* which the minister was about to introduce that day in the legislature. The position was offered as being at the deputy minister level, on an equal footing with the chairs of the Police Commission and the Law Reform Commission. This status implied, and specific contractual promises were made concerning, eventual increases in salary. The *Landlord Tenant Act* was enacted and brought into force; Clark was appointed rentlesman by Order in Council on June 28, 1974.

In the opinion of the court, Clark worked with devotion to his duties and concern for his office. The salary increase he had been promised should have taken effect in October 1974 but was never provided. From then until the next general election, held on December 11, 1975, Clark dealt with the Deputy Attorney General, the Attorney General and even the Premier in person but none of the promises made to him regarding salary or benefits were ever fulfilled. In the election, the Social Credit Party came to power. Thereafter, Clark dealt with the new Attorney General and eventually with the Minister of Consumer and Corporate Affairs, to whose portfolio the administration of the *Landlord Tenant Act* was transferred. Further promises were made. Despite Clark's repeated attempts, the contract with him was never put in writing. The chairs of the Police Commission and the Law Reform Commission received increases but the rentlesman did not. On December 5, 1977, the Cabinet rejected Clark's claim and on January 31, 1978, after Clark had allowed sufficient time for the government to find a successor, he resigned effective May 1, 1978. He then sued in order to recover the monies due to him in light of the agreement he had originally struck in 1974.

The court started its *ratio* by describing Clark's treatment at the hands of the two successive governments as "shabby." It went on to demolish every point raised by the defence. Citing the case of *Verreault*, it affirmed that the rules of agency did indeed apply to government contracts and found that here, the Attorney General had acted as agent for the Crown in entering into the contract with Clark. It also found that there was Cabinet authority for the contract. In addition, it held that the Attorney General's common law authority to contract was supplemented by statutory authority to contract, contained in the *Attorney-General Act*[50] and that this was supplemented by a provision in the *Landlord Tenant Act*[51] authorizing the appointment of the rentlesman. The court made two specific findings relating to Clark's circumstances. First, it perceived an implied term of the contract obliging the government to make an Order in Council appointing Clark "in the terms and conditions as agreed."[52] Moreover, it held that the Crown could not be permitted to fall back on a restrictive interpretation to hold the contract with Clark invalid and therefore to breach its terms with impunity.

More generally, the court derived the lessons of principle from Clark's conflict with the province in the following terms.

> Needless to say, it is the duty of the Government to resist claims against the public purse where proper legal defences are available. However, before subjecting the plaintiff to the expense of this trial, the question

---

[50] R.S.B.C. 1960, c. 21, s. 4(2).
[51] S.B.C. 1974, c. 45, s. 49(1).
[52] (1979), 99 D.L.R. (3d) 454 at 463.

which the Government should have asked itself on the undisputed facts of this case, is not: can we in law defend the non-fulfilment of this agreement, both by ourselves and by the former Government; but rather, can we defend this action in justice and in good conscience? On the facts herein, the answer is obvious.[53]

This test of "justice and good conscience" is the one to apply in looking not only at matters of contracting by Ministers but also at the adherence of Ministers to legal norms and standards. Political conscience or discretion cannot be substituted for application of the law, especially not by an Attorney General.

---

§ 11.7.2
Singh v. Canada (Minister of Employment & Immigration)
Supreme Court of Canada; April 4, 1985
(1985), 17 D.L.R. (4th) 422

With this case, the Supreme Court of Canada provided an extremely valuable instruction to Ministers not only in respect to their obligation to apply the law, but also regarding the manner in which they are bound to do so. This prescription was necessary and timely in light of the fact that the entire legal system had recently been reformed by the incorporation into it of the *Canadian Charter of Rights and Freedoms*. Of particular interest in this regard was the fact that Ministers needed to be judicially informed about the difference between this new *Charter* and the *Bill of Rights* which had preceded it, but which was a very different instrument.

Singh and a number of other applicants had sought Convention refugee status in Canada. The Minister of Employment and Immigration had rejected their claims. The Immigration Appeal Board and the Federal Court of Appeal had rejected their appeals. The Supreme Court, through a panel of six judges, unanimously sent the matter back for redetermination.

The substance of the applicants' claim was founded on security of the person, protected by section 7 of the *Charter*. In examining this concept, the court held that its meaning had changed with the adoption of the *Charter* and that the restrictive attitude which had characterized

---

[53] *Ibid.* at 464.

its interpretation pursuant to the *Bill of Rights* ought now to be re-examined. The thrust of this argument was that the courts should adopt a more liberal, encompassing, broader notion of security of the person in determining whether Ministers had acted in conformity with legal norms. Here, the court used analogies from American law to explain its new position, although reluctantly. In this connection, it referred to the doctrine according to which the power to expel or exclude aliens was an attribute of sovereignty and noted the deference of the courts to the political departments of government. It concluded, however, that despite this, the Fifth and Fourteenth Amendments to the *U.S. Constitution* were available as constitutional protections to aliens subject to removal. In the Canadian context, this meant that the remedies sought by the present applicants should be available to them.

Having set the stage by stating which philosophical stance it preferred, the court found that the decisions reached by the Minister were contrary to the *Charter*'s section 7 protection; the core of the matter was whether they could be saved under section 1. In defence of the administrative scheme in place pursuant to the *Immigration Act, 1976,*[54] the Minister pleaded that his system had received the approbation of the office of the United Nations High Commissioner for Refugees, and that it was similar to mechanisms in place in Commonwealth and Western European countries.

> He further argued that the Immigration Appeal Board was already subjected to a considerable strain in terms of the volume of cases which it was required to hear and that a requirement of an oral hearing in every case where an application for redetermination of a refugee claim has been made would constitute an unreasonable burden on the board's resources.[55]

The court totally rejected this "me too" type of reasoning and it was here that it effectively told Ministers not only that they should act in conformity with the law, but also how that should be done. The Supreme Court in particular dealt final blows to the arguments of administrative convenience and of costs as oppositions to conformity with constitutionalized legal norms.

---

[54] S.C. 1976-77, c. 52.
[55] (1985), 17 D.L.R. (4th) 422 at 468.

The issue in the present case is not simply whether the procedures set out in the *Immigration Act, 1976* for the adjudication of refugee claims are reasonable; it is whether it is reasonable to deprive the appellants of the right to life, liberty and security of the person by adopting a system for the adjudication of refugee status claims which does not accord with the principles of fundamental justice.

Seen in this light I have considerable doubt that the type of utilitarian consideration brought forward by Mr. Bowie can constitute a justification for limitation on the rights set out in the Charter. Certainly the guarantee of the Charter would be illusory if they could be ignored because it was administratively convenient to do so. No doubt considerable time and money can be saved by adopting administrative procedures which ignore the principles of fundamental justice but such an argument, in my view, misses the point of the exercise under s. 1. The principles of natural justice and procedural fairness which have long been espoused by our courts, and the constitutional entrenchment of the principles of fundamental justice in s. 7, implicitly recognize that a balance of administrative convenience does not override the need to adhere to these principles. Whatever standard of review eventually emerges under s. 1, it seems to me that the basis of the justification for the limitation of rights under s. 7 must be more compelling than any advanced in these appeals.[56]

The court went on. Citing a speech of the chair of the Immigration Appeal Board, it qualified the existing system of refugee determination as dissatisfying and unsatisfactory. The essence of its holding was that the standard which the refugee determination process would have to meet in order to ensure that the Minister in charge of it was in compliance with the *Charter*, based on fairness and justice. As a result of this ruling, the system was in fact changed.

---

§ 11.7.3
Mulroney v. Coates
Ontario High Court of Justice; April 8, 1986
(1986), 27 D.L.R. (4th) 118

The obligation of members of the executive government to observe legal norms should also be looked at as their subjection to the law, rather than their exemption from it or their evasion from it. This

---

[56] *Ibid.* at 468-9.

requirement is all the more significant when it is applied in the highly controversial circumstances engendered by a political scandal.

The Progressive Conservative government of Prime Minister Mulroney was elected with an overwhelming parliamentary majority on September 4, 1984. Coates, a Member of Parliament from Nova Scotia, was made Minister of National Defence. It was only a few months thereafter that, while on an inspection of a Canadian military base in West Germany, Coates and a number of officials with him went to a night club near the base. In February 1985, the *Ottawa Citizen* published an article reporting on Coates' visit and alleging that it may have posed a security risk. Coates promptly resigned as Minister and in April 1985, he brought an action in damages for libel against the newspaper and its publisher, in his home province.

In the context of that litigation, Coates applied for the issue of letters of request for the examination on discovery, in Ontario, of the Prime Minister, the Deputy Prime Minister, the Clerk of the Privy Council, as well as ten of their civilian and military officials. The Nova Scotia court issued the orders sought. The present judgment was the decision of the applicable Ontario court on the application of the proposed deponents to set aside the summonses issued to them. Among the several grounds of this application to set aside, the one which concerns us is whether there exists, and if yes to what extent, a prerogative or an immunity which protects officers of the Crown from having to testify. This was the first scandal to affect the newly elected government and Mulroney was loath to be dragged into the litigious aspect of it; he had either demanded or accepted Coates' resignation and he was intent on leaving the matter at that, the political level. With his style of governance, moreover, the prospect of giving testimony in a legal proceeding did not appear palatable or convenient to him.

The Ontario court started by considering the procedure which the Nova Scotia authorities had followed. It found that,

> Such examinations have come to be regarded as an essential part of the due process of justice in civil proceedings before that court, and that any inability to conduct such examinations for discovery through the refusal of consent or the refusal of letters of request by a compatible judicial

> authority would impair or impede the due process of justice in civil
> proceedings pending before that court.[57]

Having so set the stage, the court proceeded to address the question
whether Mulroney and the others proposed deponents could claim
Crown immunity. It cited British precedent for the proposition that
there was no general testimonial immunity for a Prime Minister and
a Minister solely because of the positions they occupied[58] and explicitly endorsed that point of view. It also looked to more recent Canadian jurisprudence[59] which stood for the proposition that Ministers
of the Crown enjoy no special privilege and are in the same position
of obligation to the law as any other subject. Notwithstanding these
examples, the court stated that there is indeed a limited immunity
from having to testify "only in so far as he (the deponent) is sought
to be examined for discovery regarding matters in which he is acting
in his capacity as a servant, agent or representative of the Crown in
right of Canada in the legal sense of that term."[60] This statement,
unfortunately, was not sufficiently explained, nor adequately distinguished from the precedents to indicate the judicial reasoning on
which it was based.

The court went on to examine the cases of the specific officials of the
Crown involved here. It dealt first with the Cabinet members. It
applied a double test to them: first, whether there was an immunity,
and, second, whether the proposed inquiries would trespass upon
that immunity.

> ... I have concluded that, with regard to three of the proposed deponents,
> discovery is sought of servants, agents or representatives of the Crown
> in right of Canada, in the legal sense of that term, along lines of inquiry
> in respect of which the individual concerned was acting exclusively in
> his official capacity. The three are Mr. Mulroney, as Prime Minister of
> Canada, in respect of whom discovery is sought to explore 10 lines of
> inquiry relating to the resignation of Mr. Coates and the investigation
> conducted regarding the possibility of a security breach; Mr. Nielson, as
> Deputy Prime Minister of Canada, in respect of whom discovery is
> sought to explore three lines of inquiry relating to the resignation of Mr.
> Coates; and Mr. Osbaldeston, as clerk of the Privy Council and secretary

---

[57] (1986), 27 D.L.R. (4th) 118 at 122.
[58] *R. v. Baines* (1908), [1909] 1 K.B. 258 (Eng. K.B.).
[59] *Canadian Javelin Ltd., Re*, [1982] 2 S.C.R. 686 (S.C.C.) [See § 11.9.A.]
[60] *Supra* note 57 at 131.

to the Cabinet, in respect of whom discovery is sought to explore five lines of inquiry relating to the investigation and security inquiry superintended by him and conducted at the request of the Prime Minister. As it has been made to appear to me that all of the lines of inquiry sought to be pursued on the examination for discovery of these proposed deponents will inevitably trespass upon ground covered by the suggested prerogative or immunity, I see no useful purpose in ordering their attendance upon examinations at which it is clear that that position will, in my view meritoriously, be asserted. I therefore consider that, in the exercise of my discretion, I ought not to order the enforcement of the letters of request with respect to the examination of the three proposed deponents named above.[61]

In particular with the court's opinion of the inevitability of the eventual trespass on the proposed deponents' immunity, one may be allowed to query the intensity of the court's analysis and its degree of deference to executive authority.

Finally, the court looked at the ten other prospective deponents to whom the summonses arising out of Nova Scotia were applicable. These were government officials and political aides, rather than Cabinet members. They were held not to be servants of the Crown in the legal sense. In respect of them, matters of immunity were deferred until the actual examinations on discovery would be held and the contents of the questions to be asked of them were more clearly defined.

§ 11.7.4[62]
Canadian Wildlife Federation Inc. v. Canada (Minister of the Environment)
Federal Court of Canada – Trial Division; December 28, 1989
(1989), 31 F.T.R. 1[63]

This case is centred on the legal validity of a ministerial decision to issue a licence for the construction, operation and maintenance of the Rafferty Alemeda damming project in Saskatchewan. The court was called upon to adjudicate whether the decision was in compliance

---

[61] *Ibid.* at 131-132.
[62] Cross-reference to § 1.3.A.4, 1.3.D.3, 2.2.E.1, 2.6.1 and 11.14.2.
[63] Affirmed (1990), [1991] 1 F.C. 641 (Fed. C.A.).

with the *Environmental Assessment and Review Process Guideline Order* (EARPGO).[64]

The Minister of the Environment had made a decision to grant a first licence on June 17, 1988. The Federal Court found fault in that the terms of EARPGO were not observed as no environmental review was conducted and quashed that licence. The court so described the legal landscape which should have appeared to the minister as a result of that ruling, pursuant to the assessment regime established by EARPGO.

> Guideline 32 continues and ends with the command to the Minister to make the Panel's report available to the public. This is the great strength of this legislative scheme. It balances the information, knowledge and ultimately the opinion of the public, against the authority of the Minister and the government of the day who may, for what they believe to be high purposes of State, quite ignore the Panel's recommendations. They may, equally of course, adopt or adapt the Panel's recommendations in order to save both the environment and the project, as they see fit and feasible.[65]

Instead of appointing an EARP panel, the minister decided to hold an inquiry on the project's environmental impacts, which was internal to his department. Following that report, the minister issued a second licence and it is the legality of that decision which was in question here.

The court held that both the manner in which that decision was reached and the substance of the decision were inconsistent with the legal requirements. The minister's decision was held to be vulnerable, first, because it was not reasoned in light of the EARPGO categories of possible environmental damage.

> Unfortunately the Minister, most likely on the advice of his advisers, did not produce a written, reasoned decision in explanation of his action, except for the press conference notes of even date, and that leaves the court bereft of any reasoned explanations. Persuasive as they were, neither the Minister's nor the intervener's respective counsel could present ingenious arguments or speculation adequate to replace a formal, written, reasoned decision signed by the Minister.[66]

---

[64] SOR/84-467.

[65] (1989), 31 F.T.R. 1 at 8, affirmed (1990), [1991] 1 F.C. 641 (Fed. C.A.).

[66] *Ibid.* at 12.

This links the decision to bad advice the minister may have received from his officials.

Ultimately, however, the decision was up to the minister himself and the court did not shy away from spelling out that the highest accountability to law, that is the greatest duty to want to obey the requirements of legislation, rather than to avoid them, was his.

> It is quite evident that the respondent's department ought to have referred the pertinent proposals, if not the whole project, to the Minister for public review by a panel constituted by him under ss. 21 and 22 of the EARP Guidelines. Given the determinations of the significant environmental effects expressed in the IEE, the Minister ought lawfully to have subjected the proposals to such public review, as it is clearly mandated by this binding, authoritative legislation. The Minister's advisers ought to have advised him to embrace the EARP Guidelines warmly, instead of seeking ways to abridge or avoid the process.

> The respondent Minister's counsel urge that, if the court finds that the Minister did not comply with the EARP, then the court should nevertheless exercise a discretion to excuse that lawbreaking. It is notionally easier to excuse an individual tangled in regulations and bureaucracy than it is to excuse a Minister of the Crown from noncompliance with relevant, binding legislation, whether regulatory or not. If there be anyone who ought scrupulously to conform to the official duties which the law casts upon him or her in the role of a high State official, it is a Minister of the Crown. That is just plainly obvious.

> But there is an irony in these proceedings which could make a cynic cackle with glee. In the first place, because the Minister did not embrace willingly the EARP Guidelines prior to April, 1989, and even subsequently, as this court finds, the devolution of events described in s. 3 of the Guidelines is now savagely distorted.[67]

---

§ 11.7.5
Bhatnager v. Canada (Minister of Employment & Immigration)
Supreme Court of Canada; June 21, 1990
[1990] 2 S.C.R. 217

A variation of the notion of the subjection of ministers to legal norms,

---

[67] *Ibid.* at 15.

duties and obligations is their exposure to contempt proceedings. This is particularly true in the case of the current practice of government, in which Ministers often direct large departments which simultaneously undertake a wide variety of program activities. Considering that contempt of court is a personal, rather than an institutional, offence, the question that must be addressed is the extent to which ministers presiding over large bureaucracies can be held so personally responsible for the failing of their staff, amounting to proceeding contrary to the rule of law and its application, as to constitute contempt.

The present case grew out of the field of immigration and it also involves the external affairs portfolio. Both departments comprise not only the Ottawa headquarters but also offices around the world. In some cases, such as here, communications among these offices break down, resulting in the commission of acts in contravention of orders of the courts.

Mr. Bhatnager, an Indian citizen living in India, had applied for permanent residence in Canada so as to be with his wife. Handling of his file had not been completed over five years. Mrs. Bhatnager applied to the Federal Court for a writ of *mandamus* to order the Minister of Employment and Immigration to process the application. As part of the court's proceedings, an order was issued to bring Bhatnager's immigration file from New Delhi to Toronto and that order was served on the solicitors of the Minister of Employment and Immigration and External Affairs. The entire file did not arrive at the courthouse in Toronto in time for the hearing of the *mandamus* application.

The foregoing facts led to a show cause hearing as to whether the two ministers' alleged failure to comply with the order to produce the file constituted contempt. The Federal Court of Canada – Trial Division held that the ministers' default did not amount to contempt; the Federal Court of Appeal stated that it did. The Supreme Court of Canada resolved the matter by a thorough analysis of all the arguments raised by Mrs. Bhatnager and concluded that the state of the law would not allow a finding of contempt either at Common Law or under the *Rules of the Federal Court*.

The point which attracted the court's closest scrutiny was whether the ministers' personal knowledge of service of the order to produce the file was necessary so that failure to so produce would constitute contempt. The court held that in Common Law, the standard had always been personal service or actual personal knowledge. Here, the ministers were not served personally and did not have personal knowledge of the court proceedings.

Mindful that ministers and their institutions were bound by legal obligations, including the duty to respect court orders, the court nevertheless took account of the reality of the functioning of large bureaucratic organizations.

> In the case of Ministers of the Crown who administer large departments and are involved in a multiplicity of proceedings, it would be extraordinary if orders were brought, routinely, to their attention. In order to infer knowledge in such a case, there must be circumstances which reveal a special reason for bringing the order to the attention of the Minister.[68]

The court made it clear, however, that this legal precision should not be considered as a limitation on ministers' accountability, nor as a loophole.

> This does not mean that Ministers will be able to hide behind their lawyers so as to flout orders of the court. Any instructions to the effect that the Minister is to be kept ignorant may attract liability on the basis of the doctrine of wilful blindness. Furthermore, the fact that a Minister cannot be confident in any given case that the inference will not be drawn will serve as a sufficient incentive to see to it that officials are impressed with the importance of complying with court orders.[69]

With respect to the *Rules of the Federal Court*, the Supreme Court of Canada held that imputation of knowledge could not be used in criminal or quasi-criminal cases in the absence of express language in the covering instrument, which it did not see here.

The requirement of ministerial knowledge as an aspect of accountability is a perennial one. This is particularly true of instances where what a minister needs to know or ought to have known relates to maladministration in his department. For example, while the Auditor General of Canada was testifying on February 12, 2004 to the House of Commons Public Accounts Committee on the Report she had just

[68] [1990] 2 S.C.R. 217 at 226 c-d.
[69] *Ibid.* at 226 f-h.

recently released dealing with the sponsorship scandal, she ventured into this topic.

> **Ms. Sheila Fraser:** In our traditional model, it is the current minister who is accountable for the actions within a department, and I question, if that is still really the expectation, is it realistic to expect a minister to know everything that is going on in a very large, very complex organization, as some of the departments are...within our system the minister of the department has responsibility of that department. I think, quite frankly, most people would not expect even the minister to know all of the day-to-day operations. Some people would call into question how appropriate it is for a minister to become involved in day-to-day operations.[70]

The thoughts expressed here are so pertinent to the application of accountability and to the obligation of members of the executive to observe legal norms that merely hours later, in question period, some of the Auditor General's words were cited by the President of the Treasury Board[71] in response to a question regarding what the Prime Minister of the day, Paul Martin, Minister of Finance at the time of the events comprising the scandal, knew about those events. Unfortunately, although such partisan use of testimony is indicative of the reality of public management, it does not help to clarify ministers' duties of a legal or conventional nature.

See also *Canada Deposit Insurance Corp. v. Oland* (1997), [1997] A.J. No. 931 (Alta. C.A.).

---

§ 11.7.6
Tetzlaff v. Canada (Minister of the Environment)
Federal Court of Canada – Trial Division; February 5, 1991
(1991), 47 Admin. L.R. 290

The sole point of this judgment is that in addition to owing a public duty to act in accordance with the law, ministers must do so in a timely fashion.

---

[70] House of Commons; Standing Committee on Public Accounts; Evidence; Thursday, February 12, 2004 at 0940.
[71] Hansard, February 12, 2004, p. 512.

This case grew out of the complex litigation relating to the construction of the Rafferty-Alameda damming project in Saskatchewan. The
Minister of the Environment made an initial decision not to appoint
an environmental assessment and review panel about this project. In
December 1989, the Federal Court – Trial Division ordered him to
appoint one and he complied. In October 1990, the panel resigned
because the work was proceeding while they were conducting the
environmental review. Tetzlaff sued to have a new panel appointed.
The minister made the appointment after the hearing of this case but
prior to the judgment. The court dismissed the application because
of the Minister's compliance but the significant element of the judgment is the commentary on observance of the law, in time. The conduct of the environmental review was said to be the legal basis for
the project and had the Minister failed to appoint a review panel,
Tetzlaff would have been entitled to an order.

> The law places a heavy burden on the Minister to assemble an environ-
> mental review panel. He was not helped by the abrupt resignation of
> the previous panel. The Court of Appeal has made it plain that the
> Minister's licence cannot long endure, if at all, in the absence of a panel,
> for what is required is that a panel must be appointed. If it be unlawful
> for the Minister to decline to appoint a panel in these circumstances, and
> it surely is, the Minister's tardiness or even genuine inability to assemble
> a panel must carry the same consequence as his or her refusal, but
> without blame.[72]

See also *Prosecution of Ministers Laurent Fabius, Edmond Hervé and
Georgina Dufoix,* Cour de justice de la République, France, Arrêt du
21 juin 1999; *Trial of the Leaders of the Khmer Rouge Movement, Cambodia;
Democratic Republic of the Congo v. Belgium,* February 14, 2002; *Natural
Resources Defense Council v. Department of Energy,* 191 F. Supp.2d 41;
February 21, 2002; *Walker v. Cheney,* 230 F. Supp.2d 51 and *Gairy and
another v. Attorney General of Grenada,* [2002] 1 A.C. 167.[73]

---

[72] (1991), 47 Admin. L.R. 290 at 298-18.
[73] All international comparisons.

11.8 ISSUE: PROFESSIONAL ETHICS OF MEMBERS OF THE EXECUTIVE GOVERNMENT[74]

§ 11.8.1
Sommers v. R.
Supreme Court of Canada; June 25, 1959
(1959), 124 C.C.C. 241

Sommers had, at relevant times, been the Minister of Lands and Forests of British Columbia. He was charged with accepting a bribe as an official of the government and with conspiracy. He was convicted at the assizes in Vancouver and by the British Columbia Court of Appeal. He appealed to the Supreme Court of Canada on the ground that a minister was not an "official" within the meaning of the *Criminal Code*.

The appeal was rejected and the minister's guilt reaffirmed. The question at issue was whether the expression of "official" extended, as Sommers contended, only to non-political officials of the permanent civil service or did it include Ministers. One of the court's tasks was to clarify the uncertainty created by the inconsistent use of designations in statutes, which was susceptible of leading to confusion. On the merits, it held that the rules which apply to public servants must also apply to ministerial officials and that the exclusion of ministers from the application of the law would represent a fundamental departure from the intent of the legislators. "At common law, corruption of an official, either judicial or ministerial, is an offence, and with respect to ministerial officers, an offence in the essence of which the distinction between political and non-political officers has no significance."[75] Even in terms of the level of punishment the court held that the same standards are to apply.

For purposes of political law, extrapolating from this judgment, what is important is not so much the rule against corruption, but rather its principle that officials or officers of the State who are elected and in the political sphere owe the same accountability to the legal regime

---

[74] Cross-reference to § 2.4 and 6.7.
[75] (1959), 124 C.C.C. 241 at 244-245.

as do those who are appointed and employed in the public administration. Members of the executive government do not enjoy a separate, different or lesser accountability to law by the fact that they are elected.

---

§ 11.8.2[76]

Report of a Commission of Inquiry into the Facts of Allegations of Conflict of Interest Concerning the Honourable Sinclair Stevens;
December 1, 1987
-and-
Stevens v. Canada (Commission of Inquiry)
Federal Court of Canada – Trial Division
(2000), [2001] 1 F.C. 156[77]
-and-
Sinclair Stevens v. Parker, Commissioner
Federal Court of Appeal
filed December 11, 1987; file A-1276-87; withdrawn May 13, 1988
-and-
Noreen Stevens v. Parker, Commissioner
Federal Court of Appeal
filed December 16, 1987; file A-1277-87; withdrawn June 30, 1988
-and-
Stevens v. Canada (Commission of Inquiry)
Federal Court of Canada – Trial Division; October 28, 2003
[2003] F.C.J. No. 1589

This case provides a number of insights into the professional ethics of members of the executive government and more particularly into objective and subjective views of the conflicts of interests of cabinet ministers.

When Brian Mulroney appointed the members of his first administration in the fall of 1984, he named Sinclair Stevens, a lawyer and businessman, to the Regional Industrial Expansion portfolio. While Stevens was a loyal Progressive Conservative, it became clear very soon after his elevation to the Cabinet that he had a rather self-serving notion as to what was permissible and what he ought not do in terms

---

[76] Cross-reference to § 11.14.10.
[77] Affirmed (2002), 215 F.T.R. 228 (Fed. T.D.).

of using his ministerial position for personal gain. As early as May 12, 1986, Stevens was forced to resign from Cabinet because of the intensity of the allegations regarding him. That resignation and the course of events which followed have led to a judicial saga between Stevens and Canada which has now lasted well over a decade and which is far from being completed. The element of greatest interest is that this conflict has led to the creation of instruments of political law which are novel to and definitive of the topic.

On May 15, 1986, the Government of Canada instituted a judicial commission of inquiry to look into the allegations respecting the conduct, dealings and actions of Stevens and to see whether he had breached the *Conflict of Interest and Post Employment Code for Public Officer Holders* which the incoming Mulroney administration had adopted in September 1985. After a study which lasted over a year, on December 1, 1988, the Commissioner, Chief Justice William Parker, viewed an exhaustive report.

The most noteworthy element of this work was the definition of the fundamental notion which was to guide the ethics of members of the executive government in administering the public trust for the public interest, namely that of conflict of interest. The report stated that a real conflict of interest consisted of the following:

> All counsel agreed that at least three prerequisites have to be established before a public office holder can be said to be in a position of real conflict of interest. They are:
>
> 1. the existence of a private interest;
> 2. that is known to the public officer holder; and
> 3. that has a connection or nexus with his or her public duties or responsibilities that is sufficient to influence the exercise of those duties or responsibilities.[78]

An alternative definition was stated:

> A real conflict of interest denotes a situation in which a minister of the Crown has knowledge of a private economic interest that is sufficient to influence the exercise of his or her public duties and responsibilities.[79]

---

[78] Report of a Commission of Inquiry into the Facts of Allegations of Conflict of Interest Concerning the Honourable Sinclair Stevens, p. 15.
[79] *Ibid*, p. 35.

The report also included the following definition of an apparent conflict of interest:

> An apparent conflict of interest exists when there is a reasonable apprehension, which reasonably well-informed persons could properly have, that a conflict of interest exists.[80]

Applying the norms derived from these definitions, referring to earlier studies and in particular to the *Starr-Sharp Report*[81] and relying on the relevant jurisprudence, Commissioner Parker concluded that during his tenure as a minister, Stevens "demonstrated a complete disregard for the requirements of the guidelines and code and the standard of conduct that is expected of public office holders."[82]

Stevens proved himself to be not only incapable of understanding the notion that incurring conflict of interests undermined his public ethics, but, by his subsequent unceasing litigiousness, showed he was unwilling to accept the fundamental standard of decency in public behaviour for the public benefit. He and his wife initiated no less than three legal actions to combat the conclusions of the report about him.

The first case, the one in the Trial Division of the Federal Court, sought to have the report set aside and declared to be of no force and effect, by reason of the fact that the Commissioner had exceeded his terms of reference and jurisdiction. Stevens also alleged that the Commissioner erred in law,

> (a) in defining what constitutes a conflict of interest within the meaning of the guidelines for public office holders;

> (b) in treating alleged breaches of the blind trust, per se, as an issue to be inquired into and reported on; and

> (c) in treating the mingling of private and public business as an allegation of conflict of interest.[83]

---

[80] Op. cit., p. 35.
[81] Ethical Conduct in the Public Sector: Report of the Task Force on Conflict of Interest (1984).
[82] Op. cit., p. 342.
[83] Statement of claim, para. 5(b); file T-2682-87.

These errors, Stevens claimed, violated his *Charter* section 7 (life, liberty and security of the person) rights. Interestingly, a prominent part of the claim related to the performance of the Commission's counsel who was said to have acted contrary to the principles of fundamental justice and had deprived the applicant of his right to a determination by a fair and impartial tribunal.

The merits of this claim have not, to this day, been adjudicated. Many interim and procedural judgments have been rendered but the heart of the matter remains to be determined. Meanwhile, ever since 1986, Stevens has been out of political life and public view and the litigation is no longer attracting the public and media interest it once did.

The action in Trial Division, filed on December 18, 1987, using section 18 of the *Federal Court Act*, was the only suit in this series which has become so permanent. Prior to its filing Sinclair Stevens and his wife Noreen Stevens, also a lawyer, had each filed a separate action in the Federal Court of Appeal, pursuant to section 28 of the *Federal Court Act*. Minister Stevens' Court of Appeal action was in essence the same as the one he had initiated in the Trial Division. By May 13, 1988, he decided to withdraw it.

Noreen Stevens' action in the Court of Appeal was based, in large measure, on grounds similar to that of the disgraced minister. In addition, though, she also complained that

> The participation by Commission Counsel in the drafting and prepara-
> tion of the Report of the Respondent violated the principles of natural
> justice and the duty of fairness applicable to the conduct of the Inquiry,
> created an appearance of unfairness, raised a reasonable apprehension
> of bias with respect to the findings of the learned Commissioner and
> deprived the Applicant of her right to a determination by a fair and
> impartial tribunal.

> The Respondent erred by rejecting the submission of the Applicant that
> Commission Counsel should not participate in the drafting and prepa-
> ration of the Report in view of the adversarial and prosecutorial role
> adopted by Commission Counsel during the Inquiry.[84]

---

[84] Originating notice under Section 28 of the Federal Court Act, paras. 8 and 9; file A-1277-87.

This action was also withdrawn. Nevertheless, Stevens' judicial pugilism continues unabated. In April 2003, he was in the Federal Court – Trial Division, seeking to find out who wrote Commissioner Parker's Report, and to determine what involvement the Commission's legal counsel had in writing and preparing it. Stevens' subpoenas designed to achieve such disclosure were quashed on grounds of the deliberative secrecy of administrative tribunals, as well as Commissioner Parker's solicitor-client privilege.[85]

---

§ 11.8.3
Vander Zalm v.
British Columbia (Acting Commissioner of Conflict of Interest)
British Columbia Supreme Court; May 15, 1991
(1991), 56 B.C.L.R. (2d) 37

There can be no clearer illumination than this case of the principles that members of the government must act in an ethical manner in the execution of their professional duties, and that they must take adequate notice of the legalities of their actions and work with legal advice.

Vander Zalm was, at material times, Premier of the Province of British Columbia. While he held that position from 1986 until April 22, 1991, during the years 1984 to 1990, he also owned a theme park called "Fantasy Gardens," in the Victoria area. The controversy which eventually gave rise to this matter originated from the sale of Fantasy Gardens. The manner in which that sale was conducted, apparently directly involving the Premier, was said to be contrary to the conflict of interest guidelines put in place in 1987 by Vander Zalm's own government. This prompted calls for the Premier's resignation.

In July 1990 the British Columbia Legislative Assembly enacted the *Members' Conflict of Interest Act*.[86] This Act was brought into force on December 21, 1990. On February 14, 1991, in response to the controversy, Vander Zalm requested that Hughes, a former Deputy Attorney General who had been appointed Acting Commissioner under the new legislation, undertake an inquiry into the Premier's behaviour in respect of the sale of Fantasy Gardens. The details of that

---

[85] (2003), [2003] F.C.J. No. 1589, 2003 CarswellNat 3373.
[86] S.B.C. 1990, c. 54.

request and of its treatment are significant. Vander Zalm was not represented by legal counsel in his approach to Hughes. Hughes expressed a preference that the inquiry be a more formal one, held under the *Inquiry Act*,[87] as that would offer greater legal protection to the rights of the parties. Vander Zalm specifically preferred that Hughes conduct the investigation as he had done while Deputy Attorney General in inquiring and reporting on allegations of breach into the conflict of interest guidelines by Ministers. This implied that Hughes' investigation would be conducted as if under the guidelines as before the enactment and coming into force of the new legislation, because the Act was not applicable for part of the time the events surrounding the sale took place. The Leader of the Opposition, Harcourt, agreed to this procedure and on that basis, Hughes proceeded.

The report was issued on April 2, 1991. It found that the Premier had played a "primary and dominant" role in the sale and that, consequently, he was in breach of the *Conflict of Interest Guidelines*. Vander Zalm immediately resigned, giving the following statement:

> Having had an opportunity to read the Hughes Report, I must now reconsider my decision of last Friday to remain as Premier until a successor is chosen. There were those who criticized me last Friday for not stepping down before now, but I felt obliged to see it through.
>
> Yesterday, in meetings with lawyers, I was encouraged by the strength of their submissions to Mr. Hughes and believed the findings would be favourable.
>
> Regrettably, the findings are not what I expected. In politics, there is no Court of Appeal in these matters. I must live by the guidelines which I initiated.
>
> In my view, there is only one appropriate course of action—I am prepared to resign now to ensure an orderly transition as quickly as possible.[88]

While the Premier made the remark about the absence of appeal in political life, he did not follow that course of action. On April 30, 1991, he petitioned the British Columbia Supreme Court for judicial review of Hughes' report. Hughes, in turn, applied for an order dis-

---

[87] At that time R.S.B.C., c. 198; now R.S.B.C. 1996, c. 224.

[88] (1991), 56 B.C.L.R. (2d) 37 at 40.5.

missing the petition on the ground that the report was beyond the court's power of judicial review, as there had been no excess of legal authority.

The court granted Hughes' application and denied the petition by Vander Zalm, thereby sealing the end of his political career in a definitive manner. It looked very closely at the manner in which the investigative mandate had been conferred upon Hughes and concluded that in this matter, he had not acted in his official capacity as Acting Commissioner of Conflict of Interest. Rather, the request was for him to investigate in the manner he had used in his previous capacity, as Deputy Attorney General.

On the issue of Hughes' appointment, the court held:

> I conclude that Mr. Hughes exercised no jurisdiction which would make his findings subject to judicial review. Such power as he had was conferred upon him by the agreement between him and Mr. Vander Zahm that he would make such inquiries as he thought fit, and render an opinion on the subject of conflict of interest. Mr. Hughes' source of power, in the words of Donaldson M.R., was Mr. Vander Zalm's consensual submission to his jurisdiction. The essence of the matter is that Mr. Vander Zalm requested Mr. Hughes to function, as he had done from time to time while Deputy Attorney General, as a respected adviser in giving an informed opinion.[89]

It was only after Hughes' investigation had started that Vander Zalm sought the benefit of legal counsel. In the course of the hearing on the application to have Vander Zalm's petition dismissed, his counsel presented the most interesting argument, that the agreement of the Premier and of the Leader of the Opposition to the form of the investigation vested that procedure with the quality of "government action," as an exercise of its prerogative. This argument was also rejected by the court, which reiterated that the determining factor in the case was the set of terms under which Hughes was appointed.

> The submission is that Mr. Hughes' position was similarly "recognised by" the Legislative Assembly because it was undertaken at the joint request of the offices of the premier and the leader of the opposition. It may be that there are circumstances in which the concurrence of the premier and the leader of the opposition could be considered as "rec-

---

[89] *Ibid.* at 43.12.

ognition" by the legislature so as to have some form of legislative effect although, except in relation to matters relating to the procedure of the house, that seems constitutionally doubtful. If there can be such circumstances, they were not present here.[90]

The characterization of Vander Zalm by Susan Delacourt, one of the country's most knowledgeable journalists, as "a politician whose rise and fall was linked to the fortunes of his own theme park,"[91] thus seems appropriate.

---

§ 11.8.4[92]

R. v. Munro

Ontario Court (General Division); November 18, 1991

(1991), 1991 CarswellOnt 3290

At the material times the accused in this criminal trial, John Munro, was the Liberal Member of Parliament for Hamilton East, Ontario, and Minister of Indian Affairs and Northern Development in the last ministry of Prime Minister Pierre Trudeau. For years, allegations of unethical behaviour had circulated around Munro in relation to his political work, and in particular regarding the way in which he was alleged to have used his ministerial position to assist him as a candidate for the succession of Trudeau as Leader of the Liberal Party in 1984. In the present case, Munro was one of several defendants accused of conspiracy to commit fraud and theft, as well as of several offences amounting to corruption. Munro applied for a directed verdict of not guilty, which was granted in part. The court found that the meetings, negotiations and other bureaucratic processes which had taken place in the normal course of departmental business had been unjustifiably strung together by the Crown.

> While the situation looked suspicious primarily because of the fact that Indian bands, some for the first time, had gotten involved in the political process and made donations, there was only suspicion and no evidence of improper behaviour with respect to a number of the allegations. The

---

90 *Ibid.* at 46.20.

91 Delacourt, Susan, *United We Fall: The Crisis of Democracy in Canada*, Viking Press, Toronto, 1993, p. 189.

92 Cross-reference to § 11.8.5.

Crown also argued that certain donations were made by the Indian bands in order to gain access to M., a government Minister.[93]

While this case indicates that the Crown must present a solid case backed by proper evidence in order to convict in such politically sensitive circumstances, it also clearly shows that ministers must make a particular effort to avoid the appearance of impropriety in the conduct of their work and in particular in regard to the financial relations of their departments with client constituencies.

---

§ 11.8.5[94]
Munro v. Canada
Ontario Court (General Division); November 16, 1992
(1992), 98 D.L.R. (4th) 662
and
Ontario Court (Divisional Court); December 16, 1993
(1993), 110 D.L.R. (4th) 380

This string of cases illustrates the public ethical dilemmas which can arise out of the failed prosecution of a former minister of the government for fraud alleged to have been committed in relation to a campaign for the leadership of a political party. The underlying case was *R. v. Munro*, in which the Crown was not able to convict the former Minister of Indian and Northern Affairs for having enlisted the help of a number of Indian bands in his campaign, in return for access and preference.

When Munro was cleared of the criminal charge, he set out to clear his reputation and to be compensated for his legal expenses, all by way of civil litigation, asking for damages of $5.7 million.

The first of the cases listed here is an action in damages claiming that the prosecution of Munro was based on malicious prosecution, negligence, abuse of process, conspiracy to injure, breach of contract and breach of fiduciary duty. Here, several of the defendants brought motions to have parties struck out and to have some of the causes of action struck out. The General Division ruled that in litigating against the federal Crown, the defendant should be the Attorney General of

---

[93] (1991), 1991 CarswellOnt 3290.
[94] Cross-reference to § 11.8.4.

Canada, rather than Her Majesty in right of Canada. With respect to the R.C.M.P., the court ruled that the members of that force are to be defended by the Attorney General of Canada and that the Commissioner, the senior officer of the force, has no vicarious liability for the actions of the policemen working for him.

With respect to Munro's argument that the prosecution against him was an abuse of process, the view of the court was that,

> There does not appear to be any dispute that the tort of abuse of process does exist. The parties seem to agree that it arises where a proceeding in court is used for a purpose other than its intended purpose. It seems to be common ground that there must be some evidence that a particular defendant committed some overt act that demonstrates the unlawful purpose which gives rise to the abuse. In the statement of claim, it is alleged that Kennedy pursued Munro for the improper purpose of denigrating Munro's good name, professional reputation and national political status, to embarrass him in his professional capacity, and further that Kennedy did so to promote his own professional standing within the R.C.M.P. Those actions are alleged as material facts on the issue of malice, but, in my view, could equally be found to support a claim for abuse of process. In my view, the statement of claim intertwines the actions of the Commissioner and Kennedy sufficiently to give rise to a claim against both. For purposes of a motion to strike, I must assume that these allegations of fact can be proven, and I should only strike where it is plain and obvious that the plaintiff cannot succeed. I am not prepared to strike that cause of action.[95]

The essence of that judgment was thus to allow the matter to proceed.

In the second judgment, the court held that while the Attorney General could now be sued for malicious prosecution,[96] he still had absolute immunity from suits alleging negligence by him or by Crown attorneys in the performance of their duties.

The litigation and discussion of these matters continued for years after the judgments referred to here. Munro applied to have his legal expenses paid by the government because of the fact that the prosecution against him resulted from his professional actions while in

---

[95] (1992), 98 D.L.R. (4th) 662 at 681a-d, reversed (1993), 110 D.L.R. (4th) 380 (Ont. Div. Ct.).

[96] This was a change in the previous law, resulting from the case of *Nelles v. Ontario*, decided by the Supreme Court of Canada at (1989), 60 D.L.R. (4th) 609 (S.C.C.).

government. The government even enlisted a former Supreme Court Judge, Willard Estey, to advise it on the matter of compensating Munro. In late 1996, the Minister of Justice, Allan Rock, in apparent contradiction of the policy on compensating public servants charged with an offence resulting from the performance of their duties, denied any compensation to Munro, admitted for political reasons which were never clarified.

Despite all the antecedents, on May 10, 1999, the parties struck a deal. In exchange for compensation of $800,000, Munro retracted his application for damages. It would appear that the decision to end the Munro litigation by compensating him comprised elements which were not disclosed by the Government of Canada. It is difficult to understand why no apology was offered to Munro, for example. He, in turn, ended the matter by issuing what the media entitled a "scathing attack" on Brian Mulroney, who was Prime Minister when Munro's prosecution failed and when he first applied to be compensated.[97]

While the resolution of this litigation and the consequential indirect clearing of Munro from suspicion seems fair, from the point of view of the development of political law, the opportunity to further develop a tort of "negligent prosecution" in a political context was foregone.

---

§ 11.8.6[98]
Tafler v. British Columbia (Commissioner of Conflict of Interest)
British Columbia Court of Appeal; May 1, 1998
(1998), 161 D.L.R. (4th) 511

Ethical problems of members of the executive government are attempted to be resolved increasingly through legislation regarding the focus of their dilemmas of an ethical nature, namely conflict between their public interests and their private ones. In that context, this case does not resolve the substance of allegations of conflict of interests involving Harcourt, the Premier of British Columbia, from November 1991 until February 1996. The interest of the case, rather, is that it

---

[97] "Munro takes swipe at R.C.M.P., Mulroney," Janice Tibbetts, *Ottawa Citizen*, May 11, 1999, p. A5.
[98] Cross-reference to § 3.13.1.

offers an analysis of the legal process for the resolution of the conflict of interests of parliamentarians adopted by that province since 1990. Moreover, it analyzes the link between the conflict of interest resolution process and administrative law in general.

In March 1995, first a radio reporter and later on a Member of the Legislative Assembly raised allegations that Premier Harcourt was tainted by a conflict of interest prohibited under the *Members' Conflict of Interest Act*.[99] Starting on March 16 and for a total of five days, the Commissioner appointed to carry out the legislation conducted interviews. These proceedings were open only to those directly involved. On March 20, Tafler, a magazine editor, applied to the Commissioner to render public the process of preparing the opinion on the basis of which the Legislative Assembly would have to make its decision about Harcourt. In effect, Tafler wanted to open the proceedings to everyone, to be able to report about it. After arguments and consideration, the Commissioner rejected the application on the ground of Parliamentary privileges, in particular that of excluding strangers, and on the basis that his proceedings were not judicial or quasi-judicial in nature. Tafler appealed to the Supreme Court of British Columbia.

The court dismissed the petition and left the Commissioner's decision in place. It is the court's analysis of the conflict of interest regulation process, rather than the outcome of this secondary proceeding in favour of publicity, which is of interest to us.

In coming to agree with the Commissioner that the preparation by him of opinions was not a judicial or quasi-judicial process, the court relied extensively on the 1978 case of *Minister of National Revenue v. Coopers & Lybrand* (1978).[100] Its initial step was to consider the language of the statute to determine where the tasks of the Commissioner lay along the continuum of functions between administrative and judicial ones. The pith and substance of the purpose of the legislation was set out in the following terms:

> From time to time allegations arise of a real, apparent or perceived conflict of interest. The issue may originate from the public, the media or members of the Legislative Assembly itself. The subject may have

---

been and has been in the past the focus of some debate and perhaps some rancour. The solution, short of resolution by the Assembly, was to be found, in the past, in caucus or in cabinet or in hopes of some effluxion of time.

In my opinion, the *Members' Conflict of Interest Act* was enacted to attempt to provide a means of resolution of the allegations of conflict of interest by the creation of a Commissioner who has the ability to obtain information and to provide a report to the Legislative Assembly about one of its members.[101]

The court also conducted a detailed reading of the provisions of the *Members' Conflict of Interest Act* in light of the criteria of examination laid out in the *Coopers & Lybrand* case and derived the following conclusions:

- the proceedings amount to a request for an opinion and there is no necessity for a hearing;

- the Commissioner may conduct a hearing, meaning that the rights and obligations of the Member against whom the allegation was made are affected by the decision of the Legislative Assembly itself, not by the Commissioner

- while the Commissioner has subpoena and contempt powers, the process he conducts is not an adversarial one; and

- what the Commissioner produces is an opinion which goes to the Speaker of the Legislative Assembly and it is only the latter which makes a decision.

The question then arises: Does the foregoing amount to the exercise by the Commissioner of a quasi-judicial function?

. . .

In the final analysis, the Commissioner investigates in a manner he decides and arrives at an opinion of the existence or non-existence of a conflict of interest. It is an information gathering process coupled with an opinion.[102]

---

[101] (1995), 5 B.C.L.R. (3d) 285 (B.C. S.C. [In Chambers]) at 293.27-28, affirmed (1998), 161 D.L.R. (4th) 511 (B.C. C.A.).

[102] *Ibid.* at 296.45 and 297.47.

On these bases, the court concluded the process adopted by British Columbia under the *Members' Conflict of Interest Act* not to be judicial or quasi-judicial. The court added that in conducting business pursuant to the Act, the Commissioner was serving the Legislative Assembly and that his actions were therefore protected from the effect of the general law or the civil law by the privileges and immunities of the Legislative Assembly itself.

> Consequently, the manner in which it chooses to deal with its members in the context is one cloaked with privilege, the exercise of which is not reviewable. The public knowledge interest will be met by the Legislative Assembly dealing in its proceedings publicly, if it wishes, with the information and the opinion it receives in the usual fashion in the legislative chamber.[103]

The conduct of the Commissioner's investigation thus continued to be barred to Tafler for purposes of reporting.

The British Columbia Court of Appeal upheld the Supreme Court ruling. In its view, the Commissioner is an officer of the Assembly, the privileges of the Assembly extend to him and therefore anything done by him pursuant to the *Members' Conflict of Interest Act* is not reviewable by the courts. The court took note of the fact that by the time this decision was rendered, Premier Harcourt had resigned; it therefore mentioned the issue of mootness but deliberately did not decide the case on that issue.

---

[103] *Ibid.* at 299.53.

§ 11.8.7[104]
Goddard v. Day
Alberta Court of Queen's Bench
(2000), 194 D.L.R. (4th) 551[105]
-and-
Carter v. Alberta
2001 ABQB 429[106]

It is fundamental to the ethical conduct of politicians and hence to their accountability to law, that they refrain from undue interference with the legal system, that they not abuse their public positions to bring personal beliefs into the political realm and that they not use defamatory tactics to underscore their political campaigns. What actions constitute such conduct? That is the subject of this case, debates before the courts of justice in Alberta and in the court of public opinion throughout Canada.

Goddard was a lawyer practicing in the City of Red Deer and a trustee of the local school board. Day had, since 1986, represented part of that city in the Alberta Legislative Assembly and was, at the relevant time, the provincial treasurer. In March 1999, Goddard was acting as criminal defence counsel for an individual charged with several *Criminal Code* offences, including possession of child pornography. On April 9, 1999, after Goddard's client had been convicted but when he had not yet been sentenced, Day wrote a letter to the editor of *The Red Deer Advocate*, the local newspaper, on his ministerial letterhead. This led first to a news story in the paper, which related, among other matters, that,

> Alberta Treasurer Stockwell Day is questioning why a Red Deer lawyer who sits on the public school board defended a pedophile's right to possess child porn. Day said Lorne Goddard, a trustee for 18 years, may have gone too far when he tried to convince a judge his client had a Constitutional right to have child porn: "Mr. Goddard must also believe

---

[104] Cross-reference to § 2.5, 6.6.

[105] And (2000), 194 D.L.R. (4th) 559 and (2001), 200 D.L.R. (4th) 752 and 2000 ABQB 799; November 7, 2000 and 2000 ABQB 820; November 15, 2000 and 2000 ABQB 970, December 20, 2000, settled, December, 2000.

[106] Affirmed 2002 ABCA 303 (Alta. C.A.), leave to appeal refused (2003), [2004] 1 W.W.R. 585 (S.C.C.), additional reasons at 2004 ABCA 99 (Alta. C.A.); May 18, 2001.

it is fine for a teacher to possess child porn—perhaps even pictures of one of his students, as long as he got the photos from someone else," the MLA for Red Deer North said in a letter to the Advocate.

. . .

Macaulay, who unsuccessfully ran for the school board in 1998 elections, told the Advocate that Goddard shirked his duty to protect children by defending Kevin Valley who was jailed twice for sex-related crimes involving young girls. Goddard said he's amazed people don't understand he was only doing his job. "Everyone has the right to a fair trial," said Goddard. As a lawyer, he is compelled to make legal arguments even if he doesn't personally agree with them.

. . .

Day said Goddard's legal arguments left the impression he supports child pornography. "He must believe it because he argued for it...if not, he needs to clarify it."[107]

Day's letter was published in full in the local newspaper, *The Advocate*, on April 17. This in turn led to news stories in the Calgary and Edmonton newspapers on April 30, 1999. Beyond the mere fact of engaging in this form of discourse, Day also took other actions. Goddard alleges that Day spoke of the matter to the Premier of Alberta and misrepresented to him Goddard's position on child pornography, leading the Premier to comment about the matter on radio.

On June 10, 1999, Goddard filed a statement of claim, starting the action in defamation. Thereupon, Day was alleged to have arranged for his legal fees to be paid by the Alberta Risk Management and Insurance Division, a part of the Ministry over which he presided. Subsequently, on September 3, 1999, Day issued a letter of apology, which contained the following text:

> Our system of justice often involves a consideration of both sides of an issue. In order to allow for a full understanding of both sides of an issue, lawyers regularly present arguments on behalf of clients though they do not personally support the views of their clients. This is basic to our

---

[107] "Day blasts trustee over pedophile case," Andrea Maynard, *The Red Deer Advocate*, April 9, 1999, reproduced in the amended statement of claim, para. 8.

justice system and I acknowledge it should not be taken to reflect on any lawyer's personal position on an issue.[108]

Later still, Day set up an internet website in which he published statements about this litigation.

The core of Goddard's action was to examine whether it is acceptable for a political figure to publicly tarnish a lawyer in the performance of his duties as a criminal defence counsel, on the basis of the politician's publicly expressed beliefs. It may be politically convenient to attribute personal motives or beliefs to a lawyer with a client accused of legally and morally reprehensible actions, but does this fall beyond political figures' accountability to the functioning of the legal system? Does the proper functioning of the legal system not require some measure of self-restraint on the part of politicians?

The action also raised a number of other aspects of the issue. First among these was the potential conflict of interest arising from the confusion of Day's personal opinions with his official functions.

> The Defendant Day intended the untrue statements to be viewed as true and more credible because they were written by a Cabinet Minister whilst purporting to write a personal letter. The Defendant Day was at all material times acting outside the course and scope of his duties and jurisdiction as a Cabinet Minister and as an MLA.[109]

Goddard pointed out that Day had the opportunity to intensify the effect of his point of view because, in his capacity as defence counsel, Goddard could not respond to Day while the case was before the court.

The key question in this case is Day's motivation. Goddard alleges that:

> Such reckless behaviour establishes a course of conduct of political self-interest, personal insincerity and reckless disregard for the Plaintiff in an attempt to avoid the consequences of his own actions. As a result, the Plaintiff is further entitled to punitive damages.

---

[108] Amended statement of claim, para. 25.
[109] *Ibid.*, para. 16.

. . .

The Plaintiff's own political aspirations in the Red Deer area have been snuffed out. He can no longer run for nomination.[110]

In short, Goddard's position was that Day made the public comments in question and undertook his subsequent courses of action in order to derive political benefit from the controversy, without regard for the effect of those comments on Goddard's present professional life or his political prospects.

On this basis, the claim for damages included special, general, aggravated as well as punitive ones, amounting at least to $600,000. The matter was still before the court in March 9, 2000, when Day announced that he would be a candidate for the leadership of the eventually to be formed Canadian Alliance political party.

Day's defence was based on a rather unusual conception that can be characterized as "parliamentarian's necessity." He indicated that:

> As an elected Member of the Legislative Assembly for Red Deer North, Mr. Day was under a legal and/or social and/or moral duty to publish the words complained of in the letter and the web site to his constituents, who had a corresponding duty and/or interest to receive them.[111]

In another instance, Day defended the statements he made by calling them "political query with the aim of determining the views of the plaintiff."[112] These two varieties of purported justifications for political speech were imaginative legal arguments, if somewhat distortive of traditional views, mixing as they do the concepts of right to speak with duty to express. It was to be interesting to see if the courts would agree that political life can impose an obligation on its participants to distort elements of the legal system.

This unusual defence is further complemented by a reference to democracy as a cloak for political speech unfettered by legal bounds.

> In the further alternative, the democratic form of government established in Canada under the *Constitution Act, 1867*, and the preamble thereof in

---

[110] *Ibid.*, para. 39 and 40(g).
[111] Amended statement of defence, para. 8.
[112] *Ibid.*, para. 18.

particular, require full debate of all issues of public interest by elected public officials and to the extent the law of defamation would impose liability on Mr. Day in these circumstances, it is inconsistent with the *Constitution Act, 1867*.[113]

In a political law perspective, Mr. Day had a view of the legal system that was coloured by what might be described as libertarian political views.

None of these events prevented the newly-formed Canadian Reform Conservative Alliance Party from choosing Day as its first leader on July 8, 2000, or prevented Day from leading the Alliance Party into the 37th federal general election of November 27, 2000.

Had Day remained Treasurer in the Government of Alberta, this entire series of events might have remained cloaked under the obscurity of primarily local concern. Surprisingly, the matter was given very little air time and was not the subject of much discussion in the media or in the Canadian Alliance Party during the leadership race. Upon Day's success in the campaign, however, when he became not only leader of a national political party but also Leader of the Official Opposition, the spotlight became very much focused on him, and on this litigation. Indeed, we may say that the more actions Day took or failed to take in this case, and the more events relating to the case unfolded, the greater was the public's, the media's and the political classes' attention to the professional ethical aspect of Day's behaviour as a political figure of national prominence.

The litigation of *Goddard v. Day* involved a number of court rulings and indeed, extended into various issues peripherally linked to the principal case.

In the first judgment, issued by the Alberta Order's Bench on October 13, 2000, the matter for decision was whether the trial, on the merits, should go before a judge alone, or a jury. At a case management meeting on January 14, 2000, Day's counsel succeeded in securing trial by jury. Here, he applied to have the trial conducted by a judge alone. The court held, although with some palpable reluctance, that the issues ought to be heard by a jury, despite the complexity and duration of the matters to be tried.

---

[113] *Ibid.*, para. 16.

The court examined the subject matter of the case in its broad perspective, providing an interdisciplinary view worthy of political law:

> [6)] I am satisfied that the evidence of the experts will at least touch upon the following issues and include complex legal matters and issues of political science which may be difficult to express in layman's terms:
>
> - the role of elected representatives;
>
> - the purview of an elected M.L.A. in Alberta in the exercise of an alleged duty;
>
> - the professional and ethical duties of a lawyer with respect to legal submissions made to a Court on behalf of a client;
>
> - the obligation of a Barrister to ensure that representations made to the Court fairly represent the law insofar as the Barrister is able to ascertain the law at the time the representations are made;
>
> - what personal beliefs a Barrister has to have with respect to the state of the law that he is advancing on behalf of his client, specifically relating to arguments that a particular Federal Statute is unconstitutional under the *Charter of Rights and Freedoms*;
>
> - the scope of parliamentary privilege and the law with respect to parliamentary privilege and the Legislative Assembly of Alberta;
>
> - the role of the Defendant, Day, as an individual rather than M.L.A. acting within the scope of parliamentary privilege when he made the alleged defamatory statements about the Plaintiff.[114]

The *prima facie* right to trial by jury prevailed. Trial on the merits was then scheduled to begin on November 6, 2000. This would have put it right in the middle of the 37th federal general election, which was to be held on November 27 of that year. To avoid the publicity necessarily attendant to a trial involving obvious political overtones and the distraction from the focus of the election campaign which the trial could have provided, Day sought, and on October 26, 2000 obtained an adjournment. The reasons for this decision were issued on November 7.

---

[114] (2001), 200 D.L.R. (4th) 752 at 754 – 755.

The Defendant, Stockwell Day, is the leader of a national political party, and is currently involved in the conduct of an election campaign, an election having been called by the Prime Minister of Canada on Sunday, the 22nd of October, 2000, with the election to be held on Monday, the 27th of November, 2000.

Having regard to the election call and the timing of this trial, it was anticipated that practically the entirety of this trial would occur during the campaign. I was satisfied that Mr. Day had no control over when an election was called and that when this matter was set for trial, it was not anticipated that an election would be called for the month of November 2000. I was further satisfied that had it been anticipated that an election would be called for the month of November 2000. Mr. Day would not have agreed to a trial *date* during the month of November 2000, and the matter would have been set for an alternative time. Finally I was satisfied that Mr. Day would not be able to fully participate in the trial having regard to his other duties. I, therefore, granted the adjournment that Mr. Day requested.[115]

In a third proceeding, the court was faced with an application by Goddard to strike a paragraph of Day's Amended Statement of Defence on the ground that it disclosed no defence in law, in response to the claim. Day was claiming that in the subject paragraph, the meaning attributed to the words and statements have a lesser defamatory meaning than that attributed to them in the Amended Statement of Claim. By now, the court stated showing its impatience with Day's use of the law for what seemed to be political tactics.

I conclude from this discussion that a Defendant is not permitted to massage and distort the statements complained of that the allegedly defamatory statements take on a meaning that is not at all defamatory. In those situations, the Defendant should simply defend on the basis that what was said was not defamatory. If the Defendant insists on attempting to justify non-defamatory statements, then the remedy for the Plaintiff is to bring an Application to have the defence of justification to a non-defamatory meaning struck out. In my view, this is one of those rare situations where an Application to strike out will be successful.[116]

Plainly, the court perceived that Day was espousing positions that were not reasonable. Moreover, it was patently linking this lack of reasonableness to the politicization of the controversy. Exaggeration,

---

[115] 2000 ABQB 799, paras. 4, 5.
[116] 2000 ABQB 820, para. 17.

and indeed distortion, in the court's eyes, were hallmarks of political speech rather than legal process.

> It is the Defendant's position that child pornography is so abhorrent to many people that the allegation that a lawyer made representations to the effect that the *Constitution* of Canada permits the possession of such child pornography would tend to cause that lawyer to be hated or despised, be the subject of ridicule, be shunned or avoided and is an imputation which tends to lower or adversely affect the person in the estimation of others. It is in that context that the Defendant, Day, suggests that the alternative defamatory meaning is defamatory.

> I do not doubt that there are some people who would follow the path suggested by the Defence in terms of their estimation of the Plaintiff. However, that is not the test. The test is whether or not it is plain and obvious that the Defence discloses no **reasonable** defence. I am satisfied that the allegation that someone is a criminal lawyer, or a politician would tend to adversely affect that person in the estimation of some other people. The same might be said of practically every appellation, which describes a position or occupation taken by a person. Those other people would not be reasonable people.

> I am satisfied that reasonable people would not hate, or despise, or subject a person to ridicule, shun or avoid that person, or consider that person to be a lesser person in their estimation because that person has made a Constitutional argument in a criminal court.

> Reasonable people are conversed about the constitutional liberties of fellow citizens. Reasonable people support the **Constitution** of Canada or at the very least, support the right of other citizens to rely upon the protection afforded by that **Constitution**.[117]

On November 15, 2000, yet another aspect of case, that of qualified privilege, was ruled upon. Part of Day's defence was that he had written his texts under the protection of qualified privilege, in his capacity as a Member of the Legislative Assembly of Alberta. Goddard brought in an expert witness to address the issues of parliamentary privilege, the scope of an MLA's duties to constituents and the defence of qualified privilege. Day applied to have the expert evidence ruled not admissible. This application was dismissed.

---

[117] *Ibid.*, paras. 21, 22, 23 and 24.

[5] It is my determination that I am unable, at this point, to rule that the expert's evidence proposed to be adduced by Mr. Ritter is inadmissible. I am satisfied that the pleadings raise at least the spectre of privilege based on Mr. Day's parliamentary functions. That, in my view, is a claim for parliamentary privilege. Mr. Day has not sought to amend his pleadings to remove that claim. Further, I am satisfied that the defence of Mr. Day clearly invokes a privilege based on duties arising from his function as a Member of the Legislature of the Province of Alberta. In my view, it is unlikely that there is a pristinely clear point at which qualified parliamentary privilege ends and privilege based on a public obligation begins.[118]

In its analysis, the court found glaring contradictions in Day's pleadings.

[16] It is Mr. Day's position that he is not advancing a defence of either absolute or qualified parliamentary privilege. In fact, he says that he is not advancing a defence of absolute privilege at all. It is, therefore, his position that any discussion relating to absolute privilege is irrelevant.

(17) I am satisfied that the Statement of Claim, or Statement of Defence, or the combination of the two, may place a matter in issue. It is accordingly necessary to review the Amended Statement of Claim and the Amended Statement of Defence to the Amended Statement of Claim. Several paragraphs of the Amended Statement of Claim are relevant to this question. Paragraph 2 of the Amended Statement of Claim states:

...and later on...

[23] In the argument presented at this motion, Mr. Day argues that he has only raised the question of a common law qualified privilege. His pleadings say otherwise. Mr. Day has claimed a qualified privilege and has indicated that the letter was written **solely** in his capacity as a Member of the Legislative Assembly of Alberta. That surely raises the issue of parliamentary qualified privilege.[119]

Significantly, the court also characterizes the full scope of the legal issues which this case raised.

[27] In my view, there is a parallel to be drawn with respect to laws which emanate from the High Court of Parliament. The study of that

---

[118] (2000), 194 D.L.R. (4th) 551 at 553.
[119] *Ibid.*

law is limited to a very small, select group of people. The decisions themselves are made by Speakers, and by Parliament itself. The decisions are infrequent and what is considered to be current law involves reaching back into history three or four hundred years. The study of this law is not part of the ordinary experience of lawyers and Judges within the Province of Alberta. The need for expertise is surely as great as the need for expertise regarding Statutory Law in Saskatchewan or British Columbia. In my view, this body of law is *sui generis*, that is of its own kind. It is analogous to the "law" of Aboriginal Title, which can only be understood with the assistance of expert evidence on its historical context (**Delgamuukw v. British Columbia**), (1997) 3 S.C.R. 1010.

[28] I find it interesting that while the Defendant, Day, takes the position that Mr. Ritter's evidence is not to be adduced, he proposes to adduce evidence of his own expert, Dr. Rodger Gibbons, whose report has also been provided to me. That Report includes discussion of the following topics:

– The traditional concept of parliamentary democracy;
– The origin of **parliamentary privileges**;
– The origin of Cabinet secrecy and enshrinement of that concept in law;
– The concept of **qualified privilege for Parliamentarians**.

[29] I find it unusual that Mr. Day would attack the evidence of Mr. Ritter and at the same time propose to adduce evidence relating to the exact same issues, but of course coming to difference conclusions.[120]

In a fifth proceeding, Day made an application for the Alberta Court of Queen's Bench to rule that there was a defence of qualified privilege for political discussion and comment made in the absence of malice. This application was also dismissed.[121] While this ruling was still preliminary and procedural, it is the one which comes closest to addressing the core of the events of the case. It is also the most significant of the judgments involved in the *Goddard v. Day* litigation saga.

---

[120] *Supra* note 118 at 555 and 556-557.
[121] *Ibid.* at 557-558.

ANALYSIS

Qualified Privilege Generally

[15] The Defendant, Stockwell Day, seeks an incremental development of the common law by the creation of a new category of occasion when privilege derives from the subject matter alone: Political information. The Defendant, Stockwell Day, suggests that political information should be broadly defined as it was in *Reynolds v. Times Newspapers Ltd.*, (1999) 4 All E.R. 609 (H.L.), as being information, opinion and arguments concerning government and political matters that affect citizens. It is suggested that malice apart, the publication of political information should be privileged, regardless of the status and source of the material and the circumstances of the publication.[122]

Goddard's position here was that Day had not advanced a factual basis for this constitutional argument, in which he claims that the *Alberta Bill of Rights* and the *Canadian Charter of Rights and Freedoms* require this incremental development. The court held that this was not fatal to Day's case. It was satisfied first, that this matter involved purely private litigation and no government action, and second, that analysis of this matter required a balancing of the value of reputation with that of freedom of expression under the *Charter*.

In addition to its examination of the Canadian situation, the court cast a comparative look at other jurisdictions. Of particular interest for us is its interpretation of the recent *Reynolds* judgment of the United Kingdom House of Lords.

[42] In *Reynolds v. Times Newspapers Ltd.*, (1999) 4 All E.R. 609, the House of Lords considered the issue of whether the common law should be extended to occasions relating to political information. It determined that the common law should not develop political information as a generic category of information whose publication attracted qualified privilege irrespective of the circumstances. It held that such a development would not provide adequate protection for reputation, which was an integral and important part of the dignity of the individual and formed the basis of many decisions fundamental to the well being of a democratic society. It, therefore, used language very similar to that used by the Supreme Court of Canada in its analysis in *Hill v. Scientology*, *supra*.

---

[122] *Ibid.* at 562-563.

...and later on...

> The House of Lords concluded that a special defence of qualified privilege for political debate should not be created:[123]

The court also looked at the positions espoused by the courts in the United States, Australia and New Zealand. It concluded that there was a particularly Canadian response.

> [54] In my view, there is an additional reason why a new category of occasion of privilege relating to political discussion should not be created. In Canada a myriad of public officials are elected. Some of those public officials are elected to High Office, including the Parliament of Canada, The Legislative Assemblies of the Provinces, and the Governing Boards of major cities. Other elected offices are generally viewed as being of lesser significance. All of the individuals involved contribute to the democratic process within Canada. To create a new category of privilege which would allow all of the people in Canada who have attained some form of political office to be subjected to defamatory remarks, in the absence of actual malice, would be a further discouragement to anyone seeking such political office. There are already many factors which discourage qualified people from seeking political office. These include generally low pay, a negative electorate and significant, to the point of invasive, media scrutiny. One must ask why would anyone ever run for any political office if, in addition to the existing discouragements towards such an enterprise, there is added a privilege which affords protection to individuals who speak falsely about you, so long as they do so in a political context. This is another factor that must be considered in the balancing of values within a free and democratic society. When one considers this factor in addition to the value of reputation and balances those factors against the freedom to publish false information about someone, whether or not that someone is fulfilling a political function, I am satisfied that freedom of expression must give way.[124]

The Court next also concluded that the right to freedom of speech confirmed by the *Alberta Bill of Rights* was not unfettered. On all of the foregoing cases, the judgment was that there does not exist in Canada a defence of qualified privilege relating to political discussion.

---

[123] *Ibid.* at 570-571.
[124] *Ibid.* at 574-575.

The final judgment was rendered by the Alberta Queen's Bench on December 20, 2000, on a renewed application to proceed to trial before a judge alone, without jury. The judge who had ruled in every phase of this action directed here that the matter proceed before him alone.

> The principle witness that the Defendant, Stockwell Day, might call is Dr. Roger Gibbons, who is a Professor of Political Science at the University of Calgary. Dr. Gibbons also deals with the questions of Parliamentary privilege and the scope of duties of an elected Member of the Legislature of the Province of Alberta. His report discusses representative government, and in my view, could be considered to be an outline for a university course respecting representative government.[125]

Given the nature of the evidence, the judge held that an investigation of the matter would be too "scientific," complicated and inappropriate for a jury.

At the general election of November 27, 2000, Day was re-elected in the British Columbia riding of Okanagan-Coquihalla, which be had first won in a September 11, 2000 by-election. The party he was leading, the Canadian Alliance, fared much worse than it had expected, however, electing a mere 66 members out of 301 to the House of Commons. Day was held mostly responsible for this result and questions were being raised as to how he would be able to fare as Leader of the Opposition. Presumably, in part, to enable him to be more effective as a federal parliamentarian, as a party leader, and as Leader of the Official Opposition, in mid-December 2000, he agreed to settle the action.

At this point, Day was in this matter so deeply that his confidential settlement proved no less a political and legal albatross than if he had continued with the action. Rather than being beset by the continuation of this litigation, Day then became mired in the revelations arising out of the manner in which the case had been conducted, and the details of the way it was settled.

It was revealed that the case could have been settled a year earlier, but that Day had refused. It then became public that the entire matter cost over $782,000 of which only $60,000 was for Goddard's damages.

---

[125] 2001 ABQB 429, para. 6, affirmed 2002 ABCA 303 (Alta. C.A.), leave to appeal refused (2003), [2004] 1 W.W.R. 585 (S.C.C.), additional reasons at 2004 ABCA 99 (Alta. C.A.).

As part of the settlement, Day was to pay over $474,000 of his own legal fees as well as for $746,000 of those for Goddard.

The revelation most hurtful to Day was that the Alberta Treasury had been forced to pay the entire amount through the province's Risk Management Fund. After months of public criticism, Day made a public apology which was of no legal consequence although it may have had political benefit. Later on, he was forced to mortgage his home to pay some of the costs.

Later still, it became known that the lawyer who had represented Day, or perhaps the law firm of which the lawyer was a member, had made a sizeable political contribution to the Canadian Alliance.

This series of events became embroiled in the Alberta provincial election of March 12, 2001. The debacle of this seemingly unnecessary but never-ending litigation contributed to the general political disruption of the Canadian Alliance and the rapid lessening of Day's hold on his own party. He was even publicly disavowed by his former Premier, Ralph Klein, who was anxious not to be tainted with the same brush as Day in the Alberta election campaign.

The final stroke of this political-legal saga was a separate legal action, started by a former Speaker of the Alberta Legislature, hoping to prevent the payment of Day's settlement by the Risk Management fund of the provincial treasury. David Carter had been Speaker of the Legislature from 1986 until 1993. In this case, he applied to the Alberta Queen's Bench for an order that the decision of the Director of the Risk Management Fund to pay the amount necessary to settle Day's defamation action was not valid, because the Director did not have the power to make that decision.

The court held first that Carter did have the requisite standing to bring this legal action, based only on his position as a taxpayer and a resident of Alberta. On the merits, however, Carter's application was also dismissed. The court felt it had to balance the application of parliamentary privilege and the consequential non-interference by the Executive branch in the internal functioning of the legislative branch, with the delegation of powers which the Legislature may have given to the executive to operate the Fund. In this instance, the court was satisfied that the Legislative Assembly had properly delegated its powers with respect to the establishment and administration of the Fund.

The most fundamental and important question that the court had to face, was whether, in writing the texts which Goddard found defamatory, Day was acting within the scope of his duties as an MLA. In this regard, the court discussed the minutes of a December 21, 1989 meeting of a Member Services Committee of the Alberta Legislative Assembly, at which the subject of defamation coverage for MLAs was debated, but its conclusions on this point are somewhat vague.

> My reading of the minutes is that the issue being discussed is whether the Committee should ask that Parliamentary Counsel develop a set of expanded guidelines as to when a member would be considered to be acting within the course of their duties as a member. It was specifically stated in that meeting that the government did provide coverage for members pursuant to a recent order of that Committee which extended coverage to members for things, which are done in the course of their duties as members. Attached as Exhibit D to Mr. Whitehouse's affidavit was an opinion from Mr. Michael Clegg, Parliamentary Counsel of the Legislative Assembly which stated that legal liability of defamation, might come within the scope of coverage provided by Government, if the act would reasonably be viewed as coming within the normal function of an MLA.[126]

On the basis of this recounting of the decision-making process, the court took an implicit view that in acting as he did, Day was within the scope of his parliamentary functions.

> In conclusion, in my view there can be no doubt but that it is the Legislative Assembly, which is speaking when any legislation is passed or regulation, prepared. The Legislative Assembly of this province has properly established a fund, which is used to protect its members for acts done outside the House, so long as the MLA was acting within the scope of his or her authority and properly performing his or her duties. It has done so by way of legislation, regulation and order. It has provided for the administration of that fund and for payments out of that fund.[127]

---

[126] *Ibid.*, para. 45.
[127] *Ibid.*, para. 49.

§ 11.8.8

Investigations of the Groupaction Contracts and the Sponsorship Program, Special Audit Report of the Auditor General of Canada to the Minister of Public Works and Government Services on Three Contracts Awarded to Groupaction, May, 2002 and Report of the Auditor General of Canada to the House of Commons, November 2003, Chapters 3, 4 and 5, on Government-Wide Audit of Sponsorship, Advertising and Public Opinion Research and Appointment of a Special Counsel for Financial Recovery, announced February 10, 2004 and Commission of Inquiry Chaired by Mr. Justice Gomery, established February 19, 2004.

-and-

LeFrancois v. Canada (Attorney General) and Via Rail Canada Inc.
Québec Superior Court; action no. 500-17-020104-041

-and-

Vennat v. Canada (Attorney General) and Federal Business Development Bank
Québec Superior Court; action no. 500-17-020135-045

-and-

Vennat v. Canada (Attorney General)
Federal Court of Canada – Trial Division; action no. T-611-04

-and-

Pelletier v. Canada (Attorney General)
Federal Court of Canada – Trial Division; action no. T-668-04

At the time of writing, this was an issue of primordial interest in Canadian public and political life. As none of the proceedings will have been completed, remedies much less having been applied, it is impossible to draw long-term conclusions from the scandal for the development of political law. Nevertheless, the matter is already instructive in respect of the professional ethics of members of the executive government, as well as in several other domains.

In the mid-1990's, roughly contemporaneously with the 1994 re-election of the Parti Québécois to government in Québec and with the 1995 Québec referendum on sovereignty federal authorities operating in a somewhat crisis-like political environment, a number of measures were adopted. Parliament enacted the so-called Clarity Legislation. The government also made the reference to the Supreme Court of Canada, on the basis of which the latter would eventually render the Québec Secession Reference decision. Together with these, the federal

government initiated an advertising and sponsorship program, based in Public Works and Government Services Canada (PWGSC). The objective of these programs was to promote the visibility of Canadian authorities and federal services, ostensibly in all of Canada, but in reality mostly within the Province of Québec.

Throughout its existence, the sponsorship program was clouded by public administration practices that respected neither the rule of law nor the norm of value for money. Several internal and external audits were conducted over the years, all of which pointed out serious difficulties but none of which seemed to lead to corrective action. In May 2002, the Auditor General (AG) presented to the Minister of Public Works a Report on three government contracts that had been awarded between 1996 and 1999 to a company called Groupaction for advertising-related services. The amounts of money involved were considerable enough to attract the attention of the AG, although relatively minuscule in comparison to the overall budget of the Department. Among her conclusions, the AG noted that "Our audit found that senior public servants responsible for managing these contracts demonstrated an appalling disregard for the *Financial Administration Act*, the Government Contracts Regulations, treasury Board policy and rules designed to ensure prudence and probity in government procurement."[128] This finding led the AG, in her explanatory press conference relating to the Report, to pronounce the now infamous condemnation: "Senior public servants broke just about every rule in the book."[129]

In response to this Report, the House of Commons Standing Committee on Public Accounts held hearings at which it examined several "suspect" public servants. The AG also referred some parts of the file to the R.C.M.P.. Over the course of the next two years, it became seemingly apparent that the breach of rules by public servants was not the only aspect of the matter and that indeed, the entire sponsorship program, rather than merely a few contracts, was in need of investigation.

---

[128] Report to the Minister of Public Works and Government Services on three Contracts, Awarded to Groupaction, Auditor General of Canada, May 2002, http://www.oag-bvg.gc.ca/domino/reports.nsf/html/02sprepe.html
[129] News Release of the Office of the Auditor General of Canada, May 8, 2002.

The AG should have issued a far broader Report in November 2003, including chapters on advertising, sponsorships and public opinion polling. In the course of the transition from the Chrétien administration to that of Prime Minister Martin, the release of this Report was delayed to February 12, 2004. Its release caused an instantaneous and enormous furore. The AG's principal findings were summarized as follows.

1. We found that the federal government ran the Sponsorship Program in a way that showed little regard for Parliament, the *Financial Administration Act*, contracting rules and regulations, transparency, and value for money. These arrangements—involving multiple transactions with multiple companies, artificial invoices and contracts, or no written contracts at all—appear to have been designed to pay commissions to communications agencies while hiding the source of funding and the true substance of the transactions.

2. We found widespread non-compliance with contracting rules in the management of the federal government's Sponsorship Program, at every stage of the process. Rules for selecting communications agencies, managing contracts, and measuring and reporting results were broken or ignored. These violations were neither detected, prevented, nor reported for over four years because of the almost total collapse of oversight mechanisms and essential controls. During that period, the program consumed $250 million of taxpayers' money, over $100 million of it going to communications agencies as fees and commissions.

. . .

4. The government's communications policy states that federal institutions must suspend their advertising during general federal elections. We noted that the policy was properly implemented.[130]

The AG's Report gave rise to a number of investigations. To date, the most intricate and interesting of these was the one conducted by the Public Accounts Committee. This body was not so much looking to assign culpability, civil or criminal, as to determine the impact of the management of the sponsorship program on ministerial and deputy ministerial responsibility. From the outset, the Committee's proceedings were the setting for attempts by political figures and public

---

[130] Report of the Auditor General of Canada to the House of Commons, November 2003, p. 1.

service officials each to shift blame on the other. The most resounding testimony of this nature was given on March 18, 2004 by the Hon. Alfonso Gagliano, former Minister of Public Works and Government Services.

My responsibility in this matter

To be responsible is to have to answer to someone for one's actions.

. . .

To whom does a politician, a Member of Parliament, a Cabinet minister answer?

The answer is manifold: as a Member of Parliament, you answer to the voters. You do so by standing for re-election and being voted in or out, depending on how they perceive you performed as their representative, how they think your party performed, etc...

As a minister, your responsibility is itself twofold: first, you answer to the man who appointed you there in the first place, the Prime Minister. Second, you answer as a group before the House of Commons: this is known as ministerial responsibility.

Then, Mr. Gagliano made the following rather astounding assertion:

A minister does not run his department: he has neither the time nor the freedom to do so.[131]

The thoughts expressed here amount to an unusual and unorthodox interpretation of ministerial responsibility, one not conducive to resolving the problems pointed out by the AG. The search for appropriate institutional remedies continues.

---

[131] Testimony of Alfonso Gagliano to the House of Commons Standing Committee on Public Accounts, March 18, 2004.

11.9 ISSUE: OBLIGATION OF HEADS OF STATE AND GOVERNMENT TO OBSERVE LEGAL NORMS[132]

11.9.A— SUBJECTION OF HEADS OF STATE AND GOVERNMENT TO DOMESTIC LAW

See *Canadian Javelin Ltd., Re*, [1982] 2 S.C.R. 686 (S.C.C.).

---

§ 11.9.A.1
Bill 150 and the Québec General Election of 1994
litigation not initiated

Pursuant to the doctrine of accountability to law, the basic duty of a Head of State or of Government is to observe and abide by the legal norms and the legally binding texts applicable in his jurisdiction in the process of governing. One aspect of the doctrine is that in the course of public life, political or partisan considerations should not prime over legal ones, so as to render law merely a tool of political will. Another purpose of the doctrine is to underline that in democratic regimes, the government itself is subject to those legal rules which guide political life. Consequently, the normal expectation which the doctrine gives rise to is that Prime Ministers and Presidents apply the laws of their own jurisdictions; it would stand to reason that this be even more so where the law in question is prepared and enacted at the initiative of the very government which is expected to apply it. This scenario is based on the assumption that the argument does not involve wilfully unjust, unconstitutional or morally objectionable laws.

The *Nixon* case was the perfect example of the application of the general rule, namely that no Head of State or of Government is above the law. In the present case, by contrast, the objective is to show that the circumstances of the constantly evolving public life of a jurisdiction can rightfully entail warranted exceptions to the general rule. The doctrine of accountability to law must be broad enough to have room for manoeuvring so that Heads of State or Government may

---

[132] Cross-reference to § 6.6 and 6.7.

govern for the benefit of the people. Such exceptions can modify the results achieved pursuant to the doctrine and maybe even the proper execution of the duties arising from it. In all cases, however, there must be questioning and awareness of the exception, analysis of the specificities of the case and properly justifiable reasons to account for the change. Let us see what gives rise to these special circumstances.

The conditions for the faithful observance of accountability to law can indeed be complicated by changing circumstances which may force re-examination of whether it is more appropriate to observe an existing legal prescription or to amend it. Thus, the principle of *"rebus sic stantibus"* can have as much relevance in political law as in the sphere of international law. Moreover, in constitutional matters, the stakes are much higher than in other domains and the adherence to existing rules of legality cannot be provided in a legalistic manner, but must reflect constitutionalism itself, which is the mutual adaptation of law and politics in the evolution of the State. In addition, the wisdom of observance of existing legal rules can be influenced by electoral situations. Even given the need for flexibility of, reliance upon and adherence to, legal norms in some specific circumstances, it is important to note that the expression of State intention in legal form be meant, at least at the time of that expression, to be binding and not a mere political statement. It is this particular element of the law-policy-politics distinction that leads us into examination of the debate about the legalities of constitutional development which took place in the Québec general election of 1994.

The origin of the discussion must be traced back to the failure, on June 23, 1990, of the Meech Lake Accord, which would have developed the 1982 constitutional amendment and made it acceptable to Québec. That failure resulted in a shock to the collective consciousness of Québec that was far more profound than that palpable in other parts of the country. It was as a direct consequence that the Liberal government of Premier Bourassa proposed Bill 90 on September 4, 1990, for the purpose of establishing a commission on the political and constitutional future of the province, the Bélanger-Campeau Commission.[133] In the debate to adopt the bill in principle, the minister in charge of the constitutional file, the Hon. Gil Rémillard, expressed the horn of the dilemma facing Québec thus:

---

[133] Projet de loi 90, *Loi instituant la Commission sur l'avenir politique et constitutionnel du Québec*, 34th Legislature, 1ere Session, 1990.

M. le Président, on se retrouve maintenant dans une situation où nous devons prendre les moyens nécessaires pour exprimer ce que nous sommes, dans un contexte qui nous permettra de protéger des acquis et de faire en sorte que notre avenir puisse être en considération de toute cette histoire que nous avons reçue en héritage et qui nous permet d'exprimer avec détermination ce que nous voulons faire.

Je disais tout à l'heure, en citant le professeur Dion, que les Québécois sont une nation et ça signifie, M. le Président, que, comme société, comme nation, comme peuple, nous pouvons exprimer librement ce que nous sommes et je me réfère au premier considérant de la loi que nous discutons aujourd'hui, M. le Président; le premier considérant de cette loi est particulièrement éloquent. Je le cite: "Considérant que les Québécoises et les Québécois sont libres d'assumer leur propre destin, de déterminer leur statut politique et d'assurer leur développement économique, social et culturel."'[134]

Rémillard pointed out that the important question left for Québec following the failure of Meech at the heart of the matter was how best to express itself.

Following publication of the Bélanger-Campeau Report, the National Assembly was presented a further bill, Bill 150, which was assented to on June 20, 1991, as *An Act respecting the process for determining the political and constitutional future of Quebec.*[135] This law continued to be referred to in popular shorthand as Bill 150. It enunciated, in its very first section, the answer of the Québec National Assembly, of the government and of a sizeable portion of the population of the province, as to how Québec should choose its political and constitutional future in the circumstances of the apparent inability of Canada to reform itself so as to satisfy Québec's aspirations.

---

[134] Débats de l'Assemblée nationale, 4 septembre 1990, p. 4333.
[135] S.Q. 1991, c. 34.

THE PARLIAMENT OF QUÉBEC ENACTS AS FOLLOWS:

CHAPTER 1

REFERENDUM ON SOVEREIGNTY

1. The Gouvernement du Québec shall hold a referendum on the sovereignty of Québec between 8 June and 22 June 1992 or between 12 October and 26 October 1992.[136]

This provision acted as an incentive for Québec to prepare the expected 1992 referendum on sovereignty. It also had the effect of a "sword of Damocles" on the political class in the remainder of the country. The vital interest of the federal government, then led by Prime Minister Mulroney, a political ally of Premier Bourassa, was to avoid a Québec referendum, or at least a referendum which Québec would hold alone and on the issue of separation. Thus in the year following the enactment of Bill 150, the federal authorities orchestrated a new accord, this one entitled the Charlottetown Accord, which they hoped would encompass measures satisfactory to Québec but would not be comprised uniquely of these, so as to prevent alienation of the other communities within Canada. Most significantly of all, Prime Minister Mulroney set out to convince Premier Bourassa that a referendum organized on a Canada-wide basis on the Charlottetown deal could satisfy the requirements of Bill 150 for a vote on the future of Québec. On August 21, 1992, Bourassa announced that he accepted. The reaction to this decision came swiftly.

It took no time for Bourassa's nationalist opponents to whip up the storm of opposition to Bourassa's deal. Their slogan had a clever appeal—it turned Bourassa's old "profitable federalism" back upon him. "At that price, it's No," the slogan said.

The two-party assault was a formidable force against the Québec premier. Bourassa had to fight his own provincial opposition leader, PQ leader Jacques Parizeau, as well as Brian Mulroney's old friend Lucien Bouchard, the leader of the breakaway group of Quebeckers who now sat as the nationalist Bloc Québécois in the House.

At one point, these Non campaigners had been the same people to taught Bourassa for abandoning a vote on sovereignty in favour of the refer-

---

[136] S.Q. 1991, c. 34, s. 1.

endum on the Charlottetown deal. Now, however, they were reaping the rewards of that Bourassa decision. "They asked us a simple question and they will get a simple answer," Parizeau said repeatedly throughout the campaign.

. . .

Bourassa and Mulroney tried their hardest to argue that the Non campaigners were trying to lure Quebeckers down the road to sovereignty, and that the only logical vote for a federalist was a Qui on the ballot. But even key members of Bourassa's own party were having a hard time buying that argument.[137]

As events would turn out, the Canada-wide referendum led to a defeat of the substantive proposals Bourassa and Mulroney had agreed to and Québec's "place within Confederation" was still not sufficiently provided for. Soon thereafter, Bourassa left the political stage and Daniel Johnson became Premier and Leader of the Liberal Party of Québec.

The next provincial general election was called on July 24, 1994, to be held on September 12, 1994. It was in the course of that election campaign that Bourassa's decision to accept the vote on the Charlottetown Accord as fulfilling the requirements of Bill 150 became the subject of political debate.

The discussion related at first to the relative merit of the position espoused by the Liberal Party and that favoured by the Parti Québécois. The Liberals argued that at the time of its adoption in 1991, Bill 150 was the proper step to take, but that in light of the imminence of a constitutional deal by 1992, changed circumstances demanded that Premier Bourassa accept the referendum on Charlottetown as being sufficient to suit the political and constitutional future of the province. The Parti Québécois, arguing from a more partisan and hence less flexible perspective, indicated that Bourassa should have simply abided by the terms of Bill 150 and held the 1992 vote on the issue of sovereignty.

Over the course of the campaign, the Péquiste argument became more specifically pertinent to the issue of accountability to law. While the

---

[137] Delacourt, S., *United We Fall: The Crisis of Democracy in Canada*, Viking Press, Toronto, 1993, pp. 176-177.

Liberals relied on the merits of intent, flexibility and results, and said their approach to federal-provincial relations produced more positive results, the PQ relied on the exact wording of Bill 150 itself, saying that the text of the law had been intended to have effect and that the referendum it had provided for should have been held because that is what the law had required.[138]

In a yet later phase of the debate, the parties came to discuss not only the difference between the intent and the text of the legislation, but the matter of whether, at the enactment of Bill 150, the government which introduced it actually had the intention of having it carried out. The debate by this point was on the very subject of the binding nature of law on the government which had introduced it and hence on the will of that government to be accountable to its own legal norms.

On one side, it was said that:

> Johnson also hinted the Liberal Party has never had any intention of holding a referendum on sovereignty, even when it adopted Bill 150 calling for a province-wide referendum if the rest of the country failed to make constitutional offers—what eventually turned into the doomed Charlottetown accord.[139]

> Campaigning in Sherbrooke yesterday, Johnson said the government's only aim with the law was to pressure the rest of Canada into offering constitutional reform, the Star's Robert McKenzie reports.

> "The strategy at the time, and what we embarked upon, was finding ways to get offers from the rest of Canada of a revision of the Canadian federation and of federalism," Johnson said.[140]

On the other side, the perspective was rather different.

> "Est-ce naif de croire que le gouvernement respecters ses propres lois? Quelle crédibilité devons-nous accorder au projet de M. Johnson de faire adopter une loi pour obliger le gouvernement à équilibrer ses budgets?" se demande Jacques Parizeau.[141]

---

[138] "Johnson breaks taboo on Constitution," *Globe and Mail*, August 19, 1994.

[139] "Johnson says he'll press for more Québec autonomy," Elizabeth Thompson, *The Gazette*, August 24, 1994, p. A8.

[140] "Liberals misled voters: Parizeau," Edison Stewart, *Toronto Star*, August 25, 1994.

[141] "La Souveraineté doit être vue comme une union," *La Presse*, 25 août 1994.

It would be an exaggeration to claim either that this debate, as described here, was the main focus of the election campaign, or that the casting of doubt on the Bourassa government's goal in having Bill 150 enacted was the reason for the Péquiste victory at the polls. Nevertheless, even if it is only through the only record of these exchanges that remains available for examination, the resulting press clippings, the significance of this analysis is to show that political parties, even in their essentially political functions as vehicles for the achievement of power, are aware of the importance and the extreme controversiality of a government's accountability to its own laws.

---

§ 11.9.A.2
George v. Harris
Ontario Superior Court of Justice; January 10, 2003
[2003] O.J. No. 26[142]

It is rare for a legal action to be so politically changed and so controversial as to have an effect on the outcome of an election. Such a singular characteristic attaches to this case.

The Progressive Conservative government of Premier Mike Harris came into office in June 1995 on a program entitled the "Common Sense Revolution." The essence of this program was a dramatic shift of the province's political life toward the right, including less tolerance for dissent, born out of the Premier's and the government's unshakeable certitude in the correctness of their motivations, whatever the social and political consequences. Against this backdrop, in the early days of September 1995, an Aboriginal community occupied the provincial park at Ipperwash. In the context of that occupation, one of the aboriginals, Dudley George, was fatally shot on September 6, 1995, by an officer of the Ontario Provincial Police (OPP). The political controversy of this matter stems from the allegation that at the time the shooting occurred, the Premier had taken personal charge of the police action.

On March 25, 1996, the administrator of the George estate sued the Premier, the Attorney General, the Solicitor General and the Chairman of the Management Board of Cabinet of Ontario in tort. He

---

[142] Additional reasons at (2003), 2003 CarswellOnt 1710 (Ont. S.C.J.) and Ontario Superior Court of Justice, September 18, 2003, (2003), 2003 CarswellOnt 3548.

contended that individually or together, these officials made the decision to use the paramilitary tactical response unit of the OPP, using force against unarmed civilians, and that this resulted in the death of Dudley George. This legal action tainted the entire tenure of office of Premier Harris, not only in his first term from 1995 to 1999, but also during his second term, from 1999 to 2002. It cannot be determined but is within the reach of reasonable conjecture, that the long-standing negative publicity affecting the Premier's re-electability, as well as the actual legal risks involved, may have contributed to Harris' decision to retire from provincial politics in 2002. Retirement would not absolve Harris of legal liability, but it could certainly ease the electoral path for the re-election of his party in a subsequent campaign. In the meantime, the incident at Ipperwash spawned various other legal proceedings. Several OPP officers were prosecuted. In February 2002, Harris launched a defamation action against the *Globe and Mail*, arising out of an article dated December 14, 2001, which had linked Harris to orders given to the OPP.

At the time Harris resigned in 2002 and was replaced by Ernie Eves as Premier, the matter was still not resolved. On September 2, 2003, Premier Eves announced that another general election would be held on October 2 of that year. The trial of one of the defendants, Robert Runcimon, Solicitor General of the time of the events leading to the action, had long been scheduled for September 22, 2003. The proximate link between such a trial and the election, that is between the legal and political aspects of the matter, was best exemplified by Runcimon's application to have the trial delayed so that it would be held only after October 3 and therefore not have an effect on the voters.

In this campaign, the case of *George v. Harris* was clearly perceived as being so relevant to the images of the competing parties as to exert a potential influence on voters' decisions. The Ontario Superior Court rendered its decision on the Runciman motion on September 18, in the form of an Endorsement. The judge recounted that Mr. Runciman, as one of the defendants, argued for a brief adjournment of the trial on the ground that he would otherwise not be able to participate in the trial as needed, given the necessary time committed to his campaign. In support of the motion, the Minister's Chief of Staff filed an affidavit indicating that the candidate was committed to attending events and canvassing in his own and neighbouring ridings each day until October 2, 2003. The plaintiffs, respondent on the motion, objected to the adjournment, arguing that it was simply a politically motivated request to prevent damaging evidence from coming out during the campaign that would prove embarrassing and harmful to Mr. Runciman and to the Progressive Conservative Party. The court granted the motion, based primarily on the proposition that every person has an inherent right to be present at a trial or at any other proceeding to which he is a party. The judge also felt that a four day delay in a trial scheduled to last for six months, in an action which had been ongoing for over eight years was not significant.

The interaction between the law and politics of the situation could not be denied. The trial was indeed postponed but, for a variety of reasons among which the shadow cast by the protracted litigation arising out of the Ipperwash events is only one. The Progressive Conservatives were swept from office. The incoming Liberal Party led by Premier Dalton McGuinty, true to its electoral promise to that effect, launched a Commission of Inquiry on November 12, 2003, to look into the events surrounding the death of Dudley George. Ironically, in one of the inquiring judge's first public statements, he indicated that former Premier Harris will likely be called to testify. At the time of writing, the matter is still ongoing.

See also *Public Inquiry into the Events Surrounding the Death of Dudley George*, established November 12, 2003; *Harris v. Globe and Mail* and *U.S. v. Nixon*,[143] 483 U.S. 203 (1974).

---

§ **11.9.A.3**[144]
Clinton v. Jones
United States Supreme Court; May 27, 1997
137 L.Ed.2d 945 (U.S. Ark., 1997)

The rule of democracy and the role of law in democracy require that a Head of State or head of a government must be subject to legal norms and requirements, as would any other citizen. It is appropriate to question, however, whether a person holding such a high office may be entitled to postpone litigation initiated against him in respect of private actions until the end of his tenure of office, specifically to enable him to fulfil his governmental functions without hindrance.

---

[143] International comparison.
[144] International comparisons. Cross-reference to § 10.7.4 and 11.10.5.

This was the question addressed by the Supreme Court of the United States in this case.

According to Jones, in 1991, prior to the assumption of the Presidency by Bill Clinton, he performed acts that constituted sexual harassment and violation of civil rights. The limitations period on such cases was three years. In 1994, merely days before the end of that period, Jones files a civil suit against Clinton, asking for damages in the amount of $700,000. There is some question as to whether Jones' action was taken independently, perhaps in response to an article in *The American Spectator* newspaper, which seemed to refer to her, or was a politically motivated scheme constituting part of the continuing right-wing attacks on Clinton, who by then was President of the United States.

There is a long-standing characteristic of American society to be more litigious than most, including the realm of public life. Going beyond that trend, in recent times, political confrontation has come to include "the rise of scandals, the rising use of law as a weapon of attack, the uniting of these two trends in lawsuits based on scandalous allegations."[145]

No matter what the circumstances or the motivations for which, this case arose, once filed, it had to be conducted by the parties so that a law-making judgment would clarify the issue. Clinton's defence was based on grounds of Presidential immunity. He also presented a motion requesting that the hearing of the motion be postponed until he is no longer President, this delay being without prejudice to the plaintiff's right to refile the suit. During the proceedings, Clinton was elected to a second term, which ended on January 20, 2001.

The United States District Court for the Eastern District of Arkansas dismissed Clinton's motion of immunity and ruled that discovery procedures could go forward. It ordered, however, that the trial itself be stayed until the end of the Clinton Presidency. The United States Court of Appeals for the Eighth Circuit affirmed the lower court ruling on the issue of immunity. More significantly, it held that the order to postpone the trial until the President would leave office be reversed, as that would have amounted to the "functional equivalent" of a grant of temporary immunity.[146] Thus, this case came to be heard

---

[145] "The Paula Jones ratchet," *The Economist*, May 31, 1997, p. 31.
[146] 137 L.Ed.2d 945 (U.S. Ark., 1997) at 957.

by the United States Supreme Court on January 13, 1997, amidst vibrant public debate and controversy, aroused not only by the rarity of cases against presidents in office, but also because of the fact that another scandal, Whitewater, was also being vigorously pursued by Clinton's political opponents.

Clinton's petition to the Supreme Court raised several interrelated issues. He alleged that a President should be immune from lawsuits in respect of unofficial conduct arising before he assumed office. What the court termed his "principal submission" was that in all but the most exceptional cases, the Constitution should be interpreted as affording the President temporary immunity, thereby justifying deferral of the trial. Given the specifics of the American constitutional system, the case also raised matters relating to the separation of the three branches of government.

The President argued that what he sought was not immunity in the sense of being above the law, but only a postponement of judicial proceedings based on the character of his office.

> As a starting premise, petitioner contends that he occupies a unique office with powers and responsibilities so vast and important that the public interest demands that he devote his undivided time and attention to his public duties. He submits that—given the nature of the office—the doctrine of separation of powers places limits on the authority of the Federal Judiciary to interfere with the Executive Branch that would be transgressed by allowing this action to proceed...We had no dispute with the initial premise of the argument. Former presidents, from George Washington to George Bush, have consistently endorsed petitioner's characterization of the office.[147]

The Supreme Court thus agreed that the Office of the President was unique, but concluded that it does not follow that the principle of the separation of powers would be violated if this action were to proceed. "Whatever the outcome of this case, there is no possibility that the decision will curtail the scope of the official powers of the Executive Branch. The litigation of questions that relate entirely to the unofficial conduct of the individual who happens to be the President poses no perceptible risk of misallocation of either judicial power or executive power."[148]

---

[147] *Ibid.* at 963.
[148] *Ibid.* at 965.

Clinton also pleaded that letting the case go forward would place a burden on his execution of the Office that would hamper the performance of his official duties. The court rejected this on the basis of a review of the relevant history. In over 200 years, only three presidents, it said, had been subjected to private actions. It concluded, with perhaps a tinge of judicial sarcasm, that a deluge of litigation was unlikely to engulf the Presidency. It held that the District Court had given undue weight to the concern that the trial of this case might generate unrelated civil actions that could hamper the President in the conduct of the duties of his office. Further, the Supreme Court made an effort to address the political circumstances in which this case had arisen. It focused, more seriously, on the risk that its decision could "generate a large volume of politically motivated harassing and frivolous litigation,"[149] but was not convinced of the seriousness of that risk. Relying on the Federal Rules of Civil Procedure as well as on precedent, the court concluded that "the availability of sanctions provides a significant deterrent to litigation directed at the President in his unofficial capacity for purposes of political gain or harassment. History indicates that the likelihood that a significant number of such cases will be filed is remote."[150] With respect to this specific case, the District Court would be able to avoid overuse of the President's time by proper management of its conduct.

The matter of the interference with the President's governance of the country through litigation was also addressed from the perspective of the relationship between the Executive and the Judiciary. The court reaffirmed that the boundaries between branches are not watertight and that there are overlapping responsibilities and interdependency. Consequently, the exercise by a federal court of its constitutional jurisdiction which takes up the President's time is not a violation of the *United States Constitution*. The courts have the authority to determine whether a President acted within the law.

> In sum, "[i]t is settled law that the separation of powers doctrine does not bar every exercise of jurisdiction over the President of the United States." Fitzgerald, 457 U.S., at 753-754. If the Judiciary may severely burden the Executive Branch by reviewing the legality of the President's official conduct, and if it may direct appropriate process to the President himself, it must follow that the federal courts have power to determine

---

[149] *Ibid.* at 969.
[150] *Ibid.* at 969–970.

the legality of his unofficial conduct. The burden on the President's time and energy that is a mere by product of such review surely ca (sic) be considered as onerous as the direct burden imposed by judicial review and the occasional invalidation of his official actions. We therefore hold that the doctrine of separation of powers does not require federal courts to stay all private actions against the President until he leaves office.[151]

Based on the foregoing reasoning, the Supreme Court held that "deferral of this litigation until petitioner's Presidency ends is not constitutionally required."[152]

Given the unanimous decision of the court, there can be no clearer judicial statement to the effect that, bearing in mind the necessity and appropriateness of safeguards against politically motivated and frivolous attacks on the Head of State, the holder of that high office is not only subject to the requirements of law, but also bound to address his opponents by judicial process within the same time frame as other citizens.

Prior to the argument of this case in the Supreme Court, media opinion as to whether the trial should go ahead or not was split along ideological lines. After publication of the judgment, the most perceptive comment was provided in the following terms.

> Despite all this, nine out of nine judges on the Supreme Court agreed that the Jones case should go ahead, only one expressed any reservations about the judgment. There was something wonderfully American about this. The principle of equality before the law is sacrosanct; even the danger of weakening the presidency cannot justify a dent in it. Mr. Clinton's lawyers stressed that the president did not claim immunity from the law, only a delay in its application; and legal delays are common. No matter; even a delay could not be allowed. America was founded, after all, to raise the principle of equality up high, and to defy the authoritarianism of Europe.

> Perhaps this is still the wisest principle of government. Attempts to protect authority at equality's expense are generally self-defeating in the end, especially in an age when egalitarian sentiment is powerful.[153]

---

[151] *Ibid.* at 967–968.
[152] *Ibid.* at 953.
[153] "The Paula Jones ratchet," *The Economist*, May 31, 1997, p. 31.

See also *Tripp v. Executive Office of the President*, 104 F. Supp.2d 30 (D.D.C., 2000) and *Prosecution of Presidents Chun Doo Hwan and Roh Tae-woo*, Supreme Court of the Republic of Korea, December 16, 1996.

---

§ 11.9.A.4
Organization for Quality of Government v. Government of Israel
High Court of Justice of Israel; June 15, 1997
limited information available

In a democracy, citizens' organizations and members of the opposition can, each for their respective reasons, take legal action to ensure that the justice system is guided by criteria of law, rather than becoming subservient to partisan political considerations. In such legal actions, even the highest elected official, the Prime Minister, can be drawn in if there is popular perception that his motives can be questioned, for example in respect of the appointment of high justice officials. Such litigation can also be the continuation of political conflict by legal means. The ultimate barrier against such politically motivated use of the courts is the same as that against the politically motivated acts complained of, namely the adherence to statute and the presentation of evidence.

A member of the Likud Party, Deri, was charged with corruption at a time when a new Attorney General was needed to conduct the prosecution against him. Deri sought to have Bar-On, a political ally, appointed by the government to the position. The issue raised the argument whether an Attorney General ought to be an eminent jurist or merely a political activist. The actual allegation was that Bar-On was appointed as part of a political deal which included a plea bargain by Deri in consideration for which Deri and the political party he led in the Kinesset would deliver support for a deal brokered by Prime Minister Netanyahu on Hebron. Prime Minister Netanyahu's Government appointed Bar-On on January 10, 1997. The High Court entertained a petition against the appointment and suspended it, whereupon Bar-On resigned on January 12.

In the midst of serious political strife resulting from this matter, the police conducted an investigation into the action of the Prime Minister and the Minister of Justice and recommended that they be charged with fraud and breach of trust. The State Attorney, in the capacity of acting Attorney General, decided to prosecute only Deri. The Organization for the Quality of Government thereupon petitioned against the Government and several members of opposition parties petitioned against the State Attorney on the ground that the Prime Minister and the Minister of Justice were not prosecuted for their conduct in the matter. The Supreme Court of Israel, sitting as High Court of Justice in first instance, rejected all the applications as not supported by sufficient evidence.

See also *Government of Germany v. Krenz*, Leipzig Court, November 7, 1999; *Attorney General of Cape Province v. P.W. Botha*, December, 1997 and *Communist Party of Chile v. Augusto Pinochet*,[154] Court of Appeal of Santiago, January 12, 1998.

---

§ 11.9.A.5
Prosecution of Prince Norodom Ranariddh
Phnom Penh Military Court; March 4 and 17, 1998
limited information available

The dispensing of justice for, and the provision for accountability to law by executive officers of the State can take place only in an environment of legitimate democracy and political stability. Where these vital elements are replaced by chaotic governance and political insecurity, trials of senior governmental officials can become more political arrangements in which there is not even a semblance of legality or justice. No theory of political law can condone as being genuine, show-trials orchestrated for purposes of the psychological face-saving of any of the participants before the citizenry and the electorate. Indeed, the essence of political law is to keep a balance between the appropriate roles of law and politics, rather than to have a legal system totally beholden to those in political authority.

Following the elections organized under United Nations auspices in 1993, in the period of 1993 to 1997, Norodom Ranariddh was First Prime Minister and Hun Sen was his Co-Prime Minister. In July 1997, Hun Sen mounted a coup which resulted in Ranariddh going to live in exile in Bangkok, although he continued to have a following within Cambodia. As a second general election was scheduled for July 26,

---

[154] Cross-reference to § 11.9.C.2.

1998, the countries assisting in the attempts to stabilize the Cambodian political situation, tried to devise a way to ensure that the election would approximately reflect the will of the people and the balance of factions in the country, including that loyal to Ranariddh.
Toward that end, it was reported in the press that the Japanese authorities brokered a complicated political deal which would include
a seemingly judicial component. Prince Ranariddh was to be charged,
tried and convicted for alleged crimes against Cambodian law. Thereafter, he was to be pardoned by his father, King Sihanouk. The clean
slate thus created would, on the one hand, serve to justify Hun Sen's
coup and on the other, enable Ranariddh to contest the 1998 election
without further hindrance.

Pursuant to this plan, on March 4, 1998, a military court in Phnom
Penh tried Ranariddh on charges of arms smuggling arising out of
the seizure, in May 1997, of a substantial shipment of weapons which
had entered the country. The court convicted him and sentenced him
to five years' imprisonment. The entire proceeding was held with the
Prince in absentia. He did not recognize the legitimacy of the court,
nor present a defence, but contended that the charge was false and
politically motivated. The trial was open to observers, including those
of Amnesty International, but neither local nor international opinion
believed that the trial was in fact a proceeding in law.

> The lamentable weaknesses of Cambodia's judicial system are well
> known. This situation is not going to improve if people simply accept
> that every judicial proceeding is simply something to be got through
> then ignored.

. . .

> The only trials which proceed promptly are those for which there is a
> political agenda. It is one more example among many of the lack of
> judicial independence. What kind of message does this send to the Cam-
> bodian people?

. . .

Amnesty International and Human Rights Watch Asia both issued pre-trial statements saying that the Prince would not receive a fair trial in the present political climate of harassment and murder.[155]

This local opinion was reflected in the reporting of the world-class media.

> The BBC's correspondent in Phnom Penh said Cambodians accept that the courts are not acting independently of second Prime Minister, Hun Sen, who came to power after a coup last year.[156]

In execution of a further part of the deal, a further and similar trial took place on March 17, 1998, in the course of which Ranariddh was sentenced to 30 years' imprisonment for conspiracy with the Khmer Rouge.

Observers of political law must recognize that even though such proceedings seem distasteful to those seeking to establish genuine principles of accountability to law on the part of the leaders of States and governments, they do take place in more than rare instances. The real way in which these proceedings ought to be analyzed is to ask whether such show-trials constitute legal proceedings at all, or are they more appropriately qualified as purely political events cloaked in judicial appearance and form. It is difficult to draw a boundary between trials which are conducted without adequate judicial and legal safeguards and political show-trials in which the legal component is merely theatrical and which serve purely political ends. As in other categories, each case deserves to be examined on its merits. In the present instance, however, the pre-prepared nature of the entire trial, the lack of independence and impartiality of the judge, the military venue, the absence and non-co-operation of the accused, the dubious nature of the charges, the speed of the proceedings, the absence of evidence as well as the advance discussion of a pardon, and in particular the politicized environment in preparation for an election in which the accused would participate, all seem to indicate that these proceedings were not really of a judicial nature at all.

In consideration of the political component of political law, from a Canadian perspective, it is worth asking whether such show-trials

---

[155] "Chorus of Criticism follows Prince's trial," Samrath Sopha and Eric Pape, *Phnom Penh Post*, March 14-27, 1998, p. 5.

[156] "Forever Cambodian PM found guilty," BBC News, March 4, 1998.

can serve a useful purpose in the sense of aiding in rendering the electoral process free and fair, and thereby be useful political, rather than legal, tools in the democratization of a country. Given the violent contestations of the outcome and the continuingly chaotic state of Cambodian public life after the election, this trial did not even seem to have served that kind of purpose.

The Cambodian view of this case may be somewhat different. That country has been devastated by three decades of war and genocide, resulting in the almost complete absence of the rule of law. In those circumstances, an internationally devised solution which enables all the participants to save face may be of use in the attempts to move toward peace, stability and particularly renewed legality.

See also *East Timor Prosecutions and Litigation*, started February 2000; *Prosecution of former President Suharto*, started in 2000 and *Prosecution of President Jacques Chirac*, Cour de Cassation, Assemblée Plénière, Arrêt no. 481 du 10 octobre 2001.

11.9.B— SUBJECTION OF HEADS OF STATE AND GOVERNMENT TO FOREIGN LAW

§ 11.9.B.1[157]
In Re Estate of Ferdinand E. Marcos Human Rights Litigation
Trajano v. Marcos
U.S. Court of Appeals, Ninth Circuit; October 21, 1992
978 F.2d 493 (9th Cir., 1992)
-and-
Hilao v. Estate of Marcos
U.S. Court of Appeals, Ninth Circuit; September 11, 1996
95 F.3d 848 (9th Cir., 1996)

There exists a general presumption against the extraterritorial application of domestic law. Were this rule to be adhered to strictly, a head of state or government who had been shown to have acted in a fashion contrary to his accountability to the legal regime of his own country, by actions taken in violation of the legal rights of his own people, could not be brought to justice and have that accountability enforced

---

[157] International comparisons.

in a foreign jurisdiction. However, there are *fora*, such as the United States, in which exceptions to the rule against extraterritoriality can be invoked, thereby reinforcing the accountability of executive governors to legal norms and preventing them from avoiding the responsibilities which flow from that accountability. The multiple litigation against Ferdinand Marcos, President of the Republic of the Philippines, after his being deposed, belongs to this category of exceptions.

The first of these cases relates to an incident which occurred on August 31, 1977, in which Trajano, a student, was kidnapped, tortured and murdered after he had asked a question of Marcos' daughter about her appointment as director of an organization. At that time, Marcos was President, his daughter Marcos-Manotoc was chair of a national public organization and oversaw the police and military who carried out the murder, and they were propped up in power by Ver, who headed the military intelligence service. The principal orchestrator of the murder, Marcos-Manotoc, was acting on behalf of Marcos.

In February 1986, all of these officials fled their country and settled in exile in Hawaii. On March 20, 1986, Trajano's mother launched an action, asking for damages for false imprisonment, kidnapping, unlawful death and a deprivation of rights, all for Trajano's estate, as well as for emotional distress on her own behalf. The U.S. District Court for the District of Hawaii held Marcos-Manotoc responsible and concluded that "the violation of fundamental human rights constitutes a tort in violation of the law of nations"[158] according to American law, and awarded damages of $4.16 million pursuant to the applicable provisions of the *Philippine Civil Code*. The U.S. Court of Appeals for the Ninth Circuit upheld. The Supreme Court denied *certiorari*, which in the Canadian context means the equivalent of refusing leave to appeal. The result was thus that the Court of Appeals judgment was determinative on the matter.

The judgment was motivated first on the ground of tort. Marcos-Manotoc pleaded her immunity under the *Foreign Sovereign Immunities Act* (FSIA) but admitted acting on her own authority, not on that of the Republic of the Philippines.

---

[158] 978 F.2d 493 (9th Cir., 1992) at 496.

Trajano, on the other hand, argues that under *Chuidian*, the FSIA does not immunize acts of individuals which are outside the scope of their official duties, and that the acts of torture and arbitrary killing (which the complaint avers occurred under Marcos-Manotoc's own authority) cannot be "official acts" within whatever authority Marcos-Manotoc was given by the Republic of the Philippines.[159]

The court concluded that Marcos-Manotoc caused Trajano's wrongful death and that that was a tort under the law of nations which was incorporated into U.S. federal common law by a statutory provision.[160]

The more contentious ground of the ruling was whether the U.S. courts could exercise jurisdiction, notwithstanding Marcos-Manotoc's argument that there was no extraterritorial jurisdiction over civil actions based on torture. In response to this, the court held that

> Regardless of the extent to which other principles may appropriately be relied upon, the prohibition against official torture "carries with it the force of a *jus cogens* norm," which "enjoy[s] the highest status within international law."
>
> . . .
>
> "Under international law, any state that engages in official torture violates *jus cogens*." *Siderman* at 717 (citations omitted). We therefore conclude that the district court did not err in founding jurisdiction on a violation of the *jus cogens* norm prohibiting official torture.[161]

This holding was reinforced by the reason that the seizure of jurisdiction over the claim by the U.S. courts could not constitute unwarranted interference with the domestic affairs of the Philippines, as the Philippine government was not objecting.

Further, Marcos-Manotoc tried to deny the jurisdiction of the U.S. by relying on *Article III* of the *United States Constitution*, saying that it would not enable the American judiciary to deal with purely foreign disputes. Relying on the writings of framers of the *Constitution*, the court upheld its jurisdiction, indicating not only that the judicial

---

[159] *Ibid.* at 497.
[160] 28 U.S.C. 1350.
[161] *Supra* note 158 at 500.

power of the federal courts extended to "all cases which concern foreigners,"[162] but also that, as international law was deemed to form part of federal common law,

> ...for a court to determine whether a plaintiff has a claim for a tort committed in violation of international law, it must decide whether there is an applicable norm of international law, whether it is recognized by the United States, what its status is, and whether it was violated in the particular case.[163]

While, from a Canadian perspective, this extension of American jurisdiction may seem intrusive into other legal systems, in a case such as this, the extraterritorial application of American law is a way of ensuring that unrestrained executive power is checked by a legal accountability mechanism where it is likely that no other legal regime would accomplish the goal.

By contrast, the *Hilao* case illustrates that while litigants may be successful in obtaining judgment against heads of state or government on substantive issues such as tortious liability for actions in contravention of accountability to law, they may thereafter be frustrated in the obtention of damages by the application of procedural rules such as those relating to the execution of judgments. This technical defeat of substantive victory is a serious restraint on the accountability of executive governors to law.

Hilao is the title of a class-action suit comprising some 10,000 plaintiffs "who suffered (or are family members of those who suffered) torture, disappearance, and summary execution during Marcos' tenure as president of the Philippines."[164] These plaintiffs sued successfully in Hawaii and won an award of nearly $2 billion.[165]

In separate and unrelated proceedings, on the basis of a request for international legal assistance, by the Republic of the Philippines, al-

---

[162] *Ibid.* at 502, citing from the correspondence of James Madison.

[163] *Ibid.* at 502.

[164] 95 F.3d 848 (9th Cir., 1996) at 850.

[165] *Hilao v. Estate of Ferdinand Marcos* (*In Re Estate of Ferdinand Marcos*, Human Rights Litigation) MDL No. 840 (D. Haw. Feb. 3, 1995). This ruling was upheld in a decision rendered on December 17, 1996 by the Ninth Circuit Court of Appeal, 103 F.3d 762 (9th Cir., 1996). Related decisions can be found at 103 F.3d 767 (9th Cir., 1996) and 103 F.3d 789 (9th Cir., 1996).

leging that certain funds on deposit in specified Swiss banks had been stolen by Marcos from the Philippines and seeking to have those funds returned, the Swiss Federal Council froze Marcos' accounts in those banks.

Hilao intended to enforce this judgment out of the Marcos funds in the same Swiss banks. Presumably because those banks did not have branches in Hawaii, the judgment of the Hawaiian court was registered in the U.S. District Court in the Central District of California, where there were branches of the Swiss banks in Los Angeles. On October 5, 1995, Hilao moved for entry of his judgment against the Swiss Bank Corporation and Credit Suisse in the amount of the judgment against the Marcos Estate, plus accrued interest. On December 11, 1995, the court ordered the banks to deposit the funds into the court registry. The banks appealed and moved to stay the judgment.

The Ninth Circuit Court of Appeal vacated the District Court's order. It signalled its awareness of the substantive merit of Hilao's claim by repeating the most damming portion of the lower court ruling.

> It states that various courts "have found that the Marcoses engaged in a sophisticated pattern and practice of secreting the assets of the defendant Estate in foreign countries;" that the Marcoses have refused to testify or produce documents about those assets; that the Banks, "aided by Swiss courts," have refused to produce any documents; and that the Estate and the Republic of the Philippines have agreed to divide the Estate's assets and that both the Swiss government and the Banks, which were found to be agents and representatives of the Marcoses, "are playing a supporting role in the attempt to consummate the agreement."[166]

Nevertheless, upon an examination of both California and federal laws on banking and civil procedure, the court concluded that neither gave the District Court authority to make the order it did. It found that the banks' refusal to produce documents and the allegation that they were acting as "agents and representatives of the Marcos Estate" did not suffice to constitute the "exceptional circumstances" which would have allowed the court to make such an order. Finally, the court declined to address the arguments dealing with the act-of-state doctrine and international comity.

---

[166] *Supra* note 164 at 855.

The struggle of the victims of the human rights abuses and the un-accountability to law of the Marcos regime did not end with the *Hilao* decision of September 11, 1996. Only two days later, they applied to the U.S. District Court for an injunction to prevent the banks from disposing of the Marcos funds and won, when the court dismissed the banks' motion to dismiss.[167] That judgment went to the Ninth Circuit Court of Appeal, which, on December 3, 1997, granted the banks' petition for writs of *mandamus* against the District Court.[168] Within the United States, the judicial struggle for enforcement had, to date, gone no further and it seemed as if the entire attempt to obtain accountability would be thwarted.

A mere few days later, however, on December 10, 1997, in an action by the Government of the Philippines against the Marcos estate, the Supreme Court of Switzerland ordered that the funds being held by the banks under its jurisdiction be put in escrow.

The regime of President Ramos, who was in office at the time of this judgment, did not seem inclined to compensate the *Hilao* claimants. In the summer of 1998, however, President Estrada was elected and in early September, he negotiated a compensation package of $170 million.

It would appear that for the assurance of accountability to law, where inability to execute judgments stands as a barrier to substantive res-olution, negotiation, that is politics, must be used to supplement litigation.

---

§ 11.9.B.2
United States v. Noriega
United States Court of Appeals, Eleventh Circuit; July 7, 1997
117 F.3d 1206 (11th Cir., 1997)

The holding of a head of state or government to account in the legal system of his own country is not only feasible, as the cases show, but also proper. Holding such an official to account to the legal system of a foreign country seems possible only where the authorities wish-

---

[167] *Rosales et al. v. Crédit Suisse and Swiss Bank Corporation*, No. CV 96-6419.
[168] *Crédit Suisse v. United States District Court for the Central District of California*, 130 F.3d 1342 (9th Cir., 1997).

ing to hold the official to account can back their legal claims with military might. As such, the procedure may seem somewhat questionable even where the head of state or government being held to account appears, *prima facie*, to be holding office unconstitutionally in light of the legal system of his own country. Among the grounds of questioning that such a procedure raises are first, whether this is a proper use of law or merely a tool of great power politics and second, whether there can be justification for such flagrant extraterritorial application of domestic legal doctrines.

Noriega was the commanding officer of the armed forces of the Republic of Panama. American authorities suspected that he was involved in the smuggling of cocaine from Colombia into the United States. On February 4, 1988, a grand jury in Miami indicted him on drug related charges. Outliving various power plays in Panamanian political life, on December 15, 1989, Noriega claimed that a state of war existed between his country and the United States. In accordance with long-standing U.S. practice in the region, the Americans invaded Panama. "Noriega lost effective control over Panama during the armed conflict, and he surrendered to United States military officials on January 3, 1990. Noriega was then brought to Miami to face the pending federal charges."[169]

The U.S. District Court for the Southern District of Florida convicted Noriega and sentenced him to very long prison terms. Noriega appealed the conviction. He also sought a new trial; that motion was denied. This judgment was rendered by the Eleventh Circuit U.S. Court of Appeals on the appeal of the conviction and on the denial of the new trial.

The principal argument raised by Noriega that is of interest in this study is his claim of immunity from prosecution in the United States as the head of a foreign state. The District Court had rejected this claim not on the basis of its analysis of Noriega's position vis-à-vis Panamanian law, but rather on the ground that "the United States government never recognized Noriega as Panama's legitimate, constitutional leader."[170] This set the stage for an explanation of American legal principles on foreign sovereign immunity.

---

[169] 117 F.3d 1206 (11th Cir., 1997) at 1210.
[170] *Ibid.* at 1211.

The court held that the exemption of the person of the sovereign from arrest or detention within a foreign territory was grounded on the implicit limitation which states accepted to their individual territorial jurisdiction. In order to lend substance to foreign head-of-state immunity in the criminal context, the court had to look to the executive branch for direction on the claim raised by Noriega. It also indicated how this was to be done.

> To enforce this foreign sovereign immunity, nations concerned about their exposure to judicial proceedings in the United States:
>
>> follow[ed] the accepted course of procedure [and] by appropriate representations, sought recognition by the State Department of [their] claim of immunity, and asked that the [State] Department advise the Attorney General of the claim of immunity and that the Attorney General instruct the United States Attorney for the [relevant district] to file in the district court the appropriate suggestion of immunity...[171]

Other courts of appeals had developed two standards for dealing with such claims. In the first, which arose out of *In Re Doe*[172] it was said that the government could either explicitly suggest immunity, expressly decline to suggest immunity, or offer no guidance. Some courts which followed that reasoning had held that in the absence of a formal suggestion of immunity, none should be recognized for a putative head of state. By contrast, in *Spacil v. Crowe*,[173] another court held that where the government either expressly granted or denied a request to suggest immunity, the courts were bound to follow the lead of the executive, but that where no such opinion was issued the courts themselves should make an independent determination on a claim for immunity. The noticeable element in this entire discussion is that it reflects only on the relationship of the American judiciary with the American executive and that whichever branch of government renders the decision on immunity claims, only American legal analysis and thinking are involved, not that of the country of origin of the claimant.

On the foregoing basis, the court decided the matter of Noriega's claim as follows:

---

[171] *Ibid.*
[172] 860 F.2d 40 (2nd Cir., 1988).
[173] 489 F.2d 614 (5th Cir., 1974).

Noriega's immunity claim fails under either the *Doe* or the *Spacil* standard. The Executive Branch has not merely refrained from taking a position on this matter; to the contrary, by pursuing Noriega's capture and this prosecution, the Executive Branch has manifested its clear sentiment that Noriega should be denied head-of-state immunity. Noriega has cited no authority that would empower a court to grant head-of-state immunity under these circumstances. Moreover, given that the record indicates that Noriega never served as the constitutional leader of Panama, that Panama has not sought immunity for Noriega and that the charged acts relate to Noriega's private pursuit of personal enrichment, Noriega likely would not prevail even if this court had to make an independent determination regarding the propriety of immunity in this case.[174]

Noriega also contended that his conviction ought to be overturned as he was brought to the United States in contravention of the *Treaty of Extradition* which existed between the two countries. The allegation was that the treaty did not allow Panama to extradite its nationals. In a rather extraordinary statement, the court rejected this ground because, it said, the provision would at most inform the U.S. of the hurdles to face in such an extradition and in any event this provision did not cover the parties' resorting to self-help or abduction. The court in effect sanctioned the abduction of Noriega by the U.S. military.

The third claim by Noriega relating to his position as head of state related to the fact that his having been brought before the American courts by an invasion of his country "was so unconscionable as to constitute a violation of substantive due process."[175] The court declined this ground of appeal as well, indicating that its power to try a person was not impaired by reason of the fact that that person had been forcibly abducted into the court's jurisdiction." Further, whatever harm Panamanian civilians suffered during the armed conflict that preceded Noriega's arrest cannot support a due process claim in this case."[176]

On April 6, 1998, the Supreme Court of the United States denied *certiorari*[177] and the matter now seems closed.

---

[174] 117 F.3d 1206 (11th Cir., 1997) at 1212.

[175] *Ibid.* at 1214.

[176] *Ibid.*

[177] 118 S.Ct. 1389.

See also *Prosecution of President Saddam Hussein*, June 29, 2001; *Prosecution of Prime Minister Ariel Sharon*, November 19, 2001; *Prosecution of Palestinian Leader Yasser Arafat*, December 20, 2001 and *Prosecution of British Columbia Premier Campbell*, January, 2003.

11.9.C— SUBJECTION OF HEADS OF STATE AND GOVERNMENT TO INTERNATIONAL LAW

See *The Prosecutor v. Jean Kambanda*, International Criminal Tribunal for Rwanda, September 4, 1998, ICTR 97-23-S.

---

§ 11.9.C.1
Ex parte Augusto Pinochet Ugarte
High Court of Justice, Queen's Bench Division; October 28, 1998
[1998] All E.R. (D) 629
and
R. v. Bow Street Metropolitan Stipendiary Magistrate
House of Lords; November 25, 1998
[1998] 4 All E.R. 897
and
R. v. Bow Street Metropolitan Stipendiary Magistrate
House of Lords; January 15, 1999
[1999] 1 All E.R. 577
and
R. v. Bow Street Metropolitan Stipendiary Magistrate (No. 3)
House of Lords; March 24, 1999
[1999] 2 All E.R. 97
and
The Kingdom of Spain v. Augusto Pinochet Ugarte
Bow Street Magistrate's Court; October 8, 1999
(2000) ILM 39, 135

In the fall of 1998, Augusto Pinochet, who had led a military coup in Chile in September 1973 and had been at helm of that country under several guises until 1990 as the leader of a brutal and bloody right-wing dictatorship, went to England for medical treatment. While he was there, on October 16, 1998, at the behest of a judge of the National Court of Spain, Balthazar Garzon, the authorities of Spain issued an international warrant for Pinochet's arrest on the ground that while head of state of Chile, Pinochet had caused the death of a number of

Spanish citizens. On October 17, the warrant was executed and Pinochet was arrested at the London Clinic. On October 22, a further warrant was issued against Pinochet in Spain. Through use of these warrants, the Kingdom of Spain was requesting of the United Kingdom that Pinochet be extradited to face trial in Spain for the murders of the Spanish citizens.

These antecedents gave rise to a political legal battle, the first phase of which, that primarily involving the United Kingdom, lasted until March 2, 2000. The highlights of this battle were court judgments which were to define and expand in the direction of greater justice the legal limits within which heads of state and government can act. Seen in one perspective, the judgments of the United Kingdom courts in this case are the most significant judicial pronouncements on the international protection of human rights since the rulings of the Nuremberg Tribunal at the end of World War II. In another light, the *Pinochet* judgments constitute a great leap forward in the definition of the accountability of heads of state and government to legal norms of governmental behaviour, by contrast to their immunity from prosecution for anything they may have done while in office.

There can be no doubt that the *Pinochet* proceedings were not only judicial and legal in nature, but also intensely political. Throughout the series of trials, judgments, appeals and reconsiderations before the courts, the political authorities of the United Kingdom, Spain and Chile were involved, in the most active way possible, in the determination of the outcome of this phase of the proceedings. Moreover, other governments such as those of France, several other European states and the United States, were immersed in the matter, either by issuing yet further warrants, by making appearances before the U.K. courts, or by conducting or resuming investigations into the activities of Chilean authorities, within Chile in respect of the foreign nationals implicated, or within the territory of the other countries so involved.

International humanitarian organizations, prime among them Amnesty International, were also active in this case. The Association of the Relatives of the Disappeared Detainees and the Medical Foundation for the Care of Victims of Torture were also involved.

On October 22, 1998, the day on which the second Spanish warrant was issued, Pinochet brought a series of applications for judicial review and for *habeas corpus* before the Queen's Bench Division of the

High Court. Considering that in extradition matters, the final decision as to whether or not to surrender the person being held was to be made by the Home Secretary, the most significant of the applications was that for *habeas corpus* addressed to the Home Secretary of the day, Jack Straw. Pinochet's argument was essentially based on sovereign immunity, namely that as the former head of state, pursuant to the U.K. *State Immunity Act, 1978,* as well as on the basis of international customary law set out in a number of scholarly works, and in reliance on precedent, he could not be made subject to the writ of British courts, and could therefore not be held liable for his actions as head of state.

The Queen's Bench issued a cleverly nuanced decision. It held that the applicant was entitled to immunity from the criminal and civil processes of English courts as a former sovereign, and that therefore the warrants against him were quashed. However, it also held that the applicant was to remain under arrest until the final determination of any appeal of this decision. Thus, the court's order of *certiorari* would not take effect until the determination of any appeal. That could take a long time and the court did not want to be rushed.

> We grant leave to the Crown Prosecution Service to appeal against our decision to the House of Lords. We do that having regard to the obvious public importance and international interest in the issue that has been raised and argued. We would not wish it to be thought that we give leave because we are doubtful as to the outcome.

> . . .

> We certify the point of law I have indicated. The certificate is that "a point of law of general public importance is involved in the court's decision, namely the proper interpretation and scope of the immunity enjoyed by a former head of state from arrest and extradition proceedings in the United Kingdom in respect of acts committed while he was head of state."[178]

The Commissioner of the Metropolitan Police and the Government of Spain appealed to the House of Lords. A panel consisting of five judges considered the matter extensively, looking at all aspects of the claim of immunity.

---

[178] [1998] All E.R. (D) 629, paras. 130, 131.

The panel split on a 3-2 basis, allowing the appeal and retaining Pinochet under arrest pending a decision to extradite him to Spain. By the time this matter was before their Lordships, the detention of Pinochet had become not only a matter of the most vital public interest (in both sense of that expression), but was a cause celebre, with competing groups of demonstrators urging their views on world-wide television audiences and competing political figures making public pronouncements. The court acknowledged the politicized nature of the issue but reinforced its duty to set that consideration aside.

> I would allow this appeal. It cannot be stated too plainly that the acts of torture and hostage-taking with which Senator Pinochet is charged are offences under United Kingdom statute law. This country has taken extra-territorial jurisdiction for these crimes. The sole question before your Lordships is whether, by reason of his status as a former head of state, Senator Pinochet is immune from the criminal processes of this country, of which extradition forms a part. Arguments about the effect on this country's diplomatic relations with Chile if extradition were allowed to proceed, or with Spain if refused, are not matters for the court. These are, par excellence, political matters for consideration by the Secretary of State in the exercise of his discretion under s. 12 of the 1989 Act.

> . . .

> Counsel for General Pinochet further put forward wide-ranging political arguments about the consequences of the extradition proceedings, such as adverse internal consequences in Chile and damage to the relations between the United Kingdom and Chile. Plainly it is not appropriate for the House to take into account such political considerations. And the same applies to the argument suggesting past "acquiescence" by the United Kingdom government.

> Concentrating on the legal arguments . . .[179]

It is perhaps symptomatic of the attitude of those supporting Pinochet and demonstrating in his favour that they never understood the independence of the British courts from the Government of the United Kingdom, nor the fact that law alone guided the justices' deliberations. Their accusations of complicity and plotting thus ring hollow.

---

[179] [1998] 4 All E.R. 897 at 941 g-h and at 946 h-j.

The decision of the House of Lords was, in the end, a monumental victory for the rule of law in governance and for the reinforcement that even heads of state and government must conduct themselves in a manner accountable to law. The ruling was based on two mutually reinforcing principles. First, it said that a head of state or former head of state could claim immunity only in respect of acts performed by him in the exercise of his functions as head of state. The key finding here was that the actions here alleged against Pinochet, namely the various abuses of human rights, the acts of torture and the hostage-takings, could not be regarded in any circumstances as being functions of a head of state.

> In my view, art. 39(2) of the Vienna Convention, as modified and applied to former heads of state by s. 20 of the 1978 Act, is apt to confer immunity in respect of acts performed in the exercise of functions which international law recognises as functions of a head of state, irrespective of the terms of his domestic constitution. This formulation, and this test for determining what are the functions of a head of state for this purpose, are sound in principle and were not the subject of controversy before your Lordships. International law does not require the grant of any wider immunity. And it hardly needs saying that torture of his own subjects, or of aliens, would not be regarded by international law as a function of a head of state. All states disavow the use of torture as abhorrent, although from time to time some still resort to it. Similarly, the taking of hostages, as much as torture, has been outlawed by the international community as an offence. International law recognises, of course, that the functions of a head of state may include activities which are wrongful, even illegal, by the law of his own state or by the laws of other states. But international law has made plain that certain types of conduct, including torture and hostage-taking, are not acceptable conduct on the part of anyone. This applies as much to heads of state, or even more so, as it does to everyone else; the contrary conclusion would make a mockery of international law.
>
> This was made clear long before 1973 and the events which took place in Chile then and thereafter.[180]

Second the House of Lords came to a restrictive view of the Act of State immunity. The justices perceived the doctrine at the foundation of this form of immunity as being a recognition in domestic law that certain questions of foreign affairs are not justiciable. However, they went on, where Parliament had shown that a particular subject matter

---

[180] *Ibid.* at 939 g-940 a.

was to be justiciable in English courts, that justiciability limited the applicability of the Act of State doctrine. In their opinion, Parliament held torture to be such a serious matter that the Act of State doctrine could not apply in such cases. Thus, where the person accused of torture was a public official, investigation into the conduct of that official was required.

> Concentrating on the legal arguments, I am satisfied that there are several reasons why the act of state doctrine is inapplicable. First, the House is not being asked to investigate, or pass judgment on, the facts alleged in the warrant or request for extradition. The task of the House is simply to take note of the allegations and to consider and decide the legal issues of immunity and act of state. Secondly, the issue of act of state must be approached on the basis that the intent of Parliament was not to give statutory immunity to a former head of state in respect of the systematic torture and killing of his fellow citizens. The ground of this conclusion is that such high crimes are not official acts committed in the exercise of the functions of a head of state.

> . . .

> Fourthly, and more broadly, the Spanish authorities have relied on crimes of genocide, torture, hostage-taking and crimes against humanity. It has in my view been clearly established that by 1973 such acts were already condemned as high crimes by customary international law. In these circumstances it would be wrong for the English courts now to extend the act of state doctrine in a way which runs counter to the state of customary international law as it existed in 1973. Since the act of state doctrine depends on public policy as perceived by the courts in the forum at the time of the suit the developments since 1973 are also relevant and serve to reinforce my view.[181]

The impact of this judgment was, in itself, profound. It restricted the domain of activity of heads of state which could be guided by political, ideological, and other considerations based on will and interest, vis-à-vis those based on law. In an unfortunate development, it turned out that Lord Hoffman, one of the three justices comprising the majority, had an interest in a charity closely allied to Amnesty International. As a consequence, Pinochet petitioned on December 10, 1998, to have the House of Lords ruling set aside. On January 15, 1999, the Lords granted that petition and referred the matter to another committee of the House for rehearing. While this partial side-

---

[181] *Ibid.* at 946 j-947 a.

1138 / LAW OF DEMOCRATIC GOVERNING – VOLUME II: JURISPRUDENCE

tracking of the litigation was damaging to the legal strength of the case against Pinochet, it in fact added to its political law dimension, in that it added a layer of political involvement.

The second decision of the Lords on the merits of the extradition case was handed down on March 24, 1999. This panel, consisting of seven judges, reaffirmed the central issue of principle by a majority of 6-1; Pinochet had no immunity in respect of acts of torture and conspiracy to torture which were allegedly committed at a time when all three of the most closely interested states, namely the U.K., Chile and Spain, had ratified it. In effect, this meant that the extradition could continue only in respect of acts of torture committed after September 29, 1988, but it did mean that the extradition could proceed.

The final judicial decision was handed down on October 8, 1999, by a Metropolitan Magistrate in the Bow Street Magistrates' Court. The court was satisfied that all the requirements of the *Extradition Act, 1989*, were met and committed Pinochet to await the decision of the Home Secretary as to whether to extradite.

On January 11, 2000, Minister Jack Straw issued a statement based on a medical examination undertaken on January 5. He concluded that Pinochet was not fit to stand trial and that he would not be extradited to Spain. On March 2, 2000, Pinochet was allowed to be flown home to Chile. In a surprising turn in his state of health, while before departing Britain he had seemed frail, upon his arrival in Santiago a day later, he looked remarkably reinvigorated.

The second phase of the Pinochet prosecution, that indigenous to Chile, has been going on ever since. On June 5, 2000, Pinochet was stripped of the immunity from prosecution which he had arranged for himself before giving up the reins of power. At the time of writing, Pinochet was conducting legal manoeuvres to avoid being tried in Chile on the charges that might have been brought against him in Spain.

Observers of political law should take note of various factual developments and diverse lines of argumentation which have been intertwined in these complex and multinational proceedings. On one level, this has been a struggle to establish and expand legal principles aiming at the accountability of heads of state and government to law. On other levels, there have been influential political arguments brought to bear on the case. Former British Prime Minister Thatcher repeatedly sought to have Pinochet set free on the exclusively political grounds that he had sided with the U.K. in the war of 1982 with Argentina over the Falkland Islands. Even the Pope was said to have intervened in Pinochet's favour.

Despite the seeming difficulty of distinguishing the core of this case from the mountains of paper relating to it, the importance and fundamental significance cannot escape. Heads of State are subject to law and accountable to it. They remain so even into retirement.

> Moreover, there is a strong countervailing argument: the ease with which dictators have escaped any consequences for their crimes has encouraged more to seize power and to commit further barbarities. Latin America, in particular, has been plagued by military coups. If a dictator forces democrats to grant him an amnesty at home, as General Pinochet did, that is where he ought to stay. The rest of the world is not bound to grant a blanket endorsement to such bad bargains. Putting ex-dictators on trial carries short-term political risks. But this bloody century has shown that the long-term risk of impunity have been far more terrible.[182]

> And the real significance of the Pinochet case goes much further than this. Although a clutch of human-rights treaties passed since the second world war have supposedly outlawed murder, torture and arbitrary arrest by governments, dictators all over the world have continued to employ such methods with impunity, safe in the knowledge that, even if they lost power, they were beyond the reach of any law. The Pinochet case has changed that forever.

> Despite all the confusion surrounding the case, there is no doubt that it constitutes a landmark in international law. Two separate panels of Law Lords, members of one of the most cautious supreme courts in the world, have found that a former head of state is not, as many previously thought, immune from prosecution for crimes against humanity.[183]

Lawless dictators, take note!

See also *Prosecution of President Muammar Khadafi*, Cour de Cassation de la Belgigne, Chambre criminelle, Arrêt no. 1414 du 13 mars 2001.

---

[182] "Ex-dictators are not immune," *The Economist*, November 28, 1998, p. 16.
[183] "Releasing Pinochet," *The Economist*, January 15, 2000, p. 21.

§ 11.9.C.2
Prosecution of Slobodan Milosevic
International Criminal Tribunal for the Former Yugoslavia
started February 12, 2002; in progress

There can be no doubt that the trial of Slobodan Milosevic, the former Head of State of Yugoslavia, is one of the most, if not the most, significant proceedings ongoing at the time of writing in the realm of accountability to law and legal accountability to democracy.

Milosevic can best be described as the leading figure among the Serbs of Yugoslavia throughout the late 1980's and the 1990's. During his tenure of office, Yugoslavia disintegrated under the pressure of Serbian nationalism and expansionism, successive civil wars involving Croatia, Bosnia-Herzegovina and Kosovo and, of particular interest, ethnic cleansing in various parts of former Yugoslavia. On May 24, 1999, the Chief Prosecutor of the *International Criminal Tribunal for Former Yugoslavia* (ICTFY) Louise Arbour,[184] issued an indictment for Milosevic. On April 1, 2001, he was arrested and extradited to the Netherlands to stand trial.

The principal document of indictment is dated June 29, 2001, and was authored by Arbour's successor as Prosecutor, Carla del Ponte. It accuses Milosevic of genocide, crimes against humanity, grave breaches of the *Geneva Convention*, as well as violations of the laws and customs of war. There are also other indictments which were issued later. Milosevic's trial opened on January 12, 2002. Its progress is slow, if deliberate; its duration is unpredictable. At present, we can lay out the significant issues at stake without yet dealing with the results for political law arising out of a judgment.

The core of the issue is the role law plays, the role law is accepted by civilized society as playing, and the role law is expected to play, in moderating political and ethnic excesses cloaked as the exercise of sovereignty, or disguised as the defence of society from alleged hostile forces. Prosecutor Del Ponte's opening address to the ICTFY contained the most powerful explanation of this position.

---

[184] At the time of writing, Arbour had finished a stint as one of the Justices on the Supreme Court of Canada and had become the United Nations Commissioner for Human Rights.

The law is not a mere theory or an abstract concept. It is a living instrument that must protect our values and regulate civilized society and for that we must be able to enforce the law when it is broken.

. . .

This tribunal and this trial in particular, gives us the most powerful demonstration that no-one is above the law or beyond the reach of international justice.[185]

The eminent truth of this statement reinforces the necessary moderating and channelling influence legality exercises within political life, up to the highest levels of governance.

This prosecution also focuses attention on the proper forum for dealing with such issues. The ICTFY was established under the *aegis* of the United Nations, on the basis of the approval of the Security Council permanent members, the Great Powers. Milosevic himself never recognized the jurisdiction of the Tribunal, but he has *de facto* been forced to attorn to it by responding to the charges against him. It was during the functioning of this tribunal that the International Criminal Court was established in Rome, potentially to handle such cases. Nevertheless, the United States has consistently opposed the setting up of any permanent tribunal, for fear of politicized prosecution involving its soldiers. Thus, although the ICTFY is continuing to function, there is doubt as to the forum which could or would handle other similar cases.

The basic principle of the subjugation of political figures, even at the highest level, to legal norms is established. The mechanics of its application are still in a state of controversy and uncertainty. The prosecution ended its case on February 25, 2004. The court then adjourned for three months to allow Milosevic to prepare his defence.

See also *Milosevic Action in Dutch National Court to Prevent Detention* and *Bosnian Case Against NATO Bombing of Serbia*, European Court of Human Rights, filed October 24, 2001.

---

[185] Transcript: Carla del Ponte's address, BBC News; February 12, 2002, http://news.bbc.co.uk/hi/english/world/europe/newsid_1816000/1816719.stm, last consulted September 8, 2004.

11.10 ISSUE: PROFESSIONAL ETHICS OF HEADS OF STATE AND GOVERNMENT

§ 11.10.1
Starr v. Ontario (Commissioner of Inquiry)
Supreme Court of Canada; April 5, 1990
(1990), 68 D.L.R. (4th) 641
-and-
Starr v. Ontario
Ontario Court (General Division)
filed July 5, 1990; file no. 51523; settled

Even in a democratic political legal regime and an open society, it is inevitable that the temptation of money, benefits and perks of all sorts will prove irresistible to some public officials and to those having close dealings with them. The question most pertinent to dealing with this reality is then not how to attempt to use law to eradicate it, as that is already the domain of criminal law, but rather how best and most properly to investigate such incidents, and how to bring to public light the facts and circumstances surrounding them. This is particularly significant in a federal state such as Canada, in which subject-matter jurisdictional issues arise. Whether in Canada or in other countries, however, only institutions which are involved in public decision-making but are bound to administer law and to interpret its ethical foundations, as well as aloof from politics, as are the courts, can determine the appropriate criteria for retaining the most senior public officials along the path of their obligations to the public they are meant to serve.

At the time of administration of the Liberal Premier of Ontario, David Peterson, Gordon Ashworth was the executive director of the Premier's Office and Patricia Starr was the president and chair of the Toronto section of a Canada-wide women's organization. Starr was also associated with a private sector company called Tridel. Starting with a February 15, 1989 story in the *Globe and Mail* there were published allegations that Start and Tridel had relationships of a financial nature with Ashworth and other elected and unelected public officials. The Premier himself was never implicated but the allegations about members of his political entourage did affect him and on June 22, 1989, Ashworth resigned.

Several investigations were initiated. Among them, on July 6, 1989, a commission of inquiry with a single commissioner, Mr. Justice Lloyd Houlden, was established pursuant to the *Public Inquiries Act*.[186] It was the terms of reference of the Houlden Inquiry which led to this litigation. The task assigned was, generally, to investigate the nature and extent of Starr's and Tridel's dealings with elected and unelected public officials, and to inquire into whether benefits or advantages were conferred on public officials. At the very beginning of the Commission's work, Starr asked the Commissioner to state a case regarding the competence of the Province of Ontario to establish the inquiry and the potential effects of the inquiry on individual rights. Upon Houlden's refusal to state this case, that is to obtain judicial clarification of the matter, Starr appealed but the Divisional Court and the Ontario Court of Appeal both denied the remedy she sought.

The Supreme Court of Canada took a different view and concluded that the inquiry was beyond the powers of Ontario to establish because of the way the commissioner's terms of reference were worded. At first impression, this judgment is based on principles of federalism. The court devoted great emphasis to the analysis of the pith and substance of the legislative provisions and to the precedents relevant to the establishment of commissions of inquiry. On these bases, it concluded that the Houlden Inquiry was in fact a substitute police investigation in respect of specific criminal offences replacing procedures that would otherwise have been conducted in the course of criminal investigation and procedure pursuant to the *Criminal Code*. That Code and the subject matter of criminal law was in the federal domain. In this regard, the fact that Starr and Tridel were named in the terms of reference, and what the court referred to as the striking resemblance between those terms and section 121(b) of the *Criminal Code* were cited as specific problems. The court concluded that there was here an encroachment on the federal criminal law power.

> In sum then, I find unpersuasive the argument that this inquiry is solidly anchored in s. 92(4), (7), (13) or (16) of the *Constitution Act, 1867*. There is nothing on the surface of the terms of reference or in the background facts leading up to the inquiry to convince me that it is designed to

---

[186] R.S.O. 1980, c. 411.

restore confidence in the integrity and institutions of government or to review the regime governing the conduct of public officials. Any such objectives are clearly incidental to the central feature of the inquiry, which is the investigation and the making of findings of fact in respect of named individuals in relation to a specific criminal office. It is to that aspect of my analysis that I now turn.[187]

In these circumstances, allowing the Commission to continue would be to assimilate the Commissioner's role to that of a judge.

The foregoing analysis by the court must be read, however, not only as an indication of what could not and ought not to have been done in the present instance by Ontario. It must be read positively, so as to derive indications regarding the proper way this, and by implication other similar investigations, should be constituted. The court picks up on some of the pleadings of counsel intervening on behalf of the Government of Ontario, who emphasized that inquiries must be aimed at the "good government of Ontario."[188] It thus mentions the integrity of the institutions of government as being required to be the central feature of an inquiry, rather than merely incidental.

Based on this kernel, the court further develops the notion of the proper role of public inquiries and of the appropriate manner in which they are to be set up.

> There is no doubt that commissions of inquiry at both the federal and provincial level have played an important role in the regular machinery of government. Their history is well documented by numerous authors:
>
> . . .
>
> Most authors seem to agree that public inquiries serve a number of functions including enabling government to secure information as a basis for developing or implementing policy, educating the public or legislative branch, investigating the administration of government and permitting the public voicing of grievances. Investigatory commissions in particular serve to supplement the activities of the mainstream institutions of government.[189]

---

[187] (1990), 68 D.L.R. (4th) 641 at 669 a-b.
[188] Ibid. at 667 e.
[189] Ibid. at 673 e and g-h.

After the Supreme Court of Canada rendered this judgment quashing the inquiry, Starr was charged with fraud, uttering forged documents and 34 counts of violating the *Election Finances Act*. In an effort to resist these charges, she herself initiated legal action against the Province, the Premier and the Attorney General on July 5, 1990, in which she sought a total of $3 million in general, special and punitive damages. In the first version of the statement of claim, she even attempted to make the Executive Council a defendant. In this action, Starr, who described herself as a politically active individual, alleged that a press release of June 22, 1989, issued by Premier Peterson constituted defamation and libel of her and "was intended to inflame public perception"[190] of her involvement in a perceived scandal. She also claimed, basing herself on the Supreme Court ruling, that the Houlden Inquiry amounted to malicious prosecution and that that Inquiry was set up for the purpose of persecuting her and causing her embarrassment, all so as "to deflect criticisms away from the defendants in the political arena in the midst of perceived government scandals."[191] This lawsuit was settled privately; we may presume that Ontario agreed to pay Starr's legal fees and expenses in relation to the inquiry.

---

§ 11.10.2[192]
Mulroney v. Canada (Attorney General) et al.
Québec Superior Court
filed January 29, 1996; file no. 500-05-012098-958
settled January 6, 1997

Brian Mulroney was Prime Minister of Canada, at the head of two successive majority Progressive Conservative governments from September 4, 1984, until June 25, 1993. During that time, the Government of Canada, under his leadership, adopted and implemented a number of policies and programs that were dramatically different from those of his predecessors. Throughout the period, among segments of the opposition parties, the media and public opinion, doubts were expressed about the public ethics of Mulroney himself and of several members of his government. In fact, a number of ministers were forced to resign in disgrace because of conflicts of interest or attempts at personal enrichment at public expense. There were also

---

[190] Statement of claim, para. 19.
[191] *Ibid.*, para. 29(a).
[192] Cross-reference to § 10.9.6.

a number of other incidents of allegations of impropriety which were not or could not be proven.

Among the unsubstantiated allegations, the most serious one by far was that against Mulroney himself, in the so-called Airbus scandal, which arose in the years following the resignation of the Prime Minister and the subsequent general election in which the Progressive Conservative Party suffered the most drastic loss in Canadian political history at the hands of the Liberal Party, led by Jean Chrétien. The matter had its roots in an investigation undertaken by the Royal Canadian Mounted Police (R.C.M.P.) and in the investigative journalism of a television program of the Canadian Broadcasting Corporation (CBC) entitled "The Fifth Estate." In March 1995, The Fifth Estate reported that Mulroney, Frank Moores, a former Premier of Newfoundland and a businessman named Schreiber were jointly involved in a scheme to collect secret commissions on the sale of 34 Airbus A320 aircraft from Airbus Industries to Air Canada. The report subsidiarily contained further allegations regarding secret commissions derived from the proposed establishment of an armaments factory by Thyssen Industrie in Nova Scotia and the sale to the Canadian Coast Guard of helicopters by the Messerschmitt Company. The R.C.M.P. made The Fifth Estate report part of its own investigation.

In order to gather evidence to see if crimes had been committed, the police needed to follow the trail of the money allegedly secreted away. Toward that end, on September 29, 1995, under the signature of the Director of the International Assistance Group in the Department of Justice, Canada sent a Letter of Request to the Competent Legal Authority of Switzerland, asking them to provide all banking information for any accounts allegedly related to the various suspect transactions, to provide documentary evidence regarding those accounts and any safety deposit boxes registered in the names of Mulroney or Moores, as well as to freeze any funds remaining in the accounts until the end of the police investigation.

The most significant, and ultimately most inflammatory passages of the Letter of Request read as follows:

> As Prime Minister, Mr. MULRONEY would have the power to control all the business of the Government of Canada except where the powers have been removed by Statute. The powers would include the ability to

have government contracts approved or to exert influence upon the Minister responsible for the approval of the contract. He would have the power to appoint and dismiss Ministers who would not cooperate with his wishes. His duties were to administer the business of government in the best interests of Canadians.

. . .

On March 13, 1985, Mr. MULRONEY appointed Mr. MOORES to the Board of Directors of Air Canada. The R.C.M.P. has reliable information that Mr. SCHREIBER was given these commissions in order to pay Mr. MULRONEY and Mr. MOORES to ensure that Airbus Industrie obtained a major contract with Air Canada for the planned upgrade of their aircraft fleet.

. . .

The RCMP has been advised that Frank MOORES went to the Schweiz-erischer Bankverein Zurich in Zurich, Switzerland in 1986 or 1987 to open two bank accounts numbered 34107 and 34117, the latter account using password "Devon." The account 34117 was opened to channel a portion of the funds to Mr. MULRONEY.

. . .

The reports then imply that the funds were transferred to MOORES' accounts at the same bank as payments for Mr. MOORES' and Mr. MULRONEY's assistance in obtaining the contract.

. . .

The RCMP has seen copies of the documents used in the preparation of the reports by The 5th Estate and Der Spiegel and believes that over 11 million Canadian dollars were paid by Airbus Industrie to IAL's account in Liechtenstein then transferred to IAL's account in Zurich between 1988 and 1991. The documents ended in 1991, however the confidential source believes that the payments continued until Mr. MULRONEY resigned from office. The agreement between IAL and Airbus Industrie is believed to have resulted in commissions of approximately 20 million U.S. dollars once all 34 aircraft had been received. A confidential source has told the RCMP investigator that 25 percent of those commissions were to pay Mr. MULRONEY.

. . .

These payments would have begun when the initial contract was signed between Airbus Industrie and IAL in March, 1985 and continue until the option to buy further aircraft expires in 1996. The contract is reported to contain a clause which states that the commissions will cease when the political situation changes in Canada. Mr. MULRONEY resigned as Prime Minister just prior to the Federal election held on October 25, 1993 and it is assumed that his resignation would have terminated the contract.

. . .

The commissions received by Mr. SCHREIBER, Mr. MOORES and Mr. MULRONEY would have increased the cost of the aircraft purchased by Air Canada thereby defrauding the Canadian public of their tax money.

. . .

The above three cases demonstrate an ongoing scheme by Mr. MULRONEY, Mr. MOORES, and Mr. SCHREIBER to defraud the Canadian Government of millions of dollars of public funds from the time Mr. MULRONEY took office in September, 1984 until he resigned in June, 1993.[193]

The contents of that Letter very quickly became public knowledge and created great sensation throughout Canada. The allegations and Mulroney's predictable outrage and denials were widely reported in the media.

The former Prime Minister did not stop at exculpatory expressions. On November 20, 1995, he initiated legal proceedings against the Attorney General of Canada, the Department of Justice lawyer who had prepared and signed the letter, the Commissioner of the R.C.M.P. and the police officer in charge of the investigation. The actual terms of the case he was making were contained in the Declaration, the final version of which was filed in Québec Superior Court on January 29, 1996.

---

[193] Letter of Request to the Competent Legal Authority of Switzerland, Department of Justice Canada, September 29, 1995, extracts from pp. 4 through 8, from the section entitled "Summary of the Facts."

Mulroney was not reticent in describing himself in the imperial style he had adopted during his time in public office.

1. Le demandeur fut Premier ministre du Canada pendant près de neuf (9) ans;

2. Il est un avocat de stature internationale et est un des associés principaux de l'un des plus prestigieux cabinets d'avocats canadiens;

. . .

4. La stature internationale du demandeur à titre d'ancien homme d'état et d'avocat universellement connu lui donne accès à un cercle select et extrêmement exclusif de chefs d'états et de décideurs d'affaires d'envergure mondiale et lui fait bénéficier d'un considérable achalandage de mandats importants et prestigieux;[194]

The core of Mulroney's case is that the allegations contained in the Justice Letter to the Swiss authorities are totally false and, because of the number of individuals and institutions who were made aware of it, they increased exponentially the risk of their divulgation to the media.

8. Cette demande d'aide, adressée par le gouvernement canadian au gouvernement suisse, contient de très graves allégations à l'encontre du demandeur, toutes totalement fausses;

. . .

11. Toutes les allégations précitées relatives au demandeur sont fausses, et ont été formulées à son encontre par les défendeurs, qui les savent générées par de la spéculation médiatique, qui se savent totalement incapables d'en prouver quelqu'une et qui se montraient totalement indifférents à l'impact désastreux qu'elles auraient sur la réputation du demandeur auprès du gouvernement suisse, auprès de la communauté d'affaires suisse qui devait nécessairement en recevoir copie et auprès de l'opinion internationale qui ne pouvait manquer d'en être saisie, considérant les circonstances ci-après décrites;[195]

Mulroney went on to deny that he had ever had a Swiss, or any other foreign, bank account, that he had received the alleged commissions,

---

[194] Déclaration précisée, January 29, 1996, paras. 1, 2 and 4.
[195] Ibid., paras. 8 and 11.

that he had in any way influenced Air Canada in its purchasing decisions or that he had collaborated in such a scheme with Moores or Schreiber.

Mulroney's position was that the justice and police authorities based their investigation on media reports, without first attempting to verify them. His Declaration detailed the attempts of his legal counsel to obtain the original text which had been sent to the Swiss authorities, which was allegedly denied, as well as the offer made on Mulroney's behalf to co-operate with the investigation within Canada, the offer which was allegedly refuted.

Mulroney took issue even with that part of the letter which set out the Prime Minister's role in Canadian governance.

> 19. La description par les défendeurs de la fonction de Premier ministre est fausse, trompeuse, non fondée en droit et représente une vision triturée du fonctionnement du gouvernement canadien, laissant l'impression aux lecteurs étrangers que l'appareil gouvernemental canadien est en fait chapeauté par l'individu détenant le poste de Premier ministre et ce, en flagrante contradiction avec la Constitution du Canada, la *Loi sur l'administration financière*, la fonctionnement, la constitution et le rôle du Conseil des ministres, du Conseil du trésor et des autres organismes du pouvoir exécutif de l'état canadien;[196]

Further, Mulroney detailed his attempts to get the Canadian authorities to withdraw, or at least to moderate the terms of the letter of September 29, 1995. He set out how, during the second week of November 1995, various media organizations became aware of its contents. On November 18, 1995, the entire letter was in fact published.

On the basis of the foregoing recital, Mulroney concluded that the justice and police officials involved intentionally and recklessly set out to harm him and to wilfully damage his dignity, honour, reputation and right to privacy. He also claimed that his rights under the Québec and Canadian Charters of Rights had been breached, without clarifying the nature of these breaches.

> 36. Les défendeurs Prost et Fiegenwald ont agi de concert, de propos délibérés, sachant que la demande d'aide allait fatalement être publiée

---

[196] *Ibid.*, para. 19.

par les médias, et en ne se préoccupant pas des conséquences dracon-
iennes qu'allait certainement avoir ladite publication dans la presse internationale;

37. Le comportement ci-haut décrit des défendeurs est extraordinaire et
exorbitant du sense commun, ces derniers ayant agi de manière à causer
préjudice au demandeur, encourant ainsi leur responsabilité;

38. Ces allégations constituent de la part des défendeurs des atteintes
illicites et intentionnelles au droit du demandeur à la sauvegarde de sa
dignité, de son honneur et de sa réputation, ainsi qu à son droit au respect
de sa vie privée;

39. L'émission de la demande d'aide, dans les circonstances, constituait
une violation flagrante par l'état canadien et par ses préposés, des droits
fondamentaux du demandeur, tant à l'égard de la *Charte des droits et
libertés de la personne du Québec* qu'en regard de la *Charte canadienne des
droits et libertés* et le demandeur este en droit de requérir, dans la mesure
du possible, pleine et complète réparation du préjudice subi, par la
condamnation conjointe et solidaire des défendeurs pour les dommages
réels subis par le demandeur ainsi que pour les dommages exemplaires
réclamés;[197]

As compensation, Mulroney demanded $25 million general compen-
satory damages and $25 million exemplary damages. This latter
amount was said to be for the purpose of ensuring that Canada would
be a democratic country subject to the rule of law. In addition, Mulroney asked the court to order that a document retracting the allegations and apologizing for them be published in the world's 50
largest daily newspapers.

The Commissioner of the R.C.M.P. and the officer in charge of the
investigation filed their defence on May 23, 1996. This was essentially
based on the facts that a police investigation on the basis of independently obtained information was in progress, that the police could
not base their investigation on media reports and rumours, and that
they therefore needed here, as in many other such cases, to obtain
information relevant to their investigation from the sources which
actually held such information. The police emphasized that they were
carrying out their professional duties and were acting in good faith.
Moreover, they pleaded that Mulroney's claim for damages was

---

[197] *Ibid.*, paras. 36 to 39.

grossly exaggerated and vexatious, in particular in light of the fact that in the pre-trial interrogatory, Mulroney admitted that he had suffered no financial loss at all.

A separate defence was filed on May 24, 1996, by the Attorney General and the Justice official who had originated the Letter requesting assistance. The fundamental element of this pleading was that the investigation required the assistance of the Swiss authorities.

> 68. Contrairement aux affirmations catégoriques du demandeur, la demande d'assistance de la G.R.C. n'est pas la simple restitution de rapports médiatiques, mais est fondée sur des renseignements indépendants jugés assez crédibles pour qu'il soit nécessaire de vérifier s'ils étaient vrais ou faux et cette demande a été précédée d'une enquête minutieuse, dont aucun détail ne peut être révélé à ce stade de l'enquête policière, et ce, pour des motifs d'intérêt public;[198]

The Attorney General also responded that every defendant acted in the execution of statutory duty, fully independently, in good faith, impartially and objectively. Very importantly, the Attorney General affirmed that the letter did not constitute an accusation or charge, and that those receiving it would have the necessary experience to understand it as such, mindful that it was a series of allegations to be proven or disproven in an investigation. He also reiterated that Canadian authorities had taken every precaution to keep the entire process confidential so as to avoid prejudice to the former Prime Minister.

An interesting element of the Attorney General's defence was the allegation that the letter was never made known to him. In order that the impartiality and objectivity of the procedure be maintained, the letter was apparently handled as a routine file. Moreover, considering that those who did participate in the preparation of the file were public servants in the execution of their duty, they could not be held liable in damages.

> 91. Aucun des défendeurs n'a commis aucune erreur de jugement ni aucune négligence professionnelle dans l'exécution de ses fonctions en rapport avec la demande d'assistance ni en rapport avec les interventions de Me Roger Tassé;

---

[198] Défense du Procureur Général du Canada et de Madame Kimberly Prost, May 24, 1996, para. 68.

96. Plus particulièrement et sans restreindre la généralité de ce qui pré-
cède, les quatre défendeurs bénéficient du soi-disant privilège qualifié
("qualified privilege") de la *common law* en vertu duquel les actes qu'ils
ont posés de bonne foi et sans malice dans l'exécution de leur devoir
d'assister la G.R.C. dans son enquête sur des actes criminels ne peuvent
donneer prise à une condamnation pour diffamation;[199]

Pre-trial procedures continued throughout 1996, as did the sustained
high level of public and media interest in the case. The action was
eventually set down for hearing by the Superior Court for January 6,
1997, and it was expected to last three months. Throughout this time,
the information requested of the Swiss authorities was not forthcoming and the police investigation was therefore not completed. Pursuant to the Swiss banking laws, secret proceedings were under way
to prevent disclosure of the information that was being sought.

To general surprise, on the day the trial was due to begin, it was
announced that on the previous day, an out-of-court settlement had
been reached. The Government of Canada issued an apology to Mulroney and agreed to pay his legal bills. In return, Mulroney withdrew
the action. It is suspected that the settlement contained other elements
but given its nature as being confidential to the parties, not everything
is known about it.

The settlement was the subject of extensive reporting. The general
sense was that the case had been mishandled, that individuals in
authority would have to pay a political price and that institutional
changes would also have to be made. The most serious comment was
made in the *Globe and Mail*:

> As befits Mr. Mulroney, who has relied on high-risk strategies in his
> career, the stakes would have been colossal had the trial proceeded.

> While labelled as a defamation suit, the case for the plaintiff relied heav-
> ily on the claim that the government acted in a negligent fashion.

> For Mr. Mulroney, who has charged that he was the victim of a reckless
> partisan action by the Liberal-led government, there was the hope that
> a victory would lead to vindication because he feels his career was
> unfairly judged by Canadian public opinion.

---

[199] *Ibid.*, paras. 91 and 96.

But had Mr. Mulroney lost the case, it could have been a grievous blow to a man who, fairly or not, is still scorned by many Canadians. A loss would have cemented the unpopularity born from a decade in office, an unwelcome twist for the still-fragile Conservative Party as it heads into the next federal election, possibly this year.

Either way, revelations made during the trial could have potentially tarnished the careers of some of the high-ranking politicians, journalists, bureaucrats and police officials who were expected to parade through the witness box.[200]

The paper also drew the most sober and somber conclusions from the Mulroney proceedings.

Clearly, the botched Airbus investigation will have reverberations throughout the criminal-justice system. There will be demand for a new, more transparent and more accountable way to investigate potential criminal activity involving the political system.[201]

The Mulroney libel action deserves extensive study as it encompasses numerous aspects of very great interest for political law.

The first aspect of the case of *Mulroney v. Canada* which has to be noted is its extraordinary nature. Never before in the course of this country's history had a litigation occurred between a head of government, active or retired, and the State itself; the case was thus unprecedented. The allegations on which the action was based, namely those in the letter addressed by the Canadian to the Swiss authorities, related to scandalous and probably criminal behaviour; not only was it unusual, but it was unique in Canadian political life that such a high public figure be open to such charges. The matter was so delicate that had the letter been sent and the action been started during Mulroney's tenure of office, a constitutional crisis may have developed. In conjunction with these characteristics, the matter was extremely controversial. At the time the letter came to public knowledge and the action was instituted, Mulroney's policies and his person still aroused the same bitter political and partisan divisions which had been perceptible in Canadian public affairs at the time of Mulroney's

---

[200] "Mulroney, Ottawa settle suit," Tu Thanh Ha, *Globe and Mail*, January 6, 1997, p. 1 at 4.

[201] "Ex-PM rolls dice, wins again," Hugh Winsor, *Globe and Mail*, January 6, 1997, p. 1 at 4.

resignation in 1993, and which had indeed contributed to his resignation. Public opinion therefore followed the matter with great intensity and partisan fervour.

Next to the controversiality of this action, its politicization was its most prominent feature. From the outset, Mulroney and that segment of public opinion which remained loyal to him perceived the investigation not as being of a legal nature, not as a means of ascertaining whether the former Prime Minister had observed professional ethics while in office and had behaved in a manner accountable to law, but rather as a politically motivated witch-hunt based on party and partisan motivation.

> He insisted, however, that the government went too far in its letter to the Swiss by making blanket statements calling him a criminal and referring to "criminal activity on the part of a former prime minister."

> "This is not an allegation. This is an indictment. This is a statement that the government of Canada has found me guilty of a crime and not only a crime but a crime in the nine years I was in office," he said. "The government has accused me, convicted me and sentenced me."

> "This is a fascist condemnation without the accused being present on the part of the government of Canada."

> . . .

> "A forceful Brian Mulroney yesterday attacked the federal government's investigation into allegations he took bribes, saying it 'reeks of fascism' and 'violates everything Canada stands for.'"[202]

> «Je regrette que M. Mulroney et ses avocats aient utilisé le processus de la cour pour déposer un document politique et faire avancer leurs positions politiques,» a indiqué M. Rock, hier, avant d'assister à la rencontre hebdomadaire du conseil des ministres.[203]

Mulroney's persistent use of hyperbole and inflammatory language contributed to the impression which he wished to create, that the investigation of him was a political ploy.

---

[202] "Mulroney says probe is 'fascist'," William Marsden, *Montréal Gazette*, April 18, 1996.
[203] "Mulroney: Allan Rock nie avoir initié l'enquête," *Le Droit*, June 5, 1996.

From the political law perspective, a closely related and fundamental aspect of the case is the participation of the Minister of Justice in the background of the investigation. The Minister, as well as his official who authored the letter, both indicated that the file had been treated as routine and that the official had not only dealt with the case alone, but had not even informed the Minister. The purpose of this position was to lend credence on the part of the Government to the position that the case against Mulroney was not politicized. While it is within the traditional independence of prosecutorial officials to avoid political influence, the common citizen may react with some scepticism to the contention that in a matter so delicate the Minister in charge of the department was not forewarned of the letter, even if he chose not to eventually be involved in its preparation and transmission. In the absence of a trial, this will unfortunately also remain in the realm of speculation.

The core factual issue at stake was whether a Prime Minister of Canada, while in office, had used his political power and legal expertise for personal enrichment, contrary to the norms of ethical behaviour and to the principles of the accountability of law of high public officials. There is much speculation about the consequences of either finding at the end of a trial, but little acknowledgement of the damage to Canada's political legal system from the mere fact that those around Mulroney and Mulroney himself had acted and had seemed to act in a manner so as to leave themselves open to such charges. Other Prime Ministers of recent decades may have had policies judged to be good or bad and may have practised politics which could be held to be wise or inappropriate. No one had brought into the system public behaviour that could engender legal charges. In order to remedy this peculiar situation, Mulroney's interest was to forestall a finding one way or the other. From the perspective of the importance of public ethics as an aspect of accountability to law, the absence of a finding may, coincidentally, have been better than a finding of Mulroney's guilt.

Another significant aspect of the case revolved around the Department of Justice letter itself. Was this text suitably and carefully enough worded? Reading of the entire document can sustain the Government of Canada's arguments that first, this was an investigatory and not an accusatory document and second, that it, just like similar documents in other cases, was to be treated as confidential by those receiving it. Whether Mulroney's assertion as to its accusatory tone could be proven in court will not likely be known. It is equally inter-esting how the document became public knowledge. Several versions of it are thought to have existed and there were at least English and German language variations of it. It is plausible that capable media researchers informed the public about it; however, there is the pos-sibility that someone in Mulroney's entourage leaked it as a way to render the libel suit possible, in the expectation or the hope that no "smoking gun" evidence could be found and no finding would come out of the process.

The final element of this case that is of interest is the settlement. It is, of course, a legal document in that it puts an end to the court pro-ceedings. Yet in the sense that all the documents which pertain to this case are both legal and political in content and context, the settlement is as well. There is neither an exoneration nor an inculpation of Mul-roney. The *quid pro quo* is the government's apology and payment of Mulroney's considerable legal fees, in return for the termination of the $50 million demand. The government's apology, it is true, does not relate to the contents or tone of the letter, but to the damages which Mulroney and his family may have suffered. In short, this is a pyrrhic victory for either side and allows both to continue to act in their respective interests. The lawsuit came to a politically acceptable conclusion.

While the January 6, 1997, settlement resolved matters between Mul-roney and the State, it did not conclude the entire Airbus affair. The prosecution of Schreiber, one of Mulroney's associates in the scheme, has continued. In fact, in order to enable the R.C.M.P. to continue to pursue this case in respect of Schreiber, the agreement with Mulroney significantly did not include revocation of the Letter of Request. The investigation was therefore not ended, nor even suspended, for years. Thus it remained possible that at some future date, the Government of Canada may find the information required for a prosecution of the former Prime Minister himself. It was only on April 23, 2003 that the R.C.M.P. announced that it was definitively closing the investigation. Nevertheless, this remains one of the cases in Canada where law and politics are most intensely blended.

> Prime Minister Jean Chrétien and former Prime Minister Brian Mulroney squared off yesterday over whether continuing the Airbus probe is po-litically motivated.

"You cannot help but to think that there is something political behind it," Mr. Mulroney was quoted as saying yesterday by spokesman Luc Lavoie. He also was quoted as saying that "the political vendetta behind this is ongoing."[204]

See also *Schreiber v. Canada (Attorney General)*[205] (1999), [2000] 1 F.C. 427 (Fed. T.D.).

---

§ 11.10.3
Report of the Commissioner of Conflict of Interest on the Activities of Don Morin,
Conflict of Interest Commissioner of the Northwest Territories
November 24, 1998
-and-
Morin v. Crawford
Supreme Court of the Northwest Territories; January 14, 1999
(1999), 29 C.P.C. (4th) 362

Participants in political life who have been successful to the extent of achieving the highest political office and who then engage in a pattern of decision-making designed to benefit themselves rather than the public which they are entrusted to govern will not hesitate to use litigation to attempt to forestall the legal sanctions which they must ultimately face. While from an objective point of view it appears that such instances are akin to abuses of the courts by politicians in disparate situations we may be entitled to contemplate whether in the subjective perspective of the offending politician, the attempt to hang on to power is a political or a legal measure. In either interpretation, where the nature of the offence is such that genuine breaches of the rules of professional ethics are concerned, attempted recourse to the law as a means of political survival will usually fail.

In the Northwest Territories (NWT) general election of October 16, 1995, the constituency of Tu Nedhe elected Don Morin, a businessman who had long also been involved in territorial politics. The specificity of the NWT political system is the absence of organized parties. Those elected to the Legislative Assembly govern by consensus. They also

---

[204] "Mulroney denounces Airbus 'vendetta'," Tu Thanh Ha and Robert Matas, *Globe and Mail*, August 19, 1999.
[205] Cross-reference to § 9.9.A and 10.9.

choose a Premier for the Territories in the same fashion. It was in this manner that Morin became Premier on November 22, 1995, taking the additional portfolios of Minister of the Executive Council and Minister responsible for Intergovernmental Affairs.

On February 16, 1998, another Member of the Legislative Assembly, Jane Groenewegen, representing the Hay River constituency, filed a complaint with the NWT Conflict of Interest Commissioner. The complaint consisted of a number of allegations that Morin had exercised his powers as a Member of the Legislative Assembly in a manner so as to benefit himself financially. The legal basis of the complaint was the *Legislative Assembly and Executive Council Act*.[206] Section 81 of that Act provides the complainant and the Member complained against to make representations to the Commissioner, while section 82 authorizes the holding of public hearings. Section 83 establishes upon the Commissioner to deliver a report to the Speaker of the Legislative Assembly.

On November 24, 1998, the Commissioner signed and dated a completed report, as required by law and took the steps necessary to deliver it to the Speaker. In order to enable her to do that, a special session of the legislature needed to be called.

The report turned out to be a scathing condemnation of Morin's actions and of the pattern of corruption he had engaged in. With respect to a number of violations of various provisions of the *Legislative Assembly and Executive Council Act*, the Commissioner indicated how Morin had used his position to betray the trust of the people to the point where he should be reprimanded on no less than seven counts, each of which the Assembly accepted. This conclusion was strengthened by the Commissioner's recommendation that where a Member uses public office to line his own pockets, he betrays the trust of the people to such an extent that his seat in the Legislative Assembly should be declared vacant.

> He brought down his own reputation and the reputation of his office of Premier. He brought down our reputation in the Northwest Territories.

---

[206] R.S.N.W.T. 1988, c. L-5, as amended.

It will take years of work to regain what he has taken away from each of us.[207]

The report went on to discuss and defend the rules involved.

There is nothing major wrong or out of date in the Northwest Territories law on this subject. The Act is clear. The basic principles are: full disclosure—so that conflicts are easy to identify; notice—so that the attention of others is drawn to your conflict and withdrawal—so that you do not become involved in advancing your own interests when you should be serving others. It is not the Act which needs changing here, it is the conduct of the Premier.[208]

The Commission even levelled criticism at Morin's conduct vis-à-vis the Inquiry, indicating that he used it as a means to attack the complainant. Both in the Assembly and at the Inquiry itself, Morin responded to assessment of his accountability to the legislation with personal and general counter threats and bravado, imagining that the questioning of his fulfilment of legal duty was politically motivated. In two separate but pithy sentences, the Commissioner summarized in popular terms the results of her Inquiry. In one part of the conclusions, she indicates that, "Mr. Morin is obliged to govern himself by the standards set out in the Act"[209] while a few paragraphs later, she says that by his performance, Morin simply missed the basic point of avoidance of conflict of interest.

From the perspective of the study, there is an even more pertinent part of the Commissioner's reasoning than her conclusions. The report draws a sharp differentiation of political from private benefit.

Political benefit

There is a clear difference between a private benefit to a Member and a political benefit for a Member which accrues through his efforts on behalf of his or her constituency, and which is acceptable and outside of the scope of conflict of interest legislation.

There is clear evidence that Mr. Morin benefited politically from the transfer of the Bison herd to Fort Resolution.

---

[207] Report of the Conflict of Interest Commissioner in the matter of alleged contraventions by the Member from Tu Nedhe, November 24, 1998.

[208] *Ibid.*, at p. 78.

[209] *Ibid.*, at p. 77.

. . .

The transfer of the herd and the resulting emotional and financial impacts was a triumph for Mr. Morin and the DKFN. But this political benefit is perfectly acceptable and within the normal realm of the political benefit that a successful project would bring for any political leader. It may or may not be open to political analysis, commentary and approval or concern, but it is not a conflict of interest.

. . .

No private benefit

A conflict of interest which would adversely affect the public's view of the integrity of the political process arises where the member directly or indirectly benefits personally through use of his or her office. Because of the emphasis in this Act on the importance of public perception, even a strong appearance of personal benefit accruing from the use of a Member's office may be sufficient to find a violation of the Act.

In the case of the Wood Bison herd, it is clear that there was no direct or indirect personal benefit to Morin arising through his involvement in this project.[210]

With respect to another of the allegations against Morin, the Commissioner is led to analyze the factors that constitute political interference in a proceeding intended by law to be conducted along politically uninvolved lines of public administration. The report, correctly, links breaches of conflict of interest rules to the destruction of public confidence in government and in politicians.

While the Commissioner's report is in itself a matter of interest for political law as being an analysis of the law-politics relationship in the field of public ethics, the case became even more worthwhile of study because of Morin's anticipatory reaction to it. On November 24, 1998, without either Morin, his counsel or the Members of the Legislative Assembly knowing what the report contained, on the day it was due to be delivered to the Speaker, Morin made two applications to the Supreme Court of the Northwest Territories. The first was for an interim injunction to restrain the Commissioner from delivering the report to the Speaker and also sought an order to deliver the

---

[210] *Ibid.*, pp. 10 and 12.

report to the court, to be sealed and held pending the outcome of the second application. That second one was an application for judicial review of the report on the ground that the Commissioner was biased. Both applications were symptomatic of Morin's politically motivated and confrontational style.

The court dismissed Morin's first application on November 25, denying the validity of every argument he raised. The first issue seized by the court was the timing of the application for injunction based on the allegation of bias. In its view, this application ought to have been made earlier, that the issues of natural justice should have been dealt with before the inquiry started, or while it was proceeding. Raising the matter on the day the report was scheduled for delivery was too late.

The second point, namely the separation between judicial and legislative functions, was much more significant in the court's view. The conflict of interest provisions in the legislation provide for the report to be dealt with, that is accepted or rejected, by the Legislative Assembly. They amount to a complete code and the court was loath to interfere into the sphere of the legislature. Thus, the court felt that the applicant ought to take his complaints to the floor of the House once the report was tabled. That was the proper alternative forum.

In this regard, the court offered some perceptive advice on the balance of convenience issue as well.

> I recognize and I appreciate that for anyone in public life, merely the publication of a report...

> I recognize that if there is, then the mere publication of the report could have serious harm to the applicant's personal and political reputation. One could say that suffering the slings and arrows of outrageous fortune is part of the job of being a politician. But on a more serious note, when I consider the question of irreparable harm and balance of convenience, I have to consider the public interest. It is not in the public interest to drag out this process. It is not in the public interest to have a process that was put into place by the legislature itself, that has now been carried on for several months, to be all of a sudden side-railed by a last-minute application. The legislators, as the representatives of the public, have put this process in place, and therefore the process should be allowed to play out. it is not in the public interest to have a cloud hanging over one of the political leaders of this territory. It is not in Mr. Morin's interest

to continue having a cloud hanging over his head, and certainly not in the interest of his constituents.[211]

In effect, the court held that the public interest in knowing the contents of such reports outweighed politicians' interest in delaying publication, which would leave everyone in uncertainty.

The final *ratio* of the decision dealt with the parliamentary privilege of the Legislative Assembly. Now that the Commissioner had written the report and only physical delivery was in question, the Commissioner's role was completed and she was *functus*. Consequently, the court had no role to play and it should not interfere in that of the legislature.

> The legislature has reserved to itself the ultimate decision on whether or not to accept any recommendation of the Commissioner.
>
> . . .
>
> They still have the ultimate power to say whether or not they accept a recommendation should there be a recommendation for a penalty. So this ultimate reservation of that power suggests to me that clearly this whole process is part of the exercise of that privilege; that the Court should be very loath to even consider entering into that area.[212]

On November 26, 1998, one day after the report was delivered, Morin resigned as Premier, although he hung onto his seat.

Morin's second application, the one for judicial review of the inquiry and its report, argued that there was a denial of natural justice. In response, the Commissioner applied for summary dismissal of the application on the ground that the court had no jurisdiction because the matter fell within the ambit of the privileges of the Legislative Assembly. The Northwest Territories Supreme Court gave the issue extensive consideration and heard not only from the parties but also from legal counsel for the Legislative Assembly itself. Ultimately, it found that the Assembly was the master of its own rules, including those in respect of conflicts of interest. The Commissioner thus got the dismissal she had sought.

---

[211] *Morin v. Crawford*, Transcript of an unedited and unreported decision delivered by Justice J. Z. Vertes, November 25, 1998, pp. 4 and 5.

[212] *Ibid.*, p. 6

Mr. Morin's counsel argued that a political forum such as the legislature is not the appropriate one in which to debate the methods and findings of the Commissioner. There is the danger of political interests influencing any decision. Counsel referred me to the comments of one of the judges on the 1878 *Landers* case (at page 213):

> "One of the most important principles underlying the successful and proper administration of justice is that those who pass upon the facts, and those who expound the law, should be without interest or prejudice; and how, then, are such principles maintained when the same excited (it might be political) majority occupied at the same time the position of accusers and judges. I am told such is the case in the House of Commons in *England*; but I answer, first, that a body like the latter, numbering hundreds, drawn from the first-class men of the kingdom, actuated by the highest aspirations, and supported, resting on and reflecting, day by day, the *highest toned public opinion*, is not to be compared with a Provincial Assembly, drawn, as a rule, not from the ranks of first-class public men, and whose numbers, being comparatively small, may be expected to become more bitterly excited by political squabbles, and whose supporters on both sides, out of the Legislature, would, in many cases, subordinate their judgments to their political proclivities, and thus a suitable controlling public opinion could not safely be relied on."

Leaving aside whatever may be meant by "first-class men of the kingdom," I think the simple response to this argument is that the legislators, as a collective body, chose this process. The members collectively bound themselves to it. The question of conflicts of interest, while of the utmost public interest, is inherently also an internal matter, one that goes to the very nature of the role of members. What Mr. Morin has been found guilty of are not "crimes," they are contraventions of internal rules of conduct. Thus those who are part of the collective body may be in the best position to make judgments on these matters.

I think it is fair to say that a political forum would rarely be considered an adequate alternative to the courts for complaints of injustice. That is certainly the case if a citizen was engaged in litigation against the state. But it may not be the case where the parties involved are either members, officers or servants of that political forum and the topic is one that relates to that forum's internal affairs. Debate on the floor of the House draws public attention to the issues and may alter the public's perception of the matters under debate. It may affect the reputation of both a member (such as Mr. Morin) and the Commissioner, for good or bad. The Assembly could be persuaded to reject the Commissioner's recommendations.[213]

See also *Democracy Watch v. Chrétien et al.*, 2004 F.C. 969, July 9, 2004; *R. v. Pilarinos*, 219 D.L.R. (4th) 165 (B.C. S.C.) and *R. v. Pilarinos*, 2002 BCSC 1267 (B.C. S.C.).

---

§ 11.10.4
Prosecution of NATO Secretary General Willy Claes
Cour de Cassation of Belgium; December 23, 1998

The lesson to be drawn from this case is that it demonstrates that issues of public professional ethics can follow senior statesmen from one rung along their careers to another. In the 1980's, Willy Claes was Economics Minister and later Minister of Foreign Affairs in Belgium. On October 17, 1994, Claes became Secretary General of the North Atlantic Treaty Organization (NATO). Notwithstanding Claes' high position in the Alliance or the fact that he was by then no longer a Belgian Parliamentarian, on October 19, 1995, the Chamber of Deputies of the Belgian Parliament voted to indict him on corruption charges; in return for the awarding of contracts in which Claes played a leading role, the Italian helicopter manufacturer Augusta and the French aviation firm Dassault had made secret payments to the Socialist Party, of which Claes was a leader. Following this renvoi by the Chamber to the highest court, on December 23, 1998, Claes was convicted of that part of the case relating to Augusta and given a three-year suspended sentence. It is an aspect of accountability to law that, following the rules of public professional ethics applicable to senior statesmen, rules which may be unwritten but are enforced nonetheless, upon his indictment, Claes had to resign immediately from his NATO position. The prosecution arose from his earlier functions, but it broke his position at NATO and ended any prospect of a return to Belgian public life.[214]

---

[213] (1999), 29 C.P.C. (4th) 362 at 393, paras. 98, 99 and 100.

[214] "Le SP n'a pas pu sauver Willy Claes entame sa course en solitaire, Son retour au sommet de la politique Belge est hautement 'improbable,'" *Le Soir*, October 21, 1995, p. 1.

§ 11.10.5[215]

Jones v. Clinton

U.S. District Court, Eastern District of Arkansas; April 12, 1999

36 F. Supp.2d 1118 (E.D. Ark., 1999)

-and-

Jones v. Clinton

U.S. District Court, Eastern District of Arkansas; July 29, 1999

57 F. Supp.2d 719 (E.D. Ark., 1999)

This case was an afterthought to the substantive legal duel which first arose from the allegations of Jones against President Clinton and which eventually led to the impeachment trial in the Congress of the United States. Nonetheless, it did provide a significant point of law in regard to the subjection of the President to the rules of contempt of court. This case was also important in that the judgment was rendered with the court's complete awareness of the political nature of the overall proceedings.

It was in the course of the substantive *Jones v. Clinton* litigation that, at a hearing held on January 12, 1998, the court first heard of allegations relating to a sexual relationship between Clinton and White House intern Monica Lewinsky. The President then denied the allegation but later admitted it in his grand jury testimony of August 17, 1998, and his subsequent address to the Nation in the media. This discrepancy led the court to consider whether Clinton had, by lying at the hearing of January 12, committed contempt. The court waited for the impeachment hearings in Congress to conclude and once these were over, it undertook its own determination on the contempt issue. The first point of unusual interest was that the court held this investigation *sua sponte*, of its own volition.

The judge asked directly whether a President of the United States could be held in civil contempt of court and be sanctioned therefore. She first addressed the constitutional aspect of the matter.

> Nevertheless, this Court has considered the matter and finds no constitutional barrier to holding the President to civil contempt of court in this case and imposing sanctions.

---

[215] Cross-reference to § 10.7.4 and 11.9.A.3.

This lawsuit involved private actions allegedly taken by the President before his term of office began, and the contumacious conduct on the part of the President was undertaken in his role as a litigant in a civil case and did not relate to his duties as President. Both the Court of Appeals for the Eighth Circuit and the Supreme Court held in this case that the Constitution does not place the President's unofficial conduct beyond judicial scrutiny. In so ruling, the Court of Appeals specifically rejected the President's argument that "because a federal court will control the litigation, the Third Branch necessarily will interfere with the Executive Branch through the court's scheduling orders *and its powers to issue contempt citations and sanctions.*" *Jones v. Clinton*, 72 F.3d at 1361 [Emphasis added].[216]

Next, she went through the points of the President's testimony with precision. She found that he gave false, misleading and evasive answers that were designed to obstruct the judicial process.

The most important point is that the court was aware of the politicized nature of the entire litigation and realized that the President had given his replies to questions because he treated the lawsuit as having been politically inspired. Was a politically motivated lawsuit justification for giving legally false or contemptuous replies to interrogatories?

> Certainly the President's aggravation with what he considered a "politically inspired lawsuit" may well have been justified, although the Court makes no findings in that regard. Even assuming that to be so, however, his recourse for the filing of an improper claim against him was to move for the imposition of sanctions against plaintiff. See, e.g., *Clinton v. Jones*, 520 U.S. at 708-09, 117 S.Ct. 1636 (noting the availability of sanctions for litigation directed at the President in his unofficial capacity for purposes of political gain or harassment). The President could, for example, have moved for sanctions pursuant to Fed.R.Civ. P. 11 if, as he intimated in his address to the Nation, he was convinced that plaintiff's lawsuit was presented for an improper purpose and included claims "based on 'allegations and other factual contentions [lacking] evidentiary support' or unlikely to prove well-grounded after reasonable investigation."*Id.* at 709 n. 42, 117 S.Ct. 1636 (quoting Fed.R.Civ.P. 11(b)(1), (3)). The President never challenged the legitimacy of plaintiff's lawsuit by filing a motion pursuant to Rule 11, however, and it simply is not acceptable to employ deceptions and falsehoods in an attempt to obstruct the judicial process, understandable as his aggravation with plaintiff's lawsuit may have been.

---

[216] 36 F. Supp.2d 1118 at 1124 (E.D. Ark., 1999).

. . .

> In sum, the record leaves no doubt that the President violated this Court's discovery Orders regarding disclosure of information deemed by this Court to be relevant to plaintiff's lawsuit. The Court therefore adjudges the President to be in civil contempt of court pursuant to Fed.R.Civ.P. 37(b)(2).[217]

With the argument of political justification being denied to the President, the court could come to no other conclusion but that of adjudging the President to be in contempt, pursuant to the Federal Rules of Civil Procedure. The Court did so, with comments it deemed necessarily added.

> The Court takes no pleasure whatsoever in holding this Nation's President in contempt of court and is acutely aware, as was the Supreme Court, that the President "occupies a unique office with powers and responsibilities so vast and important that the public interest demands that he devote his undivided time and attention to his public duties." *Clinton v. Jones*, 520 U.S. at 697, 117 S.Ct. 1636. As noted earlier, however, this Court has attempted throughout this case to apply the law to the President in the same manner as it would apply the law to any other litigant, keeping in mind the duties and status of the Presidency and the "high respect" that is to be accorded his office. See *Clinton v. Jones*, 520 U.S. at 707, 117 S.Ct. 1636. In that regard, there simply is no escaping the fact that the President deliberately violated this Court's discovery Orders and thereby undermined the integrity of the judicial system.[218]

In a further Order focused on the issue of the sanctions to be imposed on the President as a result of the contempt finding, the court made additional telling observations. It agreed that the discovery had been conducted with intensity and contentiousness. It referred to the President's replies as contemptuous even though the plaintiff had characterized them as contemptible. The underlying action having been dismissed, it decided to rely on compensatory punishment only. It did feel, however, that sanctions were appropriate not only to redress the President's wilful misconduct but also to deter others who, in emulating the President, would engage in misconduct that would undermine the integrity of the judicial system. This having been clarified, the court reiterated that "it takes no pleasure in imposing con-

---

[217] *Ibid.*
[218] *Ibid.*

tempt sanctions against this Nation's President and, no doubt like many others, grows weary of this matter."[219]

11.11 ISSUE: OBLIGATION OF GOVERNMENT TO OBSERVE LEGAL NORMS

11.11.A—PREVALENCE OF LEGAL NORMS OVER OTHER WRITTEN NORMS

See *Carey v. Ontario* (1983), 1 D.L.R. (4th) 498 (Ont. C.A.), reversed [1986] S.C.J. No. 74 (S.C.C.) and *Commission of the European Communities v. Greece*,[220] European Court Reports, 2000, page I – 5047, Case C-387/97.

11.11.B—APPLICATION OF LEGAL NORMS EVEN IN THE ABSENCE OF TEXTS: «PRINCIPES GÉNÉRAUX DU DROIT»[221]

See *Affaire Syndicat général des ingénieurs-conseils*, Conseil d'État, le 26 février 1959; *Affaire Fédération nationale des syndicats de police*, Conseil d'État, le 24 novembre 1961 and *Affaire Demoiselle Arbouset, Conseil d'État*, le 2 mars 1973.

11.11.C—PREVALENCE OF LEGAL NORMS OVER POLITICAL INTERESTS

See *Alberta Teachers' Assn. v. Alberta*, 1 Alta. L.R. (4th) 361 (Alta. Q.B.) and *Legal Consequences of the Construction of a Wall in the Occupied Palestinian Territory (Request for an Advisory Opinion)*,[222] International Court of Justice, Advisory Opinion, July 9, 2004; General List, No. 131 and *Beit Sarrik Village Council v. The Government of Israel*, HCJ 2056/04, Supreme Court of Israel, June 30, 2004.

---

[219] 57 F. Supp.2d 719 (E.D. Ark., 1999) at, p. 18 of unedited version.
[220] International comparison.
[221] International comparisons.
[222] International comparison.

11.11.D—APPLICATION OF DOMESTIC LEGAL WRIT TO FOREIGN GOVERNMENTS

See *Bouzari v. Iran (Islamic Republic)* (2002), [2002] O.J. No. 1624 (Ont. S.C.J.), affirmed (2004), 2004 CarswellOnt 2681 (Ont. C.A.) and *Arar v. Syria and Jordan*, case in progress.

11.12 ISSUE: DIFFERENCE BETWEEN PRIVATE LEGAL OBLIGATION AND PUBLIC ACCOUNTABILITY TO LAW[223]

§ 11.12.1
Link Organisation Plc. v. North Derbyshire Tertiary College and Others
United Kingdom Court of Appeal; August 14, 1998
[1998] EWCA Civ 1400

Link is an organization that provides educational services, while the College is authorized by the United Kingdom authorities to offer vocational qualifications for persons at work. The College drew most of its funding from the Further Education Funding Council (the Council), a public body established pursuant to the *Further and Higher Education Act* of 1992. In July 1995, Link contracted to provide certain educational services to the College. The parties got into a dispute about the performance of the contract and started litigation in the High Court of Justice about the issues of remuneration for the services rendered by Link, and whether the contract was beyond the powers of the College. In order to get around the absence of privity of contract between Link and the Council as the College's funding agency, Link applied to bring the Council in as a defendant to this action. Link's application was aimed at binding the Council in relation to the issues arising out of Link's contract with the College, in a claim that the Council had acted in breach of public law if it refused to fund the obligation on the part of the College toward Link. The High Court agreed to Link's application and that is the ruling under appeal here.

---

[223] Cross-reference to § 1.4, 3.10, 3.11 and 11.13.

The Court of Appeal concentrated first on a proper analysis of the nature of the action.

> Properly understood, therefore, the statement of claim does not seek to make any claim in private law against the Council; and does not on its face make any claim against the Council in public law, as opposed to seeking to establish various matters that, taken together, are expected by Link to have conclusive effect in any foreseeable public law proceedings.

> Two things follow from that analysis. The first is that the joinder of the Council has to be viewed as the asserting of a claim in public law by means of a writ action. The second is that in assessing whether that claim is properly brought, it is necessary to scrutinise the statement of claim to see whether it indeed asserts anything in the nature of a public law claim against the Council.[224]

More importantly still, the court used this case to set out the distinctions between private legal obligations and duties in public law. On the substantive terms, it said that the nature of the legal problem involving is different. The College was potentially liable for its failure to make payments under a private law contract. By contrast, what the Council could hypothetically be responsible for is its failure to act in compliance with the terms of a statute; the test here was whether the Council's conduct was reasonable. In this instance, the attempt to join the Council as a defendant was premature as it "cannot properly be forced into making decisions on at present hypothetical funding issues by being threatened, on public law grounds, in private law proceedings against one of its funded organisations."[225]

Not only is the nature of the case different in private and public law, but so are the procedure and the remedy. In private law, the method of action is by writ. In public law, the claim is for judicial review. In private law, only one who is a party to a contract has *locus* to obtain a declaration, unless exceptional circumstances exist. Conversely, one who is not a party cannot have *locus*, or standing to participate in an action, forced on him by being made a party.

> It has to be accepted that the courts' original [ie private law] jurisdiction to grant declarations is at present narrower than their supervisory [ie

---

[224] [1998] EWCA Civ 1400, p. 5.
[225] *Ibid.*, at p. 7.

public law] jurisdiction. Except in proceedings by the Attorney-General, it is confined to situations where the plaintiff can show that his private rights have been infringed, are threatened with infringement or that he has suffered special damage in consequence of some breach of public duty by the defendant.[226]

In sum, a litigant cannot assert a public law right through a private law action. While some of the procedural aspects of this case may be particular to the legal system of the United Kingdom, the principle to be derived from it, namely that the accountability to law of public institutions and of public officials must be enforced by public law litigation, rather than attempts to use private law remedies, can be taken as more generally applicable throughout democratic legal systems.

11.13 ISSUE: POLITICAL UNPOPULARITY OF LEGAL NORMS[227]

---

§ 11.13.1
Reference re Electoral Divisions Statutes Amendment Act, 1993 (Alberta)
Alberta Court of Appeal; October 24, 1994
(1994), 119 D.L.R. (4th) 1

This was a reference by the Government of Alberta to the highest court of the province, to ascertain whether the electoral boundaries redistribution plan devised by a 1992 Select Committee of the Legislature, which was enacted into law in early 1993, was in conformity with the standards required pursuant to the *Canadian Charter of Rights and Freedoms*. While that case has value as precedent in the issue of redistribution, the evidence regarding the manner in which the Alberta authorities proceeded led the court to even more fundamental and profound considerations on the place of legal norms and values in a political system, on the acceptance by parliamentarians of such norms and values and on their ultimate accountability to observe constitutional and legal parameters in political life.

---

[226] *Supra* note 224, p. 8, quoting from Woolf & Zamir, The Declaratory Judgment, 2nd edition.

[227] Cross-reference to § 1.4, 3.10, 3.11 and 11.12.

The court answered the first question of the reference, as to the *Charter* compliance of the redistribution plan, by indicating that, in the absence of sufficient information, it could not give a reply. The formal version of this part of the answer was qualified by a sentence at the very beginning of the judgment, which, even though couched in judicially cautious terms, left no doubt as to the dissatisfaction of the court with the manner in which the redistribution had been handled. "Despite some hesitation, the court has again decided to refuse to condemn Alberta's electoral boundaries."[228] The "again" in this sentence recalls that the same court had had to refuse to condemn an earlier redistribution plan in a 1991 ruling.[229]

The formal reply to the initial question of the reference continued with a further, very telling sentence: "We do think, however, that there may have been regard for irrelevant considerations."[230] In the context of this study's attention to accountability to the law, this part of the court's reply to the first referred question should be read together with the response of the court to the second issue which it was asked to address, namely to discover in what particulars the electoral division submitted infringed or denied the rights or freedoms guaranteed by the *Charter*. Here, the court gave its most forceful reply, ostensibly in regard to the process of redistribution, but more generally and more pertinently on the issue of accountability to the law:

> Unpopularity of Charter rights is not a valid factor when assessing Charter rights.[231]

This part of the reply was also supported by a statement in the body of the judgment:

> Constitutional rights must be respected even if to do so is momentarily unpopular. We suggest a renewed effort for the next election.[232]

The facts which led to this ruling deserve to be set out. Alberta's electoral divisions had, for a long time, been divided principally along the lines of urban and rural constituencies. Over the past several

---

[228] (1994), 119 D.L.R. (4th) 1 at 2h.
[229] *Reference re Electoral Boundaries Commission Act (Alberta)* (1991), 86 D.L.R. (4th) 447 (Alta. C.A.).
[230] *Supra* note 228 at 19d.
[231] *Ibid.* at 19e.
[232] *Ibid.* at 3b.

decades, the rural areas of the province had been over-represented and as urbanization intensified, the historical distortion became ever more serious. In the years prior to this reference, the courts had been asked to grapple with the matter of the constitutionality and the equitable nature of representation in the Legislature several times. In this instance, the primary documents placed before the court were the report of the 1992 Select Committee of the Legislature which devised the redistribution scheme, and the 1993 statute which gave it force of law.[233]

The court's *ratio* motivating its inability to determine whether the redistribution plan was in conformity with the *Charter* or not, was that the report of the Select Committee merely drew the boundaries of the electoral divisions but provided no reasons for the way these divisions were arranged. The court could thus not look into whether the Select Committee, or the Legislature to which that Committee reported, had used reasons deemed proper in light of the *Charter* and in light of the way the Supreme Court of Canada had indicated the *Charter* should be interpreted on this issue.[234]

Going beyond the absence of formal written reasons, the court did perceive evidence that the Select Committee and the Legislature may have had regard for considerations irrelevant to the *Charter* in drawing the boundaries and that such considerations may have corrupted the constitutional and legal merit of the entire redistribution scheme. What were these irrelevant considerations? They were the unpopularity of the *Charter*-mandated criteria, political sentiment, ideology and electoralist considerations.

In the *Carter* case, the Supreme Court had indicated that while the rule as to representation in Canada was not the "one person – one vote" doctrine evolved in the U.S. system, Canada's brand of "effective representation" entailed that divergences among constituencies could be justified on grounds of geography, community history, community interest and minority representation.

---

[233] *Electoral Divisions Statutes Amendment Act*, 1993, S.A. 1993, c. 2.

[234] *Reference re Provincial Electoral Boundaries*, [1991] 2 S.C.R. 158 (S.C.C.). This is commonly called the *Carter* case after Professor Roger Carter, Q.C., who was the named respondent in conducting the reference.

In the present case, the Alberta Court of Appeal had before it evidence that the considerations which had animated the Select Committee and the Legislature had included:

- public support for the *status quo,* because of community sentiment and familiarity of electors with their Members of the Legislative Assembly;

- the protest of forming communities, based on the rural traditions of the province's population;

- the fear of loss of traditional ridings and of being drowned in huge new ridings;

- the concern of elected officials for the comfort zone of a vocal portion of the electorate;

- the demands upon parliamentarians who would have to travel far from the Legislature; and, ultimately

- the desire to avoid the massive surgery of redistribution designed to achieve effective representation by correcting the widespread and significant imbalance in voting power.

The court reacted to the seeming influence of these considerations in the preparation of the redistribution scheme with a vigorous defence of the *Charter* and a strong statement of the requirements for parliamentarians to observe the legal milestones it constructed.

> While we hesitate to make a firm statement in the absence of detailed reasons, we fear there may well have been regard for an irrelevant consideration. This serious concern proceeds from this basic idea: we do not think it a correct approach to the Charter to exclude unpopular alternatives simply because they are unpopular.
>
> It is one thing to say that, on the facts and for a given community, a deviation becomes a practical necessity; it is quite another to say that existing deviations must remain because significant numbers of voters otherwise will be unhappy. The only fit response to that, in general, should be to remind voters, with Burke, that "the people never give up their liberties but under some delusio (sic)."

While some deviations in Alberta are no doubt inevitable, we see evidence that the practical necessities raised by the principle of effective representation did not, alone, guide the hand of the legislators. On the contrary, what seems to have motivated this scheme at least in part was the acknowledgement that, whether or not some disparities were warranted, change would be made slowly so as not to offend unduly the political sensibilities of some electors.[235]

By contrast to the way the authorities of the province had arrived at the redistribution statute to be referred to the court, the interventions of the Alberta Association of Municipal Districts and Counties, of the Liberal Party of Alberta, of the New Democratic Party of Alberta and of the Alberta Civil Liberties Association were noted by the court. While support for, and opposition to, the redistribution scheme was split among these intervenors, all of their submissions were well grounded in the *Charter*.

The court concluded by reiterating that it would have its own role to play in ensuring that all parties clearly understood through its judgments that legal considerations must take precedence over political ones in applying constitutionally-mandated procedures of governance.

We accept also that part of the problem may have been a lack of clarity in the 1991 decision, which seems to have led some to think that we accepted, as a valid Charter factor, a sensitivity to the complaints of certain voters about the practical effect of enforcement of Charter rights.[236]

A proper reading of this case invites this conclusion: it is one of the pillars of the democratic system that in circumstances in which constitutional and legal considerations compete with political ones, even the governors of the people, the parliamentarians, are accountable to the legal system, despite the potentially greater popularity of political expediencies.

By the time the next provincial election took place on March 11, 1997, a further redistribution scheme had in fact been worked out.

---

[235] *Supra* note 228 at 14 h, 15 a-c.
[236] *Ibid.* at 18 g.

See also *RJR-Macdonald Inc. c. Canada (Procureur général)*, [1995] 3 S.C.R. 199 (S.C.C.) at 328-329.

---

§ 11.13.2
R. v. Bryan
Manitoba Court of Appeal; February 4, 1999
(1999), 170 D.L.R. (4th) 487[237]

The Canadian Wheat Board and the market management system established by the Board have been in existence for several decades. One of the mechanisms put in place by the applicable legislation[238] is the Board's position as the sole authorized exporter of grains from Canada. Farmers wishing to export are required to sell their produce to the Board, which then sells to foreign, including American, buyers. During the latter half of the 1990's, partially as a result of the psychological impact of the *Free Trade Agreement* and of the subsequent *North American Free Trade Agreement*, and partially as a result of the desire of individual grain growers for more directly channelled income, the Board's export monopoly became increasingly unpopular with, and contested by, farmers. When, in response to their demands, the Board refused either to breach the terms of its own legislation by allowing farmers to export cross-border individually, or to seek legislative amendments to enable farmers to achieve the same purpose, several farmers decided to challenge the Board's export monopoly by trucking their products to prospective U.S. buyers without the requisite permits. Bryan was one of those. In consequence, he was indicted of offences under the *Customs Act*.

At the hearing on February 19, 1998, Bryan gave notice that he would challenge the constitutional validity of the legislation. He sought to have sections 32, 45 and 46(d) of the *Canadian Wheat Board Act* and section 4 of the Canadian Wheat Board Regulations, on which the *Customs Act* provisions under which he was charged rested, declared *ultra vires*, as well as to have them declared inoperative, invalid and unenforceable as contrary to sections 1(a) and 2 of the Canadian *Bill of Rights*. The ruling was based primarily on the court's acceptance of

---

[237] Leave to appeal refused (2000), 253 N.R. 194 (note) (S.C.C.).

[238] *Canadian Wheat Board Act*, now R.S.C. 1985, c. C-24, originally S.C. 1935, c. 53. That legislation was in some measure a follow-up to the *Canada Grain Act*, S.C. 1925, c. 33, which established the Board of Grain Commissioners for Canada.

the Crown argument that the monopoly of the Board was validly based on subsection 91(2) of the *Constitution Act, 1867*, the trade and commerce clause. The court also denied the constitutional challenge based on the *Bill of Rights*.

The *Bryan* case was the latest in a number of decisions in which the courts responded to economically and even more politically motivated challenges to the powers of the Wheat Board's legislated monopoly, based on the unpopularity of the law and the scheme it affirmed. In the context of the grounds on which Bryan's constitutional challenge was based, the court thus also took direct notice of the fact that the accused disagreed with the general goals and purposes of the Act. Considering the trend, the court could not ignore that this argument was part of the broader dissatisfaction with the Board's monopoly position which the Act protested. In earlier cases, various other pleadings had been attempted to overturn the monopoly. Here, the court repeated the relevant words from an earlier case in which the Federal Court had held that:

> The applicant has strongly held views about the Canadian Wheat Board's monopoly over the export of wheat. However that is a policy matter and any change must be one for Parliament to make. The role of the Court is to interpret and express the existing law. Under existing law, the applicant's wheat is that contemplated by the *Canadian Wheat Board Act* and unless he obtains a licence from the Board by meeting its requirements, he may not export such wheat.[239]

Here, as in the earlier cases, the arguments against the validity of the legislation that were based on its unpopularity were dismissed.

Before the Manitoba Court of Appeal, Bryan couched his reasoning in more legally cognizable arguments; he pleaded essentially that the relevant provision of the *Canadian Wheat Board Act* was *ultra vires* the Parliament of Canada. He attempted to show that in the context of modern economic and political changes, the Wheat Board had become the dominant marketer of grain in the world and that the trade and commerce power was not sufficient for the federal government

---

[239] *Jackson v. Canada (Attorney General)* (1997), 7 Admin. L.R. (3d) 138 (Fed. T.D.), affirmed (2000), 25 Admin. L.R. (3d) 247 (Fed. C.A.), leave to appeal refused (2001), 270 N.R. 192 (note) (S.C.C.); quoted at [1998] 6 W.W.R. 616 (Man. Q.B.) at 623, affirmed (1999), 170 D.L.R. (4th) 487 (Man. C.A.), leave to appeal refused (2000), 253 N.R. 194 (note) (S.C.C.).

to acquire ownership of a producer's grain on a compulsory basis. The court unhesitatingly rejected this argumentation. Among a variety of other motives based on statutory and jurisprudential reasoning, the court subtly referred to Bryan's political and economic argument.

> The purpose and effect of s. 45 of the *Act* has not essentially changed. The globalization of trade and the political and economic changes that have taken place in Canada and elsewhere since *Murphy* and *Klassen* were decided do not impact on the constitutional validity of the legislation. To the extent that the merits or desirability of such legislation may have changed (and I make no comment in that regard), this is a matter for Parliament and not the courts.

> Section 45 is one of the three supporting pillars of the *Act*—the others being the role of government and the pooling concept. It cannot be severed from the remainder of the legislation without severely destabilizing the overall statutory scheme.[240]

On February 3, 2000, the Supreme Court of Canada dismissed Bryan's application for leave to appeal.[241]

---

§ 11.13.3
Driskell v. Manitoba (Attorney General)
Manitoba Court of Queen's Bench; August 23, 1999
[1999] 11 W.W.R. 615

The purely legal issue for resolution in this case was the right of prison inmates to vote. A provision in the *Manitoba Elections Act*[242] disqualified inmates serving five years or more from voting in a provincial election. Two inmates who fell into this category challenged the constitutionality of the legislation. The court conducted a thorough review of the jurisprudence which, it must be noted, was

---

[240] (1999), 170 D.L.R. (4th) 487 at 496, leave to appeal refused (2000), 253 N.R. 194 (note) (S.C.C.).

[241] At the time of writing, the status of the Canadian Wheat Board was again in doubt, on both domestic and international levels. Within Canada, various farmers expressed the wish to bypass it and Alberta was progressing to legislate on their behalf. In WTO negotiations in early August 2004, Canadian authorities were bargaining the CWB's ordered marketing scheme in return for other countries' reduction of agricultural subsidies.

[242] R.S.M. 1987, c. E30, s. 31.

becoming extensive. It concluded first that the *Elections Act* was not *ultra vires* the province and that this ground of attack failed. However, pursuing on the Crown's concession that the disqualification infringed section 3 of the *Charter*, the court also held that it was not justified under section 1. The objective enunciated for the legislation, namely maintenance and enhancement of the integrity of the electoral process, were found to be vague and poorly defined "although in principle laudable."[243] It also lacked rational connection and proportionality.

This case is one of a long string of judicial pronouncements on inmates' rights, resulting from the consistent refusal of legislative bodies in Canada to accept the *Charter* position on this issue, as enunciated by the courts. Parliamentarians are, in turn, pushed by significant segments of the electorate. In popular parlance, inmates' right to vote had become a political football. The inmates would not desist any more than right thinking citizens outraged by their desire to vote.

These circumstances led the court to assess the circumstances of this judgment as including the following:

> The application places into apparent conflict what are normally complimentary and fundamental pillars of our precious, democratic and free society.
>
> . . .
>
> This application is not a contest between the legislature on the one hand and the courts or the applicants or the *Charter* on the other.[244]

Recognizing that this controversy involved the relationship of legislatures and the judiciary, the court referred to the guarantee for every citizen of the right to vote a core element of the democratic system, subject only to some regulations on capacity and procedure. In protesting that cornerstone, the court was determined to consider the matter according to its proper, that is constitutional and legal criteria. To do this, it analyzed a report prepared by a Committee of the Alberta Legislative Assembly.

---

[243] [1999] 11 W.W.R. 615 at 637, para. 107
[244] *Ibid.* at 620, paras. 2 and 7.

They quoted with approval Chief Justice Fraser and Cote J.A. in *Byatt v. Alberta* (1998), 158 D.L.R. (4th) 644, 661 indicating that the "competing interests here are the serving prisoners on one side, and all other citizens on the other." This narrow view ignores the fact that loosening the rules under which government takes away the vote of (government deemed) undeserving people, threatens the vote of all citizens.[245]

Going beyond this analysis, the court also commented on the reasons for which it found the Committee's report unacceptable.

a) Most people feel prisoners should not vote. Clearly, individual and minority rights in the *Charter* cannot be subject to a popularity test.

b) The legislature should decide the issue. This is couched as "deference to the legislature." This is just a variant of (a) and it is a circular argument. The legislative will cannot on its own cancel *Charter* protection against legislative will.[246]

From the foregoing, it is clear that in matters of public controversy where the legislature adopts the political position that is based on its assessment of the popular will and where the judiciary adopts the legal position grounded on the application of constitutional and legal norms, there is a close linkage between the struggle between branches of government for supremacy over an issue and the political unpopularity of legally required resolution of those issues.

See also *R. v. McSorley*, 2000 BCPC 114 (B.C. Prov. Ct.) and *Commonwealth v. Woodward*,[247] 7 Mass. L. Rep. 449 (Mass. Super., 1997).

11.14   ISSUE: ROLE OF LAWYERS IN GOVERNMENT[248]

See *P.S.A.C. v. Canada (Treasury Board) (Ball, Reinhardt and Bonin)* (October 28, 1985), Doc. 148-2-109, [1985] C.P.S.S.R.B. No. 239 (Can. P.S.S.R.B.).

---

[245] *Ibid.* at 628-629, para. 59.
[246] *Ibid.* at 629, para. 62.
[247] International comparison.
[248] Cross-reference to § 3.10, 3.11, 8.9 and 8.10.

§ 11.14.1
Johnston v. Prince Edward Island
Prince Edward Island Court of Appeal; February 14, 1989
(1989), 73 Nfld. & P.E.I.R. 222

This case deals with the doctrine of solicitor-client privilege as it applies to the government's legal advisors and to the link between that doctrine and the confidentiality of Cabinet documents.

Johnston applied to the Supreme Court–Trial Division for a declaration invalidating certain legislation, and for damages. In the course of those proceedings, Johnston sought access to 34 documents showing matters discussed at Cabinet meetings. Among these, four were legal opinions prepared by Department of Justice lawyers for the Executive Council or Cabinet of the province. Upon the refusal of the Clerk of the Executive Committee to disclose them, Johnston applied to the Trial Division for an order to have the subject documents provided. The Crown claimed privilege. On the ground that the information in the four documents was readily available to a reasonably competent member of the Bar, the court decided to allow disclosure.

The Crown appealed and by this judgment the Appeal Division overturned and maintained the Crown's privilege. Johnston's arguments included that the documents ought to be produced for reasons of public policy, as well as that they were really Cabinet documents and the Crown ought to have sought their protection on that basis. The court specifically rejected the reasoning of the first judgment. It relied, rather, on the general principle stated in the *Crompton* case, to the effect that in this respect, government lawyers are in the same position as their private sector counterparts. The criteria that matters in adjudicating on solicitor-client privilege were that the documents constituted communications between lawyers and their clients, that they entailed seeking or giving legal advice, that they were intended to be treated as confidential and that they did not fall into any category of exceptions to the general rule, such as being for the purpose of facilitating the commission of a crime. The Court of Appeal did not accept Johnston's argument that the facilitation of tortious behaviour should be considered an exception similar to criminal behaviour, as there was only an allegation of such behaviour, but no proof.

The court also considered the public policy issue raised by the fact that the documents requested were for the Cabinet, in the following words:

> The public policy argument arises when a claim for public interest immunity is made, but I do not see where it arises with respect to the documents in question where the solicitor-client privilege is claimed. There is a difference between the solicitor-client privilege, and the claim for public interest immunity and they can not be treated in the same manner. The claim for public interest immunity applies to Cabinet documents which are outside the scope of the solicitor-client privilege.[249]

See also *Nelles v. Ontario*, [1989] 2 S.C.R. 170 (S.C.C.).

---

§ 11.14.2[250]
Canadian Wildlife Federation Inc. v. Canada (Minister of the Environment)
Federal Court of Canada – Trial Division; December 28, 1989
(1989), 31 F.T.R. 1

The essence of the lawyer's function is to tender legal advice and to conduct legal representation, all in the interests of the client. Concomitantly, the lawyer, in his capacity as an officer of the court, must try to ensure that his client abides by the rule of law and observes the requirements of the law. In the public sector, legal advisors must also bear in mind the close link between observance of the law and the service of the public interest. Where lawyers patently act otherwise, the courts will not hesitate to instruct them as to their duty.

In this case, the Minister of the Environment had issued a licence pursuant to the *International River Improvements Act*[251] for the construction, operation and maintenance of the Rafferty-Alameda damming project on the Souris River in Saskatchewan. The Federal Court's Trial Division had quashed that licence and the appeal of that decision had been dismissed. The Minister then initiated an environmental review within his department and proceeded to issue a second licence, all this without conducting a review under the *Environmental*

---

[249] (1989), 73 Nfld. & P.E.I.R. 222, 229 A.P.R. 222 at 227 [24].
[250] Affirmed (1990), 41 F.T.R. 318 (note) (Fed. C.A.). Cross-reference to § 1.3.A.4, 1.3.A.4, 1.3.D.3, 2.2.E.1, 2.6.1 and 11.7.4.
[251] R.S.C. 1985, c. I-20.

Assessment and Review Process Guidelines Order (EARPGO).[252] The present litigation was an attempt to quash that second licence by way of *certiorari* and *mandamus*. The court characterized the issue as being whether the minister had complied with the EARPGO in deciding to issue the second licence and in issuing it. It concluded that he minister had reached the wrong conclusion about the applicability of EARPGO and ought to have conducted that kind of environmental and review process. More significantly, the court also expressed its belief that the minister had been brought to this decision and explicitly rebuked them for their role.

> It is quite evident that the Respondent's department ought to have referred the pertinent proposals, if not the whole project, to the Minister for public review by a panel constituted by him under § 21 and 22 of the EARP Guidelines. Given the determinations of the significant environmental effects expressed in the IEE, the Minister ought lawfully to have subjected the proposals to such public review, as it is clearly mandated by this binding, authoritative legislation. The Minister's advisers ought to have advised him to embrace the EARP Guidelines warmly, instead of seeking ways to abridge or avoid the process.

> . . .

> The evidence discloses that construction is well under way, so there is little doubt that irrevocable decisions have long since been taken while the EARP Guidelines have been circumvented. In effect this appears to be the principal reason for counsel's asking the court to exercise its discretion in favour of dismissing the applications for relief which the applicants with their perfectly solid standing, have brought against the Minister.[253]

While the court refers only to "the Minister's advisers" but does not pinpoint his lawyers, it must be taken for granted that the latter, whose task it is to tender advice on the interpretation and application of the law, must have been included in the ambit of this public criticism.

There is a dynamic in governance, involving the interaction between public servants and public service lawyers and their political masters. While the court could not venture into second guessing how the

---

subject advice came about, a thorough analysis must contemplate the possible scenarios. The advice may have been offered voluntarily, it may have been offered in the belief that is what the minister preferred or it may even have been sought or induced in the terms which were ultimately used. No matter which fact pattern occurred, this result should not have been reached.

The court's resolution of the issue clearly reflected its reticence vis-à-vis the advice of the legal advisers of the minister. In setting aside the second licence unless an EARP panel was appointed by the minister, the court expressed its scepticism.

> The Minister's respective counsel must be taken at their word. Assuming that it is now not reasonably practical to quash or set aside the second licence issued on August 31, 1989, and that the Minister and the intervener are quite earnest in wishing to see the project proceed without further interruption, what is the best way to unscramble the omelette which has been made of the EARP Guidelines in this case?
>
> It is a truism that what the court may order in broad, sweeping strokes, it may also order in more compact, neatly configured measures. It appears that some form of order nisi is called for here, especially at this time of year when the profound frigidity of the outdoors may be causing some diminution of the pace of work in the Souris River Basin.
>
> Therefore the court will order that the licence issued on August 31, 1989, will be quashed and set aside at close of business on Tuesday, January 30, 1990, unless in the meanwhile the Minister appoint an Environmental Assessment Panel pursuant to the EARP Guidelines, to conduct a public review of those aspects of the Rafferty-Alameda Project proposals in relation to which significant (including "moderate") impacts, being adverse environmental effects are identified...[254]

---

§ 11.14.3[255]
Tremblay c. Québec (Commission de la Fonction publique)
Québec Superior Court; May 14, 1990
[1990] R.J.Q. 1386

Tremblay was a Crown prosecutor and a member of the Québec

---

[254] *Ibid.* at 16.
[255] Cross-reference to § 3.11.1.

public service who, for his entire career, had specialized in criminal law. On April 6, 1988, he announced to his superior, that he intended to be a candidate in the upcoming federal general election. The Deputy informed him that pursuant to section 8 of the *Act respecting Attorney General's Prosecutors*,[256] his candidacy would entail his dismissal from the public service. The writs were issued for the election to be held on November 21, 1988. On October 19, Tremblay became a candidate and on the following day, he was dismissed. On June 22, 1989, the Québec Public Service Commission upheld the dismissal. Tremblay appealed that ruling to the Québec Superior Court.

The essence of this judgment was to determine whether section 8 of the *Act respecting Attorney General's Prosecutors* contravened section 3 of the *Canadian Charter of Rights and Freedoms*, dealing with the democratic rights to vote and, by necessary extension, to be a candidate, as well as section 15 of the *Charter*, on equality before the law.

These facts afforded the court an opportunity to delve into the functions and duties of government lawyers, as well as to see whether the exceptional standards the Québec legislation attempted to apply to Crown prosecutors were justified or not.

The human relations regime applicable to government lawyers in Québec was the same as that found in federal public service and in that of most other provinces. This regime is based on the incompatibility of public service work with undertakings of a partisan political nature. Thus, when a government lawyer other than a Crown prosecutor wanted to enter the political fray, he would have to seek a period of leave without pay from his employment. This procedure is meant to preserve the professionalism of all public servants to whom it applies, and the apolitical nature of their work. With respect to government lawyers, it is also designed to safeguard the independence of the judicial system from political interference, its impartiality and its integrity. The implication of these rules as far as government lawyers are concerned is that their accountability to the legal system is incompatible with the assumption of partisan political positions.

Québec's law treated Crown prosecutors differently from the province's other lawyers. Through the imposition of a system of automatic removal from office in case of candidacy at an election, the province

---

[256] L.R.Q., c. S-35.

sought to lend even greater weight to the unique attachment of prosecutors to the administration of justice. Given that this standard effectively constituted a bar to prosecutors' exercise of the democratic rights guaranteed to them by section 3 of the *Charter*, the court held the measure to be too restrictive and therefore contrary to the *Charter*. Moreover, the measure could not be saved under section 1 of the *Charter* as a reasonable limitation on democratic rights; the solution envisaged was not proportional to the goal sought to be achieved. In this, the court compared prosecutors to judges and said that the background of many of Québec's magistrates as politicians did not prevent them from adjudicating with impartiality and equity. Even if the court held section 8 to be too severe, it reiterated the importance for Crown prosecutors of both the substantive and perceptual aspects of their functions: in prosecutions, impartiality and the perception of impartiality are the key to a justice system based on legal, rather than political criteria. The fact that sole regard of prosecutors must be for the law was explicitly acknowledged.

In the analysis of the appellant's equality rights under section 15 of the *Charter*, the court recognized prosecutors as a discrete and isolated minority within the public service. While accepting the necessity for the protection of this minority's accountability to the law alone, it held that that accountability could be sufficiently protected by placing Crown prosecutors under the same regime as other government lawyers in respect of their prospects as candidates for office. The standard imposed on prosecutors by section 8 was thought to be discriminatory.

---

§ 11.14.4
Venczel v. Assn. of Architects (Ontario)
Ontario Supreme Court (Divisional Court); September 26, 1989
(1989), 45 Admin. L.R. 288[257]

In a short ruling that nonetheless is a definitive statement of this point of law, the Ontario Divisional Court has set out the obligation of lawyers conducting governmental work to exercise restraint and not to usurp the functions and attributions of their clients. In this instance, the mandate was the hearing of a statutory administrative tribunal,

---

[257] Additional reasons at (1990), 45 Admin. L.R. 288 at 289 (Ont. Div. Ct.).

but the rule can be extrapolated to other areas of governmental work by lawyers.

The Ontario Association of Architects initiated disciplinary proceedings against Venczel, one of its members, because he had affixed his seal to a design that had not been entirely prepared under his supervision. The Association's discipline committee had retained counsel to give it legal advice during the hearing. In the course of that hearing, the counsel "went far beyond the role of counsel advising the committee and actually participated...as a member of that committee."[258] Venczel was found guilty of professional misconduct and appealed on the ground that the committee's counsel had acted beyond his mandate.

The court concluded that the discipline committee had sought to obtain the advice of counsel rather than to abdicate to him its own obligation of conducting the hearing. The necessary corollary to the committee's abdication was the counsel's seizing of control of the proceedings. He ought not to have acted as *de facto* chairman, argued with counsel for the parties, made rulings, purported to make a finding of fact, nor acted as spokesman for the committee. The accused was entitled to know whether he was tried by the committee or by someone hired by the committee to assist it.

See also *Cross c. Teasdale*, [1991] R.J.Q. 1826 à 1832 (Que. C.A.) and *R. c. Montour*, [1991] R.J.Q. 1470 (Que. S.C.), affirmed (1998), 1998 CarswellQue 888 (Que. C.A.), leave to appeal allowed (1999), 237 N.R. 399 (note) (S.C.C.).

---

§ 11.14.5
Kearney v. R.
New Brunswick Court of Appeal; February 25, 1992
(1992), 70 C.C.C. (3d) 507[259]

The subject-matter of this case was the prosecution of a Crown prosecutor on charges of sexual assault. The case was determined on the application of the accused for a stay of the proceedings against him.

---

[258] (1989), 45 Admin. L.R. 288 at 289, additional reasons at (1990), 45 Admin. L.R. 288 at 289 (Ont. Div. Ct.).
[259] Reversed (1992), 76 C.C.C. (3d) 480 (S.C.C.).

In the realm of political law, the greater significance of the decision by the New Brunswick Court of Appeal is its commentary on the accountability of the Attorney General to law, and on the character-istics of the office he holds.

After Kearney was charged with having committed offences while he was a Crown prosecutor, the matter of his employment with the Department of the Attorney General and Minister of Justice was con-sidered by the Attorney General himself, the Deputy Attorney Gen-eral and the Director of Public Prosecutions. Against the latter's ad-vice, the decision was made to terminate Kearney's employment. This decision leaked to the media. Kearney thereupon applied to the Queen's Bench to have his prosecution stayed, on the grounds of section 7 [legal rights] and section 11 [criminal proceedings] of the *Charter*. The trial judge issued the stay. The Court of Appeal, by a 2-1 majority, upheld it. It based its decision in part on distinguishing the case from *R. v. Vermette*,[260] stating that the public comments in that case had been made by the Premier, who was not involved in the prosecution. The Supreme Court of Canada reversed the judg-ments below in an extraordinarily terse ruling.[261] The justices held that the *Vermette* judgment did apply and sent the matter back for a new trial.

The parts of the Court of Appeal judgment that interest us begin with the indication that the powers of the Attorney General spring from section 92(14) of the *Constitution Act, 1867*, from legislation and from the common law. In our democratic society, this official holds a unique position as the head of the administration of justice. The control functions of the Attorney General discussed are his powers to prosecute, to stay proceedings and to discontinue proceedings once they are launched.

> In New Brunswick, the Attorney-General is appointed to office at pleas-ure by the Premier of the government of the day. The political office of Attorney-General has been under fire for many years. When I refer to "political office" I mean it in the broad sense of the word "political," not just party politics.[262]

---

[260] (1988), 50 D.L.R. (4th) 385 (S.C.C.).
[261] (1992), 76 C.C.C. (3d) 480 (S.C.C.).
[262] (1992), 70 C.C.C. (3d) 507 at 518 h, reversed (1992), 76 C.C.C. (3d) 480 (S.C.C.).

The court goes on to point out the Attorney General's position as being the guardian of the public interest, as needing to be insulated from political considerations, as requiring impartiality of decision-making, and as needing to be conscious of the public perceptions of his decisions in regard to prosecutions. Significantly, the core of the function of the Attorney General is not even, in the court's view, winning or losing. Rather, the important element is seen as the up-holding of the presumption of innocence of the accused. These elements of the Attorney General's work are, sometimes explicitly, sometimes implicitly, made applicable by the court to the Deputy Attorney General and to all prosecutors working with them.

Most importantly, from this litany of characteristics of the office, the court reaches the following conclusion about accountability to law.

> I return now to the thread of remarks quoted from Professor Edwards' Viscount Bennett lecture. First, however, let me refer to the historical background of immunity of the Crown. Paul Lordon, Q.C. in his book *Crown Law* (Toronto, Butterworths, 1991), says at p. 563:
>
>> "Historically the axiom that 'the King can do no wrong' has been interpreted as attributing absolute perfection to the sovereign. On the other hand, Professor Hogg offers an interpretation of the maxim as being that 'the King was not regarded as above the law; on the contrary, he was regarded as under a duty—an unenforceable duty, to be sure—to give the same redress to a subject whom he had wronged as his subjects were bound to give each other.'"
>
> I point this out because the Attorney-General is, as well, answerable to the law.[263]

Here the Attorney General was held not to have observed that accountability insofar as Kearney's rights were concerned. The Court of Appeal thought that the image of the department was placed above the *Charter* rights of the accused and that this had amounted to an abuse of process. It also felt that "The Attorney General's argument...is an example of the damper of jurisprudence of conceptions and shows an uncompromising oversight as to the consequences "of their [his and the Deputy's] actions on the principles of fundamental justice."[264]

---

[263] *Ibid.* at 526 b-d.
[264] *Ibid.* at 521 d.

The effect of the Supreme Court's reversal of this judgment must be understood with caution. While the *ratio* set out in the preceding paragraph was overturned, the highest court did not contradict either the descriptions of the functions of the Attorney General and his lawyers nor the idea of their particular accountability to law.

---

§ 11.14.6
Bovbel v. Canada (Minister of Employment & Immigration)
Federal Court of Appeal; February 24, 1994
[1994] 2 F.C. 563[265]

Upon application by Bovbel, the Convention and Refugee Determination Division of the Immigration and Refugee Board (IRB) determined that he was not a Convention refugee. Before the Federal Court Trial Division and the Federal Court of Appeal, the most important ground of appeal from the Board's decision related to the practice of the IRB in having drafts of the decisions submitted to its own legal counsel. Bovbel alleged that this practice of legal verification of Board decisions constituted a breach of natural justice. The Trial Division held that the existence of the Board's "Reasons Review Policy" constituted a breach of the rules of natural justice, even in the absence of evidence as to its application. It felt that the policy endangered the independence of Board members and created a reasonable apprehension of bias. The Court of Appeal did not agree. On the basis of the divergent reasonings on this issue, this case became focused on the functions of lawyers as advisors of quasi-judicial tribunals such as the Immigration and Refugee Board.

The Court of Appeal first examined the IRB's Reasons Review Policy in some detail. The primary focus of that policy was the identification of errors of law, the bringing to Board Members' awareness of existing jurisprudence and the tendering of advice on legal issues arising from a case. The court specified that the procedure prescribed by the policy was to encourage Board Members, who are Order-in-Council appointees not necessarily legally trained, to submit their reasons for decision to the staff of the Board's legal services, who are public service lawyers, who act as general legal advisors but who do not

---

[265] Leave to appeal refused (1994), 179 N.R. 65 (note) (S.C.C.).

participate in the Board's hearings. The court also recounted the goals of this policy as being:

1. To ensure that the reasons are written in an appropriate style and form.

2. To ensure that the reasons address the issues which need to be dealt with.

3. To ensure that decisions of the IRB, IAB or the courts are not overlooked by the panel.

4. To ensure that the decisions which depart from procedure are made knowingly and after full consideration of the existing jurisprudence.

5. To ensure that the reasons are consistently of as superior a quality as possible by drawing upon the legal unit's knowledge and expertise.

6. To ensure that the legal unit is aware of the decisions being made so that the bank of jurisprudence is updated and complete.[266]

Delving deeper into the IRB's policy instruments, the court examined the relevant portions of the Convention Refugee Determination Division Member's Handbook, which clearly explained for the benefit of Members the role of their own legal advisors. The general tasks of the Legal Services Branch were listed as the provision of legal assistance which a panel may require; the provision of opinions on legal matters, on request; and the provision of written opinions on legal issues raised at a hearing. The role of a legal advisor was compared to that of a specialized researcher for Board Members. Within this overall context, the court cited the reference to the specific work of lawyers in the process of commenting on reasons for decisions prepared by Board Members.

A legal adviser peruses the draft reasons with certain objectives in mind. These are mainly:

(a) to ensure that the reasons address the issues which need to be dealt with, and

---

[266] [1994] 2 F.C. 563 at 566 d-h, leave to appeal refused (1994), 179 N.R. 65 (note) (S.C.C.).

(b) to ensure that decisions which depart from precedent are made knowingly and after full consideration of the jurisprudence.[267]

The court even went on to reproduce verbatim the portion of the Handbook in which the administrative routing of written reasons was set out. It even examined yet another of the IRB's policy instruments, the Case Processing Manual.

In order to understand the court's view of the proper nature of legal work in a quasi-judicial tribunal like the IRB, it is vital to extract the three key concepts from this body of policy instruments. The first is that in the interpretation of the Court of Appeal, the prescription for use of the Reasons Review Policy is not mandatory. Board Members were, as a general rule, expected to have their draft reasons reviewed, but were not obliged to do so. Secondly, in the view of the court, once legal counsellors did become involved, the nature of their advice was to relate to issues of law. They were "not expected to discuss the findings of facts made by the members but merely, if there was a factual inconsistency in the reasons, to look at the file in order to determine, if possible, how the inconsistency could be resolved."[268]

Most importantly, the cardinal rule regarding the extent of legal advice in an institution such as the one dealt with here, is that,

> While the Board's lawyers may give advice, it is the panel members themselves who must decide the case. Members, of course, are free to accept or reject the advice of legal advisers, as the members see fit.[269]

Bearing in mind the distinction between the functions of Board Members appointed by the government and those of their public service legal advisers, the court elegantly summed up its *ratio* for refusing Bovbel's pleadings of breach of natural justice as follows.

> There is no doubt that the participation of "outsiders" in the decision-making process of an administrative tribunal may sometimes cause problem. The decisions of the tribunal must, indeed, be rendered by those on whom Parliament has conferred power to decide and their decisions must, unless the relevant legislation impliedly or expressly provides otherwise, meet the requirements of natural justice. However,

---

[267] *Ibid.* at 568 b.
[268] *Ibid.* at 573 b.
[269] *Ibid.* at 567 f.

when the practice followed by members of an administrative tribunal does not violate natural justice and does not infringe on their ability to decide according to their opinion even though it may influence that opinion, it cannot be criticized.[270]

The court then reinforced its ruling by repeating a position of one of its own earlier decisions in a similar case.

> The Refugee Division is a lay tribunal required to decide claims which, as I have observed, involve the life, liberty and security of the person. It must do so within the framework of extensive, confusing, and sometimes confused, jurisprudence. It is required to give written reasons for decision not favourable to claimants. The desirability of legal review of those reasons is manifest. Having come to a decision on what is essentially a question of fact: whether the claimant has a well-founded fear of persecution for a reason that engages the Convention refugee definition, a tribunal does not, in my opinion, offend any tenet of natural justice by taking advice as to legal matters contained in its reasons.[271]

---

§ 11.14.7
Shaffer v. The Queen
Tax Court of Canada; September 8, 1994
not reported; file no. 94-539 [IT] I

The lawyers of the government take part in all law related activities of the State and represent the legal interests of the State. In many instances, they engage in representation against the interests of their fellow citizens who may have breached legal norms. Such lawyers are to be held to a high standard of expertise regarding the state of the law and of the other instruments relating to governance. Given their proximity to the processes of governance and that access to information about these, they must be both presumed to have the requisite knowledge to engage in this type of practice and the professional accountability to abide by legal norms which they help to enforce for the rest of society. These were the bases on which the Tax Court of Canada dismissed appeals against reassessments by a number of the lawyers of the Department of Justice, including Shaffer, in respect of deduction from personal taxable income of fees for mem-

---

[270] *Ibid.* at 570 h-571 a.
[271] (1993), [1994] 1 F.C. 330 (Fed. C.A.), quoted in [1994] 2 F.C. 563 at 571 d-f, leave to appeal refused (1994), 179 N.R. 65 (note) (S.C.C.).

bership in the Bar, when those fees were paid by the Department. In this case, it is the Minister's Reply to the Notice of Appeal which is most indicative of the proper view of the duty of lawyers in government employment. In addition to the usual pleading as to what the appellant should have known, the Minister states that the reason why that knowledge was expected of the appellant was that

> The Appellant is employed by the Department of Justice as a senior counsel for the senior assistant Deputy Minister's office;

> . . .

> [H]is academic education, general knowledge and contacts should have prevented him from making these claims;

> [T]he Appellant had easy access to any information or documentation regarding professional dues deductions and should have verified that his claims were legitimate;[272]

The Minister's pleading meant that in Shaffer's specific circumstances, the fact that the Department of Justice did not inform him of its policy on such deductions was not an excuse sufficient for exoneration. Government lawyers had the opportunity and therefore the duty to inform themselves and comply. The court agreed.

---

§ 11.14.8
Public Disavowal of Legal Advice by the Premier of Alberta
March 11, 1998

Given the interdisciplinary nature of political law, not all decisions constituting its jurisprudence must necessarily be rendered by the courts. Precedents can also be set by the public actions of parliamentarians that touch on the legal system and its interaction with the making of policy and the development of politics. So it is with the case of Premier Ralph Klein of Alberta and his public disavowal, on March 11, 1998, of legal advice which had led to the presentation before the provincial legislature of Bill 26, the *Institutional Confinement and Sexual Sterilization Compensation Act*.

---

272 Reply to the Notice of Appeal, paras. 3 a), d), i) and ii).

Bill 26 was prepared for the purpose of limiting the compensation payable by the Province of Alberta to individual Albertans who, during the period from 1928 to 1972, were forcibly sterilized in provincial institutions pursuant to a number of provincial statutes authorizing such procedures. One such person had been awarded one million dollars' compensation by the courts and the province intended to limit its financial exposure in respect of the other such former patients. As drafted, the Bill included section 3, which provided that it would operate notwithstanding sections 2 and 7 to 15 of the *Canadian Charter of Rights and Freedoms* and the Alberta *Bill of Rights*. Since the advent of the *Charter*, this was the first legislative proposal put forward by Alberta which included use of the notwithstanding clause (NWC). Bill 26 was discussed in the Progressive Government caucus on March 9, 1998. The Premier and allegedly half the members of caucus were present. The presentation was made by the province's Justice Minister, Jon Havelock. According to press reports, the Bill was characterized as balancing the interests of prospective claimants for adequate compensation with that of all Albertans in protecting the province's treasury. The inclusion of the NWC was said to be a legal technicality, a tool to "bullet-proof" the legislation from being susceptible to be declared contrary to the *Charter* by any court. On March 10, 1998, Bill 26 was read for the first time in the Legislative Assembly of Alberta.

The reaction of outrage on the part of the public and of the media was instantaneous and vociferous. As a direct consequence, on March 11, 1998, barely one day after the Bill's tabling, the Premier issued a statement in the Legislature to the effect that the government would proceed no further with this bill.

The first political law aspect of this controversy which deserves scrutiny is inclusion of the NWC in Bill 26. In the 16 years since the fundamental revision of the Canadian legal system through adoption of the *Charter*, the mechanism has hardly ever been used. The effect of the NWC is to subtract a statute from judicial review as to its conformity with the *Charter*. Its impact is thus to place, in respect of that statute, the value of the political goal sought to be achieved by the government that has had it enacted higher than the value of constitutional validity and legality which the criterion of Charterability is meant to ensure. Moreover, use of the clause reverses in favour of the executive branch of government, and of the legislative branch under its effective control, the onus of the supremacy of the judiciary as the guarantor of legal legitimacy which was the intention of the framers of the *Charter*, and which was the consequence of the *Charter*. The use of the NWC had intended to be reserved for matters of overriding public policy necessity and for the major benefit of the people, as opposed to the merely strategic (and publicly political) goal of limitation of governmental expenditures. Here, it was patent that the NWC was being used for a purpose other than that which it was originally intended to address. Because of the particular circumstances, in that the Bill dealt with the rights of an already deeply aggrieved minority, its attempted use was doubly offensive.

From the available evidence, the best explanation as to the willingness of the government to use the NWC can be found in the conception of the Minister of Justice about the role of the legal system vis-à-vis the political outlook of the government and his specific attitude regarding the *Charter*.

> What we have witnessed, then, was no accident. It was not an overreaction in a moment of crisis, based on a hasty misreading of the law. It was a deliberate frontal assault on the Charter; and everything it stands for...Havelock has made no secret of his distaste for the document or its values, not to mention the independence of the judiciary.

> He had railed against the legal system's "seeming preoccupation with the rights of the accused," and the incursion of judicial discretion "into areas which traditionally have been the preserve of duly elected representatives," even wondering aloud whether the answer might be to "repeal or amend the Charter."[273]

Apart from this rather unique anti-legal system ideological perspective of the Minister of Justice, there was also speculation that the attempt to use the NWC in Bill 26 may have been linked to Alberta's position in the case of *Vriend v. Alberta*, then before the Supreme Court of Canada. This could of course not be substantiated.

The public reaction on the issue of the NWC confirmed the profound attachment of the Canadian public to the *Charter* as the highest substantive embodiment and also as the most prominent symbol of the principle of legality. Henceforth, it would be more difficult for any

---

[273] "Clause is about denying rights to a defenceless minority," Andrew Coyne, *Edmonton Journal*, March 12, 1998, p. A-17.

Minister of Justice to carve out a political niche from constitutional protection, in which legality would not prevail.

Analysis of this case must also reflect the manner in which Premier Klein made the announcement that his government would not proceed with the legislative process on Bill 26. He indicated that, while it was his own political sense that had failed him in this manner, he and the caucus had depended on the advice of lawyers. He also made it appear publicly that the reason for his wrong political decision was that he had been given bad legal advice, or a combination of bad legal and political advice by them. Several comments must be made about the Premier's remarks in regard to the role of lawyers in government as an aspect of the principle of accountability to law. For the sake of clarity, it must be emphasized that in this instance, the accountability to law being examined here is that of Premier Klein.

The public repudiation of legal advice contained in and implied by the Premier's statement constitutes, most prominently, a breach of the constitutional convention of ministerial responsibility. Traditionally, ministers comprising a government should accept responsibility for their political decisions based on officials' advice which is deemed to be non-partisan, rather than blame public service advisers for their input into such decisions. This convention applies most clearly to the head of a government. The resolution chosen by Premier Klein to the situation created by Bill 26 was completely political in nature: he decided to withdraw the bill. If the problem had really been related to the advice proffered, it could have been corrected more appropriately either by deletion of the NWC from the bill or by a serious regard at the method through which officials tendered their legal advice and at how that advice was politically vetted. Thus, the effort to avoid blame is not only politically motivated but also seems entirely gratuitous. The matter must also be set in its proper context. At the time these events were unfolding, there was consideration that if Jean Charest would leave the leadership of the federal Progressive Conservative Party for that of the Liberal Party of Québec, Mr. Klein could be one of the contenders to replace him. The Premier's reaction may thus be explained by his desire to remain politically unharmed even at the cost of breaching convention.

Even more significantly, the Premier's statement undeniably amounted to a breach of the duty of accountability to law by an elected public official in several respects. First, the comments constituted a

public disavowal of legal advice based on the idea that reliance on
law was a bar to sound political decision-making, when clearly this
was not the true state of affairs. The original decision to frame Bill 26
was a political one made by the Premier and it was to include in the
legislative proposal a legal mechanism that was legally discriminatory and politically unpopular, and therefore harmful to him in his
political capacity. Given that the decision on Bill 26 was political in
nature, the attempt to blame the unpopularity of the measure on its
questionable legal component alone is wholly unjustified. In plain
language, the Premier used the law as an excuse for his political
responsibility.

Moreover, Klein's statement also breached his accountability to law
by seeming to discredit the legal system. He attempted to shift blame
on his legal advisers despite the fact that there is no real evidence
either that they recommended the use of the NWC rather than merely
informed him of its availability, or that the advice to use the clause
came from them, as opposed to coming from the policy or political
advisers, or even from the Minister of Justice himself.

The most compelling portrait of the probable interaction among the
participants in the making of the decision on Bill 26 was painted in
an editorial of the *Globe and Mail*, which said:

> "Cash issue settled," the advisers must have then moved on to the thorny
> question of how to reconcile this compensation package with the rights
> of individuals to pursue their cases in court."

> "We'll make the bill say that they can't go to court to seek damages,"
> one adviser must have suggested, "like that Pearson Airport bill."

> One assumes that someone—perhaps the legal scholar at the ta-
> ble—must have raised the matter of the Charter of Rights.

> Obviously, someone else replied, "No problem. We'll just use the not-
> withstanding clause."

> Perhaps the legal scholar then left the room or was momentarily di-
> verted. Presumably no one was there to warn these political geniuses
> that the notwithstanding clause, though useful in issues such as the

balancing of collective rights against the Charter's individual rights, is intended to be invoked only in extraordinary situations.[274]

In democratic systems, heads of governments' accountability to law also involves the responsibility for managing the governmental system in such a manner that its legal and political components complement each other and converge and be seen to converge, rather than the opposite. In this context, Premier Klein's disavowal of the lawyers' advice was generally harmful, because it intensified the false appearance of dichotomy between legal and political considerations in public decision-making, instead of striving to unite the two.

This was not the only occasion on which Premier Klein found it politically expedient to be publicly critical of legal matters. In fact, in the summer of 2001, the Premier had a very visible dispute with the province's judges, in particular with Chief Justice Catherine Fraser.

During the first week of July, the Chief Justice announced that the Calgary branch of the Court of Appeal would move to Edmonton to resolve the consequences of sick building syndrome in the courts' Calgary premises. Klein attacked the decision, stating his opinion that this was a tactic by members of the judiciary to obtain more luxurious and expensive premises in Calgary.

Unlike the Premier's freedom to treat his government's lawyers in a high-handed fashion, in this case, he seems to have received advice from his Minister of Justice to moderate his anti-judicial rhetoric. On July 26, 2001, Klein apologized.

> Justice Minister David Hancock said Wednesday that Klein has sent a letter to Alberta Chief Justice Catherine Fraser to smooth relations with the judges. "It was important to clarify that the premier meant no disrespect to the court," Hancock said in an interview.
>
> "He intended no offence. If there was any offence taken he would apologize for the comments."
>
> Fraser could not be reached for comment.[275]

---

[274] "A political disability breeds sterile ideas," *Globe and Mail*, March 12, 1998, p. A-18.

[275] "Klein apologizes for criticizing appeal court judges over toxic office space," John Cotter, *CP newswire*, July 26, 2001.

The very next day, however, the Premier deflated the value of his apology. His remarks indicated not only his ignorance of the bonds and the bounds between law and politics, but also his lack of understanding of the necessary self-restraint of judges' public speeches.

> Alberta Premier Ralph Klein said he has the right to chide judges who speak out on political issues outside court. But he also acknowledged Thursday his apology to Alberta's chief justice for suggesting earlier this month that appeal court judges in Calgary have been faking illness to get more expensive office space.
>
> Klein said those remarks were in response to comments made by a judge about the office space controversy.
>
> "I was speaking my mind," he said to reporters in Calgary. "When a judge goes into a public forum, then I assume he or she is in a political forum."[276]

Klein was forced to make yet another apology under pressure from the Bench and the Bar of Alberta.

> "On July 9, 2001, in response to questions from the press at my annual Stampede Breakfast in Calgary, I made certain impromptu statements which I now realize conveyed untrue and disparaging imputations against the Hon. Chief Justice of Alberta, Catherine Fraser, and other Calgary justices of the Alberta Court of appeal," Klein said in a written statement.
>
> "I want Albertans to know that I unreservedly accept that the chief justice and the other Calgary justices of the Alberta Court of appeal have at all times acted ethically and honestly in their negotiations with the government for new premises in Calgary.
>
> "I sincerely apologize to the chief justice and to the other Calgary justices and regret any embarrassment caused by my answers to the news media on July 9, 2001."
>
> The statement was a response to a letter from a lawyer for the judges calling the remarks inflammatory and demanding a public apology.

---

[276] "Klein says he can chide judges who make comments outside of court," *Ottawa Citizen*, July 27, 2001.

Klein had already said he was sorry in a letter to Fraser, but that did not satisfy the judges.[277]

---

§ 11.14.9[278]
Stevens v. Canada (Prime Minister)
Federal Court of Appeal; June 5, 1998
[1998] 4 F.C. 89

This case derives from the actions of Stevens when he was a minister in the government of Prime Minister Mulroney, and from the consideration of his actions by a Commission of Inquiry. The principal issue relating to Stevens' actions is dealt with under the category of Professional Ethics of Members of the Executive Government. Here the Federal Court of Appeal looked at the solicitor-client privilege of the legal counsel to the Commission of Inquiry as it applied to his billing accounts, and at the protection of that information from disclosure under the *Access to Information Act*.[279]

In all of the proceedings relating to the investigation of the allegations against him, Stevens took a highly confrontational approach to the government. During the work of the Commission of Inquiry, the relationship between Stevens and the legal counsel to the Commission was noticeably adversarial. The head of the Commission, Parker, was later said to have indicated that the counsel would not be involved in writing the Commission's report. That report, which was submitted to the House of Commons on December 3, 1987, was so critical of Stevens that he challenged its findings in court and alleged that the counsel was in fact involved in writing it. In order to ascertain whether this allegation was true, Stevens sought to obtain the counsel's billing accounts.

In this decision, the court determined that in respect of solicitor-client privilege of a lawyer's bills of accounts, the relationship was no different where the government was the client than if an individual or another person was the client. The protection of the relationship was in favour of the client and in that respect, the protection to be afforded

---

[277] "Premier Klein apologizes to Alta. judges for suggesting they faked illness," *Ottawa Citizen*, August 3, 2001.

[278] Cross-reference to § 11.8.2.

[279] R.S.C. 1985, c. A-1.

the government was no less than that to be given any other client. The purpose of this doctrine was the fair and proper administration of justice.

There is one aspect of the solicitor-client relationship in which lawyers' work for the government is particular. That is that for policy reasons aiming at greater transparency of its operations, the government may, in its capacity as the client, exercise its discretion to release more information than others would or than is legally necessary.

> ...a government body may have more reason to waive its privilege than private parties, for it may wish to follow a policy of transparency with respect to its activity. This is highly commendable; but the adoption of such a policy or such a decision in no way detracts from the protection afforded by the privilege to all clients.[280]

Considering that that is what happened here, Stevens' appeal of the decision originally rendered by the Information Commissioner not to require disclosure of the Commission counsel's billing accounts, upheld by the Federal Court Trial Division, was dismissed.

See also *McRae v. Canada (Attorney General)* (1998), 61 B.C.L.R. (3d) 83 (B.C. S.C.), additional reasons at (1998), 9 C.C.L.I. (3d) 215 (B.C. S.C.).

---

§ 11.14.10
Review of the Nova Scotia Public Prosecution Service
Kaufman Inquiry
Final Report; June 9, 1999[281]

The evidence of several major situations points to serious weaknesses in the justice system of Nova Scotia. In 1990, the Royal Commission on the Donald Marshall, Jr., Prosecution tabled its final report, outlining the structural problems inherent in the administration of justice. The commissioners' most damaging analysis was that,

> [o]fficials in the Department of the Attorney General are more concerned about the career of a politician than the reputation of an Indian; they are quick to write superficial and unprofessional opinions that support not

---

[280] [1998] 4 F.C. 89 at 121.
[281] Cross-reference to § 9.5.7 and 11.8.2.

investigating or charging a politician yet search for reasons to limit the compensation paid to an Indian for years of wrongful imprisonment; and they require substantially more likelihood of conviction before charging a politician than an Indian.[282]

This report led to the establishment of a Public Prosecution Service by statute and the consequential separation of this function from the Department of the Attorney General. Nevertheless, during the 1990's, the problems of managing prosecutions continued. In particular, the examples and the assumptions regarding political interference in the domain of prosecutions persisted. In response to the difficulties raised by the public perception of political tainting of the justice system, for example, in the prosecution of the executives of Westray Mining and in that of former Premier Gerald Regan, on July 10, 1988, a further inquiry was initiated by the Attorney General. This inquiry presented an interim report on January 20, 1999, and a final report on June 9, 1999.

The Kaufman Inquiry's terms of reference mandated it to:

• consider prosecutorial independence and public accountability;

• examine the business element of the Service; and independence and efficiency of operations and communications.

The fundamental issue was stated to be proper management of the Prosecution Service, but underlying everything was the matter of overt and covert political interference. With this combination of issues, Mr. Justice Kaufman's reports provide a wealth of material defining and clarifying the accountability of government lawyers to the legal system and on that of the political class to avoid interfering in the work of prosecutors. A month after Kaufman handed in his final report, a general election was held in Nova Scotia and a new majority Progressive Conservative government was elected. By November 1999, the incoming Justice Minister, Michael Baker, undertook publicly to appoint a new and permanent Director of Public Prosecutions, to widen the budget flexibility of the Public Prosecution Service, thereby freeing it from government constructs, and to enable Crown prosecutors to engage in collective bargaining.

---

[282] Report of the Marshall Commission, Vol. I, p. 220, cited in the Interim Report of the Review of the Nova Scotia Public Prosecution Service, Hon. Fred Kaufman, p. 2.

The first aspect of the Service broached by Kaufman was the thorniest, that of its independence; here of course, independence means freedom from political interference. Even in a jurisdiction where the Public Prosecution Service is separate from the Attorney General's department, the Attorney General is the chief law officer of the Crown and the notion of independence does not connote independence of prosecutors from the minister responsible for them before the House of Assembly. In the interim report, Kaufman used the position of a judge to illustrate the core of the notion of "independence."

> While *political independence*—freedom from direction, control or influence by politicians—is perhaps, the most important element of judicial independence, it is by no means the only one:
>
> . . .
>
> The point is that "independence," even when established by statute, is never absolute, and so it is with the DPP and PPS. It is, therefore, important to clarify to which relationships, and with respect to which functions, this independence is intended to apply.
>
> . . .
>
> I accept what Dr. Gillis said as being an accurate reflection of the realities of political life—that the independence of offices and institutions cannot usefully be discussed in purely abstract terms; such discussions, to be realistic, must take into account other competing claims on the public purse, and this no matter how anxious a government may be to do the "right" thing. It follows also that the independence of an institution can be curtailed through control of its budget, and this applies particularly to situations where additional funds are needed to finance cases such as *Westray*.[283]

In the final report, he further qualified this aspect of government lawyers' obligations.

> I believe that regular meetings between the Attorney General and the DPP are essential. The Attorney is entitled to know what's going on in the Service. This is not a licence to meddle; it is, rather, a recognition of the fact that the Attorney General is the Minister responsible for public prosecutions and that it is the Attorney General, not the DPP, who answers to the legislature. I do not see this as a derogation from the

---

[283] Interim Report, pp. 3-4.

DPP's statutory rights, for even if advice is given by the Attorney, the Director need not accept it, unless "instructed" in writing to do so. Indeed, I was told there were times when the DPP found meetings with the Attorney General helpful—a caring voice from outside the Service with words sometimes of caution and often of encouragement.

I therefore recommend that the Act be amended to require that not less than once a month meetings be held between the Attorney General and the Director of Public Prosecutions to discuss policy matters, as well as existing and contemplated major prosecutions.[284]

As a note of both caution and advice, Kaufman indicated that the conduct institutionalized at such meetings is not a licence for the Minister to meddle, meaning that he should not use the occasion for politically suitable decisions.

This entire subject-matter was further developed within the Final Report, through a background paper prepared for Kaufman by Canada's foremost authority on the role of prosecutors, Dr. Philip Stenning. His finding was devastating of the system, in that he found that the Attorney General had the right to intervene on grounds he alone deemed appropriate, by instruction which prosecutors were not at liberty to ignore, either in all prosecutions or in specific cases.

> Such provisions, I would argue, are calculated to engender confusion and uncertainty on the part of the public and the media (not to mention the public prosecutors themselves) about the supposed "independence" of the DPP and the PPS, and the role of the Attorney General. While the emphasis in Section 2 of the Act on the importance of the independence of the DPP and the PPS to "ensure fair and equal treatment in the prosecution of offences" gives the impression that the intent was to secure a substantial measure of actual independence from the AG for the DPP and the PPS, the specifics of the subsequent provisions of the legislation make it clear that this is not in fact the case. While the talk of "independence" suggests that it would rarely if ever be proper for an Attorney General to intervene personally in a directive (or even influential) way in any particular case, the specifics of the legislation make it clear that it is lawful for the AG to do so *in any case at all*, at his or her discretion. The vaunted "independence" of the DPP and the PPS turns out to be potentially almost wholly illusory (although of course this may not actually have been (and apparently has not been) the case in practice).[285]

---

[284] Final Report, pp. 13-14.
[285] *Ibid.*, Appendix D, p. 351.

Kaufman was no less thorough on the issue of accountability, as well as with respect to the linkages between independence and accountability. His conclusion, in sum, leans toward the position that Crown Attorneys should be free from direction, control and influence both from outside the Prosecution Service but also, in regard to individual cases, from within.

On the managerial aspects, Kaufman made a number of further recommendations. The one to retain in particular is that the Public Prosecution Service should, in response to unforeseen circumstances, be able to overspend its annual budget so as to continue its functioning.

---

§ 11.14.11
Olympia Interiors Ltd. v. R.
Federal Court of Appeal; September 13, 1999
(1999), [2000] 1 C.T.C. 256[286]

Olympia was charged with offences under the *Excise Tax Act*,[287] brought to trial and the charges were later stayed. Simultaneously, proceedings of a civil nature were under way to recover funds the Crown believed were owed to it. In this action, Olympia alleged that the prosecution had been malicious and claimed that the Crown servants involved had acted in misfeasance and abuse of authority.

The interest of the case is that it examines the method of operation of Crown prosecutors in light of the major cases dealing with malicious prosecution and abuse of power.

The rules on malicious prosecution were set out by the Supreme Court of Canada in *Nelles v. Ontario*,[288] which talked about basing prosecutions on an honest belief in the guilt of the accused, founded on reasonable grounds, in opposition to the absence of reasonable and probable cause for bringing the action, or in the absence of malice, namely a primary purpose other than that of carrying the law into effect. The rules on malice by a public body were set out in the even

---

[286] Leave to appeal refused (2000), 252 N.R. 393 (note) (S.C.C.), reconsideration refused (June 22, 2000), Doc. 27550 (S.C.C.).

[287] R.S.C. 1985, c. E-15, as amended.

[288] (1989), 60 D.L.R. (4th) 609 (S.C.C.).

more important case of *Roncarelli v. Duplessis*[289] as simply acting for a reason and purpose knowingly foreign to the administration.

While this court felt that the prosecutor did have reasonable and probable cause, it did acknowledge the potentially confusing perception in the mind of the accused who felt targeted in both criminal and civil procedures, but said that that perception did not amount to malicious prosecution.

> In this case one other possible basis for questioning the purposes of the Crown's prosecution arises from Ms. David's perception that the criminal proceedings were initiated to compel payment of taxes, a civil matter. It is not surprising that a litigant who is not a lawyer is confused by proceedings on the civil enforcement side, to assess and compel payment of taxes owed, and proceedings of a criminal nature under the *Act* to impose penalties by fine or imprisonment for tax evasion, fraud or flagrant disregard of a taxpayer's obligations. Both sorts of proceedings are provided under the *Excise Tax Act*, and in this case both were directed to deal with Olympia's situation, concurrently, at least for some time."

> . . .

> In only one aspect might it appear to the plaintiffs that the case is supportive of their claims, that being the finding that one particular process followed was an abuse of process, i.e., the use in the investigative phase by the audit and enforcement unit of an audit to seek information to support a stalled special investigation for possible criminal prosecution. In the case at bar the plaintiffs allege that the criminal prosecution was an abuse of process because it was for the purpose of collecting a civil remedy, taxes, interest and financial penalty outstanding. There is no evidence to support that as the purpose of the prosecution. Here the routine audit process was underway before any special investigation was commenced for possible criminal prosecution. Once the latter was underway the investigation went forward quite independently and expeditiously on reasonable and probable grounds that supported the warrant authorizing search and seizure and, subsequently supporting prosecution. Those in the technical and regular audit services were not involved in or kept informed of the investigation, and the prosecutor Ms. Woolcott testified that she declined to be involved in the civil process.

---

[289] (1959), 16 D.L.R. (2d) 689 (S.C.C.).

LEGAL ACCOUNTABILITY TO DEMOCRACY / 1209

I find there was no abuse of process. In particular, I find that the prosecution in this case was for the purpose of criminal prosecution under the *Act*, not for purposes of collecting outstanding taxes and interest, or monetary penalties applicable to outstanding tax payable balances.[290]

The effect of these remarks is that while Crown attorneys and prosecutors are bound to use the law solely for the purposes for which it was intended, the full use of the judicial arsenal of the State thought to be an offender does not constitute malicious prosecution.

The court also reviewed the law on abuse of power, including the element of a public officer intending to injure, or acting knowingly without authority in law. It concluded that the official involved acted pursuant to the *Department of National Revenue Act*[291] and the *Excise Tax Act*.[292]

The Federal Court of Appeal dismissed an appeal as having failed to identify any reviewable error.

See also *Babcock v. Canada (Attorney General)*, [2002] 3 S.C.R. 3 (S.C.C.) and *Herzig v. Canada*, 2001 FCT 39 (Fed. T.D.), affirmed 2002 FCA 36 (Fed. C.A.), leave to appeal refused (2002), 301 N.R. 394 (note) (S.C.C.) and 2001 PSSRB 68 (Can. P.S.S.R.B.) and 2002 FCA 36 (Fed. C.A.), leave to appeal refused (2002), 301 N.R. 394 (note) (S.C.C.) .

---

§ 11.14.12[293]
Alfred Crompton Amusement Machines Ltd. v.
Customs and Excise Commissioners (No. 2)
United Kingdom Court of Appeal, Civil Division; February 17, 1972
[1972] 2 All E.R. 353[294]

The Crompton company disputed the Commissioners' assessment of its business and brought the matter to arbitration. The central issue of the proceedings became the question of privilege. Crompton

---

[290] [1999] 3 C.T.C. 305 (Fed. T.D.) at 326, para. 60, and 327, paras. 62-63, affirmed (1999), [2000] 1 C.T.C.256 (Fed. C.A.), leave to appeal refused (2000), 252 N.R. 393 (note) (S.C.C.), reconsideration refused (June 22, 2000), Doc. 27550 (S.C.C.).

[291] R.S.C. 1985, c. N-15, as amended.

[292] R.S.C. 1985, c. E-15, as amended.

[293] International comparison.

[294] Affirmed [1973] 2 All E.R. 1169 (U.K. H.L.).

sought access to the documentation which lay behind the Commissioner's decision. For some of those documents the Commissioners relied on legal professional privilege in obtaining legal advice, in anticipation of litigation and to provide evidence and information for the arbitration. For some of the other documents, the Commissioners relied on Crown privilege, indicating that the public interest required them to keep confidential the papers they had received from third parties. In determining whether the Commissioners could avail themselves of this type of privilege, the Court of Appeal was brought to look at the distinction between independent lawyers and those employed by the various government departments. It upheld the privilege. The ruling afforded Lord Denning, Master of the Rolls, to portray in most eloquent terms the specific characteristics of legal work in the employ of government and the specific duties incumbent on such lawyers.

Salaried legal advisers

The law relating to discovery was developed by the Chancery courts in the first half of the 19th century. At that time nearly all legal advisers were in independent practice on their own account. Nowadays it is very different. Many barristers and solicitors are employed as legal advisers, whole time, by a single employer. Sometimes the employer is a great commercial concern. At other times it is a government department or local authority. It may even be the government itself, like the Treasury Solicitor and his staff. In every case these legal advisers do legal work for their employer and for no one else. They are paid, not by fees for each piece of work, but by a fixed annual salary. They are, no doubt, servants or agents of the employer. For that reasons the judge thought that they were in a different position from other legal advisers who are in private practice. I do not think this is correct. They are regarded by the law as in every respect in the same position as those who practise on their own account. The only difference is that they act for one client only, and not for several clients. They must uphold the same standards of honour and of etiquette. They are subject to the same duties to their client and to the court. They must respect the same confidences. They and their clients have the same privileges. I have myself in my early days settled scores of affidavits of documents for the employers of such legal advisers. I have always proceeded on the footing that the communications between the legal advisers and their employer (who is their client) are the subject of legal professional privilege; and I have never known it questioned. There are many cases in the books of actions against railway companies where privilege has been claimed in this way. The validity of it has never been doubted. I speak, of course, of their communications in the capacity of legal advisers. It does sometimes happen that such a legal adviser does work for his employer in another capacity, perhaps of an executive nature. Their communications in that capacity would not be the subject of legal professional privilege. So the legal adviser must be scrupulous to make the distinction. Being a servant or agent too, he may be under more pressure from his client. So he must be careful to resist it. He must e an independent in the doing of right as any other legal adviser. It is true, as the Law Reform Committee said in their report in 1967 that the "system is susceptible to abuse," but I have never known it abused. So much so that I do not think the law should be changed in the way that the judge would have it. There is a safeguard against abuse.[295]

With respect to the legal professional privilege, the Court accepted the Commissioner's point of view as it found that the documents were used to enable the Commissioners to form their own opinion of the justice of the company's claim to deductions. At the same time, these papers were material which the Commissioners could place before their solicitors if the matter led to legal conflict, as they anticipated it might.

With respect to the Crown privilege, the court did not accept the Commissioners' line of argumentation. It saw the need to balance the public interest in favour of confidentiality with the public interest in seeing that justice be done. The fact that the Commissioners had received these documents from third parties was not conclusive. On such claims, the ultimate defender of public interest is the Attorney General, who must show that the information contained in the documents needs to be withheld. That test is not met here. Nevertheless, the court found that as the documents had been made available to the Commissioners in confidence, they ought to be protected by privilege on this alternative ground.

---

[295] [1972] 2 All E.R. 353 at 376 e-377 a, affirmed [1973] 2 All E.R. 1169 (U.K. H.L.).

§ 11.14.13[296]
Waterford v. Commonwealth
High Court of Australia; June 24, 1987
(1987), 71 A.L.R. 673

The fact that the relation of government lawyers to the departments they work for and the public policy benefit of protecting that relationship are both common features of democratic systems of governance is well illustrated in this case. In 1982, Waterford sought access to documents on unemployment insurance which were part of the 1982-83 Budget Papers of Australia. Access was denied. He then requested access to the documents of the Department of the Treasury which related to the processing of the first request, namely the internal working documents which set out the advice of the Department's legal counsel. This request was also denied; the Federal Court and, here, the High Court, dismissed Waterford's appeals. The court characterized the issue in the following manner:

> The central question at issue in this appeal is whether it is open to the Commonwealth to claim legal professional privilege in the circumstances of this case, that is to say in respect of documents the subject matter of which is legal advice obtained from within the Government and concerned with proceedings pending in the tribunal.[297]

This court relied on the *Alfred Crompton* case and also cited Canadian, Irish and American parallel jurisprudence.[298] It held, in very wide terms which it related to the modern practice of governance, that the solicitor-client privilege relating to the government's own lawyers must be allowed to flourish.

> In our opinion, given the safeguards to which reference is made in the various citations, there is no reason to place legal officers in government employment outside the bounds of legal professional privilege. The proper functioning of the legal system is facilitated by freedom of consultation between the client and the legal adviser.

---

[296] International comparison.

[297] (1987), 71 A.L.R. 673 at 675.46.

[298] *Shell Canada Ltd. v. Canada (Director of Investigation & Research)* (1975), 55 D.L.R. (3d) 713 (Fed. C.A.); *Geraghty v. Minister for Local Government* (1975), I.R. 300; *National Labour Relations Board v. Sears, Roebuck & Co.*, 421 U.S. 132 (1975) and *U.S. Steel Corp. v. United States*, 730 F.2d 1465 (1984).

. . .

> To our minds it is clearly in the public interest that those in government who bear the responsibility of making decisions should have free and ready confidential access to their legal advisers.[299]

The court went on deliberately to reinforce its point.

> The growing complexity of the legal framework within which government must be carried on renders the rationale of the privilege, as expressed in *Grant v. Downs*, increasingly compelling when applied to decision makers in the public sector. The wisdom of the centuries is that the existence of the privilege encourages resort to those skilled in the law and that this makes for a better legal system.[300]

The court found the foundations of this privilege both in common law and in the statute. It resisted all of the appellant's attempts to limit it.

A noteworthy aspect of the court's discussion of the issue dealt with the necessity for the legal adviser to retain his independence, even through a relationship of employment. For the lawyer in government, the dilemma is between providing such legal assistance as the client needs on one hand, and respecting the rules of professional ethics and discipline on the other. One member of the court acknowledged that this dilemma was genuine for lawyers employed by their clients, but concluded that the matter was resolved because the independence of government lawyers in giving legal advice was protected by the Attorney General "as the first law officer(s) of the Crown, and is buttressed by the laws relating to the public service and sometimes by specific legislation."[301]

See also *In re: Sealed Case No. 99-3091*, United States Court of Appeal – D.C. Circuit, September 13, 1999.

---

[299] *Supra* note 297 at 677.15 and 33.
[300] *Ibid.* at 678.46 to 679.1.
[301] *Ibid.* at 685.24.

11.15 ISSUE: STATE SUPPORT FOR PUBLIC PARTICIPATION IN THE POLITICAL/LEGAL SYSTEM

Wilson & Lafleur Ltée. c. Société québécoise d'information juridique (Soquij), [1998] R.J.Q. 2489 (Que. S.C.), reversed [2000] R.J.Q. 1086 (Que. C.A.) and *CCH Canadian Ltd. v. Law Society of Upper Canada*, 2004 SCC 13 (S.C.C.).

---

§ 11.15.1
R. v. Kanayok
Nunavut Court of Justice; July 15, 1999
not reported; Rankin Inlet file 199 – 59548 (N.C.J.)

At the time the facts of this case arose, the location where they occurred was in the Northwest Territories. On April 1, 1999, that location became the Nunavut, a separate territory within Canada. This circumstance is not only of historical interest. The purpose of the establishment of Nunavut was to enable the Inuit people, in the majority within this Territory, to exercise greater influence over their own lives through governance. That public policy goal permeates this judgment.

The case arose out of the 1997 federal general election. Kanayok, a unilingual Inuit, reluctantly accepted to act as official agent for John Turner, Reform Party candidate in the electoral district of Nunavut. At that time, this electoral district was one of two constituencies comprising the Northwest Territories; today, it is coterminous with the Nunavut Territory. After the election, Kanayok did not file the election expenses returns required under the *Canada Elections Act*. The court found him guilty. However, in pronouncing sentence, it indicated that in its opinion, the Office of the Chief Electoral Officer should provide to the people of Nunavut documentation relating to the electoral process that reflects the language of common use in the Territory, namely Inuktitut; that it should make available appropriate training for those involved in the electoral process, such as official agents, and that it should provide information in Inuktitut on its toll free information lines. The court's perspective was that in order for the electoral system to be fair and open to the people of Nunavut and to keep the Canadian parliamentary and democratic process up to its internationally recognized level of fairness, it should adopt the system to local circumstances within Canada, perhaps even beyond the federal Official Languages legislation.

See also *New Brunswick (Minister of Health & Community Services) v. G. (J.)*, [1999] S.C.J. No. 47 (S.C.C.); *Winters v. Legal Services Society (British Columbia)*, [1999] S.C.J. No. 49 (S.C.C.) and *British Columbia (Minister of Forests) v. Okanagan Indian Band* (2001), 208 D.L.R. (4th) 301 (B.C. C.A.), leave to appeal allowed, [2002] 4 C.N.L.R. iv (note) (S.C.C.), leave to appeal allowed (2002), [2001] S.C.C.A. No. 629 (S.C.C.), affirmed (2003), 2003 SCC 71 (S.C.C.)

---

§ 11.15.2[302]
Centre for Legal Research and Another v. State of Kerala
Supreme Court of India; May 2, 1986
[1987] L.R.C. (Const.) 544

Part IV of the *Constitution of India*, entitled "Directive Principles of State Policy," sets out certain principles that are fundamental in the governance of the country. These are to be applied in legislating, even though they are declared not to be justiciable. Several of these principles deal with the role of law in the management of the State, as for example the goals of achieving a uniform civil code throughout the country and that of separating the judiciary from the executive in the public service of the State. By the *Constitution (42 and Amendment) Act 1976*, Article 39A was included in this Part of the *Constitution* in the following terms:

> *Equal justice and free legal aid*. The State shall secure that the operation of the legal system promotes justice, on a basis of equal opportunity, and shall, in particular, provide free legal aid, by suitable legislation or schemes or in any other way, to ensure that opportunities for securing justice are not denied to any citizen by reason of economic or other disabilities.[303]

---

[302] International comparisons.
[303] Constitution of India, article 39A.

The Centre for Legal Research petitioned to determine whether the government of the State of Kerala should provide financial support to voluntary organizations or social action groups engaged in legal aid programmes and, if so, to what extent and under what conditions.

The Supreme Court declared that "the State Government undoubtedly has an obligation...to set up a comprehensive and effective legal aid programme in order to ensure that the operation of the legal system promotes justice on the basis of equality."[304] It characterized such legal aid schemes as a social entitlement of the people, in which the people are participants, rather than mere beneficiaries. Securing their participation is best achieved by operating the programmes through voluntary organizations and social action groups which have their finger on the pulse of the people, which know the unmet legal needs of the people and which can best determine the measures aimed at social or distributive justice to them.

The court emphasized that the State should lay down norms in the selection of organizations and groups to support and that it must, in particular, encourage and support legal aid programmes run by groups that are totally free from government control. Most significantly, it felt that such programmes should adopt a dynamic posture, and that their strategy should include the promotion of legal literacy and the encouragement of public interest litigation.

This judgment reinforces constitutional recognition of legality as a fundamental principle of democratic governance. Going beyond the general declarations based on the rule of law that are used in many jurisdictions, this court specifies the duty of the State in enhancing the legality of government as including the dissemination of knowledge of the law among the population, and the development of the legal framework of government through public interest litigation. The ruling, bold in its expansion of governmental accountability to law, is even more significant in that it was given by the Chief Justice of India.

---

[304] [1987] L.R.C. (Const.) 544 at 545 b.

INDEX

A

- Aboriginals, 1.11.2, 2.2.E.10, 2.4.1, 3.3.C.1, 3.3.C.3, 4.10.3, 4.13.C.1, 5.3.5, 5.12.1, 8.2.C.3, 11.3.A.1, 11.8.5
- abortion, 10.7.1
- Action Démocratique du Québec, 5.9.8
- agriculture, 1.21.2
- Airbus, 11.10.2
- alcohol, 1.13.A.1, 8.8.1
- Algonquin College, 4.4.4
- Alliance Québec, 3.6.4, 9.3.A.3
- APEC (Asia-Pacific Economic Cooperation), 3.14.2, 9.9.B.1
- APEC (Association for the Preservation of
- English in Canada), 6.6.C.2
- Auditor General of Canada, 9.4.1, 11.7.5, 11.8.8
- Australia, 1.11.7, 5.8.5, 6.2.6, 11.14.3

B

- Bahamas, 10.9.2
- Bélanger-Campeau Report, 11.9.A.1
- Bloc Québécois, 1.2.3, 1.14.4, 3.3.A.2, 3.3.B.1, 3.3.B.2, 3.12.C.1, 4.4.1, 4.4.2, 6.6.C.1, 6.6.D.1, 6.6.D.2, 10.9.5, 10.9.7
- broadcasting, 1.2.2, 1.11.1, 1.11.3, 1.11.7, 1.12.2, 1.14.4, 1.21.1, 3.12.B.1, 3.14.1, 3.14.2, 5.8.1, 5.8.2, 5.8.5, 5.9.1, 5.9.2, 5.9.3, 5.9.4, 5.9.5, 5.9.6, 5.9.7, 5.9.8, 5.9.9, 5.9.10, 5.9.11, 8.2.C.2, 10.4.4, 10.5.1, 10.9.2, 10.9.3, 10.9.5, 10.9.9
- bribery, 11.6.1
- budget process, 7.6.1, 8.6.6, 10.12.3
- business incentives, 9.8.A.5

C

- Cambodia, 11.9.A.5
- Canada West Foundation, 4.13.D.1
- Canadian Bar Association, 3.8.2
- Canada-U.S. Free Trade, 6.7.A.1
- Canadian Forces, 3.12.C.1
- Canadian Reform Conservative Alliance, 6.8.B.1, 11.8.7
- Charlottetown Accord, 3.12.B.1, 4.10.3, 4.13.C.1, 4.13.D.1, 11.9.A.1
- Christian Heritage Party of Canada, 6.4.A.3
- citizenship, 3.4.2
- Clarity Bill, 2.4.6
- Colorado, 8.7.2
- Common Sense Revolution, 3.10.5, 7.4.1, 11.9.A.2
- Communism, 3.5.1, 3.15.1
- Communist Party of Canada, 6.4.A.1
- conflict of interests, 1.8.B.4, 3.13.1, 11.10.3
- Conservative Party of Canada, 6.8.B.1
- constitutional amendment, 1.2.1, 1.3.D.1, 1.12.1, 4.2.1, 4.12.1, 8.2.A.1, 8.2.B.1, 11.2.A
- contracting, 11.14.1
- copyright, 8.7.1
- criminal prosecutions, 1.3.C.1, 1.3.D.3, 1.5.1, 1.5.3, 1.8.B.2, 1.11.3, 1.13.A.6, 2.2.E.4, 2.2.F.1, 3.3.C.1, 3.3.C.2, 5.5.C.1, 5.8.3, 6.2.3, 6.2.4, 7.5.1, 8.3.1, 8.3.2, 8.3.3, 8.3.4, 8.3.5, 8.8.1, 10.8.3, 10.10.3, 10.10.4, 10.11.1, 10.11.2, 10.11.3, 10.11.4, 10.12.1, 10.12.2, 10.12.3, 10.13.1, 11.6.1, 11.7.1, 11.8.1, 11.13.2, 11.14.5, 11.14.11, 11.15.1
- Crown prosecutors, 3.11.1, 9.5.7, 11.14.3
- customs, 9.8.A.4
- Czech Republic, 3.5.13

D

- defamation, 6.6.C.3, 6.6.C.5, 6.6.D.1, 10.4.4, 10.5.1, 10.9.5, 10.9.6, 10.9.7, 10.9.8, 11.8.7
- defence, 2.4.3, 9.9.B.1, 9.9.C.2, 9.9.C.3
- diplomatic & consular relations, 11.3.B.1, 11.3.B.2
- disallowance or reservation, 8.8.1
- divorce, 1.11.4, 1.11.5

E

- education, 1.13.A.2, 1.13.A.5, 1.8.B.1, 1.13.A.4, 1.13.A.7, 1.14.6, 1.14.8, 2.2.B.2, 2.2.E.10, 2.2.I.1, 2.2.I.2, 3.4.1, 3.10.5, 4.11.C.2, 5.8.4, 7.4.1, 8.3.6, 8.8.3, 11.2.B.1
- employment equity, 7.2.1
- employment insurance, 10.4.2
- energy, 9.4.1, 10.8.2
- energy transmission, 8.6.2
- environmental assessment, 1.3.A.4, 1.3.A.6, 1.3.D.2, 1.8.B.2, 1.8.B.4, 1.11.2, 1.13.A.6, 2.2.E.1, 2.2.E.6, 2.6.1, 9.6.1, 11.7.4, 11.7.6, 11.14.2
- État de droit, 1.5.1
- European institutions, 3.10.6
- extradition, 3.10.3

F

- Fair Share Saskatchewan program, 9.4.3
- farming, 9.2.3, 9.2.4
- Fiji, 4.9.1
- finance, 1.8.B.6
- fisheries, 2.2.E.4, 3.3.C.3, 9.8.A.3, 9.8.A.6, 9.8.A.7, 9.9.A.1, 9.9.C.2
- flag of Canada, 3.3.A.2
- forestry, 2.2.E.9
- French language, 3.4.1, 3.14.1, 7.3.1, 9.3.A.3, 10.4.5
- fraud, 11.4.1

G

- government contracting, 9.8.B.1
- Green Party, 1.11.3, 1.21.1, 5.9.5

- G.S.T. (Goods and Services Tax), 3.12.D.1, 6.7.A.2, 8.5.3, 8.5.4, 10.4.3
- Groupaction, 11.8.8

H

- health, 1.3.A.3, 1.5.2, 1.13.A.5, 1.16.1
- Hong Kong, 4.6.2, 4.6.3, 4.6.4, 4.7.1
- honours & titles, 10.8.4
- House of Commons, 8.2.B.1
- Hungary, 3.15.1

I

- ICTFY (International Criminal Tribunal
- for the Former Yugoslavia), 11.9.C.2
- immigration, 1.4.1, 1.8.B.5, 2.2.E.2, 2.2.E.3, 2.2.E.8, 3.16.1, 3.16.2, 8.6.4, 8.8.4, 9.3.A.1, 9.5.1, 10.10.2, 11.7.2, 11.7.5, 11.14.6
- India, 5.10.1, 11.15.2
- impeachment, 10.7.4, 10.7.5
- intellectual property, 1.13.A.2, 8.7.1, 9.4.6
- initiatives, 6.6.D.5
- international relations, 1.3.A.1, 2.4.3, 9.10.A.1
- International Court of Justice, 9.9.C.3
- international trade, 9.10.A.1
- international tribunals, 10.10.4
- Israel, 11.9.A.4

J

- judicial investigations, 5.13.1, 6.5.2
- judges as litigants, 5.5.A.2

K

- Kaufman Inquiry, 11.14.10

L

- labour relations, 1.13.A.3, 1.9.1, 1.14.7, 1.14.8, 2.2.A.1, 2.2.G.1, 8.2.C.1, 8.6.3, 9.5.3, 9.5.5

• law societies, 1.7.1, 1.8.D.1, 1.9.2, 8.5.6
• legislative counsel to Parliament, 8.10.1
• Liberal Party:
•• British Columbia, 1.11.5, 3.3.C.3
•• Canada, 1.14.3, 4.4.2, 4.13.C.2, 6.2.2, 6.3.1, 6.3.3, 6.4.B.1, 6.7.A.2, 8.3.7, 9.5.1, 10.4.3, 10.8.2, 11.8.4
•• Nova Scotia, 6.2.4
•• Québec, 4.4.1
• Lortie Royal Commission, 2.4.5, 6.2.2

M
• malicious prosecution, 11.14.11
• Meech Lake Accord, 3.3.B.1; 3.6.3, 3.12.B.1, 4.10.1, 4.10.2, 4.10.3, 4.13.B.1, 4.13.B.2, 4.13.B.3, 4.13.C.2, 4.13.D.1, 4.13.D.2, 9.11.1, 11.9.A.1
• ministers of Canadian governments:
•• Lloyd Axworthy, 4.4.3, 9.9.B.1, 11.3.A.3
•• Joe Clark, 4.10.3, 9.4.4
•• Robert Coates, 11.7.3
•• Sheila Copps, 6.6.C.3, 6.7.A.2
•• David Dingwall, 9.5.2
•• Charles Drury, 3.8.1
•• Alfonso Gagliano, 11.8.8
•• Joe Greene, 2.7.1
•• Ray Hnatyshyn, 9.2.2.
•• Otto Jelinek, 9.8.A.4
•• Doug Lewis, 3.10.4
•• Mark MacGuigan, 8.2.B.1
•• John Manley, 3.3.A.1
•• Marcel Masse, 9.2.2
•• Bill McKnight, 9.2.2
•• Ann McLellan, 2.4.6, 4.4.5
•• John Munro, 6.4.B.1, 11.8.4, 11.8.5
•• André Ouellet, 3.8.1
•• Lucienne Robillard, 5.5.A.1
•• Allan Rock, 2.4.6, 4.3.1
•• Sinclair Stevens, 6.8.B.1, 11.8.2, 11.14.9
• Minnesota, 6.8.A.2

• monarchy, 3.3.A.1
• Montesqieu, 3.10.6
• Montfort Hospital, 4.2.3
• Montreal, 2.2.F.1, 6.4.B.2
• multiculturalism, 3.3.A.1
• municipal affairs, 1.3.A.7, 7.3.1, 8.9.1

N
• NAFTA (North American Free Trade Agreement), 1.4.1, 9.10.A.1, 11.13.2
• Namibia, 3.11.2
• NATO (North Atlantic Treaty Organization), 3.3.C.1, 3.15.1, 9.9.C.1, 9.9.C.3, 11.10.4
• NCC (National Citizens' Coalition), 5.5.C.2, 6.7.A.4, 10.9.4
• National Party of Canada, 1.14.4, 5.9.6, 6.4.A.2
• Nationalist Party of Canada, 6.2.3
• Natural Law Party of Canada, 5.9.7
• New Democratic Party:
•• Alberta, 11.13.1
•• British Columbia, 3.3.C.3, 6.7.A.4, 11.7.1
•• Canada, 1.14.4, 6.2.2, 6.4.B.1, 6.6.C.2, 9.5.4
•• Ontario, 9.5.5, 9.8.A.2, 10.13.1
• New Zealand, 6.7.A.5, 10.9.9
• Newfoundland as an independant colony, 4.11.C.1, 10.8.1
• newspapers, 2.4.5, 3.14.3, 5.10, 10.9.4,10.9.7
• Nisga'a Final Agreement, 3.3.C.3, 3.14.3

O
• oath of office of parliamentarians, 3.3.B.1
• Ottawa, 9.5.4

P
• Pakistan, 4.6.5
• Parliament Hill, 1.3.D.3, 8.3.3, 8.3.4, 8.3.5, 10.11.2

• Parliamentarians as litigants, 5.3.3, 5.5.B.2, 5.7.B.2
• parliamentary privilege, 1.2.2, 1.12.2, 11.5.1
• Parti Québécois, 4.4.2, 4.13.B.1, 5.9.8, 6.6.C.5, 10.12.2, 11.8.8, 11.9.A.1
• patriation, 1.2.1, 4.2.1, 4.12.1, 4.13.A.1, 8.2.A.1, 8.2.B.1
• police, 3.12.B.2, 3.14.2, 5.5.B.1, 6.6.C.4, 8.3.1, 8.3.5, 9.9.B.1, 10.12.2, 11.8.5, 11.8.8, 11.10.2
• political questions doctrine in the U.S., 2.4.3, 10.8.5
• postal service, 2.2.H.1, 9.4.2, 10.5.1
• premiers of Canadian provinces and territories:
•• Lucien Bouchard, 4.2.3, 4.3.1, 4.4.1, 4.4.5, 6.6.C.5, 9.3.A.3, 10.9.5
•• Robert Bourassa, 3.12.B.1, 11.9.A.1
•• John Buchanan, 8.5.1
•• Gordon Campbell, 3.3.C.3
•• Glen Clark, 6.7.A.4, 9.8.B.1, 9.9.C.2
•• William Davis, 1.11.1
•• Grant Devine, 3.10.4, 9.4.3
•• Ujjal Dosanj, 6.7.A.4
•• Maurice Duplessis, 2.7.1, 10.8.4
•• Ernie Eves, 8.6.6
•• Mike Harcourt, 3.13.1, 6.7.A.4, 11.8.6
•• Mike Harris, 3.10.5, 4.2.3, 6.7.A.3, 8.3.6, 8.6.6
•• Joseph Howe, 3.3.B.1
•• Daniel Johnson, 5.9.8
•• Ralph Klein, 9.4.5, 11.8.7, 11.14.7
•• Jean Lesage, 4.4.2
•• René Lévesque, 10.9.5, 10.12.2
•• Peter Lougheed, 10.4.4
•• Frank McKenna, 4.13.C.2
•• Dalton McGuinty, 8.6.6
•• Frank Moores, 10.9.6, 11.10.2
•• Don Morin, 11.10.3
•• Jacques Parizeau, 3.3.B.2, 6.6.C.5
•• Brian Peckford, 9.5.6
•• Tony Pennikett, 4.10.1, 4.13.B.1
•• David Peterson, 11.10.1

•• Bob Rae, 1.14.7, 6.7.A.3, 6.7.B.2, 10.4.1, 10.4.2
•• Gerald Regan, 6.6.C.4
•• Ross Thatcher, 3.10.4
•• Bill Vander Zalm, 8.5.2, 10.9.1, 11.8.3
•• Clyde Wells, 9.5.6
• presidents of the United States:
•• James Adams, 3.9.2
•• Bill Clinton, 5.9.10, 8.6.7, 10.7.4, 11.9.A.3, 11.10.5
•• Richard Nixon, 11.9.A.1
•• Ronald Reagan, 2.4.3
• prime ministers of Canada:
•• Kim Campbell, 10.4.1
•• Jean Chrétien, 4.13.D.1, 6.4.B.1, 6.7.A.2, 9.5.2, 9.9.B.1, 10.4.1, 10.8.4, 11.8.8
•• Joe Clark, 10.8.2
•• Sir John A. Macdonald, 3.6.2
•• Paul Martin, 11.7.5, 11.8.8
•• Brian Mulroney, 1.3.D.3, 1.8.B.2, 2.4.5, 4.10.3, 6.7.A.1, 6.8.B.1, 8.3.4, 8.5.3, 8.5.4, 9.4.4, 9.5.7, 10.9.4, 10.9.6, 11.7.3, 11.8.2, 11.9.A.1, 11.10.2
•• Pierre Elliott Trudeau, 1.2.1, 1.2.3, 2.4.3, 2.7.1, 3.8.1, 4.12.1, 4.13.C.2, 8.2.B.1, 8.6.5, 10.8.2, 11.8.4
• prisons & prisoners, 5.4.1, 11.13.2
• Progressive Conservative Party :
•• Canada, 1.14.4, 6.2.1, 6.4.A.4, 6.4.B.2, 6.6.D.2, 6.7.A.1, 6.8.B.1, 9.5.1, 10.8.2
•• Newfoundland, 10.9.6
•• Nova Scotia, 6.6.C.4
•• Ontario, 6.7.A.3, 7.2.1, 10.4.1
• public opinion polling, 5.10.1
• public servants, 1.8.B.4, 2.2.E.7, 5.5.B.1, 5.5.C.1, 9.4.5, 9.4.7, 9.6.2, 9.6.3, 11.3.A.2, 11.3.B.1, 11.8.8

Q

• Québec secession, 1.2.3, 2.4.6, 4.2.2, 4.3.1, 4.6.1, 10.2.1, 11.2.C.1
• Queensland, 6.2.6

R

- racism, 2.2.E.10, 6.2.3, 6.2.4, 6.2.5, 6.6.C.1, 6.6.C.2, 6.6.C.5, 6.6.D.1, 8.3.7
- Rechtsstat, 1.5.2
- redistribution, 2.4.4, 3.2.1, 3.6.1, 3.6.2, 5.3.1, 5.3.2, 5.3.3, 5.3.4, 5.3.5, 5.3.6, 8.8.2, 10.8.5, 11.5.2, 11.13.1
- referendum, 3.6.3, 3.6.4, 3.12.B.1, 4.3.1, 4.4.1, 4.4.2, 4.4.4, 4.4.5, 4.6.1, 4.11.C.1, 4.11.C.2, 5.2.1, 5.5.A.3, 5.8.4, 8.8.3, 10.8.1
- Reform Party:
- • Canada, 1.14.4, 3.3.B.2, 3.9.1, 3.12.C.3, 4.4.1, 4.13.D.2, 6.3.2, 6.3.4, 6.6.C.1, 6.6.D.2, 6.8.A.1
- • Manitoba, 6.3.2
- retirement, 1.8.A.3, 1.3.A.5, 1.8.B.1, 1.13.A.4, 1.13.A.5, 1.13.A.7
- Royal Commission on New
- Reproductive Technologies, 9.4.4
- Russia, 4.8.1, 10.7.5

S

- school board elections, 10.10.3
- Scotland, 5.9.9
- securities regulation, 2.2.E.5
- Senate, 1.2.1, 4.2.1, 8.2.A.1, 8.2.B.1, 6.3.4, 4.13.D.1, 4.13.D.2, 8.2.A.1, 8.2.B.2, 8.6.5
- State – sponsored crime, 10.10.4

T

- taxation, 1.19.1, 2.2.B.1, 3.12.D.1, 9.3.A.4, 9.11.1, 9.11.2, 9.11.3, 11.14.7
- telecommunications, 2.4.1
- terrorism, 10.11.1, 10.11.3
- Toronto, 1.8.A.1, 1.14.5, 3.12.B.2, 5.5.B.2, 6.3.1, 6.4.B.1
- transportation, 1.3.D.1, 1.8.B.3, 2.2.C.1, 2.2.D.1, 4.11.A.1, 4.11.B.1, 4.11.B.2, 6.5.1, 7.7.1, 9.8.A.2, 9.8.B.1, 10.10.4

U

- United Kingdom, 1.11.6, 2.4.7, 3.10.6, 4.5.1, 6.4.B.3, 6.7.B.3, 7.5.1, 8.5.6, 8.7.3, 11.9.C.1, 11.12.1, 11.14.2
- United States, 3.9.2, 5.2.2, 5.3.6, 5.9.10, 5.9.11, 6.6.D.5, 6.8.A.2, 8.2.C.3, 8.3.8, 8.6.7, 8.7.2, 9.9.A.1, 9.9.B.2, 10.2.2, 10.7.4, 10.8.5, 10.10.1, 11.9.A.3, 11.9.B.1, 11.9.B.2, 11.10.5
- university elections, 10.7.3
- U.S. federal rules of evidence, 10.7.4
- U.S.S.R., 10.7.5

V

- Vancouver, 6.3.3., 8.6.2
- Venezuela, 5.12.2

W

- weights & measures, 10.8.3
- welfare assistance, 1.8.A.1, 11.3.A.1
- welfare institutions, 9.7.1
- Western Guard Party, 6.2.5
- Westray mining disaster, 11.14.10
- wheat, 11.13.2
- whisleblowing, 11.3.A.3
- women, 6.4.B.3
- workplace harassment, 10.7.2

NUMBERS

- 6 and 5 legislation, 3.7.1, 9.8.A.1